From Hittite to Homer

This book provides a groundbreaking reassessment of the prehistory of Homeric epic. It argues that in the Early Iron Age bilingual poets transmitted to the Greeks a set of narrative traditions closely related to the one found at Bronze Age Hattusa, the Hittite capital. Key drivers for Near Eastern influence on the developing Homeric tradition were the shared practices of supralocal festivals and venerating divinized ancestors, and a shared interest in creating narratives about a legendary past using a few specific storylines: theogonies, genealogies connecting local polities, long-distance travel, destruction of a famous city because it refuses to release captives, and trying to overcome death when confronted with the loss of a dear companion. Professor Bachvarova concludes by providing a fresh explanation of the origins and significance of the Greco-Anatolian legend of Troy, thereby offering a new solution to the long-debated question of the historicity of the Trojan War.

MARY R. BACHVAROVA is Professor in the Department of Classical Studies at Willamette University, Oregon. She was trained both in classics and in the languages and cultures of Anatolia and the Near East. She is the co-editor, with B. J. Collins and I. C. Rutherford, of *Anatolian Interfaces: Hittites, Greeks and Their Neighbours* (2005). She has also written a new translation of Hurro-Hittite narrative songs in the recently published *Ancient Mediterranean Myths: Primary Sources from Ancient Greece, Rome, and the Near East*, edited by C. López-Ruiz (2013).

CAMBRIDGE
UNIVERSITY PRESS

University Printing House, Cambridge CB2 8BS, United Kingdom

One Liberty Plaza, 20th Floor, New York, NY 10006, USA

477 Williamstown Road, Port Melbourne, VIC 3207, Australia

314-321, 3rd Floor, Plot 3, Splendor Forum, Jasola District Centre, New Delhi - 110025, India

79 Anson Road, #06-04/06, Singapore 079906

Cambridge University Press is part of the University of Cambridge.

It furthers the University's mission by disseminating knowledge in the pursuit of education, learning and research at the highest international levels of excellence.

www.cambridge.org
Information on this title: www.cambridge.org/9781108994101

© Mary R. Bachvarova 2016

This publication is in copyright. Subject to statutory exception and to the provisions of relevant collective licensing agreements, no reproduction of any part may take place without the written permission of Cambridge University Press.

First published 2016
First paperback edition 2021

A catalogue record for this publication is available from the British Library

Library of Congress Cataloging in Publication data
Bachvarova, Mary R., author.
From Hittite to Homer : the Anatolian background of ancient Greek epic / Mary R. Bachvarova.
    pages cm
Includes bibliographical references and indexes.
ISBN 978-0-521-50979-4 (Hardback: alk. paper)   1. Epic poetry, Greek–History and criticism.   2. Homer. Iliad.   3. Hittites–Religion.   4. Gilgamesh.   5. Hittite literature–History and criticism.   I. Title.
PA3106.B33 2015
881.009–dc23   2015013725

ISBN 978-0-521-50979-4 Hardback
ISBN 978-1-108-99410-1 Paperback

Cambridge University Press has no responsibility for the persistence or accuracy of URLs for external or third-party internet websites referred to in this publication, and does not guarantee that any content on such websites is, or will remain, accurate or appropriate.

From Hittite to Homer:

The Anatolian Background of Ancient Greek Epic

MARY R. BACHVAROVA

CAMBRIDGE
UNIVERSITY PRESS

To G. D. S. A.

Contents

List of maps [page xi]
List of figures [xii]
List of tables [xiv]
Acknowledgments [xv]
List of abbreviations [xvii]
Notes on the text [xxii]
Maps [xxxiv]

1 Introduction [1]
   Status quaestionis [1]
   The world of the Hittites [5]
   An outline of the book [12]

2 Hurro-Hittite narrative song at Hattusa [20]
   Introduction [20]
   Members of the genre of Hurro-Hittite narrative song [23]
   The formal features of Hurro-Hittite narrative song [35]
   Bilingual poets [46]
   The functions of Hurro-Hittite narrative song [49]
   Conclusion [52]

3 Gilgamesh at Hattusa: written texts and oral traditions [54]
   Introduction [54]
   The Akkadian *Epic of Gilgamesh* [56]
   The Akkadian *Epic of Gilgamesh* in the Hittite archives [60]
   The Hittite *Song of Gilgamesh* [63]
   The Hurrian *Song of Gilgamesh* and *Song of Huwawa* [72]
   Conclusion [76]

4 The Hurro-Hittite ritual context of Gilgamesh at Hattusa [78]
   Introduction [78]
   Background [79]
   The Hurro-Hittite pit ritual involving the story of Gilgamesh [81]
   Gilgamesh in Mesopotamian rituals [85]
   Pit rituals [86]
   The *Purification Ritual for the Former Gods* [95]
   Odysseus' *katabasis* [99]
   Myth and ritual: the chicken and the egg? [108]
   Conclusion [110]

5 The plot of the *Song of Release*   [111]
   Introduction   [111]
   The opening   [113]
   The assembly scene   [117]
   The hospitality scene   [124]
   The parables   [129]
   Conclusion   [131]

6 The place of the *Song of Release* in its eastern Mediterranean context   [132]
   Introduction   [132]
   The assembly scene in its Near Eastern context   [133]
   The assembly scene of the *Song of Release* and the *Iliad*   [139]
   The hospitality scene of the *Song of Release* in its eastern Mediterranean context   [142]
   The messenger scene in the *Song of Release* in its eastern Mediterranean context   [145]
   Conclusion   [146]

7 The function and prehistory of the *Song of Release*   [149]
   Introduction   [149]
   The *Song of Release* and royal ancestor veneration   [149]
   The origin of Hurro-Hittite narrative song   [156]
   Conclusion   [165]

8 Sargon the Great: from history to myth   [166]
   Introduction   [166]
   The Anatolian reception of legends of Sargon   [167]
   From history to myth, from oral to written   [178]
   The *šarrena* ritual   [182]
   King lists and genealogies as indexes for world history   [187]
   Naram-Sin and Hector   [191]
   Conclusion   [196]

9 Long-distance interactions: theory, practice, and myth   [199]
   Introduction   [199]
   Wandering seers or Orientalizing construct?   [200]
   Push–pull factors encouraging long-distance interactions   [206]
   Long-distance elite interaction and transmission of narratives   [211]
   Medicine, long-distance travel, and cosmogonies   [213]
   Conclusion   [217]

10 Festivals: a milieu for cultural contact   [219]
   Introduction   [219]
   Hittite festivals   [221]
   Feasts and festivals in second-millennium Greece   [226]
   A festival of Mycenaean Thebes   [229]

First-millennium Greek festivals [232]
The Delia [236]
The Milesian New Year festival [241]
Apollo as a vector for transmission of cult [243]
The *Chaoskampf* myth in its festival setting: Syro-Anatolia [250]
Conclusion [263]

11 The context of epic in Late Bronze and Early Iron Age Greece [266]
Introduction [266]
Ancestor veneration and mortuary ritual in the Mycenaean period [268]
Elite competition and epic in post-palatial Greece [273]
The Protogeometric period: the age of nostalgia [278]
Hērōes and *meropes anthrōpoi*: the shared concept of divinized ancestors among Early Iron Age Greeks and Syro-Anatolians [285]
The *Odyssey* as a narrative of long-distance elite interactions [295]
Conclusion [299]

12 Cyprus as a source of Syro-Anatolian epic in the Early Iron Age [301]
Introduction [301]
Cyprus in the Late Bronze Age: a member of the brotherhood of Great Kings [303]
The arrival of the Greeks in Cyprus [306]
Cultural continuity in Syro-Anatolia [310]
Iatnana, Danuna, and the House of Mopsus [316]
Contact between Greece and Cyprus in the Early Iron Age [321]
Cypriot epics about Aphrodite? [323]
Conclusion [329]

13 Cultural contact in Late Bronze Age western Anatolia [331]
Introduction [331]
Contacts among Ahhiyawa, west Anatolia, and the Hittites in the Late Bronze Age: the beginnings of a cultural memory about the Trojan War? [333]
Transmission of Hittite cultural features to west Anatolia in the Late Bronze Age [342]
Transfer of people and cultural features between Greece and Anatolia [344]
Conclusion [347]

14 Continuity of memory at Troy and in Anatolia [349]
Introduction [349]
Reminiscences of Bronze Age Troy in the Homeric tradition [351]
Cultural continuity and Greek migrations in Early Iron Age west Anatolia [356]
Troy across the end of the Bronze Age [361]
Troy as a place of remembrance [367]

Genealogical and dynastic ties with the Bronze Age Anatolian Past [373]
Continuity of elite mortuary practices in Syro-Anatolia, Mopsus'
  ḫešti-house, and Karatepe [379]
Conclusion [393]

15 The history of the Homeric tradition [395]
Introduction [395]
The date of "Homer": an overview [396]
The upper and lower limit for the creation of a Greek epic about Troy [400]
The refining of the pre-Homeric Greek epic tradition: competition
  among Aeolic and Ionic poets [402]
Conclusion [416]

16 The layers of Anatolian influence in the *Iliad* [418]
Introduction [418]
Relations between Achaeans and Anatolians as portrayed in the *Iliad* [421]
Bilingual Anatolian epic poets [426]
A Phrygian–Aeolic tradition about the fall of Troy? [429]
A pro-Trojan *Iliad* [432]
Lycian influence on the *Iliad*: a Milesian setting? [438]
Lycian hero worship in the *Iliad*: the death of Sarpedon [445]
Apollo's role in the transfer and transmission of the *Iliad* [449]
Conclusion [453]

Appendix: Contraction and the dactylic hexameter [458]
References [465]
Subject index [565]
List of Hittite texts by CTH *number* [637]
Index of tablets and inscriptions [642]
Concordance of tablets from Ugarit [649]

List of maps

Map 1 Bronze Age Greece and the Near East   [*page* xxxiv]
Map 2 Early Iron Age Greece and Anatolia   [xxxvi]
Map 3 Hattusa. Based on Neve (1993), Fig. 27 by H. Özel.   [xxxviii]

List of figures

Figure 1   The *āpi* at Urkesh. Photograph by Kenneth Garrett, used by kind permission. [*page* 88]
Figure 2   The KASKAL.KUR at Boğazköy. Photograph by Jürgen Seeher, used by kind permission. [91]
Figure 3   The Ayia Triada Sarcophagus. American School of Classical Studies at Athens, Alison Frantz Photographic Collection. [92]
Figure 4   Bilingual edition of the *Song of Release*, obverse of Bo 83/604, photograph by Erich Neu. Hethitologie Portal Mainz, Photoarchiv. [112]
Figure 5   Silver stag *bibrû* from Mycenae. Athens National Archaeological Museum, no. 388. [208]
Figure 6   Chamber A at Yazılıkaya. Photograph by Horst Ehringhaus, from Ehringhaus (2005), p. 21, fig. 30. [225]
Figure 7   Yeniköy Stele. Ankara Museum of Anatolian Civilizations, Turkey 12467. [244]
Figure 8   Schimmel Rhyton. Drawings by Andrea Foust. [245]
Figure 9   Apollo Philesius. British Museum 1824,0405.1. Courtesy of the Trustees of the British Musem. [248]
Figure 10 Mycenaean Vessel with an Anatolian God from Miletus. From Weickert (1959/60), Tafel 72.1. Courtesy of the Deutsches Archäologisches Institut. [250]
Figure 11 Storm-god at Malatya fighting sea-snake. Drawing by Andrea Foust. [259]
Figure 12 Stele at Grave Circle B. From Marinatos (1990). Drawing from squeeze by A. Sakellariou. [270]
Figure 13 Tanagra Larnax. From Aupert (1975), fig. 118. [271]
Figure 14 Warrior Vase from Mycenae. National Archaeological Museum, Athens (photographer: Giannis Patrikianos). © Hellenic Ministry of Culture and Sports /Archaeological Receipts Fund. [276]
Figure 15 Cypriot Kalathos from Kouklia. From Iacovou (1988), Fig. 71. [277]
Figure 16 Geometric *skyphos*. Eleusis Museum. © Hellenic Ministry of Culture and Sports /Archaeological Receipts Fund. [279]

Figure 17 Troia (top view). Redrawn with permission from the Troia project. [364]
Figure 18 Troia (side view). Redrawn with permission from the Troia project. [366]
Figure 19 West Sanctuary at Troy. [368]
Figure 20 Stone circles at Troy, in West Sanctuary. Courtesy of The Department of Classics, University of Cincinnati. [369]
Figure 21 Karatepe South Gate, Forecourt. From Çambel and Özyar (2003). [385]
Figure 22 Karatepe South Gate, Left Chamber. From Çambel and Özyar (2003). [387]
Figure 23 Karatepe South Gate, Right Chamber. From Çambel and Özyar (2003). [388]
Figure 24 Karatepe, Orthostat 11. From Çambel and Özyar (2003). [389]
Figure 25 Karatepe, Boat Scene, North Gate, Right Chamber. From Çambel and Özyar (2003). [390]
Figure 26 Tell Halaf, Orthostat. From Moortgat, A. (1955), Tafel 102, A3, 176. [391]

List of tables

Table 1 Bronze Age chronology: Greece and the Near East   [*page* xxiv]
Table 2 Equations among Near Eastern and Greek gods   [xxxii]
Table 3 Scheme of four versions of the third tablet of the
        Song of Gilgamesh (*CTH* 341.III.3)   [70]
Table 4 Layers of Anatolian influence on the *Iliad* and the *Odyssey*   [455]

Acknowledgments

This book has taken many years to complete. It began its life as a PhD thesis in the now defunct Committee on the History of Culture at University of Chicago (2002), with a dissertation committee of Shadi Bartsch, Christopher Faraone, Harry Hoffner, Jr., and Calvert Watkins. I thank all of them for taking on duties that lay outside their home departments, and in the case of Prof. Watkins, his home institution.

The current monograph retains very little of the original PhD thesis unchanged, other than the basic point that the *Song of Release* shows striking parallels to the *Iliad* (also published in Bachvarova 2005a and 2008a). During the course of reworking my ideas into their current form I have incurred debts to various institutions: In 2009–10 I spent a sabbatical year in Cincinnati, using the libraries of the University of Cincinnati Classics Department and Hebrew Union College. Willamette University also gave me a generous semester of Junior Leave in 2007, and the Center of Ancient Studies and Archaeology at Willamette awarded me a fellowship in 2008 that allowed me a course reduction for one term. I continued to use the Oriental Institute Research Archives and the Regenstein Library at the University of Chicago even after completing my degree. The electronic resources of the Hittitology Portal of Mainz University and the Oriental Institute Research Archives made it possible to stay abreast of the relevant bibliography. The staff at the Hatfield Library, especially in the Inter-Library Loan office, were extremely helpful, supplying me promptly with any books and articles I requested.

I thank A. R. George for permission to quote from his translation of the *Epic of Gilgamesh*, Andrea Foust for doing some important illustrations, Dr. Morena Stefanova for providing excellent photos of the Schimmel rhyton from the Metropolitan Museum collection, and Brandon Guyton for preparing mock-ups of the maps.

I am very grateful to the colleagues who have read all or part of earlier versions of this book: John Franklin, Carolina López-Ruiz, Sarah Morris, Kurt Raaflaub, and the two anonymous readers for Cambridge University Press. Ann Suter read through the entire final manuscript very carefully, making many improvements in wording and helping me to clarify details of my exposition. I have consulted with many colleagues over the years, but I thank in particular Ian C. Rutherford for his continued support; Maureen Basedow for discussing with me the West Sanctuary and sector D9 at Troy; Carolyn Aslan, H. Craig Melchert, and Christopher Roosevelt for sharing forthcoming articles; Alexander Herda for his thoughts on Miletus; Rostislav Oreshko for his thoughts on Karatepe; and Eva von Dassow for her help at the last minute with chronological issues. I would also like to express my gratitude for their inspirational influence to two scholars who have recently died: Joan Goodnick Westenholz, who worked on the oral milieu of Sargonic legend, and Calvert Watkins. It was an undergraduate class with Cal that demonstrated to me the kinds of results that can come from comparative philology and suggested the potential fruits of comparing Greek and Hittite texts.

Finally, I thank my mother-in-law, Dr. Jane Shelton Anderson, for welcoming our entire family, including Lady and Bear, into her home during my sabbatical year, and my mother, Prof. Rosemary Faulkner (Bachvarova), for her many years of personal and financial support and help with Sam and Oliver.

This book is dedicated to my husband, Dr. Gregory D. S. Anderson, who has made many personal and professional sacrifices to support my career and take care of our family.

Abbreviations

Bibliographic Abbreviations
Abbreviations of Greek authors follow the conventions of H. G. Liddell, R. Scott, H. S. Jones, and R. McKenzie, *A Greek–English Lexicon* (1996, Oxford), except as cited below. Latin authors are cited according to P. G. W. Glare, *Oxford Latin Dictionary* (1982, Oxford).

ABoT	Ankara Arkeoloji Müzesinde bulunan Boğazköy Tabletleri (1948). Istanbul.
BAM	F. Köcher (1916–80) *Die Babylonisch-assyriologische Medizin in Texten und Untersuchungen*. Berlin.
Brill's New Pauly	H. Cancik *et al.* (eds.) (2002–) *Brill's New Pauly*. Leiden and Boston.
CAD	*The Assyrian Dictionary of the Oriental Institute of the University of Chicago* (1964–2010). Chicago.
CHD	H. G. Güterbock, H. A. Hoffner, Jr., and T. P. J. van den Hout (1989–) *The Hittite Dictionary of the Oriental Institute of the University of Chicago*. Chicago.
CTH	E. Laroche (1971) *Catalogue des textes hittites*. Paris. The *CTH* numbering of Hittite texts follows the electronic database KhT.
EA	J. A. Knudtzon (1964) *Die El-Amarna-Tafeln*. Aalen.
Erg.	*Ergänzungslieferung*
ETCSL	Electronic Text Corpus of Sumerian Literature (www-etcsl.orient.ox.ac.uk/)
FGrH	F. Jacoby (ed.) (1923–58) *Fragmente der Griechischen Historiker*. Berlin and Leipzig.
HED	J. Puhvel (1984–) *Hittite Etymological Dictionary*. Berlin.
HEG	J. Tischler (1983–2001) *Hethitisches etymologisches Glossar*. Innsbruck.
HFAC	G. Beckman and J. Hoffner, Harry A. (1985) "Hittite Fragments in American Collections." *Journal of Cuneiform Studies* 37: 1–60.

hHAp	Homeric Hymn to Apollo
hHAphr	Homeric Hymn to Aphrodite
HT	L. W. King (1920) *Hittite Texts in the Cuneiform Character in the British Museum*. London.
IBoT	*Istanbul Arkeoloji Müzelerinde bulunan Boğazköy Tableteri(nden Seçme Metinler)*. Istanbul.
KAI	H. Donner and W. Röllig (1962–4) *Kanaanäische und aramäische Inschriften*. Wiesbaden.
KAR	E. Ebeling (1919, 1923) *Keilschrifttexte aus Assur religiösen Inhalts I, II*. Leipzig.
KBo	*Keilschrifttexte aus Boghazköi*. Leipzig, Berlin.
KhT	Konkordanz der hethitischen Keilschrifttafeln (www.hethport.uni-wuerzburg.de/hetkonk/)
KRI	K. A. Kitchen (1993–2008) *Ramesside Inscriptions Translated and Annotated: Translations*. Oxford and Cambridge, Mass.
KTU	M. Dietrich, O. Loretz, and J. Sanmartin (1995) *The Cuneiform Alphabetic Texts from Ugarit, Ras Ibn Hani and Other Places*. Münster.
KUB	*Keilschrifturkunden aus Boghazköi*. Berlin.
LKA	E. Ebeling (1953) *Literarische Keilschrifttexte aus Assur*. Berlin.
NF	*Neue Folge*
RAC	T. Klauser *et al.* (1950–) *Reallexikon für Antike und Christentum*. Stuttgart.
RE	A. Pauly and G. Wissowa (1958–1978) *Real-Encyclopädie der classischen Altertumswissenschaft*. Stuttgart.
RlA	E. Ebeling *et al.* (1932–) *Reallexikon der Assyriologie und vorderasiatischen Archäologie*. Berlin.
StBoTB	Studien zu den Boğazköy-Texten, Beiheft. Wiesbaden.
TUAT	O. Kaiser *et al.* (1982–) *Texte aus der Umwelt des Alten Testaments*. Gütersloh.
VBoT	A. Goetze (1930) *Verstreute Boghazköi-Texte*. Marburg.
YOS	*Yale Oriental Series*. New Haven.

Other Abbreviations

A	Tablets in the Asiatic collection of the Oriental Institute, University of Chicago

Abbreviations

Aa	personnel tablets, textile workers
Ab	personnel tablets, textile workers
An	personnel tablets
Aq	personnel tablets
Av	personnel tablets, allocations of grain
BA	Bronze Age
BM	Museum siglum of the British Museum in London
Bo	Tablet siglum of (unpublished) texts from Boğazköy
bott.	bottom
col.	column
Cypr.	Cypriot
De	sheep tablets
E	grain tablets
EC	Early Cypriot
ED	Early Dynastic
EG	Early Geometric
EH	Early Helladic
EIA	Early Iron Age
EPG	Early Protogeometric
EM	Early Minoan
F	fragment
FF	fragments
Fn	rations/offerings/allocations of grain
Fp	rations/offerings/allocations of olive oil
Fq	rations/offerings/allocations of barley and flour
Fr	rations/offerings/allocations of olive oil
Ft	rations/offerings/allocations of olive oil
Ga	offerings (coriander)
Geo	Geometric
Gp	allocations of wine, barley flour, cyperus
HH	Hurro-Hittite
Hitt.	Hittite
HL	Hieroglyphic Luwian
Hurr.	Hurrian
IE	Indo-European
IM	Museum siglum of the Iraq Museum in Baghdad
K	Museum siglum of the British Museum in London (Küyünjik)
KN	Knossos
L	letter

LBA	Late Bronze Age
LC	Late Cypriot
LH	Late Helladic
LM	Late Minoan
MB	Middle Babylonian
MBA	Middle Bronze Age
MC	Middle Cypriot
MG	Middle Geometric
MH	Middle Helladic
MH	Middle Hittite
MS	Middle Script
Msk	Tablet siglum of texts from Meskene
MY	Mycenae
Myc	Mycenaean
NA	Neo-Assyrian
narr.	narrative
NE	Near Eastern
NH	New Hittite
NS	New Script
OB	Old Babylonian
OH	Old Hittite
OS	Old Script
PG	Protogeometric
PIE	Proto-Indo-European
PY	Pylos
RS	Museum siglum of the Louvre and Damascus (Ras Shamra)
Sa	chariot and armor tablets
SB	Standard Babylonian
Sc	chariot and armor tablets
SM	Submycenaean
Σ	scholia
T	testimonium
TC	Tablet siglum of the Takahashi Collection
TH	Thebes
Tn	vessel tablets
TT	testimonia
trans.	translation
translit.	transliteration
Un	miscellaneous provisions tablets

V	lists without ideograms
VAT	Museum siglum of the Vorderasiatisches Museum, Berlin (Vorderasiatische Abteilung. Tontafeln)
Wu	sealings on nodules
YHSS	Yassıhöyük Stratigraphic Sequence

Notes on the text

There is much that the theorizing of Classical scholars can provide to Near Eastern scholars, and Classical scholars have not yet plumbed the depths of the material offered by Near Eastern texts. I intend this volume to serve as a research tool for students and scholars just moving into the field of comparative philology of the eastern Mediterranean area. Thus, I do not presume that readers are aware of the history of or current state of research on a particular question, or the controversies that I skim over in the main body of the text, and I make sure to provide the background scholarship throughout the notes. However, in order to reduce the size of the notes, I tend to refer to the most recent works and to works written in English.

When quoting Hittite texts in the original, Hittite is written in lower-case italics, words that were written in Akkadian (but presumably pronounced in Hittite) are transliterated into upper-case italics, and words written with Sumerian logograms (Sumerograms) are transliterated into upper case. Square brackets indicate where signs have been lost because of damage to the tablet, while partial square brackets indicate partially legible signs. Raised Sumerograms are determinatives, written before (sometimes after) a noun in the Hittite tablets, indicating its class (divinity, male, female, wooden, stone, etc.). They were not pronounced aloud. I transliterate ḫ as "h" and š as "sh," except when š is used in a Hittite and Hattic word, in which case I transliterate it as "s." The divine name *Išḫara* is thus spelled "Ishhara," king *Pitḫana* as "Pithana," and the town *Purušḫanda* "Purushanda." I follow conventional modern spellings with some widely recognized Near Eastern names, such as Alalakh. Similarly, I use Latinate spellings of commonly known Greek names. For texts from Hattusa, I cite column and line numbers. Single-column tablets are cited by obverse and reverse. The raised slash after numbers indicates that they occur after a break of indeterminate length; two raised slashes indicates the line numbering resumes after two breaks of indeterminate length, and so on. Different exemplars of the same text are distinguished by letters: A, B, C, etc.

For editions of Classical Greek texts, I refer to the editor's last name after the text citation, if there are questions of fragment numbering or editing the text. References to editions of Linear B texts can be found in *A Companion to Linear B: Mycenaean Greek Texts and their World, Vol. 1*, ed. Y. Duhoux and A. Morpurgo Davies (Leuven). I cite Hittite texts by their *CTH* number, but in practice the website Konkordanz der hethitischen Keilschrifttafeln (www.hethport.uni-wuerzburg.de/hetkonk/) is the proper source to find out more about a specific Hittite text, where they can be looked up by their *CTH* number, by their excavation number, or by their publication number. Although the *CTH* numbering groups texts by genres, readers who are not Hittitologists will not recognize the conventions. Thus, I take care to provide a title for each text. In addition, I refer specifically to the line numbers of fragments, rather than using the composite text line numbering often used in transliterations, because I feel it is important to respect variation that occurs between versions of a particular text. I then cite the transliteration (which may not cite the passage in the same way), and a specific translation if I do not translate the passage myself. This should make it easy to find the text citations, even if the reader does not know the language in question, although it adds to the bulk of the footnotes. Ugaritic texts from Ugarit are cited by their *KTU* number, but I also provide a concordance for the ritual texts with their excavation number. Texts from Ugarit in other languages are cited by their excavation number.

With regard to the terminology used to refer to groups of people, when I say "Anatolian," I mean people living in Anatolia, but not including Greek-speakers. I thus group together people speaking various languages, not necessarily related. "Anatolian languages," however, are a specific subgroup of Indo-European languages found in Anatolia. When I say "Greeks," I mean speakers of Greek, without intending to imply a sense of belonging to a national group. When I say "Mycenaean," I mean people participating in the culture we label Mycenaean, without intending to imply that they spoke Greek.

Finally, I provide two aids for those struggling with the many unfamiliar names: Table 1 is a synchronistic chart of the Bronze Age rulers referred to in the text, and Table 2 provides the correspondences among Near Eastern and Greek gods.

Table 1. *Bronze Age chronology: Greece and the Near East*

Greece (periods)[1]	Greece (pottery sequences)[2]		Cyprus[3]		Troy[4]		Miletus[5]		Arzawa[6]	Central Anatolia	
EBA 1	EH I	3000–2650			I	3000–2550					
EBA 2	EH II	2650–2250			II	2555–2300	II	3rd mill.		Anatolian EBA III **Alaca Höyük**[10] Royal Graves	2400–2100
					III	2300–2200					
EBA 3	EH III	2250–2100/2050	EC I–II	2250–2000							
					IV	2200–2000					
MBA	MH	2100/2050–1700									
	MH I										
			EC III – MC I–II	2000–1750/00	V	2000–1750	III	2000–1800		**Kanesh**[11] II	1970–1835
	MH II									Ib	1835–late 18th cent.
										Hurmeli	?–1790
										Inar	1790–1775

Bronze Age chronology

East Anatolia, North Syria, North Mesopotamia				Babylon		Assyria		Egypt
Ebla/Tell Mardikh[7]			**Urkesh[8]**					
IIa	3000–2400							
			āpi built	Gilgamesh of Uruk[9]	2600			
IIb1	2400–2300							
				Akkade				
				Sargon	2340–2285			
IIb2	2300–2000			Rimush	2284–2276			
			Tupkish	Manishtushu	2275–2261			
			Tishatal ?	Naram-Sin	2260–2224			
			Isharkinum	Sharkalisharri	2223–2199			
				(six more kings)	2198–2160			
				Gudea of Lagash	2130–2110/2115			
				Utu-hegal of Ur	2119–2113			
				Ur III				
				Ur-Namma	2112–2095			
				Shulgi	2094–2047			
				Amar-Sin	2046–2038			
				Shu-Sin	2037–2029			
				Ibbi-Sin	2028–2004	**Old Assyrian empire**		
						Puzur-Assur Ishalim-ahum	from 2025	
IIIa Ibbit-Lim	2000–1800					Ilushuma		
						Irishum I	1974–1935	
			Atalshen			Ikunum	1934–1921	
						Sargon I	1920–1881	
				1st Dynasty of Babylon	1894–1750	Puzur-Asur II	1880–1873	
						Naram-Sin	1872–?	
			Aleppo			Shamshi-Adad I	1833–1776	
		Mari						
		Yahdum-Lim	1815–1799	Sumu-Epuh	1810–1780			
IIIb	1800–1600	Yasmah-Addu	after 1798					
				Hammurapi	1792–1750			

Table 1. (cont.)

Greece (periods)[1]	Greece (pottery sequences)[2]		Cyprus[3]		Troy[4]		Miletus[5]		Arzawa[6]	Central Anatolia	
										Warsama	1775–1750
										Anumhirbi of Hassu	
	MH III				VIa	1750–1300	IV	1800–1450		Pithana of Kussara Anitta of Kussara	1750–1725
										Zuzu of Alahzina	1725–?
LBA 1	LH I	1700/1675–1635/00	MC III–LC I		VIb/c					**Hattusa**[13] **Labarna**	?–1650
										Hattusili I	1650–1620
	LH IIA	1635/00–1480/70			VId						
	Santorini eruption	ca.1642–1612								Mursili I	1620–1590
										Hantili I	1590–1560
										Zidanta I	1560–1525
										Ammuna Huzziya I	
										Telipinu	1525–1500
					VIe					Alluwamna	1500–1400
LBA 2	LH IIB	1480/70–1420/10									
										Tahurwaili Hantili II Zidanta II	
			LC IIA–IIC Early	1450–1300	VIf		V	1450–1315			
										Huzziya II Muwattalli I	
LBA 3	LH IIIA1	1420/10–1390/70			VIg						
	LH IIIA2 Attarisiya	1390/70–1330/15			VIh				Assuwa Confederation Kupanta-Kurunta of Arzawa Madduwatta Kupanta-Kurunta of Arzawa	Tudhaliya I/II	1400–1350
										Arnuwanda I	
										Hattusili II?	
									Tarhuntaradu of Arzawa	Tudhaliya III	

East Anatolia, North Syria, North Mesopotamia					Babylon		Assyria		Egypt	
	Mari Zimri-Lim	1776–1761	**Aleppo** Yarim-lim I	1780–1765						
			Hammurapi I	1765–1745	**Old Babylonian Kingdom**	1762–1675				
					Samsuiluna	1749–1712				
	Alalakh[12] VII Yarim-Lim I	1720–1670	Abba-AN I	1745–?	**2nd Dynasty of Babylon**					
			Yarim-Lim II	1710	Abi-eshuh	1711–1684				
	Ammiqatum	1670–1625	Niqmi-Epuh	1670						
			Irkabtum	1645	Ammisaduqa	1646–1626				
			Yarim-Lim III	1635						
			Mitanni	1630–1233	Samsuditana	1626–1595				
	Hammurapi									
	VI	16th cent.								
Kizzuwatna[14] Pariyawatri Ispudahsu										
									Thutmose I	1504–1492
	V	early 15th cent.							Thutmose II	1492–1479
					Kassites	1475–1155			Hashepshut	1479/73–1458/57
Eheya Paddatisu Pilliya	Idrimi	1490–1460	Parattarna I						Thutmose III	1479–1425
	IV	mid. 15th – 14th cent.	Parshatatar							
Talzu	Niqmepa	1460–?	Shaushtatar							
	Ilimilimma II?	1420	Parattarna II						Amenhotep II	1428–1397
Sunassura			Artatama I							
									Thutmose IV	1397–1388
					Kurigalzu I				Amenhotep III	1388–1351/0
			Shuttarna II		Kadashman-Enlil I	1374–1360				

Table 1. (cont.)

Greece (periods)[1]	Greece (pottery sequences)[2]	Cyprus[3]	Troy[4]	Miletus[5]	Arzawa[6]	Central Anatolia	
			Kukkunni			Suppiluliuma I	1350–1322
	LH III B 1330/15 –1200/ 1190						
						Arnuwanda II	1322–1321
					Uhhaziti of Arzawa Mashuiluwa of Mira Kupanta-Kurunta of Mira	Mursili II	1321–1295
		LC IIC Late T– IIIA 1300– 1125/00	VIIa 1300–1180	VI 1315–1200			
Tawagalawa			Alaksandu			Muwatalli II	1295–1272
				Atpa	Piyamaradu Masduri of Seha River Land	Mursili III Hattusili III	1272–1267 1267–1237
			Walmu		Alantalli of Mira Tarkasnawa of Mira Tarhunnaradu of Seha River Land	Tudhaliya IV	1237–1209

East Anatolia, North Syria, North Mesopotamia			Mitanni	Babylon		Assyria		Egypt	
			Artashshumara	Burna-Buriash II	1359–1333	**Middle Assyrian Kingdom**[15]	1353–1056		
	Carchemish[16]		Tushratta			Assur-uballit I	1353–1318		
	Sharrikushuh	ca. 1340						Amenhotep IV/Akhenaten	1351–1334
			Shattiwaza					Smenkhare	1337–1333
				Kurigalzu II	1332–1308			Tutankhamun	1333–1323
								Ay	1323–1319
								Haremhab	1319–1306 or 1319–1292
	Sahurma					Enlil-nerari	1317–1308		
				Nazimaruttash	1308–1282	Arik-den-ili	1307–1296	Ramses I	1306–1304 or 1292–1290
	Amurru					Adad-nerari I	1295–1264	Sethos I	1304–1290 or 1290–1279
	Benteshina								
	Shapili			Kadashman-Turgu	1282–1264			Ramses II	1290–1224 or 1279–1213
	Benteshina restored			Kadashman-Enlil II	1264–1255	Shalmaneser I	1263–1234		
				Kudur-Enlil	1255–1246				
				Shagarkti-Shuriash	1246–1233				
Tarhuntassa[17] Kurunta	Shawushkamuwa			Kashtiliash IV	1232–1225	Tukulti-Ninurta I	1233–1197		
			Ugarit Niqmaddu III		1215–1200			Merneptah	1224–1205 or 1213–1204/3

Table 1. (cont.)

Greece (periods)[1]	Greece (pottery sequences)[2]	Cyprus[3]	Troy[4]	Miletus[5]	Arzawa[6]	Central Anatolia
						Arnuwanda III 1209–1207
		Eshuwara				Suppiluliuma II 1207–?
LH IIIC	1200/ 1190– 1050		VIIb1 1180–1130	VII begins 1200		
		LC IIIB 1125/00– 1050	VIIb2 1130–1050			

[1] This chart follows the Aegean high chronology and the Near Eastern high middle chronology. Periodization of the Bronze Age is only given for Greece, as the classification varies for different parts of the Near East. The Aegean high chronology is based on radiocarbon dating of the Santorini eruption to sometime between 1642 and 1612 BCE (Manning and Kromer 2011). The Middle Bronze Age Near Eastern chronology comes from astronomical information, the *Kanesh Eponym Lists* best preserved in copies from Kanesh 1b (Barjamovic, Hertel, and Larsen 2012), the radiocarbon dating of wood from the Warsama palace at Kanesh (Barjamovic, Hertel, and Larsen 2012 : 28–35, with earlier refs.), and some synchronisms internal to the Near East, e.g., the death of Shamshi-Adad I in the eighteenth year of Hammurabi's reign and the destruction of Babylon, under the rule of Samsuditana, by Mursili I. The fall of Babylon is conventionally dated to 1595 BCE by the high middle chronology. Our current knowledge would also allow for the low middle chronology with dates for the key Middle Bronze Age events eight years later (fall of Babylon 1587 BCE). The choice between the high middle and low middle chronologies hinges on which eight-year Venus cycle one chooses to link to the "Year of the Golden Throne," the eighth year of Ammisaduqa of Babylon in the omen compendium *Enuma Anu Enlil*, Tablet 63, omen No. 10. See Nahm (2013) and T. de Jong (2012–2013), arguing for the low middle chronology, based on the mention of a solar eclipse in the year after the birth of Shamshi-Adad I in the *Mari Eponym Chronicle*, which T. de Jong associates with an eclipse he calculates to have occurred in 1838 BCE, Nahm to an eclipse of 1833, and atmospheric effects from the Santorini eruption that de Jong argues are alluded to in the Babylonian Venus observations for years 12 and 13 of Ammisaduqa, thus fixing the Santorini eruption at 1628/7 (T. de Jong and Foertmeyer 2010). The arguments of Nahm and de Jong are plausible, but I have chosen to adhere to the high middle chronology here because the eight-year difference does not impact any of the synchronisms between Greece and the Near East, and because the high middle chronology is well-known and will allow readers outside the field the ability to correlate the dates mentioned here with those that have been widely cited, while those who are well-versed in the chronological issues can adjust as necessary. Readers interested in the disputes about Middle Bronze Age chronology will find earlier references in T. de Jong (2012–2013) and Manning and Kromer (2011). If references are not given, dates come from *Brill's New Pauly*, Supplement 1: *Chronologies of the Ancient World: Names, Dates, and Dynasties* (ed. W. Eder and J. Renger, 2007). When kings' reigns are determined solely by a synchronism with another king, I normally do not give dates. I do not take into account the results of radiocarbon dating in the Egyptian dates, which suggest the dates are some twenty years too low (see Shortland and Bronk Ramsey 2013). Finally, I do not give entire dynasties, but focus on the kings who are mentioned in this volume.

[2] BA Greece dates from Manning (2010).
[3] Cyprus dates from Knapp (2013: 27, with earlier references).
[4] Troy dates from Jablonka and Rose (2011), Rose (2014); subdivisions and dates for Troy VI from Pavúk (2007).
[5] Miletus dates from Niemeier (2007a; 2009).
[6] Synchronisms from Bryce (2005) and Beckman, Bryce, and Cline (2011).
[7] Ebla dates from Matthiae (2008).
[8] Urkesh dates from Buccellati and Kelly-Buccellati (2009).
[9] Date based on synchronism with Enmebaragesi of Kish, a historical connection that George (2003: 103–4) makes clear should be taken with a grain of salt.
[10] Dating from Sagona and Zimansky (2009: 213–16).
[11] Kanesh dates from Barjamovic, Hertel, and Larsen (2012, esp. p. 4, fig. 13).
[12] Rough dates of Alalakh levels from Mullins (2010: 61–3).
[13] Hittite dates and reigns from Bryce (2005: xv), omitting Kurunta.
[14] Synchronisms with Hittite kings follow Bryce (2005).
[15] The Middle Assyrian Kingdom dates cited differ by ten years in the different recensions of the *Assyrian King List*. I use the later dates here, as they match the Hittite chronology better (synchronism between Suppiluliuma II and Tukulti-Ninurta I).
[16] Carchemish reigns from Bryce (2005; 2012: 84–6).
[17] Synchronisms with Hittite kings follow Bryce (2005), with rough approximation of Hartapu's reign based on Hawkins (2000: 429) and Bryce (2005: 352–3).
[18] Malatya reigns from Bryce (2012: 101–4).

East Anatolia, North Syria, North Mesopotamia	Carchemish	Ugarit			Babylon	Assyria		Egypt	
Hartapu, son of Mursili (III?)	Talmi-Teshshub		Ammurabi	1200–1180					
	Kuzi-Teshshub	early–mid 12th cent.	Malatya[18]					Ramses III	1188–1155 or 1183–1151
	Ir-Teshshub,	later 12th cent.	PUGNUS-mili Runtiya, Arnuwanti I,						
	Ini-Teshshub I	late 12th–early 11th cent.	PUGNUS-mili II			Tiglath-Pileser I	1115–1076		

Table 2. *Equations among Near Eastern and Greek gods*

Type	Sumerian	Akkadian	West Semitic/ Syrian	Hurrian	Hittite	Luwian	Hattic	Greek
Sun-god	Utu	Shamash	Shapash (goddess)	Shimige	Istanu	Tiwaz	Estan (goddess)	Helios
Storm-god	Ishkur	Adad	Dagan (Ebla) Hadad/Addu Baal ('lord')	Teshshub	Tarhun	Tarhunt	Taru	Zeus
Sea-god	(a.ab.ba)	Tiamat	Yam	Kiashe	Aruna			Poseidon
Moon-god	Nanna	Sin	Yarih	Kushuh	Arma	Arma		Selene (goddess)
Chthonic god of agriculture	Dumuzi	Dagan	Dagan	Kumarbi	Halki (goddess)		Telipinu	Demeter (goddess)
Father/grandfather god	Enlil	El	El	Kumarbi				Cronus
	Enki	Ea						
Underworld goddess	Ereshkigal	Allatum		Allani	Lelwani Sun-goddess of the Earth Sun-goddess of Arinna		Sun-goddess of Arinna (Wurusemu)	

Goddess (of sexuality)	Inanna	Ishtar	Ishhara Ashtarte Asherah	Shawushka	Anzili	Aphrodite
Former Gods	Anunnaki (among the Hittites)			*am(m)ate= na en=na*	*karūiliēš šiuneš tatinzi maššaninzi*	Titans
Plague/war god	Nergal	Erra	Mot (death) Reshep (plague god)		Sandas Iyarri	
Tutelary deity					LAMMA (a class of gods, not a specific god) Appaluwa	Kurunta/ Runtiya	Apollo
Mother/ grandmother goddess	Ninhursag				DINGIR.MAḪ 'the Great Goddess' Hannahanna DINGIR.MAḪMEŠ 'the Great Goddesses' group includes Anzili	Demeter
Mountain Kel Dağ (Turkish) Ğebel al-Aqra (Syrian)			Sapon	Hazzi		Casius
Snake monster	Asag	*bashmu*	Tunman	Hedammu	Illuyanka	Typhon Python

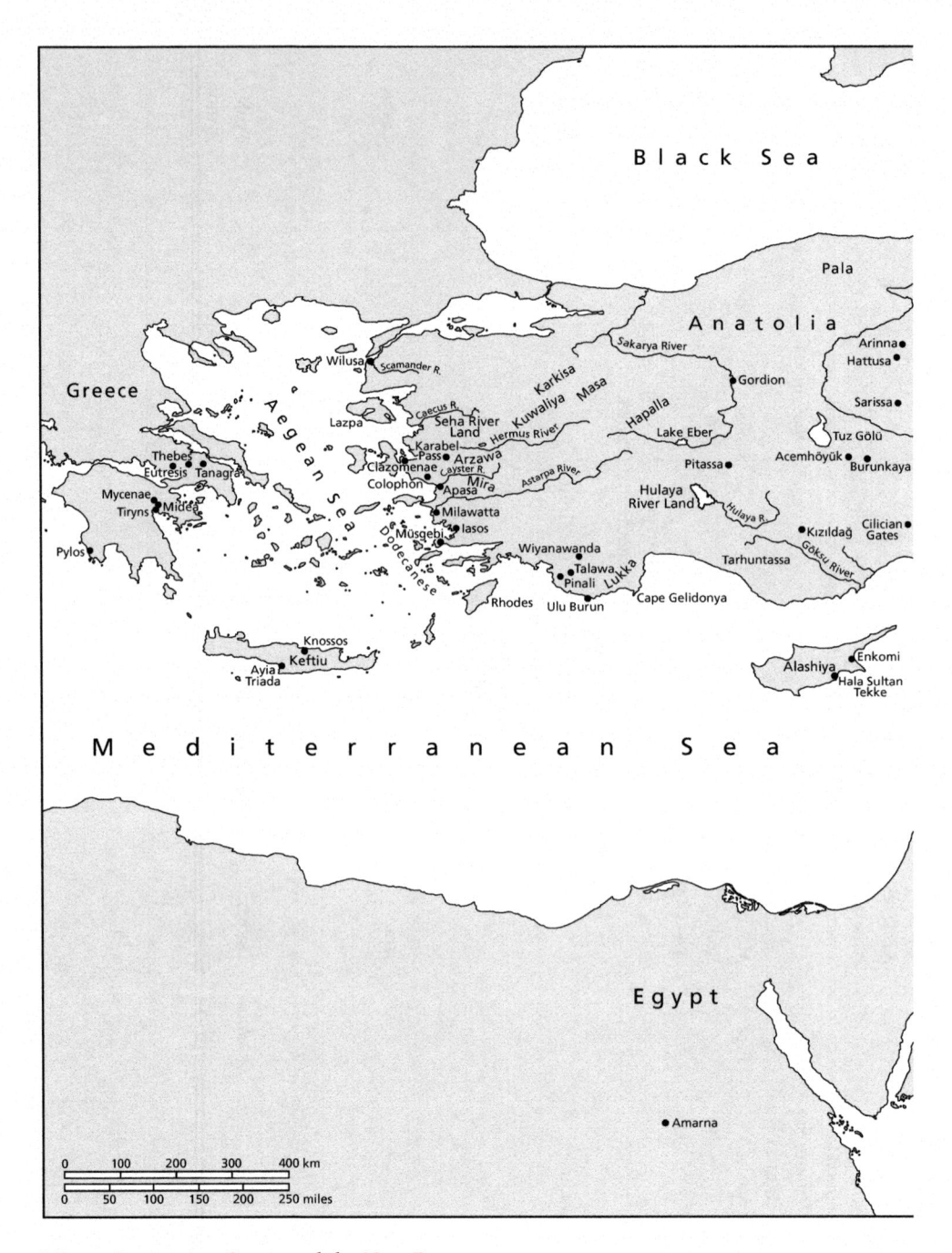

Map 1: Bronze Age Greece and the Near East

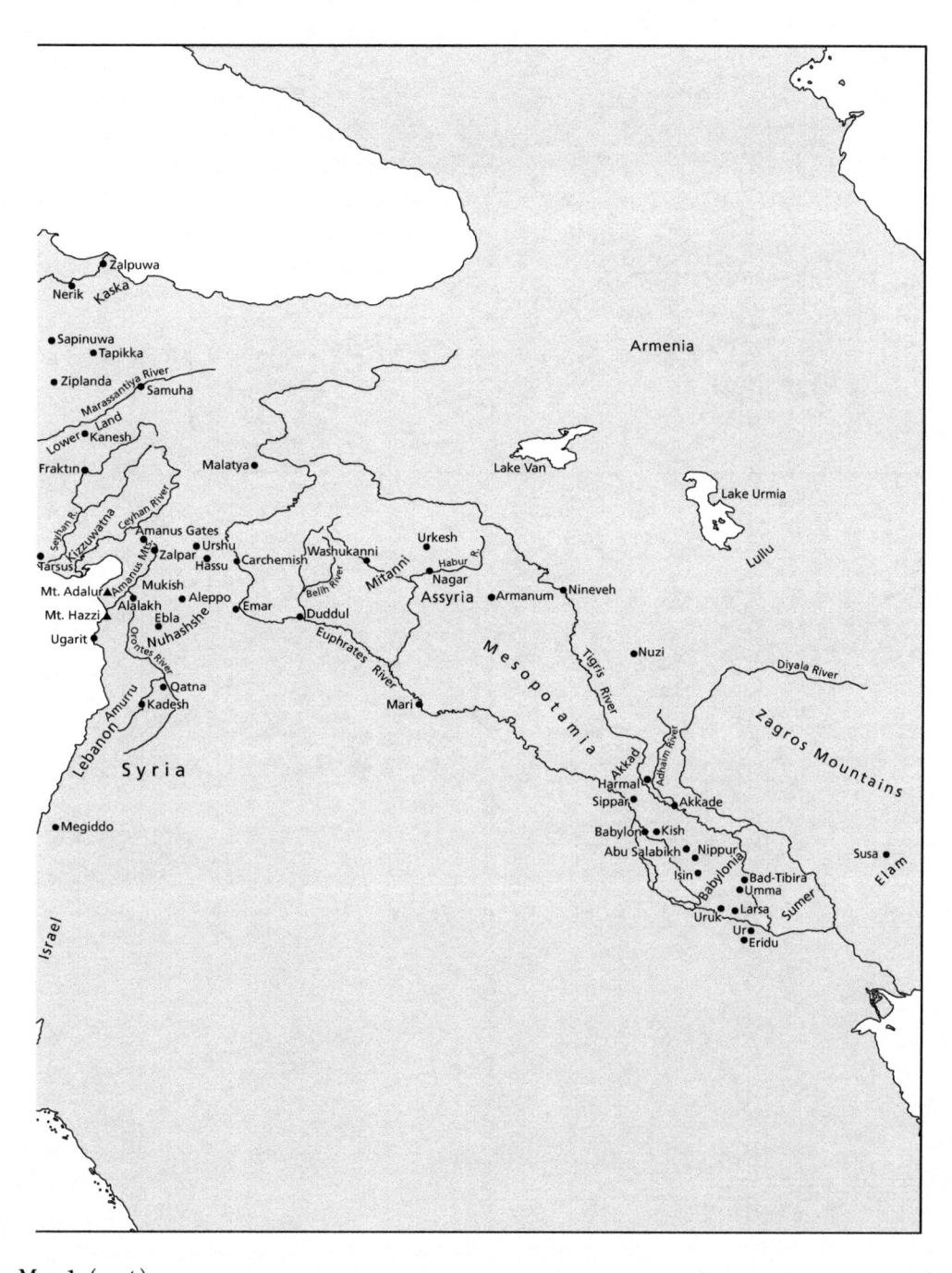

Map 1: (*cont.*)

Map 2: Early Iron Age Greece and Anatolia

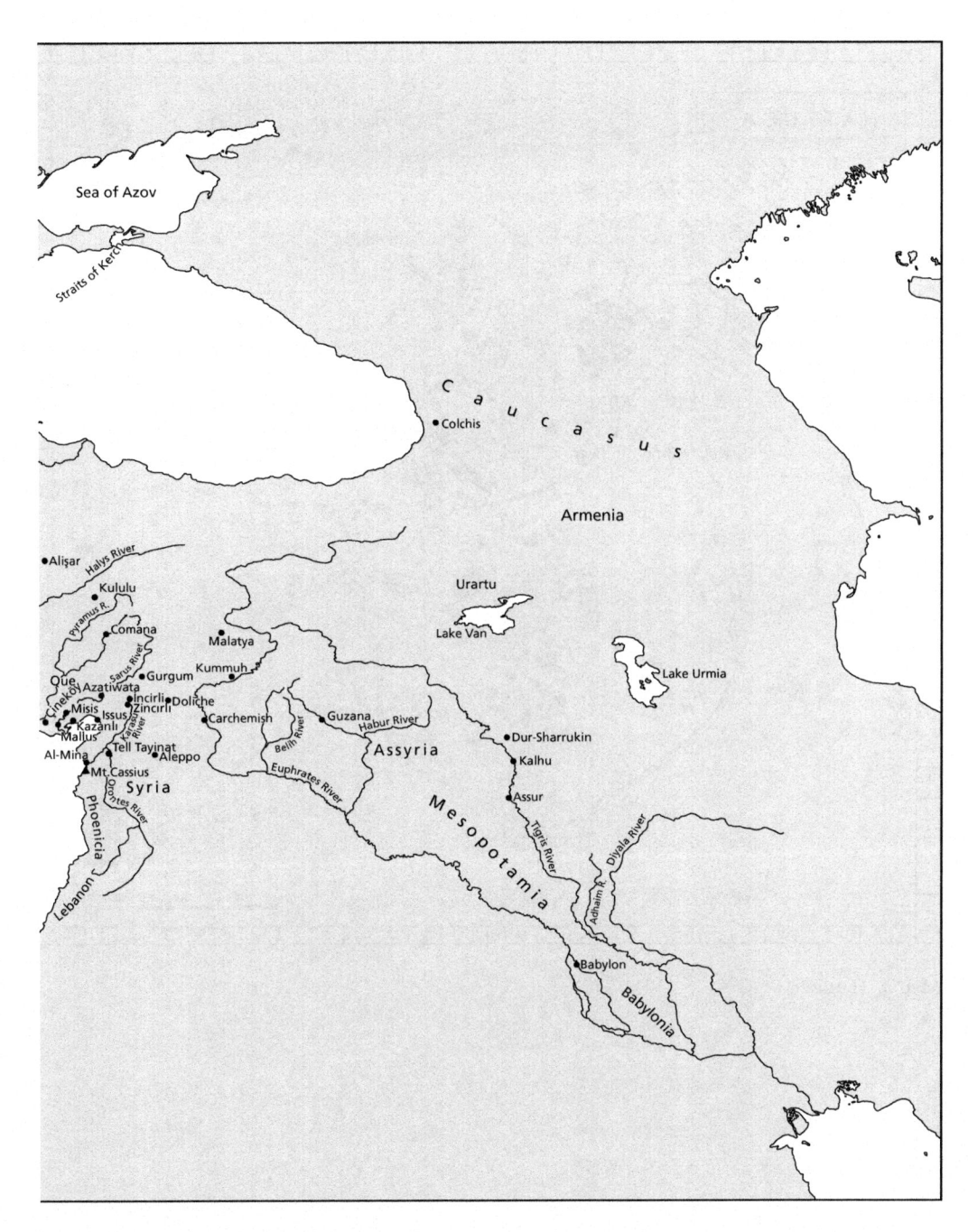

Map 2: (*cont.*)

Map 3: Hattusa

He saw the secret and uncovered the hidden,
> he brought back a message from the antediluvian age.

He came a distant road and was weary but granted rest,
> [he] set down on a stele all (his) labours.

He built the wall of Uruk-the-Sheepfold
...

See its wall which is like a *strand of wool*,
> view its parapet which nobody can replicate!
...

Go up on to the wall of Uruk and walk around,
> survey the foundation platform, inspect the brickwork!
...

[*Find*] the tablet-box of cedar,
> [*release*] its clasps of bronze!

[*Open*] the lid of its secret,
> [*lift*] *up* the tablet of lapis lazuli and read out
> all the misfortunes, all that Gilgameš went through!
>> Standard Babylonian *Epic of Gilgamesh* I 7–28
>> (trans. George 2003: 539)

1 | Introduction

Status quaestionis

Scholars of the ancient world have long since recognized that the Akkadian *Epic of Gilgamesh* has striking parallels with Homer's *Iliad* and *Odyssey*. But, how could Greek poets have learned of the legendary deeds of the third-millennium Mesopotamian king? And, why were the Greeks interested in a story like his or in any of the other Near Eastern stories that have been shown to have influenced the poetry of Homer and Hesiod? In this book I present an entirely new approach to the first question by focusing on the second one, and I look for answers in Anatolia and Cyprus, where Greeks were in intense contact with Near Eastern cultures for hundreds of years before Homer's time, rather than in Mesopotamia, with which they had no direct contact. I rely primarily on the information provided by the tablets found in the libraries of the second-millennium Hittites, whose capital Hattusa was located in central Anatolia. Here the stories of Gilgamesh's deeds have been found in three different languages, along with narratives of how the gods established the current world order, and stories of the Akkadian conqueror Sargon the Great's voyages into the unknown and of his grandson Naram-Sin's failings, all of which I shall argue played a role in shaping the Greek tradition of epic.

All our knowledge of the ancient literature that influenced Greek epic is preserved for us by scribes, but the world of the Late Bronze Age and Early Iron Age Greeks was an oral one, and the Hittite libraries are an unusually good source of oral-derived literature, allowing us to reconstruct in part the Near Eastern oral traditions to which the Greeks had access. In fact, bilingual Syro-Anatolian oral poets must have been the key means for the transfer of the art of Near Eastern narrative song to the Greeks, and in showing that I arrive at a new model for cross-cultural interaction in the eastern Mediterranean in the Late Bronze Age and Early Iron Age.

Near Eastern influences on Greek literary and cult practices have become a popular topic for Classical scholars in the last decades; this interest has been driven in large part by the work of Walter Burkert and Martin L. West. Burkert's *Orientalizing Revolution* (1992, a revised version of the book originally published in German in 1984) popularized the avenue of inquiry among Classicists of this era, and West's *The East Face of Helicon* (1997a) crowned decades of his publications on the subject,[1] presenting a vast number of striking verbal and thematic correspondences between Near Eastern, especially Semitic, texts and Greek texts. In addition, Sarah Morris (1992a) has discussed the relationship between Greek and west Semitic art, material culture, and poetry from an archaeologist's perspective. However, relatively few scholars interested in the interactions between Greece and the Near East have focused on Anatolian influence on Greek culture, despite evidence of intensive contact between Greek-speakers and Anatolians beginning in the Late Bronze Age and continuing into and beyond the Classical era.[2] When Classicists have paid attention to Bronze Age Anatolia, their interest is motivated by a long-standing fascination with the Trojan War and the ever-intriguing question of whether the events described by Homer in the *Iliad* have any basis in fact.

When in 1924 Emil Forrer realized that men of Ahhiyawa (cf. the Homeric Achaeans) were mentioned in the Hittite tablets, and Paul Kretschmer connected Alexander (Paris) of Ilium to the king Alaksandu of Wilusa with whom the thirteen-century New Hittite king Muwattalli made a treaty, some embraced the news enthusiastically as evidence for the historicity of the Homeric tradition.[3] However, opinion soon turned against using Hittite texts to understand the *Iliad*, in part because of the vehement objections of the Hittite scholar Ferdinand Sommer and in part because of legitimate skepticism towards somewhat naïve attempts to find the "kernel of truth" in the story of the Trojan War.[4] As it became more acceptable to see Semitic culture as an important influence on the Greeks, the Hittites received even less attention from Classicists, victims of a backlash against the glorification of Indo-European culture.[5] Thus, scholars divided themselves into two camps, with those who supported using Hittite texts to understand Greek culture finding themselves in the

---

[1] Including his editions of Hesiod's *Theogony* (1966) and *Works and Days* (1978), and his *Greek Philosophy and the Orient* (1971a).

[2] S. P. Morris (2001a; 2001b) has been the exception, turning her attention to Anatolia as a key place of contact. Burkert (2004) is still focused on the Neo-Assyrian period and directly afterwards. Lane Fox (2009) focuses on mercantile connections between Euboea and north Syria in the same period.

[3] Forrer (1924a; 1924b), Kretschmer (1924). For a synopsis of the early discussion see Beckman, Bryce, and Cline (2011: 1–3).

[4] Sommer (1932; 1934). Looking for the kernel of truth: Page (1959).

[5] Burkert (1992: 1–8) presents a balanced discussion of the history of the changing attitudes of Classical scholars towards the contribution of the Near East.

minority while the majority looked to texts in Akkadian, Ugaritic, and Hebrew to elucidate the prehistory of the Greek literary tradition, focusing especially on that part of the Neo-Assyrian period which corresponds to the Greek Orientalizing era, narrowly defined as 750–650 BCE.[6] In this framework the numerous correspondences between Semitic and Greek poetic phrases, myths, and religious practices are typically explained as the result of direct borrowing.[7] The minority who advocate looking to Anatolia as an important site for transfer of Near Eastern culture to Greek-speakers have generally been Hittitologists, Anatolian archaeologists, or Indo-Europeanists, such as G. Huxley, Hans Güterbock, Jaan Puhvel, and Calvert Watkins.[8]

Furthermore, until the late 1990s knowledge of Anatolian political geography was not detailed enough to withstand the attacks of dissenters who argued against the equations of Ahhiyawa with Mycenaean Greeks, and Wilusa with Ilium. Their objections, however, have since been invalidated by new archaeological finds and the decipherment of key Hieroglyphic Luwian inscriptions.[9] Armed with the Hittite administrative documents and our current understanding of the Linear B texts and Mycenaean civilization, the Homerist Joachim Latacz has re-opened the question of whether the Homeric tradition preserves a memory of an historical event in the Late Bronze Age that was immortalized in song by Mycenaean bards, to which he answers a resounding "yes."[10] I myself am much less sanguine about the possibility of genuine memories of Bronze Age events. In this book I focus primarily on epic traditions, that is, traditional storylines in which legends about the past meant to explain the present were cast. That is, I am more interested in ancient historiography (if we can use this term for orally transmitted stories) than ancient historical events.

Indeed, the libraries and archives at the Hittite capital of Hattusa, modern-day Boğazköy, have much more to offer to Classicists interested in the prehistory of Greek culture than new leads on the possible historical

---

[6] Burkert (1992: 5). S. P. Morris (1992a: 101–49), on the other hand, considers that the term "Orientalizing" applies already in the Mycenaean period through the Dark Age, into the Archaic period.
[7] The position is defended by M. L. West (1988: 169–70; 1997a: 587, 625–30), but he is open to formative contact with speakers of Luwian and Hurrian (M. L. West 1997a: 589).
[8] Huxley (1960), Güterbock (1983a; 1984; 1986; 1992), Puhvel (1983; 1988a; 1988b; 1991; 1992; 1993), Watkins (1970; 1986; 1995: 135–51, 277–91, 448–59; 1998; 2000a; 2000b; 2008).
[9] I choose not to re-engage the question of whether Wilusa is Troy, because I consider it closed. See Bryce (2005; 2006, esp. pp. 77–86) on the political geography of western Anatolia.
[10] Latacz (2004). The latest German edition is Latacz (2005).

events behind Homer's Trojan War, interesting as that question may be. Cuneiform documents in seven different languages provide a unique window into a Late Bronze Age Mediterranean culture created from early Proto-Indo-European concepts, indigenous Anatolian practices, Mesopotamian learning, and west Semitic and Hurrian traits. We can compare different forms of the same stories and ritual activities passing through different avenues, via oral or written transmission, and through the mediation of different peoples, speaking Luwian, Hurrian, west Semitic, or Akkadian. The models we derive from the Hittite data can then be applied to Greek materials, to elucidate exactly how Near Eastern and indigenous motifs and narrative patterns could have been adopted and adapted by Greek-speakers. Thus, the Hittite material is an unparalleled resource for any scholar interested in cultural contact in the ancient world.

Furthermore, the numerous correspondences between Hittite and Greek ritual and literary themes and motifs indicate that Anatolia must have been an important channel by which the literary and religious traditions of the wider Near East reached the Greeks, whether in the Mycenaean period, the Early Iron Age, or later. In some cases the texts from the Hittite archives present interpretations of themes or put together motifs in ways that stand midway between the Greek and Mesopotamian traditions.

Finally, Hurro-Hittite narrative poetry, attested almost exclusively in the Hittite archives and one of the main focuses of this book, presents a precious witness for the prehistory of the Homeric tradition.

I am interested not only in the content of the texts, but also in how the correspondences between the two sets of texts came into being – how Greeks came into contact with Near Eastern epic, why Greeks were interested in it, and the means by which the narratives were converted into Greek narratives. Therefore, in this book, I present both the texts that were found in the Hittite libraries and their context: their function, the gods to whom they were attached, the values they espoused, the milieus in which they were performed, and how they moved around and were adapted to new audiences. I have focused on several key factors: the value placed on exotic objects and knowledge from far away and long ago, the desire of local courts and polities to connect themselves to world history, the transfer and syncretism of gods, the opportunity for contact among proficient performers afforded by festivals and other public displays, and the role of healing rituals and royal ancestor veneration. All of these can be subsumed under one rubric: legitimization of authority. Throughout I apply my findings on the second-millennium material to analyze the prehistory of Homer's epics, showing how each factor worked synergistically with the others to promote the transfer of epic narratives from east to west, first to the Hittites and then eventually to the Greeks.

The evidence I analyze in this book for the most part is not meant to invalidate earlier discussions of east–west interaction, only to add more pieces to the puzzle, although I would emphasize the following: my focus is on oral transmission of Near Eastern motifs rather than transmission via writing; I do not believe that the Orientalizing period as defined by Burkert was the most important period of Near Eastern influence on Homeric poetry; and I am skeptical of direct contact between Assyrians and Greeks as a crucial vector of transmission of Mesopotamian literature, as opposed to a more indirect route that passed plots and motifs from Akkadian through the Hurrian, west Semitic, non-Greek language(s) of Cyprus, and/or Anatolian languages before they reached Greek-speakers.

Finally, a methodological note: although the ultimate end point of my investigation is the time of Homer and Hesiod, I am often forced to use evidence from later periods because of the large gap in the data between *ca.* 1175 and 700 BCE. Many of my conclusions rely on the assumption that if conditions or features were present both in the Late Bronze Age and in the Early Iron Age, then they can be surmised to be survivals from the Bronze Age and operating during the gap between the end of the Bronze Age and the beginning of documentation again in the Iron Age, even though the gap extended across several centuries.

The world of the Hittites

I begin with some background information about the Hittites. Speakers of the Anatolian branch of the Indo-European language family, they entered Anatolia some time in the third millennium BCE, probably from the west.[11] In the second millennium we see two major Anatolian languages: Luwian and Hittite. Luwian-speakers appear to be concentrated in the west and south, and Hittite-speakers were concentrated around the Old Assyrian merchant colony of Kanesh (Hittite Nesa, modern Kültepe), the city after which the Hittites named their own language *nešili*, and they extended east

---

[11] Steiner (1990), *pace* Stefanini (2002). For more details on Hittite civilization, consult especially Bryce (2002; 2005), Collins (2007b), Klengel *et al.* (1999), and the relevant articles in Sasson (1995). For a well-illustrated introduction to the site of Hattusa see Seeher (2002). For a grammar of Hittite, see Hoffner and Melchert (2008).

to the upper Euphrates.[12] The Hittites first enter world history in the form of names found in the Akkadian records from Level 11 of Kanesh, which was destroyed *ca.* 1835 BCE.[13] They re-appear in the archives of their capital Hattusa, modern-day Boğazköy, located in central Anatolia in the bend of the Kızıl Irmak River. Originally the site of an Assyrian merchant colony, Hattusa had been razed by Anitta of Kussara, the first Hittite king to leave a record of his achievements; but, some seventy years after Anitta's reign, *ca.* 1650 BCE, Hattusili I seized power and set up the city anew. The Hittites became players in the international zero-sum competition for wealth, prestige, and power when king Hattusili I began to assert Hittite hegemony in north Syria as far as Aleppo, and then across the Euphrates, eventually all the way to Babylon, which was sacked by his grandson and adopted son Mursili I in 1595 BCE (according to the "high middle chronology").[14] The Old Kingdom lasted about 150 years, after which Hittite power and resources were reduced by intradynastic strife and the pressure of population groups to the north and east, especially the Kaska (whose linguistic affiliations are unknown), and the Hurrians.

Hittite hegemony expanded anew *ca.* 1400 BCE under the first New Kingdom ruler, king Tudhaliya I/II,[15] moving east and south as the Hittites spread their control to Kizzuwatna (Plain Cilicia). Tudhaliya also turned to the west, where he took on the Assuwa confederation and scuffled with the "men of Ahhiyawa." The Middle Hittite period, which refers to a stage of the Hittite language, starts a generation later with Arnuwanda I.[16]

The Hurrian Mitanni confederation or empire in northeast Syria was terminated by king Suppiluliuma I (1350–1322 BCE), whose reign marks the beginning of the linguistic period called New Hittite. However, western Anatolia proved to be perennially troublesome, despite the break-up of the large Arzawan state by Suppiluliuma's son Mursili II into three or four smaller states interlinked with each other and with the Hittite royal family through dynastic marriages.

By 1300 BCE the north Syrian lands of Carchemish, Aleppo, Emar, Amurru, and Ugarit were under Hittite control and interlinked through royal marriages, some more closely than others. Cyprus had been pulled into

---

[12] Singer (1981).
[13] For a clear overview of the history of Kanesh, see Barjamovic, Hertel, and Larsen (2012: 43–52).
[14] For the high middle chronology, see the notes to the Bronze Age chronological chart included in this volume (Table 1).
[15] It remains uncertain whether the well-known king Tudhaliya was the first or second of his name to reign in the second half of the fifteenth century. See Bryce (2005: 122–3).
[16] Melchert (2007).

the Hittite orbit, and the Hittite empire considered itself to be on par with Assyria and Egypt, Muwattalli II, son of Mursili II, defeating Ramses II at the battle of Kadesh in 1274 BCE. Muwattalli experimented with transplanting the Hittite capital to Tarhuntassa, strategically located on the coast in Rough Cilicia, but his brother Hattusili III soon returned it to Hattusa.

Hittite power reached its peak under Hattusili III, although it began to decline almost immediately under his son and successor Tudhaliya IV, who undertook a major building spree continued by his son Suppiluliuma II, renovating the capital extensively. The Hittite empire fell *ca.* 1180 BCE, perhaps in part because of the internal strife which had consistently plagued the royal family throughout its history, and in part for whatever causes left other famous east Mediterranean empires and cities vulnerable to the so-called Sea Peoples.[17] But, the capital was vacated peacefully and deliberately by Hittite officials,[18] some people continued to live there, and it was eventually settled by the Phrygians. Hittite traditions survived at least to some degree in the Neo-Hittite states of southeast Anatolia and northwest Syria, such as Adana, Tabal, Hilakku, Que, Kummuh and Karatepe, Carchemish, Malatya, and Sam'al; these are the Hittites of the Hebrew Bible. *Ca.* 700 BCE the Neo-Hittite states (Hatti) were finally subsumed into the Assyrian empire.[19]

The primary site in which Hittite texts are found is Hattusa, which contained several archives and libraries, the most notable of which are the storerooms near Temple 1, the Haus am Hang, and archives A, E, and K in the citadel Büyükkale (Map 3).[20] Three other spots in east-central Anatolia have provided a number of Hittite texts: Ortaköy (Hittite Sapinuwa), Maşat (Tapikka), and Kuşaklı (Sarissa).[21] A small number of tablets in Hittite, letters or ritual and literary texts, have also been found in north Syria (Emar and Ugarit) and Egypt (Amarna).

The majority of the texts found in the various archives of Hattusa are New Hittite (1320–1190 BCE), with some Middle Hittite (1400–1320 BCE),

---

[17] On whom see Chapter 12, 314–15.   [18] Seeher (2001).
[19] On continuity in north Syria leading into the Iron Age, see Bryce (2012) and the discussions of the historical contexts of each set of inscriptions edited in Hawkins (2000); also Chapter 12 of this book. On the Neo-Hittites as the Hittites of the Hebrew Bible, see Bryce (2012: 64–75) and Collins (2007a; 2007b).
[20] See Seeher (2002) for a description of the various sites in which tablets were found. Van den Hout (2002a; 2006; 2009b) discusses the text collections and what they can tell us about Hittite administration and the organization of the archives.
[21] A few texts dating to the Middle Hittite period have also been found at Kayalıpınar (Samuha) (Rieken 2009), and two Late New Hittite texts have been found at Oymaağaç, which has been supposed to be ancient Nerik (Czichon 2008; Czichon *et al.* 2011: 213, 219).

and fewer Old Hittite (1650–1400 BCE) texts, while the texts from Sapinuwa and Tapikka are Middle Hittite, and those from Sarissa are Late New Hittite. It must be emphasized that the terms Old, Middle, and New Hittite refer to linguistic features in the texts and are not tied to cultural or political developments.[22] Paleographically Hittite texts have been divided into Old, Middle, and New Script, based on sign forms and overall ductus: how close together the signs are written, how much the signs are slanted, and how close to the edges of the column the lines begin and end.[23] Since many texts are copies of older ones, texts can show Old Hittite grammatical forms with New Script paleography; very few texts show Old Script ductus. It has been recently suggested that the distinction between Old Script and Middle Script is not as sharp as once thought; if Old Script is merged with Middle Script and only securely datable texts are taken into consideration, Hittite texts in the Hittite style of cuneiform writing are first clearly attested no earlier than 1500 BCE.[24]

The specific details of how the Hittites learned how to write on clay tablets in the Mesopotamian cuneiform script are still unclear. We do know of Akkadian scribes in Hattusa who taught their sons how to write,[25] but how men like them got there is a subject of speculation. It has been suggested that scribes who were brought back from the campaigns of Hattusili I in northern Syria introduced cuneiform to Hattusa.[26] Certainly the Old Assyrian script standard for the texts found at Kanesh is not the precursor of the Hittite Old Script. Hittite cuneiform resembles most closely the north Syrian variant of Old Babylonian script, suggesting that the script was already being used in Anatolia before Hattusili I.[27] Finally, we now know that there were already scribes in the court of Hattusili I who knew how to write in Akkadian before he had completed his campaigns in north Syria, as shown by the *Tikunani Letter* addressed to Tunip-Teshshub and written in vivid Akkadian, which was probably sent by Hattusili

---

[22] Furthermore, Middle Hittite should be considered a transition stage between Old and New Hittite rather than an independent stage unto itself (Melchert 2007).

[23] Van den Hout (2009b: 73).

[24] Van den Hout (2009a; 2009b, with earlier references) and Wilhelm (2010a). The final word on this debate has not been spoken. See Archi (2010) for a dissenting view.

[25] Beckman (1983b). [26] Rüster and Neu (1989: 15, with earlier references).

[27] Klinger (1998), who also notes that classic Akkadian texts and learning only appear in abundance in the Middle Hittite period. The Hittite script is most similar to the script of Alalakh VII (17th cent. BCE, van den Hout 2009b: 87, with earlier references). The redactional history of texts earlier than Hattusili I, such as *CTH* 1: *Proclamation of Anitta* (trans. H. A. Hoffner, Jr. in Hallo and Younger 1997: 182–4), is still unexplained. On the prehistory of the text and Kültepe Ib (1835 to late 18th cent. BCE) as the seat of Anitta, see Bryce (2005: 35–7).

I shortly before he destroyed Hassu in his campaigns into north Syria.[28] Certainly, Akkadian texts at Hattusa were written in more than one ductus, which do not necessarily correspond with the contemporaneous Hittite ductus, indicating that they were written by scribes who came from different scholastic traditions, and were not necessarily trained at Hattusa.[29]

Hattusa (in Akkadian *Ḫatti*) was a multilingual, multicultural site. Hittite, the language most frequently used in the texts, was an Indo-European language, but the Anatolian branch to which it belongs diverges markedly from other Indo-European languages, showing that it separated off quite early from the rest of the family. Hittite was used to record ritual and religious texts such as purification rituals, descriptions of festivals, prayers, vows, omens, and oracular responses, as well as instruction texts, letters, treaties, annals, law collections, and other administrative texts, and finally myths and other narratives – what we would call literature.[30] The other Indo-European Anatolian languages attested at Hattusa are Luwian and Palaic, the latter relatively closely related to Hittite, associated with northeast Anatolia (Paphlagonia), and recorded only in a few ritual texts.[31] Some non-Anatolian language texts are found at Hattusa. There are some Sumerian texts, mostly scholastic in nature, while Akkadian was used for international correspondence and treaties, as well as prayers, medical texts, omen compendia, and other types of learned texts, including classic stories of Gilgamesh, the gods, and Akkadian heroes such as Sargon the Great and his grandson Naram-Sin. The substrate language Hattic (*ḫattili* in Hittite, tentatively linked to northwest Caucasian languages) appears in a few ritual and omen texts,[32] and Hurrian, a language related to Urartian and possibly linked to northeast Caucasian languages,[33] was also used in rituals, omen texts, and in a genre of narrative song that shares striking parallels with Greek hexametric poetry and is a major focus of this book.

Hurrian is otherwise found in the *Mitanni Letter* sent by king Tushratta to Pharaoh Amenhotep III at Amarna in Egypt (*ca.* 1388–1351/0 BCE), and

---

[28] The *Tikunani Letter* (*CTH* 187: *Fragmentary Royal Letters*) is published, edited, and translated by Salvini (1994). The implications are noted by Devecchi (2005: 25).
[29] Klinger (2003).
[30] The fullest collection of translations of Hittite texts is in the German series *Texte aus der Umwelt des Alten Testaments*, general editors R. Borger *et al.* (*TUAT*); Haas (2006) is a collection of the Hittite texts that have literary qualities. One useful source in English is *The Context of Scripture*, edited by W. W. Hallo and K. L. Younger (1997, 2000, 2002).
[31] On Palaic see H. C. Melchert in Woodard (2004: 585–90).
[32] On Hattic see Klinger (2007), Schuster (1974; 2002), and Soysal (2004a).
[33] On Hurrian see Wegner (2007).

at a few other sites, such as Nuzi, Mari, Urkesh (Tell Mozan), and Ugarit, but it is best attested at Hattusa. Hurrian names first appear in the record around 2300 BCE and references to Hurrians and documents in Hurrian become more frequent over the course of the first half of the second millennium. Their primary area of settlement was northern Iraq (Subartu), western Iran, and southeast Turkey into north Syria. Urkesh at the upper reaches of the Habur River was an important Hurrian city in the Ur III period (end of third millennium BCE), and at that point the Hurrians controlled Nineveh. In the seventeenth century they are well attested at Alalakh VII in north Syria, and by the sixteenth century various polities appear to be working as a larger confederation – if not empire – called Mitanni, the upper echelons of which were intermixed with Indo-Iranians. The site of its most important city Washukanni has not yet been confirmed, but it may be Tell el Fakhariya.[34] As Hattusili I expanded his empire east, he came into conflict with the Hurrians, but in the end they proved to be important intermediaries of Mesopotamian traditions and north Syrian practices for the Hittites, although influence from both cultures had already reached Anatolia by the Old Assyrian period (ca. 1970 BCE) through the network of Assyrian merchant colonies, especially Kanesh. We have evidence that some Hittite royalty and high officials in the Middle Hittite period spoke Hurrian; for example, the priest Kantuzzili is the author of an invocation of Teshshub and Hebat in Hurrian.[35] This is the period in which strong Hurrian influence on Hittite religious and magical practices becomes evident, a development that is to be connected in large part with the annexation into the Hittite empire of the Cilician state of Kizzuwatna, whose cult center was Kummani, mother city of the Classical Comana, where Luwians and Hurrians had blended to form a characteristic southeastern Anatolian culture as the Mitanni hegemony faded away.[36] And, by 1375 BCE at the latest, Hittite kings could bear two names, one Hittite and one Hurrian,[37] an acknowledgment of the mix of ethnicities in the royal line.

---

[34] On the Hurrians see Kuhrt (1995: 283–300), Wilhelm (1989; 1996), and the articles collected in Buccellati and Kelly-Buccellati (1998). On Mitanni see the comments of von Dassow (2008: 68–90).

[35] *Hurrian Ritual for the Royal Couple*: CTH 784 = KUB 27.42 (translit. Haas 1984: 113–19, No. 11), see Singer (2002b: 30).

[36] Trémouille (2000) provides an excellent overview of Hurrian myth and ritual as attested in Hittite texts. See Beal (1986) and Desideri and Jasink (1990: 51–109) on the history of Kizzuwatna. On Comana, see Lebrun (2001), equating with Kummani, and Trémouille (2001: 65–6). See Bryce (2003a: 88–9) on the mixing of Luwians and Hurrians in Kizzuwatna.

[37] E.g., Tashmi-Sharri = Tudhaliya III, see Bryce (2005: 430 n. 91).

Luwian, the other well-attested Anatolian language besides Hittite, appears not only in cuneiform texts, but also – in a slightly different dialect – inscribed on stone in an unrelated writing system. This Hieroglyphic Luwian script (also called Anatolian hieroglyphs), which bears some formal resemblance to Aegean scripts such as Cretan Hieroglyphic,[38] seems primarily to have been used to write on waxed wooden tablets, all of course lost to us, for daily economic records and possibly personal correspondences.[39] It first appears on seals.[40] Hieroglyphic inscriptions become more common in the Late New Hittite period and continue to 700 BC in southeastern Anatolia and northern Syria.[41] Hieroglyphic Luwian is therefore the only Anatolian language attested before, during, and after the Greek Dark Ages. Of the first-millennium languages, Lycian A is closely related to Luwian, Carian is a less closely related Luwic language, and Lycian B (Milyan) shares features of both Lycian A and Carian.[42] Lydian probably represents a distinct branch in the Anatolian family, while Pisidian and Sidetic are at least Anatolian languages, although their exiguous remains leave their relationship to the other branches unclear.[43]

Because the center of Hittite territory was central and eastern Anatolia, while Lydian, Luwian, and the Luwic languages were spoken in western Anatolia and along the Anatolian coast,[44] the speakers of the latter languages were the ones most likely to be in direct contact with

---

[38] Hawkins (1986: 374).

[39] Waal (2011). On wooden writing boards, see Chapter 16, 424, n. 19.

[40] See Bryce (2005: 125–6), Hawkins (1997). An inscription on a silver bowl refers to an event from the Old Kingdom, but see Chapter 13, 347–8, on the bowl. Also note that a Syrian cylinder seal has turned up in Level Ib of Kanesh, with three hieroglyphic Luwian signs carved on it (Collon 1987: 57, No. 233), and two more signs are found on a clay vessel from the same level (Hawkins 2011a).

[41] See Hawkins (2000) for an edition with translation and discussion of the Iron Age Hieroglyphic Luwian inscriptions.

[42] Yakubovich (2010: 135–6).

[43] On the Luwians see Melchert (2003d), and Yakubovich (2010), and on the relationship between Luwian and the first millennium Anatolian languages see Melchert (2003c: 175–6). On the position of Lydian see Melchert (2003a). *The Cambridge Encyclopedia of the World's Ancient Languages* (ed. Woodard 2004) is a useful source for what we know about most of relevant Early Iron Age languages spoken in ancient Anatolia. Carian is discussed in detail by Adiego (2007). Although we know very little about it, we think it was a Luwic language: that is, not a descendant of Luwian, but relatively closely related (Yakubovich 2010: 90–6). Phrygians are first attested in Anatolia in the Early Iron Age; the Phrygian language belongs to the same branch of Indo-European as Greek. On the Phrygians, see further Chapter 14, 357–8. See the overview of the peoples of Iron Age Anatolia in Popko (2008).

[44] The judicious review of the evidence by Yakubovich (2010: 75–160) shows that Luwic language(s), i.e., languages belonging to the same branch as Luwian, but not Luwian itself, can be detected in

Greek-speakers, but the texts we can compare with the Greek materials are nearly all Hittite.[45] It is important, therefore, to understand the ways in which the Hittites related to their neighbors to the west, in order to explain how the traditions we find at Hattusa could have made their way to other parts of Anatolia. We must acknowledge furthermore the mediating role of people speaking lost, poorly attested, or undeciphered languages, including Eteocyprian and the Tyrrhenian languages,[46] and perhaps the languages of such mysterious peoples as the Pelasgians, the original settlers of Greece in early Greek thought,[47] the Gergithes, and the Leleges, these last often named along with the Carians as peoples displaced by the arrival of Ionians in Anatolia.[48]

An outline of the book

In this book, I do not plan to provide the final word on the topic of the Anatolian background to Greek literature and religion. Rather, I hope to lay the groundwork for others to build on. I have three goals: to show how Greek epic in the widest sense, comprising all narrative poetry composed in hexameters – not just Homer but Hesiod's works and the Homeric Hymns – drew on Syro-Anatolian predecessors;[49] to provide an improved methodology to analyze the relationship between the cultures on each side of the eastern Mediterranean, from the Aegean Sea to the coast of north Syria; and to present some possible ways how and reasons why transmission of oral texts and textual motifs east to west could have occurred.

---

second-millennium west Anatolia. On the difference between Luwic and Luwian, see Yakubovich (2010: 6–9).

[45] The lack of attested Late Bronze Age texts in west Anatolia must be due in large part to the use of the perishable medium of waxed wooden tablets (Hawkins 1986: 373).

[46] On the Anatolian provenance of the Tyrrhenian languages, see Chapter 14, 361–2.

[47] Georges (1994: 163–5, with n. 148).

[48] Gergithes: Hdt. 5.122, 7.43; Hodot (2001: 171–3). Strabo (13.1.58–9) provides us with the most abundant information on the Leleges. According to Homer the Leleges belong in the southern Troad near Mt. Ida; they also occupy Pedasus near the Satnioeis (*Il.* 20.86–96, 21.86–7). Pherecydes (*FGrH* 3 F 155) puts them in Caria and the adjoining islands. Alc. F 337 Lobel-Page mentions the city Antandrus, next to Cilicia, as a possession of the Leleges. (All are quoted by Strabo 13.1.50–1, 14.1.3.) They also were given a mainland Greek origin. "The L[eleges] were most likely a people of Balkan origin who probably in the course of the last great migrations around the turning of the 2nd to the 1st millennium were on the one hand driven to the Troad and south-western Asia Minor, and on the other hand to western central Greece" (F. Gschnitzer, "Leleges," in *Brill's New Pauly* 7.380–1). Also see Descat (2001).

[49] In Chapter 2, 22, with n. 9, I define the epic genre.

I begin by describing the Hurro-Hittite narrative tradition that I argue is the closest of the extant Near Eastern material to the Greek hexametric tradition, and its cultural context. I next present the theoretical framework in which I am working. I argue that shared gods, festival settings, magico-medical rituals, and ancestor veneration were the key factors for transfer of epic motifs from east to west. Then I focus on the Greek reception of Syro-Anatolian epic in the Early Iron Age, beginning with mainland Greece and Euboea, then examining Cyprus and Cilicia, and finally western Anatolia. Much in this section is conjectural, but it is appropriate to draw out what we can from the data available, primarily archaeological but also from the hexametric texts themselves, to propose specific suggestions for the mechanics and milieus of transmission, rather than to fall back on vague statements that cannot be tested.

Chapter 2 is devoted to a general overview of Hurro-Hittite narrative poetry. The Hurrian and Hittite narrative songs from Hattusa that offer precursors to both Homer's and Hesiod's works belong to a single genre defined by meter, motifs, and phraseology. Texts in this oral-derived genre include, besides the well-known Kumarbi cycle (which has been compared to Hesiod's *Theogony*), *Atrahasis*, the *Song of Gilgamesh*, and the *Song of Release*. The last has striking similarities to the plot of the *Iliad*. I show that this genre shares formulas and type scenes with Homeric epic, and that it exhibits the kind of variation expected of oral-derived literature. I argue further that the genre crossed from Hurrian into Hittite by the same sort of mechanism seen for the Serbian–Albanian epic tradition and for Central Asian epic: bilingual bards. It is possible to determine or at least surmise that some of the texts were performed at festivals, while others were used as mythical exempla in rituals and prayers, providing means and motivations for the incorporation of foreign epic traditions first by the Hittites and then by the Greeks.

The legend of Gilgamesh made obvious contributions to both the *Iliad* and the *Odyssey*, and it is important to establish that the *Song of Gilgamesh* was an oral-derived text and a full-fledged member of the genre of Hurro-Hittite song in order to support my contention that it was a close relative of this particular tradition – not the texts preserved by Mesopotamian scribes – that exerted a formative influence on Greek epic. Thus, Chapter 3 provides a comparative analysis of the Akkadian *Epic of Gilgamesh* found at Hattusa and the Hittite and Hurrian *Songs of Gilgamesh*. I discuss the connections between the *Song of Gilgamesh* and other Hurro-Hittite texts, and the variation in the Hurro-Hittite Gilgamesh tradition that shows the *Song of Gilgamesh* was not simply translated by scribes out of Akkadian, but was the product of bards who could perform in Hurrian and/or Hittite.

Judge of the dead and legendary inventor of ancestor veneration, Gilgamesh was a key mediator between the living and dead. Thus, he was not only treated as a figurative ancestor by local courts wishing to connect themselves to the distant past and to world history, but also appealed to in private rituals to communicate with angry ghosts thought to plague the living. The ritual use of the Gilgamesh story added value to it, making it into an esoteric good analogous to an exotic pharmacological ingredient in a medical potion, which helped to motivate its transmission westwards. Chapter 4 examines a fragment of a Hurro-Hittite purification ritual that makes use of Gilgamesh's story, comparing it with a relatively well-preserved pit ritual that alludes to the Kumarbi cycle, the Hurro-Hittite *Purification Ritual for the Former Gods*. The latter ritual has been compared to Odysseus' *katabasis* in the *Odyssey*, which has also been compared with Tablet XII of the *Epic of Gilgamesh*. The Hurro-Hittite pit ritual involving Gilgamesh allows us to provide a single source for both sets of parallels. Odysseus' visit to the underworld has long been recognized as a relatively late addition to Homeric epic, introducing an egregious inconsistency to the plot, for Odysseus accesses the underworld at the far northern edge of the Black Sea at the Straits of Kerch, which requires him to be transposed from the far west to the far east in the blink of an eye. I argue that the twofold connections of the Homeric episode point to the late absorption into the *Odyssey* of an Anatolian myth about the edges of their world, which was attached to an Anatolian version of a widespread rite used to contact the dead.

In Chapter 5 I analyze the Hurro-Hittite *Song of Release*, which combines elements found in Mesopotamian and Hurrian myths to create an original work with striking similarities to Homer's *Iliad*. I argue that the text tells how the north Syrian city Ebla was punished because its assembly refused to release the captive people of Ikinkalis to serve the cult of the dead kings of Ebla.

In Chapter 6 I situate the *Song of Release* in the larger tradition of eastern Mediterranean epic narrative, comparing it to *Gilgamesh and Akka*, *Atrahasis*, Ugaritic epics, and the *Iliad*, and showing that it stands halfway between Mesopotamian epic and Greek epic. This relatively neglected story in the Hurro-Hittite narrative tradition provides key evidence that the strain of Near Eastern epic with which Greek-speakers came into contact was not the Mesopotamian one, but one closely related to the Syro-Anatolian oral tradition indirectly reflected in the tablets found at Hattusa.

In Chapter 7 I argue that the *Song of Release*, like the *Epic of Gilgamesh*, drew on rites of royal ancestor veneration. These performances occurred in both funerary and festival contexts. Thus, ancestor veneration provides a larger context to be considered when trying to understand the motivations for the Hittites to adopt Hurrian epic, while funerals and festivals provided opportunities for new audiences to access it. I return to these points in the final section of this book when I argue that these same venues and motivations played a role in the transfer of Near Eastern epic to the Greeks. A discussion of the means of transmission of Hurrian epic to Hattusa points to two more key factors that are also applicable to the later transfer of Near Eastern epic to the Greeks: the transfer of gods and dynastic ties.

The texts from Hattusa reveal that a key push–pull factor for the transfer of epic was a fascination with the distant past and with faraway prestigious kingdoms. In Chapter 8 I examine the reception and use of the heroic legends about the Akkadian kings Sargon the Great and Naram-Sin by the Hittites, looking at the narratives and the rituals that refer to them. Sargon appears in a variety of Akkadian and Hittite prose texts at Hattusa, but also in a tiny scrap of Hurrian epic that shows that he was glorified in the same genre as Gilgamesh, which allows us to surmise that his grandson Naram-Sin was also glorified in Hurro-Hittite narrative song. Sargon provided a positive example for the great deeds of Hittite kings who wished to earn their place in world history, and the storyline attached to him of how he explored and conquered distant lands was one framework within which the Hittites turned recent history into myth, while Naram-Sin's hybris provided a negative example. Certainly the legends of the Sargonic kings were well known in scribal circles, but, as with Gilgamesh, we can catch a particularly clear glimpse at Hattusa of an orally transmitted tradition about those Old Akkadian kings. Writing came late to the Hittites and the Hittite court put unusual weight on orally transmitted knowledge, as opposed to scribal learning. Thus, we have unparalleled access at Hattusa to the orally transmitted stories that later influenced Greek myth. Because the famous storyline attached to Naram-Sin re-appears in the *Iliad* attached to Hector, we can surmise that the Greeks were engaged in the same process and used narrativizations of events provided by their Near Eastern neighbors in similar ways. Therefore, the *Iliad* can be seen as an amalgamation of motifs from two different Hurro-Hittite narratives in addition to the Gilgamesh story. Finally, a Hurrian rite invoking Sargonic kings, along with other far-flung legendary kings and characters from Hurrian narrative song, gives more information on how royal ancestor veneration interacted with epic. It also shows how genealogies and king lists interacted with longer narratives and cosmogonies to create a framework for the understanding of the very earliest history of the world, and suggests that the Hesiodic genealogical work, the *Catalog of Women*, had a Near Eastern analog too.

I present my theoretical framework for the transfer of epic from east to west in Chapter 9. I first critique the popular model of "wandering charismatics" as vectors of transmission of verbal art and magico-religious techniques from east to west. I substitute two models that are better attested, the verbal artist or healer who was a luxury commodity traded among kings, and long-distance elite interactions within a guest-friendship network. I argue that stories were transmitted from the Near East to Greece because they were considered to be valuable commodities whose bearers controlled access to prestigious esoteric knowledge, and I show that the value attributed to stories about the beginning of the world and long-distance travel motivated the borrowing of narratives that thematized the transcendence of the barriers of space and time, and made them powerful medicines.

In Chapter 10 I focus on the chief milieu that is clearly attested as a place in which exchange of songs, texts, and ideas took place across geographic and cultural barriers: festivals that drew a supralocal audience, a milieu found both in the Late Bronze Age and in the Greek Archaic period. I link these settings to particular practices whose similarities on either side of the eastern Mediterranean can be explained as transmitted by these means, such as performing with song and dance the story of the Storm-god or Apollo killing a malevolent monster, often a snake, which enacted an ideology of kingship in which the king was demonstrated to be responsible for controlling chaos and ensuring the fertility of the land. I show that political ambitions were a highly important push–pull factor in the transfer of cultural forms across space at festivals, one that can be demonstrated on either side of the Dark Age. A local polity's desire to assert its right to membership in the supralocal elite of its day encouraged participation in the fashions of public life, expressed through feasts and festivals. The transfer of a god, such as Apollo or the Storm-god of Aleppo, or a shared god facilitated the transfer of festivals honoring him or her, or the performances characteristic of the god's cult. Finally, we can see that Archaic Greeks had etiologies for performances in their festivals that attributed them to non-Greeks, for example at the Delian or Pythian festivals in honor of Apollo, showing that transfer across linguistic barriers of songs was a plausible scenario for them.

Since there are no Greek texts between the fall of the Mycenaean civilization and Homer, we must rely on archaeology to show us the cultural values and practices that encouraged the borrowing of Near

Eastern epic when Greek-speakers came into close contact with Near Easterners after the end of the Bronze Age. In Chapter 11 I use funerary rituals and grave offerings to argue that hero worship and the heroic values celebrated in epic had their roots in the Mycenaean period, and that they continued to develop, absorbing Near Eastern elements, as Greeks shifted to a less centralized, highly competitive clan-based society, in which prestige accrued to long-distance "warrior-traders" who could demonstrate their participation in a network of elites that extended from Greece to Cyprus. It was along this network that one stream of Near Eastern epic flowed to Greece, via Cyprus. The deposition of exotic and antique goods in warrior graves in Greece presents a material correlate to the texts from Hattusa that express the same interest in linking to places far away and times long ago. Finally, the competitive ethos depicted in the chariot-racing imagery on grave goods and monuments helped to drive the evolution of Greek epic, as bards performing at funeral games and other occasions that drew supralocal crowds sought to produce an appealing song by incorporating particularly interesting new details from other bards. It is the *Odyssey* that best depicts the world of long-distance elite interactions in which Homeric epic began to take the form in which we know it, while similarities between the Greek *hērōes* and west Semitic *m^erappîm*, divinized ancestors who were considered to be healers, encouraged the transfer of narratives attached to ancestor veneration and explaining the distant past. These were particularly appealing to Greeks in the transition to the Iron Age when they began to build a collective memory about a lost age of heroes, symbolized by the Mycenaean ruins conspicuous in the Greek landscape.

In Chapter 12 I turn to Cyprus (Alashiya) and Cilicia as loci of transmission of Syro-Anatolian epic. The island shows long-term ties with Syria and the cultural mixing and syncretism that encouraged the amalgamation of north Syrian and Cypriot religion and verbal art during both the Late Bronze Age and the Early Iron Age. Cultural continuity in Neo-Hittite north Syria and Cilicia allowed for the preservation of texts and beliefs attested at Hattusa even after the fall of the Hittite empire, so that Greeks in Cyprus could have access to them in the Early Iron Age and the Archaic period, whether through speakers of Anatolian languages or through Eteocypriots or Phoenicians. When Greek-speakers and peoples with Aegean connections began to settle in Cyprus and Cilicia after the collapse of the Mycenaean palatial culture, as part of the movements of the Sea Peoples, they maintained ties with Greek-speakers in Greece and in western Anatolia. A sense of shared identity developed among Greek-speakers in Greece, west Anatolia, Cilicia, and Cyprus, as shown by the myth of Mopsus, the legendary founder of the historical House of Mopsus in Adana/Danuna/(A)hhiyawa, and by the Assyrian name for Cyprus, Iatnana 'island of Danuna'. This allowed for a conduit between Cilicia and Cyprus for stories about Syro-Cilician gods to reach Cypriot Greek-speakers, and this could have been one way in which the snake-killing stories known from Ugaritic and Hittite texts reached Greek-speakers to combine with Greek traditional stories. Finally, stories about Aphrodite, a Cypriot goddess whose personality is an amalgamation of Helladic, Indo-European, and Near Eastern traits, clearly contain Near Eastern elements best explained as absorbed into the Greek narrative tradition on Cyprus. On the other hand, the *Homeric Hymn to Aphrodite*, set on Mt. Ida, shows Near Eastern influence also came via western Anatolia. Like the *Odyssey*, then, the *Hymn to Aphrodite* shows two layers of Near Eastern influence, the later one coming specifically from Anatolia.

The rest of the book is devoted to the cultural milieu of western Anatolia. In the final chapters, I build upon the conclusions drawn in previous chapters as I try to answer two questions by connecting them: Why was the Trojan War so resonant that it became the focus of the narrative tradition that Homer drew upon, and how were Near Eastern elements grafted onto the Greek epic tradition in the *Iliad*?

I set the scene in Chapter 13 by discussing how contact in the Late Bronze Age allowed for transmission of cultural traits found at Hattusa, including narrative traditions, to west Anatolian polities, and what kinds of interactions between Mycenaeans and Anatolians could have been remembered after the end of the Bronze Age.

In Chapter 14 I discuss how such memories and recollections of legendary personalities from Bronze Age Syro-Anatolia could have been retained, pointing to cultural continuity, specific practices such as maintaining dynastic lists, and maintenance of stories attached to legendary figures. I discuss the figure of Mopsus again, this time focusing on how a shared Greco-Anatolian hero could have allowed for the merging of Greek and Near Eastern narratives in the Early Iron Age. We only have scraps of the Greek epics that told of Mopsus, so we can go no further than to note the importance of this legendary figure in building a shared Greco-Anatolian legendary history. But, the pictorial program on the orthostats of Neo-Hittite Karatepe, in which Azatiwazas celebrated how he upheld the House of Mopsus, demonstrates how royal ancestor veneration could have served as a context for the performance of epic.

In the final two chapters I excavate the text of the *Iliad*, as it were, examining in Chapter 15 how competition among Aeolic and Ionic poets made the *Iliad* the primary vehicle for Greek identity, and providing a window of 1160–1050 BCE for the beginning of a Greek epic about the fall of Troy. In Chapter 16 I expose the layers of Anatolian influence on the text. The *Iliad*, when its Anatolian context is taken into account properly, offers us a wealth of information on how Greeks maintained connections across the eastern Mediterranean, and how Achaeans and Anatolians maintained memories of Troy and a sense of their shared Greek–Anatolian identity. It was described with stories of ties of marriage and immigration (applied to Greeks, Phrygians, Carians, and Lycians), and through a single yet multi-faceted narrative about the fall of Troy, which enshrined the sense of loss and nostalgia both Greeks and Anatolians felt, surrounded by the ruins of Bronze Age kingdoms.

2 | Hurro-Hittite narrative song at Hattusa

> I sing of him, excellen[t] Silver. Wise men [told] me [the story of] the fath[erless boy . . .].
>
> *Song of Silver* I i 7–8[1]

Introduction

The first part of this book surveys a set of mythological and mythologizing narratives attested at Hattusa, discussing in some detail issues that have important implications for our understanding of the prehistory of Greek epic, such as their relation to the oral traditions and how and why they were transferred westwards. A total of five different but more or less interconnected traditions that influenced Greek epic can be detected at Hattusa.[2] There is a native Hittite tradition represented by the *Legend of the Queen of Kanesh* and other mythico-historical narratives, which I do not discuss here. There are the two classic and widely attested Akkadian narratives *Atrahasis* and the *Epic of Gilgamesh*. In addition, the genre of Hurro-Hittite narrative song encompasses more than ten songs identified so far, some with Hurrian versions, and they evince multiple recensions or textualizations.[3] Within the genre I include the *Song of Gilgamesh*, a variant version of *Atrahasis*, the *Song of Release*, the *Song of Birth*, the *Song of Hedammu*, the *Song of Ullikummi*, the *Song of the Sea*, the *Song of Silver*, and the *Song of Keshshi*, a fragment mentioning Sargon the Great,

---

[1] *CTH* 364.1.A = *HFAC* 12 i 7–8. Laroche (1965; 1968) originally provided a transliteration of many of the texts discussed in this chapter, but all the mythological texts have recently been transliterated on KhT. I only cite transliterations in this chapter if they were not transliterated as part of the "Mythen der Hethiter" project on KhT, or if they differ significantly, and I have chosen to follow them over KhT. Many of the relevant texts have been translated by Hoffner (1998a). For translations with recent bibliographies also see M. Bachvarova in Chavalas (2013: 272–90) and in López-Ruiz (2013), and Haas (2006, German). In this chapter I only cite translations if they are not in Hoffner (1998a) or supersede his translations.

[2] Surveyed by Beckman (2005).

[3] The term textualization can refer to either an individual oral performance or a single writing down of an oral text (Honko 2000a).

and *Elkunirsa and Ashertu*. Possibly, Hittite narratives such as the one involving a hero with the Hurrian name of Gurparanzah that takes place in the court of Akkade and the *Tale of Appu* should be included in the genre. In addition there are narratives in both Hittite and Akkadian involving the Akkadian conqueror Sargon the Great and his grandson Naram-Sin, including *Sargon, King of Battle*, the *Cuthean Legend of Naram-Sin*, and *Naram-Sin in Asia Minor*. And finally, there is the Luwian "Wilusiad."

The possible existence of a "Wilusiad" is well known to Homerists. It was posited by Calvert Watkins on the basis of an incipit among a series of incipits for Luwian "Thunder Songs" in the description of the *Festival of Istanuwa*. The choral song begins, "When they came from high Wilusa" (*aḫḫa=ata=ta alati auienta Wilušati*).[4] While the epithet "steep" or "high" is coupled in formulas with city names in the *Iliad*, the collocation does not, to my knowledge, appear in Near Eastern poetry. This single line is an important piece of evidence that Hittites participated in the network of traveling poets who were the ancestors of the poets working in the oral tradition that eventually produced the *Iliad*. The formula, which ended up in Homeric poetry, reached the Hittite capital from northwest Anatolian Istanuwa via a transferred festival. Songs could have been transmitted back and forth between west Anatolia and Hattusa by the same sort of performers and scribes who brought to Hattusa the literary traditions of its southern and eastern neighbors, performing in Hittite and other languages, for the same reasons and in the same milieus – competitive emulation and transfer of divinities driving the movement of performers among the courts in Anatolia.

I will argue this point in some detail in subsequent chapters, but now we turn to the tradition of Hurro-Hittite narrative song (Sumerogram SIR$_3$, Hitt. *išḫamāiš*, Hurr. *ḫalmi*), which is just as important as the tradition the

---

[4] *Festival of Istanuwa*: CTH 772.1 = KBo 4.11 rev. 46 (translit. Starke 1985: 341). This Thunder Song is for Suwasuna, a god only attested in this festival and related texts. See Watkins (1986: 713–17; 1995: 144–8) on the phrase. Istanuwa appears to be near the Sangarius River, since the ritual mentions a toast to it (CTH 772.2 = KUB 35.135 iv 16′–17′, translit. Starke 1985: 322, see Hutter 2003: 239). Also note another lacunose line discussed by Watkins (1986: 713–15), which he restores as "When the man came from steep [Wilusa?]" *ālati=tta āḫḫa* LÚ-*iš auita* [*Wilušati*] (*Luwian Moon Incantation*: CTH 766 = KUB 35.103 iii 11, translit. Starke 1985: 223). There has been much skepticism about the formula. Neumann (1999: 21, n. 20) suggests reading the phrase as "when they came from the ... meadowland," while Starke (1997: 473, n. 78) argues that *ala-* means "sea," and thus translates, "when they came from the sea, from Wilusa." Watkins (1987b; 1987c: 312; 1995: 144–51, with n. 19), however, has shown that *ala-* does indeed mean "steep" or "high," as seen from the fact that it modifies "rock face" (*uwāniya-*) in *Ritual of Puriyanni against the Impurity of a House*: CTH 758.1.C = KUB 35.54 iii 18 (translit. Starke 1985: 68).

Luwian incipit represents, though much less well known as a whole to Classicists. In large part this is because of the current state of research on the genre. At this point Hittitologists do not all agree that there is a single genre; that it represents a bilingual oral tradition, rather than texts translated by scribes into Hittite; or that the Hittite versions are poetic. I have discussed elsewhere in detail the evidence that there is a single genre, and that the genre was the product of a bilingual oral tradition that may have started out as the property of the Hurrians, but thrived in its new Hittite milieu.[5] In this chapter I will only summarize the evidence, providing some comparisons between Hittite and Greek poetic formulas and type scenes.

The results set the stage for some far-reaching conclusions. The influence of the Gilgamesh story on Homeric epic has long been acknowledged, in the fantastic wanderings of Odysseus and in the intense friendship between Achilles and Patroclus in the *Iliad*,[6] as has the connection between the Kumarbi cycle and Hesiod's *Theogony*.[7] But, most Classicists do not know that both stories were told within a single genre in Syro-Anatolia.[8] Indeed, there has been a tendency to separate the Greek hexametric narratives into different genres, distinguishing heroic epic from folktale (*Iliad* and *Odyssey*) within the oeuvre of Homer, and Homeric epic from Hesiod's cosmogonic, didactic, and genealogical works (*Theogony*, *Works and Days*, and *Catalog of Women*), while the Homeric Hymns are put into yet another category of religious narratives praising the gods.[9] In fact, according to its formal features, Greek hexametric poetry was a single genre, as was Hurro-Hittite narrative song, and both sets of texts encompass the same types of subgenres: heroic, theogonic, didactic, genealogical, and praise of individual gods.[10] Thus, after it is established that the *Song of*

---

[5] Bachvarova (2014). [6] M. L. West (1997a: 402–17). [7] For references see n. 14.
[8] Bryce (1999: 262) did note the significance of the presence of the Gilgamesh story at Hattusa.
[9] The term "epic," like other terms drawn from ancient Greek literature, such as "lyric," "tragedy," and "hero," has been applied with more or less success to any number of narrative traditions, and there have been attempts to separate "epic" from "folk tale," "heroic" from "romantic," and so on, on the basis of aesthetic judgments that have little or nothing to do with the notions of genre held by the original audiences and composers. The questions of genre and of the applicability of modern notions of genre have exercised the minds of many an Assyriologist. See, for example, Edzard (1994), listing "fairy tale" motifs in *Gilgamesh and Huwawa*; *Gilgamesh, Enkidu, and the Netherworld*; and the Lugalbanda stories; and an extended discussion of how to define genre in Longman (1991: 3–21). See Gilan (2010) on the classification of Near Eastern, especially Hittite, narratives, insisting there is no such thing as heroic epic at Hattusa. I do assume that the concept of "hero" has some cross-cultural meaning in the eastern Mediterranean. See Chapter 11.
[10] Foley's study of some narrative sequences shared by the Homeric Hymns and Homeric epic shows the common origin of the two supposedly separate genres (Foley 1997: 151–3). Clay

Gilgamesh, the Kumarbi cycle, and the *Song of Release* belong to a single tradition, it becomes clear that Homer, Hesiod, and the Homeric Hymns could have borrowed much of their Near Eastern material through a single channel as a single unified tradition that looked much like the Hurro-Hittite narrative tradition found at Hattusa, an assumption strengthened by the fact that Hurro-Hittite formulas can also be found in Greek hexametric poetry. A theory that can present a single source for a large number of the parallels between Near Eastern narrative poetry and Greek hexametric poetry as a whole, even if transmitted via multiple locations and at different times, has superior explanatory power to the piecemeal theories offered so far attempting to explain each parallel individually.

On the other hand, the temptation to draw a straight line between texts should be avoided, between the Kumarbi cycle and the *Theogony*, for example, or between the *Song of Gilgamesh* and the *Iliad* or *Odyssey*. Nor should it be assumed that the process of transmission was as simple as our incomplete evidence suggests. Multiple, repeated layers of transmission should be assumed, for the most part east to west, but also west to east, although the nature of our evidence complicates our ability to see the latter. Furthermore, we should be careful to avoid the simplistic assumption that what can be detected in the preserved documents is a truly representative sample of the stories told in eastern Mediterranean narrative traditions, although I will argue in subsequent chapters that in fact it was the themes themselves of the Near Eastern stories that show clear parallels to Greek hexametric poetry which drove the stories' transmission.

Members of the genre of Hurro-Hittite narrative song

I here provide an overview of the genre, its members, and its stylistic features. I touch on the evidence that the written texts refract an oral tradition.[11] I also discuss the cult context informing and motivating the performances of some of the songs.

(2006: 4–6) lays out the evidence internal to the Homeric texts that narratives about gods were rated on the same level as narratives about heroes and were performed in the same contexts. See Graziosi and Haubold (2005) on the unity of Greek cosmogonic and heroic epic. Nagy (2010: 79–127) shows that performers of hymns to gods were not differentiated from performers of epic. For example, Demodocus sings a hymn about Aphrodite, then performs a segment of the Trojan War epic.

[11] I borrow the term "refract" from Sourvinou-Inwood, who uses it to explain the relationship between "real-life" rituals and iconography or myths connected to the rituals, one in which the

I begin by describing the texts that belong to the genre of Hurro-Hittite narrative song, summarizing their plots and pointing out some interesting connections with other narrative traditions in the area. First the Kumarbi cycle. Modern scholars have grouped together a series of songs telling of conflicts between gods for control of heaven into a single cycle: the *Song of Birth*, *Song of the Sea*, *Song of Hedammu*, and *Song of Ullikummi*.[12] All are found in both Hurrian and Hittite versions. In nearly all cases the Hittite version is substantially better preserved than the Hurrian one. This is a set of songs with an international theater of action: Mesopotamian, Hurrian, north Syrian, and Hittite places and gods make their appearance. The cycle as a whole has been compared to the *Theogony*, while the individual songs are perhaps best compared to the Homeric Hymns, the more elaborate of which tell famous stories about the gods.[13] The theogonic storylines have roots that go back as far as the Sumerian tale *Enki and Ninhursag*, some of whose themes the Akkadian *Epic of Creation* shares, and they have many branches, including the Akkadian *Atrahasis*, Orphic cosmogony, and the theogonies of the Phoenician Sanchuniathon (whose *floruit* is unclear) and the sixth-century Pherecydes of Syros.[14] I agree with Anna Maria Polvani, however, that we should be careful to avoid a too rigid and systematic

---

ritual is not directly represented, but alluded to by an iconographic or mythological "schema." See for example Sourvinou-Inwood (2003: 85–8). Here I use to it to refer to the relationship between "facts" and the evidence available that does not directly represent the facts, but alludes in some way to their existence.

[12] The order follows Rutherford (2001b). On the use and origins of the texts grouped within the Kumarbi cycle also see Archi (2009).

[13] Epic performances began by invoking a god; the Homeridae began with Zeus (Pi. *N.* 2.3), and Thucydides (3.104) calls the *Homeric Hymn to Apollo* a *prooimion*, 'opening' to another song, presumably an epic performance. But, we should expect that the longer hymns stood on their own too. See Maslov (2012) for a discussion of the term *prooimion*, showing that it did not originally refer to the Homeric hymns.

[14] Lesky (1950; 1955) brought the story of the Kumarbi cycle to the attention of Classicists. M. L. West (1997a: 276–305) not only reviews the comparisons made with the *Epic of Creation* (also called *Enuma Elish*) and the Kumarbi cycle but also discusses a wealth of other details that have Near Eastern analogs. Rutherford (2009a) is a recent discussion of the parallels and how the storyline reached the Greeks. Sanchuniathon and Pherecydes of Syros are both epitomized by Philo of Byblos in his *Phoenician History*. The material from Philo comes to us by way of Eusebius. It is presented and discussed by Baumgarten (1981) and Attridge and Oden (1981). M. L. West (1966: 24–30; 1971: 1–75), Walcot (1966), and Kirk, Raven, and Schofield (1983: 50–71) discuss the stories of Sanchuniathon and Pherecydes in light of the Babylonian texts and the Greek parallels, while Schibli (1990) deals with Pherecydes alone. A translation and discussion of the Orphic cosmogony in the Derveni papyrus may be found in Betegh (2004), while all the Orphic material is collected by Bernabé (2004; 2005). Discussion of all these sources appears in López-Ruiz (2006; 2010). Translations: *Enki and Ninhursag* (Old Babylonian, see Attinger 1984: 2): ETCSL t.1.1.1; *Epic of Creation* (from the second half of the second millennium): Foster (2005: 436–86); *Atrahasis* (already attested in the Old Babylonian

ordering of the texts, since there is no evidence that the narratives themselves were conceived of by scribes as chapters in a book with a fixed plot, nor is there any evidence that they were composed by a single poet equivalent to Homer; indeed, there are sufficient stylistic, thematic, and linguistic differences to cause us to consider them to be the product of more than one individual.[15]

Still, some narratives clearly presuppose others. Thus, the *Song of Birth* starts off the action, telling of the primeval conflicts between the gods Alalu and Anu, then Anu and Kumarbi, the latter leading to the conception of the Storm-god of Kummi – in Hurrian Teshshub, in Hittite Tarhun – through the ingestion of Anu's sperm by Kumarbi.[16]

The *Song of the Sea*, performed in a ritual for Mt. Hazzi, the home of Ugaritic Baal and known in Greek as Mt. Casius, tells of the conflict between Teshshub and the Sea, in which the Sea unleashes a great flood. The tale parallels the Syrian story about the battle between Baal and Yam. It should come before the *Song of Hedammu*,[17] since it explains why the

---

period): Foster (2005: 227–80). López-Ruiz (2013: 1–62) now conveniently collects translations of these texts and other relevant texts and discusses the texts.

[15] Polvani (2008), discussing how some texts of the Kumarbi cycle show closer affinities to Mesopotamian analogs and to each other than others. See Starke (1990: 306, with n. 1048) for the unusual number of Luwianisms in one version of the *Song of Ullikummi* (*CTH* 345.3.1.A = *KBo* 26.65+), as an example of the linguistic differences not only between texts, but between textualizations. Also see n. 60 below.

[16] Often called the "Song of Kingship in Heaven" or the "Song of Kumarbi" by modern scholars, a newly joined fragment to the first tablet allows us to reconstruct the actual title of the work as the "Song of Going out," i. e., the "Song of Birth" (*KUB* 33.120 + *KBo* 52.10 iv 28′ = *CTH* 344.A, see Corti 2007). For a possible Hurrian version see *Mythological Fragments*: *CTH* 370.II = *KUB* 47.56, mentioning Anu, Alalu, and Kumarbi (see translit. and discussion in Salvini and Wegner 2004: 17–18, 38, No. 7). The theme of the conception and birth of Teshshub and his various rivals can be compared to the difficult births of Zeus, Athena, and Apollo, and to *How Sosruquo Was Born* (Abaza Saga 86, trans. Colarusso 2002: 185–7). We are not absolutely sure of Kummi's location, but it is somewhere in the mountainous northeast Tigris region, and from its earliest attestation it is strongly associated with Teshshub. At Hattusa it is mentioned in Hurro-Hittite songs and rituals (Mayer 2002; Wilhelm 1994: 317–18).

[17] A possible Hittite textualization of *Song of the Sea*, booked under *Fragments of the Kumarbi Myth*: *CTH* 346.9.A = *KBo* 26.105, tells of a massive inundation by the sea, whom Kumarbi tries to appease with offerings; see Haas (2006: 151–2). A Hurrian textualization of the *Song of the Sea* begins širadili kiaže "I shall recount the sea," and is labeled in the colophon DUB.I.KAM ŠA A.A[B.BA] "first tablet of the sea"; other Hurrian fragments may belong to the same text (*Fragments of the Kumarbi Myth*: *CTH* 346.II = *KUB* 45.63, *VBoT* 59, translit. Salvini and Wegner 2004: 46–8, Nos. 12, 13, discussion pp. 21–2). The song may also be mentioned in a library catalog listing tablets of rituals and noting that the relevant tablet has disappeared: ⌜DUB.I⌝[+(x).KAM Š]A A.AB.BA šarā=ma=at ŪL artari "1 [+ ?] tablet(s) of the sea, but it is not available" (*Tablet Catalog of the DUB.x.KAM Type*: *CTH* 276.2 = *KUB* 30.43 iii 2′–3′, ed. with discussion Dardano 2006: 38, 42–3). The song was performed in *Ritual for Mt. Hazzi*: *CTH* 785 = *KUB* 44.7 (Rutherford 2001b: 598); on the ritual and Mt. Hazzi see further Chapter 10, 256–8.

Sea would take the side of Kumarbi and give him his daughter in order that the sea monster Hedammu be conceived to fight Teshshub.[18] In the Hittite versions Hedammu is defeated when *IŠTAR* seduces him, and in response Kumarbi creates – by ejaculating onto a rock – the deaf and dumb rock monster Ullikummi ('destroy Kummi!'[19]), who will be impervious to her wiles, as told in the *Song of Ullikummi*.[20] In the Hurrian versions she is the goddess of magic Shawushka, while in the Hittite versions the Akkadogram *IŠTAR* conceals the name of the Anatolian goddess Anzili.[21] In addition to the Hittite fragments, there are up to eight Hurrian fragments, and the Hittite and Hurrian versions diverge too much for the one to be considered simply a translation of the other.[22]

We have other fragments of narratives that do not necessarily fit in the cycle, but contain characters and formulas common to the genre and either describe or allude to the conflicts of various gods with the Storm-god. For example, one fragment recounts how Mt. Pishaisha happens upon a naked and sleeping *IŠTAR* and sleeps with her, just as the gardener did with Inanna in the Sumerian *Inanna and Shukaletuda*. Like Inanna, the goddess is enraged, and the mountain pleads for his life and offers to tell her a story that alludes to two matches between the Storm-god and a rival, in one case the Sea, in the other Mts. Namni and Hazzi.[23] The story of the mountains' rebellion against the Storm-god is told in another fragment that also mentions Eltara, who is presumably an analog of El, a member of the earlier generation of Mesopotamian gods.[24] A third fragment, *Ea and the Beast*, involves some of the same characters that appear in the Kumarbi

---

On the widespread and ancient story of the Storm-god in conflict with the sea, see Schwemer (2008b: 24–7).

[18] *CTH* 348. For the Hurrian version see Salvini and Wegner (2004: 19, 40–1, Nos. 8, 8a). Schwemer (2008b: 6) thinks the *Song of the Sea* was the final episode of the cycle.

[19] Salvini (1977: 85).

[20] *CTH* 345. For the Hurrian version of the *Song of Ullikummi* see Salvini and Wegner (2004: 19, 41–2, No. 9).

[21] See Wilhelm (2010b) showing that the goddess hiding behind the Akkadogram *IŠTAR* is the Anatolian goddess Anzili, and Bachvarova (2013a) on the implications of the equation. On the Hurrian goddess of magic Shawushka, see Wegner (1981), and for the citations of Anzili in the Hittite versions of the Kumarbi cycle, see Bachvarova (2013a: 27). A table of equations of Near Eastern gods is provided in Table 2.

[22] Giorgieri (2001).

[23] *Fragments Mentioning Ishtar (Mt. Pishaisha)*: *CTH* 350.3.A = *KUB* 33.108 (trans. M. Bachvarova in Chavalas 2013: 284); *Inanna and Shukaletuda* (trans. ETCSL t.1.3.3). See Rutherford (2001b: 602), Haas (2006: 212–13), Singer (2007: 634–5), and discussion by Bachvarova in Chavalas (2013).

[24] *Mythological Fragments*: *CTH* 370.1.63.A = *KBo* 22.87; see discussion by Polvani (2008). Eltara appears in rituals directed at the Former Gods, the gods deposed by the Storm-god, but he is

cycle, such as Ea and the river Tigris, along with an unnamed beast, who proclaims his privileged knowledge of upcoming events, the doings of an unnamed god who will overcome the other gods. It picks up the themes of kingship of the gods in heaven, the defeat and underground exile of a god, impregnation by spit, pregnancy, and birth.[25]

Two additional songs have been suggested to belong to the Kumarbi cycle, the *Song of LAMMA* and the *Song of Silver*, but the remains of the *Song of LAMMA* do not allow us to fit it tightly into the master plot of Teshshub's fight for power. In it, the tutelary deity, made king in heaven, does not carry out his duties; therefore, humans no longer make sacrifices to the gods. Because the song refers to both LAMMA (the "tutelary deity") and Hebat, the patron deities of Carchemish, the narrative could originate from there.[26] Similarly, in the extant remains of the *Song of Silver* there is no obvious mention of a conflict between the semi-divine hero and his half-brother Teshshub. The story opens with a proem that is typical of Hurro-Hittite song: "I sing him, excellen[t] Silver."[27] Mocked by the other children for having no father, Silver confronts his mother and learns his father is Kumarbi. A half-divine figure is also found in the Old Hittite myth *Illuyanka*, and they form striking parallels with Gilgamesh on the one hand and Greek heroes on the other. We can only understand a few more points in the narrative. Silver sets off to Urkesh, Kumarbi's home in northeast Syria, but he cannot find his father there. He pulls down and threatens the sun and the moon, exhibiting, perhaps, the same kind of hybristic behavior that led to Bellerophontes' demise, for the Greek hero attempted to ride Pegasus up to the gods' seat Olympus. Further parallels have been found with the myth of the half-divine Phaethon, who attempts to ascend to heaven in the chariot of his father, the sun.[28]

---

not mentioned otherwise in Hurro-Hittite song, and his existence does not fit well with the genealogy laid out in the *Song of Birth*. On the Former Gods see Chapter 4, 94.

[25] *CTH* 351.1.A = *KBo* 31.95+: *Fragments Mentioning Ea* (*Ea and the Beast*, ed. and discussion Archi 2002a); see further Haas (2006: 143–4; 2007a: 347).

[26] *CTH* 343, see Haas (2006: 146–7) for an interpretation and Archi (2009: 218) on the connection to Carchemish.

[27] *CTH* 364.1.A = *HFAC* 12 i 7.

[28] On *Illuyanka* see Chapter 10, 252–6. For Bellerophontes' ascent to heaven, see Pi. *I.* 7.43–8 (not found in Homer: see Chapter 16, 424–6). See James and van der Sluijs (2012) on the parallels with the Phaethon story, Gantz (1993: 31–4) for the Greek sources for Phaethon. On references in the *Song of Silver* to the mountainous homeland of the Hurrians north of Urkesh, see Buccellati and Kelly-Buccellati (2009: 67–9). Possible parallels to the opening scenario of the *Song of Silver* are found in Caucasian myth: Circassian Saga 39: *The Ballad of Ashamaz* (trans. Colarusso 2002: 172–3); Abaza Saga 72: *Chwadlazhwiya's Tale* (trans. Colarusso 2002: 290–6).

Moving on to songs that definitely do not belong to the Kumarbi cycle, the *Song of Keshshi* (Hurr. 'hunter'[29]) deals with a hero who lives among humans, like Silver.[30] It tells the story of the hunter Keshshi, married to the beautiful but false Shinda(li)meni, and her evil brother, Udibsharri. The narrative is extant in Hurrian, Hittite, and Akkadian, the latter attested in a single fragment from Amarna in Hittito-Egyptian ductus. Six of the fragments at Hattusa are in Hittite, while eighteen (including one duplicate) are in Hurrian. It is very unfortunate that we can understand so little of this narrative, one version of which was made up of at least fifteen tablets and was well over 6,000 lines,[31] for its length indicates its importance to its audience and tellers. It has been shown that there are significant differences between the longer Hurrian and shorter Hittite versions.[32]

We pick up the narrative already in progress in the Hittite version, where we learn that Keshshi is so smitten with his wife that he neglects the gods, failing to provide them with their food and libations, and no longer goes out to hunt. His mother complains that he does not care for her any longer, and pays attention only to his wife, so Keshshi takes up his spear and heads to the mountains to hunt. During his extended time in the mountains he suffers from hunger and thirst and falls ill. He has a series of seven ominous dreams, which his mother will interpret for him. Keshshi's divine father intervenes in the action in some unclear way, as do his divine ancestors. The dreams of Keshshi parallel those of Gilgamesh when he is on his journey to the Cedar Mountains to do battle with Huwawa, but Gilgamesh's dreams are not included in the corresponding section of the extant Hittite versions of the *Song of Gilgamesh*.[33] In the Hurrian version of the *Song of Keshshi*, other gods are involved, including IŠTAR, the Sun-god, and the Moon-god. We can recognize a scene involving an assembly of elders, to which Keshshi's wife is called to be accused by Keshshi, and various omens are discussed in other parts of the text, along with Keshshi's pleas for success in hunting. The story shares elements of the Greek myth of Meleager, who violates the taboo against engaging in heterosexual sex while hunting by courting Atalanta.[34]

---

[29] Wilhelm (1999).

[30] CTH 361. For a transliteration and discussion of the Hurrian version see Salvini and Wegner (2004: 23–7, 56–69), with new pieces in Dijkstra (2008). For the Hittite version see translations of Haas (2006: 206–10) and Bachvarova in Chavalas (2013: 284–7).

[31] Cf. colophon of CTH 361.II.2 = KUB 47.2 left edge 9–11: "Fourteenth tablet of the Song of Keshshi, not finished," and discussion and translit. of Salvini and Wegner (2004: 23, 25, 60, No. 27).

[32] Dijkstra (2008), Haas (2006: 208). [33] Haas (2006: 209–11).

[34] On Meleager see Felson-Rubin and Sale (1983).

The *Song of Gilgamesh* will be discussed in some detail in the following chapter. I will point out only two important facts here: Any theory of the introduction of Hurro-Hittite song to Hattusa needs to take into account the fact that the *Song of Gilgamesh*, the Kumarbi cycle, and the *Song of Release* all belong to the genre, rather than treating each separately. Secondly, there is enough of the Hurrian version to show that it differed significantly from the Hittite version. Neither version was simply a translation of the Akkadian *Epic of Gilgamesh*; both were tailored to meet the preferences of its Anatolian audience. The variations alone, which are typical of oral traditions, differentiate it from the Standard Babylonian *Epic of Gilgamesh*, a product of the scribal schools.

A similar argument can be made concerning the fragments of *Atrahasis* found at Hattusa. Another widely attested narrative in the Akkadian tradition, with Old Babylonian, Middle Babylonian, Late Babylonian, and Neo-Assyrian versions, *Atrahasis* is a product of a long-standing tradition, containing within it the plot line of the older Sumerian *Flood Story*.[35] It tells one key episode in the Mesopotamian cosmogonic myth, the invention of humans to do manual labor for the gods and the gods' attempt to destroy them when they become too numerous, sending a flood that destroys all of mankind except for the clever Atrahasis and those he brought on board his boat; humans are saved because Atrahasis is careful to follow the advice of the god Enki. The similarities with the Biblical story of Noah and the ancient Greek myth of Deucalion are obvious.[36] Parts of a version of *Atrahasis* were incorporated into the Standard Babylonian *Epic of Gilgamesh*, related by its hero, here named Utnapishtim, to Gilgamesh,[37] and already in the early second-millennium Sumerian *Death of Gilgamesh* reference is made to Gilgamesh's journey to Ziusudra, the Sumerian

---

[35] In the *Flood Story* (trans. Black et al. 2004: 212–15), humans are created to relieve the gods from the burden of irrigation work, but then grow too numerous. All but Ziusudra, aided by Enki, are destroyed in a flood. A related text is the Babylonian *Epic of Creation*, in which the father god Apsu is offended by the clamor of the younger gods, and calls an assembly in which, against the desires of their mother Tiamat, he decides to destroy the younger gods. But, Ea saves them by putting Apsu to sleep and capturing him, then goes on to produce Marduk, whose creation corresponds to the creation of man in *Atrahasis*. Marduk is so disruptive to the older gods that they decide to do battle against him to free themselves from "this unremitting yoke" (OB I 122, trans. Foster 2005: 443). Tiamat wins the battle and ends the problems by creating another set of beings, one of whom now is in control of both the army and the assembly. Eastern Mediterranean texts telling of the Deluge are collected and discussed in López-Ruiz (2013: 63–106).

[36] See M. L. West (1997a: 489–93). [37] See Foster (2005: 227–8).

equivalent of Utnapishtim, so it seems likely that the flood story had already been pulled into the Gilgamesh myth at that point.[38]

I argue that the Hittite scraps of *Atrahasis* should be grouped in the genre of Hurro-Hittite narrative song, and I explore here some of the variations in the narrative, insofar as its fragmentary nature will allow, which show that it was not a canonical written text solely the province of learned scribes, although our only access to it is through scribes.[39]

A possible Middle Babylonian version in a Hittite hand is found in Hattusa, but it consists only of a single fragment mentioning Atrahasis, too small to be placed.[40] Two New Hittite exemplars can also be found, one a copy of an older Middle Hittite tablet.[41] In the latter tablet the text is laid out in two columns per side, and its colophon runs across the column division, a phenomenon typical of bilingual tablets, suggesting that there was an Akkadian or – more likely in my opinion – a Hurrian version in the lost facing column.[42] This fragment contains a scene in which Enlil is informed by his vizier Nusku that some of the gods refuse to do hard labor any more, which follows quite closely the Standard Babylonian version. The scanty fragments of the other Hittite version, laid out with one column per tablet side, indicate that it deviated from the Akkadian version in important details, including the types of disasters visited on humans by the gods – here one involves a plague of ants – but especially in the addition of a new character, the father of Atrahasis, a human named Hamsha or "Fifty" (also a term for Enlil) in direct communication with Kumarbi, who may or may not be replacing Enlil.[43]

---

[38] Trans. George (1999: 198–9). Also see George (2003: 97–8) for the possible inclusion of the Ziusudra episode in an early version of *Gilgamesh and Huwawa A*.

[39] I will treat parallels between *Atrahasis* and the Hurro-Hittite *Song of Release* in Chapter 6.

[40] *CTH* 347 = *KBo* 36.26. Soysal (2013: 698) has recently suggested that the fragment *KBo* 47.147 (*CTH* 832: *Hittite Fragments with Various Contents*, translit. Groddek 2011a: 130–1) mentions Atrahasis in an OB spelling of the initial syllable (ᵐ*Wa-tar-ra-ḫa-ši-iš*). He suggests it is a version of *Atrahasis*. It could also be a historiola referring to the myth embedded in an incantation, as is *KUB* 8.62, discussed in Chapter 4.

[41] Polvani (2003: 538–9) notes that *CTH* 347.2.A = *KUB* 36.74 shows signs of being a NH copy of a MH version because of the use of older sign forms (copied therefore from the tablet itself, not by dictation), and suggests that it and the MB version represent a tradition which could have been imported directly from Babylon, after Mursili I seized the city. See translation and discussion of the Hittite version in Haas (2006: 277–9); translit., trans. and discussion in Polvani (2003). Translations of the Akkadian versions found at other sites are provided by Foster (2005: 227–80).

[42] See Haas (2006: 278).

[43] *CTH* 347.1.A = *KBo* 53.5 + *KUB* 8.63, and see Haas (2006: 278) and J. L. Miller (2005) on Hamsha. The "Land of Fifty" appears in *Gula-AN and the Seventeen Kings*, one of the Akkadian narratives concerning the rebellion against Naram-Sin. The geonym is otherwise unattested. See

Parallels with the Kumarbi cycle with regard to vocabulary items in fact suggest that the Hurro-Hittite text under discussion is a separate story that incorporates elements of *Atrahasis* (as the Mesopotamian *Epic of Gilgamesh* did), along with elements found in other Hurro-Hittite narratives. Although Hurrian versions have not yet been found, Hurrian influence in at least one of the Hittite versions is indicated by the presence of Kumarbi.[44]

The Akkadian narrative about Atrahasis found at Ugarit exhibits similar variations. The story is preserved in a fragment containing only part of the first and fourth columns of the tablet, which mentions the main character.[45] On the one hand there is a clear reference to the gods' decision to flood the earth, and to the scene in which Enki/Ea circumvents the stricture imposed upon him not to reveal the gods' plans to any humans by speaking to a reed wall in his temple, knowing full well that Atrahasis can overhear him. Here the Mesopotamian storyline seems to be followed quite closely. On the other hand, the poorly preserved fourth column mentions "your wife" and "life" two times in the accusative; the direct speech thus has affinities with Gilgamesh's dialogue with Utnapishtim and the sage's sympathetic wife concerning his desire for eternal life, and here the narrative seems to deviate significantly from the Mesopotamian storyline. Like the Boğazköy text discussed above, which seems to be part of a bilingual tablet, it has been suggested from the layout of the piece, marked with horizontal lines dividing it into short paragraphs, that the tablet from

---

J. G. Westenholz (1997: 252–3) *ad* i 19'. Archi notes that in the *Song of Birth*, Enlil and Kumarbi are two separate gods (2004b: 321), but it is impossible to decide here whether or not Kumarbi is replacing Enlil.

[44] Polvani (2003: 537–8). The use of the rare Luwian word *ḫaršantan* (a part of a vehicle) in it, similar to the term ᴳᴵˢ*ḫaršandaḫit* 'vehicle part' in the *Song of Ullikummi*, speaks to "the formation of, if not a real and proper poetic literary language, at least a lexical formulary peculiar to mythological texts," as Polvani (2003: 537) observes (*CTH* 347.1.A = *KUB* 8.63 i 14'; *CTH* 345.1.2.A = *KUB* 36.12 iii 7', trans. M. Bachvarova in López-Ruiz 2013: 158). The older Hittite fragment of the *Atrahasis* contains the puzzling phrase, "we (will) saw the burden" (*aimp[a]n ardumeni*) in *CTH* 347.2.A = *KUB* 36.74 iii 2'. The verb root *ard-* ('saw') is otherwise confined to the *Song of Ullikummi*, in the significant word *ardāla* (*CTH* 347.2.A = *KUB* 36.74 iii 2'; *CTH* 345.1.3.1.A = *KBo* 26.65 ii 18'; *KUB* 33.106 iii 52', trans. M. Bachvarova in López-Ruiz 2013: 160, 162), the only occurrences of the neuter plural noun; see Polvani (2003: 533). It is the primeval saw taken from the sealed storehouse of the gods to cut the monster Ullikummi from the earth. The term *aimpa-* ('burden') is also favored in the Kumarbi cycle and ancillary texts, appearing once in the *Song of LAMMA* and twice in the *Song of Birth*, there referring to the burden put inside Kumarbi when he swallows Anu's "manliness" (*CTH* 343.1.A = *KUB* 33.112 iv 10', fragmentary context, trans. Hoffner 1998a: 47; *CTH* 344.A = *KUB* 33.120 i 30, 34, trans. M. Bachvarova in López-Ruiz 2013: 141).

[45] RS 22.421 (ed. Nougayrol in Nougayrol *et al.* 1968: 300–4, No. 167; trans. Foster 2005: 255).

Ugarit was a bilingual, with Sumerian, Hurrian, or Hittite on the missing side.[46] Finally, even though it can be linked to an ongoing oral tradition, *Atrahasis* was also part of the Hittite-influenced scribal schooling at Ugarit, illustrated by a trilingual scholastic text *LÚ.DINGIR.RA* found at Ugarit in Sumerian with Akkadian and Hittite translations, which was imported from Hattusa.[47] All this adds up to suggest that Hittite scribes were taught to write using well-known myths, as Akkadian scribes were. But, I argue that the Hurro-Hittite myths were derived quite directly from an oral milieu.

The *Song of Release*, a Hurro-Hittite song discovered in the late twentieth-century excavations at Hattusa, is the most extensively attested, with approximately one hundred fragments representing perhaps three different versions, one of which was more than five tablets long.[48] They were all found in a single area of the Oberstadt, a part of the capital only recently excavated, primarily in Building 16, but also in Building 15. Possibly all the tablets were originally stored in a single *pithos* jar, along with a Middle Babylonian version of *Gilgamesh*, a Luwian song from the *Festival of Istanuwa*, and a Hattic passage of the type performed in the *purulli* festival.[49] Quite a suggestive grouping! Five different languages, two texts with a tight connection to live performances, one that was confined to the world of the educated scribe, and then the *Song of Release*. The *Song of Release* is among the earliest attested of the Hurro-Hittite narratives. The ductus and the language of the Hittite side show that the written version is a product of the Middle Hittite period (*ca.* 1400 BCE).[50] But, as far as we know, it was not copied in later times, for the attestations are confined to this single cache.

Besides possibly *Atrahasis*, the *Song of Release* is the only Hurro-Hittite text written down in bilingual format, a format otherwise seen at Hattusa in the Old Hittite *Hattusili's Testament* (an admonitory historical text in Hittite and Akkadian), some Hattic passages, and some examples of

---

[46] Kämmerer (1993: 193–5), suggesting Sumerian could be on the missing side.

[47] RS 25.421 (eds. J. Nougayrol, No. 169, and E. Laroche, No. 2, in Nougayrol *et al.* 1968: 310–19, 773–9), and see Neu (1995a: 126–7) on *LÚ.DINGIR.RA* at Ugarit.

[48] CTH 789. On the number of versions see Archi (2007b: 189). For bibliographic details see Chapter 5, 111, n. 2.

[49] Klinger (2001b: 205–6); *Epic of Gilgamesh*: CTH 341.1 = *KBo* 32.128–33 (translit. and discussion Wilhelm 1988); *Festival of Istanuwa*: CTH 772 = *KBo* 32.126 + 126a (translit. Starke 1985: 366–7, with p. 359); *Hattic Songs of the Women of Tissaruliya*: CTH 741.1.C = *KBo* 32.121 (translit. Klinger 1996: 717–18). On the *purulli* festival see Chapter 10, 252–4. On this remarkable find, see P. Neve and H. Otten in Neve (1984; 1986).

[50] Neu (1996: 3–7).

teaching texts in the Mesopotamian scribal tradition.[51] We do find that treaties can appear in two versions, one Hittite and one Akkadian, as can Old Hittite historiographic documents. Thus, *Hattusili's Annals* exist in a Hittite and an Akkadian version, as does the *Telipinu Proclamation*.[52] With respect to *Hattusili's Testament* and the Hattic–Hittite bilinguals, the two versions are sufficiently similar to be considered an original text accompanied by a translation, rather than two independent partially or nearly coinciding productions, unlike other Hurro-Hittite songs that have been found in both Hittite and Hurrian versions. The *Song of Release* is a more complex case; I will argue later in this chapter that it reveals the existence of a bilingual oral tradition.

The plot of the epic will be discussed in greater detail in later chapters of this book, in which the significance of its ties to other eastern Mediterranean narratives will be explored more fully, but I point out some key features here that show its importance for the prehistory of Greek epic. The *Song of Release* tells the story of the destruction of the north Syrian town of Ebla, brought on by the refusal of its council to release certain captives from the town of Ikinkalis, despite the attempts on the part of their king Meki to persuade them to accept the admonitions of the Storm-god. Here we have a plot with remarkable resemblances to that of the *Iliad*, both with respect to the overall plot concerning the conflict over Helen, and with respect to the conflict that sets the action in motion in Book I, when Achilles and king Agamemnon quarrel over the return of the concubine Chryseis to her father who has come to ransom her. However, in contrast to the *Iliad*, in which the notion of leadership is explored through the characters of Agamemnon and Achilles on the one hand, and Priam, Paris, and Hector on the other, the *Song of Release* unequivocally takes the side of the king, whose special relationship with the Storm-god enables him to relay the words of the god demanding the release of the captives, with the

---

[51] See Cooper (1971) for a listing of the bilinguals including Akkadian and/or Sumerian. The Akkadian/Hittite bilinguals include omen texts, hymns, and a wisdom text also found at Ugarit. The Sumerian/Akkadian texts are incantations. The Sumerian/Akkadian/Hittite trilinguals are a hymn and wisdom literature. Many of the Hattic/Hittite bilinguals or "quasi-bilinguals," which consist of passages quoted as part of rituals, especially building rituals, and songs, especially antiphonal songs involving groups of young women, are collected in Schuster (1974; 2002). There are Hurrian/Hittite bilingual or quasi-bilingual incantations. That is, they exist in some copies with Hurrian *legomena*, while in others the *legomena* are in Hittite, for example, CTH 780: *Ritual of Allaiturahhi* (see Haas and Wegner 1988: 5).

[52] It is generally believed that the Akkadian version of *Hattusili's Annals* is dependent on the Hittite one, rather than vice versa, but see Devecchi (2005: 26–32) for discussion with counter-arguments. For more details on the *Annals*, see Chapter 8, 149, with n. 44.

conditional promise of prosperity for the city if it obeys, and utter destruction if its council refuses.[53] The message in the threat of the destruction of the city is underlined repeatedly in an accompanying set of parables in which different creatures are punished for their lack of gratitude to their mentors.

Four more possible members of Hurro-Hittite song are *Elkunirsa and Ashertu*, *The Heroic Deeds of Gurparanzah*, the *Tale of Appu*, and the *Song of Oil*. *Elkunirsa and Ashertu* tells the earliest known version of the Potiphar's wife tale (also found in the myth of Bellerophontes). It follows the standard verse structure for Hurro-Hittite narrative song, and it was used somehow in a purification ritual. It tells of how Ashertu, rebuffed by the Storm-god, threatens him, but is punished by him with her husband's permission. Then, she seems to reconcile with her husband and is free to retaliate against the Storm-god, although he is warned by his sister, IŠTAR. The story breaks off here, and the back side of the tablet presents a purification ritual, which describes IŠTAR begging for the life of her brother.[54] *The Heroic Deeds of Gurparanzah* tells of how Gurparanzah, king of Ailanuwa, won the hand of Tadizuli, daughter of the king of Akkade, in a contest with bow and arrow at a feast at court, a scene with obvious parallels to Odysseus' contest with the suitors of his wife.[55] The *Tale of Appu* is about a rich but childless man who, through the Sun-god's intervention, produces two sons, named Good (ḫandanza) and Bad (ḫuwappaš), who end up fighting over their inheritance and taking their case to the gods.[56] We can compare, perhaps, the legal conflict between Hesiod and his brother Perses over their inheritance in the *Works and Days* (27–46). Finally, some scholars have proposed that one Hurrian fragment be assigned to a *Song of Oil*. In it, Oil is personified and engages in a dialogue with the Hurrian goddess Shawushka, possibly telling of how he fought a lion.[57]

---

[53] Bachvarova (2005a). [54] CTH 342. See Bachvarova (2013a: 30–3).

[55] S. P. Morris (1997: 621). The scene in the *Odyssey* has also been compared to Egyptian scenes; see Walcot (1984). Compare also the bride contest in the Turkic epic *Alpamysh* (Reichl 1992: 143–70, 339, 351). Levaniouk (2011: 234–5) focuses on the parallel of the eagle as a good omen in *Alpamysh* and *Odyssey*, which is also found in *Gurparanzah*. See partial trans. by M. Bachvarova in Chavalas (2013: 287–90).

[56] CTH 360. See Haas (2006: 194–9) for German translation and comparative discussion, also Hoffner (1998a: 82–5) for an English translation.

[57] See Giorgieri (2001: 136; 2009) on *KBo* 27.217 (discussion and translit. Salvini and Wegner 2004: 19–20, 42–4, No. 10), with duplicates, classified as *CTH* 345.II.2.A: *Song of Ullikummi* in the KhT. The examples discussed here do not exhaust the possible members of this genre. We have a variety of unplaced fragments, some of which could be the remains of otherwise lost

The copying down of Hurrian and Hittite narrative songs clearly did not happen at a single point in time according to a single process. The *Song of Release* is a one-off Middle Hittite production in a unique format, in which the Hittite side follows closely the Hurrian, with no later copies. The Hittite *Song of Keshshi* is extant only in New Hittite copies,[58] while two of the Hurrian fragments are of Middle Hittite date. The *Song of Silver* is similarly extant in New Hittite copies with pre-New-Hittite linguistic features.[59] No Hittite piece of the *Song of Gilgamesh* is earlier than the New Hittite period, but two Hurrian fragments date to the Middle Hittite period. The Kumarbi cycle is of New Hittite date, both the Hittite and the Hurrian versions, but the *Song of Birth* has Old Hittite features.[60] Further study may allow us to distinguish between older features that are the result of scribes copying older texts and those that are the result of the retention in the poetic language of archaisms that gave the poet more flexibility when composing.

The formal features of Hurro-Hittite narrative song

Indigenous genres, we can agree, should be defined by indigenous classifications as revealed, for example, in terminology, collecting of texts in particular locations in an archive or library, or grouping of texts together in lists.[61] To differentiate among genres we can also use such factors as method of composition, occasion of performance or use, audience, and performers. Finally, we can use the specific formal characteristics of the texts and performances themselves. Of course, because of the nature of our access to the evidence in question here – it is incomplete and furthermore which texts have been recovered is to some degree random – many of these criteria cannot be exploited fully. The key criteria for grouping texts into genres therefore must be shared formal features. The shared verse structure, formulas, and poetic techniques allow us to delimit a single oral-derived genre of Hurro-Hittite song that crossed linguistic barriers at

---

songs, cf. the fragments edited in Polvani (1992), ones booked under *CTH* 349 and 370 on KhT, and comments by Beckman (2005: 261).

[58] Haas (2005: 361) states that they show evidence of being copies of MH precursors.
[59] Hoffner (1988: 162).
[60] Haas (2006: 130), Melchert (2005: 453), who also discusses the fact that different Hurro-Hittite songs have different amounts of Luwianisms (also n. 15 here). On the dating of the tablets from Hattusa by script, spelling, and ductus, see Chapter 1, 8.
[61] See Dardano (2006) on Hittite tablet catalogs; van den Hout (2002a) and Archi (2007b: 192–6) on how the tablets were organized in the archives; Hutter (2011) on *Sammeltafeln* (tablets containing more than one text).

Hattusa, combining indigenous Anatolian themes with Hurrian, Syrian, and Mesopotamian ones.[62]

Poetic figures characteristic of Hurro-Hittite song – parallelism, ascending cola, simile and metaphor, assonance and alliteration – are typical of Near Eastern literary texts in general.[63] Some features of the Hittite versions of the songs are also found in Hittite texts that are derived from Hattic precursors. Thus, the inverted word order of the Hittite versions of Hurro-Hittite song is also found in translations of Hattic texts; it is a marker of Hittite "translation literature" that signals more broadly the artistic use of language.[64] Clitic doubling, in which characters in a sentence appear both as nouns and as members of the enclitic chain (made up of pronouns, local particles, and the quotative particle, attached to the first word of a sentence), a poetic device which translates roughly as, "the mountain, it does X ...," is another turn of phrase in the Hittite songs that is found in Hittite translations of Hattic liturgical phrases.[65]

The term "song" (Hitt. *išḫamāiš*) is a native one, appearing in at least some of the colophons, as well as in self-referential descriptions of the mode of performance,[66] just as *Atrahasis* and the *Epic of Creation* were classified as songs (Akk. *zamāru*).[67] The performer is identified as a LÚNAR 'musician, singer' (Hitt. LÚ*kinirtallaš*, literally 'lyre player'[68]) in the colophons of two of the tablets of the *Song of Release* and within the

---

[62] On Hurro-Hittite song, see Hoffner (1998a: 66–7; 1998b: 180), Neu (1996: 7), and Watkins (1995: 247–8). On the poetic techniques characteristic of the *Song of Release* and Hurro-Hittite poetry in general, see Neu (1988b: 246–8). These correspondences between various Hurro-Hittite songs are evidence that they are indeed members of a single literary genre. Archi (2007b: 197–201) has already pointed out some of the oral features of Hurro-Hittite song. He argues for Hittite oral poets: "transmission from the Hurrian to the Hittite can therefore have been achieved only orally. Therefore, the Hittite singers received these poems either directly from Hurrian singers, and then translated them into their own language or, more frequently, reworked the available written versions whilst respecting the literary form" (Archi 2009: 210). As will be seen below, I have a different idea of how the Hurrian songs made their way to the Hittite language.

[63] Haas (2006: 123–4). [64] Sidel'tsev (2002).

[65] Melchert (1998) argues that clitic doubling is unique to Hittite, but D. R. M. Campbell (2007: 58) notes that clitic doubling with the absolute case pronoun is common in Hurrian.

[66] Schuol (2004: 141), and cf. the openings of *Ullikummi*: CTH 345.1.1.A = KUB 33.96 i 4, *Silver*: CTH 364.1.A = HFAC 12 i 7, and *Gilgamesh*: CTH 341.III.1.A$_1$ = KUB 8.57 i 1–2, see Chapter 3, 64–5, and Chapter 5, 113–14, with n. 7.

[67] Cf. the end of the OB *Atrahasis*: "This [my] song (is) for your praise" (trans. Foster 2005: 253) and the end of the SB *Epic of Creation*: "Let them sound abroad the song of Marduk,/ How he defeated Tiamat and took kingship" (trans. Foster 2005: 485).

[68] According to the lexical list *Sa Vocabulary* LÚNAR = LÚ*kinirtallaš*: CTH 299.5 = KBo 1.52 i 15′–16′ (translit. and trans. Landsberger and Hallock 1955: 64), see Schuol (2004: 163–4).

song itself, reference is made to the (poor) pay of the singer.[69] To be sure, we moderns might not consider the ᴸᵁNAR's mode of performance to be "singing." It has been proposed that the Hurrian voluntative verb *šidatili*, used in the opening lines of the *Song of Release*, is related to the Hurrian noun *šīri* 'number' and thus should mean 'I shall recount'.[70] However, at Mari, the *muštawûm*, who recites or declaims (*uštawûm*), is grouped with musicians (*nārum*),[71] indicating that this mode of performance was considered to be as artfully produced as a musician's. Finally, as Gregory Nagy has pointed out, cross-cultural evidence shows that while the category of song is distinct from everyday speech, it is not necessarily melodic as we in modern Western culture would define it.[72]

The noun *išḫamāiš* is formed from the verb *išḫai-/išḫiya-*'bind', i.e., 'bound speech';[73] compare the Sumerian sign SIR₃ (ŠIR) 'song', which also stands for KEŠDA 'knot, bind'. The Hittite term reflects a common Indo-European metaphor for poetic verses and narratives as products of craftsmen, using images of spinning, weaving, or sewing to describe the process of linking together the words and formulaic expressions into a highly worked and ornamented whole. Examples include the metaphor of the *rhapsōidos* 'song-stitcher', who combines sections (perhaps with a collaborator) as if creating a piece of clothing; the Greek term *oimē* 'song', cf. *oimos* 'thread'; Gr. *humnos* from *huph-* 'weave'; and the Indic term *sūtra* 'thread', on which the words are strung like beads, from the same verb root as *išḫamāiš*, PIE *sh₂ey-* 'bind'.[74] The technological image of a woman or man artistically transforming the raw material of language into an object of beauty implies a process that requires a level of training, if not professionalism, from the poet. Indeed, the Hittite versions of Hurro-Hittite song are just as artistically polished as the Hurrian ones. Certainly, whoever was responsible for the Hittite versions of the songs needed to have achieved some level of proficiency in the poetic language used in order to produce

---

[69] *KBo* 32.13 bott. edge 2; 66 2' (translit. and trans. Neu 1996: 227, 526). On the poor (?) pay of the singer, see *KBo* 32.16 iii 4' (translit. and trans. Neu 1996: 278–9, with discussion pp. 8, 284). On the term ᴸᵁNAR and his songs in Hittite texts see Schuol (2004: 136–47, 163–72).
[70] See Neu (1996: 257–8). At Ugarit *šr* is 'sing' and in Akkadian *šērum* is 'song'.
[71] Ziegler (2007: 50–1).   [72] Nagy (1990b: 19–51).
[73] Haas (2005: 361) and Bader (1989: 23, 269, n. 114).
[74] Nagy (1996a: 83–91; 1996b: 61–76; 2009: 229–32; 2010: 278–308). Schmitt (1967: 296–301) and Durante (1971, 1976: 2.167–79) discuss the metaphors of building, weaving, and sewing together songs in Vedic, Greek, and Germanic. On attempts to connect Hitt. *išḫamāiš* with Indic *sāman*, and Gr. *oimos* see *HEG* (I-K: 379–80) and Maslov (2012: 200–2), covering the scholarly discussion although preferring the etymology "path, way" for *oimos*. The weaving image is also used in Sumerian: *šir tag.tag* (Alster 1992: 48, n. 97).

the formulaic phrasing and prosodic patterns that define the genre. If indeed scribes rather than an illiterate singer were responsible for producing them, they were steeped in the oral tradition from which the textualizations of both Hurrian and Hittite songs were derived.

In the rest of this section I discuss further evidence of variation (beyond the differences between the Hittite and Hurrian versions mentioned so far), which is a marker of oral-derived texts. I then touch on formulas shared among Hurro-Hittite narrative songs, some of which are also found in Greek epic. Next, I touch briefly on the prosody of the Hurrian and Hittite versions. Finally, I move on to a comparative discussion of the bilingual Serbian–Albanian epic tradition. This last will show that we should consider the Hurrian and Hittite epic narratives as representing instantiations of two nearly convergent but ultimately independent formulaic systems developed by bilingual poets, such as found in Central Asia.

Over the past eighty years the question of orality has both inspired and plagued the field of epic studies. When a performer utilizes a chapbook, has read an authoritative version, takes notes in order to help his memory, or performs with the awareness that his performance will be published in print form, is it real "folk" epic? Currently most scholars of modern traditional epic accept that none of these factors precludes calling a performance "authentically oral."[75] In fact, my primary concern here is not whether the texts under scrutiny are authentically oral, that is, produced via composition in performance by an illiterate performer. With the evidence at hand, it is not possible to draw a firm line between texts that were composed in performance and ones that were written by scribes. It is not impossible that some performers were literate (although to be sure there are no clear examples, at Hattusa at least, of literate singers), and scribes were surely well aware of the oral tradition, even if they were not master bards themselves.[76]

---

[75] See generally Finnegan (1980), who has, however, been criticized for defining "oral" literature too broadly, encompassing anything that is performed aloud. For a comparative analysis of Balinese performance traditions, in which training for improvisational oral performances includes use of written materials, see de Vet (1996), who in her later work delves into the intellectual trends that influenced Parry, showing that his theory of oral poetry was based on now outmoded notions contrasting oral and literate modes of thought (de Vet 2005). Powell (2002: 4–17, 21–3, 56–71), although revisiting the oral-literate dichotomy, remains particularly concerned with the concept that certain types of texts can only be produced with writing, even as he notes the ways in which the two concepts have been misused.

[76] More relevant to those who study ancient epic, since all our sources are perforce written, is the work on "textualization" of epic, that is, how an orally produced narrative reaches a written form, and to what degree the writing and editing of the text affect its initial production and final written form. See Honko (2000a) and more generally the contributions to his edited volume (2000b).

When a performer is sufficiently proficient in the formulaic phraseology in which the story is told, he or she in a sense produces the text anew each time it is performed, even if he or she perceives himself or herself to be repeating it "exactly." When scribes absorb enough of the oral traditions to be affected by them, and are able to expand and contract episodes to cater to their audience, and to vary their wording – whether consciously or unconsciously – according to the formulaic systems of the genre, even if they intend to reproduce a known text "exactly," it results in what Paul Zumthor has labeled *mouvance*.[77] Because *mouvance* in written texts is indicative of a living oral tradition, it is one important, if indirect, indication that there was an active oral tradition from which written versions of the songs we have were drawn. John Miles Foley has explicated the category of "*oral-derived texts*, that is, the manuscript or tablet works of finally uncertain provenance that nonetheless show oral traditional characteristics,"[78] which is applicable to Homer and much European narrative poetry dating to the medieval period, while in his posthumous book Albert Lord acknowledged the possibility of "transitional texts," composed by literate, even well-educated, poets steeped in the oral tradition.[79] The concept of oral-derived or transitional literature is eminently applicable to the material under discussion here, though it needs some reshaping to fit the second-millennium context of the texts under examination, for it is highly unlikely that any of the Hurro-Hittite narrative songs found in Anatolia were copied to disseminate works of literature *qua* literature to a wider audience.

I present an example from the *Song of Ullikummi* of the kind of scene-level variation expected from oral-derived literature.[80] Here the brothers of the goddess Anzili come to her and the three go off to observe the monstrous being growing from the mountain. I have underlined the relevant variations:

The first version:

>   i 15′   ... Tarhun a[nd] Tashmisu
>   took each other [b]y the h[and.] [Fro]m the *kuntarra*-
>   building,
>   from the temple they went forth [...], while Anzili from
>   heaven

---

[77] Zumthor (1987: 160–72; 1992: 46–9), with reference to medieval manuscripts of troubador poetry. This kind of variation is fundamentally different from the errors made by Mesopotamian scribes copying out memorized texts, which are discussed by Delnero (2012).
[78] Foley (1990: 5, emphasis in the original, also see his pp. 1–8).   [79] Lord (1995: 212–37).
[80] Already noticed by Güterbock (1952: 10–11), with further discussion of variants at Güterbock (1951: 143). Also see Bachvarova (2014).

with heroicness cam[e] away. [An]zili to her mind
spoke in turn. "Wher[e] are they running inside,
20'   the two brothers?" She sw[ift]ly(?)[81]
stood, Anzili. Before her two [brothers] she rose up.
They t[o]ok each other by the hand.
They went up to Mt. Hazzi.[82]

The second version:

iv 3'   [They] hurr[ied] (?)
         [t]ook each other [by the hand]
5'   [   ] they went f[o]rth
         [   ] they walked
         [   ] with [heroic]ness s/he came back.
         [   ] she saw. Anzili
         [   ] "Wh]ere they inside
10'   [   ] I will proceed to [c]ome. Anzili
         [   ] before her brother she stood up.

         [   ] began. "Where are you (s.) running? [ ]
         [   ] "W]hat path is it? Tell it to me.
         [   ] Tarhun an[swered] Anzili
15'   [   ] "... to me Istanu (the Sun-god) answered ..."
         [   ]
         [s/he do]es [something]
         [   ] Th]ey
         [   ] they went up [to Mt. Hazz]i.[83]

In the beginning of the passage in question, the differences, as far as the lacunae allow us to see, are minor, but the second of the two versions then presents a speech by Anzili that is not in the first; although the end of the second passage has a large gap, it is clear that those missing lines contained material not in the first version. Thus, the second version is expanded compared to the first version.

We can see larger-scale variation in the *Song of Hedammu* as well, for there are at least two different Hittite versions represented among the extant fragments; Version "X," most of one entire tablet, describes in detail the seduction of Hedammu by Anzili, while fragments of another tablet, "Version Y," include not only the seduction scene, but also a discussion involving Ea, scolding Kumarbi and Tarhun for the damage they are doing to humans with their fighting; it must also include a meeting between

---

[81] So García Trabazo (2002: 213).   [82] *CTH* 345.1.2.A = *KUB* 36.12 + *KUB* 33.113 i 15'–23'.
[83] *CTH* 345.1.1.D/2.C = *KUB* 33.92 iv 3'–19'.

Kumarbi and the Sea. So, it goes through the plot much more swiftly than "Version X."[84]

We move to examining some shared formulas in Hurro-Hittite song, comparing them to formulas and type scenes in the later Homeric tradition. As McNeill has noted, there are in fact striking similarities in style between the Late Bronze Age narrative tradition and Homer:

> The Hittite epic shares with all the other main epic traditions of the ancient Near East – Sumerian, Akkadian and Ugaritic – the habit of employing constantly recurring phrases of varying length, conventionally described by modern scholars as "formulae." Each tradition has a considerable number of stock phrases – noun-epithet combinations, whole verses, and even groups of verses – that are likely to occur in any poem belonging to it. Similarly, repetitions of single verses or groups of verses are apt to occur within a short space in an individual poem, though the verses concerned are not used outside it. What is particularly striking – though by no means a coincidence – is that this feature is shared by the Greek Iliad and Odyssey of Homer.[85]

The parallels with Greek epic suggest that it should be considered to be a relative of the Hurro-Hittite tradition, and that bards performing songs, rather than merchants *vel sim.* recounting basic plots, were the means by which Near Eastern epic motifs reached the Homeric tradition. Since for the most part it is the Hittite versions of the songs that have been sufficiently preserved to track shared formulaic patterns, the emphasis here will be on the Hittite material. In any case, it is important to show that the Hittite versions in particular have a formulaic quality in order to combat the

---

[84] I have translated what can be reconstructed of the two versions, with the aid of parallel passages, in López-Ruiz (2013: 144–53), along with other fragments. I arrange the version as follows: "Version X," with the extended telling of the seduction: A = *KUB* 33.85 (+) *IBoT* 2.135 (+) *KUB* 33.86 + 8.66 (+) 36.57 (+) *KBo* 26.74 (+) 19.110 (+) 26.75; B = *KUB* 33.88; C = *KBo* 22.51; D = *KUB* 36.95 + 56. "Version Y," the more swift-moving version: A = *KBo* 26.72 (+) *KBo* 19.109 + 109a + Bo 6404 + *KUB* 33.84; B = *KBo* 56.6 + *KUB* 8.65; C = *KUB* 33.100 + *KUB* 36.16; D = *KUB* 33.103; E = *KUB* 33.116; F = *KUB* 33.122; G = *KBo* 26.71 + *KUB* 12.65 + *KBo* 26.112 + Bo 69/546; H = *KBo* 26.73; I = *KBo* 19.111. In this book, however, I do not use the classification system given above. Instead I continue to use the numbering scheme of KhT for the *Song of Hedammu*.

[85] McNeill (1963: 237–8). Also see M. L. West (1997a: 169, 220) and Burkert (1992: 114–20) on formulas in Near Eastern epic. Lesky (1955) also compared some phrases of hexametric poetry to Hurro-Hittite poetry. Haas (2006: 126–8) compares the style and use of formulas in Hurro-Hittite and Homeric epic. Also see Archi (2007b: 199–200) for more examples of formulas and type scenes, and further discussion of formulas and type scenes in Hurro-Hittite narrative song in Bachvarova (2014). See Chapter 1, 3, n. 8, for references to Puhvel's work on further parallels in phraseology between Greek epic and Hittite.

commonly held notion that they are simply scribal translations of Hurrian texts. However, I must first point out that previous research on the roots of written Akkadian and Sumerian poetry in oral tradition has been hampered by an excessively close adherence to the Parry–Lord "oral formulaic" theory, in which the hallmark of oral poetry is the use of the formula, or "a group of words which is regularly employed under the same metrical conditions to express a given essential idea."[86] In fact, the word-patterning is not necessarily so rigid. For Near Eastern poetic narratives it is better to look for formulaic expressions, a formulaic template.[87]

I mention here a few such shared expressions. The most frequently seen stock epic phrase in Hittite is "X began to speak (in turn)" (X (āppa) memiškiwan daiš), using the supine construction with frequentative verb so common to artful Hittite narrative.[88] In Hurrian the phrase is alu=m=ai=n kad=i=a 'saying it, s/he declares', or alu=i=b ḫill=i(=b) 's/he said, s/he spoke'.[89] Every speech then elicits a reaction, whether rejoicing, anger, or sadness. This reflects the importance of speaking and speech-acts in the narrative tradition; the poem shows that words are powerful in order to invest itself with greater significance.[90] A similar formula appears in Akkadian narrative poems such as the *Epic of Gilgamesh*, particularly in the later sections of the Standard Babylonian version: "A opened his mouth to speak, saying to B."[91]

Stock characters have stock epithets, such as "Teshshub, great/heroic lord/king of Kummi," found in the Hurrian *Song of Gilgamesh*, the opening line of

---

[86] Parry (1930: 272). First articulated by Parry in 1928, see Parry (1971); also see Foley (1988: 20–35). On issues with the definition of the formula and the excessive reliance on oral formulaic theory in analyzing Homeric poetry see Hoekstra (1965: 7–30). One attempt to apply oral formulaic theory to Mesopotamian texts is the collection of articles in Vogelzang and Vanstiphout (1992).

[87] As described by Lord (1960: 4).

[88] *Appu* varies with "X began to ask." (*CTH* 360.1.A = *KUB* 24.8 i 27). See Melchert (1998: 483–4).

[89] Giorgieri (2001: 141); Salvini (1977: 76–7; 1988: 166–8).

[90] The formulas that introduce speeches and reactions to them are discussed by McNeill (1963: 238, 240–1), who cites Greek equivalents of the type, "answering him spoke swift-footed Achilles" (*Il.* 1.84); and Archi (2007b: 199). Also see Burkert (1992: 116), Haas (2006: 125, 127), and M. L. West (1997a: 196–8). The introductory form "begin to speak" is found in one non-poetic Hittite text, the *Testament of Hattusili I*: *CTH* 6 = *KUB* 1.16 iii 56 (translit. Sommer and Falkenstein 1938: 14), where it is meant to mark high style. Based on the citations in the *CHD* (M: 255) the formula appears in the *Song of Silver, Keshshi*, the Kumarbi cycle, including *Ullikummi, Gilgamesh, Appu*, and *Telipinu Myth (Mugawar)*. More detailed statistics on ways of introducing speeches in Hittite poetry may be found in De Vries (1967: 110–19).

[91] A *pāšu ipušamma iqabbi izzakkara ana* B (Tigay 1982: 233). In Ugaritic it appears as "He lifted up his voice and cried," for example in *Aqhat* (*KTU* 1.19 iii 13, trans. N. Wyatt 2002: 304).

the *Song of Release*, and the *Song of Ullikummi*.[92] Shawushka is "Queen of Nineveh," Kumarbi is "Father of the Gods," and Ea is "King of Wisdom."[93]

Finally, the most striking example of shared formulas was found by Erich Neu. It is a three-line passage from a Hurrian textualization of the *Song of Keshshi*, which corresponds nearly identically with a few lines from the *Song of Release*. The lines are too fragmentary to understand, but the passage is from the speech threatening Ebla.[94] Unfortunately, it is impossible to situate this passage in a particular episode of *Keshshi*, because so little of it has been preserved.

One formula that alliterates beautifully in Hittite, "Dark Earth" (*danku tekan/ dankuš daganzipaš*; Hurr. *timeri eže*[95]) is found not only in Hittite epic narratives, but also in *mugawar* invocations[96] and incantations, and was used in Hattic as well (*ištarrazil*[97]). Like inverted word order, it seems to be a marker of stylized speech more generally. It is found in the poetic speech of other Indo-European languages, and in Greek it is used by both Homer (*gāia melaina*, *Il.* 2.699, etc.) and Sappho (*gān melai[n]an*, F 16.2 Lobel-Page).[98]

There are other sets of Hittite formulas that have Greek counterparts which have been elaborated: A formula shared by the Hittite *Gilgamesh*, *Hedammu*, and *Ullikummi*, "his tears flowed like canals,"[99] has been compared to "Agamemnon stood pouring tears like a black-watered fountain, which pours dark water down a rock too sheer for goats."[100] In the *Song of Ullikummi* Kumarbi says to his vizier, "Take your staff with your hand and pu[t] the swift winds o[n yo]ur [feet] as shoes,"[101]

---

[92] *Song of Ullikummi*: CTH 345.I.1.A = KUB 33.93 + KUB 17.7 iii 32′. For *Song of Gilgamesh* see Salvini and Wegner (2004: 16–17). For *Song of Release* see Chapter 5, 113.
[93] See Haas (2006: 124–5) and Archi (2007b: 199) on these noun–epithet combinations.
[94] Neu (1993a: 114–18). Release: CTH 789 = KBo 32.214 i 8′–11′ (translit. Neu 1996: 550), KBo 32.107 (translit. Neu 1996: 544); Keshshi: CTH 361.II.5 = KUB 47.5 iv 13–15 (translit. Salvini and Wegner 2004: 64–5, No. 30).
[95] *Song of Release*: CTH 789 = KBo 32.13 i/ii 10 (translit. Neu 1996: 220–1).
[96] On the Anatolian *mugawar* invocation for a disappeared god, see Chapter 4, 103–4, with n. 115.
[97] Schuster (1974: 107–8) and Soysal (2004a: 506).
[98] See Oettinger (1989–1990), arguing it is borrowed from Hurrian (disproved by Soysal 2002: 330), Dunkel (1993: 103), and Haas (2006: 128). Alcaeus F 130B.14 Lobel-Page: *me[l]ainas* ... *khthonos*.
[99] Gilgamesh: CTH 341.III.3.A = KUB 8.48 i 18–19 (Gilgamesh reacts to Enkidu's dream about his impending death); Hedammu: CTH 348.I.5.A = KBo 19.112 rev.? 18′ lacunose; Ullikummi: CTH 345.I.2.A = KUB 33.113 i 16′–17′. Noted by Klinger (2005: 119–20), who also provides more examples. Also see Chapter 5, 127–8, with nn. 63–4, for other shared formulas.
[100] *Il.* 9.13–15; *Il.* 16.3–4 (Patroclus); McNeill (1963: 239).
[101] CTH 345.I.1.A = KUB 36.7a iii 39′–41′ + 17.7 iii 10′–11′. See McNeill (1963: 238–9). Also see Archi (2007b: 199) on this as a formulaic expression.

phrasing repeated in the many instances in which a character departs to a new location. In Homer, the shoes are winged, the wind carries the messenger, and the sequence has again been elaborated:

> (Hermes) tied his beautiful sandals under his feet, immortal, golden, which carried him both over the water and over the limitless earth with the breath of the wind. He seized his staff, with which he enchants the eyes of men, whomsoever he wishes, and again wakes up even the sleeping; holding this with his hands he flew, powerful Argeiphontes.[102]

Another, more extensive, example of a Hittite formulaic template is the negative reaction to a speech, as passages from the Hittite version of the *Song of Release* and the *Song of Birth* show.[103] A set of formulaic phrases develops a specific narrative sequence: a character hears a curse, feels sick inside of himself, then responds with a curse of his own. Below are two variants of this scene from the Hittite side of the parables associated with the *Song of Release*:[104]

> And, when the mountain heard, his heart was sickened inside him, and the mountain cursed the deer in return, "The deer whom I fattened, now he curses me in return. Let the hunters also bring him, the deer, down ..."[105]

> The craftsman heard, and his heart f[elt] bad inside him. [The craftsman] says before his mind, "Why does the tower which I built curse me?" The craftsman spoke a curse [against the tower], "Let Tarhun also strike it, the tower ..."[106]

A third example from the *Song of Release* combines the formulas of the first part of the first passage quoted above, and a variant of the craftsman's response from the second passage:

> When the smith heard, his heart was sickened inside him.
> The smith began to speak before his heart, "Why does the copper which I poured curse me in return?" The smith said a curse against the cup. "Let Tarhun also strike it, the cup ..."[107]

---

[102] *Il.* 24.340–5 = *Od.* 5.44–9.
[103] On reactions leading into direct speech, see Vogelzang (1990), whose examples show that Hurro-Hittite negative reactions fit within broader Near Eastern conventions.
[104] Also compare *CTH* 789 = *KBo* 32.14 left edge 1–3 (translit. Neu 1996: 95; trans. M. Bachvarova in López-Ruiz 2013: 299), concerning the woodsman and the piece of wood.
[105] *KBo* 32.14 ii 9–14 (translit. Neu 1996: 75, 77; trans. M. Bachvarova in López-Ruiz 2013: 297).
[106] *KBo* 32.14 rev. 44–6 (translit. Neu 1996: 91; trans. M. Bachvarova in López-Ruiz 2013: 298).
[107] *KBo* 32.14 ii 50–6 (translit. Neu 1996: 81, 83; trans. M. Bachvarova in López-Ruiz 2013: 298).

The comparable example from *Song of Birth* quoted below comes at the end of a damaged passage, from which the full context cannot be gleaned, but Tarhun has heard that the gods led by Kumarbi are resolved to do battle with him. Tarhun is upset at the news and reminds his bull Sherish how he had cursed his foes already and has driven off Kumarbi (perhaps). Sherish replies with concern, "Why are you cursing them?," warning that Ea can hear him. Then, the curses seem to be conveyed to Ea, because we have a series of third-person imperatives, and Ea replies in words very similar to those of the offended craftsmen in the *Song of Release*:

> When Ea h[eard] the word[s], in his heart he felt bad. Ea began to speak in turn to the Tutelary Deity of the Steppe, "Don't you say curses repeatedly to me! He who cursed me, [...] curses me! You who [(verb) (object)] to me in turn, you curse me! Underneath a pot of beer [(subject?) (verb)], that pot boils over!"[108]

Ea, probably speaking to the second of Tarhun's bulls, Tauri, seems to be warning him that by repeating the curses of Tarhun, he himself is cursing Ea and will therefore be punished. The scenario is the same as that in the parables: a superior learns of the rebelliousness of one of his subordinates, expressed in a curse uttered by the subordinate. However, the craftsmen do in fact curse their artifact effectively in return, while Ea probably only threatens to curse Tauri. Further, the craftsmen's dismay is expressed only to themselves, while Ea speaks aloud to Tauri.

This same motif of a negative reaction to a speech can be found in many other works in the eastern Mediterranean epic tradition, including the *Iliad*, for example at 1.188–92:[109]

> So he (Agamemnon) spoke; and the son of Peleus felt pain, and in his shaggy breast his heart was in doubt, whether, drawing his sword from beside his thigh, to move aside the others and kill the son of Atreus, or to check his anger and restrain his passion.

Further, the second part of the sequence of formulas found in the parables, the speaking to oneself in response to something said, is found in the *Iliad*:

---

[108] *CTH* 344.A = *KUB* 36.31 5′–7′ + *KUB* 33.120 iii 67′–72′ (trans. M. Bachvarova in López-Ruiz 2013: 143).

[109] Compare what Sargon says in the Late Assyrian version of *Sargon, King of Battle*, when he has heard how his merchants have been ill-treated by the ruler of the Anatolian city Purushanda: "When Sargon heard the word of the merchants, his heart was grieved ..." (4′, translit. and trans. J. G. Westenholz 1997: 136–7). The sequence is also found in a lacunose passage in the *Song of Birth*: *CTH* 344.A = *KUB* 33.120 iii 19′–21′ (trans. M. Bachvarova in López-Ruiz 2013: 143).

"Angered, (Odysseus) spoke to his great-hearted soul, 'Woe is me, what do I suffer? ...'"[110] The details of the curse and counter-curse, however, are unique to the Hurro-Hittite tradition and speak to the Hittite obsession with magical speech.

Turning now to the prosody of Hurro-Hittite epic, the Hittite incarnation of Hurro-Hittite epic has been shown by Ian McNeill to fit "the familiar meter of the Sumerian and Akkadian epics, which has four stresses and is divided into two cola of two stresses each."[111] Stephen Durnford and Craig Melchert have since refined McNeill's results. Durnford argues that not all words in a Hittite poetic phrase carry stress, but rather that only nouns, verbs, and predicate adjectives must be stressed; adjectives and genitives preceding a head noun are unstressed. Melchert demonstrates that lack of stress is optional, and that the combination of supine and finite verb can count as a single stress unit.[112]

The prosody of Hurrian, on the other hand, has not yet been explored to any great extent. Any metrical analysis of Hurro-Hittite poetry requires fully preserved paragraphs, since the tablets are not laid out with a single stiche per tablet line, and finding a full paragraph preserved is a rare circumstance indeed! Only the text of the *Song of Release* is sufficiently well preserved for analysis of the Hurrian version. My survey of the evidence from it has shown that the Hurrian side of the *Song of Release* conforms to the same rules of prosody that the Hittite side does.[113] Nearly all complete paragraphs in the Hurrian side of *Song of Release* can easily be read as made up of lines consisting of four stressed words setting off semantically coherent phrases. My attempt to evaluate Hurrian meter thus lends support to McNeill's theory that the similarity between the Hittite epic meter and Mesopotamian epic meter indicates the Hittites borrowed the verse form from the Hurrians, who in turn had borrowed it from Mesopotamian sources.[114]

Bilingual poets

The shared poetic language of Hurro-Hittite narrative song indicates a long-standing tradition, already full-grown at its first recording in the

---

[110] *Il.* 11.403–4. On the Hittite and Greek formula, "he spoke to himself," see Dunkel (1993: 105–6). Also see M. L. West (1997a: 199 with earlier refs.) on negative reactions to speeches, and speaking to oneself. He cites these two Iliadic passages, comparing the latter to the *Epic of Gilgamesh*, SB x 11–12 (translit. and trans. George 2003: 678–9).

[111] McNeill (1963: 240).   [112] Durnford (1971) and Melchert (1998; forthcoming).

[113] Bachvarova (2011).

[114] McNeill (1963: 242). On the transfer of poetic prosodic patterns across languages, see Bachvarova (2004).

Middle Hittite *Song of Release*. This allows us to surmise a lively oral tradition extending back in time before that. What we are seeing with the *Song of Release* is the first writing down of an existing bilingual tradition. I turn now to evidence from the former Yugoslavia and Central Asia of how oral epic can cross linguistic barriers, which could help explain the mechanisms of transfer of epic, not only from Hurrian to Hittite, but ultimately from one or more Syro-Anatolian languages into Greek.

The Hurro-Hittite tradition is comparable, for example, to the Balkan epic tradition about the brothers Mujo and Halil that was shared by Bosnian Serbs and Northern Albanians, as meticulously analyzed by John Kolsti and Stavro Skendi. Indeed, Kolsti's analysis of the bilingual tradition provides insight into how the Hurro-Hittite poetic tradition could have developed. While Skendi considers the Albanian version of the tradition to be completely derivative, offering good evidence of the strong influence of specifically Serbian motifs and formulas on the Albanian version,[115] Kolsti shows that the bilingual singer is not simply translating from one language to another. Rather, he is able "to develop a given theme on the basis of two distinct formulaic patterns."[116] Kolsti's study of the two traditions, focusing particularly on the *Legend of Kosovo* and sections of *Mujo and Halil*, for which versions in both northern Albanian and Serbian were available, notes the many points at which they coincide, from characters and motifs to themes and entire narratives, proposing that bilingual singers skilled in composing in both languages were responsible for transmitting themes, motifs, and formulaic expressions across the linguistic barrier.[117]

> Ugljanin has little difficulty in expressing the ideas "mounted" and "dismounted" in Albanian, because the Albanian tradition provides him with formulas. When the formulaic patterns in Albanian and Serbo-Croatian do not coincide, either because of vocabulary or rhythmic patterns . . ., the bilingual singer recreates formulas which he has learned through the years from Albanian singers . . . But in many instances Albanian and Serbo-Croatian formulas do correspond. That is, the bilingual singer may use similar words and grammatical constructions to express a given idea in the two languages. This in no way implies,

---

[115] Skendi (1954: 99–116).
[116] Kolsti (1990: 129). "The Albanian variants, it is clear, share many common elements with the Bosnian songs, or even the popular written songs. But this in no way proves that the Kosovo *songs* originate in the Serbian Christian oral tradition. The Kosovo songs from Old Serbia . . . point to a firm Albanian Moslem oral tradition little influenced by the Serbian Christian written tradition" (Kolsti 1990: 194). I discuss the relevance of the Serbian–Albanian epic tradition in more detail in Bachvarova (2014).
[117] A decasyllabic verse cognate with the Slavic *deseterjac* was in widespread use in northern Albania, used by both Muslims and Catholics (Kolsti 1990: 3–7; *contra* Skendi 1954: 174, 196).

however, that the singer translates such formulas from one language to another; it simply means that Albanian and Serbo-Croatian formulas may coincide.[118]

While versions of the narratives in each of the languages differ in the same ways that different versions in the same language do, with expansion and contraction of sections and addition or omission of episodes and motifs, versions in different languages can also be nearly identical sometimes.[119] Some features, however, do not cross cultural barriers. For example,

> Ugljanin refers to [the hero] Mujo's sister as "the white" Ajkuna, *Ajkunen te bardh*. This is a common Albanian epithet used to describe a woman ... [I]t is curious to note that Ugljanin avoids this epithet when he sings of Ajkuna in Serbo-Croatian.[120]

In the light of these comparative examples, we should be careful not to assume that where the Hittite version differs from the Hurrian version of the *Song of Release*, the one text in which one can fruitfully do a line-by-line comparison, the Hittite version is inaccurate.[121] Furthermore, all Hurrian poetic figures did not need to be imitated exactly. The Hittite poetic language was free to develop or exploit characteristically Hittite figures. While the *Song of Release* was written down paragraph by paragraph, switching back and forth between the two languages, a tour de force in collaboration by the singer(s) and scribe(s), the Hittite versions of other songs were composed in an essentially different manner, separately from the Hurrian ones, and the fragments we have of the Hurrian versions show that they differ, sometimes significantly. This indicates that the Hittite tradition, even if it was originally derived from the Hurrian one, eventually could stand on its own.

Further insight into how bilingual epic singers worked in multilingual contexts is given by Karl Reichl's work on Turkic epic. He shows that they were responsible for transferring the epic cycle *Köroğlu/Göroglï* from Azerbaijan to the Turkmens, Uzbeks, Uighurs, the Arabs in Bukhara, and Tajiks, among others.[122] He is able in some cases to pinpoint from

---

[118] Kolsti (1990: 44–5, and see his pp. 13–57).   [119] Kolsti (1990: 136–7).
[120] Kolsti (1990: 37).
[121] De Martino (1999) presents a close comparative study of the poetics of the Hurrian and Hittite sides, but is thinking in terms of translation (and mistakes in translation), not of a poet who can work creatively in two languages. He is followed by Archi (2007b: 190). Also see Wilhelm (1997: 283–4) for "mistakes." See my discussion in Bachvarova (2014).
[122] Reichl (1992: 66–75, 249–61, 319–33). Also see Reichl (2001: 41–9), surveying the different versions of *Alpamysh* in different Central Asian languages.

which language to which language the transfer happened, for example, from Turkmen to Karakalpak, or from Uzbek to Tajik. He can even pinpoint particular performers who served as nodes by which transfer across languages occurred, either because they themselves could perform in more than one traditional epic language, or because their students could. Thus, a single man can be responsible for the transfer of an epic from one language to another, and only a few bilingual bards could have a major effect. Another key point from his study is that the teacher-to-student transfer of an epic tradition consists of the ability to perform specific epics, rather than the ability to perform epic more generally. We do not need many bilingual bards like the one(s) responsible for the textualizations of the *Song of Release* in Hurrian and Hittite to transfer the storylines we know were transferred from Hurrian to Hittite or another Syro-Anatolian language (including possibly a non-Greek Cypriot language) in the second millennium, or from a Near Eastern language to Greek in the Early Iron Age. I argue that this was the process by which the Near Eastern epic plot lines, type scenes, and formulas made their way to Greek hexametric epic.

The functions of Hurro-Hittite narrative song

I present here a brief overview of the milieus and motivations of the Hurro-Hittite narrative songs mentioned in this chapter. Volkert Haas has suggested that all Hittite myths, including Hurro-Hittite narrative songs, had a ritual function,[123] and I argue that the ritual context of the texts provided one of the key means by which such texts were transmitted to Greek-speakers, for it both provided an opportunity for hearing the text and provided the text with some value and thus motivated the borrowing. I do not mean to imply that texts were not performed purely for entertainment as well, in more informal settings within the family or among friends, or as a part of feasts and celebrations not sponsored by the state; such settings were surely also milieus in which Greek-speakers would have had access to Syro-Anatolian mythology and epic. However, I speak here primarily of what is visible to us in the archaeological record, in the tablets whose copying and storage served the Hittite state and the monumental

---

[123] Haas (2006: 131). J. Lorenz and Rieken (2010), on the other hand, argue that their primary function was teaching scribes to write. I see the use of epic texts in the scribal curriculum as deriving from their cultural importance; when scribes were taught to write with these texts, they were also taught the key values of the social order for which they worked.

ruins that represent physical settings for performances. Furthermore, although there was indeed a particularly clear connection between myth and ritual in the Hittite texts,[124] it is not safe to assume that outside of the circle that produced those texts or among the Greeks the connection was always equally strong. However, it is possible to postulate functions for most Hurro-Hittite songs, each serving different purposes, often more than one. In some cases the song empowers or reminds the gods of their duties, in others it provides an etiology for a practice. Two songs can be connected to ancestor veneration. On the temporal plane, the songs assert the right of the Hittite king to rule his people, admonishing them to be obedient to their ruler. They define his role as just benefactor of his people, whose righteous actions earn the approbation of the gods and ensure prosperity for the land. Thus, the versions of the narratives preserved by the Hittite scribes speak to the needs and propaganda purposes of the court that sponsored them.[125]

Some textualizations could have been performed as one of the offerings to a god in festivals or in cult observances. As noted earlier, the *Song of the Sea* is attested to have been performed in a festival setting. In the opening of the *Song of Birth* the Former Gods are called to listen.[126] This may indicate that the setting for the performance of the song was a ritual propitiating the Former Gods. The *Song of Birth* could have been used to accompany a ritual with incense, which plays a central role in the song and would have been considered to be a messenger to the gods in the ritual.[127] Sacrifices to the *kunkunuzzi*-stone are described in the Hittite *Song of Birth*,[128] perhaps another etiology here for another part of the ritual, an offering to a baetyl stone, in which the song could be performed. In the *Song of LAMMA* there is an etiology for the mule halter belonging to Tarhun, apparently a cult object, suggesting a context for performance in which offerings were being made to Tarhun.[129] In addition, Haas compares the "hymnic" opening of *Appu* praising the Sun-god to those found in Babylonian epics,[130] and in fact the frame does provide us with valuable information as to the function of this so-called folk tale: It is a suggestive recounting of the Sun-god's past deeds that reminds him of his abilities and empowers him, appropriate for a ritual in his honor. A fragment

---

[124] Popko (1995: 82), Oettinger (2004).
[125] Archi (2009) argues that the texts were intended to be recited on ritual occasions.
[126] *CTH* 344.A = *KUB* 33.120 i 1–4 (trans. M. Bachvarova in López-Ruis 2013: 140).
[127] Salvini and Wegner (2004: 17–18).   [128] Haas (2002; 2006: 139–40).
[129] Haas (2006: 144).   [130] *CTH* 360.1.A = *KUB* 24.8 i 1–6; Haas (2006: 195).

grouped with the *Song of Hedammu* mentions a festival in the town of Duddul, ordered by [Kumarbi], honoring Mukishanu. There are sixty youths and sixty maidens from Duddul, the men carrying weapons; they are given lapis lazuli containers of wine.[131] This Hurrian festival may have been considered to be related in some way to a festival or cult actions during which this particular textualization was performed.

Many of the textualizations can be connected to a purification ritual. A Hurrian text assigned to the *Song of Birth* seems to be connected to a Hurrian *itkalzi* ritual.[132] It is very easy to postulate a ritual function for the *Song of Oil* since oil was used frequently in purification rituals; Giorgieri suggests the song should be connected to the *Ritual of Allaiturahhi*, in which oil is used to purify the patient against the "fear of lions,"[133] while Ilya Yakubovich connects it to ceremonies of anointing for kingship and purification.[134] If, as I have argued elsewhere, *Elkunirsa and Ashertu* is an example of the genre, we have a clear instance of Hurro-Hittite song used in a purification ritual.[135] In Chapter 4 I will discuss the use of the storylines of *Song of Gilgamesh* and the Kumarbi cycle in purification rituals. Although the rituals do not directly quote from a particular Hurro-Hittite song, they do allude directly to them. The *Song of Keshshi* could have been used in a ritual for easy birth, since Shindalimeni/Shindamani, Keshshi's wife, appears elsewhere as a character in a Hurrian childbirth incantation (unfortunately mostly incomprehensible).[136]

The *Song of Release* and the *Song of Gilgamesh* can both be connected to ancestor veneration, but in very different ways. I will explore fully the possible ritual context for each in subsequent chapters.

Finally, the protagonist of the *Song of Silver* can be connected to either purification or to ethnic consciousness. Haas considers the name Silver to

---

[131] *CTH* 348.1.22.A = *KBo* 26.82 (trans. M. Bachvarova in López-Ruiz 2013: 147–8); a festival is mentioned in *CTH* 348.1.24.A = *KBo* 26.117. See Polvani (1992: 447) and Pecchioli Daddi and Polvani (1990: 133), connecting this fragment to the *Song of Hedammu*. Duddul/Tuttul is mentioned in *CTH* 348.1.2.A = *KUB* 8.67 iv 4' (trans. M. Bachvarova in López-Ruiz 2013: 148), apparently the place where Hedammu is raised; see Siegelová (1971: 78–9). It is near the mouth of the Belih River, a tributary of the Euphrates (del Monte and Tischler 1978: 446), and is the home of Dagan (who was syncretized with Kumarbi), cf. the Sargon inscription quoted at the beginning of Chapter 8.
[132] *Mythological Fragments*: *CTH* 370.11 = *KUB* 47.56 (translit. and discussion Salvini and Wegner 2004: 17–18, 38–9, No. 7). On the practitioners of the *itkalzi* ritual see Chapter 4, 86.
[133] Giorgieri (2009). On *CTH* 780: *Ritual of Allaiturahhi*, see recently Bachvarova (2013a: 33–7), with further bibliography.
[134] Yakubovich (2005: 134).   [135] Bachvarova (2013a).
[136] *Ritual of Shalashu*: *CTH* 788.7 =*KBo* 27.176 10' (translit. and discussion Haas and Wegner 1988: 29–30, 419, No. 98), see Haas (2006: 209).

allude to the use of the metal as a *materia magica* in purification rituals,[137] but Silver might also be some kind of national hero, for the rebus-writings for Hatti and Hattusa contain the Sumerogram for silver: ^{URU}KÙ.BAB-BAR-*TI*, ^{URU}KÙ.BABBAR-*ša*;[138] thus, the Hattic word for silver must be *ḫatt(uš)*. Therefore, there was a (folk-)etymological connection between the mineral and the name of the Hattians, and the royal name Hattusili means 'he of the silver place'. The metal trade may have been one of the earliest ways Hattians became part of an international network, and they could have developed a sense of ethnic or national identity as the inhabitants of a place renowned for its silver. Indeed, inscriptions and legends of Sargon the Great and Naram-Sin refer to the Silver Mountains "as the border land of the Old Akkadian realm,"[139] and the Silver Mountain appears as a distant location near the merchant colony of Purushanda in Anatolia in the *Cuthean Legend of Naram-Sin*.[140] The connection seems to be refracted in the first-millennium epithet of the northern Anatolian Halizones from Alybe/Chalybe (cf. the modern name of the Halys River), the "birth(place) of silver" (*argurou genethlē*, Il. 2.857).[141] The *Song of Silver*, therefore, could be the story of the eponymous hero of Hattusa.

Conclusion

I have shown that Hurro-Hittite narrative song is a genre defined by a common prosodic structure, shared formulas, themes, and characters. I postulate a series of bilingual traditions responsible for the transfer of Mesopotamian-influenced epic from east to west: a Mesopotamian Sumerian–Akkadian one, a northern Mesopotamian Akkadian–Hurrian one, a Syrian Akkadian–west Semitic one out of which Ugaritic narrative poetry developed, and an eastern Anatolian Hurrian–Hittite one. These are the traditions we can assume from the evidence, but there must have been others: Hurrian–Luwian, Hurrian–west Semitic, Hurrian–Eteocypriot, and

---

[137] Haas (1982: 167–8, 177); also see Haas (2003b: 214–17) on silver as *materia magica*.
[138] Hoffner (1968b: 41–2, with earlier references), *HEG* (A-H: 211–12). Gabeskiria (2005) argues unconvincingly against this etymology. The Hittite word for silver is *ḫarki-* 'white'. In Hurrian it is *išḫoni/ušḫoni*.
[139] J. G. Westenholz (1997: 311–12).
[140] SB 47–50 (translit. and trans. J. G. Westenholz 1997: 310–13). Cf. the Sargon inscription quoted at the beginning of Chapter 8.
[141] Also see Watkins (1986: 707–8, n. 13). Bryce (2006: 139, with earlier references) discusses and dismisses any connection between the Halizones of Alybe/Chalybe and the Hittites.

Conclusion

west Semitic–Eteocypriot are all possibilities At some point there were bilingual Greek–Anatolian, Greek–Eteocypriot, and possibly Greek–Phoenician[142] traditions of performance that were the means by which the Hurro-Hittite tradition reached Greece, and this mechanism of transfer explains the parallels in phraseology between Homeric and Hittite epic discussed in this chapter. The languages involved within Anatolia most likely would not have been directly descended from Hittite. Rather, they would have been Phrygian, Lydian, or Luwic languages. This means that I will need to explain how the Hurro-Hittite narrative tradition, or something very similar to it, moved to western Anatolia, a subject I will discuss in Chapter 13.

This chapter has laid the groundwork for the more detailed discussion of the stories about Gilgamesh, Ebla, Sargon, and Naram-Sin to follow. I have defined the genre of Hurro-Hittite narrative song and provided some preliminary discussion of its functions and transfer to Anatolia. In the next chapter I discuss in detail the evidence that the *Song of Gilgamesh* is oral-derived, both in its Hurrian and in its Hittite manifestations. This will support my larger contention that transmission of Near Eastern epic to the Greeks was by means of oral poets, not scribes translating texts.

---

[142] In Chapter 12, 322, n. 100, however, I argue that putative Phoenician–Greek poets were not a key means by which epic traditions were transmitted directly to Greece, beyond transfer within Cyprus.

3 | Gilgamesh at Hattusa: written texts and oral traditions

> I [will pra]i[se] him, G[ilgamesh,] the hero.
>
> *Song of Gilgamesh* I i 1–2[1]

Introduction

Gilgamesh appears to have been a historical figure reigning in Uruk around 2600 BCE, but it is to the Ur III scribal schools (*ca.* 2000 BCE) that we owe the first written versions of narratives about him in Sumerian.[2] Already in the second millennium BCE the Gilgamesh tradition had spread widely in written form, and the epic has been found at quite a few Near Eastern sites, but, as Gary Beckman notes, "almost a century of excavation at the Hittite capital has yielded more textual sources for Gilgamesh than are known from all other Late Bronze Age sites combined."[3]

Despite the lack of evidence of transmission to Greek-speakers through written texts in Akkadian (or any other Near Eastern language) of narrative motifs that clearly originated in the Near East, scholars used to think in terms of transmission of a specific fixed text to explain the relations among the myths,[4] an approach modeled on how literate Romans worked with fixed Greek texts.[5] Although Walter Burkert has argued that "the eastern epic, at least in Mesopotamia, is based in a fixed tradition of writing,"[6] we should understand that even though the written texts may be the only sources through which we can have access to the wider tradition,

---

[1] *CTH* 341.III.1.A₁ = *KUB* 8.57 i 1–2 (following translit. of Laroche 1965, 1968: 121). The following study of the *Epic of Gilgamesh* has been greatly facilitated by the masterly edition with commentary of the Akkadian versions by George (2003).

[2] George (2003: 101–12). The oral narrative tradition that lay behind the *Epic of Gilgamesh* was a major influence on later storytelling traditions of the eastern Mediterranean world, leaving its mark not only on Greek epic, but also on the Hellenistic *Alexander Romance*. Dalley notes additional parallels with the Qumran Book of Enoch, and even with the stories collected in *One Thousand and One Arabian Nights* about Buluqiya and Sinbad (Dalley 1989: 47–8; 1998a: 43; 1998b: 170–2).

[3] Beckman (2003: 41). [4] Walcot (1966: 53–4).

[5] This approach is effectively criticized by Haubold (2002). [6] Burkert (1992: 115).

they represent the tip of the iceberg of a primarily oral culture. We might postulate transmission of texts into Greek across linguistic barriers via scribal training, on the model of what we can clearly see happening with transfer from Sumerian to Akkadian in the ancient Near East, as has been argued by Burkert,[7] but I know of no provable or even likely examples from the Greek Archaic period or earlier.[8] Oral transmission between verbal artists simply must have been the most common way stories and songs crossed barriers,[9] although oral performers were not unaware of the written texts, since written texts were recited or read at public occasions, such as healing rites, coronation ceremonies, and New Year ceremonies.[10] Furthermore, the written tradition was not only derived from oral tradition, but continued to be influenced by it as scribes composed and wrote down new versions of famous stories.

In fact, there is clear evidence that the narrative tradition with which Greek-speakers came into contact included at least one element that is not found in the Standard Babylonian version of the *Epic of Gilgamesh*, but appears in earlier attested Sumerian stories about the king of Uruk. If we acknowledge that the Cyclops episode in the *Odyssey* does not merely

---

[7] Burkert (1983c: 55; 1992: 25–33, 92, 95). Similarly, Bryce (1999) suggests that Anatolian scribes brought the Near Eastern literary tradition to Mycenaean Greece.

[8] Burkert (2004: 30–2; in large part reiterating Burkert 1992: 91–3) still persists in arguing for transmission from a fixed literary text in the Greek early Archaic period in his analysis of the relationship between *Epic of Creation* and the reference to Tethys and Oceanus as "primeval couple" (30) in the Deception of Zeus episode in *Iliad* 14. Arguing that the name of Tethys is the same as that of Akkadian Tiamat, he states, "Note that there can be no question of Bronze Age borrowing in this case. Four hundred years of oral tradition in Greece would have led to stronger distortion in the process of assimilation; it is even not at all clear that the *Epic of Creation* is old enough for Bronze Age transfer" (31–2). Actually, it has been persuasively argued that the *Epic of Creation* does date to the Late Bronze Age (Dalley 1989: 228–30; Foster 2005: 436). Because Burkert conceives of a fixed text influencing the formation of another text, he must argue that *Tiamatu* could be pronounced *Tiawatu*, basing his claim on some variant spellings of the goddess' name, and discounting M. L. West's objections (1997a: 147–8, n. 200) that the writings *Tiawatu, Tāwatu* are learned false archaisms substituting *wa* for *ma*, based on the scribes' knowledge of the sound change *w>m* between vowels. (There is no sound change *m > w* in the relevant period.) Also he must elide the chronological problem of Ionic *ā > ē*, on which see the Appendix, 463. Lejeune (1972: 235, with notes) does point out that *a* is replaced with *e* in certain borrowed words, but only from Iranian; the Greek *e* reflects a closed pronunciation of the Iranian vowel. That Eudemus of Rhodes (F 150 Wehli) spelled the name of the "Babylonian" goddess "Tautu" reflects a later sound change in Akkadian. In sum, there is no good evidence for transmission from a written Akkadian text to the Greek tradition.

[9] M. L. West (1997a: 593).

[10] See Annus (2002: 122–3), Burkert (1987b: 23–4; 1992: 124–7), and M. L. West (1966: 15–16) on public performances of written texts. For more on the interaction between oral and written texts see Chapter 8, 180–2. For the *Epic of Creation* being read aloud in the *akītu* festival, see Chapter 10, 262.

represent a widespread folk motif, but is specifically indebted to the Huwawa episode in Gilgamesh's story, then we should also acknowledge that the tricks Odysseus plays on the one-eyed monster correspond to the tricks that Gilgamesh plays on the guardian of the forest in the Sumerian lays *Gilgamesh and Huwawa A* and *B*, which are not included in the Standard Babylonian version.[11] We can best explain the inclusion of this element in the *Odyssey* by suggesting that it remained in the eastern Mediterranean oral narrative tradition for more than a thousand years.

Thus, any evidence on the relationship among the written versions we have and the oral versions that were the means by which Greek-speakers gained access to the Gilgamesh tradition is particularly valuable. In this chapter I explore some of the variations in the Akkadian, Hittite, and Hurrian Gilgamesh narratives at Hattusa in order to get at the oral traditions behind the written texts.

The Akkadian *Epic of Gilgamesh*

For the Akkadian tradition of the Gilgamesh story we can distinguish, first, a poorly preserved Old Babylonian stage, in which the Huwawa episode was most favored by scribes, but the process of combining some of the episodes known from the various Sumerian lays involving Gilgamesh into a single narrative was well under way;[12] second, a Middle Babylonian stage, also poorly preserved, of which the Akkadian texts at Hattusa are examples, along with tablets from Nippur, Ur, Megiddo, Emar, and

---

[11] On the folk tale elements of the Cyclops episode, including the tricks played on the Cyclops, see Hansen (1997: 449–51, with earlier references). For the Sumerian stories see translations on ETCSL t.1.8.1.5, t.1.8.1.5.1.

[12] Fleming and Milstein (2010) have argued that we can distinguish two OB epics about Gilgamesh, one focused primarily on the Huwawa episode, the other focused more on the intense relationship between Enkidu and Gilgamesh. The jumping-off point for this theory is a small detail in the description of Enkidu's life before he met Gilgamesh. The Penn tablet has him frolicking with wild beasts, while the Yale tablet presents him as a herdsman (Fleming and Milstein 2010: 10–11). (The two tablets are written by the same scribe, and Yale picks up directly after the Penn tablet (tablets II and III).) Even if we do not agree that there is a real significance to these differences, the two scholars make many insightful points about the differing ways Enkidu is portrayed in the twelve OB tablets available to us, in comparison to the Sumerian lays *Gilgamesh and Huwawa A* and *B* and the SB version. Certainly they are correct to lay emphasis on the facts that the primary interest of nine of the ten OB texts other than Penn and Yale is the Huwawa episode (Fleming and Milstein 2010: 5–7) and that the most-copied Sumerian Gilgamesh text by far is *Gilgamesh and Huwawa A* (Fleming and Milstein 2010: 69–70).

Ugarit;[13] and third, the Standard Babylonian version in twelve tablets, the final tablet of which is a close prose translation of a large part of the Sumerian *Gilgamesh, Enkidu, and the Netherworld*, appended to an already complete narrative.[14] This is the version best known to non-specialists. A Neo-Assyrian catalog names Sin-leqi-unninni as its author.[15]

As the Standard Babylonian epic opens, King Gilgamesh, the part-human part-divine child of the goddess Ninsun, has been exercising the young men of Uruk with sports and abusing the young women to such a degree that the residents of Uruk complain to the gods, who decide to create Enkidu to be his equal. When the shaggy Enkidu, living among wild animals, repeatedly foils the snares of a hunter, the man is advised by his father to complain to Gilgamesh. The king then sends out Shamhat, a "harlot," to seduce the wild man. Once introduced by Shamhat to the human experience of sex, Enkidu is rejected by his former wild companions, losing his supernatural speed and strength but gaining human understanding. Shamhat tells him of the dreams that Gilgamesh has had of Enkidu's existence, then clothes him and feeds him the civilized foods of bread and beer. Soon enough Enkidu learns of Gilgamesh's demands on the brides of Uruk. Angered, he arrives in Uruk during some sort of celebration and challenges Gilgamesh to a wrestling match. Gilgamesh beats him and the two become fast friends.

After a poorly preserved episode involving Gilgamesh's mother describing Enkidu's uncouth upbringing and Enkidu's despondency at her comments, Gilgamesh suggests that the two seek out and kill the forest monster Huwawa. There is some discussion with Enkidu and the elders of Uruk, who attempt to dissuade Gilgamesh, and with Ninsun, who bewails the restlessness of Gilgamesh and calls on Shamash, the Sun-god, to protect him, alluding to the hero's future role in the underworld as ruler and judge of the dead.[16] The pair set off into the wilderness of the Cedar Mountains, a journey punctuated by a series of seven dreams, each of which Enkidu interprets favorably for Gilgamesh.

---

[13] For the MB text at Ugarit, see George (2007). Claims of a narrative involving Gilgamesh and the city of Aratta from Ebla were ill-founded (George 2003: 5–6). The hero's name is used in Elamite onomastics; this indicates the easternmost extension of his legend (W. G. Lambert 1960: 47).

[14] George (2003: 49).

[15] See George (2003: 28–33). The Neo-Assyrian catalog of texts and their authors from Assur is the only source that explicitly links the scribe with the composition, listing "the Series of Gilgamesh" as "that of the mouth of Sin-leqi-unninni, the in[cantation-priest]" (K 9717.10, ed. W. G. Lambert 1957: 11).

[16] See George (2003: 461).

The Huwawa episode, one of the high points of the narrative, is contained in Tablet v. The heroes reach the forest, home of the gods, and observe the gigantic cedars, the bushy undergrowth, and the tracks of Huwawa. The next bit of narrative is poorly preserved, but they seem to draw their weapons, and Enkidu offers encouragement, saying that two are more effective than one. When the narrative picks up again, Huwawa is berating Gilgamesh for following the advice of Enkidu, and Enkidu for turning against him, the monster threatening to cut Gilgamesh's throat. Gilgamesh needs more encouragement from Enkidu, then they join battle with Huwawa, splitting apart the mountains Sirara and Lebanon and creating the Levantine rift valley. A dark cloud surrounds them, but the Sun-god releases the thirteen winds against Huwawa, who is no longer able to move either forward or backwards, allowing Gilgamesh to strike him with his weapons. The monster begs for his life, offering to guard the trees for the king, while Enkidu advises Gilgamesh against such a course of action, and Huwawa – even though he expresses aloud his wish that he had killed Enkidu before – asks Enkidu to plead for him. Again Enkidu insists that Gilgamesh kill the monster before the gods find out what they are doing. After more rounds of arguing between Huwawa and Enkidu, the monster finally curses Enkidu, and Enkidu demands that Gilgamesh silence him. Gilgamesh stabs him in the neck, and that is the end of Huwawa. The heroes cut down a number of the gigantic cedars and bring them back to Uruk to build a huge door for the temple of Enlil.

Gilgamesh subsequently attracts the amorous attention of Ishtar but rejects the goddess, well aware of the fate of her previous lovers. She seeks revenge by obtaining the Bull of Heaven from her father Anu and unleashing it against Uruk, but Gilgamesh and Enkidu defeat the bull, and Enkidu further insults the goddess by throwing its haunch at her. While Ishtar mourns the fallen animal, Gilgamesh has its horns crafted into containers to hold the oil used to anoint the statue of his dead father, the hero Lugalbanda. Enkidu, however, has a dream that tells him he is doomed by a decision of the gods. The dream swiftly comes true.

Gilgamesh extravagantly mourns his best friend's demise, creating a lavish statue of Enkidu to receive funerary offerings, then sets off weeping into the wilderness to find an answer for his fear of death. Journeying to the farthest edge of the world, he encounters Shiduri, the wise alewife, in a stunningly beautiful garden of jewels, who tells him to cross the ocean that encircles the world with the aid of the boatman Urshanabi to Utnapishtim, the Mesopotamian Noah; the only survivor of the Deluge can inform him how to bear death. Gilgamesh does indeed find Utnapishtim and his wife beyond the edge of the world, and hears the story of the Deluge, which is also told in the Akkadian *Atrahasis*. (In fact, the narrator at one point slips by calling Utnapishtim Atrahasis!) Gilgamesh loses his chance for everlasting life, unable to complete Utnapishtim's test of staying awake for seven days and nights. However, Utnapishtim's wife persuades him to tell Gilgamesh how to retrieve the plant of everlasting youth from the bottom of the sea. Again, Gilgamesh loses his chance to escape old age when a snake steals the plant while he sleeps. When Gilgamesh reaches Uruk again, he realizes that although he will not live forever, Uruk and its walls will be his eternal monument.

Although violating the narrative unity of the epic, Tablet XII relates to its main theme of mortality. Enkidu is alive and goes down into the underworld to retrieve some sporting equipment of Gilgamesh. His description of the varying conditions of its residents makes clear the importance of tending one's ancestors through offerings of food and drink, to keep them comfortable in the afterlife.

The *Epic of Gilgamesh* in both the Middle Babylonian and Standard Babylonian versions frames itself as an archaeological artifact buried in the ancient walls of Uruk, a precious lapis lazuli tablet hidden away in a closed tablet box. The reader must find and open the box to gain access to its secrets, the story of Gilgamesh, the hero who learned "the totality of wisdom about everything, he saw the secret and uncovered the hidden" – just as the reader is imagined to have done to retrieve the tablet he metaphorically holds in his hand. "[H]e brought back a message from the antediluvian age. He came a distant road and was weary but granted rest, [he] set down on a stele all (his) labors."[17] In this self-consciously written text, the emphasis is on the scribe and his institution, which can last across dynasties and transmit privileged information to new generations of rulers, allowing them to learn from the mistakes of their predecessors. Yet, embedded within the *Epic of Gilgamesh* is an acknowledgment of the importance of orally transmitted wisdom, coming from the mouth of the antediluvian sage Utnapishtim. We should not underestimate the significance of oral wisdom for the "average" person living in the Late Bronze Age, although it is utterly lost to us. Nor should we give

---

[17] SB I 6–10 (trans. George 2003: 539). On the MB passage (from Ugarit), see George (2007). We do not have any OB version of the first tablet, only an OB incipit, "surpassing all kings," in the colophon of the OB Pennsylvania tablet, corresponding to the I 29 of the SB version (George 2003: 22). Also see Chapter 8, 178–9, on the *Cuthean Legend of Naram-Sin* framing itself as a written work.

too much weight to the self-promoting claims of the written texts produced by men who operated within a very circumscribed circle, although they are all we have.

The Akkadian *Epic of Gilgamesh* in the Hittite archives

The *Epic of Gilgamesh* was one of the texts used to train scribes to write and use proper Akkadian. This was surely the function of the Middle Babylonian examples from Hattusa and its vassal state Emar, where the epic represents one of the texts with which young scribes practiced after having learned the lexical lists,[18] along with omen compendia, medical incantations, mythico-historical texts concerning the exploits of Sargon the Great and his grandson Naram-Sin, and wisdom texts. Yet, the tablets from Hattusa betray the story's origin in an oral milieu by their differences from each other, showing that the Middle Babylonian stage of the epic was not yet represented by a single codified text, any more than the Old Babylonian stage was.[19]

There are at least three separate Middle Babylonian exemplars of the *Epic of Gilgamesh* (*CTH* 341) at Hattusa.[20] One (Boğ₃) is just a small fragment, speaking of a dream in direct speech, perhaps one of the dreams that Gilgamesh had on the way to the Cedar Forest.[21] The most recent find at Hattusa is six pieces, possibly all from a single "big library tablet" (Boğ₁), found in Temple 16 along with the *Song of Release*.[22] They are the earliest attestation of the *Epic of Gilgamesh* at Hattusa, dating, like the rest of the tablets from the find, to the Middle Hittite period and written in Middle Script, and therefore 100–150 years earlier than the other two exemplars. Moreover, Beckman comments that "the language of this earlier Akkadian edition does not display the characteristics of Hittite Akkadian,"[23] while George notes, "The edition of Gilgameš that these fragments represent was written in regular couplets of good Babylonian poetry, as far as one can tell from the larger pieces."[24] Whoever composed the text was quite competent in Akkadian and must have been taught by a man fluent in literary Akkadian.

---

[18] George (2003: 287, 306, 327).   [19] See n. 12.
[20] On the find locations see J. Lorenz and Rieken (2010: 221–2).
[21] *CTH* 341.1 = *KUB* 37.128 (translit. and trans. George 2003: 325–6).
[22] George (2003: 307). See Chapter 2, 32, on the find spot.   [23] Beckman (2003: 42).
[24] George (2003: 309–10).

Four of the fragments are small flakes, while two of the fragments offer a more substantial piece of the text, which George assigns to the first tablet of the series, a supposition that requires the beginning of the epic to be much compressed when compared to the other Akkadian versions, both the Old Babylonian and the Standard Babylonian ones. Best-preserved is the episode in which the harlot clothes Enkidu, the crowd of shepherds compares him to Gilgamesh, and Enkidu consumes his first civilized food, but there are traces of the first meeting between the two heroes, Gilgamesh's declaration that he will seek out Huwawa with the attempt by the elders of Uruk to dissuade him, the killing of Huwawa, and the gods' judgment against Enkidu.[25] As George notes,

> The text is often very close to the Pennsylvania and Yale tablets (OB II–III) and may derive directly from late Old Babylonian or early Middle Babylonian originals that belonged to the same tradition. However, MB Boğ₁ can deviate significantly from the older version, and when it does it sometimes exhibits phrasing found in the later, Standard Babylonian text.[26]

The third exemplar (Boğ₂) is "composed in the local variety of peripheral Akkadian."[27] It is part of a large tablet of either six or four columns written in New Script; this format implies an advanced school text. If it is a teaching text, the teacher who was responsible for the textualization did not come directly from Mesopotamia. The first and sixth (or fourth) columns are preserved, the one telling of a dream of Gilgamesh as he proceeds to the Cedar Forest, the other recounting how Gilgamesh spurns Ishtar and she sends the Bull of Heaven. George suggests that this is the second tablet in its series. If so, the narrative is again much compressed when compared to either the Old Babylonian series represented by the Pennsylvania and Yale tablets or the Standard Babylonian version. George notes about the text:

---

[25] *CTH* 341.1.A–D = *KBo* 32.128-33 (translit., trans., and discussion George 2003: 307–17); also see Klinger (2001b: 205).
[26] George (2003: 310–11). Also see Wilhelm (1988) for a close analysis of similarities and differences between this version and other Akkadian ones. The six-column OB Penn tablet, labeled the second tablet in its series, begins with Gilgamesh's dreams about Enkidu (see trans. of George 2003: 173–81). The six-column OB Yale tablet continues the story, beginning with the aftermath of the wrestling match between the two heroes, and ends with the preparation for the journey to the Cedar Forest (trans. George 2003: 195–207).
[27] Beckman (2003: 42), *CTH* 341.1 = *KUB* 4.12 (translit., trans., and discussion George 2003: 317–25).

> It is ... afflicted by errors of transmission, particularly on the reverse, where there are several clear cases of textual corruption. Sometimes the tablet is well enough preserved to show that the text is poetry, though in western style the beginnings and ends of the lines of verse do not necessarily coincide with the beginnings and ends of lines of tablet.[28]

George has made a detailed comparison of the wording with which one of Gilgamesh's dreams (the third in the Standard Babylonian version, the second in the Boğazköy version) is described in the Boğazköy text and in the Old Babylonian tablet (of unknown provenance) that is our primary early source for this passage. I place his translations of one section of the relevant passages side-by-side here, in which Gilgamesh describes how he is crushed by an avalanche in his dream, only to be saved by the Sun-god:

Old Babylonian Schøyen$_2$	Middle Babylonian Boğ$_2$
5 With my shoulder I propped up a mountain;	13′ In my dream, my friend, a mountain [...]
6 the mountain collapsed on me, pressing me down.	14′ it threw me down, it held (me by) my feet... [...]
7 Feebleness enclosed my legs,	
8 a radiant brightness overpowered my arms,	15′ A radiant brightness overpowered my arms.
9 There was a man, like a lion [he drew] near me,	There was a man [...,]
10 shining brightest in the land and most [comely] in beauty.	16′ the most handsome in the land and his beauty [...]
11 he took hold of my upper arm,	[...]
12 from under the mountain itself he pulled me forth.	17′ From beneath the mountain he pulled me out and [...]
	18′ He gave me water to drink and my heart grew [calm (...)]
	[On] (19′) the ground he set [my] feet.[29]

George notes the slight changes in phrasing, and the "additions" and "subtractions" to the text in the Boğazköy version here and elsewhere in the passage, commenting, "Here one should bear in mind that the Boğazköy tablet may not report the text fully," and, "it seems that the Middle

---

[28] George (2003: 318–19).
[29] OB Schøyen$_2$ 5–12 (updated trans. George 2009: 31), MB Boğ$_2$ = *CTH* 341.1 = *KUB* 4.12 i 13′-19′ (trans. George 2003: 319–21, with my updatings based on his 2009 translation of the Schøyen$_2$ tablet). Also see George (2003: 44–5).

Babylonian version is longer because it conflates this passage with another dream."[30] In the latter, supplied by Old Babylonian Harmal₁, Gilgamesh wrestles a bull, but is saved by the Sun-god. Thus, OB Harmal₁ 9, "[he gave] me water to drink from his waterskin,"[31] corresponds to Boğ₂ 18′.

George appears to be working under the assumption of a fixed text, judging the scribe on his accuracy in transmitting that text without changes.[32] However, the slight changes in wording, expansions, and compressions that differentiate the two versions are in fact canonical signs of composition in performance, as discussed in the previous chapter.[33] While George is certainly correct to surmise that the scribe at Hattusa who produced Boğ₂ was copying from another tablet, I suggest that the textualization represented by Boğ₂ was initially carried out by a scribe in close contact with the living Akkadian oral tradition.

The Hittite *Song of Gilgamesh*

The Hittite *Song of Gilgamesh* is extant in some forty small fragments.[34] The pieces were found in at least three different places. Some of the tablets are New Hittite, others Late New Hittite.[35] Thus, we can be confident that there were multiple copies – in fact, versions – of the *Song of Gilgamesh*, recorded and/or used by different people and made over more than one

---

[30] George (2003: 45).   [31] Trans. George (2003: 249).
[32] Also see George (2003: 22–3, 25–6, 31) on the multiple OB versions of Gilgamesh and on MB variations; here too he shows a certain reluctance to accept that unity and excellence can be the product of a tradition, not a person. Similarly, many Classicists assign to Homer the credit for creating the *Iliad* and the *Odyssey* from a long-standing narrative tradition, but see Foley (1999: 50) on crediting a legendary author living a few generations before the present with crafting the narrative being performed: "I interpret this legendary singer as an anthropomorphization of what we name by the abstraction 'tradition', as a representational strategy that allowed *guslari* [bards] to talk about what they and their peers jointly inherited and continued to practice." See in more detail Foley (1999: 51–63), and on Homer see Jensen (1980: 157–8) and Nagy (1990b: 78–81; 1996a: 27; 1996b: 76).
[33] Fleming and Milstein (2010: 164–7) also examine differences in the descriptions of the dreams, but they are thinking in terms of scribal compositions.
[34] The Hittite version has been translated by Beckman (2001a). For a German translation with discussion see Haas (2006: 273–7), and for important discussions of the Gilgamesh tradition at Hattusa see Archi (2007b: 186–8), Beckman (2003), Klinger (2005), and del Monte (1992a, with Italian translation). Transliterations of all the passages of the Hittite *Song of Gilgamesh* cited in this chapter may be found on KhT *sub CTH* 341 (Rieken et al. 2009ff.). I include the exact *CTH* numbering for ease of reference.
[35] Beckman (2003: 42). The find spots include the storerooms near Temple 1, quadrant K/18 of the Unterstadt, and Archive K in Büyükkale (the citadel, see Map 3).

generation. Just as it is clear that the relationship between the Middle Babylonian Boğ₂ and other earlier and later versions of the *Epic of Gilgamesh* cannot be described in terms of a manuscript stemma, it is equally obvious that the Hurrian and Hittite versions are not just translations of a fixed Akkadian text, but vary in points both small and large, taking into account the interests of a western audience. This indicates a semi-independent east Anatolian–north Syrian narrative tradition about the Sumerian hero's exploits, one that belongs to the larger Hurro-Hittite genre of narrative song.

It should be noted that my discussion of the *Song of Gilgamesh* does not conform to the view held by many scholars of the relationship among the versions of the Gilgamesh story in Akkadian, Hittite, and Hurrian. Beckman, for example, argues:

> It is just not credible that the concise Hittite-language edition represents either a direct reflection of oral tradition or an independent composition based on the Old Babylonian materials. Rather, the Hittite editor/translator must have begun with an Akkadian *Vorlage* very much like the work generally credited to Sîn-leqe-unninnī, but lacking [certain] elements.[36]

Given the state of our knowledge of the Gilgamesh tradition at Hattusa, however, it is currently impossible to claim any of the Akkadian exemplars as the basis for a Hittite or Hurrian translation.[37] Jörg Klinger thinks the Hittite song is a translation of a Hurrian version, claiming that there are more similarities between the Hittite and Hurrian exemplars than between the Hittite and Akkadian exemplars,[38] but, as I will show, there are remarkable differences between the extant Hittite and Hurrian versions.

Fragments of at least four different tablets, each covering parts of the beginning of the story, have been found,[39] and it has been postulated, based on the number and scope of the fragments, that the full text would have covered three tablets. With all due caution in light of possible variation among the versions, we can piece together the following connected narrative from the various fragments.

The Hittite version opens differently from the Middle Babylonian and Standard Babylonian versions, which are presented as revered written documents. The first line of the Hittite *Song of Gilgamesh* appears to refer to Gilgamesh, the "hero" (UR.SAG, lit. 'head dog', i.e., supremely manly),

---

[36] Beckman (2003: 49).   [37] Klinger (2005: 115–16).
[38] Klinger (2005: 117–19, 122), followed by Archi (2007b: 188). Haas (2006: 273) sees the Hurro-Hittite *Gilgamesh* as at least partially independent of the Akkadian *Gilgamesh*.
[39] Beckman (2003: 42), Otten (1958a: 94).

in the accusative. A first-person verb starts the beginning of the first line. We may fill in the lacuna to produce a verb of speaking. The proem thus conforms to that of the Hurro-Hittite *Songs of Release, Ullikummi,* and *Silver,* calling attention to the bard's oral performance: "I [will pra]i[se] him, G[ilgamesh,]/ the hero."[40]

According to this version, Gilgamesh was created by DINGIR.MAH 'the Great Goddess', and wandered all over until he settled in Uruk; in fact, Ninsun, Gilgamesh's mother in the Akkadian versions, does not appear at all in the extant fragments. Subsequently, the young men in Uruk endure Gilgamesh's abuse until the gods themselves come to the place of assembly and decide to take action (rather than responding to the prayer of the people of Uruk).[41] The Great Goddess creates Enkidu in the steppe, where he lives among the wild beasts, foiling the traps of a hunter, here specifically named Shangashu (Akk. 'killer').[42] Shangashu goes to complain to Gilgamesh, who sends out the harlot Shamhat to seduce him.[43] Very little of the next episode is preserved, other than a reference to the festive garments that Enkidu has donned(?).[44] We next glean that Enkidu goes to confront Gilgamesh when he hears from Shamhat how Gilgamesh sleeps with all the brides, but they end up eating and drinking together. At this point they have a conversation[45] that apparently inspires Gilgamesh to announce at another feast to which his soldiers have been summoned (rather than an assembly as in the Akkadian version) that he wishes to see Huwawa.[46] We do not know whether Enkidu attempted to dissuade him,[47] how Enkidu's helping role was conceived, or whether the Sun-god was called upon at this point to aid the heroes.

---

[40] [*wa-*]*al-l*[*a-aḫ-ḫi-*]*ya-an* ᵈG[ILGAMEŠ-*un*]/ UR.SAG-*in* (*CTH* 341.III.1.A₁ = *KUB* 8.57 i 1–2, following translit. of Laroche 1965, 1968: 121). On such openings, see Chapter 5, 113–14.

[41] *CTH* 341.III.1.A₁ = *KUB* 8.57, with Ea (+) Eb = *KBo* 10.47a i (+) 47b. The Sumerogram in the singular, DINGIR.MAH 'Great Goddess', typically refers to the specific goddess Hannahanna 'grandmother', who can appear in disappearing god myths (Popko 1995: 87–8; on the myth, see Chapter 4, 104, n. 115). In the plural, the Sumerogram refers to a group of goddesses that can include Anzili. See Chapter 4, 94. See Beckman (2003: 43–4, 46) on the differences between the Akkadian and Hittite versions of *Gilgamesh*.

[42] See Beckman (2003: 51) on his name.

[43] Pieced together from *CTH* 341.III.1.A₂ (+) A₃ (+) H = *KUB* 17.2 (+) 8.56 (+) *KBo* 26.101 and Ea (+) Eb (+) Ee = *KBo* 10.47a (+) b (+) e, col. i.

[44] *CTH* 341.III.1.Ef = *KBo* 10.47f ii.

[45] *CTH* 341.III.1.B = *KUB* 8.55, with C = *KUB* 8.51 ii, F = *KUB* 36.72 ii. Beckman (2003: 45) comments that here the "Anatolian writer ... displays his ignorance of the putative *droit de seigneur* exercised by the Sumerian king." But, as George (2003: 170–1) points out, already in the OB version the practice is so carefully described as to imply that it was "strange also to the poet's Old Babylonian audience."

[46] *CTH* 341.III.1.J = *KUB* 60.14, Eg = *KBo* 10.47g iii 1′–3′.

[47] Possibly Enkidu's answer is contained in the fragment *CTH* 341.III.20.A = *KBo* 19.115.

After this fairly brief telling of the events leading up to the confrontation in the mountains with the monstrous guardian of the gigantic cedar trees, the pace of the story slows, and that episode is recounted in some detail. The heroes set off on their journey, offering sacrifices at the bank of the Mala River (the Euphrates),[48] a significant border for the Hittites.[49] Gilgamesh's set of dreams is not included in the Hittite version, nor is the earlier set in which Enkidu comes to his notice, although the *Song of Keshshi* contains an analog of the series of dreams that Gilgamesh has on the way to confront Huwawa.[50] On the sixteenth day they reach the heart of the mountains, where Huwawa spots them. Gilgamesh sees Huwawa's tracks and is afraid, but Enkidu encourages him.[51]

The tablets we have been following so far break off here, but the same scene is continued in three separate exemplars.[52] Now the Sun-god of Heaven talks directly to the heroes, unlike in the Akkadian versions, and the two men have seized their axes and have got to work cutting down the cedars, when Huwawa notices them and is filled with anger.[53] The Sun-god encourages them to slay Huwawa before he goes into his house, but Huwawa threatens to drag them up to heaven and to strike them on their skulls, driving them into the "Dark Earth."[54] The monster launches his assault as promised but fails to overcome them. The two men drag Huwawa by the hair and somehow equids are involved, all elements not found in the Akkadian versions. Next, Gilgamesh is overcome by a cloud of dust and calls out to the Sun-god, weeping. The god sends eight (rather than thirteen) winds against Huwawa, who cannot move backwards or forwards. He soon capitulates (without even being struck by Gilgamesh) and offers to serve as Gilgamesh's slave, felling the cedars that he has grown. Enkidu, however, advises Gilgamesh to show no mercy.[55]

Slight variations among manuscripts in the passage under discussion show that the text retains the flexibility proper to oral tradition. These variations in the Hattusa versions of the story of the battle between Gilgamesh and Huwawa should be thought of as choices made by composers who

---

[48] *CTH* 341.III.1.F = *KUB* 36.72 iii.
[49] Beckman (2003: 44). Also see Chapter 8, 177 on the significance of the Euphrates for the Hittites.
[50] See Chapter 2, 28.   [51] *CTH* 341.III.1.Eg = *KBo* 10.47g iii 4′–28′, L = *KBo* 19.114.
[52] *CTH* 341.III.1.C = *KUB* 8.51 (+) 53 iii, iv; Ed (+) Ec (+) Eh = *KBo* 10.47d (+) c (+) h iv; D = *KUB* 33.123.
[53] *CTH* 341.III.1.C = *KUB* 8.51 iii 1′–12′, Ed (+) Ec = *KBo* 10.47d (+) c iv 1–7.
[54] See Beckman (2003: 47). Archi (2007b: 200) sees Babylonian models for such scenes.
[55] *CTH* 341.III.1.C = *KUB* 8.53 iv 13′–31′; D = *KUB* 33.123; Ec + Eh = *KBo* 10.47 c + h iv 8–30, following Beckman (2001a: 162).

were working with a known "mental text" in a long-standing oral tradition, rather than original experiments. I provide a translation of lines iv 16–32 of the best preserved version, with significant differences underlined:

> iv 16 ... To the[m Huwawa ...]
> says, "Upwards you (indirect/direct object) [...]
> You in heaven upwards [I will] car[ry ...]
> And [y]our skulls I will strike. You (i./d.o.) [...]
> 20 in the Dark [Ear]th I will move [...]
> He upwards [...]. Them [in the] sk[y ...]
> The skulls [he] st[ruck.] He downwards [...]
> he did not move. [They seize]d Huwa[wa ...]
> B[y] the hair [...] they did [X ...]
> 25 "Furthermore, you (object) [...]
> Horses (nom./acc.) [...] the[y] wash [...]
> And the dust whi[ch ... a]rises, [...]
> Heaven is n[ot vis]ible. [...]
> [Gilgamesh] looked upwards at the Sun-god of Heaven [...]
> 30 He cr[ies out ...] of [the ...]
> [he] sa[w ... His te]ars ... [like] can[als]
> [flo]w.[56]

Compare now the next best preserved version. Lines 2′–15′ cover the same material:

> 2′ ["U]pwards you (object) [...]
> [up]wards I will carry [...]
> You (object) in the Dark [Earth ...]
> 5′ I will move. You (object) upwards [in the sky]
> I did not move. [Your] skulls [I will strike(?)]
> the cliff/rock [in front of][57] me, my foot (acc.) [...]
> You (object) in the Dark E[arth ...]
> I did not move." Th[ey] seized [...]
> 10′ ["] by the hair [...]
> Furthermore, to them sweat wh[ich ...]
> [h]orses the[y] will plant [...]
> [wh]ich (pl.) ... arises [...]
> [is not v]isible. To himself/themselves [...]
> 15′ [... he] look[ed] upward ...[58]

---

[56] *CTH* 341.III.1.Ea + Eh = *KBo* 10.47a + h iv 16–32, with C = *KUB* 8.53 iv 6′.
[57] Supplied by 1.G = *KUB* 36.73 3′.   [58] *CTH* 341.III.1.K = *HT* 10 2′–15′.

Even in its fragmentary condition the tablet shows minor but interesting variations when compared to the previous version in the wording of Huwawa's threats, with some additions and re-ordering in the second of the two.[59]

We next find out from another fragment that "they hold him (Huwawa) down low";[60] presumably the heroes are pushing the monster to the ground to kill him. In a fragment from a tablet continuing the story, Gilgamesh and Enkidu cut down the cedars, apparently intending to build a gate for Enlil's temple. The fragment breaks off when they are removing their garments to purify themselves. The Mala River is again a landmark on their return trip.[61] A fragment of a different tablet contains a conversation between IŠTAR and Gilgamesh, in which Gilgamesh describes a lavish palace he will build for her.[62]

The remains of the final section of the Hittite versions include Enkidu's baneful dream of the gods sitting in council and deciding his fate. Ironically, this episode, which has been used to argue for influence from the Akkadian *Epic of Gilgamesh* on the Homeric tradition because of its parallels with the death of Sarpedon,[63] is only preserved at Hattusa. The last line of Tablet VI of the Standard Babylonian version does give us the first line of the seventh tablet: "My friend, for what reason were the great gods taking counsel?"[64] And, the small MB Akkadian fragment Boğ₁ (f) preserves a few words of the episode: "they spoke" (*i-ta-a-mu*, 2′), "case" (*di-ni*, 6′), and "t[hey] d[ecided] the case of Enkidu" (*di-in* ᵈ*en-ki-du ip[á-ra-su]*, 9′).[65] So, we can be sure that the episode did appear in the MB and SB versions. But, exactly what was said among the gods and by whom we do not know, so we cannot see how the Hittite version differed. What we can say is that the Hittite version conforms to Hittite conventions. Two gods plead the two sides of a mortal's case, with Anu arguing against Enkidu before Enlil and Ea, while the Sun-god of Heaven serves as Enkidu's advocate. Anu points to the heroes' crimes of killing Huwawa

---

[59] Del Monte (1992a: 288–9) translates the two versions separately so that the differences are clear. Archi (2007b: 187) comments on the differences. A further minor variation can be detected in *CTH* 341.III.1.G = *KUB* 36.73 4′, which uses the phrase *dankui daganzipi kattanda* (MI-*i* KI-*pí* GAM-*an-da*) 'downwards into the Dark Earth' instead of *dankuwai* [*takn*]*ī* 'in the Dark Earth' (*KBo* 10.47d + c iv 20), *daganzipi* alliterating effectively with *kattanda*. I have discussed these passages in Bachvarova (2014).

[60] *CTH* 341.II.21.A = *KUB* 8.54 i 3 (trans. Beckman 2001a: 162).

[61] *CTH* 341.III.2.A = *KUB* 8.52 (+) 23.9.   [62] *CTH* 341.III.2.B = *KUB* 8.58.

[63] See Chapter 16, 445.

[64] Translit. and trans. George (2003: 630–1): *im-tal-li-ku* (*malāku* 'take counsel', 'give counsel').

[65] *KBo* 32.129 = *CTH* 341.I.1.C (translit. and trans. George 2003: 314–17).

and the Bull of Heaven, but the Sun-god states that he was the one who commanded them to do it. Enlil scolds the Sun-god for supporting them in their crime, and Anu decides that of the two, it is Enkidu who will die. The scenario of gods arguing a human's case in assembly, with one deity serving as defense lawyer, is common in Hittite prayers and substitution rituals attempting to remove guilt and pollution from a human, possibly inspired by an evil dream, also imagine a scenario of an intercessor pleading the human's case to the gods.[66] Enkidu could be considered to be a ritual substitute for Gilgamesh, according to Hittite expectations.

The wanderings of Gilgamesh involve at a minimum the visit to Ziduri, the boatman Urshanabi, and the visit to Utnapishtim. There are at least two scenes in Gilgamesh's wandering not found in the Akkadian version, visits to the Moon-god and the Sea-god; the latter scene ends with someone uttering a curse, a favorite activity of characters in Hurro-Hittite song.[67] On the other hand, when the hero asks the alewife the road to Utnapishtim, he does so in wording very close to that of the Standard Babylonian version.[68]

There seems to be considerable variation in the tablets covering the final sections of Gilgamesh's story, in terms of the level of detail with which the story is told, as shown by Table 3.[69] The very beginning of exemplar A is preserved, in which Enkidu tells Gilgamesh of the bad dream that foretells his death. A small bit of the beginning of column ii in A mentions a "vizier." This suggests that Gilgamesh is now wandering, making visits to the gods, since viziers appear in the hospitality scenes of Hurro-Hittite narratives. We are unable to discern how much more of the narrative was covered in this tablet, but to reach the story's end the final three columns would need to cover the visit to Ziduri, the meeting with the Urshanabi, the visit to Utnapishtim, and the hero's return to Uruk, episodes which covered more than two full tablets in the Standard Babylonian version.[70]

Only the rightmost edge remains of column iv on the reverse of exemplar C, with room for about three signs each, some twelve lines extending to the bottom edge, with a four-line space apparently left blank. Here we can see a conversation is in progress, there is mention of Ullu, who must be

---

[66] For examples of rituals involving juridical scenarios, see Chapter 4, 96, and Chapter 7, 154. For the motif in prayers, see Bachvarova (2006). For Hittite dream divination, see Mouton (2007).
[67] *CTH* 341.III.3.D = *KUB* 8.59. Noted by Haas (2006: 273) as evidence of some independence from the Mesopotamian Gilgamesh tradition.
[68] *CTH* 341.III.12.A = *KBo* 54.2; see Soysal (2004b).
[69] The variation is discussed in more detail in Bachvarova (2014).
[70] *CTH* 341.III.3.A = *KUB* 8.48 + *KBo* 19.116 (+) *KUB* 8.49.

Table 3. *Scheme of four versions of what we assume is the third tablet of the Song of Gilgamesh (CTH 341.III.3), arranged from most condensed version to most prolix*

Col.	A = KUB 8.48 + KBo 19.116 (+) KUB 8.49	C = KUB 8.50 + KBo 22.91	B = KUB 17.3	E = KUB 33.124
i	first 22 lines preserved (2 paras): **Enkidu's bad dream foretelling his death**		passage near top edge preserved (2 paras): **Enkidu's bad dream**	
ii	first 4 lines preserved: **mention of vizier** indicates a hospitality scene, therefore Gilgamesh is wandering	first 15 lines preserved (2 paras): **Gilgamesh runs wailing into the mountains, kills two lions with other animals**	passage near top edge preserved (3 paras): **tearful reaction of Gilgamesh** (to Enkidu's death?)	
iii		last 21 lines preserved (2 paras): **meeting with Urshanabi, who advises him to cut punting poles**	9 lines near bottom edge preserved (2 paras): **Moon-god demands Gilgamesh offer him two lions that he has killed, beginning of visit to Ziduri**	
iv	colophon preserved (incorrectly states "1st Tablet")	rightmost edge of last 12 lines preserved, blank space of approximately 4 lines at bottom: **conversation, with mention of Ullu and assembly** (of Uruk?)		last 5 lines and colophon preserved: **conversation with Urshanabi, mention of "stone images,"** which are destroyed by the hero before he receives Urshanabi's help

the equivalent of Utnapishtim (the name is derived from the Akkadian distal pronoun[71]), and of an assembly.[72] Does the song end with Gilgamesh calling Uruk into assembly to tell them about Ullu? In any case, it is hard to imagine that column iv of exemplar B could cover the same material that is covered in column iv of this version in equivalent detail, if B contains the ending of the story.

The best-preserved piece of exemplar B is made up of nine lines of the bottom of column iii, extending almost to the bottom edge and containing an encounter with the Moon-god, who demands that Gilgamesh make two lions he has killed into offerings for him, and the beginning of his visit to Ziduri.[73] In order for the narrative to be completed, column iv would have to include the end of the Ziduri episode, the meeting with Urshanabi, the Utnapishtim episode, and the return to Uruk. The close of the story is relatively compressed compared to the first of the tablets discussed here, unless a large space was left blank in that one. Or, the narrative of exemplar A continues onto another tablet, in which case the latter part of the narrative would be considerably more extensive than in exemplar B.

Finally, exemplar E only contains the final five lines of column iv on the reverse and a bit of the colophon, which tells us it is not the final tablet of the series. The fragment preserves the conversation with Urshanabi, which marks the beginning of the final stage of Gilgamesh's voyage to Utnapishtim. In it there is some talk about the "stone images,"[74] which we know in other versions had served as the boatman's crew but were destroyed by the excessively impetuous hero. If this is the second tablet, the earlier parts of the story would be relatively condensed compared to the other Hittite versions. If the third, then the narrative would be comparatively prolix.

In sum, in the Hittite *Song of Gilgamesh* we see a particular interest in the Huwawa episode,[75] with a compressed narrative of the events before it,

---

[71] Beckman (2003: 47, 51–2, with earlier refs.).   [72] *CTH* 341.III.3.C = *KUB* 8.50 + *KBo* 22.91.

[73] *CTH* 341.III.3.B = *KUB* 17.3. Two other fragments not translated by Beckman (2001a) preserve parts of his visit to the alewife: *CTH* 341.III.5.A = *KUB* 36.65 (here she is called Nahmezule); *CTH* 341.III.12.A =*KBo* 54.2; see Haas (2003c) and below on the alewife's name.

[74] *CTH* 341.III.3.E = *KUB* 33.124.

[75] Gilgamesh's visit to the Cedar Forest was located in Syro-Anatolia in the Babylonian versions, that is, to the west of Mesopotamia rather than to its east, as it was in the Sumerian versions (George 2003: 93–4; Fleming and Milstein 2010: 9). In the Hittite versions we see the same interest in the Huwawa episode that Fleming and Milstein (2010) have shown was prevalent in the OB period (see n. 12) (Beckman 2003: 44; Tigay 1982: 111–18). In contrast Uruk, which was so important in the Akkadian versions, was downplayed (Beckman 2003: 44). Similarly, in the MB Emar$_2$ version, among Ishtar's former lovers, enumerated by Gilgamesh when he rejects

and a relatively unstandardized telling of the episodes that follow; some of the differences between the Hittite and Akkadian versions of the epic show the Hittite version has been made to fit with the overall expectations of Hurro-Hittite narrative song.

The Hurrian *Song of Gilgamesh* and *Song of Huwawa*

Of the Hurrian versions five small fragments are preserved, belonging to at least three different textualizations. (This surmise is based on the different spellings of the hero's name.)[76] Two fragments are part of the episode involving Ullu, possibly from the fourteenth century; thus, they are at least a century older than the Hittite versions of the song and date roughly to the period of the earliest Akkadian version at Hattusa.[77] One of them is labeled in the colophon "[. . .] of Gilgamesh,/ [ ] not finished."[78] In it the Hurrian Fate-goddesses (Hutena)[79] and a person named Irri[b-. . .] are mentioned. In column ii of the other fragment Teshshub, great lord of Kummi, is mentioned, followed by the name of Gilgamesh three times in quick succession. Teshshub is the star of Hurro-Hittite epic in general, but the Storm-god is not a featured player in the Mesopotamian epic. In column iii appears the Iranian city Susa, indicating that the theater of action ranged beyond Mesopotamia to the east.[80] Finally, in column iv

---

her advances, is a Sutean, a native of the region of Emar. George (2003: 331–3) is noncommittal on whether this is an addition to the Emar version "pandering to western tastes," or was later omitted from the SB version.

[76] The Hurrian version is edited and commented on by Salvini and Wegner (2004: 16–17, 31–7), whose text numbering I include in the parenthetic references below. The observation on the spelling of the name of Gilgamesh comes from Archi (2007b: 187). When the find spots are known, the fragments come from Büyükkaya or Temple 1. I do not include the following fragments: a fragment assigned to the Hurrian *Song of Gilgamesh* (*CTH* 341.II.4 = *KUB* 47.10, No. 4) mentioning Ea, but without any clear ties to the Gilgamesh story (Salvini and Wegner 2004: 17); and a fragment (*CTH* 341.II? = *KUB* 47.16, MH, No. 44), referring to Teshshub, "great lord of Kummi" (5′, 7′), but no characters from the known versions of Gilgamesh. Kelly-Buccellati (2006) argues that Gilgamesh and Enkidu are depicted on a stone plaque of local manufacture found at Tell Mozan (Hurrian Urkesh), showing a younger kilted man turning towards an older bearded and naked man whom he holds by the wrist. If so, then it shows that Gilgamesh was known by the Hurrians already *ca.* 2300 BCE, well before epic narratives about Gilgamesh are attested; see 54.

[77] *CTH* 341.II.1 = *KUB* 8.60 (+) 47.9 (No. 1); *CTH* 341.II.3 = *KBo* 19.124 (+) 33.10 (No. 3, found near Temple 1). On the dating see Beckman (2003: 42).

[78] *CTH* 341.II.1 = *KUB* 8.60 left edge.   [79] See Haas (1994: 309, 372–3).

[80] Susa is otherwise mentioned in the Hittite corpus only in an evocation in the Kizzuwatnean ritual *CTH* 481: *Expansion of the Cult of the Goddess of Night* (*CTH* 481.B = *KBo* 15.29 iii 12′, translit. and trans. J. L. Miller 2004: 292).

Ullu and Shawushka are mentioned. It is hard to see any resemblance with other versions of the *Epic of Gilgamesh*. A third fragment of New Hittite date mentions [Huwa]wa and a mountain,[81] while a fourth mentions Gilgamesh and [Teshshub, great lord of] Kummi.[82]

The fifth fragment, dated to the thirteenth century, is labeled "Fourth tablet of Huwawa, not finished,"[83] a clear indication that this narrative diverged significantly from the Standard Babylonian *Epic of Gilgamesh*, since in it the Huwawa episode occurred relatively early in the narrative, and was not its only subject. (The Hurrian material thus offers support to the bold theory of Daniel Fleming and Sara Milstein that there existed an Old Babylonian Akkadian epic solely about Gilgamesh's defeat of Huwawa.[84]) The fragment opens with a formulaic speech introduction, then mentions "fine oil." The intelligible parts of this tablet differ markedly from the commonly known versions of Gilgamesh, for we can see in column i, along with Gilgamesh and Enkidu, the words "to/for the young woman" (Hurr. *šiduri*) and (?) "to/for the woman," and someone (one of these females?) repeatedly says, "... you will kill my brother!"[85] Presumably she is trying to protect someone, perhaps even Huwawa, although his name does not appear in the fragments. The episode has some parallels with the scene of IŠTAR pleading for the life of her brother in the incantation associated with *Elkunirsa and Ashertu*.[86] The alewife, here called Nahmazule, appears speaking in column iv, and Teshshub of Kummi, the Hurrian Sun-god Shimige, and Ea all appear in the closing lines of column iv. At the least there has been syncretism between Mesopotamian and Hurrian gods,[87] and perhaps we can be so bold as to see a blending of elements of the Hurrian myths found in the Kumarbi cycle with elements of the Gilgamesh tradition.

While it is possible to detect Hurrian influence in the Hittite *Song of Gilgamesh* because of the use of Hurrianized forms of the names Enkidu, Huwawa, and Utnapishtim, the case of the alewife, whose name in Hittite is Ziduri, is more complicated.[88] In the Old Babylonian sources she is not given a name, but in the Standard Babylonian version she is called Shiduri, which is in fact a Hurrian noun meaning "young woman." As George

---

[81] *CTH* 341.II.5 = *KUB* 47.15 (= No. 5).
[82] *CTH* 341.II = TC-4F5h (+) *KBo* 53.232 (translit. Salvini and Wegner 2004: 75, No. 51), see Nakamura (2007).
[83] *CTH* 341.II.2 = *KUB* 8.61 + *KBo* 8.144 left edge (= No. 2), see Beckman (2003: 42).
[84] See n. 12.   [85] See Salvini and Wegner (2004: 16).   [86] See Chapter 2, 34.
[87] Salvini (1988: 159).
[88] *Enkita-* and *Huwawai-* (Beckman 2003: 50–1; Haas 2003c: 130; Klinger 2005: 118); ⌈ú-da⌉-na-pí-iš-t[a(-) (Soysal 2007).

comments, "In this analysis the Hurrian word would have been taken into use as a personal name by speakers of Akkadian in the third millennium; just such a name often occurs in north Mesopotamia of the early second millennium."[89] The relevant section is not preserved in the Akkadian versions at Hattusa. The Hurrian version only uses *šiduri* as a common noun. The alewife is also called Nahmi/azule in the Hittite versions and only by this name in the Hurrian versions, receiving the feminine determinative in Hittite and the divine determinative in Hurrian.[90] Thus, in the Hittite versions she has two appellations, just as the antediluvian sage Utnapishtim is also called Ullu.[91] And, while the Hurrian language has contributed her name to the Standard Babylonian version, the Hurrian version uses an entirely different name not known to the Mesopotamian tradition.

One wonders whether the *Song of Huwawa* might end with Gilgamesh sparing Huwawa's life, or perhaps his death was presented as a tragic event. Of course, in our current state of knowledge any proposal concerning the *Song of Huwawa* can be no more than speculation, but the Mesopotamian sources suggest that he did not die in every version of his showdown with Gilgamesh.[92] Certainly in the Sumerian *Ballad of Early Rulers*, Huwawa, "caught in submission" (12), is mentioned as a hero on par with Alulu, Etana, Gilgamesh, and Enkidu.[93] Furthermore, Jacob Klein has suggested

---

[89] George (2003: 149). Additionally, esoteric material drawn from the western edge of the Mesopotamian world, attached to famous landmarks, has been incorporated in the SB version, like the incorporation of north Syrian ideas about the mountains of Lebanon in the etiology of the rift between Sirara and Lebanon (SB v 133–4, translit. and trans. George 2003: 608–9), and the location of the home of the gods on a mountain summit, not to be found elsewhere in Mesopotamian literature (SB v 6, translit. and trans. George 2003: 602–3). See George (1990).

[90] Haas (2003c), Klinger (2005: 118). Hitt.: *KUB* 36.65 3′: ᶠ*Nahmizulen* (translit. E. Rieken *et al.* 2009ff. on KhT); Hurr.: *KUB* 8.61 + *KBo* 8.144 iv 22′: ᵈ*Nahmazulel* (translit. Salvini and Wegner 2004: 34). ᶠ*Ziduriš*: Hitt. *KUB* 17.3 iii 9′ (translit. E. Rieken *et al.* 2009ff. on KhT). The *šiduri* in *KUB* 8.61 + *KBo* 8.144 i 4′ (translit. Salvini and Wegner 2004: 33) saying "you will kill my brother" must be a "young woman" (Haas 2003c).

[91] See Soysal (2004b). However, his suggestion, based on the use of the two names in two different versions of the Hittite narrative, "that two different textual origins (Akkadian and Hurrian) of the Hittite translations of Gilgameš Epic are conceivable" (10), should be laid aside. Although Ullu(ya)'s name is derived from Akkadian, he appears in a Hurrian-influenced *ambašši* ritual (see discussion in Chapter 4, 81–4), while Utnapishtim's name appears in the Hurrianized stem form.

[92] In addition, of the three OB tablets that preserve bits of the Huwawa episode, one hints at a different unfolding of the monster's death, since someone is killed without much ado (IM obv. 15, trans. George 2003: 269): "If it is Ḫuwawa then we must accept that this account of his death is very different from that found in OB Ishchali" (George 2003: 267).

[93] See Alster (2005: 288–322) for this scholarly text found in Mesopotamia, Emar, and Ugarit. Klein (1999: 207) discusses the difficulties of translating this phrase.

that one of the Sumerian hymns of the Ur III king Shulgi (*ca.* 2050 BCE), dating to the same era in which the Sumerian Gilgamesh lays are hypothesized to have been written down, refers to a version of the Huwawa episode in which Gilgamesh brings the captive Huwawa back to Uruk.[94] Finally, it has been suggested by Dietz Otto Edzard that the two Sumerian *Gilgamesh and Huwawa* lays had opposite endings; while in version A Huwawa is killed, in the lost ending of version B he may have been spared. As Edzard notes, there is certainly not enough room in version B for an ending similar to that of version A.[95] Since some Old Babylonian literary catalogs list both version A ("The lord to the Living One's Mountain")[96] and version B ("Ho, hurrah!"),[97] in this era at least some scribes-in-training would have known both possible endings, although version A was considerably more popular than version B. Both endings could have been known in the oral tradition.[98]

Certainly it is clear, despite the fact that the actual death of Huwawa is not preserved in any Hittite examples of the first tablet, that he was killed in the Hittite *Song of Gilgamesh*, for the Hittite fragments involving the council of the gods and Nahmizule refer to this event. Because the murder of the protector of the Cedar Forest is a key motivation in the gods' later decision to cause Enkidu to die, it is integral to the trajectory of the full-length Gilgamesh narrative. However, if the focus is shifted to Huwawa, the formidable north Syrian foe of Gilgamesh, the overall trajectory of

---

[94] *Shulgi O* 100: "your captured hero" (*ur-sag dab₅-ba-zu*), apparently about Huwawa, mentioned at 95 (see ETCSL t.2.4.2.15). See discussion of Klein (1976: 273, 290–1). For the date of the Sumerian Gilgamesh lays, see George (2003: 7).

[95] Edzard (1993: 11, 56–7). [96] Trans. George (1999: 150).

[97] Trans. George (1999: 161). There are four catalogs which do so: ETCSL 0.2.01: *Old Babylonian Catalog from Nippur* (N2); ETCSL 0.2.02: *Old Babylonian Catalog in the Louvre* (L); ETCSL 0.2.03: *Old Babylonian Catalog from Urim* (U1); ETCSL 0.2.04: *Old Babylonian Catalog from Urim* (U2). On evidence for the scribal curriculum from literary catalogs, see Black *et al.* (2004: 301–4).

[98] We can compare the variant endings of the Huwawa episode to the "forked pathway" of the early modern Return Songs of Serbian epic (Foley 1999: 137), which share much in common with the story of Odysseus' return to a household where suitors are importuning his wife. As Foley (1999: 115–67) shows, there are two possible endings to the Return Songs, one in which the wife or fiancée proves faithful like Penelope, and one in which she turns out to be a latter-day Clytemnestra. There seem to have been comparable variants in the story of the Trojan War, at least in the Greek tradition after Homer. Pausanias (8.12.6) tells the Mantinean version of the story, in which Penelope was expelled by Odysseus for being unfaithful, while Theopompus states it was Odysseus who left once he found out (Σ *ad* Lycophron 806 = *FGrH* 115 F 354), and Apollodorus (*Epit.* 7.38) says she was killed by Odysseus for sleeping with Amphinomos. Also cf. Σ *ad* Lyc. 772 = Duris *FGrH* 76 F 21: Penelope slept with the suitors and gave birth to Pan.

Gilgamesh's story is no longer important, and the Hurro-Hittite poet could cater to his audience's interest in their native son Huwawa.[99]

One might compare the different depictions of Naram-Sin in the Akkadian *Cuthean Legend of Naram-Sin* and in the Sumerian *Curse of Akkade*, two narratives that tell from two perspectives the same event, the fall (or near-fall) of Akkade because of the mistakes of its king Naram-Sin. In the Sumerian version, Akkade is destroyed – this despite the fact that we have clear historical evidence it survived Naram-Sin – because of the hybris of Naram-Sin, who ignored the will of the gods and tore down the Ekur temple in Nippur. In the Akkadian version, the city is nearly destroyed, but Ishtar comes to help Naram-Sin at the last moment, and Naram-Sin himself is portrayed as well-meaning, if deluded, and deeply concerned with his kingdom's welfare.[100]

Conclusion

The variation in the versions of the Gilgamesh story found at Hattusa point to a living bilingual oral tradition based on the Mesopotamian tradition, but reshaped to appeal to a western audience and to fit with the Hurro-Hittite mythological tradition. The Gilgamesh tradition was open to being reshaped at the hands of individual bards who wished to appeal to the particular point of view and sympathies of their particular audiences, a process found in the oral epic traditions of other parts of the world also. The "mental text" then was not solely the province of learned scribes, although our only access to it is through scribes.

---

[99] Similarly, the different tellings of the Indic epic *Ramayana* present different characterizations and emphases on different characters, depending on its audience. The Sanskrit version is focused on the experiences of Rama and his wife, Sita, who was kidnapped by the *rākṣasa* ('demon') Ravana, who may be seen as representing the Dravidian population of India in conflict with the northern Aryans. Rama only wins her back after a battle with the forest demon, whose advances his loyal wife has fended off. The Tamil version, however, has much more sympathy for Ravana. The Tamil *Ramayana* is by the ninth-century CE author Kampar. See Ramanujan (1991) on the different versions of the *Ramayana*; Richman (1991) on politicized modern interpretations of the *Ramayana*, taking Rama as representing northern, Aryan peoples and Ravana as southern, Dravidian peoples; Sundaram (1989: ix–xi) on Kampar's sympathy for Ravana.

[100] The *Curse of Akkade* is edited and translated on the ETCSL website, and a translation is also provided in Black *et al.* (2004: 116–25). The *Cuthean Legend of Naram-Sin* is edited and translated by J. G. Westenholz (1997: 263–368). I study the effect of different audiences on the viewpoint of a narrative with respect to the Naram-Sin stories and apply the findings to the *Iliad* in Bachvarova (2008a). Also see Chapter 16, 432–5.

We turn now to an interesting fragment that tells us a little about the *Sitz im Leben* of the Mesopotamian hero in Anatolia. It shows how the function of the Gilgamesh epic in ritual could have fostered its transfer to the Greek epic tradition, and how treating the epic solely as a literary text prevents us from fully comprehending its significance to its original audience.

4 | The Hurro-Hittite ritual context of Gilgamesh at Hattusa

"... and Gilgamesh ga[ve] him life [ ] ..."
- from a Hurro-Hittite pit ritual involving Gilgamesh[1]

Introduction

The *katabasis* episode in Book 11 of the *Odyssey* is generally acknowledged to be indebted to the story of Enkidu's visit to the underworld told in the final tablet of the Standard Babylonian *Epic of Gilgamesh*,[2] but it also has been compared to the Hurro-Hittite *Purification Ritual for the Former Gods*.[3] It is in fact possible to link the Mesopotamian epic hero and the Hurro-Hittite ritual by way of a fragment of an incantation used in a pit ritual of the same type as the *Purification Ritual for the Former Gods* that alludes to the part of the Gilgamesh story in which he seeks the aid of Atrahasis (*KUB* 8.62). I argue therefore that the *katabasis* episode in the *Odyssey* derives from an eastern Mediterranean narrative tradition very similar to that found at Hattusa, where pit rituals had already incorporated elements of the Gilgamesh story. In addition, it is not coincidental, in my opinion, that the ritual for Odysseus is carried out in the very part of the overall narrative that has another strong parallel with the Gilgamesh story, the Cyclops episode. This suggests that the Cyclops episode came to the *Odyssey* tradition through the same channel as the *katabasis* episode.

I begin with some background on how the figure of Gilgamesh was useful for those who were interested in communicating with or propitiating the dead. I then present a translation of the fragment of the ritual mentioning Gilgamesh. I put the fragment in context by surveying pit rituals in the second millennium BCE in general and evidence for continued use of pit rituals in the first millennium. These widespread rituals were connected with the appeasing of legendary heroes, and thus were complementary to the use of narratives that commemorated the dead.

---

[1] Classified as *Song of Gilgamesh* on KhT: *CTH* 341.III.6.A = *KUB* 8.62 iv 13'.
[2] M. L. West (1997a: 415–16).   [3] Steiner (1971).

I next examine the relatively well-preserved *Purification Ritual for the Former Gods*, in order to understand the process of bricolage that permitted the Mesopotamian hero to be used in a Hurro-Hittite ritual, and the ways in which Hurro-Hittite ritual and narrative could interact. I then analyze the *katabasis* episode in *Odyssey* 11, combining it with other pieces of evidence to argue that the section of the *Odyssey* beginning with the loss of all but one of Odysseus' ships at the hands of the Laestrygonians and ending with his visit to the underworld came from an Anatolian epic tradition.

Background

Gilgamesh played a privileged role in enabling interactions with the dead and underworld gods. The hero was considered to be the judge and ferryman of the dead, and was called on in exorcisms and healing spells,[4] and the Sumerian *Death of Gilgamesh* already promises that Gilgamesh will rule and judge the dead with Ningishzida and Dumuzi.[5] The stories connected to Gilgamesh addressed the concerns of patients who imagined that their sickness was caused by the ill will of ghosts or sorcerers. While the Standard Babylonian epic tells of Gilgamesh's quest for eternal life, motivated by the death of his best friend Enkidu, the earlier Sumerian *Death of Gilgamesh* describes how mourning rites that would appease dead ancestors were first established for him.[6] The Standard Babylonian epic alludes to Gilgamesh's role in establishing rites for the dead when it mentions how he made the horns of the Bull of Heaven into containers for offerings for his dead father Lugalbanda, and describes the elaborate statue he crafted to commemorate his dead friend, while the Sumerian story of *Gilgamesh, Enkidu and the Netherworld*, added on as Tablet XII to the Standard Babylonian epic, vividly pictures the suffering of the dead who lack descendants to provide them with proper offerings of honey, ghee, and cool water. Furthermore, the *Gilgamesh Epic* provides an etiology for the wrestling competitions celebrated in the Abu-festival, or festival of the offering pit, when the spirits of the dead came to visit their living relatives and were remembered and placated with offerings of food and

---

[4] George (2003: 127–35); W. G. Lambert (1960: 39–41).
[5] George (2003: 128). The first evidence of offerings for the deified Gilgamesh appears in the mid third millennium (George 2003: 122–7).
[6] George (2003: 126).

drink, then sent back into the underworld.[7] It is therefore appropriate to ask, as George does,

> Could it have been that Tablet XII – or maybe the entire series of twelve tablets – was put to ritual use, sung or recited, for example, at funerals and in memorial cults? Was it perhaps performed at the funerals of kings?[8]

While George argues that the Sumerian and Akkadian narratives of Enkidu's visit to the underworld were "literary, not sacred," and suggests that "one or both texts came in due course to be put to use in ways that were not originally intended,"[9] I would propose that the long-lasting influence of Gilgamesh's story is inextricably connected to the importance attached to royal ancestor veneration, and that recitation in secular contexts does not preclude performance on more solemn occasions, just as Greek epic is both associated with hero worship and considered to have been sung at feasts and festivals.[10] It is plausible to suggest that versions of Gilgamesh's story were performed in the court of the Ur III king Shulgi, who claimed the deified king as a relative,[11] so he was a literary character, but Gilgamesh was also appealed to and propitiated so that he would intercede on behalf of the patient and banish impurity and malevolent ghosts to the underworld. While lesser ghosts afflicted individuals, a royal death contaminated the state and was treated with a large, state-level mortuary ritual *cum* festival. Given the possible use of the Standard Babylonian *Epic of Gilgamesh* to propitiate the royal dead in what was essentially a large-scale purification ritual, it is indeed frustrating that the identification of Sin-leqi-unninni, the legendary composer of the epic, as a *mašmaššu*-priest, or incantation-priest who engaged in ritual purifications, is not secure because of damage to the Neo-Assyrian catalog listing legendary authors and their works in which his name appears.[12]

---

[7] On the wrestling competitions in festivals, see M. E. Cohen (1993: 463) and George (2003: 126–7, 168–9).

[8] George (2003: 54).   [9] George (2003: 53).

[10] While the setting for song within Homer's epics indicates that they were performed at social occasions such as banquets, the rise of epic has been connected with the rise of hero worship. See Chapter 11 for a full discussion.

[11] The Ur III kings, especially Shulgi, were very attracted to the myth of Gilgamesh. The self-deified king Shulgi considered himself to be the brother of Gilgamesh and the son of the goddess Ninsun and the hero Lugalbanda (*Shulgi O* 50, 139; *Shulgi P* C.22–3, 38, trans. ETCSL t.2.4.2.15, 16), see Michalowski (1988).

[12] A *mašmaššu* "wipes away" (*mašāšu*) impurity (Cunningham 1997: 14–15). The catalog is edited and discussed by W. G. Lambert (1962), and see Chapter 3, 57, n. 15. Seleucid era *kalû*-priests (lamentation-priests) at Uruk claim him as ancestor (Beaulieu 2000), but it is unlikely that the partially preserved professional designation should be restored as U[Š.KU] (= Akk. *kalû*), instead of M[AŠ.MAŠ] (George 2003: 28, n. 74).

I will follow this line of reasoning further in later chapters, delving into the Near Eastern background of Greek hero worship and how it provided a vector for transfer of epic. Here I content myself with one suggestion, which I will pick up again in the final chapters, that the necromancy episode in Book 11 of the *Odyssey* shows that the close connection between propitiation of the dead and epic was maintained across time and space.

The Hurro-Hittite pit ritual involving the story of Gilgamesh

A fragment of a tablet from Hattusa, published as *KUB* 8.62, provides the key evidence for the use of the Gilgamesh narrative in Hurro-Hittite ritual.[13] It mentions Gilgamesh and Ullu(ya); however, it lacks any of the markers of Hurro-Hittite song, as far as we can tell, such as pleonastic marking of subject with pronominal enclitics, inverted word order, or the formulaic speech introduction *memiškiwan daiš* "he/she began to speak," and it contains several *hapax legomena*. It refers to the Hurrian *ambašši* ritual, a purificatory holocaust offering, and the extant passages can plausibly be described as the *legomenon* of a pit ritual requesting life for a client, or perhaps the entire city of Itla, a location mentioned only in this tablet.

I begin with a translation of *KUB* 8.62:

§1′ i 1′ [...]
The wildlife of the [st]eppe [does/did] no[t ...]
[...] go[e]s. ... [...]
bows down. Him (acc.)[14] st[eppe ...].

§2′ 5′ Of the w[h]ole steppe [...]
the *tarlā*-bird (acc.), the *tārumaki*[-bird ...].
the god Ullu ... down [...].

§3′ (In) the city Itla [...]
washes in front. (For) himself/yourself/myself [...]

---

[13] It has been assigned to the third tablet of the *Song of Gilgamesh* by Beckman (2001a: 165); see the critique of Klinger (2005: 118, n. 24, with earlier references), who points out that the mention of Ullu both at the beginning of the tablet and in the fourth column prevents this tablet from fitting into the framework of what we would expect the third tablet to contain. Friedrich (1930a: 65–7, 79) suggested that this tablet represents a different story altogether, while Kammenhuber (1967: 56) argued that it is a separate version of the Gilgamesh story based on a Hurrian version. Beckman now believes that the text does not belong to the *Song of Gilgamesh* (oral communication 5/9/08).

[14] I have been referring to the entity who is the beneficiary with the English masculine gender pronoun, but the Hittite common gender pronoun could refer to anything construed as animate in Hittite.

10′ Come! (For) himself/yourself/myself the wooden ḫupp[ar-vessel . . .]
Fire . . . bur[ning . . .].[15]
of bread the scen[t . . .].
of hot bread the s[cent . . .].
They come/will come (or: will proceed to do something) [. . .]

§4′ 15′ Eat! Drink! Eat your [fill! Quench your thirst! . . .]
Illness (neut. nom./acc. or comm. acc.) the city Itl[a . . .].
Ladder (acc. pl.) . . . from/with [. . .].
When/As a single (acc.) sick[ness . . .]
in sickness, for Ullu [. . .].

20′ Ullu . . . of the circle (of gods) [. . .]

§5′ When/As the circle (of gods) (acc.) [. . .]
(of?) this very heap of fat le[ave . . .]
Promise life for him. Living [. . .]
like us [. . .]
25′ important/weighty (neut. nom./acc. sing.). But the name for y[ou . . .]
[. . .] of the cit[y] Itla [. . .].

§6″B 4′ . . . Anzili (IŠTAR-iš) . . .
§7″ A iv 1′[...]
The eagle (nom.) . . . the lamb (acc.) [. . .]
ga[ve] a family to him/her [. . .]
The god Susarwa (gen.?) [. . .]
5′ there was life. U[llu . . .]
(one) of life let him/it be. The Sun-god (nom.) [. . .].
But let him be living. The god T[a-. . .].

§8″ Five (acc.) zandanatar (neut. nom./acc. sing.) upon [. . .]
ambašši-ritual zatraš (nom. sing.? gen.? dat./loc. pl.?) [. . .]
10′ to Ullu the hand (acc.) up[on]
be living, Ullu, further! [. . .]
like us, wh[ich . . .]
and Gilgamesh (nom.?) ga[ve] him life [. . .]
and Gilgamesh life in the futu[re . . .] (or: in retu[rn. . .])
15′ one of life let him be. Kumarbi[16] [. . .]
Now also let him be living [. . .]

---

[15] war[. . .]: perhaps the beginning of a form of the verb war- 'burn', or of the noun waršula-, translated here (12′, 13′) variously as "drop" or "scent," or the verb waršiya-'be calm'.

[16] KhT takes as vocative, not nominative, and groups with the preceding sentence.

§9″ Six (acc.) *zandanatar*[17] upo[n ...]
     ambašši-ritual *anapāš*[18] [...]
     [...] he too[k] up [...]
20′ [...][19]

The first two preserved paragraphs allude to the steppe and its wildlife. One possible inference is that the wilderness is portrayed in a state of lack, as in the Telipinu myth told in Anatolian *mugawar* invocations. The return of the absent god is needed to restore nature to its proper condition.[20] In the first paragraph of column i, someone bows, the gesture of a penitent or pleading worshipper. In the second paragraph, two otherwise unattested types of birds are mentioned; the *tārumaki*-bird may be a woodpecker, and the *tarlā*-bird is possibly a stork.[21] Ullu appears for the first time. The third paragraph, mentioning the otherwise unknown city Itla, refers to purificatory cleansing with the verb *arri*, often used to describe how the client is washed. Now ritual offerings are described temptingly; the fragrance of newly baked bread beckons to the gods, a group of which are described as approaching. This could either be a description of the ongoing ritual or an allusion to a previous occasion that is meant to provide an example to the deities invoked, who are called to eat and drink of the offerings in the fourth paragraph. Now the city Itla is coupled with illness. Perhaps there is a plague in the city, or the city is involved in a historiola (a story embedded in an incantation). The ladder mentioned at this point is a piece of paraphernalia used in pit rituals, an important piece of evidence for the type of ritual being enacted. Ullu in turn is coupled with a mention of the

---

[17] Neut. nom./acc. sing.?   [18] Nom. sing.? Gen.? Dat./loc. pl.?
[19] *CTH* 341.iii.6.A = *KUB* 8.62, with unpublished duplicate B = Bo 5700, translit E. Rieken *et al.* 2009 ff., on KhT. Gurney (1986: 61) has suggested that another small fragment (*CTH* 341.iii.14. A = Gurney 5) could follow this passage. I provide a translation of §§3″–4″, rev. 2′–10′:

   Gilgamesh the god/goddess [...]
   On which [day] they engendered me/ they were born for me [...]
   I (will) know by a sign [...]
   On that day [...]
   But, to a single [...]

   And my god, the god [...]
   was angry, and the god [...]
   formerly [...]
   400 years [...]
   ...

[20] See trans. of the Telipinu myth (*CTH* 324) by M. Bachvarova in López-Ruiz (2013: 453), and further references to discussions of the ritual below, 104, n. 115.
[21] See *HEG* (T/D: 184, 239–40, with earlier references).

"circle," or group of gods. In the fifth paragraph an analogy is set up: as some event occurred before, so may it occur now. An offering, now of fat, is again mentioned, and in turn a request is made, "Promise life for him." The story of Utnapishtim, granted eternal life by the gods, provides the context to understand the mythical allusion. Now someone is overtly named, just as in more extensively preserved purificatory rituals the practitioner "says the name of the client of the ritual."[22]

In column iv of the reverse the text is picked up again. We seem to be in the middle of a mythologeme in which Anzili (IŠTAR-iš) and a god Susarwa (only attested here) play a part, involving the granting of life, as life was granted before. The Sun-god is mentioned, then a god T[a...], perhaps Tashmishu, the brother of Teshshub, or Takidu, one of Hebat's attendants. The seventh paragraph of those preserved continues the theme, now introducing Gilgamesh, who seems to be an agent who has given someone a family, and is expected to now give life. Kumarbi also appears, and there is explicit mention of an *ambašši* ritual and an inanimate thing called *zandanatar*, fitting Anatolian morphology for abstract nouns. The term only appears here and assonates with the term *zatraš*, also hapax, as is *anapāš*, which occurs in the equivalent position in the following paragraph, where the passage breaks off.

The *ambašši* ritual mentioned in *KUB* 8.62 is closely connected to Hurrianized north Syria and southeast Anatolia. The term is an abstract noun derived from the Hurrian verbal root *am*-'burn', and the ritual of fully immolating an animal offering has been connected to holocaust rituals mentioned in the Hebrew Bible.[23] In the Hittite texts it is commonly combined with other purificatory techniques, including pit rituals, the most famous example being the *Purification Ritual for the Former Gods*.[24]

The poor condition of the key tablet in which the pit ritual involving Gilgamesh is described is extraordinarily frustrating, but we can at least flesh out its ritual context and apply what we know about allusions to Gilgamesh in Mesopotamian rituals to understand how his story may have been used in the pit ritual.

---

[22] *Ritual of Allaiturahhi*: CTH 780.ii.Tablet 6'.B = *KBo* 33.119 13' (translit. Haas and Wegner 1988: 158, No. 24).

[23] Schwemer (1995).

[24] The *ambašši* and pit ritual also can be elements in an extended complex ritual, such as *CTH* 481: *Expansion of the Cult of the Goddess of Night*, used when the goddess was divided and transferred from the Kizzuwatnean town of Samuha. On the ritual see J. L. Miller (2004: 259–439) and Beal (2002).

Gilgamesh in Mesopotamian rituals

Outside of Hattusa, Gilgamesh appears in a few Neo-Assyrian incantations of prescriptions against ghosts, called on to judge the victim's case along with the Sun-god Shamash,[25] or to witness a transaction with a ghost who receives a gift and in return is forced to swear that he or she will take the evil away. He appears along with Shamash, the Anunnaki or Former Gods (on which more below), and ghosts who are related to the victim.[26] He is also found fairly frequently in incantations against illness.[27] A typical example exhorts Shamash and Gilgamesh, "I, your servant, may I live; and furthermore, may I be healthy, your praise I will utter,"[28] words similar to the incantation in *KUB* 8.62.

At Hattusa Gilgamesh is mentioned in at least three incantations of Mesopotamian origin. Two are syllabic Sumerian incantations against sorcery in Middle Babylonian script, possibly imported from Babylon.[29] Gilgamesh also appears in an Akkadian ritual against sorcery at Hattusa, in the form of a doll, as he sometimes does in Akkadian rituals of the *maqlû* type, a ritual that was performed at the end of the month of Abu, when it was intended to expel ghosts from the world of the living.[30] As is typical of the Mesopotamian texts found at Hattusa, there is no evidence that these particular texts were actually used, or of influence from these texts on the extensive incantation literature attributed to performers at Hattusa, although certainly Mesopotamian influence can be detected more generally in Hittite incantations.[31]

---

[25] *KAR* 227 iii 14 (with duplicate) (translit. and trans. Scurlock 1988: 352–3, Prescription 85; Ebeling 1931: 131).

[26] *KAR* 227 iii 25–50 (translit. and trans. Scurlock 1988: 357–61, Prescription 87).

[27] Examples in Ebeling (1931: 124–7, 130–3).

[28] VAT 13657 iii 50–1 (translit. Ebeling 1931: 132).

[29] *Sumerian Incantations*: CTH 800 = *KBo* 36.13 right col. 15′ (George 2003: 132; Wilhelm 1991: iv). The second set of Sumerian incantations, *KUB* 30.1–4, belongs to at least two separate tablets. *KUB* 37.108–10 probably belong to one of these tablets, but no direct join has been made. Only *KUB* 30.1 has been edited (Geller 1989; also see the earlier edition of Falkenstein 1939). In versions found elsewhere this second incantation twice mentions Gilgamesh breaking the sorcerers' spell, although these lines are not preserved in the Boğazköy version (31, 41′ in Geller's composite edition, 1989: 196–7, 198–9).

[30] *Akkadian Incantations*: CTH 812 = *KBo* 36.29 iv 7′ (translit. Schwemer 1998: 78). There are at least five copies of the incantation. See discussion of Schwemer (1998: 78, with earlier references) on Gilgamesh as king of the dead and his appearance in incantations. On this text, also see the comments of Farber (2001). On dolls of Gilgamesh in *maqlû* ('burning') incantations and the association of *maqlû* with Abu, see Abusch (1974: 259–61), M. E. Cohen (1993: 455, 457, 463–4, with earlier references), and Parpola (1983: 203–4), commenting on No. 208 = K 649 (ed. Parpola 1970: 154–5).

[31] See most recently Haas (2007b).

Gilgamesh also is mentioned (without the divine determinative) at Hattusa in a Hurrian incantation that accompanies offerings to the gods, possibly in his role as judge in the underworld.[32] This important passage, noticed by Volkert Haas and Hans-Jochen Thiel,[33] has been joined by Detlev Groddek to another fragment mentioning Shawushka that includes the tablet's colophon, where we glean that the ritual is attributed to an "Old Woman of Kizzu[watna]."[34] A few lines of the Hurrian Gilgamesh incantation parallel an incantation from another Hurro-Hittite ritual text attributed to such a practitioner.[35] This is significant because the latter includes a pit offering to the Former Gods of a type similar to the *Purification Ritual for the Former Gods*. Thus, the fragment of the Hurrian incantation mentioning Gilgamesh is also an incantation for a Hurro-Hittite pit ritual, like *KUB* 8.62.

Pit rituals

The pit rituals at Hattusa are one sub-type of the Hurro-Hittite purification rituals performed by an exorcist (^{LÚ}AZU/^{LÚ}ḪAL) and/or an "Old Woman" (^{MUNUS}ŠU.GI). The male practitioner is particularly associated with *itkalzi* 'mouth washing' and the *itkaḫi* 'purification' rituals from Sapinuwa in northeast Anatolia,[36] while some of the rituals in which the female performers appear come from Kizzuwatna in Cilicia or from Mukish in northern Syria.[37] The pit rituals attested at Hattusa are also a sub-type of a general practice found in Mesopotamia, Syria, and Greece in the Late Bronze Age.

One key Near Eastern term for the pit is found in Akkadian (*abu/apu*), Hurrian (*āpi* /ābi/), Hittite (*āpi* or *āpiti*),[38] Ugaritic (*ảp*), and Hebrew

---

[32] *Fragments of Hurro-Hittite Rituals and Incantations*: CTH 790 = KUB 32.46 obv. 20′: *kal-ga-a-mi-šu-un-na* (translit. Haas and Wegner 1988: 443, No. 107). This text is labeled in the KhT as CTH 701.f.22: *Drink Offerings for the Throne of Hebat*.
[33] Haas and Thiel (1978: 36, 193–4); Haas (1994: 334–5).
[34] CTH 701.f.22 = KBo 33.115 i 5′, iv 2′ (translit. Haas and Wegner 1988: 493, No. 133). The join is noted on KhT *ad loc*. On the Old Woman, see Chapter 8, 182, with n. 69.
[35] CTH 790 = KUB 32.46 obv. 15′–17′ ‖ KUB 27.34 iii 12′–14′ (translit. Haas and Wegner 1988: 443, 341, Nos. 107, 75).
[36] Haas (1984: 10–11). As noted in Chapter 2, 51, Salvini and Wegner (2004: 17–18) have suggested that an *itkalzi* ritual could have been the context for the *Song of Birth*.
[37] Haas and Thiel (1978: 16–18), Haas and Wegner (1988: 4).
[38] For other Hittite terms see Collins (2002: 225).

('*ôb*).[39] Festivals, offerings, and other rituals involving the *abu* are well attested from the end of the third millennium onwards. Rites for the *a-ba-i* are attested at Ebla, dating to *ca.* 2300 BCE. Jacopo Pasquali and Piergiorgio Mangiarotti suggest this is a pit.[40] If so, it would be the earliest attestation of the term. An elaborate installation in stone of a deep chamber in the ground at the Hurrian city of Urkesh shows how important pit rituals were among the Hurrians (Fig. 1).[41] Here a large quantity of animal bones was found, especially of year-old pigs, but also of sheep, bovines, dogs (mostly puppies), and equids.[42]

The *abu*-festival is first attested in the Ur III period at Ur and Mari.[43] Furthermore, a month *Ab/p šarrāni* 'Pit(-festival) of the (dead) kings' is attested from the Old Assyrian period.[44] The Neo-Assyrian sources show a

---

[39] See Ebach and Rüterswörden (1977), Hoffner (1967), and Loretz (2002). Ebach and Rüterswörden (1977: 213–14) suggest that Mycenaean *Upoyo Potniya* 'Lady of Upo' (PY Fn 187.8, Fr 1225, 1236) was the 'Lady of the Pit', but other scholars present different etymologies; see Aura Jorro (1985, 1993: 2.388).

[40] Pasquali and Mangiarotti (2005).

[41] M. Dietrich and Loretz (2004), Kelly-Buccellati (2002; 2005), Buccellati and Kelly-Buccellati (2004); Buccellati (2005: 10–11). The Buccellatis suggest that the *āpi* could date as far back as the ED period, the start of the third millennium (2009: 38–9).

[42] The statistics are provided by Di Martino (2005). The *ảp* is mentioned in Ugaritic texts, both mythological and ritual, where it is part of a complex of Hurro-Hittite funerary practices incorporated into the royal cult (*Keret*: KTU 1.16 i 3, 17, ii 39, translit. and trans. N. Wyatt 2002: 219, 222, 230: "entrance," see M. Dietrich and Loretz 2004). Niehr identified Room 28 in the Royal Palace as a *ḫešti*-house. This is a small room to the north of Courtyard II in the *zone funéraire* of the palace. It was accessed via the even smaller Room 27, which connects to the courtyard and other parts of the palace. Under the floor of Room 28 are a tomb and a small cave that has a hole at the back wall, which may have served as an access point to the underworld (Niehr 2007: 224, with earlier references), and a pit that would have been covered with a wooden cap and reached via an entrance to the east. This, Niehr (2006b: 10–11; 2007) suggests, was an *ảp*. See further Chapter 14, 382, n. 139. On the *ḫešti*-house, see Chapter 7, 151, with n. 8.

[43] On the month of Abu and other festivals for the dead, see M. E. Cohen (1993: 259–61, 454–81).

[44] CAD A/1: 2, Donbaz (1992: 123), M. E. Cohen (1993: 460). An offering of porridge "at the entrance to the *abi*" is noted in an OB text from Sippar (*YOS* 12.345, quoted from M. E. Cohen 1993: 460–1). An offering not in the pit, but right in front of it, is made to lure out the entities below. A list from Assur mentioning offerings for the "*āpi* of the House of Kings" – that is, the royal tomb – and dating to the twelfth century indicates that pit rituals propitiating dead royalty were well established in the latter half of the second millennium in Mesopotamia (A 842, Middle Assyrian, ed. and discussion Donbaz 1992). At Emar, offerings to the *abû* (*sic*) along with various forms of Ashtarte, who is bewailed, are made in the month of *Abû* ('father'). The month belongs to the wider north Syrian calendrical tradition; see Fleming (2000: 75). Also see Loretz (2002: 512) on "Ashtarte of the pit." See Fleming (2000: 174–89) for the rituals of the month of *Abû*, and Loretz (2002: 495–9), surveying the scholarly discussion of the Emar material. "At Emar, the word *abû* refers to the entire shrine, without regard for its shape. It is true that pits were discovered by the excavators on the flat open space behind the temples of the storm-god and Aštart at the western height of the tell. However, the compound preposition *ana pānī* 'before', which describes the placement of offering materials, is not what we would expect

Fig. 1: The *āpi* at Urkesh, *ca.* 2300 BCE

focus on funerary offerings during the *abu*-festival,[45] and Neo-Assyrian rituals against ghosts take advantage of the easy passage in and out of the underworld afforded to ghosts in the month of Abu.[46]

Rituals involving the *abu* are also found in Neo-Assyrian sources, although not all are necromantic. They typically involve offerings into a pit that is then closed up. In a substitution ritual that may be a part of a burial ritual for a woman of the palace, possibly Esharra-hamat, the first wife of Esarhaddon, a pit is dug, oil and honey are poured into it, and the women of the palace call out, "Come!" Then, a figurine is buried, the pit is closed, and offerings are made to Antum, the female counterpart to Anu and one of the gods of the earlier generation; to Gilgamesh; and to a ship

with offering deposited in a hole" (Fleming 2000: 188). This issue is resolved by the evidence from Hittite pit rituals, in which offerings are placed before the pit in order to lure up the god. See below.

[45] M. E. Cohen (1993: 461).

[46] Scurlock (1995) discusses the use of rituals in Abu that refer to the Ishtar and Dumuzi myth. A festival in which the dead come up to visit the living bears an obvious resemblance to the Athenian Anthesteria, but it was celebrated in the dry months of the summer, when nothing grows, rather than in the spring.

made of a grain paste, which symbolizes the dead person's journey to the other world. The ceremony is meant to remove the impurity caused by death.[47]

Finally, 1 Samuel 28, in which King Saul encounters the ghost of Samuel, presents a famous – if disputed – example of a necromantic ritual involving an 'ôb.[48]

The Hurrian-influenced pit rituals at Hattusa come from a widespread practice of accessing the underworld via pits, typical of cultures in which the dead are buried underground. For example, pits are used in later Neo-Assyrian rituals to get rid of ghosts or to make use of them, whether for divination or to carry off evil.[49] Impurity may be put in a pit by burying a pot with a figurine representing the evil;[50] or offerings are made into a pit.[51] There is no written evidence for a "pure" Hurrian pit ritual, although the archaeological evidence from Urkesh shows that sacrifice of animals into the pit was an important element. In the rituals attested at Hattusa, whatever peculiarities the Hurrian practice involved were combined with the customs of Anatolia, where there was an indigenous tradition of interacting with the underworld at the sinkholes so characteristic of the geology of the region, where rivers can dip in and out of the ground.[52] The river is useful not only for rituals to contact the human dead or

---

[47] K 164 (translit. and trans. Ebeling 1931: 59–65), see Donbaz (1992), Ebach and Rüterswörden (1977: 212), Nasrabadi (1999: 36–40). On boats in funerary imagery, including the Ayia Triada sarcophagus, see Gallou (2005: 43–9). In another ritual from Assur, soothing blood, honey, oil, beer, and wine are poured into the pit, then a singer invites the gods to eat the meat which is offered. The meat is put into the pit, then offerings of honey and oil are made. In the second, after the singer performs, honey, oil, beer, and wine are poured into the pit, then the pit is filled in by the singer, and the king seals it by stepping on it (*KAR* 146 iii 10′–29′, iv 23′–30′, translit. and trans. Ebeling 1952: 142–8; re-edited by Menzel 1981: T98–101 = Nr. 45, whose line numbers I follow). See Ebach and Rüterswörden (1977: 210–11, with other examples) and M. E. Cohen (1993: 459).

[48] Schmidt (1995) argues that the Hebrew Bible pit rituals reflect first-millennium practices retrojected into the past, but Loretz (2002) effectively argues that they reflect a long-standing Near Eastern tradition.

[49] Scurlock (1988: 103).

[50] *BAM* 323 36–8 (translit. and trans. Scurlock 1988: 217–18, 221, Prescription 56).

[51] *CT* 23.15–22+ i 33′–9′ (translit. and trans. Scurlock 1988: 167–9, Prescription 14; Ebeling 1931: 148, No. 30.F).

[52] On the KASKAL.KUR as a sinkhole (Turkish *düden*), see E. I. Gordon (1967). On the geology of Anatolia and its influence on their conception of the gods, see Deighton (1982). Collins (2002: 226, 233) shows that the pit rituals found in the Hittite sources had both indigenous and exogenous origins. The concept of a river leading underground as a way to access the underworld is connected to the concept of the underworld as a place of primordial waters, on which see López-Ruiz (2010: 114–15).

underworld gods; it also brings up and exposes hidden evil in the form of mud, and it can wash away and carry away evil.[53]

In Hattusa there are three artificial KASKAL.KURs ('roads to the underworld'). One is near Temple 1, an artificial cave over a natural spring.[54] The other two are in the Südburg and date to the final period of Hittite hegemony. Of the two in the Südburg, Chamber One is built into the bank of a dam, while the better preserved Chamber Two is "an open-ended vaulted chamber ... built into the side of a tumulus" that forms the northern bank of a large artificial pool (Fig. 2). The construction, labeled in Hieroglyphic Luwian DEUS.VIA+TERRA 'divine road to the underworld', leads laterally under the bank with a figure of the deified king Suppiluliuma I ('he of the pure pool') carved on one wall and a Hieroglyphic Luwian inscription lauding the deeds of Suppiluliuma II on the other. The Sun-god stands at the far end ready to intercede with Former Gods on behalf of the king.[55] There is a shallow trench for offerings before the Sun-god, while in a building nearby is a large stone-lined pit, which Billie Jean Collins suggests "must have been a ritual pit for communicating with the Underworld. Two miniature bronze axes, models of the implements that would have been used to dig the pit, were found lying

---

[53] The "Old Woman" Tunnawi(ya), one of the more famous sorcerers among the Hittites (Dardano 2006: 49–50, with earlier references; J. L. Miller 2004: 452–8), makes this clear: "As you, spring, bubble mud back up from the Dark Earth, for this person, the client of the ritual, remove likewise evil impurity from her(/his) limbs" (*Ritual of Tunnawiya*: CTH 409.1.A = *KUB* 12.58 i 12′–14′, translit. Goetze 1938: 6, 8). The "Old Woman" uses clay from the spring and the river bank to make models of the evil tongues she wishes to nullify, and of two cows, presumably corresponding to the fertile cow she manipulates in the ritual, to render the client fertile again. Later she throws ritual paraphernalia made impure by contact with the client into the river. While Tunnawi(ya) is associated with indigenous Anatolian rituals and uses incantations with clear Indo-European origins (Watkins 1995: 249–50; M. L. West 2007: 336–8), the "Old Woman" Allaiturahhi from Syrian Mukish is portrayed as conceiving of springs in the same way, cf. *Ritual of Allaiturahhi*: CTH 780.11.Tablet 1.H = *KUB* 58.74 ii? 13–16 (translit. García Trabazo 2005: 192), see translation of *CHD* (Š: 77).

[54] Neve (1969–1970; 1993: 75, 80), Seeher (2002: 25).

[55] Hawkins (1990: 314), compared by Kelly-Buccellati (2002: 143) to the Urkesh structure. Also see the descriptions of Seeher (2002: 84–91) and Neve (1993: 69–80). It is debated whether the image represents Suppiluliuma II or his divinized ancestor Suppiluliuma I. I follow Singer (2009: 180) and Hawkins (1995b: 19). A Divine Road to the Underworld is listed in the *Alaksandu Treaty* among the Wilusan gods witnessing the transaction (*CTH* 76.A = *KUB* 21.1 iv 28, translit. Friedrich 1930b: 80; trans. Beckman 1999b: 92), and a possible KASKAL.KUR has been excavated at Troy; it was used first during Troia vi/vii, and washtubs were added much later (Korfmann 1998: 57–61). Homer alludes to the spot as the place where Trojan women were wont to wash their laundry (*Il.* 22.147–56), so apparently he is not aware of a possible earlier function. The Trojan feature was also compared by Kelly-Buccellati (2002: 143) to the construction at Urkesh.

Fig. 2: The KASKAL.KUR at Boğazköy, Exterior View (*ca.* 1200 BCE)

nearby."[56] We may compare the model of the ladder that was used in the Gilgamesh ritual.[57]

It can be argued that Bronze Age Greece had its own style of necromantic pit ritual, not related to the Hurro-Hittite pit rituals. In Mycenaean Greece there is some evidence of *bothroi* or ritual pits near graves in which offerings were repeatedly deposited over an extended period of time.[58] Of course we cannot assume that the offerings were meant to raise the dead, and the ceremonies' locations were fixed by their proximity to the tomb, thus differing from the pit rituals discussed here. In addition, a necromantic ritual may be shown on the Ayia Triada sarcophagus, dating to the end of the third millennium (Fig. 3). On the right half of one side are depicted three men offering two tied-up calves and a model boat to a smaller male figure whose arms are concealed within his garment. It seems that the artist intends to show him emerging from the ground because his garment does not end at the ground line and his feet are not visible.[59] If it is a pit ritual,

---

[56] Collins (2006: 176). See Neve (1993: 52, with fig. 142).   [57] See 83.
[58] Gallou (2005: 21–2, 88, 98–9).
[59] Laffineur (1991) attempts to argue that the sarcophagus depicts a precursor of the necromantic ritual of *Odyssey* 11.

Fig. 3: The Ayia Triada Sarcophagus (LM IIIA2, *ca.* 1390/70–1330/15 BCE): The dead man rises from the ground to the right

then the pit is a permanent built structure like those at Urkesh and Hattusa, as the smaller figure is between a stepped altar made of bricks and a building façade, either a temple or a tomb.

Nearly all of the evidence for Greek pit rituals in the first millennium comes from literary depictions, but Clement of Alexandria's (190 CE) exhortation to turn away from the "mouths of pits (*barathrōn*) full of the marvelous (*terateiā*)"[60] shows that they were indeed carried out in the real world, although one should not assume that there was an unbroken chain of transmission of a Greek ritual from the third millennium or even from the early first millennium BCE.

Some analogs from Anatolia indicate that the practice of pit rituals to eliminate evil was maintained across the Dark Age. There are the "ritual dinners" found in sixth-century Sardis. Almost thirty of them have been found buried in private houses. "In every recognizable instance a standard service of four vessels – jug, dish, *oenochoe*, and *skyphos* – and an iron knife were neatly placed together; the vessels hold a standard meal

---

[60] *Protrepticus* 11 (ed. Marcovich 1995: 19; trans. Ogden 2001: 53).

consisting of a whole puppy, bread(?), and wine."[61] Noel Robertson has convincingly compared them to Hurro-Hittite rituals, and his argument can be bolstered by the evidence of the use of puppies in Hittite purificatory rituals.[62] The knife included in the deposits could have been used to kill the puppy, and it also could have been used to dig the pit, as in some of the Hurro-Hittite rituals.[63] At Ephesus puppies were found buried in one or more pits (900 BCE), and at the shrine of Artemis at Hyampolis a similar deposition of puppies was found.[64]

Hattusa provides many detailed descriptions of pit rituals, some of which present striking similarities to *Odyssey* 11,[65] although the pits in the rituals found at Hattusa were not used for necromancy, as they were in the Greco-Roman sources and by the witch of Endor that Saul consulted – that is, they were not used to raise the dead in order to ask them questions about the future. Rather, they were used to bury impurity or to communicate with underworld deities,[66] or the patient himself or herself could be conceived of as if buried like a dead body underground, and thus s/he must be "taken from the earth."[67] At times the pit could be used to lure out a god who was conceived of as being angry and hiding in the underworld, a variation on the Anatolian *mugawar* invocation.[68] Copies of the

---

[61] Robertson (1982: 122).   [62] Collins (1990).

[63] These pit dinners were described and analyzed in detail by Greenewalt (1978), who weighs the possibilities of the two suggested connections, but prefers to compare a rich stew associated with the Lydians called *kandaulos*. Pedley (1974) argued that the "dog dinners" reflect Carian practices, as Hecate was a Carian goddess, and dogs were sacrificed to her. Whether these pit sacrifices were in fact connected either with Hecate or with Hipponax's "Hermes the dog-throttler, Candaules in Lydian" (Hipponax F 2.1 Degani), as has been suggested, lies beyond the scope of this study, but on the etymology of Candaules see Chapter 14, 374.

[64] See Forstenpointner, Weissengruber, and Galik (2005).

[65] The Hittite pit rituals and their wider east Mediterranean context have been studied well by Collins (2002), Ebach and Rütersworden (1977), and Loretz (2002).

[66] In *Mastigga's Ritual against Family Quarrel*, representative of Kizzuwatnean rituals, a pit is used to bury evil (*CTH* 404.1.1.A = *KBo* 39.8 ii 26–54, translit. and trans. J. L. Miller 2004: 73–8, translit. A. Mouton 2010ff. on KhT). See R. Parker (1983: 229) on the Greek use of such techniques to dispose of impurity.

[67] On the "take from the earth" rituals, see Taracha (1985), collecting attestations; Taracha (1990; 2000). (Taracha translates Hittite *taknaz dā*-as 'take off the earth'.) They can vary quite a bit from each other, but often involve digging "storage pits" (ÉSAG), within which a smaller hole is dug and miniature beds with coverings are placed for the underworld gods (Taracha 1990: 179). They can be associated with indigenous Anatolian performers like Tunnawi(ya) (*CTH* 409: *Ritual of Tunnawiya*, ed. Hutter 1988), and with Hurrian performers, like the woman Ashdu (*CTH* 490: *Ritual of the Hurrian Woman Ashdu against Witchcraft*, ed. Haas and Wegner 1988: 251–315, Nos. 50–67).

[68] *Offering and Prayer to the Storm-god of Nerik*: *CTH* 671.A = *KUB* 36.89, ed. with trans. and commentary by Haas (1970: 140–74), partial English trans. Hoffner (1998a: 22–4), and discussion by Mazoyer (2003b: 217–19).

Hurro-Hittite rituals show us how the Hurrian practices became Hittite, for the earliest ones, from the Middle Hittite period, contain incantations only in Hurrian; then follows a stage in which the incantations appear in Hurrian with Hittite translations; and finally, only the Hittite version is copied.[69] The transition from Hurrian to Hittite implies that the incantations were most effective if actually understood by all involved, rather than being mumbo-jumbo, an esoteric language of the gods, as found in spells in the Greek magical papyri.[70] Furthermore, even with our imperfect knowledge of the narrative traditions at Hattusa we can detect allusions to narratives in the incantations that enhanced their efficacy.

The pit could be used to communicate particularly with the Former Gods (*šiunēš karūiliēš*).[71] As the *Song of Birth* explains, the Former Gods have been deposed by the newer generation of gods. Called as witnesses in treaties and in purification rituals, by the Middle Hittite period they are equated with the Mesopotamian Anunnaki (^{d}A.NUN.NA.KE$_4$).[72] They are called in Hurrian the "grandfather-gods" (*am(m)ate=na en=na*), while in Luwian they are called "father gods" (*tatinzi maššaninzi*). The sphere of influence of the Former Gods overlaps with that of the Former Kings, the dead ancestors of the royal family.[73].

Some pit rituals communicating with the Former Gods use a model ladder, like the ritual involving Gilgamesh and Ulluya. One particularly clever example is part of a larger ritual of the "drawing paths" type in which the exorcist (^{LÚ}AZU) is drawing the MAḪ-goddesses and the Fate-goddesses of the gods, and the MAḪ-goddesses of the body of a person, (and?) the goddesses Zukki and Anzili.[74] Ten pits (*āpi, āpiti*) are dug, nine of them for the nine Former Gods.[75] When the tenth is cleared out, offerings are put into it. Then (a model of) a silver ladder and a silver

---

[69] Haas and Thiel (1978: 8–9). [70] On which see Chapter 9, 214.
[71] In the *Ritual of Hantitassu of Hurma*, an indigenous Anatolian ritual (J. L. Miller 2004: 447–50) performed when a man or woman's years are "mobilized/disturbed," a pit is used to make contact with the Former Gods (*CTH* 395 = *KBo* 11.14 iii 5′–31′, translit. and trans. Ünal 1996: 22–4, 30).
[72] The story told about the Anunnaki-gods' conflict with the Igigi-gods in the Akkadian *Atrahasis* cannot be reconciled with the Kumarbi cycle. On the Hittite Former Gods and the equation with the Anunnaki, see Archi (1990), Bachvarova (2006: 142–3), and Haas (1994: 108–15).
[73] See Gonnet (1995: 193–5), noting that the adjective *karūili-* 'former' or 'primeval' is applied to the deified dead kings as well as the Anunnaki-gods. Also see Chapter 7, 153–5, on the Former Kings, and Bachvarova (2013a: 36–40). On the Hurrian term *am(m)ate=na en=na* see Wilhelm (2009: 66, with n. 26).
[74] Evocation Rituals for DINGIR.MAḪ.MEŠ and the Fate-goddesses: *CTH* 484.1.A = *KUB* 15.31 i 1–2 (translit. and trans. F. Fuscagni 2011ff. on KhT).
[75] See Collins (2002: 225) on the number of Former Gods.

toggle-pin ornament are put into the first pit, and on the toggle-pin hangs an ear (perhaps of metal or of dough).[76] A headdress is bound to the ear that is put in the tenth pit.[77] The symbolic model and offerings make very clear the message the humans are trying to convey to the gods: "Come up and listen to us, we have some lovely gifts for you." In another example, the *Ritual Mentioning the Former Gods*, a ritual of the type performed by Old Women, the pit is dug with a knife, and a ladder, here made of copper, is put down into it, while a Hurrian invocation to a number of Former Gods is uttered.[78]

We should expect that the pit ritual mentioning Gilgamesh followed similar lines, and it is likely that the pit was conceived of as a way to reach him, as well as a place in which to store safely out of sight the pollution taken off the patient. The hero would have been invoked and given offerings, along with other divine figures.

The *Purification Ritual for the Former Gods*

The Gilgamesh ritual may have used some of the same actions as those found in the *Purification Ritual for the Former Gods*, known to Classicists because of its similarity to the necromantic episode in the *Odyssey*. It was used "when they purify a house of blood, impur[ity], threats and oaths."[79] The methods by which the evils are removed are quite elaborate, and the pit ritual is only one of a wide variety of symbolic gestures, including throwing, breaking, binding, grinding, striking, washing, and pegging. Besides analogic magic the ritual practitioner, an exorcist (LÚAZU or

---

[76] An ear-shaped loaf was used to extract the goddess from ritual pits and a fire in the *Ritual for Ishtar of Nineveh*: *CTH* 716.1.A = *KBo* 2.9 iv 12 (translit. F. Fuscagni 2009ff. on KhT, trans. B. J. Collins in Hallo and Younger 1997: 164).

[77] *CTH* 484.1.B$_2$ = *KUB* 15.32 ii 4′–16′; with A = *KUB* 15.31 ii 10–21 (translit. and trans. Fuscagni 2011ff. on KhT).

[78] Ishhara, her father Enlil and mother Abadu, Nara, Namshara, Minki, Amunki, Amizadu, Alalu, [Au]nnamu, Iyandu (*CTH* 449: *KBo* 17.94 iii 29′–32′, translit. Haas and Wegner 1988: 354, No. 77). A list of equipment for a "take from the earth" *Ritual of the Hurrian Woman Ashdu against Witchcraft* includes a copper ladder (*CTH* 490.1.A.1 = *KUB* 59.75 i 22′, translit. and trans. Haas and Wegner 1988: 263, No. 53).

[79] *CTH* 446.A = *KUB* 7.41 i 1–2 (translit. Otten 1961: 116). The text is extant in multiple copies, many of which were recognized after Otten's edition was published; the earliest ones date to the Middle Hittite period (A = *KUB* 7.41, F = *KBo* 57.57, J = *KBo* 51.38). *CTH* 446 has been translated by B. J. Collins in Hallo and Younger (1997: 168–71). Also see the synopsis in Haas (1994: 282–9) and the German translation by J. L. Miller in *TUAT NF* 4: 206–17.

LÚHAL), uses legal language as if the underworld gods were judges to whom he is arguing a case for his client,[80] and he tells a historiola about Anzili,[81] concealed behind the Akkadogram *IŠTAR* or the Sumerogram GAŠAN ('lady'). We assume she is standing in for the Hurrian goddess of magic Shawushka. As will be discussed below, one of the *legomena* clearly presupposes knowledge of the events and themes of the Kumarbi cycle, in which Anzili played an important role.[82] While Andrea Trameri has shown that the text is a composite of rituals put together by scribes,[83] the small-scale variation in the *legomena* between the different copies shows that the scribes who made the copies were sufficiently knowledgeable in the orally transmitted formulaic phraseology to unconsciously expand and contract the phrasing of the incantations.

In the first of two pit rituals within the larger ritual, the exorcist "goes to the riverbanks" (i. e., the pit on the riverbank) with offerings, including a lamb, which he "slaughters down into the hole (*pattešni*)."[84] The exorcist then proclaims, "Let the Sun-goddess of the Earth open up the gates, let out the Former Gods and the Sun-goddess of the Earth!" He calls upon each of the Former Gods of the riverbank by name; the list shows interconnectedness with Hurro-Hittite narrative song: "Aduntarri the exorcist (LÚHAL), Zulki the dream-interpretess, Irpitiga the lord of the earth, Nara, Namshara, Minki, Amunki, Abi (the pit)."[85] The list corresponds in part to that given in the damaged opening of the *Song of Birth*, in which the gods are called on to listen to the song, and they are among those called on

---

[80] I have compared this section of the ritual to the trial scene in Aeschylus' *Eumenides* (Bachvarova 2006: 145–7).

[81] Cf. ᵈGAŠAN-*li* (*CTH* 446.B = *KBo* 10.45 ii 36, translit. Otten 1961: 124).

[82] On the connections between the *Song of Birth* and the *Purification Ritual for the Former Gods*, see Haas and Wilhelm (1974: 50–3) and Archi (1990: 119–20).

[83] A. Trameri, oral presentation, "Ritual Texts and Ritual Practice in the Hittite Tradition: Text Transmission and Composition Aspects of the Incantation CTH 446," in the symposium "Exploring Ritual in the Ancient Near East and Mediterranean: Performance, Texts, and Material Culture," May 16, 2014, Institute for the Study of the Ancient World, New York University. Key pieces of evidence that indicate compiling from different rituals include the writing of the name of the Former Gods, either ᵈA.NUN.NA.KE₄ or *karūiliēš* DINGIR.MEŠ, in sections deriving from different written texts, and confusion on where the practitioner is and where he is coming from. I thank Trameri for discussing his findings on the text with me and for sharing with me his unpublished M.A. thesis on the topic (Trameri 2012).

[84] *CTH* 446.B = *KBo* 10.45 i 32′–5′ (translit. Otten 1961: 118, 120). Compare the same expression "slaughter (down) into a pit" in the *Death Rituals*: *CTH* 450.1.7e.A = *KUB* 39.4 obv. 13 (translit. Kassian, Korolëv, and Sidel'tsev 2002: 322), *CTH* 450.1 = *KUB* 34.65 i 23″ (translit. and trans. M. Kapełuś 2011 on KhT). See *HED* (H: 248–52) for further examples in ritual contexts.

[85] *CTH* 446.B = *KBo* 10.45 i 39′–45′ (translit. Otten 1961: 118, 120).

in the Hurrian *Ritual Mentioning the Former Gods*.[86] Furthermore, the list of the Former Gods also follows a Mesopotamian tradition that can be traced back to Gilgamesh himself, a tradition of appeasing and propitiating those who have crossed to the other side, for in the Sumerian *Death of Gilgamesh* the hero makes offerings to a similar set of named underworld gods.[87]

Later on in the ritual, the exorcist will explicitly refer to the story of how Kumarbi and his coevals were replaced by the Storm-god:

> He (the exorcist) takes three birds. Two birds he offers to the Anunnaki, but one bird he offers to the deified pit. He speaks as follows: "You are the former ...,[88] not for you is an ox (or) a sheep set. When the Storm-god drove you down under the Dark Earth, he set for you this offering."
> He [co]oks the birds with the fire, he sets them before the god.[89]

This phraseology about "sending into the Dark Earth" copies the beginning of the *Song of Birth*:

> (A i 12–15) As just nine years were counted off, Alalu was king in heaven, and in the ninth year Anu [w]ent in batt[le] against Alalu. He defeated him, Alalu, and he ran away before him, and he went down into the Dark Earth. He went down into the Dark Earth, while Anu seated himself on the throne.[90]

---

[86] [Mink]i, Ammunki, Ammezzadu, and the father and mother of Ishhara (Enlil and Abadu) (*Song of Birth*, *CTH* 344.A = *KUB* 33.120 i 1–5, translit. E. Rieken *et al.* 2009ff. on KhT). Also see Haas (2006: 134) and Wilhelm (2009) on the names of the Former Gods, including the appearance at Emar of Alalu and Ammezadu. See n. 78 for the gods invoked in *CTH* 449.

[87] Ereshkigal, Namtar, Dimpiku, Neti, Ningishzida, Dumuzi, Enki, Ninki, Enmul, Ninmul, Endukuga, Nindukuga, Endashuruma, Nindashuruma, Enmutula, Enmeshara, "maternal and paternal ancestors of Enlil; ... for the Anuna gods of the Holy Mound, for the Great Princes of the Holy Mound, for the dead *en* priests, the dead *lagar* priests..." (trans. ETCSL t.1.8.1.3. Nippur version 8–23); see Haas (1994: 110–11, 132), who also compares the Sumerian *Death of Ur-Namma* (*Ur-Namma* A, trans. ETCSL t.2.4.1.1), in which the dead king, founder of the Ur III dynasty (2112–2095 BCE), makes offerings to a series of the gods of the underworld, including Gilgamesh, when he arrives below.

[88] The text has the sequence *ka-ru-ú-i-li-eš-ša(-)mi-i[t]*; the word signified by the signs after *karūiliēš* is not intelligible.

[89] *CTH* 446.B = *KBo* 45.10 iii 41–8 (translit. Otten 1961: 130–2). The mythological fragment *Ea and the Beast* makes use of the same phraseology. The beast prophesies to Ea that the god who will seize power over heaven "will drive (the rest of the gods?) ... down under the Dark Earth" (*dankuwai taknī kattanta ... pennai*, *CTH* 351.1.A = *KUB* 36.55 ii 10′–11′, translit. E. Rieken *et al.* 2009ff. on KhT). The phrase is enough to conjure up the full story of the Storm-god's rise to power. Haas (2006: 144; 2007a: 347) points out the reference appears in both *CTH* 446 and *Ea and the Beast*; note that the transliteration of Rieken *et al.* excludes any reference to a ritual substitute (*tarpalli-*, *contra* Archi's 2002a analysis) and therefore any reference to substitution ritual. On the mythological fragment, also see Chapter 2, 26–7.

[90] *CTH* 344.A = *KUB* 33.120 i 12–15 (translit. E. Rieken *et al.* 2009ff. on KhT; trans. M. Bachvarova in López-Ruiz 2013: 141).

Now, having called up the Former Gods that were mentioned at the beginning of the *Song of Birth* from the place whither the Storm-god had sent them, the exorcist tells them,

> I, a human, did not come at random. I did not come in strife. In the house there are placed blood, tears, oath of the god, strife, sins. Heaven above is angry, and the earth below is angry.
>
> And you, Former Gods, the Storm-god the exorcist (^{LÚ}AZU), sent from the earth, and he said this word to you.[91]

At this point the exorcist repeats his request that the gods purify the house, putting it in the mouth of the Storm-god, and makes further offerings.

The exorcist, going to the water with offerings in hand, "speaks as follows: 'With respect to which matter I have come, let the spring, the water, ask me. But with me comes Anzili from the green fields.'"[92] He now tells a historiola about the goddess. She demands water from the springs, with which she will purify the sins and evils of the cursed house. The spring responds, "[Draw] water seven times... [ ], draw water eight[93] times [ ] pour it. But, the ninth time, which water ..., draw that [ ], take it for yourself."[94] The series of increasing numbers follows the figure of speech found in *KUB* 8.62, in which five *zandatar* are mentioned, then six, before the fragment breaks off. This particular parallel suggests that the Gilgamesh incantation follows some of the same templates as the *Purification Ritual for the Former Gods*.

Based on the parallels in some of the wording of *KUB* 8.62 and the incantation from the *Purification Ritual for the Former Gods*, we may be justified in thinking not only that both rituals addressed divinities construed as belonging to the remote past, but also that the Gilgamesh ritual

---

[91] *CTH* 446.B = *KBo* 10.45 i 45′–52′ (translit. Otten 1961: 120). Haas (2007a: 347) argues that when the Storm-god is referred to as a ^{LÚ}HAL (interpreted by him to mean 'seer'), the title alludes to his role in reading liver omens as illustrated in the *CTH* 313: *Prayer to Adad* (ed. and German trans. Archi 1983; trans. Haas 2006: 249–51), which is based on an Akkadian version, and thus the reference should be taken as an allusion to Mesopotamian myth. B. J. Collins in Hallo and Younger (1997: 169) translates as "exorcist of the storm-god," but Haas' interpretation makes sense, since Aduntarri was earlier called a ^{LÚ}HAL and Zulki a dream-interpreter.

[92] *CTH* 446.B = *KBo* 10.45 ii 21–5 (translit. Otten 1961: 122).   [93] The text has "seven."

[94] *CTH* 446.E = *IBoT* 2.128 rev. 2′–7′, filled in with *CTH* 446.B = *KBo* 10.45 ii 36–8, in which, however, the spring's response is significantly briefer (partial translit. Otten 1961: 124). Similarly, nine pits were dug for the underworld gods in *CTH* 484: *Evocation Ritual for DINGIR.MAḪMEŠ and the Fate-goddesses* discussed above (see 94–5), and in *CTH* 447: *Ritual against Underworld Powers*, nine sheep are sacrificed, and offerings are made nine times (see edn. of Popko 2003a). Nine pits are dug in the necromantic ritual portrayed in Statius' *Thebaid* 4.443–72.

referred to Hurro-Hittite narrative song, as the ritual for the Former Gods did, rather than treating Gilgamesh only as a hero of a Mesopotamian epic. Possibly the client and/or practitioner did not even know the Akkadian epic existed. However, the fact that Gilgamesh was called upon in Mesopotamian purification rituals must have ultimately been a factor in the prehistory of the Hittite performer's invocation in the pit ritual, insofar as the magico-medical tradition informing his craft had a Mesopotamian element to it. As far as we can see there was no interest in maintaining some kind of "ethnic purity" in any of the pit rituals. Rather, a web of allusions is woven, drawing threads from different knowledge systems in order to make the ritual as compelling as possible. The comments of David Frankfurter on the Late Antique Philinna spell are applicable here: "far from being dependent on any single macro-myth, [it] is evidently a pastiche of mysterious images and Mediterranean motifs composed ingeniously to 'tap into' *several* authoritative symbol systems."[95] Such a blending must have been going on in the Gilgamesh pit ritual, in which the Mesopotamian hero is mentioned along with Hittite Anzili and Hurrian Kumarbi.

Odysseus' *katabasis*

Although far from identical, the ritual in *Odyssey* 11 as described by Odysseus shares key elements with the Hurro-Hittite *Purification Ritual for the Former Gods*: in both cases the pit is dug at a riverbank with a knife or sword,[96] a sheep is slaughtered down into it, and a holocaust is carried out.[97] *Odyssey* 11 shows that the ritual propitiating the spirits of the underworld maintained its close connection with epic narrative into the Greek Archaic period, but because all descriptions of Greek pit rituals postdate Homer, we cannot decide whether or to what extent Odysseus' *nekuomanteia* reflected current practice or influenced later practice.

Here is how Odysseus describes it:

---

[95] Frankfurter (1995: 474–5). Also see Fauth (1995) for a full-length study of the syncretism of Egyptian, Near Eastern, pagan Greek, Judaic, Christian, Gnostic, and Mithraic belief systems in Late Antique religion and magic.
[96] On lakes or rivers being suitable places to contact the dead in Greco-Roman culture, see Ogden (2001: 43–51).
[97] Kullmann (1995: 148) argues for further parallels with *Gilgamesh*, comparing the voyage across the Ocean to Utnapishtim. Ogden (2001: xxiii–xxv, 43–60) provides a good discussion of *Od.* 11.

(The ship) arrived at the edges of the deep-flowing Ocean. There exist the people and city of the Cimmerians, enveloped in mist and cloud; not ever does blazing Helios see them with his rays, not when he moves towards starry heaven, nor when he turns again towards the earth from heaven, but dire night stretches over the miserable mortals. We beached the ship there, hauling it up, and we took out the sheep, and we ourselves went to the side of the current of the Ocean, so that we could reach the place that Circe advised us of[, where the Pyriphlegethon and Cocytus, which breaks off from the water of the Styx, flow into the Acheron, and there is a cliff and the meeting of the two loud-sounding rivers[98]].

There, Perimedes and Eurylochus held the sacrificial victims[, a ram and a black ewe[99]]. But I, drawing my sharp sword from beside my thigh, dug a pit (*bothros*) a cubit-length in each direction; around it we poured a libation to all the dead, first with honey mixed (with milk), afterwards with sweet wine, the third in turn with water; they sprinkled on it white barley. I beseeched much the unsteady heads of the dead, (promising them) that I would, once I had come into Ithaka, offer a sterile cow, whichever is the best, in my house, and that I would fill the fire with good things, and that I would sacrifice separately to Teiresias alone the all-black sheep that is outstanding in our herds. After I had prayed to them, the companies of the dead, with vows and prayers, taking the sheep, I cut their throats into the pit, and the cloudy-black blood flowed. The souls of dead corpses gathered up from out of the Dark Place. Brides and youths, and old men who had withstood much, and tender maidens, having a mind whose grief was fresh; many wounded by bronze spears, men slain by Ares, having gory armor; they moved around the pit in large numbers in various directions with a divine clamor, and green fear seized me. Then indeed, urging my companions, I ordered them, having cut up the sheep that lay there, their throats slit with the pitiless bronze, to burn them up, and to pray to the gods, powerful Hades and praiseworthy Persephone. But, I myself, drawing my sword from beside my thigh, sat there, not allowing the unsteady heads of the dead to come closer to the blood before I perceived Teiresias.[100]

While the parallels are striking, it is true that the Homeric rite differs from Hurro-Hittite pit rituals in that Odysseus does not communicate with deities, but with dead humans, including his own mother. In my opinion, however, the discrepancy has been over-emphasized.[101] Odysseus'

---

[98] *Od.* 10.513–15.   [99] *Od.* 10.571–2.   [100] *Od.* 11.13–50.
[101] Based on Homer's depiction of the rest of the ghosts, Johnston (1999: 83) argues that "at the earliest stage, the Greeks presumed that most of the dead were feeble and unable to affect the living." Relying on Schmidt (1995), she claims, "there is no evidence at all for necromancy in

katabasis acted as a purification ritual cleansing him of his crime against the Cyclops, and propitiation of the dead is certainly an important component of the ritual.[102] In any case, as Daniel Ogden points out, Odysseus obtains information about the future – the typical goal of Greek necromancy – only from Teiresias, who as a prophet would have had access to such information while alive.[103]

Finally, none of the dead whose stories Odysseus hears belongs among the ordinary dead. They are all heroes or heroines, and therefore they may have been conceived of by the audience of the *Odyssey* as closer to chthonic divinities, like the Hittite Former Kings who were invoked or alluded to in rituals, than to their own dead kin. If Circe, *mutatis mutandis*, fulfils the role of an Old Woman, advising Odysseus on exactly how to perform the ritual,[104] then Teiresias should be compared to the divine seers the Hittite exorcist calls up from the underworld.[105] In addition, the catalog of heroes has a parallel in Tablet VIII of the *Epic of Gilgamesh*, where a report on the great heroes of old whom Enkidu saw in the underworld in a dream is now lost but can be assumed.[106] On the other hand, the catalog of heroines that caters to Arete, queen of the Phaeacians, whose goodwill Odysseus needs, is a

---

the other eastern Mediterranean cultures (including the Levant, Egypt, and Anatolia) until about the time of Esarhaddon's reign" (Johnston 1999: 88). It is true that ghost prescriptions are not found earlier than the Neo-Assyrian period (Scurlock 1988: 5). Ogden (2001: 133) admits the possibility that Greek necromantic practices were borrowed from Mesopotamia in the Orientalizing period, but notes, "We may in any case presume that there was, at some level, a very ancient east Mediterranean necromantic *koinē*." He covers Greco-Roman necromantic practices, including pit rituals (163–79), thoroughly, but does not delve into Hurro-Hittite practices; nor does Johnston in her otherwise excellent discussion. See van den Hout (1994: 45, with earlier references) for Hittite attempts to communicate with the dead.

[102] When Odysseus blinded the Cyclops he provoked the anger of his father Poseidon, who was preventing the hero from returning home. Teiresias, after he lays out his future course to Ithaca and his destruction of Penelope's suitors, instructs Odysseus to journey inland with his oar until no one recognizes it for what it is and there erect a monument to Poseidon, with appropriate sacrifices, thus laying to rest the god's anger (*Od.* 11.100–37); see Steiner (1971: 275–8), also see Ebach and Rüterswörden (1977: 215).

[103] His unique abilities are underlined by Circe, "Son of Laertes, whose race comes from Zeus, much-contriving Odysseus, now do not remain in my house any longer if you don't want to; but first it is necessary to complete another road and to come into the house of Hades and praiseworthy Persephone, in order to consult the soul of Theban Teiresias, the blind seer, whose intelligence is steadfast; to him alone, although dead, Persephone granted thought. Shades know nothing" (*Od.* 10.488–95); see Ogden (2001: xxiv).

[104] *Od.* 10.505–40. On Circe compared to Shiduri, see M. L. West (1997a: 404–10).

[105] Steiner (1971: 274). The Greek seer also parallels the various priests and priestesses to whom Gilgamesh promised gifts in the hereafter in the *Death of Gilgamesh* (see n. 87).

[106] George (2003: 483).

specifically Greek element; it is in the mold of the Hesiodic *Catalog of Women*.[107]

The location of the episode, at the farthest reaches of civilization, signals the supposed exotic nature of the rite, and connects "out there" with "down below." Odysseus himself, the client of the ritual, journeys out from the home of the practitioner Circe, as opposed to the Hurro-Hittite practitioners, whose rituals were brought to the Hittite capital. This is because the episode self-referentially alludes to one of the ways in which the narrative of a hero's journey to the edge of the world was used, to purify the patient and to soothe spirits in the other world.[108]

The visit to the underworld is certainly integral to the narrative as it stands, placed at the midpoint of the epic when Odysseus has reached the farthest limit of his travels and now may begin the return journey to regain his identity, his household, and his wife. However, it is clear that it is a late addition to the Homeric tradition.[109] Martin West has observed that, while the visit to the underworld was a central part of the tradition of Odysseus' trials, its placement at this point in the narrative, as well as to the east of Greece, is part of a set of changes to a fairly fixed narrative tradition:

> [T]he necromantic consultation of Teiresias has been transplanted to a new and inappropriate setting. It would naturally have been undertaken at one of the sites in central Greece that were dedicated to such purposes. The seer's advice falls into two parts. The first part (11.100–17), designed for its present position in the middle of Odysseus' wanderings, is a warning against harming the Cattle of the Sun; this is strictly superfluous, as it will be later repeated by Circe. The second part (118–37) concerns the journey that Odysseus must undertake much later, after he has got home and killed the suitors. We may suspect that in an earlier *Odyssey* the hero obtained this guidance at a time nearer to when he would need it.[110]

The new location is part of an illogical transfer of the action from the west of Greece to the east for a set of episodes that includes the attack of the Laestrygonians at Telepylus, which appears to be the port of Balaclava in the Crimea, and the landing at Circe's Aeaean island. The place at which

---

[107] On the internal audience see Doherty (1995: 65–86), and see Rutherford (2000) on the similarities between the Hesiodic *Catalog of Women* and the catalog of heroines in the *Odyssey*.
[108] See Chapter 9, 216, 218.
[109] See the survey of scholarly views by A. Heubeck in Heubeck and Hoekstra (1989: 75–7).
[110] M. L. West (2005: 60). M. L. West notes that the lying tales Odysseus tells actually refer to this alternate version of events. See Marks (2003) on how lying tales in the *Odyssey* refer to other versions of the narrative.

Odysseus digs his pit to call up Teiresias is "precisely at the Cimmerian Bosporus [= Straits of Kerch]. On both sides of the strait there are hellish vistas of mud volcanoes with eruptions of naphtha."[111]

While some have explained the dislocation of the action as the result of Odysseus circumnavigating the world, which the poet glosses over for his own reasons, others see influence from an early oral version of the Argonaut Jason's voyage into the Black Sea.[112] The knowledge Homer shows of the far northeast, which is assumed to have been extracted from a lost *Argonautica*, has been attributed to Greek explorations of the Black Sea coast, which eventually led to colonization, especially by Miletus,[113] events which cannot be pushed back much farther than 650 BCE; this interpretation therefore supports a late date for the *Odyssey*. Scholars have gone so far as to postulate a Milesian author for the lost *Argonautica*.[114]

An entirely different interpretation is possible if we accept that the Homeric tradition was influenced by a native Anatolian tradition, or, to put it more forcefully, that the Homeric tradition as embodied in the *Iliad* and *Odyssey* is the final product of repeated interactions between Greek and Syro-Anatolian epic traditions. We do not have to assume that the Greeks themselves had voyaged extensively along the coast of the Black Sea. Rather, it was native Anatolians, fascinated with the northern edge of their land, who developed stories about significant geographic points along the sea's coast and incorporated the locations into already established stories.

Indeed, we can discern the dim outline of such an Anatolian narrative tradition in the story of Jason and the Golden Fleece, which has long been acknowledged to have second-millennium Anatolian parallels. The Golden Fleece, which Jason must retrieve from Colchis, on the eastern coast of the Black Sea, can be compared to the sacred fleece hunting bag (*kurša*) that

---

[111] M. L. West (2005: 55).
[112] M. L. West (2005: 39–47). The best evidence: Circe herself mentions the voyage of the Argonauts (12.69–72); Circe's Aeaean island can be connected with Aea, the island where the Golden Fleece was found; the Siren episode alludes to an earlier version of the *Argonautica* in which Orpheus, one of the Argonauts, bests the bird-women in singing. M. L. West (2005: 62–3) argues that the earlier *Argonautica* could have incorporated elements of the Gilgamesh narrative, although all his suggestions are conjectural, and he admits, "we shall have to suppose that the *Odyssey* poet was in a position to draw independently on a version of the Gilgamesh epic" (M. L. West 2005: 63). If we were to think of borrowing from the Gilgamesh tradition, then I would think more in terms of transmission of motifs and bundles of motifs than influence from a fixed narrative.
[113] See articles in Bol, Höckmann, and Schollmeyer (2008).
[114] M. L. West (2005: 58, with earlier references).

must be retrieved in *mugawar* invocation rituals to restore prosperity. It hangs on an *eya* tree (perhaps an evergreen oak or yew). In addition, the serpent that guards the oak tree on which the Golden Fleece hangs in a grove sacred to Zeus has been compared to the snake in the Old Hittite *Illuyanka* myth, whom the Storm-god must battle to maintain agrarian fertility.[115]

Another, more obscure, hint that Anatolians maintained legends about the lands on the Black Sea that were known to the Homeric tradition is the epithet used at *Iliad* 2.857 for Alybe (Chalybe), the home of the Paphlagonians and Halizones. As noted earlier, it is called "the birthplace of silver" (*argurou genethlē*), perhaps a reminiscence of the (folk-) etymology of Hattusa as "Silver Place."[116] The epithet "birthplace of silver" follows the same pattern as the well-known (although much later attested) characterization of Zeus Dolichenus, the Syro-Anatolian Storm-god that came to represent the might of the Roman army, as *natus ubi ferrum nascitur/oritur* 'born where iron is born'.[117] Given that the northeastern edge of Anatolia was famed as an iron-producing region, it was a place that should have been known as a "birthplace of iron." Indeed, a connection has been made between Hittite *ḫapalki* 'iron', Greek *khalups* 'iron', and Chalybe.[118] It may be that, in an effort to keep the action in the long-ago Bronze Age, the poet modified the traditional epithet accordingly, replacing it with another traditional epithet that originally belonged to central Anatolia. Of course in this speculative discussion we are assuming very old narrative traditions about significant Anatolian places, which were not necessarily related to the Trojan War.[119]

---

[115] The Anatolian *mugawar* invocation for a disappeared god can be applied to various gods, including the Storm-god, the vegetation-god Telipinu (*CTH* 324), and the grandmother-goddess Hannahanna. It has been compared to the myths of Dionysus and Demeter. Gaster's (1950) work was an early and important comparative study. Also see Bachvarova (2008b: 31–2), Burkert (1979b: 123–9, 138–42), Haas (2006: 103, 106, 108), Tassignon (2001); trans. M. Bachvarova in López-Ruiz (2013: 451–8). On the *kurša* see Bawanypeck (2005b: 185–7), Bremmer (2008: 312–14), Güterbock (1989), Haas (1975; 1978). On Anatolian elements of Jason's story see Bremmer (2006), Collins (2010: 61), extending Bremmer's conclusions on the connections with west Anatolian scapegoat rituals, and Haas (1975; 1978). Haas (1977) suggests the *eya* is an evergreen oak. Puhvel (*HED* E/I: 253–7) suggests a yew. See Haas (1994: 701, n. 31) for earlier discussions, and Mazoyer (2003a). On the Illuyanka myth see Chapter 10, 252–6. For the *mugawar* equipment see Fig. 8.

[116] See Chapter 2, 52.

[117] See M. Theotikou in Schütte-Maischatz and Winter (2004: 25–9). On Zeus Dolichenus see briefly Chapter 10, 259, n. 181.

[118] Blakely (2006: 207–8), Laroche (1973: xix), M. Theotikou in Schütte-Maischatz and Winter (2004: 27, n. 90; 29).

[119] Strabo (12.3.24, 14.5.28) mocks earlier accounts of the Halizones and discusses the various examples of wealth accrued from mines in Anatolia and Thrace: Tantalus and the Pelopidae,

Finally, perhaps to be associated with Anatolian traditions about the edge of the world at the Sea of Azov are stories of battles against the Amazons, distorted reflections of the Iranian tribes that came down from Central Asia. The first-century historian Nicolaus of Damascus (born 64 BCE) says, for example, that Smyrnaean Magnes, the beloved of Gyges and "famous for his poetry and music," "sang in epic (*en tois epesin*) of the excellence (*aristeiān*) of the Lydians in chariot battle against the Amazons."[120]

Certainly, the positioning of the place where Odysseus enters the underworld is from an Anatolian perspective, not a Greek one, for it is emphatically described as north of Anatolia, not east of Greece, in a place that "not ever does blazing Helios see . . . with his rays." The description of polar winter darkness may be indebted to Anatolian formulaic descriptions of places on the fringe of the world, for Giovanni Lanfranchi argues that the image of the Cimmerians, an Iranian people from southern Siberia, living in perpetual darkness has its roots in legends about Sargon the Great who voyages to unknown lands, making his way through darkness into the light.[121] As we will see, Sargonic legend had a place in Hurro-Hittite narrative; thus, the description might be considered one more piece of evidence that this section of the *Odyssey* was influenced by an epic tradition fairly closely related to the Hurro-Hittite tradition found at Hattusa.

We do not know anything about Odysseus' visit with Teiresias in the earlier version of the story that has been reworked into what we have now. Certainly, the episode could have very old roots, since it refers to necromantic practices that seem to have been in use in Bronze Age Greece. One might expect that the original Odyssean ritual followed standard Greek necromantic practice. That is, the spirit was called up to the surface of the earth, and there was no glimpse of the underworld's other denizens, as in Tablet XII of the *Epic of Gilgamesh*. It seems that not only did the similarities with Tablet XII and with the Hurro-Hittite pit rituals come into the epic together, but also the alteration away from the original mainland-Greek-style necromantic ritual occurred when Odysseus' *katabasis* was moved to the Black Sea, when a popular version of the episode that stemmed from the native Anatolian tradition of epic song was incorporated. As noted earlier, the episode in fact is part of a complex of

---

Cadmus, Priam, Midas, and Gyges and his descendants. His examples suggest an interest that could have inspired epic narratives.

[120] *FGrH* 90 F 62 = *Suid.* s.v. *Magnēs* (Adler M 21), see Högemann (2002: 1129–30).
[121] Lanfranchi (2001–2002). See further Chapter 8, 171, with n. 21.

episodes that are situated on the Black Sea, and among these we must include the Cyclops episode, which incorporated elements of the Gilgamesh tradition and the Caucasian myth of a one-eyed monster that likely came through Anatolia, rather than directly to Greece. For, the Cyclops episode has a set of striking parallels with Caucasian stories of Uryzmaeg, in which the hero cleverly tricks the one-eyed giant, blinding him with a torch.[122]

The Cimmerians likely replaced the more familiar Cheimerians, who resided near the mouth of the Acheron River in western Greece,[123] when the episode was transferred to the east. The allusion to the Cimmerians has also been used to argue for a late date for the *Odyssey*, since their earliest mentions in Assyrian texts are from the end of the eighth century.[124] Three letters of Sennacherib to Sargon II mention that the Urartian king Rusa I was defeated by the *Gimirrāya* when he attempted to invade their territory.[125] By 714 BCE, then, they had made it to the south side of the Caucasus. By the beginning of the seventh century they had reached Asia Minor, and in 644 they captured Sardis.[126] However, an Anatolian could have heard of them well before they had reached his land or even crossed the Caucasus, through their activities on the northern side of the Black Sea. Certainly, Homer's description of their land at "the edge of the deep-sounding Ocean, . . . enveloped in mist and cloud" fits the northern coast of the Black Sea better than Armenia, and if West is right to find it significant that "[t]he Pontic reference points are clustered in a particular sector in the north: the Crimea; the straits of Kerch; perhaps the interior of the Sea of Azov,"[127] then the Cimmerians should be placed there as well, on the far side of the Caucasus, where equestrian nomads are attested archaeologically by the ninth century.[128] The mention of the Cimmerians,

---

[122] Ossetian: *Uryzmaeg et le géant borgne* (trans. Dumézil 1965: 55–9); also Circassian Saga 37: *A Cyclops Bound atop Wash'hamakhwa*, Abaza Saga 52: *How Sosruquo Brought Fire to His Troops*, Ubykh Saga 86: *The Birth of Soseruquo* (trans. Colarusso 2002: 170, 200–2, 387–97). The story was also attached to Sinbad, another great traveler; see Dalley (1989: 48). M. L. West (2007: 297–9, with earlier references) mentions a possible Indo-European heritage for the one-eyed monster.

[123] Ogden (2001: 44).

[124] On the Cimmerians in the *Odyssey*, see A. Heubeck in Heubeck and Hoekstra (1989: 77–9).

[125] Parpola (1987: 29–33, Nos. 30–32).

[126] See A. Kammenhuber, "Kimmerier," in *RlA* 5.594–6 and I. von Bredow, "Cimmerii," in *Brill's New Pauly* 3.335–7. See Lebedynsky (2004: 7–35) for a full discussion of textual attestations of the Cimmerians. See Ivantchik (1993) for translations of the relevant Akkadian texts. There is no archaeological evidence that can be attributed to the Cimmerians per se at any point. See the discussion of Tsetskhladze (1999: 482–6).

[127] M. L. West (2005: 58).   [128] Lebedynsky (2004: 78–94).

then, is better used to argue for the incorporation of an Anatolian myth into the *Odyssey*, rather than to argue for a late date for the epic as a whole.

Finally, as Douglas Frame has elucidated, an older layer of Greek ritual and myth, ultimately of Proto-Indo-European origin, can be detected in the *katabasis* episode, which has an affinity with the Near Eastern myths and rituals discussed here. Frame ingeniously shows that there are elements of Proto-Indo-European solar myth in the episode, in which the rising of the sun is connected with a return from death; thus, the twin horsemen, in Vedic the Nasatyas, in Greek the Dioscuri, who symbolize the setting and rising sun, are magic healers. In this framework, the crossing to the otherworld is not effected by entering a pit or traveling via an underground river, but by the sun dipping below the horizon, clarifying the point of Homer's pleonastic description of the place of the ritual: "not ever does blazing Helios see them with his rays, not when he moves towards starry heaven, nor when he turns again towards the earth from heaven, but dire night stretches over the miserable mortals." It is a place of sunless death, but Circe, as daughter of the sun (*Od.* 10.138), knows how to make sure that Odysseus can return from the underworld and to his former life.[129] The solar myth, like the story of Gilgamesh, treats the return from long-distance travel as a return from the dead, and the mythical frameworks, diverse as their origins may be, could be implemented for the same purpose, healing the sick.

The intersections between the Gilgamesh story and the motifs of Proto-Indo-European solar myth that Frame has shown to lie behind elements of the *Iliad* and the *Odyssey* do not end there, however. Frame argues that the alternation between life and death by the solar twins, with Polydeuces giving up eternal life for his twin Castor, so each can live in turn, the one substituting for the other, is related to the substitution of Patroclus for Achilles, dying in his place, which represents a reworking of the Anatolian practice of ritual substitutes. It also connects to the relationship between Gilgamesh and Enkidu, the one semi-divine and not having experience of death, and the other dying in his place, according to the decision of the gods.[130] We get here a glimpse of some of the associations that eased the

---

[129] Frame (2009: 38–94).
[130] Frame (2009: 75–9, 117–30), arguing that Nestor and his "twin" Periclymenus are forms of the solar divine twins; Polydeuces giving up eternal life for his dying brother, each living in turn: Pi. *N.* 10.5–59; *Od.* 11.298–304. On Frame's larger argument that mythology concerning Nestor is cryptically alluded to throughout the Homeric poems, see Chapter 15, 913. Nagy (1990a: 129–30 with earlier refs.) argues that Patroclus is a ritual substitute for Achilles, connecting the Greek word *therapon*, which seems be used in the meaning of its Hittite

borrowing of specific Near Eastern storylines into Greek epic, because they could be seen to share certain concerns and narrative patterns already present in the Greek tradtion.[131] Thus, the ritual in *Odyssey* 11, like the *Purification Ritual for the Former Gods*, also combines several different but relatable "authoritative symbol systems," Helladic, Indo-European, and Near Eastern.

Myth and ritual: the chicken and the egg?

Ogden has remarked on the "developing tendency [among the ancient Greeks] to associate a specialization in necromancy with aliens,"[132] and points to the first traces of the association in the *Odyssey* and Aeschylus' *Persians*. But, one can guess that a belief that performers who come from the "furtherworld" were particularly able to carry out rites to contact those in the netherworld was already a factor in the spread of innovative twists on the commonly practiced pit rituals in the second millennium. It continued to be a factor in the further development of pit rituals into the Early Iron Age, encouraging the transfer of storylines that informed and were informed by rituals invoking the dead, especially (fictional) royal ancestors.

In Chapter 2 I noted that Hurro-Hittite epic incorporated allusions to rituals, just as in this chapter I have shown that Hurro-Hittite ritual incorporated allusions to the Gilgamesh narrative and the Kumarbi cycle. While the stories may have been transmitted by a different set of performers from the performers of the incantations which allude to them, singers rather than incantation specialists, each set was quite aware of the material the other group controlled. We know, for example, that an ^{LÚ}A.ZU ('exorcist') was present in the *Ritual for Mt. Hazzi*, when the *Song of the Sea* was sung.[133] The *Ritual of Allaiturahhi* may incorporate a Hurro-Hittite narrative, the *Song of Oil*, and it makes reference to Mt. Pishaisha, a character from Hurro-Hittite song.[134] *Elkunirsa and Ashertu* was embedded in a purification ritual. These songs may have been

cognate *tarpalli-* 'ritual substitute' when applied to Achilles' friend. On Enkidu as ritual substitute for Gilgamesh in the Hittite *Song of Gilgamesh*, see Chapter 3, 69 and on Hittite substitution rituals, Chapter 7, 154.

[131] One question remains to be answered: Exactly when and in what context did the *katabasis* scene in the *Odyssey* absorb Syro-Anatolian features? This will be discussed in Chapter 11, 298–9.
[132] Ogden (2001: 95).   [133] *CTH* 785 = *KUB* 44.7 i 11′–14′ (translit. Rutherford 2001b: 598).
[134] *CTH* 780.I.A = *KUB* 45.21 rev. 29′ (translit. Haas and Wegner 1988: 50, No. 1). On the *Song of Oil*, the *Ritual of Allaiturahhi*, and Mt. Pishaisha see Chapters 2, 26, 34, 51, and 7, 154–5.

performed by bards within the rituals, which were intended for a wealthy client, but it could be that the exorcist or Old Woman who carried out the ritual actually was capable of performing the narrative. Extended versions of the stories could only be performed in settings that allowed for a leisurely unfolding of the narrative, at the court or home of a wealthy patron, or in a festival when the gods or dead were welcomed in the same manner as an honored guest from afar, flattered and propitiated so that any resentment might be dispelled. But, shorter versions or condensed allusions to the narratives in private rituals could serve the same function, in addition providing suggestive storylines to guide the god or dead hero in the act of healing the patient.

While pit rituals were a multifarious phenomenon widespread in the Late Bronze Age, the story of Gilgamesh, who invented the funerary offerings that kept the dead happy in the afterlife, who journeyed into the "furtherworld" to make contact with a sage from primeval times blessed with eternal life, and who was the judge of the dead, provided a particularly appropriate accompaniment to them, whether in the festivals during the month of Abu or in private rituals. The very popularity of pit rituals in the eastern Mediterranean allowed for the borrowing of specific regional details, including the stories attached to the rituals. Finally, it appears from the archaeological evidence that pit rituals survived in Anatolia into the first millennium. These are the factors that enabled the double set of parallels in *Odyssey* 11 to the Gilgamesh story and to the Hurro-Hittite purification rituals to develop.

Because allusions to storylines in rituals need to be stories known to the client in order to be effective, we cannot say that the ritual was the primary way in which the story deriving from the Mesopotamian *Gilgamesh* epic was brought to the attention of Greek-speakers. Rather, what we see is a symbiotic relationship between the storylines that presuppose the values encoded in the rituals, and the rituals, which make themselves more effective by using storylines that allude to the ritual practices themselves. Whereas Gilgamesh was evidently sufficiently familiar to Hittite royalty (for whom most of the rituals preserved at Hattusa were intended) to retain his identity, by the time of Homer his specific character was effaced, although his storyline remained relevant. This implies that the story had been incubating in the (Greco-)Anatolian narrative tradition for at least several generations, long enough for any memory of its original hero to have passed from the audience's common knowledge, rather than being borrowed directly into the Homeric tradition shortly before the *Odyssey* reached its final form.

Conclusion

Throughout this work I argue that the epics found in the Hittite libraries made their way to Anatolia and then to Greece through contact with performers versed in the stories praising particular gods and heroes whose characteristics and stories had analogs in Greek religion. This model of transmission should replace not only that of transmission between scribes by means of written texts, but also the implicitly secularized model in which Late Bronze Age and Early Iron Age performers are compared to modern traditional Yugoslav or Turkic bards whose epics primarily promote a sense of national, ethnic, or clan identity, rather than being interwoven with religious practices. Certainly expression of group identity was an important function of ancient eastern Mediterranean epic, but its magico-religious element, which found expression in the Kumarbi cycle, the Ugaritic *Baal Cycle*, Hesiod's *Theogony*, and the Homeric Hymns, should not be downplayed.

In the following chapters I argue that one of the main topics of the Hurro-Hittite *Song of Release* is royal ancestor cult. Furthermore, internationally recognized techniques of royal ancestor worship were a way for the living to connect themselves to the distant past, along with performance of epic stories about the legendary times when the gods were born and heroes walked the earth. In subsequent chapters I will explore more fully the interaction among epic narratives, worship of gods and royal ancestors, and the articulation of group identity through the creation of a shared legendary past.

5 | The plot of the *Song of Release*

> I shall sing of Teshshub, p[owerful] lord of Kummi. I shall exalt the young w[oman], the doorbolt of the earth, Alla[ni].
>
> *Song of Release* I i 1–3[1]

Introduction

The discovery of the first fragments of the *Song of Release* (SIR₃ *parā tarnumaš*) in 1983 in Buildings 15 and 16 of the Oberstadt of Hattusa was the most momentous event in the last fifty years for those who study ancient epic. More fragments were found in 1985, and the hand copies were swiftly published in *Keilschrifttexte aus Boghazköi* 32 by Heinrich Otten and Christel Rüster (1990), followed by an edition, translation, and commentary by Erich Neu (1996).[2] The narrative was more than five tablets long in at least one of its textualizations.[3] It is the only Hurro-Hittite song preserved in a bilingual format, with the Hurrian version in one column of the tablet and the Hittite version in the other (Fig. 4). As noted earlier, two fragmentary colophons attribute the song to an unidentified singer.[4] The narrative could be refracting a known historical event, the destruction of the north Syrian city Ebla at the hands of the Old Hittite

---

[1] *CTH* 789 = *KBo* 32.11 i 1–3.
[2] The text has been fully edited and translated as much as possible by Neu (1996). I use his edition throughout. I do not reference his transliterations individually in this or the following two chapters. I have provided the fullest English translation currently available with some discussion of my overall interpretation, which differs in some important details from earlier ones: M. Bachvarova in López-Ruiz (2013: 290–9). Wilhelm (1996; *TUAT Erg.*, 82–91) provides important discussions of the ordering of the tablets. I translate here the Hittite version when available, since, although the Hurrian version can claim primacy, our understanding of it comes mostly from comparison with the Hittite version. For interpretations of the text other than the ones addressed in this chapter see Astour (2002: 141–64) and Archi (2002b). Some five or six tablets in total give us a worthwhile chunk of text. A further fifteen or sixteen smaller pieces give us tantalizing glimpses of other parts of the narrative and about eighty more, even smaller pieces (including the parables) add little else to our knowledge, but indicate that the text was very repetitious and/or there were multiple copies or versions.
[3] Cf. the colophon of *KBo* 32.15, left edge: "Fifth tablet of release, no[t finished]."
[4] See Chapter 2, 36–7.

Fig. 4: Bilingual Edition of the *Song of Release*, obverse of Bo 83/604 (published as handcopy *KBo* 32.15), assembly scene, Hurrian on the left, Hittite on the right

king Hattusili I or his successor Mursili I (Tell Mardikh IIIb, *ca.* 1600 BCE, some 200 years earlier than the textualizations of the epic we have), and the story refers to the captives from another town, Ikinkalis, the capture of which is commemorated in the *Annals of Hattusili I*.[5] Thus, among the Hittites the song could have served to commemorate a great deed from the past that showed how they entered on the world stage; at the very least it resonated with their memories of the event.

---

[5] The destruction of Tell Mardikh IIIb has been attributed to either Hattusili I or his grandson Mursili I, during the Hittite forays into north Syria, although there is no textual evidence relative to this event in Hittite texts, other than the mention of a "man of Ebla" in one fragmentary OH text describing military successes (*Res Gestae of Hattusili I*: CTH 14.III.B = *KUB* 40.4 ii 6′, translit. and trans. de Martino 2003: 108–9). See Klengel (1992: 82) and Matthiae (1981: 113; 2007). See Haas (2006: 177) and Matthiae (2007) on the relationship between the destruction of the city and the composition of the epic. On Ikinkalis in the *Annals of Hattusili I* see Chapter 7, 157. On the claimants for the earlier destruction of Tell Mardikh IIb1, see Chapter 8, 175–6.

The fragments preserve the opening lines, a messenger scene among the gods, a hospitality sequence in which the Storm-god and his brother visit Allani and the Former Gods in the underworld, and an argument in the assembly of Ebla in which the Storm-god (in the Hurrian version Teshshub, in the Hittite version Tarhun) is involved, demanding the release of captives from the town Ikinkalis and declaring a conditional blessing or curse on Ebla. In addition, a relatively well-preserved series of parables was found together with the fragments that belong to the *Song of Release*, each making the same point, that ungrateful subordinates will be punished. The parables' relationship to the Ebla storyline is unclear.

The striking similarities of the *Song of Release* with the plot, themes, and motifs of the *Iliad* went unrecognized at first as scholars explored its connections with the Hebrew Bible. In fact, they were led astray to some degree when some scholars postulated that the text told of a release from debts, an interpretation that enhanced its already clear parallels with Leviticus.[6] I present in this chapter my interpretation of the song, along with the parables, which informs my subsequent analysis of its relationship to other eastern Mediterranean epic narratives.

The opening

The poem begins with a hymnic opening typical both of Hurro-Hittite songs and of Homeric narratives:[7]

>   (*KBo* 32.11 i 1–3) I shall sing of Teshshub, p[owerful] lord of Kummi. I shall exalt the young w[oman], the doorbolt of the earth, Alla[ni].
>
>   (i 4–6) And along with them I shall tell of the young woman Ishhara, the word-mak[er,] famous for wisdom, goddess.
>
>   (i 7–9) I shall tell of Pizikarra . . . Eb[la . . .] who will bring . . . Pizikarra des[troy . . .] (from?) Nuhashshe. And Ebla [. . .]
>
>   (i 10–13) Pizikarra, the Ninevan [. . .] he bound [. . .] bound [. . .] to the gods [. . .]

---

[6] Leviticus 24:10–26; see Neu (1993b), Hoffner (1998b: 180–3), and discussion by Bachvarova (2005b: 47–8, with earlier references).

[7] On the "I shall sing . . ." opening in Hurro-Hittite narrative song, see de Martino (2000: 300–1), Haas (2006: 127), Hoffner (1988), and Chapter 2, 36, n. 66. The "I shall sing (or tell) . . ." opening is discussed in some detail by Wilcke (1977: 153–5, 175–86, 200). It is found in poems classified as hymns, as well as narrative poems dealing with the heroic deeds of gods and men. Also see M. L. West (1997a: 170–3) and De Vries (1967: 127–34) on openings.

The openings of the Homeric epics and hymns are strikingly similar, presenting a thumbnail sketch of the plot; compare the *Odyssey* (1.1–5):

> Recount to me the man, Muse, the wily one, who wandered very much, once he had sacked the holy city of Troy; the cities of many men he saw and learned of in his mind, and many were the pains he suffered in his heart on the sea, when trying to keep his life and the homecoming of his companions.

And, compare further the *Hymn to Demeter* (1–5):

> I begin by singing of Demeter, the lovely-haired august goddess,
> her and her slender-ankled daughter whom Aidoneus
> snatched, for deep-thundering wide-seeing Zeus gave her,
> playing apart from golden-crowned Demeter of gleaming harvest.

The opening of the Standard Babylonian *Epic of Anzu* follows an identical trajectory, self-referentially mentioning the singer's performance and giving a brief synopsis of the plot:

> I 1 Son of the king of the inhabited world, splendid one, beloved of [Ma]mi,
> The mighty one will I ever sing, divine firstborn of [En]lil,
> Ninurta, the splendid one, beloved of Mami,
> The mighty one will I ever praise, divine firstborn of Enlil.
> 5 Born (in) Ekur, leader of the Anu[nna-gods], Eninnu's hope,
> Who [wa]ters pen, garden, town, street, and city,
> Wave of battles, dancer (in combat), sash of valor,
> Whose tireless onset raging fiends dread,
> Hear the praise of the mighty one's power!
> 10 It is he who in his fierceness bound and fettered the stone creatures,
> Overcoming soaring Anzu with his weapon,
> Slaying the bull man in the midst of the sea.[8]

The *Song of Release* thus presents a conventional eastern Mediterranean hymno-epic opening.

Allani (Hurr. *allai=ni* 'the lady') was an underworld goddess,[9] and Ishhara was the chief goddess at Ebla in the third millennium, when it was at its peak of power. There Ishhara was closely connected to the king; later she was partially assimilated to Ishtar/Shawushka of Nineveh,

---

[8] SB *Epic of Anzu* I 1–12 (trans. Foster 2005: 561–2).
[9] See U. Lorenz (2008); she corresponds to the Hittite Sun-goddess of the Earth.

possessing Ishtar's connection to sexuality and Shawushka's healing powers. At Hattusa, where she is particularly associated with the north Syrian city Ashtata/Emar, she first appears on a Middle Hittite treaty in her capacity as guarantor of oaths.[10] Clearly, Ishhara was at home both in Ebla and at Hattusa.

After a gap of approximately fifty lines,[11] a dialogue between Teshshub and Ishhara closes column iv of the first tablet, but a recent join by Meindert Dijkstra has helped to fill in the gap,[12] for a fragment describing how Tarhun sends his brother Suwaliyat to Ebla with a message for Ishhara must belong at the bottom edge of column ii on the obverse:

> (KBo 32.37 4'–7') [...] in the night [.... E]arly in the morning [...] message rep[ort-... Tarh]un aro[se] from his bed [...]
> (8"11') [... sw]iftly he crossed [...] And Tarhun [...] release (obj.) [... "... l]et go!" And, Tarhun [began] t[o] speak [words] t[o Suwal]iyat.
> (12'–19') "[...] loyal Suwaliyat, hold [your ear c]ocked! Swiftly go to the city of the throne (Ebla), and go [to the house] of Ishhara.[13] You go and stress these wo[rds in] front of [Ishhara ...] I, far away, you be[fore ...] you ... I [will] bring [...]. Call [...] to you!"

The rousing of the Storm-god early in the morning with an urgent message apparently has something to do with the issue of a release of prisoners. His response is to send Suwaliyat immediately to Ebla to convey a message to Ishhara, involved presumably because of her connection with Ebla. Perhaps the message to Ishhara asks her to return with Suwaliyat for a meeting

---

[10] *Treaty between Arnuwanda I and the Kaska*: CTH 139.1.B = KBo 8.35 ii 10' (translit. Christiansen 2012: 179; see Prechel 1996: 91). On the connection between Shawushka and Ishhara, see Prechel (1996: 41–2, 69). See Matthiae (2010: 284–6) and Prechel (1996: 5–22) on Ishhara at Ebla, and Prechel (1996: 90–133) on Ishhara in Hattusa. A Hurrian text at Emar mentions Ishhara of Ebla (Msk. 74.224, obv. 10'), while she is known as a goddess of Emar in Hittite texts (*Mursili II Concerning the Tawananna Affair*: CTH 70.1.A = KUB 14.4 iv 17–18, translit. and trans. de Martino 1998: 30, 38). In Alalakh, IŠTAR can refer to the local goddess Ishhara (Wegner 1981: 176–7), just as the Akkadogram can conceal Anzili at Hattusa; also see Chapter 12, 323, n. 103.

[11] On the length of the gap see Haas (2006: 179).

[12] Cited on the KhT *sub KBo* 32.11. See already Neu (1996: 40–1) on this fragment possibly belonging with *KBo* 32.11. Wilhelm (*TUAT Erg.*, 86) suggests this fragment should be paired with *KBo* 32.10, discussed below in the context of the song's opening. Other joins to this tablet by Dijkstra (*KBo* 32.63, 209, 32, 67) add some new information: The Sun-god is involved from the beginning of the story. Pizikarra appears again, along with a mention of destroying in the third person: *KBo* 32.32 right col. 3'–5': "Pizi-.../ he destroyed.../ he injured..." *KBo* 32.67 also contains a dialogue between Teshshub and Ishhara, referring to "spears" (7'). The Sun-god also appears in *KBo* 32.31 + 208 i 13, a dialogue which mentions "not returning," and "freeing" (i 12, iv 13', Hurrian only).

[13] Archi (2002b: 23): "Išhara [w]ent? [already there.]"

with the Storm-god, one culminating with a discussion of the problem of the prisoners who must be released. Perhaps she is involved in punishing the Eblaites for their violation of a treaty with Ikinkalis?

Next we move down to the end of column iv of *KBo* 32.11. Although little of the beginning of the passage is comprehensible, the pronoun "I" appears, someone is not listening, and the topic is freeing.[14] Ishhara mentions the request of another person, perhaps the request for freedom on the part of the people of Ikinkalis, while Teshshub discusses the future destruction of Ebla with her:

> (*KBo* 32.11 iv 12′–15′) Ish[hara s]ays words to [Te]shshub. S/he asks, ask[s …] … Ishhara asks, ask[… "…] I shall give [….."]
>
> (iv 16′–21′) Teshsh[ub says] words to Ishhara, "And [n]ow des[troy] Ebla […] … Ishhara […] he will destroy. Who[15] … them/it […] Ishhara. Ebla … them [….] And, the countries are destroyed, destroy[ed …"]
>
> *(Colophon:)*
>
> (iv 22′) First tablet of the Song [of] Release o[f …][16]

In various small fragments from other tablets there are hints of the battle that was the downfall of Ebla, but the denouement of the story is lost.[17] The man named Pizikarra from Nineveh mentioned in the opening lines of the *Song of Release* as "destroying Ebla"[18] could be the hero of the story, perhaps chosen by the Storm-god to destroy the town. Indeed, Paolo Matthiae argues that Pizikarra was an historical Hurrian king of Nineveh in an alliance with the Hittite king who conquered Ebla.[19] But, we cannot connect him directly to the Ebla storyline as it stands. He does appear in a small Hittite fragment that seems to help set the scene for the narrative,

---

[14] *KBo* 32.11 iv 6′, 7′, 9′.   [15] Interrogative pronoun; following Wegner (2007: 85).

[16] Haas (2006: 179) completes the colophon: "o[f Tarhun]" (Š[A ᵈIM-*aš*]) to fit his interpretation of the text as telling how the Storm-god was held captive in the underworld (see below).

[17] *KBo* 32.215 r. col. 10′ preserves the expression *me-n*]*a-aḫ-ḫa-an-*[*ta*] *za-aḫ-ḫ*[*i*(-)…, "do battle [ag]ainst" or – reading the second word as the noun *zaḫḫ*[*iya*] – "in battle [ag]ainst." This fragment, which could either be narrative or direct speech, also mentions "oath," "slaves," and "in priso[n]" (*KBo* 32.215 right col. 7′, 12′, 17′). It could belong to a scene otherwise not preserved, or it could belong to the same scene as *KBo* 32.17, which mentions "E[bla]," "Zaz[alla]," "[I] sa[id]," "fie[ld]," "he di[d]," "agai[nst]," and "Teshshub, lord "(*KBo* 32.17 iii 3′, 4′, 7′, 11′, 14′, 12′, 13′, iv 12′, Hittite and Hurrian). Also, *KBo* 32.18 (Hittite), in direct speech, the first paragraph addressed to Meki, [Star] o[f] Ebla, refers to an "ar[my]." In the second paragraph, the speaker mentions Tarhun and "against … bows[tring]."

[18] *KBo* 32.11 i 8, cf. Neu's (1996: 41–2) discussion of the incomplete verb form *pa*-X = *paḫ*- 'destroy'.

[19] Matthiae (2006a: 46–8; 2007; 2008: 17, 231–2).

along with Purra, who is one of the people of Ikinkalis whose release the Storm-god requests.[20] The fragment begins with a curse mentioning the land Lullu(wa), a mythically far-off mountainous place,[21] and describes the Sun-god, "shepherd of all," taking notice of a situation:

> (*KBo* 32.10 ii 1–3) [... the lan]d of Lulluwa [... let] not good, let not [...] let him/it not find.
> (ii 4–6) [...] shepherd of all [...] from the sky the Sun-god (nom.) [...] began [to do something].
> (ii 7–10) [...] the Great King of [Kumm]i [...] slay[...] repeatedly [... the land of L]ulluwa [...] not [...]

The fragment breaks off here, but we pick up the thread again on the reverse:

> (iii 2′–7′) Piz[ikarra ...] in pr[ison ...] But of Purra [...] bound (neut.) to the stone, the destruction of Purra, god ⸢X⸣, god ⸢Y⸣ of Kummi has bound destruction to the *kunkunuzzi* stone.[22]

It appears, then, that Purra lost his life in the course of the story. It may be that the all-seeing Sun-god is the first to notice a serious problem on earth, as in the *Song of Ullikummi*.[23] Is it the Sun-god who sends the message to the Storm-god in the opening tablet?

The assembly scene

The thread of the Ebla storyline is picked up in the middle of a speech in *KBo* 32.19 demanding the release of the people of Ikinkalis, and especially of Purra, the man who seemed to meet his death in the small fragment discussed above.

---

[20] Several MH letters to a man named Purra were found at Ortaköy, so it was a name that contemporary men could bear. See Ünal (1998: 31).

[21] The name Lullu(bu) first appears in the third millennium referring to somewhere southeast of Lake Urmia at the northern part of the Zagros mountains of Iran, but "[i]n the second millennium, the term Lullubu lost its specific ethnic and geographical identity and was extended to any barbarian mountaineer" (J. G. Westenholz 1992: 136). See further details in Eidem (1992: 50–4), and Eidem and Læssøe (2001: 30–1).

[22] On the stone see below, 121–2. On the final line, in which Neu (1996: 457) saw mention of IŠTAR and the Storm-god, see Wilhelm (*TUAT Erg.*, 86).

[23] The Sun-god intervenes from on high when he notices the rapidly growing rock monster Ullikummi and when Gilgamesh and Enkidu battle Huwawa: *Ullikummi*: CTH 345.I.1.A = *KUB* 33.93 + *KBo* 26.58 iv 33′–36′, D = *KUB* 33.92 + 36.10 iii 18′–22′; *Gilgamesh*, Chapter 3, 67.

(*KBo* 32.19 ii 1–4) "Re[lease in goodwill] the sons of the city Ikinkal. Release e[specially Purra], the one to be given back,[24] (who) [give]s to eat [to the nine kin]gs.

(ii 5–10) "[And,] Ikin[kalis in the city of the throne gav]e [to eat] to three kings. B[ut], (in) Ebla, [in the city of the throne he] ga[ve] to eat [t]o six kings. But, now he [gets] u[p] before [y]ou, [Mek]i.[25]

(ii 11–15) "If [you (pl.) make] re[lease] in Ebla, [the city of the throne,] if you [make] r[elease, I will] exalt your weapons like [X].

(ii 16–19) "Your [weapons] alone will begin [t]o [defeat] the enem[y], [while] your plowed fiel[ds will go and thrive for you] in prai[se.]

(ii 20–23) "Bu[t] if y[ou] don't [ma]ke release in [Eb]la, in the city of the throne, then (when it is) the seventh da[y], I will come to you, yo[urse]lves.

(ii 24–26) "I will destroy the ci[ty] of Ebla. As if it had n[ever] been settled, so I will make it!

(ii 27–31) "I will smash the [lower] walls of the city of Ebla like a c[up]. And, I will trample the upper wall [li]ke a clay pit!"[26]

The tablet becomes too fragmentary for continuous translation, but we can discern "[bef]ore (him) he speaks" (ii 45), marking the end of the speech. Although the speaker of these words is not mentioned in the remains of the tablet, it can be surmised that it is Tarhun arguing on behalf of Purra, who seems to be the leader of the people of Ikinkalis, while Purra stands before Meki, the "tenth" king of Ebla.[27] Tarhun comes to the defense of the people of Ikinkalis and threatens to curse Ebla, like the "gods of the city" who curse a man that turned against his city in one of the parables, using the same imagery found in the curse the smith cast on the cup.[28]

---

[24] Hurr. i 3: "Purra, the war prisoner," *āzzīri*, cf. Akkadian *asīru*. The Hurrian thus makes clear the people of Ikinkalis are not debt slaves (Otto 2001: 527–8).

[25] No subject is named in the second paragraph. Neu (1996: 407–8) argues the subject has changed to the Storm-god. Wilhelm (1997: 288–9) prefers to assume that Purra is still the subject. This fits with the Near Eastern custom of a subordinate standing before his superior and with the grammar of the Hurrian.

[26] *KBo* 32.19 ii 1–31, filled in with the better-preserved Hurrian side, i 1–31, and with parallel passages *KBo* 32.19 iii 27'–51'; *KBo* 32.29, 22, 24 + 216. I follow the order of Wilhelm (1997: 292), who places *KBo* 32.19 and 20 before 15. Haas (2006: 177–92) orders as follows: 13 (hospitality scene), 15, 19.

[27] Neu (1996: 407–8) assigns i/ii 11ff. to the Storm-god, quoting himself, while Haas (2006: 184–5) attributes these lines to Purra.

[28] *KBo* 32.14 i/ii 55–60. Smashing a pot is in fact a typical cursing gesture. A similar image appears in *Song of Ullikummi*, when Kumarbi decides that his son Ullikummi should destroy the Storm-god and the rest of the gods: "let him sha[t]ter them [like] empty vessels" (*CTH* 345.

The names of three of the earlier nine kings are provided in another partially preserved overlapping passage from *KBo* 32.20, which contains more of the beginning of the demand. Unfortunately, only the Hurrian side is preserved, leaving the highly repetitive passage nearly incomprehensible, but the kings' names are Hurrian, and two of them are compounds with "Ebla": Aribibla ('who gave Ebla') and Paibibla ('who built Ebla').[29] In column i on the obverse can be discerned, "for eighteen/eighty years ...," "they brought as king Paibibla to the throne...," "on the eighteenth/eightieth year,"[30] then the next king is introduced with the same phrases, so it seems that a series of kings' reigns is being described, apparently nine of them, since the list ends with Meki as the tenth at the bottom of column iv on the reverse. Comments on Purra are interspersed. This looks distinctly as if the bard is drawing on a king list of the sort found at third-millennium Ebla, as well as at Hattusa.[31] Then the narrative segues into the passage translated above, from *KBo* 32.19.[32] Somehow Purra and other servants are involved with a series of kings of Ebla, and the Storm-god has taken notice of the situation.

In due course I will offer a solution to the puzzle of what Purra's role is and why the Storm-god is so concerned about his plight, but we return now to *KBo* 32.19. Meki, having been instructed by Tarhun about the potential consequences of not releasing the citizens of Ikinkalis, conveys the words of Tarhun to the assembly, as indicated by the very damaged reverse of the tablet. There the Hurrian side shows us that the Storm-god's speech is repeated, while the Hittite side shows us that it is in a message conveyed to the assembly, probably by Meki. His request that the people of Ikinkalis be released fits with the mercifulness that Hittites expected of their kings.[33]

1.1.A = *KUB* 33.93 iii 25', translit. E. Rieken *et al.* 2009ff. on KhT; trans. M. Bachvarova in López-Ruiz 2013: 155).

[29] Neu (1996: 441–8).

[30] *KBo* 32.20 i 5'–6', 11'. On the passage see Wilhelm (1997: 289–92; *TUAT Erg.*, 87).

[31] See Archi (2001a) on the king lists from Ebla; more discussion in Chapter 7, 150. In between we learn about something "of Purra," "with a gift," "loosing" (a verb), and Teshshub, "lord of Kummi," as an agent (*KBo* 32.20 i 8'–10'). On the reverse side, iv 6'–7', 9', 12' (filled in with *KBo* 32.26 l. col. 5'), there is mention of "giving to a lord," a "song," and of a "female slave," and we learn that "Teshshub knows."

[32] *KBo* 32.20 iv 15'–21' match *KBo* 32.19 i 1–10 (21' different phrasing, but same meaning); only a few signs are preserved of 22'–24', but they do not match what follows in *KBo* 32.19. *KBo* 32.20 then breaks off.

[33] The name M[eki] may appear in the context of an assembly of elders (*KBo* 32.19 ii 51, iii 1, 2), and the words of the Storm-god, preserved in i 1–25, are repeated in iii as reported speech, cf. quotative particle *wa(r)* at iii 9', 26', 27', 28', 32', which is lacking in i 1–25 (Wilhelm 1997: 286).

The action in Ebla is next picked up in *KBo* 32.16, of which only the Hittite side is decipherable. The speaker Zazalla, son of Pazzanikarri, is introduced responding antagonistically to the king:

> (*KBo* 32.16 ii 6–10) But [i]f there is one who speaks greatly in [the ci]ty,[34] [whose wo]rds no one turns aside, Zazalla is the one who speaks greatly. In the place of assembly, his words [n]o one overcomes.
>
> (ii 11–13) [Zazal]la began [t]o speak to Meki, "Why [do you] speak humility,[35] star of Ebla, Me[ki]...?"[36]

The rest of *KBo* 32.16 is very damaged, but the obverse of *KBo* 32.15, the "fifth" tablet of the *Song of Release*, runs parallel to *KBo* 32.16 ii 17–iii 18′.[37] Here Zazalla (or another member of the anti-release party) rebuts the words of Meki,[38] arguing that if Tarhun were in want, each would contribute whatever he might need; if someone were depriving the god, the Eblaite council-men would mitigate the god's suffering:

> (*KBo* 32.15 ii 7′–9′) "[Ea]ch will give half a shekel [of gold], [w]e [will each give] him [one shekel] of silver. But, if he, Tarhun, is hungry, we will each give one measure of barley [to the g]od.
>
> (ii 10′–13′) "[Ea]ch will pour a half measure of wheat, [a]nd each will pour for him one measure of barley. But if [Tarhun] is naked, we will each clothe him with a fine garment. The god is (like) a human.

Meki, as the representative for Tarhun's side, is comparable to the Hebrew Bible prophets who utter the word of God, but are ignored. On the mercy of Hittite kings see Bryce (2002: 31).

[34] Following the transliteration of Neu (1996: 275), rather than Wilhelm (1997: 279; followed by Haas 2006: 182), who sees a mention of Pazzanikarri and Zazalla, both opposing Meki ([ᵐ*pa-az-z*]*a-n*[*i-ka*]*r*ʾ*-ri-ma* instead of [*nu ma*]-*a*ʾ-*an* [UR]U-*ri-ma*), but leaves unexplained the lack of a nominative ending on the father's name.

[35] See Hoffner (1998a: 74), translating the verb as a second person singular.

[36] KBo 32.16 ii 6–13, filled in with *KBo* 32.54 6′–9′. The topos of the peerless speaker is typical of Homer. Thus we are told of Thoas in the *Iliad*, "in the assembly few of the Achaeans bested him when the young men competed with words" (*Il.* 15.283–4), also see *Il.* 2.370–2 (Dickson 1995: 12). And, Nestor tells Diomedes: "in council among all your peers you are the best, no one will fault your speech, as many are the Achaeans, nor will (any one) speak against it" (*Il.* 9.54–7). See Bachvarova (2005a: 137–8). Compare also the praise of Ishtar in the Akkadian *Hymn to Ishtar*: "She it is who stands foremost among the gods,/ Her word is the weightiest, it prevails over theirs" (25–8, trans. Foster 2005: 86).

[37] In the parallel passages consisting of the first three lines partially preserved near the top of *KBo* 32.15 and *KBo* 32.15 i/ii 14–16, appear "who...," "of Teshshub," "he seizes," "his horn," and "he speaks facing."

[38] Haas (2006: 182) attributes *KBo* 32.15 ii 4′–17′ to Zazalla, then – with no overt change of speaker – ii 18′–iii 7 to Meki. Neu (1996: 482) assigns iii 5–7 to the Storm-god. But, as Wilhelm (1997: 282) points out, in Hurro-Hittite epic a change of speaker is normally carefully marked.

(ii 14′–17′) "But, if he, Tarhun, is cursed, each of us will give him one *kupi*-vessel of fine oil, we will (each) pour out for him fuel, and we will free him from deprivation. The god is (like) a human."

But, under no circumstances will he agree to releasing the people of Ikinkalis. They serve as cupbearers, cooks, washers, and spinners. Meki should release his own servants, send off his son and wife!

(*KBo* 32.15 iii 8–11) When Mek[i] he[ard] the word, he b[eg]an to wail. [He] wai[ls ...], Meki. He [di]d obeisance a[t] the feet of [T]arhun.

(iii 12–14) Meki, bowing to Tarhun, spoke the words, "[L]isten to me, Tarhun, great ki[n]g of Kummi.

(iii 15–20) "I will [gi]ve it, (i.e.,) compensation,[39] but m[y c]ity will not give i[t].[40] Nor will Zazalla, son of Pazz[anik]arri give relea[se]." Meki (tried to?) purify his ci[ty] from sin,[41] the ci[ty of Eb]la. He (tried to?) throw aside the sins for the sake of his city.[42]

(iii 21–4) [...] Because the Great King of Kummi [...] the Great King of Kummi, [...]. Before the stone [...][43]

The stone mentioned in the final line preserved could be the same as the *kunkunuzzi* stone, to which "the destruction of Purra is bound" in the fragment discussed earlier, and/or it may be a baetyl representing the Storm-god.[44]

---

[39] *parišsan*. I owe this translation of the noun to Cyril Brosch (oral communication 9/2011).

[40] Hurr. iv 15–16: "I will give it, my city will not give it, i.e., release."

[41] Hurr. iv 18–19: "Meki took away [...] Ebla [...]." Compare *CTH* 446: *Purification Ritual for the Former Gods*, "Purify evil, impurity, blood, oath of the god, sin, curse away from the house and city" (B = *KBo* 10.45 iv 13–15, with C = *KUB* 41.8 iv 12–14, translit. Otten 1961: 136; see trans. B. J. Collins in Hallo and Younger 1997: 171).

[42] Compare *CTH* 383: *Prayer of Hattusili III and Puduhepa to the Sun-goddess of Arinna*, begging her to take into account all the benefits the Storm-god of Nerik has received from the Hittite king and forgive him whatever sins he might have committed: "throw aside that sin for the sake of your beloved [son], the Storm-god of Nerik" (*CTH* 383 = *KUB* 14.7 iv 3–4, translit. Sürenhagen 1981: 96). Also, in a fragment assigned to the Kumarbi cycle by Polvani (1992: 449–50), Takidu, the divine servant of Hebat, goes to Shimmurra to ask a woman named Kutiladu to "let go the sin" (*waštul tarnaš*, *Fragments of the Kumarbi Myth*: *CTH* 346.12.A = *KBo* 26.88 iv 1–3, translit. and trans. E. Rieken *et al.* 2009ff. on KhT). Also cf. the *Telipinu Myth* (*Mugawar*), in which he is asked to let go (*tarna*) his anger and other emotions (*CTH* 324.1.A = *KUB* 17.10 iii 24–5, translit. E. Rieken *et al.* 2009ff. on KhT, trans. M. Bachvarova in López-Ruiz 2013: 456).

[43] *KBo* 32.15 iii 8–24, filled in with the Hurrian side: iv 8–19.

[44] *Kunkunuzzi* is a hard stone, perhaps basalt, of which Ullikummi is made and on which Kumarbi breaks his teeth when he tries to swallow one in the manner of Cronus, in an episode that serves as an etiology for baetyl worship (*Song of Birth*: *CTH* 344.A = *KUB* 33.120 ii 42–73, translit. E. Rieken *et al.* 2009ff. on KhT; trans. M. Bachvarova in López-Ruiz 2013: 142–3). It

While *KBo* 32.15 is missing most of its upper half, and *KBo* 32.16 is missing a good part of the lower half and also lacks most of the Hurrian side (columns i and iv), it can be seen that *KBo* 32.16 offers a different version of this scene, important evidence that the *Song of Release* is an oral-derived text. Whereas *KBo* 32.15 lists the cupbearer, cook, and spinner as examples of the servants who will not be released (ii 27′, 28′, iii 1–2), when the story is picked up in *KBo* 32.16, on its reverse, the list includes two other servants, the meal-grinder and water-drawer, who are not in the list of *KBo* 32.15. The speech ends, and Meki "repeatedly cries out" ([*ui*]-*uiškizzi*, *KBo* 32.16 iii 11′) and attempts to conciliate Tarhun. I surmise this is the speech of Meki, quoting to Tarhun what has been said in council, which is preserved in *KBo* 32.15. Tarhun responds by demanding again that the people of Ikinkalis, who serve the nine kings their food in the afterlife, be freed. At a minimum, then, in *KBo* 32.16 the speech of the side opposing the release of the captives contains either more or different examples of the types of servants who will not be released than *KBo* 32.15. For this reason I suggest that *KBo* 32.16 and *KBo* 32.15 present two different versions of the same sequence.[45]

Some scholars have argued that the suffering of the naked, cold, and hungry Storm-god described in the speech in assembly is purely hypothetical, to be compared to the suffering of the people of Ikinkalis.[46] Others connect it to the hospitality scene in the underworld; thus, Volkert Haas argues that the description of his suffering state refers to his piteous condition just after being released from the underworld, which parallels the condition of the people whose release he demands.[47] The unnamed speaker in the assembly, probably Zazalla, either denies that there is any correlation between the enslaved state of the people of Ikinkalis and the

---

also appears in an ominous dream of Keshshi, falling from the sky (*Keshshi: CTH* 361.i.1.A = *KUB* 33.121 iii 7′, translit. E. Rieken *et al.* 2009ff. on KhT; trans. M. Bachvarova in Chavalas 2013: 286; there B is erroneously listed as A). See Neu (1996: 461) and in more detail Haas (2002; 2006: 210). Even if all aspects of its significance are not clear to us, we can recognize that mention of the *kunkunuzzi* stone is characteristic of Hurro-Hittite songs. On baetyls, see Chapter 10, 242, with n. 114.

[45] In order to reconcile the larger trajectory of *KBo* 32.16 with *KBo* 32.15 and 19, it must be assumed that there were at least two rounds of back-and-forth between the council and the god – Meki repeating the god's conditional threats to the council, then conveying the words of the council to the god, and the god repeating his threats again – but word-for-word repetition of the quoted speech would still be expected, not such variation in the examples. Von Dassow (2013) offers a close analysis of the differences between the two tablets. She does not treat the variation as evidence of an oral derivation for the song, but argues that *KBo* 32.16 is a scribal compilation drawing sections from different part of a fixed text, and that it was used in scribal training.

[46] Neu (1993b: 347–8; 1996: 482–3).   [47] Haas (2006: 183).

Storm-god's suffering, claiming that the latter's condition can be improved simply by offerings of material goods, not services on the part of the people of Ikinkalis, or he argues that for the Storm-god he would do much, but for the kings he will not release the captives. Lack of context makes it difficult to choose between the two alternatives.

I have argued elsewhere that the god would in fact be in danger of suffering if his cult were neglected, that the kings mentioned here are dead, and that the people of Ikinkalis are meant to serve their cult. The Storm-god's hypothetical suffering is not meant to parallel the suffering of the people of Ikinkalis; it parallels instead the suffering caused to the dead kings by neglect of their cult, brought about by the fact that the people of Ikinkalis who have been conquered by Ebla are required to work for the members of Ebla's assembly instead of attending to the dead kings' cult.[48]

There certainly would be repercussions for humans if either the gods or the royal dead were neglected. Neglect of the gods was a subject frequently alluded to in Hittite prayers.[49] Thus, in the Middle Hittite *Prayer of Arnuwanda and Ashmunikal for the Sun-goddess of Arinna*, the king and queen argue that the Hittites take the best care of the gods, but the Kaskean enemy is preventing the servants of the gods from serving them properly by oppressing them with *šaḫḫan* and *luzzi* (governmentally imposed services and payments in return for land use and corvée labor).[50] Since Hittite kings ensured that the gods were receiving their due by limiting the amount of *šaḫḫan* and *luzzi* that was required of those subjects who cared for their cult, they could make a great show of freeing the inhabitants of a captured town from such duties so as to better serve the gods, as Hattusili I did in his *Annals* after conquering the town of Hahhu. There he used a phrase similar to the phrase used in the title of the *Song of Release*, *parā tarna-*:

> I, the Great King, the *Tabarna*, took the hands of the female slaves from the millstone, and the hands of the male slaves from the sickles. [I] freed

---

[48] Bachvarova (2005b: 54–5). I was surer then that the god was indeed in want and needed the services of the people of Ikinkalis. Wilhelm (1997: 290-2) argues that Purra was able to serve ten kings in succession because of his supernatural longevity. Neu (1996: 481–2) argues that the kings belong to various regions subordinate to Ebla. Von Dassow (2013: 159) argues that the people of Ikinkalis have been held in subjection for several generations, covering the reigns of nine kings.

[49] Cf. in the *Song of Hedammu*, Ea warning Tarhun that the gods will suffer if he and Kumarbi kill off too many mortals in their battle for supremacy (*CTH* 348.I.1.D = *KUB* 33.103 obv. ii 1–8, filled in with C = *KUB* 33.100 + 36.16 iii 8′–16′, E = *KUB* 33.116 ii 1′–8′, translit. E. Rieken *et al.* 2009ff. on KhT; trans. M. Bachvarova in López-Ruiz 2013: 150).

[50] *CTH* 375.1.A = *KUB* 17.21 i 9′–27′, with B = *KUB* 31.124 i 5′–7′ + Bo 8617 (translit. von Schuler 1965: 152, 154; trans. Singer 2002b: 41). See discussion of Bachvarova (2005b: 51–2).

(EGIR-*an* [= *appantan*] *tarnaḫḫ*[*un*]) them from *šaḫḫan* and *luzzi*.[51] I ungirded their belts. I released them to my lady, the Sun-goddess of Arinna, in perpetuity.[52]

In addition, Arnuwanda and Ashmunikal used the phrase *parā tarna-* when they issued an edict freeing from municipal obligations those cities, craftsmen, and workers of the land who were dedicated to the Stone House (mausoleum) of the king: "let them be free from *šaḫḫan* and *luzzi* ... Let no one change their status (*parā⸗ma⸗aš⸗kan lē kuiški tarnai*)."[53] Here *parā tarnai* clearly does not mean "free," but "change someone's status."[54] I contend that the change of status in the *Song of Release* is of the same sort as that commanded in the edict of the royal pair: transfer of services to the royal dead from serving the living elite of Ebla.

This is as far as the Ebla storyline can be followed in the *Song of Release*, but the opening of the first tablet and various fragments indicate that Meki's attempts to appease the god failed and that the dispute played itself out in Ebla's destruction. In the end, the *Song of Release* is a piece of admonitory history illustrating the importance both of obeying the king and of caring for the royal dead.

The hospitality scene

A set of fragments from a single tablet (*KBo* 32.13+) preserves a hospitality sequence among the gods. It begins with the arrival of the Storm-god and his brother Suwaliyat. Teshshub/Tarhun is welcomed by his hostess, the underworld goddess, in Hurrian Allani, in Hittite the Sun-goddess of the

---

[51] Akk.: AMA.AR.GI-*šunu aštakan* 'I made a release', with no mention of the goddess (*CTH* 4.I.A = *KBo* 10.1 rev. 14, translit. Devecchi 2005: 54).

[52] *Hattusili's Annals*: *CTH* 4.II.A = *KBo* 10.2 iii 15–20 (translit. de Martino 2003: 68). See Bachvarova (2005b: 52–3) and Neu (1988a: 20–1; 1993b: 332–3; 1996: 11–12). On possible echoes of Sargonic legend here, see Chapter 8, 177–8.

[53] *Ashmunikal's Instructions for the Workers of the Stone-House*: *CTH* 252.A = *KUB* 13.8 obv. 1–9 (translit. Otten 1958b: 106; trans. Bachvarova 2005b: 53). On the Stone House see van den Hout (2002b) and Chapter 7, 152.

[54] This is why I avoid translating the title of the song SIR₃ *parā tarnumaš* as "The Song of Liberation" or "The Song of Freedom," as some have done, for the people of Ikinkalis are not in fact set free. They are turned over from one type of service to another. Von Dassow (2013: 153–5), comparing the Hurrian expression corresponding to Hittite *parā tarna-* in the *Song of Release* with its Akkadian equivalent *andurāram wuššurum*, argues that the Hurrian phrase means "to effect a restoration" or "to decree (an edict of) release."

Earth, with a chair and footstool. He then is entertained by her personally with abundant meat and drink, the Former Gods seated to his right.[55]

I translate the Hittite version inscribed on the main fragment here:

> (*KBo* 32.13 ii 1–8) When Tarhun went, he went inside the palace of the Sun-goddess of the Earth. His throne [was X]. When Tarhun the king went in from outside, Tarhun sat aloft on a throne the size of a field of an IKU, and he raised his feet on a stool of the size of a field of seven *tawallas*.
>
> (ii 9–14) Tarhun and Suwaliyat[56] went under the Dark Earth. The Sun-goddess of the Earth girded herself up. She turned before Tarhun. She made a fine feast, the doorbolt of the earth, the Sun-goddess of the Earth.
>
> (ii 15–20) She slaughtered 10,000 oxen before great Tarhun. She slaughtered 10,000 oxen. She slaughtered 30,000 fatty-tailed sheep, and there was no counting for those kids, lambs, and billy goats, she slaughtered so many.
>
> (ii 21–7) The bakers prepared (food) and the cup-bearers came in, [wh]ile the cooks set forth the breast meat. They brought them (the pieces) with bowls [. . .]. The time of eating arrived, and Tarhun sat to eat, while she seated the Former Gods to Tarhun's right.
>
> (ii 28–34) The Sun-goddess of the Earth stepped before Tarhun like a cupbearer. The fingers of her hand are long, and her four fingers lie below the cup, and the drinking-vessels with which [she gives] to drink, inside them lies goodness.

How the hospitality scene in the *Song of Release* fits into the rest of the story has been a matter of speculation. Does it set up the destruction of Ebla, or does it close that episode? If the feast follows the Ebla episode, it could mark a reconciliation between the gods of the underworld and heavens, as Erich Neu and Walter Burkert have suggested.[57] Haas and Ilse

---

[55] The other fragments besides *KBo* 32.13 (joined by M. Dijkstra 1/7/13; see KhT *ad loc.*) belong to the back side of the tablet: 105 (not edited in Neu 1996), in Hittite, mentions wine, eating (a repeated action, 2x), drinking (3x), and a cup (4x); 65, in Hittite and Hurrian, mentions wine and Teshshub; 72 (Hittite) involves Suwaliyat and someone else visiting Allani's palace in the Dark Earth by "three paths." The back side of *KBo* 32.13 fits after this fragment and is very damaged. We can pick out from the Hittite version "they [d]ivide," "when it was di[vid]ed," and "in front of Tarhun he/she stepped forth." The next paragraph opens with the name of the Storm-god, then a second singular verb form. It is direct speech, probably spoken by Tarhun, then the Sun-goddess of the Earth appears in the nominative and, "b[owing, begins t]o speak." *KBo* 32.82 (Hittite) mentions the Moon-god and "in the [Dar]k Earth."

[56] Hurr. i 9: "Teshshub with Shattahamo." See Neu (1996: 244–6).

[57] Neu (1993b: 345–6) and Burkert (1993). Such a celebratory feast would fit in with the Ugaritic example from the *Baal Cycle* discussed in Chapter 6, 143. Neu suggested that the release of the men of Ikinkalis is part of the festivities, since this is typical of jubilees. According to him, the

Wegner interpret the episode quite differently, comparing it to the plot of the Sumerian stories of *Ereshkigal and Nergal*, in which Nergal descends to the underworld to challenge Ereshkigal but is seduced by her. They see Allani as a seductress who lures the Storm-god into the underworld to imprison him by causing him to eat food that bewitches him.[58] Haas suggests that the Storm-god, having been trapped in the underworld by Allani, just barely escapes, leaving behind Suwaliyat as his substitute.

This last reconstruction parallels the plot line of the very damaged end of another Hurro-Hittite story, *Elkunirsa and Ashertu*, in which, as far as can be seen, the Storm-god, tricked by Ashertu, possibly by consuming food and drink offered by her, seems to end up in the underworld, his body parts sullied (by evil words?). Other fragments of the incantations accompanying *Elkunirsa and Ashertu* show that the Storm-god is purified by human conjurers, from (false) oaths, and [evil] words, among other things, allowing him to leave the underworld.[59] The advantage of this reconstruction of the *Song of Release* is that it helps to solve the puzzling use of the term "cursed" in the assembly scene to describe the Storm-god and explains Meki's purification on behalf of his city. However, the timeline seems confused. Once the god has returned from the underworld, he should no longer be suffering.

My analysis of the function of the hospitality scene in the *Song of Release* is based on parallels drawn from *Appu*, *Ullikummi*, and *Hedammu*. It indicates that the feast sets up the destruction of Ebla, as each case of hospitality among the gods in the Hurro-Hittite examples outside of the *Song of Release* is followed by a conversation, usually about a recently arisen problem, that sets the next stage of the plot in motion.[60]

---

festival of Allani is described as an example of a symbolic reconciliation between heavenly and chthonic gods.

[58] Haas and Wegner (1991: 386; 1997: 442–3), Haas (1994: 552). Compare also *Inanna's Descent* or the Greek story of Persephone. De Martino (2000: 303, 304, 308–10), building on this suggestion, sees her to-and-fro motion before the Storm-god as an alluring dance. He then connects this episode to the Ebla storyline by proposing that the Storm-god's experience as a prisoner made him sympathetic to the plight of the people of Ikinkalis. Hitt. *weḫ-* 'turn' is a term used for dancing (de Martino 1989: 8). But, compare perhaps the formulaic hospitality scene from the Abkhaz tale *Sasruquo's Sorrow*: When the hero appears at the house of an old woman, she plays hostess: "She spun swiftly about and in the flash of an eye had prepared a meal for him" (Saga 79, trans. Colarusso 2002: 353).

[59] *CTH* 342.1.2.A = *KUB* 12.61 iii (translit. E. Rieken et al. 2009ff. on KhT). See Bachvarova (2013a: 30–2).

[60] Haas (2006: 180–1) places *KBo* 32.13 after the opening and before the Ebla scenes. Wilhelm (*TUAT Erg.*, 83–4) places it between the debate in the assembly and the demand of the Storm-god, but acknowledges that the question of its relation to the Ebla episode remains unanswered.

In the *Tale of Appu*, when the Sun-god returns to heaven having promised a childless man that he will beget a son, the Storm-god, seeing him approaching from a distance, immediately senses he has a problem on his mind and says to his vizier, "He comes for the first time, the Storm-god, the shepherd of the lands. The land is not destroyed somehow? The cities wouldn't be laid waste somehow? The troops wouldn't be defeated somehow?"[61] Then, he orders his cooks and cupbearers to welcome him with food and drink. This scene has strong parallels with the beginning of the hospitality scene in the *Song of Ullikummi* in which Tashmishu wonders to Tarhun what disaster motivates the Sun-god's visit. (It turns out to be the existence of Ullikummi.)[62]

The three hospitality scenes from the fragments of the *Song of Hedammu* all occur as the context for addressing a problem, as the gods take sides over whether Kumarbi or the Storm-god should be king in heaven. The first (fragmentary) hospitality scene occurs in the context of marriage negotiations between the Sea-god and Kumarbi arranging the transfer of Sea-god's daughter, Shertapshuruhi, to Kumarbi. The Sea-god comes to visit, props up his foot, and accepts a drink. Then he offers his daughter, describing her enormous length and width, telling Kumarbi to come fetch her in seven days, a typical length of time. [63] The child produced in this marriage, Hedammu, will solve the problem of finding a worthy adversary for the upstart god Tarhun. In the second hospitality scene, Anzili warns Tarhun about Hedammu, refusing all hospitality until she has conveyed her urgent message.[64] The ultimate purpose of the third

---

[61] *CTH* 360.1.A = *KUB* 24.8 ii 14–18 (translit. E. Rieken *et al.* 2009ff. on KhT).

[62] *CTH* 345.I.1.A = *KUB* 33.96 + 93 + 7a iv 44′–48′ (translit. E. Rieken *et al.* 2009ff. on KhT; trans. M. Bachvarova in López-Ruiz 2013: 156). See Haas (2006: 196–7), noting the structure and function of the type scene.

[63] Whereas the huge dimensions here refer to the daughter of the Sea-god (*CTH* 348.I.6.B = *KUB* 33.109 i 7–8, translit. E. Rieken *et al.* 2009ff. on KhT; trans. M. Bachvarova in López-Ruiz 2013: 146), in the *Song of Release* they refer to the size of the furniture and the large amounts of food Allani serves. Other examples of vast measurements in Hurro-Hittite epic: *Song of Gilgamesh*: *CTH* 341.III.1.A₁ = *KUB* 8.57 i 7–9 (translit. E. Rieken *et al.* 2009ff. on KhT; trans. Beckman 2001a: 158), of Gilgamesh (parallels in the MB version from Ugarit and the SB version: George 2007: 247–8); *Song of Ullikummi*: *CTH* 345.I.1.B = *KUB* 33.98 + 36.8 i 15–16 (translit. E. Rieken *et al.* 2009ff. on KhT, trans. M. Bachvarova in López-Ruiz 2013: 154), of the rock Kumarbi impregnates. Also see de Martino (2000: 319). In Ugaritic, the vast dimensions are applied to furniture: *Baal Cycle*: *KTU* 1.4 i 27–43 (trans. N. Wyatt 2002: 91–2). Also see M. L. West (1997a: 122).

[64] *CTH* 348.I.5.A = *KBo* 19.112 rev.? 1′–15′ (trans. M. Bachvarova in López-Ruiz 2013: 154). A similar sequence of hospitality offered but refused occurs in the *Song of Ullikummi*: *CTH* 345.I.1.A = *KBo* 26.58 + 36.7a iv 51′–4′ (trans. M. Bachvarova in López-Ruiz 2013: 148). On hospitality scenes in Hurro-Hittite epic, also see Haas (2006: 125–6) and Archi (2007b: 199).

hospitality scene, again between the Sea-god and Kumarbi, is unclear, yet it can be recognized that important matters are to be discussed. Kumarbi sends his courtier Mukishanu to convey a message to the Sea-god:

> (1.F ii 6′–9′) [Mukishanu] heard [the wor]ds. He p[romptly stood] up. [He] made his way away under river and earth. Arma, Istanu, and the gods of the earth, did [not s]ee him. [He] went down to the Sea.
>
> (28.A iii 5′–16′) Mukishanu began to speak in turn the words of Kumarbi to the Sea, "Come, the father of the gods, Kumarbi, calls you, and for which matter he calls you, it is an urgent matter. Come promptly. Come away under river and earth. Let not Arma, Istanu, and the gods of the earth see you." When the great Sea heard the words, he stood up promptly, and he w[ent] away down by the path of earth and of river. He completed it at one go. He came up to Kumarbi from below, from the pillar(?), from the earth, to [his] throne. They set a throne for the Sea, for him to sit. The grea[t Sea] sat on his throne. He [s]ets a laid table for him, t[o] eat. And the cup-bearer give[s] him sweet wine to drink. Kumarbi, the father of the gods, and the great Sea [s]i[t]. They eat (and) drink their fill.
>
> (28.A iii 17′–18′) Kumarbi began to [s]peak words to his vizier, "Mukishanu, my vizier, which words I speak to y[ou], hold your ear cocked to my words ..."[65]

This hospitality sequence shares many of the motifs found in the passage from the *Song of Release*, including the entrance, the chair and footstool, the food, and the cupbearer serving the drink. However, the tablet that presents the equivalent scene starts after the beginning of the sequence, which should contain the message that sends Tarhun on his mission, and it ends at the point right before the end of the sequence preserved in the *Song of Hedammu*, in which the messenger, having duly eaten and drunk, accomplishes his mission.

We might therefore expect that the feast of Allani also sets the stage for the next phase of the story, providing the opportunity for deliberation concerning the course of action to be followed. I suggest that the feast occurs in the underworld because the nine deceased kings mentioned in the text are suffering from neglect of their cult. In fact, the Former Gods who join the Storm-god at the table of Allani, who was closely associated

---

[65] *CTH* 348.I.1.F = *KUB* 33.122 ii 6′–9′; 28.A = *KBo* 26.71 + *KUB* 12.65 + *KBo* 26.112 + Bo 69/546 iii 5′–18′ (translit. E. Rieken *et al.* 2009ff. on KhT; trans. M. Bachvarova in López-Ruiz 2013: 150–1)

with royal ancestor cult,[66] may be interceding for the deified dead kings. Ishhara is also linked with the Former Gods in other Hurro-Hittite texts, both songs and incantations, and is closely connected to Allani.[67] These connections mean that Ishhara must have been involved with the Storm-god's journey to Allani's underworld abode.[68] Possibly she sends him there at the end of the conversation that closes *KBo* 32.11, just as the Sun-god had sent the Storm-god to her.

The parables

The parables that were found together with the fragments of the *Song of Release* explain how a series of greedy animals, such as a roe deer, a dog, or a pig, or ungrateful built objects, such as a cup or a tower, turn on their benefactors or creators and insult or curse them, then are cursed in return and destroyed.[69] After each parable the narrator is careful to explain that the characters represent rebellious or ungrateful humans, a son or an administrator raised to a lofty position. However, although two of the tablets (*KBo* 32.12 and 14) containing parables are comparatively well preserved, their place in the narrative is unclear. Certainly, although *KBo* 32.12 is tagged as the "second tablet," it cannot follow directly after the end of KBo 32.11, which is labeled as the "first tablet." Gernot Wilhelm argues that the parables do not belong in the narrative of the *Song of Release*, suggesting they belong to a different work entirely, with the colophon-less *KBo* 32.14 belonging to a preliminary draft and *KBo* 32.12 representing a

---

[66] Taracha (2000: 192–3).
[67] See Prechel (1996: 97–9); Archi (2002b: 33) on her relationship with the Former Gods; Prechel (1996: 99–100, 107–16) on her relationship with Allani. Also see Chapter 4, 95, on *CTH* 449: *Ritual Mentioning the Former Gods*, in which Ishhara is invoked along with the Former Gods.
[68] This sequence follows quite closely the narrative structure suggested by M. L. West (1997a: 173–4) for how stories are set in motion.
[69] See trans. by M. Bachvarova in López-Ruiz (2013: 297–9). The parables, with their animal characters and overt morals, have been compared to Aesop's fables and the much-translated story of Ahiqar. See Oettinger (1992). Also comparable is the Sanskrit *Pancatantra*, the structure of which in fact may shed some light on the structure of the *Song of Release*, for in the Sanskrit composition narratives told by intradiegetic narrators are embedded within the frame narrative, in multiple layers. Finally, the parables bear some similarity in their message to the OH *Palace Chronicles*, a series of disconnected tales of how greedy or untrustworthy subordinates were disciplined by the Hittite king, often with picturesque punishments that occasionally equated them with animals (*CTH* 8–9, trans. Haas 2006: 54–9). I study the relationship of the parables to the "heroic" section of the *Song of Release* in some detail in Bachvarova (2010), discussing the use of animal imagery in Hittite historical texts and Homeric epic. Also see Otto (2001) for a unified interpretation.

final draft.[70] There is no overlap in content between *KBo* 32.14 and *KBo* 32.12.

I agree more with Alfonso Archi, who thinks that *KBo* 32.11 and 12 belong to "two different series" of the *Song of Release*.[71] If the parables are indeed part of the *Song of Release*, they must belong to a different textualization than *KBo* 32.11.[72] Parallel tablets of the *Song of Release* do not begin and end at the same point in the narrative,[73] and it furthermore seems that different versions of the epic contained expanded or contracted motifs and scenes, a canonical characteristic of oral composition in performance, as discussed earlier.[74] It is therefore plausible to assume that *KBo* 32.12 at least belongs to a different telling from *KBo* 32.11, and we do not need to assume that *KBo* 32.12 and 14 belong to the same version. Rather than thinking in terms of a polished final written version produced from rough drafts, we should be thinking of multiple textualizations. Indeed, the fact that the hand of more than one scribe can be discerned in the tablets[75] fits with the proposal that more than one textualization was being carried out.

The parables do in fact support and enhance the message of the story of Ebla's destruction. They explain the message of the rest of the epic, in which the Eblaite king Meki is overruled by his assembly, which sides with the powerful speaker Zazalla, preferring to continue to exploit the captive people of Ikinkalis by having them do menial labor for them rather than to release them to serve the royal dead. Because the dead kings' approval is needed to legitimate the current king, any neglect of their cult puts Meki's kingship and therefore the prosperity of the entire kingdom in danger, a fact conveyed quite clearly by the parables. As the benefactors of the community of Ebla, the royal dead fit the roles of the insulted mentors in the parables just as the Storm-god does, and they match the "gods of the father" who punish the rebellious son in the cup parable.[76] At the very least, therefore, we can say that the parables, even if they were not part of every performance of the *Song of Release*, are compatible in themes and

---

[70] Wilhelm (*TUAT Erg.*, 84), a position followed by Otto (2001: 529). Neu (1993b: 340) considered the parables to be told as part of the festivities of a Jubilee year.

[71] Archi (2007b: 189), however, does agree with Wilhem that *KBo* 32.14 is a draft, suggesting it is "a third manuscript."

[72] On the term "textualization," see Chapter 2, 20, n. 3.   [73] See Wilhelm (*TUAT Erg.*, 82–3).

[74] At the bottom edge of the reverse of *KBo* 32.14, it seems that the scribe and the bard, seeing they are running out of room, drastically contract the last two parables, the bard shortening them to make them fit and the scribe squeezing them into the space available (Bachvarova 2014: 94).

[75] Neu (1996: 5), Archi (2007b: 189).

[76] *KBo* 32.14 iii 1–5 (trans. M. Bachvarova in López-Ruiz 2013: 298).

message with the *Song of Release* and belong to the same narrative tradition.

The epithets given to Ishhara in the opening lines of KBo 32.11 could signal that she is the narrator within the epic who tells the parables that fill the tablets *KBo* 32.12 and 14, since these are called "wisdom," in Hurrian *mādi* and in Hittite *ḫattātar*, and Ishhara is singled out for praise as "word-mak[er],/ famous for wisdom" (*tive tān-*[...]/ *mādi amudōvadi*).[77] If the parables are part of the *Song of Release* there was a conflation in the parable section of the real poet performing the story and a mythical character closer to the action, whether it was Ishhara or a different character inside the story who told these parables.

Conclusion

I have presented as thorough an analysis as possible of the meaning of the *Song of Release*, but we are left with many questions tantalizingly unanswered. What is sure, however, is that here we have an oral-derived text about the destruction of a famous Near Eastern city, and this plot line needs to be taken into account by scholars interested in Near Eastern influence on the Homeric tradition. In the next chapter we will deepen our understanding of this narrative tradition by examining the relationship between the *Song of Release* and other narrative songs of the eastern Mediterranean area in the second and first millennia BCE.

---

[77] *KBo* 32.11 i 5–6, see Neu (1996: 39–40, 127). The first epithet is similar to one she receives in a Hurrian incense prayer from Ugarit, *madi kad=i* 'speaker of wisdom' (RS 24.285.4, translit. and trans. M. Dietrich and Mayer 1994: 94). The latter epithet is also similar to the Hittite epithet *ḫattannaš ḫaršumnaš* EN-*aš* 'lord of wisdom and the headwaters' (e.g., *Song of Birth*: CTH 344. A = *KUB* 33.120 ii 5, iii 15′; translit. E. Rieken *et al.* 2009ff. on KhT; trans. M. Bachvarova in López-Ruiz 2013: 141, 143). This applies particularly to Kumarbi; see Beckman (1986: 27–8), Haas (2007a: 347), Wilhelm (2002: 62–4, discussing Ea), and *HED* (H: 261–2).

6 | The place of the *Song of Release* in its eastern Mediterranean context

> Who, then, brought the two together to battle in strife? The son of
> Leto and Zeus. For he, angered by the king, raised up an evil sickness
> and the host was perishing, because the son of Atreus dishonored
> Chryses, his priest, for he came to the swift ships of the Achaeans,
> in order to free his daughter, carrying an incalculable ransom, having
> in his hands the wool fillets of far-darting Apollo on his golden staff,
> and he entreated all the Achaeans, but especially the sons of Atreus,
> the two commanders of the people ...
>
> *Iliad* 1.8–16

Introduction

As noted at the beginning of the last chapter, the discovery of the *Song of Release* in the 1980s has opened a new phase in the study of the Hurro-Hittite tradition of narrative poetry. We now can deepen our understanding of how Greek epic could have borrowed and adapted Near Eastern motifs by seeing how the *Song of Release* reworked motifs attested in Mesopotamian and Ugaritic poetry. Furthermore, the *Song of Release* gives us opportunities to discern additional examples of traditional elements that were adapted and reworked in Homeric poetry, such as the assembly scene in the beginning of *Iliad* 1, and the overarching Iliadic theme of the capture and return of Helen. I will show in the end that the *Song of Release* lies midway between the broader Near Eastern epic tradition (including both the Mesopotamian and Ugaritic strands) and the Homeric tradition, reworking epic motifs and themes to fit a Hittite context, and introducing narrative sequences that do not occur in the wider Near Eastern tradition, but do appear in Homer.

I first compare the assembly scene of the *Song of Release* to similar scenes in other Near Eastern mythical narratives, especially *Atrahasis*, as well as in the *Iliad*. Next, I move on to the hospitality scene among the gods, comparing it to scenes in the *Baal Cycle* and in the *Iliad*. I close with a discussion of the messenger scene, comparing it to passages in *Atrahasis* and the *Iliad*.

The assembly scene in its Near Eastern context

While arguments presented by two opposing humans, discussions concerning freeing oppressed workers, and arguments or discussions *between* a human and his assembly can be found separately in Near Eastern literature, the *Song of Release* is the only eastern Mediterranean narrative known to me dated earlier than the *Iliad* in which two humans argue before a human assembly over releasing a captive. Gods, humans, and abstract things can engage in arguments, but the extant examples present them as appearing before a single divine judge or an assembly of gods, not an assembly of humans. For example, in Sumerian disputations opposite principles argue against one another, and animals can also debate against each other, threatening and insulting each other.[1] Hittite literature provides us with an example of two humans arguing a case in the *Tale of Appu*, but the "good" brother and the "bad" brother do so before the Sun-god in a civil court case, not before an assembly, and not arguing over a political or military decision. The Hurrian version of the *Song of Keshshi*, as far as we can make it out, does seem to present a confrontation between Keshshi and his wife in front of the elders of their community,[2] but the three best parallels in other respects from the wider Near Eastern literature to the assembly scene in *Song of Release* are in the Gilgamesh tradition, in the Hebrew Bible, and in the Akkadian narrative *Atrahasis*, all of which present arguments about people being forced to work against their will. Only the *Song of Release* presents those people as war captives, as Chryseis is in the *Iliad*.

---

[1] Cf. for example the *Disputation between Heron and Turtle* (trans. Black et al. 2004: 235–40).
[2] *Tale of Appu*: CTH 360.1.G = *KBo* 19.102 (+) 26.85 + *ABoT* 1.48, D = *KBo* 19.108 (translit. E. Rieken et al. 2009ff. on KhT; trans. Hoffner 1998a: 84–5). On the opposing brothers see Haas (2006: 194); to his list of examples add Perses and Hesiod in *Works and Days* 27–46, arguing before the corrupt *basileis*, and see Chapter 2, 34. Keshshi: CTH 361.II.2 = *KUB* 47.2 (discussion and translit. Salvini and Wegner 2004: 25, 59–60, No. 27). The Hebrew Bible does provide quite a few examples of human assemblies (see Sutherland 1986 for discussion). Elders in assembly debate with Gilgamesh and Enkidu about his journey to Huwawa in *Epic of Gilgamesh* SB II 260–III 12, supplemented with the OB version (trans. George 2003: 569–75). Assembly of gods: *Anzu* OB version, tablet II (trans. Foster 2005: 556–60); *Song of Hedammu*: CTH 348.1.7.A = *KUB* 33.110 ii 5′ (translit. E. Rieken et al. 2009ff. on KhT; trans. M. Bachvarova in López-Ruiz 2013: 150); *Baal Cycle*: *KTU* 1.2 i 15–49 (trans. N. Wyatt 2002: 58–63). For a discussion of the assembly of gods in the Hebrew Bible, see Mullen (1980); assembly of gods in Greek: *Il.* 4.1, 20.4–30; Aesch. *Sept.* 220, also see M. L. West (1997a: 112, 173–4, 177–81, 193–5) and Burkert (1992: 117). Neu (1996: 480–1) discusses the assembly scene in the *Song of Release* and how it reflects Ebla's real-life assembly.

In the Sumerian lay *Gilgamesh and Akka*, Gilgamesh argues directly with his assembly of elders over the imposition of corvée labor on his people by king Akka of Kish. He succeeds in a second assembly in winning over the young men of Uruk, who then go to fight against Kish.[3] Here is an argument in assembly over whether men of a particular town should do forced labor for the men of another town, preceding a battle that decides the matter, but the debate is not between two men in front of the assembly, but between Gilgamesh and the assembly.

At 1 Kings 12:1–20, after King Solomon dies, his son Rehoboam is about to become king, and Jeroboam, who had been promised that he would some day be the leader of most of the tribes of Israel, returns from Egypt and asks Rehoboam before the people of Israel who have gathered in assembly that Rehoboam be more merciful towards them than his father was:

> "Your father made our yoke heavy. Now therefore lighten the hard service of your father and his heavy yoke on us and we will serve you." He said to them, "Depart for three days, then come again to me." So the people went away.
>
> The King Rehobo'am took counsel with the old men, who had stood before Solomon his father while he was yet alive, saying, "How do you advise me to answer this people?" And they said to him, "If you will be a servant to this people today and serve them, and speak good words to them when you answer them, then they will be your servants for ever." But he forsook the counsel which the old men gave him, and took counsel with the young men who had grown up with him and stood before him. And he said to them, "What do you advise that we answer this people who have said to me, 'Lighten the yoke that your father put upon us'?" And the young men who had grown up with him said to him, "Thus shall you speak to this people who said to you, 'Your father made our yoke heavy, but do you lighten it for us'; thus shall you say to them, 'My little finger is thicker than my father's loins. And now, whereas my father laid upon you a heavy yoke, I will add to your yoke. My father chastised you with whips, but I will chastise you with scorpions.'"[4]

Two sides of an issue are presented by two different constituencies to Rehoboam: whether to be merciful to an oppressed and overworked people.

---

[3] 1–47, see trans. at ETCSL t.1.8.1.1. Further discussion of the role of the assembly in this poem may be found in D. Katz (1987) and Riley (2000). Also compare 2 Samuel 16:15–17:14, the dispute of Hushai and Ahithophel before "all the men of Israel." I owe this reference to Prof. H. A. Hoffner, Jr.

[4] Trans. May and Metzger (1973: 434–5).

The wrong decision is made, to continue to oppress them, and that will lead to the downfall of the leader who made the decision. As in *Gilgamesh and Akka*, the young men are portrayed as more impetuous than the older men, but here this proves to be disastrous for the king who follows their advice. In *Gilgamesh and Akka*, the king is debating about whether his own people should give in to demands for corvée labor, while in 1 Kings 12 Rehoboam is debating over whether to continue to oppress another people. In a typically biblical topos, God is portrayed as influencing even the unreasonable decision of Rehoboam, so that Rehoboam may be punished as he deserves. Neither Gilgamesh nor Rehoboam is rebuffed and overruled as Meki was by his assembly; rather each of them is free to make his own decision. These examples make clear how striking this plot twist in the *Song of Release* must have been to the Hittite audience, serving as an adequate explanation of why Ebla deserved destruction. Just as *Gilgamesh and Akka* and the Hebrew Bible make different culturally and historically determined uses of the same motif of arguing in assembly over relieving an overburdened people of excessive labor, the Hittite text reworks this same idea to fit with Hittite concerns, in order to send a clear message to the immediate subordinates of the Hittite king not to cross his word.

The Near Eastern text that shows the closest parallels to the assembly scene of the *Song of Release* is the Akkadian narrative *Atrahasis*, which tells the story of the invention of mankind to do manual labor for the gods and the gods' attempt to destroy them when they become too numerous, with a flood which destroys all of mankind except for the clever Atrahasis and those he brought on board the boat Enki advised him to build. The Akkadian *Atrahasis*, like *Gilgamesh*, is attested at a variety of sites peripheral to Mesopotamia, including Ugarit and Hattusa, and as discussed earlier, variant versions in Hittite have been found in Hattusa. By comparing *Atrahasis* with the *Song of Release*, it can be seen quite clearly how Hurro-Hittite poets reworked a Near Eastern narrative sequence known to them for a Hittite audience, producing a song that shows strong affinities with the *Iliad*.[5]

First of all, there is a clear connection between the *Song of Release* and *Atrahasis* in the odd expression uttered by the speaker in the assembly of Ebla, "The god is (like) a human."[6] The phrase has a parallel in the equally

---

[5] I compare the OB version of *Atrahasis*, since it is both relatively well preserved and antedates the *Song of Release*. On *Atrahasis* also see Chapter 2, 29–32.
[6] *KBo* 32.15 ii 13', 17': AN UŠ UN, the first two signs of which could be read DINGIR-*uš* for Hittite *šiunuš* 'god' (nom. sing.). UN could stand for Hittite *antuḫšaš/antuwaḫḫaš* 'person, human',

puzzling opening line from *Atrahasis*: "when the gods (were like) man,"[7] referring to the menial labor the gods are forced to engage in until they invent humans to do it for them. In addition, the line is comparable to a set of phrases in the parables of the *Song of Release*, in which the narrator makes clear that the animal or object he has been telling a story about in fact represents a human, e.g.: "But it is not a cup. It is a man."[8] In the assembly scene of the *Song of Release* the point is that the Storm-god can suffer like a man.

Atrahasis opens with an untenable situation: the Anunna-gods[9] are forcing the Igigi-gods to do corvée labor, digging irrigation ditches. The Igigi-gods attack Enlil's house (I 39ff.), and this triggers a debate between the Anunna-gods, who gather in assembly:

> I 99   (Enlil) sent and they brought Anu down to him,
> 100   They brought Enki before him.
>   Anu, king of [hea]ven, was present,
>   The king of the depths, Enki, was [ ].
>   With the great Anunna-gods present,
>   Enlil arose, the debate [was underway].
> 105   Enlil made ready to speak,
>   And said to the great [gods],
>   "Against me would they be [trying this]?
>   "Shall I make battle [against my own offspring]?
>   "What did I see with my very own eyes?
> 110   "Battle ran right up to my gate!"
>   Anu made ready to speak,
>   And said to the warrior Enlil,

---

although, as Hoffner (1998a: 79, n. 54) points out, the Sumerogram is used for the Hittite word only in New Hittite, and we are still lacking a phonetic complement marking the nominative case. The Hurrian side has preserved only *ene* 'god' (*KBo* 32.15 i 12′), in the absolutive case, which shows that the noun can only be the subject of an intransitive sentence or the object of a transitive one. Hoffner and Wilhelm both prefer the latter interpretation. Wilhelm (1997: 280) takes *ene* with what goes before and transliterates the three signs on the Hittite side as DINGIR.UŠ-*un*, an accusative form, calling the sequence "unklar." The *CHD* (P: 62) follows a similar tack: "We will release him, the ^{d}UŠ, from depravation [*sic*]," and Hoffner (1998a: 75) translates the phrase as, "We will bring him back from dire need, (namely) the ... god."

[7] *Inūma ilū awīlum* (translit. W. G. Lambert and Millard 1969: 42). However, the grammar of the Akkadian line is difficult. For example, the seemingly nominative *awīlum* can be read as a locative with comparative meaning (W. G. Lambert and Millard 1969: 147). See the discussion in Foster (2005: 229, n. 1), and see Alster (2002) for a rich discussion of the opening line of *Atrahasis*.

[8] *KBo* 32.14 iii 1.

[9] They are the Anunnaki; in Mesopotamian thought they were not clearly the earlier generation of gods that they were among the Hittites.

> "The reason why the Igigi-gods
> "Surrounded(?) your gate,
> 115 "Let Nusku go out, [let him learn their cause],
> "[Let him take] to [your] so[ns]
> "[Your great] command."
> Enlil made ready to speak,
> And said to the [courtier Nusku],
> 120 "Nusku, open [your gate],
> "Take your weapons, [go out to the group].
> "In the group of [all the gods]
> "Bow down, stand up, [and repeat to them] our [command]:
> ..."[10]

Nusku conveys the question to the Igigi-gods and then their response back to Enlil:

> "'Our forced labor [was heavy], the misery too much!
> '[Now, every] one of us gods
> 'Has resolved [on a battle] with Enlil.'"
> When he heard that speech,
> Enlil's tears flowed down,[11]

As in the *Song of Release*, an urgent problem is discussed before an assembly and a message is brought back: the Igigi-gods feel cruelly oppressed and demand to be released from the excessive labor imposed upon them by the Anunna-gods. However, in *Atrahasis* the attack triggers the debate, while in the *Song of Release* the result of the debate seems to trigger the attack. In *Atrahasis* Enlil's response to the news that his house is under siege is exactly what Meki's was when he heard the unwelcome words of Zazalla: tears. Unlike the assembly of Ebla, the assembly of the gods decides to take effective action to resolve the situation, deciding that the Anunna-gods must kill one of their own as a scapegoat and thus create man to relieve the Igigi-gods of their labor. "The great Anunna-gods, who administer destinies,/ Answered 'Yes!' in the assembly."[12] Thus, the Igigi-gods, freed from forced labor, call off the attack. In contrast with the *Song of Release*, Zazalla refuses to free the servants who do his menial labor, and as a result the attack threatened by the Storm-god is carried out, with disastrous consequences for Ebla.

---

[10] A I 99–123 (trans. Foster 2005: 232–3). [11] A I 163–7 (trans. Foster 2005: 243).
[12] A I 218–19 (trans. Foster 2005: 236).

In a thousand years or so, the gods are faced with a new problem, overcrowding by humans.[13] They first decide to reduce the population with disease. Atrahasis, however, is aided by the advice of the Prometheus-like trickster Enki, who tells him to withhold offerings to his own gods and goddesses, and instead to ply Namtar ('fate') with gifts so that he might be persuaded to stay the plague he has sent. Like the Anunna-gods, Atrahasis' assembly is easy to persuade. They turn to the new god Namtar, honoring him lavishly at the expense of their old gods.[14] Just as in the *Song of Release* the Storm-god is portrayed as dependent on man for his sustenance, after the flood when Atrahasis is able to offer sacrifice again, the gods gather around the food like greedy flies, hungry after a long fast, a truly cynical image of the exalted gods![15] In the *Song of Release*, on the other hand, Zazalla refuses to be persuaded and carries the day. While he offers to honor the Storm-god lavishly if it proves necessary, he will not comply with the god's express wish to free the captives, since it impinges on Zazalla's life of ease. In all three cases, the decision made is self-serving. In *Atrahasis* the gods manage to avoid doing the manual labor necessary to support themselves by creating humans, while Atrahasis' people choose to direct their sacrifices to a new god, casting aside their old gods to save themselves. Zazalla's selfish decision, however, brings on the destruction of his city.

The *Song of Release* utilizes many of the narrative sequences found in *Atrahasis*: one set of beings oppressing another with coerced labor, decisions reached in assembly, and interaction between a leader of the people and his god, although the themes and motifs are presented in quite a different light, fitting with Hittite concerns. In the Akkadian text, the oppressors are gods who decide to free another set of gods only because they can create a new set of human slaves to replace them, while in the *Song of Release* a conquering city exploits a conquered one. Although in both *Atrahasis* and the *Song of Release* a human has an especially close connection to a god, the relationship between god and human is portrayed differently in each narrative. In *Atrahasis*, the eponymous hero is wholly supported by Enki, who shows him how to survive the punishment of the gods so that the human race may continue; in the *Song of Release*, while Meki does seem to have a special relationship with the Storm-god, since he conveys his message to the assembly and then presents before him

---

[13] Compare the opening of the Homeric *Cypria*; see Burkert (1992: 100–4) and Chapter 12, 327.
[14] A I 364–412 (trans. Foster 2005: 239–40).   [15] A III iv 16–v 35 (trans. Foster 2005: 251).

the results of the decision taken by the Eblaite assembly, he is still unable to protect his city against the god's wrath.

The assembly scene of the *Song of Release* and the *Iliad*

So much for the similarities and differences between the assembly scene in the *Song of Release* and its predecessors in the Near Eastern narrative tradition. The Greek tradition about the Trojan War also shows a remarkable affinity to the *Song of Release*, both at the level of the overall plot, of a city destroyed because its assembly refuses to release the captive Helen,[16] and in the scenes from *Iliad* 1 depicting the conflict in assembly between Achilles and Agamemnon over the captive Chryseis, which triggers the withdrawal of Achilles from the battlefield, thus setting the plot in motion. Helen's abduction in fact merges a Greco-Aryan epic storyline of retrieving an abducted wife, also found in the two Sanskrit epics *Mahabharata* and *Ramayana*, with a Near Eastern epic storyline about the release of captives,[17] while Chryseis also combines the two storylines, but with more emphasis on the fact that she is a war captive from another city.

The opening scenario contains the plot of the fall of Troy in miniature. Chryseis' father arrives in the Achaean camp, dressed in his priestly garb, and entreats:[18]

> (1.17–21) "Sons of Atreus, and the other well-greaved Achaeans, may the gods, who have Olympian abodes, grant that you sack Priam's city, and come home safely. May you free my own daughter, and take the payment, respecting the far-darting son of Zeus, Apollo."
>
> (22–32) Then all the other Achaeans approved of respecting the priest and accepting the payment; but it did not please the son of Atreus, Agamemnon; he sent him away badly, and laid on him this heavy command, "Let me not meet you, old man, by the hollow ships, either lingering now or coming back again in the future, lest your staff and fillet of god fail to protect

---

[16] The Trojan assembly was bribed to vote against the release of Helen: *Il.* 3.204, 11.122–42; see Sale (1994: 65–80).
[17] See Jamison (1994) on the Greco-Aryan tradition. As Rinchindorji (2001) shows, marriage by abduction – usually positively portrayed – is also a major theme in Central Asian epic.
[18] For a more detailed discussion see Bachvarova (2005a). Also see M. L. West (1997a: 273–4, 348) for Near Eastern parallels to Chryses' speech calling on Apollo and reminding him of the services he has provided the god, and on the motif of Apollo's arrows sending the plague. Matthiae (2007; 2014) has also noticed the striking parallels with the *Iliad*. He further suggests comparing Ishhara in the *Song of Release* to Aphrodite in the *Iliad*. Both goddesses share a connection with Ishtar and are on the side of the sacked city.

you. I will not release her, rather old age will come upon her in my house in Argos, far from her fatherland, going back and forth before the loom and sharing my bed; but go, don't annoy me, so that you may go safer."

Chryses leaves in fear and grief and calls out to his god, "Listen to me, silver-bowed one, you who haunt Chryse and very holy Cilla, and rule Tenedos with strength, Smintheus, if I ever roofed over a shrine pleasing to you, or if ever I burned fatty thigh pieces of bulls and goats, grant my wish. May the Danaans pay for my tears with your weapons!"[19] Thus appealed to by his priest, Apollo causes the Achaeans as a whole to suffer for their leader's decision, as the Eblaites must when their assembly rejects the demand of the Storm-god.

These two events are linked in the two stories in opposing ways, however. In the *Iliad*, the god is appealed to successfully by the priest, who pointedly refers to his past services for the god, to punish those who insulted him by insulting his servant. In the *Song of Release*, the god is unsuccessfully appealed to by Meki not to punish those who insulted him. In the *Song of Release* Meki seems to serve as the Storm-god's messenger, conveying his words verbatim to the assembly, then returning to the god's presence with news of the decision taken by Zazalla. He seems to have the ear of the Storm-god, much as Atrahasis is the confidant of Enki. In the *Iliad*, when the priest of Apollo comes to plead his case, he does not serve as the god's representative, and only after the priest is rejected does Apollo become involved, at his request.

The plague, conceived of as the missiles of the god, devastates the Greek host for nine days, and finally another assembly is called to ferret out the source of impurity that has provoked this disaster at the hands of Apollo. Now Achilles attempts to address the situation in terms similar to those a Hittite or an Akkadian would use, wondering at first if Apollo feels slighted by the Greeks' neglect and requesting that omens be sought:

> (1.58–67) Standing up among them, swift-footed Achilles spoke, "Son of Atreus ... let us ask some seer or priest or dream-reader, for even dreams come from Zeus, who might say why Apollo is so angry, if perhaps he finds fault with a vow or hekatomb, if perhaps he wants, having partaken in the savor of sheep and perfect goats, to ward off the plague from us."[20]

---

[19] *Il.* 1.37–42.
[20] Compare *CTH* 373: *Kantuzzili's Prayer to the Sun-god* (translit. García-Trabazo 2002: 273–87; trans. Singer 2002b: 31–3), pleading with his god to reveal the source of his anger and protesting that he has served him faithfully, which is based on Mesopotamian hymns to the

The seer Calchas, at the instigation of Achilles, makes an attempt to divine the god's thoughts and states correctly that he is angered specifically over the captive Chryseis. Agamemnon then responds angrily to the suggestion in words very similar to those of Zazalla at Ebla:

> (1.131-9) "Don't in this way, noble though you may be, god-like Achilles, try to deceive with cleverness, since you will neither divert me nor persuade me. Do you indeed wish, while you yourself hold a prize, for me to sit here lacking one? Do you order me to give her back? But if the great-hearted Achaeans will give the prize, choosing according to wish, so that it will be compensation – if they don't give, I myself will choose either your prize or, going to Ajax, or Odysseus' I will take and lead away; he will be angered, whom I visit."

Zazalla similarly responds to the demand he let the captives go with a rhetorical question and demands in his turn that his opponent give up someone of his own instead:

> (*KBo* 32.15 ii 20′-21′) "... Does your mind rejoice inside you, Meki?[21]
>
> (ii 22′-25′) "First of all, your heart will not rejoice inside you, Meki, while, secondly, inside Purra, who is to be given back, his mind will <not> rejoice.[22]
>
> (ii 26′-29′) "In the case we let those ones go, who will give to us t[o] eat? They are cupbearers for us, and they give out to us. They are cooks for us, and they wash for us.
>
> (iii 1-4) "And, the thread which they spin is [thick] like the hair [of an ox.] But, if for you releasing [is desirable,] re[lease] your male and female servants!
>
> (iii 5-6) "Surrender your son! Send [...your] wife!"[23]

It is only natural that a dispute between two powerful antagonists would play itself out in such language, but even the premise of the Iliadic dispute is similar in many details to the situation in the *Song of Release*, as far as can be made out from the latter's frustratingly fragmentary remains. In both cases humans debate the release of war captives in acrimonious terms, and the unwise but powerful speaker prevails, while the other speaker is unable to carry his side, even though he has a better

---

Sun-god, and the Akkadian *Poem of the Righteous Sufferer* (trans. Foster 2005: 392-409). See Singer (2002b: 30-1). Also see the discussion in M. L. West (1997a: 124-8) on this motif.

[21] The Hittite version corresponds to a Hurrian negative.
[22] Hurr. i 22′-24′: "Secondly (the heart) of Purra is not pleased. We are not releasing the sons of Ikinkalis in goodness."
[23] *KBo* 32.15 ii 20′-iii 6, filled in with Hurrian side, i 20′-iv 6.

understanding of what the god demands and the danger of opposing him. A god is angered over the servant who is not freed, and the humans debate in assembly whether the god is in fact angered because of their neglect. The humans in possession of the servants argue that they cannot do without their services, and demand that their opponents do without their own helpers instead. However, Apollo's anger stems from the dishonor done to his priest rather than the fact that his own demand has been rebuffed.

In the end, Chryseis is in fact returned and Agamemnon directs that the girl Bryseis be taken from Achilles. Achilles then goes in tears to complain to his mother, the goddess Thetis, and she in turn goes to Zeus to ensure that Achilles is compensated for this insult. As in *Atrahasis*, a human with direct access to a divinity is able to convince the divinity to help, in stark contrast with Meki's inability to protect his city. Thus the narrative of the *Iliad* is set on its course with this double enactment of a debate over freeing a prisoner and compensation for her. While it was difficult for the Achaean elders to persuade Agamemnon, since he was the one who had to give up something in order to please Apollo – who after all in the *Iliad* is not on the Achaean side – and in the *Song of Release* Meki is completely unable to win over Zazalla, in contrast in *Atrahasis* the elders quickly accept the suggestion of their leader and turn from their own gods to placate Namtar, who seems not to have an already established place of worship in the city. However, this decision costs them nothing. In the *Song of Release*, meanwhile, the Storm-god's anger, caused by the Eblaites' refusal to release the men of Ikinkalis, results not in a plague but in their city being sacked. So, in the *Iliad*, the problem of the god's anger had not already occurred before the assembly of Achaeans was called, but, as in the opening of *Atrahasis*, is imminent, "at the gates," as Enlil puts it. In *Atrahasis*, the siege and the plague are in two separate episodes and managed successfully each time, but in the *Iliad* the siege is ongoing, and the plague and the further setbacks when Achilles withdraws from the field are episodes punctuating the eventually successful siege after which Helen is retrieved.

The hospitality scene of the *Song of Release* in its eastern Mediterranean context

The hospitality scene in the *Song of Release* has close parallels both with Homeric hospitality scenes involving humans, especially in the *Odyssey*, and with scenes in Ugaritic narrative poems involving gods alone and gods with men.[24]

Among the frequent hospitality and feasting scenes in the Ugaritic material, I give the example that is closest to the scenes I discuss from the *Song of Release* and the *Iliad*, the celebration of Baal's victory over Yam:

> i 2   Radaman served Vali[ant] Baal;
>   he waited on the Prince, Lord of Earth.
>
>   He arose and served,
>   5   and gave him to eat:
>
>   he carved a breast in his presence,
>   with a jaw-shaped knife fillets of fatling.
>
>   He busied himself and poured,
>   and gave him to drink:
>
> 10   he put a cup in his hands,
>   a goblet in both his hands –
>
>   a great chalice, mighty to behold,
>   a drinking-vessel of the inhabitants of heaven,
>
>   a holy cup, which women might not see,[25]
> 15   a goblet which (even) a wife could not look upon.
>
>   A thousand measures it took from the winevat,
>   ten thousand (draughts) it took from the barrel.
>
>   He arose, intoned and sang,
>   The cymbals in the minstrel's hands: ...[26]

The opening of this passage is missing, so it is unclear whether more of the motifs from the feast of Allani appeared here, like the chair and footstool which the visitor uses, but it can be seen that the host hurries to serve the guest personally. The vast measurements found here are applied to the size

---

[24] There is an extensive secondary literature on hospitality and feasting scenes in Homer (see Reece 1993); Lloyd (1990) discusses them in Ugaritic narratives; M. L. West (1997a: 179, 201–3) has further discussed the themes of hospitality and feasting in Greek and Canaanite narrative poetry. Also see references in Chapter 5, 127, n. 64.

[25] Or: "A goblet Athirat may not eye" (trans. S. B. Parker in S. B. Parker 1997: 106, with n. 35).

[26] *Baal Cycle*: KTU 1.3 i 2–19 (trans. N. Wyatt 2002: 70–1). Other examples of feasting in Ugaritic: *Keret*: KTU 1.15 iv 1 – vi 8 (funeral feast for Keret, trans. N. Wyatt 2002: 214–19); *Aqhat*: KTU 1.17 v 14–31 (Danel welcomes Kothar-and-Hasis, trans. N. Wyatt 2002: 268–9).

of the cup which is special in other ways too, like Allani's, while in the *Song of Release* it applies to the number of animals slaughtered for the feast.[27]

Hospitality scenes are frequent in Greek epic, the most famous hospitality scene in the *Iliad* being the embassy to Achilles by Odysseus, Ajax, and Phoenix in Book 9. Its function within the narrative offers telling parallels to Hurro-Hittite hospitality scenes. When the three arrive at Achilles' tent, Achilles greets them, brings them in, and seats them "on couches with purple coverings."

> (9.201–4) And right away he called to Patroclus who was inside, "Set out a bigger bowl, son of Menoitios, and mix (the wine) stronger, and get ready a cup for each; for men who are most dear to me come into my house."
>
> (205–19) So he spoke, and Patroclus obeyed his dear companion. Right away he threw down a great meat-tray in the light of the fire, and then he put on it the back of a sheep and of a fatty goat, and on it the chine of a fatty pig, rich with lard. Automedon held it for him and then shining Achilles cut it up. . . . Patroclus, taking the bread, laid it out on the table in beautiful baskets, then Achilles served the meat. He himself sat across from godlike Odysseus at the opposite wall.[28]

As in both the Ugaritic and Hurro-Hittite examples, the guest is seated on a regal seat, the host serves the guest personally, and the food mentioned is meat, bread, and wine. The guests come upon Achilles playing his lyre and "singing the glories of men" (9.189), a self-referential moment showing Achilles' obsession with glory and his self-imposed idleness. This is a variation of the usual sequence of events, in which song follows the meal, as in the example from the Ugaritic *Baal Cycle*, a scene of joyous celebration after Baal's triumph over Yam, and in Odysseus' extended fantastic tale of his adventures at the feast of the Phaeacians.

However, in the *Iliad* the purpose of the hospitality scene is not to provide an occasion for joyous celebration, but to provide an opportunity to solve the problem presented by Achilles' withdrawal from the battlefield.[29] As I have already shown, the pattern of a problem presented

---

[27] Other Ugaritic passages supply the image of putting one's feet up on a footstool, applied to El receiving Anat (*Baal Cycle*: *KTU* 1.4 iv 29, trans. N. Wyatt 2002: 99), and Danel getting good news (*Aqhat*: *KTU* 1.17 ii 11, trans. N. Wyatt 2002: 263). N. Wyatt (2002: 263, n. 55 with earlier refs.) points out that this is a gesture confined to kings and gods. Further, as Reece (1993: 21) mentions, in Homeric epic, the "most elaborate expression for seating" includes the footstool on which the guest's feet rest.

[28] *Il.* 9.185–219.

[29] Foley (1999: 171–87) examines Homeric feast scenes from a similar angle, arguing the feast "betokens *a ritualistic event leading from an obvious and pre-existing problem to an effort at mediation of that problem*" (174, emphasis in the original). The banquet on Olympus in the *Iliad*, with Hephaestus as cupbearer, also has a parallel with the scene in *KBo* 32.13, the rightwards

to one's host after dining and drinking is found repeatedly in the Hurro-Hittite songs, making it possible to postulate that the purpose of the Storm-god's visit to the goddess of the underworld in the *Song of Release* is to discuss the problem posed by the Eblaites' exploitation of the captives of Ikinkalis. The embassy to Achilles varies this traditional pattern when the mission of Odysseus and his companions fails to resolve the problem.

The messenger scene in the *Song of Release* in its eastern Mediterranean context

In the messenger scene of the *Song of Release* the Storm-god, roused from bed by a messenger, talks with his brother Suwaliyat, and sends him to Ebla to talk to Ishhara. Although messenger scenes are common enough in eastern Mediterranean epic,[30] the best comparandum to the sequence of being wakened for a message comes from *Atrahasis*, and like the narrative sequence postulated above, the scene occurs early in the story, presenting Enlil with the problem of the rebellious Igigi-gods:

> 72   It was night, half-way through the watch,
>   Ekur was surrounded, but Enlil did not know!
>   . . .
>
> 76   Kalkal woke [Nusku],
>   And they listened to the clamor of [the Igigi-gods].
>   Nusku woke [his] lord,
>   He got [him] out of bed,
>   "My lord, [your] house is surrounded,
>   . . . "[31]

---

circling of Hephaestus as he pours the wine (*Il.* 1.595–8), just as the gods are seated in order moving rightwards in the *Song of Release*. Similarly, in the *Baal Cycle*: *KTU* 1.4 v 46–7, the guest sits to the right of the host (trans. N. Wyatt 2002: 103; discussion in Lloyd 1990: 182).

[30] On messenger scenes, see M. L. West (1997a: 190–3, 229) and McNeill (1963: 241). In other Near Eastern epics, it is common for a hero to wake from a puzzling dream and seek an interpretation of it and advice on a course of action. This inverts elements of the scenes we are discussing here. Rather than being awakened with a message, the hero wakes having been given a message. Both Gilgamesh (SB I 245–300, trans. George 2003: 553–7) and the hunter Keshshi (*CTH* 361.I.1.A = *KBo* 57.15 + *KUB* 33.121 + 36.62, 2.A = *KUB* 17.1 iii, trans. M. Bachvarova in Chavalas 2013: 286–7) wake and ask their mother for an explanation of their dreams as a prophecy for the future. An early example of a dream motivating future action is in the Sumerian *Gudea Cylinder A* (trans. ETCSL t.2.1.7). For this motif also see M. L. West (1997a: 185–90).

[31] I 72–80 (trans. Foster 2005: 232).

Enlil, terrified at the news, follows Nusku's suggestion to convene an assembly, in which the gods decide to send out Nusku to learn what grievance had compelled the Igigi-gods to lay siege to his house.

Compare also the sequence of one god waking, then awakening another god, then the convening of an assembly, to *Iliad* 10.1–179. While the scenes from the *Song of Release* and *Atrahasis* come from the life of the gods, in the *Iliad* this same sequence applies to the human realm and is multiplied as a series of repeated motifs. (I quote only the first episode in the sequence.) As Book 10 opens, Agamemnon paces restlessly during the night, pondering what he can do to turn the tide away from a Trojan victory. He first searches out his brother Menelaus and is pleased to find him awake too. They then decide to go to awaken other leaders of the Greeks so they can convene and discuss the matter:

> (10.137–42) First then Gerenian Nestor the horseman roused from sleep Odysseus, matching Zeus in his intelligence, calling him; swiftly the cry entered his mind, and he came out of his tent and spoke a word to them, "Why do you wander in this way alone through the army, along the ships, in the ambrosial night? Has so great a need come?"
>
> (143–7) Then Gerenian Nestor the horseman answered him, "Odysseus, descendant of Zeus, son of Laertes, many-wiled, don't be angry; for such a pain has come upon the Achaeans. But come with us, so that we can wake yet another, to whom it is appropriate to give counsel, on whether we should flee or fight."
>
> (148–50) Thus he spoke, and wily Odysseus, going into his tent, put an elaborate shield across his shoulders, and went with them. They went to Diomedes, son of Tydeus . . .

When compared to the examples from *Atrahasis* and the *Song of Release*, this scene reveals itself as an elaborate version of a traditional narrative sequence, otherwise unattested in the Greek epic tradition.

Conclusion

I have offered here some preliminary conclusions on the structure of the *Song of Release* and how it fits into the larger picture of Near Eastern epic. Various branches of Near Eastern tradition can be picked out, with the Hurrian branch probably in contact with the Ugaritic branch in north

Syria, while Hurrian bards definitely drew upon the Akkadian tradition, itself built on an originally Sumerian tradition. We have evidence for transmission into Hittite of a sub-branch of the Hurrian tradition, and we may expect that the Hurrian tradition was also transmitted to Luwians in Cilicia, where there was intense contact between Luwian-speakers and Hurrian-speakers.[32]

A diachronic view of the tradition can also be gained, showing how later branches re-used traditional motifs appearing in earlier ones, moving closer to the form attested in Greek epic on the level of plots, motifs, and formulas as branches developed in locations closer to Greece. The Akkadian *Epic of Gilgamesh* itself borrows and reworks themes and motifs found in the earlier Sumerian literature. For example, it inverts the oppression by corvée labor theme found in *Gilgamesh and Akka*; it includes the flood story from a version of *Atrahasis*;[33] and it uses the creation of man sequence to introduce Enkidu.[34] In the same way, the Hurro-Hittite Kumarbi cycle re-uses elements of the succession of gods theme, but also adds new elements, ones later found in Hesiod's *Theogony* and in Phoenician texts.[35] The *Song of Release* re-uses many elements of *Atrahasis*, but moves most of them to the human sphere, most importantly the discussion in the assembly, creating a "Homeric" scene of two humans arguing before their assembly over the release of servants captured in war and the need for compensation.

Finally, we can draw some conclusions on the types of alterations that were carried out as poets reworked the inherited tradition to create new stories, or to present a traditional story to a new audience. As is well known, episodes can be expanded or compressed, or combined to make a new storyline. But, the variations discussed in this chapter also show us that a single theme or plot line is made up of a bundle of motifs, the realization of any one of which is always in tension with other possible realizations known to the audience. A plot line can end in success or in failure, as with the embassy scene in the *Iliad*. A character can be good or bad, even if s/he carries out the same function, as with the Achaeans attacking Troy in the *Iliad* when compared to the Igigi-gods in *Atrahasis*. I call this type of relationship between instantiations of motifs a "toggle switch": a meaning, role of a character, or a result is flipped to its opposite.

---

[32] Chapter 1, 10.   [33] Tigay (1982: 214–40).   [34] Tigay (1982: 192–7).
[35] See Chapter 2, 24–5, n. 14, for references on the parallels between Hesiod and the theogonies of the Phoenician Sanchuniathon and Pherecydes of Syros.

Having done a study of the formal parallels between the *Song of Release* and earlier Near Eastern texts, which presents internal evidence for the prehistory of its narrative tradition, I turn now to a study of the external evidence for its prehistory, examining more closely how and why the *Song of Release* arrived at Hattusa.

7 | The function and prehistory of the *Song of Release*

Introduction

In this chapter I discuss how the *Song of Release* could have been imported to Hattusa and its possible function there. The discussion of its background complements my discussion of the reception of the legends of the Akkadian emperors Sargon and Naram-Sin in the following chapter. Understanding the appeal of these two narrative traditions and the ways in which they made their way to Hattusa can help explain how the same narratives could move even farther west and eventually be absorbed into the Homeric tradition.

I begin by providing some background on royal ancestor veneration among the Hittites, and I discuss how it may have informed their understanding of the plot of the *Song of Release*. I then argue that when Teshshub of Aleppo was imported to Hattusa by Hattusili I, so was the *Song of Release*, because it was performed within the Storm-god's cult.

The *Song of Release* and royal ancestor veneration

In this section I explore the assembly scene in the light of royal ancestor veneration at Ebla and Hattusa. The interpretation I offer here elucidates the performance setting and the Hittite audience's response to the song, which in turn leads to a better understanding of possible mechanisms of transmission.

Royal mortuary cult was a common enough phenomenon in the ancient Near East, one with which nearly any Middle or Late Bronze Age audience would have been familiar, for throughout the Near East kings sought the legitimizing support of their dead predecessors. This concern was particularly overt in a royal funeral, but in addition there was a constant cycle of meals and other offerings to assure them they were not forgotten. The parallels between third-millennium Eblaite and second-millennium Ugaritic practices of feeding the royal dead show that there was a common north Syrian practice going back to the Middle Bronze Age, which was analogous, but not necessarily identical, to the Mesopotamian practice of *kispum*, making offerings of food and drink to statues or statuettes of ancestors.[1]

At Ebla, architectural remains indicate that large-scale banquets were held for the royal dead, who were present in the form of statuettes tucked into cellae with altars for offerings. Lists of offerings for royal ancestors parallel the list of kings provided in the *Song of Release*.[2] Besides lists of offerings performed at Ebla, offerings to royal dead made in a series of different towns were recorded in the descriptions of royal weddings. The fact that buildings associated with royal ancestor veneration, such as the É ma-tim ('house of the dead'), were dispersed in various towns throughout the core of the Eblaite kingdom[3] explains why in the *Song of Release* the people of Ikinkalis would be involved in the care of the dead kings of Ebla, cooking food and serving it, and making textiles. At Ebla, as at Ugarit, one building associated with ancestor cult was called the House of the Stars. If the dead kings of Ebla, as well as live kings, could receive the epithet "star," it is important that Zazalla calls Meki "star of Ebla," for the epithet could have hinted at his future role as honored royal ancestor, although a Hittite audience may not have been aware of the connotation.[4]

A variety of sources sheds light on the Hittite practices of royal ancestor veneration,[5] which was associated with several different types of buildings.

---

[1] Matthiae (1979: 567–8). Also see Vidal (2005). On royal ancestor veneration and *kispum* in Mesopotamia see Hallo (1992), Spronk (1986), and Tsukimoto (1985). For royal funerary cult at Ugarit see Levine and de Tarragon (1985) and del Olmo Lete (1999: 166–253). On veneration of ancestors among non-royal families in Ugarit, Emar, and Israel, see Schloen (2001: 342–7) and van der Toorn (1994; 1995). Legitimation of authority: see A. C. Cohen (2005: 43–4, 109–10) on ED offerings to royal predecessors, not just ancestors, which were continued across changes in dynasties, from which it may be inferred that "the cult of the dead predecessors played an important part in maintaining authority" (110). At Ugarit: *A Funerary Ritual in Poetic Form*: KTU 1.161 (translit. and trans. Pardee 2002: 85–8), invoking the *rapa'ūma* at the enthronement of Ammurapi. Whitley (1995: 44–6) provides a theoretically informed analysis of the relationship between cult of the dead and "control over crucial resources."

[2] On the king list in the *Song of Release* see Chapter 5, 119; on royal ancestor veneration at Ebla see Archi (1986; 1988; 2001a; 2007a: 49), connecting it to Hittite and north Syrian practices, Guardata (1995), Haas (1994: 238–9), Matthiae (1979; 1990: 348–54; 1997), and Oesch (1996: 46–7). On the royal ancestor lists, see especially Archi (2001a) and Bonechi (2001). Similar lists are found at Ugarit. One Ugaritic king list was found in the House of the Hurrian Priest: *Rites Involving the Royal Shades of the Dead*: KTU 1.113 (translit. and trans. Pardee 2002: 195–202). Also see discussion by Vidal (2000; 2006).

[3] See most recently Vidal (2005).

[4] See Taracha (2000: 200). The epithet "star of Ebla" was used as a royal title in north Syria during the nineteenth century BCE (Archi 2001b), and "star" was used as a laudatory term for kings in other parts of the Near East (Michalowski 2003). Del Olmo Lete (1999: 205–6) argues for the astral associations of dead kings at Ugarit.

[5] See Archi (2007a), Gonnet (1995), Haas (1994: 243–8, 804–6), Kümmel (1967: 15–16), Otten (1958b: 110–15), Singer (2009), and Taracha (2000: 192–202) on royal ancestor cult at Hattusa.

It was a crucial element in the state-sponsored festivals originating from Hattusa, and it was carried out in locations inside and outside of Hattusa. For example, in the spring AN.TAḪŠUM festival, offerings were made to a statue of Hattusili I,[6] and in the fall *nuntarriyašḫaš* festival offerings were made at the House of the Grandfathers[7] and at the *ḫešti*-house, a place in the capital's citadel Büyükkale associated with the underworld gods, especially the underworld goddess Lelwani,[8] Ugarit also provides documentation for feeding of royal ancestors, parading their statues, and fêting them with music and song in festival settings.[9]

At Hattusa, the recipients included the most important early kings: Hattusili I, Mursili I, Tudhaliya I/II, and Suppiluliuma I.[10] These lists of offerings to the kings and royalty of the Old Kingdom, an invaluable source

---

[6] *AN.TAḪŠUM Festival, Sixteenth Day: Temple of Ziparwa, Sungoddess of the Earth*: CTH 612.b. A = KBo 4.9 iii 11–12 (translit. and trans. Badalì, Zinko and Ofitsch 1994: 32–3); also see Zinko (1987: 33).

[7] On the House of the Grandfathers see Kapelus (2007); on rites there in the *nuntarriyašḫaš* festival see Nakamura (2002: 83–4).

[8] Nakamura (2002: 120). In the AN.TAḪŠUM festival the dead year was laid to rest in the *ḫešti*-house: *AN.TAḪŠUM Festival, Eleventh Day*: CTH 609.3 = IBoT 2.1 vi 8′–14′ (translit. Haas and Wäfler 1976: 71–2), *AN.TAḪŠUM Festival, Outline Tablet*: CTH 604.A = KBo 10.20 ii 11–13 (the eleventh day, translit. and trans. Güterbock 1960: 92, 96). See discussion of Haas and Wegner (1992: 246–50). On the *ḫešti*-house see Groddek (2001), Haas and Wäfler (1976; 1977), Popko (2003b: 317–18), Singer (2009: 170), Taracha (2009: 49–50), Torri (1999: 5–33), and Zinko (1987: 28–9). The KI.LAM harvest festival included a visit to the Stone House and the *ḫešti*-house. On the *ḫešti*-house in the KI.LAM festival see Singer (1983: 112–15). A catalog mentions two different tablets about the "Festival for the *ḫešti*-house" directly after four different tablets having to do with the KI.LAM festival (*Tablet Catalog, x DUB UMMA/mān Type*: CTH 278.1 = KUB 30.68 ii 3″–9″, translit. and trans. Dardano 2006: 194–5). Similarly *Various Tablet Catalogs*: CTH 282.22 = KBo 31.31 (translit. Dardano 2006: 268). The *purulli* festival (a New Year's festival) could be celebrated in the *ḫešti*-house (*Purulli Festival*: CTH 674.1 = IBoT 2.17 2′–5′, translit. Haas and Wäfler 1976: 74; discussion Haas and Wäfler 1977: 95). See Chapter 10, 253, with n. 148; also Torri (1999: 7).

[9] Bonatz (2000a: 133–5), Niehr (2006b: 7–13; 2007), Struble and Rimmer Hermann (2009). Evidence for veneration of royal ancestors in a festival context is not as clear as at Hattusa, despite Spronk's claim (1986: 155, 195) that the *rapaūma* were invoked during the Ugaritic New Year's festival; see review by M. S. Smith and Bloch-Smith (1988) and del Olmo Lete (1999: 26, 39). In the month of H[iyaru] the divinized royal ancestors are included among the gods who receive offerings (*Ritual for a Single Month*: KTU 1.112, translit. and trans. Pardee 2002: 36–8); see del Olmo Lete (1999: 232–46), suggesting that statues of the deified dead were ritually transported with those of the gods. He argues further that the *Rituals for Two Months*: KTU 1.105 (translit. and trans. Pardee 2002: 41–3) involved funerary offerings in the month of Hiyaru (del Olmo Lete 1999: 247–53). In other texts they were called to participate in feasting with music. In one case the kings are referred to generally; in another the kings are specifically listed (*A Divine Drinking Rite and Blessing*: KTU 1.108, *Rites Involving the Royal Shades of the Dead*: KTU 1.113, translit. and trans. Pardee 2002: 192–210).

[10] CTH 660: *Offerings for Royal Statues*, some texts of which are edited by Groddek (2004b: 112–26), and *King Lists*, one of which is edited and translated in Nakamura (2002: 268–75, CTH 661.5 = KUB 11.8 + 9). A more complete edition of the texts and an early discussion were published by Otten (1951). In a ceremony enacted by the Hittite queen, six dead queens were

for early Hittite history, were maintained because invoking the names of the dead was a central act of commemoration, as it was in Mesopotamian *kispum* rites.[11] Statues of deified dead kings received offerings in the Storm-god's temple, indicating that there was a connection between the Storm-god, symbol of kingly power, and royal ancestor veneration, and that the Hittite audience would consider the intervention of the Storm-god on behalf of the dead kings in the *Song of Release* appropriate.[12]

The natural stone features of Yazılıkaya, situated within walking distance of Hattusa (see Map 3), were turned into a grand space for the mortuary cult of Tudhaliya IV and for the celebration of festivals. Thus, Yazılıkaya allows us to imagine one way in which ancestor veneration was carried out in a festival context. Here the living rock walls of the main chamber were carved with reliefs of the Hurro-Hittite gods processing towards one end, while the twelve Anunnaki-gods (Former Gods) appeared in a group on their own wall.[13] The side chamber, Chamber B, depicts the deified Tudhaliya in the embrace of his god, Sharruma, along with the underworld god Nergal in the form of a sword. The niche would have contained his cremated remains. This must have been Tudhaliya's Stone House (É.NA$_4$) or mausoleum.[14] The base of a monumental statue of Tudhaliya IV remains.[15]

While no Hittite royal cemeteries contemporaneous with the thirteenth-century descriptions of funerary rituals have been found, within Hattusa a few

---

given offerings and called the Sun-goddess of Arinna, that is, equated with the queen of the underworld (Nakamura 2002: 90).

[11] Finkelstein (1966: 114–16). On *kispum* see further Chapter 8, 186, n. 90.

[12] The copies of *CTH* 660 that provide us with the information about the location of the statues in the temple of the Storm-god by mentioning offerings to other divinities in the same location, are all New Hittite (Popko 2002: 77–8; Archi 2007a: 53). Only one shows evidence of an OH forerunner (*CTH* 660.9 = *KBo* 39.90, translit. Groddek 2004b: 120–1), but the remains of this particular tablet do not provide any information from which we can glean the setting. On statues of the dead, see further Chapter 8, 186, with n. 91.

[13] Singer (1986) has suggested that the main chamber represents the *ḫuwaši* (baetyl) of the Storm-god; others have suggested it was the site of the spring AN.TAḪŠUM festival: Otten (1956), referring to New Year's Festival: *CTH* 600 = *KUB* 36.97, which describes all the gods entering the house of Tarhun; also see Bittel (1975) and Seeher (2002: 124–54).

[14] Van den Hout (2002b: 77–80), based on the fact that É.NA$_4$ was where the actual remains were stored. Singer (1986: 251; 2009: 183–4) argues Room B is the ^{NA_4}*ḫekur*, while Tudhaliya's *ḫešti*-house was among the buildings in front of the rock monument, while Bonatz (2007a: 115–18) argues Room B is his ^{NA_4}*ḫekur*, but he does not speak of the *ḫešti*-house. The term ^{NA_4}*ḫekur* refers to the outward form of a monument for the dead and overlaps with the term É.NA$_4$. On the relationship and differences among the three structures, see Archi (2007a: 50–3), Singer (2009: 169–72) and van den Hout (2002b).

[15] See Bonatz (2007a: 116–17).

monuments used for mortuary ritual can be distinguished:[16] Tudhaliya's ^{NA_4}ḫekur SAG.UŠ 'eternal rocky peak', which his son Suppiluliuma boasts he has built, may be the rock outcropping Nişantepe at Hattusa, where a Hieroglyphic Luwian inscription telling of Suppiluliuma's deeds was inscribed;[17] the KASKAL.KUR ('road to the underworld') in the Südburg;[18] and several chambers in the Oberstadt: Houses A, B, and C, all associated with Temple 5, one of which bears a relief of a Tudhaliya (see Map 3).[19] In all, we get a sense of an all-pervading concern for care of the royal ancestors, one that literally shaped the landscape of Hattusa. The multiplicity of types of sites suggests that several different types of ancestor worship were being accommodated and used, that the Hittite practices had heterogeneous origins.

The edict of Arnuwanda and Ashmunikal (*ca.* 1400–1350 BCE) shows that towns outside of Hattusa were involved in royal ancestor worship,[20] and there is archaeological evidence of late New Kingdom regional ^{NA_4}ḫekurs at Sirkeli and Fraktın, with settlements to house their attendants.[21] In addition, mentions of *zawallis*, vengeful ghosts (of kings), in specific towns show that dead Hittite kings could be upset about neglect of their cult outside of Hattusa.[22] Thus, even if the requirement that the people of Ikinkalis care for the kings of Ebla was based on an Eblaite practice, a Hittite audience would have been able to understand why they would be expected to tend to the dead kings of their capital city.

Certainly the Hittite audience – in fact most Near Easterners – would have been aware that royal ancestors have the power to curse the

---

[16] The only cemetery in the environs of Hattusa is the non-royal burial ground Osmankayası (18th–14th cent.), where both cremation and inhumation were carried out, and there is evidence of animal sacrifice, libation, and broken vessels, all conforming to the Hittite descriptions of royal funerary rites in later periods. See Bittel *et al.* (1958) and Singer (2009: 174–5) for suggestions for the sites of royal ancestor veneration.

[17] *Inscription of Suppiluliuma II Concerning the Conquest of Alashiya*: CTH 121 = KBo 12.38 ii 17′–21′ (translit. Güterbock 1967: 193; trans. H. A. Hoffner, Jr. in Hallo and Younger 1997: 193), see Güterbock (1967: 197–8), van den Hout (2002b: 74–80) on Nişantepe and the Hieroglyphic Luwian version of *CTH* 121, arguing that it is the ḫekur of Tudhaliya IV. Singer (2009: 182–3) argues that it is more likely that it was for Suppiluliuma II.

[18] See Chapter 4, 90–1.

[19] See Bonatz (2007a: 119), Neve (1987: 64, 67–8), and H. Gonnet in Neve (1987: 70). It was either of Tudhaliya IV or of Tudhaliya I/II; see Singer (2009: 180, with earlier references).

[20] Discussed in Chapter 5, 124. On the mention of É.NA$_4$s for kings in towns other than Hattusa see van den Hout (2002b: 84–6). Singer (2009: 171–2) argues against the notion that "immediate members of the Hittite royal family would have been left permanently far from the central Stone House in Hattusa."

[21] See van den Hout (2002b: 90–1); and see Bonatz (2007a: 113–15) on the Fraktın relief as representing the dead royal pair Hattusili III and Puduhepa.

[22] Archi (1979: 88–92; 2001a: 5, n. 14).

inhabitants of a city from beyond the grave and to grant or withhold kingship, and that the success of the harvest depends on their good will.[23] Several Hittite purification rituals provide important context that explains how the Hittite audience would have conceptualized the dead kings' interest in the current king's welfare.[24] In the Middle Hittite *Ritual for the Sun-goddess of the Earth*, for example, performed in response to an inauspicious dream the king had in the House of the Grandfathers, the king presents the model substituting for him to (the statues of) his "grandfathers and grandmothers" and calls on them to intervene with the Sun-goddess of the Earth for him, asking that his sin be ignored.[25] In a New Hittite *Substitution Ritual for the King*, performed in response to an unpropitious lunar omen, the king (?) goes to the mound of the Moon-god as night falls to plead his case, taking the (statues of the) "[For]mer Kings," who seem to be expected to intercede for him in the underworld and to witness the transaction.[26] The king imagines the Sun-god to have put him into the hands of the underworld gods and the queen of the underworld Ereshkigal (Anatolian Lelwani), and asks that the human substitute he has prepared take his place.[27]

In the Hurro-Hittite *Ritual of Allaiturahhi*, where the "powerful kings" appear in an underworld setting in a historiola meant to present an example for a polluted patient who wishes to be cleansed and made

---

[23] Gonnet (1995: 192–5), Archi (1979; with comments of van den Hout 1998: 82–3). On the fourteenth day of the Hittite funerary rituals the participants in fact promise the deceased that he will be properly honored in ancestor cult and in turn express their expectation that he will ensure that his descendants control the throne: *Death Ritual: CTH* 450 = *KUB* 39.8 iii 29″–36″ (translit. and trans. Kassian, Korolëv and Sidel'tsev 2002: 572–5).

[24] One difficult example is *Mastigga's Ritual for Family Quarrel*, which addresses the impurity left behind after a politically motivated assassination or other untoward incident (Hutter 1991: 38). After sealing the impurity in an ox horn, the Old Woman says, "When the Former Kings come back, and they turn their attention to the law of the country, only then let this seal be moved'" (*CTH* 404.II.A = *KBo* 2.3 iv 26–31, translit. A. Mouton 2010ff. on KhT; translit. J. L. Miller 2004: 105). Hutter (1991: 38–9) argues that the Former Kings are the recent predecessors of the clients of the ritual, called to witness the ritual and to judge the merits of the political dispute as rulers who had been demonstrably successful. Beckman ("Mythologie. A. II. Bei den Hethitern," in *RlA* 8.571) associates these Former Kings with the Former Gods, differentiating them from "departed mortal rulers."

[25] *CTH* 448.4.1.b.A = *KUB* 42.94 iv? 15′–25′, with duplicates (translit. and trans. Taracha 2000: 50–3).

[26] *CTH* 419.A = *KUB* 24.5 + 9.13 obv. 6′ (translit. and trans. García Trabazo 2010: 32–3): [*karūil*]*iuš labarnaš*. Singer (2009: 174, n. 22) disputes the reconstruction, proposing [*tarpall*]*iuš labarnaš* '[substit]utes, kings', an unusual collocation.

[27] *CTH* 419.A = *KUB* 24.5 + 9.13 rev. 13–18 (translit. and trans. García Trabazo 2010: 44–5). The use of a human substitute indicates Babylonian influence (Taracha 2000: 220–1). On Lelwani see Torri (1999).

confident again, there is a close connection between the Storm-god and the Former Kings. It seems that they are expected to help the patient, probably a member of the royal house, and that the Storm-god, who is addressed directly by the practitioner, is meant to intercede with the "powerful kings" for the patient. In the historiola the underworld goddess Allani is described as giving a salve to the Storm-god to cure his sister Anzili in the underworld, and perhaps the Storm-god is expected to receive the cure from the "powerful kings" to release the royal patient from his fears.[28]

It thus seems highly likely that the purification ritual Meki engages in at the conclusion of the assembly episode would have been imagined by the Hittites to involve the dead kings, who have been angered by their mistreatment, and the singer's audience would not have been surprised that Meki's attempt to propitiate the Storm-god failed once the assembly had refused to release the people of Ikinkalis. In addition, given this context, when the audience heard that the council of Ebla refused Meki's request, passed on from the Storm-god, to ensure that the former kings get their due, they would have believed the council was in effect denying Meki's right to kingship.

The *Song of Release* made sense to a Hittite audience, then, and was not simply a piece of esoteric imported literature. It may be that the *Song of Release*, with its insistence on the proper performance of ancestor cult, found a place in royal ancestor veneration in the Middle Hittite period, when the *Song of Release* was deemed worthy of recording, perhaps during those sections of festivals that were focused on propitiating royal ancestors elsewhere. Many have suggested that narratives exalting the deeds of kings of yore were performed in rituals commemorating royal ancestors. Such a setting has been inferred for the *Epic of Gilgamesh* in the Middle Babylonian period,[29] and Jean-Marie Durand and Michaël Guichard have suggested that the *Great Revolt against Naram-Sin* and the *Eponym Chronicle* were recited during the *kispum* offering for Naram-Sin and Sargon at eighteenth-century Mari.[30]

---

[28] CTH 780.II.Tablet 6.A = *VBoT* 120 ii 5′–22′ (translit. Haas and Wegner 1988: 133–4, No. 19). The earliest versions are Middle Hittite. For the interpretation presented here see Bachvarova (2013a: 35–7).

[29] See Chapter 4, 80. In Chapter 4, 95–9, I discussed allusions to Hurro-Hittite narrative songs in rites meant to harness the supernatural powers of the dead to cure a patient.

[30] Durand and Guichard (1997: 43–4). Copies of both texts were found at Mari. On the Mari version of the *Great Revolt* see J. G. Westenholz (1997: 230–7). For the *Eponym Chronicle*, see trans. by Glassner (2004: 160–4). Also see Chapter 8, 187–91, on chronicles and king lists.

In Chapter 4 I discussed the possibility that bards could have performed in healing rituals invoking the dead, or that the ritual practitioners themselves were capable of performing episodes from epic. We can see that men classified as singers (^{LÚ}NAR) do play a role in the cyclical Hittite royal ancestor cult: In the *nuntarriyašḫaš* festival, a singer plays the large lyre (^{GIŠ} ^{d}INANNA GAL, *ḫunzinar*) and calls out the name of the king Labarna as the offerings are made.[31] In the Hittite royal funerary ritual, singers also play an extensive role, frequently performing on the large lyre; on some occasions a singer plays the harp (^{GIŠ}TIBULA) and calls the name of the deceased king.[32] Of course, different singers would have specialized in different types of songs, and there is no way to confirm or disprove that the singer who called on the deceased kings was also proficient in narrative song. Although no audience for the Hittite funerary rituals is ever mentioned, it can be assumed that the audience participated in the main meal of each day, along with the performers, and it was composed of a similar array of people to those who attended the *šalli aššeššar* ('Great Assembly') of a festival.[33] Whatever songs were performed then, this would have been an occasion at which they could be heard by a supralocal audience of administrative officials and diplomats.

The origin of Hurro-Hittite narrative song

I have so far discussed the implications of the theme of ancestor worship for the *Song of Release*'s Hittite audience. I now turn to how the role of the Storm-god, the appearance of war captives from Ikinkalis, and the setting in Ebla can help elucidate the prehistory of the text. The meter and formulary systems discussed in Chapter 2 that characterize Hurro-Hittite song show that the genre had a long prehistory of oral performance prior to its earliest appearance in written form and argue against the assumption that it arrived only in the Middle Hittite period, via the heavily

---

[31] *King Lists*: CTH 661.5 = KUB 11.8 + 9 iv 20′–5′ (translit. and trans. Nakamura 2002: 272–3).
[32] *Death Rituals*: CTH 450.1.7e.A = KUB 30.25 + KUB 39.4 rev. 19–20 (translit. and trans. Kassian, Korolëv and Sidel'tsev 2002: 330–1). See Schuol (2004: 103–4, 107) on the large lyre and harp in the death rituals. The Hittite term *ḫunzinar* comes from Hattic 'large lyre', cf. w. Sem. *kināru/ kinor* (Lawergren 1998: 58–9).
[33] On the need for an audience for funerary ritual, "in which individuals could materialize ideology, and in which social groups could thereby advance their interests," see A. C. Cohen (2005: 147–54; quote from 43). There is explicit evidence for diplomats at funerary rituals in eighteenth-century Mari (Sasson 2004: 197–9). On the Great Assembly see Chapter 10, 225.

Hurrianized region of Kizzuwatna, which was at that time firmly under Hittite sway, and when intermarriage of Hittites and Hurrians began to make Hurrian names common among the elite.[34] Further internal evidence allows us to make the argument that Hurro-Hittite song reached Hattusa in the Old Hittite period (perhaps at that point only in Hurrian).

Because the *Song of Release* refers to events and places significant in the Old Kingdom, Neu suggested that the transfer of the storyline to Hattusa occurred in the time of Hattusili I.[35] In the *Annals of Hattusili I*, the Old Hittite king boasts of conquering the town of Ikinkalis (Ikakali).[36] The only other time the town appears in a Hittite text outside of the *Song of Release* is in a tiny fragment, in which Mt. Hazzi also appears.[37] It is dangerous to draw far-reaching conclusions from such a small piece, but it is surely significant that the mountain that plays such an important role in the Kumarbi cycle and in festivals in which kingship in heaven and on earth was celebrated through Hurro-Hittite narrative song,[38] is linked to the town that plays such an important role in the *Song of Release*, which

---

[34] On the rise of Hurrian influence in the Middle Hittite period, see Hoffner (1998b: 175–84), Richter (2002: 297–9), and Wilhelm (1989: 20–30). Beal (2003: 17–21) argues that in the Old Hittite period there was a Hittite king with a Hurrian name PU-Sharruma, assuming Sharruma was a Hurrian god. In fact, Sharruma most likely originated as a Cilician god who was brought into the Hurro-Hittite pantheon as the son of Teshshub and Hebat (Schwemer 2001: 484–7; Haas 1994: 390–2, seeing him as a regional god; Trémouille 2006: 193–5, observing that there is no evidence to link the god specifically with an ethnic group). Wilhelm (2010a) in his edition of a recently discovered Hurrian omen text (CTH 774: *Hurrian Omens* = KBo 62.54) notes that the omen tradition arrived somewhat earlier and separately from the Kizzuwatnean influence. The omen text is designated OH in the KhT and is possibly in the same hand as OH *Hurrian Omens*: CTH 774 = KUB 8.47 (translit. de Martino 1992: 35–6, No. 6; see Wilhelm 2010a: 623–4). Given that a MH fragment of a *Moon Omen Compendium* is signed by a Hurrian scribe [K]uzi-Teshshub from Nuhashshe (CTH 533.8 = KUB 8.29 iv 1'–3', translit. and trans. Riemschneider 2004: 96–7), also named as the original author of a NH *Omen Compendium Concerning the "Presence"* (CTH 549.c.A = KBo 10.7, translit. and trans. Riemschneider 2004: 25–32; see Laroche 1970: 127), we may consider the Hurro-Hittite omen tradition to be imported directly from north Syria. In other words, we can see different paths for Hurrian influence, and one is clearly earlier than Middle Hittite. The *Song of Release* could belong to this strain of Hurrian influence.

[35] Neu (1995b: 15–16; 1996: 483).

[36] Hitt.: CTH 4.II.A = KBo 10.2 i 17–18 (translit. de Martino 2003: 36); Akk.: CTH 4.I.A = KBo 10.1 obv. 8 (translit. Devecchi 2005: 36; trans. G. Beckman in Chavalas 2006: 220). Wilhelm (2008: 193) suggests that Ikinkalis "has to be looked for south of the Antitaurus and west of the Euphrates."

[37] Only a few signs of three lines can be read: Hazzi appears in 1' and [Iki]nkal in 2' and 3' (CTH 832: *Hittite Fragments with Various Contents* = KBo 39.273, translit. Groddek 2004b: 335); see Haas (1994: 13, n. 42).

[38] See further Chapter 10, 258–60.

explores the topic of legitimate kingship through the negative example of Meki. Ebla itself is mentioned in a fragment of an Old Hittite historical text concerning the campaigns in north Syria, which mentions Urshu, Hassu, Aleppo, Zalpa(r) and Yarim-Lim III, king of Yamhad in north Syria.[39] The fact that the place names Ebla and Ikinkalis are found particularly in historical texts from the Old Kingdom supports the suggestion that the *Song of Release* was known in Hittite territory at this early date.

Finally, through comparison of a set of Old Hittite historical-admonitory texts, including the *Annals of Hattusili I*, *Testament of Hattusili I*, and the *Palace Chronicles*, with the parables associated with the *Song of Release*, I have shown that the Hurro-Hittite song makes use of phraseology, themes, images, and motifs already well established in the Old Kingdom, the literature of which was dominated by the persona of Hattusili, who left vividly phrased admonitory texts rich in animal imagery to preserve his wisdom (*ḫattātar*), insisting that his word be followed even after his death and describing the picturesque punishments that befell rebellious and corrupt subordinates. All of these themes and images are echoed in the *Song of Release*, both in the parables and in the episode in the Eblaite assembly.[40] It is difficult to explain this as pure coincidence. Again, at a minimum, it indicates that Hattusili's concerns and management tactics found confirmation in the *Song of Release*, and that even if the song was not specifically tailored to a Hittite audience, they would have found it perfectly comprehensible in light of their own values. We should also entertain the suggestion put forward by Paolo Matthiae that the song was in fact specially composed to celebrate Hattusili's achievements,[41] rather than reworked from an earlier version already extant, as I am suggesting. The *Song of Release* may bear the mark of the Middle Hittite political landscape in the reference to the region Nuhashshe in its opening lines, for it seems that the area around Ebla was only known by this name from the fifteenth century on,[42] but this mention could be explained as an adaptation to new circumstances that would be expected from a flexible oral tradition.

---

[39] *Res Gestae of Hattusili I*: *CTH* 14.III.B = *KBo* 12.13 + *KUB* 40.4 (translit. and trans. de Martino 2003: 104–9).

[40] *CTH* 6: *Testament of Hattusili I* (trans. Haas 2006: 59–65; P. Goedegebuure in Chavalas 2006: 222–8); *CTH* 8–9: *Palace Chronicles* (trans. Haas 2006: 54–9). See Bachvarova (2010). Neu (1995b: 17, 21), on the other hand, notes that the parables have similarities with MH instruction texts.

[41] See especially Matthiae (2007).

[42] *KBo* 32.11 i 9; noted by Archi (2002b: 24), and see Klengel (1992: 152) on Nuhashshe.

I propose that the introduction of the *Song of Release* to Hattusa was tied to the introduction of the cult of the Storm-god of Aleppo under Hattusili I. Although the evidence is frustratingly incomplete, we can build a partial picture of references to Ikinkalis, Ebla, and gods associated with Ebla in Hurrian and north Syrian rituals, suggesting that, like the Kumarbi cycle, the *Song of Release* was embedded in a Hurro-Hittite ritual complex that connected Hattusa to Ebla via Aleppo and other significant north Syrian landmarks, through imported cults and rites.

More generally, there is some reason to infer that Hurrian religious practices arrived in Hattusa earlier than the Middle Hittite period, in particular the worship of Teshshub of Aleppo, from the description Hattusili I gives of his exploits in eastern Anatolia and northern Syria in his *Annals*. In the *Annals* Hattusili boasts that he has taken the following gods from the east Anatolian town of Hassu and brought them to the temple of the goddess Mezzulla:[43] the Storm-god, lord of Mt. Armaruk; the Storm-god, lord of Aleppo; Mt. Adalur; and the goddesses Allatum, Liluri,[44] and Allanzu, "the young woman of Hebat."[45] A final item Hattusili includes among the booty are two silver bulls, corresponding to the pair of divine bulls who attend Teshshub.[46] Allatum is the same as the Hurrian underworld goddess Allani who welcomes the Storm-god to her abode in the *Song of Release*. Adalur is a mountain in the Amanus range,[47] and Armaruk is best identified with Mt. Armarik, modern Ğebel Seman. Armarik can be seen from Ebla and is in fact mentioned in the third-millennium archives of Ebla as a divinity entitled to offerings. There he is associated with a mountain god in the form of an eagle (Hurr. *ešuwan*), after which the Syrian (*ḫ*)*išuwa* festival is named, which was celebrated at Hattusa to legitimate the ruling Hurro-Hittite dynasty. In the festival Eshuwan received offerings in Allani's temple at Hattusa, next to Kura,

---

[43] Hitt.: *CTH* 4.II.A = *KBo* 10.2 ii 26–8, 38–40, filled in with B.c = *VBoT* 13 4′–6′, 14′ (translit. de Martino 2003: 54–60); Akk.: *CTH* 4.I.A = *KBo* 10.1 obv. 37–8, 43–4 (translit. Devecchi 2005: 46–8; trans. G. Beckman in Chavalas 2006: 221).

[44] On the north Syrian goddess Liluri see Haas (1994: 409–10, 854–5, 869–71).

[45] *Contra* trans. of G. Beckman in Chavalas (2006: 221); see the *šarrena* ritual = *Historical-Mythological Hurrian Texts*: *CTH* 775.D.1 = *KUB* 27.38 iii 8–9, discussed in Chapter 8, 182–7, where Allanzu is called ᵈ*Ḫebat=(v)e šiduri* 'young woman of Hebat'.

[46] On the divine bulls see Haas (1994: 319–20) and Schwemer (2001: 477–84).

[47] In texts from Hattusa Adalur is only mentioned in *Hattusili's Annals*. It is where the troops of Aleppo who had come to help defend Hassu were defeated (*CTH* 4.I.A = *KBo* 10.1 obv. 32–33, translit. Devecchi 2005: 44), not mentioned in the Hittite version, see trans. G. Beckman in Chavalas (2006: 220–1, with note 34). On its exact location see Wilhelm (1992: 29), although J. L. Miller (2001: 84–6) prefers "southern Kara Dağ ... between the Karasu and Afrin rivers" (85).

one of the chief gods of Ebla, and the Hurrian Fate-Goddesses.[48] Finally, Ebla appears with Aleppo in a fragment of a Hurrian ritual concerned with kingship, one of only two times Ebla is mentioned in Hittite texts outside of the *Song of Release*.[49]

These references give us hints that the *Song of Release* was embedded in a network of cult practices associated with Ebla that could be used to legitimate kingship, which reached eastern Anatolia and eventually Hattusa via the Hurrians.[50] Wilhelm observes:

> [The *Song of Release*] may have been handed down to subsequent generations by oral tradition for a long time. It is likely, however, that it forms a part of old traditions about earlier events in the lands south of the Anatolian plateau and the Taurus chain. . . .
>
> A good candidate for a Hurrian-speaking area where such traditions may have been preserved is the powerful and wealthy kingdom of Ḫaššum itself.[51]

I would reframe Wilhelm's hypothesis slightly by agreeing, first, that the song was traditional, but suggesting that what we have represents a version tailored to please a Hittite audience. It is not impossible that epic

---

[48] Haas (1981: 251–3); Wilhelm (1992). Mt. Armaruk is mentioned in a Hittite treaty as a landmark marking the border of Carchemish in the direction of Mukish: *Treaty between Suppiluliuma I and Sharri-kushuh of Carchemish*: CTH 50 = KUB 19.27 obv. 8' (translit. Haas 1981: 252). It is also referred to in the Hurrian *itkalzi* rituals: *Itkalzi Ritual*: CTH 777.4 = FHG 21 i 9 (translit. Haas 1984: 69, No. 6); *Fragments of Itkalzi Ritual Mentioning Tashmi-sharri and Taduhepa*: CTH 778 = KBo 33.8 ii? 4', 9' (translit. Haas 1984: 305, No. 65); also *Hurrian Fragments*: CTH 791 = KUB 45.73 6' (translit. Trémouille 2005: 29, No. 43). Armarik is also mentioned at Ebla in a spell against snakes along with Adarwan, "lord of the eagle" (Haas 1981: 253), another mountain god who may be connected to the mountain god in the form of an eagle for whom the (ḫ)išuwa festival was named. The festival was performed for the Storm-god of Mt. Manuzzi, whose Hurrian name was Eshuwan. Offerings to Eshuwan in the festival: *(Ḫ)išuwa Festival*: CTH 628.Tablet 5.C = KBo 7.45 + KBo 20.114 i 5'–6'. See the translit. and trans. of Wilhelm (1992: 26–7). Liluri, one of the deities captured by Hattusili I, was a chief honorand, while the Storm-god of Aleppo and his pair of bulls, Sherish and Hurri (or Tilla), were among the many gods to receive offerings. On the pair of steers honored in the (ḫ)išuwa festival, see Haas (1994: 319). On the (ḫ)išuwa festival see further Chapter 10, 258–61.

[49] *Fragments of Hurro-Hittite Rituals and Incantations*: CTH 790 = KUB 45.84 obv. 16', 18' (translit. Trémouille 2005: 40–1, with comments p. xix, No. 65, NH). It also mentions Lullubi, which appears in the *Song of Release* (see Chapter 5, 117, n. 21) and the Hurro-Hittite *šarrena* ritual, discussed in Chapter 8, 184. According to Wilhelm (2008: 192), the text mentions "the gods of the father" and heaven and earth, and is concerned with kingship (and queenship). Compare to the *šarrena* ritual for dead kings.

[50] Wilhelm (2008: 190) suggests that Hurrian names associated with Hassu, including that of its king Anumhirbi ('Hirbi pleased him'), indicate Hassu was Hurrianized in the Old Hittite period.

[51] Wilhelm (2008: 193). Note, however, that he speaks of the traditions as "written in Hurrian." Also see Wilhelm (1992: 31) on possible worship of north Syrian gods attested at Ebla in Hassu.

narratives about the destruction of Ebla were first spun in the third millennium after the conflagration that destroyed Tell Mardikh IIb1, for which both Sargon the Great and his grandson Naram-Sin are made to claim responsibility,[52] since the names of the two human protagonists who spar in the Eblaite assembly, the king Meki, "star of Ebla," and Zazalla, are steeped in Eblaitic tradition, and Ikinkalis (Agagalis) is mentioned in texts from Ebla.[53]

Of course, we cannot know what this earlier epic song about the fate of Ebla would have looked like, but I have shown that the Middle Hittite epic we have caters to the Hittite dynasty's strong interest in royal ancestor cult, and that its title echoes significant phraseology deployed by Hittite kings to proclaim their pious deeds towards the gods and dead. It could be that the song was originally composed by Hurrians at Ebla, since Matthiae reports the presence of Hurrian names in the few tablets that come from the city destroyed by the Old Hittite king.[54] I would further suggest that the earlier song was particularly connected with the cult of the Storm-god, and spread with the cult of the prestigious Storm-god of Aleppo (originally Haddad/Adad), who also was worshipped in third-millennium Ebla.[55] In Hattusa the Storm-god of Aleppo was firmly associated with Hurrian ritual. The syncretism of the Storm-god of Aleppo and Hurrian Teshshub of Kummi effected by the Hurrians allowed for the possibility for a Hurrian song to be developed about Teshshub of Kummi's participation in the fall of Ebla, one that mingled Mesopotamian, north Syrian, and Hurrian themes and

---

[52] See Chapter 8, 145–6.
[53] The name or title Meki comes from the west Semitic *melku* 'king', and appears in an inventory text of Drehem from the Ur III period (the year Amar-Sin 7) to designate the *ensi*, or ruler, of Ebla; on the Ibbit-Lim statue at Ebla as an epithet of Ibbit-Lim himself; as a title of the Eblaite king Ibbi-Damu, attested in a seal from Old Assyrian Kanesh, and in an unpublished letter from Mari referring to a king from an unknown area, who refused demands for metal from king Aplahanda of Carchemish, who is known to have corresponded with Yasmah-Addu of Mari (Astour 2002: 133–41, 148; Owen and Veenker 1987). Otten (1988b: 292, n. 17) has connected the name found in the letter to the Meki in this text, arguing that the events could be dated to the time of Shamshi-Adad (also Archi 2002b: 25–7). It is disputed whether the three mentions of Meki all refer to the same person or show that Meki was maintained as a traditional title for kings in Ebla and perhaps the surrounding area. On the name Meki at Ebla and in the *Song of Release* also see Neu (1996: 406–7), Pettinato (1991: 20–4, 183–4). On the significance of the term "star" see above, 150. On the appearance of Zazalla in the Ebla archive of Tell Mardikh IIb1 (*ca.* 2300 BCE) see Neu (1996: 480, with earlier references); Astour (2002: 149). For Agagalis at Ebla, see Pettinato (1991: 193).
[54] See Matthiae (2007: 10–11), citing communications by J.-J. Durand.
[55] Offerings were sent from Ebla to the Storm-god in Aleppo as well as made to him at Ebla. On the connections between Ebla and Aleppo see Archi (1999) and Matthiae (2003). For further details on the worship of the Storm-god of Aleppo at Ebla, see Chapter 10, 257.

formal features.[56] It can be objected that Teshshub of Aleppo should not be conflated with the "powerful lord of Kummi" who plays such an important role in the *Song of Release*, but such careful distinctions are not valid for a people who came to see "Teshshub of Aleppo of/in Hattusa" as their city god.[57] Certainly, Teshshub of Aleppo is equated with the Teshshub of Kummi born from the head of Kumarbi in a New Hittite Hurrian *Invocation of Teshshub of Aleppo* performed in an *itkalzi* ritual, which says, "Your father, An(i), engendered you, ... your mother Kumarbi bore you, for Aleppo, to the throne."[58]

Other evidence for early interaction of the relevant sort between Anatolians and Hurrians is the cult functionary ᴸᵁ*ḫalliyariš*, who is mentioned in festival descriptions particularly from the Old Hittite period, for Dennis Campbell suggests that the term could be built off the Hurrian root *ḫal-* 'sing' (cf. Hurr. *ḫalmi* 'song').[59] The ᴸᵁ*ḫalliyariš* always appears in a group and usually plays the lyre.[60] If this etymology is valid, then the ᴸᵁ·ᴹᴱˢ*ḫalliyareš* indicate that early Hittite contact with the supralocal musical culture of Syro-Mesopotamia was mediated by Hurrians.

It is probable that Hurrian-speaking attendants, indeed singers, accompanied the statues of Hurrian gods brought to Hattusa by Hattusili.[61]

---

[56] The name of the Storm-god is frequently hidden behind the Sumerograms ᵈU/10 or ᵈIŠKUR/IM, but the Storm-god of Aleppo was surely named Teshshub rather than bearing his west Semitic name Adad when he first arrived at Hattusa. There is no relevant evidence for Hurrian presence from Aleppo itself. There were numerous Hurrian names in nearby Alalakh ᵥɪɪ, part of the kingdom of Yamhad, of which Aleppo was the chief city (von Dassow 2008: 15–16, 70). It was attacked by Hattusili I on the same campaign as Ikinkalis (*Annals of Hattusili I: CTH* 4.ɪɪ.A = *KBo* 10.2 i 15–18, translit. de Martino 2003: 34, 36; trans. G. Beckman in Chavalas 2006: 220). The cult of the Storm-god in the Near East is fully discussed in the magisterial work of Schwemer (2001), with Schwemer (2007), and also by Haas (1994: 314–39). On the worship of the Hurrianized west Semitic Storm-god at Hattusa see Schwemer (2001: 494–502) and Bachvarova (2009: 34–5, with earlier references).

[57] *Liver Oracle*: *CTH* 570 = *KUB* 5.6 iv 9 (translit. and trans. Beckman, Bryce, and Cline 2011: 204–5); see Popko (2002: 74) and Schwemer (2001: 496). Taracha (2008) argues for the additional identification of Teshshub of Kummani with Teshshub of Aleppo.

[58] *Hurrian Fragments*: *CTH* 791 = *KUB* 47.78 i 12′–15′ (eds. Thiel and Wegner 1984: 189, 196–213; translit. Trémouille 2005: 9, No. 8, following the interpretation and translation of Wilhelm 2003: 394–5).

[59] *ḫal=iri* > *ḫal=(i)l* > *ḫall-*, cf. "active participle" formant *-iri* (D. R. M. Campbell, email communications, July 23 and 24, 2010).

[60] On the ᴸᵁ*ḫalliyari*-see Schuol (2004: 162), Klinger (1996: 752–3), suggesting a Hattic connection, and *HEG* (A–H: 131).

[61] One would expect that it would be standard procedure to take such valuable booty, as shown by complaints in the MH *Prayer of Arnuwanda I and Ashmunikal to the Sun-goddess of Arinna* that temple personnel, including the ᴸᵁNAR ('singer'), were captured and enslaved by the enemy (*CTH* 375.1A = *KUB* 17.21 ii 10′–11′, translit. von Schuler 1965: 154; trans. Singer 2002b: 41). See

Certainly gods expected the forms of worship to which they were accustomed.[62] A [LÚ]NAR performs Akkadian incantations and songs for the imported goddess Pirinkir; he must have been trained in her cult.[63] The festival of Istanuwa included Luwian "Songs of Thunder" for the Luwian Storm-god of the Vineyard.[64] At an earlier time in Kanesh a musician of the Storm-god is attested, and at contemporary Ugarit there are singers of Ashtarte and of the Moon-god.[65] Within the Hurrian cult at Hattusa there is mention of specific songs attached to particular gods.[66]

Of course, just because a king dragged off the statue of a foreign god, it does not follow that the god was integrated into state worship. However, the Old Hittite *Puhanu Chronicle* confirms that the Storm-god of Aleppo was in fact incorporated into the circle of gods whose worship was sanctioned by Old Hittite kings and in turn upheld their claims to kingship.[67] This text, which presents a series of dramatic vignettes with few obvious connections among them, remains difficult to interpret, but the Hittite campaigns into north Syria and against the Hurrians seem to be mythologized, and the Storm-god of Aleppo plays an important role in the action. In one scene a bull with a crumpled horn is described, which seems to be a statue belonging to the cult of Teshshub of Aleppo brought back as booty,[68] perhaps one of the very figurines Hattusili boasts of carrying off from Hassu. The damage suffered by the image is explained as the result of his efforts on behalf of the Hittites when they crossed the Taurus mountains on campaign to Syria. In the next section it is explained that at first the

---

Schuol (2004: 169). Koitabashi (1998: 365–7) shows that in Ugarit also, singers were attached to a temple.

[62] See further Bachvarova (2009: 36–7).
[63] *CTH* 644: *Fragments of Rituals Mentioning Pirinkir* (ed. Beckman 1999a).
[64] See Chapter 2, 21.   [65] Koitabashi (1998: 365–6).
[66] In the *Drink-Offerings for the Throne of Hebat*, "the singer ([LÚ]NAR) steps forward and sings the song of the god," and in a parallel passage, it is specified that the singer steps forward and sings the song of the Storm-god (*CTH* 701.d.4 = *KUB* 12.11 ii? 29′–31′, translit. Salvini and Wegner 1986: 306, No. 46; *CTH* 701.a$_1$.1.B = *KBo* 23.15 iii 17′–18′, translit. Badalì 1991: 191).
[67] *CTH* 16 (NS, with OH linguistic features), German trans. Haas (2006: 47–51); partial trans. H. A. Hoffner, Jr. in Hallo and Younger (1997: 184–5). See Gilan (2004a) for one recent transliteration, translation, and analysis, with references to earlier discussions. I follow much of his interpretation here. See Richter (2002: 306–10), Schwemer (2001: 494–5; 2008a: 153), and Singer (1994), all arguing for the early adoption of Teshshub of Aleppo in Hattusa. Most scholars have argued that Teshshub of Aleppo arrived at Hattusa at the beginning of the Empire period, for example Haas (1994: 553–4), J. L. Miller (2004: 461–2), and Popko (1998).
[68] Gilan (2004a: 278).

Storm-god of Aleppo ran from the Hittites, then he was brought over to "our" side because the Hittite king obeyed the command to worship him.[69]

Mysterious as this text is, one thing is certain: the fact that this text was created during the Old Kingdom and copied into the New Hittite period indicates that the introduction of the Storm-god of Aleppo occurred in the Old Kingdom and was considered exceedingly important. It makes most sense to suggest that the event corresponds to the event mentioned in *Annals of Hattusili I*. The spread of the worship of Teshshub of Aleppo throughout a large part of the Near East was motivated by his strong connection with kingship, and this must have been the reason for his incorporation into the Hittite pantheon at a very early period, during a time in which the Hittites were first attempting to define their position on the world stage.

Two phases can be distinguished, then, in the transmission of Hurro-Hittite song to the court of Hattusa. In both cases many of the texts in the performers' repertoire were informed in part specifically by the cult of Teshshub and more generally by the cult practices they brought with them. The *Song of Release* belongs to the earlier phase; it arrived with Hattusili I's importation of Teshshub of Aleppo and was thematically related to the king's activities in Syria. The second phase begins with the New Kingdom and the dynastic marriages with Kizzuwatna (Plain Cilicia), and it is connected to the importation of performers who took part in a set of festivals that supported an ideology of kingship, which will be discussed in a later chapter.[70] The second phase was also when it was decided to write down the songs, which had originally only been orally performed. Perhaps the *Song of Release* was written down when it started to be performed in the Hittite court to commemorate deeds from Old Kingdom times, perhaps in the context of venerating kings from that earlier era, so as to justify the current interest of Tudhaliya

---

[69] *CTH* 16.b.A = *KBo* 3.40 rev. 8'–11', with duplicate *CTH* 16.a.C = *KBo* 13.78 rev. 6'–10' (translit. and trans. Gilan 2004a: 268–70). Gilan (2004a: 274–6) sees a dispute between the Sun-goddess of Arinna, as leader of the Hittite army, and the Storm-god of Aleppo, in which the Hittite king, pregnantly referred to as the Sun-god (cf. the king's usual appellation "My Sun-god"), is opposed to the Storm-god of Aleppo. In one of the scenes a man complains that he is being mistreated and speaks of an adversary that has been led to Arinna (*CTH* 16.a.A = *KUB* 31.4 + *KBo* 3.41 obv. 1–14, translit. and trans. Gilan 2004a: 265, 267). The mention of Arinna calls to mind the Sun-goddess of Arinna, to whom the booty which Hattusili brought from Syria was dedicated.

[70] On importation of festivals see Chapter 10, 258–60.

I/II in north Syria by referring to the earlier exploits of his royal ancestors in the same region.[71]

Conclusion

I have argued that the tablets on which the *Song of Release* is preserved present to us an oral-derived text. Its purpose, to honor the Syrianized Hurrian Storm-god, Teshshub of Aleppo, explains why and how it came to Hattusa. In the later parts of this book I will continue to argue that importation and syncretization of gods motivated the transfer, reworking, and combining of storylines attached to them. In addition, the *Song of Release* gained meaning from its audience's knowledge of the practices of royal ancestor veneration and reinforced the need to commemorate the royal dead properly. The fact that the practices portrayed in the song, the actual practices attested from third-millennium Ebla, and those from second-millennium Hattusa were so similar is not irrelevant, for, as will be discussed in the following chapter, internationally recognized techniques of royal ancestor veneration were used by local courts to connect themselves to world history. And, knowledge of world history spread by means of the epics and legends found throughout the Near East that eventually reached Greece.

---

[71] It has been suggested that the *Song of Release* supported the ambitions of king Tudhaliya I/II "to repeat Mursili I's great deeds in upper Syria" (Matthiae 2006b: 85; also see Matthiae 2007: 20–1). On Tudhaliya's campaigns in Syria see Bryce (2005: 123, 140–1).

8 | Sargon the Great: from history to myth

> Sargon, king of the world, was victorious (in) 34 battles. He destroyed their (city) walls as far as the shore of the sea . He moored the ships of Meluḫḫa, Magan, and Tilmun at the quay of Agade. Sargon, the king, bowed down to the god Dagān in Tuttul. He (the god Dagān) gave to him (Sargon) the Upper Land: Mari, Iarmutti, and Ebla as far as the Cedar Forest and the Silver Mountains. 5,400 men daily eat in the presence of Sargon, the king to whom the god Enlil gave no rival. As for the one who destroys this inscription, may the god Anum destroy his name.
>
> *Sargon Inscription* 11.1–42[1]

Introduction

In this chapter I explore the reception and use of legends about the Akkadian conqueror Sargon the Great and his grandson Naram-Sin, both by the Hittites and by the Greeks. Just as the Hittite court narrativized historical events using Sargonic legend as a model,[2] a similar process occurred, I suggest, when the Homeric tradition later absorbed the storylines of Anatolian myths and legends to structure the Greek communal memory of their legendary past in Anatolia. Furthermore, the function of Sargonic legend for the Hittites may shed light on *why* Near Eastern mythico-historical narrative poetry ("epic") continued to spread farther west. When the Hittite court co-opted Sargonic legend, I will argue, it was able to link itself to the widely recognized world of Mesopotamia; Sargon also provided a role model for the first Hittite Great King, Hattusili I, and later kings of the Hittite empire.

The Hittites show they were well aware of the implications of the historiographic tradition, which on the one hand provided admonitory examples for

---

[1] Trans. Frayne (1993: 28–9).
[2] My discussion of the reception of Sargonic legend in Anatolia is based on the insightful studies of van de Mieroop (2000) and Beckman (2001b). Also see Bachvarova (2012a) for discussion of the reception of Sargonic myth at Hattusa, with special attention paid to the *šarrena* ritual discussed below.

current rulers, empowering the performers who were masters of such privileged access to the past, and on the other legitimated kingship by the association with legendary kings. All these factors may have given cachet to storytellers performing the mythico-historical traditions represented by legends about Sargon and Naram-Sin not only at Hattusa, but also in courts west of Hattusa. I suggest that bards continued to maintain their prestige by claiming privileged knowledge of stories about the distant past and faraway places into the Early Iron Age, and they continued to deploy variations of the same storylines. This explains how motifs and storylines attached to the Sargonic kings are also found in Homeric epic, even as the indivual characters of Sargon and Naram-Sin were effaced. In particular, as I will show, the story of Hector is derived from the primary storyline associated with Naram-Sin, that of a king unable to interpret the omens of the gods correctly, who is therefore responsible for the destruction of his city.

Finally, as I argued in Chapter 3, the most likely means of transmission of such narratives from Near Easterners to Greeks was oral performance rather than a written text. In order to understand how the storylines discussed here reached Greek-speakers, it is necessary to continue to explore the relationship of written texts to oral traditions. The legends of Sargon and Naram-Sin provide an opportunity to do so. I focus particularly on how written and oral traditions about Sargonic heroes interacted with each other, to help explain how we can use written texts to get at oral traditions. I also discuss evidence for Hurro-Hittite oral traditions about the Akkadian kings that connect them to the Kumarbi cycle. I argue that this evidence, from an invocation ritual for dead deified kings (the *šarrena* ritual), can be combined with the evidence of a small fragment of a Hurrian narrative song about Sargon to show that both Akkadian emperors were sung of in the same genre of narrative song to which the Kumarbi cycle, the *Song of Gilgamesh*, and the *Song of Release* belonged. This ritual also shows how local courts could insert themselves into world history by placing an ancestor into a king list that included famous kings from far away and long ago. Lastly, it allows us to discuss the interplay between extended narratives and the king lists or genealogies that served as indexes, so to speak, or large-scale frameworks structuring relations between individual narratives.

The Anatolian reception of legends of Sargon

Sargon (2340–2285 BCE), having seizing the throne of Kish in an apparent *coup d'état*, was the first to unify southern and northern Mesopotamia into a single empire. His exploits and those of his grandson Naram-Sin (2260–2224 BCE), whose supposed failure as a leader served as a foil to his grandfather's successes,[3] excited the imagination of succeeding generations well into the first millennium BCE.[4] Scribes continued to copy inscriptions extolling their deeds, some of them, such as the inscription quoted at the beginning of this chapter, claiming to have been originally inscribed on votive statues of the kings.[5] Their names appear in quite a few historical omens, which were tidbits of admonitory history.[6] And, both kings were featured in a variety of full-length mythico-historical "legends,"[7] some purporting to be transcriptions from *narûs* (stelae),[8] but still betraying influence from otherwise lost oral traditions about the Sargonic kings.[9] In fact, although the legends of Sargon the Great are well known to us because of the interest scribes took in them, we can also discern a strong, adaptable, and multilingual oral tradition telling of his deeds and voyages, especially in Anatolia. Sargonic legend interacted with the Gilgamesh tradition and inspired the Hittite king Hattusili I as he aspired to place his kingdom on the world stage.

---

[3] Beckman (2001b: 87–8).
[4] Nearly all of the texts concerning the reigns of these two kings post-date them by several centuries. An insightful overview of the primary sources, their claims, and the issues with them is provided by van de Mieroop (1999: 59–76). Also see J. G. Westenholz (1997: 1–3; 2010). There are two schools of thought concerning the claims presented in the legends of Sargon and Naram-Sin. While some consider the traditions to contain a kernel of truth (e.g., J. G. Westenholz 1998: 13–14), others think that the events and ideas current at the time that the tablets were written influenced the narratives (e.g., Liverani 1993: 52–6).
[5] See Jonker (1995: 110–14) on copying the inscriptions, sometimes collected in so-called *Sammeltafeln* (compilation tablets). Gelb and Kienast (1990: 129–56) present an overview of the sources of copied inscriptions.
[6] Van de Mieroop (1999: 32–3). The Sargon omens are collected in Lewis (1980: 135–40).
[7] See J. G. Westenholz (1997: 21–3) on the term "legend." I use it for convenience rather than because I fully agree with the division of myth, legend, and epic, which represents our modern categories, not the indigenous Late Bronze Age genre categories. I do feel uncomfortable applying the term "epic" for quite short texts that are not necessarily part of a larger "mental text." (See Chapter 2, 22, for more discussion of the term "epic.")
[8] J. G. Westenholz (1997: 16–20) reviews the study of *narû*-literature.
[9] See J. G. Westenholz (1983: 331; 1992, especially p. 144; 2011: 285–6). Many of the examples of Sargonic legends "should be regarded as either exercise compositions made once and for all by the student on the basis of the ancient stories, or adaptations by the scribes of the stories for some contemporary purpose, all based on an essentially oral tradition" (J. G. Westenholz 1983: 331). The stylistic differences between the different tales show they do not belong to a single formally defined genre. See the discussions of each legend in J. G. Westenholz (1997). On the other hand, two pseudo-letters from Sargon that turn into scholastic lists are clearly for the entertainment of scribes (ed. and trans. J. G. Westenholz 1997: 141–69).

One focus of Sargonic legend was his travels to Anatolia, and Sargon's exploits there situated the Hittites on the periphery of an empire whose center was Akkade,[10] just as the Cedar Forest episode in the Gilgamesh tradition placed the Hittites on the edge of the world explored by the legendary king of Uruk. The Hittite reception of Sargonic legend thus gives a window into how a peripheral kingdom might react to and manipulate the conceptions projected onto it by the center, and it can provide us with some valuable analogies with which we can reconstruct the Greeks' reaction to their position on the periphery of the Near Eastern world and how it might have shaped the absorption of elements of the Near Eastern narrative tradition into Greek epic.

Several lines of transmission to Anatolia can be traced for stories about Sargon: one via the Old Assyrian merchant colonies in Anatolia, in particular Kanesh, a second from scribal schools of Mesopotamia and/or north Syria, and a just barely detectable orally transmitted tradition from the Hurrians, probably coming from north Syria, which is revealed by the fragment of a Hurro-Hittite song mentioning Sargon and the *šarrena* ritual.[11]

Evidence for the first line of transmission comes from a tablet from the merchants' colony of Anatolian Kanesh, modern Kültepe, which shows that the deeds of Sargon were commemorated in Anatolia already in the Old Assyrian period.[12] The *Old Assyrian Sargon Legend*, certainly not part

---

[10] There is evidence that Naram-Sin, at least, did extend his reach quite far west. Archaeological evidence in the form of stamped bricks bearing Naram-Sin's name shows that his building projects extended to Tell Brak/Nagar. A stele depicting eastern Mediterranean goods and people as booty and captives from a campaign of Naram-Sin indicates that his army managed to reach the Mediterranean shore (Mellink 1963; A. Westenholz 1999: 47–8; J. G. Westenholz 1998: 13–14). Inscriptions referring to Naram-Sin have been found on Cythera and at Kourion on Cyprus, but how they got there is unknown (Dalley and Reyes 1998: 87). Also see Alster and Oshima (2007: 5, n. 27) for further material evidence of Sargonic forays to the west.

[11] J. G. Westenholz (2011: 286–91) discusses all the possible lines of transmission, including some not touched on here.

[12] This is a very difficult text. I make no claims to understand it. See van de Mieroop (2000) and Alster and Oshima (2007, with further references), who provide transliterations with translations and full discussions; Foster (2005: 71–5), noting correspondences with *Gilgamesh* that he considers to be parodic; and Cavigneaux (2005), with additional comparisons to *Gilgamesh*. I use Alster and Oshima's translation here. It is evident that in Old Assyrian times Sargon and his grandson were considered worthy of imitation, as two Old Assyrian rulers bore their names. See Kuhrt (1995: 82–6) on the (sparse) evidence for the Old Assyrian kings. These two kings' reigns roughly coincide with level II at Kültepe, the period in which this text was written down. See van de Mieroop (2000: 136) on the conflating of Sargon of Akkade and Sargon I of Assyria.

of a fixed scribal tradition, is presented as the first-person boast of Sargon about various exploits – some rather odd. This erudite and punning text mimics claims made by Sargonic inscriptions. For example, the Sargon inscription quoted at the beginning of this chapter boasts, "He (the god Dagān) gave to him (Sargon) the Upper Land: Mari, Iarmuti, and Ebla as far as the Cedar Forest and the Silver Mountains.[13] 5,400 men daily eat in the presence of Sargon, the king to whom the god Enlil gave no rival."[14] The Kültepe text similarly proclaims:

5–7   From sunrise to sunset I took possession of the land, and
8–9   in a single day I delivered battle to 70 cities.
10–11 I captured their princes and destroyed their cities.
11–13 I swore by Adad, the lord of strength, and Ištar, lady of battle.
...
19   ... 1,000 oxen and 6,000 sheep
20   I used to slaughter every day.
21–2 7,000 were my "heroes" (*qá-[r]a-du*), who used to eat ribsteaks every day before me ...[15]

The locations of many of the various places Sargon boasts he has conquered in the autobiographical pseudo-inscription fall within the ambit of Kanesh, in eastern Anatolia and northern Syria; besides Kanesh they include Amurru, Hahhu, Hatti, and Alashiya (Cyprus). Moreover, the text from Kültepe makes reference also to specific themes and places featured in the Sargon and Naram-Sin legends found at Hattusa; for example, Sargon's extended stay of "seven years, a month, and fifteen days" at the lavish meal (according to one reading of the pun in l. 42)[16] bears comparison with Sargon's extended stay enjoying the riches of Purushanda in *Sargon, King of Battle*.[17] It is certainly possible that there was some continuity in the transmission of Sargonic legends in Anatolia across the gap in our information between *ca.* 1900 BCE and *ca.* 1600–1500 BCE. It

---

[13] Possibly the Taurus Mountains. See the discussion of silver sources based on lead isotope analysis in Yener *et al.* (1998: 550–5). And, on Anatolia as a place famed for silver, see Chapter 2, 51–2.

[14] *Sargon* 11.20–8 (trans. Frayne 1993: 28–9); see van de Mieroop (2000: 150–1).

[15] Trans. Alster and Oshima (2007: 10). For the boast concerning the large numbers of animals slaughtered for the feast, compare the hospitality scene in the *Song of Release*, KBo 32.13; see Chapter 5, 125.

[16] The relevant phrase *ina ikiltim* can mean 'in darkness' or 'at eating', see trans. Alster and Oshima (2007: 10, with p. 14).

[17] See van de Mieroop (2000: 149–53), comparing themes and places that appear in the tablet to those in other Sargonic legends. Also see Torri (2009: 112–13), comparing the *Old Assyrian Sargon Legend* with *Sargon, King of Battle*.

could have been solely in writing and the province of scribes, possibly entertaining themselves by composing one-off texts, but we should also accept the likelihood of orally told legends within Anatolia,[18] in addition to the later transmission directly from Mesopotamia through scribes. This has long been acknowledged, as has the possibility of transmission via north Syrian scribes, where kings were also emulating Sargon and Naram-Sin.[19]

I turn now to the Akkadian texts at Hattusa that appear to have been brought there by the scribes. The legend *Sargon, King of Battle* is well represented at Hattusa. It is one of at least four extant narratives ranging in date from Old Babylonian to Late Assyrian that tell a roughly similar story of Sargon making a bold voyage into the unknown.[20] He, like Gilgamesh, enters deep into a hostile forest, battles darkness, and travels to the end of the world to plunder the natural resources of strange lands.[21]

---

[18] Beckman (2001b: 89), van de Mieroop (2000: 142–4, 157–8), J. G. Westenholz (2010: 38–9).

[19] Scribes were possibly included among the deportees from Babylon that Mursili I took to the land of Hatti (*Telipinu Proclamation*: CTH 19.II.A = KBo 3.1 i 30–1, translit. Hoffmann 1984: 18; trans. P. Goedegebuure in Chavalas 2006: 230). Cf. Beckman (1983b: 100, 102–4) on scribes from north Syria and some coming directly from Mesopotamia. Also see Chapter 1, 8–9. Beckman (2001b: 86) focuses on scribes as the conduit of knowledge about the Sargonic kings. A son of a Babylonian scribe wrote down CTH 819 = KBo 19.99, a version of the *Cuthean Legend of Naram-Sin*. See n. 108 below. See Steiner (1999: 430–3, 436–7) on the north Syrian kings' imitation of the Sargonic kings, one of the ways in which the Hurrians would have had access to the Sargonic tradition. This theory is critiqued by J. G. Westenholz (2011: 287).

[20] *Sargon, the Conquering Hero* (OB, often grouped with MB *Sargon, King of Battle*, translit. and trans. J. G. Westenholz 1997: 59–77; trans. Foster 2005: 107–12); *Sargon in Foreign Lands* (OB, translit. and trans. J. G. Westenholz 1997: 78–93); *Sargon the Lion* (OB/MB, translit. and trans. J. G. Westenholz 1997: 94–100); *Sargon, King of Battle* (MB and SB, translit. and trans. J. G. Westenholz 1997: 102–39).

[21] In *Sargon in Foreign Lands*, reaching the Cedar Forest is a momentous occasion (i 12′–15′, translit. and trans. J. G. Westenholz 1997: 82–3). Sargon sits in darkness in the *Old Assyrian Sargon Legend* (41–3, see Alster and Oshima 2007: 4, 14). He battles darkness in the forest in *Sargon the Conquering Hero* (59–64, translit. and trans. J. G. Westenholz 1997: 70–1) and *Sargon in Foreign Lands* (iv 9′–11′, translit. and trans. J. G. Westenholz 1997: 90–1). A cloud of dust darkens the scene when Gilgamesh fights Huwawa (*Epic of Gilgamesh* SB v 135–6, translit. and trans. George 2003: 608–9), and he goes through darkness when traveling the path of the sun to the end of the world (SB ix 138–71, translit. and trans. George 2003: 670–3). See Chapter 4, 105, for a parallel with the *Odyssey*. The opponent of Sargon in *Sargon, King of Battle* and *Sargon the Conquering Hero* is connected to Utnapishtim, the antediluvian sage at the end of the world whom Gilgamesh seeks. He is called Nur-Daga[n] (Hittite *Sargon, King of Battle*: CTH 310.4 = KBo 13.46 ii 8′; see Güterbock 1969: 18), Nur-daggal (Akkadian *Sargon, King of Battle*, EA 359, translit. and trans. J. G. Westenholz 1997: 108–31), or Uta-rapashtim (Akk. *Sargon the Conquering Hero* 58, translit. and trans. J. G. Westenholz 1997: 68–9). Sargon, Nur-Dagan, king of Purushanda, and Utnapishtim all appear together in the Late Babylonian *Map of the World* (obv. 10′, translit. and trans. Horowitz 1998: 22–3), an Akkadian text that explores the concept of the outer limits of the world. On the conflation of Ut-napishtim, Uta-rapashtim,

Hittite scribes also brought the story to Egyptian Amarna, where the best preserved exemplar is found. In Middle Babylonian, it bears clear marks of Hittite mediation in the ductus and Akkadian dialect.[22]

In the Amarna version of *Sargon, King of Battle*, the action begins when Sargon declares his desire to attack a city (Kanesh?; the signs are damaged), but his soldiers shrink from the challenge of the arduous journey, and the king turns his attention to Purushanda, a merchant colony in Anatolia that once was an enemy of Anitta (*ca.* 1725 BCE), the first Hittite king to leave a record of his achievements.[23] Meanwhile, merchants urge the king on, and he asks for directions to this place where he has never gone. The similarities to the prelude of Gilgamesh's visit to the Cedar Forest are manifest.[24] Anatolia's wealth of minerals and exotic trees is described, and the land is perhaps comparable to Shiduri's jeweled garden at the edge of the world.[25] After a break, the action picks up at the court of Nur-daggal in Purushanda. The king doubts that Sargon will be able to negotiate his way across the river and through the tangled underbrush and mountainous terrain, but Nur-daggal is quickly proved wrong and must pay his respects to Sargon, who enjoys his time at the palace so much that he stays for over three years. The description of the road to Purushanda, which is only found in the version of *Sargon, King of Battle* from Amarna, can be

and Nur-daggal, see George (2003: 152), van de Mieroop (2000: 137–8), and J. G. Westenholz (1997: 57–8, 102–3). For more on his name see below, n. 31. Interactions between Sargonic legend and the *Epic of Gilgamesh* are discussed by Foster (2005: 72), Glassner (1985), van de Mieroop (1999: 65, 70–1; 2000: 133, 138).

[22] EA 359 (translit. and trans. J. G. Westenholz 1997: 108–31; Izre'el 1997: 66–75; discussion J. G. Westenholz 2011: 291–2). The unpublished M.A. thesis of Gilan (2000) provides an insightful analysis of the Sargonic legends at Hattusa, and a useful new edition of the Hittite *Sargon, King of Battle* text. I thank him for making it available to me. The text is composed in MB peripheral Akkadian: "In general, it seems to reflect features of the Syro-Anatolian dialects of Akkadian" (J. G. Westenholz 1997: 105). It is in a variation of the older Hittite hand (see Gilan 2000: 28, *pace* Izre'el 1997: 71), as is in fact typical of the Amarna tablets (Wilhelm 1984: 650–1). Beckman went as far as suggesting to J. G. Westenholz (1997: 105) that the tablet was imported from Anatolia. Gilan (2000: 27–8) reviews the discussion perceptively. There is another Akkadian fragment of *Sargon, King of Battle* at Amarna: EA 375 (translit. and trans. J. G. Westenholz 1997: 132–3; Izre'el 1997: 87–8).

[23] *CTH* 1: *Proclamation of Anitta* (trans. H. A. Hoffner, Jr. in Hallo and Younger 1997: 182–4) speaks of how he conquered it. On Anitta, see Chapter 1, 8, n. 27. It has been argued that Purushanda is the site Acem Höyük, but Barjamoviç (2010: 14) argues that it is a site northwest of the Eber Lake, Bolvadin Üçhöyük.

[24] *Epic of Gilgamesh* SB II 213–301 (translit. and trans. George 2003: 566–71).

[25] SB IX 172–93 (translit. and trans. George 2003: 672–5). We may also compare *CTH* 822: *The Merchants' Tale* (ed. and trans. Košak 2003; trans. and discussion Haas 2006: 220), a small fragment of a story possibly embedded in a ritual (so Košak), in which merchants describe their wares.

compared with that of the road to the Cedar Forest in the Hittite *Song of Gilgamesh*,[26] and it shows that some kind of interaction between the two traditions could have occurred specifically in Syro-Anatolia. Because "[a]t the beginning of the Hittite kingdom Purušḫanda had been a powerful and dreadful adversary" of Anitta, Giulia Torri suggests this story is the product of Anatolian and specifically Hittite interest in Sargonic legend.[27]

The Hittite versions of *Sargon, King of Battle* found at Hattusa "seem to be free adaptations of the same legendary material."[28] In the best preserved of the six Hittite exemplars (none of which is particularly well preserved),[29] some differences from the Amarna text can be picked out, the most interesting changes being the addition of dreams. One is sent to Sargon to start the action,[30] while to Nur-daggal[31] is sent a lying dream like that of Agamemnon's in Book 2 of the *Iliad*, in which the goddess Ishtar promises

---

[26] *EA* 349 rev. 5′ (translit. and trans. J. G. Westenholz 1997: 122–3); *Song of Gilgamesh*: *CTH* 341 III.1.Eg = *KBo* 10.47g iii 12′–14′ (translit. E. Rieken *et al.* 2009ff. on KhT). See Beckman (2003: 44, n. 56). The equivalent description in the SB version (v 9, translit. and trans. George 2003: 602–3) is much briefer.

[27] Torri (2009: 114), arguing that Anitta's conquest of Purushanda inspired the story about Sargon's conquest of the merchant colony; see further J. G. Westenholz (2011: 290–4). In *Sargon the Conquering Hero* and *Sargon in Foreign Lands*, he goes not to Purushanda but to Marhashi and/or Shimmurra, the gateway to Hurrian territory. Note that the two SB exemplars from outside Amarna are only small fragments, with no mention of place names, so we cannot state where Sargon was presented as going in these versions. The OB (late seventeenth-century) fictional letter from Ur purporting to be from Sargon (translit. and trans. J. G. Westenholz 1997: 148–69) mentions the Anatolian town, showing that interest in Purushanda was not simply the result of MB interest in Anatolia (Gilan 2000: 34). Torri (2009: 115–16) suggests that the letter could show that an OH legend of Sargon warring against the Hittites' traditional enemy made its way to Mesopotamia. The *Old Assyrian Sargon Legend* from Kültepe shows that Anitta could have had access to stories about Sargon, and that new stories, which anachronistically catered to the interests of Old Assyrian merchants, could have been transmitted back to Mesopotamia by the merchant network (van de Mieroop 2000: 143–5).

[28] J. G. Westenholz (1997: 102).

[29] *CTH* 310 = *KBo* 54.1 (translit. Groddek 2010a: 1), *CTH* 310.1 = *KBo* 3.9, *CTH* 310.2 = *KBo* 3.10, *CTH* 310.3 = *KBo* 12.1 (translit. Rieken 2001: 578–9), *CTH* 310.4 = *KBo* 13.46 (partial translit. Meriggi 1968: 261–2), *CTH* 310.5 = *KBo* 22.6+ (partial translit. Groddek 2008: 13–19, 79, 90; Rieken 2001: 578–9), *CTH* 310? (311?) = *KBo* 57.269, a small fragment mentioning merchants (translit. Groddek 2011b: 139–40). Most have been transliterated, translated, and commented on by Gilan (2000). Also see trans. and discussion of Haas (2006: 68–71). All are New Hittite except for *KBo* 12.1, which is Late New Hittite and riddled with false archaisms (Rieken 2001).

[30] *CTH* 310.5 = *KBo* 22.6 i 6′ (translit. Rieken 2001: 578; trans. Haas 2006: 69).

[31] Labeled here Nurdahhi (*KBo* 22.6 i 22′), which could be interpreted as Hurrian Nawar-tahe 'man of Nawar'. Archi (2000; 2007b: 197) thus suggests that the Hittite *Sargon, King of Battle* comes from a Hurrian version, arguing that scribes replaced the Hurrian name Nawar-tahe with Nur-Dagan. (The signs GAN and ḪÉ are very similar.) J. G. Westenholz (2010: 45, n. 17; 2011: 288), pointing out that another Hittite version calls him Nur-Dagan (see n. 21), prefers an opposite scribal error, starting from the Akkadian Nur-Dagan 'light of Dagan'. It is possible that a Hurrian-speaking Hittite scribe was responsible for the error.

him victory in battle.[32] Such differences suggest that, although these texts were produced by scribes, possibly for their own entertainment, they picked up on a flexible oral tradition that was known beyond scribal circles.

Finally, although the Hittite *Sargon, King of Battle* does not belong to the genre of Hurro-Hittite song,[33] Sargon, "lord of Akkade," does appear, along with Shawushka of Nineveh, a child, and a man named Ashnuri, in a Hurrian fragment that shows characteristics of the genre.[34] This scrap is vitally important because it confirms that, although as a rule Akkadian legends about Sargon were not composed in the literary hymno-epic dialect used for the *Epic of Gilgamesh*,[35] Sargon could appear in the same Hurrian narrative tradition that praised Gilgamesh and sang of the destruction of Ebla. It can be surmised that the stories told of him were not wildly different from those that are preserved, focusing on his prowess as a conqueror of and voyager into unknown lands. This fragment is one of the two pieces of evidence for an orally transmitted Hurrian tradition about the Sargonic kings, the other being the *šarrena* ritual, to be discussed in a later section of this chapter.

Parallels among Sargonic legend, the Gilgamesh story, and the *Song of Release* give the impression that we are looking at the tip of a second-millennium iceberg of oral legends feeding off each other to build a thematically coherent ancient mythical history. It is exactly in this history that the Hittites were interested in participating. Several parallels between the Sargonic and Gilgamesh traditions have already been mentioned, and from their earliest attestations the traditions concerning Sargon and Naram-Sin can be seen to be interacting with the Gilgamesh tradition. Thus, Naram-Sin boasts of killing a wild bull,[36] as Gilgamesh and Enkidu

---

[32] CTH 310.5 = KBo 22.6 i 21′–8′ (translit. Rieken 2001: 578; trans. Haas 2006: 70).

[33] Frequentatives are used *ad sensum* (KBo 22.6 i 9′, iv 19′, 22′), and *memiškiwan daiš* appears only once (KBo 22.6 i 17′, translit. and trans. Güterbock 1969: 19, 21), otherwise forms of the verb *te-* are used. There is no inverted word order or clitic doubling, and it is not scannable. Thus, it shows none of the markers of Hurro-Hittite narrative song, on which see Chapter 2, 36, with n. 62, and 42–3.

[34] *Hurrian Mythological-Historical Fragments*: CTH 775.D.2 = KUB 31.3 (translit. Salvini and Wegner 2004: 37–8, discussion p. 17, No. 6), briefly mentioned by J. G. Westenholz (2011: 288). The scrap shares vocables with other mythical-historical texts: *a-za-al-ti-li, i-ša-am-me-e-ni, ḫa-a-ni, ma-an-zu-u-ra, pa-ri-ya, ša-a-wa_a-a-al-li, zu-ú-ul-tu*. It is possible to reconstruct the introduction to direct speech [*alumai=n*] *qatiya* (see Trémouille 2000: 136, with earlier references, on the formula and Chapter 2, 42 here), and the voluntative verb *azaltili* must belong to a direct quote.

[35] Although the two SB exemplars of *Sargon, King of Battle* are not in the hymno-epic style, they do have some poetic features (J. G. Westenholz 1983: 335; 1997: 105–7; Izre'el 1997: 72–3).

[36] *Naram-Sin* 23.9–14 (translit. and trans. Frayne 1993: 127), found in two OB copies.

killed the Bull of Heaven; both leaders boast of ruling the Cedar Forest or Mountains;[37] and, Naram-Sin boasts of cutting down cedars for building projects as Gilgamesh did.[38] In turn, the story of Gilgamesh's deeds seems to be influenced by the Sargonic kings' legendary accomplishments, for in the Akkadian versions of the epic the location of the Cedar Mountains, the home of Huwawa, has been moved to the west, where Naram-Sin sought his cedars, in the Amanus mountain range between north Syria and southeastern Anatolia, whereas in the Sumerian lay *Gilgamesh and Huwawa* it had been to the east, in Iran.[39]

In addition, Sargonic legends and/or a local Syro-Anatolian version of the Gilgamesh story mentioning Ebla may have interacted with the narrative tradition that resulted in the *Song of Release*. Inscriptions attributed to both Sargon and Naram-Sin claim that each conquered Ebla, sometimes specifying "as far as the Cedar Forest,"[40] while in at least one Old Babylonian version of the *Epic of Gilgamesh*, the heroes come near Ebla as they approach the Cedar Mountains.[41] It is impossible to confirm which Sargonic king could in fact be responsible for the destruction of Ebla in the second half of the third millennium, and indeed the city's destruction may merely have been incorporated into Sargonic legend,[42] but the Hittite king

---

[37] *Sargon* 11.20–6; 12.13′–21′ (translit. and trans. Frayne 1993: 28–31), both part of an OB *Sammeltafel* extant in two copies; *Naram-Sin* 25.1–16 (translit. and trans. Frayne 1993: 130), found in two OB copies; 26 i 21–9 (translit. and trans. Frayne 1993: 132–3). A year name commemorates the voyage of Naram-Sin to the Cedar Forest (translit. and trans. Frayne 1993: 86). Another year name commemorates his cutting down cedars either in the Amanus Mountains (so Frayne 1993: 86) or in Lebanon (so George 2003: 94).

[38] *Naram-Sin* 29 rev. 8′–10′ (translit. and trans. Frayne 1993: 140). Other Mesopotamian kings also boasted of cutting down cedars for building projects, see George (2003: 93–4).

[39] On the shift of the locations of the Cedar Forest from east to west, influenced by Sargonic exploits, see George (2003: 20, 93–4) and Chapter 3, 71, n. 75. In the Sumerian version, the Sun-god Utu is supposed to take particular interest in Gilgamesh's activities in the Cedar Mountains (e.g., *Gilgamesh and Huwawa A* 1–12, trans. Black et al. 2004: 344). The Zagros mountains are the home of Utu. But, an OB text states that Huwawa's dying cries broke apart Mounts Sirion and Lebanon (Ishchali 31′, translit. and trans. George 2003: 262–3, discussion 266). In the SB version the heroes come near Mount Lebanon (iv 4, translit. and trans. George 2003: 588–9), and their fighting breaks apart Sirara (the SB form of the mountain's name) and Lebanon (v 134, translit. and trans. George 2003: 608–9).

[40] *Sargon* 11.20–8, 12.13′–18′ (translit. and trans. Frayne 1993: 28–31); *Naram-Sin* 26 *passim*, 27 (translit. and trans. Frayne 1993: 132–6); 1004 (translit. and trans. Frayne 1993: 163); 2005 (translit. and trans. Frayne 1993: 167).

[41] Schøyen$_2$ 26 (translit. and trans. George 2003: 234–5), most likely from Babylonia (Larsa, George 2009: xvi). See George (2003: 94, 225–6) and George (2009: 29–36) with an updated discussion and edition with translation.

[42] The dating of the relevant archaeological layer, Tell Mardikh iib1, has been disputed. See summary of Klengel (1992: 22–3) and comments of van de Mieroop (1999: 60). Astour (1992; 2002: 58–76) argues that the destruction, which he views as caused by an accidental fire,

who later destroyed Ebla again *ca.* 1600 BCE would have been well aware of the mythico-historical import of his deed.[43]

Hattusili was certainly well aware of the Akkadian conqueror's exploits and vied with him in the working of great deeds, for the *Annals of Hattusili I* compare the Hittite king to Sargon, both implicitly and explicitly.[44] Beginning in the third person, then changing into a first-person narrative, the *Annals* present a litany of cities attacked and sacked, and precious, highly crafted goods brought back from various cities, especially from Hattusili's campaigns in eastern Anatolia and north Syria, a telling contrast to the precious raw materials brought back from the edge of the world by Gilgamesh, Sargon, and Naram-Sin. The periphery is raiding the center, not the other way around. Hattusili dwells particularly on the destruction of Hahhu and Hassu, two cities that were part of the Old Assyrian network of trading colonies and were mentioned in the legends concerning Sargon and Naram-Sin.[45] Just as Sargon is compared to a lion in his legends, so Hattusili twice compares himself to a lion,[46] and Hattusili closes the episode of his destruction of Hahhu with a supreme boast:

---

should be dated before the time of either Naram-Sin or Sargon, and further that "Naram-Sin's Ebla, always mentioned together with Armanum, is in all likelihood not the north Syrian Ebla at all" (Astour 2002: 65). Archi and Biga (2003) detail a set of synchronisms between Mari, Babylon, and Ebla to argue that Ebla was destroyed by Mari about ten years before Sargon seized power. Over the years Ebla's excavator, Paolo Matthiae, has debated whether Naram-Sin or Sargon was the most likely conqueror. Currently he considers Sargon to be in fact responsible for the destruction of Tell Mardikh IIb1 (Matthiae 2006b; 2007; 2008: 96–8).

[43] See Chapter 5, 111–12, on the Hittite destruction of Tell Mardikh IIIb.

[44] The *Annals of Hattusili I* (*CTH* 4) describe the events of five years, not necessarily contiguous. The *Annals* are found in two separate, slightly deviating versions in Hittite and Akkadian (the latter in only one copy). It is a matter of dispute which version is the original and which the translation, a question made more difficult by the fact that the Akkadian version, found only in a NS tablet, shows evidence of being redacted over time, see Devecchi (2005: 26–32) and, in more detail, Melchert (1978). The Hittite version has been edited and translated by de Martino (2003: 21–80); the Akkadian version by Devecchi (2005); an English translation is provided by G. Beckman in Chavalas (2006: 219–22). The *Annals of Hattusili I* are the first example of annalistic history at Hattusa, and the genre could be related to Middle Assyrian annalistic history (Klinger 2001a: 285; Tadmor 1977).

[45] In *Sargon, the Conquering Hero* the golden armor of Sargon's soldiers comes from Hassu (48–9, translit. and trans. J. G. Westenholz 1997). Hahhu is mentioned in the OB *Gula-AN and the Seventeen Kings* (5', translit and trans. J. G. Westenholz 1997: 250–1), and the *Old Assyrian Sargon Legend* (62, translit. and trans. Alster and Oshima 2007: 10–11).

[46] *Sargon the Lion* obv. 16'–17', rev. 9' (translit. and trans. J. G. Westenholz 1997: 96–9); *Annals of Hattusili I*: *CTH* 4.II.A = *KBo* 10.2 ii 18, iii 1 (translit. de Martino 2003: 52, 64; trans. G. Beckman in Chavalas 2006: 221). On Hattusili's use of the lion simile see Collins (1998).

No one [before had crossed] the Euphrates.[47] I myself, the Great King, T[abarna, on foot] crossed it. My armies crossed [behind me] on foot. Sarg[on had cross]ed it, he defea[ted] the troops of Hahhu, but he di[d] nothing [to Hahhu]. He did not burn it down with fire. He did not [...] to Tarhun of Heaven. And, I, the Great King, Tabarna, destroyed Hahhu. I [burned] it down with fire, and the smoke to [the Sun-god in] heaven [and to the Storm-god I sent up as incense]. I hitched the king of Hassu and the king of Hahhu to a carriage.[48]

Hattusili is obviously responding to the legendary boast of the Akkadian king found in *Sargon, the Conquering Hero*: "Lo, the king who wants to equal me, where I have gone, let him also go!"[49] The crossing of a river, breaching a natural barrier, is a topos found in the Hittite *Sargon, King of Battle* and in the Hittite *Song of Gilgamesh*,[50] and for the landlubber Hittites it served the same function as Gilgamesh or Odysseus crossing the sea at the edge of the world.

Earlier, we discussed echoes in the *Song of Release* of Hattusili's boasts of giving the citizens of Hahhu their freedom.[51] At a minimum, Hattusili's invocation of the topos of the merciful king shows his knowledge of the conventions of the international brotherhood of Great Kings. It may be

---

[47] Hittite: Mala (a tributary of the Euphrates); in the Akkadian version it appears as Purattu (J. L. Miller 2001: 85, suggests this is the modern Afrin).

[48] CTH 4.II.A = KBo 10.2 iii 29–42 (translit. de Martino 2003: 72–6), filled in with the aid of duplicates and the Akkadian version, CTH 4.I.A = KBo 10.1 rev. 18–25 (translit. Devecchi 2005: 56). While no extant piece of *narû*-literature refers to Sargon crossing the Euphrates, Naram-Sin does boast of reaching the sources of the Tigris and Euphrates, and of crossing the two rivers: *Naram-Sin* 2 ii 7–15; 29 rev. 3'–7' (translit. and trans. Frayne 1993: 91, 140). A year name also commemorates his journey to the sources of the Tigris and Euphrates (translit. and trans. Frayne 1993: 86). As Steiner (1999: 433–4) notes, the yoking of the two kings matches Sargon's yoking of Lugalzagesi of Umma (*Sargon* 1.23–31, translit. and trans. Frayne 1993: 10).

[49] 120–3 (trans. J. G. Westenholz 1997: 77), see Beckman (2001b: 91), Gilan (2000: 17), Güterbock (1964), Haas (1993: 139–42), and van de Mieroop (2000: 134–6).

[50] *Sargon in Foreign Lands* refers to "my Euphrates" (ii 21, translit. and trans. J. G. Westenholz 1997: 88–9), and Sargon makes a point of crossing the Euphrates in *Sargon, King of Battle* (EA 359 rev. 4', translit. and trans. J. G. Westenholz 1997: 121), but in the Hittite version he crosses the Aranzah, which is either the Marat Su or the upper Tigris, where he stops to make sacrifice (KBo 22.6 i 16'–20', translit. and trans. Güterbock 1969: 19, 22), see J. G. Westenholz (1998: 8). Gilgamesh and Enkidu cross the Mala River, where they make sacrifice in the *Song of Gilgamesh* (CTH 341.III.1.Eg = KBo 10.47g iii 2', CTH 341.III.2.A = KUB 23.9 7, translit. E. Rieken et al. 2009ff. on KhT). See Beckman (2003: 44), who notes there is no reference to a river-crossing in the Akkadian *Epic of Gilgamesh*. As Steiner (1999: 430–6) shows, the *Annals of Hattusili I* use other motifs and phrases paralleling Sargonic inscriptions and literary narratives.

[51] See Chapter 5, 123–4.

that Hattusili was aware that such a deed was attributed to Sargon, for this seems to be a standard motif of the Mesopotamian king's legacy. At least, in the legends concerning Naram-Sin's defeat of a coalition of rebellious states, Naram-Sin highlights the ingratitude of the lands that rebelled against him by pointing out the clemency of his predecessor Sargon towards Kish:

> ... my fore(father) Sargon
> after he had conquered Uruk,
> had established the freedom (*andurār*) of the population of Kiš(i),
> had shaved off their slavemarks,
> (and) had broken their shackles.[52]

From history to myth, from oral to written

Our sources, of course, for Sargonic legend are the tablets and inscriptions of the scribal schools, which make quite clear their devotion to the written word. Thus, the native title of the Standard Babylonian *Cuthean Legend of Naram-Sin* was "Open the Tablet Box."[53] Its opening echoes the beginning of the Standard Babylonian *Epic of Gilgamesh*, framing itself as a copy of an inscription on a stele:[54]

> Open the tablet-box and read out the stela (*narû*),
> [which I, Naram-Sin], son of Sargon,
> [have inscribed and left for] future days.[55]

Naram-Sin blames the early Sumerian hero Enmerkar for not leaving a written record of his times from which Naram-Sin could learn. The lack of

---

[52] The *Great Revolt against Naram-Sin* OB 16–20 (translit. and trans. J. G. Westenholz 1997: 240–3), see Charpin (1998: 13–14, 16), Potts (2001: 402, n. 14), and J. G. Westenholz (2010: 32) on Naram-Sin's mention of Sargon's mercy, which also appears in an OB copy of a Naram-Sin inscription (ix 32–x 14, translit. and trans. Wilcke 1997: 25, 28). As usual there are differing views on the history of the *Great Revolt*. Some view the different versions, which cannot be reconciled to a single stemma, as evidence of oral tradition (J. G. Westenholz 1997: 231); others focus on the role of scribes in producing the versions (see Charpin 1998: 15–16, with earlier references). Unfortunately, the fragments of the Hittite text telling a version of this story that caters to an Anatolian audience, *Naram-Sin in Asia Minor*, do not include this passage.

[53] See J. G. Westenholz (2011: 293).

[54] J. G. Westenholz (1992: 142–5) discusses the self-reference as a written text in Naram-Sin texts. See Chapter 3, 59, on the opening of the *Epic of Gilgamesh*.

[55] 1–3 (trans. J. G. Westenholz 1997: 301).

example has prevented him from engaging in hero worship or veneration of ancestors.[56] He ends his story:

> wise scribes,
> let them declaim your inscription (*narû*),
> You who have read my inscription
> and thus have gotten yourself out (of trouble),
> you who have blessed me, may a future (ruler)
> Bless you![57]

Yet, as I have shown, knowledge of Sargonic legend clearly extended beyond scribal circles, presenting a model to be emulated by the first Hittite kings when they went beyond the borders of Anatolia. I explore briefly in this section the relation between the written texts and oral performance and/or traditions generally in the ancient Near East and specifically at Hattusa in order to further expand the discussion presented in Chapter 3, where I discussed evidence for an oral tradition about Gilgamesh lying behind the written versions. This discussion helps to explain how the deeds of Sargonic kings could have been incorporated into the Hurrian oral tradition, as well as why Hattusa in particular has proved to be such an important source for orally derived texts, including Hurro-Hittite song and the *šarrena* ritual.

While Hattusili I, like Naram-Sin, presents his *Annals*, in which he boasts of outdoing Sargon, as a written work, the *Annals*' oral milieu can be discerned within the *Annals* in the use of the first person, as if direct quotes from the king were combined with the scribes' third-person account. One can imagine *Hattusili's Annals* being recited or read aloud at a feast in which Hattusili's victorious soldiers compare their own performance to those of Sargon's soldiers (a scenario that assumes they were in fact privy to Sargonic legend). The Hittite *Sargon, King of Battle* ends with a variation on the usual boasts of cutting down great trees to use as timbers in the temples of the god, when Sargon, at the request of his "heroes" (UR.SAG), cuts down a tree growing at Nur-daggal's palace entrance to be made into a dining table where they can meet and reminisce

---

[56] 1–30 (trans. J. G. Westenholz 1997: 301–7).
[57] 175–80 (trans. J. G. Westenholz 1997: 331). See J. G. Westenholz (1993) on the notion of writing down one's deeds on a *narû* for others to read and remember one by. See Michalowski (1991: 53–4) and Franke (1989: 14–16, 19) on scribes' adherence to a tradition of commemorating kings, and the dependence of kings on scribes for administrative knowledge. Jonker (1995: 95–104) discusses the development of a sense that written texts could be used to preserve quasi-historical information across generations in her analysis of the *Cuthean Legend*.

about their exploits. Perhaps we have a topos here alluding to one of the typical occasions for such a story. Certainly, Hattusili's comments in his *Annals* about Sargon defeating the troops of Hahhu, but doing nothing to the town, bring to mind the words of Sargon's soldiers in the Hittite *Sargon, King of Battle*, when he proposes returning home after his prolonged sojourn in Purushanda: "We conquered the land, but we did nothing to it."[58]

Hattusili makes a point of mentioning the gold statue he has made of himself for the Sun-goddess of Arinna, on which are inscribed his deeds.[59] In this he is again imitating Sargon, for his deeds too were inscribed on statues of himself.[60] Perhaps Hattusili learned of the practice from Babylonian scribes. But, to understand the topos fully we need to contemplate exactly how inscriptions were seen to function. Furthermore, while it can be taken as given that a contemporaneous oral tradition would have had an impact on the written tradition, could the opposite be true? To what degree were written texts conceived of as independent of oral performance?

Jacob Klein's analysis of the move in the Ur III period (*ca.* 2000 BCE) from the preservation of the memory of great deeds by means of orally transmitted song, to inscriptions on statues and in public places, to tablets copied by scribes is highly instructive.[61] That the deeds were orally transmitted is made clear by the protests of King Shulgi that he has never neglected the songs of his predecessors, but has made sure that they were still sung.[62] Meanwhile,

> to lighten their task somewhat the kings had their hymns written on statues. These were the statues which had stood permanently in the temples and "sang" the deeds of their creators to the gods. This increased the chances that their memory would remain "alive", but unfortunately made them more fragile.[63]

---

[58] *CTH* 310.5 = *KBo* 22.6 iv 11′–12′ (translit. Rieken 2001: 578; trans. Haas 2006: 71).
[59] *CTH* 4.II.A = *KBo* 10.2 iii 21–2 (translit. de Martino 2003: 68, 70; trans. G. Beckman in Chavalas 2006: 221).
[60] Dedication of statue of self: *Naram-Sin* 26 (translit. and trans. Frayne 1993: 132–5, see his comments at p. 132); *Sargon* 14 (translit. and trans. Frayne 1993: 32–3); gold statue placed before god/king: *Naram-Sin* 1001 (translit. and trans. Frayne 1993: 160), a copy of a label of a gold statue of Naram-Sin for a deity from a *Sammeltafel*.
[61] Klein (1989: 301), followed by Jonker (1995: 85–9). Also see Ludwig (1990: 67–9) on the inscribing of praise songs on stelae to keep them ever alive.
[62] *Shulgi B* 270–80 (trans. ETCSL t.2.4.2.02).   [63] Jonker (1995: 86).

Shulgi came up with a solution to the common concern that a ruler's deeds would be erased with his inscriptions (evident in the closing curses against those who might efface the text), and in so doing he "took a decision which fundamentally influenced the nature of contact with the remains of the past. He it was who commissioned the *edubba*, 'the tablet house', the scribes' academy, which was in his service, to multiply his own songs and to take care that they were propagated."[64] Thus, by the end of the Ur III period a threefold set of techniques was used to preserve the past: orally transmitted songs, inscriptions, and the copying in scribal schools of tablets containing narratives based on either or both of these modes of remembering. It is this last mode of remembering that provides the chief access to the tradition, but we should not assume that scribes were the primary mode of disseminating Sargonic legend in the third and second millennia.[65]

The work on early inscriptions in ancient Greece also has some applicability here, for it shows that "[m]uch if not all of the early writing put on stone was meant to represent statements which were to be uttered aloud, usually in verse: so here writing is the servant of the spoken word, a means of communicating what would usually be sung or said."[66] In a world in which reading was perforce done aloud,[67] the primary purpose of the Akkadian inscriptions that accompanied depictions of great deeds on the walls of palaces and temples, or on statues or other votive offerings presented to deities, was not to be copied by scribes, but to serve as a perpetual declaration of the deeds and piety of the subject, able to be read aloud by priests and visitors, who would thus re-enact and re-activate the offering and/or boast.[68] This must have been true for Hattusili I's inscribed statue for the Sun-goddess of Arinna. Through this means, illiterate performers of "folk epic" would have had a chance to absorb the latest court propaganda. In light of this, we can feel fairly confident that even scribal exercises about Sargon were not completely divorced from the oral world

---

[64] Jonker (1995: 87).

[65] Compare Thomas (1992: 34–6, 69–70) on the continued importance in Greek legal procedure of oral memory, even after the advent of writing. Also see J. G. Westenholz (1992: 145–7) for evidence of oral performance of written texts. A more complex question is the degree to which performers in the third and second millennia BCE were literate and how often illiterate performers were taught to perform a text written by a scribe, issues that unfortunately cannot be examined in any detail here. See at least the contributions in Vogelzang and Vanstiphout (1992), and Black *et al.* (2004: xlviii–xlix).

[66] Thomas (1992: 62). See further Day (1989), P. Pucci (1988), Svenbro (1993: 1–63), and Thomas (1992: 61–5).

[67] Grayson (2000).   [68] Franke (1989: 18–20).

of myth, legend, and epic, not only drawing from orally performed narratives, but also representing texts that could feed the oral tradition.

Finally, an understanding of the Hittites' view of the use of writing shows some of the reasons why they created the unique set of texts found at Hattusa that allow us to discern, although only dimly, this otherwise lost repertoire of illiterate bards and storytellers that is the basis of the comparative research presented here. Without the continuous tradition of more than a thousand years of scribal learning, the "high culture" of the Hittite temple and king's court was far less invested in the notion of scribes as transmitters of the vital inherited information that can be seen in the Akkadian versions of the Gilgamesh and Naram-Sin legends. A relatively high value was given to the work of illiterate oral performers, as can be seen, for example, with the spells of the "Old Women," to whom many magic rituals were attributed.[69] Scribes were responsible for recording their performances for posterity, and in some cases it can be shown that the scribes altered a ritual description to fit new circumstances, although they were careful not to take credit for this new version, instead investing it with the authority of a legendary named performer.[70] Nevertheless, we are presented with an unusual selection of oral-derived texts that allows us to hear the voices of illiterate singers, spell-casters, and storytellers, however indirectly, a group of texts, including the oral-derived Hurro-Hittite narrative songs, unparalleled in the Near Eastern archives outside of Hittite sites, which otherwise would be inaccessible to us.

The *šarrena* ritual

An important witness to the oral tradition about Sargon and his grandson Naram-Sin, which provides further evidence beyond the small fragment discussed earlier that Sargonic heroes were incorporated into the traditions of Hurro-Hittite song, is a Middle Hittite ritual calling upon Sargon and his descendants, as well as other characters from Hurro-Hittite song, and which refers to them as ^{d}*šarrena* ('deified kings').[71] It also provides

---

[69] On the "Old Woman" as respected practitioner of magic, see B. J. Collins in Chavalas (2013: 246–7).

[70] J. L. Miller (2004: 253–4, 472–511) reviews previous discussions by Hittitologists on how ritual texts were written down and argues that scribes bear more responsibility for their final form than previously supposed. Christiansen (2006: 1–30) also discusses how and why the Hittite ritual texts were written down and used. Also see Chapter 4, 96, n. 83.

[71] The Akkadian term *šarru* is used elsewhere to refer to royal ancestors, for example, in eighteenth-century Mari and Hurrian Nuzi (1500–1350 BCE); see Wilhelm (2003: 394, n. 5).

information on the *Sitz im Leben* of the mythical narratives, and the values and practices that informed them and made them precious commodities. The ritual in question manifestly wishes to situate the Hittite king within the larger framework of the mythical history of the ancient Near East, alluding both to Sargonic legend and to the narratives of Hurro-Hittite song, using the former kings to legitimize the kingship of the present ruler. It evinces the same interest in far-flung places found in Sargonic legend, listing kings ruling the edges of the earth, but again, like the *Annals of Hattusili I*, the angle of view is from the periphery into the center.

The *šarrena* ritual is described in Hittite and its songs are quoted in Hurrian.[72] The performer (unfortunately his or her title is lost) makes dolls out of red, white, and blue wool, perhaps meant to imitate the statues and statuettes used in ancestor cult, both royal and non-royal. He or she repeatedly invokes the ^{d}*šarrena* by name. When we first pick up the song, the deified kings are the topic: "[...] of the deified kings, those of Atalshen. // [...] of the deified kings, those of the Sea-god,[73] [...] of the deified kings..." We know of an Atalshen who was the king of Urkesh and Nawar/Nagar (Tell Brak), the first Hurrian king to leave behind an inscription (dated perhaps to the end of the Ur III period).[74] The Sea-god, meanwhile, is one of the Storm-god's opponents in the Kumarbi cycle.

The next paragraph moves into a past-tense narrative, with mention of Teshshub's companions, the mountains Hazzi and Namni. It should be noted that a Hurrian *Song of Kingship* (*šarrašiyaš*) and the *Song of the Sea* were performed in rituals involving Mt. Hazzi. This mountain, home of Baal and later Zeus Casius, was closely connected to legitimate kingship through the story of the Storm-god's defeat of the forces of chaos.[75]

Column i breaks off here. In column ii the topic is a series of gods: Sharruma; the goddesses Ninatu, who is a companion of Shawushka, Takidu, Hebat; and the Moon-god Kushuh. The Moon-god "speaks

---

It has been Hurrianized to an *i/e*-stem and the Hurrian pluralizing suffix -*na* has been added. For further discussion of the divinized *šarrena* at Hattusa, see Bachvarova (2013a).

[72] *Hurrian Mythological-Historical Fragments*: CTH 775.D.1 = *KUB* 27.38 (translit. Haas and Wegner 1988: 384–90, No. 87, discussion pp. 25–6). I have discussed this text in Bachvarova (2012a). Important discussions appear in Houwink ten Cate (1992b: 110–11), de Martino (1993), and Wilhelm (2003).

[73] See Rutherford (2001b: 604), Wilhelm (2003: 394, n. 5), for this interpretation.

[74] Kuhrt (1995: 285) suggests he should be dated *ca*. 2150 BCE. Buccellati and Kelly-Buccellati (2009: 41) tentatively place him in the Ur III or Isin-Larsa period. Cf. Nawar-tahe in *Sargon, King of Battle*, discussed in nn. 21, 31.

[75] On the *Song of the Sea*, see Chapter 2, 25–6, and Chapter 10, 256. On the *Song of Kingship*, see Chapter 10, 256–7. On Mt. Hazzi see Chapter 10, 256–8.

wisdom" (*madōli*).[76] The text continues without a break into the third column, and Allanzu, "young woman (*šidūri*) of Hebat," now appears. She was one of the deities taken by Hattusili I when he first brought Teshshub of Aleppo to Hattusa.[77] Then, the song turns to the *šarrena*, who are "wise," as are the "besworn ones," that is, the ones who have taken an oath, perhaps as judges.[78] The paragraph closes with the name of the deified Naram-Sin,[79] also wise.

The next paragraph opens by asserting Sargon is wise. Here column iii breaks off. When we pick up the thread again in column iv, the participant(s) in the ritual are exhorted to see a series of kings. Some of them are known to us as historical figures, and taken as a group they show how kingship in Hatti was legitimized by being incorporated into the network of the brotherhood of Great Kings immortalized in Sargonic legend. The kings in the first two decently preserved paragraphs of column iv are Audaluma, "lord, lord of Elam, king," Immashku, "lord of Lullu," and Kiklipatalli, "lord of Tukrish," located north of Elam.[80] The "wailing-priest of Ea" did something in the story.[81] As always, our poor understanding of Hurrian lexemes is extremely frustrating, but it is logical that an expert in ritual mourning would appear in an invocation of dead kings.

In the following paragraph characters now appear who are well known from Hurro-Hittite narrative song: "[See, (there is) S]ilver, lord, king, (the one whom) ... brought forth.[82] See, (there is) lord Hedammu,

---

[76] Kushuh plays a role in the Hurrian *Song of Keshshi*: CTH 361.ɪɪ.1, 3, 5, 9 = *KBo* 7.70 6′, *KUB* 47.4 i 4″, *KUB* 47.5 i 6′, *KBo* 35.43 i 7′ (translit. Salvini and Wegner 2004: 48, 61, 63, 67, Nos. 14, 28, 30, 34). Possibly, his presence there has something to do with Shindalimeni's function as mythical midwife, since the moon was closely associated with pregnancy (cf. *armai-* 'to be pregnant', from *arma-* 'moon': see Dardano 2010: 77).

[77] Cf. the same phrase in *Annals of Hattusili I*; see Chapter 7, 159.

[78] See Haas and Wegner (1988: 26).

[79] See de Martino (1993: 128) on the accurate use of the divine determinative for Naram-Sin, who was apotheosized while still living. Sargon, however, was not considered to be a living god, so does not receive the divine determinative in the *šarrena* ritual.

[80] Elam is mentioned in the Late Babylonian *Sargon Geography* (35). Lullu is mentioned in the *Old Assyrian Sargon Legend* (51) and the *Sargon Geography* (12). On Lullu(bu) as a faraway, mountainous place, see Chapter 5, 117, n. 21. Tukrish is mentioned both in the *Sargon Legend* (62) and the *Sargon Geography* (34) (*Old Assyrian Sargon Legend*, translit. and trans. Alster and Oshima 2007: 9–11; *Sargon Geography*, translit. and trans. Horowitz 1998: 68–71). See van de Mieroop (2000: 140–2, 151–3), who compares the places mentioned in this text with those in the *Sargon Legend* and other legends of the Sargonic kings.

[81] *lallar(i)=ne=ž* ᵈÉ.A-*we=n(i)=eš* ... *milulādo*, iv 16–17, cf. Akk. *lallarum*.

[82] *uštae/* [x-r]*a-at(-)ḪUR-ri* (iv 19–20, following translit. of Wilhelm 2003: 393), cf. *ušt-*'set out, bring forth' (Trémouille 2005: 327).

king, (the one whom) Kumarbi engendered."[83] In a mindset within which dead kings interacted with the Former Gods displaced and overthrown by Teshshub,[84] it made perfect sense to group Teshshub's defeated rivals Hedammu and Silver with other dead kings.

Set off in their own paragraph are Manishtushu, "lord, [king,] elder son of Sargon," and the son of Naram-Sin, Sharkalisharri, "[king,] the one who gave his land to another."[85] A storyline involving Sharkalisharri's role in the fall of the kingdom of Akkade is probably alluded to here. Indeed the kingdom abruptly declined after his reign.[86] Then follows a paragraph on the lord of Illaya, a land to the southeast of Hattusa, and on the lord of Hatti.[87] After a mention of the Hurrian Sun-god Shimige in the next paragraph, the text breaks off.

The *šarrena* ritual derives much of its power from Hurro-Hittite narrative song, in which "historical" personages, gods, and other mythical characters all appeared. By mentioning epic characters, characters involved, on the one hand, in the *Chaoskampf* myth used to legitimize kingship,[88] and, on the other, in legends of conquering and civilizing the farthest edges of the world, the ritual alludes to epic themes familiar to its audience, situating the Hittite court in the wide sweep of history from the beginning of the world and to its farthest corners. A connection between cosmogonic and genealogical myth, the one leading into the other, is characteristic of histories that are meant to justify the present order.[89]

---

[83] Similarly, the Hurrian *Invocation of Teshshub of Aleppo* explicitly refers to the story of Teshshub's unusual birth told in the *Song of Birth*: "Your father An(i) engendered you, ... your mother Kumarbi bore you" (*Hurrian Fragments*: CTH 791 = KUB 47.78 i 12′–14′, translit. Trémouille 2005: 9, No. 8). See further Chapter 7, 162.

[84] The Former Kings are discussed in Chapter 4, 94, with n. 73, and Chapter 7, 154–5.

[85] I combine elements of the translations of de Martino (1993: 130) and Wilhelm (2003: 395, n. 10). Wilhelm (2003: 395, n. 10), noting that the term *šarri* normally applies to a deified king, views iv 11, in which Audaluma is clearly so designated, as an exception, and objects to filling in the end of iv 22, 24, 26, 28 with [*šarra*]. I do not find his objection cogent.

[86] In the scribal tradition, however, Nippur's point of view won out, one in which Sargon was portrayed positively and Naram-Sin negatively (and inaccurately), as the one responsible for the fall of Akkade, while the other members of the dynasty were ignored. Naram-Sin stopped being remembered as the grandson of Sargon and became his son to tighten up the opposition between successful conqueror and failed ruler. With the mention of Manishtushu and Sharkalisharri we see a different strain of remembrance. For once, orally transmitted memory seems to be more accurate than the written tradition (J. G. Westenholz 2008). On the decline of Akkade after Sharkalisharri, see A. Westenholz (1999: 56–7).

[87] Illaya appears in various Hittite administrative and religious documents (del Monte and Tischler 1978: 138).

[88] See N. Wyatt (1998) and Chapter 10, 251, 256–7.   [89] Eliade (1963: 21–3).

Cosmogonic myth thus plays out on two interacting planes, the natural and the political, and this results in the combining of characters from the Kumarbi cycle and from human history.

Finally, the rites in which offerings are made to the *šarrena* may have been recognized by the Hittites as analogous to the Mesopotamian *kispum* ritual, in which food offerings were made to statues of the dead, including legendary figures such as Gilgamesh, Sargon, and Naram-Sin.[90] But, even if the directing of ancestor veneration towards legendary or fictional figures was ultimately derived from Mesopotamian practice, it is more likely that the performer of the *šarrena* ritual saw him- or herself as utilizing north Syrian rites of royal ancestor veneration, which were also performed before statues, sometimes life-sized, sometimes quite small, which may be represented by the wool dolls made by the performer of the *šarrena* ritual.[91] Earlier we noted the suggestion that two Mesopotamian texts found at Mari, the *Great Revolt against Naram-Sin* and the *Eponym Chronicle*, were performed at *kispum* rituals for Akkadian kings, and that the *Epic of Gilgamesh* may have been performed at the funerals of kings.[92] The *šarrena* ritual is another example of a text revealing the reciprocal, symbiotic

---

[90] The Ur III kings, who claimed a family relationship with Gilgamesh, made offerings, some in connection with ancestor cult, to Gilgamesh (George 2003: 124–5). Sargon received *kispum* offerings already in Ur III Nippur. J. G. Westenholz (2008) discusses evidence for shrines and offerings made to Sargon, Manishtushu, and Naram-Sin in the Ur III period. And, the list of *kispum* offerings at Mari during the reign of Yasmah-Addu (son of Shamshi-Adad I of Assyria) segues from Sargon and Naram-Sin to the lineage of Shamshi-Adad, reflecting the desire of the Mariot kings to establish a connection with the Sargonic dynasty. On *kispum* at Mari see Durand and Guichard (1997: 28, 41–3, 63–6, with edition of the relevant text at pp. 66–70), Dercksen (2005: 121–3, with earlier references), and, most recently, Archi (2001a: 10), Jacquet (2002), and J. G. Westenholz (2010: 37); on offerings to Sargon and Naram-Sin at Mari see Jonker (1995: 52–4, 225–6). Not all are persuaded that *kispum* was actually offered to Sargon and Naram-Sin at Mari, see Fleming (1999: 160–2).

[91] On north Syrian mortuary ritual and royal ancestor veneration in the Late Bronze Age see Vidal (2005) and Niehr (2006b). It is true that the NH king Hattusili III sent a letter to the Babylonian king Kadashman-Enlil II asking him to send craftsmen to Hattusa to make a statue of a dead ancestor (*Letter from Hattusili III to Kadashman-Enlil*: CTH 172 = KBo 1.10 rev. 58–61, translit. Hagenbuchner 1989: 287; trans. Beckman 1999b: 143). The request suggests that he wished to incorporate a Mesopotamian touch into the Hittite rite of commemoration. But, making offerings to statues of the royal dead was common practice in Ebla and other parts of north Syria. On the statues and statuettes at Middle Bronze Age Ebla, see Matthiae (1979: 568; 1990). At Alalakh the fifteenth-century king Idrimi had his statue in a temple. See Fink (2007: 198) and Chapter 14, 381. On the statues of the dead as a Syro-Hittite phenomenon, see Bonatz (2000a: 129–38) and Struble and Hermann (2009: 29–39). On the use of statues in royal ancestor veneration, see A. C. Cohen (2005: 104–5, for the Early Dynastic period) and Hallo (1988). Also see Chapter 14, 379–81. So, if the custom was imported, then it is most likely that the Hurrians would have brought it from north Syria.

[92] See Chapters 4, 80, and 7, 155.

relation between narrative song – "epic" – and fictional royal ancestor veneration that later also existed between Greek epic and Greek hero worship.

The dead kings seem to derive a major part of their authority from their wisdom, possibly used in the *šarrena* ritual to make a judgment with reference to the performer's claims (now lost) concerning Hattusa's right to preferential treatment or to empower them to cure a patient; privileged knowledge of the past allows one to understand the present better and to predict the future. In turn, the importance of wisdom, to which the audience gains access through the poet's performance, is a self-aggrandizing theme of Hurro-Hittite narrative song. Thus, the parables in the *Song of Release*, put into the mouth of a narrator within the story, repeatedly describe themselves as wisdom (*mādi, ḫattātar*), and Ishhara is called "famous for wisdom" (*mādi amudōvadi*) in the opening lines.[93] Lastly, according to my interpretation, Ebla is destroyed because its foolish council refuses to allow Ebla's dead kings their due, ignoring the parables' chief pearl of wisdom, the advice to treat one's mentors with appropriate respect.[94] Oral bards, then, offered a rival claim to scribes for special access to knowledge of the past. Moreover, it was they, not cuneiform scribes, who transmitted the cultural memory of their ancient history across the end of the Bronze Age in Anatolia.

King lists and genealogies as indexes for world history

Not only the content, but also the format, of the *šarrena* ritual tells us about how world history was structured in the oral tradition. I argue that we can use the *šarrena* ritual to see how several types of texts, typically treated by modern scholars as separate genres, were linked together into a single coherent whole covering the ancient history of the world. We need

---

[93] See Chapter 5, 113, 131. For a discussion of *ḫattātar* see Beckman (1986: 26–30).

[94] Finally, the *Song of Silver* opens with a preface declaring that someone's (one supposes Silver's) "[wis]dom [is greater?] than th[eir] wisdom," [*ḫat*]*tatar⸗šet ḫat<ta>annaš⸗š*[*maš* . . .] (*CTH* 364.1.A = *HFAC* 12 i 4, translit. E. Rieken et al. 2009ff. on KhT). In the next paragraph it is plausible to reconstruct: "Wise men [told] me [the story of] the fath[erless boy]." *nu⸗mu ḫaddanteš* LÚ.MEŠ-*uš wan*[*numiaš* DUMU-*aš* . . . *memir* (*HFAC* 12 i 8); see the tentative transliteration of Hoffner (1988: 144), and his translation in Hoffner (1998a: 48), and the German translation of Haas (2006: 148). If the story itself is presented as passed down from wise men and is about a hero who is surpassingly wise, it is no surprise to see Silver, who may have been considered to be the eponymous hero of Hattusa itself (see Chapter 2, 51–2), grouped with wise kings of old in the *šarrena* ritual.

to examine this whole as a unified system, not pull out single texts, in order to understand why the Greeks would be interested in making use of various elements of the Near Eastern narrative tradition. The invocation of the non-Hittite kings in the *šarrena* ritual is presented as a list with brief allusions to their deeds or provenance, using the same schematic form in which world history was presented in the Mesopotamian king lists. The king lists of the Mesopotamian chronicles incorporated local royal genealogies into supralocal genealogies stretching back to antediluvian times to express the relationship between local and supralocal history, between the heroes of yore and present-day kings.[95] The famous heroes of Sumerian legend, such as Etana, Akka (the opponent of Gilgamesh), Enmerkar, Lugalbanda, and Gilgamesh himself, along with the all-important Akkadian dynasty begun by Sargon, were folded into the dynastic lists of the Sumerian *Chronicle of the Single Monarchy*, for example, without regard to historical synchronisms.[96]

Connections among narratives about the very earliest history of the world and king lists are not only found in the *šarrena* ritual, for the king lists themselves can refer to the time before kingship existed. Thus, the Old Babylonian Sumerian *Royal Chronicle of Lagash* prefaces the usual list of rulers with the tale of how, after the flood, the gods taught the people of Lagash agriculture and saved them from drought and famine.[97] The *Chronicle of the Single Monarchy*, for its part, begins before the flood, "when kingsh[ip] had come down from heaven" (l. 1).

The Kumarbi cycle also draws on the king list tradition, but uses it for a different purpose, to present a series of divine kings ruling over heaven, and the *Song of Birth* pushes history even further back, when kingship was still in heaven, while echoing exactly the phraseology of the *Chronicle of the Single Monarchy*. It is clear that the beginning of the *Song of Birth*

---

[95] Wilcke (1988; 1989). On the king lists and chronicles see the excellent introduction to Glassner's edition and translation (2004); also see Jonker (1995: 140–52, 213–34), discussing their connections to *kispum* and as historiographic works. On the Hittite lists see Chapter 7, 151–2.

[96] Trans. Glassner (2004: 118–27). Glassner (2004: 95–9) suggests the *Chronicle* is based on a tradition from the time of Naram-Sin, but that our version goes back to Utu-hegal (twenty-second century BCE).

[97] Trans. Glassner (2004: 144–9). This same structure was followed by Berossus (*FGrH* 680 F 1b) ca. 1,500 years later in his *Babyloniaka*, the "histories about heaven and the sea and the first birth/creation (*prōtogoniās*) and kings and their deeds" – compare the title of the *Song of Birth*. He begins by telling how the earth was formed, how mankind was invented by the gods, and how they were endowed with the gifts of civilization by the fish-man Oannes, then he moves on to what we would call history with a chronology of kingly reigns. See translation and discussion of Verbrugghe and Wickersham (1996).

draws on the blueprint also used in the chronicle. The *Chronicle of the Single Monarchy* begins:

> When kingsh[ip] had come down from heaven, kingship (was) at [Eri]du. At Eridu, Alulim <was> king; he reigned 28,800 years; Alalgar reigned 36,000 years; two kings reigned 64,800 years. Eridu was abandoned; its kingship was taken to Bad-tibira.[98]

The *Song of Birth* similarly presents a genealogy of the first kings of heaven by naming a series of rulers, the length of their reigns, and who ruled next after their defeat:

> (A i 7–11) Long ago, i[n f]ormer years, Alalu was king in heaven. Alalu was on the throne, and powerful Anu, their foremost, (that) of the gods, stood before hi[m], and he kept bow[i]ng down at his feet, and he kept putting drinking cups in his hand.
>
> (A i 12–17) As just nine years were counted off, Alalu was king in heaven, and in the ninth year Anu [w]ent in batt[le] against Alalu. He defeated him, Alalu, and he ran away before him, and he went down into the Dark Earth. He went down into the Dark Earth, while Anu seated himself on the throne. Anu was sitting on the throne, and powerful Kumarbi kept giving him to drink. He kept bowing down at his feet and putting drinking cups in his hand.
>
> (A i 18–19) As just nine years were counted off Anu was king in heaven, and in the ninth year Anu went in battle against Kumarbi …[99]

Strikingly, the first god who held "kingship in heaven," Alalu, has a name nearly identical to that of the first human ruler named by the chronicle, Alulim of Eridu.[100] It is after this brief synopsis in list-like form of the earliest history that the *Song of Birth* presents a full-blown exposition of the Storm-god's rise to power.

In fact, there is an interplay between more schematic list-like chronicles and more expansive narratives, each only fully meaningful to an audience who could situate a particular story in the *longue durée* covered by the lists and genealogies and recognize their allusions. We can see this in the *šarrena* ritual with the brief mention of Sharkalisharri's role in the demise

---

[98] G I 1–9 (trans. Glassner 2004: 119).
[99] *CTH* 344.1.A = *KUB* 33.120 i 7–19 (translit. E. Rieken *et al.* 2009ff., trans. M. Bachvarova in López-Ruiz 2013: 140–1).
[100] As noted by Haas (1994: 83, n. 19). See in more detail Bachvarova (2012a: 112–13). On Alalu as an underworld deity in Mesopotamia and as a Former God in Emar and Hattusa, also see Wilhelm (2009: 62–3, 66–7), who, however, wishes to distinguish between Alalu and Alulu.

of the empire of Akkade and the allusion to Hedammu's parentage, which would bring to mind the entire stories and only have meaning to an audience that already knew them. The use of a list to serve as a table of contents for the legends that made up the early history of the world is also found the Syro-Mesopotamian wisdom text, the *Ballad of Early Rulers*, which impresses upon its audience the fleetingness of human life and encourages its hearers to drink and be merry (a message comparable to that of Shiduri in the *Epic of Gilgamesh*):[101]

> Where is Alalu, the king who reigned 36,000 years?
> Where is Entena (=Etana) the king, the man who ascended to heaven?
> Where is Gilgameš who, like Ziusudra, sought the (eternal) life?
> Where is Huwawa, who was caught in submission?
> Where is Enkidu, whose strength was not defeated(?) in the country?
> Where are those kings, the vanguards of former days?[102]

Finally, we can see this same use of a list mentioning famous heroes to serve as a table of contents in the genealogies of Greek epic. Thus, the genealogy of Aeneas is a synopsis of a series of stories: Dardanus, sired by Zeus, founded Ilium; his son, Erichthonius ('truly native'), was the richest of men, owner of a vast herd of mares, with whom the North Wind (Boreas) fell in love; Erichthonius sired Tros, who had three sons, Ilus, Assaracus, and Ganymede (Priam's uncle, Aeneas' grand-uncle), the most beautiful of men, who was abducted by Zeus to be his cupbearer.[103] Hesiod's *Theogony* is also formatted as a genealogy, pausing along the way to present extended versions of specific stories, and the sixth-century Hesiodic *Catalog of Women*, which continued the *Theogony*, follows the same format, but with much more emphasis on the genealogical side and the stories of particular heroines only briefly told.[104]

What we can conclude, in short, is not only that Naram-Sin and other Sargonic kings were praised in Hurro-Hittite song, but that the genre of king lists was not solely a scribal exercise, perhaps to be read aloud on a specific occasion. We can assume that genealogical or dynastic lists complementary to narratives were part of the oral repertoire. That is why a list

---

[101] For an interpretation of the text, including a discussion of its thematic correspondences with the *Epic of Gilgamesh*, see Alster (2005: 294–7).

[102] *Ballad of Early Rulers* (Standard Sumerian version) 9–13, trans. Alster (2005: 301–2). Versions were found at Emar and Ugarit (*ca.* 1300 BCE). OB exemplars appear to have come from Sippar, and there is a Neo-Assyrian version (Alster 2005: 288–99). Also see Chapter 3, 74, n. 93.

[103] *Il.* 20.213–40.   [104] On genealogical literature, see West (1985: 3–27).

of (fictional?) Eblaite kings could have been considered to be appropriate for incorporation into the *Song of Release*.[105] Compare also the inclusion of the Catalog of Ships and the catalog of Trojan allies in the *Iliad* for the interaction between narrative and list in Greek epic. Thus, the narratives borrowed by the Greeks did not stand on their own. They were part of a larger systematizing of world history, in which narratives were related to each other by means of fairly flexible lists. A local court could insert their own dynasty, attach themselves to a particular story, or co-opt a storyline for themselves in order to mark their place on the world stage.

Naram-Sin and Hector

I turn now to the *Cuthean Legend of Naram-Sin*. I argue, based on the appearance in the fragment of Hurro-Hittite song mentioned above of Sargon, who was closely connected to his grandson in the Mesopotamian imagination, and the mention of both Sargon and Naram-Sin in the *šarrena* ritual, which incorporated a variety of other characters from Hurro-Hittite narratives, that a version of this storyline was performed in the Hurro-Hittite tradition. It was preserved in the oral tradition of epic along with versions of the storylines of the *Song of Gilgamesh* and the Kumarbi cycle. The *Song of Release* was subsequently reworked into Hector's story in the *Iliad*.[106] The *Cuthean Legend* is a relatively well-preserved text, attested first in the Old Babylonian period, with the latest version in Standard Babylonian found at several sites, including Assurbanipal's library at Nineveh.[107] It was a particularly popular story, and at Hattusa early versions of the story are inscribed on a prism in Middle Babylonian. There are as many as four Hittite exemplars.[108] As with the Sargon stories at Hattusa, the Naram-Sin

---

[105] For parallels between how king lists order and frame historical events and how it is done in other Mesopotamian texts, such as the *Lament for Sumer and Ur*, the *Sumerian Sargon Legend*, and the Etana stories, see Wilcke (2001); also see Wilcke (1988) on the interplay among lists, omens, and narratives.

[106] This section presents some of the same arguments found in Bachvarova (2008a), where I discussed in addition how the same story was told in the Sumerian *Curse of Akkade*, but from a very different point of view, in which Naram-Sin was considered blameworthy, and Akkade was destroyed.

[107] J. G. Westenholz (1997: 296–7). It was the one story about a Sargonic king that had "serialized and standardized editions" (J. G. Westenholz 2011: 293).

[108] See J. G. Westenholz (1992: 133–4) on its popularity and her list of texts (J. G. Westenholz 1997: 5). Akkadian texts about Naram-Sin at Hattusa: *narû*-prisms (MS): *CTH* 819: *Akkadian Fragments = KBo* 19.98 (No. 21A: *Naram-Sin and the Enemy Hordes*, translit. and trans. J. G. Westenholz 1997: 280–93) and possibly *KBo* 19.99 (not translated by J. G. Westenholz; its

story was not simply a Mesopotamian scribal exercise translated out of Akkadian into Hittite, for it displays at least one distinctively Hittite detail: when Naram-Sin complains to Ishtar after he loses a major battle against the enemy hordes, she instructs him to purify himself, then engage in dream-incubation, invoking (*mugai-*) his gods in his sleep. The *mugawar* is a peculiarly Anatolian ritual.[109]

According to the Akkadian *Cuthean Legend*, Naram-Sin, by not following the advice of his diviners, nearly lost Akkade to the invading Gutian hordes, more beast than human. He suffered a near-complete defeat, only turned around by the intervention of Ishtar. Naram-Sin is portrayed as a good ruler, concerned with the prosperity of his people, yet his actions only led to the destruction of his kingdom. Three years in a row Naram-Sin sent out his troops, only to have them utterly defeated. Although he asked the gods for their advice, he repeatedly rejected the omens transmitted by extispicy (divination by means of an animal's exta), refusing to keep his army within the walls of his city.

Two more rounds of omens are sought until, finally, Ishtar decides to help him with some good advice, to leave the enemy alone, for the gods will deal with them in the future. When Naram-Sin takes Ishtar's advice, Akkade is spared, and Naram-Sin orders that a tablet be prepared and a stele be made, which will convey his warnings to future rulers to strengthen their fortifications and stay inside their walls, putting aside their weapons and allowing the enemy to kill and to roam about at will. The major theme

---

remains are so exiguous its exact content cannot be ascertained); also see Beckman (1983b: 103–4) and J. G. Westenholz (2011: 289) on the scribe who wrote down *KBo* 19.99, the son of a Babylonian scribe, already mentioned in n. 19. Hittite texts about Naram-Sin at Hattusa (translit. Güterbock 1938: 49–80; trans. and comparative discussion Haas 2006: 72–6): *Naram-Sin in Asia Minor*: *CTH* 311: *KBo* 22.85 (translit. Groddek 2008: 83), *CTH* 311.1 = *KBo* 3.13 (J. G. Westenholz's No. 18: *Great Revolt against Naram-Sin*), *CTH* 311.2.A = *KBo* 3.16 + *KUB* 31.1 + *IBoT* 4.7 (partial translit. Groddek 2007: 5), *CTH* 311.2.B = *KBo* 3.18 + 17 + 19 (grouped by J. G. Westenholz under No. 21B). For important discussions of the material from Hattusa, see Hoffner (1970) on the Hittite versions, but assuming a scribe translating an Akkadian text (see J. G. Westenholz 1997: 328, on l. 164, for one correction of Hoffner's interpretation), van de Mieroop (2000: 138–40), and Beckman (2005: 257–8). I use the SB version here, as it is the most complete (translit. and trans. J. G. Westenholz 1997: 300–31).

[109] *CTH* 311.2.A = *KBo* 3.16 iii 5–13 with duplicate *CTH* 311.2B = *KBo* 3.18 + *KBo* 3.19 iii 9–17 (translit. Güterbock 1938: 54, 56; trans. Haas 2006: 75). On the *mugawar*, see Chapter 4, 104, n. 115. See Mouton (2007: 15, 109–10) on dream-incubation (another Anatolian practice) in the Hittite Naram-Sin legend. Anatolian focus in the *Great Revolt against Naram-Sin*: *CTH* 311.1 = *KBo* 3.13 obv. 11' (translit. Güterbock 1938: 68; trans. Haas 2006: 73): two of the rebellious kings are Pamba, king of Hatti, and Zipani, king of Kanesh, who do not appear in any other versions. See van de Mieroop (2000: 139–40), J. G. Westenholz (2011: 294–8, with earlier references).

of the work is the ruler as receiver of omens that presage his success or failure in actions that have consequences for his people. Clearly in the written text there was a self-aggrandizing message from the omen-readers, who were skilled scholars and scribes, to their royal patron.

The theme of the ruler who fails to interpret omens correctly is manipulated to very different ends and in a very elaborate way by Homer to achieve maximum pathos and to fit with the concerns of his audience. We can see in Homer a more sophisticated discussion of the responsibilities of the gods and humans in the fall of a city, one that allows the audience insight into the thinking of the gods to which other characters within the story are not privy, allowing us to evaluate the humans' actions in a way they themselves cannot. This is true with regard to the rulers on both sides of the conflict. For, like Hector, Agamemnon rejects the interpretation of his seer, refusing to release Chryseis to please Apollo and thus relieve the Achaeans from the plague sent by him, and Agamemnon is also tricked by Zeus with a lying dream that convinces him to make an attack on Troy, promising him victory (2.1–36). The manipulation of this convention is far more pathetic, however, in the case of Hector, who we know will be tragically maneuvered into the position in which he must be killed in defense of his city because of his ill-placed faith in the support of Zeus.

James Redfield, in *Nature and Culture in the Iliad: The Tragedy of Hector* (1994), argues that Hector is the real hero of the *Iliad*. It is his death, after all, that culminates the story, and the restoration of his body to his father by Achilles marks the end of the Achaean hero's wrath. Redfield traces the trajectory of Hector's tragic error, beginning at the end of Book 8 when Hector announces that the Trojans will win and that he relies on Zeus for support. Hector is thinking of the moment when Zeus thundered thrice, driving Diomedes off (8.167–244), and the Achaeans were routed, leaving the Trojans in complete control of the plain before Ilium. Yet, Hector's confidence is expressed directly after we the audience have been allowed to witness a scene among the gods in which they discuss exactly for how long he will be allowed to win, and why. And, the scene closes with the gods rejecting the sacrifices the Trojans make to them, since the city of Troy was hateful to them. Hector's confident decision to keep his men outside the walls of Troy for the night then allows Diomedes and Odysseus to wreak havoc in the camp.[110] Apparently Hector is not aware of the advice given to Naram-Sin, to remain inside the city and let the enemy do their worst outside.

---

[110] M. L. West (1997a: 374) cites a different set of Near Eastern parallels to the Doloneia.

Hector becomes more and more deluded during the course of the next few days, and a key turning point is the first time he rejects the cautious advice of the seer Poulydamas interpreting a bird omen, and refuses to retreat rather than attack:

> (12.230–43) Hector of variegated helm spoke to him, looking at him from under his brows, "Poulydamas, now those things you speak are not dear to me. You know how to think other advice (*mūthon*) better than this. If in earnest you tell that truthfully, then the gods themselves indeed have lost their minds, who would advise to forget the plans of loud-thundering Zeus, which he himself promised to me and agreed to. You yourself advise me to trust in slender-winged birds, which I don't care about at all, don't pay any attention to... Let us trust in the plan of great Zeus, who rules all mortals and immortals. There is one bird that is the best, to defend our fatherland..."

Hector's reply is strikingly similar to that of Naram-Sin's in the *Cuthean Legend*:

> What lion (ever) performed extispicy?
> What wolf (ever) consulted a dream-interpreter?
> I will go like a brigand according to my own inclination.
> And I will cast aside the (oracle) of the god(s): I will be in control of myself.[111]

This entire sequence of events is reprised in Book 18. Patroclus has been killed, Achilles has announced his intention to kill Hector, and the reply of Thetis, that this means his own death is imminent, presupposes that he will be successful. It has become clear to Achilles that the gods' intervention, the advice to avoid battle (the same advice that Hector ignores, causing his own destruction), which seemingly was to give him more honor, has been at the cost of his friend's life. He laments in words which many scholars have noticed bear remarkable resemblance to the words of Gilgamesh mourning the death of Enkidu.[112] In this context, in which once again the intentions of the gods are made clear to the audience, Hector again disagrees with Poulydamas' cautious advice and insists that Zeus supports him.

> (18.310–13) So Hector spoke, and the Trojans shouted assent, foolish ones, for Pallas Athena took from them their minds, for they agreed with

---

[111] SB 80–3 (trans. J. G. Westenholz 1997: 317). [112] E.g., M. L. West (1997a: 340–4).

Hector who advised badly, but no one did with Poulydamas, who advised a good plan.

The delusion of the Trojans is reminiscent of the wrong decision made by the Eblaite council in the *Song of Release*, who ignore the advice of their king, the go-between for Teshshub, and take Zazalla's side.

Hector rejects cautious advice – now from his parents – most pitifully for the third and final time in Book 22. Hector refuses to retreat, but:

> (22.98–107) Anguished indeed, he spoke to his great-hearted soul, "Woe is me, if I take shelter in the tower and walls, Poulydamas would be the first to place shame on me, who advised me to lead the Trojans to the city at the fall of baneful night, when shining Achilles rose up. But I wasn't persuaded; indeed it would have been much better. But now, since I have destroyed the host with my recklessness, I am ashamed before the Trojan men and women with their trailing robes, lest some other person, who is less than me, might say, 'Hector, trusting in his strength destroyed his people'."

Compare what Naram-Sin says to himself in the *Cuthean Legend*, when for the third year in a row his massive troops sent against the enemy are all slain and he realizes his grievous error:

> What have I left to the dynasty!?
> I am a king who does not keep his country safe
> and a shepherd who does not safeguard his people.
> How shall I ever continue to act so that I can get myself out (of this)!?[113]

Hector goes on with a distinctively Greek answer, evoking the honor and duty of a Homeric warrior: "So they will say; but it would be much better for me, standing face to face in battle, to kill Achilles and return or to die myself with glory for the city" (22.108–10). In fact he is unable to follow through on this brave thought, because "trembling seized him" (136), and he turns tail and runs. As Naram-Sin puts it, "Terror of lions, death, plague, twitching of limbs, panic, chills" (SB 94–5). The Greek gods, interested spectators, realize this is the moment of truth, and, untypically, hesitate (22.167–85).[114] Yet, as Naram-Sin says in the *Cuthean Legend*, "Above, in co[uncil,] the flood was decided" (SB 97). Hector must die.

---

[113] SB 90–3 (trans. J. G. Westenholz 1997: 319).
[114] This scene is a doublet of the scene among the gods when they decide that Sarpedon must die (*Il.* 16.431–61) and descends from the scene in the *Epic of Gilgamesh* in which the gods debate whether he or Enkidu must die (M. L. West 1997a: 179–80, 343–4), on which see Chapter 3, 68–9.

Conclusion

Hattusili's patterning of his own exploits after those of Sargon leads us to think about how fitting local history into world history, contemporary events into the *longue durée*, enabled historical events to be turned into myth, a process that was surely at work in the prehistory of the story of the Trojan War, as it was during the Persian War.[115] The scribes and diviners who were trained in the art of writing on clay and in proper Akkadian by copying Naram-Sin's and Sargon's inscriptions and omens, and in some cases their legends, were being inculcated into Mesopotamian culture by learning about the successes and the failures of the great heroes of the past. The scribes wrote of the exploits of their own kings following the frameworks they learned as part of their scribal training; such narratives also served as inspiration for future kings. Similarly, oral poets must have fit historical events into a framework the meaning of which their audience understood, and not just narratives but also lists or catalogs.

The discussion of Sargonic legend showed how there was mutual influence between the Gilgamesh and Sargonic traditions, giving us a window onto how oral poets and storytellers fed off each other's work to develop a thematically coherent picture of their legendary past that eventually was to play such an important role in the development of Greek mythology. At the same time, the discussion of the influence of the king lists on the *šarrena* ritual and the *Song of Birth* showed that such lists served as a kind of skeleton providing a solid large-scale structure to the flesh of the individual narratives. That dynastic lists or genealogies serving as memnonic devices for the recollection of episodes of mytho-history could do more than preserve names will become an important point in the final chapters, in which I argue that first-millennium Anatolians bridged the gap across the end of the Bronze Age with dynastic lists, including one that remembered Alaksandu of Troy.

Epic presented itself as wisdom in the form of admonitory history about the deeds of Great Kings and heroes, and (fictional) royal ancestor veneration allowed local courts to draw on the legitimizing power of those same kings and heroes.[116] Indeed, for a local court to join the group

---

[115] See Boedeker (2001a; 2001b) and Chapter 16, 418–19, on the mythologizing of the Persian War in the fifth century BCE.
[116] Helms (1988: 148–9) offers a supporting analysis within an anthropological framework of "the association of elites, particularly rulers of centralized societies, with geographically distant

of Great Kings, it had to join its past to theirs.[117] One way to do this was to take on the responsibility of feeding the dead of other dynasties, in order to become in a sense a member of their family;[118] thus, performing *kispum* for legendary kings was a commonly used strategy on the part of dynasties that wished to be part of world history. Indeed, the interest of Syrian courts in joining world history should be viewed as encouraging the incorporation of Sargonic legend into Syrian epic, the same tradition that commemorated the destruction of Ebla, as indirectly revealed by the appearance of Sargon in a Hurrian epic song.[119] While the Hittite royal family did not attempt actually to connect its genealogy with that of renowned Mesopotamian kings, in the *šarrena* ritual it is clear that the king of Hatti was included in the larger group of prestigious *šarrena* that indeed comprised Sargonic, Hurrian, and other kings of realms distant in space and time. And, they appear to be receiving offerings. I argue that this same desire to seek prestige through a connection to world history was at work spurring the transfer of Syro-Anatolian ways of remembering the remote past to the Greeks, helping to reshape Greek royal ancestor veneration into hero worship, by attaching Near Eastern storylines to Greek heroes, thus deeply affecting Greek heroic, cosmogonic, and genealogical epic.

This chapter offers further evidence that the texts attested at Hattusa that can be shown to have parallels with Greek myth ultimately came from

---

places or peoples, as evidenced in mythical tales or historical episodes in which rulers or ruling dynasties were derived from external sources."

[117] See Assmann (2003) on the connection between collective memory and a group identity.

[118] This is explicit at Emar and Nuzi: see van der Toorn (1994; 1995).

[119] This urge to connect a royal lineage with the broader world through eponymous ancestors is also found in the *Assyrian Royal Chronicle*, originally from the time of Shamshi-Adad I, in which the king list is prefaced by a list of "seventeen kings who dwelt in tents" (10, trans. Glassner 2004: 137), among whom are Amorite tribes, geographical names, such as the Haneans, and eponymous ancestors, such as Ditanu. There has been much discussion of the historical significance of the early sections of such lineages, and the west Semitic ethnic consciousness of which they were the product. See, for example, Finkelstein (1966) and Vidal (2006, with earlier references). A text belonging to a *kispum* ritual originally from the sixteenth century BCE similarly begins its list of invokees with eponymous ancestors, then segues into historical figures, finishing by naming the troops of Amurru, Hana, and Gutium (Amorite peoples), soldiers killed in battle, then more generally all the dead: "you who have no one to make a food-offering or to invoke your name, come, take your share of this meal and this drink, and bless Ammī-ṣaduqa, son of Ammī-ditāna, king of Babylon" (BM 80328 38–43, trans. Glassner 2004: 71). See edition of Finkelstein (1966) and discussion of Glassner (2004: 71–3). For discussion of Ditanu and the Greek Titans, see Chapter 11, 290.

an oral milieu. In addition, the effacing of the particular identity of Naram-Sin, like that of Gilgamesh, indicates that the narrative tradition evolved for a period of time without any contact with the Mesopotamian tradition. This storyline was not incorporated directly into the Homeric tradition from a written Neo-Assyrian text.

I have now presented the last major piece of evidence for my claim that a unified genre of Syro-Anatolian narrative song very similar to that found at Hattusa was responsible for the major storylines of Homeric and Hesiodic epic. The questions now to be answered are why, how, and when the influence occurred; this will be the focus of the rest of this book.

9 | Long-distance interactions: theory, practice, and myth

> Eumaeus: "Who would in fact call another guest from elsewhere, himself going to him (*epielthōn*), if he weren't one of those who are craftsmen (*dēmioergoi*), a seer (*mantin*) or healer of ills or carpenter, or even a divine singer, who can please by singing? For these ones among men are invited/summoned (*klētoi*) over the boundless earth."
>
> *Odyssey* 17.382–6

Introduction

In this chapter I begin to answer the question of why Near Eastern narratives would have been interesting to a Greek audience, as well as providing suggestions on some ways the transfer occurred. I make no claim that the milieus I explore were the only settings in which east and west interacted, and I acknowledge that stories and elements of stories moved in ways invisible to the record, told by merchants abroad perhaps, or within households established by mixed marriages, as opposed to bards performing polished verbal art,[1] but I do present several viable frameworks explaining where and how interaction between epic traditions (defined broadly to include all the types of narratives found in Greek hexametric poetry) and transfer of epic material took place.

I think of the artists responsible for the interchange less as independent agents than as representatives of a group: a nation, a region, an ethnos, a socio-economic class. Embedded in multiple interlocking institutions and networks, they responded to external constraints and demands, carrying out the aims of their societies as they strove to achieve success and recognition. Thus, I move away from treating texts as literary products of artists who had the kind of artistic freedom found among modern authors. A viewpoint that treats the texts that I have been discussing up to this point as literature, i.e., entertainment for a literate elite, not only discounts the significance of their oral milieu, it separates the texts we have from the

---

[1] As argued by Lane Fox (2009).

milieus in which they were produced, and fails to take into account their range of possible functions, all of which can help us to understand why these texts were considered valuable enough to be borrowed.

In this chapter I first critique the widely espoused theory of wandering craftsmen as transmitters of cultural features from east to west. Then, I provide another framework within which east–west transmission of epic in the Late Bronze Age and Early Iron Age can be studied, concentrating on long-distance elite interactions, which were carried out by the transfer of performers, especially singers and healers, between courts, as well as by the movement of elites themselves. That is, I de-emphasize the "free will" of the performers and focus more on why their "product" was considered desirable by their patrons. I continue to develop the themes from the last chapter, in which I discussed how local courts legitimized themselves by connecting themselves to world history and legendary heroes from the distant past and far away. In this chapter I examine how the worth attributed to esoteric goods and long-distance travel encouraged contact and therefore transfer of verbal art, and I explore how the high value put on long-distance travel motivated the spread of certain stories. I close with an analysis of how the efficacy imputed to the exotic encouraged the spread of healing incantations and the historiolae used in them, which themselves made use of the theme of the long-distance journey.

Wandering seers or Orientalizing construct?

Walter Burkert has presented two means by which Near Eastern cultural traits could have reached Greece, but his suggestion that Akkadian epic entered the Homeric tradition by being translated by bilingual scribes has not been embraced as enthusiastically as his theory of freely moving craftsmen of verbal art and ritual technology bringing stories and magico-religious practices to the west in the Orientalizing period. This has caught the imagination of Classical scholars and been given great explanatory power in subsequent discussions of textual and cultural links across the Mediterranean. By simply referring to the theory as a given, Classical scholars have been able to avoid the question of why and how, and to move directly to a discussion of the motifs or practices under consideration.[2] However, a re-examination of Burkert's theory as a whole is certainly overdue. Burkert claims:

---

[2] For Burkert's thoughts on bilingual scribes as transmitters of Near Eastern epic, see Chapter 3, 55, n. 8. While M. L. West has been criticized for merely providing a list of

In fact successful charismatic specialists became, as they can today, widely sought-after personalities; they could cross frontiers even more easily and more often than other craftsmen with simpler skills. Being the mobile bearers of cross-cultural knowledge, the migrant charismatics deserve particular attention as to cultural contacts. In fact they represent the intellectual elite of the time with a chance to achieve international status.[3]

In the first place, there are problems in the terminology used. In the ancient world charismatics and trained specialists belonged to two different categories: doctors and diviners required specialized training, while "charismatics" (like the prophets of the Hebrew Bible) had an inborn talent that gave them a direct line to the gods. The prophet is labeled in Akkadian *muḫḫû(tu) maḫḫû(tu)* 'frenzied one', or *ragginu (raggintu)* 'shouter'.[4] Cristiano Grottanelli, who provides the most detailed analysis of the Near Eastern charismatic prophet, describes his unique trait as a "special relationship with the supernatural, and this relationship is expressed, very concretely, by the working of miracles."[5] The term for diviner, *bārû*, on the other hand, literally means "examiner." As André Finet remarks, "With him there is no inspiration, neither visions, nor dreams."[6]

Secondly, we need to be careful in distinguishing how these men and women moved. Were they able to move freely, were they sent from one patron to another, or were they invited by a patron? Imprecision on this point is a consistent problem in scholarly discussions.[7] The question is

---

correspondences, without explaining the significance of them, he certainly does offer some discussion of the variety of ways in which stories crossed geographic and linguistic barriers (1997a: 586–630).

[3] Burkert (1992: 42).

[4] López-Ruiz (2010: 190) has also noted the confusion in terminology. There were female ecstatics as well as male ones. At Mari a particular kind of ecstatic was called the *āpilu* 'answerer', and the *nābûm* is also found there, cognate with Old Testament *nāvî'* (Grabbe 1995: 108). On the *bārû* and other diviners, see Oppenheim (1969). See Sweek (2002) on the different types of Near Eastern prophet and their relationship to the state, also Nissinen (2000, esp. pp. 107–11, contrasting scholar and prophet; Nissinen in Nissinen, Seow, and Ritner 2003: 6–7, 16, 97–100, 179–80). Burkert (1983b; 1992: 46–53) argues that the techniques of the *bārû*, who practiced liver divination, were borrowed by the Greeks directly from Mesopotamia in the Orientalizing period. In fact, the correspondences between the Greek and Akkadian terminology are not as impressive as he claims. I argue rather that the Greeks learned of hepatoscopy from Anatolians or in Cyprus; see Bachvarova (2012b: 157–8).

[5] Grottanelli (1982: 662).

[6] "Pas d'inspiration chez lui, ni de visions, ni de rêves" (Finet 1966: 87).

[7] Including the otherwise fine discussions of Bremmer (1996), Nagy (1990b: 56–7), and Rollinger (1996: 202–10).

closely tied to their social status. Furthermore, if they were free to move on their own initiative, was it because they operated on the fringes of society or because they were embedded in a trans-generational supralocal community of elites? In fact, what does "elite" really mean in this context? In the modern academic world with which Burkert implicitly makes an analogy, elite status is based on our intellectual merits and our productivity, and is aided by personal charisma – in the commonly used sense, rather than that of Max Weber (whom Burkert follows), who uses it in the sense of "calling."[8] In much of the rest of the modern world, it is based on a combination of conspicuous consumption and family background, whom one knows, as well as, of course, personal charisma. The latter set of standards matches more closely the expectations of the ancient world, from the Late Bronze Age through the Archaic period. Furthermore, as I will show, some of the standard examples of mobile prophets – Elijah, Elisha, Homeric *dēmiourgoi*, Epimenides, and Melampous – have been misidentified.

While the Late Bronze Age letters reveal to us a "brotherhood of Great Kings,"[9] within which physicians, exorcists, augurs, and even gods were sent back and forth as diplomatic gifts on a par with luxury drinking vessels, and precious raw materials,[10] the Old Testament prophet served a higher master, Yahweh. The narrative of 1 and 2 Kings, which tells of Elijah and Elisha, is shaped by a Deuteronomistic point of view, in which the faith of a series of kings of Israel is shown to be consistently wanting, especially in comparison with Elijah's and Elisha's close relationship with God. Elijah obeyed God's command to travel to such-and-such a place and visit the court of such-and-such a king, rather than requests from mere mortals.[11] Elisha, the chosen successor of Elijah, had more control over his own actions and movements, but he worked within an organized group of prophets from a fixed abode, like the prophets at eighteenth-century Mari,

---

[8] On Weber's use of the term "charismatic," see Cryer (1994: 243).
[9] Zaccagnini (1987: 62–3). Also see Bryce (2003b: 76–85).
[10] On the transfer of skilled personnel such as craftsmen, augurs, and doctors as part of the reciprocal gifting between Egypt or Babylon and Hattusa, Cyprus, and Ugarit in the Late Bronze Age, see Zaccagnini (1983: 250–5; 1987: 59–60), who discusses the inability of craftsmen to move legitimately on their own across international borders in the Middle and Late Bronze Ages. On the transfer of the gods of Ahhiyawa and Lazpa, see Chapter 13, 346. Visit of IŠTAR of Nineveh to Amarna: *EA* 23:13–32 (trans. Moran 1992: 61), see Haas (1979: 401), Wegner (1981: 65–7), Beckman (1998: 3).
[11] 1 Kings 17–19, 21:17–19, 2 Kings 1–2, 4–10. Similar is the scenario of Numbers 22, in which Balak, king of Moab, repeatedly sends messengers with money to ask Balaam to curse Israel, but God forbids the prophet from doing so.

who were typically attached to temples of the specific gods for whom they served as mouthpieces.[12] Elisha traveled with the king on campaign or was near enough to his court to know of events and concerns there, and to show repeatedly that he was empowered by Yahweh.[13] Finally, the point made by these stories from the Hebrew Bible is highly contingent on the overall point of 1 and 2 Kings, and should not be applied across the Mediterranean to the figure of the Greek seer.[14]

On the Greek side, the one example from Homer commonly cited as reflecting "free artisans moving from one client to another seeking better economic gain,"[15] which is quoted at the beginning of this chapter, does not in fact refer to wandering craftsmen, but to craftsmen invited or summoned, like those traded among the Great Kings of the Near East. Thus, in Book 17 of the *Odyssey* the swineherd Eumaeus refers to craftsmen, seers, and singers as summoned (*klētoi*) at the request of a patron.[16] Similarly, the movements of the legendary healer Epimenides in the early sixth century were by invitation or by order of the god, and in any case he did not travel beyond Greece to other countries.[17] Certainly the healers

---

[12] On the prophets of the Hebrew Bible as "cult functionaries" see Cryer (1994: 245–50).
[13] 2 Kings 2:15–19.   [14] See the critique of Nissinen (2000: 111–14).
[15] Zaccagnini (1983: 258), similarly Grottanelli (1982: 664, citing Zaccagnini) and Burkert (1992: 42, citing Grottanelli): "In the more marginal regions where the power of the kings was less, the independence of the seer was correspondingly enhanced. He could travel freely on his own initiative, as is seen in both Greece and Israel. As was the case with local craftsmen, free enterprise developed in the Greek world in particular." M. L. West (1997a: 611): "In the freer conditions of the Greek world skilled émigrés might make their own way from town to town, doing their best to acquire a reputation."
[16] *Od.* 17.382–6. The adjective *klētos*, from *kaleō* 'call', conventionally translated in the passage opening this chapter as "welcome," occurs only twice in Homer, here and at *Il.* 9.165, where Nestor tells Agamemnon, "but come on, let us send *klētous*, who will go quickly to the shelter of Achilles, son of Peleus." The translation "summoned" fits best here, as it does in the compound adjective applied twice to the allies of the Trojans, *poluklētoi* 'called from many places' (*Il.* 4.438, 10.420). At *Od.* 19.134–5, Penelope says, "I did not busy myself with guests, suppliants, or heralds at all, who are *dēmioergoi*," describing three different types of travelers. The *xenoi* ('guests') travel freely, while the heralds are sent and the suppliants are driven by circumstances beyond their control. Tandy (1997: 166–9) also debunks the construct of the itinerant singer, showing that there is no evidence internal to the *Iliad* or *Odyssey* for such singers. And see Muhly (2005), making many of the same points I make here. Thamyris, the "archetypal wandering poet," mentioned in the *Iliad* (2.591–600) as voyaging from the house of Eurytus in Oechalia, was actually a poet of the sort referred to by Eumaeus; see Wilson (2009).
[17] Plato, *Laws* 642d, "according to the proclamation (*manteion*) of the god"; Plu. *Sol.* 12.4, "sent for" (*metapemptos*); D. L. 1.109–10 (= Epimenides *FGrH* 457 T 1), because of an oracle by the Pythia. Similarly with Thaletas, the healing musician: he was sent among the Lacedaemonians "according to the oracle" (*kata puthokhrēston*, [Plu.] *Mus.* 1146c, Philod. *Mus.* 18.36–9). The standard example of a Greek healer who crosses international borders is Democedes, whose story is told in Herodotus 3.125, 129–137. He may have traveled within the borders of the

were able to move freely, but it is the value attributed to them that motivates an invitation, and I prefer to focus on why they were valued and therefore invited, rather than their own "free will."

The Archaic hero Melampous was indeed a mobile healer, but he was a different kind of seer from the *dēmiourgos*: he was an agent of long-distance elite interactions embedded in a social network cemented by marriages and guest friendships and disturbed by conflicts over women, goods, and power.[18] From a distinguished family in Pylos, Melampous was the nephew of Neleus, its king, and traveled all the way to Thessalian Phylace to undergo an ordeal in order to win Neleus' daughter for his brother Bias. Thrown into prison, as he fully expected to be because of his mantic powers, he eventually secured his release and the attention of the king because of his ability to understand the language of birds, those mediators between heaven and earth, a talent which also enabled him to cure the king's son of his impotence. For this he was given the cattle that Neleus had demanded as the price for his daughter.[19] Thus, Melampous' freedom of movement came from his elite social standing, and he utilized his mantic powers to abet his brother's quest for improved status.

At some point itinerant philosophers and magicians did become a recognized class of workers. When and under what circumstances are in fact questions worth re-opening, but they lie beyond the scope of this study. We should be careful not to project back before the Classical period characters like the wandering charlatans alluded to by Plato and Hippocrates, without actual evidence, which is currently not forthcoming.[20] It is true, on the other hand, that we should not assume that lack of evidence means that they did

---

Greek world freely, but Democedes ended up in Persia because he had been taken captive (Moyer 2006). Similarly, the poet of *hHAp* 174–5 describes himself as traveling a circuit, not crossing international borders. Empedocles wanders because he has been cast out like an exile, since he has committed murder (31 B 139 Diels-Kranz).

[18] Bremmer (1996: 100). We can cobble together a good part of early versions of Melampous' story from Homer's brief telling at *Od.* 11.281–97, 15.225–42, supplemented by the material from the scholia, which they drew from Pherecydes of Athens (*FGrH* 3 FF 33, 114), and fragments of Hesiod's *Catalog of Women* (FF 35, 79, 80 Most). Melampous was an interesting enough figure to have an entire narrative poem composed about him that was attributed to Hesiod. The *Melampodia* is unfortunately nearly completely lost (Hes. FF 206–15 Most). See Gantz (1993: 185–8) for a full discussion of the sources. Also see Finkelberg (2005: 80–6), for a different interpretation of his story.

[19] In the *Odyssey* we are told that he was forced to flee Pylos and traveled to Argos, where, as we learn from Pherecydes, he cured the daughters of king Proetus of their madness, caused by either by Hera or by Dionysus, in turn for a share of the kingdom and the hand of one of the king's daughters.

[20] Hipp. *Morb. Sacr.* 1.4 vi 354 Littré and Pl. *Rep.* 364b (Burkert 1983b: 116, 119; 1992: 125).

not exist. As Burkert justifiably suggests, "We cannot expect to find many archaeologically identifiable traces of such people."[21]

It is worth digging a little further into the theoretical underpinnings of Burkert's theory. The image of the "migrant craftsman" relies on one key claim made by Grottanelli:

> The pattern consisting of the concentration of healers and diviners (and also of texts on such special crafts) at court is dominant before the Iron Age. The crisis or collapse of the Ancient Oriental palace organization implies that the healers and diviners are "free" to move about and to offer their services on the "market." It is this new situation that accounts for the figures I have described so far ..., for only in the new Iron Age situation are the "healer-saviours" at the same time "free" and unattached, and "liminal" in the sense that their special skill and power set them apart.[22]

We should be acutely aware that the construct of a free-market economy arising after the fall of the palace economies, in which skilled labor moved on its own initiative, is just that, a theoretical construct based on a now outdated Orientalizing (in Edward Said's sense[23]) contrast of "free" west and "enslaved" east,[24] what Ian Morris and J. G. Manning have called the "divided Mediterranean model."[25] Yes, the Late Bronze Age palaces maintained control of the movement of high-value raw materials and the work of highly skilled craftsmen; the palaces created the demand for the craftsmen's products; and the palaces often provided for their day-to-day maintenance. Yes, the collapse of the palace-controlled chains of production and trade routes created new opportunities; this was perhaps the root cause, for example, for the rise of innovations such as iron-working, based on a widely available raw material.[26] However, that is a very different proposition from craftsmen "'free' to move about and offer their services on the 'market'," as Grottanelli puts it. Indeed, I wonder whether the model was influenced by events in the mid twentieth century, which saw the flight of skilled labor and academics from Nazi Germany, war-torn Europe, and the countries of the Soviet bloc to the free markets of other parts of Europe and America.[27] The "itinerant craftsman" theory seems to

---

[21] Burkert (1992: 51)   [22] Grottanelli (1982: 665).   [23] Said (1978).
[24] Moyer (2006: 225–7).   [25] I. Morris and Manning (2005).
[26] Concomitantly, there was a reduction in the importance of bronze, which required two different raw materials to be brought together that were not widely available and were not found in the same locations.
[27] Compare M. L. West's summary (1997a: 611) of Burkert: "He also invokes a particular historical factor tending to promote westward migration in the eighth and seventh centuries:

derive much of its explanatory power from our own recent experience rather than evidence from the ancient world. That is not to assert categorically that there were no migrant or itinerant craftsmen. Rather, a focus on the motivations of their patrons will provide a better explanation for how and why their products moved across geographical and linguistic barriers.

Push–pull factors encouraging long-distance interactions

More recently, studies of the archaeological evidence for interactions between east and west have focused on

> some of the cultural exchange taking place in the Middle and Late Bronze Age as located in a desire to enhance prestige through the acquisition and display of the foreign, the exotic, and the monumental ... The status attached to the acquisition of and control over exotic goods and symbols may have also served as an ideology to legitimize political power.[28]

This approach builds on the insights of anthropologists such as Arjun Appadurai, who, in the valuable introduction to his edited volume *The Social Life of Things: Commodities in Cultural Perspective*, analyzes the concept of the "politics of value," arguing, "[t]he long-distance movement of precious commodities entailed costs that made the acquisition of them *in itself* a marker of exclusivity and an instrument of sumptuary distinction."[29] He suggests:

> I propose that we regard luxury goods not so much in contrast to necessities (a contrast filled with problems), but as goods whose principal use is *rhetorical* and *social*, goods that are simply *incarnated signs*. The necessity to which *they* respond is fundamentally political.[30]

This way of looking at interaction between east and west, which focuses on the values encouraging long-distance interactions, has abundant support in the sources available to us from the Bronze Age; they show how exotic

---

the expansion of the Assyrian empire to the Mediterranean, with all the destruction, dispossession, and social upheaval that that process entailed."

[28] Hitchcock (2005: 693, with earlier references). Also see the insightful article of Colburn (2007, with earlier references) and the overview of the significance of foreign craftsmanship in the Bronze Age eastern Mediterranean by Brysbaert (2008: 77–85).

[29] Appadurai (1986: 44).

[30] Appadurai (1986: 38). Also see Helms (1988: 119–29) on the prestige gained by control over foreign goods.

goods were used to implement the ideology of kingship, and how long-distance travel was valorized as a "journey for power."

In the Late Bronze Age, trade of luxury goods between royal houses was framed as gift exchange among "brothers."[31] The gift's pedigree as an imported item was key in adding value to the item; thus, the giver makes a point of who gave the gift in question to him.[32] We not only can use this information to trace the specific connections that were made, we can also provide a cultural context for the archaeological evidence of foreign objects, presumably gifts, that are found in Bronze Age Greece, since we may assume that the objects made the recipient feel that he or she was a player in the supralocal eastern Mediterranean community.[33]

Marian Feldman has written of a phenomenon that grew out of the exchange of luxury goods within the brotherhood, the creation of a consciously hybrid "International Style." The themes of the International Style are victory and prowess in battle, and fertility and prosperity. "Both themes resonate deeply with an iconography based on the ancient Near Eastern concept of kingship in both its military and protective aspects."[34]

Collecting and displaying exotic goods was clearly an important strategy for promoting an ideology of kingship, which was enhanced by proclaiming membership in the brotherhood of Great Kings, within which were included the Mycenaeans. A spectacular collection of luxurious items, which, if not imported or made by imported craftsmen, certainly attempted to incorporate foreign styles, comes from Shaft Grave IV at Mycenae (LH I).[35] Besides the Anatolian stag *bibrû* pictured in Fig. 5,[36] the items show connections to Egypt, Libya, the Levant, even as far away as Central Asia. A Mycenaean scepter among them suggests that the mortuary display of foreign goods was meant to support a claim of kingship.[37] In turn, "It is clear that Mycenaean pottery can be associated with Levantine cult practices,"[38] especially at Ugarit, where a large number of Mycenaean vessels were found in the Temple aux Rhytons.[39] At Hazor, Mycenaean

---

[31] Zaccagnini (1987), Bryce (2003b: 96–106).
[32] In *Fragments of Hittite Letters*: CTH 209.12 = KBo 2.11 rev. 11′–14′ (translit., trans., and discussion Hoffner 2009: 352–3), the sender, possibly the king of Arzawa, tells the Hittite king that he has sent him two vessels of silver and gold given to him from Egypt.
[33] Karantzali (2001: 79). [34] Knapp (2008: 161). See Feldman (2006).
[35] Colburn (2007: 208–9), Laffineur (2005), Vermeule (1972: 95–100). See Burns (2010) generally on the topic of trade in exotic goods in the Mycenaean period, and more specifically his pp. 80–6 on the Shaft Graves and the significance of the exotic goods buried in them.
[36] On which see further Chapter 13, 345. [37] See Kilian (1988: 294) on the scepter.
[38] Wijngaarden (2002: 115). [39] Also see Wijngaarden (2002: 120–1).

Fig. 5: Silver stag *bibrû* found in Shaft Grave IV from Mycenae (made *ca.* 1970–1835 BCE, buried *ca.* 1700–1600 BCE)

vessels were particularly used for elite dining and drinking,[40] and at both Ugarit and Hazor, "Mycenaean pottery was suitable to be included in funerary strategies of display."[41] The use of heirloom Mycenaean vessels shows their prestige and suggests the possibility that specific objects carried with them their biography.

Within such a framework it is easy to understand why foreign performers, healers, and craftsmen could be collected like esoteric objects to enhance the prestige of local courts, an impulse that can be seen in third-millennium

---

[40] Wijngaarden (2002: 118–19).
[41] Wijngaarden (2002: 122). Also see his pp. 122–4 on funerary use of Mycenaean vessels in the Levant.

Ebla,[42] the early second-millennium court of Mari,[43] the Neo-Assyrian courts,[44] the court of Polycrates, tyrant of Samos (535–522 BCE), where Anacreon of Teos and Ibycus of Rhegium both took up residence, and the court of the Lydian king Croesus in Sardis (560–546 BCE), which Herodotus (1.29) says all the leading Greek sophists made a point to visit.

We turn now to a second push–pull factor encouraging movement of stories and their performers, the valorization of long-distance travel. The anthropologist Mary Helms has presented an influential exploration of "the wide-spread association of political 'elites' with foreign or distant goods and information." As Helms notes, "The combination of travel experience with trade, religiosity, esoteric knowledge, and advisory services to eminent rulers ... is ... characteristic of ... specialists in geographic distance."[45] Such a valuation results in the concept of the "journey for power," as Robert Penglase has termed it in his discussion of parallels within a set of myths from the Greek and Near Eastern sides of the Mediterranean.[46] Helms' findings on "the political and ideological contexts or auras within which long-distance interests and activities may be conducted"[47] can help scholars of the ancient world not only to interpret myths about long-distance travel that distill a *Weltanschauung*, but also to assess the real-life valuation and motives of their tellers.[48] This approach thus takes us beyond how they and their tellers traveled and interacted with each other, to why specific storylines were considered worth borrowing. It also allows for the possibility that the elites themselves could be transmitters of stories, not just "professional" bards or exorcists.

Certainly, in the earliest Akkadian literature swift long-distance travel was already valorized. In the late third millennium the work of traders no less than conquerors was considered a heroic achievement; *The Valorous Sun*, a difficult text found at both Abu Salabikh (near Nippur in Mesopotamia) and Ebla, honors the Sun-god for his care of merchants and even describes the god himself as engaged in trade across the sea:

> 16 He sustains campaigners and traveling merchants in foreign lands,
> The foreign lands render up lapis and silver
>   to the traveling merchant,

---

[42] Tonietti (1998).

[43] Ziegler (2006; 2007: 14, 19–20). Also see Koitabashi (1998: 365–6) on foreign musicians appearing at Ugarit.

[44] Franklin (2008: 193–4).   [45] Helms (1988: 94).   [46] Penglase (1994).

[47] Helms (1988: 4).

[48] Lane Fox (2009: 186–209) approaches traveling heroes from a very different angle.

>   The cedar forest yields unworked timber, boxwood, cypress,
>   (standing tall like) splendid standards,
>   Fit for a nobleman to adorn his house.
> 20 He loads his barge with aromatics, oils, honey,
>   the goods that merchants bring,
>   And incense of the gods, juniper, almond, and . . .-oil.[49]

The primeval hero of the first dynasty of Uruk, Lugalbanda, when offered his heart's desire by the giant Anzu-bird, preferred over all things supernatural speed, which he used first to catch up with his army, after having been left in the wilderness of the mountains, then to make the trip back from Aratta (Iran) to Uruk, where he was able to meet with Inanna, so that he might learn of the particular sacrifice she desired and ensure victory for his troops.[50] In the second millennium the youthful god Ninurta, who has strong parallels with Heracles,[51] made a "journey for power" to the chaotic edge of the world, slaying there a series of monsters including the serpentine Asag and returning to establish civilization in Sumer.[52]

In the Mesopotamian worldview the outer edges of the world were a primeval space to be conquered and exploited for its esoteric luxury raw materials. Legends about Sargon the Great focused on his arduous voyages to the west, where he conquered foreign lands, took back booty and tribute, and kept open trade routes for his merchants, and the Late Babylonian *Map of the World* shows that Sargon maintained his reputation as a world traveler well into the first millennium.[53] Gilgamesh too was a great explorer and culture hero, crossing the waters of death to visit the antediluvian hero

---

[49] *The Valorous Sun* 16–21 (trans. Foster 2005: 51). Not only was the Mesopotamian Sun-god the patron god of traders, but divinized traders were even in his retinue, according to Early Dynastic lexical lists (W. G. Lambert 1989: 4–5).

[50] *Lugalbanda and the Anzud Bird* (trans. Black et al. 2004: 22–31), found in OB copies of an original that probably dates to the Ur III period, drawing on even older material (Wilcke 1969: 3–4). Lugalbanda is sometimes named as the father of Gilgamesh. Also note the supernatural speed of the messenger who travels the long distance between Aratta and Uruk in *Enmerkar and En-suhgir-ana* (trans. Black et al. 2004: 3–11), and king Shulgi's boasts about his supernatural ability to cover long distances in *Shulgi A* (trans. ETCSL t.2.4.2.01, discussion in Klein 1981: 180–1). Compare Helms' discussion on supernaturally high-speed travel symbolizing control over distance (1988: 61–4).

[51] Annus (2002: 119–20), Burkert (1979b: 80; 1987b: 14–18).

[52] See the Sumerian *Ninurta's Return to Nibru* (also called *Angim*) and *Ninurta's Exploits* (*Lugal-e*) (trans. Black et al. 2004: 163–86).

[53] There Sargon is mentioned along with Utnapishtim and Nur-daggal (Nur-Dagan), the Anatolian king whom he defeated in the second-millennium legend *Sargon, King of Battle*. See the edition and translation of Horowitz (1998: 20–42). Also note the *Sargon Geography*, in which Sargon is given dominion over the entire world (ed. and trans. Horowitz 1998: 67–95). For more detailed discussion of Sargonic legends, see Chapter 8, 169–72.

Utnapishtim on the edge of the world.[54] Here we can see quite clearly that geographical distance was equated with distance across time, for there Gilgamesh was able to access knowledge about the world that existed before the current population of humans came into being.

In later Greco-Roman thought the edges of the earth continued to be inhabited by primitive, utopian, or monstrous beings – a world beyond contemporary civilization,[55] one explored by Odysseus in his own epic journey.[56] Long-distance or supernatural travel is a staple theme of Greek epic, including the lost *Arimaspea*, which tells wondrous stories of what Aristeas supposedly saw among the Hyperboreans,[57] and the *Argonautica*, which tells the tale of a voyage to the Black Sea to find the Golden Fleece, an object with Late Bronze Age Anatolian analogs.[58] The popularity of such stories speaks to the mystical value of long-distance travels among first-millennium Greeks.

Long-distance elite interaction and transmission of narratives

Helms has framed esoteric knowledge as one more exotic good to be traded:

> In traditional societies goods derived from a distance or transported a long way will probably be high in value and low in bulk. There can be little quarrel with any of these points as generalities, particularly if we recognize that one of the more frequently exchanged types of long-distance goods is esoteric knowledge which is, by definition, rare, strange, in a sense cunning, can be very durable especially in oral societies, and represents the highest degree of portability and lowest possible bulk of any transported good.[59]

To Helms' seminal analysis of long-distance travel of ideas in traditional societies we can add the suggestion that mythic narratives were in fact a highly valuable luxury good to be traded over long distances and collected as "markers of exclusivity." They represent one element driving the supraregional popularity of some of the cult places discussed in this book, such as the Syrian Mt. Casius and Greek Delos,[60] magnets for supraregional performers and fabled in legends.

---

[54] George (2003: 95–8). [55] See Romm (1992). [56] Colburn (2007: 203–7).
[57] See testimonia and fragments collected in Bernabé (1987: 144–54). Herodotus (4.14.3) attributes the epic to Aristeas of Proconessus.
[58] On the Golden Fleece see Chapter 4, 104, with n. 115. [59] Helms (1988: 118–19).
[60] On Delos as a place of contact, see Chapter 10, 236–7; on Mt. Casius, see Chapter 10, 258.

While I, like Gregory Nagy and John Miles Foley, discount the notion that one single poet of exceptional genius must have been responsible for the *Iliad* and the *Odyssey*, I do think single poets in privileged positions that allowed them contact with more than one social world could be disproportionately important agents in the transmission of a striking feature of verbal art, whether a single innovatory detail or an entire narrative, to a new milieu, filling a role similar to that described in William Labov's and Jonathon Marshall's models of linguistic influence. According to Marshall, whereas people embedded in strong social networks are less influenced from the outside, people with strong ties beyond a particular social network in which they are embedded are more influenced linguistically by the outside, both because of their attitude and because of their situation.[61] Labov shows how linguistic innovations are spread by individuals occupying key nodes in networks of relationships.[62]

In the Late Bronze Age and Early Iron Age, two groups were particularly likely both to be influenced from the outside and to exert disproportionate influence within their network: traveling performers and members of the elite. Traveling performers, however they moved around, were part of multiple networks. Their families, whether literal or figurative, may have been the source of their original training, but they were also part of a wider network of performers, and their travels gave them opportunities to absorb new ideas and bring them to new audiences. They needed to be flexible and responsive to their regional audiences, providing the impetus to incorporate the novel as well as the local, since display of the local myths of other groups could help to establish them as wielding the "authority of distant knowledge."[63] The elite in their turn, who were disproportionately influential in their own local world because of their high status, were able to mobilize resources to stage public ceremonies that drew people from near and far, a fertile milieu for interaction and influence among performers and audiences. Furthermore, the performers were traveling within a supralocal social network of elites that speeded new ideas along the same tracks by which the elite themselves traveled, and some of the elite could have been able to perform the valued texts or the rites, as Melampous is portrayed doing.

---

[61] Marshall (2004). This has been shown to be a factor affecting the degree of language shift for individuals.
[62] Labov (2001).   [63] The term is from Helms (1988: 131).

Medicine, long-distance travel, and cosmogonies

An additional factor in the popularity of certain storylines transmitted by long-distance travel throughout the eastern Mediterranean in the Late Bronze Age and the Early Iron Age was their supposed efficacy against disease when used as historiolae in magical rituals, that is, as suggestive storylines that helped to guide the thoughts and actions of their audience, whether human, divine, or demonic.[64] As I will show in this section there was a particularly close connection between medicine and long-distance travel, whether in the person of the doctor himself or herself, or in the use of suggestive storylines that illustrated how time and space could be bridged, bringing the far near, expelling evil, and attracting good, or in the form of exotic ingredients in the pharmacological repertoire, including incantations and stories, such as the story of the Cow-Maiden, *Elkunirsa and Ashertu*, *Gilgamesh*, and cosmogonic myth.

An interest in exotic spells is already evinced in the Old Babylonian "Subarian" (Hurrian) medical spells, which are garbled nonsense as far as we can tell, but presumably tapped into the same healing powers invested in the Hurrian goddess Shawushka (Ishtar) housed at Nineveh.[65] The Keftiu ("Cretan") spells in a New Kingdom Egyptian medical papyrus (*ca.* 1350 BCE) against the "Asian" sickness battle a foreign disease with a foreign spell.[66] Hittite diplomatic letters reveal requests for doctors from Babylon and Egypt.[67] Furthermore, at Hattusa there was an extensive collection of white magic incantations attributed to performers from a variety of locales, sometimes clearly representing local traditions, e.g., Arzawa, Kizzuwatna, or Mesopotamia.[68] Legendary healers like the Cretan seer Epimenides and the Lesbian poet Terpander, called in to save Athens and Sparta respectively

---

[64] On historiolae see Frankfurter (1995) and Sanders (2001).

[65] On Shawushka see Chapter 2, 26, with n. 21.

[66] The London Medical Papyrus (BM 10059) contains a total of seven spells; the other six are in northwest Semitic. See Arnott (1996), Ritner (2001); and Redford (2005–2006), who suggests reading the Keftiu spell as a combination of Greek and Akkadian phrases.

[67] Ramses II responds to Hattusili III, saying he will send a doctor (LÚ*ā*[*ši*]*pu*) [and exorcist (LÚA.ZU)] for his sister who is unable to bear a child (*Letter from Ramses II to Hattusili III*: *CTH* 163 = *KBo* 28.30, translit. Edel 1994: 1.178–80, No. 30; trans. Beckman 1999b: 137–8). The pharaoh sends a doctor with medicine for Kurunta to Tudhaliya IV (*CTH* 163 = *KUB* 3.67, translit. and trans. Edel 1994: 170–1, No. 72). Hattusili III discusses with Kadashman-Enlil II doctors from Babylon who were not returned promptly (*ašûm* and *āšipu*, *Letter from Hattusili III to Kadashman-Enlil II*: *CTH* 172 = *KBo* 1.10 rev. 34–48, translit. Hagenbuchner 1989: 285–6; trans. Beckman 1999b: 142–3).

[68] On Arzawan and Luwian magic, see Bawanypeck (2005a; 2005b: 241–8) and Hutter (2001; 2003: 232–56); on Kizzuwatnean magic see most recently Strauss (2006). The situation with the

from plague or strife, were effective in part purely because they came from far away.[69] Herodotus' interest in exotic *pharmaka* pervades his work,[70] while much later a fascination with exotic vocables drove the inclusion of the so-called *voces magicae* in Late Antique Greco-Roman spells.[71]

A particularly clear example of a widespread story closely connected to healing rituals and probably spread by means of these same healing rituals is the tale of the pregnant cow Geme-Sin ('Girl of the Moon-God Sin'), found in Sumerian, Akkadian, Ugaritic, Hittite, and Hurrian birth incantations (the last both at Hattusa and elsewhere), and, as I have argued elsewhere, in Greek birth incantations as well. The Akkadian myth leads the birthing mother through the steps of the cow's story, first the secret impregnation by the Moon-god Sin, then her pregnancy, and finally the moment of birth.[72] Just as Sin notices the suffering of the writhing cow in

---

Akkadian incantations found at Hattusa is a bit more complex; it is probably necessary to distinguish between texts used to teach scribes and texts that were actually put to use. Among the latter we should put those with instructions in Hittite and incantations in Akkadian, like *CTH* 432: *Ritual against Depression* (ed. and trans. Beckman 2007) and *CTH* 718: *Ritual for Ishtar/Pirinkir, with Babilili Incantations* (see Beckman 2002). Other texts entirely in Akkadian that could have been actually used include *CTH* 810: *The Moon-god and the Cow* (see Röllig 1985, discussed below), *CTH* 811: *Akkadian Prescription against Fever* (ed. and trans. Meier 1939); and those booked under *CTH* 812: *Akkadian Incantations*, many of which are discussed by Schwemer (1998; 2004).

[69] Supposedly the Spartans would send for foreigners (*xenous andras*), when told to do so by the Pythia, to cure them of illness or madness, including Terpander, Thaletas, Tyrtaeus, Nymphaeus, and the "Lydian" Alcman (Ael. *VH* 12.50, *Suid.* s.v. *meta Lesbion ōidon* (Adler M 701) = Terpander TT 7, 9 in D. A. Campbell 1988: 298–301).

[70] See Thomas (2000: 72–4, 286–8).

[71] Versnel (2002) presents a perceptive study of the function of *voces magicae*, as well as providing a thorough bibliography on the subject.

[72] See the translation of the Neo-Assyrian version of the Cow-maiden story in Foster (2005: 1007–8), and the editions and discussions of Röllig (1985) and Veldhuis (1991), also Stol (2000: 59–72). Texts using at least some elements of the plot line at Hattusa: in Akkadian, *CTH* 810: *The Moon-god and the Cow*, see n. 68; in Hittite, *CTH* 363.1.A: *The Sun-god, the Cow, and the Fisherman* (translit. E. Rieken et al. 2009ff. on KhT; trans. Hoffner 1998a: 85–7; German trans. and discussion Haas 2006: 199, 202–6, with earlier references). Also see Hoffner (1981) and Singer (1995: 125–6). There is some possibility that *CTH* 363 is a continuation of *CTH* 360: *Tale of Appu* (on which see briefly Chapters 2, 34, and 5, 127). *CTH* 363 follows *CTH* 717: *Hurro-Hittite Prayer to Ishtar* (ed. and trans. Güterbock 1983b), but whether the two were thought of as somehow related is debated. *Incantations with Luwianisms*: *CTH* 767.7 = *KUB* 44.4 + *KBo* 13.241 (ed. and trans. Beckman 1983a: 176–99; ed. Starke 1985: 233–6, with discussion pp. 208, 210; trans. and discussion Bachvarova 2013b, and in Chavalas 2013: 297–8); also see Giorgieri (2004). Hurrian incantations: *Fragments of Hurro-Hittite Rituals and Incantations*: *CTH* 790 = *KBo* 27.117 and *Ritual of Shalashu*: *CTH* 788 = *KUB* 47.19 (translit. Haas and Wegner 1988: 415–17, 420–1, discussion pp. 29–30, Nos. 97, 99); also see Haas (1988b: 134–5). See Sanders (2001) for a discussion of the transmission of the story as a birth incantation, Bachvarova (2001) for a full discussion of the parallels between the incantation and the story of Io as told in Aesch. *Supp.* 291–319, 531–89.

labor and sends down goddesses with specific instructions to relieve her pain through massage and application of cooling water, so the human healer will aid the laboring woman to bring forth a healthy son. The corresponding Greek myth about Io tells how she was raped by Zeus and subsequently tormented by the gadfly sent by Hera, in flight from which she traversed most of the known world, going through Asia Minor, the Caucasus, and Syria before she ended up in Egypt,[73] where Zeus brought her to bear by the touch of his healing hand. The earliest well-preserved version of the story in Greek is told by her descendants, the Danaids, in Aeschylus' *Suppliants*, a play rife with birth motifs.[74] I thus suggest that the Greeks learned this story in the same way as the Hittites did, through its use in birth incantations.

Io's journey, which does not have a counterpart in the Near Eastern versions of the story, has many resonances. It represents the laboring mother's journey through childbirth, but it also picks up a motif found in other incantations, in which a character's search for a cure takes him to many different places, the motif representing the healer's access to knowledge from far-off places. For example, in the Ugaritic *Horanu and the Mare* a mare whose daughter's foal has been bitten by a snake takes a message asking for help against the snake bite to a series of deities' homes throughout the known world, from Crete to Syria to Mesopotamia, but only the healer Horanu can help by going to the Tigris River to get the supplies needed to carry out the ritual.[75] This is perhaps an allusion to Nineveh on the Tigris, the home of Hurrian Shawushka, a goddess of magic and healing.[76] In Io's case, her journey represents the foreign origin of the incantation. Io's voyage also reveals a sense of connectedness across the Mediterranean, which is mirrored in her genealogy linking Greece to Egypt, Libya, Arabia, Phoenicia, and Cilicia.[77]

---

[73] Aesch. *Supp.* 538–62. In *PV* 700–35, she encounters Prometheus beyond the Black Sea, where he prophesies that she will go through Scythia, the Caucasus, and along the mythical edges of the world. In Hes. *Aegimius* (F 230 Most) she at least travels through Euboea (M. L. West 1985: 145–6). Apollodorus (*Bib.* 2.1.3) also has her travel all over the known world.

[74] Bachvarova (2001).

[75] *KTU* 1.100 (translit. and trans. Pardee 2002: 172–9); also see N. Wyatt (2002: 385).

[76] On Nineveh as the home of Shawushka, see Beckman (1998) and Reade (2005).

[77] The stemma of Io as laid out in the *Catalog of Women* presents an elaborate genealogical network connecting east and west, one that incorporates many stories with a Near Eastern influence (Bachvarova 2001: 84–5; M. L. West 1985: 42, 76–82, 144–54, 165, 177–8; 1997a: 442–52). On available evidence for her family tree in the *Catalog* see Gantz (1993: 202–12). From the fragments we can pick out the following relevant members of her line: Belus (w. Sem. 'lord'), father of Aegyptus and Danaus; farther down the line was Perseus, while Agenor (Gr. 'lord'), son of Libya, produced Phoenix, father of Adonis (w. Sem. 'lord' again). Phoenix's

The Hurro-Hittite story *Elkunirsa and Ashertu* is another example of a historiola imported as part of a healing ritual that makes a point of its exotic origin. The story exhibits obvious west Semitic traits, and it was embedded in a purification ritual, which makes a point of mentioning sorcerers from Levantine Amurru, and it appears that the practitioner who tells the story is equating himself or herself with the powerful, exotic foreign sorcerer within the incantation.[78]

The Gilgamesh story exhibits a slightly different relationship with healing rituals. As discussed in Chapter 4, it informed the rites that called on the dead or underworld gods to help the patient, and the patient needed to know the story in order to appreciate its applicability. However, the story itself tapped into the powers bestowed by the "journey for power" by presenting itself as conveying knowledge about primeval times brought back from the edge of the world. The Odyssean *katabasis* episode both incorporates an exotic story about travel to the edge of the world and the ritual context that gave it meaning.

Cosmogonies share some of the same properties as stories about long-distance traveling; because horizontal distance was equated with vertical distance geographic remoteness meant nearness to the divine or supernatural.[79] In particular, cosmogonic myth has a special affinity for healing rituals. Burkert observes: "A new and proper order has to be created or recreated from its very foundations. Something has gone wrong, as sickness and pain indicate; so one should begin afresh from the beginning."[80] The Akkadian cosmogonic story *Atrahasis* was used for barren women.[81] Cosmogonic elements are not alien to Akkadian incantations: for example, an Old Babylonian incantation against infant illness

---

daughter was Europa, who was raped by Zeus as a bull, his theriomorphic form drawn from the iconography of the Syro-Anatolian Storm-god. The fifth-century historian Pherecydes of Athens, in his own telling of genealogies, says that Phoenix, son of Agenor, was married to Cassiepeia, daughter of Arabus, and they had three sons, Cilix, Phineus, and Doryclus (*FGrH* 3 FF 21, 86; also Hesiod FF 72–107 Most). Her complex international family tree thus shows an awareness of fellow Greeks settled in Cilicia, and reflects the practice of long-distance elite marriages, in which both female and male outsiders married into local aristocracy. See Finkelberg (2005: 33–7) on Io's family tree signaling intermixing of Greeks with other populations.

[78] See Bachvarova (2013a: 32) and discussion in Chapter 2, 34. [79] Helms (1988: 4–5).
[80] Burkert (1992: 125).
[81] Michalowski (1992: 237), Reiner (1960), who also mention that written versions of *Erra and Ishum* (probably from the eighth century BCE, trans. Foster 2005: 880–911), telling the story of Erra's near-destruction of the world, were used as house amulets against the plague. Hdt. 1.132.3: the Persian *magos* performs their theogonic story (*epaeidei theogoniēn*) at their sacrifices. See Eliade (1963: 24–32) on the use of cosmogonic myth in healing rituals.

recounts the creation of the worm that is conceived of as causing the illness, and then how Damu and the Doctor-goddess Gula vanquished it:

> Anu begot heaven, heaven brought forth earth,
> Earth bore stench, stench bore mud,
> Mud bore fly, fly bore worm.
> the worm, daughter of Gula, is clad in a traveling cloak,
> She is blood-soaked,
> ... the child's blood, she extinguished his eyes.
> Damu cast the spell and Gula killed(?) [the worm],
> ... he slaughtered them ... [ ]
> He (the child?) opened his mouth, took the breast,
>   raised his eyes and [saw].
>
> (The spell is not mine: It is the spell of Damu and Gula,
>   Damu [c]ast and I took.)[82]

Furthermore, cosmogonies shared the same cachet as stories about long-distance travel and were therefore transferred by the same means as stories about bridging horizontal space. Indeed, as will be discussed in the following chapter, among the chief storylines transmitted from east to west were ones about the creation of the world and the conflicts between the generations of gods at its beginning. Finally, as Carolina López-Ruiz notes:

> the crafts performed by three out of four of Homer's craftsmen (poets, healers, and diviners), depend on a special type of knowledge about the origin of the cosmos and the gods. Furthermore, they share the capacity of *using* that privileged knowledge for healing and purificatory purposes (physical and spiritual) and, in certain circles, for religious initiation.[83]

Conclusion

The perspective presented here shows that an important but neglected factor in the transmission of cultural traits from east to west was the valorization of long-distance interaction and esoteric goods, considered

---

[82] *Against Infant Illness* (*YOS* 11.5 1–8, trans. Foster 2005: 180). Other examples of "cosmogonic" incantations translated by Foster are the OB *Incantation against a Mote in the Eye* and the NA *Incantation against a Mote* and *Incantation against Toothache* (Foster 2005: 181, 969, 995), see comments by Foster on p. 43, with earlier references. Also see Frankfurter (1995: 463–6) for a survey of earlier scholars' analyses of the use of cosmogonic myth in incantations.

[83] López-Ruiz (2010: 189). López-Ruiz (2010: 182–95) discusses the performance context of cosmogonies.

to be particularly valuable and efficacious. It provides reasons for the parallels between Greek and Near Eastern epic, not only explaining why esoteric stories were interesting to the Greeks, but also why particular stories were so popular. Theogonies and stories describing momentous voyages to the edge of the world and the powerful knowledge and precious goods brought back by the hero, whether Gilgamesh or Sargon, bridged the vast gap that separates the present from the distant past, all the way to the beginning of time and the creation of the world. Indeed, the linking of mythic time and space strengthened the conceptual link between the hero traveling to distant places and the mythic past in which he lived. Stories that described how to reach across the divide between living and dead or explained the fate of those who had died were also popular, both because they dealt with a realm even more mysterious than the ends of the world and because they promised to help the living gain the favor of the dead by remembering them, and therefore be cured and protected by them. For this reason, they informed Near Eastern rituals of (fictional) royal ancestor veneration and healing and purification rituals, rituals that gave opportunities for Greek-speakers to observe performers of verbal art and to borrow elements seen to be efficacious or compelling.

Finally, we may extend the notion of Feldman's "International Style" from physical artifacts to narratives. Feldman argues the "International Style" celebrates and legitimizes kingship, and presents a style instantly recognized as prestigious and marking participation in the network of supralocal elites. We can see the same goals and features in the narratives we have discussed so far, and I will argue in the following chapter that we can see them with regard to supralocal festivals in the eastern Mediterranean. They followed easily recognizable patterns that showed to their audiences that the local court or polity was a legitimate member of the elite, and the commonalities and the common goals of the festivals, as well as the narratives told within them, aided in the borrowing of specific details that performers or their patrons saw to be especially impressive or pleasing.

10 | Festivals: a milieu for cultural contact

> I have never sailed the broad sea by ship, except to Euboea from Aulis, where once the Achaeans, waiting out the winter, gathered together a large host, from holy Hellas to Troy with its beautiful women. There I crossed into Chalcis to the funeral games (*aethla*) of battle-minded Amphidamas; the many prizes that the children of the great-hearted one set had been announced ahead of time. There I say that, having won with my song, I carried off a tripod with handles.
>
> Hesiod *Works and Days* 650–7

Introduction

One of my main focuses in this book is the role of official, "state-sponsored" religion as a mechanism of intentional, formalized transfer of verbal art among performers across linguistic and geographic boundaries, rather than more casual transfers by merchants or mixed marriages, or transmission by lone wandering performers invisible to the record. Once again, I must insist that this should not be taken as a denial that other methods of transfer were operational or important to the development of Greek epic. Rather, I am taking advantage of what is visible to us in the texts and the archaeological record. However, I do think that scholars have failed to recognize how important state-sponsored religion must have been in fostering the spread of epic narratives and motifs. State-sponsored festivals served multiple functions, religious, social, and political: propitiating the gods and ensuring the proper flow of the seasons, building community and affirming identity, and asserting and displaying a court's right to rule, and its membership in the supralocal elite. The ideology of kingship required an audience drawn not only from within the community but also from among outsiders – diplomats and other elites – to convey its message, and the political function of festivals provided a motivation and means for exchange of verbal art, including the precursors of Homer's and Hesiod's poetry, beginning in the Late Bronze Age and (*mutatis mutandis*) continuing into the Archaic period.

Festivals are in fact unique in that they are both examples of what was transferred and mechanisms by which transfer occurred, as performers and their sponsors gained access to and strove to emulate new, effective, and fashionable musical styles and narrative content.[1] The process of exchange within the eastern Mediterranean (including the Aegean) was made easier by the similarities between Greek and Near Eastern festivals, which partook of a festival culture common to the Mediterranean world.[2] They were sufficiently similar to permit non-local audience members to make fruitful analogies between their own customs and those they were witnessing, and to allow for non-local performers to be integrated into local festivals.[3] And indeed, the Late Bronze Age Near Eastern sources show us some situations that would have produced chances to see performers from other regions, and the motivations to emulate the best of what a performer saw, whether he or she was driven by a personal desire for prestige or as part of a top-down program to integrate a local court with the wider supralocal community of elites. The same processes of emulation and display worked to encourage borrowing of prestigious, internationally recognized or exotic performance types, including music, dance, and song lyrics, both in Late Bronze Age Anatolia and in the time when we start to have written sources for the Greek world. These processes led to the commonalities I discuss throughout this book.

I begin by discussing some fairly typical examples of Hittite state-sponsored seasonal festivals, particularly the KI.LAM festival. I then make some comparisons with festivals from second-millennium Greece, showing how similar Mycenaean practices were to them. The same factors that encouraged the transfer of verbal art among the Hittites were at work in Greece. I pay special attention to the Linear B records from Thebes, which have not yet been discussed satisfactorily with this in mind.

Next I focus on continuity, change, and accommodation in first-millennium Greek festivals, with case studies of the contributions of non-local performers in the Delian festival and accommodation of indigenous practices in the Milesian New Year festival. I close this section with an excursus on how the spread of specific versions of the Greco-Anatolian god Apollo caused the spread of narratives attached to him.

---

[1] My argument overlaps somewhat with that of López-Ruiz (2010: 35–7), who speaks of sanctuaries (where festivals were held) as sites of cultural exchange.

[2] On the similarities see van den Hout (1991–1992: 101).

[3] When I speak of festivals as means of transfer, I do not mean to imply that the same kinds of "sanctuary networks" and "elite movement" (on which see Hornblower and Morgan 2007: 34) were in operation in the Late Bronze Age and Early Iron Age Aegean as in the Archaic and Classical periods.

I end with a study of the *Chaoskampf* motif, enacted through song, dance, and story in festival contexts, which provides a particularly clear example of transfer of song and verbal art by means of festivals. I first compare narratives connected to Hittite festivals to the stories of Apollo and Pytho, and Zeus and Typhon, then I look at how the spread of the Storm-god of Aleppo caused the spread of *Chaoskampf* narratives attached to him because of their role in legitimizing kingship, and at how the *Chaoskampf* motif played out in other ways in Syro-Anatolian festivals. Finally, I compare the rites of the Mesopotamian Akitu festival with the Panathenaea.

Hittite festivals

The peculiar Hittite obsession with collecting and describing festivals allows us a picture of how festivals operated that is unmatched by any site other than Hattusa in the ancient world.[4] Even so, the Hittite descriptions of festivals are not completely satisfactory for our purposes. They generally tell us when singers performed and occasionally provide us with an incipit (which matches up frustratingly rarely with the texts we actually have), while shelf catalogs may give the title of a text performed in a particular festival. But, the texts themselves were normally recorded separately, and only occasionally are we provided with a clear performance context. For the most part we are left to make the connections between text and performance context ourselves. Certainly we should not assume that the texts we have were actually performed as written. It is in fact difficult to decide whether the records of festivals are meant to be descriptive or prescriptive. But, we can surmise that texts like the ones we have were performed in festivals that looked in their broad outlines like the festival descriptions, and we can search for and attempt to explain parallels between Greek and Hittite festival activities and the myths attached to them.

---

[4] Other Near Eastern sites offer far less evidence, and the Greek sources – almost all post-Classical – are frustratingly uneven and incomplete. The epigraphic evidence in Greek consists of dedications, a few calendars, and laconic instructions describing disbursements, obligations, and privileges, while Greek literature provides us with stunning works of verbal art – tragedy, comedy, and bits of the lyric poets, especially Pindar – which were clearly performed in festivals, but with little indication of how the contemporary audience viewed the relationship between text and context. Descriptions of festivals or parts thereof are typically either chance allusions in discussions of other matters, or the work of antiquarians such as Pausanias and the scholiasts, who must be treated with caution when reconstructing a picture of the rites in question in earlier periods.

Spring and fall festivals were used to strengthen the solidarity of the core of the Hittite kingdom,[5] propitiating the gods and the royal dead on behalf of the royal family.[6] In some festivals, such as the spring AN.TAḪŠUM ('crocus') festival[7] and the fall *nuntarriyašḫaš* festival ('festival of haste'),[8] the royal family, together and separately, traveled by chariot to a variety of towns and mountains mostly within a day's ride of Hattusa to participate in a series of local festivities, returning between trips to Hattusa to visit the temples there.[9] In this way, the link between the center and its hinterland was enacted, asserting the hegemony of Hattusa over Hittite territory.

The fall KI.LAM ('gatehouse') festival, on the other hand, was centripetal; it displayed the unity of all parts of the core of the Hittite empire by bringing in regional performers and administrators to the Hittite capital, including male choruses and choruses of maidens,[10] each ceremonially presenting the results of their labor that sustained the kingdom, whether crops, handiworks, or song and dance.[11] Lasting three days, the festival moved through a series of temples belonging to specific gods and other public places.[12] Largely the same events were repeated each day, although some were curtailed on the second day in order to make room for a rite for

---

[5] See Gilan (2004b: 197–9, with earlier references). For an overview of second-millennium regional festivals in Anatolia, see the *Cult Inventories under Tudhaliya IV*, edited, translated, and discussed by Hazenbos (2003; 2004).

[6] For offerings to the dead in festivals at Hattusa and Ugarit, see Chapter 7, 151–2.

[7] The AN.TAḪŠUM festival lacks a full edition. See Haas (1994: 772–826), Taracha (2009: 138–40), and Zinko (1987) for summaries, and discussion in Haas and Wegner (1992).

[8] On the *nuntarriyašḫaš* festival see Nakamura (2002) and Haas (1994: 827–47). It was celebrated after the king had returned from campaign. The title fits what we know of the connotations of the traditional Mediterranean harvest, which is a time in which the farmer and his helpers work non-stop to get in the grain.

[9] On the king's travels in the AN.TAḪŠUM and *nuntarriyašḫaš* festivals, see Popko (2009: 9, 78–82).

[10] See discussions of specific examples in Rutherford (2004a; 2005a; 2008). The ceremonies may have been taken on the road to the towns themselves as well (Haas 1994: 767–71).

[11] The KI.LAM festival texts have been edited and commented on in detail by Singer (1983; 1984b); also see Groddek (2004a). A description of the three days of the ceremony in Hattusa is provided in Singer (1983: 57–133), and also see the overview by Haas (1994: 748–71). I ignore possible differences between the "Great Festival" and the "Regular Festival." There is some uncertainty on the timing of the festival, in large part because it is unclear how to translate *mašiyanki* in a reference to the festival: "His Majesty performs the festival in the *respective* (or: at *any given time* in the) year" (*Oracle Concerning the Celebration of Various Festivals*: *CTH* 568.A = *ABoT* 1.14 iii 12–13, trans. Singer 1983: 134–5, with my emphasis; see further Houwink ten Cate 1988: 191–2, with note 53). Houwink ten Cate (1988: 191–4) argues that the KI.LAM festival was appended to the *nuntarriyašḫaš* festival, at least after cult reforms in the New Hittite period, but Nakamura (2002: 126–30) argues that, while components of the KI.LAM festival were incorporated into the *nuntarriyašḫaš* festival, they were not core elements.

[12] For a short discussion of Hittite processions, see S. de Martino in Sasson (1995: 2666–7).

the Grain-goddess Halki. There were chanting, singing, dancing, and playing of the lyre.[13] The king and members of his family, particularly the crown prince and the queen, could be called upon to perform, often in their capacity as priest or priestess.[14] There was a foot-race, as is typical of Hittite festivals. (Athletic competitions were quite prominent in the local festivals.)[15] The regional AGRIGs (overseers of the royal storehouses[16]) supplied breads, drink, and animals, from one to three each, to various delegations of participants from outlying towns, a practice with feudal overtones strongly reminiscent of that discernable in the Linear B records of feast provisioning.[17] Smiths and other participants also provided provisions for specific parts of the multi-day festival.[18]

The latent theme is the human ability to turn products of nature into things of culture. The representation of mastery over nature is shaped by an evolutionary anthropological framework spanning several stages of the evolution of human culture, from hunting wild animals to agriculture, with its need to predict the seasons, to metallurgy. Dominion over humans is mapped onto domination over nature, the parallel justifying Hittite hegemony over central Anatolia. Thus, a mimetic scene shortly before the Great Assembly acts out a historical event, the defiance of the people of the Hattic town Tissaruliya,[19] whose representative refuses an invitation

---

[13] On dance in Hittite festivals see de Martino (1989). On music and musical instruments in Hittite festivals see Badalì (1989; 1991), de Martino, "Musik A. III. Bei den Hethitern," in *RlA* 8: 483–8, and Schuol (2000). On songs see Rutherford (2008).

[14] See Taggar-Cohen (2005: 369–434, 444–5).

[15] The entertainment at the regional seasonal festivals included boxing, wrestling, fighting, pressing stones (weight-lifting?), and throwing them. See Hazenbos (2003: 167–72), and Hutter-Braunsar (2008). C. W. Carter (1988) and Puhvel (1988b) both discuss the athletic competitions found in Hittite festivals. For racing in the KI.LAM festival, see Singer (1983: 103–4); for racing in the AN.TAḪŠUM festival, see *AN.TAḪŠUM Festival, Outline Tablet*: CTH 604.A = KBo 10.20 i 19–23 (the second day) (translit. and trans. Güterbock 1960: 91, 96). On horse racing in the AN.TAḪŠUM festival, see Hutter-Braunsar (2008: 28–9). Footracing is among the earliest and most common events in Greek festivals (Instone 2007: 75).

[16] Singer (1983: 57; 1984a: 98–9, 108, 126–7).

[17] Singer (1983: 151, 157–61, 168–70; 1984a: 106, 119–20), texts transliterated in Singer (1984b: 102–19). See Ardzinba (1982: 248) on the feudal aspect of gift-giving in the Hittite festivals.

[18] *Nuntarriyašḫaš Festival*: CTH 626 Outline.7 = KBo 13.257, recording festival provisions (translit. and trans. Houwink ten Cate 1988: 192, with discussion pp. 191–3; Nakamura 2002: 74–5); mentions of the KI.LAM festival and the smiths restored in lacunae because of parallels from *Recurring Festival* (EZEN$_4$ SAG.UŠ): CTH 629 = KUB 25.27, a detailed list of provisions for rites for Halki (translit. and trans. Nakamura 2002: 76–7), and *Oracle concerning the Celebration of Various Festivals*: CTH 568 = ABoT 14 iii 8–24 (translit. and trans. Singer 1983: 134–5). Also see Rutherford (2005a: 626–7).

[19] The men of Tissaruliya perform Hattic songs during the festival and receive supplies (Singer 1983: 158, 166; Rutherford 2005a: 631). Supplies: CTH 627 = KUB 58.48 iv 2′–16′, see van den Hout (1991–1992) for translit., trans., and discussion.

to eat and drink with the king. It apparently ends with the submission of the town to Hittite rule. As Calvert Watkins sees it, "This dramatic vignette might have concluded with a symbolic re-enactment of the resolution of those conflicts in the cultural symbiosis of Hittite and Hattic which is attested by the continued performance of the ritual itself."[20] With similar intentions, the fall festival of the Storm-god Iyarri of Gursamassa showed the men of the rebellious west Anatolian Masa, equipped only with reeds, fighting to a foregone conclusion with the men of Hatti, armed with wooden staves.[21]

Continuity with the older Hattic cultural layer is asserted through ceremony and language. Stag standards carried in the processions through Hattusa must have been similar to those found in Alaca Höyük (2400–2100 BCE).[22] Most of the songs in the KI.LAM festival are in Hattic, a language that perhaps was already dead except in small pockets. It was used by the Hittite court in liturgies performed by groups from specific towns, such as Tissaruliya and Anunuwa.[23]

Hattic exclamations and recitations in Hattic punctuate the ceremonies, while gods with Hattic names are featured, all legitimizing the empire established by the Hittites by harking back to the indigenous traditions of Hattic Anatolia.[24] But, in one New Hittite description, a god with a Hattic name (Wahisi) is serenaded in Hurrian.[25] Thus, we can see the incorporation into the festival of a new regional tradition, despite the conscious archaizing. All this adds up to show that the centralized Hittite administration made sure to maintain archaic and local traditions, bringing in local performers and using them to honor particular gods in the manner to which they were accustomed, but also adapting the festivals over time to integrate singers from new areas.

---

[20] Watkins (1995: 143). Also see Gilan (2001: 122–3) and Rutherford (2005a: 631): "it would be the etiology of a regular cultic journey from Tiššaruliya to Ḫattuša."

[21] *Cult Inventories under Tudhaliya IV*: CTH 525.2 = KUB 17.35 iii 9–15 (translit. and trans. C. W. Carter 1962: 129–30, 143). See Archi (1973: 25–6) and Puhvel (1988b: 28–9). See Chapter 13, 334, on Masa. See Gilan (2001) and Hutter-Braunsar (2008: 25–6, 31–3) for other examples of mock or not-so-mock fights in festivals. See Rutherford (2005a: 630–1) on other etiologies based on mythico-historical conflicts.

[22] Singer (1983: 93–4).

[23] Anunuwa: CTH 627.1.a.A = KBo 10.23+ vi 1–8, etc. (translit. Singer 1984b: 15); see Singer (1983: 28–9) and Rutherford (2005a: 629). The people from Anunuwa seem to be well respected for their singing, as they turn up elsewhere performing their music.

[24] Gilan (2004b).

[25] CTH 626.1.j.A = KBo 10.25 v 2′–3′, filled in with E = KBo 11.42 left col. 2′ (translit. Singer 1984b: 51); see Singer (1983: 102). See Archi (2004a) on the relationship between singers in various languages and the gods they sing for.

Fig. 6: Chamber A at Yazılıkaya: A space in which to celebrate festivals. The gods process along the right edge and the left back, towards the central scene on the right back.

The invitees to the "Great Assembly" (*šalli aššeššar*) of the festival were made up of the king's family, the priests of the towns Arinna and Ziplanda (with attendants), the priests of Hatti, the "lord of Hatti," the priestess of Halki, performers, residing foreign delegates, and others classified simply as dignitaries (LÚ.MEŠDUGUD). Their rank specified the order in which they filed in and out of the tent set up for the Great Assembly with which the first day of the KI.LAM ceremony culminates, outside of Hattusa at the *ḫuwaši*-stone (baetyl) of the Storm-god, perhaps the monument Yazılıkaya carved out of living rock (Fig. 6, see Map 3).[26] There they witnessed offerings to a series of gods accompanied by musical performances.[27]

At Hattusa "residing foreign delegates" (Akk. *ubārum*) were regular attendants at Hittite festivals,[28] and in general, participation by allies was

---

[26] See Singer (1986). On Yazılıkaya as a *ḫuwaši*- stone, see Chapter 7, 152, n. 13; on baetyls see this chapter, n. 114.

[27] *KI.LAM Festival*: CTH 627.1.j.B = *KBo* 27.42 ii 21–67 (translit. Singer 1984b: 57–8; description Singer 1983: 73, 77).

[28] Bodi (2003) calls the *ubarūtu* "resident aliens." I follow Na'aman (2005). See Rutherford (2005a: 625, 632, with earlier references), Süel (1976–1977), and Neu (1970: 76–9) for *ubarūtu* in Hittite contexts.

expected in Near Eastern festivals. In early eighteenth-century Mari allied princes attended important festivals,[29] and the king of Alashiya was forced to apologize when he failed to send a messenger to Amarna to attend a festival.[30] In another Amarna letter, from the Babylonian king Kadashman-Enlil I to the pharaoh Amenhotep III, he complained, "When you celebrated a great festival, you did not send your messenger to me, saying, 'come t[o eat an]d drink'. N[or did you send me] my greeting-gift in connection with the festival."[31] The presence of the foreign delegates and other diplomats signaled the membership of the two courts in the brotherhood of Great Kings. The desire to show full understanding of the conventions and lifestyle of the international elite would have driven the competitive emulation of the ceremonies witnessed in allies' courts, motivating the transfer of performers and the imitation by local performers of the best of their competitors' performances.

Feasts and festivals in second-millennium Greece

The evidence available on the Mycenaean side consists of the disbursement records of the Linear B tablets, depictions of feasting and related activities in Mycenaean frescos, and the archaeological remains of feasting. The feasts have received theoretically-informed analyses by Mycenologists, showing how they were used to mobilize the labor force by creating obligations and loyalty, while hierarchy was enforced by grades of exclusivity in the feasting.[32] I do not attempt to survey the full range of evidence, but I do pick out some particularly apposite examples. To repeat, the point of the comparison in this chapter is not to sort out what commonalities are due to a common pre-Hellenic heritage, borrowing, or independent developments, but to show similarities that allowed for the transfer of verbal art, including an interest in presenting a local court or polity to a larger group of political peers.

That the Mycenaean calendar was arranged around the yearly sequence of festivals is indicated by month names referring to the festival cycle,[33] including: *di-wi-jo-jo me-no* (KN Fp 5), *diwioyyo mēnos* 'month of (the

---

[29] Durand and Guichard (1997: 39–40).   [30] EA 34 (trans. Moran 1992: 105–6).
[31] EA 3.18–20 (trans. Moran 1992: 7).
[32] See especially Halstead (1999: 39–40), and the articles collected in Halstead and Barrett (2004), Hitchcock, Laffineur, and Crowley (2008), and Wright (2004a). On accounts of banqueting and other religious activities by Mycenaean palaces, see especially Bendall (2007: 59–65).
[33] See Weilhartner (2005: 21–8). For other possible examples see Constantinidou (1989: 14).

event having to do with) Zeus'; *wa-na-se-wi-jo* (PY Fr 1215), *wanassēwio-* '(month) of the Mistress'; *pa-ki-ja-ni-jo-jo* (PY Fr 1224), *pa-ki-ja-nioyyo mēnos* '(month) of the sacred place Pa-ki-ja-ni-ja'; *di-pi-si-jo* (PY Fr 1240), *dipsio-* '(month) of the thirsty (i.e., the dead)';[34] *wo-de-wi-jo-jo me-no* (KN Ga 953 = 955), *wordēwioyyo mēnos* 'month of the rose (festival)'.[35] Several Mycenaean festivals are also specifically named in the Linear B records.[36] So far, no overlap between the names for months and festivals across the various Mycenaean sites has been found, so we cannot surmise that separate polities were united by a common sacred calendar, as various groups of first-millennium Greeks were.

Festival imagery is frequent in Mycenaean and Minoan art. Processions are depicted in Minoan and Mycenaean frescos, made up of men, women, and children carrying containers, statues, conical rhyta, and other offerings, along with lyre players and other musicians.[37] The depictions of bull-leaping in Minoan festivities may be compared with the bull-leaping shown in Hittite relief sculptures, and the practice is mentioned in the Luwian festival of Istanuwa.[38] Depictions of foot-races and boxing on Mycenaean vases attest to the cultural importance of other types of athletic competition. A fragment of a Minoan steatite vase shows a running man in

---

[34] See Hannah (2005: 16–17, 27–9), Trümpy (1997: 2). Weilhartner (2005: 126) takes as the recipient, not the date.

[35] See Aura Jorro (1985, 1993: 2.438–9) and Weilhartner (2005: 127), pointing out that it follows the morphology of other festival names.

[36] *po-re-no-zo-te-ri-ja* (PY Un 443), *po-re-no-zōstēriā* '.... Girding' (see Palaima 1999: 455); *te-o-po-ri-ja* (KN Ga 1058), *theophoriā*, 'Carrying (the Statuettes of) the Gods'; *wa-na-se-wi-ja* (PY Fr 1221, also cf. Fr 1215), *wanassēwiā*, '(Festival) of Wanassa'; *di-pi-si-je-wi-jo* (PY Fr 1218), *dipsiēwio-* '(Festival) of the Thirsty Ones'; *re-ke-to-ro-te-ri-jo* (PY Fr 343, 1217), *lekhe(s)-strōtērio-*, 'Spreading of the Bed', possibly for a sacred marriage ritual, as suggested by Constantinidou (1989: 19–25); *me-tu-wo ne-wo* (PY Fr 1202), *methuos newo(yyo?*, genitive of time within which?) '(Festival) of New Wine'; *to-no-e-ke-te-ri-jo* (PY Fr 1222) has been given several different interpretations: *throno-helkētērion* 'Strewing of the Throne', *throno-ekkheutērion* 'Anointing the Throne', *stono-egertērion* 'Raising of Lamentation', and *thoino-ekhetērion* 'Sacred Banquet/Sacrifice'. See Gallou (2005: 56–7, 82–3) and Palmer (1963: 250–5). Another possible festival name appears in PY Fr 1231: *po-ti-ni-ja, di-pi[-si-]jo-i, [/ ke-se-ni-wi-jo* [ ] OLE S 1[/ *vacat* [ ] *vacat* [. "For Potnia, for the thirsty ones, 9.6 [+?] liters guest-oil." Or: "For Potnia, for the thirsty ones, in the Guest Festival/Ritual, 9.6[+?] liters oil." See Weilhartner (2005: 123) on the problems analyzing the text. Also see Constantinidou (1989: 14–18).

[37] See Immerwahr (1990: 114–21) and Hägg (2001). Processions with offerings in festivals are discussed by Gallou (2005: 105–10).

[38] Tablet of *Lallupiya*: CTH 771.1 = KUB 35.132 iii 1 (translit. Starke 1985: 346). See Gilan (2001: 117, n. 33), Güterbock (2003), Hutter-Braunsar (2008: 33–4), Marinatos (1993: 218–20), Taracha (2002; 2004), J. G. Younger and Rehak (2008: 169, 180–1, with earlier references); *pace* Soysal (2003; 2004c). A *krater* with a bull-leaping scene has been found in fourteenth-century Alalakh as well (Yener 2009).

front of an altar and a sacred tree, implying a festival context.[39] Depictions of chariot-racing competitions in Mycenaean festivals are small in number, but enough to show that such competitions occurred.[40]

Contributions from outlying regions and various social strata to centralized Mycenaean feasts, and palace contributions to regional feasts served to integrate the center with outlying regions.[41] The feasting at Knossos, Pylos, and Thebes that involved individual animals and comestibles provided from a variety of towns and by important personages such as the so-called "collectors" implies a scenario in which adult men (with at least some women and other dependents) gather from a variety of localities and eat and drink.[42] The Wu nodules from Mycenaean Thebes (end of LH IIIB1, *ca.* 1250 BCE), which record incoming shipments for a feast, indicate that animals and therefore people travelled long distances to be at feasts. The nodules show contributions of livestock to be consumed from a Theban (*te-qa-jo*, TH Wu 47) and a Samian (*sa-me-we*, TH Wu 59, cf. the islands Same or Samos – neither one close to Thebes), and contributions arrived from as far away as Carystus (*ka-ru-to*, TH Wu 55) and Amarynthus (*a-ma-ru-to*, TH Wu 58) in Euboea.[43] One might expect that people from these areas also attended the feast itself.

Our best depiction of the Mycenaean feast comes from a set of frescos in the Throne Room (6) of Pylos, a relatively exclusive location for feasting, as opposed to that carried out in Court 63, or the feasting for *hoi polloi*, who did not even enter the palace.[44] Hall 5, leading into the Throne Room, depicts a procession of both sexes, who are carrying various containers with a larger-than-life bull in their midst, moving towards the focus of the public display, the ruler on his throne before the sacred hearth.[45] In the Throne Room itself, lions and griffins flank the throne, fragments of a painting of a stone vase, implying libation rituals, were found, deer frolic in the wild near the throne, symbolizing the hunt and the world beyond

---

[39] Rystedt (1986) and Evans (1901: 101–4).
[40] Rystedt (1999: 95–6); note that one of the depictions she discusses has also been analyzed as a funeral game, see Chapter 11, 269, n. 9.
[41] Palaima (2004) and Bendall (2004: 108–11, 128).
[42] The texts are discussed by Killen (1992; 1994; 1996; 2001; 2004).
[43] Edited in Melena and Olivier (1991: 33–50) and Weilhartner (2005: 205–12); see Palaima (2004: 103, 106).
[44] Bendall (2004: 120–4), Wright (2004b: 41–6).
[45] Kilian (1988: 293); for the focus on throne and hearth at Tiryns and Pylos see Wright (1994: 54–7). On the sacred hearth see Wright (1994: 57–60). For evidence of involvement of the *wanax* in Mycenaean religious rites see Palaima (2006b: 64–6) and Mazarakis Ainian (1997: 305–7); for his role as priest and contributions to festival provisions see Palaima (1995: 130–4).

civilization, and an outsized lyre player sits on a mountainous rock above pairs of men seated at small tables toasting each other. The bird flying away from the lyrist's mouth seems to represent the song on his lips.[46] These peaceful scenes contrast with the "Homeric" battle scene in Hall 64, through which a clear message was sent to those feasting in the adjoining Court 63, of dominance by one man over another. The "Mycenaean" warriors wear boar's tusk helmets (antiques by the date of the painting), and the darker enemy wear sheepskins.[47] It is hard to avoid the supposition that songs or skits were performed during festivals there underlining the iconographic message, as in the KI.LAM festival.

On the other hand, the frescos in the Throne Room of Knossos show a mix of Mycenaean and Minoan iconography, with the empty throne to receive the goddess, flanked with griffins, combining the motifs of Minoan epiphany and Mycenaean seated ruler.[48] A similar process of integration and homogenization must have gone on in Mycenaean festivals that linked outlying regions with the central palace, incorporating non-Mycenaean peoples into the Mycenaean world, as occurred among the Hittites.[49]

The Minoan frescos from Thera, Rooms 4 and 5 in the West House, combine nautical festival imagery on the south wall of Room 5 with a naval action (a battle?) on the north wall in which foreigners are carefully distinguished from Minoans by the color of their skin, haircuts, and outfits. The strong narrative component has caused Sarah Morris to compare it to Homer's story of the Greek nautical expedition against the Trojans, while Nanno Marinatos has underlined the signs of a spring festival, the butterflies and lilies.[50] Here we can see the multiple functions of a seasonal festival when it was under the control of the ruling elite, which used a regularly recurring rite meant to ensure the prosperity of the community to express hegemony and exalt in their power over those who were not members of the dominant group.

A festival of Mycenaean Thebes

The Theban Linear B tablets (end of LH IIIB2, *ca.* 1200 BCE) have been daringly analyzed by their editors, Vassilis Aravantinos, Louis Godart, and

---

[46] The frescos are dated to LH IIIB. A full description is provided in Lang (1969: 192–6). J. Carter (1995: 294) suggests it represents the epiphany of the deity.
[47] Davis and Bennett (1999: 107–12), Yalouris (1989).   [48] Coldstream (1977: 6).
[49] On which see Davis and Bennet (1999).
[50] S. P. Morris (1989). See N. Marinatos (1984: 34–44, 52–61) for a religious interpretation of the imagery of the fresco.

Anna Sacconi, who claim that sacred feasts for Zeus "protector of the harvest" (*o-po-re-i, opōrei*, from *Opōrēs*), Demeter (*ma-ka, Mā Gā*), her daughter (*ko-wa, korwa*), and assorted sacred animals were the occasion for the disbursements.[51] While their interpretation has been criticized,[52] some kind of ceremonial event did occur on at least some of the days during the period covered by the tablets, as John Killen has shown by comparing the Theban Fq, Ft, and Gp tablets with tablets from Pylos and Knossos.[53] The Fq and Gp tablets name many single men, with occasional females and groups of craftspeople, as is common in records of disbursements for feasts.[54] The Fq tablets record small disbursements of grain to individuals and some groups, probably daily supplementary rations[55] for two weeks of a multi-day summer festival celebrating the harvest. The Gp tablets record disbursements of wine. Also relevant are the Av tablets, lists of men, singly or in groups, sometimes including disbursements of grain.[56]

It is best to view most, if not all, of the recipients as actually employed in carrying out the festival, not the spectacle's audience.[57] I suggest that it was a harvest festival based on the fact that some of the recipients in the grain ration texts are winnowers (*akhneusi*),[58] who are unlikely to have been employed year-round. In ancient Greece the threshing and winnowing of wheat started towards the end of June but could take place as late as the end of August; the barley harvest was completed a month or so earlier. Farmers would have the most leisure to celebrate a festival in July or August.[59] Other possible supporting evidence for the timing of the festival

---

[51] Aravantinos, Godart, and Sacconi (2001: 317, with earlier references; 2003). Those who follow the editors' theory include Hiller (2006: 71–2), Meier-Brügger (2006: 114–15), and Ruijgh (2004; 2006). Duhoux (2008: 349–89) provides editions of Fq 126, 130, 254 [+] 255, with a detailed discussion of the interpretative issues of the texts as a whole; also see Melena's editions (2001: 49–50).

[52] Palaima (2000–2001; 2003a; 2003b), arguing that the Fq tablets record "simple daily allotments of grain in return for service" (2006a: 144). Duhoux (2008: 351–3) and S. A. James (2002–2003) both argue for secular occasions.

[53] Killen (2006, with earlier references), also Chadwick (1996–1997) and see the sober assessment of Weilhartner (2005: 194–5).

[54] Killen (2006: 88). [55] S. A. James (2002–2003: 406, with earlier references).

[56] On the relationships between the Fq, Av, and Gp texts, see Hiller (2006: 72–4, with chart pp. 76–7), Killen (2006), and Lejeune (1997).

[57] Compare Shelmerdine (2008: 401) with respect to the recipients in the PY tablets.

[58] Palaima (2003a: 115); that is, *a-ke-ne-u-si* should be transcribed as *akhneusi*, not *hagneusi* 'pure ones' as suggested by the editors (Aravantinos, Godart, and Sacconi 2001: 180). Neither term is attested as a substantive in later Greek, although *Hagneus* appears as a man's name (Neumann 2006: 136).

[59] Brumfield (1981: 40–3), Petropoulos (1994: 28). Compare, for example, the Athenian Skira (June/July) and the Cronia (July), both festivals related to the harvest (Parke 1977: 29–30, 156–62).

is Av 104 [+] 191.1, tabulating groups of "grain-pourers" (*si-to-ko*[*-wo*], *sitokhō*[*woi*]).[60] The Theban winnowers certainly bring to mind the depiction of winnowers celebrating on the Minoan Harvest Rhyton from Ayia Triada, shown singing in a closely packed procession led by a man in a shaggy garment.[61]

There is evidence that non-residents, including an Anatolian, attended the feast at Thebes; in particular, among the men and youths listed in the Fq tablets appear a Milesian,[62] "Smintheus,"[63] a Trojan(?),[64] and "the son of the Lacedaemonian."[65] Unlike the "Lacedaemonian's son," the Milesian seems to have some standing in his own right, but his position near the bottom of tablets indicates that he was not terribly important.[66] Are the Milesian and the Lacedaemonian whose son appears in the Theban tablets – or the son himself – actually from these locations? Did the Milesian arrive especially for these meals,[67] or was he already ensconced at Thebes for a long or short stay? Was the Milesian a Mycenaean who had visited or lived for an extended period of time in Miletus, or was he a Mycenaean who was involved in trade with Miletus? The inventory of geographical names found in the Linear B tablets shows Thebes had a wide range of influence;[68] it is thus possible that the Lacedaemonian's son or the Milesian, Trojan, and Sminthian were actually from the towns they were named after in the records.[69]

---

[60] See Aravantinos, Godart, and Sacconi (2001: 173–6), who see the term as meaning "servants of (the Goddess of Grain) Sito" *Sītō-kowoi*, and the editions with discussion of Weilhartner (2005: 194–5) and Melena (2001: 31), with a slightly different interpretation. I follow the interpretations of Weilhartner and Melena for the meaning "grain-pourers." Compare their mention in a similar record from Pylos, An 292. On the different suggestions for the meaning of the term, see Aura Jorro (1985, 1993: 2.298–9).

[61] See J. G. Younger and Rehak (2008: 178–9, 181).

[62] Fq 177.2, 198.5, 214.[12], 244.2, 254[+]255.10, 269.3, 276.6. Aravantinos, Godart, and Sacconi (2001: 358) likewise see him as an envoy invited to the feast. For other examples of people named after Miletus in Linear B texts, see Aura Jorro (1985, 1993: 1.453–4).

[63] Av 106.3. The cult of Apollo Smintheus was celebrated at Tenedos (*Il.* 1.38). Strabo (13.1.48) enumerates a variety of places called Sminthia in Anatolia.

[64] Gp 164. So Aravantinos, Godart, and Sacconi (2001: 290); see Aura Jorro (1985, 1993: 2.365, 368) on *to-ro-o* (*Trōhos* 'of Trojan'), and *to-ro-wo* (nom./dat.). Palaima (2007: 200–3) advocates for 'man of Tlos'.

[65] At least eight times, mostly Fq tablets. On the reading *ju* for *65, leading to the interpretation of "son," see Palaima (2006a) and Duhoux (2008: 353–9).

[66] On the significance of the position of the names on the tablets see S. A. James (2002–2003: 407–12).

[67] As Aravantinos, Godart, and Sacconi (2001: 358) suggest.

[68] Aravantinos, Godart, and Sacconi (2001: 355–8), Milani (2005).

[69] Strabo and Homer mention a legendary Cretan town Miletus (*Il.* 2.647, Str. 10.4.14), but I do not think it is relevant here, because the geographic range of towns mentioned at Thebes does not otherwise include Crete, but does include Anatolia.

It would not be surprising if Thebes engaged in the same type of diplomacy with other Mycenaean kingdoms and kingdoms farther afield that was the practice among the Near Eastern Great Kings, who invited dignitaries from other courts to attend festivals. The men with designations that mark them as foreign could be official representatives, they could be performers, or they could have served some other purpose in the festival, enhancing it by their foreign connections. Whatever their capacity, if Anatolians attended Mycenaean festivals, then we must allow for the possibility of the transfer of Mycenaean and Anatolian features back and forth across the Aegean in the Late Bronze Age.[70]

First-millennium Greek festivals

In this section I look at first-millennium Greek festivals. Although comparison with the second-millennium data allows us to examine changes that can be connected to broader societal changes, there is a basic continuity in procedures of the festivals that suggest that they remained important milieus for contact and exchange of verbal art during the some 600 years intervening, for which we have little or no data.

Classical Greek festivals, both local and Panhellenic, were the product of the reworking of Mycenaean-era festival practices.[71] Public religion was articulated at the level of the polis, at once acknowledging socio-economic, local, and clan divisions within the city, and situating each unit in a larger whole,[72] with noble families asserting themselves through control of hereditary priesthoods.[73] As in Mycenaean times, the center's control over the periphery was demonstrated in cult by processions bringing offerings of victims, cloth, and agricultural products or a god to or from outlying shrines.[74] The procession itself articulated the social order, as different age classes, social groups, and regional units processed in groups. Panhellenic festivals, such as the Olympian, Pythian, Nemean, and Isthmian games, drew on the same forms and themes as local festivals

---

[70] For further discussion of this festival, see Chapter 13, 345–6.
[71] See R. Parker (2005), Robertson (1992), and Scullion (2007) for important surveys of Attic and Greek festivals. Mazarakis Ainian (1997: 376–80) discusses the decentralization of cult practices following the end of the Mycenaean palatial culture.
[72] Sourvinou-Inwood (1990). [73] R. Parker (1996: 23–4).
[74] R. Parker (1996: 25–6; 2005: 178–80).

intended for a local audience, but opened them to the larger group of all Hellenes.[75] And, by the Archaic period, societal changes were driving an ever-increasing obsession with competition, expressed both in athletics and in artistic contests,[76] which must have increased the rate of change in music and verbal art, and encouraged emulation, conditions favorable for the rapid spread of fashionable features of verbal art from one location to another.

At the few sites where we can unequivocally argue there was continuity of cult activity from the LH IIIC period across the Dark Age – for example, Phocian Kalipodi, Laconian Amyclae, Isthmia, and Olympia – we can see a variety of developments, but in each case religion was made to serve political ends.[77] We can surmise that the involvement of the elite in festival competitions was a by-product of the use of such gatherings as a space for competitive display among the elite, which was already obvious in the mortuary offerings and iconography of the post-palatial period. Hesiod boasts how he won a tripod at the funeral games of Amphidamas in the *Works and Days* (654–9), and many have assumed that the song that took the prize was the *Theogony*, which presents its implied audience as mourning a recent loss, casting itself as "forgetfulness of evils and an end of worries" (55), and insisting that the singing of "the glories of earlier men and the blessed gods" helps anyone who has fresh sorrow by distracting him from his pain (98–103). This is certainly a claim appropriate for a funeral game. In fact, funeral games were a type of festival, and, as Gregory Nagy underlines, most of the Panhellenic games that appeared in the Archaic period presented themselves as having been derived from funeral games.[78] Moreover, the connections between Greek festivals and hero

---

[75] Sourvinou-Inwood (1990). Osborne (1993) discusses the notion of competitive festivals. Also see Instone (2007) on the development of Panhellenic festivals. Morgan (1989: 203–5) sees the early stages in the development of the Panhellenic games as the result of intrastate competition, while only later in the sixth century did they become the setting for interstate competition and peer polity interactions, fostering emulation and transfer of ritual practices.

[76] Murray (1993: 202–13).

[77] Morgan (1996) has undertaken a comparative study of these four sites: Amyclae was where Apollo Amyclaeus and Hyacinthus were worshipped. With its worship of Hyacinthus as a dying or disappearing god, the site may indeed represent true continuity in cult (Eder 1998: 137–8), with the addition over time of a political function as a meeting place. See Pettersson (1992: 9–41) interpreting the evidence. Isthmia, Kalipodi, and Amyclae seem to have been natural meeting places for local chieftains, ideal places for competitive display and building community. The use of Olympia as a place for local leaders to gather may demonstrate a holdover from the Mycenaean palaces' use of local shrines to strengthen the connections between center and periphery.

[78] Nagy (1999: 117).

worship have parallels in the incorporation of ancestor veneration into the large state-sponsored Hittite festivals.

One way in which the processes of self-definition and creating a sense of community were realized was through *theōriai*, state delegations that attended festivals and visited sanctuaries to sight-see and observe, sometimes taking on a more active role by displaying their skill in choral song and dance.[79] The treaty between the Spartans and Athenians in 421 BCE shows that *theōriā* was a religious obligation.[80] Whether this practice was a holdover from the Late Bronze Age or created anew, it provided the same mechanism by which innovations in song could be heard and emulated that we saw at Hattusa.

I turn now to how the Greek settlement of Ionia allowed for transfer of festivals and festival practices between mainland Greece and Anatolia. In the Early Iron Age many Greeks who were settling on the Anatolian coast consciously maintained a sense of their Greekness in contrast to the native peoples, even while integrating elements of Anatolian religion, leading to the proliferation of Anatolian-flavored local Artemises, Apollos, Zeuses, and mother-goddesses in various guises.[81] The accommodation of Anatolian religious practices would have allowed for the absorption of Anatolian festivals and elements of them into festivals brought from Greece, and the integration of indigenous performers into the rites therein, while artists would have been quick to borrow particularly effective or appealing elements of others' performances that they had the chance to witness and to bring them back to their home territory.

By the Archaic period, the Ionian, Doric, and Aeolian polities of Anatolia were expressing unity with their mainland brethren by the conscious cultivation of shared festivals. Shared month names in the Attic and Ionic calendars indicate that the beginnings of a regional sacred calendar had

---

[79] On *theōriā*, see Rutherford (2004b), with cross-cultural parallels, Elsner and Rutherford (2005), Kowalzig (2005), Rutherford (2009b).

[80] Quoted by Th. 5.18: "Concerning the common shrines, it shall be possible, for whoever wishes, to sacrifice and to seek an oracle and to visit as a pilgrim (*theōrein*) according to ancestral custom, both by land and by sea." See Dillon (1997: 103–4).

[81] On Anatolian Artemis, e.g., of Ephesus, see Barnett (1948: 20–1), Burkert (1999), S. P. Morris (2001a; 2001b), Weißl (2004). On Anatolian Zeus: e.g., Carian Zeus, associated with Mt. Latmus, worshipped at Mylasa: Paus. 8.10.3, Str. 14.2.23, Hdt. 5.119–21, Plu. *Mor.* 301f–302a, Benda-Weber (2005: 70–1), Carstens (2008a), Işik (2000), Laumonier (1958: 39–126, Pl. III), Peschlow-Bindokat (1996). The Anatolian Mother-goddess: for the development of the Phrygian *Matar Kubeleya*, known to the Greeks as Cybele, see Berndt-Ersöz (2006: 200–5), Mellink (1983), Roller (1994; 1999: 46–53; 2006: 128–30). On Cybele and Kubaba in general see Bryce (2005: 353–4), Hutter (2006), Munn (2006), Popko (1995: 100–1), and Roller (1999). Also see Chapter 12, 328, n. 126.

been established before Greeks left for Anatolia *ca.* 1050 BCE.[82] Key Ionian festivals were the Apatouria and the Panionia. Herodotus (1.143.3, 147.2) notes that the Anatolian cities that belong to the Panionic League (the Dodecapolis) and celebrate the Panionia consider themselves of the purest stock, and that a subset of Ionians, who were supposed to have come from Athens, also celebrate the Apatouria. As I will discuss in Chapter 15, the Homeric tradition of the *Iliad* and *Odyssey* probably evolved out of epic performances at the Panionia in the late eighth and early seventh centuries BCE.[83]

The Apatouria (from **sm-ph₂tor-u* 'of the same father'), celebrated in Pyanopsion (September/October) in Athens, was used by phratries ('brotherhoods'), in which membership was inherited through one's father, to mark the passage through the age classes of males, and the festival was organized and celebrated at the phratry level. Here we see the interweaving of familial, ethnic, and political ties.[84] In the case of the Apatouria, it seems likely that the transfer of the festival went from east to west, since the month Apatourion (which corresponded to the Athenian Pyanopsion) only existed in Ionia, and the festival name had an Ionic form, even in Athens.[85]

The Ionians also shared the Dionysian Anthesteria and the Lenaea festivals with their mainland brethren.[86] And, Athens shared with the Ionian city-states the Apolline Thargelia festival, which involved a scapegoat ritual thought by many to have Anatolian roots. In Ionia the name is *targēlia*, with no aspiration of the initial dental stop. Robert Beekes sees the variation in the form as evidence that it is a pre-Greek term.[87] Although

---

[82] Huxley (1966: 30–4), Hannah (2005: 28–9), Trümpy (1997: 10–31, especially p. 18). On the Early Iron Age Greek migrations to Anatolia, also see Chapter 14, 358–61. On the dating used here, see Chapter 11, 267, n. 3.

[83] See 413–14. Nagy (2010: 54; also see 137–8) argues, "The festival of the Apatouria seems to be a traditional setting for the performance of epic poetry in Ionian cities, including Athens." He adduces *Vita* 2.29–32 West, in which Homer is invited to the Apatouria in Samos, but he does not perform epic or give any formal performance. And, Nagy refers to a comment in Plato *Timaeus* 21b about boys in rhapsodic contests in the Athenian Apatouria, on which see further Nagy (2002: 53–6). On Homer as the archetypical poet who performs at festivals, see Nagy (2010: 52–8).

[84] See S. D. Lambert (1993: 143–89).

[85] The form exhibits psilosis (loss of initial *h-*) and Ionic treatment of the intervocalic combination of resonant and semivowel (**orwi > ouri*, not Attic *ori*). See Beekes (2010: 114), Chantraine (2009: 92), and Huxley (1966: 31).

[86] On the sharing of cults among cities see Hornblower and Morgan (2007: 20–1).

[87] Beekes (2010: 534). Thargelia shared: Deubner (1966: 179–98, esp. 181–2 on celebration in Ionia); scapegoat ritual: Bremmer (2008: 169–214, esp. 179). The earliest datable attestation is Hipponax (sixth cent., F 107.49 Degani), with the mention of the *pharmakos*.

the shared heritage that was fostered by the Ionian Dodecapolis and common celebration of certain festivals, both among Ionians and between Ionians and specific parts of mainland Greece, has been shown to be a patent fiction, that did not decrease its symbolic significance.[88] Whether shared Attic and Ionian tribe names indicate that the particular tribes were already in place before the Ionian migration, or that the groupings were borrowed either by Athenians or by Ionians,[89] they are evidence for a conscious cultivation of ethnic unity.

Furthermore, it is safe, I feel, to retroject the use of shared festivals to create a shared identity to an early stage of Iron Age Greek settlement in Anatolia, as it would have been one of the chief ways that the Greek identity of Aeolis and Ionia was created, even if we cannot declare definitively that it would have been in operation immediately after the end of the Mycenaean period, or that the particular festivals and the particular polities involved in them were always identical throughout the Dark Age. In this context Anatolian traits that had been absorbed into Aeolic and Ionic festivals would have had a chance to travel westwards to mainland Greece, including epic or theogonic performances, or performances of precursors to the Homeric Hymns.

The Delia

The Delian festival is another example of a festival that connected Ionians from Anatolia to their mainland peers. Probably taking place on the seventh day of Thargelion (late May), it celebrated the birth of Apollo.[90] It used myth and performances drawing people from throughout the Aegean to position Delos within the larger Greek world and to celebrate the wide variety of peoples who attended it. Delos was already settled in the Mycenaean period, but in the Geometric period there is an increase in the archaeological finds, which should be connected to its rise as a cult site. Homer shows that it was already well known in his time as an internationally famous place, since Odysseus when he first meets Nausicaa makes a point of comparing her to the palm tree there, to which Leto clung when giving birth to Apollo, a way of telling the princess he belongs to the civilized world (*Od.* 6.162–5).[91] Delos was a contested space in the sixth century, coveted by both the Peisistratids of Athens and Polycrates of

---

[88] Kowalzig (2005: 48–56).   [89] See R. Parker (1996: 17) for an overview.
[90] Ferrari (2008: 127–8).   [91] Bruneau and Ducat (2005: 32–3).

Samos. In the fifth century, it served as the center for the Delian League, an alliance of Ionian city-states led by Athens, which relied on legends of the Ionian migrations to assert kinship with the Ionian *poleis* it wished to control.[92]

Our earliest description of the Delia comes from the *Homeric Hymn to Apollo*, and Thucydides quotes from the hymn to argue that mainland Ionians and Athenians gathered at Delos in the olden days to celebrate the festival; later, he says, islanders and Athenians participated (probably the mainland Ionian cities were occupied by barbarians[93]), although the festival as a whole was less elaborate; then, the Athenians made them more splendid again.[94]

In the *Homeric Hymn to Apollo* (146–64), the poet speaks of the god and the human audience at the Delian festival enjoying the performances by the local girls, who are able to sing of the birth of Apollo in such a way that all participants can understand, no matter what their native language:[95]

> But you, Phoebus, take pleasure in your heart most in Delos, where for you the trailing-robed Ionians gather with their children and their modest wives. They, commemorating you, enjoy boxing, choral dancing, and song, whenever they stage a competition ... In addition to this a great wonder, the fame of which will never perish, are the Delian girls, attendants of the Far-shooter; when first they hymn Apollo, and then in turn, commemorating them, Leto and arrow-shedding Artemis, they sing the song (*hūmnon*) of men and women of old, pleasing the tribes of men. And they know how to imitate the dialects (*mimeisthai phōnās*) and the chattering (*krembaliastun/bambaliastun*) of all men; each one would say that he himself is speaking; so closely matching their speech is the beautiful song.

The girls' supernatural ability to be understood by all addresses the problem of not comprehending a performance in a foreign language, which in turn suggests that the Delia was known for performances in languages other than Greek or for non-Greek audiences. In addition to the displays

---

[92] Athenians founding the Delian League in 478 BCE: Th. 1.95–7, Arist. *Constitution of the Athenians* 23.4 (Athenians form alliances with Ionians, attracting them away from their alliance with Sparta); Athens as origin of the Ionian migrations: Hdt., e.g., 1.146.2, 147.2.

[93] See Nagy (2010: 218–21) and Chapter 15, 416, n. 76.

[94] Cited by Th. 3.104 to prove that the contests revived by the Athenians in the fifth century had been celebrated since ancient times.

[95] Ferrari (2008: 12–13, with n. 39, 128). The earlier scholarship on the question of whether the girls are presented as performing in Greek or an Anatolian language is covered by Clay (2006: 50, n. 102).

by visiting poets and in-residence performers, which illustrated the international and cosmopolitan nature of the cult, it is probable there were choruses of state delegations at Delos, both competitive and non-competitive.[96]

Situated in the center of the Cyclades, close to Samos, Delos was strategically located to link Anatolia with the Aegean islands and mainland Greece, and the island attracted myths that told of voyages connecting various parts of the Greek world, such as the story told in the first half of the *Homeric Hymn to Apollo*, of Leto's travels in the Greek islands, Thrace, and southwest Anatolia, in search of a place where she could give birth to her child; the myth of Theseus' trip from Crete to Greece (also motivated by Athenian control of Delos[97]); and the story of the Hyperborean maidens, who were supposedly the first to sacrifice to Apollo. Even in the time of Herodotus (4.33) their offerings, supposedly from the far north, beyond the furthest northeast boundary of Greek colonization,[98] arrived in Delos each year to commemorate the maidens who died there.[99] There are various features of the "northern" maidens that in fact connect them to Anatolia. Herodotus (4.35) says that the Hyperborean maidens were Hyperoche and Laodice, but that it is said that before them Arge and Opis, who can be seen as goddesses of childbirth, came with the gods themselves. The story alluded to is therefore a distorted reflection of, or reworks elements of, the myth of the birth of Apollo, the focus of the Delia.

> Women beg for them, naming them in a hymn composed by the Lycian man Olen, and from them the islanders and the Ionians learned to hymn Opis and Arge, naming them and begging. This Olen also made other ancient hymns, when he came from Lycia, which are sung in Delos.

The name Opis was also attached to Artemis of Ephesus.[100]

It is always difficult to tell how such legends refract fact, but I suggest that there was a sense that the Delian hymns were thought to have an Anatolian flavor; certainly a hymn invoking two goddesses of childbirth is comparable to an Anatolian *mugawar* invocation performed by an "Old Woman" practitioner for the goddesses Anzili and Zukki to aid a laboring

---

[96] Plutarch (*Nicias* 3.4–6) mentions that the Athenian chorus processed into Delos via a grand sea-bridge built by Nicias. There were prizes for choruses, and some scraps of lyric imply performance there (Rutherford 2004b: 82–9).
[97] See Nagy (2010: 18), with earlier references.   [98] Georges (1994: 2–3).
[99] See Sale (1961).
[100] Call. *Dian.* 3.204, 240; Antimachus F 99 (Matthews 1996). See Matthew's commentary (1996: 266–7), and S. P. Morris (2001b: 137).

woman.[101] The hymn of the "Lycian" (or Hyperborean) Olen[102] that invoked Opis and Arge can then be seen as impelling the movement of Opis and Arge from their Anatolian home by luring them with an "Anatolian" song familiar to them. The parallels that apparently were perceived between the Delian hymns and Anatolian songs could have been the result of a shared heritage, or because of an actual transfer of song. It was plausible, at least, to the Greeks that a foreign poet would supply the script for one of the major performances of the Delian festival.

The Chian poet of the *Homeric Hymn to Apollo* describes Delos as one stop on his festival circuit (164–74). In the seventh century, poets did cross over from Anatolia to perform in festivals on the Greek mainland. Thus, the Lesbian Terpander, according to legend, was the first to win the Dorian Carnea and the "Lydian" Alcman composed for it. This was a seasonal festival marking the end of summer and the beginning of winter, which took place in the month of Carneus (late autumn) for Apollo Carneus. The Carnea was widespread in Dorian territory, then was transferred to Thera and onwards to Cyrene by the Aegeidae to assert political ties between Thera and Cyrene.[103] Such transfers must have been commonplace in the early days of Greek immigration to Anatolia, both giving the Greeks a comforting sense of the familiar and maintaining ties with the mainland.

In a *Homeric Hymn to Aphrodite* (6.19–20), presented as a prelude to an epic performance, the poet asks the goddess, "grant that I carry off victory in this contest, and prepare my song."[104] But, there is evidence that the figure of the poet performing competitively at festivals goes back much earlier than the Archaic period: Homer's name, it has been suggested, is

---

[101] *CTH* 333: *Disappearance and Return of Anzili and Zukki* (ed. and trans. Beckman 1983a: 72–83). For a brief comment on the ritual see Bachvarova (2013a: 26).

[102] For Olen's ethnicity, see Hdt. 4.35.3, Call. *Ap.* 4.304–6, Paus. 1.18.5, 5.7.8, 8.21.3, 9.27.2, 10.5.7–8, *Suid.*, s.v. *Ōlēn* (Adler Ω 71): "the Dymaean (a city in Achaea), or Hyperborean, or Lycian, an epic poet. But it is likely that he was Lycian, from Xanthus, as Callimachus shows and Polyhistor in his books about Lycia." On Olen see Benda-Weber (2005: 271–2).

[103] Terpander at Carnea: Hellanicus *FGrH* 4 F 85a. Alcman mentions the Carnea: Σ *ad* Theocritus 5.83 = F 52 Page; Ferrari (2008: 127–35) also argues that Alcman F 1 was performed at the Carnea. Date of Carnea: Ferrari (2008: 129–35). Transfer of Carnea to Thera, then Cyrene: Pi. *P.* 5.72–81, 99, Hdt. 4.149, Call. *Ap.* 2.71–96. See Pettersson (1992: 58–60) and Calame (2003: 84–6). The festival shows the standard features of a seasonal Aegean festival, thus providing a familiar frame of reference, but with unique characteristics. There was feasting with supplies provided by the *karneātai*, unmarried men representing the tribes, three from each tribe in each of nine tents, and there was a race in which the *staphulodromoi* 'grape-vine-runners', chosen from among the *karneātai*, chased a man decked out in wool fillets. On the Carnea more generally: Scullion (2007: 193–5), Pettersson (1992: 57–72).

[104] On poetic competition in festivals, see Martin (2000: 410–18).

back-formed from the name *Homēridai*, of the clan who considered themselves to be the legitimate heirs of the Homeric tradition. The clan name is related to *homārios* 'place of union'; compare the Vedic cognate *samaryam* 'festive gathering', at which poets performed. Thus, poetic performances were inextricably bound up with festival display. Similarly, the poet's name Thamyris/as, a "Thracian" poet mentioned in *Il.* 2.594–600 who boasted that he could out-perform the Muses,[105] comes from Aeolic *thamuris* 'assembly'. The competitive format for festival performances is manifest by the Archaic period, directly referred to by Hesiod in his *Works and Days* (656–8) when he exulted in his victory in the funeral games for Amphidamas, and it is portrayed in the contest between Homer and Hesiod in *Vita* 1 West. The very fact that in the earliest reference from the *Iliad* the competitive context is referred to so obliquely shows that the contest format was already taken for granted. That competition would have been a key motivator to change and improve one's song, possibly by incorporating the best of what one's competitors have to offer.

Thamyris' supposed Thracian ethnicity, which contradicts his Aeolic name, enshrines the value invested in the foreign poet, which I suggest could explain why Alcman, who composed songs performed in Spartan festivals, was considered by many ancient scholars to be Lydian.[106] In addition, some credited Olympus, who was given a Phrygian or Lydian origin, with the first performance of the *puthikos nomos*. This musical piece commemorated the combat between Apollo and the Pytho at Delphi.[107] It is not impossible that the legends crediting Anatolian poets with etiologies for performances refract an earlier period in which Greeks looked to Anatolians for guidance and inspiration in music and song. We know they did do this in the Archaic and Classical periods, when we have access to better evidence, as shown by the naming of several of the musical rhythms and modes after Anatolian ethnic groups.[108]

---

[105] Durante (1971, 1976: 2.185–204), Frame (2009: 581, with note 146, 632–6), M. L. West (1999: 375–6), Wilson (2009: 50–1, 'the one who brings people into a group *through song*', emphasis in the original). Nagy (2010: 254–64 with n. 11, 377) prefers to focus on the significance of another meaning of *homēros*, 'hostage'.

[106] For Alcman's ethnicity see the testimonia in D. A. Campbell (1988: 336–51).

[107] [Plu.] *Mus.* 1131d, 1136c; see Rutherford (2001a: 25–7). On Olympus see testimonia in D. A. Campbell (1988: 272–85).

[108] M. L. West (1992a: 387–90) details the importation of musical styles and technology from the Near East through the Archaic period. He has discussed the influence of the Near East in general on Greek music. Among the instruments imported from Anatolia that were part of the mainstream of Greek music were lyres, harps, and different types of aulos (M. L. West 1992a: 70–2, 81–2, 90–2). The aulos first appears at the end of the eighth century, a time of contact with Midas' Phrygia, and the use of the aulos was considered Phrygian. On the Phrygian

The Milesian New Year festival

The results of the process of integration and accommodation within first-millennium Anatolia can be glimpsed by means of an inscription from Miletus, the so-called Molpoi Decree, covering some details about local festivals, especially the Milesian New Year festival.[109] The festival follows patterns familiar to Greek festivals, and the similarities between this festival and the ones recorded at second-millennium Hattusa are also manifest. There were a race and choral competition at Miletus, followed by the procession connecting Miletus and Didyma, which Alexander Herda suggests goes back at least as far as the Late Geometric period (*ca.* 700 BCE).[110]

The festival formalizes the contribution of different family groups by drawing *proshetairoi* ('colleagues') from three tribes: the Hoplethes (an Ionian *phulē*), the *Oinopes* ('of wine-colored face', a racial term?) and the *Boreis* ('northerners'? or named after Borus, a son of Neleus?).[111] The *molpoi* ('singer-dancers') procession proceeded from the shrine of Apollo Delphinius and ended up in Didyma at the shrine of Apollo Didymeus, god of prophecy, stopping at seven stations to sing paeans at the shrines of various divinities.[112] The procession began at one of a pair of small

---

connections of the aulos see West (1992a: 330–2) and Berndt-Ersöz (2006: 168). There were Lydian, Phrygian, and Ionian scales and modes (M. L. West 1992a: 174–5, 177–83). The Lydian mode appears in the beginning of the seventh century (M. L. West 1992a: 331–2). The Lesbian Terpander was given credit for a variety of musical innovations, including citharodic nomes, the seven strings on the *phorminx*, which he must have gotten from the Near East, and the *barbitos*, a type of Assyrian harp (Franklin 2008).

[109] The original inscription was from the second half of the sixth century BCE; the final version is from *ca.* 200 BCE. The festival occurred between the seventh and tenth days of Taureon (April/May). English translation in Gorman (2001: 176–81); see her discussion at pp. 181–6. The text has been edited and discussed by Herda (2006a). Also see Herda (2008; 2011) for further discussion (his Eng. trans. in Herda 2011).

[110] Herda (2006a: 175–8; 2008: 22).

[111] At Miletus there were also three other Ionian tribes, the Argadeis, Geleontes, and Aegocoreis. These four (Hoplet(h)es, Argadeis, Geleontes, Aegocoreis) were the original tribes at Athens before the Cleisthenic reforms (Hdt. 5.66); at Miletus the six tribes probably took turns contributing to the festival (Herda 2006a: 31–3; 2011: 63). Georges (1994: 17) suggests 'northerners' for *Boreis*. On Borus (mentioned by Hellanicus, *FGrH* 323a F 23, as the grandson of Neleus) and the *Boreis*, who are found at Ephesus as well, see Crielaard (2009: 54) and Janko (1992: 341). Janko also points out a Maeonian Borus in the *Iliad* (5.44).

[112] Herda (2008: 18–20) presents a summary of his detailed discussion of the procession in Herda (2006a). On Apollo of Didyma and the sanctuary see Fontenrose (1988). On possible cult activities in the Mycenaean period, see Schattner (1992). For a general discussion of religion as revealed by the Iron Age archaeological remains in Miletus and Didyma, see Gorman (2001). On Anatolian influence see Greaves (2010: 192–3). See Johnston (2008: 82–90) on the oracle of Apollo at Didyma.

stone cubes called *gulloi*[113] which might be descendants of Hittite *ḫuwaši*-stones or baetyls, attention-focusing devices that sometimes could be small enough to put on a table.[114] The procession then moved on to the shrine of Hecate, then to that of Dynamis, then through a sacred oak grove to a shrine of the nymphs, divinities with Anatolian roots.[115] The procession proceeded to a riverbank to honor the river-god and founder-hero Celadus and Hermes, then to Apollo Phylius, then to Apollo *Keraiïtēs*, and finally ended up at the second *gullos* in Didyma. Herda's analysis of the function of the procession could equally well describe the earlier ritual journeys of the Hittite king and his retinue: "[The stations] symbolize the rooting of the Milesians in an originally foreign territory, they symbolize the divine sanctioning of the taking of the land."[116]

According to Pausanias (7.2.6), the sanctuary of Apollo at Didyma was older than the migrations of the Greeks to Anatolia. The name of the founding hero *Brankhos*, first prophet of Didyma, from whom the Branchidae priests of the Didymean oracle claimed descent, could be of Anatolian origin.[117] The hymn of Branchus, attested quite late as an incomprehensible liturgy, seems to position itself as in an indigenous language, paralleling the use of Hattic in Hittite festivals and the *grammata Ephesiaka* for Artemis of Ephesus. According to the early Christian writer Clement of Alexandria, it "was spoken by Branchus when purifying the Milesians from plague. He says to them, as he waves over them laurel branches, 'Sing (*melpete*), oh children, of the (male) far-worker (*hekaergon*), the (female) far-worker (*hekaergan*).' The people, so to

---

[113] Hesych. s.v. *gullos*: "a cube, four-sided stone." On the *gulloi* see Gorman (2001: 173) and Herda (2006a: 254). Small stones found at Knossos have been interpreted as portable versions of baetyls (Nilsson 1950: 258). For portable stones in Greek festivals see Clinton (1992: 121–3), discussing the *Hieros Lithos* and the priest called the *Lithophoros* at Eleusis.

[114] They were an important component of Anatolian religion in both the second and first millennium and were called *waniza* in Hieroglyphic Luwian (Hutter 1993: 96–9). On baetyls see Carstens (2008a), Fick (2004), and Hutter (1993), and for baetyls in Minoan cult, Marinatos (2004: 32–6) and Warren (1990). For Hittite *ḫuwašis* small enough to fit on a table, see *Fragments Naming the Ašuša(tal)la-People*: CTH 665 = KUB 35.133 i 15'–17' (translit. Starke 1985: 278), see Hutter (1993: 92–3).

[115] On the Anatolian worship of springs, see Egetmeyer (2007: 219, n. 76), Haas (1994: 464–6), and Robert (1955: 217–19, 299). Second-millennium spring-goddesses were typically paired with local storm-gods as purveyors of ground- and rainwater (see Popko 1994: 35, 37–9; 1995: 72–3).

[116] "[Die Stationen] symbolisieren die Verwurzelung der Milesier in einem ursprünglich fremden Territorium, symbolisieren die göttliche Sanktionierung der Landnahme" (Herda 2008: 23).

[117] Herda (2008: 21–2, with note 68).

speak, struck the lyre: '*bedu zaps khthōm plēktron sphinx knaxzbikh thuptēs phlegmo drōps.*'[118]

This festival takes advantage of the commonalities in the Aegean festival culture, while incorporating some indigenous regional peculiarities, even stressing the town's non-Greek heritage as a way of commemorating the union of Greeks and the indigenous population in the region.

Apollo as a vector for transmission of cult

> Oh lord, you hold Lycia and lovely Maeonia and Miletus, the desirable city on the sea, and again you yourself rule greatly Delos, surrounded by waves; and the very famous son of Leto playing on his hollowed-out phorminx towards rocky Pytho...
>
> *Homeric Hymn to Apollo* 179–83

The *Homeric Hymn to Apollo* recognizes the wide scope of Apollo's fame, and the worship of Apollo was a prime vector for transfer of regional details of broadly congruent cult practices back and forth across the Aegean. With Apollo, in fact, we have an example of a god who already in the Late Bronze Age was important to both Greek-speakers and Anatolians.

Regarded by many modern scholars as the quintessential Greek god with deep Indo-European roots, Apollo has also been argued to be a pre-Greek or Semitic god adopted by the Greeks via Cyprus.[119] Hittitologists, meanwhile, focusing on Apollo's role as archer and fighter of plague, connect him to second-millennium Anatolian ^{d}LAMMA ŠA LÍL 'tutelary deity of the steppe', who is associated with the bow and with deer (see Figs. 7, 8), and to the plague gods who are called upon by Arzawan augurs

---

[118] Clem. Al. *Strom.* 5.8.48–9; the *grammata* are mentioned by Callimachus in *Iambus* IV, F 194.28–31 Pfeiffer; see Preisendenz, "Ephesia grammata," in *RAC* 5.518. On Branchus see Fontenrose (1988: 106–9).

[119] On Apollo as a Greek/Indo-European god see Burkert (1975), Watkins (1995: 149, with earlier references; 1998: 209–10). E. L. Brown (2004) attempts a Luwian derivation of his name. Beekes (2003b) argues he is a pre-Greek god. Egetmeyer (2007) shows that Apollo cannot be a post-Mycenaean import to Greece. Faraone (1992: 57–66, 125–32, with discussion of the history of the scholarship on Apollo) compares him to the Mesopotamian plague god Erra, also found in Hittite rituals (Haas 1994: 210–11, 368–9; Kümmel 1967: 100–3). The west Semitic god Reshep was syncretized with Apollo as archer god at Cyprus, where Reshep is first attested in the seventh century (Lipiński 1995: 185, 187–8). On Apollo's relationship with Reshep see B. C. Dietrich (1978). Also see Schretter (1974), who connects Apollo to Nergal and Reshep. On the relationship between Apollo Amyclaeus and Reshep see S. P. Morris (1992a: 113). On Reshep and Apollo see further Chapter 12, 313, 319–20.

Fig. 7: Yeniköy Stele (*ca.* 15th–14th century BCE)

from southwest Anatolia in Hittite texts.[120] They have obvious links with the Apollo who sent the plague on the Greek army and was propitiated according to the advice of the Greek augur Calchas in the beginning of the *Iliad* (1.43–100).[121] Certainly, Apollo Philesius at Didyma (Fig. 9) resembles iconographically the Anatolian LAMMA-god. Representations of his statue on coins and a relief sculpture show him holding a model of a stag,

---

[120] On Arzawan rituals against plague see Hutter (2003: 235–6). The Arzawan augurs' rituals are edited and translated by Bawanypeck (2005b).

[121] Hutter (2003: 236–7) notes the connection between Apollo and west Anatolian augurs' rituals and plague rituals involving ᵈLAMMA ŠA *kurša* 'tutelary deity of the sacred hunting bag'; the fact that Calchas is acting the part of an Arzawan augur is discussed by Högemann and Oettinger (2008). Also see Hutter (2001: 231), noting the general connection between Apollo and Arzawan plague gods. For further connections between Apollo and Hittite plague gods, see Mastrocinque (2007: 201–8). D. Smith (2013) has recently pointed out some intriguing parallels between omens concerning the flight of birds from the Akkadian terrestrial omen compendium *Šumma Ālu* and Homeric bird omens. Based on this evidence, he argues for a direct Mesopotamian origin for Homeric augury. As he himself points out, however, Hittite scribes had knowledge of Mesopotamian-style augury. There is no reason not to assume that Arzawan augurs came into contact with and assimilated elements of Mesopotamian augural knowledge. Furthermore, D. Smith considers solicited vs. unsolicited omens to be an important distinction. But, the solicited *ḫurri*-bird omens he discusses as his primary example from the Hittites are not augural, but extispicy. Hittite augural reports are observational, not solicited. For further discussion of Arzawan augurs, see Mouton and Rutherford (2013).

(a)

Fig. 8: Schimmel Rhyton: Forepart of red deer (*Cervus elaphus*) (13th century BCE).

and Pliny describes the bronze statue of a nude Apollo holding a stag that can rock back and forth in his hand.[122]

The *Treaty between Muwattalli II and Alaksandu of Wilusa* shows that Apollo (*Appaliunaš*) was an important god in second-millennium Troy.[123]

---

[122] *NH* 34.75. See Fontenrose (1988: 115–16) on the statue. See Herda (2006a: fig. 11a; 2008: fig. 5) for the relief sculpture. See Bielefeld (1962) on the statue's Anatolian characteristics.

[123] *CTH* 76.A = *KUB* 21.1 iv 27 (translit. Friedrich 1930b: 80; trans. Beckman 1999b: 92). There is an inconvenient lacuna before the divine name ʳᵈʾ *Appaliunaš*, and the poorly drawn hand copy by Albrecht Götze in *Keilschrifturkunden aus Boghazköi 21: Historische Texte* (1928, No. 1) misrepresents the remains of the broken sign before the *ap*. A photo of the relevant

(b)

Fig. 8: (*cont.*) On the right worshippers approach two LAMMA-gods, the first libating, the second one offering a round bread, and the third, a kneeling page, with the vessel for libations. The larger seated goddess with hawk and bowl to receive a libation is labeled Ala. The male deity with throwing stick and hawk on the back of a fallow deer (*Dama mesopotamica*) is labeled DEUS.CERVUS$_x$ ('Divine Stag'). On the far left, the implements of a *mugawar* invocation: the *eya* tree and the *kurša* bag hanging on the wall, next to a quiver filled with arrows and two spears. On the ground are the trophies of a hunt: the head, skin, and hooves of a fallow deer.

In addition, a clear link can be found between the first-millennium Apollo and one particular second-millennium god, *Appaluwan* (acc. sg.), who is given offerings in an Arzawan-style (west Anatolian) ritual against plague.[124] The name of this otherwise unattested god is too similar to that of Apollo to ignore, and if the two names are in fact related, then any hope of arguing for a Greek etymology of the god's name must finally be put aside. The best way to explain the alternation of *li/l* in *Appaliuna-* and *Appaluwa-* is by recourse to Robert Beekes' reconstruction of a palatal *l* in the phonemic inventory of his "unitary pre-Greek";[125] thus, Beekes'

section of the tablet is now available on an internet database, the Mainzer Photoarchiv, showing that the remains of the sign are consistent with the divine determinative. The photo is accessible via KhT *sub KUB* 21.1. Thus, we may confidently state that the god of the Wilusans is an ancestor of the god who supports the Trojans in the *Iliad*.

[124] *Fragments of Purification Rituals*: CTH 456 = KBo 22.125 i 9′, 10′ (translit. Groddek 2008: 116–17). Also noted by Ian Rutherford (pers. comm.).

[125] Beekes (2010: xvii, 118–19).

(c)

Fig. 8: (cont.)

suggestion of a pre-Greek origin for Apollo is vindicated. Beekes argues that the pre-Greek language he postulates as the source of the Greek god's name was spoken in Greece, along the southwest coast of Anatolia, and perhaps Cilicia.[126] The god of the *Alaksandu Treaty* must represent the Graecized version of the pre-Greek god, with the suffix-*ōn* added by the Mycenaean Greeks when adopting the pre-Greek god; then "Trojan"-speakers (speakers of a language indigenous to second-millennium Troy) made his Graecized name Anatolian again by treating it as an *a*-stem noun.[127]

Possibly the god was brought to Troy by Mycenaeans. One can reconstruct *A]-pe-ro₂-n[e* in a Linear B offering list, a reconstruction that would, if correct, confirm that an ancestor of Apollo was indeed already worshipped in second-millennium Greece.[128] But, surely he was also already

---

[126] Beekes (2010: xv).
[127] On the possible linguistic affinities of "Trojan," see Chapter 14, 361–2.
[128] KN E 842.3; *ro₂* = /lyo/. See Aura Jorro (1985, 1993: 2.113). See Beekes (2003b) on problems with Burkert's derivation of Apollo's name, and Nagy (2004: 138–43), supplying an alternate Greek etymology, but without taking into account *Appaluwa*. In the Hittite spelling of the Mycenaean Greek names *Aléksandros* (cf. *A-re-ka-sa-da-ra*, MY V 659, 2) and *Apélyōn* (cf. Cypr. *Apeilon*) in "Trojan," we can see that Greek accented *-e* is realized as *-a*, whereas unaccented *-o* is realized as *-u*.

Fig. 9: Apollo Philesius of Didyma, holding a deer in his hand (bronze copy of an original by Canachus, *ca.* 520 BCE)

present in southwestern Anatolia, as the Hittite plague ritual shows. Gods who were considered effective healers were particularly mobile, and it looks as if Apollo/Appaluwa was already a healer in the Late Bronze Age, and already moving back and forth across the Aegean. The Hittite texts confirm for us strong continuity in Apollo's character across the Dark Age.

Didymean Apollo may directly continue the Arzawan Apallu, or be related to him in the same way as the Wilusan Appaliuna: a shared god that underwent his own developments in Greece, then was transferred to Anatolia to merge again with his "brother." It may be significant that a Mycenaean sherd depicting a LAMMA-god with his horned headdress and holding a bird of prey, another characteristic animal of the divinity, was found at Bronze Age Miletus (see Fig. 10, and the deities with the hawks in Fig. 8). The Apollo *Keraiïtēs* of Didyma, or Horned Apollo, was explained by Callimachus as commemorating Apollo's attempt to milk a billy-goat,[129] and many see him as an initiatory god related to the Doric Apollo *Karneios* ('of the ram'). But, he may also refract Near Eastern iconography in which gods are distinguished by their horned headgear (cf. Figs. 8 and 11, the Storm-god at Malatya), as may be the case for Apollo *Keraiatās* in Cyprus.[130] In addition, the name of the LAMMA-god Kurunta (Luwian Runzas) means "having horns/antlers,"[131] so the Greek epithet may simply be a translation of the indigenous god's name. One can see how complex the interactions could have been between mainland Greek gods and the gods that Greek-speakers encountered in Anatolia, with similarities encouraging connections between the two sets of gods and new interpretations being put on old iconography.

A similar equation must have been made between Apollo and Delphinius, whose cult is found on both sides of the Aegean.[132] The term *Delphinios* may be descended from a pre-Greek language,[133] and Walter Burkert has attempted to link the name to that of the Anatolian vegetation-god Telipinu,[134] but the epiclesis also could be fruitfully related in the Greek mind to dolphins (*delphis*), and to Apollo's cult place Delphi, even if the connections were not justified etymologically.

Delphi became an important cult center in the late ninth century, and the cult of its local Apollo, Pythius, was established in more than one place in Crete by the late seventh century. Eventually the cult of Apollo Pythius was established throughout the Greek world.[135] Its spread is refracted in the journey Apollo makes throughout Greece before he settles in Delphi, where he slays Pytho, as described in his Homeric hymn, and it allowed for the spread of the snake-slaying story with it. As with the hymns of Olen at Delos, authorship by

---

[129] Call. *Iamb.* F 217 Pfeiffer.
[130] Herda (2006a: 319–26, 439–40; 2008: 19). See Knapp (2008: 277–9) and S. P. Morris (1992a: 113–14) on Apollo Keraiatās and the late thirteenth–early twelfth-century statue of the Horned God from Enkomi.
[131] Haas (2003a: 301), Melchert (1994: 256). Cf. Reshep *šprm* "of Horned Animals" (?), mentioned at Karatepe as the Phoenician equivalent of Luwian Runzas; see Chapter 12, 313, n. 61. The connection between horns and Apollo was carried to an extreme with the large altar for Apollo at Delos built entirely out of ram horns (Call. *Ap.* 2.60–4): see Bruneau and Ducat (2005: 50–1).
[132] Graf (1979: 3–4). [133] Graf (1979: 4–7, 21).
[134] Burkert (1979b: 134). On Telipinu see Haas (1994: 442–5) and Mazoyer (2003b), although I am not persuaded of all his claims.
[135] Davies (2009: 62–3).

Fig.10: Mycenaean Vessel with an Anatolian God from Miletus (LH IIIB–C, 1230–1190 BCE). To the left we can see the Hittite horned headdress belonging to divinities. To the right is the end of a bird's beak, which could belong to a hawk on the divinity's arm (cf. Fig. 8).

a foreigner, the "Lydian" Olympus, was plausible, and the Greeks saw the story as derived from Anatolia, not transferred in the opposite direction.

The *Chaoskampf* myth in its festival setting: Syro-Anatolia

The transfer back and forth across the Aegean of cult features that became associated with Apollo was fostered both by the shared features in the Anatolian and Greek gods that were the result of their common origin and by the shared identity of the Greeks, consciously kept alive on both sides. This allowed for the transfer of specific versions attached to Apollo of the multifarious genre of *Chaoskampf* myths. I argue in this section that the types of festivals discussed above were a key milieu allowing for the display and pick-up of regional variants of the stories attached to Apollo, specifically the snake-slaying story, just as festivals for the Storm-god, recognized by the Greeks as Zeus, allowed for transfers of the *Chaoskampf* myth attached to Zeus, as told in Hesiod's *Theogony*.[136] A scholion to Pindar *Nemean* 2.1d quotes three lines from "Hesiod" in which he boasts of competing with Homer by singing novel songs about Apollo. This festive and competitive setting is what I envision driving the incorporation of

---

[136] Significantly, Apollo is called *hieron menos Hēelioio* 'divine strength of the sun' in the *Homeric Hymn to Apollo* (371) when he slays the Pythian snake, indicating how there could be some overlap between Apollo *lukeios*, the bringer of light, and Zeus the sky-god, allowing for the transfer of storylines between the two. (This reference refutes the claim by Burkert 1985: 149, with n. 55, that Apollo was only equated with the sun in the fifth century.) Whereas Zeus maintains the connection to the theme of just kingship equaling the control of chaotic forces, Apollo continues the connection with the conquest of dark winter, as his festivals often marked the new year (Levaniouk 2011: 320).

appealing details gleaned from performers from other locations.[137] In the Near East, *Chaoskampf* myths, of which the snake-slaying story is but one instantiation, were performed or recited, sometimes as epics, at state-sponsored festivals because the various stories about the Storm-god battling chaotic monsters upheld the ideology of kingship.[138] They explained how agrarian prosperity was fostered by a powerful king supported by the gods, enhancing the message of the festivals in which they were performed and achieving the twin religious and political goals of persuading the gods and the human audience of the righteousness of the king. For this reason the ideology of kingship was a driving force in the spread of the *Chaoskampf* myth in the second millennium, as local kings made use of an internationally recognized storyline. In the first millennium, the story maintained its effectiveness even as kingship disappeared in Greek *poleis*.

The motif of a god or hero slaying a snake, which frequently appears in eastern Mediterranean cosmogonic myths, has many manifestations, layers, and applications, and it overlaps with a widespread Indo-European storyline. In Greek myth Apollo kills the Python in order to establish the Delphic oracles, Heracles kills the many-headed Hydra, and Zeus must overcome Typhon in order to establish himself as supreme god.[139] One striking feature of the stories attached to Apollo and Zeus is their Anatolian connection with both the Illuyanka myths and the *Song of Hedammu*. In this section I discuss first the Illuyanka myths, their parallels with Greek myths, and their festival setting. I then discuss the Kumarbi cycle, first the parallels between the Storm-god's fight with Hedammu and Zeus' fight with Typhon, then evidence for performance of Hurro-Hittite song in a festival setting. I continue the exploration of the significance of place by discussing how the landmark Mt. Hazzi/Sapon/Ǧebel al-Aqra provided a focus for the myth across time. Finally, I turn to the theme of legitimate kingship, embodied in particular by the Storm-god of Aleppo, as a motivating factor in the spread of the *Chaoskampf* myth within the festival setting.

---

[137] Hes. F 297 Most, see Nagy (2010: 116–17) and Martin (2000).
[138] See Taracha (2009: 92) and N. Wyatt (1996: 155–8; 1998).
[139] On snake-slaying stories see Dijkstra (2005), Fontenrose (1959), Kirk, Raven, and Schofield (1983: 66–8), Schwemer (2001: 118–19, 226–37), and M. L. West (1966: 379–81; 1971: 20–5; 1997a: 300–4). On the Indo-European stories see García Trabazo (1996), J. Katz (1998; 2005: 28–9), Watkins (1995: 297–468), and M. L. West (2007: 255–9). See N. Wyatt (1996: 122, 127–218) for a review of the *Chaoskampf* myth and its meaning. Also see M. S. Smith (1994: 110–13) on the "conflict myth" in Mesopotamia and Syria.

Several versions of or allusions to the *Chaoskampf* myth are recorded in the official libraries of Hattusa. I begin with the most famous examples, the Kumarbi cycle and the Illuyanka myths recited in the *purulli* festival. I continue by discussing several other examples, showing how their spread was connected to the spread of an ideology of kingship from north Syria to Anatolia. I then move to first-millennium examples from Delos, Assyria, and Athens.

The *purulli* festival, celebrated in the spring (at least in the Empire period, *ca.* 1250 BCE), was a Hattic festival for the land.[140] Those tablets that are specifically identified as descriptions of the *purulli* festival show the standard ceremonies of a Hittite festival, including the Great Assembly.[141]

It is explicitly stated in the frame of the two versions of the Illuyanka ('snake') myth that was used in the *purulli* festival celebrated in Nerik, a city in north central Anatolia:

> [T]hus Kell[a, the anointed priest[142] o]f the Storm-god of Nerik,[143] the story of *purulli*, [... o]f Ta[rhun] of Heaven: When they speak as follows: "Let the land thrive (and) prosper. Let the land be protected." So that it thrive and prospers, they celebrate the *purulli* festival.[144]

Nerik was lost to the Kaska enemy from the time of the Old Kingdom king Hantili II to the reign of Hattusili III. It seems that the two versions were collected at Hattusa in an effort to keep the celebration alive.[145] We should

---

[140] Cf. the Hattic word *wur* 'land' (Hoffner 2007: 130–1 with earlier references); Hattic songs performed in the *purulli* festival: *Hattic Songs, Women of Tissaruliya*: *CTH* 741.2 = *KBo* 23.103 iv 14′–19′: "When the king comes to the regular festival to Ziplanta, the maidens sing these songs and when the king celebrates the *purulli* somewhere they sing these very songs on the first day" (translit. Klinger 1996: 710; also see Rutherford 2008: 77). On the *purulli* festival see Haas (1994: 696–747), but note that a large number of the texts he considers to belong to the *purulli* festival do not refer explicitly to it, but only refer to Nerik, Telipinu, the *eya* tree, or the *kurša* bag (the last two are ritual objects that appear in the Telipinu myth, but also are used in other contexts, cf. Fig. 8). On the *purulli* festival and its celebration in different situations see Klinger (2009).

[141] *CTH* 674: *Purulli Festival*, most transliterated by Haas (1970: 252–4); also *CTH* 674.1 = *IBoT* 2.17 2′–5′ (translit. Haas and Wäfler 1976: 74).

[142] The "anointed priest" (^{LÚ}GUDU$_{12}$ or *kumra*) officiated in rites from the Hattic cultural layer.

[143] This local Storm-god from the Hattic town of Nerik was named Nerak or Nerikkil, but it is unclear what he is called in the story, since his name is hidden behind the Sumerian sign for "Storm-god."

[144] *Illuyanka*: *CTH* 321.A = *KBo* 3.7 i 1–8, with F = *KBo* 12.83 i 1–5 (translit. E. Rieken *et al.* 2009ff. on KhT; trans. M. Bachvarova in López-Ruiz 2013: 137). See the recent commentary and discussion of Hoffner (2007). On the etymology and meaning of the term *illuyankaš* see J. Katz (1998).

[145] Hazenbos (2003: 193–6), Hoffner (2007: 120–2). Klinger (2009) shows that we should not entirely believe the claims of Hattusili III that he revived the festival in Nerik, for there is some evidence that it had continued to be celebrated there.

be careful, however, not to assume too tight a connection between all versions of the *purulli* festival and the Illuyanka story.[146] During the lengthy period before Hattusili III was able to celebrate the festival at Nerik again,[147] it was celebrated in other towns, but not necessarily in honor of the Storm-god. For example, Mursili II celebrated it in the *ḫešti*-house in Hattusa for Lelwani,[148] and in Utruna Muwattalli II celebrated it for Telipinu.[149] One suspects that these festivals did not refer to the Illuyanka myth at all.

The two versions of the myth represent two separate transcripts. When and how they were collected and grouped together we do not know, only that the language of the stories appears to be older than that of their frames, and that the stories show evidence of being copied directly from an Old Hittite exemplar in their linguistic forms.[150] In one of the two versions, the Storm-god, defeated by the snake, achieves his victory through Inara, the goddess who protects wild animals. She recruits the human Hupasiya to help her, allowing him to sleep with her as a reward, then hosts a feast at which the snake and his children over-indulge and thus are unable to get back into their hole, giving Hupasiya an opportunity to tie up Illuyanka so that the Storm-god can kill him. The rest of the story, before it breaks off, focuses on Hupasiya, whom Inara ensconces in a specially built house, ordering him not to look out the window through which he can see his wife and children. Of course, the mortal eventually

---

[146] Popko (1995: 149) proposes multiple local *purulli* festivals.
[147] "(The king) will come to Nerik, he will build the city. Forth from Nerik I will consult an oracle: whether I should immediately strike the enemy or immediately celebrate the *purulli* festival and lead away back (to Nerik) the god." (*Oracle for an Itinerary in the Kaska Territory*: CTH 562.1 = KUB 22.25 obv. 19′–21′, translit. Haas 1970: 44–5, n. 3). The real-world action of the return of the festival to Nerik corresponds to action on the divine plane in the frame closing the story, which speaks of the gods visiting the Storm-god of Nerik (*Illuyanka*: CTH 321.D = KUB 12.66 iv 8′–17′, translit. E. Rieken et al. 2009ff. on KhT; trans. Bachvarova in López-Ruiz 2013: 139); see Taracha (2009: 103–4).
[148] "But when spring occurred, because I celebrated the *purulli* festival as a great [festival] for the Storm-god of Hatti and for the Storm-god of Zip[landa], and I did not celebrate in the *ḫešti*-house for Lelwa[ni] the *purulli* festival as a great festival, I went up to Hattusa, and I celebrated for Lelwani in the *ḫešti*-house the *purulli* festival as a great festival. When I had carried out in the *ḫešti*-house the great festival, I made a review of the troops in Arduna" (*Comprehensive Annals of Mursili II*: CTH 61.ɪɪ.10 = KBo 2.5 iii 13′–24′, translit. Götze 1933: 188, 190).
[149] *Cult Inventories under Tudhaliya IV*: CTH 525.7 = KUB 42.100 iv 12′–21′ (translit. and trans. Hazenbos 2003: 20, 24). (Now classified in KhT as CTH 673: *Tablet of the Pardon by the Storm-god of Nerik*.)
[150] All eight copies are NH; see Hoffner (2007: 120–2). Note that the two Hittite versions should not necessarily be considered "old" and "new" versions (Beckman 1982: 24, with n. 87; Watkins 1992: 320).

does so and begs to return to his family. He then seems to be sent off in disgrace by the goddess.

The closing bracket to the first version of the Illuyanka story is unfortunately not fully intelligible because of gaps in the text, but it is clear that the prosperity of the land depends on a successful celebration of the festival, and that the king's interaction with the wilderness-goddess Inara, whatever it is, legitimates his kingship:

> (A ii 15′–20′) Inara [went] to Kiskil[ussa]. As she se[t] her house [and] the [course] of the flood [in] the hand of the king, therefore we enact the f[i]rst *purull*[*i*], and the hand [of the king does X to the house] of Inara and the course of the flood.
>
> (21′–24′) Mount Zaliyanu is fore[most] of all. When the rain pours in Nerik, the [M]an of the Staff sends thick bread from Nerik.
>
> (25′–26′) He requested rain from Mount Za[liyan]u, and he brings it, [thick . . .] bread, to him.[151]

Inara must represent ground water, while the mountain fosters the heavenly water distributed by the Storm-god. The ritual is part of a contractual agreement between gods and humans in which worship and offerings are compensated with adequate rain.

In the other version, it is specified that when the Storm-god is defeated, he loses his heart and eyes. The god then engages in an elaborate subterfuge to retrieve them, first begetting a son with the daughter of a poor mortal, then sending him to marry the daughter of Illuyanka, instructing him to ask for the stolen body parts as a dowry; in return the son joins the snake's family instead of paying a bride-price. In the battle that follows, the son, now no longer part of the Storm-god's family, nobly requests to die with the enemy.

It has been surmised from a passage in a festival for the goddess Teteshapi naming the character of the "daughter of the poor man," whom the Storm-god marries, that the story was enacted in some sort of ritual drama in the *purulli* festival:[152]

---

[151] *CTH* 321.A = *KBo* 3.7 ii 15′–26′ (translit. E. Rieken *et al.* 2009ff. on KhT; trans. M. Bachvarova in López-Ruiz 2013: 138). Also see the interpretations in the transliterations and translations of Beckman (1982: 14–15, 19) and Haas (2006: 99–100), who see Inara placing the kingdom in the hands of the king, while Hoffner (1998a: 12) sees the king establishing Inara's temple.

[152] Haas (1988a: 286; 1994: 703, n. 44), Pecchioli Daddi (1987a: 55–6; 1987b: 368). Popko (1995: 149) and Taggar-Cohen (2005: 411) are skeptical.

> The daughter of a poor man [...] the NIN.DINGIR ('Lady of the God') dance[s] in front of [...] The sons of the palace hold the NIN.DINGIR. The man of the staff holds the da[ughter of a poor man [...[153]

If so, then the story told in the festival for Teteshapi was quite different from either of the variations discussed above, since both Inara and the daughter of the poor man appear – and the poor man himself;[154] such variation would after all not be surprising, given that there are already significant differences between the two versions we have. In fact, one of the notable features of the *Chaoskampf* myth is how many variations of it we can find in the Hittite documents.

The story of Typhon as told by Apollodorus in his *Bibliotheca* (1.6.3), Nonnus' *Dionysiaca* (1.137–2.569), and Oppian's *Halieutica* (3.15–25) has particularly close ties with the Illuyanka myth. Apollodorus' and Nonnus' versions show similarities with the second version: Typhon cuts out Zeus' tendons (*neura*) and hides them in his lair, and a helper or helpers must retrieve them so Zeus can defeat the monster in a second battle.[155] On the other hand, Oppian's version is strikingly similar to the version involving Hupasiya, for Typhon is lured from his cave by a meal to be attacked by Zeus.[156] Meanwhile, the story of Zeus and Typhon (Typhoeus) in Hesiod's *Theogony* 820–70 has connections with the *Song of Hedammu* in the general theme of a battle between a sea-snake and the Storm-god, while the volcanic nature of the monster that comes through in the imagery of earthquake and forest fire hot enough to melt ore seems to draw on the theme of *Song of Ullikummi*, in which the thunder and lightning of the Storm-god is pitted against the newly formed rock monster.[157]

In most versions of the battle between Typhon and Zeus, the monster is given a childhood in Cilicia, where his lair is the Corycian Cave.[158] Here

---

[153] *Festival for the Goddess Teteshapi*: *CTH* 738.1.12 = *KBo* 25.48 iii 6'-9' (translit. Pecchioli Daddi 1987b: 378, n. 87). On the NIN.DINGIR priestess, a member of the royal family, see Taggar-Cohen (2005: 384–422; 2006).
[154] *CTH* 738.2.C = *KBo* 21.90 23' (translit. and trans. Taggar-Cohen 2005: 430–1).
[155] Gantz (1993: 49–51) lists the ancient sources for the tale. On the correspondences between *Illuyanka* and Apollodorus' version, see Burkert (1992: 103; 1979b: 7–9; 2004: 40), Watkins (1992).
[156] Houwink ten Cate (1961: 209). [157] Also see López-Ruiz (2010: 93–4).
[158] Pi. *P.* 1.31–2, 8.21, Aesch. *PV* 351–2; Apoll. *Bib.* 1.6.3 and Oppian *Hal.* 3.15 specify the Corycian cave (not the same as the Corycian cave on Mt. Parnassus), which Strabo describes (13.4.6, 14.5), also clarifying that Cilicia is the location of the Arimoi, who are mentioned in *Il.* 2.783 with reference to the place of Typhon's death (Watkins 1992: 321). Also see Bremmer (2008: 319–20), Casabonne in Casabonne and Porcher (2003: 131–2), and Lane Fox (2009: 293–8) beautifully describing the cave.

the evidence for cult continuity is particularly strong, because lists of the priests employed at the cave have been preserved for us. Tarhunt is a frequent component of their names.[159] The second-century BCE poet Oppian, who told a version of the story of Zeus and Typhon, was a native of Corycus.[160] It is certainly plausible, as Robin Lane Fox suggests, that a descendant of the *Chaoskampf* story, blending in its own unique way elements found in the various versions we have discussed here, continued to be told at the Corycian Cave.[161] The Zeus and Typhon episode could have entered Greek hexametric poetry via Greco-Anatolian poets, possibly residing on Cyprus or in Cilicia, who adapted a descendant of the tradition made manifest to us by the texts found at Hattusa for a new audience and merged it with Greek epic.

While we do not know the performance setting of the *Hedammu* or *Ullikummi*, at least one otherwise lost episode of the Hurro-Hittite *Chaoskampf* story told in the various songs grouped by modern scholars into the Kumarbi cycle was sung in cult contexts that are typical of festivals. A fragment that mentions Mt. Hazzi tells us that a Hittite version of the *Song of the Sea* was performed during a ritual: "the *Song* [o]*f the Sea* [they/he] sing(s)/ ['(when the Storm-god)] overcame (*tarahta*) [(the Sea)],'"[162] with a pun on the Hittite name of the Storm-god, Tarhun.[163] The events of the *Song of the Sea* probably occurred directly before the Storm-god's battle with the sea-snake told in the *Song of Hedammu*.[164] Here we can imagine a battle between the Storm-god and Sea taking place in sight of Mt. Hazzi, a scenario also well known from the mythology of Ugarit, which looked out at Mt. Hazzi, the Ugaritic Mt. Sapon.

In addition, another fragmentary text tells us that the *Song of Kingship*, which only exists for us as an incipit but presumably belonged to the tradition of Hurro-Hittite narrative song, if not from the Kumarbi cycle, was performed by a group of male singers at a sacrifice for Teshshub that also involved Mt. Hazzi in some way, either as the location for the rite or as

---

[159] Houwink ten Cate (1961: 190–1, n. 7, 202, 204–6).
[160] *Hal.* 3.8, 208–9, see Houwink ten Cate (1961: 207) and Lane Fox (2009: 286–7).
[161] Lane Fox (2009: 297–8). Bremmer (2006) further suggests that elements of the story of Jason and the Golden Fleece were made known to the Greeks through the *purulli* festival.
[162] *Ritual for Mt. Hazzi: CTH* 785 = *KUB* 44.7 i 11′–12′; Mt. Hazzi mentioned in colophon, vi 3′ (translit. Rutherford 2001b: 598). The mountain was worshipped in more than one festival; citations in del Monte and Tischler (1978: 106–7) and del Monte (1992b: 38).
[163] See Gilan (2004a: 279).   [164] See Chapter 2, 25–6.

the main dedicatee. Perhaps this group of bards performed serially episodes from the song.[165]

At Ugarit a rich lore is attached to Mt. Sapon, as the scene of battles between the Sea-god Yam and the Storm-god Baal, which influenced even Egyptian myth.[166] Visible from the sea and from Ugarit, on the current border between Syria and Turkey, the mountain was an important landmark for sailors and a stable locus for the *Chaoskampf* story across many centuries.[167] Knowledge at third-millennium Ebla of the story of the Syrian Storm-god's fight with Yam is indicated by the use there of the royal name Yigris-Halab, the first part of which corresponds to Ugaritic *Ygrš*, the name of the Storm-god's mace used against the monster; thus, the name means "Baal's mace of Aleppo."[168] The myth was also well known in eighteenth-century Mari, and was already used to legitimate kingship, for it was mentioned as a familiar story in a prophecy at Mari with regard to Zimri-Lim's kingship.[169] The importance of Mt. Hazzi in the Hittite rituals that use the *Chaoskampf* myth supports a north Syrian origin for the Hurro-Hittite instantations of the myth found at Hattusa.[170]

We can see continuity into the first millennium in the story's use in Syro-Anatolian cult. At Malatya there is a Neo-Hittite representation of the Storm-god slaying a huge snake coming out of the waves, which dates to some time between 1050 and 850 BCE (Fig. 11),[171] and the cosmogony of

---

[165] *Ritual for Mt. Hazzi*: CTH 785.B = KBo 8.88 obv. 8 (NH); CTH 785 = KBo 8.86 obv. 5′; Mt. Hazzi mentioned in colophon, rev. 4′ (MH?, translit. and trans. Haas and Wilhelm 1974: 260–3; translit. Haas 1998: 170–2, Nos. 100, 101); see Houwink ten Cate (1992: 116–17). The *Song of Kingship*, on which see de Martino (1993: 124), is not the same as the *Song of Birth*, also known as the "Song of Kingship in Heaven" among modern scholars. See Chapter 15, 414–15, for competitive collaboration among poets in festival settings.

[166] Typhon is syncretized with Seth (Hecat. FGrH 1 F 300, M. L. West 1997a: 304), and Baal Sapon is incorporated into the Egyptian pantheon by the thirteenth century (Koenig 2007: 229–30). M. L. West (2002a: 111–12) notes that the conflict between the Titan Aigaion, son of Pontus (the sea), and Zeus, told in Eumelus' *Titanomachy* (F 3 West), could be derived from the conflict between the Storm-god and the Sea.

[167] Lane Fox (2009: 243–52).

[168] C. Gordon (1998: 342). See Bonechi (2001: 55) for citations.

[169] See Durand (1993: 43–5) on A 1968.

[170] The gods observe from Mt. Hazzi the stone monster Ullikummi growing in the *Song of Ullikummi*: CTH 345.2.A = KUB 33.113 i 10′ (translit. E. Rieken *et al.* 2009ff. on KhT; trans. M. Bachvarova in López-Ruiz 2013: 157).

[171] See Akurgal (1962: 81–2), although note that he is incorrect to assign the image specifically to *Illuyanka*, as opposed to *Hedammu*, because *Illuyanka* is associated with north Anatolia, as shown by the towns referred to in it. In the first version of *Illuyanka*, Ziggarata is the home of Hupasiya, Kiskilussa is the place of the battle, Inara builds her house at Tarukka, and Nerik

Pherecydes of Syros includes a snake-slaying episode.[172] Mt. Hazzi/Sapon is Mt. Casius, where Zeus and Typhon have their first battle in Apollodorus (*Bib.* 1.6.3).[173] In fact, the name Typhon may be a Graecized version of the mountain's west Semitic name Ṣapōn,[174] while Casius may be the Greek version of its Hurrian name Hazzi.[175]

In Chapter 7 I discussed the introduction of Hurro-Hittite song to the Hittite court. I suggested that two phases in the introduction of Hurrian narratives to the Hittite court can be distinguished, one in the Old Kingdom and one at the beginning of the New Kingdom. The *Song of Release* arrived with the original introduction of Teshshub of Aleppo by Hattusili I from Hassu. As Itamar Singer has shown, the original location of the action of the Hurrian *Chaoskampf* myth was at Lake Van, and when the Hurrians moved into Syria, some of the landmarks in the story were replaced with north Syrian ones, in particular Mt. Hazzi.[176] The stories were then imported to the Hittite capital after the subordination of Kizzuwatna that led to dynastic marriages between the Hittite court and Hurrianized Cilicia. In both cases the stories were useful to the ideological program of the Hittite court, a function that would have been articulated through the rituals or festivals in which they were performed, and the Storm-god was the main character in both narrative traditions.[177] Meanwhile, other north Syrian festivals imported through the same channel, such as the (ḫ)išuwa festival and the ḫiyar(r)a or "donkey" festival for

---

receives rain from Mt. Zaliyanu. The story is thus localized to north central Anatolia. The second version of *Illuyanka* mentions that the battles occur near the sea; what body of water is referred to is unclear, but it is more likely to be the Black Sea than the Mediterranean (*pace* Houwink ten Cate 1961: 213). Nerik is the town that seems to benefit from the ceremony, and in the frame of the second story, the gods of the town of Kastama are granted special privileges, while Tanipiya benefits from a grant by the king.

[172] Mentioned by Celsus: Kirk, Raven, and Schofield (1983: 66, no. 57).

[173] Herodotus (3.5) connects the region around Mt. Casius with Typhon (Porzig 1930: 382). The mountain is called Kel Dağ in Turkish, while its Syrian name is Ǧebel al-Aqra. Some of the more important recent studies on Typhon/Sapon/Hazzi/Casius include Haider (2005), Healey (2007), Lane Fox (2009: 242–314), and N. Wyatt (1995).

[174] The name Typhon also chimes with that of Apollo's opponent Pytho, with metathesis of the consonants. If we believe these two names are related, then the mountain continued to have some influence on the story, even as the locus of the story moved elsewhere. However, see Watkins (1995: 461–2) for Indo-European etymologies of the two names, certain for Pytho, possible for Typhon.

[175] Healey (2007: 142–3, with earlier references). [176] Singer (2002a).

[177] Further on the Storm-god of Aleppo at Hattusa in Bachvarova (2009: 34–5), where I discuss his cult at Hattusa as an example of the transfer of a god with his personnel; also Chapter 7, 159–64.

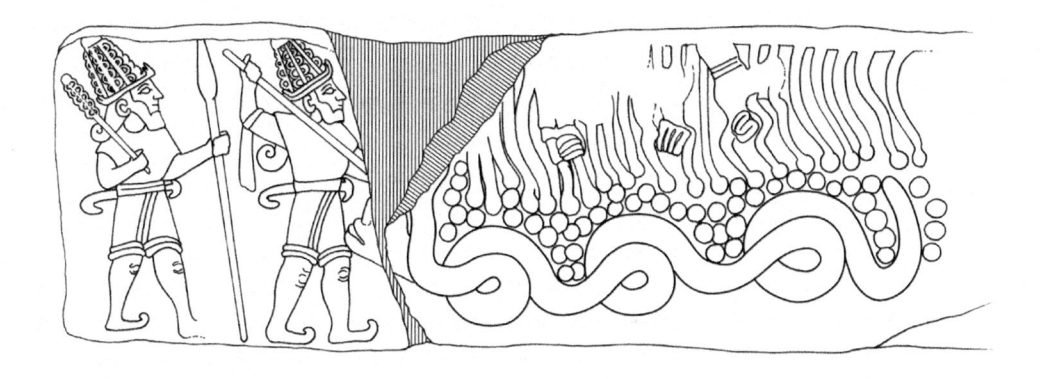

Fig. 11: Storm-god at Malatya fighting sea-snake (ninth century BCE)

the Storm-god of Aleppo, promoted the ideology of kingship at Hattusa through other forms of the *Chaoskampf* motif.[178]

The Syro-Anatolian Storm-god, especially in the specific manifestation of Hadad/Teshshub of Aleppo, was immensely popular as a symbol of righteous kingship already in the third millennium BCE, when he received offerings sent from Ebla.[179] The Storm-god's power over fertilizing rain represented the king's responsibility for his land's prosperity, and his thunder and lightning symbolized the king's prowess in war, while the stories of the Storm-god's struggle for kingship in heaven reflected the human king's labors to maintain his supremacy.[180] The west Semitic/Syrian Storm-god Hadad of Aleppo eventually was equated with the Hurrian Storm-god Teshshub, who himself was equated with the Anatolian Storm-god – Hattic Taru, Hittite/Luwian Tarhun(na)/Tarhunt.[181]

The Storm-god of Aleppo was the only non-Anatolian god to receive offerings in the AN.TAḪŠUM and *nuntarriyašḫaš* festivals.[182] He

---

[178] On the possible transfer in the other direction of a Hittite-style festival to north Syrian Emar, see Archi (2001c) and Fleming (1996). Prechel (2008), however, argues that the tablets found in Emar describe private rites, not public festivals, noting the lack of correspondences with commonly worshipped gods at Hattusa.
[179] See Schwemer (2001: 211–21, 489–502).
[180] Schmitz (2009b: 134–7) discusses evidence of the link between kingship, the Storm-god of Aleppo, and the *Chaoskampf* motif in the Near East.
[181] The Storm-god of Aleppo proved to be a popular and long-lasting god in the Near East, eventually becoming Zeus Dolichenus, the god of the Roman troops. See Bunnens (2004).
[182] AN.TAḪŠUM Festival, Outline Tablet: CTH 604.A = KBo 10.20 iii 19 (twenty-first day) (translit. and trans. Güterbock 1960: 94, 97). On the Storm-god of Aleppo and other gods in the *nuntarriyašḫaš* festival, see Nakamura (2002: 131–2).

maintained his regional identity; as mentioned earlier, a liver oracle even names the Storm-god of Aleppo of/in Hattusa,[183] and people from Aleppo were involved in his worship at Hattusa.[184] Thus, we may infer that a distinct Aleppan style of worship was maintained for him in Anatolia, perhaps from the time when Hattusuli I first brought him as booty from his campaigns to the east of Anatolia. As mentioned earlier, that the worship of Teshshub of Aleppo had a Hurrian mythological component relating the *Chaoskampf* myth is shown by the fact that he was invoked in a Hurrian prayer reminding him of his birth from Anu and Kumarbi, which is told in the *Song of Birth*.[185] One can view this information from another angle: the ideology of kingship embodied in the personality of the Storm-god was necessarily expressed through narrative, so when the god was transferred, narratives came with him.

The *(ḫ)išuwa* festival was a Luwian- and Hurrian-influenced, north-Syrian-derived festival that "cultivated the memory of the roots of the dynasty."[186] Its Cilician context is indicated by the mention of Adaniya and Tarsus, men from which attended the festival, along with men from other Cilician towns.[187] It was celebrated for the Storm-god of the mountain Manuzzi and in it Mt. Hazzi, along with many other mountains, received offerings, as did Teshshub of Aleppo. A contest with the Storm-god was featured, acted out by the king to the accompaniment of musicians:

> ... on the [roof], facing the door [...], three harpists dance before the god like a battle. They fight with the permission of the Storm-god. The harpists sing a *kuwayaralla* of battle and the harpists strike the harp and the tambourine. And, one of the harpists stands in the doorway of the god (and) blows the horn. And, one *purapši*-man who is standing on the roof facing the king speaks as following a *kuwarayalla*, "Oh king, do not fear. The Storm-god places/will place the enemy and the enemy lands beneath your feet. You will smash them like empty vessels of clay. And he has given you, the king, life, prosperity, a victorious weapon into perpetuity, the favor of the gods forever. Do not fear anything. You have vanquished."[188]

---

[183] See Chapter 7, 162. [184] Souček and Siegelová (1974: 44).
[185] See Thiel and Wegner (1984) and Chapter 7, 162.
[186] Taracha (2009: 138). A colophon states it came from Kizzuwatna: (*Ḫ)isuwa Festival: CTH* 628 = *KBo* 33.178 rev. 2′–10′ (translit. and trans. Wegner and Salvini 1991: 40–1). The festival is analyzed by Wegner and Salvini (1991: 6–11) and Haas (1994: 848–75); also see Bachvarova (2009: 41–2).
[187] *CTH* 628.Tablet 12.A = *KUB* 20.52 i 17′, 21′ (translit. Groddek 2004c: 91–2). See Rutherford (2005a: 623) for discussion.
[188] (*Ḫ)išuwa Festival: CTH* 628.Tablet 10.A = *KBo* 15.52 + *KUB* 34.116 v 1″–2″, with duplicate *CTH* 628.Tablet 10.F = *KBo* 20.60 v 4′–11′ (translit. Groddek 2010b: 370–1). My translation is

Here the Storm-god is clearly the king's model for divinely legitimized kingship.

The ḫiyara festival for the Storm-god of Aleppo was a widespread festival that originally marked the renewing of treaty obligations with the sacrifice of a donkey, then became attached to the god no later than the Old Babylonian period, spread with the god, and evolved in each location.[189] At Ugarit, Baal ('Lord') of Aleppo was one of the chief recipients of sacrifices during the month of ḫiyaru (April/May, named after the festival), along with Baal of Sapon. The Hurrian-influenced list of deities also includes Šarrašiya.[190] Thus, we can see that the festival's focus was legitimization of kingship, for Šarrašiya is a personification of the same abstract term used in the title of the Hurrian *Song of Kingship* (šarrašiyaš). It was "a term ... frequently used ... as 'offering term' in Hurro-Hittite rituals: šarrašiya 'for kingship'. ... The sacrifice to this deity directly after the two storm-gods seems to suggest that the ḫiyara festival at Ugarit was especially performed with regard to (the Aleppine) Baʿlu's kingship over the gods."[191] It is likely that one use of the Ugaritic *Baal Cycle*, like that of the Kumarbi cycle, was to provide a narrative backdrop to the festival in Ugarit.[192] Thus, at Ugarit the contest affirming the Storm-god's kingship, expressed through a narrative, translates into a legitimization of the local king's rule, as at Hattusa.

Some versions of the stories discussed here were also told during Greek festival celebrations. The *Homeric Hymn to Apollo* was performed at the Delia at least once, in 522 BCE,[193] and the story of Apollo's fight with the snake Pytho was a focal point in the musical contests of the *puthikos nomos*

---

modified from Bachvarova (2009: 42), where the passage is discussed in more detail. There, however, I presented a different interpretation of the passage. I am now persuaded by the interpretation of Groddek (2010b: 390–1).

[189] Already in the Old Babylonian period the Storm-god of Aleppo was honored in a festival in the month of Hiyaru. On the ḫiyara festival see Schmitz (2009b: 135–6) and Collins (2010: 60), commenting on earlier scholars' work.

[190] *Rituals for Two Months*: KTU 1.148 rev. 28 (translit. and trans. Pardee 2002: 44–9). The reading of the Ugaritic trty as representing šarrašiya has been clarified by the equivalent entry in a parallel Akkadian *Deity List*: RS 92.2004 obv. 8 (translit. and trans. Pardee 2002: 17–19). Embedded in the ritual is a Hurrian hymn invoking Ea, Hebat of Aleppo, and other gods (Lam 2006).

[191] Schwemer (2008b: 11). See *CHD* (Š: 245) for citations of šarrašiya. A Hurrian ritual of anointing for kingship, the *Hurrian Ritual for the Royal Couple*: CTH 784 = KUB 27.42 rev. 15′ (translit. Haas 1984: 118, No. 11), refers to "Teshshub of Kingship"; see Yakubovich (2005: 125).

[192] N. Wyatt (1996: 155–8; 1998) has indeed suggested that the Baal cycle was used to legitimize kingship, linking the enthronement of the human king to the pervasive motif of enthronement in the Ugaritic Baal myths.

[193] See Chapter 15, 398.

in the Pythian games at Delphi during the sixth century.[194] Thus, the form, the function, and the context of the Hittite and Greek stories match. The use of the *Chaoskampf* motif in festivals was in fact quite widespread. Both the Panathenaea and the Mesopotamian *akītu* festival (celebrating the fall equinox) use other versions of the *Chaoskampf* myth as a background to the festivities. By the sixth century, Athena's role in the Gigantomachy, one episode of the Greek version of the *Chaoskampf* myth in the *Theogony* (617–733), was celebrated in the Panathenaea by being depicted on the *peplos* presented to her. Her role has parallels with the role of Marduk in *Enuma Elish* (the *Epic of Creation*), which the head priest of Marduk's sanctum recited from beginning to end in Babylon during its version of the *akītu* festival. The *Epic of Creation* tells how Marduk was created at the request of the gods and went on to defeat the monsters born from Tiamat (the sea), and to take back the tablet of destiny. The fight was depicted on the doors of the *akītu*-house at Assur, as the equivalent event in Greek myth was on the pediments and metopes of many a public building in Greece, including at the Peisistratid temple in Athens.[195]

In sum, whereas Walter Burkert, in his seminal study of the parallels between the *Epic of Creation* and Homeric poetry, looked to literary transmission, because copying such texts was part of the Mesopotamian scribal training,[196] or to the use of cosmogonic motifs in purificatory rituals, practiced by lone wandering seers,[197] I argue rather that the correspondences in form and function point to the transmission of motifs out of which such texts were built through their public

---

[194] M. L. West (1992a: 212–14). There was also a festival in Thessaly associated with Apollo's snake-slaying: see Davies (2007: 56).

[195] On the theme of Athena's role in the Gigantomachy in the Panathenaea, see Frame (2009: 403–7, with earlier references), Nagy (2009: 553–63). On the giants woven into the *peplos*, see Eur. *Hec.* 467–74 with scholion, further references in Burkert (1983a: 156, n. 92). On the Panathenaea more generally, see R. Parker (1996: 75–9, 89–92) and Robertson (1992: 90–119). For the recitation of the *Epic of Creation*, see trans. of W. Farber in *TUAT* II, "Texte zum Akitu-Fest (Neujahrsrituale)," p. 217 (II.ii 63–8), fourth day of the eleven-day festival. Although the performance is explicitly attested only by the first millennium because this is when our earliest description of the festival dates from, we can expect it to have been recited much earlier. The fight between the generations of gods described in the *Epic of Creation* was imagined to occur in the *akītu*-house, located just outside the towns that celebrated the festival. See M. E. Cohen (1993: 404–5), Pongratz-Leisten (1994: 71–84). Depiction of the theomachy on the doors of the *akītu*-house: M. E. Cohen (1993: 423). See M. E. Cohen (1993: 400–53) for a discussion of the *akītu* festival.

[196] Burkert (1992: 95). Also see my comments on his analysis of the parallels between the *Epic of Creation* and the Deception of Zeus episode in the *Iliad* in Chapter 3, 55, n. 8.

[197] Burkert (1992: 125), and see Chapter 9, 200–6.

performance in festivals, although surely there was a reciprocal relationship between their efficacy as historiolae in incantations and their appeal as public performances, as shown by the incorporation of the ritual context of performance of a story about a journey to the edge of the world into the *Odyssey*.[198]

Conclusion

The very rich Hittite sources explain how festivals were an important milieu promoting transfer of song and verbal art, showing that festivals could be imported from other regions, that performers from notable regions could be brought in to festivals, and that some festivals went on tour. The festivals might be associated with a particularly notable landmark or with a particularly popular deity. The Mycenaean sources show commonalities with Hittite festivals not only in the overall program, but in the attempt to forge close links with areas outside the chief towns, and to accommodate indigenous practices of places taken over by the Mycenaeans.

It is not impossible that contact and borrowing between Greek and Near Eastern epic in festival contexts occurred in the Late Bronze Age, but the evidence for this kind of contact is better for the first millennium BCE. Analogous processes were at work in first-millennium Greek festivals, providing the opportunity to borrow appealing details in verbal art from one tradition to another. The festival circuit supplied non-local performers with venues throughout the eastern Mediterranean, as reflected in the stories of performers such as Terpander, Olen, Olympus, and the poet portrayed in the *Homeric Hymn to Apollo*. The story itself of the hymn explains on the mythological level facts of which everyone was aware: Apollo's cult was widespread throughout Greece and the coast of Anatolia. Myths of the arrival of Dionysus in Athens and the establishment of Demeter's cult in Eleusis, told in the *Homeric Hymn to Demeter*, even if we should not take the etiologies literally, provided similar explanations of

---

[198] M. L. West (1997a: 602) does suggest, "We can imagine performances at festivals or at private celebrations. When a *nâru* ['singer'] was received in another city, it seems likely that he would have sung there. When the king led his armies on campaigns to east, west, or north, as happened regularly under the Assyrian empire, there might well have been singers in attendance to divert them in the evenings with songs of every sort, including, perhaps, celebrations of previous military triumphs. Some singers might have stayed with garrisons in conquered territories."

how their cults became so widespread, and Herodotus (2.171.2–3) was able to believe that the Thesmophoria was brought from Egypt by the Danaids.[199] Again, we do not need to trust his judgment, just to acknowledge that fifth-century Greeks were open to such etiologies. They did not feel the need to deny that they shared in common festival practices with other parts of the Mediterranean, and they realized that festivals could be transferred to new locations.

The festival context is particularly useful for explaining parallels between the Homeric Hymns and Near Eastern narratives, since at least two of them can be safely connected to festival contexts: the *Homeric Hymn to Apollo* and the *Homeric Hymn to Demeter* (which draws on the same Anatolian disappearing-god storyline used in the Eleusinian Mysteries and the Thesmophoria, also applied to Dionysus[200]). In fact, Nagy argues that "the god who presides over the given festival that serves as the setting for the performances of that given epic will be named as the primary god of the *prooimion* [Homeric hymn]."[201] So, we could invoke the festival setting to explain parallels between hexametric stories about other gods and Near Eastern stories and narrative songs, not only about Apollo, Zeus, Dionysus, and Demeter, but also about Aphrodite, as will be discussed in Chapter 12. Festivals also would have been settings for the performance of heroic epic, as in the Panathenaea, both as an expression of pride (whether to proclaim their national superiority or membership in the brotherhood of great powers) and to complement ancestor veneration, which often took place in festivals.[202] In the final chapter I will explore the effect of the Panionic performance setting on the *Iliad*'s storyline.

We should not view the stories and rituals as inextricably connected, however. That is, we should not insist that the stories could only be performed in the rituals or festivals, nor that the rites required these stories and only these. With regard to the *Chaoskampf* myth in second-millennium Hattusa, for example, surely many members of the audience would have been familiar with the stories from having enjoyed their performances in other contexts, not all of them sponsored by the Hittite

---

[199] See Rutherford (2005b: 131).
[200] See Clinton (1992) and Suter (2002: 6–7, 214–18, 221–4) for the relationship between the *Homeric Hymn to Demeter* and the Thesmophoria and Eleusinian mysteries. On the Anatolian background of the Demeter myth, see Chapter 4, 104, n. 115.
[201] Nagy (2010: 105).
[202] On the Hittite offerings to royal ancestors, see Chapter 7, 151; on offerings to collective ancestors in Iron Age Greek festivals see Chapter 11, 287, n. 82.

court. What is important to my overall argument is that we have examples of particular stories being performed in particular festivals and rituals, and the stories' performers found the means to travel to Hattusa and to support themselves at least in part because of the interest the Hittite court took in their work.

11 | The context of epic in Late Bronze and Early Iron Age Greece

> First the immortal ones having Olympian homes made the golden race of *meropes* humans. They were ruled by Cronus (*epi Kronōi ēsan*), when he was king in heaven (*ouranōi embasileuen*); and they lived like gods, having a spirit without care, far away from pain and bitterness ... Then, once the earth covered over this race, they became *daimones* through the plans of great Zeus, noble guardians of mortal men on the surface of the earth, ... givers of wealth; and they had this as their kingly prize.
>
> Hesiod *Works and Days* (109–26)

Introduction

In previous chapters I have discussed the values that promoted the transfer of specific kinds of storylines and the performers who possessed knowledge of them, pointing to festivals as a key milieu for the transfer. I have suggested that it was not impossible that transfer occurred as early as the Bronze Age. However, it is easier to find evidence to support this claim in the Early Iron Age, and we can actually discern how eastern epic storylines were grafted onto the Greek epic tradition, whose antecedents can be traced back into Mycenaean times,[1] and even all the way back to the Greco-Aryan phase.[2]

---

[1] See Latacz (2004: 212–49; 2005: 342–50), and his "Epic. II. B," in *Brill's New Pauly* 4.1042–8, and Ruijgh (1995: 73–91; 1997), although I do not agree with all their arguments; also Bartoněk (2003: 462–70), Horrocks (1980; 1987; 1997: 201–3), Janko (1992: 10–12), Kirk (1960: 175–7; 1985: 8), Pavese (1980), and M. L. West (1988: 156–9). Key evidence: metrically irregular words and phrases that fit the meter when their Mycenaean-era (sometimes even earlier) forms are restored; tmesis and optional use of the augment, both of which are archaic features; the mention of Mycenaean-era objects, such as the boar's-tusk helmet, silver-riveted sword, and tower shield. Some scholars refer to this early layer as "Achaean" (Ruijgh 1995: 3; 1997: 33), or Arcado-Cypriot (Householder and Nagy 1972: 62–6), pointing to forms only found in Arcado-Cypriot, the first-millennium dialect group most closely related to the Mycenaean Greek of Linear B. But, see Haug (2002: 39–69, with earlier references) critiquing the linguistic evidence used to argue for a continuous tradition from Mycenaean Greek and Peters (1986) on the "Achaean" layer.

[2] See M. L. West (2007: 68, 447–503) and Jamison (1994; 1997; 1999) for parallels between Greek and Indic narrative traditions at the level of theme and storyline, some of which, however, could possibly be explained by later indirect contact between traditions. On the Greco-Aryan origin of the hexameter, see the Appendix.

In the rest of this book I work through the evidence, first from Greece, Cyprus, and Cilicia, then from western Anatolia. The archaeological evidence discussed in this chapter and the ones following begins with the Mycenaean period and extends through the post-palatial period (LH IIIC, 1200/1190–1050 BCE) and the Protogeometric period (ending *ca.* 950 BCE), and into the beginning of the Geometric period, just before the time of the "Panionic Homer" (by the end of the eighth century BCE).[3]

In this chapter I first examine the transition from the palatial society of Late Bronze Age Greece to the warrior-trader elite of the Early Iron Age, focusing on mortuary rituals as evidence, both because they are archaeologically salient and because they are one of the key drivers of transfer of the specific Near Eastern storylines that appear in hexametric epic. In Late Bronze Age and Early Iron Age Greece the mortuary display and repeated rites of commemoration for the elite dead, which I have earlier shown interacted with and promoted the transmission of legends to Anatolia, are archaeologically visible through monuments, offerings, and the debris of feasting. They demonstrate not only that these were festive occasions – if not festivals per se – but also that Greeks were engaged in competitions of martial and athletic prowess, of wealth and social status. It is likely that these contests also included displays of skill in dancing, playing music, and singing, including performances of narrative song, both in the Late Bronze Age and Early Iron Age. And, as stated earlier, festivals in Classical Greece often presented themselves as commemorating an important dead hero.[4]

In addition, the mortuary depositions and rituals tell us about how the afterlife of ancestors was conceived of, what their interests were considered to be, and therefore what kinds of storylines were appropriate for them and would be considered appealing to them. In this way, we can begin to understand how Greek hero worship shaped and was shaped by Near Eastern epic traditions. Finally, the archaeological evidence can suggest how the distant past was conceived of, and therefore what storylines might be considered pertinent for narrativizing cultural memory.

As I will show, the tradition of performing epic was maintained across the end of the Bronze Age to the Early Iron Age in Greece and the Near

---

[3] Using the latest results of ^{14}C dating, dendrochronology, and pottery seriation, Weniger and Jung (2009) have dated the beginning of the Protogeometric period and beginning of Greek migrations to Anatolia to 1070/40 BCE, but here I continue to use the conventional date of *ca.* 1050 BCE. I fold Submycenaean into LH IIIC, because not all locations show a Submycenaean phase. Note that 1050 BCE was the beginning of the Iron Age in Greece, but in Syro-Anatolia the beginning of the Iron Age is conventionally dated to 1175 BCE. For the concept of the Panionic Homer, see Chapters 15, 413–14, 16, 443–5.
[4] See Chapter 10, 233.

East. Beginning in the Protogeometric period, a motivation for and means of transfer of stories from the Syro-Anatolian epic tradition to the Greek epic tradition were provided by long-distance elite interactions extending from Greece – especially obvious on Euboea – to Cyprus, and from Cyprus to Cilicia and north Syria. These interactions were intertwined with competitive emulation among elites, articulated through hospitality, drinking, and feasting (both mortuary feasting and festivals). At Lefkandi in particular, a fascination with antique and exotic eastern goods suggests these Euboeans could have been interested in how their eastern neighbors understood their past and in their stories about major personalities. This would explain why Near Eastern storylines left a lasting impression on the Greek version of ancient history. It is at this point in time and at this location, I will argue, that Greeks would have begun to apply Near Eastern storylines about certain heroic figures to their own legendary figures. This claim is similar to an argument that has been made by others, but I focus on the tenth century, not the Orientalizing period, and on transfer via Cyprus, not directly from Phoenicians.

By the Protogeometric period the Greeks manifest a nostalgia for the greatness of their Mycenaean past, exhibited to them in the form of grand ruins and tumuli. Concomitantly the Greeks began to rework their rites of ancestor veneration to incorporate a collective memory of a legendary age of greatness, and their inherited conception of the *hērōs* was reshaped into what we know as hero worship, eventually articulated in part by means of their epic tradition. The story of the Ages of Man in the *Works and Days* suggests that at this point the Greeks looked to the east for inspiration in creating a cultural memory about ancient times beyond their experience. Again, my argument has some similarities with earlier attempts to make connections between this Greek myth and Near Eastern conceptions of the remote past, but I focus not on the concept of the Golden Age, but on a different parallel, arguing that the Greeks equated their *hērōes* with the equivalent figure in west Semitic mythology, the *mᵉrappîm* ('healers'). Finally, I will discuss how elements of the story of Gilgamesh's journey were reworked into a precursor of Homer's *Odyssey* to express the values of the warrior-trader elite attested in the mortuary offerings at tenth-century Lefkandi.

Ancestor veneration and mortuary ritual in the Mycenaean period

I begin with the Mycenaean period, discussing what we know about elite ancestor veneration. As Chrysanthi Gallou has shown in her extensive study of Mycenaean attitudes towards the dead, cyclical mortuary rites indeed existed,[5] and they strongly suggest that certain storylines or themes expressed the right of local lineages to hegemony, as well as a desire to show the dead they were remembered.

There is ample evidence from Early Mycenaean times for mortuary display that expressed the power of elite families, often of more than one family per town, suggesting competition within the elite for status. The monuments were placed prominently at the base of a settlement, where all who approached could see them, indicating the relationship between familial and political might.[6] The association of tombs with altars shows that a claim to temporal power through a lineage was articulated as control over religious activities.[7]

Secondary burial points to at least one occasion after the initial display of mourning during which the elite dead were remembered with lavish public ceremony. In addition, at Mycenae, Thebes, and Midea there is important evidence, alas scanty, in the palatial period for repeated, cyclical commemoration of the elite dead involving conspicuous consumption and competitive display, gatherings of large groups, and feasting and drinking.[8] The evidence suggests that the dead were considered to enjoy the drinking and all the entertainment associated with it beyond the grave. We know that competitive display in mortuary ritual was actualized in athletic competitions, including bull-leaping, sword-fighting, and chariot-racing, the premier event in later Greek competitions, because such competitions are depicted side-by-side with mourning rituals in vase paintings and *larnakes* (chests for bones).[9] The speeding chariots depicted

---

[5] Gallou (2005), Gallou and Georgiadis (2006), *contra* Sourvinou-Inwood (1995: 89–94). On Mycenaean burial practices see Cavanagh and Mee (1998).
[6] Deger-Jalkotzy (1995: 371–2).   [7] Gallou (2005: 21–5).
[8] Grave Circles A and B at Mycenae (LH I) are our best evidence for repeated commemoration of the dead. They are highly visible, carefully incorporated into the public architecture, and associated with the "Cult Center" and palace in the LH IIIB period. Channels cut into the rock allowed libations to be poured underground at Grave Circle B (Gallou 2005: 16–30, 87–8, 138), and the space was a place to congregate, as shown by the remnants of repeated feasts. There was also a space for public gatherings at the tombs in Thebes. And, the Dendra "Cenotaph," a LH III A1 tomb at Midea, has evidence of repeated sacrifice, feasting, and libations (Gallou 2005: 127–9). There is an abundance of drinking vessels in high-status burials (Wright 2004b: 26–8).
[9] See Gallou (2005: 125–7), and Gallou and Georgiadis (2006: 139–40), citing scenes on *larnakes* and a LH IIIB2 *krater* from Tiryns depicting a chariot race with an enthroned female in the background toasting with a chalice, on which see Rystedt (1999: 96), writing of a "civic feast/ funeral," and Kilian (1980). As Rystedt (1999: 95) notes, the depiction of chariot-racing and sword-fighting in funerary contexts was maintained into the Geometric period.

Fig. 12: Stele at Grave Circle B (LH I, *ca.* 1700–1600 BCE), showing chariot-warrior running over a man with a figure-eight shield, with a lion chasing a deer below

on stelae at Grave Circles A and B suggest both chariot warriors in battle and the racing associated with the funeral games of those who were buried there (Fig. 12).[10] Gallou notes that the open spaces associated with tombs, most obviously at Thebes, were suitable for athletic events.[11] Competitive display in singing and music is not clearly attested, but may be assumed.[12]

In some locations at least, the elite dead were considered to participate actively in the celebrations. At Mycenae, for example, grotesque statuettes found in a temple near Grave Circle B may represent the dead,[13] like the statues and statuettes that received offerings from their descendants in the Near East. One of the Tanagra *larnakes*, found in a Mycenaean cemetery in Boeotia, shows a long-robed priest carrying a figurine and facing a procession of mourners (Fig. 13). The scene depicts how the statuettes could be

---

[10] Gallou (2005: 125, with earlier references). Late Minoan *larnakes* show the deceased transported by chariot (Watrous 1991: 301). Chariot racing in particular was associated with mortuary ritual in the Indo-Iranian culture of the Central Asian steppe, and at the beginning of the second millennium the new technology of light, fast war-chariots riding on spoked wheels spread rapidly to other Indo-European peoples, including the Greeks. On the spread of war-chariots and chariot racing from the Pontic–Caspian steppe, along with other forms of funerary display, including song, see Anthony (2007: 397–411). It is likely that chariot racing in funeral contexts came to the Greeks along with the spoke-wheeled war-chariot.

[11] Gallou (2005: 126–7).

[12] See Cavanagh and Mee (1998: 105–7) on the display of power through funerary ritual and on the Mycenaean funerary imagery that indicates dancing. Voutsaki (1998) provides a good discussion of the ways in which mortuary display can be competitively used by elites to consolidate their power and to establish a group identity, with their lineage at the top.

[13] Gallou (2005: 24), van Leuven (1989: 199–200).

Fig. 13: Tanagra Larnax, found in Dendron in Boetia, showing a priest on the right, carrying a statue, facing four mourners (LH IIIA–B 1420–1200/1190 BCE)

used in repeated post-funerary rites of ancestor veneration.[14] Finally, the records at Pylos reveal a cult of the Thirsty Ones (the dead who were thirsty for libations) and offerings of oil for them,[15] including one record which implies welcoming them, for PY Fr 1231 mentions *ke-se-ni-wi-jo* 'of a guest', i. e., 'welcoming', either referring to a type of oil or to a festival.[16]

Large-scale feasting and drinking were consciously used by the elite to harness the "bodily memory" of the living participants. The pleasurable sensations of repletion and intoxication were used to impress on the participants' minds a lineage's claims to superiority,[17] which were legitimated through their privileged access to ancestors. These claims must have influenced the types of verbal art performed on such occasions and the

---

[14] Immerwahr (1995: 116, with Fig. 7.5b). On statues or statuettes of the dead in Bronze Age Syro-Anatolia, see Chapter 8, 186, with n. 91.

[15] Mention of a festival (or shrine) for the Thirsty Ones (*di-pi-si-je-wi-jo*, PY Fr 1218, see Gallou 2005: 62–3), a month of the Thirsty (*di-pi-si-jo* PY Fr 1240), offerings of oil to the *di-pi-si-jo-i* in six different tablets (Gallou 2005: 97–8; Aura Jorro 1985, 1993: 1.175–6). Also see Chapter 10, 227.

[16] Compare the later Greek *theoxeniā* in which gods, or more commonly heroes/heroines, were invited to dine with the worshipper, on which see Jameson (1994).

[17] Hamilakis (1998).

values encoded in them, making epic performers all the more conscious of epic's function to remember great deeds of the past, and explaining the appeal of stories that showed how time and space were transcended. As Sofia Voutsaki argues, "mortuary ritual creates social reality by creating the spatial and temporal schemes that divide and order the cultural universe."[18] Its counterparts in verbal art were cosmogonies and genealogies, key tools to explain a local polity's position in the history of the world.

Mortuary ritual in Mycenaean Greece allowed for amalgamations of Minoan and Mycenaean features and was open to foreign influence. For example, Sarah Morris, when comparing the statuettes of ancestors from Mycenae to figurines from Egypt, Cyprus, and the Levant, notes "the centrality of the cult of the dead in Mycenaean culture, a concern largely absent in Minoan Crete," and suggests the statuettes represent "an Orientalizing innovation."[19] And, the blend of Minoan and Mycenaean iconography on the Ayia Triada limestone *larnax* (LM IIIA2, *ca.* 1390/70–1330/15 BCE, see Fig. 3) is discussed by Brandon Burke, who points out that the vessels being used in the ceremony depicted on it are archaic and "Minoan," as is the clothing of some of the participants.[20] The obvious iconographic message of blended traditions on the *larnax* must have been matched by the message conveyed by the music and verbal art supporting the *drōmena* during which this item was manipulated.[21]

There is a possibility that mingling of mortuary traditions was also occurring in western Anatolia. The Mycenaean-style tombs along the coast of southwestern Anatolia and the nearby islands, at Müsgebi, Miletus, and Ephesus, and on Lesbos, Carpathus, Rhodes, Astypalaia, Cos, Calymna, and Samos, indicate that some inhabitants, whether migrants or native-born, preferred the Mycenaeans' forms of funerary architecture over Anatolian forms.[22] In addition, some Mycenaean funerary rituals definitely

---

[18] Voutsaki (1998: 44). [19] S. P. Morris (1992b: 209).
[20] Burke (2005). Wright (1994: 51, 54; 1995a; 1995b: 69–72) argues that Mycenaean drinking ceremonies draw on the behaviors of the Minoan elite, but maintains that the Mycenaean elite used Minoan ceremonies and objects as foreign, elite goods to differentiate themselves from commoners, rather than legitimating ownership of land by co-opting autochthonous rituals. See Chapter 4, 91–2, for further discussion of this *larnax*.
[21] The *larnakes* themselves have been argued to be reworkings of Egyptian funerary furniture by Watrous (1991), who finds Egyptian parallels for the procession and the presence of the deceased at the ceremony, and points out that the boat carried in procession towards the deceased depicted on the Ayia Triada *larnax* is also found in Egyptian funerary scenes. Also see Chapter 4, 89, with n. 47, on boat imagery in funerary ritual.
[22] Georgiadis (2009); for Rhodes, Karantzali (2001). For the possibility that the Late Bronze Age cist tombs on Lesbos are Mycenaean, see Teffeteller (2013: 576–7).

made their way to Anatolia in the Late Bronze Age, as shown by the broken and "killed" weapons at Ialysus on Rhodes and at Miletus.[23] As Mercourios Georgiadis stresses about the southeastern Aegean,

> The local idiosyncracies emphasize the amalgamation of Mycenaean elements with local traditions in the eschatological and metaphysical beliefs and practices, from LH IIB until LH IIIC ... What is unique in the area is the role and importance of the ancestors in everyday life of the local community.[24]

We may suspect that along the west Anatolian coast already in the Late Bronze Age, stories about legendary characters, ancestors, and the remote past were being used in mortuary ritual to negotiate local identities in the face of competing claims of those invested in either an indigenous Anatolian identity or a Mycenaean identity, the latter represented by the men of Ahhiyawa mentioned in Hittite texts.[25] We cannot tell how current any of these stories remained until Greek-speakers re-settled the coast (1050 BCE), but the legends of "Minoan" settlement from Crete in Anatolia, preceding the post-Trojan war settlement of Greek-speakers (the *nostoi*), imply some level of social memory within Anatolia of events of the Bronze Age that is best explained through an unbroken use of the legendary past to legitimate claims and ponder the intricacies of the opposition of native to immigrant.

Elite competition and epic in post-palatial Greece

With the fall of the Mycenaean palaces, the superficially homogeneous supralocal culture that is implied by the Linear B tablets and archaeological finds ended and was followed by the post-palatial period. For a brief time (LH IIIC Middle/Developed) regional polities in mainland Greece, the Aegean coast, and the islands flourished. To this period has been dated the reworking of the Linear B term *qa-si-re-u* into its Homeric meaning of "king," as regional chiefs now assumed the mantle of leadership.[26] The

---

[23] Hamilakis (1998: 122).   [24] Georgiadis (2003: 110). Also see Carstens (2008b: 59–70).
[25] For a detailed discussion of Ahhiyawa and Mycenaean activities in Bronze Age Anatolia, see Chapter 13.
[26] On the *qa-si-re-u*, see Aura Jorro (1985, 1993: 2.189–90), Carlier (1995), Deger-Jalkotzy (1998–1999; 1998b: 124), Mazarakis Ainian (2006: 182), Middleton (2010: 92–7), and Palaima (1995: 123–5; 2006b: 68–9). See Chapter 12, 309, for discussion of the use of this term on Cyprus. On the post-palatial period, see Crielaard (2006: 277–85), Deger-Jalkotzy (1991a; 1991b; 1994; 1995; 1998a; 2002: 48–9, 53), Lemos (1998: 45–9; 2002: 215), and Middleton (2010). Also see Thomatos (2006) and Deger-Jalkotzy (1998a) for the Aegean islands.

southeast Aegean suffered less than mainland Greece from the fall of the palace culture, and Georgiadis surmises that west Anatolian polities were also able to flourish with the cessation of Hittite involvement in their area.[27] Miletus remained part of the Mycenaean world,[28] and Troy, Iasos, and probably Müsgebi continued to produce Mycenaean pottery through the LH IIIC period, indicating continuity into the eleventh century.[29] Athens, which "looks like the largest site in eleventh-century central Greece," Perati in Attica, Lefkandi, which remained relatively unharmed during the transition to the Iron Age, Cycladic Naxos, and Rhodian Ialysus all flourished.[30] Thus, by the end of the LH IIIC period the Aegean had moved away from a relatively homogeneous *koinē* towards relatively independent regions, which remained, however, in contact with each other.[31] It is at this time that we see evidence for the spread of Aegean-influenced groups into Cyprus, Cilicia, and the Levant, whom scholars generally connect to the Sea Peoples mentioned in twelfth-century Egyptian texts.[32]

On the mainland the continued high value placed on feasting and drinking is shown by the dinnerware buried with the elite dead in the eleventh century.[33] Evidence for long-distance trading between Greece and the east is greatly reduced, but the numerous depictions of ships on pottery show that short-range travel remained important.[34] Now is when we see the first beginnings of the development of certain "Homeric" themes in art and social practices: the fascination with a lost past and individual prowess in battle. The "Homeric" rite of cremation was more widely practiced than before.[35]

As Joseph Maran has shown, beginning in the twelfth century, the elites at Tiryns, Mycenae, and Midea were trying to tap into the still-remembered power and glory of the palatial culture, constructing buildings on and oriented towards the ruins of Mycenaean palaces. At Tiryns there is evidence they also manipulated antique symbols of power, such as tripods

---

[27] Georgiadis (2003: 114). [28] Deger-Jalkotzy (2002: 55).
[29] Welwei (1992: 55–6). On the locally made LH IIIC pottery at Troy, see Chapter 14, 362. See Carstens (2008b: 70–1) on the Submycenaean necropolis at Çömbekçi with rectangular or circular cist tombs containing both cremations and burial. For further discussion of cultural continuity in west Anatolia across the end of the Bronze Age, see Chapter 14.
[30] On Athens see I. Morris (2000: 202–3, esp. 203), Thomatos (2006: 253–4, 259). On Lefkandi specifically, see Crielaard (2006: 272–85), Lemos (2002: 218), Thomatos (2006: 258). On Ialysus see Benzi (2013: 512–19); there is a decline there after the LH IIIC Middle.
[31] Deger-Jalkotzy (2002). [32] See Chapter 12, 314–15.
[33] Muhly (2003: 26), with parallels from the Levant. [34] Deger-Jalkotzy (2002: 55).
[35] Thomatos (2006: 258, 260), Cavanagh and Mee (1998: 93–4).

or scepters. He states, "the specific way of relating to the palatial past ... aimed at the perpetuation of power within the same family... I would conclude that, at least temporarily, certain families succeeded in consolidating their leading role by claiming descent from the strong kings of palatial times."[36] Maran further argues that in the twelfth century there were two competing ways of accumulating prestige: those who were descended from local inhabitants connected themselves through genealogies and control over antique prestige objects to an area's glorious past, while those who had arrived more recently "may instead have opted to gain symbolic capital in different ways, for instance by drawing on their relation to distant elites to receive exquisite foreign cultural forms and to display them in practices."[37] That is, the latter group flaunted their connection to long-distance exchange and networks.

In fact, both strategies can be seen at work in the goods found in graves in Greece. Antique or heirloom items show an interest in maintaining ties with the glorious Mycenaean past, used to consolidate the local elites' power.[38] Eastern imports in Greece tended to be antiques brought at an earlier time or the result of individual interactions with or via Cyprus, rather than large-scale trade. Burials in the large graveyard of Perati, for example, contained Egyptian cartouches, antique amulets from Syria and Cyprus, an antique Mitanni cylinder seal and one from Cyprus, and the earliest iron knives found in Greece, made in Cyprus.[39]

Further evidence for the values of the elite comes from the paintings on vessels, which exhibit their users' interest in what we would consider Homeric, heroic activities. The same themes continue to be important into the Geometric period. The post-palatial images include chariots with racing and soldiers in battle, hunting with chariots, choral dancing, funerary rituals with mourning women, and soldiers departing while women bid farewell or mourn (Fig. 14). Particularly evocative are an LH IIIC Middle representation of a

---

[36] Maran (2006: 143). He argues that the continued use of the symbols of Mycenaean power has created the illusion of extensive continuity in the archaeological record. But, "the break caused by the catastrophic end of palatial rule selectively suspended the communicative memory within the highest level of society and led to a situation in which core characteristics of the palatial past, though it had just ended, nevertheless seemed so distant that this past immediately became the focus of cultural memory" (Maran 2011: 173).

[37] Maran (2011: 175).

[38] Crielaard (2006: 281), Deger-Jalkotzy (1991b: 148–9; 2002: 58–63), Maran (2006: 141–3), Thomatos (2006: 258–60). Middleton (2010: 101–7) points out that warrior graves are concentrated in areas that were not part of the palatial system in the Mycenaean period, arguing against assuming warrior graves are for *basileis*, as Deger-Jalkotzy does.

[39] Iakovides (1980), Deger-Jalkotzy (2002: 61, 66–8), Crielaard (2006: 281).

Fig. 14: Warrior Vase from Mycenae (LH IIIC, *ca.* 1150 BCE): A mourning woman bids good-bye to a line of departing warriors

man playing a phorminx from Tiryns and an eleventh-century "warrior-musician" with phorminx from Kouklia (Palaepaphos) (Fig. 15), who brings to mind Achilles playing his luxurious lyre and singing of the "glories of men" while Patroclus listens.[40] At feasts, festivals, and funeral games, epic must have been featured as it had been before the end of the palatial culture, but it now would have begun to express a fascination with bygone glories and to frame the emerging cultural memories in light of contemporaneous achievements in the competitive arena and on the battlefield.

At the end of LH IIIC Middle/Developed (1150/40 BCE) the contraction of relations across space was matched by a contraction of relations across time. As Eva Rystedt notes when she contrasts the Dark Age with the Late

---

[40] *Il.* 9.186–91, see Deger-Jalkotzy (1994: 20–2; 1998b: 124–5). For scenes from the post-palatial period see Crouwel (2006a; 2006b), Deger-Jalkotzy (1991a: 64–6; 1991b: 148; 1994: 20–2, with fig. 4; 1998b: 125), Vermeule and Karageorghis (1982: 67–8 on Cyprus, 120–41 on the mainland).

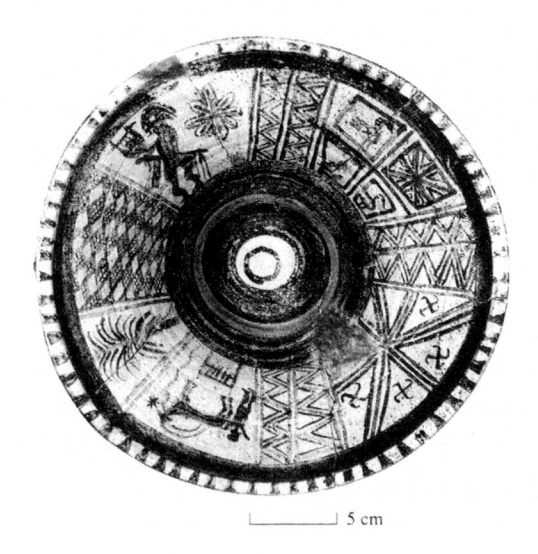

Fig. 15: Cypriot Kalathos from Kouklia, early eleventh century BCE, warrior playing a lyre on upper section of rim

Bronze Age, "a settled and expanding society in which leadership had had a chance to root through iterative power transmission could be thought of as one in which the forward-and-backward extensions of time from the present and its memorial/immemorial dimensions were taken care of," while one without the advantages of permanence would not have been able to maintain family tombs across generations, or to rely on repeated gatherings in a single spot as venues in which the current elite's ties to a legendary past could be reinforced.[41] On the other hand, the tradition of performing epic was portable and durable, even while the individual stories told in the form of epic were radically changed as they were adapted to new values and concerns.[42]

Sigrid Deger-Jalkotzy has argued that it was at the end of the postpalatial period that Greek epic became fascinated with the hero as an individual warrior and his exploits on the battlefield. In fact, this is one of the salient differences between Homeric and Near Eastern epic. While Gilgamesh is spoken of as a great warrior in the Akkadian epics, he is not portrayed as engaging in combat with other humans on the battlefield.[43]

---

[41] Rystedt (1999: 97).
[42] As Patzek (1992: 73–98) has argued, there is no evidence that actual memories of historical events in the Mycenaean period could have been retained in the Greek epic tradition.
[43] In the Sumerian *Gilgamesh and Akka*, he blasts the enemy with his radiance, but he is not described as actually fighting (see trans. at ECTSL t.1.8.1.1).

It is true that we are missing the key battle scene from the *Song of Release*, and it may be that individual hand-to-hand combat was its focus, given that Pizikarra is singled out as the crucial individual in the sack of Ebla. In fact, fighting between champions did actually exist in the Late Bronze Age Near East.[44] It could be, therefore, that Anatolian epic developed this motif on its own. But, the theme was already apparent in the battle scenes depicted in Mycenaean frescos and other media, and more emphasis appears to have been put on it in the post-palatial period with the concomitant decline in the centralized power structure of the palaces, as shown by the increase in warrior graves and in depictions of individual military prowess in vase paintings.[45] These are the values and storylines that Greek-speakers brought with them when they began to settle in Anatolia in the Protogeometric period.

The Protogeometric period: the age of nostalgia

With the final demise of Mycenaean culture at the close of the LH IIIC period, there was a general decrease in prosperity, a reduction in settlements on the mainland, and large-scale population shifts, including the beginnings of a new wave of settlement on the coast of Anatolia and the islands, which extended to Cyprus. In the Protogeometric period we see a settled population living modestly without much social complexity,[46] although continuity from the post-palatial period into the Geometric period in the types of imagery on pottery indicates maintenance across the divide of the relevant cultural traits.[47] The images include funerary scenes with mourning women; battles on land and at sea; chariots, some in battle, some in funeral processions; and ceremonial drinking, hunting, and

---

[44] In the *Apology of Hattusili III*, the king describes one of his exploits as general, boasting that he routed the enemy Kaska by taking on and slaying their champion: CTH 81.B = KBo 3.6 ii 22–4 (translit. Otten 1981: 12; trans. T. van den Hout in Hallo and Younger 1997: 201); see Hoffner (1968a), and for further Near Eastern examples of single combat see Vanschoonwinkel (2005: 357–60).

[45] See Deger-Jalkotzy (1999) on the increased emphasis on individual prowess and warrior values in LH IIIC; and the references in n. 40 to her argument that the new emphasis on "heroic" values influenced the inherited tradition of Greek epic. See Davis and Bennet (1999: 107–12) and Hiller (1999) on Mycenaean depictions of combat, and Papadopoulos (2009) comparing LH IIIA and B with LH IIIC depictions.

[46] See Lemos (2002: 191–225) and I. Morris (2000: 195–207). [47] Dakoronia (2006: 174–5).

(a)

Fig. 16: Geometric *skyphos* from Eleusis, MG II (800–760 BCE), showing land and naval battles

choral dancing, sometimes with lyre players (Fig. 16).[48] As noted earlier, one would expect the loss of complex, expensive forms of royal ancestor veneration that depended on long-term, multi-generational residence in a single site. As society became more settled again, a renewed interest in and opportunity for such elaborate rites would have contributed to the development of hero worship as we know it. In this context, we can understand how urgent the Greeks' desire was around the beginning of the first millennium to build a connection to their distant past. What they needed were meaningful storylines with which to articulate their cultural memory.[49]

Whereas Sigrid Deger-Jalkotzy and Maran focus on the post-palatial period as a key era for the development of heroic epic, Ian Morris looks to the Protogeometric period, during which he sees "a broad rethinking of identities, which transformed mythological, historical, and geographical

---

[48] For the Geometric period see Coldstream (2006) and Deoudi (1999: 54). The continuity "suggests that burial rites remained constant and essentially unchanged in major aspects from Mycenaean to Geometric times" (Eder 2006: 555).

[49] My thoughts share some features in common with the theory of G. Lorenz (1996), who thinks that in the Geometric period Greeks in contact with the Near East realized the poverty of their ways of remembering the past and incorporated elements of Near Eastern ancestor veneration, but I see an earlier period as the relevant time.

(b)

Fig. 16: (*cont.*)

categories. This left its traces on the earliest surviving Greek poetry, written down some 300 years later."[50] The sense of an irretrievably past glorious age that pervades Greek epic, in which the semi-divine heroes lived and to which contemporary humans can never return stems, he argues, from this time. Thus, Hesiod places the age of heroes between the Bronze Age and the contemporary Iron Age, inserting them into an already well-formed myth about the Ages of Man, Gold, Silver, Bronze, and Iron. "If located in terms of absolute chronology, the heroes live at the cusp of the historical Iron Age."[51]

I agree with Deger-Jalkotzy and Maran that the cultural memory of a heroic past could have begun already in the post-palatial period, but it is in the Protogeometric period, I argue, that we can expect Near Eastern conceptions of the legendary past to begin to shape this cultural

---

[50] I. Morris (2000: 229), also cf. I. Morris (1988: 750; 2000: 231). Thus, like Deger-Jalkotzy, he sees nostalgia for the past as shaping epic. Lemos (2002: 216) in turn looks to the Subprotogeometric period as the key time for formation of epic as we know it. Calligas (1988) uses similar nostalgia for lost glory to explain the interest in epic, but in the eighth century. S. Sherratt (1990) subsumes the twelfth to early eighth century into a single second period of "active generation," in which Mycenaean epic was reworked, with end of the eighth century as a third period of formation.

[51] Antonaccio (1994b: 407).

memory, for this is when once again contacts began to be established with the east, particularly in Euboean Lefkandi and via Cyprus.[52] These conceptions could then spread within the Euboean cultural *koinē*, demonstrated by pottery, clothing fasteners, and mortuary customs, that was established in Boeotia and Thessaly and extended into the Cycladic islands.[53] The power obtained through long-distance exchange manifests itself in the archaeological record in the exotic objects traded as part of the intense competition and networking among the elite. These goods may have been instrumental in consolidating the power of local *basileis*, as they stepped in to fill the void left by the breakdown of the centralized palatial system, and as Maran has suggested, this strategy may have been used in the post-palatial period by those who were not able to claim a connection to long-standing local lineages.[54] At Lefkandi their deposition in graves increased over time from the Middle Protogeometric onwards, but these kinds of goods can already be found beginning in the Submycenaean period.[55]

In addition, the earliest evidence of the kind of behaviors we associate with Homeric epic comes from Lefkandi, and we can see quite clearly how a fascination with the past was connected with a fascination with the east and with heroization. Here were found the cremated remains of a warrior, wrapped in cloth and deposited in a bronze amphora, matching closely the detailed description of Patroclus' funeral in *Iliad* Book 23. A richly dressed woman was laid alongside him, and a pair of sacrificed horses with a chariot was placed nearby. All were buried within a large apsidal building, the ruins of which formed a conspicuous mound (*ca.* 1000–950 BCE).[56] The interest in the past and the exotic is indicated by key objects: the woman buried with the ashes of the man wore a nearly 1,000-year-old Babylonian necklace,[57] and the antique amphora in which the ashes of the man were placed came from Cyprus. The graveyard next to the "*hērōon*" shows a desire on the part of later generations to associate themselves with whomever they thought was buried there.[58] While the earliest graves, Early

---

[52] Crielaard (2006: 286–7).   [53] Lemos (1998; 2002).
[54] Maran (2011: 175), and see 274–5 in this chapter.
[55] See Crielaard (2006: 286–7), Mazarakis Ainian (2006: 193–4) for Lefkandi; for the elite network involving Greece, especially Lefkandi and Knossos, and Cyprus see Crielaard (1998).
[56] Popham, Touloupa, and Sackett (1982) compare to the funeral of Patroclus. Also see Antonaccio (2002), I. Morris (2000: 218–21, 235–7), and Popham and Lemos (1995) for nuanced analyses of the material. G. Lorenz (1996: 31–2) provides a review of scholarly opinions concerning the possibility of hero worship at Lefkandi. On Lefkandi see further S. Sherratt (2006).
[57] Popham (1994: 15).   [58] See most recently Crielaard (2006: 288–9).

Protogeometric ones, predate the graves in the *hērōon*, the burials extend into the Middle Protogeometric, and some actually set into the tumulus are Subprotogeometric II or later, that is, 900–825 BCE.[59] This cemetery is the wealthiest among the cemeteries at Lefkandi and contained a variety of imports, some Levantine, others Cypriot, some of which were antiques, including pottery, faience, a cylinder seal, bronze bowls, and jewelry.[60] The same fascination with antiques and exotica is evinced in Homer's epics,[61] for such items of gift exchange are described in Homer, such as the *krater* given to Telemachus by Menelaus, who tells him it was given to him by the king of Sidon and made by Hephaestus.[62] And, compare the heirloom boar's-tusk helmet deposited in Tomb 201 at Knossos with Meriones' helmet, the previous owners of which have been carefully remembered.[63]

Ian Morris argues that the increased use of iron over bronze, especially for weapons, took on a symbolic significance for Greeks.

> [B]ronze was the metal of the past ... This means either that when people turned away from bronze at the end of the eleventh century they were aware of drawing a line between themselves and the past, or (perhaps more likely) that with the hindsight of a generation or so, central Greeks realized that one more symbolic tie to antiquity had been cut.[64]

Morris goes on to argue that "iron symbolically cut its users off from the east. It was a product of the local soil."[65] However, many of the iron knives found in warrior's graves actually came from Cyprus or take Cypriot-influenced forms.[66] Alexander Mazarakis Ainian thus argues:

> the excavations at Lefkandi have shown that there was a dramatic increase of the Cypriot and Levantine imports from the mid-10th century onwards ... It is beyond doubt that from that point onwards exchanges with the eastern Mediterranean, and Cyprus in particular, were intensified. One of the motives for the maintenance of these contacts was

---

[59] Antonaccio (2002: 21).   [60] Popham (1994: 17–22), and Popham and Lemos (1995).
[61] Grethlein (2008).
[62] *Od.* 4.615–9; also cf. the Sidonian *krater*, a prize at Patroclus' funeral games (*Il.* 23.740–9), brought by Phoenician traders to Thoas and used to ransom one of Priam's sons, and the *depas* Priam brings to Achilles, which he had received from the Thracians (*Il.* 24.228–37).
[63] It was stolen from Amyntor in Eleon by Autolycus, who gave it to Cytheran Amphidamas in Scandeia, who gave it to the Cretan Molus as a guest-gift, who gave it to his son Meriones (*Il.* 10.261–70); see H. W. Catling (1995: 127) and in Coldstream and Catling (1996: 534–5) on the latest known boar's-tusk helmet.
[64] I. Morris (2000: 209–10, 218), building on Lorimer (1950: 453).   [65] I. Morris (2000: 218).
[66] Crielaard (1998: 191, with earlier refs.).

presumably the need for metals. Today several scholars believe that the Greeks derived their knowledge of metal technology from Cyprus.[67]

Mazarakis Ainian goes on to suggest about the cremated warrior at Lefkandi:

> We could perhaps identify the eminent warrior of Lefkandi ... as a leader who excelled not only in war but also in long-distance trade, through which the supply of metals and costly objects was secured. The Cypriot bronze ash-urn, apart from being an antique, perhaps underlined this eastern connection.[68]

I agree with Mazarakis Ainian that iron-working and iron knives did not, as Ian Morris suggests, symbolize the local soil for the Greek elite, but connections to the east, especially Cyprus. However, Mazarakis Ainian's focus is on the possibility of immigrant craftsmen arriving by the trade route maintained by such leaders and of "[s]ecuring trading partnerships through marriage."[69] In the older paradigm of Near Eastern influence on Greek epic this would be sufficient evidence to postulate transmission of epic motifs, for we would be thinking about the immigrant poet as a craftsman who translates his work into another language, and/or of informal communication of storylines within a bilingual home. I have argued earlier in this book that poets who could perform in the formulary system of two different languages transferred epic storylines in epic form in Hittite Anatolia. I am looking now for such a scenario involving the Syro-Anatolian languages and Greek, and a shared value system among peoples that speak different languages, which would provide a context that fostered poets who could perform the same narratives to audiences speaking different languages but in the same types of milieus as part of a supralocal elite "etiquette." As I will argue in the following chapter, Cyprus provided one appropriate milieu that allowed for the transfer of epic storylines from one or more Syro-Anatolian languages into the formulary system of Greek epic. The archaeological data as it currently stands points to Lefkandi as the earliest place at which the Cypriot epic tradition could reach mainland Greek bards, whether because a Cypriot bard traveled to Lefkandi or

---

[67] Mazarakis Ainian (2006: 194). Mazarakis Ainian goes on to make reference to the theory of Burkert (1992) concerning itinerant craftsmen from the Near East "in the later Dark Ages," which I consider to be less relevant to the prehistory of the Homeric epics, as laid out in Chapter 10. As touched on in Chapter 12, 309, Iacovou (2006: 327–8) argues that Greek *qasireus* were able to spearhead migrations to Cyprus because of their role in the distribution of bronze, which gave them knowledge of Cyprus as the place from which copper came.

[68] Mazarakis Ainian (2006: 194).   [69] Mazarakis Ainian (2006: 195).

because a Lefkandi traveler learned a Cypriot epic while in Cyprus and brought it back to Euboea.[70]

In addition, the evidence must extend beyond evidence of contact and show shared values among the supralocal warrior elite. The deposition of antiques and Near Eastern artifacts in graves in Greece suggests that spatio-temporal distance gave prestige, and such a value system would have motivated an interest among Greek elites in demonstrating a connection with the wider world of the eastern Mediterranean. These are the kinds of factors that show Syro-Anatolian narratives, bound up with their techniques of ancestor veneration, were appealing and worth borrowing. In addition, the shared practice of cremation in Greece and Cyprus suggests the elite warrior-trader class of both places shared common values concerning eschatology and treatment of the dead.

Furthermore, it appears that these values were shared not only among Greek-speakers, but also with residents of Syro-Anatolia. The "Homeric" practice of cremation seen at Lefkandi became popular in mainland Greece starting in the LH IIIC period. It is typical of the warrior tombs of the eleventh and tenth centuries at Cyprus as well, and is also found at Knossos.[71] Elite dead were also cremated in Iron Age north Syria and eastern Anatolia,[72] and cremation can already be found in Bronze Age Alalakh VII (beginning of the sixteenth century) and Hattusa.[73] Cremation is expensive, therefore reserved for those with means. Thus, it can easily become a marker of elevated social status.[74] Furthermore, the burning of the body can be considered to release the soul from the shackles of the physical body upwards to heaven in the smoke that rises from it, so cremation could reflect a specific eschatological view. Even if cremation for elite mortuary rites was not borrowed by Greeks from Syro-Anatolia, the shared practice could indicate a shared conception of how treatment of

---

[70] As has been suggested for craftsmen by Popham (1994: 22) and H. W. Catling in Popham (1980: 96). But, Coldstream (2007: 136), noting that there is sufficient depth of settlement at the site to assume an indigenous tradition, disputes the inference.

[71] Crielaard (1998: 188–9). For cremation of leaders at Early Iron Age Thermon, see I. Morris (2000: 227–8).

[72] E.g., Carchemish, Tell Halaf (Guzana, tenth through the second half of the ninth century), Sam'al (Zincırlı, mid eighth century). See Chapter 14, 380–1.

[73] Alalakh: Novák (2003: 65). The Homeric ritual has also been compared to the Hittite royal funerary rites, which prescribe burning the body, gathering up the bones, wrapping them in a cloth, and placing them in a container. See Rutherford (2007: 229 with earlier references). The relevant section is Day 3¹ of the *Death Rituals* (*CTH* 450.I, see translit. and trans. by Kassian, Korolëv and Sidel'tsev 2002: 257–330).

[74] Crielard (1998: 188–9).

the corpse affected the dead's experience of the afterlife. The recognition that they held this practice in common could have encouraged Greeks in Cyprus to borrow Syro-Anatolian concepts about the dead and elite ancestors, merging them with long-standing Greek concepts about *hērōes* and then transporting these ideas westwards to mainland Greece.

Hērōes and *meropes anthrōpoi*: the shared concept of divinized ancestors among Early Iron Age Greeks and Syro-Anatolians

The Near Eastern, specifically west Semitic, notion of divinized ancestors as great figures of bygone days who could act as healers and needed to be celebrated in epic song had great influence on the Greeks' framing of their distant past. In this section I first review the development of hero worship in Greece, then propose that Hesiod's Ages of Man myth, told in the *Works and Days*, the opening lines of which were quoted at the beginning of this chapter, shows evidence for influence in the use of the term *meropes*, which refers to men of bygone days. This word comes from the west Semitic *m^{e}rappê* 'healer', which is in turn related to the Ugaritic and Hebrew terms *rapa 'ūma* and *r^{e}pā 'îm* 'divine ancestors', who represented heroic royal ancestors in the west Semitic imagination in the Late Bronze Age and the Early Iron Age, and who, like Gilgamesh, had the power to intervene for the suffering patient.[75] More corroborating evidence for this influence comes from other terms and names borrowed from west Semitic referring to beings belonging to the very beginning of history, such as the Titans and Iapetus. With the addition of the influence from the Kumarbi cycle and *Illuyanka* on the *Theogony*, we can single out a stream of influence on Hesiod, coming from Syro-Anatolia via Cyprus to Euboea in the beginning of the Early Iron Age.

Evidence for worship of heroes is already found in Mycenaean texts,[76] for a *ti-ri-se-ro-e* (*tris(h)ērōs*) 'thrice hero' received offerings at Pylos, while

---

[75] Annus (1999).
[76] Although there has been much discussion of the history of the practice, most of the scholarly analyses, valuable as they are, that connect it to the rise of the polis (de Polignac 1995: 128–50), claiming of land in the face of population pressures by claiming ownership of an ancient tomb (Snodgrass 1982; 1988; against whom see Whitley 1988), and so on, are irrelevant to the discussion here, because I am looking at an earlier period than that of the *Iliad* and *Odyssey* – we are looking at the prehistory of the epics, not their immediate context, influence, or afterlife – and my focus is on a time period earlier than the first archaeological evidence for tomb worship or hero worship in Greece, which begins in the eighth century BCE. The earliest explicit evidence for worship of a Homeric hero in the first millennium comes from Therapne

at Knossos a fragment of a tablet seems to record that a hero received a chariot.[77] The fragment is highly suggestive, given the use of chariots in funerary cult, both for races and as offerings.[78] Exactly what kind of divinity the *tris(h)ērōs* was we do not know, but he was connected with the prosperity of a household, for in the tablet PY Tn 316, the divinities given offerings at the shrine in *Pa-ki-ja* along with *tris(h)ērōs* were *Potnia, Ma-na-sa, Poseidāheiā* (presumably the consort of Poseidon, whose shrine is the next on the list to receive offering), and *Do(m)potās*. All received various types of gold vessels, and the goddesses also received women.[79] Striking is the repeated appearance of *pot/s-* 'master, mistress', and the grouping of *tris(h)ērōs* with the Master of the House (cf. later Greek *despotēs*). It is hard to avoid the conclusion that these were offerings connected at least in part to celebrating the lineage of the royal house, which in turn suggests that at least one important trait of the later *hērōes* was established already in the Late Bronze Age.

Mazarakis Ainian notes the importance of ancestor veneration in the Early Iron Age: "if we count the instances of 'tomb cult', almost 50% of the EIA cult places so far identified were addressed to heroes and ancestors (especially in the 8th c., but not exclusively)."[80] The ancestors were not just the recently deceased, but nameless predecessors from the

---

in Laconia, directed towards Menelaus (Antonaccio 1995: 155–66; Snodgrass 1988: 24–5). The Polis cave in Ithaca, which eventually was considered to be the cave in which Odysseus hid the gifts of the Phaeacians when he returned to his homeland, was a cult place in use continuously from the Bronze Age, and bronze tripods were deposited there in the eighth century, but explicit reference to Odysseus is only quite late and can be explained as directly inspired by the *Odyssey* (Antonaccio 1995: 152–5). (Malkin 1998: 94–119 sees this site as containing the earliest evidence for cult of a Homeric hero, arguing that we should assume the tripods were always dedicated to Odysseus.) Nagy (1999) and Seaford (1994: 106–43) both argue that local hero cult was derived from ancestor cult when private, family-based rites were moved into the public realm. Nagy further argues that Panhellenic Homeric epic deliberately avoids mention of local hero cult. Malkin (1987: 263–6) argues that the transition from private ancestor cult to public heroic cult first occurred in the eighth century, in colonies for their founders, then was transferred back to the mainland; Antonaccio (1999) argues against his position. See Antonaccio (1994b, with earlier references) for a history of the study of hero worship and Boehringer (2001: 25–46) for a survey of the scholarship on the term *hērōs* and hero worship in the Archaic and Classical periods. The etymology of the term *hērōs* and its possible connection to Hera remain disputed (G. Lorenz 1996: 20–21). For further reference on the history of the scholarship see n. 82.

[77] PY Tn 316.5 (golden vessels for divinities), Fr 1204 (rose-scented oil). See Aura Jorro (1985, 1993: 2.353–4), Gallou (2005: 96). Chariot offering: KN Sc 244:]*no*/ *e-ro-e* BIG[A.

[78] Gallou (2005: 49).   [79] Duhoux (2008: 321–35) and Melena (2001: 68–70).

[80] Mazarakis Ainian (1997: 380). Also see Mazarakis Ainian (1999; 2006) for surveys of the cult of the dead in Protogeometric and Geometric Greece, and in the eighth century in particular.

Mycenaean Age, probably already called *hērōes*, represented by tombs and ruins of fortifications at Thermon in Aetolia and on Naxos, for example.[81]

Remarkably, there is little clear reference to hero worship within Homer, which is a problem for those who wish to connect epic with the hero worship attested in inscriptions and literary sources.[82] However, both Homer and Hesiod use the term *hērōs*, and in Homer, living heroes use the term with reference to each other.[83] And, it seems clear that hero worship is presupposed: the term demi-god (*hemitheos*) is used, and there are casual references to tumuli by which heroes will be remembered by name.[84] Thus, the tomb (*sēma, tumbos*) of Ilus, the eponymous hero of Ilium, is mentioned several times in the *Iliad*, and Ilus himself is described as "divine" (*theios*), "ancient elder of the people" (*palaios dēmogerōn*), and

---

[81] At Thermon, Early Geometric and Geometric offerings and sacrifices have been found in the Early Mycenaean ruins, ending in the late ninth century. The chief's apsidal house developed into a place for ancestor worship, with graves inside, while a later building was placed on top of the graves (Mazarakis Ainian 1997: 125–35; I. Morris 2000: 226–8). On Naxos in the Protogeometric period there are traces of repeated rounds of burnt offerings on top of Mycenaean remains. While the Mycenaean graves were invisible, the fortification wall was obvious to the worshippers (I. Morris 2000: 246–9).

[82] Coldstream (1976, with earlier references) argued that Homeric epic was responsible for the spread of hero worship in the eighth century, a theory debunked by Snodgrass (1988). As Deoudi (1999) makes clear, however, heroic epic and the rise of hero worship must be considered together. Deoudi (1999: 40–55) discusses the manifestation of heroic values in the Geometric period, which indicates a desire to refer to and imitate the world depicted by Homer. I. Morris (1988) connects the rise of tomb cult in the eighth century to epic as two manifestations of a Greek interest in their past, which were used to gain power in the present through an appeal to the heroic age and its heroes. Also see Hiller (1983), who shows that hero cult was both independent of and motivated by the spread of Homeric epic. By the sixth century, hero worship and tending of ancestors were separate phenomena, although there was probably interaction between the two cult practices. *Tris(h)ērōs* has been compared to the later Greek *tri(to)patores/pateres* 'great-grandfathers, collective ancestors', who seem to represent the three-generation limit of individual memory. The collective ancestors received offerings during ceremonies of phratries and clans, often as a preliminary to a festival, according to evidence that comes mostly from Athens and areas under its influence and begins in the sixth century. Lexical texts tell us that they received offerings for childbirth and at marriage, and that they were conceived of as winds (*anemoi*), representing the immaterial and uncatchable form of ghosts. They were involved in a purification ritual described in a fifth-century lead tablet from Selinous in Sicily (Antonaccio 1995: 245, 264–5; Hemberg 1954; Jameson, Jordan and Kotansky 1993: 29–31, 107–14; Johnston 1999: 51–8), which shows us that they can be polluted and require purification, although we do not know whether this comes from their own sin, or from a recent death or murder within the family. They receive a libation of wine "through the roof" (A.11), possibly the roof of a tomb.

[83] Snodgrass (1988: 20–1). See I. Morris (2000: 233–5) critiquing M. L. West's (1978: 370–3) discussion of supposed differences between Homer's and Hesiod's view of the *hērōs*.

[84] *Il.* 12.23: *kai hēmitheōn genos andrōn*, about the many warriors who would die during the Trojan War. Hadzisteliou-Price (1973), Lateiner (2002: 53–5), G. Lorenz (1996: 23–5).

"ancient son of Dardanus."[85] Moreover, Hector boasts that if he kills the Achaean champion put up against him, the Achaeans can heap up his tomb (*sēma*) on the Hellespont so that those who pass it in the future will say, "'This is the tomb of a man who died long ago whom once, although he was outstanding, shining Hector slew.' So some day someone will say, and my glory (*kleos*) will never die."[86] These are clear references to Mycenaean tombs (or features taken to represent them) as locations for hero worship, and it is clear that they were thought to have been built in the time of the heroes commemorated in Homeric epic.

The Trojan War was the watershed marking the end of the heroic age when gods and humans interacted directly,[87] and Homer was aware of an era of general destruction following the war, for in the *Iliad* Hera promises that after the fall of Troy Zeus can feel free to destroy Argos, Sparta, and Mycenae.[88] Thus, Homer took for granted some of the basic elements of hero worship, acknowledging it as a way of remembering the past that goes together with epic, just as the funeral games of Patroclus are complementary to the epic describing his death.[89]

As noted earlier, Hesiod's Ages of Man myth inserts the age of heroes between the Bronze and Iron Ages. According to I. Morris, "this was a classic foundation charter, naturalizing the evident decline in power and sophistication since Mycenaean times and promoting the stability of the new elites. There was no point struggling against the limitations on mortals, since they were Zeus's will."[90] Moreover, one cannot retroject the myth of ages before the Iron Age: as Ludwig Koenen observes, the key opposition, based on historical fact, is bronze versus iron, so the myth of the Ages of Man could not have existed before the Iron Age.[91]

Koenen sees the possibility of Near Eastern influence on the historiographic framework used:

---

[85] *Il.* 10.414–16, 11.166, 371–2, 24.349, see Hadzisteliou-Price (1973: 138–9) and Boardman (2002: 55). Other landmark tombs and their physical correlates are discussed by Luce (2003).

[86] *Il.* 7.86–90.

[87] Burkert (1995: 227). In a Hesiodic fragment (F 155.94–119 Most), Zeus decides to destroy the race of heroes with the Trojan War (González 2010), and in the opening of the *Cypria* (F 1 West), Zeus decides to lighten the human burden on the earth, carrying out his plan by killing the heroes in Troy (see Chapter 12, 301, 327). Koenen (1994: 26–30) offers a rather different explanation of this fragment. The Trojan War serves the same purpose as the Great Flood in Mesopotamian myth.

[88] *Il.* 4.50–2, Hiller (1983: 12).   [89] Grethlein (2007).

[90] I. Morris (2000: 232). See I. Morris (2000: 228–33) for his interpretation of the myth, and Antonaccio (1994b: 405–8) for additional discussion and references to earlier scholarship on Hesiod's myth of the Ages of Man.

[91] See Koenen (1994: 24–5, with n. 59).

We have distinguished two layers – Hesiod's story and an older amalgam of tales. They combine the narration of past history, depicted as a mythic series of successive cycles, with prophecies that reflect the ideologies of Egyptian and Near Eastern kingship and that culminate in the salvation of mankind through the just king. Sandwiched between is another layer. I have already argued that the heroic age, lacking any metallic identifier, was added by Hesiod to the pre-existing cycle of the ages – gold, silver, bronze, and iron. The need for such tampering indicates that the series of the metallic ages is itself pre-Hesiodic.[92]

While Koenen considers Hesiod himself to have added in the age of heroes,[93] I agree with Morris that "central Greece between 1025 and 925, when iron had most power as a symbol distancing the modern world from the past, is the most likely context for the creation of something like Hesiod's myth."[94] Counting off the three-generation horizon of historical memory from the end of the post-palatial period, placed at *ca.* 1050, brings us to 960 as the earliest time in which the end of the Bronze Age could be remembered as part of the legendary, rather than historical, past,[95] and it is at this point that the myth of four ages could most likely come into being – the time of the Lefkandi hero – and then later, at the time the graves were inserted into his tumulus, the heroic age would have been inserted into the myth of ages.

My own argument for possible Near Eastern influence – specifically west Semitic, to use a linguistic designation, north Syrian if we prefer a geographic designation – on the Ages of Man myth rests on the significance of the infrequent epic expression *meropes* (*anthrōpoi*), which is used three times in Hesiod's story of the Ages of Man, each time in a programmatic statement about one of the races.[96] As Amar Annus has shown, the Greek

---

[92] Koenen (1994: 24).

[93] Koenen (1994: 24). Morris' phrasing on this point is not specific: "I suggest that central Greeks added races of heroes and iron to an older east Mediterranean tradition about three metallic races to a create a coherent genealogy" (I. Morris 2000: 234). It leaves undecided the question of whether the two races were added together, or one after the other, although implying the former possibility.

[94] I. Morris (2000: 234).

[95] On the "floating gap" that lies beyond the third generation, before which mythical or legendary events are placed, see Assmann (2008: 112–13), Vansina (1985: 23–4, 168–9).

[96] The focus of M. L. West (1978: 174–7; 1997a: 312–19) was on the concept of a series of metallic ages in other mythologies (no example, however, is mentioned that is earlier than Hesiod). Koenen (1994: 11–26; also Most 1997) is rightly skeptical of Near Eastern influence here. *Meropes anthrōpoi* in the *Works and Days*: "the golden race of *meropes* humans first ..." (109); "father Zeus made another race, the third, of *meropes* humans of bronze" (143–4); "but Zeus

term *merops* comes from the west Semitic *m^{e}rappê* 'healer'.[97] At Ugarit the cognate term *rapa 'um* is applied to the epic heroes Danel and Keret, and the legendary west Semitic ancestor Ditanu is mentioned as the most important of the *rapa 'ūma* in the poem *Keret* and in the *Funerary Ritual in Poetic Form*. He has his own temple, and his healing powers are called upon in an incantation. Ditanu also appears in king lists recited in rituals of royal ancestor veneration at Ugarit, and he is one of the seventeen kings who lived in tents mentioned at the beginning of the *Assyrian Royal Chronicle*,[98] so his name metonymically represents the genealogical tradition of a local court positioning itself in world history by connecting its own dynasty to internationally recognized legendary dynasties.

Ditanu gave his name to the Greek Titans, who represent one reworking of the west Semitic genealogical tradition involving these mythical ancestors. They are the "earlier generation" of gods defeated and imprisoned by Zeus in Tartarus, as told in Hesiod's *Theogony*. In the Septuagint, *r^{e}pā 'îm* is translated as either *gigantes* or *titanoi*, an acknowledgment on the part of the translators of the parallels that can be drawn between the *r^{e}pā 'îm* and the Greek conception of the earlier generations of gods. In the Hebrew Bible, though, with the excising of any reference to the practice of ancestor veneration among the Jews, the divinized ancestors were reshaped into men of ancient times and legendary foes of the Israelites.[99]

Whereas the sequence of Uranus, Cronus, and Zeus has particularly close parallels with the *Song of Birth*, the Titans episode adds west Semitic

---

will destroy this race (the fifth) of *meropes* humans..." (180), out of a total of twenty-one appearances of *merop-* in Homer, Hesiod, and the Homeric Hymns, including the personal names Merops and Merope.

[97] See Annus (1999), building on the earlier work of Astour (1964: 239, 245–9), who connects the term specifically to Meropie, an alternative name for Cos, the island of doctors.

[98] *Assyrian Royal Chronicle* B i 5 (translit. and trans. Glassner 2004: 136–7); on this text also see Chapter 8, 197, n. 119. *Keret*: KTU 1.15 iii 2–4, 13–15 (trans. N. Wyatt 2002: 210, 212); *Ritual for a Single Month*: KTU 1.114 (translit. and trans. Pardee 2002: 34–5); *Funerary Ritual in Poetic Form*: KTU 1.161 3, 10 (translit. and trans. Pardee 2002: 87); *Consultation of Ditānu with a View to Healing*: KTU 1.124 (translit. and trans. Pardee 2002: 170–9); see Loretz (1993: 289–93) suggesting it is a necromantic rite, also N. Wyatt (2002: 423–5). Ditanu's name has been etymologized as "aurochs" (*CAD* D: 164–5) or as a geographic term (Tidnum, see Chavalas 1994: 122, n. 130, with earlier references); also see Vidal (2006: 168–9).

[99] Annus (1999), Noegel (1998), N. Wyatt (2007). Burkert (1992: 94–5) presents an alternative, less plausible explanation of the Titans' name, having to do with the apotropaic use of clay (*titu*) figurines. Hesiod's folk etymology derives *Titanos* from *titainō* 'stretch, strain' (*Th.* 207–10). On the reworking of the status of the *r^{e}pā' îm* in the Hebrew Bible, see Loretz (1994).

elements to the Hurrian story of the defeat of the Former Gods.[100] The interaction between the genealogical/dynastic list tradition and narratives about the Former Gods, discussed in Chapter 8, helps to explain how Ditanu transitioned from being a legendary ancestor in a dynastic list to one of the Greek Former Gods. In addition, the *Works and Days* makes use of the phrase "king in heaven," a phrase that metonymically refers to Near Eastern mythology about the beginning of the world that was used both in king lists and in the *Song of Birth*, when discussing the first men, the Golden Race who lived "when Cronus was king in heaven."[101] The phraseological parallel shows the continuity of the narrative tradition.

The borrowed word *merops*, with its particular portmanteau of ritual and mythico-historical referents, represents another Greek adaptation of the west Semitic tradition of venerating legendary ancestors, in this case with the recognition of their role as healers in magical rituals, which matched their own conception of *hērōes*. It appears three times in the Ages of Man myth in the phrase *genos meropōn anthrōpōn*. In two of the three other times the term appears in Hesiod it refers to the counting off of generations, and in one case it refers to Zeus destroying the race of heroes with the Trojan War, a motif adapted from the Near East, as discussed in the following chapter. Thus, for Hesiod at least, the term is still closely bound to its original use in west Semitic to refer to men from long ago – for Hesiod, before the Trojan War.[102] This supports my contention that the Greeks looked to the Near East for inspiration when building anew a sense of their place in world history and a connection to the glories of their

---

[100] See further López-Ruiz (2010: 113–17; 125–6) on the Titans and west Semitic elements in Hesiod's cosmogony. Bremmer (2008: 81–7) proposes that the Titanomachy was the myth providing background for the Cronia, a festival performed particularly in Asia Minor in honor of Zeus' father Cronus, whose story parallels that of Kumarbi, Teshshub's father. However, as Mondi (1984: 343) points out, Cronus does not play a role in the Titanomachy. The two episodes in which Zeus asserts his primacy, in one case over his father, in the other over the Former Gods, "present diachronically independent mythological narratives."

[101] *Op.* 111. See discussion of this phrase in Chapter 8, 188–9. On Cronus as a Titan, see *Th.* 207–10, 851; López-Ruiz (2010: 117). According to López-Ruiz (2010: 117), the Ages of Man myth "seems to preserve an alternative tradition whereby he played a positive and prominent role"; "Hesiod's views again coincide with the Northwest Semitic traditions of Ugarit and Philon about the ancestral god El" (118).

[102] FF 90.20, 155.98, 212.5 Most. Similarly, in *Il.* 1.250 it refers to the two generations Nestor has outlived. The *Iliad* prefers collocations with *polis/poleis*. Koller (1968) has tried to argue that that was the original pairing, seeing *merops* as a non-Greek ethnic term and comparing it to non-Greek *ethnica* ending in *-ops*. It may be that the collocation was originally associated specifically with men from Cos, an island famed for its healers, as found in *hHAp* 42 (Annus 1999: 14–15; Astour 1965: 245–9). See Annus (1999) for further discussion of the hero Merops, heroine Merope, the bird named *merops*, Meropie, and Merops as a king of Cos.

remote past, visible all around them in the form of Mycenaean-era ruins. Some Greeks made an equation between the Greek *hērōes* and what they saw as equivalent figures from north Syria. And, they borrowed the Near Eastern notion of ancient times as divided into discrete units with different ruling lines dominating in turn, integrating the Near Eastern conception with a Greek perception of a sharp contrast between a time when bronze was prevalent and their current world in which iron was the chief fabric for tools and weapons.

I have shown that there was interaction between the list tradition of the Sumerian *Chronicle of the Single Monarchy* and the Hurro-Hittite *Song of Birth*, while characters of the Hurro-Hittite story of how the Storm-god took control of kingship in heaven were included in the list of legendary kings of far-flung realms in a Hurro-Hittite ritual. A similar interaction between genealogy and cosmogony can be found in Genesis and in the linking of Hesiod's *Theogony* and the Hesiodic *Catalog of Women*, which was grafted onto the end of the story of Zeus' rise to power.[103] I argue in fact that there are connections both broad and narrow between the Greek and west Semitic understandings of the beginnings of the world as they knew it, which can be partially explained as the result of transmission of stories that informed rites of ancestor veneration, including stories told about the legendary ancestors' place in the earliest stages of the world, when gods and men still associated face to face. Cyprus would have been a particularly convenient location through which Greeks could absorb elements of the west Semitic practice.

In the case we are discussing here, we can pick out influence specifically from a west Semitic language in the terms *merops* and *Titanos*, as well as two more terms, *ōgugos* and *Iapetos*. *Ōgugos* is connected to the most important of Koenen's examples of Near Eastern influence on the Ages of Man myth, the elements found in the Mesopotamian narrative *Atrahasis*, with Enlil's three attempts to destroy mankind by plague, drought, and famine before he sends the flood, a sequence that parallels the destructions of the silver, bronze, and heroic races.[104] First of all we can argue that the Near Eastern influence is not just thematic, but necessarily involves a narrative, insofar as the motif requires three successive stages. In fact, the parallels between Noah's flood, which draws on the same flood story found in *Atrahasis* and *Gilgamesh*, and Greek flood stories have long been noted.[105]

---

[103] Most (2006: xlvii–xlix).
[104] See trans. of OB version by Foster (2005: 239–44); Koenen (1994: 20–2).
[105] See Chapter 2, 29–30.

Secondly, although the Hesiodic *Catalog of Women* does not refer to Deucalion's flood, the term *ōgugios* was already applied to the "undying water of the Styx" in the *Theogony*, which requires knowledge of a story about the Boeotian king "Ogygos' role as survivor of the primal flood."[106] This story draws quite directly on the story of

> Og of Bashan[, who] is recorded in the Bible as having been the last of the Rephaim, the denizens of the underworld (Jos 12,4). In the talmudic and midrashic tradition, however, Og of Bashan is recorded as having survived the deluge by sitting on top of Noah's ark. Whether the Aegean and biblical floods are the same, of course, is impossible to know, but that both names identify giants who survive primal massive inundations is compelling.[107]

Moreover, Genesis shows other interesting parallels with Hesiod's *Theogony*. Both texts work from the origin of the world to human genealogies that define contemporary relationships among ethnic groups. Both are interested in the role of woman in human society (casting her as a necessary evil). And, both view early human history as a process of decline in morality and reduction in human lifespan, with a transition from a state of intimacy with the gods (or God), punctuated by a period in which the gods (or sons of God) had sexual intercourse with humans, producing, in the words of the Bible, "the mighty men that were of old, the men of renown," who correspond to the semi-divine Greek heroes.[108]

Finally, there is the striking correspondence between the names of Noah's son Japeth and the Titan Iapetus in Genesis 10:1–5, which, like the *Catalog of Women*, connects east and west through a genealogy using geographic names. Japeth was the father of Javan, whose name represents the Levantine term for westerners (cf. Gr. Ionian). In Apollodorus, who is drawing on the Hesiodic catalog, Ion was the descendant of Iapetus by way of Prometheus and his son Deucalion.[109] Javan's sons are to be located in Cilicia and the Greek islands, including Elisha, who should be connected

---

[106] Noegel (1998: 414); *Th.* 805–6. *Pace* M. L. West (1997a: 489–93), who states that the flood story did not reach Greece until after 550 BCE. For a careful discussion of the sources on Ogygus' flood see Fowler (2013: 118–20). Also note another interesting use of the name in epic: Ogygia is the mythical island of Calypso (e.g., *Od.* 1.85).

[107] Noegel (1998: 414).

[108] Gen. 6 (trans. May and Metzger 1973: 8). See Bremmer (2008: 96–7).

[109] Apollod. *Bib.* 1.7.2–3; see J. P. Brown (1995: 82–3). On the use of the term Yawan (Javan), see Chapter 12, 319, with n. 84. Bremmer (2008: 81) and M. L. West (1997a: 289–90) note the similarity in the names, but do not push the connection.

with Alashiya.[110] The Cypriot and Cilician connection to Javan supports my argument that Cyprus was a key locus for the transmission of west Semitic concepts and Syro-Anatolian ideas in other languages. Although there is no reason to exclude influence from Greek genealogies on Genesis, the position of Iapetus as a member of an important Greek genealogy indicates influence on the Greek side not only from Syro-Anatolian concepts mediated by a west Semitic source, but also from narratives that linked specific characters together, as the Greeks fleshed out a coherent framework for their legendary past.

As I will show in the following chapter, in the Early Iron Age many west Semitic speakers were embedded in the Neo-Hittite culture found in east Anatolia and north Syria. And, in Chapter 14, there will be a detailed discussion of the evidence for use of genealogies and the public practice of royal ancestor veneration by Neo-Hittite royal houses, which will help to explain how the practices we can see in Neo-Hittite Anatolia could be made known to Greek-speakers or to the people who served as intermediaries introducing the practices to Greek-speakers. At this point my discussion of influence coming from eastern Anatolia and/or north Syria requires an important reminder: it is not appropriate to put the categorizations "west Semitic" and "Mesopotamian" or "Anatolian" side-by-side. The latter are geographic terms, the former a linguistic one. In the Bronze Age many west Semitic speakers were brought into the orbit first of Mesopotamian-derived cultural practices, then of the Hittite empire. Although the examples we have been discussing in this chapter show influence via a west Semitic language, examples discussed earlier show influence from Hittite Anatolia on Hesiod's *Theogony* and the *Works and Days*.[111] In addition the cultures of western Anatolia and east Anatolia–north Syria differed from one another. The route via Cyprus and Euboea brought east Anatolian–north Syrian storylines to Greece, some of which were mediated by west Semitic speakers, others by speakers of other languages. Some of these storylines, whatever the intermediary language to Greek, originally came from Hittite Anatolia, others came from north Syria, and some of these had their ultimate origin in Mesopotamia or underwent influence from Mesopotamian-derived concepts before they reached the Greeks.

---

[110] Elisha ~ Alashiya: López-Ruiz (2010: 235, n. 119), Saporetti (1976: 88).
[111] See Chapter 2, 34, for connections between the *Tale of Appu* and Hesiod's *Works and Days*, and Chapter 10, 250, 255, for influence from *Illuyanka* and *Song of Hedammu* on the *Theogony*.

The *Odyssey* as a narrative of long-distance elite interactions

Turning from stories about distant times to stories about voyaging to faraway places, I show how the warrior-trader values discussed earlier in this chapter that are displayed in the *Odyssey* explicate the milieu in which and reasons why some of the Near Eastern motifs found in the *Odyssey* were incorporated into Greek epic. We can suggest that the story of the *Odyssey* developed first on mainland Greece and Euboea, incorporating a first round of Near Eastern elements via Cyprus there, then as the Greek epic poets in Anatolia began to dominate the market, the *Odyssey* absorbed a second round of Near Eastern influence within Anatolia. The Early Iron Age Euboeans were heavily involved with trade, and their pottery with its characteristic painted pendant semi-circles is found as far east as Cyprus and the Levant, even in the tenth century. The archaeological data have therefore been used by many, including Martin West, to argue that Near Eastern elements in Greek epic were brought via the Euboean trade route from north Syria, Cyprus, and Cilicia and absorbed in Euboea, although West argues that the Orientalizing period was the relevant era.[112] The Euboean route is particularly plausible for the storylines valorizing long-distance elite interactions.

In the Early Iron Age, Greeks engaged in the "journey for power," bringing back esoteric goods and knowledge, and they equated the empowering journey across space with empowering ties to the distant legendary past, the time of their heroes, just as Near Easterners in the second millennium did. Thus, it is surely not coincidental that some of the

---

[112] For Euboea as important in the formation of epic, see Lane Fox (2009), Powell (2002: 116–17, 127–33, 193–6), and M. L. West (1988: 165–72; followed by Lemos 2002: 216–17), arguing for Euboean (west Ionic) forms in the language, and pointing to the hero of Lefkandi and to contact with the east; and Ruijgh (1995: 47–50), seeing "Euboean" elements in the language of Homer arising from a visit paid there by the bard. Some supposedly west Ionic elements in Homer are easy to explain away: For example, the appearance of west Ionic *xeno-* instead of east Ionic *xeino-* from *xenwo-*requires us to assume that Homer's works were always written using the spelling conventions used now. It is likely, though, that that the texts were first written using an alphabet and writing conventions that did not distinguish between short and long *e* and *o* (later spelled ε, ει, η; ο, ου, ω), or single versus double consonants. See Cassio (2002), Chadwick (1990: 174–5), Chantraine (1958: 5–14), Horrocks (1997: 194–5), Janko (1992: 33–7), and M. L. West (2000: 30). The appearance of *p* instead of *k* for original labiovelars before *o*, as opposed to the usage of Herodotus and Ionic poets, is either a desire to avoid a strongly marked regionalism, or because it was a northeast Ionic feature, not generalized throughout east Ionic (Chadwick 1990: 175; W. F. Wyatt 1992: 172–3). For more detailed attempts to argue for west Ionic forms see Peters (1998) and the critique by Cassio (1998). Also Chapter 15, 408, n. 44.

stories transmitted focused on exactly those themes.[113] The desire for innovations expressed, for example, by the popularity of iron knives from Cyprus in elite warrior graves would have been a factor promoting the transmission of novel stories.

The overarching plot and themes of the *Odyssey* speak to the values of the warrior-traders that motivated the spread of Near Eastern epic motifs in mainland Greece and Euboea. The work is an extended meditation on hospitality, on the guest–host relations that are inherited from father to son, and on the hazards of and empowerment resulting from a long voyage. At each stop on the journeys of Odysseus and his son Telemachus guest-gifts of the type found in Greek warrior tombs from the Mycenaean period and onwards are offered, with detailed descriptions of their craftsmanship and heritage.[114] While Telemachus travels within the familiar terrain of mainland Greece, re-activating the ties that his father had made, Odysseus moves in a much wider circle, testing the limits of the known world, encountering the Cyclops, who is emphatically beyond the pale of the civilized world that practices the etiquette of guest friendship, and the Phaeacians, who in contrast act as full-fledged members of the international elite despite their remoteness.[115]

Odysseus' story has been connected to Greek expansions westwards, whether in search of trade in the Mycenaean period and Early Iron Age or colonizing in the Archaic period. Although the exact locations of many of the places and landmarks Odysseus sees are still controversial, it is agreed that his wanderings have a westward orientation,[116] while his homeland Ithaca lies off the west coast of Greece. The eastward orientation of certain of his adventures is thus evidence of changes made to the plot. The metal trade connecting the Levant, Cyprus, Greece, and Italy and lands beyond is refracted in the portrait of Athena, posing as the Taphian Mentes, a *xenos* of Telemachus through their fathers' guest friendship, and claiming to be stopping through Ithaca on an expedition trading iron for bronze in Temesa (*Od.* 1.178–94).[117]

---

[113] See Chapter 9, 209–17.   [114] See Grethlein (2008: 37).

[115] Where exactly it is that the Phaeacians are supposed to live is a matter of debate. Two cogent suggestions are Corfu (Corcyra) and Magna Graecia in southern Italy (Wolf 2006). Others see the Phaeacians as representing the Ionians (Frame 2009: 521–4, 551–2).

[116] See Wolf (2006).

[117] See Mazarakis Ainian (2006: 194). Crielaard (1998: 191–9) shows how trade networks connected Cyprus to Italy, Sardinia, and Spain. There was a Tamassos in Cyprus, but the place name in the *Odyssey* may refer to another town of the same name in Italy (S. P. Morris 1992a: 117–19; Winter 1995, 267–8, n. 43). Trade expeditions brought Greeks into contact with

In the social world depicted in the *Odyssey*, Odysseus shows that he is a member of the international "club" in Scheria by competing as an athlete and displaying his prowess in telling tales. If we are to believe the *Odyssey*, one venue for the performance of narratives about gods and heroes was a gathering at a nobleman's house, with elite visitors, both local and from far away,[118] and this gathering was not necessarily much different from a festival, with competitions of song and sport, and sacrifices to the gods.[119]

Significantly, it is the performance of epic song that is used to demonstrate the Phaeacians' belonging. Their bard Demodocus' choice as one of his performances of a Homeric hymn singing of the sexual peccadilloes of Aphrodite (accompanied by a troop of dancers) is far from accidental. Of course, it speaks to the internal audience of Odysseus, concerned whether his wife has remained faithful while he is gone, but it also chooses the goddess whose cult has expanded all over the known world from the east,[120] and Demodocus makes a point of mentioning, not only Paphos, where Aphrodite's temple was kept ready for her visit, but also Thrace, the home of Ares, and Lemnos, where Hephaestus was especially honored, showing the Phaeacians' knowledge of the eastern edge of the Greek world. Demodocus demonstrates that the Phaeacians are aware of the significant events of their contemporary time by singing of the events at Troy, and Odysseus in turn lets them know he was among those who fought there, secure in the knowledge that he will be recognized. Odysseus challenges the bard by requesting the specific episode about the Trojan horse, saying if he sings it "appropriately" (*kata moiran*), "I will straightway tell (*mūthēsomai*) all men that the god has graciously bestowed divine song on you" (8.496–8), and the bard rises to the challenge.

In turn, Odysseus' visit to the court of Scheria exemplifies the way in which songs and narratives moved around through long-distance elite interactions. With his exotic story recounting how he made his way to the edge of the world and back, Odysseus implicitly competes with and

---

Phoenicians intent on the same goals, although the Phoenicians were a bit more enterprising, leaving the safety of the calm Mediterranean to head out into the Atlantic Ocean to Spain and even farther north. In the *Odyssey* some Phoenicians are portrayed quite negatively, corrupt traders who seize the unsuspecting and sell them into slavery (14.288–97, 15.403–84). On the other hand, Menelaus boasts that the *krater* he gives to Telemachus was a gift from the king of Sidon (4.614–19). The ambivalent portrayal reflects a complex relationship among the seafaring peoples, a portrayal which conceals opportunities for transfer of Syro-Anatolian epic storylines from the Near East. See Winter (1995) for one interpretation of the portrayal of the Phoenicians.

[118] Murray (2008: 165–9). [119] On the Phaeacian feast as a festival see Nagy (2010: 79–127).
[120] On Aphrodite see Chapter 12, 323–5.

bests the local bard.[121] The example of Odysseus also suggests that some members of the Early Iron Age Greek elite could have been themselves responsible for putting exotic stories into circulation. He was not the only hero who could tell epic, for Achilles too is described as singing the famous deeds of men of yore (Il. 9.189). As suggested earlier, it is in this way that individual poets could be important in the development of the Homeric tradition, by serving as key nodes in networks of relationships.[122]

We now can briefly outline the layers of formative influence from Near Eastern myth on the *Odyssey*, schematized in Table 4, a chart that puts the textual history of the *Odyssey* next to that of the *Iliad*. The story of a wandering hero who encounters monsters on the edge of the world, proves himself, and returns from the world of the dead, seems very old, and many of the elements shared between the *Epic of Gilgamesh* and the *Odyssey* could have been in the Greek tradition long before any influence from *Gilgamesh* specifically. Some of the motifs that had their origin in Sargonic or Gilgamesh myths could have come directly across the Mediterranean from Syro-Anatolia, via the same route and for the same reasons that trade connections with Cyprus were cultivated by Greek warrior-traders. And, the Greeks themselves used the stories to provide a mythological background to their journeys westwards, to areas wild and unexplored, in the opposite direction of the "civilized" eastern centers of Neo-Hittite, Cypriot, and eventually Neo-Assyrian power.

The *Odyssey* may have originally addressed the values of the heroic trader, lauded as far back as *The Valorous Sun*[123] and driving the interest in Sargonic legend in the Old Assyrian period,[124] but as the values of the Greek aristocratic class changed and trade was viewed more negatively, the role of the hero would have lost its trader aspects. In addition, the wandering hero was given the departure point of Troy in order to link his story to the master narrative that subsumed all other legends. This change is the result of the rise in popularity of the Troy narrative in the Greek epic tradition, certainly not to be dated much before 950 BCE and probably a bit later.[125] Finally, one section of the wanderings of Odysseus was shifted to the far northeast on the other side of the Black Sea, as an Anatolian narrative tradition about the edges of the Anatolian world, itself

---

[121] Nagy (2010: 91–3).   [122] Chapter 9, 212.
[123] On *The Valorous Sun*, see Chapter 9, 209–10.
[124] On the connection between the Old Assyrian trade network and Sargonic legend, see Chapter 8, 169–70, 173, n. 27.
[125] See Chapter 14, 367–71.

indebted to *Gilgamesh*, was pulled into the *Odyssey*. This tradition included not only Odysseus' *katabasis*, but also the Cyclops story, which has parallels in Caucasian mythology.[126] This only could have occurred after the east Ionic version of Greek epic had attained supremacy on the supralocal festival circuit, as will be discussed in Chapter 15, reshaping a story that was the property of the mainland Greek tradition.

One last point needs to be made about Odysseus' storytelling: the distant origins of the Cyclops story are acknowledged by placing its events on the edge of the world.[127] Odysseus' tale about faraway places, told to the Phaeacians at the edge of the world, is therefore constructed out of the very stories that were moved around across vast distances.

Conclusion

In this chapter I focused on the circumstances that inspired mainland Greeks and Euboeans to make use of Near Eastern narrative traditions, possibly beginning as early as the eleventh century BCE but surely before 825 BCE, the date of the latest of the graves associating themselves with the *hērōon* at Lefkandi. When it is possible to distinguish the source of the influence, it is a blended Hurrian-west Semitic tradition, which would have been at home more in north Syria than in Anatolia. It is not completely impossible, however, that the source was Cilicia, on the eastern coast of which Phoenicians were settling by the ninth century and possibly as early as the eleventh century.[128] As I will argue in the next chapter, whether the source came from Cilicia or from Syria, the archaeological evidence points to Cyprus as the intermediary between either region and Greece, rather than direct transmission to Greece.

With regard to the *Odyssey*, it is possible to distinguish at least two temporally distinct strains of Near Eastern influence, even if they involve the same Near Eastern storyline, the Gilgamesh tradition. The later one,

---

[126] The parallels include the episode with the Cyclops, which has been compared to Gilgamesh's battle with the forest monster Huwawa (Chapter 3, 55–6); the episode in the underworld, which resembles Enkidu's descent into the underworld in Tablet XII of the SB *Epic of Gilgamesh* (Chapter 4); and Calypso and Circe, who share features with Shiduri (West 1997a: 404–12). For the Caucasian parallels, see Chapter 4, 106.

[127] As Christol (1997: 360) observes, "Le héros achéen doit franchir les bornes du monde connu pour affronter des géants anthropophages, Lestrygons ou Cyclopes. Pour le héros narte, il suffit de sortir de son village."

[128] Lipiński (2004: 109–43). For Neo-Hittite Cilicia, see Chapter 12, 310–16.

I have argued, must have come through western Anatolia. It is logical, although not absolutely necessary, to assume that the earlier strain came via the same route as the Hurrian–west Semitic influence on Hesiod, that is, via Cyprus. I will argue in Chapter 15 that Anatolia established its claim to being the premier milieu for composition in performance of Greek epic by the end of the eighth century. That means the earlier strain of influence arrived before then, when Euboea was involved in trade with Cyprus.[129]

The earlier strain of Near Eastern influence arrived early enough to allow the *Odyssey* to reach a sufficiently set form so that the change required to insert the Cyclops and *katabasis* episodes would noticeably disrupt Odysseus' journey, with Odysseus inexplicably transferred from the west of Greece to the northern edge of the Black Sea. I see no means to define exactly when, except for my contention that Greeks on the mainland and Euboea were motivated to tap into the Near Eastern framing of the legendary past in the Protogeometric period when they began to create their legends of the heroic age. In contrast, I will show in the final two chapters that it is possible to pinpoint quite exactly when a Greek epic about Troy came into being, to 1160–1050 BCE, and that, although we can pick out different strains of Near Eastern influence in the *Iliad*, the storylines about the destruction of a city should not be assumed to be passed to Greek epic anywhere else than in Anatolia. But first, we must examine more closely how and why Cyprus could serve as a conduit for Near Eastern influence from Cilicia and north Syria to Greek epic.

---

[129] On Euboea's role in direct trade with the Near East, see Boardman (1990: 178–82), J. Luke (2003), and Vanschoonwinkel (2008). On the flow of goods from the Levant to mainland Greece in the tenth and ninth centuries, see S. Sherratt and A. Sherratt (1993: 364–6). The Levantine site al-Mina has been singled out as an example of Greek, specifically Euboean, direct trade with the east (e.g., Boardman 1999: 38–54; 2006: 513–16; Lane Fox 2009: 86–107), but in fact, the settlement only begins *ca.* 770 BCE (J. Luke 2003: 12), and there is some debate about whether Greeks actually settled there (Boardman 1990; Descoeudres 2002; Gates 2010: 42–3; Niemeyer 2004). A detailed survey of the evidence by J. Luke (2003) shows that it is unlikely. She characterizes it as a port of trade through which Greek goods came, not a Greek settlement. On the varying interpretations of the Greek pottery at al-Mina also see Niemeier (2001: 12–14), in a more general discussion of evidence for Archaic Greeks in the Levant, and Waldbaum (1997: 1–4), in the context of the history of archaeological research in the Levant. Thus, even the relatively vague timeline I propose here means that the direct contact with the Levant shown by al-Mina is not germane, and that is why the focus must be Cyprus as a mediator of contact with Syro-Anatolia.

12 | Cyprus as a source of Syro-Anatolian epic in the Early Iron Age

> There was (a time) when a myriad of races <always> roaming across the earth weigh<ed> down the breadth of the <deep>-chested land. But, Zeus, seeing, took pity, and in his close-packed mind he planned to lighten the all-feeding earth of humans by hurling the strife of Ilian war, until he emptied the burden through death. And, because the heroes were being killed in Troy, the plan of Zeus was being carried out.
>
> *Cypria* F 1 West

Introduction

Cyprus must be highlighted as a key locus of interaction between Greek-speakers and the west Semitic, Hurrian, and Cilician strains of the Near Eastern narrative song tradition. Interactions between Cyprus and Syria and Cilicia on the one hand and between Cyprus and Greece on the other were important vectors for the transmission of Near Eastern epic to Greece,[1] because here there was an early opportunity for the Greek and Near Eastern practices that have been shown to be connected to the performance of epic to blend, resulting in the merging of epic traditions. Cyprus can be pinpointed as the source of several specific motifs featured in Greek hexametric poetry that have a special association with Aphrodite, although theogonic stories and storylines assigned to Zeus and Apollo may have passed through the island too.

The particular circumstances of Cyprus – its location, its wealth of copper, and the fact that, in the words of John Coldstream, "Cyprus ... experienced an age no darker than subfusc"[2] – meant that it was one of the most important nodes of interaction across the end of the Late Bronze Age and into the Iron Age. The island offered a favorable milieu for the

---

[1] As Bremmer (2008: 337) put it, "The 'via fenicia' probably converged with the 'via cilicia' on Cyprus." The time period he was thinking of was the Orientalizing era, but the statement holds true for earlier times. The Bronze Age dates for Cyprus cited here come from Knapp (2013: 27).
[2] Coldstream (1998: 5).

continued "professional" development of epic, because kingship, temples, and their ceremonial trappings, presumably including patronage of singers and priests, were maintained into the Early Iron Age.[3] The processes of interaction left their mark at many levels of Greek civilization, from material culture to religion to their legends and verbal art.

On the one hand, Cyprus participated in religious and cult practices of the north Syrian mainland. Placed on the farthest edge of the Mesopotamian world, we may expect that, like the Hittites, Cypriots co-opted for themselves stories in which they were the periphery to be explored, which later were one of the inspirations for Odysseus' voyages. On the other hand, as contacts between Greece and Cyprus developed anew after the fall of the palatial civilization, there was an interest in and the means to incorporate elements of Near Eastern epic into Greek epic that had made their way to Cyprus, as part of a larger complex of practices that displayed membership in a supraregional Greek elite through funerary ritual and hospitality, with feasting, wine-drinking, and song.

The survival of certain important Cypriot gods and their syncretism with Greek and west Semitic gods may have provided the opportunity for narrative songs similar to those found at Hattusa and Ugarit to influence the Greek tradition of narrative song. In addition, Cilicia also shows strong cultural continuity, even as Mycenaeans settled there after the collapse of the Hittite empire. A sense of shared identity among Greeks, creating a community that extended from Cilicia to Cyprus to Greece, could have encouraged the transfer of elements of east Anatolian cultural practices westwards.

In this chapter I first discuss conditions in Cyprus from the Bronze Age to the Early Iron Age, then continuity of culture in Cilicia and in north Syria after the fall of the Hittite empire. Then, I turn to evidence that Greek-speakers who had settled in Cicilia at the end of the Bronze Age maintained a connection to Cyprus, while Greek-speakers in Cyprus maintained a connection with the Greek mainland. These are the conditions that allowed for the spread to Greece of the Near Eastern genealogical tradition, the concept of healer ancestors discussed in the previous chapter, and the Near-Eastern-inspired narratives about Aphrodite that I discuss in the final section of this chapter.

---

[3] On the beginning of the Iron Age in Cyprus see Steel (2004a: 187–213); on Early Iron Age Cyprus see Knapp (2008: 281–97, 368–72) and V. Karageorghis (1990; 1994a, ed.).

Cyprus in the Late Bronze Age: a member of the brotherhood of Great Kings

From its earliest mentions in Near Eastern literature as the farthest point west known to the audience, in *The Valorous Sun* and the *Old Assyrian Sargon Legend*,[4] Cyprus reveals itself to be a key node in interaction between east and west.[5] The conditions required for the transfer of epic narratives were present here: the development of a hybrid culture through cultural mixing, leading to syncretism of gods and driven by competitive emulation and use of exotica to bolster local hegemony.

Alashiya was a player in international diplomacy in the Late Bronze Age, even a member of the brotherhood of Great Kings.[6] Suppiluliuma II claimed to control Alashiya,[7] but Cyprus shows extensive contact with Mycenaeans,[8] and the sea barrier allowed it to maintain more autonomy than Kizzuwatna (Plain Cilicia) or north Syria, the former completely integrated into the core territory of the Hittites and the latter divided into secundogenitures and vassal states such as Ugarit. Alashiya's king called the pharaoh brother,[9] and the kings of Ugarit, Niqmaddu III and

---

[4] On *The Valorous Sun* see Chapter 9, 209–10. This third-millennium text aggrandizing the work of long-distance traders describes the Sun-god voyaging to visit his newly established temple on "the other side of the sea" (vii 1), which its editor equates with Cyprus (W. G. Lambert 1989: 25). On the *Old Assyrian Sargon Legend* see Chapter 8, 169–70.

[5] The long-running debate over whether Alashiya was indeed in Cyprus has finally been ended by analysis of the clay of a letter sent from Alashiya to el-Amarna that shows it is from Cyprus. Amarna: *EA* 37 (trans. Moran 1992: 110); Ugarit: L.1: *Letter from the King of Alashiya to the Ammurapi* (translit. and trans. J. Nougayrol in Nougayrol et al. 1968: 85–6), with RS 20.238: *Letter from Ammurapi to the King of Alashiya* (translit. and trans. J. Nougayrol in Nougayrol et al. 1968: 87–9), the reply explicitly addressed to the king of Alashiya. See Goren et al. (2003); Goren, Finkelstein and Na'aman (2004: 57–75). See Knapp (1985: 236–41) on the other evidence linking Cyprus and Alashiya and his up-to-date discussion in Knapp (2008: 298–345). In Linear B texts the ethnonyms *a-ra-si-jo* and *ku-pi-ri-jo* both appear. They could refer to separate regions in the island, or could simply be two different designations for the same place. On the terms, see Shelmerdine (1998: 295–6) and Knapp (2008: 303–7). Cyprus may have been divided into several smaller states in the Late Bronze Age (Keswani 1996; Steel 2004a: 181–2; Webb 1999: 3–5), but see Knapp (2008: 335–41), arguing for a single state. Cyprus shows contact with both Syria and Anatolia from at least the Neolithic period.

[6] Knapp (2008: 324–36) reviews the evidence for relations between Alashiya, Hattusa, Ugarit, and Egypt. Also see de Martino (2008) for a recent review of the Hittite evidence.

[7] For the claim of New Hittite hegemony in Alashiya, see *Inscription of Suppiluliuma Concerning the Conquest of Alashiya*: CTH 121 = KBo 12.38 (ed. Güterbock 1967; trans. H. A. Hoffner, Jr. in Hallo and Younger 1997: 192–3).

[8] Steel (2004a: 170), Iacovou (2008: 629–31).

[9] *EA* 39 (trans. Moran 1992: 112), Knapp (2008: 318).

Ammurapi, both called the king of Alashiya "father."[10] Alashiya was a major trading partner with Ugarit, where documents in a variant of the Cypro-Minoan script have been found.[11]

From the archaeological record we can see that Cyprus developed a "hybridized" material culture, "a mixture of local, Levantine, Egyptian, and Aegean elements."[12] Some Alashiyan names in Late Bronze Age documents can be given Akkadian, west Semitic, Anatolian, or Hurrian etymologies, most notably a high official from Cyprus named Eshuwara, a Mitanni Hurrian name of Indo-Iranian origin meaning 'lord' (cf. Sanskrit iśvaraḥ).[13] We would expect that the name made its way into Cypriot circles via contact with Hurrianized north Syria when the region was part of the Mitannian complex of city-states. The nexus of interactions among Hurrians, western Semites, and Cypriots is encapsulated by the small shallow silver bowl of the kind used in ceremonial wine-drinking, found at Hala Sultan Tekke on Cyprus and dating to the end of the Anatolian Bronze Age (LC IIIA:1 context, ca. 1200 BCE), with an alphabetic cuneiform inscription proclaiming its owner as Aky, son of Ykhd, that is, a man with a Hurrian name whose father bears a west Semitic name.[14]

The collecting and display of exotic luxury goods to enhance prestige were in full force in Late Bronze Age Cyprus, including items used to adorn one's person, from make-up and scented unguents to clothes and jewelry; symbols of power, such as cylinder seals;[15] and drinking sets. They show that the Cypriot elites were interested in boasting of their connections with north Syria, Egypt, and the Greek mainland.[16] Priscilla Keswani discusses the Cypriot interest in foreign priestly or royal clothing (long spotted robes), chariots, weapons, images of warriors and men dominating animals or monsters. She notes that already in the Middle Bronze Age, Cypriot elites were fascinated by the power of the exotic, and that this was a pattern that continued into the later period, but with a

---

[10] Knapp (2008: 333), Singer (1999: 675–8). The letters from Alashiya at Ugarit are discussed by Yon (1999: 117–18) and Malbran-Labat (1999).

[11] Freu (2006: 209–13).   [12] Voskos and Knapp (2008: 663).

[13] See RS 20.18: *Letter from Eshuwara, Pidduri of Alashiya, to Ammurapi* (translit. and trans. J. Nougayrol in Nougayrol et al. 1968: 83–5). Astour (1964) discusses possible etymologies of Alashiyan names; also see Knapp (2008: 319, 322–3). Eshuwara is a ^{LÚ}*pidduri*, a word of disputed etymology used only to refer to an office-holder from Alashiya; see *CHD* (P: 368).

[14] Åström and Masson (1982); see Knapp (2008: 289, 323).

[15] For the hybrid iconography of seals and their use to reinforce an elite ideology, see Knapp (2008: 153–8, 167–72) and Webb (2002; 2005).

[16] Knapp (2008: 160), Steel (2004a: 165).

heightened emphasis on the control exerted by heroes or kings over the cosmic or natural order. This in turn suggests a closer identification with, or perhaps a more sophisticated manipulation of, the Near Eastern ideology of kingship and political legitimacy in the wake of several centuries of prolonged sociopolitical interaction.[17]

Furthermore, on Cyprus we can see how the local court's desire to join the brotherhood of Great Kings played out on the level of the material culture. The development of monumental architecture beginning in the seventeenth century and gaining steam in the thirteenth century can be seen in this light.[18] Large-scale building projects involving the investment of considerable manpower, they were both an expression of power and the material result of it. They housed or served as the backdrops for feasting, cult activities, and various types of public displays of power and identity, on the one hand affirming the uniqueness of Cyprus, on the other asserting its right to a place in the brotherhood.[19] Keswani points out that the

> new complex of ideology and prestige symbolism ... was strongly influenced by external contacts that introduced not only new types of status goods but a familiarity with other political systems and politico-religious cosmologies. That elements of this knowledge were in turn incorporated and adapted into the ideological and symbolic systems of Cypriot communities is evident from the diverse Near Eastern, Egyptian, and Aegean affinities of Late Cypriot art and architecture ...[20]

By the ninth century, with the Phoenician presence well established on Cyprus,[21] narrative traditions would have flowed directly from the Levant. It is the relatively well-attested connections between Cyprus and Ugarit that allow us a glimpse of one route by which a version of Near Eastern narrative song could eventually make its way to Greek-speakers, first being transferred to Cyprus at some time in the Late Bronze Age, then crossing the Mediterranean to Greece centuries later in the first quarter of the first millennium. There is evidence that there was syncretism between Alashiyan and Ugaritic gods, an important vector for transmission of verbal art, for a letter from Ugarit names a series of Alashiyan gods, but using west Semitic names: the Storm-god Baal of Sapon, the Sun-goddess Shapash,

---

[17] Keswani (2004: 139). Also see Knapp (2008: 160–2).   [18] Knapp (2008: 209–10, 242–8).
[19] See Knapp (2008: 201–49) for a full theoretical discussion of the meaning of monumentality in Bronze Age Cyprus.
[20] Keswani (2004: 157).   [21] On which see below, 307.

Ashtarte, Anat, "and all the gods of Alashiya."[22] It is easy to make connections between Ashtarte and the later Aphrodite,[23] and between the Storm-god and the later Zeus worshipped at Salamis on Cyprus. It is possible that the syncretism caused the importation of festivals, such as the *ḫiyara* or *(ḫ)išuwa* festivals, both connected with the Storm-god and with Mt. Sapon/Hazzi, as it did at Hattusa.[24]

We would expect the form of Near Eastern narrative song transmitted to Cyprus to be very close to the west Semitic tradition evinced in Ugarit. But, it is also possible that Hurrian narrative song arrived via Ugarit, where Hurrians were a major presence, leaving their impact on the musical tradition and religious practices there,[25] especially given the fact that the *Song of LAMMA* focuses on the gods of Carchemish and therefore may have originated near to Ugarit.[26] Certainly, a clever Cypriot priest would have taken care that the gods were entertained with the most prestigious, internationally accepted form of narrative song, and an ambitious epic performer on Cyprus would have made sure to present his audience with a story that combined the exotic with the familiar, which placed their local court in the wider context of world history, fitting both recent and legendary events into narrative frameworks that the audience's cultural knowledge imbued with a meaning transcending time.

The arrival of the Greeks in Cyprus

There is some evidence beyond that of material culture that shows Greek-speakers arrived in Cyprus shortly after the end of the Mycenaean palace culture and retained some of its administrative structures. More secure is the evidence for maintenance of Cypriot administrative structures across the transition to the Early Iron Age.[27]

---

[22] *Letter from an Official in Alashiya to Ammurapi*: RS 18.113A + B (trans. D. Pardee in Hallo and Younger 2002: 104); see Budin (2003: 133–4) and Knapp (2008: 181, 320–1).

[23] Budin (2003: 225–8) sees parallels between Aphrodite and the west Semitic Ashtarte, although the young hunting goddess of the second millennium also has obvious parallels with the later Artemis.

[24] See Chapter 10, 260–1.

[25] M. Dietrich and Loretz (1999: 59–75), M. Dietrich and Mayer (1995; 1997a; 1997b: 79), Pardee (1996), Van Soldt (1999: 42–3), N. Wyatt (1999: 580). The only annotated musical scores from the Late Bronze Age are Ugaritic tablets in Hurrian; there are Hurrian incense prayers calling gods from their preferred haunts; and we have mentioned the offerings to the divine Šarrašiya, and the Hurrian royal funerary rituals.

[26] See Chapter 2, 27.   [27] Iacovou (2006).

At the end of the Late Bronze Age the major sites in Cyprus did not experience the same level of destruction as in Greece and parts of Syro-Anatolia, and certain sites show continuity of settlement across the end of the Bronze Age, in particular Enkomi, Palaepaphos, Hala Sultan Tekke, and Kourion.[28] It is at the beginning of LC IIIA that we see widespread destruction of sites.[29] Trade in Cyprus towards the end of the Bronze Age was more focused on Syria and Palestine,[30] but by the end of the LC IIIA period (1125/1100 BCE) ties between Cyprus and the Aegean had been renewed, surely in part the result of an influx of Greek-speakers.[31] Phoenicians arrived no later than the ninth century, when evidence for their presence is widespread, especially at Kition,[32] and most likely they were an important factor well before. By then most of the rest of Cyprus was Hellenized, while most of the Eteocypriot inscriptions we have come from Amathus, which proclaimed its local identity in a bilingual Cypriot-Eteocypriot inscription as late as the fourth century BCE.[33]

While it is clear that Greeks arrived in sufficient numbers and with sufficient prestige to impose their language on parts of the island, when they first started to Hellenize the island and whether their arrival left any mark on the archaeological record have been subjects of dispute. The conclusions of earlier scholars that there is clear evidence of the arrival of Greeks have been called into question and emphasis has been put on the continuity in material culture even in the face of obvious changes. The appearance of locally made LH (Myc) IIIC:1b ceramics, which used to be considered simply Mycenaean, are now considered to have more complex origins, although their Aegean influence is not denied, nor their connection to the Sea Peoples.[34] Thus, while some archaeologists focus on the

---

[28] See Iacovou (2006: 325–6; 2008: 631) on continuity, including large-scale "politico-religious" public buildings that expressed political control over cult. Also see Steel (2004a: 188). The settlement of Enkomi eventually changed over to Salamis and that of Hala Sultan Tekke to Kition, because of the silting over of their harbors.

[29] See Steel (2004a: 188) on the disruptions at the end of LC II.

[30] Steel (2004a; 210), S. Sherratt (2003a).   [31] Deger-Jalkotzy (2002: 52–3, 66–70).

[32] Lipiński (2004: 42–6). Negbi (1992: 604–6) argues for Phoenician presence on the island in the twelfth century based on the Near Eastern-style temples at Enkomi and Kition. For later phases of Phoenician involvement in Cyprus see Lipínski (2004: 51–76).

[33] Egetmeyer (2009: 71–2; 88–90), Iacovou (2006: 321; 2008: 643), Lipínski (2004: 41–2).

[34] See Iacovou (2008) for a discussion of the Hellenization of Cyprus; Iacovou (2013: 607–12) on the LH IIIC:1b pottery in Cyprus. Most agree that there is little archaeological evidence for an influx of Greek-speakers at the end of the Late Bronze Age (Deger-Jalkotzy 1994: 16–20; Iacovou 2008: 631–2; contra V. Karageorghis 1990). But, for the view that Mycenaeans leaving Greece were indeed responsible for the destructions and changes in Cyprus, see, for example, Coldstream (1989a; 1998: 6–7), Iacovou (1999), V. Karageorghis (1994b). For a point of view

destructions and changes in material culture, according to others, "[t]he major innovation of the LC IIIA phase does not appear to be one of settlement but rather the associated cultural package – pottery, domestic architecture, weaponry and prestige symbolism."[35]

Louise Steel summarizes the evidence thus:

> Cyprus seems to have undergone two major periods of upheaval, the first in the 12th century, after which Cypriot culture continued and flourished with very little overall change but with possible infiltration of new ethnic groups, and the second in the 11th century, which involved a fundamental overhaul of the geopolitical and socio-economic structure of the island. The new society which emerged in the LC IIIB–CG [Cypriot Geometric] I was largely characterized by warrior burials and what have been described as "Homeric" lifestyles.[36]

The new ethnic groups involved in the first discontinuity would have included – besides the Aegeans – Levantines and possibly Cilicians, while the second discontinuity can be fairly securely related to the arrival of the dialect of Greek that came to be Cypriot. It can be dated linguistically to after Arcado-Cypriot, a subgroup closely related to the dialect used in the Linear B documents, had differentiated itself and before the deposition in CG I (1050–1000 BCE) of the iron spit at Palaepaphos, on which a certain Opheltas had his name inscribed in the distinctive Arcado-Cypriot genitive, *O-pe-le-ta-u*. Some time before the eleventh century, then, a dialect of Greek directly related to the later Cypriot dialect was sufficiently prestigious to be fixed in a version of the local writing system.[37]

---

that focuses on continuities and hybridization, rather than migration, see Steel (2004a: 187–206), Voskos and Knapp (2008), and Knapp (2008: 249–80), with a detailed discussion of the history of the scholarly debate. Also see Baurain (1997: 138–42) on the scholarly approaches to the Greek settlement of Cyprus. On the Sea Peoples see below, 313–15.

[35] Steel (2004a: 188).   [36] Steel (2002: 111, refs. omitted).

[37] As Linear B uses the masculine *a*-stem genitive in unaltered-*āo*, the Arcado-Cypriot change of word-final-*o* to-*u* is later than the codification of Linear B, but the uniformity of Linear B surely masks much linguistic diversity within second-millennium Greek. As a product of a scribal culture, Linear B did not necessarily reflect ongoing changes in the spoken language, thus we cannot categorically claim that the Arcado-Cypriot-*au* and other innovations that distinguish the subgroup date to later than the Linear B documents. See Deger-Jalkotzy (1994), reviewing the linguistic evidence. Iacovou (2003: 80) argues, "The survival, on the easternmost island of the Mediterranean, of a dialect that is considered the only direct descendant in historic times of Mycenaean Greek implies that its introduction took place before the development of the historic Greek dialects." She stresses the archaic features of the language, which she ties to the maintenance of archaic cultural features. However, it is typical for archaisms to be preserved on the periphery. Secondly, many believe that the main divisions of the Greek dialects were already in place in the Late Bronze Age. Thirdly, Arcado-Cypriot is not a direct descendant of the Greek

Maria Iacovou suggests that the Mycenaean *qasireus*' involvement in bronze-working explains why Greek-speakers migrated to Cyprus at the end of the Bronze Age. "[T]he *qa-si-re-u* [was] the one local functionary who, on the evidence of his association with the 'distribution of bronze', could have gained intimate knowledge of the land from where the raw product was primarily imported."[38] The success of Cyprus in maintaining economic prosperity during the transition to the Early Iron Age was due to its continued involvement with the metal trade as it transitioned from supplying copper for bronze to iron-working.[39] At Cyprus the term *basileus* (*pa-si-le-wo-se*) was used to designate kings,[40] while *wanax* and *wanassa* were used for members of the ruling family.[41] Iacovou has used these data to argue that the Greek-speakers who moved to Cyprus established their own administrative structures there. However, it may be that the Greeks did not introduce their own Mycenaean-derived administrative structures, but applied their own terminology to adopted Cypriot forms.

Continued use of the Cypro-Minoan script until as late as the Cypriot Geometric I period, when it was used to inscribe Opheltas' *obelos*,[42] suggests that the indigenous administrative structures supporting kingship were maintained in Cyprus, since the chief function of writing in the Near East was administrative, although Markus Egetmeyer emphasizes that "the script was not restricted to the administrators or officials, ordinary people were also able to write in the syllabary."[43] The continuity of Late Bronze Age social structures, whether originally indigenous or imported, allowed the courtly and temple settings to survive, in which professional

---

dialect preserved in Linear B; it simply belongs to the same subgroup (Bartoněk 2003: 463, 481–2; Householder and Nagy 1972: 58–62). What we can glean from the close relationship between Arcado-Cypriot and Linear B is that Arcado-Cypriot comes from the same region as the Bronze Age dialect that was the basis for the codified language we call Linear B. No special relationship between Arcado-Cypriot and the palatial culture of Late Bronze Age Greece can be assumed. Deger-Jalkotzy discounts the objection that Linear B may not reflect the state of the Greek language at the time it was being written (but see the Appendix, 462, here), and distinguishes between an earlier arrival of Mycenaeans in the post-palatial period and the later arrival of speakers of the Cypriot dialect (after LC III Middle). Voskos and Knapp (2008: 674–5) and Knapp (2008: 283–4, 288–90) caution against reading too much into this artifact, which does not indicate Greek hegemony in eleventh-century Cyprus.

[38] Iacovou (2006: 327, her references omitted).
[39] Iacovou (2006: 327–30). Mazarakis Ainian (2006) also considers the control *basileis* had over metal-working to be the root of their power. On the importance of iron-working in Cyprus, see V. Karageorghis (1994b: 5–6).
[40] The first attestation of the term in Cyprus dates to the seventh century (Iacovou 2006: 319).
[41] Palaima (2006b: 54).   [42] Olivier (2013: 16–19).
[43] Egetmeyer (2009: 80). The likely ancestor of the Cypriot syllabaries was Cypro-Minoan.

Eteocypriot, if not Greek, singers and priests could maintain a high level of performance.

Cultural continuity in Syro-Anatolia

North Syria and the southeastern part of Anatolia also show obvious evidence of cultural continuity, even as we see mixing with newly arrived populations, including people ultimately from Greece who maintained a relationship with Greek-speakers in Cyprus, providing opportunities for the exchange of information between Cilicia and Cyprus.[44] After the fall of the Mycenaean and Hittite empires in the early twelfth century, descendants of the Hittites and their Anatolian relatives continued to reside in northern Syria and southeastern and east central Anatolia, where monuments exhibit Hieroglyphic Luwian inscriptions and Neo-Hittite iconography. Some Hittite secundogenitures remained intact, in particular at the Neo-Hittite states of Malatya and Carchemish. J. D. Hawkins in fact suggests that the use of the title "Great King" by Kuzi-Teshshub (early to mid twelfth century BCE) of Carchemish, the son of Talmi-Teshshub, a direct descendant of Suppiluliuma I and Suppiluliuma II's viceroy, shows that he had elevated himself from vassal king to continuator of the Hittite empire after it had crumbled in Anatolia proper. The Iron Age kings of Malatya also claimed Kuzi-Teshshub as ancestor.[45] What had been the Hittite Lower Lands now fell between Phrygia to the northwest, and Que and Hilakku to the south. The region was divided up into a number of separate small kingdoms at first; they had developed into Tabal and Tyana by the time of Sargon II.[46] The title "Great King, Hero" continued to be used through the second half of the eighth century, suggesting that the first-millennium kings there considered themselves to be legitimate heirs of the Hittite empire, as at Carchemish.[47]

---

[44] On the continuation of the Neo-Hittite states, their role in northern Syria, and their eventual demise, see Jasink (1994) and Bryce (2012). On continuity and change across the end of the Bronze Age in Syro-Anatolia, see Harmanşah (2013: 15–71). On continuity and change in first-millennium Syro-Anatolian religious iconography, see Bonatz (2007b). On post-Hittite Anatolia generally, see Yakar (1993). On EIA Syria see the contributions in Bunnens (2000). Hawkins' (2000) comprehensive work on the Iron Age Hieroglyphic Luwian inscriptions provides valuable discussion of their context, with reference to his more detailed earlier discussions. Hawkins (2002) provides a convenient synopsis of his current views. Also see references in Chapter 1, 7, n. 19.

[45] Hawkins (1995a).   [46] See Bryce (2005: 353–4) and Hawkins (2000: 425–33).

[47] Hawkins (2000: 429–30). Also see Freu (2005).

Within Anatolia Luwian remained an important administrative language at Karatepe at the end of the eighth century BCE; at Tyana midway between the Kızıl Irmak and the south coast, with inscriptions dating to approximately 725 BCE; and at Kululu in Tabal, a site to the southeast of the bend of the Kızıl Irmak, which has yielded lead strips recording economic transactions in Hieroglyphic Luwian dated to the end of the eighth century BCE.[48] The economic records and letters on lead strips in Hieroglyphic Luwian from Kululu and Assur show that literacy in Hieroglyphic Luwian existed over a wide area and was current at least through the late eighth century, overlapping with alphabetic writing.[49] Meanwhile, Phoenicians were settling on the eastern part of the coast of Cilicia by the ninth century and possibly as early as the eleventh century, with a particularly strong presence at Tarsus beginning *ca.* 850 BCE.[50]

The inscriptional and iconographic evidence from eastern Anatolia and northern Syria after 1000 BCE reveals a multilingual, multicultural society of Phoenicians, Arameans, Assyrians, and Luwians. Bilingual Phoenician–Luwian inscriptions are found at İvriz and Karatepe, while at Tyana both Hieroglyphic Luwian and Phoenician are attested; at Aleppo inscriptions in both Hieroglyphic Luwian and Aramaic are found; Sam'al (modern Zincirli) mixed Neo-Hittite monumental sculpture with Phoenician and Aramaic inscriptions; and İncirli has provided a trilingual Hieroglyphic Luwian, Neo-Assyrian, and Phoenician inscription. Furthermore, in the ninth and eighth centuries BCE inscriptions in Aramaic appear at the behest of kings with Anatolian names. In fact, what the Greeks considered to be Phoenician culture overlaps to a large extent with what we call Neo-Hittite culture,[51] an amalgamation of west Semitic traits, already evident in the Late Bronze Age texts from Ugarit, and the remains of the Hurro-Hittite culture exemplified by the texts from the libraries of Hattusa, as conditioned by its north Syrian milieu.[52] This area was called Hatti by the

---

[48] Hawkins (2000: 17–22, 425–33).   [49] Hawkins (2000: 433).   [50] Lipiński (2004: 109–43).

[51] On the Greek use of "Phoenician" to designate residents of north Syria and eastern Turkey see Röllig (1992: 93–4).

[52] Carchemish has abundant attestations of Hieroglyphic Luwian. At Zincirli attestation of Hieroglyphic Luwian is confined to a single signet ring (Hawkins 2000: 20, 576; van Loon 1990: 1). On interactions among Arameans, Phoenicians, Assyrians, and Neo-Hittites, see Dalley (2000), Greenfield (1998), Ikeda (1984), Lipiński (2000), Nóvak (2005), and Röllig (2000). On Hurro-Hittite religious beliefs in Neo-Hittite states see Trémouille (2006). On the mutual influence of Aramaic and Neo-Hittite religion in northern Syria see Hutter (1996). On the mix of Phoenician and Hieroglyphic Luwian in inscriptions of southeast Anatolia and north Syria, starting in the ninth century, see Lipiński (1985) and Röllig (1992), who argues that Phoenician scribes could have transmitted Mesopotamian culture to eastern Anatolia.

Assyrians and is the home of the Hittites of the Hebrew Bible.[53] Hieroglyphic Luwian disappears from the record at the end of the eighth century, but Luwian names appear into the Achaemenid period (fourth century BCE). Thus, when the Euboeans traded at al-Mina in the eighth century,[54] they came into close contact with people whose culture was Neo-Hittite. One striking retention from the Bronze Age mentioned earlier is the story of the Storm-god fighting a sea-snake, as shown by the *ca.* ninth-century orthostat from Malatya depicting the combat (Fig. 11).

Cilicia is divided by the Lamus River into Rough and Plain Cilicia.[55] Rough Cilicia, called Hilakku by the Assyrians, corresponds to the New Kingdom Tarhuntassa (Luwian 'that of Tarhunt'). In the first quarter of the thirteenth century Muwattalli II had relocated the Hittite capital there; at that point the Hittites were focused squarely on the southeast as they fought with Egypt for north Syria.[56] His brother Hattusili III, after he usurped the throne from Muwattalli's son Mursili III/Urhi-Teshshub, installed his nephew, Mursili III's brother Kurunta (Ulmi-Teshshub), in Tarhuntassa as the king of a vassal state, returning the Hittite capital to Hattusa. But, apparently Kurunta styled himself a Great King, as did other descendants of Mursili III during and after the fall of the Hittite empire. In particular, a certain Hartapu, "son of Mursili, Great King," declares himself a Great King in inscriptions found on the border of Tarhuntassa and the later Tabal, as well as at Burunkaya, which is squarely in Tabal. However the political situation was viewed by the Hittite kings, it is clear that Rough Cilicia managed to separate itself from the Hittite empire as it crumbled, and it continued to function as a political entity after the empire collapsed, as did smaller administrative units in Tabal, providing some cultural continuity beyond the Late Bronze Age.[57]

---

[53] On the Neo-Assyrian use of the term "Hatti," see Chapter 1, 7, with n. 19.

[54] On al-Mina see Chapter 11, 300, n. 129.

[55] On Early Iron Age Cilicia, see Casabonne (2004a: 21–89), Desideri and Jasink (1990), Hawkins (2000: 38–45), Jasink and Bombardieri (2008), the articles collected in Jean, Dinçol, and Durugönül (2001), and Lane Fox (2009: 74–83).

[56] Bryce (2005: 230–3, 269–71) and Singer (2006a). The boundaries of Tarhuntassa are given in the *Bronze Tablet Treaty*: see Chapter 13, 334, n. 10.

[57] See Hawkins(1994) and van den Hout (2001), who suggest that Kurunta actually managed to take Hattusa for himself briefly, while Singer (1996) argues that Tarhuntassa had become a fully independent kingdom (but see the cogent objections of van den Hout 2001: 215–20). The dating of the relevant inscriptions of Hartapu, BURUNKAYA, KIZILDAĞ 1–3, and KARADAĞ 1–2, are disputed, since the Kızıldağ inscriptions look older than the accompanying image, which appears to be of eighth-century date. An earlier date makes him contemporary with Suppiluliuma II or directly after. Possibly there was a second rebellion that was quelled by Suppiluliuma (Jasink 2001c), or Tarhuntassa really had become another kingdom, as suggested

Plain Cilicia, to the east of Rough Cilicia across the Lamus River, was first called Adaniya and then Kizzuwatna by the Hittites and Adaniya (*ádny*) in Ugaritic.[58] At the end of the Middle Bronze Age Kizzuwatna was allied with the Hurrian Mitanni kingdom, but by the reign of Tudhaliya I/II it was fully incorporated into the Hittite kingdom.[59] An important area of cultural contact between Luwians, Hurrians, and Hittites in the Late Bronze Age, it controlled key routes inland across the Amanus and Taurus Mountains to the Anatolian plateau from the Mediterranean and north Syria, via the Cilician Gates, the Amanus Gates, and the Göksu, Seyhan, and Ceyhan Rivers.

There is much evidence for religious continuity in Plain Cilicia. As elsewhere in Anatolia, second-millennium deities survived, albeit in altered form. Most notably, the Storm-god continued to be worshipped at Corycus, the home of Zeus' enemy Typhon,[60] and the LAMMA-god Runzas was syncretized with Reshep, just as Reshep was syncretized with Apollo in Cyprus.[61]

LH IIIC:1b pottery and "Hellado-Cilician" or "'Cilician painted wares' of Cypriote type" appear in Cilicia after the collapse of the Hittite empire.[62]

---

by Singer. See Bryce (2005: 319–21, 351–3; 2012: 21–2, 28–30) and Hawkins (1992; 374: 429–30) for Kurunta as Great King of Tarhuntassa and Hartapu as a member of the line of Mursili III, van den Hout (2001) for Kurunta as (briefly) Great King of Hattusa. For the inscribed image of Hartapu, see Chapter 14, 374. For the continued functioning of smaller centers now free of Hittite hegemony in southern Cappadocia, see Mora and d'Alfonso (2012). This process of devolving to regional centers may be compared to the Post-Palatial period in Greece.

[58] On the Hittite terms for Plain Cilicia, see Hawkins (2000: 38–40); Ugaritic: Bordreuil and Pardee (2004).

[59] See Beal (1986), Desideri and Jasink (1990: 51–109), Freu (2001), Jasink (2001a), Trémouille (2001), and Yakar (2001) on the early history of Kizzuwatna. As Beal (1986: 426) shows, Adaniya was subject to the Hittites in the time of Hattusili I, since he was able to cross it safely in his campaigns into north Syria. Subsequently, "Adaniya seems to have successfully revolted and become the independent country of Kizzuwatna in the dark days of Ammuna." The information comes from the *Telipinu Proclamation*: CTH 19.II.A = KBo 3.1 ii 1–4 (translit. Hoffmann 1984: 26; trans. P. Goedegebuure in Chavalas 2006: 231).

[60] See Chapter 10, 255–6. For further discussion of religious continuity in Cilicia, see Lebrun (1992; 1998b; 2001).

[61] In KARATEPE 1 §XL, 212 (translit. and trans. Hawkins 2000: 53) Runzas (cf. Hittite Kurunta) corresponds to Phoenician Phu/A II, 10–11 (translit. and trans. W. Röllig in Çambel 1999: 52–3): Reshep *sprm* 'of Horned Animals(?)'. The epithet is so interpreted because the divinity is depicted standing on a gazelle (Lipiński 1995: 183–4, 187) or sometimes a stag (Cornelius 1994: 112–24). Karatepe provides the earliest attestation of Reshep in Phoenician (Lipiński 1995: 187). The LAMMA-god also was equated with Reshep by scribes in Ugarit (Barré 1978; Lipiński 1995: 179–80). See Kestemont (1986) on how second-millennium gods were reworked into their first-millennium counterparts at Karatepe.

[62] The first term comes from French (2013: 480–1), the second from Goldman (1963: 93).

The pottery appears especially at Tarsus,[63] which had been an important administrative center for the Hittites.[64] In addition, excavations have revealed late Mycenaean pottery also at Soli and Kazanlı,[65] and more excavation in Cilicia is likely to increase the number of sites with evidence of Aegean connections. Their implications have certainly been a matter of debate. While Christopher Mee took the late Mycenaean pottery at Tarsus as evidence of Greek settlement, the site's excavator, Hetty Goldman, focused on the evidence for complex interactions among multiple ethnic groups, pointing to the important role of Cyprus in mediating the interactions.[66] The pottery does indicate that at the end of the Bronze Age some people with Aegean connections settled in Cilicia. These people seem to have quickly assimilated Anatolian culture and lost any archaeologically visible traces of "Greekness."[67] They are often considered by modern scholars to be the Sea Peoples mentioned in Egyptian inscriptions as attacking the Near East from ships, who have been blamed for the fall of

---

[63] On the late Mycenaean pottery at Tarsus, besides the references below, see Yasur-Landau (2010: 160–1, 337) and Mommsen, Mountjoy and Özyar (2011), showing that the LH IIIC pottery is locally made and the Cypriot-style pottery is from Kouklia. See Vanschoonwinkel (1991: 321–2) for a nuanced discussion of the data, also Yakar (1993: 14–18). According to Strabo (14.5.12), Tarsus was founded by Argives led by Triptolemus, searching for Io. Nonnus *Dion.* 18.289–305 mentions Heracles as founder. Late sources tell us that Perseus was the founder of Tarsus, as opposed to Triptolemus or Heracles, but this was probably to establish a connection with the Persians when Tarsus was under Achaemenid rule. See Casabonne and Marcinkowski (2004: 155–61). According to Herodotus (6.54), in the fifth century the Persians explicitly rejected any kinship with the Greeks through Perseus, insisting that he was Assyrian.

[64] On Tarsus in the Hittite period, see Beal (1986: 424–5), Yakar (2001: 39–40), Lebrun (2001: 91–2).

[65] Soli has a pre-imperial phase and an imperial phase starting *ca.* 1400 BCE. Ceramics characteristic of Hittite centers have been found there, along with a bulla and sealing with Anatolian names in Hieroglyphic Luwian (Yağcı 2007). There is a small amount of LH IIIC pottery with Cypriot influence (Yağcı 2003). For the small amounts of late Mycenaean pottery at Kazanlı, see S. Sherratt and Crowel (1987), emphasizing relations with Cyprus. Jean (2003) emphasizes the possible evidence of destructions that could be connected to the advent of the Sea Peoples. Also see the recent survey by French (2013).

[66] Mee (1978: 150), Goldman (1963: 154–5). For other parallels among pottery and architecture at Tarsus, Cyprus, and Philistine settlements, see Kling (1984: 37–8) and Steel (2004a: 199). For a discussion of Greek and Cypriot influences in the area in the Early Iron Age, also see Jasink and Bombardieri (2008).

[67] However, some still argue that Greek-speakers did not settle in Cilicia at all at the end of the Bronze Age (Meyer 2011). In first-millennium Cilicia Luwian names are frequent, and some names might be of Hurrian origin. See Casabonne (2004b: 3), Goetze (1962), and Houwink ten Cate (1961: 190–2). There is no obvious evidence of Greek names among ordinary people, although Schmitz (2009a) attempts to analyze three personal names in a list from Tarsus tablet No. 7 (ca. 708–658 BCE) as Greek. It may be true that there was no effective colonization by Greeks, as also noted by Arslan (2003), but that does not mean that Greeks did not settle there (Gates 2010).

the Mycenaean palace culture and Ugarit, even the Hittite empire as a whole.[68] Certainly the Egyptians are referring to the archaeologically visible population movement of people with Aegean/Mycenaean traits into Cilicia and the Levant; those who settled in Syria and the Levant gave their name to the Philistines.[69]

Among the Sea Peoples were people called Ahhiyawans, a name used by the Hittites to refer to Mycenaeans they encountered in west Anatolia; the pharaoh Merneptah mentions the Aqajawasha (*'A-q3-3-jj-w3-3-š3-3*) as "the foreign people of the sea." It has been suggested that the Ahhiyawans moved east from what became Ionia, where Hittite documents show us Ahhiyawans were active, if not all the way from mainland Greece.[70] Inscriptions from eighth-century Cilicia show Ahhiyawans moved there. In a bilingual Hieroglyphic Luwian–Phoenician inscription at Çineköy a king Warikas describes himself as a descendant of Mopsus, and refers to his country with Phoenician ethnonym *dnnym*, which corresponds to Hieroglyphic Luwian *Hiyawanis* (*Hi-ya-wa/i*[-*ni*-]*sá*), derived from *Ahhiyawa* via "an irregular change in a borrowed word," as Ilya Yakubovich suggests.[71] In addition, in the late eighth-century bilingual inscription from Karatepe, 15 miles north of Çineköy and probably a bit later than the Çineköy

---

[68] See Killebrew (2005: 230).

[69] Killebrew (2005: 201–34), building on the work of earlier scholars, has shown that the Philistines were Aegean peoples with ties to Mycenaean culture. Yasur-Landau (2010: 114–20, 163) has argued the Sea Peoples would have more conveniently traveled overland across Cilicia through the Cilician Gates into the Levant. Also see the articles collected in Killebrew and Lehmann (2013).

[70] On the relations between the Ahhiyawans and Hittites, see Chapter 13. The Aqajawasha: *Libyan War Stele from Kom el-Ahmar (Menuf)*: KRI 4.4, §22 (trans. Kitchen 2003: 19); see Haider (1988: 49–50, 77), Lebrun and De Vos (2006: 49–50), and Jasink and Marino (2007: 410–11). Jasink and Marino believe that Late Bronze Age Ahhiyawa was in west Anatolia and the off-lying islands. They see the population movement as originating there, and not necessarily involving speakers of Greek. I agree that the Ahhiyawans who moved to Cilicia could have come from west Anatolia, but I think the evidence shows the dominant language spoken by them was Greek. For a discussion of Mycenaeans in Anatolia in the Late Bronze Age, see Chapter 13.

[71] Yakubovich (2010: 152, n. 93). Others have argued the loss of initial *a* was by regular Luwian aphaeresis. The aphaeresized form *Hiyawa* already appears in the second-millennium mentions of Ahhiyawans in two Akkadian letters at Ugarit (*Fragments of Akkadian Letters*: CTH 208 = RS 94.2530, from Suppiluliuma II to Ammurapi, and 94.2523, from Benti-Sharruma to Ammurapi, translit. and trans. Beckman, Bryce, and Cline 2011: 254–62). See Lackenbacher and Malbran-Labat (2005: 230–40) and Singer (2006b) for discussions of the content and significance of the letters. Many have attempted to separate Hiyawa from Ahhiyawa, arguing that it is a place in Anatolia already attested in the Late Bronze Age (e.g., Hajnal 2003: 35–8, 40–2; 2011; Lane Fox 2009: 218). See most recently Gander (2012: 282), who discusses the possibility of aphaeresis, then dismisses it; Oreshko (2013a) shows why it is an adequate explanation. On the supposed occurrence of ^{URU}*Hiyaw*[*a* in the MH *Annals of Arnuwanda I* (CTH 143.1.A = KUB 23.21

inscription, the Phoenician ethnonym, which is clearly based on the name of a city controlling Plain Cilicia, consistently corresponds to the Hieroglyphic Luwian ethnonym *Aḫiyawani-* and geonym *Aḫiyawa-*.[72] Warikas has been linked with the historical figure Urikki of Que, known from tribute lists from the reign of Tiglath-Pileser (738/7–728 BCE).[73] The Assyrian term Que must be derived from *Aḫḫiyawa/Ḫiyawa*.[74]

Iatnana, Danuna, and the House of Mopsus

The continued use of the term Hiyawa, although transferred to Cilicia, of itself strongly suggests some maintenance of an ethnic identity by the Aegean peoples who had settled there at the end of the Bronze Age. But, it is a complex question whether a shared identity among Greek-speakers could have served as a conduit of Cilician practices to Cyprus, which were subsequently passed farther west to Greece. The possibility is suggested by the fact that the Neo-Assyrian name for Cyprus is Iatnana 'island of Danuna',[75] while Danuna is a term that was applied to Plain Cilicia by

---

obv. 6′, ed. Carruba 2008: 66, with discussion), see Yakubovich (2010: 151–2, n. 92). I am unable to see the trace of any sign after the-*ya* in the photos posted on the Mainzer Photoarchiv (accessed via hethiter.net). As Oreshko points out, a placement of Hiyawa in Cilicia in the time of the letters makes little sense, because the letters discuss the fact that a Hiyawan is waiting in Lycia for a large shipment of metal ingots (so Singer 2006b) from Ugarit. A Cilician would have no need to wait next door in Lycia, while Mycenaeans clearly navigated along the coast of Lycia when engaged in the copper trade, cf. the Ulu Burun and Cape Gelidonya shipwrecks, both loaded with copper. See Bass (1967) and Pulak (1998; 2005). On the possibility of Mycenaeans aboard the Ulu Burun ship see especially Pulak (2005).

[72] E.g., HL KARATEPE 1 §II, 10, *á-*429-wa/i-ní-í-sá*(URBS); §III, 14, *á-*429-wa/i-ia*(URBS) (translit. Hawkins 2000: 49); Phoen. Ph/A I 2, 4, *dnnym*; geonym *'dn* (translit. W. Röllig in Çambel 1999: 50). I follow Oreshko (2013a), who offers a new interpretation of the Hieroglyphic Luwian sign *429, which appears in the word *a-*429-wa* at Karatepe, corresponding to the Phoenician *'dn*, and has been assumed to represent /dana/ to bring the Luwian word into alignment with the Phoenician: *a-tana-wa*. Oreshko argues that it is more plausible to assume that the sign in question represents /hiya/. The sequence /dana/ or /tana/ is normally spelled *ta-na*, and it is more reasonable to assume that the geonym is the same as that attested in the Hieroglyphic Luwian version of the Çineköy inscription: *Ḫiyawa* (there spelled *ḫi-ya-wa/i-*).

[73] No. 11.8′, No. 14.11, No. 27.4, No. 32.3, No. 35 iii 8 ("Iran Stele") No. 47 rev. 7′ (clay tablet with "Summary Inscription") (transcript. and trans. Tadmor and Yamada 2011: 38, 46–7, 70, 77, 87, 122). For discussions of the dating and various views on political context of the Çineköy and Karatepe inscriptions see Bryce (2003a: 104), Hawkins (2000: 44–5), Lanfranchi (2005; 2007; 2009), and Gander (2012: 294–7), the last arguing for dating Karatepe before Çineköy.

[74] Lebrun and de Vos (2006: 47–50).

[75] Knapp (2008: 343–4), Saporetti (1976: 88). The term was used by Sargon II and Esarhaddon.

the late eighth century. There is some support from Greek legends about settlement in Cilicia and stories about the Danaids. But, before we discuss these, we must address how to interpret the terms Adana and Danuna, both of which could be connected to the Greek ethnonym *Danaoi*. This has been a problem that has exercised many a scholar over the years and is tangled up with the question of the significance of the Greek colonizing hero Mopsus.

Rostislav Oreshko has recently proposed a new perspective on the problem, which results from his realization that in the Hieroglyphic Luwian version of the Karatepe inscription, which dates to some time between the mid eighth century and the early seventh century BCE,[76] the reading of Adanawa is spurious. He thus keeps distinct the Adana/Adaniya originating in Cilicia, and the T/Dan-originating in Greece. When discussing the terms, Oreshko, careful to separate geonyms from ethnonyms, argues that the Phoenician ethnonym *dnnym* should not be conflated with the Phoenician and Hieroglyphic Luwian geonyms ʾ*dn* and *Adana*. He argues that the Phoenician ethnonym *dnnym* should be linked to the Egyptian term *d3-jnjw-n3* /danunə/, /danonə/, included by Ramses III in the alliance of his enemy, the Sea Peoples.[77] In turn *d3-jnjw-n3* should be connected to the Egyptian term Tanaya, which was applied to parts of mainland Greece.[78] This term is clearly connected to the Homeric *Danaoi*.

---

[76] The dating of the material from Karatepe is not as clear as one would like. The paleography of the Phoenician inscriptions place it between the second half of the eighth century and the beginning of the seventh century (Röllig in Çambel 1999: 79), and the sign values of the Hieroglyphic inscriptions are consistent with such a date (Hawkins 2000: 44).

[77] Danuna: *D3-jnjw-n3*, e.g., *Campaign against the Sea Peoples: Medinet Habu, Pylon II Presentation Scene* (*KRI* 5.8) §37.1 (trans. Kitchen 2008: 31). Of the four attestations in the inscriptions of Ramses III, the short form Danu appears in *Sea People's Campaign, Medinet Habu: Great Inscription of Year 8* (*KRI* 5.9) §40 (trans. Kitchen 2008: 34). See Oreshko (unpublished). The term Danuna that appears in an Akkadian letter in Amarna (*EA* 151.49–55, trans. Moran 1992: 238) cannot refer to Cilicia, because it has a king (Forlanini 2005: 111–12; Oreshko unpublished). Hawkins (2000: 39, n. 19) and Jasink (2001a: 53–4) rightly disagree with the view represented by Forlanini (2005: 111–14) that this Danuna was in Syria, but the issue of the king, whom the letter speaks of as dead and succeeded by a son, cannot be explained away. Danuna appears in an Akkadian letter at Hattusa, unfortunately in a fragmentary context (*Fragments of Akkadian Historical Texts: CTH* 216 = *KBo* 28.25 rev. 7ʺ translit. and trans. Edel 1994: 84–5, No. 31). KhT considers *KBo* 28.24 to be indirectly joined to *KBo* 28.25 (translit. and trans. Edel 1994: 80–5, No. 30), but Oreshko discounts the join.

[78] The annals of Thutmose I (1504–1492 BCE) record gifts brought by an envoy from a land *tj-n3-jj-w* 'Tanaya' across the "great green," or Mediterranean Sea, including a silver jug made in the Keftiu (Cretan) style. Kelder (2010: 36); see Cline (1994: 114–16) for citations. The place names grouped under *tj-n3-jj-w* in a list, either describing envoys from Greece or a voyage in the Aegean, at Kom el Hetan, the mortuary temple of Amenhotep III, indicate that it referred to a large part of the Peloponnese and Cythera. See Edel and Görg (2005: 167–213) for discussion;

The similarities between the two terms Danuna/Danaoi and Adana could have encouraged a sense of connection between the two groups of people, one the Ahhiyawans in Greece or west Anatolia, the other Ahhiyawans based in Cilicia. In addition, it is now possible to explain the mythical movements of king Danaus and his fifty daughters, descendants of the Argive cow-maiden Io, who supposedly returned to Argos from Egypt (one branch in her many-limbed family tree that connected Greece to the rest of the eastern Mediterranean), as refracting knowledge of a relationship between Greeks on the Greek mainland and in diaspora.[79]

Greek legend also preserved traces of this move in the myth of the seer Mopsus.[80] The first datable mention of the Anatolian Mopsus in Greek is by Callinus of Ephesus (fl. *ca.* 650 BCE) via Strabo (14.4.3) who indirectly mentions the competition between Calchas and Mopsus at Clarus and Mopsus' subsequent colonizing activities in eastern Anatolia and Syria. Strabo (14.5.16) later states that Mopsus founded Mallus in Cilicia with the seer Amphilochus, then killed him in a duel.

King Warikas' name has been identified as Greek *Rhakios* (<*Wrakios*), the father of Mopsus in most versions of his myth.[81] As for Mopsus, the name is attested both in Linear B documents (*mo-qo-so*) and in the Middle Hittite *Madduwatta Indictment* (*Muksus*), unfortunately in a fragmentary context.[82] The former shows that Mopsus was a name used by Mycenaeans

---

Cline and Stannish (2011), Kelder (2010: 37–9), Kitchen (2007: 9–10). Kelder does not attempt to address the significance of the similar term in Amenhotep's list of Sea Peoples. The two terms differ in that the term *d3-jnjw-n3* is extended with the suffix *-nā*, which is found in other Greek geonyms, apparently feminine adjectives used elliptically (e.g., with an understood *gē* or *polis*, such as *Mukēnē*; see Oreshko unpublished). One can explain the difference by transmission through different linguistic intermediaries for the two terms, but what exactly the intermediary language was remains unclear.

[79] On whom, see Chapter 9, 215. According to Apollodorus (*Bib.* 3.1.1), the brother of Io's descendant Europa, Cilix, settled in Cilicia after giving up on his search for his sister who had been abducted by Zeus, while Europa's other brother Phoenix settled in Phoenicia. On the settlement of Tarsus by Argives in search of Io, see n. 63.

[80] For more on Mopsus, see Chapter 14, 382–6, 392–3. Before the publication of the Çineköy inscription with its explicit mention of Hiyawa many doubted that a grain of truth lay behind the myth of Mopsus (Burkert 1992: 52–3; Scheer 1993: 153–272; Vanschoonwinkel 1990; 1991: 314–30). Scholarship after its publication is more willing to accept there is some fact behind it (Casabonne 2004a: 74–7; Finkelberg 2005: 150–60; Lemaire 2006; López-Ruiz 2009; 2010: 38–43, Oettinger 2008).

[81] Rhacius is mentioned in the *Epigonoi* F 4 West and competes with Apollo as the father of Mopsus in various legends (Apollo as father of Mopsus: Apoll. *Epit.* 6.2–4, drawing on the *Nostoi*; Strabo 14.5.16). See Forlanini (1996a) and Jasink and Marino (2007: 408–9) on Rhacius/Warikas.

[82] KN De 1381.B, PY Sa 774; *CTH* 147 = *KUB* 14.1 rev. 75 (translit. and trans. Beckman, Bryce, and Cline 2011: 94–5).

(although the name cannot be given a Greek etymology), the latter supports a direct connection between the people active in Late Bronze Age western Anatolia and those that settled in Cilicia.[83] The connection was maintained by the continued use of the dynastic name Mopsus and was refracted in the myths that Mopsus migrated from Clarus to Cilicia.

Let us return now to the significance of the Assyrian term Iatnana referring to Cyprus. The Semites lumped together a variety of people from Cyprus and the lands west of Syria under the rubric of "Ionian," but there is no reason to assume they used it to refer exclusively to Greek-speakers.[84] A similarly vague designation could explain the broad use of Danuna in Neo-Assyrian texts. The term might refer to people who were once connected with Cilicia but not necessarily descended from Greek-speakers, or it could show that the Greek-speaking community at one point extended from Cilicia to Cyprus. The first analysis is supported by the general Cypriot influence on Early Iron Age pottery in Cilicia,[85] the latter analysis is supported by the Cypriot influence specifically on the LH IIIC1:b pottery found in Cilicia. If either of these two alternatives is true, that suggests a flow of people between Cilicia and Cyprus and a desire for a shared identity that would have facilitated the transfer of Cilician-style performances and regional Cilician motifs in the worship of gods that fit common divine archetypes, like Apollo/LAMMA, the Storm-god, or the goddess of sexuality. Although in the end the Greek-speakers were fully assimilated in Cilicia, even a narrow window of time in which this shared identity existed would have been sufficient to transmit storylines found at Hattusa to Greek-speakers in Cyprus.

In Cyprus, the continuity in specific sites led to syncretisms with the original divinities associated with them, allowing for the preservation and reworking of their narratives, precursors to the Homeric Hymns, which were likely performed in festival settings. For example, Kourion was a home of Apollo, who, as noted earlier, was syncretized with the west Semitic god Reshep, even as a fourth-century statue from Tamassos proclaimed some continuity of memory back to the Bronze Age with the epithet Apollo Alasiotas, i.e., Apollo of Alashiya.[86] Meanwhile, the Cypriot

---

[83] As noted by Tekoğlu and Lemaire (2000: 983–4).

[84] The terms *Yawan* and *Yaw(a)naya* are so used by the Assyrians, especially Sargon II. See Casabonne (2004b), Kuhrt (2002), Rollinger (1997; 2007).

[85] See, for example, at Sirkeli, Kilise Tepe, Mersin, Kinet Höyük (Ahrens *et al.* 2008, with further references).

[86] Reshep *'althyts* = Apollo *a-la-si-o-ta-i*: the Phoenician portion of the bilingual inscription is translated by N. Walls in Knapp (1996: 60), and the Greek by O. Masson (1983: 226–8).

horned Apollo might be compared to the Phoenician Reshep *ṣprm* 'of Horned Animals(?)' at Karatepe, who represents the Luwian LAMMA-god Runzas.[87]

Finally, in Cyprus, Salamis was the home of a Zeus with similarities to the Syro-Anatolian Storm-god,[88] and Philip Schmitz has argued that the Storm-god at Karatepe had a Greek epithet, *korunētērios* (Phoen. *krntryš*) from Greek *korunē* 'mace', cf. *korunētēs* ('mace-warrior') used by Homer (*Il.* 7.9, 138).[89] Schmitz points out that one type of Neo-Hittite depiction of the Storm-god of Aleppo (later tenth century BCE) shows him carrying, not the thunderbolt, but a mace. The mace (Hitt. ^{GIŠ}*ḫattala*) was also a characteristic attribute of Teshshub of Aleppo in the second millennium at Hattusa and extends back to the third millennium elsewhere. At Yazılıkaya Teshshub is depicted carrying his mace (Fig. 6); he stands on his bull facing Hebat on her feline.[90] If we accept the etymology, the use of the term indicates that Greek-speakers were well established in Cilicia and well assimilated to local religious practices involving the Storm-god.[91] The

---

[87] As Röllig (2011: 127) notes; see above with n. 61, and on the Cypriot horned Apollo, see Chapter 10, 249.

[88] Yon (1980). Bulls, the animal associated with the Storm-god, remained important in Cypriot cult in the period after the collapse of the Near Eastern states (LC III) (Steel 2004a: 204).

[89] *krntryš*: Phu/A II 19, III 2-3, 4; Pho/B 6, 8; PhSt/C III 16, 17, 19. The fact that the Hieroglyphic Luwian version of the passage in question does not include the epithet indicates that the conception could have been confined to the Greek-speakers (or Phoenicians, if we assume that Phoenician was commonly spoken there), another sign that some Greek-speakers maintained a level of independence in their traditions after settling in Cilicia.

[90] Schmitz (2009b: 129–31). In fact, at Aleppo the epigraph DEUS.MATTEA should either be read "Divine Mace" (so Hawkins 2011b: 40) or, as I would suggest, "God of the Mace." See picture in Gonnella, Khayatta, and Kohlmeyer (2005: 99, fig. 138). See Bunnens (2006: 60–1, 79) and Chapter 10, 257, on the mace of the Storm-god of Aleppo; at Hattusa, see Popko (1998) and Archi (2009: 220.) The competing interpretation of *krntryš*, by K. L. Younger (2009), builds on a suggestion of Lipiński (1995: 239–40). He connects the *bʿl kr* (Baal *kr*) of the Phoenician Cebelıreis Dağ inscription on the western edge of Rough Cilicia, mentioning a king named Wariyka (*wryk*) as a patron (ca. 625–600 BCE, ed. and trans. Mosca and Russell 1987), to the ^{d}*Ku-ra* attested at Ebla and the Kur(r)a found in the first millennium in cuneiform texts, as well as in west Semitic names, whom Lipiński considers to be a god of agriculture and the harvest. There is then no satisfactory suggestion for *ntryš*. Röllig (2011: 127–8) admits the Greek etymology is appealing, and that the statue of the Storm-god at Karatepe could have held a mace, but finds K. L. Younger more persuasive.

[91] In addition, the Phoenician-style nursing goddess in a Greek-style chiton, next to a palm tree, an image with roots in Egyptian iconography (Röllig 2011: 127), is easily associated with the Greek myth of the goddess Leto giving birth to Apollo, clinging to a palm tree on Delos. Also cf. the palm tree in the iconography of Artemis of Ephesus (S. P. Morris 2001b: 145, Fig. 7). She could be a goddess derived from the second-millennium Luwian goddess *anniš maššanaššiš*, who was syncretized with Leto in fourth-century Lycia. Cf. the Lycian goddess *ēni mahanahi* 'mother of the gods'. Discussion in Bryce (1983).

story of Zeus and Typhon, with its connections to Cilicia and north Syria, could have been told in the cult of Zeus at Salamis, and it may be that the story of his son's feat of slaying the Python also comes from a story that spread from Cyprus to the rest of Greece, although it is not impossible that it arrived in Greece directly from Cilicia.[92]

Contact between Greece and Cyprus in the Early Iron Age

In the eleventh and tenth centuries BCE, Cyprus and Euboea represented the two poles on either end of the Greek-speaking eastern Mediterranean, with convenient stopping points in Rhodes and Knossos,[93] and the Levant representing the exotic east. Intense competitive emulation, both the cause and the result of similar social conditions and contact, explains similarities among the artifacts and practices attached to elite warrior graves in Lefkandi, Knossos, and Cyprus at this period, whose occupants were cremated and which contained many antique and imported goods.[94] The shared values and practices were conducive to the spread of epic throughout the area via long-distance elite interactions articulated through guest–host relations involving occasions at which epic was performed. Furthermore, in this period Cypriots gained the upper hand in their relations with the mainland. As Jan Crielaard points out with regard to the shared elite culture, "considering the Cypriot origin of a number of prestige goods in the Greek warrior tombs and the earlier use of iron in Cyprus, it seems that local Cypriot élites were dominant in these relationships and may have even acted as role models for the emergent aristocracies in Greece."[95] Thus, we have a situation in which an Early Iron Age Cypriot elite, some portion of which spoke Greek, could have been instrumental in transmitting originally Near Eastern practices to their Greek-speaking brethren back in Greece.

---

[92] As suggested in Chapter 10, 256.
[93] See A. Sherratt and S. Sherratt (1991: 357–8) on how the trade route was shaped by geography and wind patterns.
[94] On relations between Cyprus and Lefkandi on the one hand and Knossos on the other see Coldstream (1998: 7–14), Mazarakis Ainian (2006: 194–5); on ancient Cypriot items in the burials at Knossos, with comparisons to Homer, see H. W. Catling (1984: 86–91), Coldstream (1989a). On such burials in eleventh- to tenth-century Cyprus and their relations with Crete and Euboea, see Crielaard (1998: 187–91), V. Karageorghis (2003: 340–3).
[95] Crielaard (1998: 191).

The conduit of information and objects was surely kept open in part because of a feeling of shared heritage among Greek-speakers, even as Cypriot Greeks were able to use their contacts with exotic locales farther east to their advantage. The maintenance of their Hellenic identity, at least in a qualified form, is manifested at the level of language by the lack of influence either from the Eteocypriot language(s) or from Phoenician.[96] It was expressed at the mythical level by foundation myths claiming that Greek heroes after the Trojan War had founded Paphos, Salamis, Idalion, and Cypriot Soli.[97] Although the legends are not attested until the fifth century or later, well after "Homer," and therefore cannot safely be taken into account in our analysis of how perceptions of ethnicity shaped the narrative tradition Homer inherited about the Trojan War, it is precisely in those areas, as Iacovou points out, that Greek was used as an administrative language, as opposed to the use of Phoenician at Kition.[98]

Finally, the "Homeric" burials in Cyprus show an interest in the culture we find in epic: cremation, horse sacrifice, chariots, accoutrements of the warrior and of feasting and drinking. The valuable contents also show an interest in the exotic, with items from Assyria, Egypt, Anatolia, and Phoenicia. The earliest burials come from Salamis, starting in the eighth century and extending through the seventh;[99] thus, they are too late for the kind of formative influence on Homer we are looking for. However, they support the claim that Cyprus could have had its own tradition of epic, competing and combining with Homer's, that is now lost to us.[100]

---

[96] Iacovou (2006: 322).

[97] On Greek foundation legends of Cyprus, see Vanschoonwinkel (1991: 293–312).

[98] Iacovou (2006: 322), pace S. Sherratt (2003b: 234–7), who argues against the notion of a shared Greek identity. Most of the names of the ten regional kings of Iatnana whom Esarhaddon (680–669 BCE) boasts of conquering can be interpreted as Greek (No. 1, v 63–71, translit. and trans. Leichty 2011: 23, = Nineveh A); see Lipiński (1991) with corrections of Radner (2010: 436).

[99] Beer (1984), Karageorghis (2003: 347–8). The Cypriot burial ground in Skales contains unusually late examples of Mycenaean-style chamber tombs with *dromoi* (Coldstream 1989b). On Skales also see Knapp (2008: 289–90), assuming a Greek identity.

[100] It is less likely that Phoenician poets transferred motifs and plot lines found in hexametric poetry directly to the Greek mainland or Crete at the beginning of the Iron Age, for there are almost no Phoenician colonies in the Aegean through the Archaic period, a fact working against M. L. West's (1988: 171) suggestion that "bilingual poets, probably easterners ... had settled in Greece and learned to compose epic in the Greek manner." See Lipiński (2004: 145–88) on Phoenician colonization in Greek territory. The earliest was in Crete at Kommos at the end of the tenth century, where there appears to have been established a Phoenician-style shrine for Ashtarte/Aphrodite (Lipiński 2004: 180; S. P. Morris 1992a: 155). Temple B (800–600 BCE) is the one with the three pillars in the style of a Phoenician temple (J. W. Shaw in J. W. and M. C. Shaw 2000: 20–1). Temple A (1020–800 BCE) is a small shrine

Cypriot epics about Aphrodite?

Cyprus was probably the avenue of transmission for the specific parallels between Greek and Near Eastern epic involving Aphrodite. The Greek Aphrodite began to develop into the form in which we know her on Early Iron Age Cyprus, when Greek-speaking migrants to Cyprus at the end of the Late Bronze Age came into contact with a goddess at Paphos.[101] The goddess of sexuality brought by the Greeks would have been an amalgamation of an Indo-European and an indigenous Greek goddess.[102] The Cypriot goddess she was syncretized with had already been blended with a Near Eastern goddess of sexuality, possibly a local version of Ishtar (or Ishhara) from Alalakh.[103] The later Greeks were well aware of Aphrodite's

---

underneath. I follow the dating of J. W. Shaw in J. W. and M. C. Shaw (2000: 1, 8–9, 14). On the putative temple for Ashtarte on Cythera as lying behind her epithet Cythereia, see M. L. West (1997a: 56–7). Budin (2003: 69–72) is skeptical of arguments for a Phoenician presence, and Lipiński (2004: 177) does not believe the legends concerning the early foundation of a temple for Aphrodite at Cythera by Phoenicians (Hdt. 1.105, Paus. 3.21.1), which are followed by S. P. Morris (1992a: 135). Breitenberger (2007: 8–13) accepts that Phoenicians established Ashtarte's cult on Cythera. On her epithet *Kuthereia*, see n. 110 below.

[101] See Budin (2003) for a study of the origin of Aphrodite that is well-informed on the Cypriot and Syrian archaeological evidence; also Budin (2002), J. and V. Karageorghis (2002), Serwint (2002), and Webb (2003). Penglase (1994: 159–79) discusses the Near Eastern origin of Aphrodite and Near Eastern elements in the *Homeric Hymn to Aphrodite*.

[102] Aphrodite's connection with the Indo-European Dawn-goddess is indicated by the parallel myths of Eos ('dawn') and Aphrodite seizing human lovers and the descriptions of the Vedic dawn goddess Ushas as a beautiful and smilingly seductive young woman that match those of Aphrodite (Nagy 1990a: 223–62; also see Janda 2005: 331–4), while the association between Aphrodite and birds (Pirenne-Delforge 1994: 415–17) can be traced back to pre-Mycenaean Greece. The connection between birds and sexuality is obvious in Neolithic statuettes from Europe (Gimbutas 1982: 112–50; 1991: 230–6), and the Minoan "Dove Goddess" seems to draw on this association. See most recently Moss (2005: 62–3, with earlier references). On evidence for dove-goddesses or bird-goddesses see further Moss (2005: 153–4, 158, 195–6) and Marinatos (1993: 156). On the association of Shawushka of Nineveh with doves (Hurr. *zinzapu*), see Beckman (1998: 6), Haas (1979: 400), and Wegner (1995: 16). On the syncretism of Ishtar with Shawushka and Anatolian Anzili, see Chapter 2, 26.

[103] The closest comparanda to the LC II (1450–1200 BCE) bird-faced figurines are found in Alalakh, where contact with Cyprus is indicated by an abundance of wine service items from Cyprus in Alalakh VI and V (sixteenth–early fifteenth century BCE according to the preliminary dating of Mullins 2010: 61–3). On the LC II figurines, see Budin (2003: 141–3). On Alalakh see Budin (2003: 202–6), arguing that the IŠTAR of Level VII was Ishhara, relying on Prechel (1996: 41–4, 68–70). (Also see Chapter 5, 115, n. 10.) The goddess is more explicitly attested in the texts from Level IV. On Cypriot ceramics starting in Level VI, see Kozal (2010), and on the Cypriot ware at Alalakh see Bergoffen (2005). On contact between Alashiya and Alalakh IV see Knapp (2008: 307–8, 318–19). Two Alalakh VII ration texts mention a man from Alashiya (see Zeeb 2001: 69). According to Budin (2004) the identification of Aphrodite with Ashtarte only occurred on Cyprus after the Phoenicians established themselves there (ninth century), building a temple for Ashtarte in Kition. By then she had become "Queen of Heaven,"

supralocal character, Sappho invoking her in the late seventh century to come to Lesbos from her homes in Crete, Cyprus, Cnidos, Palermo, and Syria.[104]

Palaepaphos, a site with strong continuity, has a particularly old temple of Aphrodite that can be traced back to the Late Bronze Age, when it was of the Near Eastern type, an open court with a small *adyton*.[105] In the temple was an imported baetyl stone, typical of Syro-Anatolian cult practice, as reported by Tacitus (*Hist.* 2.3).[106] According to the Roman historian, "ancient memory" (*vetus memoria*) tells that Paphos was founded by a certain king Aërias; the more recent story says the temple was consecrated by Cinyras, and the goddess arrived there after being born from the sea. The Cinyrades were her priests, and the king of Paphos was a priest-king in the Near Eastern mold, although whether this was a holdover from the Late Bronze age or an innovation brought by the Phoenicians we cannot say.[107] Yet another tradition names the Argive Agapenor as the founder of Paphos. Pausanias (8.5.2) says that he founded the city and Aphrodite's temple after being diverted on his return from Troy by a storm. Before that, he says, she was worshipped by the natives at Cypriot Golgoi.[108] If we are willing to push back into the ninth century the competing claims between separate ethnic groups about a shared legendary past, then we can suggest that they were instantiated in competing epics in Greek, Eteocypriot, and/or Phoenician deploying the figure of Aphrodite.

More than one scholar has suggested there was a (Greek) Cypriot tradition of epic, possibly with a particular emphasis on Aphrodite, and they have noted clear Near Eastern influence on the scenes that would belong to this putative tradition.[109] The hypothesis is all the more believable when we recall that Cinyras' name comes from the west Semitic word for lyre, an instrument that was divinized at Ugarit. He was not only the founder of her temple at Paphos, but also her lover and the father of

---

matching Aphrodite's epithet *Ouraniā*. Indeed, Herodotus (1.105.2–3) mentions a temple of "Heavenly Aphrodite" in Ashkelon as the oldest of the goddess' shrines. According to him, "the shrine in Cyprus is from there, as the Cypriots themselves say, and the Phoenicians who founded the one in Cythera were from this part of Syria."

[104] Sappho FF 2, 35 Lobel-Page, T 47 (ed. and trans. D. A. Campbell 1987: 40–1) = Men. Rh. 334.31–2 Spengel.
[105] V. Karageorghis (1983: 370) and Maier (1999). On the long history of worship of a goddess at Paphos see J. and V. Karageorghis (2002).
[106] Webb (2003: 18), J. and V. Karageorghis (2002: 274). On baetyls as a Syro-Anatolian cult item, see Chapter 10, 242, with n. 114.
[107] Maier (1989). [108] See J. and V. Karageorghis (2002: 273–4). [109] Richardson (1989).

Adonis.[110] Thus, the figure of Aphrodite, like that of Zeus and Apollo, can be cited as a vector for transmission of Near Eastern epic traditions to the Greeks via Cyprus. There are three examples that are brought forward: the fight between Aphrodite and Diomedes in the *Iliad*, the opening lines of the *Cypria*, and dressing scenes involving Aphrodite. This last example, when more closely examined, offers a chance to trace a complex path of transfer and reworking of a Near Eastern narrative motif that includes Lesbos and the Troad.

The fight in *Iliad* 5 between Diomedes and Aphrodite, who is referred to in Homer here and only here as Cypris, is the best example of a Near-Eastern-derived epic episode attached to Aphrodite in the Homeric tradition. It has obvious links with both Anat's fight with Danel and Ishtar's with Gilgamesh. In Tablet VI of the Standard Babylonian version of the *Epic of Gilgamesh*, Ishtar takes notice of the hero after his great victory against Huwawa, the guardian of the Cedar Forest, and she propositions him. He insultingly spurns her, reciting a litany of the men she has seduced and destroyed, and she rushes back to heaven and demands that she be avenged from her father An ('Heaven') and mother Antu ('Mrs. Heaven'), who allow her to loose the Bull of Heaven on Gilgamesh's land.[111] The episode, apparently very popular, was transferred to Anat in Ugaritic epic and reshaped to conform to the personality of the impetuous young goddess of war and hunting. When the hero Aqhat refuses her demand for his bow, she rushes to her father El ('God') and threatens to bash his head in if he does not get the bow for her.[112] In Greek epic, the episode became even more embarrassing for Aphrodite, most of whose instantiations had lost Ishtar's privilege of governing the violent passions of war. When insulted by a mortal, no threats or retribution for her. After Aphrodite confronts Diomedes who is menacing her son Aeneas on the

---

[110] On Cinyras in Homeric sources, see M. L. West (1997a: 628–9). He becomes the father of Adonis in later sources (Ov. *Met.* 10.270–502, Apollod. *Bib.* 3.18.2). Cinyras was partially syncretized with the west Semitic craftsman god Kothar, still kept separate at Ugarit, whose name lies behind the Greek term *kitharis/kitharā* 'lyre' (Franklin 2006; forthcoming). In fact, Aphrodite's epithet *Kuthereia* is best explained as built off of Kothar's name, "She of Kothar," or Kothar's consort. Later, as is typical of the Greeks, the epithet is given a geographical meaning, and is associated with her flourishing cult on the island of *Kuthēra* to express the Greek understanding of the relationship between local and supralocal manifestations of the goddess of sexuality (M. L. West 1997a: 56–7).

[111] The sequence is substantially unchanged from the Sumerian lay *Gilgamesh and the Bull of Heaven* (trans. ETCSL t.1.8.1.2).

[112] *Aqhat*: KTU 1.17 vi 8–1.19 i 19, trans. N. Wyatt (2002: 271–94), and see his discussion at pp. 275–6, n. 116, with earlier references. On Anat see Selz (2000: 35–7).

battlefield, the hero insults and wounds her, sending her crying back to Zeus ('Sky') and Dione ('Mrs. Sky'), while Athena and Hera laugh at her, and Zeus gently scolds, "Not to you, my child, have been given the deeds of war, but, you, follow after the lovely deeds of marriage; all these things will be a concern for rushing Ares and Athena" (5.428–30). The poet thus draws attention to the change in her personality and the transfer of her powers to Athena and Ares.

The parallels among these three passages from the *Epic of Gilgamesh*, the *Iliad*, and the Ugaritic *Aqhat* have long been discussed, but primarily as a literary phenomenon, the product of poets.[113] The scene of Aphrodite complaining to her parents while Athena and Hera laugh at her was one of the Iliadic scenes with Near Eastern parallels about which Martin West claimed, "There is a freshness and vividness about all this as it appears in the *Iliad* which suggests that it is comparatively modern material"; "we must surely postulate poets educated in the Levant who subsequently became Hellenized and practiced in Greece."[114] It is of course dangerous to apply our own standards to Homeric poetry in order to make an argument for the late date of transmission of the motif in question. And, on analogy with my scenario for transmission from Hurrian to Hittite for narrative song, I would slightly reframe West's last statement to say that one or more bilingual poets able to perform in the formulary systems of the poetic language of both Greek and Eteocypriot or Phoenician, or perhaps another Near Eastern language, were responsible for the transfer.

In addition, some scholars have suggested that we can see evidence for a local Cypriot epic tradition in the lost *Cypria*, which contains at least one Near-Eastern-derived motif.[115] Our primary source for the epic is a summary by Proclus from his *Chrestomathy*.[116] Its authorship was disputed, but one claimant was Stasinus of Cyprus, who was sometimes considered to be the son-in-law of Homer.[117] According to Proclus' summary, it told of the origin of the Trojan War, which included how Aphrodite bribed Paris to choose her as the most beautiful of the goddesses, promising him

---

[113] Burkert (1992: 96–9), M. L. West (1997a: 361–2). [114] M. L. West (1988: 170, 171).
[115] Burkert (1992: 100–4; 2004: 37–40), focusing on Cyprus "under Assyrian sovereignty," M. L. West (1997a: 480–2).
[116] Provided in M. L. West (2003: 66–81). See Burgess (2001: 17).
[117] See the testimonia collected in M. L. West (2003: 64–7). Herodotus (1.117) denied Homer's authorship, showing that in the fifth century the *Cypria* was attributed to Homer, but already disputed. Athenaeus cites Stasinus, "or whatever his name," as the author (8.334b), but later mentions either Hegesias or Stasinus (15.682e).

Helen.[118] It opened with a blatantly Near Eastern motif, quoted in the opening of this chapter, the relief of earth's suffering by reducing the human population, which is found in *Atrahasis*.[119] While the *Cypria* itself must have come into being after the master narrative of the Trojan War had become the framework to which all early Greek history had to be attached, it is not impossible that it contained elements that drew on local Cypriot myths, which had been given new life by being attached to the Trojan War.

The final scene from hexametric poetry involving Aphrodite that has a Near Eastern parallel is the dressing type scene found in the *Cypria*, the *Homeric Hymn to Aphrodite*, and the *Iliad*. It seems, at least, to appear in the *Cypria*. Athenaeus (682df) quotes a passage from the *Cypria* describing Aphrodite being dressed in clothing made by the Graces and the Seasons (*Hōrai*), which are scented with all manner of flowers (F 5 West). Then, her divine attendants ornament themselves with garlands and perform in a chorus with "smile-loving," "golden" Aphrodite "on the many-streamed mountain Ida" (F 6 West), which is where the action of the *Homeric Hymn to Aphrodite* takes place.[120]

The *Hymn to Aphrodite*, which tells in some detail the conception of Aeneas, also contains such a scene.[121] Struck with desire for Anchises at Zeus' instigation, the goddess goes to Paphos to be dressed and don her golden ornaments, then hurries back to Troy and Mt. Ida (58–69). In the *Iliad* (14.153–15.219) the episode in which Hera seduces Zeus also occurs on Mt. Ida. Hera's dressing has clear parallels with the type scene in the *Hymn to Aphrodite*, and then she asks Aphrodite for her magical girdle (14.166–221).[122] All these scenes parallel Sumerian descriptions of how Inanna is dressed when she goes to meet her bridegroom.[123] The Homeric hymn shows the most details of the Mesopotamian traditions about Ishtar/Inanna: besides the elaborate dressing of the Mesopotamian goddess, it

---

[118] Burgess (2001: 135–40) argues that the *Cypria* could have told the entire story of the Trojan War, then was edited down to fit into the Trojan cycle.

[119] *Cypria* F 1 West, see Burkert (1992: 100–6), Marks (2002: 19), and M. L. West (1997a: 480–2). See Chapter 6, 138, on the motif in *Atrahasis*.

[120] F 7 West, which describes her jeweled necklace, may be part of a dressing scene. Compare the dressing scene in the *Song of Ullikummi*, in which Anzili is ornamented with golden baubles (*CTH* 345.1.2.A = *KBo* 26.64 + *KUB* 36.12 ii 5′–12′, translit. E. Rieken et al. 2009ff.; trans. M. Bachvarova in López-Ruiz 2013: 158).

[121] Faulkner (2008: 18–22), with a full range of parallels, Penglase (1994: 165–76), M. L. West (1997a: 203–5). The story is alluded to in the catalog of Trojan allies: Aeneas is described as born from Aphrodite, who bedded the mortal Anchises in the folds of Mt. Ida (*Il.* 2.819–21).

[122] Burkert (1992: 88–91) discusses the Deception of Zeus episode in the *Iliad*, including other possible evidence for Near Eastern influence, as does M. L. West (1997a: 382–5).

[123] Burkert (1992: 91–4), Richardson (1989: 126), M. L. West (1997a: 382).

also includes the feigned innocence of Inanna and the dangers that a goddess' attention holds for a mortal man.

Dating to some time in the seventh century, the *Homeric Hymn to Aphrodite* was probably composed in northwest Anatolia. It is hard to avoid the conclusion that, like the mention of the survival of Aeneas' lineage beyond the Trojan War in the *Iliad*, the hymn was intended to flatter a clan of Aeneidae, who participated in a rivalry among local royal dynasties that claimed descent either from Aeneas or from Hector.[124] However, Phrygian influence on the story of Aphrodite's seduction of Anchises has been also suggested, for Mt. Ida was the home of the Idaean Magna Mater. Aphrodite presents herself as a Phrygian who can also speak "Trojan" (113–16). As Andrew Faulkner notes, this fits with a place of composition where such bilingualism was prevalent.[125] If Aphrodite corresponds to the Phrygian Magna Mater or Kubaba, Anchises would be substituting for the young god with which Cybele was frequently paired.[126] For the Phrygians the Idaean Mother was the Mother of Midas.[127] Thus, the frame of the story explaining the birth of Aeneas, in which the seduction was embedded, could have had a Phrygian source intended to provide a divine origin for the Phrygian dynasty. If so, we can postulate a competing use of the same storyline, grounded in local mythology, by a Greek-identified dynasty, which would explain the fact that the storyline

---

[124] Faulkner (2008: 4–10). On the continuance of Aeneas' family, see Chapter 15, 410, 412.

[125] Faulkner (2008: 47–50) on the issues of dating and location.

[126] On the Idaean Mother see Munn (2006: 73). On the relationship between Aphrodite and Kubaba see Munn (2006: 114–20). Berndt-Ersöz (2004; 2006: 162–4) suggests that the Phrygian "Young Male God," associated with the bull, was assimilated to the Anatolian Storm-god and then to Zeus. A strong Syro-Anatolian component can be detected in the Phrygian *Matar Kubeleya*, known to the Greeks as Cybele (Bryce 2005: 353–4). The relationship between Kubaba and Cybele has been much disputed. Roller (1994; 1999) denies any important connection between the two beyond the iconographic, while Hutter (2006), Laroche (1960) and Munn (2006: 120–5) consider them to be more or less closely related. Munn (2008: 161) has provided a neat solution to the problem: *Kubeleya* is a Phrygian adjective built from an adjective in *-li*, the standard way to form the genitival adjective in Lydian, a sequence of derivations that marks the syncretism of the Syrian goddess first with an Anatolian goddess, and then with a Phrygian divinity. "*Matar Kubeleya* in the Phrygian inscriptions therefore designates 'the Mother of the place of Kubaba', or 'the Mother who is identified with the place of Kubaba'." On how the figure of *Matar Kubeleya* shows that religious practices attested at Bronze Age Hattusa continued into the Classical period in Phrygia, see Hutter (2006), Popko (1995: 187–91), Roller (1999: 42–4), and references in Chapter 10, 234, n. 81. Perhaps the contribution of Kubaba to the Anatolian deity of wild spaces and wild animals was the ability to confer kingship, paradoxically the ultimate mark of civilized order. See Munn (2006) for a full discussion of these themes.

[127] Munn (2006: 79–88), Hyg. *Fab.* 191.1, 279.6. It was Midas, Berndt-Ersöz (2006: 209–11) suggests, who made *Matar Kubeleya* the chief deity of the Phrygians.

ended up recorded as a Greek Homeric hymn, and we might argue that a poet able to perform in both Phrygian and Greek was originally responsible for the amalgamation of the two plot lines, although in fact it would have been sufficient for a Greek poet to simply know of the hero's-birth plot line. We have no Phrygian hymns to the gods, so we have no means of arguing either position further. Finally, the close parallels in phraseology with Lesbian poetry "are substantial enough to suggest that the poet of *Aphr.* was in contact with a body of poetry which was also available to Sappho and Alcaeus."[128] In this light, the poet's vantage point on the topography of the Troad with regard to the seduction scene in the *Iliad* (14.282–93) is interesting, because the view towards Mt. Ida must be from Methymna on Lesbos, perhaps supporting the notions that the Greek version of the seduction scene originated in Aeolian Lesbos and that the Iliadic scene is a remnant of an Aeolian epic tradition about Hera, who was worshipped at Lesbos as the "Aeolian goddess," where she oversaw beauty contests in her sanctuary and absorbed elements of the Near Eastern goddess of sexuality.[129]

This dressing/seduction motif is unusual in that we can follow its trajectory in some detail: it came to Cyprus, ultimately from Mesopotamia, probably by way of a west Semitic tradition from north Syria; then it moved on to Lesbos. When the Aeolian storyline moved from the island to the coast of western Anatolia, it was merged with another version, which already existed in west Anatolia, that was attached to an Anatolian divinity, Phrygian Cybele, who was not a highly sexual goddess, but more of a maternal fertility goddess. That is, she was associated with procreation, rather than the intimacies of the sexual act. Phrygians and Greeks may have used competing versions of the birth story to legitimize local dynasties. This is how the Phrygian frame of the birth story was added to the Aeolic core of the seduction scene. As with the *Odyssey*, we can distinguish two phases of Near Eastern influence, one via Cyprus, the other within Anatolia.

Conclusion

One possible route along which narrative songs moved to Cyprus was via Cilicia, another surely was from Syria and the Levant, while the route from

---

[128] Faulkner (2008: 47).
[129] See Nagy (2010:182–3) on the vantage point, arguing the scene originates in an Aeolian *Iliad*. Hera is the "Aeolian goddess" in Alc. F 129.6 Lobel-Page; Alc. F 130B.17–20 Lobel-Page mentions the ritual *ololugē* in a beauty contest; Σ A *ad Il.* 9.129 and D *ad Il.* 9.129–30 mention a (beauty) contest among the Lesbians in the precinct of Hera (Nagy 2010: 237).

Cyprus to Euboea must have been one of the paths by which elements of Near Eastern narrative poetry spread to mainland Greece. But, in both the *Iliad* and the *Odyssey* Cilicia barely warrants a mention,[130] and Cyprus remains distant, a faraway place that Menelaus visits on his return voyage from Troy.[131] It is western Anatolia where the action of the *Iliad* takes place, where Homer is purported to originate,[132] and where the Ionic dialect, an important component of the Homeric dialect, was spoken. Homer has good knowledge of Anatolian customs,[133] and he seems to have visited the ruins of Troy.[134] It is in this milieu that the epic story of the fall of Troy achieved such prominence in the cultural memory of the Greeks (and Anatolians) and was able to reach such an acme of poetic perfection. Therefore, in the final chapters I turn to a close examination of the Anatolian context of the *Iliad*.

---

[130] The "Cilicians" only appear twice in the *Iliad*; they are important enough to be the people of Hector's wife, Andromache (6.397, 415), but it appears that this Cilicia is situated in west Anatolia (see Chapter 15, 411, n. 62).

[131] *Od.* 4.81–5. Odysseus, lying to Antinous in his own house, claims he was given as a slave to a king of Cyprus after having been captured in Egypt (*Od.* 17.415–44). In the *Iliad* Cyprus is only directly mentioned once, as the home of king Cinyras, who sent Agamemnon a guest-gift of a beautifully worked breast plate "for (even) as far as Cyprus reached the great glory (*kleos*) of the expedition to Troy" (*Il.* 11.19–28, see Richardson 1989: 124).

[132] Homer is placed in Smyrna and/or Chios in the earliest citations (Simonides F 8.1 West, Pi. F 264; see further Chapter 15, 412, n. 66), the latter the home of the Homeridae (*hHAp* 172). See Ruijgh (1995: 16–17) on Homer's Ionic origins. See Graziosi (2002) for the ancient view of Homer's birthplace and date. On Homer as a construct, see Chapters 3, 63, n. 32; 10, 239–40; 15, 396–7.

[133] See Kirk (1985: 5–6), Starke (1997: 460–6), and Watkins (1986; 2000a).

[134] See Chapter 14, 370–1.

13 | Cultural contact in Late Bronze Age western Anatolia

> Thus speaks My Sun, Muwattalli, king, Grea[t King of the la]nd of Ha[tt]i, beloved of the Storm-god of Lightning (*piḫaššaššiš*), son of Mursili, Great King, hero:
>
> In the old days, when Lab[arna], the father of my fathers, conquered all [the lands of Arzawa and] the land of Wilu[sa and] enslaved [them], the land of Arzawa rebelled from it, [but] from whatever [king] the land of Wi[lusa] defected, since the matter is long ago, [I do] n[ot know]. Even if the land of Wilusa [defec]ted [from] the land of Ha[tti], despite being far away, (the people of Wilusa) were on friendly terms to the kings of the land of Hatti, just as they were before, and [messengers] visited [them].
>
> *Treaty between Muwattalli II and Alaksandu of Wilusa*[1]

Introduction

In the previous chapters I have made arguments explaining why and how Near Eastern storylines about theogonies, the goddess of sexuality, and long-distance travel made their way to Greek epic from Cyprus and north Syria in the Early Iron Age. I also suggested there is some evidence for contact within Anatolia shaping a relatively late stage in the development of the *Homeric Hymn to Aphrodite* and the *Odyssey*. I now turn to the *Iliad*, a story set in Anatolia with multiple Near Eastern antecedents, all of which can be found at Hattusa. There is no reason to separate the locus of transmission of the Near Eastern storylines about the destruction of a fabled city to the *Iliad* from the locus of the action and every reason to contend that the places are the same.[2] In addition, I argue that the content motivated the borrowing of the Near Eastern storyline. When the Greeks learned of it, the story was not simply about the sack of a city in general, but specifically about the sack of Troy.

---

[1] *CTH* 76.B = *KUB* 21.5 i 1–9, filled in with G = *KUB* 21.2 + *KUB* 48.95 i 1–12 (translit. Friedrich 1930b: 50).
[2] Högemann (2000) argues effectively against the notion that the story of the *Iliad* originated on the Mycenaean mainland.

Kurt Raaflaub states, "collective memory... concerns itself with the past only insofar as this past is relevant and meaningful to the present."[3] In the Greek collective memory (as preserved for us), the Trojan War marked the end of the heroic past and the beginning of the contemporary age. But, in what milieu did a battle between Achaeans and Anatolians become such an important touchstone? The intense interaction between Greek-speakers and Anatolians at close quarters in western Anatolia in the Early Iron Age certainly provided an appropriate context. According to Pericles Georges:

> The Greeks' mythopoietic appropriation and representation of the foreign help explain how the first miracle of the Ionian civilization occurred, the miracle by which the Greeks of Asia remained Greek.
>
> They remained Greek because their poets and storytellers held them to their identity under very unpromising conditions. For much mixing of blood and culture accompanied the building of Ionian society. Among aristocracies and peasants alike, no line of separate blood or unacceptable custom firmly divided the Greek and native people; family bonds between Greeks and natives had been formed, in some cases, as far back as the age of migration.[4]

What Georges does not consider is the possibility that Anatolians – Carians, Lydians, Lycians, and Phrygians – were also actively engaged in mythologizing their relations with the Greek-speakers who settled their shores, that the creation of a past shared by Greeks and Anatolians was a communal enterprise. He views Homer's poetry as having a solely Greek heritage, used solely to create a Greek identity,[5] an opinion that is invalidated by the undeniable influence from Syro-Anatolian epic.

The questions, then, are the following: What kinds of interactions were occurring between Greeks and Anatolians that made a story about their traditional enmity centering on Troy good to think with in the Early Iron Age? How were the traditional epic storylines found at second-millennium Hattusa, along with "facts" about the dynasty of Bronze Age Troy and its chief god, preserved across the end of the Bronze Age to reach the Homeric tradition? Finally, how were they transmitted to Greek-speaking poets?

In this chapter I begin to answer these questions by looking at contact between Mycenaeans (men of Ahhiyawa) and Anatolians in the Late Bronze Age, some memory of which remained in the collective

---

[3] Raaflaub (1998a: 183).   [4] Georges (1994: 13). See further Georges (1994: 13–46).
[5] Georges (1994: 14).

consciousness of the Greeks and Anatolians who later resided in the Troad. I also discuss contacts among Anatolians that could explain how a close relative to the epic traditions found at Hattusa could have made its way to western Anatolia, to survive there after the fall of the Hittite empire.

Contacts among Ahhiyawa, west Anatolia, and the Hittites in the Late Bronze Age: the beginnings of a cultural memory about the Trojan War?

In this section, I review the political geography of western Anatolia in the second millennium, which shows that the area, including the later Ionia and Aeolis, participated at least to some degree in the same cultural world as the Hittites, and that the Ahhiyawans, who have been plausibly linked to Mycenaean Greeks,[6] were actively involved in Late Bronze Age Anatolian affairs. Dim memories of contacts in this time, especially around Wilusa, the later Troy, must have helped to shape the later Homeric tradition.

Although the courts of western Anatolia (greater Arzawa) were joined to Hattusa by diplomatic and family ties, much of what we know about the Arzawan lands comes from Hittite documents recording their constant conflicts with the Hittites, sometimes supported by the men of Ahhiyawa, and the vassal treaties which repeatedly tried to end the conflicts. We thus get a sense of the competitive, fractious environment in west Anatolia, the in-fighting and intermarriages among the ruling families, and the dependence of western Anatolia on the administrative practices established by the Hittites. These complex interactions would have driven the assimilation and emulation of the practices recorded in the libraries at Hattusa on the one hand, and the adoption of Mycenaean drinking, feasting, and mortuary practices on the other,[7] settings which would have been instrumental in spreading songs to new performers and audiences.

Western Anatolia was not devoid of political development in the Late Bronze Age (see Map 1). Several peer polities, including Wilusa, existed

---

[6] Most agree that Ahhiyawa is located in mainland Greece. Kelder (2010) specifies Mycenae as the most likely candidate. Latacz (2004: 238–44) argues that it was Thebes, as does Niemeier (2007b: 72–3). See Beckman, Bryce, and Cline (2011: 3–6), reviewing the arguments. Gary Beckman, Trevor Bryce, and Eric Cline have recently published translations with discussions of the some twenty-nine Hittite texts mentioning Ahhiyawa in *The Ahhiyawa Texts* (2011).
[7] On the significance of Mycenaean mortuary practices in the southeast Aegean see Chapter 11, 272–3.

there, while others, like Masa,[8] Karkisa,[9] and Lukka (roughly the equivalent of Early Iron Age Lycia, although more extensive),[10] while they may not have attained a complex hierarchical state structure, had defined identities in the eyes of the Hittites. The Hittite historiographic and administrative texts show us that there was extensive contact between the Hittites and their neighbors to the west, of the kind that would have allowed for transfer of gods and performers of narrative song and other forms of verbal art. The Hittite texts show that the men of Ahhiyawa were interested in the Anatolian coast and were active militarily and politically in Anatolia, sometimes on friendly terms with the Hittites, sometimes supporting rebels.[11] From the perspective of the west Anatolian polities, in turn, the men of Ahhiyawa were useful allies in their attempts to negotiate political power and to resist Hittite hegemony.

Indeed, there is a possibility that Ahhiyawans encouraged the Assuwa rebellion, the major political upheaval at the beginning of the Empire period.[12] In the time of Tudhaliya I/II a large part of western Anatolia was united into the Assuwa confederation,[13] a group of twenty-two lands, among which was Wilusiya. This is the earliest mention of Wilusa, later known as Ilium. Also mentioned is Taruisa, whose name corresponds to the place name Troy.[14] The hint that the Ahhiyawans may have been

---

[8] On Masa see Wittke (2004: 185–90). Some have equated it with the later Mysia (see Roosevelt 2009: 18, with earlier references).

[9] For Karkisa, see Chapter 14, 361, n. 52.

[10] Lukka lay directly to the west of Rough Cilicia, as shown by the *Bronze Tablet Treaty* between Tudhaliya IV and Kurunta of Tarhuntassa (*CTH* 106.A.1 = StBoTB 1 i 14–ii 20 translit. Otten 1988a: 10–16; trans. H. A. Hoffner, Jr. in Hallo and Younger 2000: 100–2). The completeness and exactness of the boundary descriptions in the *Bronze Tablet Treaty*, discovered in 1986, put the understanding of Anatolian political geography on a new footing. See especially Starke (1997: 448–50). On Lukka, see Bryce (2006: 81–2, 144–5, 148–50).

[11] As Bryce (2006: 105) sees it, "Kings of the land called Ahhiyawa constantly sought to roll back Hittite authority in western Anatolia by supporting local anti-Hittite insurgents and uprisings in preparation for the expansion of their own authority in the region."

[12] As suggested by F. Starke *apud* Teffeteller (2013: 579).

[13] Assuwa has been plausibly connected to the later Greek geographical term *Asiā*, see Watkins (1986: 709; 1998: 202–4), showing that in Homer *Āsiā* is scanned with initial long vowel, the reflex of Mycenaean *Aswiā*, and therefore should not be equated with Assos. Also cf. *Il.* 2.461: "In the Asian meadow, about the stream of Caustrius" (= BA Astarpa?).

[14] Most of the place names listed as part of Assuwa are otherwise unattested, but the list begins with [Art]uqqa and certainly ends with Taruisa and Wilusiya (*Annals of Tudhaliya I/II: CTH* 142.2.A = *KUB* 23.11 ii 14′–19′, translit. and trans. Carruba 2008: 36–9). Artukka appears elsewhere with Arzawa and Masa (MH *Annals of Arnuwanda I: CTH* 143.1.A = *KUB* 23.21 rev. 16′–23′, translit. and trans. Carruba 2008: 68–9). See Starke (1997: 456 and n. 91) for further references. If the list began with [Lu]qqa, the few identifiable geographic names found on the list appear in the reverse order of the list of Trojan allies in *Il.* 2.816–78. So S. P. Morris (2001a:

supporting the confederation comes from a fragmentary New Hittite letter from the "[kin]g of the [l]and Ahhiyaw[a]," possibly Tawagalawa, and probably to Muwattalli II, elder son of Mursili II, which discusses past history involving disputed possession of islands, Assuwa, Tudhaliya, and a marriage alliance. One interpretation is that the Ahhiyawans and Assuwans had been allied through a dynastic marriage that involved a gift of island territory.[15]

After the defeat of the Assuwa confederation, Arzawa was the major political force in western Anatolia.[16] It is clear that Arzawan kings did not find Hittite hegemony particularly appealing, as shown by two Hittite letters found in the Egyptian Amarna archives, to and from Tarhuntaradu, king of Arzawa;[17] in the letter from Amenhotep III (*ca.* 1388–1351/50 BCE) the pharaoh seems to exult over political unrest in Hatti and discusses a marriage alliance.[18] Yet, the Arzawan scribe writing for Tarhuntaradu requests that the Egyptian scribe write only in Hittite, rather than Akkadian, the usual language of international diplomacy.[19] This suggests a lack of independent west Anatolian administrative structures. And, Hittite rather than Akkadian was always used in the treaties between Hattusa and Anatolian principalities.[20]

---

425), Watkins (1998: 202). As Bryce (2006: 129) notes, however, "Otherwise, the correspondence between the two lists of allies is very slight." Taruisa corresponds to *Troiā*, while Wilusiya is a Luwian adjectival form of Wilusa (see Yakubovich 2010: 126–7 on Luwian mediation of west Anatolian place names in Hittite texts), but in the *Annals* they must refer to two separate places. Bryce (2006: 108–9) suggests that they were "adjoining but separate countries ... Wilusiya may subsequently have absorbed its neighbour, though local traditions (we may surmise) preserved the latter's name through the following centuries until it re-emerged as an alternative to Ilios in the Homeric tradition." In the *Iliad* Troy referred to a larger district belonging to the city Ilium (del Valle Muñoyerro 1999; Hajnal 2003: 31–2). Latacz (2004: 92–100) reviews the discussion of the equation of Taruisa and Troy and the issue of the use of both Ilios and Troia in Homer. Note, however, that he sides with Starke (1997: 456) on the equation of Assuwa with Assos.

[15] *Letter from the King of Ahhiyawa to the Hittite King*: CTH 183 = KUB 26.91 (translit., trans. and discussion Beckman, Bryce, and Cline 2011: 134–9). For Tawagalawa as king of Ahhiyawa, see J. L. Miller (2010: 164–8) and Alparslan (2005). The suggestion that the Ahhiyawan king sending the letter was Tawagalawa comes from Teffeteller (2013: 572–4). Also see Latacz (2004: 243–4).

[16] On Arzawa see Bryce (2003a: 35–40) and Yakubovich (2010: 78–96).

[17] Not to be confused with the later Tarhunnaradu who appears in the "Offenses of the Seha River Land" = CTH 211.4: *Fragments of Annals*, on which see below, 341. Both letters (cited below) are in Middle Script.

[18] *Letter from Amenhotep III to Tarhuntaradu*: CTH 151 = VBoT 1 (translit., trans., and discussion Hoffner 2009: 273–7, EA 31). See Yakubovich (2010: 82–3).

[19] *Letter from Arzawa to Amenhotep III*: CTH 152 = VBoT 2 14–25 (translit., trans., and discussion Hoffner 2009: 269–72, EA 32).

[20] Bryce (2006: 116–17).

In addition the fourteenth-century *Madduwatta Indictment*, a draft of a diplomatic letter by Tudhaliya I/II's son Arnuwanda I, sheds light on the problems the Hittites continued to have in the area.[21] The Hittite king runs through a long list of treacherous acts committed by the Anatolian freebooter Madduwatta, despite the repeated help of the Hittite king, who had assigned to him a border district of his choice to govern.[22] Among his crimes Madduwatta took over large parts of Arzawa; he had the inhabitants of Pitassa, located between Hatti and Arzawa,[23] swear loyalty to himself; he acted treacherously in multiple battles, causing the death of important Hittite leaders; he took in Hittite fugitives; and, he tried to assassinate Kupanta-Kurunta, king of Arzawa,[24] even as he was forming a marriage alliance with him

The *Madduwatta Indictment* shows that Ahhiyawans had been meddling in the political affairs of Anatolia in the reign of Arnuwanda I. Madduwatta is reminded how the Hittite king's father took care of him when Attarissiya, the "man of the city Ahhiya,"[25] chased him out of his country (which is left unspecified) after their friendship had soured, and the Hittite king complains that Madduwatta is continuing to mount raids against Alashiya, which the king considers his territory, as he and Attarissiya had done when the two were still allies.

However, the campaigns of Mursili II (1321–1295 BCE), described in his *Annals*, effectively broke the power of Arzawa for the next generation;[26] Arzawa was no longer a political entity in the eyes of the Hittite kings, and western Anatolia had been split into a confederacy bound to Hatti by ties of marriage and allegiance, made up of Hapalla, Mira-Kuwaliya, a kingdom located between the Karabel pass and the Meander River,[27] and the Seha

---

[21] CTH 147 = KUB 14.1+ (translit. and trans. with discussion Beckman, Bryce, and Cline 2011: 69–100).

[22] The governor of a border district had his seat in a fortified city of a rural province and guarded the Hittite border against enemy incursions. See Beal (1992: 426–36).

[23] On Pitassa see Heinhold-Krahmer (1977: 355–8). It cannot be the same as the later Classical Pedasa near Mt. Ida, or any of the other places with similar names, on which see E. Olshausen, "Pedasa," in *Brill's New Pauly* 10.674. The name simply means "land of the plain."

[24] Not the same man as the ruler of Mira-Kuwaliya with whom Mursili II made a treaty.

[25] CTH 147 = KUB 14.1 i 1, etc. (translit. and trans. Beckman, Bryce, and Cline 2011: 70–1).

[26] CTH 61.I: *Ten-Year Annals of Mursili II* (translit. and trans. of relevant parts in Beckman, Bryce, and Cline 2011: 10–27).

[27] Mira-Kuwaliya was within the original Arzawa proper, and the Seha River Land lay to the north, according to the borders in the *Treaty between Mursili II and Kupanta-Kurunta of Mira-Kuwaliya* (CTH 68.C = KBo 5.13 i 29′–34′, translit. Friedrich 1926: 116; trans. Beckman 1999b: 76). The Astarpa River is mentioned along with the land of Kuwaliya as the border; it probably is the Meander River (see Starke 1997: 450–1), although Hawkins (1998: 22) argues that it is the

River Land-Appawiya, the land of the Hermus or Caecus River, whose territory roughly matches later Lydia.[28] These three regions formed one contiguous unit, sometimes called by scholars "greater Arzawa," with Wilusa introduced as a fourth member of the alliance in the *Treaty between Muwattalli II and Alaksandu of Wilusa (ca. 1275).*[29]

As in previous times when the Hittite and Ahhiyawan kings and Madduwatta and Mira were linked through marriages, alliances continued to be sealed with dynastic marriages, but they did not always ensure the loyalty of a vassal. Thus, king Mashuiluwa of Mira(-Kuwaliya) attempted to incite both the population of Pitassa and the people of Hatti to rebel against Hatti, despite a marriage alliance with Muwatti, the sister of Mursili II. After Mursili replaced him with Kupanta-Kurunta,[30] the resulting dynasty of Mira did remain loyal to the Hittites and continued to intermarry with the Hittite royal family. Its members were liable to be called upon in matters beyond their borders of concern to the Hittite empire, for Alantalli, a king of Mira, is named among the witnesses of the *Bronze Tablet Treaty*, which specified the extent of the land of Tarhuntassa and the rights of its king Kurunta. Thus, Alantalli, like other members of the extended Hittite royal family, served as a local representative of Hittite hegemony.[31] The royal family of the Seha River Land, like that of Mira, was bound by ties of marriage to the Hittite royal family; Masduri, the king of the Seha River Land, who also makes an appearance in the witness list of the *Bronze Tablet Treaty*, was married to Massanuzzi, the sister of Muwattalli II.[32]

Yet, Mursili II indicates that rebels in western Anatolia were still receiving aid from Ahhiyawa, and that Ahhiyawa had an interest in Miletus. In the

---

Akar Çay (Cayster River). The inscription by king Tarkasnawa located on the Karabel pass along the road between Ephesus and Sardis mentions Mira and probably marked its border with its northern neighbor, the Seha River Land (Hawkins 1998).

[28] On the location of the Seha River Land see Hawkins (1998: 23–4), Roosevelt (2009: 16–21), and C. Luke and Roosevelt (forthcoming). Kaymançı, west of the Gygaean Lake, could have been the capital of the kingdom.

[29] Heinhold-Krahmer (1977: 326).

[30] *Treaty between Mursili II and Kupanta-Kurunta of Mira-Kuwaliya*: CTH 68, §§2–8 (translit. Friedrich 1926: 106–16; trans. Beckman 1999b: 74–5). Also see Yakubovich (2010: 84).

[31] The witnesses included Ini-Teshshub and Benteshina, the kings of Carchemish and Amurru, the latter married to Gassuliyawiya, the daughter of Hattusili III, and the former the great-grandson of Suppiluliuma I and probably linked to Hattusili III more directly by marriage as well (*CTH* 106.A.1 = StBoTB 1 iv 31, 36, translit. Otten 1988a: 26, and see p. 53; trans. H. A. Hoffner, Jr. in Hallo and Younger 2000: 106). On Gassuliyawiya, see Singer (1991). On Ini-Teshshub see Bryce (2005: 313, with n. 87).

[32] StBoTB 1 iv 32 (trans. and translit. Otten 1988a: 26–7). On Massanuzzi see Bryce (2003b: 121–2; 2005: 254).

third year of the *Ten-Year Annals of Mursili II*, a conflict with the Arzawan king Uḫḫaziti is described, and the *Comprehensive Annals of Mursili II* open the account of the third year of his reign with a victory over the rebellious town Millawanda/Milawatta (Miletus), which had sided with Ahhiyawa.[33] Milawatta was located close to the mouth of the Meander, a key route inland, but out on the tip of a peninsula and isolated from the rest of Anatolia by a mountain range, so it is not surprising that it was relatively independent from Hittite or Arzawan control and open to Mycenaean settlement.[34]

Mursili's attack on Milawatta was connected with his ongoing campaign against the Arzawan king Uḫḫaziti, and it was one of several events that culminated in Uḫḫaziti fleeing from Apasa (Ephesus) across the sea to an island.[35] There, "in the sea" (*aruni anda*), he took refuge with his sons Piyama-Kurunta and Tapalazunauli until he died, in the fourth year of Mursili's reign.[36] Later on in a frustratingly damaged context we read, "He (the son of Uḫḫaziti) from the sea/ [... w]ith the ki[ng of the la]nd Ahhiyawa/ [...-ed. And,] I sent [...] by bo[at]." Did the son of Uḫḫaziti take refuge in Ahhiyawa?[37] In turn, a fragmentary prayer suggests that a queen from the time of Mursili II was exiled to Ahhiyawa, "[b]eside/ [the

---

[33] It must be admitted that *Mursili's Comprehensive Annals* are frustratingly fragmentary here: *nu⸗kan* KUR ᵁᴿᵁ*Millawanda* ANA LUGAL KUR *Aḫḫiu*[*wā* ......]/ *nu⸗kan* ᵐ*Gullan* ᵐ*Mala-LÚ-in* ÉRIN.MEŠ A[NŠE.KUR.RA.MEŠ⸗*ya par*]*ā n*[*eḫḫun n⸗aš* KUR ᵁᴿᵁ*Millawanda*]/ GUL-*aḫḫir*. "The land of the city Millawanda to the king of the land of Ahhiya[wa...]/ [I] se[nt fort]h Gulla, Malaziti, troops [and] ch[ariotry. The land of the city Millawanda]/ they attacked" (*CTH* 61.II.2.A = *KUB* 14.15 i 24′-26′, translit. Beckman, Bryce, and Cline 2011: 29).

[34] The archaeological evidence from Miletus shows first a Minoan settlement, changing to a Mycenaean settlement, Miletus v (second half of the fifteenth to the late fourteenth century BCE); towards the end of the LH IIIA:2 period a layer of destruction follows, which coincides with the date of Mursili II's sack of Milawatta *ca.* 1315 BCE. Miletus VI (late fourteenth century to 1100 BCE) could show casement-walls typical of the Hittites, although the evidence uncovered is meager. Niemeier (1998: 27–40) discusses the evidence in some detail; also see Niemeier (2007a; 2007b: 77, 83–4). Hope Simpson (2003: 215–20) argues that archaeological evidence for Ahhiyawan control or for Hittite occupation after the destruction is not as strong as has been painted. On Miletus see most recently Niemeier (2007a).

[35] *Ten-Year Annals of Mursili II*: *CTH* 61.I.A = *KBo* 3.4 ii 15–32 (translit. and trans. Beckman, Bryce, and Cline 2011: 15–16). On the equation of Apasa and Ephesus, see Büyükkolancı (2000). There has been little ability to look for evidence of Bronze Age settlement beneath the lavish ruins from the Classical and Hellenistic period at Ephesus, but Mycenaean pottery (LH IIIA:2) has been found in Ephesus, suggesting a Mycenaean presence in this period (Hope Simpson 2003: 212). Further excavations in the area of the Ayasoluk hill show continuous settlement from the Early Bronze Age through Hellenistic times (Büyükkolancı 2000; 2007; Weißl 2004: 473). Also see Muss (2007: 170–5) on a Minoan-style cult statue found in the Artemision, and Bammer and Muss (2007) on a Hittite-style sacred spring at Ayasoluk.

[36] *CTH* 61.I.A = *KBo* 3.4 ii 50–2 (translit. and trans. Beckman, Bryce, and Cline 2011: 18–19).

[37] *KBo* 3.4 iii 2–4 + *KUB* 23.125 iii 5′–7′ (translit. Beckman, Bryce, and Cline 2011: 22). Teffeteller (2013: 572) suggests he goes to Lazpa.

sea]."[38] Ahhiyawa was continuing to play both sides, it had diplomatic ties with both the Hittites and southwest Anatolian polities, and its distance could be used to advantage by both.

It is not surprising, therefore, that Hattusa and Ahhiyawa were not fully trusting of each other. In the *Tawagalawa Letter*, a New Hittite king (probably Mursili's younger son Hattusili III) complains to the king of Ahhiyawa about two men, one named Piyamaradu, probably a member of the west Anatolian elite,[39] and his son-in-law Atpa, the ruler of Milawatta. The Hittite king has a conciliatory tone and puts the blame for any misunderstanding on the messenger going between them.[40] According to Jared L. Miller's interpretation, Tawagalawa, the brother of the Ahhiyawan king addressed in the letter and a former Great King himself, had actually intervened on the ground in Lukka and at Millawanda.[41]

The fact that an Ahhiyawan king was personally involved in Anatolian affairs shows that at one point Ahhiyawa controlled part of the coast of west Anatolia.[42] A small fragment of a boundary agreement refers to Tarhuntassa, Mira, and Ahhiyawa on successive lines,[43] and the archaeological evidence for Mycenaeans in Anatolia matches fairly well with the territories mentioned in the agreement. While evidence for Mycenaean

---

[38] *CTH* 214.12.A (*Fragments of Historical Texts*)/389 (*Fragments of Prayers*) = *KUB* 14.2 rev. 4–6 (translit. and trans. with discussion Beckman, Bryce, and Cline 2011: 158–61, 273).

[39] F. Starke ("Mira," in *Brill's New Pauly* 9.48–51) suggests that Piyamaradu of the *Tawagalawa Letter* is the son of Piyama-Kurunta, son of king Uhhaziti of Arzawa. Certainly he bears an Arzawan dynastic name. In the unpublished MH letter from Ortaköy a man named Piyamaradu is mentioned as one of four sons of a Kupanta-Kurunta, a name also used by the king of Arzawa and a later king of Mira-Kuwaliya, along with a Masduri, a name later used by a king of the Seha River Land (Süel 2001).

[40] *KUB* 14.3 ii 13: *kinuna-wa-mu* ŠEŠ-*YA* ⌈LUGAL⌉ GAL⌉ *ammel*⌈?⌉/ *annauliš IŠPUR* (translit. Beckman, Bryce, and Cline 2011: 106). "Now my brother, ⌈Great⌉ King⌉, my⌈?⌉/ equal, has written to me." See Güterbock (1983a: 201).

[41] *CTH* 181 = *KUB* 14.3, the third tablet of the letter (translit. and trans. with discussion Beckman, Bryce, and Cline 2011: 101–22; German trans. J. L. Miller with important new readings in *TUAT NF* 3: 240–7; also see Hoffner 2009: 296–313). Also see the discussion in Latacz (2004: 123–5). J. L. Miller's (2010: 164–8) interpretation picks up on the idea of Alparslan (2005). To avoid this conclusion, Beckman, Bryce, and Cline (2011: 105–6) must interpret a key sentence: "When Tawagalawa himself, (as the representative of?) the Great King..." (i 71). The name Tawagalawa has been equated with Eteocles (*Etewoklewēs* 'true glory') The inference is supported by the appearance of the name *E-te-wo-ke-re-we-i-yo-*in Linear B (PY An 654.8–9, Aq 64.15).

[42] So Jasink and Marino (2007); Jasink (2001b: 601), seeing Anatolian Ahhiyawa as not part of a mainland Mycenaean state.

[43] *Fragments of Historical Texts*: *CTH* 214.16 = *KUB* 31.29 (translit. and trans. Beckman, Bryce, and Cline 2011: 174–5). Discussed by Bryce (2005: 224).

settlement is most abundant at Miletus, it is also found at Troy, Smyrna, Clazomenae, Colophon, Ephesus, Iasos, Müsgebi, Cos (Seraglio), and Rhodes, to mention just the most notable sites, and it is particularly concentrated between Halicarnassus and Miletus, and from Rhodes to Samos.[44] The letter from the king of Ahhiyawa discussed earlier indicates that the partition of the islands off the coast of this territory happened in the time of Tudhaliya I/II, and Ahhiyawans continued to claim the islands into the reign of Muwattalli II. However, archaeological evidence for intensive and permanent settlement by Mycenaeans is only found along the small portion of the Anatolian coast between Halicarnassus and Miletus.[45] It is significant that it overlaps with the southern portion of the later Ionia.

Even if the Mycenaeans were able to control some part of the western Anatolian coast and even if the west Anatolian principalities were still interested in escaping the domination of the Hittites, they were at this point dependent on Hittite administrative structures. A letter in Akkadian found at Hattusa, from Ramses II (*rexit* 1290–1224 or 1279–1213 BCE) to Kupanta-Kurunta of Mira-Kuwaliya, indicates that during the time of Hattusili III international diplomacy with west Anatolia was conducted via Hattusa and not directly between Arzawan kings and other countries.[46]

Still, during this time, the Ahhiyawans were continuing to work to foment rebellion against Hattusa. In the *Milawatta Letter* we learn that the king of Wilusa, Walmu, has been deposed. It may be that the Ahhiyawans helped the rebels, but clearly the insurrection was not successful. The

---

[44] Bryce (1989: 1–2). For Mycenaean settlement in Anatolia see Niemeier (1998: 27–41; 2007b: 43–60, with a rich bibliography on all the relevant sites), and Hope Simpson (2003: 214–15). Kelder (2010: 121–36, 140) reviews the Mycenaean pottery found in Anatolia. For Mycenaean tombs in Anatolia see Georgiadis (2009) and further discussion in Chapter 11, 272: Teffeteller (2013) argues for a Mycenaean presence at Lesbos. Mountjoy (1998: 34–45; 1999a: 967–9) defines the area as part of an "east Aegean-west Anatolian interface." Mountjoy (1998: 47–51) denies that Ahhiyawans were Mycenaean colonists, seeing them rather as "local inhabitants who had undergone Mycenaean acculturation to varying degrees" (51). It remains unclear, though, how this acculturation could occur without the intimate contact of Mycenaeans settling there, teaching their foodways and other social practices that leave archaeological traces. Georgiadis (2003: 111) also prefers to think in terms of a Mycenaean "sociocultural identity," contrasting with a Hittite one. And, see the review of Minoan and Mycenaean settlement and influence in Bronze Age Caria in Carstens (2008b: 57–9). A detailed review of the archaeological evidence of Mycenaean trade in the Near East is provided by Cline (1994: 68–77).

[45] Niemeier (1998: 17; 2007b: 88).

[46] *Letter from Ramses II to Kupanta-Kurunta of Mira-Kuwaliya*: CTH 166 = KUB 3.23+ (translit. Edel 1994: 1.74–77, 2.125–30, No. 28; trans. Beckman 1999b: 130–1).

letter's recipient, probably Tarkasnawa, king of Mira,[47] has taken Walmu in and the Hittite king, probably Tudhaliya IV, orders that he be handed over to him so that he may be put back on the throne as a loyal vassal.[48] Another New Hittite document, "The Offenses of Seha River Land," probably from the time of Tudhaliya IV, describes the Ahhiyawan king as supporting the Seha River Land in its attempt to rebel against Hatti. The rebellion was again quelled by the Hittite king, who installed a new king of Seha River Land in place of Tarhunnaradu.[49] Gary Beckman, Trevor Bryce, and Eric Cline suggest, "It may well be that Ahhiyawan support for the rebellion finally induced Tudhaliya to force a military showdown with the Ahhiyawan regime – an action that may have resulted in the elimination of Ahhiyawa's sovereignty over Milawata, and the end of an effective Ahhiyawan political and military presence anywhere in western Anatolia."[50]

In closing, I am not concerned with whether all or even most Ahhiyawans or settlers from Greece in Anatolia spoke Greek or were integrated into the Mycenaean palace economy. What is significant is that ancestors of the Iron Age Greeks were already interacting and blending with Anatolians in the Late Bronze Age, producing hybrid items like the Mycenaean-style sword captured by Tudhaliya I/II in his war against Assuwa and the Mycenaean vessel depicting an Anatolian god found at Miletus (Fig. 10),[51] and setting the stage for the later, more intense phase of interaction and intermingling of cultural practices in the Early Iron Age. Thus were established the cultural memories of dynastic marriages and conflicts that were refracted in Greek mythology informing the Homeric tradition of the Trojan War. While it is not impossible that the cultural memory of contact in the Late Bronze Age resided with Greeks, I will argue in the following

---

[47] Hawkins (1998: 19).
[48] *CTH* 182 = *KUB* 19.55 + 48.90 rev. 32'–44' (translit. and trans. Beckman, Bryce, and Cline 2011: 128–9). Note that there is a new join, *KBo* 18.117, not included in their edition (M. Weeden, August 9, 2012; see KhT *ad loc*).
[49] *Fragments of Annals*: *CTH* 211.4 = *KUB* 23.13 (translit. and trans. Beckman, Bryce, and Cline 2011: 154–5).
[50] Beckman, Bryce, and Cline (2011: 156–7). That the Ahhiyawan king lost control of the coast of western Anatolia after the *Tawagalawa Letter* was written is suggested by the *Milawatta Letter*, for the king mentions, "when we, my majesty and my son, set the border of Milawatta" (*CTH* 182 = *KUB* 19.55 + 48.90 rev. 45', see translit. Beckman, Bryce, and Cline 2011: 128–9, with discussion p. 131). This indicates that the addressee is in charge in Milawatta and allied with the Hittite king.
[51] A sword found at Hattusa bears an Akkadian inscription commemorating the defeat of the Assuwan confederacy by Tudhaliya I/II. This sword, although not of canonical Mycenaean design, at least shows Mycenaean influence. See Cline (1994: 73, with earlier references; 1996). On the vessel from Miletus see Niemeier (2007b: 84).

chapter that it is quite clear that cultural memories were retained also among Anatolians, later to be communicated to Greeks.

Transmission of Hittite cultural features to west Anatolia in the Late Bronze Age

I have discussed the evidence for political and military contact among Anatolians, the dynastic marriages, alliances, and attempted resistance to Hittite hegemony. I now turn to how this contact allowed for transfer of the verbal art attested at Hattusa to western Anatolia in the Late Bronze Age, where Greek-speakers could come into direct contact with it both in the Late Bronze Age and in the Early Iron Age. Furthermore, I expand on Chapter 10's discussion of evidence for contact between mainland Greece and Anatolia. It shows there is a small possibility that the right kind of contact between Mycenaeans and Anatolians occurred to allow for the transfer of Near Eastern epic traditions to Greek-speakers and even to Greece already in the Late Bronze Age.[52]

The interaction between Hattusa and the west Anatolian principalities – whether we think of it as competitive emulation or as peer polity interaction – provided the sociopolitical context for transfer of techniques of verbal art via transfer of gods, magical rituals, and festivals from the Hittites to west Anatolia. The Hittites were interested in the religious and magical techniques of west Anatolia and considered even the inimical lands there to participate in the supralocal religious culture that connected Anatolia to north Syria and Mesopotamia. They thought that the international gods they invoked to come to Hattusa might be keeping themselves in Arzawa, Masa, Karkiya (Karkisa), or Wilusa.[53] They imported the Luwian festival from Istanuwa in which the "Wilusiad" was performed,[54] and they brought in ritual healers and augurs from Arzawa.[55]

We can safely assume that the same transactions occurred in the opposite direction as well, which we cannot directly see simply because we have found no archives or libraries from western Anatolia of the sort found at Hattusa, Sapinuwa, or Tapikka. Given the intense interactions at the elite

---

[52] Chapter 10, 231–2.
[53] *Ritual for IŠTAR of Nineveh*: CTH 716.1.A = KUB 15.35 i 25′–7′ + KBo 2.9 i 1′–13′ (translit. F. Fuscagni 2009ff. on KhT; trans. B. J. Collins in Hallo and Younger 1997: 164); *Evocation Rituals*: CTH 483.1.A = KUB 15.34 i 52–65 (translit. and Spanish trans. García Trabazo 2002: 582–7; German trans. Haas and Wilhelm 1974: 188–9).
[54] See Chapter 2, 21.   [55] Bawanypeck (2005a, esp. p. 13), Collins (2010).

level between the Hittites and western Anatolian polities, both competitive and cooperative, leading to the interdynastic marriages mentioned earlier, we can surmise first that the kings of Mira-Kuwaliya, the Seha River Land, and Wilusa were all eager to show they were, if not equal, at least approaching the plane of the Hittite king in their ceremonial life, and also that this eagerness would motivate importation of gods and other religious customs. Although so far only a few inscriptions and monuments have been found in western Anatolia dating to the Late Bronze Age, they are in the Hieroglyphic Luwian script, they follow the same artistic styles as used by the Hittites, and they were carved in living rock just as among the Hittites,[56] so we can detect some interest in sharing in the elite practices of the Hittites.

We do know that the oversight of local temples and cult activities engaged in during the reign of Tudhaliya IV reached as far as the region of Eskişehir, west of Gordion. The records, which cover the towns of the core of the Hittite empire, list the local temples, the gods within them and their representations, the supplies allotted, and the personnel supposed to be on site. In some cases the local seasonal festival is described, and this includes the ritual combat between the men of Masa and the men of Hatti in the festival of Gursamassa, somewhere near the border of Masa and Mira, which has been discussed earlier.[57] There are two possible pieces of evidence that texts known to us from Hattusa made their way to western Anatolia and remained extant into the Iron Age: "the association of Typhon with the Katakekaumene area of Lydia"[58] and a myth localized at Pessinus which reworks elements of the Kumarbi cycle. In it the destructive monster Agdistis is born from the sperm of Jupiter ejaculated on a rock on a mountain (cf. the *Song of Ullikummi*). Then, the monster, made drunk and trapped in a snare by Dionysus, castrates himself in his struggles (cf. *Illuyanka* and the *Song of Birth*).[59]

---

[56] See map in back leaf of Ehringhaus (2005) for the distribution of the monuments. I have mentioned the one at the Karabel pass (this chapter, 337, n. 27).

[57] *Cult Inventories under Tudhaliya IV*: CTH 525.2 = *KUB* 17.35 (translit. and trans. C. W. Carter 1962: 123–53); see Chapter 10, 224. Key landmarks mentioned in the inventory texts are also found in historical and administrative texts concerning activities in west Anatolia. See Forlanini (1996b), Hazenbos (2003: 198): *Cult Inventories of the Storm-god*: CTH 509.2 = *KBo* 2.16 (translit. and trans. Hazenbos 2003: 115–16); CTH 509.1 = *KBo* 2.1 (translit. and trans. C. W. Carter 1962: 51–73; trans. H. A. Hoffner in Hallo and Younger 2002: 63).

[58] Rutherford (2009a: 31-2) makes this point; Str. 12.8.19 (= Xanthus of Lydia, *FGrH* 765 F 13a).

[59] Arnobius *Adversus Nationes* 5.5–6, trans. López-Ruiz (2013: 492–3). This is the prologue to the birth of Attis, the beloved of Cybele. On the parallels, see Burkert (1979b: 110), Lancellotti (2002: 20–5), and Haas (2006: 172–4).

Transfer of people and cultural features between Greece and Anatolia

In turn, similar interactions would have been going on between Ahhiyawa and Apasa, Milawatta, and Wilusa, to speak only of the Anatolian polities for which sufficiently intense elite interactions with Ahhiyawa can be clearly demonstrated by archaeological and textual evidence. If religious customs, including festivals and elements of festivals, were brought to Greece by these mechanisms, they would have been layered onto indigenous pan-Aegean practices shared by mainland Greece and Anatolia, and onto practices brought back and forth by earlier contacts in the Early and Middle Bronze Age.

The Late Bronze Age written and archaeological evidence indicates that high-level diplomatic contact occurred between Ahhiyawa and the Hittites, of the sort that I have shown fostered long-distance elite interaction and trading of proficient performers and gods (who would have been accompanied by attendants). The *Tawagalawa Letter*, along with another fragmentary New Hittite letter, makes clear that at times at least Ahhiyawans were sufficiently friendly with the Hittites to be involved with them in the gift exchange engaged in by the Late Bronze Age brotherhood of Great Kings, for both texts make a point of mentioning the gifts that were not received, showing that it was in fact expected that the Ahhiyawans would send them.[60] Vessels associated with the consumption of wine were prestigious gifts, and a New Hittite inventory mentions a copper vessel from Ahhiyawa, possibly a gift that was part of a set for serving wine.[61]

In addition, a shared etiquette for elite drinking and feasting had developed throughout the Aegean. Drinking sets of the Mycenaean type or showing Mycenaean influence suggest that the coast of west Anatolia and Cyprus were at least peripherally involved in Mycenaean-style feasting.[62] The small amount of locally produced Mycenaean dinnerwares

---

[60] *CTH* 181 = *KUB* 14.3 i 53–5 (translit. and trans. Beckman, Bryce, and Cline 2011: 104–5); *Fragments of Hittite Letters*: *CTH* 209.12 = *KBo* 2.11 rev. 11′–14′ (translit. and trans. with discussion Beckman, Bryce, and Cline 2011: 146–8).

[61] *Inventory of Clothing and Fabric*: *CTH* 243.6 = *KBo* 18.181 rev. 33′ (translit. and trans. Beckman, Bryce, and Cline 2011: 180–1).

[62] Wright (2004b: 14), discussing evidence for shared practices of supralocal "elite feasting," includes "perhaps some settlements on the western Anatolian coast" in the "characteristic archaeological culture" of Mycenaeans. See below on Troy. Also see Steel (2004b: 172–7) on Mycenaean influence on Cypriot drinking; see V. Karageorghis (1982: 77–80) for a discussion of the vessels themselves.

from Troia VI (1750–1300 BCE),[63] along with fragments of imported Mycenaean dinnerware, is evidence that Mycenaean dining practices were considered to be worth imitating by some at Troy.[64]

In turn, the avid interest in such vessels from Anatolia on the part of Mycenaeans is evinced by the fact that the Mycenaean and Homeric term *depas* 'two-handled cup' is borrowed from Luwian *tapiš* (Hittite *tapišana*).[65] The particularly lovely artifact depicted in Fig. 5, a silver drinking vessel in the shape of a stag on all fours from Shaft Grave IV at Mycenae, is surely of Anatolian provenance. It is an heirloom that is a good 150 years older than its context,[66] and it represents the type of object that would serve as a guest-gift, but whether directly from Anatolia or via an intermediary there is no way to ascertain.[67]

Low-level Anatolians certainly made their way to Mycenaean sites. In ration lists from Pylos appear groups of Anatolian women, "possibly slaves, from other sites on the Asiatic coast and an offshore island (*ki-ni-di-ja* = woman from Knidos, *ze-pu₃-ra₃* = woman from Zephyros = Halikarnassos?, ... and *ra-mi-ni-ja* = woman from Lemnos."[68] Even if we cannot directly connect any single event that is described in the Hittite texts with the appearance of these Anatolians in Linear B texts, we must not dismiss the inference that unrest in Anatolia involving Mycenaeans was responsible for their departure from their homeland.

In addition, the high-level diplomatic contacts between Ahhiyawans and Anatolians that are indicated by the Hittite letters may be corroborated by the Theban ration lists discussed earlier, which were intended to feed people attending a multi-day festival. They include Smintheus

---

[63] Mountjoy (1997) on the pottery. Locally produced: Mommsen, Hertel, and Mountjoy (2001: 181–94, 202–3); Mommsen and Mountjoy (2006). I use the dating of Jablonka and Rose (2011: 898).

[64] Pavúk (2005), Rose (2008: 409).   [65] Watkins (2007a: 319–21).

[66] It is most similar to vessels from Kültepe II (1970–1835 BCE). There may have been an attempt to convert the stag *bibrû* to a two-holed Mycenaean-style rhyton by drilling a hole through its nose. On the *bibrû* see Koehl (1995). It is not unusual to see modifications to imported vessels, for example, ostrich egg rhyta from Africa and an alabaster jar from Egypt (Burns 2010: 94). On the dating of the shaft-graves see Dickinson (1977: 40–51) and Warren and Hankey (1989: 96–7).

[67] A cache of one mina's worth of Near Eastern seals, some of them re-cut in Cyprus, was found at Mycenaean Thebes. They could be considered a gift from a Hittite or Alashiyan king. It has also been proposed that they are from Tukulti-Ninurta I, under the assumption that Assyria was courting Ahhiyawa to form an alliance against the Hittites (Porada 1981–1982).

[68] Niemeier (1998: 40), PY Aa 792, Ab 189.B; Aa 61; Ab 186.B. Also see S. P. Morris (2001a: 424–7), Nikoloudis (2008: 46–8), Palaima (2007, with earlier references) for discussion of these examples and for additional examples of anthroponyms derived from Anatolian place names.

(*si-mi-te-u*, cf. Sminthia), Trowos *(to-ro-wo,* 'Trojan' or 'man from Tlos'?), and, most frequently, a Milesian (*mi-ra-ti-jo*), who appears seven times.[69] His appearance is not entirely surprising, given Miletus' close ties with Ahhiyawa.

Evidence for movements between Anatolia and Mycenaean Greece of craftsmen, who would have been sent as "gifts" between kings,[70] include the monumental lion gate and the Cyclopean walls of Mycenae, which bear such close similarities to Hittite constructions that it can be inferred they were built under the guidance of Hittite craftsmen sent by the king. The fortifications of Tiryns also bear the mark of Hittite craftsmanship.[71] In turn, fragments of Mycenaean-style frescos have been discovered at Hattusa.[72]

Mention of a *Potniya Aswiya*, 'lady of Assuwa', in a Linear B document from Pylos could be evidence of transmission of Anatolian cult to Mycenaeans, possibly as a result of the alliance between Assuwa and Ahhiyawa that had been sealed by a dynastic marriage.[73] The cult personnel who probably accompanied the Aswiyan Lady would have been versed in Anatolian songs celebrating her; perhaps they are the attendants mentioned in the texts who are also provided with similar offerings.[74] It even seems that this goddess was paired with a second Anatolian import, a *ma-te-re te-i-ja* 'mother of the gods' or 'divine mother'.[75] In turn, an oracular inquiry from the time of Mursili II shows that a god from Lazpa (Lesbos) and a god from Ahhiyawa made their way to the Hittites as part of an effort to free the king from illness.[76] The oracle inquiry asks whether to perform a three-day festival and libate in the manner of Hattusa when the gods are brought.[77] While it remains unclear whether cult personnel accompanied the Ahhiyawan god to perform a healing ritual the god was known for, this is a plausible conclusion, based on the analogy with the Arzawan augur

---

[69] See Chapter 10, 231.   [70] See Chapter 9, 202, 207–9.
[71] Maran (2004), Niemeier (2008: 329–30). According to legend Lycian giants built the walls of Tiryns (Str. 8.6.11; Apoll. *Bib.* 2.2.1). See further Bryce (2006: 102).
[72] Brysbaert (2008: 102), Niemeier (2008: 330).
[73] PY Fr 1206 (Watkins 1986: 709; 1998: 203, with earlier references; S. P. Morris 2001a).
[74] S. P. Morris (2001a: 423–4) discusses whether these attendants (*a-pi-qo-ro-i* or *amphipoloi*, PY Fr 1205) should be considered divine or human. If human, they – or their ancestors – could have accompanied the goddess from Anatolia.
[75] PY Fr 1202a, see S. P. Morris (2001a: 423–5, 429 with n. 40) and Muss (2007: 182–3).
[76] On Bronze Age Lazpa see Mason (2008), K. and S. Tausend (2006), and Teffeteller (2013).
[77] *Liver Oracle: CTH* 570 = *KUB* 5.6 ii 57′–64′ (translit. and trans. Beckman, Bryce, and Cline 2011: 192–5); see Bachvarova (2009: 32), where I suggest that cult personnel may have come with the gods. As S. P. Morris (2001a: 428–9, 433) shows, these transfers can be matched by examples drawn from Greek and Latin literature.

who performed healing rituals involving Appaluwa, who would have been his local version of the Tutelary Deity of the Steppe.[78]

Conclusion

This is the evidence known so far for the kinds of interactions in the Late Bronze Age that could have provided the basis for legends of contact between Anatolians and Greek-speakers in the Iron Age. Moreover, the contact between west Anatolia and the Hittites on the one hand and between west Anatolia and Ahhiyawa on the other could have provided the means for the narratives found in the texts at Hattusa to make their way to Greek-speakers. Given the evidence discussed earlier connecting the popularity of Hurrian narrative song at the Hittite court with the creation of dynastic ties with the Hurrian ruling house in Kizzuwatna,[79] it is not entirely impossible that Greek epic and a version of Hurro-Hittite epic (introduced to Wilusa through its dynastic ties to Hattusa) had already come into contact in the Late Bronze Age. Thus, traditional storylines about the fall of a city (any city, not necessarily Troy) could have first crossed into the Greek epic tradition in the Bronze Age in the context of the negotiation of local identities in the southeast Aegean discussed earlier.[80] But, I argue that the more likely scenario is that both the traditional storyline and the reminiscences of Bronze Age Troy were retained, not in a specifically Greek epic tradition, but in the collective memory and epic traditions of west Anatolians.

I have already discussed the fact that we know a song about Troy was performed within the cult of Istanuwa in northwest Anatolia.[81] In addition, there is a hint that the destruction of Troy was considered an event worthy of commemoration as befitted its status as a strategically located city already with a long history going back to the Early Bronze Age. The place Tarwisa (Troy) appears in a Hieroglyphic Luwian inscription on a silver bowl, as *Tara/i-wa/i-za*.[82] The inscription dates the year in which the bowl was made to the following event: "When Tudhaliya, *Labarna*, struck the land of *Tara/i-wa/i-za*."[83] If the Tudhaliya mentioned on the bowl is the

---

[78] See Chapter 10, 246–8. Also cf. the visit paid by Shawushka of Nineveh to Amenhotep III (Chapter 9, 202, n. 10).
[79] See Chapter 7, 157, 164.   [80] Touched upon in Chapter 11, 273.   [81] Chapter 2, 21.
[82] Hawkins (1997); also see Bryce (2006: 109).
[83] ANKARA 2 §§2–3, modified from trans. Durnford (2010: 55). While Starke (1997: 474, n. 86a) disagrees on phonological and historical grounds, see Hajnal (2003: 32–5) for a clear

Middle Hittite Tudhaliya I rather than the New Hittite Tudhaliya IV, this would be our earliest Hieroglyphic Luwian inscription outside of seals and pot marks by at least a hundred years. Stephen Durnford neatly solves the problem of dating by offering the suggestion that the inscription commemorates a legendary event, the memory of which was transmitted orally.[84] From this insight comes the further suggestion that Troy was sufficiently famous already in the Late Bronze Age for its fate to be the subject of legend. It is possible then that the storyline originally attached to Ebla or to Akkade was used as a framework for a song about Troy already in the Late Bronze Age. The question now is, how and why was Troy still remembered in the Iron Age as a city that underwent a legendary destruction?

---

explanation of the relationship between *Taruiša*, *Tara/i-wa/i-za* and *Troiē*. Simon (2009), however, is not persuaded and argues the silver bowl refers to an entirely different place in Urartu, $^{KUR}Tar(a)iu$.

[84] Durnford (2010).

14 | Continuity of memory at Troy and in Anatolia

Socrates: But what in fact is it that they (the Spartans) hear most happily from you and praise? You yourself tell me, since I haven't found out.

Hippias: Concerning the families (*genōn*), oh Socrates, of heroes and men, and foundations, how cities were established in the old days (*to arkhaion*); in sum, they listen most happily to all knowledge of the distant past (*arkhaiologiās*), so that I have been forced for their sake to learn thoroughly and pay special attention to all these sorts of things.

Plato *Hippias Maior* 285d

Introduction

In this chapter I piece together some suggestive material from Early Iron Age Troy and from later sources about western Anatolia, and I make cautious use of the Neo-Hittite material to argue, first of all, that there was an effort to remember and memorialize a legendary Bronze Age past among Syro-Anatolians as there was among Greeks, which would allow for some facts about Bronze Age Troy to be retained, and secondly, that royal ancestor veneration continued to be an important means of defining a community's identity and to be connected to epic narration. This is much more obvious for eastern Anatolia, but there are sufficient hints from western Anatolia to support the contention, which helps to explain how memories of Bronze Age Troy made their way into epic narratives about the doings of legendary heroes there.

I begin by differentiating authentic from spurious reminiscences of Late Bronze Age Greco-Anatolian relations around Troy in the *Iliad*. Then, I turn to the question of how any authentic memories could have been retained. I examine evidence for cultural continuity in west Anatolia and the transition from the Bronze Age to the Iron Age at Troy. I concentrate especially on evidence that the ruins of Bronze Age Troy became a focus of cult ritual as early as *ca.* 1050 BCE, while the later rituals were clearly Greek-style ancestor veneration.

I then look at evidence of attempts to maintain continuity of dynastic names among the Iron Age descendants of the Hittite empire, which suggests an interest in maintaining a connection to their past. With regard to genealogies from the Troad, on the other hand, or to specific suggestions of how memories would have been retained across the end of the Bronze Age and in what form, we are lacking any direct evidence. But, I can discuss Lydian dynastic naming practices and the evidence they provide for memories of west Anatolian Bronze Age dynasties being kept alive, as well as the manipulation of fictional genealogical connections to situate the Lydian court in world history, which show the retention of the same values and uses found at Bronze Age Hattusa for elite ancestor veneration.

Finally, I move to discuss evidence of continuity of ancestor veneration rites in Syro-Anatolia, which serves as background for a close analysis of the iconographic program at Karatepe involving the Greco-Anatolian hero Mopsus. The loss of writing in western Anatolia meant the end of Hieroglyphic Luwian inscriptions, and in any case, the habit of carving extended inscriptions and erecting orthostats with elaborate iconographic programs, which can already be found in the Empire period among the Hittites and remained an important propaganda tool among their Neo-Hittite successors, had never taken hold in western Anatolia.[1] Thus, we do not have the kind of archaeological evidence from western Anatolia that is available for north Syria and Cilicia, most notably at late eighth-century Karatepe. But, we can infer that there were commonalities between the practices well attested in eastern Anatolia and those we can only surmise for western Anatolia. At Karatepe we can see that public rites of ancestor veneration included festive activities with songs, possibly with plot lines about martial prowess. These are some of the milieus conducive to the transfer of "heroic" epic storylines.[2] While those songs performed at Karatepe have not been preserved, the *Iliad* provides an indirect glimpse of the ones that would have been performed at Troy on equivalent festive occasions honoring legendary ancestors.

---

[1] The Neo-Hittite reliefs possibly inspired the Neo-Assyrian kings to make use of palace reliefs (B. Brown 2010: 17, with earlier references). In fact, Harmanşah (2007; 2013: 183–5) and Aro (2009) argue it could be possible to trace Syrian influence on Assyrian monumental art as far back as Tiglath-Pileser I.

[2] As opposed to theogonic stories or songs about the deeds of gods, if we wish to distinguish between the various types of Greek hexametric narratives that show parallels with Syro-Anatolian narratives from the second millennium BCE.

Reminiscences of Bronze Age Troy in the Homeric tradition

I turn first to the cultural memories of Bronze Age Troy, and to what degree they contain a "kernel of truth."[3] The two memories that are undeniable are the name Alexander as the alternate for Paris and the allegiance of Apollo with Troy, as shown by the *Treaty between Muwattalli II and Alaksandu of Wilusa* (ca. 1275 BCE). As discussed earlier, the characterization of Apollo in the *Iliad* as a bow-bearing plague god who can be appeased according to the advice of an augur shows the god retains important elements of the character of the Bronze-Age Apallu, and the form of Appaliuna's name in the treaty indicates that he has been Graecized.[4] The name of the Wilusan king with whom Muwattalli made the treaty is clearly the same as *Alexandros*, and it can be given the good Greek etymology of "warding off men."[5] Alaksandu's name strongly implies a marriage alliance between Greeks and Anatolians in Wilusa. In the context of the supporting role played by Ahhiyawa in the west Anatolian polities' attempts to throw off the Hittite yoke,[6] such an alliance would be far from surprising.

The names *Paris* and *Priamos* meanwhile sound very much like (hypocoristic) Anatolian names containing the component *pariya*-'exceeding, outstanding'.[7] Thus, the Homeric Paris had both a Greek name, known to the Hittites, and an Anatolian one. The prince is called Alexander by Greeks, the gods, and Trojans when they speak to Greeks; he is called Paris by Trojans speaking to other Trojans.[8] This fits neatly with the proposed origins of his two names,[9] suggesting that at one point in the

---

[3] For an overview of Bronze Age Troy, see Rose (2014: 8–43).
[4] For more detailed discussion of Appaliuna/Apollo, see Chapter 10, 245–8.
[5] Watkins (1998: 207). On Alaksandu, see Güterbock (1986: 223–4), who notes that the female equivalent, Alexandra, appears in Linear B (*a-re-ka-sa-da-ra*, MY V 659.2).
[6] See Chapter 13, 334–41.
[7] Watkins (1986: 709–12, with earlier references), who compares the name Paris to Pariyamuwa (also see Starke 1997: 458).
[8] I. J. F. de Jong (1987).
[9] Watkins (1986: 704–5) suggests that Alaksandu "was for him his 'international name'," and that double names are perhaps the result of intermarriage or guest friendship. He goes on to discuss the double name of Hector's son Astyanax/Scamandrius (Watkins 1986: 706; also Watkins 1998: 208–11), for which Nagy (2010: 203–7) has an alternate explanation, see Chapter 15, 412. Priam also has another name, Podarces (Gr. 'swift-footed'), which he changed to Priam when he acceded to the throne, according to Apollodorus (*Bib.* 3.12.5). Suter (1991b), following Homer's explicit statement about alternate names in other cases, argues rather that Paris is the hero's divine name and Alexander his human one. On the notion of the language of gods and men, see Chapter 16, 427–8.

development of the Homeric narrative, the Trojan prince was considered to be of mixed heritage, although that "fact" may long since have been forgotten by the eighth century BCE. His double name is also a reminiscence or continuance of the dynastic custom in Bronze Age Anatolia of carrying two names to mark a dual heritage,[10] a custom that continued into the Lydian Mermnad dynasty with, for example, Meles/Myrsus and Myrsilus/Adyattes.[11]

The names of the Wilusan king and god show that the Homeric tradition preserved at least two details that can be traced back to the second millennium, and other elements of the *Iliad* are likely to represent accurate reminiscences from the Bronze Age. Particularly cogent is Joachim Latacz's comparison of the grouping of two obscure towns in the Boeotian section of the Catalog of Ships, Eutresis and Eleon (*Il.* 2.500, 502), which contribute to the contingent from Thebes, with the appearance of two towns in a Linear B tablet from Thebes, TH Ft 140, a list of towns providing olives and grain: *e-u-te-re-u* and *e-re-o-ni*.[12] Indeed, Sarah Morris has pointed out that the fleet depicted in the frescos at second-millennium Thera can be seen as a pictorial equivalent to the Catalog of Ships,[13] so the ship catalog on its own could represent a very archaic genre.

But, I disagree with Latacz, who, setting the origin of the Greek epic about the fall of Troy at a date between 1450 and 1050 BCE, contends that it is a reminiscence of a real conflict between Troy and the Greeks and maintains that the situation portrayed in the two catalogs of Greek and Trojan allies and throughout the epic is based on facts from the Mycenaean

---

[10] For example, the Hittite king Tudhaliya III had the Hurrian name Tashmi-Sharri, and Tudhaliya IV used the Hurrian name Hishmi-Sharruma before his ascension. Other examples of Hittite kings bearing dual names are Muwattalli II, also known as Sharri-Teshshub and Urhi-Teshshub, who used the name Mursili (III) during his brief reign, while the king of Carchemish Piyassili was also known as Sharri-Kushuh. It is true that names alone, while they indicate ethnic mixing, cannot be used to prove that their bearers continued to speak the language from which their name was derived. For example, the ruling family of the Mitanni Hurrians carried Indo-Aryan names; thus, Kili-Teshshub used the throne name of Shattiwaza (more examples in Derakhshani 1998: 152–7). Yet, there is no evidence that the ruling family of Mitanni continued to speak Indo-Aryan, even while some Indo-Aryan cultural traits and vocabulary items made their way into Mitanni Hurrian; nor do we have any evidence that Hurrian was spoken extensively by the ruling families of the Hittite empire. But, the double names do indicate first of all that the ethnic designation was prestigious.

[11] For Meles/Myrsus see Hdt. 1.7.4, 1.84. For Myrsilus see below, 374–5.

[12] Latacz (2004: 244–7); see the transliteration and translation of Aravantinos, Godart, and Sacconi (2001: 263–4).

[13] S. P. Morris (1989).

period.[14] The poet doubtless intends to portray Anatolia before the first-millennium Greek migrations. Of the Greeks, only Tlepolemus, son of Heracles, is mentioned as having migrated to Rhodes in the Catalog of Ships (2.653–70). The catalog tells us that the Greeks only possessed, besides Rhodes, some of the other Dodecanese islands off the coast of Anatolia between Miletus and Lycia: Syme, Nisyros, Carpathus, Casus, Cos, and the Calydnae islands, which were ruled by other sons of Heracles (2.671–80). Lesbos was not in the possession of the Greeks, for Achilles names the island as the westernmost possession of Priam, whose territory extended as far as Phrygia and the Hellespont (24.544–6), and Agamemnon tells us he sacked and plundered the island with Achilles.[15]

However, the *Iliad* cannot represent accurately the situation in the Mycenaean period. For example, Latacz argues that when the Ahhiyawans lost control of Miletus, they lost their toehold on the Anatolian coast and thereupon turned their focus on Troy; that apparently explains why Miletus is not in the possession of the Achaeans in our version of the *Iliad*. But, the situation was surely far more complex than that. As Wolf-Dietrich Niemeier notes, even after the Hittites sacked Miletus v, domestic architecture, pottery, and evidence of cult show that the inhabitants maintained a Mycenaean identity.[16] Mycenaeans were already settled in southern Ionia, or at least people were there who were making and using Mycenaean pottery and tombs, and there they stayed even when Ahhiyawa no longer exerted political control over them, if it ever did more than in word. In addition, Ephesus played an important role in Mycenaean–Anatolian relations, yet it is never mentioned in the *Iliad*. This omission could be explained by consideration of a putative first-millennium Panionic audience, with Miletus, rather than Ephesus, originally controlling the Panionia.[17] Therefore, even if the *Iliad* was intended by the poet to reflect the political situation of west Anatolia at the end of the heroic age (the beginning of the twelfth century) and was based on a continuous tradition of remembering the Late Bronze Age past of west Anatolia, the actual

---

[14] Latacz (2004: 211–49, 267–74, 283–7; 2005: 342–5). See the discussion of Kirk (1985: 262–3), arguing against the possibility of a Mycenaean-era list of Trojan allies, and Kullmann (1999a: 49–51).

[15] *Il.* 9.129–30, also 664–5. Also see Chapter 15, 411, on the implications of the audience's knowledge that the island would later be Aeolian.

[16] Latacz (2004: 238 with n. 51, 205–6), Niemeier (2009: 16–18).

[17] The lack of any mention of Ephesus may perhaps be explained by the rivalry between Ephesus and Miletus for primacy among the Ionians, which Miletus seems to have won with regard to Homer. On the rivalry see Frame (2009: 528–41), Str. 14.1.3, and Chapter 16, 444, on Ephesus replacing Miletus as the premier city in the Panionic League.

identity-making engaged in by the people who lived then would have been much more complex, and the cultural memory of the Bronze Age was repeatedly reworked in light of succeeding political considerations. The provably accurate memories about Troy are solely the dynasty name Alexander and its city god Appaliuna.

For these reasons, I will not take a strong stand on the historicity or dating of the Trojan War.[18] Certainly we can see that the Ahhiyawans were interested in controlling Wilusa as part of their activities in southwestern Anatolia. Besides their possible interference in the war with Assuwa, in the *Tawagalawa Letter* Wilusa seems to be an area of conflict between Ahhiyawa and Hattusa.[19] Thus, Troy was a space contested between Anatolians and Greeks already in the Late Bronze Age. At this point, if I were forced to choose a significant event, the garbled memory of which ultimately lay behind the tradition of the Trojan War, I would opt for the destruction either of Troia vih (1300 BCE, but it probably was destroyed by a large earthquake) or of Troia viia (1180 BCE), which fell at the end of the Bronze Age, after which there was a sharp decrease in the population.[20] Whether the destruction was caused by a natural event, by Mycenaeans, or by another group (the Sea Peoples?) is not very important, in my opinion,[21] given the evident lack of concern for historicity in the narrative traditions of the eastern Mediterranean; for example, the celebrated "fall of Akkade," attributed to Naram-Sin in lament and legend, did not occur in his reign.[22] When we have external sources against which to check the

---

[18] See Latacz (2004: vii–xi, 20–91) for a discussion of how the controversial question of the historicity of the Trojan War was re-opened among German scholars. Nor will I weigh in on the debate concerning the size and importance of the city, so vehemently argued by Korfmann, the excavator of the site, and his supporters on the one side, and Kolb and his faction on the other. See, for example, Easton *et al.* (2002), defending Korfmann, with the response of Hertel and Kolb (2003), or Kolb (2004), with the response of Jablonka and Rose (2004).

[19] The Hittite king tells the king of Ahhiyawa what he should write to Piyamaradu: "The king of Hatti – about which matter concerning Wilusa we were inimical, in this matter he has swayed me" (*CTH* 181 = *KUB* 14.3 iv 7–9, translit. Beckman, Bryce, and Cline 2011: 116).

[20] I follow the dates of Jablonka and Rose (2011: 898). On Troia vi and vii see Rose (2008: 409–13). On the transition to Troia vii, see Becks (2003: 49–50). On the decrease in population after the fall of Troia viia, see Aslan (2009b: 268). Note that Troia viib1 should probably be subsumed under viib2 (Aslan 2009a: 146–7). See below for further discussion.

[21] See Bryce (2006: 180–94) for the most reliable and up-to-date review of the Late Bronze Age data for a putative war between Mycenaeans and Anatolians at Wilusa. Bryce (2006: 64–7), while admitting that there is little conclusive evidence that the conflagration which destroyed Troia vih was caused by enemy action, suggests that this level fits with the traditional dating of the war, while Troia viia, more clearly the victim of war, was "too late to be linked with a concerted Mycenaean invasion from the Greek mainland" (67).

[22] See Chapter 8, 185, with n. 86.

veracity of an epic storyline, it is clear that epic traditions garble the "facts" in pursuit of presenting a different sort of truth. As Kurt Raaflaub observes,

> The *Chanson de Roland* turns history upside down and creates a crusader attitude where none was warranted. The *Nibelungenlied* combines protagonists who were irreconcilably separated by place and time. Serbo-Croatian epics dwell on a great national event, but populate it with figures who were never there, and with a traitor who was none.[23]

What is clear, however, is that the story of the fall of Troy follows traditional Near Eastern narrative patterns that can be traced back to the beginning of the second millennium,[24] and it is more interesting to me to trace how the knowledge of these storylines was retained and transmitted, rather than how knowledge of a putative historical event survived the end of the Bronze Age. In fact, the stories found in the *Song of Release* and the *Cuthean Legend of Naram-Sin* have survived remarkably well, both in terms of the overall trajectory of their plots and in terms of the phrasing of key scenes. Two factors must have been operating to ensure they were retained across the Bronze Age in the repertoire of Anatolian epic poets and then passed to Greek bards. First of all, the storylines had to continue to be meaningful to new audiences, both the situation of a city attacked by foreigners who came from afar, and the moral culpability of the ruling class that created the situation leading to the destruction, whether it was a council that could be blamed or an individual member of the royal family. Secondly, the tradition from which the Greeks adapted the storylines needed to be prestigious enough to make them willing to use the new, Near-Eastern-derived material in reworking their own inherited storylines, as represented, e.g., by Nestor's epyllia (*Il.* 7.132–57, 11.670–762), reminiscences of his youthful prowess in cattle-raiding or fighting a nearby – not distant – city for resources.[25]

---

[23] Raaflaub (2006: 454). See his more detailed discussions in Raaflaub (1998b: 395–6; 2005: 63–5). Astour (2002: 154–6) argues effectively against attempts to argue that Meki represents a single historical king. See Alster and Oshima (2007: 6–8) on distortion and anachronism in Mesopotamian epic and legend.

[24] See Chapter 6, 139–42, on the parallels with the *Song of Release*; Chapter 8, 191–5, on the parallels with the *Cuthean Legend of Naram-Sin*.

[25] Raaflaub (2003) argues that these passages represent the older form of Greek epic narratives. On Nestor as a hero of an otherwise lost ancient Pylian tradition, see Hainsworth (1993: 296–8). Furthermore, Raaflaub claims that a conflict between two cities across the sea from each other would have been unimaginable until shortly before the time that Homer composed the *Iliad*. According to him, any epic tradition of such a conflict would not have survived across the Dark Age, and the concept of an alliance of Greeks fits with Panhellenic impulses appropriate to the

The primary change in perspective when the storyline represented by the *Song of Release* was reworked was to focus on the attackers, rather than the besieged. While we do not have enough of the *Song of Release* to see where the narrator's sympathies lie, we might suspect, given the sympathetic portrayal of Meki, who is intent on protecting his city from the stupid decision of his assembly, that the narrator was focused on the consequences to Ebla rather than on glorifying the army that carried out the Storm-god's purpose. In other words, the story moved from appealing to an Anatolian audience, who saw themselves in the defeated city-dwellers, to appealing to a Greek or mixed audience. This, along with the use of Naram-Sin's storyline, points definitively to a contested tradition about the blame for the destruction of Troy, in which at first those who identified with the Trojans used inherited storylines to express the culpability of the invading attackers, who stood for the contemporary Greeks who were moving into the Troad. Then, the Greeks co-opted and turned around the story to present themselves as wronged. The questions that still remain to be answered, are how, when, and why a story about Troy entered the Greek epic tradition, and what kinds of archaeological and textual evidence can be brought to bear to flesh out this picture.

Cultural continuity and Greek migrations in Early Iron Age west Anatolia

There was continuity of culture in west Anatolia despite various disruptions, beginning with the disturbances that archaeologists relate to the movements of the Sea Peoples, because of which, according to Ramses III's claim, Arzawa, along with Hatti, Qode, Carchemish, and Alashiya, was destroyed.[26] Although Hittite cuneiform disappears from our view with the fall of the Hittite empire,[27] Anatolian languages such as Lydian, Carian, Lycian, Sidetic, and Pisidian were spoken in Anatolia even after the Classical period, and their speakers came into close contact with Greeks,

---

Archaic era, not earlier. See Chapter 11, 277, n. 42, on the loss of cultural memory at the end of the Late Bronze Age in Greece.

[26] *Sea Peoples Campaign, Medinet Habu: Great Inscription of the Year 8* (*KRI* 5.9) §39 (trans. Kitchen 2008: 34). See Hawkins (2000: 39). On the transition to the Early Iron Age, see the articles collected in Oren (2000) and Ward and Joukowsky (1992). For an overview of the history of Early Iron Age Anatolia, see Kuhrt (1995: 547–72). Also see references in Chapter 12, 310, n. 44. Qode is the Assyrian term for the earlier Kizzuwatna.

[27] On which see Seeher (2001) and Singer (2000).

who later defined themselves as Aeolian or Ionian, when they began to settle along the Anatolian coast again in the Protogeometric period (1050 BCE). Gordion, Sardis, Ephesus, Miletus, and Troy all show evidence of continuous or near-continuous settlement from the Hittite period to the Classical period. Thus, the social context certainly could have allowed for the retention of the storylines into the Early Iron Age and then their subsequent transmission to the Greeks.

One group new to the archaeological record in Anatolia is the Phrygians, who appear in the eleventh century. They were an Indo-European people speaking a language to be grouped with Greek and Armenian.[28] Phrygian culture and religion assimilated many practices and beliefs of the indigenous peoples the Phrygians encountered when they entered Anatolia, and they proved to be an important means by which Greeks assimilated Anatolian gods and religious customs, for example, Cybele.[29] Gordion, the center of Phrygian territory, had been a satellite of the Hittite empire in the Late Bronze Age. It was situated on a major east–west route from the central Anatolian plateau to the Sea of Marmara,[30] and knowledge of the Hittite administrative system there is shown by sealings from Hittite seals at the site.[31] We see a change of population with the collapse of the Hittite empire marking the arrival of the Phrygians (end of YHSS 8, *ca.* 1200 BCE), but no evidence of destruction is found, and the Phrygian population seems to have lived side-by-side with the earlier population,[32] a situation conducive to continuity and blending of traditions.[33]

At its height at the end of the eighth century, the Phrygian kingdom under Midas (*ca.* 700 BCE), or Mita of the Mushki, as the Assyrians called him, encompassed Boğazköy and Alişar, reaching from Dascylium to Tyana.[34] The name Midas is attested for a king of Pahhuwa in Hittite

---

[28] On the Phrygian language see C. Brixhe in Woodard (2004: 777–88). On the Phrygians, see the contributions in Kealhofer (2005), plus Popko (2008: 127–34), Voigt and Henrickson (2000a; 2000b), Wittke (2007). Berndt-Ersöz (2006) provides many examples of continuity between Hittite and Phrygian religion. See Hutter (2006) on the Phrygian religious culture as a blend of Balkan and Anatolian features.

[29] See Chapter 12, 328, with n. 126.   [30] Voigt and Henrickson (2000b: 42).

[31] Voigt and Henrickson (2000b: 42).

[32] Voigt and Henrickson (2000b: 42–6); see the chronology of Voigt (2005: 27).

[33] Voigt and Henrickson (2000b).

[34] The relationship between the Phrygians and the Mushki lies beyond the scope of this study, but see most recently Bryce (2012: 40), Fiedler (2005), and Wittke (2004). See Muscarella (1998) on interactions between Phrygia and Assyria. See Berges in Berges and Nollé (2000: 469–73) on interactions between Phrygia and Tyana. On the Midas who appears in Assyrian sources also see Chapter 16, 435.

times,[35] and although Pahhuwa was well east of Phrygia,[36] the continued use of the royal name suggests an interest in maintaining ties with earlier Anatolian dynasties.

Phrygian inscriptions dating to the sixth and fifth centuries BCE have been found in Dascylium, and even in Strabo's time a variety of Balkan and indigenous Anatolian peoples speaking their own languages were still present in the Troad. Thus, there was ample opportunity for contact between Phrygians and Greeks in the Troad, and acculturation and blending of the incoming Greeks with the Phrygians and other peoples residing in the area is suggested by their adoption of native names for towns in the area.[37]

Lydia, also called Maeonia, was a region within which the earlier Seha River Land fell. Sardis, the capital of Lydia, was a site at which Mycenaeans and Anatolians had come into contact just as later Greeks intermingled with Lydians, and the city shows some evidence of continuity of cult. The excavators of Sardis see Mycenaean and Cycladic influence on pottery, as well as Hittite influence, in the Late Bronze Age, and they point to evidence of occupation from the Bronze Age continuing into the Iron Age, even with a disruption possibly caused by the movements of Phrygians and possibly signaling the advent of Lydian-speakers to the city.[38]

Aeolis and Ionia, the areas in which new settlements by Greeks were most dense, match well those areas in which Mycenaean/Ahhiyawan activity had been concentrated; between Miletus and Halicarnassus the presence of people originating from Greece was continuous from the Bronze Age.[39] The coincidence with the evidence for Mycenaean contact is certainly in part due to the fact that these are the areas which are most convenient to access by island-hopping from the Greek mainland. But, it also suggests some cultural memory of earlier contacts that encouraged re-settlement of familiar lands, perhaps reflected in the later Greek legends of conflicts, migrations, and settlements on either side of the Trojan War, for

---

[35] CTH 146: *Mita of Pahhuwa* (trans. Beckman 1999b: 160–6). See Mellink (1965).
[36] Del Monte and Tischler (1978: 296).
[37] Str. 12.44.4, Chiai (2006). Also see Chapter 16, 430–1, for Phrygians in the *Iliad*.
[38] Hanfmann (1983: 17–25), Roosevelt (2009: 19–22). The most important Anatolian gods attested in both the Hittite documents and Lydian texts are the plague and warrior god Sandas, the goddess Kubaba, originally from Carchemish, passed on by the Phrygians (Popko 1995: 181–6; see further Chapter 12, 328, n. 126), and Men, who continues the Anatolian Moon-god Arma (de Hoz 1999: 38).
[39] Niemeier (2007b: 88); Crielaard (2009: 56–7). Herodotus (1.142) places some of the Ionian towns in Lydia (Ephesus, Colophon, Teos, Clazomenae, and Phocaea), some in Caria (including Miletus and Priene), and includes the islands Samos and Chios.

example, the settlements of Miletus and Colophon by Cretans in the time of Minos.[40]

Aeolis, the coast of Anatolia facing Lesbos, was not a political entity, but represented the territory of those who considered themselves to be Aeolian Greeks, an identity, like that of the Ionians, forged in Anatolia and Lesbos.[41] The strong Anatolian element detectable in Late Bronze Age Lesbos continued into the Early Iron Age, even after Greeks settled there in the Geometric period. (Protogeometric finds are sparse, but there are some Mycenaean-style tombs.) Some Lesbian towns have Anatolian names, such as Arisbe/a, the third syllable of which can be compared with the *-pa* of Lazpa, and Mytilene, the name of which was built off of the dynastic name Muwattalli.[42]

The legends of an Aeolian migration that occurred before the Ionians' arrival cannot be taken at face value; although the arrival of the Aeolians has been tied to the appearance of "Aeolian" Grey Ware in the Protogeometric period, the pottery is in large part based on local predecessors that go back to the Late Bronze Age. One simple fact that cannot be denied is that people who left inscriptions in a dialect classified as Aeolic settled in Lesbos and the Troad.[43] In addition, we need to take into account the cultural memory passed down to the time of Strabo (13.1.3), who says, "The Ionian (colonization) . . . was farther away from the Troad, but the one of the Aeolians was throughout it; for as a whole it is scattered from the Cyzicene to the Caecus, and it reached still further to the part between the Caecus and the Hermus River."

---

[40] Paus. 7.2.5, 3.1, Str. 14.1.6 = Ephorus *FGrH* 70 F 127; 14.1.21. See Bachvarova (2015: 134–41) and Chapter 13, 341.

[41] Hall (2002: 71–3). Aeolis was differently described at different periods. Herodotus (1.149–51) provides a list of twelve cities that extended along the coast between Cyme and Smyrna (although he states that the Ionians had taken the latter from the Aeolians) and mentions settlements in Lesbos and Tenedos. See Rose (2008: 402).

[42] Mason (2008). Spencer (1995: 300) stresses the implications of the Near Eastern influence on the Archaic temple of Lesbian Klopedi in particular and on the Aeolic architectural style in general: "It is more easy to understand the adoption of this peculiar eastern motif in Lesbos if one considers the eastern contact visible in other aspects of the island's culture in this archaic period." See Betancourt (1977: 17–49) on the Near Eastern origins of the Aeolic volute column; also see Rose (2008: 416). See Teffeteller (2013: 574–8) for continuity of culture across the end of the Bronze Age on Lesbos.

[43] See Hertel (2008: 187–93) connecting "Aeolian" Grey Ware with the Aeolic migration. See R. M. Cook and Dupont (1998: 135–6) on "Aeolian" Grey Ware (further discussion of Grey Ware below, 365), Hodot (1990: 31–40; 2001, chart on p. 157) for Aeolic inscriptions from the Troad, which start with a graffito from the end of the eighth century found at Larissa. See Rose (2008: 402–3, 405) and H. N. Parker (2008: 432–4) on the construction of Aeolian identity, Aeolians, and the supposed Aeolian migration.

Legends of an Ionian migration, in turn, were promoted by Athens, which by the sixth century was interested in justifying control over Ionia by asserting Attic–Ionic kinship.[44] Greek pottery is in evidence in Early Iron Age Ionia starting in the Protogeometric period, indicating trade contacts at the minimum, and here Greeks were to be found in abundance in the Archaic period.[45] From these Greeks, with an admixture of non-Greeks, was forged the Ionic identity.[46]

Both Ephesus and Miletus, in Iron Age Caria/Ionia, must have been important nodes of interaction between Greeks and Anatolians, and places in which cultural characteristics retained from the Bronze Age could have been passed to the Greeks. At Ephesus the Artemision was in continuous use from the Bronze Age. Legend says that when Androclus arrived at Ephesus from Athens he drove out the Leleges and either the Carians or the Lydians,[47] and Early Protogeometric finds with strong connections to Athens provide support to the tale.[48] There is good evidence of cult practices continuing from the Late Bronze Age, including Artemis of Ephesus herself.[49] Although Submycenaean pottery has been found in Miletus, Greek settlement in the Early Iron Age is only clearly evident beginning in the Protogeometric period,[50] and some of the Early Protogeometric pottery is even from Athens.[51] Because it appears that the Bronze Age land Karkisa was not on the coast, as later Caria was, it can

---

[44] Carlier (1984: 432–5), Sakellariou (1990: 137–8, with references to his earlier work). Also see Chapter 10, 234–6, for cultivation of a shared identity across the Aegean.

[45] R. M. Cook and Dupont (1998: 11–14), Huxley (1966: 23–5), Lemos (2002: 211–12), Niemeier (2007b: 88–90). On the (mis-)use of the locally made Protogeometric pottery in the tumulus tombs at Assarlık to argue for the Ionian migration see Carstens (2008b: 78–9).

[46] As Kowalzig (2005: 51) puts it, "'Ionia' was a social and political term, not geographical or ethnic, delineating the group of those who had mutually supported each other in carving out for themselves a comfortable position in the politically complex area which they 'agreed' to become Ionia." On the development of the Ionian identity, see Hall (2002: 67–71) and Crielaard (2009). See Kowalzig (2005: 49–51) for problems with the concept of an Ionian identity, and see Chapter 10, 235, for this identity being maintained through the common celebration of the Panionia.

[47] Str. 14.1.3 = Pherecydes FGrH 3 F 155, Paus. 7.2.8. On Ephesus also see Kerschner et al. (2000), S. P. Morris (2006: 70–1) and Chapter 13, 338, n. 35. On the Artemision see Bammer (1990: 142).

[48] Kerschner (2006).

[49] See Greaves (2010: 190–2): spring worship, a bronze statuette of a Hittite priest, possible influence on statuary, oracle. Artemis: see references in Chapter 10, 234, n. 81.

[50] Boardman (1999: 28), Greaves (2002: 75–7, 90), and Niemeier (2007a: 16–18), noting that the gap in settlement could not have been more than 100 years, and referring to data, to my knowledge as yet unpublished, from the Submycenaean and Protogeometric periods. On nearby Didyma see Chapter 10, 241, with n. 112.

[51] Kerschner (2003: 246).

be proposed that the Carians migrated to Miletus after the end of the Bronze Age, and the Greeks began settling there again in the Iron Age along with or directly after the arrival of this new ethnic group.[52]

Troy across the end of the Bronze Age

Turning now to Troy specifically, we begin with the linguistic situation in second-millennium Wilusa. Ilya Yakubovich has shown that the assumption that western Anatolia was primarily Luwian-speaking is too simple. We should imagine one or more Luwic languages in the area in addition to proto-Lydian and the Tyrrhenian languages, possibly along with other unattested languages of unknown affiliation. We cannot determine definitively what language was spoken in second-millennium Wilusa. While it is plausible to assume that it was a Luwic language,[53] it also could have been an early form of Lydian, for Robert Beekes argues effectively that the Lydians were displaced from the area around Troy and pushed down into Classical Lydia by the immigrating Phrygians at the end of the Late Bronze Age. In turn, one group of the original inhabitants of Lydia, the Tyrsenoi, left Anatolia entirely for the west to become the Etruscans of Italy. The theory is supported by legends, the earliest of which comes from Herodotus, claiming a "Lydian" origin for them, the presence of residual pockets of Tyrsenoi around Troy, and the seventh-century inscriptions found on the island of Lemnos written in a language clearly related to Etruscan.[54] The three Tyrrhenian languages (Etruscan, Lemnian, and Raetic) share

---

[52] On the possibility that Karkisa matches later Caria, see Herda (2009) arguing that it does, and Bachvarova (2015: 130–2), placing it farther inland. See Hawkins (1998: 29), Melchert (2003b: 7) on difficulties defining the exact extent of Karkisa. As noted earlier, Herodotus (1.142) puts Ephesus in Lydia. Miletus was a Carian city after the Late Bronze Age (Herda 2009: 43–60). Niemeier (2009: 21–4) emphasizes rather continuity of Greek settlement.

[53] See the comments of Melchert (2003e: 11–12) and Yakubovich (2010: 117–29). Starke (1997: 456–7) and Bryce (2006: 75–6, 117–22) argue that it was Luwian specifically.

[54] Hdt. 1.57, 94.5–7; D. H. 1.25–30, arguing against the theory. Tyrrhenians in Lemnos: Str. 5.2.4, Th. 4.109. See Beekes (2003a; 2003c). Some of his arguments are rather tendentious. Also, he makes use of the equation of Maeonia and the second-millennium place name Masa, following Starke's location for this west Anatolian political entity in Phrygia/Bithynia (Starke 1997: 451), although admitting that the position of Masa can only be conjectured. See the critique of Yakubovich (2010: 113–17). More likely the name Maeonia is connected to the city name Maddunassa (Roosevelt 2009: 18, with earlier references). But, Beekes does critique effectively the modern theories that the Tyrsenoi in northwest Anatolia and the outlying islands are recent arrivals, since there are too many different sites where they lived, many in less than prime land for new settlers. Also see Roosevelt (2009: 18–22) for a judicious review of the evidence for the movement of Lydians into historical Lydia. Also see Melchert (2008: 154, with earlier references). See Rix (1968) on the relationship between Lemnian and Etruscan, Rix (1998) on

areal features with the Anatolian languages in phonology, morphology, and morphosyntax.[55] And, there is a connection between the name of the Luwian Storm-god Tarhunt ('the powerful one'), and the Etruscan names Tarquinius (cf. *Tarquinius Superbus* 'Tarquin the Proud', the epithet serving as a translation of his Luwian name) and Tarchon, the Etruscan founding hero.[56]

Beekes' argument that proto-Lydians had inhabited the Troad is supported by Gunther Neumann's study of the linguistic affinities of the Trojans. For example, the Lydian *-li* derivational suffix, used to form patronymics and genitival adjectives, can be found in a set of names associated with the Troad, such as *Trōilios* and *Daskulion*.[57] Another reasonable suggestion, made recently by Alwin Kloekhorst, is that the language spoken at Bronze Age Troy was related to Etruscan.[58] However, besides Alaksandu, who has a Greek name, we know the names of only two other second-millennium Wilusan rulers, Kukkunni and Walmu, the latter having a name possibly related to Hitt. *walwa-* 'lion', and the former having a shape like other Anatolian names.[59] Neither has a secure etymology.

While there is "some limited evidence for local production of wheel-made painted pottery in the Mycenaean LH IIIC style,"[60] the appearance of Handmade Coarse Ware and Knobbed Ware at Troy suggests that a new population arrived, probably from Thrace, at the beginning of Troia vɪɪb1 (*ca.* 1180 BCE) and with increasing evidence in the material culture for a new population in Troy vɪɪb2 (*ca.* 1130 BCE). Were they Phrygians? The

---

the relationship between Raetic and Etruscan, and further van der Meer (2004, with a review of the literature) on the Tyrrhenian language family. Oettinger (2010), however, has used the fact that Lemnian (attested sixth century BCE) is more closely related to Etruscan than Raetic (attested third century CE) to argue anew the claim that the Etruscans come from Europe, not Anatolia. Genetic studies of Etruscan cattle, mitochondrial DNA, and Y-chromosomal DNA have supported the Anatolian origin of the Etruscans (Barbujani 2005; Pellecchia *et al.* 2007; Piazza *et al.* 2007), although more recent research has suggested a very early arrival, in the third millennium (Ghirotto *et al.* 2013). See Bachvarova (2012b: 149–51), in which I present this argument in expanded form.

[55] Noted briefly by Watkins (2001: 50–1, 56) and discussed in some detail by Bachvarova (2007b), focusing on the similarities between Hurrian *Suffixaufnahme*; Anatolian genitival adjectives, especially in Luwian and Lydian; and double case-marking in the Tyrrhenian languages.

[56] On Tarhunt, Tarquin, and Tarchon see Beekes (2003c: 30–1).

[57] Neumann (1999). Also see Carruba (2006). [58] Kloekhorst (2012: 49–50).

[59] Kukkunni's name (*CTH* 76.B= *KUB* 21.5 i 18, translit. Friedrich 1930b: 52; trans. Beckman 1999b: 87) is comparable to the name of the Trojan ally Cycnus: see Güterbock (1986: 224–5, with earlier references, Watkins (1986: 704). For possible Iron Age attestations of the name see Oreshko (2013b: 357).

[60] Aslan, Kealhofer, and Grave (2014: 295), citing Mommsen and Mountjoy (2006: 108, 111, nos. 72, 73).

earlier people, however, did not completely vanish from the archaeological record.[61] Carolyn Chabot Aslan points out,

> Previous local Bronze Age types of Grey and Tan Ware ... continued, although they were much reduced in number. Even so, the continuation of the previous ceramic tradition suggests that some local potters were still producing wheel-made wares ... The large numbers and new shapes of handmade utilitarian ware vessels may be indicative of a wider shift in subsistence and food production and cooking practices.[62]

So, we have here a new population mingling with the older residents while new foodways are accommodated. This could have been an important stage in the development of a cultural memory of a glorious past for Troy, associated with the royal ancestor name Alaksandu.[63]

According to Strabo, "the current Ilians say the city was not rendered completely invisible after the sack by the Achaeans, and that it was never abandoned."[64] In fact, the hiatus in settlement between Troia VIIb2 (beginning 1130 BCE), which may have been destroyed by an earthquake,[65] and Troia VIII has now been proved to be illusory, based on secure stratigraphy from the sector D9 on the southern side of the mound (see Fig. 17).[66] The

---

[61] Aslan (2009b: 268–9); Grave et al. (2013: 1775): continued use of the same clay source for the new types of cooking wares "presupposes that some part of the Trojan population must have survived the end of the Troy VIIa settlement and continued to live there." Aslan (2009a: 145–8) argues that it is invalid to distinguish two waves, one attached to Coarse/Barbarian Ware in VIIb1 and one attached to Knobbed Ware in VIIb2. That is, there may be only one ceramic phase here. Rose (2014: 38–9), in contrast, states, "Troy VIIb2 ..., however, is a different case. In these levels Carl Blegen recorded striking changes in the assemblages he discovered, including a preference for stone orthostats in house construction, and molds for tools and weapons that can be paralleled in southeastern Europe. There are also changes in the ceramic record, in that Handmade Burnished Ware was now employed for both cooking and table ware."

[62] Aslan (2009a: 148). Also see the cautious discussion of Aslan, Kealhofer, and Grave (2014).

[63] Rose (2014: 39–40): "It is worth noting that the demographic shift posited for Troy during the twelfth century B.C. does appear to have occurred to Gordion." He calls attention to the tradition recorded by Strabo (12.8.3) that Phrygians, when they came into Anatolia from Thrace, killed the king of Troy.

[64] Str. (13.1.40). As he points out, this runs counter to what Homer himself says. See further Chapter 15, 412.

[65] So Mountjoy (1999b: 333–4).

[66] "There is evidence for two Protogeometric phases following the VIIb2 phase" (Aslan 2009a: 148). One of these is now classified as Troia VIIb3, the other as the beginning of Troia VIII. Phases of D9: Phase 1: *ca.* 1050–950 (PG), Phase 2: *ca.* 950–800 (LPG-EG), Phase 3: *ca.* 800–700 (Geo), Phase 4: *ca.* 700–650/625 (Geo/Archaic transition); Phase 5: *ca.* 625–600/575 (Early Archaic), Phase 6: *ca.* 600/575–550 (Middle Archaic), Phase 7: *ca.* 550–500/480 (Late Archaic) (Aslan 2002: 82). See Basedow (2006; 2007; 2009) disproving decisively Blegen's postulation of a hiatus in settlement, and Rose (2014: 44–5) on how Korfmann's excavation team realized that Blegen was incorrect.

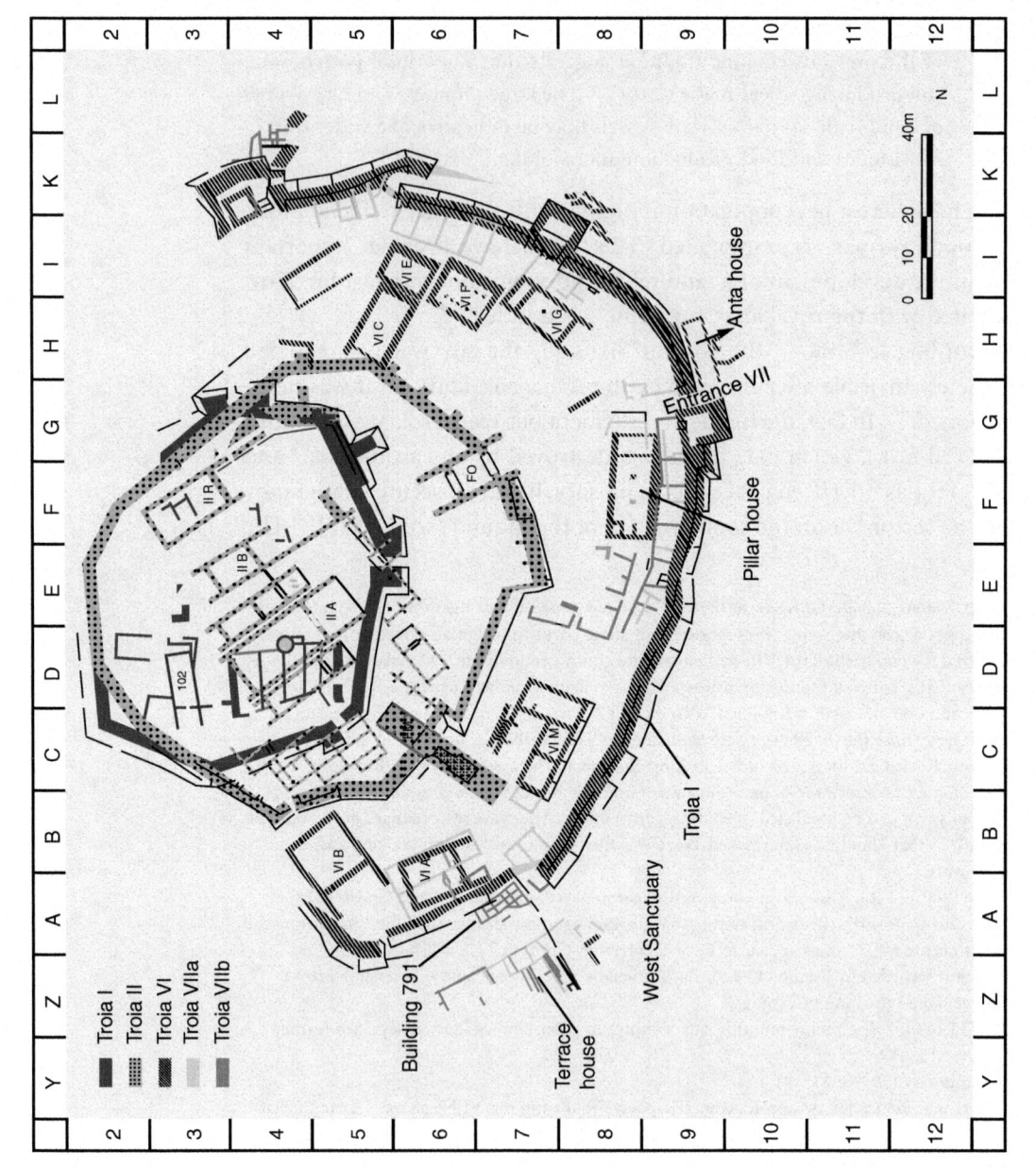

Fig. 17: Troia (top view)

side view of the mound of Troy in Fig. 18 shows why there has been some confusion about the transition from the Late Bronze Age to the Early Iron Age, for the renovations of the site in the Hellenistic period cut off the relevant layers, and Schliemann's dig did further damage. Thus, evidence for this period can only be found at the edge of the citadel. But, despite the "overall sense that that the population has decreased somewhat" after Troia vııb2, the finds in D9 reveal continuity in human presence into the Iron Age.[67]

Troia vııb3 (beginning 1050 BCE) displays the same pottery as in the previous level of Troia vıı, but now with Protogeometric pottery as well.[68] Dieter Hertel associates Troia vııb3 (his "vııı early") with Aeolic settlement because of the appearance of "Aeolian" Grey Ware.[69] However, Aslan asserts concerning the Grey Ware, "Many of the shapes were continuations from the previous period, but there are a few Grey Ware cups ... that have the same shape as painted cups found at Greek mainland sites such as Athens and Lefkandi"[70] (neither of which were Aeolic areas). Almost all the Protogeometric pottery and Gray Ware that has undergone neutron activation analysis was locally made.[71] As will be discussed in the following chapter, the Boeotian connections of Hector are our best evidence that early Greek visitors or settlers at Troy were from an Aeolic area.[72]

With only small areas of Troy along the edges of the mound able to be investigated,[73] we cannot yet determine how large the settlement was, nor the relations between Greeks possibly immigrating to the site and other people who had been previously living there. However, Aslan states, "At no point in the Protogeometric through Geometric periods at Troia is there evidence for a significant influx of Greek-style pottery."[74] The evidence so far, confined only to the edge of the mound, does not allow us to rule out a possible gap in settlement later in the ninth century,[75] and there is clear evidence of actual settlement only in the second half of the eighth century.[76]

---

[67] Aslan (2009a: 148).
[68] See Aslan (2002; 2009a: 148–51, with earlier references) on the pottery; Rose (2008: 412–13) for an overview.
[69] Hertel (2008: 5–8).
[70] Aslan (2009a: 149). Also see Aslan (2002: 91–2; 2009c), Basedow (2007: 50), Rose (2008: 412; 2014: 47), discounting the supposed Aeolian connection. Also see comments of Jablonka (2002) on Hertel's analysis.
[71] Aslan, Kealhofer, and Grave (2014: 293, 297); Mommsen, Hertel, and Mountjoy (2001). Also see below, n. 94 in this chapter.
[72] Chapter 15, 405–6.   [73] Aslan (2009a: 148).   [74] Aslan (2009a: 150).
[75] Aslan (2009a: 150; 2009b: 268).   [76] Rose (2014: 50).

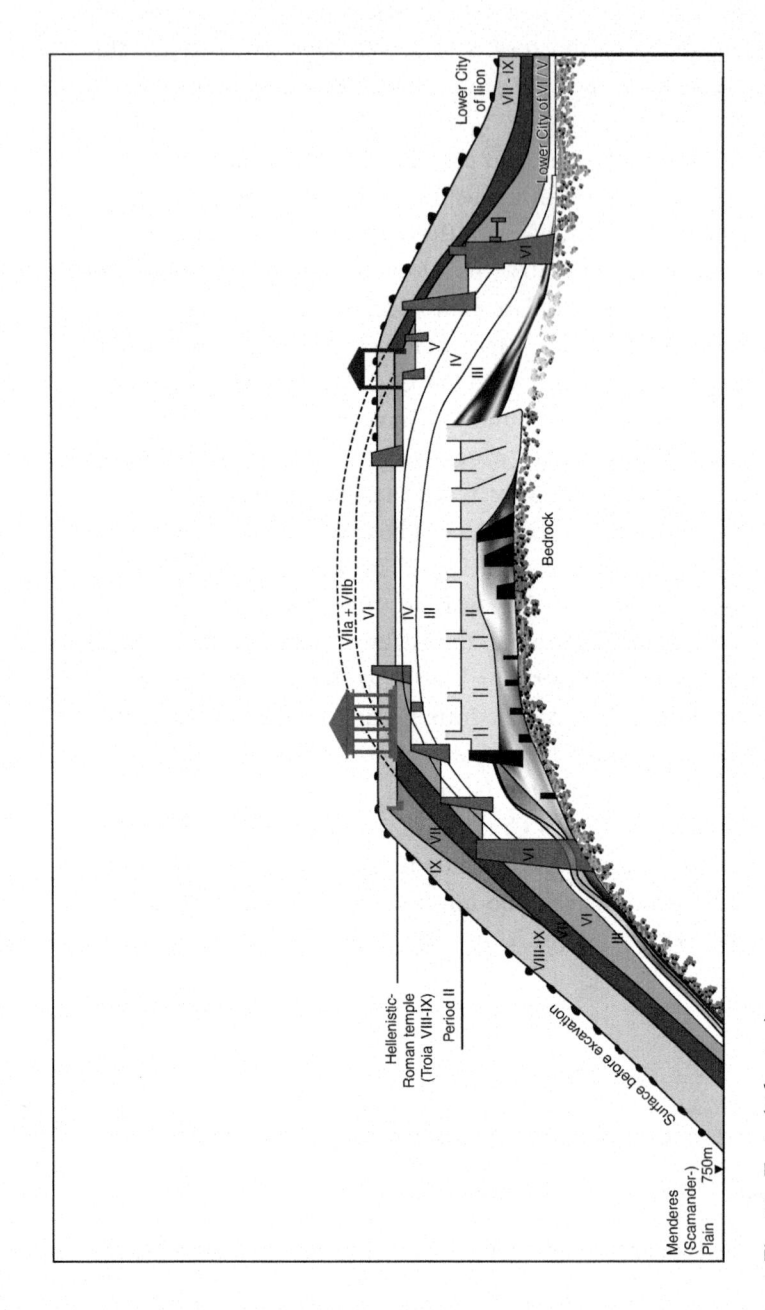

Fig. 18: Troia (side view)

Troy as a place of remembrance

According to Aslan,

> The combined evidence from the late Protogeometric material from the West Sanctuary indicates ritual activity had begun at least by this period, perhaps involving ritual feasting as indicated by the sets of kraters and cups. Impressive Bronze Age remains, including the Troia VI fortification wall and a large Bronze Age building, were located in the area of the West Sanctuary..., and it is likely that the partial ruins of these structures formed the focus for the ritual activity perhaps connected to Bronze Age heroes.[77]

As Maureen Basedow puts it, it was "an active period of ritual culture at Troy."[78] And, as in mainland Greece, memories of the legendary past were attached to prominent ruins.[79]

According to Basedow we may divide the Early Iron Age cult structures in the West Sanctuary into the following phases: Phase 1a (1050–950, PG/MPG), Phase 1b (950–875, LPG/EG), Phase 2 (825/800–725), and Phase 3 (750–650, LG).[80] The Terrace House (Hof Building) of Phase 1 (Fig. 19) was focused towards the ruins of the Late Bronze Age walls. As Rose comments, the ruins of a thirteenth-century structure, abandoned for 130 years, were now being used as a site for cult, but without being rebuilt. In it "[a] wealth of small finds, probably dedications, were found. They suggest the existence of cult activity at least by the early twelfth century B.C."[81] The objects include a bronze figurine of the Syro-Hittite striding god type.[82] In Phase 1b, offering pits appear around the Terrace House, with burnt bones, cult ceramics – for example, a fenestrated stand and strange pronged objects perhaps meant to be dressed as figurines – and some Grey Ware.[83] Sherds of a locally made Mycenaean *krater* (LH IIIB) should be interpreted as pieces of an heirloom, possibly a votive offering

---

[77] Aslan (2009a: 150; her references are omitted here). Also Aslan and Rose (2013: 6–15).
[78] Basedow (2009: 132). Also see Basedow (2006: 20).
[79] The parallels with mainland Greece are noted by Rose (2014: 49–50).
[80] I use the dates of Basedow (2009: 135), but with the date of *ca.* 1050 BCE for the beginning of Phase 1, and descriptions given by Basedow (2006; 2007; 2009), refined by the new interpretation of the West Sanctuary presented in Rose (2014: 47–51).
[81] Rose (2014: 47), citing forthcoming works by C. Aslan and P. Hnila; also Rose (2014: 24).
[82] Published by Mellink and Strahan (1998). Rose (2014: 24, 25, 35, 296, n. 15) alternates between calling the figurine a divinity and a worshipper.
[83] On which see Aslan (2009a: 149–50; 2002: 92).

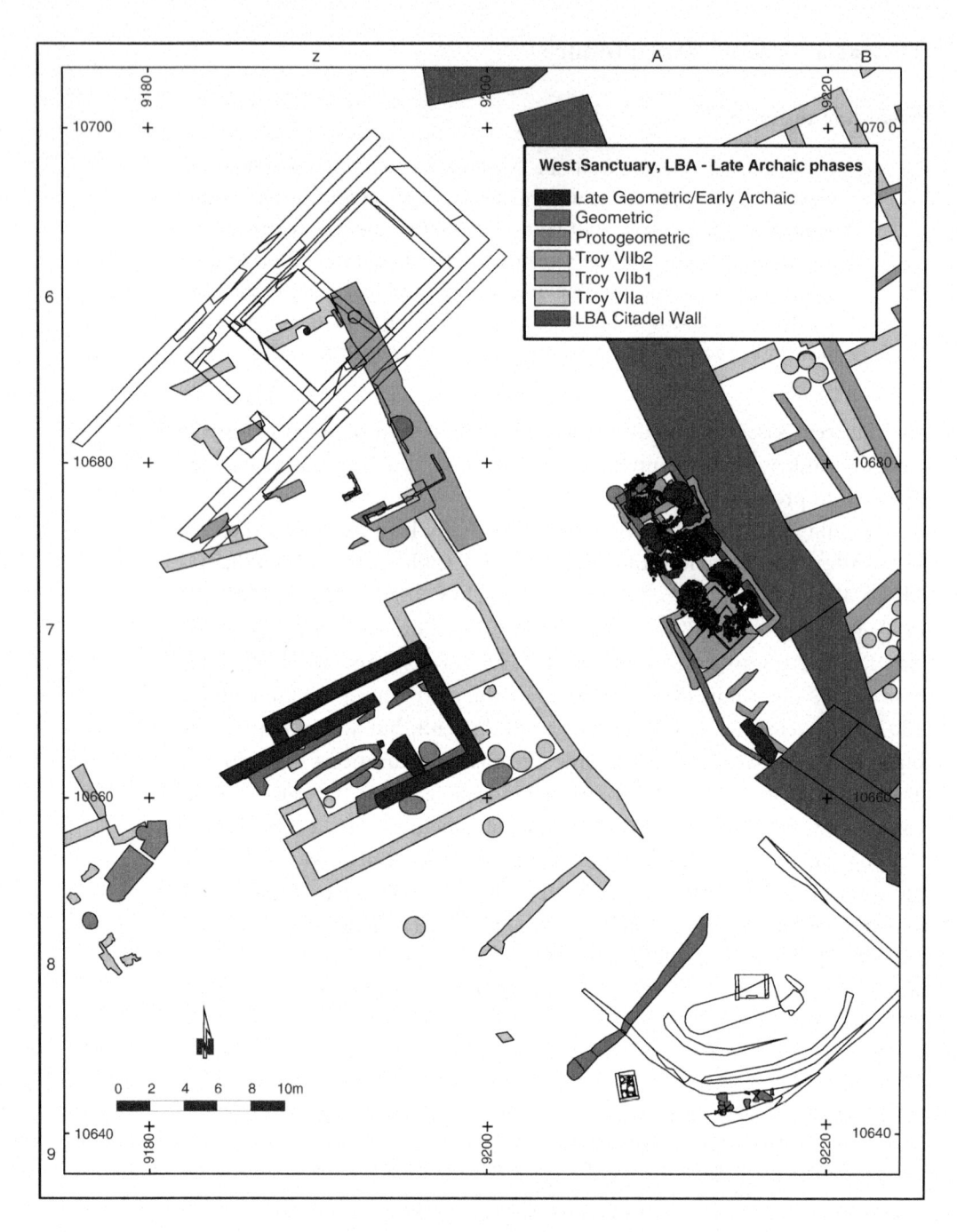

Fig. 19: West Sanctuary at Troy: Terrace House area, walls in dark grey, with ash-filled apsidal structure inside. Postholes for offering table at rear of building appeared in Geo period.

Fig. 20: Stone Circles at Troy, in West Sanctuary

excavated from a nearby Late Bronze Age cemetery.[84] The orientation of the building towards the Bronze Age wall and these offerings already show an interest in a glorious, now lost, Trojan past starting at the close of the Bronze Age.

In Phase 2 an apsidal construction appears in the house, filled with ashes. There are postholes for a triangular offering table, installed near the end of the phase. In Phase 3 the hypaethral structure was replaced with a long, narrow, roofed building, with the east end remodeled near the end of the phase into an apsidal shape. Inside there is a large deposit of bronzes. A stone statue base is placed before the offering table.[85]

By Phase 3 we find the first stone circles on the terrace built on top of earlier structures and pressed up against the remains of the Bronze Age citadel wall (Fig. 20). These replace the Terrace House as the site of cult activities. "Some were surrounded by orthostats, and each was clearly the

---

[84] On the *krater* see Mountjoy (2005). On the interpretation see Basedow (2007: 51, 52, with nn. 14, 19). The preserved pieces show the undecorated bottom of the vessel was cut off before it was broken up.

[85] I summarize the analysis of Phases 2 and 3 by Basedow (2009: 135, 139) here, with additional information from Aslan and Rose (2013: 14–15) and Rose (2014: 50–1).

locus of a fire judging by the layer of black earth on top of them."[86] The stone circles were rebuilt repeatedly over the course of the Geometric period and proliferated on the terrace on top of Building 850, itself built on top of Building 791 in the West Sanctuary. They total some twenty-eight in all and were used until *ca.* 650 BCE.[87] The drinking sets associated with the stone circles are Late Geometric to Early Archaic (750–650 BCE), but a drinking set from the Middle to Late Protogeometric period was also deposited below the circles, and "the existence of a drinking set predating the stone circles indicates that drinking or other rituals next to the citadel wall were already in place in the Late Protogeometric phase."[88] Differences among the circles suggest they each belonged to a specific family.[89] At this point, then, the commemoration of Troy's past could have been articulated at the clan level.

Finally, remains of feasting and drinking dating to *ca.* 700 BCE have been found at an additional site appropriate for ancestor veneration, a Late Bronze Age cremation area just outside the walls of Troy, the "Place of Burning."[90]

The circular stone platforms provide evidence for a shared cult context by which an epic centered on a legendary conflict for territory between Greeks and Anatolians could flow back and forth between Greece and Anatolia, for they represent a supraregional practice of remembering the legendary past and its dead in Greece and along the west coast of Anatolia.[91] The circles are often found with remains of repeated sacrifice or feasting. Aslan's and Basedow's suggestions that parts of the older Troy served as the focus of ancestor veneration should be connected to Manfred Korfmann's suggestion that Homer saw the Late Bronze Age ruins of Troy

---

[86] Rose (2014: 50).
[87] So Rose (2014: 53) on the end date for their use. Hertel (2003a: 86–90) had suggested they date from the tenth century to the fifth century. See further Aslan (2011: 412–17).
[88] Aslan and Rose (2013: 14–15).   [89] Aslan (2002: 84), Basedow (2006: 20).
[90] Aslan (2011), Rose (2014: 51).
[91] On the stone circles at Troy see Aslan and Rose (2013: 11–14, with earlier references) and Basedow (2006). For the phenomenon more widely, see Antonaccio (1994a: 50–1; 1995: 199–207, 250, 256), Hägg (1983), Mazarakis Ainian (1997: 122–3, 380), and catalog in Deoudi (1999: 89–91). I mention only a few examples here: At Nichoria in Messenia a Protogeometric chieftain's house (end of the tenth century–beginning of the ninth) contains such a round platform (Mazarakis Ainian 1997: 74–80; 2006: 185, 187). At Mycenae, there is a round platform with Geometric-period pottery at Grave Circle B (LH II), associated with a LH IIIA chamber tomb (Tomb 220). At Asine in the Argolid, the Geometric-period platforms (*ca.* 800 BCE) near the Geometric necropolis are linked with Middle Helladic tombs. There is also a platform over a tenth-century Protogeometric apsidal building. At Kalabaktepe a Geometric-period oval construction surrounds round platforms. At Miletus at the temple of Athena there is an oval platform from the Late Geometric Period oriented towards the Mycenaean fortifications.

and reconstructed in his mind the ancient city.[92] If, as Barbara Patzek emphasizes, mythico-historical memories were attached to physical objects, such as boar's-tusk helmets, bronze weaponry, or conspicuous tombs, then the ruins of Troy would serve as a large-scale mnemonic device attracting cultural memories,[93] including those of Mycenaean activities at Bronze Age Troy. This ritual activity must have played a role in shaping the Greek legend of the Trojan War, providing a setting for performance and a context that gave the story significance. Basedow argues,

> [C]omparanda suggest that it is the Greeks who are providing the physical structure for the Early Iron Age cults. That there are early cults associated with the prehistoric landscape of Troy, which is now not an abandoned ruin during the Iron Age, as previously thought, is a revelation and impetus to refer Homeric questions regarding composition, geography and sources to the Trojan Iron Age site, rather than the Bronze Age.[94]

The Greek-style pottery found at Troy, although not found in large amounts, has been taken as indicating that the people in Troy had links to Thessaly, whose Phthian hero Achilles played such an important role in the Greek tradition about the fall of Troy.[95] With the local imitation of a

---

[92] Korfmann (2002). He, however, assumes Homer visited Troy while it was unoccupied. Hertel (2003a: 186–218) provides a detailed, if hypothetical, sketch of development of the legend of the Trojan War based on the features visible to the later inhabitants and visitors.

[93] Patzek (1992: 181–5); Grethlein (2010: 132). "At what time the story of an east-west conflict was first linked to the topography of Troy is unclear, but the ruined citadel walls were continuously visible through the seventh century A.D. . . . These were almost certainly the best-preserved ruins of a Late Bronze Age place along the western coast of Asia Minor, so if one were looking for a citadel to link a war between Greece and a coastal Anatolian stronghold, Troy would have been the logical choice. That choice must have been made by the eighth century B.C." (Rose 2014: 42). My perspective differs from the relatively noncommittal view of Rose in that I see the choice of Troy's ruins to be the focus of legends about the Bronze Age as not fortuitous, but based on the status of the city as a contested space both in the Bronze Age and in the Iron Age, which resulted from its desirable location at an entry point from Europe into Asia that controlled access to the Black Sea.

[94] Basedow (2007: 55).

[95] In 1998, R. W. V. Catling, using the material available to him at that point, divided the Protogeometric and Subprotogeometric pottery into four groups. Catling's (1998) analysis remains the framework for later studies, but his conclusions have been modified, both in terms of dating (Aslan 2002: 84–5, in a study of the stratigraphy of area D9) and by neutron activation analysis studies (Mommsen, Hertel and Mountjoy 2001); see Hertel (2003b: 112–18, 127–9) and overview of Rose (2008: 412–13). We must not think only in terms of importation, since the two examples of Group III (large amphorae like Groups I and II, but of a different fabric and paint, ca. 1020–900 BCE) that underwent neutron activation analysis proved to be locally made. In addition, Rose (2014: 46–7, with p. 296, n. 8) reports unpublished NAA results on Group I from C. Aslan and P. Graeve that indicate they were also locally made. Clearest are the

Thessalo-Euboean Grey Ware cup, a type connecting Thessaly and Euboea with the northeast Aegean and northwest Anatolia, there was enough to allow R. W. V. Catling to argue for "a network of contacts linking the northeast Aegean to the Thessalo-Euboian area where Lefkandi, as one of the leading mercantile centres in the Aegean, was the focus of commercial and cultural exchange, and Skyros was the bridge between the two regions."[96] Irene Lemos pushed Catling's conclusions farther by using the archaeological data to infer a route for the transfer of epic from Greece to Anatolia. "It is clear that such links could have provided the means for the transmission of a poetic tradition from Thessaly and Euboea to the eastern Aegean islands and to the sites located on the western coast of Asia Minor."[97]

But, Aslan, Lisa Kealhofer, and Peter Grave offer a different interpretation of the evidence, taking into account the clear cultural continuity at Troy and the local production of Protogeometric ware, which militate against trade or migration being the primary reason for the changes in pottery styles, arguing rather for a northeast Aegean "cultural interaction zone":

> We are not certain why the Trojan inhabitants shifted their attention away from northern connections via Thrace and revitalized a north-east Aegean interaction zone. Protogeometric inhabitants of Troy were signalling a certain status, identity or connectivity through the use of new styles of vessels, as well as perhaps new ritual practices. Trade and cross-community migration must have taken place within this interaction zone, but the evidence does not support a one-sided model of Greek migration or Greek traders, but rather a model of local inhabitants making material cultural choices to create new cultural identities in a changing sphere of interaction.[98]

This model of a cultural interaction sphere fits well the model of bilingual poets working out a shared but contested past that I have proposed to explain the influence of Near Eastern epic on the poetic tradition which

---

affiliations of Catling's Group I, neck-handled amphorae with ribbed handles and decorated with concentric circles (PG, 1025–950 BCE), some from Phase 1 of D9 (corresponding roughly to Phase 1b of the West Sanctuary), which show connections with Chalcidice, south-central Macedonia, central Greece, Lemnos, and Clazomenae (Aslan, Kealhofer, and Grave 2014: 284–5). One fragment of the Group II amphorae (PG, larger and squatter than Group I, *ca.* 800–675 BCE according to Catling, with parallels from the northwest Aegean, from Lefkandi to Thasos, probably originating near Thessaloniki) comes from the "highest layer" of Phase 2 at D9 (*ca.* 800 BCE) (Aslan 2002: 85). Five sherds share a different paint and fabric (Group IV, late tenth–early ninth century). Two of these show Euboean-style pendant semi-circles.

[96] R. W. V. Catling (1998: 179).   [97] Lemos (2002: 217).
[98] Aslan, Kealhofer, and Grave (2014: 302).

eventually produced Homer's *Iliad*. However, it must be emphasized that the evidence from epic, to be discussed in the following chapter, shows that Greek-speakers had already formed an epic about Troy by the Protogeometric period, and this allows us to go beyond the cautious formulation of Aslan, Kealhofer, and Grave to confirm that Greek-speakers were among those coming to Troy, treating it as a site of veneration, and using a mythohistorical narrative about its Bronze Age past to build their own (Greek-speaking) ethnic identity, one which emphasized their connection with their brethren remaining in Greece.

In Chapter 11 we discussed how mainland Greeks, driven both by a fascination with the east and by a desire to reconstruct a lost past, adopted conceptions about generations of men of long ago from the Near East, particularly Syro-Anatolia. At Troy the process of creating a past worked somewhat differently, because it was truly a shared past. Here Greeks were coming into a space occupied by Anatolians, or possibly by people who considered themselves to have a mixed Greco-Anatolian ancestry, and they joined in celebrating a famous set of ruins that perhaps were already being treated as an object of veneration by the local residents. But, as with Hesiod's Ages of Man, the Greek-speakers adopted the storylines deployed by Near Easterners to create a narrative about an event that ended the time of heroes and began the present day.

Genealogical and dynastic ties with the Bronze Age Anatolian Past

Whereas Greek identity-making seems to have centered on specific heroes whose martial exploits were commemorated in song and legend and Greek remembrance of their Bronze Age past focused on physical remains (monumental ruins or heirloom objects), Anatolian polities seemed to have anchored themselves to a legendary past through royal genealogies and veneration of royal ancestors and founders, continuing the Bronze Age practices discussed in Chapters 7 and 8. It is in the mingling of those two ways of remembering the past that Greek epic absorbed Near Eastern influence.

In north Syria the continued use of Hittite dynastic names shows an interest in maintaining a connection to past glories even after the fall of the Hittite empire. For example, the ruling family of Kummuh (Commagene) "shows in its onomastics a distinct tendency towards the famous names of the Hittite empire with its Qatazili-Hattusilis,Ušpilulume-Suppiluliuwas and Muttallu (Muwatalis)."[99] In Gurgum a commemorative inscription on a lion that was placed at the gate to the citadel by Halparuntiyas III and dated to the end of the ninth century recites his lineage back to the sixth generation,[100] showing a careful maintenance of the knowledge of his genealogy back to the turn of the millennium, likely including the recitation of a dynastic list as part of ancestor veneration. The lost statue that was mounted on the lion's back was probably that of Halparuntiyas himself,[101] and the inscription rendered in a more permanent form the public acts that would have occurred before it.

On the rocky peak of Kızıldağ on the border of Tabal and Hilakku, an inscription of Hartapu, son of a Great King Mursili – possibly the deposed Mursili III – received an incised image of Hartapu seated on a throne with shallow cup in hand to receive offerings. David Hawkins suggests that it was placed there by Wasusarmas, king of Kululu, in the mid eighth century as a display of power and an effort to link himself to the former Great King Hartapu as a legendary ancestor.[102]

In western Anatolia any cultural memory of the Hittites seems to have been erased, so completely in fact that one suspects the erasure was purposeful.[103] But, the Luwian-derived dynastic name Mursili remained important among both Greeks and Anatolians. The chariot-driver helping Pelops, who came from west Anatolia to participate in the competition for the hand of Hippodameia, was named Myrtilus, and Myrsilus was the name of a tyrant of Lesbos, and also of a ruler of Sardis, whom Herodotus tells us was called Candaules by the Lydians (cf. Luw. ḫantawata/i- 'king'[104]), while according to Nicolaus of Damascus, the Lydian ruler Candaules was called Sadyattes/Adyattes. It may be that the tyrant's double name (plus title) arose from the double-naming practice that is found among the Hittites.[105]

---

[99] Hawkins (2000: 333). Dale (2011: 18) gives further examples. Bryce (2012: 61–2), on the other hand, does not wish to attribute any significance to the re-use of the names.

[100] Maraş 1 (translit. and trans. Hawkins 2000: 261–5). See discussion of Swartz Dodd (2005).

[101] Hawkins (2000: 262).

[102] See Plate 236 in Hawkins (2000) and discussion of Hawkins (1992: 271–2). This monument was also discussed in Chapter 12, 312.

[103] The Keteioi, Amazons, and Halizones have been suggested as possible matches for the Hittites (Bryce 2006: 130–5, 139).

[104] Yakubovich (2010: 94–5, 98), Dale (2011: 17).

[105] Hdt. 1.7.2, *FGrH* 90 FF 46–7, see Dale (2011: 17). Myrtilus charioteer of Pelops: Paus. 6.20.17. Pherecydes (*FGrH* 3 F 37) tells us Myrtilus, Oenomaus' charioteer, helped Pelops cheat and win the chariot race for Hippodameia's hand. Myrtilus was the "son of Hermes" according to the scholiast to Apollonius of Rhodes 1.752. Pindar *O*. 1 avoids repeating the story of the treacherous Myrtilus, who was murdered by Pelops. Myrsilus of Lesbos: Alcaeus F 70.7 Lobel-

The use of the name Myrsilus suggests that residents of west Anatolia had some means of retaining ancient dynastic names, which could have been introduced to the region through dynastic marriages with Hatti, if they were not already used by local dynasties.[106] It is easy to imagine that one way the names were remembered was through king lists recited before the statues of ancestors or in places devoted to royal ancestor worship. Possibly a House of the Grandfathers (É [= *parnaš*] *ḫuḫḫaš*) was one of those places.[107]

An interest in claiming the power of ancestors is certainly apparent in the the onomastics of Bronze Age west Anatolian elites, for *ḫuḫḫa-* is found both in compound names (Uhhamuwa, 'strength of the grandfather/ancestor') and by itself. Since the naming practice continued into the Iron Age, we can suggest that the interest in the legitimizing approval of ancestors remained alive. Thus, when the name *Ḫuḫḫaš* was taken by Gyges, who ruled Lydia *ca.* 680–644 BCE according to Assyrian documents, the Mermnad usurper's name asserted the continuity of the earlier dynastic line. Moreover, the form *Gugēs*, with initial velar, is Carian, not Lydian.[108] This suggests that local dynasties made use of supralocally recognized forms of dynastic names rather than local forms.

The widespread knowledge about Gyges as dynastic founder and legendary royal ancestor indicates that his dynasty understood the importance of making mythical dynastic connections with its glorious Bronze Age past as well as with other internationally significant courts, and of public display of royal ancestor worship, as did the first-millennium Neo-Hittites. Hipponax groups the monument of Gyges with the monuments of Tous and Mytalis, Mytalis clearly continuing the Bronze Age dynastic name Muwattalli.[109]

Page. Lydian Myrsilus the son of Myrsus: Hdt. 1.7.2. For examples of toponyms with the name Mursili in west Anatolia, see Dale (2011: 18–19). Dale (2011: 19, 22) also argues for the legitimating use of a Late Bronze Age dynastic name, but suggests the possibility that the term Mursili had become a title, not a personal name, in order to explain some inconsistencies in the references to Myrsilus by Alcaeus.

[106] The latter suggestion comes from R. Oreshko, pers. comm. July, 2013.
[107] See Chapter 7, 151–2, on Hittite king lists and the House of the Grandfathers.
[108] Hdt. 1.12. Also cf. the Hittite name *Ḫuḫḫa-* and the name *Uḫḫaziti* ('grandfather-man'); P. Högemann, "Gyges," in *Brill's New Pauly* 5.1048–9; also see Dale (2011: 17, n. 13). On the name in Anatolian onomastics, see Yakubovich (2010: 91, 93, 95) and Lipiński (2004: 113). On the usurper Gyges' name also see Roosevelt (2009: 19). On Greek *gugai* 'grandfather' as derived from an Anatolian language see van Windekens (1957–1958). (This indicates bilingual households.) Similarly, Sarpedon, the Lycian hero, has the Carian form of his name (Yakubovich 2010: 138–9; Bachvarova 2015: 150–1); for more on his name, see Chapter 16, 439, n. 75.
[109] Hippon. F 7 Degani. See discussion of O. Masson (1962: 134). On Gyges' methods of consolidating his power and achieving international recognition, see Roosevelt (2009: 22–4).

Lake Gygaea, represented by the nymph who was the mother of the two leaders of the Maeonians "born beneath Mt. Tmolus" in the *Iliad*,[110] was a well-known landmark near Sardis, modern Marmara Gölü, near Bin Tepe ('thousand mounds'), the Lydian necropolis that included the tumulus of Adyattes. The lake brings to mind Anatolian sacred pool complexes,[111] while the location of the necropolis, overlooking the ruins of several important sites belonging to the Bronze Age kingdom of the Seha River Land, has caused the archaeologists currently undertaking a survey of central Lydia, Christina Luke and Christopher H. Roosevelt, to suggest:

> The monumentalizing of Bin Tepe with tumuli by Lydian kings can be understood now not only as intending to make links with a generic idea of 'ancestors', or even with the specific Maeonian heroes of Homer, ... but also, perhaps, as an active self-association with the collectively remembered importance of the very specific network of Bronze Age power centered on the Gygaean Lake.[112]

Finally, among the suggestions for the referent of Japeth's son Magog in Genesis is Lydia (cf. Akk. *māt Gugi*, 'land of Gyges'), although later Jewish and Christian comentators interpreted Gog and Magog to refer to Scythians, i.e., people from north of the Black Sea.[113]

Gyges/Magog was not the only ancestor used to connect the Lydian court to world history. The sixth-century tradition of twenty-two generations of Lydian dynastic names reported on by Herodotus, which takes the Lydian kingdom back to the fall of the Hittite empire, *ca.* 1185 BCE, connects Lydia first to the Dorian Heraclids and then to the Neo-Assyrian empire via eponymous heroes. It begins with Heracles' son Alcaeus, then Belus, Ninus, and Agron, the first Heraclid king of Sardis. (Before that, he says, the descendants of Lydus, son of Atys, ruled.) Note the use of the all-purpose Belus (w. Sem. 'lord'), also used in the line of Io in the Hesiodic *Catalog of Women*.[114] Herodotus clearly had at his disposal a Lydian king list, and Walter Burkert has provided a perceptive analysis of the political

---

[110] *Il.* 2.865–6. Also *Il.* 20.390–1. Kullmann (1999b: 70) sees the mention as evidence for a late date for Homer, after Gyges' rule, but as mentioned, he could be using a dynastic name.

[111] On Hittite sacred pool complexes (*šuppi luli*, cf. the king's name Suppiluliuma), see Harmanşah (2011: 634–8) and Chapter 4, 90–1.

[112] C. Luke and Roosevelt (forthcoming).

[113] Jerome, *Commentary on Ezekiel* 38:2, Josephus, *Antiquities* 1.123; see Yamauchi (2003: 22–4). On other descendants of Noah see Chapter 11, 293–4.

[114] Chapter 9, 215–16, n. 77. See Roosevelt (2009: 19–20) on the Lydian dynastic tradition representing the establishment of a new kingdom at the end of the Bronze Age.

context that motivated the list, first looking at the connection with Nineveh:

> If there is any sense in this – and reconstructed genealogies do make sense – it resides in the interrelations of Lydia and Assyria. Now these relations are directly attested in the annals of Assurbanipal: "Guggu king of Luddi, a province on the other side of the sea, a distant region, whose name the kings who went before me, my fathers, had not heard mentioned, Assur the god who created me, revealed the honored name of my majesty to him in a dream, saying: 'Lay hold of the feet of his highness, Assurbanipal' ... On the (same) day that he saw this dream, he sent his couriers to me to ask my peace..."[115] To phrase things differently: Gyges, the new king, murderer of his predecessor, is anxious to achieve recognition by the Eastern superpower, using the diplomatic forms expected at Nineveh, including the tale of the king's dream. Evidently it was in this situation that a genealogy made sense that traced Lydian kingship back to the earliest times of Nineveh.[116]

Burkert then discusses the connection to Heracles:

> If this reelaboration is ... presumed to make sense, the reference is easy to find: derived from Herakles, Lydian kingship gains equal status with other Heraklid dynasties, the most prominent of which was that of Sparta. In fact it was Croesus, king of Lydia, who sought relations with the West – with Greece – and made a pact with Sparta (Hdt. 1.56ff., 1.70).[117]

Thus, by the end of the seventh century local Anatolian courts were using the same means to connect themselves to the wider world that we find in Hesiod and hints of in Homer. It not only can be traced back to a more general Near Eastern practice, but also can be specifically localized to Bronze Age Hattusa. I would suggest that the Lydians did not borrow the idea from the Assyrians, but made use of an inherited Anatolian practice, which would have spread west in the Late Bronze Age, when west Anatolian courts were in reality linked by marriage to the Hittite court and had the means, motive, and opportunity to borrow techniques of ancestor

---

[115] *Assurbanipal Prism B* §§ 909–10 (trans. Luckenbill 1968: 352).
[116] Burkert (1995: 229–30).
[117] Burkert (1995: 231). Also see Georges (1994: 22–3). Burkert argues that the Heraclid genealogy was not followed by other historians. While Heracles' time in Lydia as Omphale's slave was a wide-spread story in the fifth century, only Panyassis and Herodotus make reference to the Heraclid dynasty. See Gantz (1993: 437, 439–42).

veneration and of organizing the past that were acknowledged ways to place one's dynasty in world history.

If the Lydian court continued a tradition established in the Late Bronze Age and found in the Hurro-Hittite texts that made quasi-genealogical connections between the Sargonic dynasty and other far-flung legendary kings, and that relied on legends to insert a local court into the wide sweep of world history, the Lydian genealogy would have been supplemented by legends. The one explaining how Heracles became involved with the Lydians appears to have been particularly popular, and it can be partially reconstructed from the fragmentary sources: The early fifth-century historian Pherecydes of Athens says Hermes took Heracles to Lydia and sold him to queen Omphale after he had killed Iole's father. Eustathius records that the fifth-century Lydian historian Xanthus wrote about Omphale, which would have been in the context of his *Lydiaca*, in which he discussed the Lydian dynasty. Finally, in his *Heraclea*, Herodotus' uncle Panyassis mentions that Heracles' son by Omphale, Acheles, "became king of the Lydians" (cf. Alcaeus, the son of Heracles named by Herodotus as the start of the Lydian Heraclid dynasty).[118]

In the *Iliad* long genealogies were particularly the property of Anatolians, such as Aeneas[119] and Glaucus, whose genealogy starts with Aeolus, then Sisyphus, Glaucus, and Bellerophontes, who sired three children, Isander, Hippolochus, father of Glaucus, and Laodameia, mother of Sarpedon (*Il.* 6.153–5, 196–206). Like the Mesopotamian and Lydian king lists, one gets the impression that the genealogy serves as an index to a series of stories, for it alludes to Bellerophontes' battles against the Solymi – his son Isander later died in battle against them (6.203–4), struck down by Ares – and the Amazons (6.184–6). Were these exploits commemorated in epic narratives? (Recall the Lydian epic about battles with Amazons.[120]) The Achaeans do not seem to have such long genealogies. Instead, the extensive genealogies are attached to objects, such as Meriones' helmet and Agamemnon's scepter.[121] Did the Greeks bring to Anatolia a different way of recalling the remote past, based on artifacts left over from legendary times? Certainly, as the boast by the sophist Hippias beginning this chapter shows, by the Classical period genealogy was considered an

---

[118] Hdt. 1.7; Panyassis: Σ bT *ad Il.* 24.616b = F 20 Bernabé; Eustathius: *ad Il.* 16.702 (1082) = *FGrH* 765 F 4 (the context is the proverbial outrages the Lydians used to commit against their women); Pherecydes = *FGrH* 3 F 82. See Georges (1994: 22–3).
[119] *Il.* 20.213–40, see Chapter 8, 190.   [120] Chapter 4, 105.
[121] On Meriones' helmet see Chapter 11, 282; for Agamemnon's scepter, Chapter 16, 422.

important branch of knowledge among the Greeks. Indeed, the biographical tradition of Homer states that the poet was originally named *Melēsigenēs* 'paying attention to genealogies',[122] which fits with what was discussed in Chapter 11 concerning the adoption by the Greeks of the genealogical framework as an outline of history seen as a *longue durée*. But, what I am suggesting here is that the Greeks arriving at the beginning of the Protogeometric period in Anatolia did not yet use this framework. In Anatolia, the narrative that ended up dominant was the Trojan War as the marker of the end of the heroic age, and its aftermath, the *nostoi*, which were used to explain the contemporary situation of Greek-speakers in diaspora. While the later *nostoi* legends were firmly embedded in a genealogical framework, in the *Iliad* genealogies are referred to, but are not the primary structuring device for world history, for the Achaeans at least.

Continuity of elite mortuary practices in Syro-Anatolia, Mopsus' *ḫešti*-house, and Karatepe

What little we can see of the Lydians' continued use of practices attested in Bronze Age Hattusa, of royal ancestor veneration, dynastic lists used as indexes for world history, and fictional genealogies connecting local courts to the international network of elites, can be fleshed out by evidence from north Syria and east Anatolia, where we have a clear example of the linking of Greek and Anatolian legendary history through the shared hero Mopsus. In Chapter 12 we discussed evidence for cultural continuity in Cilicia and north Syria, focusing on the retention of cultural practices. Here I specifically examine mortuary practices. Because some of the materials used to carry out elite ancestor veneration were imperishable, we have ample evidence for continuity with regard to the practice in Early Iron Age north Syria and east Anatolia,[123] which can be used to better understand the ritual background of the legendary ancestor Mopsus, shared by Greeks and Anatolians, who is mentioned at Karatepe. In turn, we can suggest that less archaeologically visible practices in western Anatolia provided ritual context and meaning for Greco-Anatolian heroes who became associated with the Trojan War.

Sam'al (Zincirli, *Bīt Gabbari* 'House of Gabbar') has the earliest evidence for the Neo-Hittite practice of ancestor veneration centered on stone

---

[122] *Vita* 1.2 West; Nagy (2010: 135–6).
[123] For the practices in the Early Iron Age, see Bonatz (2000b), Niehr (1994; 2001; 2006a), Struble and Rimmer Hermann (2009),

statues, dating to the end of the tenth or beginning of the ninth century BCE.[124] Gabbar is a generic name meaning 'strong, heroic man', and the second of the five "early kings" of Sam'al listed in the ninth-century genealogy provided by Kilamuwa (Kulamuwa) is named Banihu 'builder'. As Alessandra Gilibert points out, the "overtly symbolic names suggest a myth of foundation."[125] In other words, Gabbar and his son are legends rather than facts. While most of the other examples of funerary monuments are contemporary with or later than the eighth century BCE, all sites show continuity with Late Bronze Age mortuary practices, including offerings to statues, cremation, and an association with the Storm-god. This allows us to project these customs back into the period between the end of the Bronze Age and the ninth century.[126] At Tell Halaf (Guzana), the evidence dates to the tenth through the second half of the ninth century.[127] At Gerçin, 7 km from Sam'al, it dates to the first half of the eighth century.[128] At Carchemish the material covers a long period, the monumental art dating as far back as the eleventh century. The first clear

[124] Gabbar's statue received offerings from his descendants (Niehr 2006a: 112–15). A high-ranking official under Panamuwa I named KTMW left a funerary stele in the eighth century depicting himself holding a phiale (Struble and Rimmer Hermann 2009: 23). Such cups held by statues in the round were often intended to receive libations (Niehr 2006a: 127). See Bonatz (2000a: 90–6) on eating, drinking, and drinking vessels on funerary stelae. The name, although written in the vowel-less Aramaic script, is clearly Luwian, as is that of his king (cf. Luwian *muwa-* 'conquer'). He speaks of a recurring feast carried out by his descendants for him and for various gods, first and foremost among whom is the Storm-god Hadad, and in addition Hadad of the Vineyard. Offerings are to be made of meat and the produce of the vineyard. The slaughtering of the victim must be done close to his "soul," imagined as being inside the stele (Pardee 2009). There is a pit in front that may be for his cremated remains. On the creation of statues and stelae for royal ancestor cult at Zincirli in the eighth century see Gilibert (2011: 125), and for non-royal funerary stelae from the late tenth to seventh centuries, see Gilibert (2011: 126–7).

[125] Gilibert (2011: 15). *KAI* 24.1–4 (translit. and trans. Tropper 1993: 30–3, K1). This Phoenician inscription is the earliest from Sam'al; Kilamuwa's reign was 840/38–815/10 BCE.

[126] On ancestor statues see Chapter 7, 150–2, and Chapter 8, 186, with n. 91; and Niehr (2006a: 118) on the association with the Storm-god. On Neo-Hittite ancestor veneration see Bonatz (2000a; 2000b). On the evidence at Tell Tayinat and Maraş in the mid ninth century, see Gilibert (2011: 125).

[127] Statues in the round have been found, male and female individuals and a couple, dating to the tenth through the second half of the ninth century, possibly associated with the Storm-god (Niehr 2006a: 119–34), but see M. Pucci (2008: 116). There is evidence of repeated offerings, and smaller statues, taken to represent relatives, were found with the larger ones. When the method of disposal of the corpse is known, it is cremation. Also see M. Pucci (2008: 118–19, 123, 124, 172–3).

[128] A long funerary inscription of Panamuwa I (*ca.* 770–760 BCE) has been found on the statue of the Storm-god in the local dialect of Aramaic (Tropper 1993: 5). Other statues representing the dead are found there too. In the inscription Panamuwa speaks of his deeds and states that he set up the statue of Hadad and his tomb next to it. The soul of Panamuwa should eat and drink with Hadad and when sacrifices to Hadad are made, Panamuwa's name should be called. See

mortuary monument is that of Watis, the wife of the tenth-century king Suhis II.[129] The custom of making offerings to the statues of the royal dead existed in southeast Anatolia as well, not just north Syria, as shown by the Hieroglyphic Luwian inscription of the funerary stele of Panunis at Kululu in Tabal, dating to the mid eighth century BCE, which speaks of eating and drinking, apparently in celebration of the dead.[130]

While certainly changes over time can be detected, the custom of providing meals to a statue or stele and antecedents of the iconography of the relief sculptures and statues in the round date all the way back to third-millennium Ebla, and the custom is attested at second-millennium Hattusa.[131] The statue of the fifteenth-century king Idrimi of Alalakh, which remained in place into the thirteenth century, presumably received offerings, as did statues at Ugarit.[132] Finally, a royal tomb from Qatna in northwest Syria provides striking evidence for commemorative meals enjoyed by both the living and the dead at the entrance of their tomb in front of their statues, a practice that apparently spanned the entire 400-year life of the palace, from the beginning of the seventeenth century until the second half of the fourteenth century BCE.[133]

The iconographic programs of Neo-Hittite monumental installations tell us that by the late tenth century BCE ancestor veneration had been established as a public activity that took place at a significant gathering point, whether city or palace gate. As Gilibert notes, "an outstanding feature and long-lasting feature of many Syro-Anatolian gates [was that] not only did they control access to and within the city, but they also served as platforms of ritual performances."[134] Marina Pucci states,

---

translation of Tropper (1993: 154–9, Inscription H=*KAI* 214), also Niehr (2006a: 117–18) and Bonatz (2000a: 69–70).

[129] Aro (2003: 314–15). At Carchemish there are both statues and stelae. One seated statue (B 48) was found on the outside of the small "Hilani" building. The Hieroglyphic Luwian inscription is illegible. Under the floor of the building a clay urn was buried in which the cremated remains would have been deposited (Gilibert 2011: 53–4; Niehr 2006a: 131–2; Woolley 1952: 179–84). In fact, because the whole floor of the room was dug up in ancient times, as was the floor of the Temple of the Storm-god, the excavator suggested that looters were after rich cremation burials underneath it. Another cremation burial with luxurious offerings was found in the North Gate (Woolley 1952: 250–1).

[130] KULULU 2 A4 (translit. and trans. Hawkins 2000: 488–9). [131] See Chapter 7, 150–2.

[132] For the Bronze Age Anatolian practices and Ugarit, see Chapter 7, 151. Idrimi: Bonatz (2000a: 132–3).

[133] See Niehr (2006b: 1–4, with earlier references), Pfälzner (2005).

[134] Gilibert (2011: 24). For the change in practices of ancestor cult, moving from a secluded private space, to a public space where many could gather in the late tenth century BCE (Carchemish and Zincirli), see Gilibert (2011: 120); M. Pucci (2008: 165–6): ancestor worship

The emphasis was on the borders of the town, on the dead ancestors and the relationship between these two elements and the local dynasty. The seat of this dynasty provided the inhabitants with a means of identification with the ruling dynasty and with the town, and distinction from the other neighboring towns, which had other dynasties.[135]

All this evidence shows that the iconographic program of Karatepe's South Gate fits into the norms for the time period and area. What is unique about Karatepe is the fact that the legendary ancestor receiving worship there is also known as a Greek hero. In addition, the evidence for ancestor veneration at Karatepe in Cilicia is the earliest we have from either Greece or Anatolia that might connect the performance of narratives about military activities and divinities with veneration for the legendary dead, as opposed to mortuary rites for the "real" and recently dead. Moreover, the veneration refers precisely to a Greco-Anatolian hero used to make a long-range connection across time and space between Ionian Clarus and Cilicia, between the aftermath of the Trojan War and current dynastic houses and cult sites: the much-discussed Mopsus.[136]

Robin Lane Fox has called attention to the similarity of the toponym *Mopsou Hestia* (Misis or modern Yakapınar), in Greek 'hearth of Mopsus',[137] and the Hittite term ^{É}ḫešti,[138] but not realizing what type of cult building the ḫešti-house was, he was unable to explore fully the implications of the correspondence. In fact, as discussed earlier, among the Hittites the ḫešti-house was a place associated with the underworld goddess Lelwani and royal ancestor veneration. It was also found at Ugarit.[139] The ḫešti of Mopsus, then, would have been the place in which offerings were

---

at gates, with statues or stelae, including Karatepe and Malatya; Bonatz (2000a: 153): ancestor worship at gates in Carchemish.

[135] M. Pucci (2008: 166). For further discussion of the use of monumental art in public spaces, especially gates, to create a space for large-scale festivals and civic rituals, beginning in the late tenth century with Carchemish and extending to the beginning of the ninth century, showing a shared "sociopolitical dynamics" at Tell Halaf, Carchemish, and Zincirli, see Gilibert (2011: 119–25).

[136] Also see Chapter 12, 318–19.

[137] Mentioned by Theopompus (*FGrH* 115 F 103) as a foundation of Mopsus.

[138] Lane Fox (2009: 217–18).

[139] On the ḫešti-house see Chapter 7, 151, with n. 8. A ḫešti-house also became a feature of north Syrian palace architecture. It is mentioned in Ugaritic texts, both mythological and ritual, where it is part of a complex of Hurro-Hittite funerary practices incorporated into the royal cult. *Keret*: *KTU* 1.16 i 3, 17, ii 39 (translit. and trans. N. Wyatt 2002: 219, 222, 230: "burial chamber"), see M. Dietrich and Loretz (2004); *A Prayer for Well-Being*: *KTU* 1.123 30′ (translit. and trans. Pardee 2002: 152), but with a different reading; see Loretz (2001) for the correct interpretation. See Niehr (2006b; 2007), suggesting the ḫešti-house is Room 28 in the Ugaritic Royal Palace and contained an *āpi*. Also see Chapter 4, 87, n. 93.

made to his statue during festivals and other occasions, and the term shows how his (supposed) descendants maintained a connection to the past by making use of the practices attested at Hattusa, whether shared already in the Bronze Age or passed via Syria in the Iron Age. The Greek reinterpretation of the term *ḫešti* from 'building for ancestor cult' to a metonym for 'house' was influenced not only by the convenient homophony of Greek *hestiā* 'hearth', but also by Semitic parallels referring to cities as the house of their founder, such as *Bīt Gabbari*.[140]

It appears that Misis was at some point well known for containing a building in which Mopsus, as legendary dynastic ancestor in Hiyawa/Que/Adana/Danuna, received rites of veneration. The practices of ancestor veneration that were carried out for Mopsus would have followed those well-attested elsewhere in the Neo-Hittite world. This is an important example of continuity of mortuary practices in a part of Anatolia where Greek-speakers came into contact with Anatolians, and is therefore relevant to my claim that the belief systems and orally transmitted texts that informed the mortuary practices were also retained and were accessible to Greek-speakers. This is an important precondition if one wishes to use texts found at Hattusa to explicate Greek epic and hero worship. Similarly, in Chapter 12 I focused primarily on evidence for continuity and contact in divine personalities to explain the oral transmission of oral texts used in cults of divinities from the Near East to Greece.

Whereas it appears that Mopsus' *ḫešti*-house was not located at Karatepe, certainly there is clear and abundant evidence for publicly performed rites of elite ancestor veneration at Karatepe, and the connection between ancestor veneration and performing narratives in a festive setting is graphically depicted in the orthostats that lined the chambers of its two monumental gates. I focus here on the best-preserved evidence, from the South Gate. There were two schools of sculptors who worked on the orthostats. The later material, with eighth-century parallels, shows more Phoenician influence (B); the orthostats carved in the older style with ninth-century parallels (A, with receding chins and large noses) probably came from nearby Domuztepe. Thus, some of the orthostats appear to be re-used from an earlier installation, and the blocks were not placed in such a way as to allow the Hieroglyphic Luwian inscriptions to be read through in order.[141] Therefore, the orthostats at Karatepe should not necessarily be

---

[140] On the House of Gabbar, see Niehr (2006a: 114–15).
[141] Winter (1979). According to her, the older group A shows "basically mythological subjects," while group B is mostly "attendants and processions" (Winter 1979: 132). On the Phoenician

assumed to tell a coherent story. However, we can see that the royal ancestor did receive sacrifices accompanied by music and singing, and the combination of divine and martial images suggests that the songs performed referred to battle victories and the gods.

On the left side of the forecourt of the South Gate is centered a rite of ancestor veneration (Fig. 21).[142] A divinized ancestor – Mopsus himself? – sits facing a table laden with food and holding a cup in his left hand and a stemmed object in his right, under which a monkey crouches, while men bring more offerings and one plies the fly-whisk (SVl 3).[143] This orthostat, belonging to the older group A, follows the iconography for mortuary ritual that can be traced back as far as third-millennium Ebla. Underneath is depicted a bovine sacrifice. On the orthostat to the left (SVl 2), belonging to the later group B, men move towards the recipient, in the top register carrying yet more offerings of food and drink, including wine in a fluted phiale and a Phrygian-style ladle with long pouring lip, showing the court's participation in the drinking fashions of the day, while on the lower register are musicians playing the tympanon-drum, double aulos, lyre, and barbiton.[144] One can imagine that the orthostat of the divinized ancestor, whom I suggest represents Mopsus, was brought from its original location and placed where it could be the center of attention in the gate house, while the newer depiction of the fête of music and song represented the current rites directed at him.

On the orthostat to the right of the recipient (SVl 4) a large god of the wild spaces is depicted standing on a steer, brandishing his characteristic hare and facing away from the feasting scene and towards a set of battle scenes in two registers (SVl 5, belonging to the older group A), the lower one presenting two antithetical horsemen separated by a man on foot with a round shield, and the upper one of a pair of antithetical foot-soldiers with "Corinthian" helmets topped with plumes or horsetails, in running position stabbing with their swords a third soldier with a peaked round helmet like those worn by the Assyrian soldiers below.[145] On the right side of the

---

influence on the reliefs, see Winter (1979: 121–4, 137–8). Re-use is not unusual: Carchemish (Gilibert 2011: 29, 42–3); Zincirli (Gilibert 2011: 72–4); Tell Halaf, Small Orthostats (Gilibert 2011: 124; M. Pucci 2008: 95, 108, 126).

[142] See the detailed description of Çambel and Özyar (2003: 95–114).

[143] See Mazzoni (2008: 3) arguing for this interpretation. On the iconography, see B. Brown (2010: 18) with earlier referemces.

[144] Compare the depiction of elegant courtly life at Zincirli, Hilani IV (Barrakib, ca. 732–711), showing ruler feasting with attendants and musicians in a row (Gilibert 2011: 130–1).

[145] Çambel and Özyar (2003: 70) compare the iconography with Greek examples. Corinthian-style helmets with plumes are common in other Neo-Hittite relief programs. Winter (1979: 120)

Continuity of elite mortuary practices 385

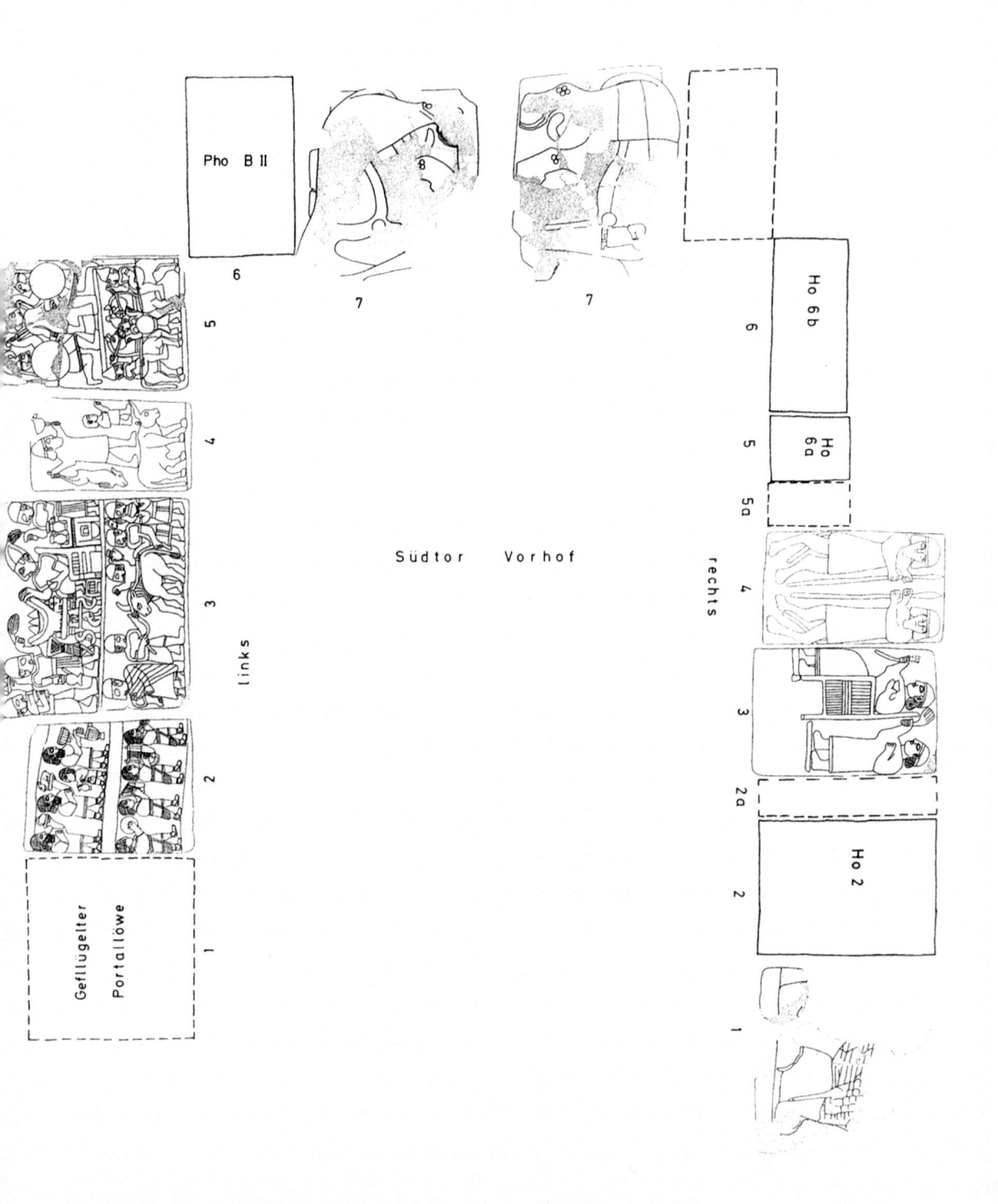

Fig. 21: Karatepe South Gate, Forecourt (end of eighth century BCE)

forecourt is a pair of men with hooved legs – mythical creatures (SVr 4), and another enthroned royal ancestor holding his cup, as large as a god, with his attendant, fly-whisk in hand (SVr 3, group B).[146] Interspersed are blocks bearing parts of inscriptions in Hieroglyphic Luwian and Phoenician in which Azatiwatas boasts of his deeds, how he founded Azatiwatayas, honored Baal *krntryš* and protected the House of Mopsus.

In the Left Chamber of the South Gate (Fig. 22) some orthostats are missing, but on those that remain we can see on the left wall men hunting small animals (SKl 1), on the back wall an offering procession (SKl 8–12), and at the right-hand corner a fishing scene (SKl 14). On the right-hand wall is another procession with rabbit offerings (SKl 15–17), possibly directed at another god of the wilderness (SKl 16).

The original order of the reliefs in the Right Chamber of the South Gate (Fig. 23) is mostly unknown, but it has a third scene of ancestor veneration across two orthostats with offerings being placed on a table; below are musicians performing and a bovine sacrifice (SKr 15, 16, group A). Other scenes have a strong narrative element: a battle scene with an archer and possibly a siege machine visible (SKr 17–18),[147] another battle scene involving charioteers and a corpse being trampled (SKr 5–7), a mostly defaced offering scene to a god (SKr 3–4), men with bows and spears (SKr 13), fish and other animals both large and small (SKr 8–10); finally, there is a damaged orthostat on which a scene of two men with a human victim hanging between them can be made out (Fig. 24, SKr 11, group B).

We have mentioned the imagery from the South Gate that signals a battle between two different ethnic groups: the antithetical warriors, and the warriors with two different types of helmets, one "Corinthian," the other Assyrian. It possibly refers specifically to conflicts with the Assyrians, who were attempting to assert control over Danuna/Que and were eventually successful under Esarhaddon at reducing Que to a province of the Neo-Assyrian empire.[148] At the North Gate, a Phoenician or Aegean warship with a battering ram is depicted, while defeated men drown in

---

sees the possibility that the helmets are derived from Greek models, which is not the same as arguing for Greek influence on the iconography.

[146] Çambel and Özyar (2003: 130).

[147] The structure, possibly made of woven withy, is suggested to be a bird trap by Çambel and Özyar (2003: 113).

[148] Because the exact date of Karatepe is disputed, we cannot definitively associate the battles depicted with an event known from the annalistic inscriptions found in Neo-Assyrian palaces, but see the references in Chapter 12, 316, n. 73, for the various reconstructions of the political situation at the time of the Karatepe inscriptions.

Continuity of elite mortuary practices 387

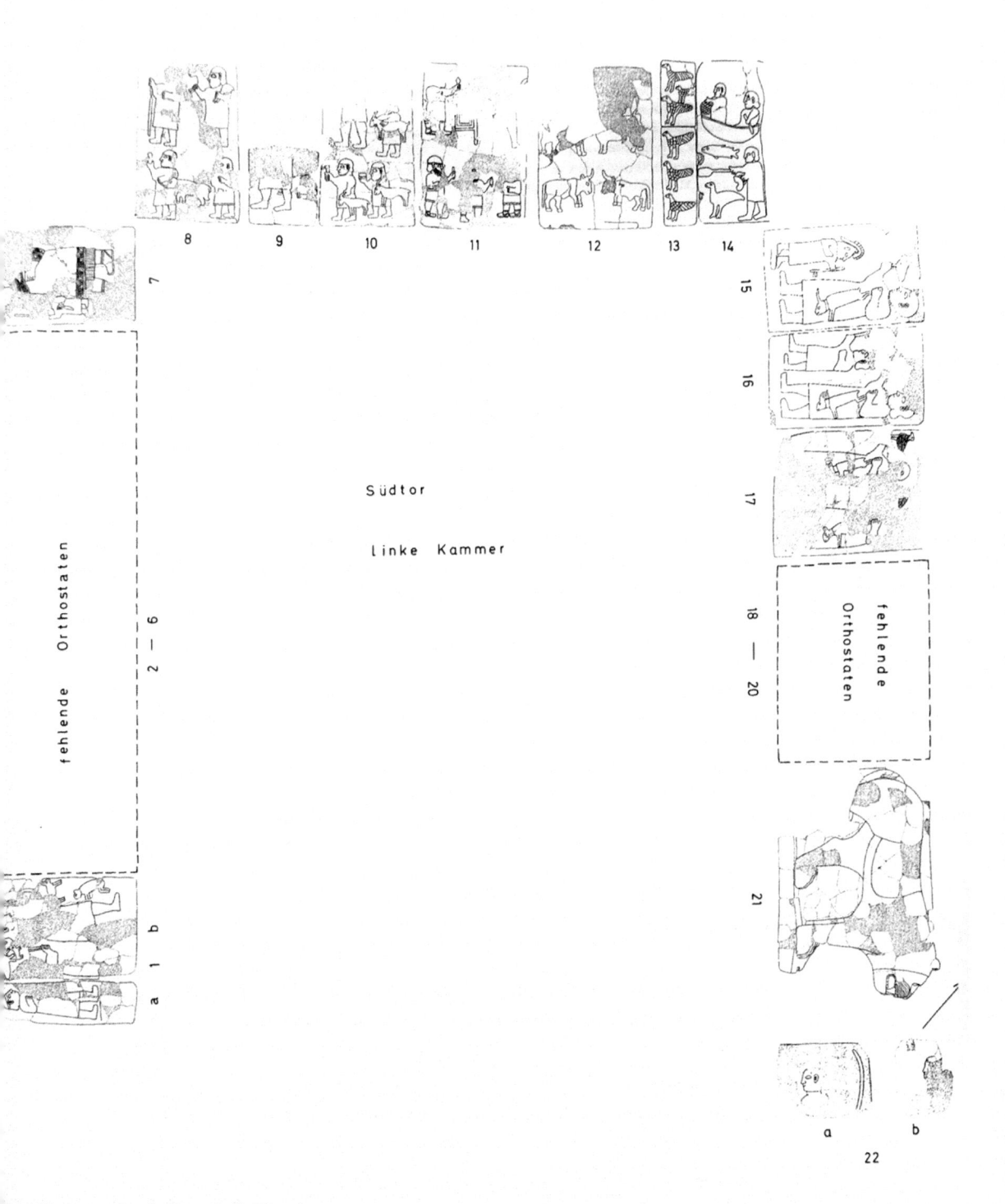

22: Karatepe South Gate, Left Chamber

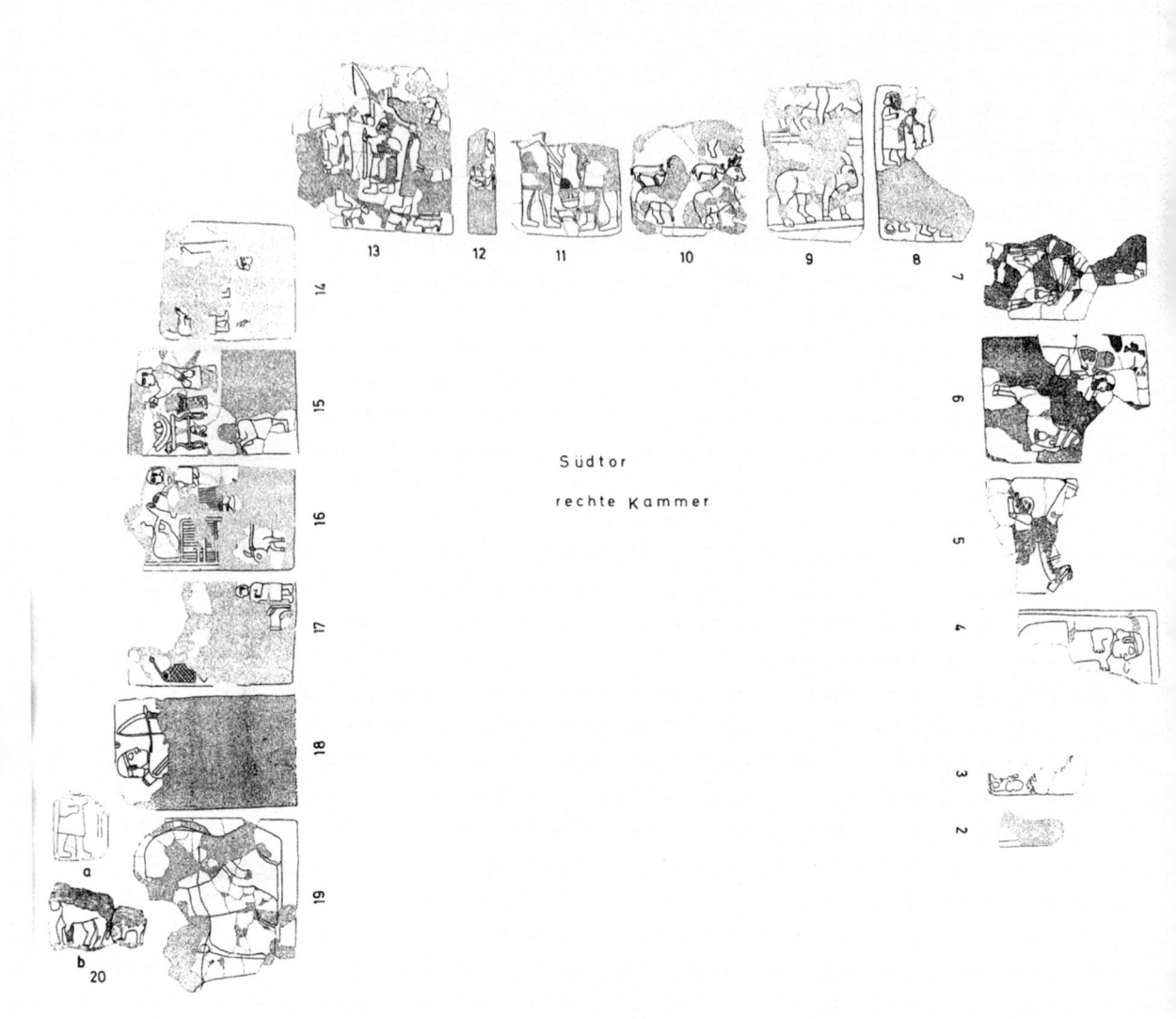

Fig. 23: Karatepe South Gate, Right Chamber

the surrounding water (Fig. 25, NKr 19, group A).[149] As Wolfgang Röllig notes, it is striking that such an image is found so far inland.[150] He sees it as evidence that Phoenicians were involved in making the reliefs. This is a reasonable claim, but in addition the scene could be understood to allude to actual events, a conflict along the coast of Que. This suggestion is

---

[149] On the ship see Çambel and Özyar (2003: 84–9, 135), Meyer (2011: 90–1), Winter (1979: 120–1).
[150] Röllig (2011: 128–9).

Fig. 24: Karatepe, Orthostat depicting two men killing upside-down victim, Orthostat 11 in South Gate, Right Chamber

supported by the accompanying hunting imagery, which is ubiquitous in Neo-Hittite and Neo-Assyrian monumental iconography. For, "Assyrian parallels show that, in the early Iron Age, military triumphs and ritual hunts went together: The victories over the enemy and that over wild animals were symbolically re-enacted and celebrated in arenas within the city, in front of crowds of spectators."[151]

As for possible references to known mythical storylines, they are far from certain but worth at least mentioning. The excavators of Karatepe suggest that Orthostat SKr 11, depicting two antithetical warriors stabbing a human victim hanging upside down between them (Fig. 24), could represent Gilgamesh and Enkidu with Huwawa. Certainly the orthostat imitates the familiar iconography of the mythological scene, which is found at Tell Halaf (Fig. 26) and Carchemish too. Other scenes that may draw on

---

[151] Gilibert (2011: 33, with earlier refs.). At Carchemish, the Long Wall of Sculpture combined a boar hunt with a military victory (Gilibert 2011: 33); similarly the hunt and military exploits were combined at the South City Gate at Zincirli (Gilibert 2011: 60). The royal hunt theme is first introduced to the Assyrian annals with Tiglath-Pileser, then found in all successors until Assurnasirpal II (ninth century). Afterwards it is found primarily in iconography, e.g., Assurbanipal's palace at Nineveh (Tadmor 1997: 328; Weissert 1997). Hunting and festive celebrations after a military victory are tightly linked (Weissert 1997: 348–9). This is found already in the *CTH* 1: *Proclamation of Anitta* (trans. H. A. Hoffner, Jr. in Hallo and Younger 1997: 182–4). Weissert (1997: 339, n. 3) provides further bibliography on discussions of the hunting motif in NA royal inscriptions.

Fig. 25: Karatepe, Boat Scene, North Gate, Right Chamber

the Gilgamesh epic are found on orthostats at Tell Halaf and Carchemish (for example, the episodes involving Huwawa and the Bull of Heaven, or Gilgamesh slaying a lion).[152] In addition, Brian Brown has suggested the iconography of royal ancestor veneration on the wall relief in Assurnasirpal II's ninth-century palace at Nimrud makes oblique reference to the legendary character Gilgamesh in the inscribing of the Sumerian sign GIŠ 'tree' (cf. the abbreviated form of Gilgamesh's name ^{d}GIŠ) on the "stylized tree" that separates two antithetical images of royal ancestors,[153] while Tallay Ornan notes that the images of Assurnasirpal slaying a bull

[152] Carchemish B11a: a male with a divine horned headdress – Gilgamesh? – stabs a lion, which is held by a man on the opposite side; B15b: two warriors identically attired are slaying a bearded captive whose face is presented in profile (see Gilibert 2011: 172). The configuration is very similar to the roughly contemporary seal No. 340 in Collon (2001); 16a: two males with horned headdresses, one with wings, slay a winged bull (Hogarth 1914). At Tell Halaf, one relief (Tafel 102 A3, 176, Moortgat 1955; Fig. 26 here) shows two warriors in profile grasping a bearded, frontally facing man by his wrists, each winding a leg around his legs, with weapons raised over his head (compare No. 338 in Collon 2001). See Çambel and Özyar (2003: 105, 133) on the parallels and possibly derivation from the Gilgamesh epic. See Ornan (2010: 249–54) on Gilgamesh imagery at Carchemish and Tell Halaf.

[153] B. Brown (2010: 32–3). For the argument that the "mirror images" represent Assurnasirpal's father Tukulti-Ninurta II and Adad-Nirari II, see B. Brown (2010: 26–8, with earlier references).

Fig. 26: Tell Halaf, Orthostat depicting two men killing captive (ninth century BCE)

and lions implicitly compare him to Gilgamesh.¹⁵⁴ If these suggestions are correct, the Gilgamesh epic remained current and widespread outside scribal circles, while the references to the narrative at the four sites show that the myth was still connected both to the ideology of kingship and to ancestor veneration, not only in Mesopotamia but also in Syro-Anatolia. This could help explain the manifest dependence of Homeric epic on the Gilgamesh epic.

Even if we discount the specific connections to Gilgamesh, these scenes appear to be snapshots of well-known storylines or standard plot sequences, which may or may not have been connected to specific, named characters. With this background, the images from Karatepe can be interpreted as follows: they depict rites of ancestor veneration and divine worship with the sacrificial offerings and musical performances involved. Among the performances were tales of battles against foreign enemies. Equations appear to have been made between contemporary events and

---

[154] Ornan (2010: 234).

legendary ones, just as has been suggested for texts that informed the iconography of Greek pottery starting in the post-palatial period.[155]

Here is not the place to explore extensively the geopolitical situation in Iron Age Cilicia at the time of the Karatepe inscription, but the seventh-century poet Callinus of Ephesus, the earliest extant Greek source for the myth of Mopsus' migration to Cilicia, was an elegiac poet, and such poets are known to have delved into legendary and recent history when discussing current events.[156] One may suggest then that an alliance prior to the time of Callinus between Danuna and the Ionians of Colophon, who claimed the shrine at Clarus, might have motivated the attention paid to the legendary ancestral connection. Some of the "Ionians" (in the Assyrian sense, i.e., westerners) whose activities are mentioned in Neo-Assyrian texts could have been Ionian (in the Greek sense) allies of Danuna/Que, for example, in the period between the time of Tiglath-Pileser III and Esarhaddon when Que was caught between the Phrygian and Urartian attempts to maintain and expand their territories in Cilicia in competition with Assyria, or when Cilicia attempted to rebel against Sennacherib.[157]

Obviously the question of whether the Cilician participants in either the battles with the Assyrians or the rites that took place in the gate houses of Karatepe considered themselves to be related to the Greeks in west Anatolia remains worthy of further investigation. If the Greek origin of the epithet *korunētērios* ('man of the mace') applied to Tarhunzas/Baal is accepted,[158] it suggests that Greek either had been or currently was spoken at Karatepe, although it was not considered appropriate for monumental inscriptions. But, given that the events considered here and the Greek epics referring to

---

[155] Chapter 11, 278–9.   [156] E. Bowie (2001, esp. p. 51).

[157] It is uncertain whether Que first moved from being a vassal state of Assyria to being a province with a governor near the end of Tiglath-Pileser III's reign, during the short reign of Shalmaneser V, or early in the reign of Sargon II, which is when the governor Assur-sharru-uṣur is mentioned in administrative letters (Nos. 1, 251, ed. and trans. Parpola 1987: 4, 196–7). See the discussion of Lanfranchi (2005). Sea battles with Sargon II: *Khorsabad Annals*, e.g., No. 2.3.117–18 (translit. and trans. Fuchs 1994: 109, 319); clay foundation cylinders from Khorsabad, e.g., No.1.1.21 (translit. and trans. Fuchs 1994: 34, 290). The battle between "Ionians" and Sennacherib is mentioned by Berossus: Alexander Polyhistor, abridging Berossus, *FGrH* 680 F 5 (6); Abydenos, using Polyhistor, *FGrH* 680 F 7c (31); both quoted in the Armenian translation of Eusebius' *Chronicle*. It is possibly part of the failed rebellion of Hilakku, led by Kirua and involving Ingira and Tarsus: *Sennacherib* 17 iv 61–91 (translit. and trans. Grayson and Novotny 2012: 135–6). See Rollinger (2001) and Lanfranchi (2000) on the Ionians in Que and fighting against Assyria. Lanfranchi argues Greek interest was motivated by opportunities for trade, while Rollinger sees the "Ionians" as less organized, more opportunistic.

[158] See Chapter 12, 320.

Mopsus are too late to be relevant to our discussion of the pre-eighth-century version of the *Iliad*,[159] I content myself with one final observation: foundations of cities were events to boast about in west Semitic and Neo-Hittite inscriptions;[160] the myth that Gilibert suggests Gabbar and Banihu stand for at Sam'al presents possible analogies to Greek colonization myths. That is, the Greeks in Anatolia may have responded to Syro-Anatolian myths about legendary founders such as Mopsus by emphasizing their own colonizer myths. This explains how a character revered by Anatolians as a founder could also be seen by the Greeks as a Greek colonizer.[161]

Moreover, while, as discussed in Chapter 12, the myths attached to Mopsus, whether Anatolian or Greek, seem to refract an actual historical event, the transfer of Ahhiyawans from west Anatolia to Cilicia at the end of the Bronze Age, what is more relevant for my discussion is that both Greeks and Anatolians were interested in maintaining a single shared cultural memory in Anatolia. But, each group whose story is available to us, separated by a substantial geographic distance, molded it to its own culturally relevant storyline. With regard to the Iliadic story of Troy, however, I argue that we see the melding of two story traditions by two peoples in close contact with each other because they lived in the same place. While Nestor's stories are representative of the epic tradition of the Greeks who came into contact with Syro-Anatolian epic, the latter narrative tradition was more focused on a distant past and the destruction of cities that had an international significance.

Conclusion

Whereas the Greeks who came to Troy must have been drawn there in part by their own cultural memories of a great city now reduced almost completely to ruins, they eventually chose to mold their understanding of its history according to the storylines deployed by the local inhabitants, who may have recognized that they themselves were a mix of Mycenaeans and Anatolians. This suggests two things: these storylines had already been

---

[159] Mopsus appeared in the sixth-century *Melampodia* attributed to Hesiod (Str. 14.1.27 = Hes. F 214 Most), the *Epigonoi* (F 4 West = Σ *ad* A. R. 1.308; the attribution to the *Thebaid* must be corrected), and the *Nostoi arg.* 2 West. On the Greek myths of Mopsus see especially the careful study of Baldriga (1994).

[160] On founding a city as a great deed mentioned in Hieroglyphic Luwian inscriptions, see Green (2010: 64–83, 259–61, 307–10), Harmanşah (2013: 134–52); on conquest: Green (2010: 288–90).

[161] This might support Malkin's theory that the earliest state-sponsored heroes were colonizers, discussed in Chapter 11, 286, n. 76.

applied to narrativize the fall of Troy, and the local traditions were prestigious enough to be considered worth adopting.

Scholars of Greek hero cult have described scenarios in which clans or tribes gathered to celebrate their eponymous hero with lamentation and/or sacrifices and competitions at his tomb.[162] The link between the performance of epic and hero-cult is much less tight. Although it is not impossible that Greek poets in the Early Iron Age performed simple lays praising their patron, as Posidonius described Celtic bards doing,[163] we need to accept that the parallels between Greek and Near Eastern narratives demonstrate a somewhat different use of narrative song, one that linked a local court to an international world of myth that stretched back into antediluvian times. In some cases the link was quite literal, through a hero or heroine who represented a foreign locale, as in Io's family tree in the *Catalog of Women*, which joined Argos to all the most important places in the known world.[164] In other cases the link was forged by the poet's use of motifs and storylines that had a prestigious, exotic, or antique pedigree, allowing the audience to participate in the latest narrative fashions and display a sophisticated appreciation of poetic art. In addition, we have seen that epic storylines and heroes that appear in epic could be involved in healing rituals, so the value of the narratives and their expert performers extended into the magico-medical realm.

While the connection between royal ancestor veneration and epic was not tight, both ways of remembering the past and legitimating the present interacted with the other. Thus, we can use evidence of royal ancestor veneration – the material remains and other sorts of evidence: genealogies, references in texts, and the values attached to ancestor veneration – as a proxy for the otherwise invisible development and spread of epic. By 700 BCE the veneration of the ruins of Troy was clearly connected to Greek-style rites of ancestor veneration, and we can presume that a Greek epic tradition about the fall of Troy was well developed by this time. In the following chapter I focus on the role of competition among Greek poets in shaping the tradition behind the Homeric *Iliad*.

---

[162] E.g., Seaford (1994: 112–20).
[163] FF 169.31, 172 Theiler. According to the Indo-European tradition that Greek-speakers brought to Greece, poets were involved in a reciprocal relationship with their patron: "the poet gave poems of praise to the patron, who in turn bestowed largesse upon the poet. To the aristocracy of Indo-European society this reciprocal relation was a moral and ideological necessity. For only the poet could confer on the patron what he and his culture valued more highly than life itself: precisely what is expressed by the 'imperishable fame' formula" (Watkins 1995: 70, see further his pp. 68–84, with earlier references).
[164] Chapter 9, 215.

15 | The history of the Homeric tradition

> (The good kind of strife) rouses a man, even if he is un-handy, to work. For, someone, looking at another – a rich man – when he is lacking work, who strives to plow and plant and then make his house in good order, as his neighbor, he envies him striving for wealth; this strife is good for mortals. The potter is angry at his fellow potter, and the builder is at the builder, and the beggar envies the beggar, and the singer envies his fellow singer.
>
> Hesiod Works and Days 20-6

Introduction

The text of the *Iliad* is the site, as it were, on which we are performing an archaeological excavation.[1] In the previous chapter I discussed the conditions in which a Greek epic about Troy could first develop. In this chapter I work through some of the key strata in the development of the Homeric story about Troy, establishing how collaboration and competition among (groups of) Greek-speaking poets created the Homeric dialect and made it dominant, concomitantly raising the status of the story of the fall of Troy to the primary framework for ancient history among the Greeks. I will argue in the final chapter that analogous processes involving competition and collaboration among Greek and Anatolian poets led to the transfer at an earlier stage of the two Near Eastern storylines I discussed in Chapters 6 and 8 to the Greek epic tradition about the fall of Troy.

I first discuss some commonly held theories about the date of Homer, before stating the approach I prefer, the one assuming a primarily oral development of the text that we know. I then set the parameters of the higher and lower ends for the creation of a Greek epic about Troy. I spend the rest of the chapter discussing the Greek cultural context shaping the Homeric tradition up to the sixth century. I argue that there were

---

[1] Comparable to Suter's study, *The Narcissus and the Pomegranate: An Archaeology of the Homeric Hymn to Demeter* (2002).

competing Greek epic traditions in Anatolia, an Ionic and an Aeolic one, both fascinated by the story of the fall of Troy and wishing to take possession of it. This competition, eventually won by Ionians by the seventh century, marked a key phase in the development of the tradition; although it left only traces on the story preserved for us, it allowed for the incorporation of Aeolicisms into Homer's Ionic dialect and it elevated the story about Troy to the dominant epic storyline expressing the Greek cultural memory about their doings in Bronze Age Anatolia. Continuing competition and collaboration among Ionic poets, I argue, especially in the context of the performance of the *Iliad* and *Odyssey* in the Panionia in the late eighth and seventh centuries, greatly speeded up the evolution of the diction and narrative content of the *Iliad* and the *Odyssey*, until they were close to the supremely sophisticated and complex works of art that are known to us. It was at this stage that the Homeric dialect became the preferred choice for Greek epic compositions, no matter what the ethnic affiliation of the poet. In the sixth century, the Homeric versions of these two stories were transferred to Athens, via Chios, for quality-controlled performances in the Panathenaea.

The date of "Homer": an overview

The versions of the *Iliad* and *Odyssey* available to the Alexandrian editors such as Aristarchus of Samothrace (220–143 BCE) represent the written texts on which our editions are based. The previous history of the two works remains a matter of debate. Walter Burkert and Martin West, assuming that a single poet was responsible for producing a unified written text of each of the two epics attributed to him, rely on mentions of features that they claim could not have been known before *ca.* 675 BCE to argue for a relatively late date.[2] However, many scholars believe that the *Iliad* and the *Odyssey* represent compositions from *ca.* 750–700 BCE. In addition,

---

[2] I mention here some of the features they single out, with some comments: Burkert (1976) argues that the mentions of Egyptian Thebes at *Il.* 9.381 and *Od.* 4.126–7 refer specifically to the Thebes of the Twenty-fifth Dynasty, sacked in 663 BCE by Assurbanipal, and should not be considered late additions. For his part, West argues that Homer echoes specific passages of the *Theogony*. For example, the reference to the son of a certain Amphidamas (*Il.* 23.87) West sees as inspired by Hesiod, who claimed to have performed at Amphidamas' funeral games, which, as noted below, are possibly datable to 705 BCE. But, both examples assume a single fixed text, rather than a more flexible tradition, made up of traditional building blocks that were available to a poet in the Homeric tradition. West (1995) argues that Poseidon's destruction of the Achaean wall (*Il.* 7.442–64, 12.17–33) presupposes knowledge of the flood as narrated in *Atrahasis* and *Gilgamesh*, and that the poet must have been inspired by Sennacherib's account of the flooding of Babylon.

many do not believe that a single poet should be considered responsible for the authoritative written version of the epics.

It is important to realize that if one follows the earlier date for "Homer," by which I mean a form of the *Iliad* and *Odyssey* close in content and dialect to that presently attested, the Orientalizing period (750–650 BCE) is not relevant to the question of Near Eastern influences on Homer, but the reverse is not true. Neither the earlier nor the later dating for Homer invalidates any part of my argument concerning Near Eastern influence on the epic prior to the Orientalizing period. Certainly ideas and motifs from the Near East did shape Greek myth and religion in the Orientalizing period, just as they left their impact on Greek art, and some of the parallels between Sappho's songs and Hittite prayers, for instance, may be the result of contact that occurred during that time.[3] Finally, the Orientalizing period is an art-historical term that was first applied by Oswyn Murray to Greek society,[4] and it is possible to re-define its upper end, as Sarah Morris has done based on archaeological and art-historical considerations.[5] This allows for a correspondence of what we can detect archaeologically and the archaeologically invisible contact during the Dark Ages in religion and literature that left its mark on Homer, irrespective of our date preference.

The earliest textualizations of episodes from Greek epic should probably be dated to *ca*. 750 BCE.[6] The two earliest examples of inscriptions that go beyond a few words both use dactylic cola, the Dipylon vase from Athens (*ca*. 730 BCE),[7] and Nestor's Cup from Pithecusae (*ca*. 720–690 BCE); the latter clearly refers to a character and object also known from Homer's

---

However, the destruction of a city by a flood or a flood-like enemy is a standard image of Emesal Sumerian *balag* laments performed by *kalû* priests, collected in M. E. Cohen (1988), and dates back to the Standard Sumerian city laments of the early second millennium; it also appears in the *Cuthean Legend of Naram-Sin* (OB 8′, translit. and trans. J. G. Westenholz 1997: 276–7). In other words, if the Greek poet was inspired by a Near Eastern example, it could have been current in the epic literature long before the Neo-Assyrian period. So, these arguments cannot be considered to be conclusive. See M. L. West (1995) for his detailed arguments for a later dating for Homer. Also see Chapter 4, 103, on his argument that the *Odyssey* is dependent on a seventh-century Milesian *Argonautica* (M. L. West 2005).

[3] On which see Bachvarova (2007a; 2009).   [4] See Murray (1993: 2, 81–101).
[5] S. P. Morris (1992a: 101–49).
[6] The strong connection between early writing and the dactylic hexameter, to which Powell (1991: 184–5) rightly calls attention, suggests that one way writing was taught was by having students write out well-known pieces of hexametric poetry, a method analogous to how writing was taught in Mesopotamia. See Burkert (1987a: 215–17). I would not agree, however, with Powell, that the alphabet was invented to write down poetry, nor with Burkert, who argues that Near Eastern poetry was transmitted via the scribal curriculum to Greek scribes (as mentioned earlier in Chapter 3, 55, n. 8, and Chapter 9, 200).
[7] ⱵΟΣΝΥΝΟΡΧΕΣΤΟΝΠΑΝΤΟΝΑΤΑΛΟΤΑΤΑΠΑΙΖΕΙΤΟΤΟΔΕ... "who now of all dancers dances most friskily, his (is) this..." See Powell (1991: 158–63).

works.[8] Both are on wine vessels, speaking to the lively, competitive atmosphere of the aristocratic symposium, and both were deposited as grave offerings, indicating the desire to imagine the dead as able to participate in the drinking and conviviality that was the privilege of the good life,[9] an attitude congenial to the performance of epics remembering dead heroes of ages long past. The audience of the cup inscriptions was surely an audience that enjoyed listening to performances of hexametric epics. However, the relationship between the earliest textualization(s) of the *Iliad* or *Odyssey* and our Homeric texts is unknowable, despite the attempt of Douglas Frame to argue that the cup specifically refers to an *Iliad* 11 substantially like that known to us from the extant text, and therefore that the "Panionic" *Iliad* (on which see below) had already taken form.[10] What we can say is that the Neleid Nestor has made his way into a supralocally recognized Ionic tradition of epic.

The *Homeric Hymn to Apollo* is one of the few texts in dactylic hexameter the date of which it might be possible to pin down securely, because its constituent parts, one for Delian Apollo, one for Pythian Apollo, were combined in 522 BCE, when a festival for Pythian Apollo was celebrated in Delos by the Samian tyrant Polycrates, but the dates of the two separate Apollo hymns – if we can talk about separate fixed texts – are less clear.[11] Another, earlier, date possibly comes from Hesiod's reference in his *Works and Days* (650–9) to the funeral games of Amphidamas, who supposedly died in the Lelantine War, thought to have occurred somewhere between 730 and 650 BCE; some date his death to *ca.* 705 BCE. Counting back from this date, Richard Janko puts the dictation of the written texts of the *Iliad* and the *Odyssey* in the second half of the eighth century BCE, based on glottochronological grounds.[12] The problems are obvious: How can we

---

[8] ΝΕΣΤΟΡΟΣ:Ε[ΣΤ]ΙΕΥΠΟΤ[ΟΝ]:ΠΟΤΕΡΙΟΝ
ΗΟΣΔΑΝΤΟΔΕΠΙΕΣΙ:ΠΟΤΕΡΙ[Ο]:ΑΥΤΙΚΑΚΕΝΟΝ
ΗΙΜΕΡΟΣΗΑΙΡΕΣΕΙ:ΚΑΛΛΙΣΤΕ[ΦΑ]ΝΟ:ΑΦΡΟΔΙΤΕΣ
"Nestor's cup is good to drink from, but whoever drinks of this cup, immediately desire of beautiful-crowned Aphrodite will seize that one." See discussions in Watkins (1976, whose reconstruction I follow); Cassio (1994), Faraone (1996), Powell (1991: 163–7), and S. West (1994). Deviations from Homeric usage can be explained as evidence for an independent tradition of incantations in dactylic hexameters.

[9] See Murray (2009: 508–10) on the role of poetry in the symposium.

[10] Frame (2009: 603–13). He also argues for a date of *ca.* 700 BCE for the inscription, based on the letter forms.

[11] Zenobius of Athos 1.62, *Suid.* s.v. *Puthia kai Dēlia* (Adler Π 3128). See Burkert (1979a), Janko (1982: 102, 112–15), and Nagy (2010: 20, 72, 221–2), following Martin (2000) in the observation that the Pythian section is "Hesiodic," while the Delian section is "Homeric."

[12] Janko (1982: 228–31). Plutarch (*Sept.* 153f) connects the Amphidamas mentioned by Hesiod to the king who died in the Lelantine War. M. L. West (1966: 43–5) and Janko (1982: 94–8) use his evidence to date Hesiod. Most (2006: xxv, n. 8) casts doubt on all aspects of this theory. "[T]he date, duration, and even historical reality of this war are too uncertain to provide very solid

assume a constant rate of change?¹³ How can we assume that each author is tapping into a unitary but evolving poetic language, which does not vary according to the background of the poet and the specific subgenre he is working in?¹⁴ How can we assume that features we know are archaisms were not being deployed in new and creative ways by the poet?

Geoffrey Kirk relies on the society and the objects depicted, external references to the story of the Trojan War, the date given by Herodotus, the development of hero cult, and the persona of the poet, all of which "are completely inadequate for any precise conclusion,"¹⁵ to arrive at a possible range of the later ninth century to the middle of the seventh century BCE for the *Iliad* and *Odyssey*.¹⁶ But, if we rely primarily on the depiction of customs in epic, then references to battle equipment and tactics that date to the seventh century or even later are evidence for a later date for an *Iliad* that looks substantially like the one we have. They include mention of massed warfare, Corinthian helmets, and the combination of pairs of throwing spears with single spears in the warrior's equipment.¹⁷

---

evidence for dating Hesiod with any degree of precision." See further discussion by Walker (2004: 156–71), dating the death of Amphidamas to around 705 BCE and explaining the Lelantine War as a multi-century conflict over the Lelantine plain; V. Parker (1997: 59–93), looking to 710–650 BCE as the date of the war and putting the death of Amphidamas at the end of the eighth century BCE or beginning of the seventh. The *hērōon* at Eretria, which has been connected to the possible heroization of Amphidamas, dates to *ca*. 680 BCE.

[13] A problem acknowledged by Janko (1992: 15).
[14] A point made by M. L. West (1995: 204–5). Also see Adrados (2005: 97–101) on the history of the discussion of the differences between the dialects of Homer and Hesiod.
[15] Kirk (1962: 287).
[16] See Kirk (1960; 1962: 282–7; 1985: 3–10). Latacz (1996: 56–65) uses Homer's worldview, and references to the Trojan War story in art and other authors, to arrive at an eighth-century dating.
[17] Possible references to phalanx warfare, the development of which has been variously dated to as early as 725, and as late as 650 BCE, and even after 600 BCE (van Wees 2000), have been debated at length; see for example M. L. West (1995: 209–10). See Kirk (1960: 179–80; 1985: 9–10) for arguments against a late date. The lines spoken by Nestor (*Il*. 7.334–5, considered an interpolation by many) referring to transportation of a warrior's cremated remains back home for burial may refer to a fifth-century Athenian custom, or it could be a reminiscence of a much older custom, explicitly attested among the Hittites for example (see Otten 1958b: 9). Van Wees (1994a; 1994b) has presented the most complete examination of battle equipment and tactics in Homer, arguing for a late date. For a review of earlier scholarly opinions on the dating of Homer see Crielaard (1995: 201–9). Arguments dating our texts of the *Iliad* and *Odyssey* much earlier than the eighth century are not convincing. Ruijgh (1995) presents the most detailed claim for a ninth-century date for Homer, following Herodotus (2.53.2), but what Herodotus actually meant by Homer being "not more than 400 years before me" is a matter of dispute. See Kirk (1985: 3–4). Ruijgh argues that Homer's language is distinctly older than that of the Ionic iambographers Archilochus, Semonides, and Hipponax, the earliest of whom dates to the seventh century, but this assumes the same rate of change for the Homeric language as for the language of iambic, which is on the whole much more colloquial. Ruijgh (1997: 35) attempts to

Finally, Minna Skafte Jensen argues strongly that the two Homeric epics we have were dictated by two different poets to scribes in Athens in 522 BCE, when Hipparchus demanded a written text be established to cross-check Panathenaic performances,[18] while Gregory Nagy has presented a different approach to the question of how to date the Homeric text, arguing that rather than thinking of a single author whose text may have suffered some alterations and interpolations over time, we can instead distinguish several stages of "crystallization" in the development of the Homeric tradition, each successively less flexible.[19] A model of decreasing flexibility over the generations up to *ca.* 700 BCE works well to explain the differences among the strata of Near Eastern influence on the text that are discussed in the final chapter, even if one prefers to think of the writing down of each authoritative text as a single unitary act occurring some time around or after 700 BCE.

The upper and lower limit for the creation of a Greek epic about Troy

We know that the story tradition about Troy is indeed very old. As mentioned in earlier chapters, the destruction of Troy/Tarwiza may have already reached legendary status among the Hittites in the Late Bronze Age, and Luwians were already singing about "steep Wilusa" in the

---

support his earlier date for Homer by arguing that Eumelus of Corinth is dependent on Homer and dates to the second half of the eighth century. Unfortunately Eumelus' date is questioned, as is his authorship of epics drawing on the Trojan war, see M. L. West (2002a) and J. Latacz, "Eumelos," in *Brill's New Pauly* 5.164. Ruijgh's argument also depends on an early date for the Greek alphabet, but DeVries (2007: 96–7) has presented a convincing case for dating its invention to *ca.* 825 BCE, based on a comparison of the letter shapes with those of the Phoenician alphabet. Since Homer apparently knows that Greeks can write with his story of Bellerophontes carrying a letter from Argos (on which see Chapter 16, 424), that section, at least, of the *Iliad* cannot be earlier than 825 BCE.

[18] Jensen (2011).
[19] See, for example, Nagy (1996a: 29–63). In Nagy (2010), following Frame (2009), he re-defines the stages prior to the Peisistratean regulation to contrast a Panionic Homer with a Panathenaic Homer. Lowenstam (1997) examines differences between artists' representations of episodes from their versions in the *Iliad* and *Odyssey*, arguing that "our Homeric poems had not become canonical in the seventh, sixth, or even early fifth centuries B. C. E." (24). He suggests that the wealth of specific detail contradicting Homer or not found in his texts points to the circulation of other versions, and lack of knowledge of Homer's versions. See Chapter 16 on variant versions of the *Iliad*. It may be, however, that the artists were simply "primarily not interested in verbal art" (Frame 2009: 610–12, n. 209, with further arguments).

fourteenth century BCE.[20] There is, however, no reason to believe that a Mycenaean epic about the fall of Troy existed. We can at least use the linguistic and metrical data internal to the Homeric tradition to arrive at the lower limit for the date at which a story about Troy was first performed as a Greek epic.

Joachim Latacz, following earlier scholars, has pointed out that in the formula *Iliou proparoithe(n)* 'before Ilium' the genitive must be scanned as *-o-o*, not as monosyllabic *-ou* (*I-li-o-o pro-pa-roi-then* -⏑⏑-⏑⏑-⏓);[21] therefore, a story about Troy must have been in existence either before the contraction of two adjacent like vowels or before the establishment of the rigid hexameter,[22] itself dependent on the process of contraction, because the substitution of one long syllable for two short syllables was a poetic exploitation of synchronic variation in the language as contraction took hold. Because the poetic analogy of two short syllables equaling one long syllable, which is the hallmark of the dactylic hexameter distinguishing it from the lyric meters from which it was derived, only makes sense once the line is perceived to contain a series of repeating dactylic feet, rather than cola of a certain number of syllables, the transition to a mora-counting meter was probably closely linked with the transition to a stichic, rather than strophic, structure. Therefore, the tradition that chose to commemorate a conflict between Greeks and Anatolians, whether real or imagined, was cast as epic at an early stage in the development of the Homeric tradition, before the stichic mora-counting dactylic hexameter had been created. According to linguistic criteria, in fact, stichic Homeric verse also developed after the Ionian migration (i.e., the Protogeometric period), because it was only at this point that the process of contraction was applicable to enough pairs of vowels to make it a productive rule for poetic composition. It is plausible to see the stichic Homeric verse as an east Ionic innovation;[23] stichic verse is characteristic of east Ionic poetry. Thus, we

---

[20] See Chapter 2, 21, and Chapter 13, 347–8. The set of fragments of the tablets describing the festival of Istanuwa include at least one in OS (sixteenth century BCE), but *KBo* 4.1 is in NS.

[21] ⏑ = short syllable, - = long syllable, ⏓ = either a long or a short syllable.

[22] Latacz (2004: 267–71), M. L. West (1988: 163). The metrical colon -⏑⏑-⏑⏑-⏑ is a variation of the eight-syllable prosodiakon rhythm, with rightwards dovetailing. The shape of the prosodakian is x-⏑⏑-⏑⏑-. When the rhythm is repeated, rightwards dovetailing (cutting the sequence one syllable to the right) gives the colon found in the formula in question: ... x-⏑⏑-x|-⏑⏑-x|-⏑⏑-x-⏑⏑-. ... On the prosodakion as an eight-syllable colon of Greco-Aryan origin and the process of dovetailing, see Nagy (1990b: 444–54).

[23] Gentili and Lomiento (2008: 266). Maslov (2013: 5–6) misses the point when he relies on evidence for the use of non-Ionic dialect forms in inscriptions in elegiac couplets or hexameters to argue that they were not Ionic verse forms. Even if the verse forms were invented by Ionic

may specify that the dactylic hexameter was created after *ca.* 1050 BCE in Ionia,[24] and that it post-dates the introduction of a story involving Troy into the Greek epic tradition.

As for the upper limit of the creation of a story about Troy in Greek epic, we can use the conventional dates for the Trojan War, which place it around the beginning of the twelfth century BCE.[25] They fall about four generations before the arrival of Protogeometric Greeks in Anatolia in *ca.* 1050 BCE. If we take the dating seriously, then we should use it, not as the date of an historical event, but to fix the upper limit of the date of the creation of the story. And, if three generations mark the horizon of "real" historical memory, and if the Trojan War was set in the legendary time beyond historical memory, minimally just beyond the three-generation limit, then the Trojan legend can be no older than *ca.* 1160 BCE (if we accept 1250 for the legendary date) or 1095 (if we accept 1185). The upper and lower limits thus create a rather narrow window of 1160–1050 BCE for the creation of the legend.

The refining of the pre-Homeric Greek epic tradition: competition among Aeolic and Ionic poets

In the previous chapter I began to discuss the Greco-Anatolian interactions that provided the settings in which the Near Eastern storylines attached to the fall of Troy would have been transmitted to Greek-speakers at this time. In the following chapter I will explore this question in more detail. Here, however, I focus on how different groups of Greek-speakers deployed the epic narrative once it was brought into being. Many Homeric scholars have long believed that the Homeric tradition had originally been cast in the Aeolic dialect and then, at a relatively late date, was transferred to the Ionic dialect, with the retention of Aeolic forms where Ionic forms were metrically inconvenient. This would mean that after the fall of the Mycenaean palaces, when dialect differentiation was well under way, an

---

poets, that does not mean that all non-Ionic poets accepted the use of the dialect as mandatory when using the verse forms.

[24] For further discussion of the history of the dactylic hexameter see the Appendix.

[25] See Burkert (1995: 223–8)) for a discussion of the dates. Ephorus (*FGrH* 70 F 223) puts it at 1149 BCE, Eratosthenes (*FGrH* 241 F 1d) at 1184/3, the Parian Marble (*FGrH* 239 §24) at 1209/8, Herodotus (2.145) can be interpreted as giving a date *ca.* 1250, and Duris (*FGrH* 76 F 41) 1334.

inherited Greco-Aryan tradition of narrative song was lost to Attic-Ionic speakers and became confined only to Aeolic bards in Boeotia and Thessaly, who then transplanted their tradition to the coast of Anatolia in the Aeolic migrations, where it was passed on to the epic-less Ionic people who also settled there.

This view was called into question repeatedly in the second half of the twentieth century, and at this point even Nagy, who believed in the putative Aeolic layer when he co-authored the 1972 book *Greek: A Survey of Recent Work* with Fred Householder, has accepted that the Ionic epic tradition represented by Homer descends directly from the second-millennium Greek epic tradition, and that no gap in the Ionic tradition can be detected in the Homeric dialect.[26]

There is no reason to assume that epic, that is, extended narrative songs, did not originally exist in all dialects of Greek.[27] The assumption of epic traditions in multiple Greek dialects surviving the end of the Bronze Age fits better the external data we have. Cornelis Ruijgh attributed the putative loss of epic in the Peloponnese partially to the Dorian invasion,[28] but are we to believe that the uncouth Dorians had not inherited the same Greco-Aryan narrative tradition that lies behind Homer? Epic hardly requires a high level of "civilization," however one might define it. Nor can the Dorian migration explain the loss of epic in all areas of the mainland and islands where Attic-Ionic was spoken, especially where there is evidence for continuity of settlement, such as Attica from LH IIB onwards

---

[26] For the arguments for the Aeolic layer see Berg and Haug (2000), Haug (2002), Janko (1982: 89–92; 1992: 15–19, with earlier references), Ruijgh (1995: 50–7), Wathelet (1970), and M. L. West (1988: 162–6; 1992b: 174–5); also see the references listed in W. F. Wyatt (1992: 168, n. 12). Janko's findings have been subjected to a searching critique by Jones (2008; 2010; 2011), who objects to the way he arrives at his statistics, as well as to his presuppositions about the Homeric language. For a continuous tradition of Ionic epic: Adrados (1981; 2005: 50–6, 87–97), Hooker (1977: 56–83), Horrocks (1987; 1997, critiqued by Janko 1998), Jones (2008; 2010; 2011), Kirk (1962: 151–2), D. G. Miller (1982), Nagy (2010: 232–3; 2011), Nikolaev (2010), Rau (2008), and W. F. Wyatt (1992), arguing that there was no Aeolic epic at all. In an otherwise fine article on the Aeolic contribution to Greek poetry and song, Maslov (2013) fails to take into consideration the implications of their arguments. See Adrados (2005: 50–3), Bartoněk (2003: 458–62), and M. L. West (1988: 162, n. 76) for full references of previous scholarship on dialectal features in Homer.

[27] As Gentili (1988: 58) points out, "The ... position would be justified only on the impossible assumption that ancient local legends pertaining to gods, heroes, and kings had been completely forgotten, to be reintroduced at a later date by Ionian bards."

[28] Ruijgh (1995: 3). The current archaeological evidence works against the notion that the southwards migration of the Dorians from northwest Greece during the Dark Age wreaked major havoc, even if it caused dialect replacement. See Eder (1998), F. Gschnitzer, "Doric Migration," in *Brill's New Pauly* 9.680–5, and Lemos (2002: 191–3).

and Lefkandi (Xeropolis) into the ninth century.[29] Moreover, what of a possible Arcado-Cypriot tradition, brought to Cyprus by the Greeks? Here was where so many of the administrative trappings of the Bronze Age managed to survive that writing was preserved across the Dark Age. Surely here a court-sponsored epic tradition could have survived.[30]

In addition, scenes that draw on the same values and customs immortalized in Greek epic are found on pottery in various locations throughout the Greek-speaking world, including Cyprus, in both the post-palatial period and the Geometric period (interrupted by a drastic decrease in figural representations in the Protogeometric period).[31] We would have to believe that epic had died away even though the conditions promoting epic and practices described in epic had not.

Finally, we need to be careful to distinguish between the desire and ability to produce narrative poetry about the past, which verge on human universals in traditional societies, and the production of hexametric poetry in particular or – narrowing it down further – an epic about a specific event, the fall of Troy, for example. The innovations that transformed inherited Greco-Aryan rhythmic patterns into the stichic dactylic hexameter would not have occurred simultaneously in all parts of the Greek-speaking world. Rather, the most likely model is one I applied earlier with regard to the transmission of innovations in the subject matter of epic, drawing on the work of sociolinguists who have been able to study how linguistic innovations radiate along social networks: innovators who are particularly well-connected and socially powerful in their community have a disproportionate effect on the local language; their solidarity with a supralocal group, as opposed to identification with a local group, is the result of social ambition and motivates the adoption of supralocal forms of speech in place of local dialects, which then, because of the speakers' prestige, are adopted by their peers in the local group because they want to imitate them.[32]

Applying this model to the spread of hexametric epic replacing putative local forms of epic in other prosodic forms, we can imagine that particularly ambitious and talented performers would make an effort to reach the

---

[29] On the continuity see Crielaard (2006), Lemos (2006), R. Parker (1996: 10–14), and Welwei (1992: 50–75), discussing the archaeological evidence and analyzing legends of the Pylian origin of the settlers of Athens (used by some scholars to support a break in continuity in Attica) as a later (fifth-century) construction.

[30] See further discussion in Chapter 12, 309–10.

[31] Discussed in more detail in Chapter 11, 278–9.

[32] See Chapter 9, 212, where I cite Labov (2001) and Marshall (2004).

widest audience possible and would be judged simultaneously on the story they told and their ability to hold an audience with their performance technique. They would be important vectors in the transmission both of stories and of innovations to the prosodic form in which they were cast, with rapid pick-up by local performers eager to attach their colleagues' success to themselves. When dialectal forms were used in place of metrically infelicitous or obsolete forms in the performer's own dialect, they would not have been borrowed at the level of phonology or morphemes; rather they were embedded in useful formulas, themselves often embedded in paragraph-level narrative units that conveyed a particularly appealing theme or motif (type scenes). The same model would apply across languages as well as across dialects, and at the level of entire stories as well as formulas.

Based on this model, I argue that the core song of the Aeolic-influenced Ionic epic tradition was originally one about the fall of Troy. That is, although I do not believe in an Aeolic layer in Homer's dialect, I do believe in an *Iliad* in the Aeolic dialect, which was eventually eclipsed by an *Iliad* in the Ionic dialect. Anatolian Aeolic (Lesbian) was spoken in the area from Troy to Larissa, at last after the eighth century (although we cannot discount the presence of speakers of other Greek dialects).[33] As Richard Janko has argued:

> Phrases like προτὶ Ἴλιον ἰρην or Ἑκτορέην ἄλοχον prove that Aeolic bards were already singing tales about a war at Troy. Local patriotism would give them good reason to develop old traditions of Mycenaean raids on the Asiatic coast; Lesbian ambitions on the Troad surely predated Pittacus' time.[34]

Secondly, the appearance of both Thessalian Achilles and Hector, who has Boeotian roots, in Homeric epic suggests the use of epic to maintain a sense of a connection between a set of Greek-speakers in Anatolia speaking an Aeolic dialect and the two regions of Greece where the mainland Aeolic dialects were spoken.[35] For this reason Dieter Hertel may be correct that the first Greeks who came to commemorate Troy as a symbol of their

---

[33] At least, inscriptions in Lesbian are found in this area after the eighth century (Hodot 1990; 2001). Also see Chapter 14, 359, n. 43.

[34] Janko (1992: 19). The formulas Janko mentions include the Lesbian-influenced forms *hīrēn* instead of *hieren*, and *Hektoreēn* instead of *Hektoriēn* (Janko 1992: 16, 17).

[35] The current view is that such Greek ethnic identities based on migration myths were relatively late developments of the Archaic period (Ulf 1996); see discussion in Chapter 14, 359–60.

glorious Bronze Age past were ancestors of the ones who later developed an Aeolian identity. Kurt Raaflaub notes,

> Hector turns out to be fighting mostly against opponents from central Greece and Thessaly; a tomb of Hector was shown at Thebes; hence it is likely that these fights originally figured in central Greek traditions and Hector was located there long before he became the leader of the Trojans.[36]

The stories of Achilles' early adventures in Anatolia, in which he sacked a variety of cities, fathered Neoptolemus, and battled the Mysian king Telephus, should be connected to the arrival of the people from mainland Greece who would become Aeolians and the beginnings of commemorating the past at Troy, as their Aeolian identity coalesced around his heroic figure and before his story became centered more specifically on one storyline, the Trojan War.[37] The theme of the wrath of Achilles – a hypothetical *Achilleid*, which many scholars have postulated was the core of Homer's *Iliad*[38] – could have been a specifically Aeolic contribution to the epic tradition about the fall of Troy. There are several additional plot elements in the *Iliad* that are best explained as vestiges of a mainland Aeolic epic tradition, including the leading position and size of the Boeotian contingent in the Catalog of Ships and the fleet's departure from Aulis in Boeotia.

Finally, there is some evidence that an Aeolic epic tradition about Troy remained alive and well on Lesbos for some time while Ionic epic was in existence, as West shows, for the Lesbian poets Sappho and Alcaeus both use peculiar hexameter-friendly Lesbian forms of Priam's name, *Perramos* and *Peramos*, the former derived from *Priamos* (as found in Homer) by the Lesbian changes *ri> ry> ery > err* and the latter allowing for more flexible placement in the hexameter.[39] Also, there is some evidence that a variant

---

[36] Raaflaub (1998b: 396). Also see Burgess (2001: 65, with n. 61), Janko (1982: 92), and M. L. West (1988: 161–2), pointing out the Thessalian connections of some key characters.

[37] Dué (2002: 63–5), Högemann (2002: 1130–2), Latacz (2004: 192–4). On Achilles' adventures also see the summary of Gantz (1993: 230–1, 576–82, 591–8) and Proclus' summary of the *Cypria* §§7, 9 West. Nagy (2010: 148–9, 250–1) suggests that Achilles was suffered to remain the star of the *Iliad* in the Panathenaic version because Thessaly was an ally of the Athenians.

[38] See most recently Hertel (2008: 207–16), M. L. West (2011: 42–7, 52–62, with earlier references).

[39] Sappho F 44.16 Lobel-Page, Alcaeus F 42.2 Lobel-Page; M. L. West (1973: 191; 2002b: 218). On the forms also see Buck (1955: 26), Hoffmann (1893: 320–1), H. N. Parker (2008: 456). Also cited by Ruijgh (1985: 167–8; 1997: 35), suggesting continued contact between Aeolic and the putative newly-formed Ionic tradition, with Homer's excellence the reason for the subsequent death of Aeolic epic.

tradition among Lesbians about the aftermath of the Trojan War remained extant after the Homeric *Iliad* rose to dominance. In Sappho F 17 Lobel-Page the Atreidae (in the plural) were stopped on Lesbos by Zeus' anger when attempting to return from Troy. In the *Odyssey* (3.130–71), on the other hand, only Menelaus, having quarreled with his brother Agamemnon about their return, went there, meeting Nestor.[40] And, the fifth-century historian Hellanicus of Lesbos states that Hector's son Scamandrius and Aeneas' son Ascanius re-founded Ilion, while in Homer's work Poseidon predicts its complete destruction.[41] If we accept that the Aeolic and Ionian traditions existed side-by-side for some time, then we can think about competition between the two groups of poets, and we should not be thinking as much in terms of individual performers as schools of performers.

It thus seems best to view the Aeolic influence as borrowings (such as the innovative dative plural in *-essi*) into an archaizing Ionic poetic dialect by bards in close contact with a prestigious archaizing Aeolic tradition in Anatolia (Lesbian). The borrowing was facilitated in part by the interpretation of some forms, such as the dative plural-*oisi* (originally locative-*oisu*) versus-*ois* (originally instrumental), or variants (such as between the various infinitive endings and between the hypothetical particles *ke* and *an*) in the epic dialect used by Ionic bards as Aeolicisms, because they were also used in a poetic dialect they considered to be Aeolic (Lesbian).[42] Eventually, however, the school of Ionic bards won out, and their dialect was then adopted for the Panhellenic performance of epic.[43]

---

[40] See A. M. Bowie (1981: 14–15).

[41] *Il.* 20.307–17, D. H. 1.45.4–48.1 = *FGrH* 4 F 31. Cf. Σ bT *ad Il.* 24.735b, which say the *neoteroi*, that is, non-Homeric epic poets, attributed the re-founding of Troy to Scamandrius. Nagy suggests that they could be thinking of the seventh-century poet Lesches of Pyrrha, who appears to have composed his *Little Iliad* in the Aeolic dialect. What we have of the *Little Iliad* (F 30 West) tells us Neoptolemus took Aeneas home as booty. For the dialect of Lesches, see A. M. Bowie (1981: 8–9), disputed by M. L. West (1988: 165). Strabo (13.1.40–2) notes the discrepancy between the Ilians' version of events and what Homer says. See Nagy (2010: 204) and the discussion below.

[42] The borrowing of forms from another dialect is paralleled in the Yugoslav epic tradition, in which a bard can select between metrically convenient Bosnian/Croatian (*iyekavski*) and Serbian (*ekavski*) forms (Foley 1999: 75–8).

[43] Compare the development of the Middle Indic literary dialects: different locations at different times provided the environment fostering the development of a school of particularly excellent performers in a specific genre, thus creating the connection between a specific Middle Indic dialect, a specific set of meters, and a specific genre, for example Maharastri for *mahākāvya* or lengthy narrative poetry created by men and Shauraseni for the poetry of courtly women. The use of a particular dialect for the genre then became codified, manifesting itself in poets' artificial use of a non-native dialect to compose in a particular genre. See Bachvarova (1997) for

If it is agreed that there are west Ionic dialectal forms in Homer, one way to explain them is also interaction among competing epic traditions in different dialects.[44] And, this could explain Arcado-Cypriot features in the Homeric dialect that are not obvious archaisms (or even some that are).[45] It may even be possible to make other fine-grained distinctions, but in a stage shortly before the final formation of the Homeric dialect the most intense interaction occurred between east Aeolic (Lesbian) and east Ionic poetic dialects, in Anatolia.[46]

Rigorous competition among oral poets in festive settings was the crucible in which Homeric poetry was refined to reach the perfection of the *Iliad* and the *Odyssey*. Looking at the Homeric dialect from this angle, we can recast the Aeolic phase in the following terms. A key influence on what would end up being Homeric poetry was an exceptionally proficient school of east Aeolic bards in Anatolia who focused on a story about Troy. Ionian bards, who had also inherited a poetic tradition going back to the Late Bronze Age, were open to borrowing innovations from their Aeolic neighbors when bards performing in the Lesbian dialect were the main

---

a cross-cultural study of how particular literary dialects become attached to particular genres. See Nagy (1985: 34–5; 1990a: 51–2; 1990b: 53) on the use of non-native dialects for poetry addressed to a Panhellenic audience. Note that I do not follow the approach that Maslov (2013: 4) rightly criticizes, which presumes that "genres came into existence in different regions of Greece and retained the original dialect when they spread to other regions."

[44] M. L. West (1988: 166–7; 1992b: 173) argues that west Ionic features show the Ionic layer developed in Euboea. Also see Chapter 11, 295, n. 112. M. L. West (1988: 167–8) has also tried to argue that there was a Doric layer too (on the Doric forms also see Cassio 1998: 18–19; Maslov 2013: 10–12, 15–16, refuting this claim), and that the Aeolic innovations were not east Aeolic, but west Aeolic, from the Greek mainland, specifically Boeotia and Thessaly, which are next to Euboea. Ruijgh (1995: 47–50) spins an elaborate tale to explain the borrowing of supposedly Euboean (west Ionic) forms, imagining that "Homère a fréquenté l'Eubée à l'invitation de rois ou de princes eubéens et . . . il a eu beaucoup de succès à leurs cours" (49), and arguing that the epic was committed to writing there. Borrowing of Euboean forms makes sense only in the context of interaction between two poetic dialects, not influence from a Euboean vernacular, as suggested by Ruijgh. Cassio (1998) espouses the notion of borrowing between the poetic dialects used to perform epic.

[45] Householder and Nagy (1972: 62–5) discuss a set of lexemes and some verbal morphology shared between the Homeric dialect and Arcado-Cypriot as archaisms from Mycenaean. Deger-Jalkotzy (1994: 21), suggesting the possibility of a Cypriot epic strain, points to the Arcado-Cyprian contribution to Homeric dialect; also see Richardson (1989). I would discount, however, the notion that because Arcado-Cypriot is closest to the Greek dialect of Linear B, therefore Arcado-Cypriot epic had the closest ties to Mycenaean culture. Also see Chapter 12, 308–9, n. 37. We do not know the relationship between the written and spoken languages in second-millennium Greece, but there is no reason to assume that the archaizing language of oral epic that goes back to pre-Greek times had a close relationship with the artificially frozen written dialect of Linear B, taught as a father language to scribes.

[46] Adrados (2005: 90, 95).

players on the supralocal circuit within Anatolia, both in the context of formulaic phrases and as useful living forms to replace obsolete ones in their own poetic dialect.[47] Eventually, the prestige of the Aeolic tradition faded, but there was no sudden termination of the Aeolic tradition concomitant with its transfer to Ionians.

Interactions between an Aeolic and an Ionic tradition allowing for the transmission of useful forms between the poetic languages would have specifically involved competing narratives of the story of the Trojan War.[48] Although there are no inscriptions from the relevant period and archaeological evidence cannot provide good evidence on the construction of ethnic identities, we can observe this competition at work quite clearly later in the Archaic period, in the descriptions of Greek historians. Whereas in the time of Strabo Troy was definitely in the Aeolic area, certainly in the late seventh century into the sixth century, as Strabo discusses, it was an area under dispute, and at that point the Trojan War was used to justify claims of both Aeolians and Ionians to the Troad.[49]

Peisistratus seized Sigeum *ca.* 625 BCE, which had originally been founded as an Athenian colony, but at that point was controlled by Mytilene.[50] According to Herodotus (5.94), before the tyrant took Sigeum back from Mytilene, Athens had attempted to deny Mytilene its claim to the town by arguing that any Hellenes who participated in the Trojan War, not just the Aeolians, had rights to the Troad, a counter-argument to a Lesbian claim that itself possibly relied on epic.[51] By the time of Sappho and Alcaeus, the ruling genos of Mytilene justified its right to hegemony through a connection to Agamemnon, so the story was already being deployed as the primary authoritative narrative of the past used to justify the present.[52]

---

[47] On the interaction between Ionic and Lesbian outside of poetry, see Horrocks (1987: 273).
[48] Nagy (2010: 143) takes a similar angle: "the Athenians' appropriation of an Aeolian Troy resulted in their appropriation of an Aeolian Homer as well."
[49] Str. 13.1.8, 38–9. See Rose (2008: 402) on how Aeolis was defined by ancient historians.
[50] Rose (2014: 64).
[51] See Strabo 13.1.38–9 on the conflict between Athens and Mytilene for the Troad, focused on their towns of Sigeum and Achilleum. On the conflict also see Tenger (1999: 121–6); on its connection to the later history of the Homeric tradition about Troy, see Nagy (2010: 142–217, 321–4). Also see Aslan and Rose (2013: 15–17) on the destruction and rebuilding of Sigeum. In an analogous case, in the sixth century the Athenians were accused by the Megarians of inserting a line into the Catalog of Ships to support their claim over Salamis: *Il.* 2.558, [Arist.] *Rh. Al.* 15.1375b30, Str. 9.1,10, see Kirk (1985: 207–9), Rose (2014: 64–5).
[52] See Carlier (1984: 458–61), Page (1955: 149–52, 170–1), Rose (2008: 402, 418). Sappho F 71 Lobel-Page mentions the Penthilidae; Alcaeus F 70.6 Lobel-Page calls the genos the Atreids. Penthilus, a son of Orestes, and/or other sons of Orestes and further descendants led the

Troy was destroyed again in the mid seventh century, and Carolyn Chabot Aslan suggests that claims for alternative sites of the legendary city arose in the aftermath; "[i]f the population of the Troad was, in fact, weakened by the events in the mid seventh century, this might explain why the Athenians saw an opportunity to move into this area shortly thereafter."[53] At that point, other cities could lay claim to the honor of being the original Troy as a way of legitimating the territorial claims of their allies or founders. According to Strabo, the walls of Sigeum were claimed to have been built by the Mytileneans using stones from the walls of Troy.[54] After Athens took Sigeum, Achilleum, where another tomb of Achilles was claimed to be located, was turned into a fortified site for the Mytileneans in the sixth century by Periander of Corinth, again purportedly using stones from Troy,[55] and "New Troy" (Neon Ilion) was built on the site of old Troy, which we now know was the Bronze Age Wilusa (the "real" Troy). New Troy is later attested to be an Aeolian city, its claim that it was never abandoned and continued the original Troy supported by Hellanicus of Lesbos.[56] Meanwhile, Strabo reports the claims of the partisan Demetrius of Scepsis (second century BCE) that Scepsis was founded by Aeneas and had been ruled by his son Ascanius along with Scamandrius. Demetrius asserts furthermore that the original Ilion was located within its territory.[57] The deployment of connections to the dynasties of Troy by competing Greek cities is analogous to the competing uses of the Dardanid genealogy by the Phrygians and the Greek Aeneidae, a competition which I have suggested shaped the storyline of the *Homeric Hymn to Aphrodite*, causing the merger of a Phrygian birth story and a Greek (Lesbian?) seduction story. Moreover, while the destruction of Iron Age Troy allowed claims to prior rights to the Troad to take a new form, as I argue in more detail in the following chapter, connections to the house of Troy had already been deployed centuries earlier by Greek dynasties and had a major impact on the Iliadic narrative.

Aeolian migration to Lesbos (Σ ad Pi. N. 11.33 = Hellanicus *FGrH* 4 F 32; Strabo 9.2.3, 13.1.3 = Ephorus *FGrH* 70 F 119).

[53] Aslan (2009c: 40). Aslan thus adds in an important piece of data that Nagy was unable to consider in his account of the conflict of the seventh and sixth centuries BCE over the Troad.

[54] Str. 13.1.38; Nagy (2010: 145, 189).

[55] Hdt. 5.94.2, Str. 13.1.38–9 = Timaeus of Tauromenium *FGrH* 566 F 129. See Nagy (2010: 178–90) and Rose (2014: 53–4, 64) for full discussion.

[56] The Ilians say it, and Hellanicus supports their claim: Str. 13.1.42 = *FGrH* 4 F 25b; see Nagy (2010: 193, 197–8).

[57] Str. 13.1.25, 35–6, 52–3 = Demetrius of Scepsis FF 26, 35 Gaede; Nagy (2010: 195–8).

However, Homer seems to be unaware of any ethnic divisions among the Greeks.[58] One possible reason is that because the action of the epic is situated before the Ionic and Aeolic migrations, any mention of either group was considered to be anachronistic.[59] Another possibility is that, because our version of the story was addressed to a Panhellenic audience, any reference to ethnic divisions among the Achaeans was considered inappropriate.[60] The Panhellenic perspective, with less emphasis on local traditions not comprehensible to all Greeks, and the presentation of the Achaeans in the *Iliad* as a single group opposed to barbarians, was the by-product of a larger movement towards Panhellenism, including the Panhellenic festivals, beginning in the eighth century.[61] However, the ethnic divisions are tacitly acknowledged, with the Aeolians clearly subordinated. As Nagy perspicaciously shows, Chryseis and Briseis, the featured captive women residing among the Achaeans, come from cities that would have been considered to be Aeolic to Homer's audience. Briseis was among a group of captive women from Lesbos, while Chryseis was captured when her husband's city, Thebe, was sacked. Andromache too came from Thebe, later an Aeolian city. Thus, "the Aeolians of Lesbos are represented as a defeated and degraded population."[62] In addition, the Homeric version of

---

[58] The Ionians "of trailing robes" are mentioned only once in the *Iliad*, in conjunction with the Boeotians, Locrians, Phthians, and Epeians (13.685–6), and they are equated with Athenians (13.689). The epithet also appears in the *Homeric Hymn to Apollo* (147), and it has been suggested that the reference is a late addition; for example, Ulf (1996: 250–1). Also see Janko (1992: 132–3). Homer shows no awareness of the Aeolians at all. Aeolians are never mentioned in the *Iliad*. In the *Odyssey* (10.55, 60) the Aeolian land is an island to the west of Greece. Homer refers to Sisyphus as a son of Aeolus (*Il.* 6.152–4), which fits the genealogy of Hesiod (F 69 Most); see Hodot (2001: 161–2). Hesiod (*Op.* 636) refers to "Aeolian Cyme" as his father's home (Hodot 2001: 161; Ulf 1996: 250), and the Lesbian king Makar is called the son of Aeolus in the *hHAp* 37. See Rose (2008) on the early use of the term Aeolian. The lack of mention of Aeolians and the single mention of Ionians is less of a problem if we assume an early date for Homer, in the eighth century BCE, rather than following the model outlined above. One could argue that the emphasis on three different Greek ethnicities developed after the time that the text of Homer had reached approximately its final form, concomitantly with the legends of Greek migrations. In this case, the Ionic poets before Homer who incorporated Aeolic forms into their dialect did not see themselves as members of a subdivision of the Greeks as a whole in competition with another major subdivision of Greeks. That is, they saw themselves as borrowing Lesbian forms, not ones that marked the large, "Aeolic" ethnic group.

[59] Nagy (2010: 226–7).

[60] Cf. Nagy (2010: 145) on Hdt. 5.94.2, concerning the Panhellenic nature of Athens' claim on the Troad.

[61] Nagy (1990b: 51–81; 1996a: 38–41, with earlier references).

[62] Nagy (2010: 241–53, esp. 250). Briseis: *Il.* 9.128–31, 270–3, 19.245–6; residing in Aeolian Lyrnessus in *Il.* 2.689–91; Chryseis from Thebe: *Il.* 2.366–9; Andromache from (Cilician) Thebe: *Il.* 6.415–16. Dué (2002) explores the stories of Bryseis, Chryseis, and Andromache as

the afterlife of Troy pointedly denies the Lesbian version of events.[63] In the *Iliad* Scamandrius is considered to be the alternate name of Astyanax, whom we know will be killed during the sack of Troy (*Il.* 6.402–3),[64] and Poseidon states that Troy will be utterly destroyed, and only the descendants of Aeneas will survive (*Il.* 20.306–17).[65] So, the text we have does seem to cater to the prejudices of an Ionic audience.

One possible reason for the ascendancy of the Ionic tradition could be that a competitive performance setting refined it to the point that it obviously was of higher quality than those of the other schools.[66] The increased creativity of the poetic tradition in its penultimate phase, which I would suggest was a by-product of increased competition among poets, explains the results of Arie Hoekstra's study of the incidence of Ionic quantitative metathesis, which appears to have arrived late in the Homeric language.[67] He shows that it came into play especially when formulas were

---

remnants of local (Aeolic) epic traditions. Also see Burgess (2001: 151–2, with n. 70; 163, with n. 121).

[63] Nagy (2010: 204–6, 321). Nagy points out that the epic also denies the Scepsian – in his eyes Ionic – version of events. When exactly Scepsis first claimed to be founded by members of the Trojan ruling house is unknown, and we do not have evidence to show that the takeover by Miletus was dated earlier than the fifth century (see Chapter 16, 436–7), so the suggestion that Scepsis represents the Ionic viewpoint requires more support from archaeological evidence before we can build further arguments upon it.

[64] Nagy (2010: 203–6; 322–3).

[65] The prophecy needed to be clarified in the eyes of a scholiast (Σ bT *ad Il.* 20.307–8a1), who adds that some say the descendants of Aeneas were thrown out by the Aeolians. Also see Chapter 16, 436, 437, nn. 61, 65.

[66] Nagy (2010: 211–14) argues that the loss of prestige of the Aeolic version can be connected to the loss of Smyrna, which claimed to be the birthplace of Homer, to the Ionians and the loss of Sigeum, where Achilles' tomb was supposed to be located. Smyrna birthplace of Homer: Strabo 14.1.37; *Vita* 2.1–3 West. Smyrna, Chios, Colophon all claim Homer: *Vita* 1.2 West; see Nagy (2010: 135) and Chapter 12, 330, n. 132. Smyrna an Aeolian city: Str. 14.1.4, Mimnermus F 9.6 West (fl. 630–600 BCE). Smyrna lost to the Ionians by 776 BCE: Paus. 5.8.7. Herodotus (1.149–50) explains that Smyrna started as an Aeolic settlement, but ended up Ionic, matching the putative progression of Homer's dialect. Archaeological evidence for this claim has been adduced: the replacement of Grey Ware, which scholars have associated with Aeolian settlement (see Chapter 14, 359, n. 43), with Protogeometric ("Ionic") ware at the site (Lemos 2002: 211); see Kirk (1962: 151; 1985: 1–3).

[67] In the process of quantitative metathesis in Attic-Ionic, $\bar{e}$ and $\bar{ẹ}$ (from etymological $\bar{e}$ and from $\bar{a}$ respectively) were shortened before following *o* or *a*; if the following vowel was short it was concomitantly lengthened. The resulting sequence of *e* + V̆ was probably normally pronounced with synizesis (as a single syllable), as a rising diphthong. See Haug (2002: 122–36) and Méndez Dosuna (1993). (Probert 2006: 85, n. 5, however, finds legitimate objections.) Thus, for first declension nouns in the genitive plural, -ᾱων > *-ηων >-εων (-*āōn* > *-*ẹ̄ōn* > -*eōn*), for the masculine first declension genitive singular, -ᾱο > *-ηο >-εω (-*āo* > *-*ẹ̄o* >-*eō*). The one expression with quantitative metathesis that turns up frequently is Κρόνου παῖς ἀγκυλομήτεω (*Il.* 2.205, etc., *Kronou pais ankulomēteō*, "child of crooked-thoughted Cronus"). Followers of

altered by being declined, a fact which he suggests may indicate that the final stage of the narrative tradition had inherited a fairly impoverished traditional language, that is, that the inherited formulary system did not have the flexibility of a repertoire of declined variations in the noun–epithet sequences.[68] As Ionic poets were spurred to become more creative, they reworked formulas to increase the variety of their phrasing.

By the late eighth century the Panionia could have provided the appropriate performance context for the *Iliad* and *Odyssey*, the large-scale festival celebrated by the twelve cities in the Panionic League providing the needed setting for the monumental size attested for the two works. In support of this claim, Frame presents a complex argument that the importance of Nestor in both the *Iliad* and *Odyssey* reflects the claims of Neleid descent for a powerful *genos* in Miletus, the city he considers to be the original key player in the formation of the Ionian Dodecapolis and the original sponsor of putative epic performances at the Panionia.[69] Certainly

---

the Aeolic phase use the lack of penetration of quantitative metathesis into the formulaic language as evidence for a late transfer from Aeolic to Ionic (e.g., Berg and Haug 2000: 18). In fact, its significance for those who argue for a continuous Ionic tradition depends on the date of the sound change. Quantitative metathesis is attested in both Attic and Ionic, and thus it could have occurred before the two dialects split and be a shared innovation (Haug 2002: 107–44; Jones 2008: 84–9). On the other hand, it is possible that Attic and Ionic could have had the processes going on side-by-side after they separated. (In that case, quantitative metathesis in both Attic and Ionic would be the result of drift.) Hoekstra (1965: 31; also see Powell 1991: 169–71) has argued for a late date for quantitative metathesis, based on the Nicandre inscription. This central Ionic inscription written in Homeric hexameters on a *korē* statue in Naxos that was dedicated at Delos, was made *ca.* 650 BCE and provides us with genitive endings spelled -ηο,-ηον (-*ēo*,-*ēon*).

[68] Hoekstra (1965: 31–41).
[69] Frame (2009: 17–18, 515–647), followed by Nagy (2010: 214, 224–32, 320–1). Aloni (2006) discusses references to local Neleid mythology, but connects their appearance in the Homeric corpus to performance at Athens. There is an oblique reference to the Panionia in the *Iliad* (20.403–5) with the mention of the bull that is forced to bellow before being sacrificed to Heliconius, as in the Panionia; Strabo 8.7.2 makes the connection; Σ bT *ad Il.* 20.404b. See Frame (2009: 18, n. 21; 515), Nagy (2010: 228–30). Frame (2009: 560–76) argues for the development of the twenty-four-book versions of the two Homeric epics in the Panionia, four books for each city in the league. Frame argues for the existence of the Panionia before 700 BCE. Although I do not agree with his argument concerning Nestor's cup, which he claims shows knowledge of the twenty-four-book *Iliad* (see above, 398), I do agree with his discussion of the significance of the fact that Melia, one of the original members of the Panionic League, is said to have been destroyed *ca.* 700 BCE (cf. Vitruvius 4.1.4–6, who calls it Melite; Frame 2009: 541–9). This assumes that the Panionia was not always celebrated at the site currently assigned to it, since archaeological remains of the Panionium at Güzelçamlı do not date before the end of the sixth century. With regard to the site of the Panionium, H. Lohmann, "Panionion," in *Brill's New Pauly* 10.446–7, argues for Çatallar Tepe, a mid-sixth-century site, possibly destroyed by the Persians at the end of the sixth century, as the site, a position not commonly followed. Herda (2006b; 2009: 37–43) discusses the circumstances of the establishment of the Panionium.

the Neleids left their mark on the legends of Ionic migrations.[70] But, these two storylines must already have been important and prestigious, since they are not obviously relevant to the ambitions of the Ionian Dodecapolis or of Miletus. And, the Neleid influence on the *Iliad* and *Odyssey* does not appreciably affect the telling of events in the narrative, unlike, for example, the sympathetic focus on Hector in the *Iliad*. The Neleid, Panionic influence must have happened at a late stage, when the basic narratives are well established. Frame envisions a scenario of competitive collaboration among poets from the various cities of the Panionic League working together through repeated performances to create and ameliorate the two poems (a process that could have lasted for decades), different poets from the twelve cities performing sections of the story at the festival. This would have led to versions of the *Iliad* and *Odyssey* fairly close to the great works we attribute to Homer.[71]

Richard Martin offers information supporting this scenario of competitive collaboration, suggesting that the various legends of contests between Hesiod and Homer were based on known practices in which bards traded the narrative thread back and forth as they worked on a single song. For example, in *Vita* 1 West (*Certamen*), Hesiod and Homer play a capping game, in which Hesiod starts with a verse or two, and Homer completes the thought with another verse or two. The contest ends with each reciting their finest passages. In addition, scholia to Pindar's *Nemean* 2.1d include a quote attributed to Hesiod, which they use to explain the term *rhapsōidos*: "In Delos then was the first time Homer and I, as bards (*aoidoi*), sang and danced (*melpomen*), stitching in novel songs a lay (*en nearois humnois rhapsantes aoidēn*)." Martin suggests this is another example of competitive collaboration.[72]

Hall (2002: 67–8) provides an even-handed discussion of the evidence. Crielaard (2009: 65) discounts the dating of the Melian War, preferring later dates to fit with his argument about Ionian ethnogenesis in the Archaic period. Frame (2009: 590–3) goes so far as to suggest the Neleid king Leodamas of Miletus sponsored the shaping of the *Iliad* and *Odyssey* into their twenty-four-book form. Leodamas could have ruled in "the latter part of the eighth century BC," if we connect his involvement in a war with Carystus in Euboea with the Lelantine War. On Leodamas, see Conon *FGrH* 25 F 1, 44; Nicolaus of Damascus *FGrH* 90 FF 52–3; Herda (1998: 16–17; 45–6). Frame is certainly not the first to make the suggestion of the Panionic stage as key for the formation of the *Iliad*, cf. Högemann (2000: 191–3); see Frame (2009: 552–3, with notes) for some earlier versions of this theory. Herda (1998) discusses the cult of Neileus at Miletus, and how his figure developed from the ancestor of a *genos* to the center of a state-sponsored cult.

[70] Frame (2009: 29–35, 515–33).   [71] Frame (2009: 557–63).

[72] Hesiod F 297 Most; Martin (2000: 415, 424). Martin (2000: 422–3) follows up on Nagy's (1996a: 83–4) discussion of the scholia to Pindar *Nemean* 2.1d: "each of the competitors sang whatever piece they wanted" (Dionysius of Argos *FGrH* 308 F 2), as opposed to rhapsodes, who

When I spent two months in Kyrgyzstan in 1995 during the thousandth anniversary of their epic hero Manas, I in fact witnessed personally and on television the serial performance of sections of the *Manas* epic in festival settings, each *manaschi* trying to outdo the last, so I find such a scenario eminently plausible.[73] Another, more collaborative scenario was described by the Kalmyk bard Nyamin Mandzhaiev, who stated that different bards specialize in particular sections of the chief Kalmyk epic *Dzhangar*. Here too a full performance of high quality by necessity involves multiple artists, each contributing the section he is considered to be most proficient at performing.[74] Thus, the scenario proposed by Frame fits modern ethnographic parallels, presenting a model that modern scholars and artists who are used to working collaboratively will also find familiar.

I close this section by briefly touching on the history of the Homeric tradition after its Panionic phase. Nagy traces the route of transfer of the Homeric tradition from Ionia to Athens via Chios. The Peisistratids seem to have been interested in asserting a claim to the unifying power of the Panionic Homeric tradition in their own supralocal festival, the Panathenaea. Their interest in the *Iliad* in particular may have been connected to their territorial ambitions in the Troad discussed earlier.[75] Although epic recitations may have been part of the festival already, once it was decided that the *Iliad* and *Odyssey* should be performed end-to-end by rhapsodes in the quadrennial Greater Panathenaea, they required a relatively set form, which was judged by the Chian Homeridae – the "Peisistratean recension," or, as Nagy prefers, the "Panathenaic regulation."[76]

---

performed in a fixed order, stitching together, as it were, pieces of a narrative to make a complete song (Philochorus *FGrH* 328 F 212; on the sewing imagery, see Chapter 2, 37). Nagy (2002: 16–17), quoting Nagy (1996b: 72–3), cites *Iliad* 9.184–91, in which Achilles is performing on his silver lyre, while Patroclus waits for him to leave off singing (*hopote lēxeien aeidōn*). Nagy considers this to represent "rhapsodic sequencing," inferring that Patroclus is waiting to take his turn.

[73] I thank the International University of Kyrgyzstan for their invitation to teach English and study Russian in Bishkek in July and August of 1995, while my husband, Dr. Gregory D. S. Anderson, studied Kyrgyz.

[74] Oral communication to Dr. Gregory D. S. Anderson in June of 2013. Mandzhiev was participating in the Smithsonian Folklife Festival, and Dr. Anderson was serving as his presenter and translator.

[75] Rose (2014: 64–5).

[76] Nagy (2002: 9–25; 1996a; 1996b); also see Seaford (1994: 144–54). A reorganization of the festival occurred under the archon Hippocleides in 566/5, turning it into a Panhellenic event (Pherecydes *FGrH* 3 F 2; Eusebius in Jerome *Chron.*, ed. Helm 1956: 102a–b: athletic competitions introduced to the Panathenaea in 566), and the regularizing of the recitation is credited to Hipparchus (d. 514), the son of the Athenian tyrant Peisistratus, if not Peisistratus himself ([Plat.] *Hipparch.* 228b: Hipparchus introduced the Homeric poems and required the

Conclusion

Nagy argues:

> the ideal point of entry for reconstructing the Mycenaean phase of Homeric poetry is the region of the Troad in Asia Minor as it existed around 600 B.C.E. Here we find evidence for competing Ionic and Aeolic traditions of poetry about an epic past, and this evidence comes not only from the Homeric poetry of the *Iliad*, albeit residually, but also from the poetry of Sappho and Alcaeus. By comparing these competing traditions, we saw how the dominantly Aeolic poetry of Sappho and Alcaeus is cognate in content as well as in form with the dominantly Ionic poetry that characterizes Homer. As cognates, these two traditions of poetry point to an uninterrupted continuum stemming from the Bronze Age.[77]

I agree that the two cognates allow us to infer "an uninterrupted continuum stemming from the Bronze Age," but Nagy seems to suggest that the story about Troy went back to the Mycenaean period, while I have suggested that the Greek epic about the fall of Troy does not date that far

---

rhapsodes to go through them in sequence; Ael. *VH* 8.2: Hipparchus "brought the epics of Homer to Athens and required the rhapsodes to sing them in the Panathenaea"). Frame (2009: 608) suggests that the Athenians originally learned about the Homeric poems (as opposed to other versions of stories about the fall of Troy and its aftermath) because they were "specially honored guests" at the Panionia, as representatives of the mother city of the Ionian migrations (Athens as mother city: Hdt. 1.146.2, 147.2). The Homeridae of Chios became the repositories of the Homeric tradition (Pl. *Ion* 530d) apparently when the center for training moved off shore of mainland Anatolia when the Ionian cities of the mainland were being sacked or taken over, first by the Lydians and then by the Persians (Hdt. 1.16–29, 161–9); see Frame (2009: 577) and Nagy (2010: 59–65), with references to his earlier discussions. Similarly, the Kreophyleioi on Samos were responsible for maintaining an epic about Heracles, *Oikhalias Halosis* (Call. *Epig.* 6 Pfeiffer). See Frame (2009: 579–82), Nagy (2010: 328–9). The earliest date possible for the Homeridae comes from a mention of Homer by the sixth-century poet Callinus as author of the *Thebaid* (cited by Pausanias 9.9.5 as Calaenus), which would imply previous existence of a guild of Homeridae with their fictional ancestor Homer. Evidence for Athenian influence on the *Iliad* and *Odyssey* includes Attic forms in the Homeric dialect (Janko 1992: 36–7; Nagy 2004: 124). See Nagy (2004: 73) on the problems with assuming the Attic forms are late interlopers and editing them out of the text. But, the proposed influence goes beyond what could be explained as alterations or interpolations to a fixed text. There are allusions to Attic cult practices, especially those relevant to the Panathenaea, in particular the *peplos* that was offered to Athena by Hecuba (*Il.* 6.63–311), which has been compared to the offering made in the Panathenaea. For the *peplos* in the Panathenaea, see Chapter 10, 262. E. Cook (1995) presents suggestive evidence for a key stage in the formation of the *Odyssey* occurring in the second half of the sixth century in Athens, because of references to the cult of Athena in Athens, for example the olive tree that serves as a post of Odysseus' bed. So, we cannot argue that the *Iliad* and *Odyssey* had achieved their final forms before they were the subject of the rhapsodic competitions in the Greater Panathenaea.

[77] Nagy (2010: 301).

back. I have discussed the role of competition among Greek poets in shaping the storyline of the *Iliad*, as well as improving its quality. However, the set of storylines they were working with had already been decided upon. There is no evidence that there was ever a Greek version of the fall of Troy that was not influenced by Near Eastern epic.

With regard to the window of 1160–1050 BCE for the first formation of the legend of the Trojan War, the lower end of the date range coincides nicely with the date of the beginning of the cult activity at Troy. The story should be seen as informing the rites practiced there. In the final chapter I will argue that an epic about the fall of Troy initially arose as the product of collaborative competition among Greco-Anatolian bards in the eleventh and tenth centuries BCE. That is, I will suggest that we can reconstruct a situation of competing versions of the narrative analogous to but earlier than the time of competition between Ionic and Aeolic bards.

16 | The layers of Anatolian influence in the *Iliad*

> Now in turn Sarpedon strongly upbraided shining Hector, "Hector, where in fact has your strength gone that you had previously? You are saying, apparently, that you will hold the city without troops and allies, alone, with your brothers-in-law and brothers, yet I am able to see or perceive none of them now. Rather, they are cowering like dogs around a lion, but we are fighting, who are 'only' your allies. And in fact I myself, who am an ally, have come from very far away; for Lycia is far off at the swirling Xanthus, where I have left my dear wife and infant son."
>
> *Il.* 5. 471–80

Introduction

After the poems attributed to Homer became popular, the mold in which Greeks cast interactions between east and west was that of the Trojan War. According to Herodotus' telling, during the Persian War Hellenes and Persians alike presented their confrontation in terms of the Trojan War, and Herodotus' history of the Persian War quite clearly means to evoke and respond to Homer's earlier telling of a great conflict between east and west. In the opening section he shows how the story of the rape of Helen was manipulated to justify the enmity between Greece and Persia, and Herodotus closes his monumental work with the gruesome execution of the Persian governor who violated the tomb of Protesilaus, the first Greek warrior to die in the Trojan War.[1] Certainly the Greeks saw the Hellenic unity presented in the campaign against Troy as an illustrative example to draw on, heroizing their contemporary fallen as they did those who fell on the Trojan battlefield.[2] The Persian king Xerxes, meanwhile, supposedly cast himself as avenging the wrongs done to the Trojans by the Greeks by making a point of sacrificing a thousand head of cattle to Athena of Ilium, and according to Herodotus, "his Magi poured libations to the heroes"

---

[1] Hdt. 1.1–5, 7.33, 9.116–22. [2] Boedeker (2001a; 2001b).

before he crossed the Hellespont into Greece.[3] I argue, however, that well before the eighth century Greeks and Anatolians were already exploring their relations with each other through the medium of epic and legend and that, while Homer's work refracts an early stage in the development of their common past, it did not begin the process.

The conversation before Homer, however, can only be reconstructed through careful excavation of his text and other sources for the early legendary history of Anatolia, for when particularly proficient Ionic bards became the model for epic poets seeking Panhellenic fame, all other voices were silenced for us. Some hints of rival Greek epic traditions about Troy have been discussed in the previous chapter. Here I focus on uncovering the Anatolian traditions and on excavating layers of Anatolian influence in the stages up to and including the putative Panionic stage. First, Anatolians played an important role in helping to form the narrative patterns used by Greek epic bards, contributing ways to frame their shared legendary past that had been preserved across the end of the Bronze Age. Then they lost any primacy they may have held in the discussion about ancient times in Anatolia, and eventually they were silenced altogether. Although their own versions of how interactions between themselves and Greeks played out are now otherwise almost completely lost to us, I argue that the story of the fall of Troy itself began as an Anatolian story, told from an Anatolian viewpoint, before it was appropriated by the Greeks. I will further argue that the storyline already existed to provide context for relations between newcomers and indigenous inhabitants before Greeks began to treat Troy as a place of remembrance in the Early Iron Age. I suggest that in the earliest stage in the Iron Age Anatolian tradition about Troy it may have been Phrygians who were the newcomers, the ones framed as attacking Troy.

The original program of the Greco-Anatolian tradition of the Trojan War was to explain the prehistory of relations between Anatolians and the newly arriving Greeks, not just to the Greeks, but to Anatolians as well, by memorializing a key legendary "event" defining their "first contact" that set the stage for their current relations. The retrojection of the political situation in the *Iliad* into a time before the migrations, as discussed in the previous chapter, was more than just epic distancing.[4] It made sense in

---

[3] Hdt. 7.42–3; see Haubold (2007) and Hertel (2003a: 226–7). According to Herodotus (5.13), a connection with the Trojans was used to justify siding with the Persians; some Paeonians who wished to join Darius' army told him they were descended from Teucrian colonists from Troy.

[4] On epic distancing see I. Morris (1986: 81–94), Patzek (1992: 186), Raaflaub (1998a: 181–2, 187 with earlier references).

the context of that original agenda, set in place well before the fifth century BCE, of explaining to both sides the circumstances of their first contact. As I will show, within the *Iliad* we can also see evidence of a way of framing their shared legendary past not as a military conflict, but as a supralocal culture that was the playing field for a network of elites competing for prestige and tied together by dynastic marriages and guest friendships. This world existed not only in legend but also in fact, and this milieu was favorable to the development of the bilingual poets who I claim were responsible for passing epic storylines from one or more Anatolian languages to one or more dialects of Greek. But, the first bilingual epic tradition about Troy was in the "Trojan" and Phrygian languages.

I move on to discuss how the pro-Trojan storyline attached to Hector was incorporated into the Homeric *Iliad*, arguing that it became prominent enough to warrant being absorbed into a Greek story which had originally focused on the Greek point of view in the context of a world in which claiming connections to autochthonous dynasties had some contemporary benefit, before the Greeks controlled the conversation about rights to coastal Anatolia.

I next discuss the reason for the prominence of the Lycians in the *Iliad*, arguing that Miletus was the key milieu for the development and transfer of myths linking heroes identified as Lycian to the Ionian Greeks. Thus, this stage in the formation of the Homeric tradition must have occurred at Miletus. In Chapter 14, I argued that we can see continuity in Anatolian mortuary rituals and the beliefs and practices attached to them, including performances of mythic storylines, across the end of the Bronze Age among the Cilicians, in particular with regard to the Greco-Anatolian hero Mopsus, and in this chapter I show that the Lycians too seem to have retained into the Iron Age certain mortuary practices descending from the Bronze Age. The way in which the death of Sarpedon is treated in the *Iliad* also shows us there was an awareness on the part of the Greeks that the Lycians engaged in practices of elite ancestor veneration analogous to Greek hero worship. This practice was complementary to the performance of epic for them, as it was for the Greeks.

Finally, while in Chapter 10 I discussed the role of the cult of the internationally recognized deity Apollo in transmitting the traditional *Chaoskampf* storyline, I close this book by arguing that the cult of Apollo was also instrumental in popularizing and circulating the story of the destruction of the city of which he was the patron god.

Relations between Achaeans and Anatolians as portrayed in the *Iliad*

The relations between Greeks and Anatolians in the legendary time posited in the *Iliad* were not framed as contact between two cultures that shared nothing in common, one moving into the space of the other. Rather, we can see that the two peoples were connected through ties of marriage and that immigration moved in both directions. Thus, the opposition of Hellenes versus barbarians that was so important to Herodotus had not yet been established as the lens through which all discussion of interactions was viewed.[5]

First of all, the linguistic differentiation between Anatolians and Achaeans was not carried through in any systematic way. Homer's categories of "Maeonian," "Phrygian," "Carian," and "Lycian" were perhaps based on the mutual unintelligibility of the four major Anatolian languages rather than on political units, and Homer himself emphasizes that the allies of the Trojans speak more than one language.[6] Trojan may have been considered a separate language by him; certainly in the *Homeric Hymn to Aphrodite* (111–15) the goddess has to explain to Anchises why she can speak Trojan although presenting herself as Phrygian. But, only the Carians are labeled as *barbarophōnoi* (*Il.* 2.867),[7] and, while some of the Anatolian allies of the Trojans may be singled out as having Anatolian names, for example, Asius, son of Hurtacus (cf. Hitt. *ḫartagga-* 'bear', also a title of a cult functionary),[8] many have obviously Greek names. Moreover, Achaeans and Trojans can share names as well. Therefore, the linguistic distinction was not crucial.

Homer does not seem particularly interested in the archaeologically attested migrations to or within Anatolia, failing to explain basic discrepancies such as the location of the Cilicians and the homeland of the Trojan ally Pandarus.[9] Instead he refers to ties created by dynastic marriages between Greeks and Anatolians. Indeed, the family of Agamemnon himself

---

[5] The fact that *barbaros* was never used by Homer was commented on by ancient historians (Th. 1.3.3, Str. 14.2.28). Also see references in n. 7 here.

[6] *Il.* 2.803–4, 4.437–8; see Watkins (1986: 706–7). Some aspects of the discussion in this section were covered in more detail in Bachvarova (2015).

[7] Georges (1994: 14–15) attempts to dismiss the epithet, but see the discussion of Brügger, Stoevesandt, and Visser (2003: 284–5).

[8] *Il.* 2.838, Watkins (1986: 708–10). For examples of names of Trojans and their allies that could have Anatolian etymologies, see Lebrun (1998a: 153–5).

[9] Cilicians: Andromache was from Cilician Thebe in the Troad (*Il.* 6.327, 415–16). Two homelands for Pandarus: see below, 443, n. 93.

is assigned an Anatolian origin. Although Homer does not emphasize it, he does tell us that Agamemnon's scepter, symbol of legitimate kingship, originally came from Zeus, who gave it to Hermes, who gave it to Pelops, who passed it down to Atreus, who, when he died, left it to Thyestes, from whom Agamemnon received it, "to rule many islands and all of Argos" (*Il.* 2.100–8). Pelops' father Tantalus, considered elsewhere to be king of either Phrygia or Lydia, is never mentioned in the *Iliad*, so we are left to infer the family connection to Anatolia in the genealogy of Agamemnon's scepter. But, the story of Pelops' sister, the perpetually weeping "Phrygian" Niobe, is told by Achilles to Priam (*Il.* 24.602–17); the tale is attached to a well-known rock formation on Mt. Sipylus in Lydia, as Achilles himself makes clear.[10]

While scholars have been interested in associating the legend of Pelops with Late Bronze Age contacts,[11] I would emphasize rather that the myth was already in the tradition inherited by Homer, and that it was uncontroversial. Thus, not all connections between Greeks and Anatolians were made via the Trojan War. There had been alternative ways of working out a legendary history providing a context to contemporary contacts, on top of which was laid the Trojan War. One way of integrating these alternate histories into the master narrative of the Trojan War was to place them before it, like Heracles' exploits in Anatolia, while the *nostoi* legends, telling of Homeric heroes' returns or colonizations of Anatolia, assigned the period of colonization to the aftermath of the Trojan War. I have argued elsewhere that the immigration and colonization storylines grew so prestigious during the Archaic age that by the time of Herodotus even Anatolians were making use of them to create a historical context for present-day relations.[12] But, Homer does name the Cretan Miletus explicitly in the Catalog of Ships (*Il.* 2.647), suggesting that a migration legend connecting Crete to the Anatolian Miletus was extant in his time. Strabo tells us that Ephorus of Cyme (400–330 BCE) says Miletus was originally founded by Cretans, brought by Sarpedon from the Cretan Miletus.[13]

---

[10] See Richardson (1993: 340–2). On the myths attached to Tantalus' line see Gantz (1993: 531–56). It is Pindar (*O.* 1) who tells us the most detailed early version of the stories of Tantalus and "Lydian" Pelops, recounting the foundation myth of the Olympian games (also mentioned by Th. 1.9.2); the latter went from Asia to the Peloponnese to woo the daughter of Oenomaus at Elis. Also see Chapter 14, 374–5, with n. 105.

[11] See Cline (1994: 69). [12] Bachvarova (2015: 129, 132, 141).

[13] See Str. 14.1.6 = Ephorus *FGrH* 70 F 127 on the Cretan Miletus and Cretans replacing Leleges at Miletus, later occupied by the Neleids. Also see 12.8.5. This story contradicts Pherecydes' version (*FGrH* 3 F 155), mentioned by Strabo earlier (14.1.3), in which Carians occupied Miletus and were expelled by the Pylian Neleus. See below for further discussion.

So, certain colonization legends were situated in the time before the Trojan War, and it appears that they were already the stuff of legend in the time of Homer.

Even if Homer preferred to elide Sarpedon's Cretan roots – which were likely well known to his audience – to present him as an Anatolian warrior, Homer does not deny him an ultimately Greek heritage.[14] Indeed, he makes a point of the guest-friend relationship between his cousin Glaucus and Diomedes to draw attention to the rupture in the community of *xenoi* that was caused by Paris' kidnapping of Helen. The meeting between Glaucus and Diomedes provides an excuse to tell the story of Bellerophontes when the Achaean warrior, impressed by the appearance of this unknown opponent, asks the Lycian who he is.[15] Glaucus replies with an extended excursus on his lineage, telling how his grandfather Bellerophontes, the son of the first Glaucus and grandson of Sisyphus, having refused the advances of the wife of his host, king Proetus of Tiryns, was the target of an assassination attempt by the duped king. Proetus tried to engineer his murder by means of a letter demanding his death "in a folded tablet" (*en pinakti ptuktōi*, 6.169) that Bellerophontes himself carried to the king in Lycia. Bellerophontes, however, impressed the Lycian king so much by completing successfully each dangerous task put to him, slaying the snake-goat-lion Chimera and defeating the Solymi and the Amazons, that he was able to marry his daughter and stay in Anatolia, receiving half of Iobates' kingdom (*Il.* 6.155–95). Thus, the connections by marriage ran in both directions, for, while Bellerophontes came from Greece to Lycia and

---

[14] The earliest extant mention of a Cretan Sarpedon is by the sixth-century BCE historian Herodorus *FGrH* 31 F 45 (Sourvinou-Inwood 2005: 269–70, n. 149; 282–3). Apollodorus (*Bib.* 2.1.4, 3.1.1–2) presents us with yet another variant of Sarpedon's arrival, as part of Io's family tree. Apollodorus, agreeing with the *Catalog of Women* (F 89 Most) and explicitly against Homer, has Europa as the mother of Sarpedon, while Homer puts him in a later generation, as a son of Laodameia and Zeus (*Il.* 6.198–9) and therefore grandson of Bellerophontes and first cousin of Glaucus. Apollodorus' version brings in Miletus as the name of the beloved over whom Sarpedon and his brother Minos came into conflict. It was the beloved who founded Miletus while Sarpedon first went to Cilicia (ruled by his uncle Cilix), then to Lycia, which he received as his share of booty when aiding his uncle in a war against the Lycians. In this way, Apollodorus reconciles multiple migration traditions. See Janko (1992: 358–9) on the Cretan connections in Sarpedon's mythology, which he argues refracts the historical settlement of Minoans at Miletus.

[15] The origin of Bellerophontes' story is discussed by Bryce (1999: 261–2), Burkert (1992: 29–30), Frei (1993a), Lane Fox (2009: 206–9), Mellink (1995: 40–1), and M. L. West (1997a: 365–7). This particular story has been singled out by Burkert as providing clear evidence of being borrowed in the Orientalizing period from the Phoenicians. On Bellerophontes see Benda-Weber (2005: 243–53), Keen (1998: 211–12).

married the king's daughter, the Lycian king's other daughter was the queen spurned by Bellerophontes in Tiryns.

The story combines elements paralleled in two tales from the Hebrew Bible with Anatolian connections, the deadly letter story of David and Uriah the Hittite (2 Samuel 11; Uriah ~ Hurr. *evri* 'lord'[16]) and the treachery of the spurned wife of Potiphar (Genesis 39). While the deadly letter motif first appears in the *Sumerian Sargon Legend*,[17] the earliest attestation of the vengeful spurned woman who persuades her husband to punish the young man who rejects her is found in the Hittite narrative *Elkunirsa and Ashertu*, itself clearly derived from a west Semitic source, as we can see from the west Semitic names of the protagonists.[18] The earliest attestations for folding waxed writing boards are primarily among the Hittites; they surely were used for Hieroglyphic Luwian, so Anatolians may have been the ones to introduce them to north Syria and the Assyrians.[19] In addition, the fire-breathing Chimera has been compared to the composite beasts found in Neo-Hittite art, as well as the lion-goat associated with the warrior-god Sandas.[20] The birth of Bellerophontes' winged horse is told in the story of Perseus (although not mentioned by

---

[16] Collins (2007b: 210–11).
[17] See Frei (1993a: 58, with earlier references) and the *Sumerian Sargon Legend* (also called *Sargon and Ur-Zababa*, trans. Black *et al.* 2004: 40–4).
[18] This story and its ritual frame are discussed briefly in Chapter 2, 34.
[19] Symington (1991). The medium was used both for accounts and for international letters. A waxed wooden writing board was found in the Ulu Burun shipwreck off the coast of Lycia, on which see Chapter 12, 316, n. 71. A discussion of writing on wooden boards by the Hittites and Luwians is provided by Payne (2008). The common format for Hittite clay tablets, with two columns per side, in fact may imitate the layout of the two "pages" of the folding wooden tablet. Bryce (1999: 261–2), suggesting that the language which Bellerophontes could not read was Hieroglyphic Luwian, posits that the story reflects the presence of Anatolian scribes in Mycenaean Greece. There is evidence for wooden writing boards in Mycenaean archives, in the form of bronze hinges (Shear 1998), but what language was written on them we do not know. Burkert (1983c: 52), on the other hand, argues that the letter must have been written on a Phoenician *deltos*, because "the one writing system which consistently used the wooden (or ivory) tablet is the Phoenician-Aramean and its dependent, the Graeco-Roman." This part of his argument is substantially repeated in Burkert (1992: 30). Although intrigued by the fact that Uriah is Hittite (a designation that refers to the Neo-Hittites in north Syria), he still eschews the conclusion that the writing board has a Luwian origin or that the story shows knowledge of Anatolian writing practices.
[20] The images are found at Carchemish and Zincirli (Burkert 1983c: 52; Frei 1993a: 47–8). On Sandas' animal, see Mastrocinque (2007). Bryce (1986: 18–19) explores, then rejects the possibility that the Chimera's fire-breathing nature mythologizes the *yanar* of east Lycia (burning plumes of gas emerging from the ground), seeing the connection as secondary. Also see Keen (1998: 211).

Homer), itself a story with Near Eastern motifs,[21] and Pegasus bears a resemblance to the winged horses found in Assyrian art. He also shares the name of the Luwian Storm-god *piḫaššaššiš* 'he of lightning', attested among the Hittites, which explains why he becomes the bearer of Zeus' thunderbolts after Bellerophontes dies.[22] Finally, Joshua Katz suggests that the hero's Greek name *Bellerophontes/Ellerophontes* means 'snake-slayer'. Therefore, parts of his myth may have been related to the Anatolian New Year's myth of the Storm-god slaying the snake, preserved in the Hittite Illuyanka stories.[23] All the Syro-Anatolian contributions to the story are explained by a Lycian origin for Bellerophontes' story.

The Chimera and Pegasus are not objects of fact. That is, the story does not intend primarily to record historical events. Rather, it shows dexterous handling of traditional motifs of the Syro-Anatolian narrative tradition. The tale of Bellerophontes and the deadly letter illustrates the ways in which long-distance elite interaction worked and was conceptualized; it also serves as an example of the kind of narrative material that was transmitted in these interactions. Bellerophontes acted according to a particular narrative pattern that had a basis in real life. For, as Mary Helms has shown, in traditional non-industrialized societies, male outsiders, considered to be endowed with special powers, are often welcomed directly into the highest echelons of society and married off to high-status local women.[24] But, the story of Bellerophontes also shares the mythic pattern of a voyage to a faraway place by a young man who overcomes obstacles that represent the relations of humans to animals and the establishment of order over chaos; it is precisely the type of story that I argued earlier is likely to be transferred across time and space.[25] Moreover, it shows quite

---

[21] Near Eastern elements in Perseus' myth: the slaying of a sea monster or snake; the *kibisis* bag, which resembles the *kurša*; Medusa, who resembles the *lamaštu* (Bachvarova 2013c: 423, 433). For the myth see Hesiod FF 77, 241 Most (the latter from the *Great Catalog of Women*?), *Il.* 14.319–20, *Theog.* 280–3, Pherecydes *FGrH* 3 F 11, Apollodorus *Bib.* 2.4.3, Pausanias 4.35.9, Strabo 16.2.28. See Gantz (1993: 300–11). On Perseus and Andromeda also see Kaptan (2000); for the Near Eastern elements, see Bremmer (2008: 337), Burkert (1992: 85–7), and M. L. West (1997a: 453–5).

[22] On the Assyrian winged horse, see Bryce (1986: 17, n. 15). For the connection with the Storm-god *piḫaššaššiš*, see Hutter (1995); Pegasus carries Zeus' thunderbolts: Eur. F 30 Jouan-van Looy.

[23] J. Katz (1998: 325–6).

[24] Helms (1988: 134–6). Finkelberg (2005: 65–108) presents a very different analysis of this story pattern, arguing that it shows matrifocal dynastic succession, which she assigns to the pre-Greek (in her scheme, Anatolian-derived) layer of civilization in mainland Greece. Our approaches, however, are not mutually incompatible.

[25] For discussion see Chapter 9, 210–11.

clearly that the complex cultural mixing in which Anatolians participated allowed them to mediate the transmission of Near Eastern narrative motifs to Greek-speakers, combining Syrian and Mesopotamian motifs with Anatolian ones.

Because Homer tells Bellerophontes' story in such a cursory way, leaving out many crucial details – for example, how Bellerophontes ended up angering the gods and was killed – it has been plausibly argued that Homer presupposes his audience's knowledge of an epic about Bellerophontes, and some have gone farther, suggesting that the story, which explains ties between Greeks and Lycians, was performed by Greek poets in the court of the Lycian king at Xanthus.[26] I suggest, rather, that one or more bilingual poets who had access to both a native Syro-Anatolian tradition and the Greek tradition were responsible for introducing the obviously Near Eastern elements to a story about a Greco-Anatolian hero.

Bilingual Anatolian epic poets

The evidence for early influence from Anatolian epic on Greek epic that I have discussed in this book is twofold: the incorporation of Near Eastern plot lines that can be found in the tablets found at Hattusa and the translation of formulas found in Hurro-Hittite narrative song. Most of this book has been concentrated on the storylines, but in Chapter 6 I discussed some shared type scenes and motifs, and in Chapter 2 I discussed some examples of shared formulas and formulaic sequences, some of which extended to several lines, such as the sending of a messenger.[27] I argue that, even if the larger-scale parallels such as plot lines could have been passed by some other means than through the epic tradition, the smaller-scale parallels are best explained as the result of bilingual poets creating phrases in the target language closely modeled on phrasing of the source language, which then became formulas in their own right.[28]

First of all, Anatolian linguistic forms in the Homeric dialect hint at the bilingual context in which bilingual poets developed their craft, since some time after Greek epic poets began to work in Anatolia, there occurred the borrowing of a small number of morphemes and particles from Anatolian

---

[26] Frei (1993a: 41–2).
[27] M. L. West (2011) has also provided a commentary on the *Iliad* detailing the numerous specific correspondences with Near Eastern formulas, type scenes, and plot sequences.
[28] See Chapter 2, 46–9, on bilingual poets.

languages into the Homeric dialect. Such small-scale borrowings include *en de* in the meaning of "therein"[29] and the originally locatival particle *tar*. The particle *tar* appears both as a rare independent particle and as part of *autar*. The latter word is embedded in formulas that calque the Luwian *kwiš tar* 'who in the world?' (Homeric *tis autar*) and Luwian *pā=tar āppa* 'but ... back again' (Homeric *autar epei* ('r') 'but then').[30] Adverbial particles such as this are particularly easy to borrow and indicate language contact that goes beyond the merely casual, but is not intense.[31] It has been argued that the frequentative use of the *-ske/o* verbal affix in past tense verbs, both imperfect and aorist, comes from Hittite. This would require more far-reaching bilingualism. Finally, the use of the patronymic adjective, while an archaic feature of Greek, is also characteristic of first-millennium Anatolian languages.[32]

The fragments of Hipponax of Ephesus show that Lydian–Greek bilingualism at least was still alive and well in the late sixth century, and bilingualism must have been common in the early days of Greek settlement in Anatolia. In addition, bilingual traditions for oral stories or incantations used in rituals could lie behind the distinction between the languages of the gods and men that is found in the *Iliad* (it is in fact found in Hattic-Hittite

---

[29] Puhvel (1993). Also see Watkins (2000b) on the repeated use of *en de* in *Il.* 5.738–42. The repeated use of *en de* is a figure that appeals to Homer: also see *Il.* 9.207–8, 18.483, *Od.* 5.265–7, 11.3–4, 12.90–1, 19.175–6. Compare, for example, no occurrences in Aeschylus, forty occurrences in Thucydides, which are all immediately followed by a dative, while in Herodotus, who writes in Ionic, sixty-seven are followed by a dative and twenty-two are used in the meaning "therein," typically in the expression *en de dē kai*. While this topic requires further study, we may preliminarily assume this is an Anatolian feature in Ionic.

[30] Watkins (1995: 150–1) and J. Katz (2007). Dunkel's (2008) objections to the equation do not address the arguments of J. Katz. For citations of *tar* in *Iliad* see M. L. West (1998: xxix) (not recorded for current editions of *Odyssey*, Hesiod, or the *Homeric Hymns*). Outside of Homer *autar* appears in a small number of Cypriot inscriptions (Egetmeyer 1992: 26). For this reason it has been considered to belong to the "Achaean" (Mycenaean) layer of the Homeric language (Ruijgh 1957: 29–55), that is, to be an extreme archaism, but one can also explain the appearance of the particle in Cypriot through contact with Luwian.

[31] Thomason and Kaufman (1988: 74, 80).

[32] Watkins (2001: 58). On the patronymic adjective also see the discussion of Hodot (2001: 174–8). The frequentative *-ske/o* is also found in Herodotus and once in Alcman (F 74 Page, Chantraine 1958: 320). The line of Alcman was cited by a grammarian precisely for the form in *-ske/o*: he used *ēske* instead of Homer's *eske* 'was'. It is considered to be an Ionic feature, and Chantraine (1958: 325) considers it to belong to the later parts of the Homeric text. See full discussion at his pp. 315–25. Certainly many of the forms are highly artificial: *naietaaske*, *peraaske* by analogy with *potheeske*. The one formula in which the frequentative *-ske/o* appears is the banal *hōde de tis eipesken*, "so someone would say." If indeed it should be considered to originate directly from Hittite (so Puhvel 1991: 13–20), a significant group of Hittite-speakers would need to have survived well past the last attestation of the language, or it would have been transmitted to Greek-speakers residing in Anatolia in the Late Bronze Age.

ritual texts and more generally in Indo-European myth).[33] Thus, bilingual performance of culturally important texts may have been common in Anatolia. The relative lack of the code-switching type of influence on the Homeric dialect suggests, however, that the number of bilingual poets was small.[34] But, the evidence from the multilingual tradition of Central Asian epic "shows that within a system in which students learn their craft from a particular teacher, only a single bilingual individual, whether student or teacher, is needed to pass an epic from one language to another."[35]

The phrases paralleling those from Hurro-Hittite epic which have already been discussed in other parts of this book are comparable to the Turkish or Albanian words or calques of Turkish or Albanian formulas in Yugoslavian epic poetry, the borrowing of the Turkish lexemes stemming from the time of the "Turkish yoke."[36] While single words may have been transmitted through knowledge of vernacular Turkish or Albanian, formulas imply knowledge of a poetic tradition.

The bilingual singer's job is easier if the verse forms coincide, as in the Bosnian/Albanian epic tradition, both versions using the Slavic *deseterjac*, and this was also the case in the Near Eastern epic traditions we have examined.[37] One might wonder whether the stichic structure of Homeric poetry, with its regular pattern of six strong positions and six weak positions, is at least in part the result of contact with the type of accent-counting stichic tradition manifested in Hurro-Hittite song, which we can assume for the Early Iron Age Anatolian traditions.[38]

---

[33] As Watkins (1970) has shown. Also see M. L. West (2007: 160–2).

[34] Code-switching is the use of more than one language in a single sentence. As noted, in the Homeric dialect we see only use of Anatolian sentential and adverbial particles on clause periphery, with borrowing of a few lexemes and calquing of a few phrases.

[35] Bachvarova (2014: 97). Also see Chapter 2, 49.

[36] See Foley (1999: 81–2, with n. 55, and earlier references). It is tempting to speculate that the Turkish influence that can be spotted in the Albanian and Serbo-Croatian songs (Skendi 1954: 143–8) originates from poets who also could perform in Turkish.

[37] See Jakobson (1966) and Vigorita (1976). Note that there is no question of the Yugoslavs borrowing their epic meter from the Turks, although they must have been strongly influenced by a robust Turkish epic tradition, as the *deseterjac* meter has an Indo-European heritage. The Albanian poet could also use an octosyllabic line. See Kolsti (1990: 4, 11, 58–86). He discounts the shorter line as "balladic," not epic, but he is intent on arguing for a bilingual *deseterjac* tradition in which Albanian was an equally important member. Also see Chapter 2, 47, n. 117.

[38] Allen (1973: 260–304; 1987: 131–9) argued for stress in Greek independent of the tonal accent, showing that the initial longum of each dactyl in the hexameter took the stress. The latter point was followed by Nagy (1974: 51–5). Devine and Stephens (1985; 1994: 85–156) showed that we should be thinking instead of a rhythmic pattern of alternating weak and strong positions, following the rules laid out by Allen with some refinements. See Bachvarova (2004) on Lydian verse as stress-counting and some discussion of previous analyses of Anatolian verse forms as syllable-counting (e.g., Eichner 1993).

With regard to the poets themselves, one would expect Phrygian–Greek, Carian–Greek, Lydian–Greek, and Lycian–Greek poets. I will dare to be more specific and suggest the possibility of a Phrygian–Aeolic tradition and a Lydian–Aeolic tradition, a Lycian–Pamphylian and Lycian–Doric tradition, and a Carian–Ionic tradition. A Lycian–Doric bard, for example, would have told of the conflicts between Rhodes and Lycia, preserved in the rivalry between Sarpedon and Tlepolemus, and perhaps his repertoire would have included the story of Bellerophontes. A Carian–Ionic bard might have focused on the local stories about Ephesus, for example, or on Carian–Greek heroes from Miletus, while there may have been a competing school of Ionic bards focusing on the Lycian Glaucids as founders of Miletus, whether started by a single master fluent in both Lycian and Ionic Greek, or by a single bilingual student who learned from a Lycian bard.[39]

A Phrygian–Aeolic tradition about the fall of Troy?

I have been arguing that the story of the Trojan War first moved to Greek-speakers from an Anatolian language. I turn now to stratifying the impact of the various Anatolian bilingual traditions on the Homeric *Iliad*. I suggest two possibilities for the earliest bilingual traditions: it may be that there were two stages, with a "Trojan"–Phrygian tradition first, and a Phrygian–Aeolic one second; or the relevant bilingual tradition could have been "Trojan"–Aeolic.[40] As discussed in Chapter 14, the evidence indicates that after Troia VIh was violently destroyed *ca.* 1180 BCE a new population came in at the beginning of Troia VIIa, while some proportion of the resident population remained and accommodated new pottery styles although maintaining some of their own dinnerware (Grey and Tan Ware). These are the circumstances in which an epic story performed during feasts that drew on inherited Near Eastern patterns could have developed about the ancient dynasty of Troy, including Alexander and possibly others that were assigned to the junior Dardanid line in the mythology, such as Aeneas, since the Dardanians also bear a name that can be traced back to the Late Bronze Age.[41]

---

[39] On the conflict between Lycia and Rhodes, and the Glaucids, see below.

[40] On the evidence that the earliest Greeks who commemorated Troy in the Iron Age identified themselves as Aeolic, see Chapter 14, 365, and Chapter 15, 405–6.

[41] Egyptian sources mention *D-3-r-d-n-jj* chariot warriors as allies of the Hittite at the battle of Kadesh (1274 BCE). See Bryce (2006: 136), Brügger, Stoevesandt, and Visser (2003: 268), Haider (1997: 117–18).

As discussed earlier, one plausible assumption about the linguistic affinities of the two groups at Troia vIIB1–2 would make the original inhabitants Lydian-speakers and the newcomers Phrygian-speakers.[42] There was in fact a special connection between Trojans and Phrygians in the *Iliad*. Hecuba's brother with the all-purpose name Asius ('Asian') is described as living "in Phrygia by the stream of the Sangarius" (16.717–19), so it seems that Hecuba herself was Phrygian.[43] Maeonia (Lydia) and Phrygia are typically grouped together in the *Iliad*, so we might infer that Homer saw both of them as the great powers of his day, and that therefore these references must date to some time before the early seventh century. Others note that contact between Greeks and Phrygians had clearly already begun in the eighth century.[44] While confusion over whether Tantalus and Niobe were Phrygian or Lydian suggests that as Phrygian standing receded before the expanding Lydian empire and their territorial control was restricted, Phrygian characters in Greek myth could be re-assigned a Lydian identity, the fact that Homer considers Niobe to be Phrygian suggests that the tradition still remembers when the Phrygians were the chief power even as far as Lydia. Of course, these modern theories about how and when the Greeks first knew of the Phrygians belong to the time before it was realized that there was no break in settlement at Troy, and therefore even if scholars agreed that the incomers at the end of the Bronze Age were Phrygian, that fact was thought to have no bearing on the appearance of Phrygians in the *Iliad* or on the question of when and where Phrygians and Greeks first came into contact.

In Homer there is no evidence that the Phrygians claimed more than a dynastic tie with the Trojans, and this might be the only relevant piece of evidence telling us about how the putative Phrygian-speakers at Troy may

---

[42] See Chapter 14, 357–8, 362–3.

[43] Also see *Il.* 3.184–7. Munn (2006: 106–14, especially p. 110), with reference to the *Homeric Hymn to Aphrodite*, proposes, "Dardanid identity was ... one of the links through which the Mermnad rulers of Lydia legitimized their appropriation of Phrygian sovereignty."

[44] Bryce (2006: 140–2), Kullmann (1999b: 65) on the Phrygian empire at the end of the eighth century BCE. See DeVries (1980) on Greco-Phrygian contact in the eighth century. Maeonia is a traditional native name for Lydia – the terms Lydia and Lydian are never used in the *Iliad* (Bryce 2006: 142–3). Helen asks Aphrodite if she will lead her even farther away from her home in Greece, "to Phrygia or lovely Maeonia" (3.400–1), and the two lands are again paired when Hector bemoans the need to sell the treasures of Troy to them (18.290–1). Contact between Greeks and Phrygians is described by Homer (*Il.* 3.184–7) as occurring by the Sangarius River. Watkins (1986: 703) sees this as a memory of the Phrygian migration, while Kullmann (1999b: 64–5) thinks it shows the extent of the Phrygian empire. Later the Phrygians would be associated (in a negative way) with the mythical Trojans (Munn 2006: 67, with earlier references; Burke 2007), as the Persians were.

have defined themselves in opposition to the newly arriving Greek-speakers interested in commemorating the ruins of Troy on their own terms. That is, they may not have presented themselves as descended directly from the Trojans of a lost heroic age, which of course, if the scenario I present is true, they would not have had the right to do. Originally the Phrygian newcomers would have been equated with the invading enemy from afar against whom the Trojans fought in that lost heroic age in the original epic storyline about Troy, then in the new Phrygian–Greek version they were tangentially attached to the losing dynasty through marriage.

This suggestion requires some real flexibility in the epic tradition. I have made the argument for flexibility in the tradition about the battle between Gilgamesh and Huwawa. I suggested that Huwawa could have been considered a local hero for Anatolians, explaining why there was a five-tablet Hurrian *Song of Huwawa*, and that the story may have had a forked pathway in the Mesopotamian tradition, with Huwawa living or dying depending on the poet's audience and aims. Certainly, it is clear that the same story could be told from different points of view, since, whereas the Akkadian *Cuthean Legend of Naram-Sin* presented the king as well-meaning but deluded and does not end with the destruction of Akkade, the Sumerian *Curse of Akkade* tells the same story from the point of view of Sumerian scribes who resented the Akkadian empire. In this version, Naram-Sin is portrayed as a bad ruler who causes his city to be destroyed by the gods because of his hybris.[45] Given this last example, I think that my surmise concerning the changing role of the Phrygians is possible.

This scenario of contact and its results has parallels to that proposed for the *Homeric Hymn to Aphrodite*, for which I argued that contact between the Greek and Phrygian traditions of narrative song caused a blending of two different storylines, although the time of contact influencing the *Iliad* would be centuries earlier than that usually assumed for the hymn.[46]

We must also acknowledge the possibility that (some of) the residents who remained in Troy across the end of the Bronze Age were bilingual in Trojan and Greek and that one piece of information attached to the memory of a Bronze Age Alaksandu was his mixed heritage. In this hypothetical scenario of contact, residents of Troy who had retained an affiliation with Ahhiyawans even through any disruptions caused by the

---

[45] See Bachvarova (2008a) and Chapter 3, 76. [46] *hHAphr*: Chapter 12, 328–9.

incomers from Thrace (possibly Phrygians) would not only have been instrumental in re-orienting the cultural interaction sphere in which Troy participated back to the northeast Aegean at the beginning of the Protogeometric period. They also would have been important players in the transfer of the Near Eastern epic storylines to Greek-speaking bards as competition for land and resources got more intense in the Troad with the Greek migrations, and storylines framing the interaction between Greek-speakers and Anatolians as hostile were called into use.

All of this is indubitably speculative, and furthermore the archaeological evidence from Troia VIIb3 does not tell us whether the people who first started to treat the ruins of Troia VI as marking a lost, glorious past were Greek-speakers or Anatolians, so we cannot confidently assert who was the first to treat Troy as a cult site. As I mentioned in Chapter 14, the Greeks themselves may have recognized the site of Troy as having some real significance in their own cultural memories of the events of the Bronze Age. However, to repeat the key point here, what we can say is that, given the continuity of settlement at Troy, it was likely not the newly arriving Greeks, but the cultural memory of the inhabitants the Greeks encountered that retained details about the dynasty at Bronze Age Troy, and those details were preserved for us by being embedded in dynastic lists and the Near Eastern storylines that shaped the storylines later attached to Achilles, Hector, and Helen.

A pro-Trojan *Iliad*

We cannot know which Near-Eastern derived frameworks were followed by the original Greek epic traditions about Troy, which I have proposed began *ca.* 1160–1050 BCE, before the stichic dactylic hexameter had been invented.[47] I now turn to how the storyline found in the *Cuthean Legend of Naram-Sin* was incorporated into the *Iliad*, an event that occurred before the Lycian influence, but after the pro-Greek version of events that reworked elements of the *Song of Release* had been well established in an earlier version of the *Iliad*. I will suggest that the incorporation of Hector's story occurred specifically in the Ionic epic tradition, after Hector had been converted from a Boeotian to a Trojan hero.[48]

The storylines from the *Song of Release* and the *Cuthean Legend of Naram-Sin* must have originally been separate instantiations of the story

---

[47] See Chapter 15, 400–2. [48] See Chapter 15, 405–6, on Hector as a Boeotian hero.

about Troy. In addition, as noted earlier, the *Cuthean Legend* presents a viewpoint sympathetic to the king of the city under siege, but it had a flip side, the version told in the Sumerian *Curse of Akkade*, in which the besieged city's leader brought just punishment on his city because of his impiety.[49] So, the storyline, if not the particular point of view as expressed in the version that was eventually incorporated into the *Iliad*, could have been deployed to please an audience who identified themselves with the attackers. The storyline attached to Hector in the *Iliad* we have, however, represents a version of the fall of Troy sympathetic to the Trojans, and therefore it would have been performed for Anatolian-identified audiences in opposition to the Greek-centric view. Then, it was pulled into the Greek-centric storyline. Although it was subordinated to the story of the wrath of Achilles, it still remained compelling, and the *Iliad* was shaped to accommodate it.

I now turn to the evidence for the relatively late incorporation of a Trojan-centric version into the *Iliad*. William Merritt Sale has studied the Homeric formulas involving Troy, and he concludes that they show the references to Troy and the Trojans had undergone reworking shortly before the final version of the *Iliad* was established. He has shown that formulas for "in/from Troy" are limited and concludes that Homer did not inherit a version in which much action took place in Troy.[50] Rather, the stage for the original Greek version of the fall of Troy was "in front of Troy." The Trojans have few epithets associated with them, which suggests that pejorative formulas were reduced or eliminated,[51] from which the conclusion may be drawn that the sympathetic attitude towards Trojans developed late in the textual history of the *Iliad* we have.[52] This certainly fits the theory of the neo-analysts. Martin West (who thinks in terms of a single poet continuously revising and expanding his magnum opus) puts it thus:

> in the expansions we meet Priam and Paris and Helen themselves, their conversation, become privy to their thoughts and feelings. We are taken inside Ilios and shown its buildings and its people, and how the invading host looked as seen from inside the walls. We are given a picture of Hector not just as a great warrior but as a husband and father, a man of tender human sensibilities as well as of courage and martial prowess.[53]

Hector's story is a key factor in stimulating sympathy for the Trojan side, and the emphasis on his tragedy should be added to the list of changes

---

[49] On the *Curse of Akkade*, see Chapter 3, 76. [50] Sale (1987). [51] Sale (1989).
[52] Sale (1994), also Högemann (2000: 191–3). [53] M. L. West (2011: 67).

made to a putative earlier version meant to appeal primarily to an audience that identified with the Achaeans. Although the story appears to be added as part of a reworking of an already extant narrative, Hector's story was woven into the larger design and has become integral to the narrative, in a fashion similar to that of the plot of Achilles' anger and his mourning over Patroclus, rather than being inserted as a single block, as Diomedes' *aristeiā* was. In fact, it is easy to imagine a version of the fall of Troy in which Hector's death was an immediate cause of the city's defeat. As it is, the lamentations of his wife and mother that close the epic not only serve as counterpoint to the mourning for Patroclus, slain by his hand, but also metonymically stand in for the lamentations for the fall of the city itself, accurately predicted by Andromache.

In addition, we can see some reworking of the character of Alexander/Paris that can be tied to the sympathetic presentation of Hector, for as Ann Suter has shown, the differential use of Paris' two names goes beyond the association of the Anatolian name Paris with Anatolian speakers. The name Alexander is more deeply embedded in the formulary system of Homeric diction, which presents him as "a rather bland, typical warrior, the noble consort of a beautiful woman."[54] On the other hand, "*Paris*' lack of a fixed position in the hexameter, its dearth of epithets, and the comparatively unformulaic nature of the lines in which it appears – all in contrast to *Alexandros* – argue for its later entry into epic diction."[55] Suter thus connects the name Paris to the late introduction of a storyline sympathetic to the Trojans into the Homeric tradition and "the desire to characterize the Trojan prince more fully, as an erotic figure and an object of abuse,"[56] two changes to the Homeric story that she considers to be interdependent. We can explain the changes to the Trojan prince's character as highlighting Hector's role as a tragic doomed figure for whom we are supposed to feel sympathy. The two different roles for Troy's leader, doomed prince who misinterprets the god's omens and feckless wife-stealer (a stock character from Greco-Aryan epic?), may have competed in the story tradition about Troy's destruction, then were incorporated into the Homeric *Iliad* in the separate but complementary characters of the two sons of Priam, with the blame placed squarely on Paris and Hector commensurately presented positively.

The combination of the two storylines required an audience that identified with both sides, the Achaeans and the Trojans, and such a

---

[54] Suter (1991a: 9). [55] Suter (1991a: 12). [56] Suter (1991a: 22).

self-identification must have been the by-product of the assertion of dynastic ties to the Trojans that would have originated in the period in which Greeks were not yet dominant over the Anatolians in the Troad, when the Greeks considered the link to provide some benefit, as opposed to the later period in which colonization narratives were the preferred way to frame past relations between Greeks and Anatolians. There is some evidence for this. While the ruling dynasty of Aeolian Cyme claimed to be descended from Agamemnon,[57] a politically motivated genealogical connection to the Trojans is seen with Hector of Chios, for example, and with the lineage of Hector and Aeneas rooting Scepsis into Anatolian legendary history.

If we believe the sources that maintain that king Agamemnon of Cyme married his daughter to the Phrygian king Midas, and we further assume that he was the same man as the Mita of the Mushki mentioned in Assyrian documents, then we can date him quite securely to the third quarter of the eighth century, as well as take note of a historical dynastic tie between Greeks and Phrygians.[58] The dynastic marriage would have set up the kind of situation that would have allowed for the kind of blending of Greek and Phrygian storylines by a bilingual epic poet seen in the *Homeric Hymn to Aphrodite*.

Pausanias, referring to the *Founding of Chios* by the fifth-century pro-Athenian writer Ion of Chios, mentions Hector of Chios in a discussion of the Ionian migration legends. He tells us the island, named after a son of Poseidon conceived with a nymph, was first settled by Oenopion ('wine-faced', i. e., dark-skinned, cf. the Oenopes clan at Miletus, but also a reference to red Chian wine), coming from Crete, along with Carians and Abantes from Euboea.[59] "From Oenopion and his sons, Amphiclus later seized rulership; he came from Istaea in Euboea following an oracle from Delphi." In the fourth generation Hector, after having taken power, threw out the Abantes and Carians. Peace having been achieved, "it then came into Hector's mind that they should join the Ionians in sacrificing at the Panionium." Assuming there is some historical kernel here, when did this Hector rule? A Chian inscription "[i]n a beautiful fifth-century hand"

---

[57] Str. 13.1.3, see Carlier (1984: 463).
[58] Aristotle F 611, 37 Rose, Pollux 9.83. See Carlier (1984: 463). I follow Berndt-Ersöz (2008) in separating the Midas who was mentioned by Neo-Assyrian sources (723–677 BCE) from the Midas who died in a Cimmerian invasion *ca.* 644/642. Lanfranchi (2000: 14–22) suggests that the earlier Midas allied himself with the Greeks to attack Que and take it from the Assyrians. The marriage then would have cemented a military alliance.
[59] *FGrH* 115 F 276; Haviaras (2007: 64–5). See Chapter 10, 241, on the Oenopes.

listing the genealogy of Hieropythus of Chios goes back fourteen generations, perhaps to 900 BCE. H. T. Wade-Gery, assuming the first generation coincides with the founding of the city and that three generations correspond to 100 years, accordingly places Hector ca. 800 BCE.[60] The Chian and Euboean connections suggest that at this point the Trojan Hector had some appeal among Ionians, even if he had originated as a Boeotian hero. And, it may be important that at this same time an Aeolian dynasty at Cyme was choosing to identify itself, on the other hand, with the victor's side.[61]

As for the pretentions of the ruling house of Scepsis to a Trojan ancestry, we return to the first-millennium BCE debate discussed in the previous chapter about who was the legitimate continuator of Troy.[62] According to Strabo:

> Palaescepsis is above Cebron at the highest part of Ida near Policha; it was then called Scepsis ..., but later they (the population) were transferred downwards 60 stadia into the town now called Scepsis by Scamandrius, the son of Hector, and Ascanius, the son of Aeneas; and these two families are said to have ruled as kings for a long time in Scepsis; but after that they converted to an oligarchy, then the Milesians joined their city and they lived democratically. But, the ones from the family were called kings nonetheless, having specific honors. Then Antigonus joined the Scepsians to Alexandrea; then Lysimachus freed them and returned them to the settlement.[63]

---

[60] Paus. 7.4.8–10; Wade-Gery (1952: 6–9, quote from 8). Assuming that the *Iliad* is the work of a single poet who lived after Hector of Chios, Wade-Gery comes to quite different conclusions from those presented here, arguing that the Trojan Hector took his name from this Chian king. Carlier (1984: 449–50) sees the king as probably being given the name because of the fame of the Trojan Hector, and rightly points out the danger of relying too heavily on the dating. On the Panionium also see Chapter 15, 413, n. 69. Obviously, if we take Wade-Gery's dating seriously and if we believe Pausanias' story, then we have an important terminus ante quem for the formation of the Panionic League.

[61] Nagy argues in some detail that Aeneas' son Ascanius was affiliated with the Ionians, while Scamandrius was affiliated with the Aeolians. This is based on the bT scholia to *Il.* 20.307–8a1: "Other people say that the Aeolians expelled the descendants of Aeneas" (trans. Nagy 2010: 198). Nagy (2010: 198–9) assumes here that the scholia are referring to the version of events as related by Hellanicus of Lesbos (*FGrH* 4 F 31), but it seems possible to assume that the scholia are responding to the version of events as told in the *Iliad*. That is, the scholia are saying there is a version of events in which Troy was not destroyed forever, but the Aeneidae settled there then were driven out by the Aeolians, which they contrast with the Romans' version, in which Aeneas ends up in Rome (as in Hellanicus' version); also see n. 65 here. In any case the legends discussed by Nagy are too late to be assumed to be relevant to the pre-seventh century, Milesian phase I am focused on.

[62] Chapter 15, 410.   [63] Str. 13.1.52.

As mentioned earlier, Strabo here is referring to the story of Demetrius of Scepsis, who was so fascinated by the Anatolians in the *Iliad* that he wrote a thirty-book study of the catalog of Trojan allies.[64] Demetrius was making the strongest argument possible for considering Scepsis to be the legitimate continuator of Trojan rule, against, one may presume, Aeolian counter-claims arguing that Neon Ilion was the legitimate inheritor of Trojan prestige. Strabo (13.1.53) reports that Demetrius goes so far as to assert that Scepsis was the royal seat of Aeneas. The rival story that had been promulgated by the fifth-century Hellanicus of Lesbos asserted that the pair of royal heirs, Ascanius and Scamandrius, actually re-settled Troy itself.[65] The site of Scepsis is generally agreed to be Kurşunlu Tepe,[66] but it has not been excavated, so unfortunately we have no date for Demetrius' story, although fifth-century coins from Scepsis are inscribed in both Ionic and Aeolic dialect (*skē/skā*), indicating that Miletus had colonized the city by this point.[67] What we can say is that Demetrius' story seems to respond to the (legitimate) claim of Neon Ilion to be the continuator of the legendary Troy. There was a political advantage to claiming a connection to the losers of the Trojan War, whether by settlers at the actual site of Troy or at another town: it established a prior claim to the Troad, and in promulgating this claim a polity might prefer a version of events about the fall of Troy that focused sympathetically on the losers' side – a *Cuthean Legend* version of events, so to speak.[68]

The competitive collaboration among poets proposed as the catalyst for the rapid improvement in the quality of the Homeric tradition would have been the means for the entry of Hector's story into the Achaean-centric epic tradition – if not at the Milesian stage in the formation of our *Iliad*, which will be discussed in the following section, then at some other venue at an earlier stage. As noted earlier, bards typically do not learn how to perform epic more generally, but how to perform a specific epic,[69] and the competitive collaborative process can involve poets performing the episodes they are known to be particularly good at.[70] Therefore, I suggest that the inclusion of Hector's storyline, which is woven through the *Iliad*, although most prominent in Books 6, 8, 12, 15–17, and 21–22, required

---

[64] Str. 13.1.45.
[65] Str. 13.1.40–2 = Hellanicus *FGrH* 4 F 31; Demetrius F 35 Gaede. Strabo (13.1.53) himself interprets the *Iliad* as saying that (only) Aeneas' descendants would re-settle Troy and distrusts the claim that a lineage could trace itself back to Scamandrius.
[66] J. M. Cook (1973: 345).   [67] Leaf (1923: 273).
[68] See Chapter 8, 191–5, on the influence of the *Cuthean Legend* on Hector's storyline.
[69] See Chapter 2, 49.   [70] See Chapter 15, 415.

extensive involvement of poets with expertise in telling his story, as opposed to, for example, Achilles' story. Furthermore, it may be appropriate to suggest that the poets devoted to telling Hector's story formed a particular school promulgating the agenda of a particular polity located on the Troad, an Ionian one.

Lycian influence on the *Iliad*: a Milesian setting?

I have suggested that the stories about the Glaucids came from a Lycian–Greek tradition, so a third bilingual tradition must have influenced Homer's *Iliad* at a relatively late stage in its development. The question is why and how this influence occurred. Trevor Bryce suggests, "the *Iliad*'s composer may have been influenced by wealthy aristocratic patrons of his own day ... [I]t may be that local rulers who claimed a Lycian ancestry influenced Homer into assigning a high profile to their alleged ancestors."[71] Herodotus, who generally is eager to present the Ionians in a bad light and to poke holes into their claims of ethnic purity, says that some of the twelve Ionian cities, after they had been established, chose as kings "Lycians" who were descendants of Glaucus, son of Hippolochus, while others chose Caucones from Pylos, descendants of Codrus (1.147).[72]

While Bryce alludes to the Glaucids of Miletus, he does not push the connection. I argue that the polity where the epics would have been performed and seen by Greek poets who could incorporate elements from them into the specific strain of Greek epic that eventually became Homeric epic was in fact precisely Miletus, where a lineage chose to claim a connection to the Lycians via a Glaucus and/or a Sarpedon, the Cretan founder of Miletus, according to some versions of the town's early history. Herodotus' story was not followed by Strabo or Pausanias, who preferred other versions that presented Neleus or Neileus (so Pausanias) leading the colonization to Miletus, but coinage from Miletus and Erythrae and mention of a Glaucid in an inscription from Magnesia show Herodotus' version

---

[71] Bryce (2006: 146). "All in all, it is possible that first-millennium Lycia had within its population an ethnic group who had links with Miletus and whose ancestral roots lay in Crete" (Bryce 2006: 147).

[72] The Caucones served among the allies of the Trojans, along with the Pelasgians and Leleges, according to *Il.* 10.429, and Hecataeus *FGrH* 1 F 119 did not consider them to be Greek, but other sources, including *Od.* 3.366, place them in the Peloponnese. See Y. Lafond, "Caucones," in *Brill's New Pauly* 3.38.

was consistent with local legends.[73] What contemporary military or political advantage the legendary connection provided we do not know, but certainly Lycians would be a natural ally for Miletus when seeking to restrict the expansion of Rhodian interests along the section of the Carian coast that would later become the Rhodian *peraiā*.[74] The Glaucus Bay mentioned by Strabo between Miletus and Lycia could have been named after Glaucus, whose bland Greek name meant 'sea-blue', or vice versa. Sarpedon's name, although Anatolian, was equally bland, meaning "of a high place," and appears to have been used by both Carians and Lycians.[75]

Originally, then, one venue that would have been appropriate for the performance of epics about the Glaucids was a festival at Miletus. I suggest that the local audience's pleasure in storylines about Bellerophontes and Sarpedon brought poets expert in their stories to the Milesian festival in which the *Iliad* was performed. They pulled the local heroes into the Iliadic storyline when it was their turn to perform a section on the Milesian stage. Sarpedon, "the last son of Zeus," the "perfect hero," whose speech to Glaucus about the rights and obligations of the warrior has been held up as the most explicit exposition of the Homeric warrior code,[76] could only be included in the *Iliad* by reworking his genealogy since he properly belonged to an earlier generation,[77] but clearly he was considered so important to the audience that it was necessary to find a way to fit him in[78] – this despite the fact that, as he himself points out to Hector in the programmatic speech quoted at the beginning of this chapter, Lycia is very far away from Troy, and the Lycians have no reason to be involved.[79]

---

[73] Str. 14.1.3; Paus. 7.2.1–6. Carlier (1984: 432–3). For more details on Miletus' founding myths see Sourvinou-Inwood (2005: 268–309). On the conflation of Neleus (*Neleus*) and Neileus (*Neileos*) see n. 95.

[74] See Held (2009) on the third-century Rhodian *peraiā*.

[75] Str. 14.2.2. The etymology of Sarpedon's name has received much discussion. Durnford (2008) argues that the name should be segmented *sar-pedon(t)*, and the meaning 'of a high place' was either a title ('commander') or an aristocratic personal name. See further Bachvarova (2015: 149–50).

[76] Clay (2009: 35); *Il.* 12.310–28; see Clay's (2009) discussion of Sarpedon's speech and his character as the perfect Homeric warrior.

[77] See Janko (1992: 358, 371–3); compare the family tree according to Homer in Benda-Weber (2005: 243) and cf. a discussion of the alternate lineage of Sarpedon at her pp. 254–6; also Bachvarova (2015: 139–40, 147–8) and n. 14 in this chapter.

[78] Janko (1992: 371) offers a different explanation: "Homer surely introduced Sarpedon from an earlier era so that Patroklos could kill a god's son."

[79] *Il.* 5.471–92; see Bryce (2006: 145–6).

As I have shown, at least one festival at Miletus, the New Year's festival for Apollo Delphinius, makes a point of incorporating indigenous traditions (such as the *gulloi* stones), while Graecizing them, and it was administered by a set of clans that included Neleids as well as local Anatolia-based ones (whether Greek-speakers or Carian-speakers).[80] This is the type of venue in which one could imagine the incorporation of the Lycian heroes into Greek epic, and we will see that in the *Iliad* there are references to the Neleids specifically in the context of the exploits of Lycian warriors. Although the inception of the specific festival for Apollo Delphinius that the second-century Molpoi Decree at Miletus refers to cannot be pushed back before the beginning of the seventh century based on the evidence now available (nor can this be ruled out), and there is no reason to assume that other Milesian festivals would not have alluded to the melding of Greek and indigenous peoples before the seventh century, just as Hittite festivals made conspicuous use of pre-Hittite and other local traditions, and Mycenaean festivals alluded to Minoan practices.[81]

Hints of what might have been contained in these epichoric legends framing the contested past of Miletus can be found in the *Iliad*. For example, Richard Janko has drawn attention to the fact that in Book 16 two of the companions of Sarpedon, sons of Amisodarus, "who raised the furious Chimaera, an evil to many men" (*Il.* 16.328–9), are slain by two sons of Nestor, Antilochus killing Atymnius and Thrasymedes killing Maris (cf. Hitt. *mariš* 'spear'). It seems possible that the two successive sets of legendary incomers were pitted against each other in mythical battles of Neleids against Glaucids. It may not be fortuitous that the two Lycian warriors here have genuine Anatolian names; they express a Glaucid claim to autochthony.[82]

Certainly, Sarpedon was a hero in Lycian sagas telling of rivalries with Rhodian Greeks. In a relatively lengthy episode in Book 5 of the *Iliad*, Sarpedon slays Tlepolemos, the leader of the Rhodian contingent, the only set of Achaeans who have already settled in the ambit of Anatolia in the Catalog of Ships. It is not implausible that, as the scholia say, the passage

---

[80] Chapter 10, 241–3. [81] See discussion in Chapter 10, 224, 229.
[82] *Il.* 16.317–29; Janko (1992: 358–9), Bachvarova (2015: 148–9). Janko: "Bryce [1986: 33] well argues that the saga arose in the Bronze Age in the area around Miletos, whence the Lukka later migrated to Lycia. That Cretans and then Mycenaeans settled in Miletos, which must equal Hittite Millawatta, is certain" (Janko 1992: 359). I am offering a different theory here, although I certainly agree with his statement that "Glaukos is a sympathetic figure, in no doubt because leading Ionian families deemed him their ancestor (Hdt. 1.147)" (Janko 1992: 382). On Atymnius' name see Janko (1992: 358–9).

reflects a long-standing enmity between Rhodes and Lycia, if not from the Late Bronze Age, when men of Ahhiyawa were indeed involved in the affairs of Lukka (although the attestations show a friendly relationship), then going back as far as the post-palatial period, when Rhodes was an important node in trade and immigration routes.[83] Burkert perceptively notes that while Tlepolemus has immigrated to Rhodes from Ephyra, the family of Glaucus and Sarpedon too is ultimately from Ephyra, since that is where Bellerophontes came from, as the scion of the royal family founded by Sisyphus, son of Aeolus. Burkert comments that their common origin "link[s] to each other difficult partners who had still to come to terms."[84]

The inconsistencies in the role and location of the Lycians in the *Iliad*, which have long been the topic of scholarly study, even in the time of Strabo,[85] are evidence for alternate tellings of the fall of Troy. Geoffrey Kirk interprets the inconcinnity between the list of Trojan allies in the *Iliad* and the role of specific ethnic groups in the rest of the epic as showing that the catalog "was the work of a singer, perhaps indeed Homer himself, who knew both the Achaean catalog and the details of the whole poem, but selected from them erratically at times, and perhaps at a relatively late stage of adjustment and refinement."[86] I frame the situation somewhat differently, arguing that the catalog draws on and reveals knowledge of an

---

[83] Σ bT *ad Il.* 5.639. See Page (1959: 147–9) and Kirk (1990: 122–3, 180–1), tracing the conflict back to the Late Bronze Age. Tawagalawa aids people of Lukka (*Tawagalawa Letter*: CTH 181 = KUB 14.3 i 1–4, translit. and trans. Beckman, Bryce, and Cline 2011: 102–3, discussion 120); a man of Hiyawa waits in Lukka for a shipment of copper overseen by Ugarit (*Fragments of Akkadian Letters*: CTH 208 = RS 94.2530 rev. 33–9, translit. and trans. Beckman, Bryce, and Cline 2011: 256–7; also CTH 208 = RS 94.2523 rev. 36–7, translit. and trans. Beckman, Bryce, and Cline 2011: 260–1). See Benzi (1988; 2013) on post-palatial Rhodes. He states, "the island was no doubt deserted before the end of LH IIIC Late" (2013: 519).

[84] *Il.* 6.153–5; Burkert (1995: 230). Because Burkert believes in a late date for Homer he suggests, "The invented Lycian genealogy may nearly be contemporary with the Lydian constructs of Gyges' epoch." I would rather underline the fact that both sides were seen as belonging to the same community; a mindset that saw no essential difference between Greeks and Lycians facilitated the creation of a bilingual epic tradition.

[85] Str. 12.8.4. The commentaries of Kirk (1985: 248–63) and Brügger, Stoevesandt, and Visser (2003: 263–88) and the discussion of Bryce (2006: 127–50) form the basis of the following discussion. The (neo-)analytical school has long assumed that the prominent role of the Lycians belongs to a later layer of the *Iliad* (M. L. West 2011: 64–5). M. L. West (2011: 23) suggests that "P," as he designates the oral poet whom he considers to have written the *Iliad*, visited Lycia and "entertained the rulers with his songs and received their hospitality, learned their legends, and repaid them by incorporating their heroes in his epic."

[86] Kirk (1985: 263). M. L. West (2011: 111–14) offers a variant of this neo-analytical approach, arguing that both catalogs were later expansions by P, and "the catalog of the Trojan allies [was] evidently constructed *ad hoc* as a foil to the Achaean catalog" (114). He has no explanation for the reference to the *barbarophōnoi* Carians of Miletus (126).

alternate telling of the *Iliad* in which the Lycians played a less important role, one pitched to a different audience. This telling belonged to the pre-Milesian, pre-Panionic phase or a non-Milesian, non-Panionic branch of the Iliadic tradition.

In the catalog Lycia takes last place, the farthest east from Troy of the allies' lands, along the coast: "Sarpedon led the Lycians, and blameless Glaucus from faraway Lycia, from the swirling Xanthus" (2.876–7). The Carians, on the other hand, receive a generous section:

> Nastes ('inhabitant') in turn led the barbarian-speaking (*barbarophōnoi*) Carians, who occupied Miletus and the mountain of Phthires, whose top is covered in leaves, and the streams of the Meander, and the high peak of Mycale. Them indeed Amphimachus and Nastes led, Nastes and Amphimachus, shining children of Nimion; and he went into battle wearing gold like a girl, foolish one, not at all did it fend off dire death, but he was laid low at the hands of the swift-footed son of Aeaces in the river, and battle-minded Achilles carried off the gold.[87]

The reference to a Carian Miletus, which other sources tell us was the hometown of the Milesian colonizer Sarpedon,[88] harmonizes with the mention of Cretan Miletus in the Catalog of Ships (*Il.* 2.647), if we assume the Carians at Miletus were supposed to have arrived after the Cretans there. This hypothetical scenario matches what I have suggested occurred historically, that is, those who were to self-identify as Carians only moved south into the area around Miletus at the end of the Bronze Age.[89]

This synopsis is not picked up or alluded to later on, and indeed the Carians are hardly mentioned in the rest of the *Iliad*.[90] Meanwhile, the surprisingly brief mention of the Lycians closing out the list does not jibe with the thematic importance of Sarpedon's death at the hands of Patroclus or the extended recounting of the story of Glaucus' ancestor Bellerophontes.[91] I contend that the poet who contributed the catalog of Trojan allies to the collaborative effort that resulted in the Panionic *Iliad*

---

[87] *Il.* 2.867–75. Both Georges (1994: 14–15) and Sourvinou-Inwood (2005: 40–2, 269) consider this story to present the Carians in a negative light. Also see Herda (2006b: 73, n. 170; 2009: 43, 68, n. 222) on a possible pejorative reference to lice (*phthires*) in the mention of Mt. Phthiron (= Mt. Latmus?) as the homeland of the Carians. Also see discussions of Kirk (1985: 260–1), Brügger, Stoevesandt, and Visser (2003: 284–7).

[88] See this chapter, 438–9.

[89] See Chapter 14, 360–1, on the Carians arriving at Miletus after the Bronze Age.

[90] Other references: Carian or Maeonian women dying an ivory cheek-piece for a bridle (4.141–2), Carians as a group in the Trojan encampment (10.428).

[91] Kirk (1985: 262).

was thinking in terms of a quite different *Iliad* in which the Carians and Nastes played a more important role (in which they were framed negatively?), whereas in the *Iliad* we have it is the Lycians, portrayed in a positive light, who are the most important allies of the Trojans. To restate, competitive collaboration explains this inconsistency, with different bards working with different local traditions; it is not the result of population movements, but rather the result of the transfer of primary control of the Iliadic storyline from the Troad to Miletus.

Finally, it appears that the term Lycian was re-defined, becoming ever narrower over time. It may be that the term was primarily an exonym, that is, used by non-Lycians, as we know the Lycians used other self-identifications, which are mentioned in the stories of Sarpedon bringing the Termilae to Lycia and Bellerophontes fighting the Solymi.[92] So, it could be that at an early period the term *Lukios* was used by Greeks to refer to indigenous peoples as far west as the Troad, which explains Homer's Zeleian Lycians. Later it was limited to people residing in what Greeks considered to be Lycia by the time of Herodotus.[93]

The effect of the Milesian milieu is evident and must be explained and harmonized with a putative Panionic stage in the shaping of the Iliadic tradition. It is true that dating the Panionia festival much earlier than the end of the eighth century remains debatable: archaeological evidence for the Panionium at Güzelçamlı does not support a date earlier than the end of the sixth century, and not all agree that the reference to the sacrificial rite to Poseidon Heliconius in the *Odyssey* (2.403–5) alludes to the distinctive practice of the Panionic sacrifice in which the bull was expected to

---

[92] Hdt. 1.173; for Bellerophontes see above. So Frei (1993b); also see Bryce (1986: 19–23) on the variety of ethnic groups subsumed under the blanket term Lycian, such as Milyans, Solymi, and Termilae, and Keen (1998: 86) on the use of *Trmmili*.

[93] See Bachvarova (2015: 129–30, 141, 150). According to Bryce, Pandarus was associated both with the Troad and with Lycia because he had entered the narrative tradition that Homer draws on before a migration from the Troad to Lycia at the end of the Late Bronze Age. This theory was originally supported by Bryce's reconstruction of a broken toponym in the list of the members of the Assuwan confederation as [L]uqqa instead of [Art]uqqa, an unlikely conjecture (Bryce 1986: 4, 8; 2006: 148), see Chapter 13, 334–5, n. 14. Now Bryce (2006: 149) argues that the connection between the Lycians and Zeleia "represents a genuine southward sea migration by a group of marauders from the north who initially plundered the Lycian coast and then subsequently settled there – Lycia's own version of the Sea Peoples." The Lukka were in fact mentioned by the pharaoh Merneptah among the "people from the sea" (*Great Libyan War Inscription, Karnak: KRI* 4.2, trans. Kitchen 2003: 2). According to Strabo (14.3.5) the Zeleian/Lycian Pandarus, son of Lycaon, was worshipped as a hero by the Lycians in Pinara. On Pandarus see Benda-Weber (2005: 268–70). On the possible Lycian etymology of Pandarus' name, see Yakubovich (2010: 138) and Neumann (2007: 278–9).

bellow before his death.[94] Furthermore, in the historical record it was Ephesus, not Miletus, that was the leading member of the Panionic League; but that was only after Miletus had been destroyed by the Persians.[95] Therefore, I follow the suggestion by Douglas Frame that "it is worth considering [the] famous cult and oracle of Apollo as the starting point of a nascent league, namely Branchidai in the territory of Miletus; this location, speculative as it is, makes good sense as a center for the earliest form of the league if Miletus was indeed the league's prime mover."[96] Then, at a later period, the Panionium was built on Mt. Mycale, and Poseidon became the chief god of the league, supplanting the patron god of Miletus, Apollo.[97]

As mentioned in the previous chapter, it is striking how little catering to the interests of a specific Greek ethnic group there is in the storyline of the *Iliad*.[98] We can no longer argue that the lack of Ionic material is the result of a late transfer from Aeolic into Ionic. What we can say is that the putative Panionic shaping of the *Iliad* was working with a well-defined tradition with little room for the incorporation of heroes interesting specifically to the Ionians. Anyway, while it would be a fascinating exercise to speculate further about the possible epic storylines that were deployed to present legends of Miletus' past, as noted earlier, what is most important for our purposes is that they were almost completely ignored in the *Iliad* that we have. The references to the Neleids, the Greek colonizers of Miletus, which Douglas Frame has excavated from the *Iliad* and the *Odyssey*, are quite oblique.[99] Their ancestor Nestor is an important

---

[94] See further details in Chapter 15, 413–14, n. 69.

[95] One question is how to assess the version of the Ionian migration according to Pherecydes of Athens. He singles out Androclus, son of Codrus, who founded Ephesus, and has Neleus originate directly from Pylos (Str. 14.1.3 = *FGrH* 3 F 155; this latter piece of information is not included by Jacoby). Frame (2009: 515–27) sees a convenient substituting of Pylian Neleus in the role of the founder of Miletus (properly Ionian Neileus). On the conflation between the two, see Herda (1998: 2, 8–14, with earlier references). Also see Nagy (2010: 215–17) contrasting Strabo with Herodotus 1.142–3, who treats Miletus as the leading city.

[96] Frame (2009: 615).

[97] Frame (2009: 614, 618) suggests that the cult of Poseidon Heliconius was taken over by the Ionian Dodecapolis after the Melian War. The attribution to Arctinus of Miletus of two now lost epics about the Trojan War, *Aethiopis* and *Iliou Persis*, may be an acknowledgment of the importance of Miletus in the development of the Homeric tradition. Eusebius mentions him in his *Chronological Canons* as active in the first and fifth Olympiads, 775 and 760 BCE (Latin trans. by Jerome, *Chron.*, ed. Helm 1956: 86b, 87a). The *Suidas*, s. v. *Arktinos* (Adler A 3960), citing Artemon (*FGrH* 443 F2), calls him a student of Homer and gives his *floruit* as the ninth Olympiad, or 400 years after the Trojan War. The issues with regard to Arctinus' dating cannot be entered into here, but see Burgess (2001: 9–10).

[98] See Chapter 15, 411.   [99] Frame (2009: 105–338).

secondary character in both the *Iliad* and the *Odyssey*, and he helps to shape key stages in the action at specific junctures in the narratives, but he is not integral to the general plots. The story about Troy did not brook any internal competition from stories about Miletus, even if it moved towards its penultimate, Panionic form at Miletus. Perhaps other Anatolian myths could remain because they were not considered to clash with the later Panhellenic refining of the epic material.

Lycian hero worship in the *Iliad*: the death of Sarpedon

A second important implication of the inclusion of Sarpedon's story in the *Iliad* is that there was an awareness within the Homeric tradition of the Anatolian equivalent of hero worship, which was equated with Greek hero worship.[100] This made it easier to transfer back and forth specific practices and performances connected to each culture's rituals honoring (fictional) elite ancestors.

Because Sarpedon's death scene in *Iliad* 16 not only has strong connections to Near Eastern epic, but also shows an awareness of and respect for Lycian rituals that honor their own heroes,[101] we can suggest that the performance of epic was complementary to such rites among the Lycians, as I have argued it was among the Greeks and Bronze Age Near Easterners. It is well known that Sarpedon's death, like that of Patroclus, draws on the Gilgamesh tradition, but in a different way. (One expects that each entered the Homeric tradition by different routes.) In the Hittite *Song of Gilgamesh* the gods discuss whether Gilgamesh or Enkidu must die as punishment for killing the Bull of Heaven, and when Sarpedon is wounded by Patroclus, Zeus debates whether to allow him to live, finally accepting Hera's admonition that he must die.[102] His stepmother says that he will be spirited off to Lycia by Sleep and Death, where his relatives "will

---

[100] Lateiner (2002: 54–5) has already suggested that Greek hero worship could have borrowed elements of Anatolian practices.
[101] *Il.* 16.419–683, esp. 431–61.
[102] M. L. West (1997a: 343–4), and see Chapter 3, 68–9, where I note that the scene is preserved primarily in the Hittite version. I lay aside here a variety of interesting problems, like the possible relationship between this scene and others in which heroes are whisked away at the moment of death, and exactly how Homer is altering the "original" story about Sarpedon's death, causing some distortion in the mythic timeline by pulling a hero from yesteryear into the Trojan War. See Janko (1992: 371–2) and Nagy (1983: 194–5). In the approach I work with, there is no need for one death scene to be dependent on the other, since both can draw on type scenes and motifs available in the wider tradition.

honor him (*tarkhūsousi*) with a tomb and stele (*tumbōi te stēlēi te*), for this is the prize of those who die" (*Il.* 16.456–7 = 674–5). Thus, Homer recognizes that there was a specifically Lycian custom of special treatment for certain dead. In the world of Homeric epic these rites are done for a man who has met the fate of an epic hero.[103] Although there is no contemporary evidence of worship of Sarpedon – or anyone else – as a hero,[104] the Sarpedoneum was located in Xanthus in the time of Appian (*B. C.* 4.78–9), and his tomb was an important enough landmark for Aeschylus to mention when tracing the route of Io's wanderings (*Supp.* 870).[105]

The rare verb *tarkhuō* must be a borrowing from an Anatolian language; compare Hittite *tarḫu-* 'be powerful, overcome', as in the name of the Storm-god Tarhunt.[106] The verb only occurs one more time in Homer, significantly in the mouth of the Anatolian Hector, fantasizing that he will slay the champion of the Achaeans and his countrymen will honor his corpse (*tarkhūsōsi*) and pile up a tumulus for him (*sēma . . . kheuōsi, Il.* 7.85–6), which will serve as a reminder of his own prowess to all who sail by. The scholia on this passage define the rare verb as "to bury" or "to do the things with regard to funerary rites (*pros kēdeiān*) as is the custom for corpses."[107] Gregory Nagy defines it as "treat like a cult-figure."[108] One could suggest a meaning of "to cause to overcome the limits of death" by ritual commemoration. I further speculate that the connection with the name of the Storm-god is not fortuitous, but somehow is related to the Storm-god's patronage of the royal dead, as seen by the housing of their statues in his temple at Hattusa.[109]

Certainly Tarhunt remained an important deity among the Lycians, worshipped as *Trqqñt*, and he also left his trace on various local Zeuses.

---

[103] Janko (1992: 372–3) sees this passage as evidence for local cult at this time.
[104] See Hülden (2006: 340–52) analyzing the evidence for actual hero worship rather than ancestor veneration, and his discussion of Lycian mortuary ritual and continued offerings for the dead at the tomb (2006: 275–340). See Benda-Weber (2005: 243–70) on Lycian heroes in Greek myth. Scheer (1993: 324–7) mentions some late evidence of Sarpedon as a god in Cilicia, alluded to less specifically by Janko (1992: 372). On Sarpedon more generally also see Keen (1998: 208–10). For possible evidence of eighth-century worship of Homeric heroes, see Chapter 11, 285–6, n. 76.
[105] See Keen (1996: 230–1; 1998: 186–7).
[106] Blümel (1926) was the first to suggest that it referred to a Lycian custom, using a Lycian verb. See Nagy (1983: 195–8, 205–6), M. L. West (1997a: 386), and most recently Watkins (2008: 136–7, with earlier references). Janko (1992: 377) is not persuaded. Hoekstra (1965: 142–3) argues that the verb harks back to Mycenaean customs. See *HEG* (T: 157–68) for a full discussion of the Hittite verb and possible cognates.
[107] Also see Kirk (1990: 245).   [108] Nagy (1983: 201).   [109] See Chapter 7, 152.

Indeed, although Lycia lacks any epigraphic sources for the period we are interested in and there is little evidence of settlement until the end of the eighth century,[110] we can still detect, on the one hand, basic continuity as indicated by place names and by continuity in gods and cult practices, and, on the other assimilation by Greeks of indigenous customs.[111] For example, the deity *ēni mahanahi* 'mother of the gods' continued the Luwian *anniš maššanaššiš*, and was later syncretized with Leto. Maliya 'mental force', a Luwian goddess of springs who bore the same name in Hittite times, was later syncretized with Athena.[112] Ea, the Mesopotamian god of wisdom, was called Iyas. Various local Artemises, local Apollos, and Hermes all continue the Anatolian LAMMA-god type, while the confusion between Lycian Apollo (*Lukios*), Apollo of Light (*lukeios*), and Apollo the Wolf-god (*lukeios*) allowed for new syncretisms in this highly adaptable Greco-Anatolian deity.[113]

As for the mortuary practices of the Lycian elite, they certainly continued elements of beliefs preserved from the Bronze Age. The Hittites considered their royal dead to ascend to heaven upon death. Stone, especially living rock and mountain peaks joining the underworld to the heavens, seems to have had some symbolic significance, possibly signifying permanence. Thus, the Eternal Rocky Peak was a location for royal

---

[110] Des Courtils (2001).
[111] Continuity in place names: In Hittite times, the enemy land Lukka lay directly to the west of Tarhuntassa and to the east of Arzawa, approximately where Lycia was, although perhaps it covered a more extensive territory inland. On Lukka see Bryce (2003a: 40–4) and Yakubovich (2010: 130–6). The later Lycaonia (**lukka-wani-* 'belonging to Lukka') fits in the Hulaya River Land. See Börker-Klähn (1993), Carruba (1996: 29), Yakubovich (2010: 137–8), preferring an association with the Lower Land. The city Attarimma located in Lukka (see the references collected in Watkins 1995: 450) has been connected to the Lycian self-designation *trmmili* (cf. Gr. Termilae), with regular Lycian aphaeresis, and three more Lycian cities from the Classical era appear in Hieroglyphic Luwian inscriptions associated with Lukka: Pinara, Oenoanda, and Tlos, corresponding to Pinali, Wiyanawanda (Hittite *wiyana* 'wine' corresponding to Greek *oinos*), and Talawa (Poetto 1993: 75–82; Yakubovich 2010: 133). For further discussion of evidence for continuity, see Benda-Weber (2005), Börker-Klähn (1993), Bryce (2006: 144–50), Çevik (2000), Frei (1993b), and Popko (2008: 93–7).
[112] On Maliya see G. Frantz-Szabó, "Malija(nni), Malimalija," in *RlA* (7:304–5), Haas (1994: 410–11), Hutter (2003: 231–2), and Lebrun (1982). The etymology comes from Watkins (2007b: 122–4). He, however, sees no reason to connect the spring-goddess Maliya with the Maliya syncretized with Athena.
[113] Bryce (1986: 172–80; 1996), Keen (1996; 1998: 193–213), Lebrun (1987; 1992; 1995; 1998b), Popko (1995: 172–6), Raimond (2004). On Apollo Lukeios or Lukios see Casabonne and Marcinkowski (2004: 146–53), Egetmeyer (2007), and Graf (1985: 220–6). The Lycian "oath gods" (*tesēti*) were related to the Hittite *šiuneš linkiyaš* or *linkiyanteš* (Bryce 1986: 174). In addition, there is some evidence for the continuation of the practice of ichthyomancy (Bryce 1996: 46–7; Lefèvre-Novaro and Mouton 2008).

ancestor cult (cf. Nişantepe in Map 3), along with the Stone House.[114] Shrines in high places cut out of the living rock were also characteristic of the Phrygians,[115] showing a continuation of the value invested in rocky high places more generally in Anatolia. Lycians used a variety of mortuary monuments among which were pillar tombs and elaborate rock-cut tombs built into cliffs designed to look like houses,[116] which may have signaled the eschatological belief that certain privileged dead ascended to the sky rather than whiling away their afterlife in the underworld. The extant examples all date to a time well after Homer, but the rock pillar tombs imitate lost wooden precursors, tracing out the characteristic joinery,[117] so it is not surprising none is extant before the sixth century.[118] Calvert Watkins suggests that the Homeric expression "tomb and stele" refers precisely to these monuments with the tomb placed on top of the pillar.[119]

Thus, some Lycian monuments represent an Iron Age Anatolian mortuary practice with roots in the Late Bronze Age, as do possibly the Gygaean monument as a descendant of the House of Grandfathers, and certainly Mopsus' *ḥešti*-house in Cilicia. The evidence from the *Iliad* and that involving Mopsus support the claim that there was a pattern of using shared Greco-Anatolian heroes to assert relationships among groups of people, both Greek and indigenous, across relatively long distances within Anatolia in the eighth and seventh centuries BCE, presumably for political or military alliances. These heroic figures also make an appearance in Greek epic. In the case of the Lycian heroes Glaucus and Sarpedon, we do not have evidence for mortuary rites directed towards them contemporary to their incorporation into Greek epic, although the fact that it is precisely Sarpedon's death scene that has Near Eastern antecedents supports the claim that narratives about Lycian heroes informed rites of ancestor veneration. And, I have shown that in the case of Mopsus, although the Clarian/Cilician hero is not attested in Homeric epic, there is indirect evidence that he was the recipient of ancestor veneration, embedded in which there were performances of narratives that had some features shared with Homeric epic, at a time roughly contemporary to its

---

[114] See Chapter 7, 152–3.
[115] Shrines to Matar Kubeleya carved in living rock on mountaintops: Berndt-Ersöz (2006: 144–6).
[116] Benda-Weber (2005: 74–75, 77, with earlier references), Hülden (2006: 340–3).
[117] Muhlbauer (2007).
[118] On the various types of tombs built by the Lycians see Benda-Weber (2005: 72–9), Hülden (2006), and Keen (1998: 182–92).
[119] Watkins (2008: 137).

Panionic stage.[120] The archaeological evidence, while not conclusive, certainly supports the conclusion that this practice played a contributing role in motivating and creating milieus allowing for the transfer of epic motifs and traditions from bards performing in Anatolian languages to Greek bards, certainly in the period in which the Lycian heroes Glaucus and Sarpedon made their way into the story of the *Iliad* (prior to the eighth century BCE?) if not earlier.

Apollo's role in the transfer and transmission of the *Iliad*

As a final contribution to the study of the prehistory of Homer's *Iliad*, I argue that the popularity of Apollo's cult in Anatolia played an essential role in the dissemination of the story of the fall of Troy. Although Zeus is mentioned as the prime mover in the opening lines of the *Iliad*, it is Apollo who is singled out as the god at home in Anatolia, and it is he who is the chief ally of the Trojans – an historically accurate depiction.

The opening lines of two variant versions of the *Iliad*, considered by the Alexandrian editors to be older than the version we have, show that Apollo played, if anything, a more important role than in the version preserved for us. One mentions him as the chief subject of the epic: "I sing the Muses and Apollo famed for his bow." The other pairs Achilles and Apollo as sharing top billing: "Now accompany me, Muses, who occupy Olympian homes, how in fact did wrath and anger seize the son of Peleus, and the shining son of Leto, for he, angered with the king..."[121] Nagy argues that the *Iliad* we have is a later version that takes as its divine subject Zeus, "as the ultimate cause of the story of the Trojan War," because our *Iliad* was the property of the Homeridae, who Pindar said typically began their performances with a *prooimion* to Zeus.[122]

---

[120] On the Gygaean monument see Chapter 14, 375. See Chapter 12, 318–19, on Mopsus migrating from Clarus to Cilicia. On Mopsus' *ḫešti*-house see Chapter 14, 382–3.

[121] Μούσας ἀείδω καὶ Ἀπόλλωνα κλυτότοξον (*Archaia Ilias*, ed. Montanari 1979: 56). ἔσπετε νῦν μοι Μοῦσαι Ὀλύμπια δώματ' ἔχουσαι/ ὅππως δὴ μῆνίς τε χόλος θ' ἕλε Πηλείωνα/ Λητοῦς τ' ἀγλαὸν υἱόν· ὃ γὰρ βασιλῆϊ χολωθείς ... (*Ilias Homerica in Cyclum Inclusa*, ed. Bernabé 1987: 64). Edition and translation also included in West (2003b: 454–5). See Cerri (2002: 16), Marks (2002: 17, n. 40), Nagy (2010: 109–10).

[122] Pi. *N.* 2.1–3; Nagy (2010: 104–5; 121; quoted here). As Ann Suter suggests to me (written communication, March 2014), an alternative explanation for the new prominence of Zeus in the opening of the *Iliad* would be the process of Olympianization, as seen in the *Homeric Hymn to Demeter*, in which Zeus was added as the prime mover of the action in a frame around the original story; see Suter (2002: 23–48) and Clay (2006) discussing more generally the process of Olympianization of the *Homeric Hymns*.

[T]he *arkhaia Ilias* 'Old *Iliad*' is without a Plan of Zeus. Although both the older and the newer *Iliad* attribute the causality of events to Apollo – it all happened because the god was angry at King Agamemnon – the newer *Iliad* subsumes the divine agency of Apollo under the divine agency represented by the Plan of Zeus, whereas the older *Iliad* does not.[123]

In fact it may be that in early versions Apollo's anger was not about Agamemnon's refusal to return Chryseis to her father, but about the attack on his prized city. I therefore surmise that Apollo took on the role of the Storm-god in the *Song of Release* when the epic storyline of a city destroyed when its assembly refused to release certain captives was first applied to Troy.

Christopher Faraone has recently argued that the opening of the *Iliad*, which I have shown is a miniature version of the story of the punishment visited on Troy because its assembly refused to release Helen,[124] was adapted from a hymn to Apollo Smintheus, a plague god who, according to Chryses, was worshipped at Tenedos (*Il.* 1.38). As Faraone points out, there are some interesting inconsistencies in the characterization of Achilles, who here supports Chryses, the priest of Apollo Smintheus, and Calchas, while "everywhere else in the poem [Achilles] seems to be an implacable enemy of the god."[125] Calchas as an augur able to explain how to cure the plague that has attacked the Achaean host had a special association with Apollo in his Anatolian LAMMA-god form. Furthermore, Calchas (or Chryses) could represent a type of performer based at Apollo's shrine in Tenedos who was in demand for his esoteric knowledge by stricken communities. Thus, this episode could have been alluded to or performed in healing rituals, as I have shown other narrative songs were in Bronze Age Anatolia,[126] and that is one way it

---

[123] Nagy (2010: 111). Nagy (2010: 117–19) goes on to argue that the invocation of Apollo should be considered "Orphic." Obviously, that interpretation does not fit with the analysis proposed here.

[124] Chapter 6, 139–42, and Bachvarova (2005a: 143).

[125] Faraone (forthcoming). Faraone goes on to note inconsistencies in content and form with the rest of the *Iliad*, which have good parallels in the hymnic corpus. M. L. West (2011: 66), who considers the opening to belong to the earliest stratum of P's *Iliad*, notes, Apollo "only emerges as the city god of Troy towards the end of ∏." The term *Smintheus* was taken to mean "mouse-god" by the D scholia on *Il.* 1.39 (= Apollonius Sophista 143, 9), and therefore relevant to Apollo's role as plague god (see Faraone forthcoming, citing Faraone 1992: 128–32), but note that the term appears apparently as an ethnonym in the Theban Linear B texts and Strabo knows of several Anatolian places called Sminthia (see Chapter 10, 231, n. 63). Thus, I agree with Aristarchus that the term was geographic (Σ D *ad Il.* 1.39), see Kirk 1985: 57), although I do not deny the relevance of the folk etymology here.

[126] Chapter 4, 81–4, 96–9, and Chapter 9, 213–17.

could have been well known outside of Tenedos and therefore considered worth incorporating into our *Iliad*.

Following Gregory Nagy's principle that "the god who presides over the given festival that serves as the setting for the performance of that given epic will be named as the primary god of the *prooimion*,"[127] we should look for a festival of Apollo as the setting for public performances of a version of the *Iliad* that opened by presenting Apollo as the prime mover of the action. In his prayer calling on Apollo to punish the Achaeans Chryses lists two other localities besides Tenedos, presumably on the Troad, at which Apollo is worshipped, his own hometown of Chryse and Cilla:

> Hear me, silver-bowed one, you who haunt Chryse and Cilla and rule very holy Tenedos with strength, Smintheus, if ever I roofed over a shrine pleasing to you, or if ever I burned fatty thigh pieces of bulls and goats, grant my wish. May the Danaans pay for my tears with your weapons. [128]

The list gives us a sense of a circuit of shrines that poets whose repertoire included a song or songs suitable for the worship of a western Anatolian version of Apollo could visit profitably. Another suitable venue might have been at a festival of the Aeolian Dodecapolis, which had come into existence before the eighth century, when Smyrna was taken from it by the Ionians. The other eleven cities were Cyme, Larissa, Neon Teichos, Temnus, Cilla, Notium, Aegiroessa, Pitane, Aigai, Myrina, and Gryneum.[129] While Neon Ilion was not a member, Gryneum was later known for its shrine to Apollo, and Strabo mentions a temple of Cillaean Apollo, located in the same Cilla referred to by Chryses, we may assume. Strabo further states that a sanctuary for Cillaean Apollo was founded by the Aeolians at Colonae when they first arrived in Anatolia as well as at Chryse.[130] A collaborative competitive performance of an extended version of the story of the fall of Troy at a major festival would allow a poet whose most well-received performance piece was the episode with which our *Iliad* now starts to kick off the competition with an adapted version of

---

[127] Nagy (2010: 105). That is, the epic performance would begin with an invocation of the appropriate god. Many of the invocations of gods preserved in the Homeric corpus are only a few lines long, calling on the deity to look upon the poet about to embark on his task with favor (Nagy 2010: 106–8). See Maslov (2012: 198) on the meaning of *prooimion* as "opening prayer, invocation."

[128] *Il.* 1.37–42.   [129] Hdt. 1.149, Str. 13.3.5.

[130] Str. 13.1.62, giving the locations of Chryse and Cilla. The shrine at Gryneum is first mentioned in the middle of the third century in an inscription of a treaty between Smyrna and Magnesia from the reign of Seleucus II (Robert 1962: 86–7).

his virtuoso hymn in honor of Apollo Smintheus drawing on the plot of the *Song of Release* and replicating the plot of the fall of Troy in miniature.

In fact, one way that Milesians would have been made familiar with the story of the fall of Troy would be at their own festivals for their chief god Apollo. The Panionia then would have incorporated the performance of an epic about the fall of Troy because it had already become well known at Miletus through performances relating to the cult of Apollo, even though according to later sources the Panionia celebrated Poseidon.[131] That is, the transfer from the Troad to Miletus occurred within the context of Apollo's festival circuit, just as the cult of Delian Apollo promoted the transfer of Anatolian songs to Greece.

After the opening books, Apollo comes to the fore again in Book 16, with its pivotal scenes of the return of Patroclus to the battlefield, the death of Sarpedon at his hands, and the resulting death of Patroclus at the hands of Hector and his Trojan companions. He protects not only the Trojans but also the Lycians, and he is acknowledged as a Lycian god. While it makes perfect sense for Apollo to be heavily involved with the Trojans, scholars have been hard-pressed to explain his involvement with the Lycians here.[132] I choose to take Glaucus' characterization of Apollo as a Lycian god seriously, and I see him as a key connecting thread between the two storylines, the larger story about Troy and the traditional scene of the death of the Lycian hero Sarpedon, transposed to this new context.

The link made by the poet is evident in the twist on the conventional "come from wherever you are" opening of Glaucus' prayer to Apollo to staunch his wound so that he can lead the fight for his cousin's body: "Hear, lord, you who are somewhere in the fertile land of Lycia or in Troy; you are able to listen everywhere to a man who suffers, as now suffering has

---

[131] Thus, there may be a kernel of truth behind Vitruvius' assertion that the Ionians when they arrived in Anatolia first built a temple to Apollo Panionius (4.1.5), although Herda (2006b: 57–8) points out that Vitruvius is probably referring to a later temple of Apollo Panionius at Clarus.

[132] Bryce (1983: 11), for example, discounts the significance of Apollo's connection with the Lycian heroes. Janko (1992: 372), referring to Cilician shrines for Apollo and Artemis Sarpedonius (D.S. 32.10.2, Str. 14.5.19): "Apollo Sarpedonios may be a syncretism based on a Cretan and Anatolian god, akin to 'Lykian' Apollo . . .; hence perhaps the role of Sarpedon's brother Apollo in sending him to Lykia." Lateiner (2002: 58): Apollo is a "Panhellenic patron of hero-cults". Clay (2009: 37) appeals to "his function as god of limits, more particularly the limits between mortality and immortality, between gods and men."

come on me."¹³³ Apollo then goes on to obey his father Zeus' command to rescue the body of his half-brother Sarpedon and make him presentable for burial before Sleep and Death return him to Lycia (16.666–84). Certainly in this section there is much made of brotherly relationships, from the two Neleids who slay the sons of Amisodarus, and the "twin brothers" (*didumaosin*, 16.672, 674) Sleep and Death, to the mention of the (other) brothers of Sarpedon, who will duly bury him (16.456, 682). This gives some motivation for Apollo's role, since he is the half-brother of Sarpedon. And, is it pure coincidence that Sleep and Death are called by a kin term that brings to mind Didyma? Apollo next appears on the battlefield to stop Patroclus' onrush against Troy, then takes on the form of Asius, the brother of Hecuba, to urge Hector against Patroclus according to Apollo's wish. (The name Asius or 'Asian' pointedly calls attention to Apollo's pan-Anatolian cult.) Apollo continues to intervene directly in the final moments of Patroclus' life, even slapping off his helmet and corselet so that the Achaean is left exposed to the Trojans' attack.¹³⁴ The entire Book 16 of the *Iliad* thus reads as the product of a poet particularly interested in incorporating one or more Anatolian-oriented storylines appealing to a Milesian audience, who takes advantage of the festival setting in which he is performing, a festival for Apollo.¹³⁵

Conclusion

In sum, we can distinguish Anatolian influence on the following layers in the development of the story of the *Iliad*, schematized in Table 4: there was a Luwian song about "steep Wilusa," extant in the Bronze Age, but perhaps not interacting with the Greek tradition until much later. Possibly the silver bowl with the Hieroglyphic Luwian inscription mentioning Tudhaliya I/II's victory over Tarwiza shows that the fall of this important west Anatolian city was already the stuff of legend in the Late Bronze Age.

---

[133] *Il.* 16.513–16. For the "come from wherever you are" opening, see M. L. West (2007: 318–23) discussing Indo-European invocations, M. L. West (1997a: 272, 589) on Near Eastern invocations, and Bachvarova (2009: 29–31) on parallels between Hittite and Greek invocations.

[134] *Il.* 16.698–801. Janko (1992: 408–10) explains the involvement of Apollo in the death of Patroclus as paralleling Achilles' death at the hands of Apollo and Paris.

[135] Why was Apollo allowed to remain such an important character in the Panhellenic *Iliad*, and why in the Panhellenic *Odyssey* did the final scenes at Odysseus' house occur in the context of a festival of Apollo (*Od.* 20.149–56, 276–8, 21.258–68)? On the latter see Levaniouk (2011). As Larson (2000: 210–22) has argued, the divinity was particularly cultivated by the Peisistratids.

When the Phrygians arrived at Troy, it may be that they began to use traditional Anatolian storylines to create a shared history about a contested past with the local inhabitants. Certainly, a Greek story taking place "in front of Ilium" was already extant at the very beginning of the Iron Age migrations. The elements of Achilles' storyline that were patterned after Gilgamesh could have developed independently of the story of Troy, in Thessaly in the context of contacts with the Near East mediated by Cyprus, but his story was eventually merged with the story of the fall of Troy. Hector has Boeotian connections and possibly had a story separate from that of the Trojan War before he was equated with the Trojan leader, but what its plot was we do not know beyond the fact that it involved single combats with local rivals. Thus, some elements of the characters of Achilles and Hector should be associated with the Aeolic contribution to the Greco-Anatolian story, vestiges of a prestigious Aeolic tradition brought over from Greece that was eventually eclipsed by the Ionic one. The specific plot line that was patterned after the *Song of Release* was one Anatolian contribution to that Greek epic tradition, merged with a Greco-Aryan epic storyline about bride-stealing. Hector, on the other hand, was featured in another epic tradition about the fall of Troy – possibly an Ionian one. This story of the fall of Troy telling of doings inside Ilium was patterned after Naram-Sin's story, with Hector taking the Sargonic king's place. This second Anatolian contribution to the Greek epic tradition about Troy crossed to Greek-speaking poets well before the eighth century, but it was merged with a pro-Greek version focused on Achilles at a relatively late stage. It had far-reaching effects on the Homeric plot line, which was reworked to culminate in his death, while the pro-Lycian components introduced in Miletus seem like relatively superficial additions to an already well-established plot line, introduced in the same setting of a festival honoring Apollo that allowed for the emphasis on the Greco-Anatolian god in the opening section of Homer's epic. In the crucible of competition among poets in festival contexts, the various versions of the *Iliad* and ancillary stories, originally in different Greek dialects and Anatolian languages, were fused together to create the *Iliad* that has proved to be one of the foundational texts of Western culture.

Table 4. *Layers of Anatolian influence on the* Iliad *and the* Odyssey

Date	External circumstances	Stage of Iliadic tradition	Stage of Odyssean tradition
		TROJAN STAGE	
	Wilusiad in Istanuwa festival; silver bowl mentioning destruction of Taruisa.	Troy already the subject of Anatolian cultural memory beyond the Troad.	
		Memories of Alaksandu and Apollo retained from the Bronze Age.	
1180	Troy's Bronze Age walls treated as cult place, locus of cultural memory, by Anatolians	Incoming Phrygians and resident Trojans begin to use traditional storylines about the destruction of a city to explain their contemporary relations.	
1160–1050	Post-palatial period in Greece. Speakers of Aeolic dialect visit Troy, are aware of Troy as symbol of lost glorious Bronze Age.	AEOLIC STAGE	
		Aeolic epic tradition, in which the heroes Achilles and Hector were featured, incorporates an Anatolian storyline about Troy.	
		One or more Anatolian storylines about destructions of famous cities can cross to Greek bards:	
		Destruction of city because assembly does not release captive(s); leader could be portrayed positively, e.g., *Song of Release*.	
		Leader fails to obey omens of gods, city is attacked by foreign invaders.	
		Two possible instantiations: one sympathetic to leader of city under attack, the other unsympathetic to the ruler; both versions sympathetic to the plight of the city-dwellers.	
		Leader refuses to keep troops safe inside city walls, but is sympathetically portrayed, e.g., *Cuthean-Legend of Naram-Sin*.	
		Leader is impious, city is punished, e.g., *Curse of Akkade*.	

Table 4. (cont.)

Date	External circumstances	Stage of Iliadic tradition	Stage of Odyssean tradition
after 1050	Mycenaean ruins treated as sites of ancestor veneration. Contraction of adjacent vowels in hiatus. Isomoraic dactylic hexameter verse invented by Ionic poets. Competition between Aeolians and Ionians for Troad.	Story about Achilles' anger influenced by the Gilgamesh tradition, possibly by contact via Cyprus reaching mainland Greece, the influence eventually reaching Iliadic tradition in Troad through bards moving back and forth from mainland to Troad. Song tradition about Troy picked up by East Ionic bards. Episode about Sminthian Apollo of Tenedos and Chryses makes use of *Song of Release* storyline (perhaps not yet part of the story about Troy).	A pre-existing Odyssean epic, embodying values of warrior-traders, is influenced in mainland Greece and/or Euboea by Sargon and Gilgamesh traditions via Cyprus. The stories of Odysseus' wanderings and the fall of Troy are linked.
		IONIC STAGE	
	Ionian bards perform episodes from the larger story about the destruction of Troy at Miletus during major festival(s) for Apollo that attract non-local performers.	East Ionic bards begin to dominate the Iliadic tradition. In the Homeric tradition Carians (of Miletus) are major allies of Trojans, portrayed negatively. Catalog of Trojans composed for this *Iliad*. Episode about Sminthian Apollo of Tenedos and Chryses can be incorporated into Homeric tradition about the fall of Troy by a bard traveling the circuit of festivals in honor of Apollo.	Cyclops story absorbs Caucasian elements (one-eyed monster). *Katabasis* at Straits of Kerch attached to Odysseus.
800	Hector of Chios. Local Greco-Anatolian dynasties are linking themselves to both sets of participants in Trojan War.	Sympathetic portrayal of Hector, following storyline of *Cuthean Legend of Naram-Sin*, already extant in the Greek epic traditions about Troy, can be incorporated into the Homeric tradition by Ionian bards and combined with Achilles' story.	

		MILESIAN STAGE
		In the context of an Apolline festival patronized by ruling families of Miletus who consider themselves descended from Sarpedon and Glaucus, the already well-known Lycian heroes are incorporated into an already well-established Homeric tradition about fall of Troy, requiring some distortion of their timeline. They replace the Carians as chief allies of the Trojans and are portrayed positively.
		PANIONIC STAGE
ca. 700	Melia destroyed; Panionia already in existence.	Monumental *Iliad* begins to take shape in context of the multi-day Panionia festival.
	Midas marries the daughter of Agamemnon of Aeolian Cyme.	Neleid patrons influence the Iliadic tradition.
		Monumental *Odyssey* begins to take shape.
		Neleid patrons influence Odyssean tradition.
		Anatolian versions of the Cyclops and *katabasis* episodes added as a block within the Phaeacian episode to Homeric tradition.
720–690	Nestor's Cup	Nestor featured in internationally famous version(s) of Ionic hexametric epic.
		→ Neleids have exerted influence on supralocal epic tradition.
		→ Panionic influence on Greek epic already begun.
end 6th cent.	Panionium at Güzelçamlı (Mykale); Poseidon chief god of Panionic League, having replaced Apollo.	

Appendix | Contraction and the dactylic hexameter

To understand fully the significance of the use of the uncontracted form *I-li-o-o pro-pa-roi-then* 'before Ilion', scanned -⏑⏑-⏑⏑-⌣,[1] for our understanding of the date by which an epic about Troy was first composed requires some explanation of the development of the dactylic hexameter.[2] The hexameter is derivable from metrical cola inherited from Greco-Aryan verse,[3] with the important change in prosody from syllable-counting to

---

[1] ⏑ = short syllable, - = long syllable, ⏔ = biceps (optionally double short or single long); -⏔ = dactyl, -⏑⏑- = choriamb, x = anceps (optionally long or short), ⌣ = either a long syllable or *brevis in longo* (a short syllable treated as long because it is followed by a pause at verse end), | = caesura, || = verse end. Some lyric meters are labeled Aeolic, but is important to note that the term "Aeolic" for a particular type of versification should not be taken as an ethnic designation. See Nagy (1974; 1990b; 1992) for a diachronic analysis of lyric meters and Cole (1988) for a unified synchronic analysis of the relationship among different lyric metrical cola.

[2] Gentili and Lomiento fix the creation of the dactylic hexameter very late, to the eighth century – that is, shortly before the compositions of Homer himself – based on the fact that formulas that do not fit the dactylic hexameter appear in hexametric poetry outside of the *Iliad* and *Odyssey*, and that the cola that make up the dactylic hexameters are paired with other cola in some poetic inscriptions (Gentili and Lomiento 2008: 264–5; Gentili and Giannini 1977). Early bards outside the Homeric tradition were described as using strophic structures, analogous perhaps to those of Stesichorus, who sang stories drawn from the tradition of the Trojan War in Doric lyric stanzas ([Plu.] *Mus.* 1132b); see Gentili in Gentili and Giannini (1977) and Gentili and Lomiento (2008: 264). However, the looser metrical constructions of the early inscriptions could also be explained as the product of poets who had not received the same level of rigorous training as the Homeridae. The significance of Stesichorus' use of extended dactylo-anapestic sequences (that is, runs of double-short alternating with single long, with some contraction and resolution: ...⌣⏑⏑⌣⏑⏑⌣⏑⏑⌣⏑⏑...) depends on whether he represents an innovation, imitating Homer's meter as he uses Homer's narrative material, or an old tradition of narrative poetry, of which the dactylic hexameter is a specialized form. Haslam (1978: 56) sees Stesichorus as combining dactylo-anapestic verse types – "a prestigious member of which was the dactylic hexameter" – and iambo-trochaic. See Nagy (1990b) for a discussion of Stesichorus as representing a tradition as old as Homer. M. L. West (1971b: 313–14) sees two traditions of narrative poetry, one freer and sung, the other stichic and recited. Similar questions of influence from Homer versus independent traditions arise with Sappho F 44 Lobel-Page, telling of the wedding of Hector and Andromache, in glyconics with dactylic expansion; see Hooker (1977: 56–8, 76–8), Horrocks (1987: 272–3), and Nagy (2010: 238–41, with references to his earlier work).

[3] Meillet (1923) suggested that the dactylic hexameter of Homer's epics may have been of foreign origin. The notion is critiqued by Peabody (1975: 22–3). Ruijgh (1995: 3, 8) found the suggestion appealing and argued for a Minoan origin. On Greco-Aryan verse see Meillet (1923), Nagy

mora-counting, in which two short syllables equals one long syllable, an analogy based on the synchronic process of contraction of two vowels in hiatus.

The derivation of the hexameter I find most plausible, espoused in different variations by Gregory Nagy, Berkley Peabody, Nils Berg, Eva Tichy, Martin West, and Bruno Gentili, sees the hexameter as built from metrical cola drawn from the same pool of possibles out of which were drawn the cola found in Greek choral lyric poetry, such as the songs of Pindar and Bacchylides and in tragedy, all of which are ultimately related to Vedic verse forms.

Compare:

–⏑⏑–⏑⏑–|⏑⏑–⏑⏑–⏑⏑–⏒||

dactylic hexameter with penthemimeral caesura

with the choral lyric sequence:

–⏑⏑–⏑⏑–|x–⏑⏑–⏑⏑–⏒||

hemiepes + paroemiac (enoplion)

Compare:

–⏑⏑–⏑⏑–⏑|⏑–⏑⏑–⏑⏑–⏒||

dactylic hexameter with trochaic caesura

with the choral lyric sequence:

xx–⏑⏑–x|x–⏑⏑–⏑⏑–⏒||

pherecratean + paroemiac (enoplion)

Compare:

–⏑⏑–⏑⏑–⏑⏑–|⏑⏑–⏑⏑–⏒||

dactylic hexameter with hephthemimeral caesura

with the choral lyric sequence:

–x–x–⏑⏑–|xx–⏑⏑–⏒||

choriambic dimeter + pherecratean

Syllable-counting is the norm in early lyric poetry outside of Stesichorus.[4] The two anceps syllables that begin the eight-syllable glyconic and the

---

(1974), Peabody (1975: 24–65), M. L. West (2007: 45–51). For evidence of continuity of the poetic tradition back to the Greco-Aryan times also see Chapter 11, 266, nn. 1–2.

[4] On his metrical structures, see n. 2.

seven-syllable pherecratean, the so-called Aeolic base, originally could be realized as ⏑⏑, ⏑-, ⏑-, or --. In the transition to the dactylic hexameter, the Aeolic base was re-interpreted as a dactyl, via the double-long variant (--, treated as a dactyl with a long biceps), enhancing the sense of a line with repeating dactylic feet and moving from a syllable-counting meter to a mora-counting meter, in which a short syllable is one mora and a long syllable is two morae. A similar process would have had to occur with the lyric cola of the final example given above; the two anceps syllables in the choriambic dimeter would have to be treated as longs amenable to resolution into two shorts, while in the pherecratean the anceps syllables would be realized as two shorts. The sequence thus moved from being conceived of as two (or three) juxtaposed cola to being analyzable as a series of repeating dactyls. The metrical lengthening and "morphological stretching" (e.g., two-syllable *andres* → three-syllable *āneres*) that occur especially in the first and fourth feet are remnants of the reworking into dactyls of the Aeolic bases of each of the two cola that made up the line.[5] The caesurae, which mark word breaks and often sense breaks, were originally the seams between cola; the irregularities in the meter coalescing at edges of the caesura are the remains of the original process of building verse lines through the simple juxtaposition of the formulaic cola.[6]

But, variations of formulas that fill each of two halves of the dactylic hexameter line, fitted either around a caesura after the third longum (penthemimeral caesura), or around a caesura after the following short syllable (trochaic caesura), show that the two halves cannot be treated separately.[7] Many essential notions are expressed across the caesura in lines that cannot be separated into constituent parts. Perhaps Ari Hoekstra's statement that "the earliest narrative poetry that has left any traces in Homer was already composed in hexameters"[8] is a little too strong, but it seems impossible that the dactylic hexameter was a very late invention relative to the final developments in the Homeric formulaic systems.

---

[5] Berg and Haug (2000), Berg and Lindeman (1992).
[6] Berg (1978), Berg and Haug (2000), Berg and Lindeman (1992), Gentili and Giannini (1977), Gentili and Lomiento (2008: 262–6), Haug and Welo (2001), Peabody (1975: 45–55), M. L. West (1973: 188). For older theories see Hoekstra (1981: 39). Nagy (1974: 37–102; 1990b: 439–64; 1992; 2004: 144–56) has argued that the stiche is most comparable to a pherecratean with dactylic expansion and stresses the stiche is derived from a concatenation of separate formulaic cola, not metrical cola. He notes that formulaic cola can straddle verses.
[7] Hoekstra (1981: 33–53).   [8] Hoekstra (1981: 53).

The most important innovation that differentiated the dactylic hexameter from other Proto-Indo-European-derived Greek verse forms was thus the shift from counting syllables to counting morae,[9] caused by the equation of a long syllable with two short syllables. But, the time in which the twenty-four-mora dactylic hexameter (counting the final two syllables as four morae) came into being is a matter of debate. Certainly some phrases referring to Mycenaean-era objects are in uncontracted dactylic hexameters,[10] and some scholars trace the meter back to the second millennium BCE.[11] But, if we believe that it is warranted to reconstruct Mycenaean-era forms for Homeric formulas, then we must accept either that the dactylic pattern had not yet been fully established, or that contraction (substituting one long syllable for two shorts) was already established, since some of the reconstructed formulas have iambo-trochaic sequences (single-short rather than double-short between longs: ⏑-x-, with long anceps) embedded within them, not just falling at colon edge, for example:

Diī mētin atalantos = Mycenaean *Diwei mētin hatalantos*[12]
⏑- - -⏑⏑-⏓||
"equal to Zeus in intelligence"
hierē is Tēlemakhoio = Mycenaean *hierā wīs Tēlemakhoyyo*[13]
⏑⏑- - -⏑⏑-⏓||
"holy strength of Telemachos"

In the first example, the third syllable is either a long anceps, in a single-short sequence, or a contracted biceps. In the second example, the fourth syllable must be analyzed in the same way. If the first analysis is chosen, the cola have a single long anceps within the phrase, not at its edge. If the second analysis is chosen, substitution of a double-short sequence for a single long syllable has occurred. I argue that the former option, which requires that the mora-counting dactylic hexameter had not yet been codified in the Mycenaean era, is the more likely. To treat the above formulas as dactylic with contraction, rather than eight- or nine-syllable

---

[9] See Peabody (1975: 28–9) on the fundamental importance of syllable-counting in Indo-Iranian verse. The replacement is also found in Stesichorus: see Nagy (1990b: 452–3). Also see n. 2 here.
[10] Janko (1992: 10–11). Also see Chapter 11, 266, n. 1.
[11] So M. L. West (1973: 188, "rather looser in technique"; 1997b: 234), Ruijgh (1985: 162–3). Criticized by Berg and Haug (2000), Berg and Lindeman (1992), and Haug (2002: 62–7). Also see the discussions of Barnes (2011) and Maslov (2011) offering differing explanations of the forms with metrical anomalies that have been used to defend the great antiquity of the dactylic hexameter.
[12] *Il.* 2.169, 407, 636, 7.47, 11.200, 10.137. Also see the interpretation of Watkins (1987a: 729–30).
[13] *Od.* 2.409, 16.476, 18.60, 405, 21.101, 130, 22.354.

cola modulating between double-short and single-short rhythm, we would have to suppose that this contraction was an allowable process. But, it should be assumed that the analogy of two shorts equaling one long only became productive during the period when two short vowels in hiatus began to undergo contraction to a single long vowel in the spoken language.[14] This is when the dactylic hexameter as presently known would have come into being, the composition technique changing from the rhythm being determined by phrases to the phrases being generated to fit into a specific rhythm.

The degree to which we can pin down when contraction of two adjacent vowels in hiatus began in the vernacular would thus affect the judgment about when the Homeric verse was created. Unfortunately, only a rough guess can be made.[15] Although Linear B does not show contraction, Antonin Bartoněk is right to doubt that the codified Linear B writing system, attestations of which cover at least 150 years and a very wide area (*ca.* 1400 BCE for the Room of the Chariot Tablets in Knossos, to *ca.* 1200 BCE in Thessaly and the Peloponnese) with only minor changes or dialect differences,[16] accurately reflects the spoken language.[17] On the other hand, the contraction found in all first-millennium dialects of Greek can for the most part be explained as simply a parallel innovation that took effect after dialect differentiation.

Contraction occurred at different times for different sets of vowels and depending on the consonant lost between the vowels (*y*, *s*>*h*, *w*), and therefore had different rates of appearance in Homer's text. For example, *e* + *e* contraction is rare, although a fairly large number cannot be resolved,[18]

---

[14] Allen (1973: 255–9; 1987: 113–14), Nagy (1974: 49–56). See Peabody (1975: 44–5) on how the sandhi rules of Sanskrit allowed for a similar substitution of one long syllable for two short ones, effecting a significant change in versification techniques in Sanskrit poetry, as opposed to Vedic. Peabody (1975: 55–64) argues that elision of vowels in short syllables, creating consonant clusters, similarly allowed for the equivalence of one long syllable and two shorts in Greek verse; he does not refer to the Ionic process of contraction of two short vowels in hiatus, dating the development to an earlier stage of the language.

[15] See discussion of Kirk (1962: 196–201).

[16] On morphological variation in Linear B, see Hajnal (2007: 148–53, with earlier references); note, however, that he is discussing sets of variants that only later were selected by different dialects, so they may not have been linked at this stage with a specific dialect. Bartoněk (2003: 451, 454–7, 462–3, 477–83, 488–9, with earlier references) discusses dialect variation in Mycenaean.

[17] As Bartoněk (1966: 71) notes, *e* + *e* and *o* + *o* contractions could have started as soon as the last quarter of the second millennium, with the loss of intervocalic *y* and *s* (> *h* in Mycenaean), even if it is not visible in the Linear B texts; and even if in Homer contractions are often not metrical.

[18] Chantraine (1958: 38–43).

while $o + o$ is always written as contracted to *-ou* (/ō/), although in some cases, as in *Iliou proparoithen*, the bisyllabic value needs to be restored.[19]

Two contractions allow us to make some comments on relative dating. First, the change $a + e > \bar{a}$ has to be after the Attic-Ionic change of $\bar{a} > \bar{e}$, which happened between the first compensatory lengthening (**ephansa* > *ephāna* > Att.-Ion. *ephēna*) and the second compensatory lengthening (**pantya* > *pansa* > Att.-Ion. *pāsa*, Lesb. *paisa*). Many date the change of $\bar{a}$ to $\bar{e}$ by referring to the Ionic term *Mēdos*, corresponding to Iranian *Mādā*, which could imply $\bar{a} > \bar{e}$ after first contact with the Medes, surely not before 800 BCE,[20] but this assumes that the foreign vowel would have been taken as a Greek $\bar{a}$, unfortunately not a safe assumption.[21]

Bartoněk, on the other hand, puts the closing of the long mid vowel space to 900 BCE, "probably due to the substratum influence of non-Greek languages spoken in Asia Minor, and maybe partly also in connection with considerable overloading in the back long-vowel row …, at first perhaps in Ionia but soon after also in the other Attic-Ionic areas."[22] Beginning with this date, he places the second compensatory lengthening in the ninth century.[23] The parallel development in both Attic and Ionic would be the result of drift or of continued close ties across the Mediterranean, as shown by shared clan names, festivals, and calendars.[24]

In the end, however, the dating of the second compensatory lengthening to the end of the second millennium or beginning of the first millennium is most logical,[25] around the time of the split between Attic and Ionic. I will accept a conventional date of *ca.* 1050 BCE for this event, based on the appearance of Early Protogeometric pottery in Anatolia. Thus, it is difficult to push the contraction of $a + e$ much before the period when the dialect split. In Homer *a*-stem verbs sometimes show contraction, sometimes not (*-a-e* versus *-ā*, *-a-eis* versus *-āis*, *-a-ei* versus *-āi*), and some of the contracted forms can be restored to their uncontracted percursors. "Still," Pierre Chantraine notes, "the number of forms that cannot be uncontracted remains large. In formulas that seem old the meter requires that the contracted form be kept."[26]

---

[19] Chantraine (1958: 44–8). [20] Horrocks (1997: 216–17), Kirk (1962: 197; 1985: 7).
[21] See Szemerényi (1968: 145) and Chapter 3, 55, n. 8. [22] Bartoněk (1966: 101).
[23] Bartoněk (1966: 104). Sihler (1995: 51) puts it at *ca.* 800 BCE. [24] See Chapter 10, 234–6.
[25] So Rau (2010: 178).
[26] Chantraine (1958: 51–2): "Toutefois le nombre des formes irréductibles reste grande. Dans des formules qui semblent anciennes le métrique impose de maintenir la form contracte."

On the other hand, the contraction of *e* + *o* occurs fairly often in Homer, although it varies according to the morphology involved.[27] It has differing results in Attic from in east Ionic, the monophthong /ō/ (spelled ου) in Attic and the diphthong *eu* in East Ionic, which shows that the contraction took place separately in Attic in the time after the Ionians left the mainland to settle in Anatolia.[28] Thus, the poetic equation of a single long syllable with two short syllables is likely to have become possible not long before the beginning of the Protogeometric period and definitely exploitable no sooner than shortly after that, and the Greek epic about Achaeans attacking Troy needs to have been in existence before then.

[27] Chantraine (1958: 58–63).   [28] Kirk (1962: 197; 1985: 6–7).

References

Abusch, I. T. (1974) "Mesopotamian anti-witchcraft literature: Texts and studies Part I: The nature of *Maqlû*: Its character, divisions, and calendrical setting," *Journal of Near Eastern Studies* 33: 251–62.

Adiego, I. J. (2007) *The Carian Language*. Leiden and Boston.

Adrados, F. R. (1981) "Towards a new stratigraphy of the Homeric dialect," *Glotta* 59: 13–27.

(2005) *A History of the Greek Language: From Its Origins to the Present*. Leiden and Boston.

Ahrens, A., E. Kozal, C. Kümmel, I. Laube and M. Novák (2008) "Sirkeli Höyük – Kulturkontakte in Kilikien: Vorbericht über die Kampagnen 2006 and 2007 der deutsch-türkischen Mission," *Istanbuler Mitteilungen* 58: 67–107.

Akurgal, E. (1962) *The Art of the Hittites*. London.

Allen, W. S. (1973) *Accent and Rhythm: Prosodic Features of Latin and Greek: A Study in Theory and Reconstruction*. Cambridge Series in Linguistics 12. Cambridge.

(1987) *Vox graeca*. 3rd edn. Cambridge.

Aloni, A. (2006) *Da Pilo a Sigeo: Poemi, cantori e scrivani al tempo dei tiranni*. Alessandria.

Alparslan, M. (2005) "Einige Überlegungen zur Ahhiyawa-Frage," in *V. Uluslararası Hititoloji Kongresi bildirileri: Çorum, 02–08 Eylül 2002, Acts of the Vth International Congress of Hittitology: Çorum, September 02–08, 2002*, ed. Y. Hazırlayan and A. Süel. Ankara. 33–41.

Alster, B. (1992) "Interaction of oral and written poetry in early Mesopotamian literature," in *Mesopotamian Epic Literature: Oral or Aural?*, ed. M. E. Vogelzang and H. L. J. Vanstiphout. Lewiston, N.Y., Queenston, Ont., and Lampeter. 23–70.

(2002) "*ilū awīlum : we-e i-la*, 'gods : men' versus 'man : god': Punning and the reversal of patterns in the Atrahasis epic," in *Riches Hidden in Secret Places: Ancient Near Eastern Studies in Memory of Thorkild Jacobsen*, ed. T. Abusch. Winona Lake, Ind. 35–40.

(2005) *Wisdom of Ancient Sumer*. Bethesda, Md.

Alster, B. and T. Oshima (2007) "Sargonic dinner at Kaneš: The Old Assyrian Sargon Legend," *Iraq* 69: 1–20.

Annus, A. (1999) "Are there Greek rephaim? On the etymology of Greek Meropes and Titanes," *Ugarit-Forschungen* 31: 13–30.

(2002) *The God Ninurta in the Mythology and Royal Ideology of Ancient Mesopotamia*. Helsinki.
Anthony, D. W. (2007) *The Horse, the Wheel, and Language: How Bronze-Age Riders from the Eurasian Steppes Shaped the Modern World*. Princeton, N. J.
Antonaccio, C. M. (1994a) "The archaeology of ancestors," in *Cultural Poetics in Archaic Greece: Cult, Performance, Politics*, ed. C. Dougherty and L. Kurke. Cambridge and New York. 46–70.
  (1994b) "Contesting the past: Hero cult, tomb cult, and epic in early Greece," *American Journal of Archaeology* 98: 389–419.
  (1995) *An Archaeology of Ancestors: Tomb Cult and Hero Cult in Early Greece*. Lanham, Md. and London.
  (1999) "Colonization and the origins of hero cult," in *Ancient Greek Hero Cult: Proceedings of the Fifth International Seminar on Ancient Greek Cult, Organized by the Department of Classical Archaeology and Ancient History, Göteborg University, 21–3 April 1995*, ed. R. Hägg. Skrifter Utgivna av Svenska Institutet i Athen 8°, 16. Stockholm. 109–21.
  (2002) "Warriors, traders, and ancestors: The 'heroes' of Lefkandi," in *Images of Ancestors*, ed. J. M. Højte. Aarhus. 13–42.
Appadurai, A. (1986) "Introduction: Commodities and the politics of value," in *The Social Life of Things: Commodities in Cultural Perspective*, ed. A. Appadurai. Cambridge. 3–63.
Aravantinos, V. L., L. Godart and A. Sacconi (eds.) (2001) *Thèbes: Fouilles de la Cadmée I: Les tablettes en linéaire B de la Odos Pelopidou: Édition et commentaire*. Pisa and Rome.
Archi, A. (1973) "Fêtes de printemps et d'automne et réintégration rituelle d'images de culte dans l'Anatolie hittite," *Ugarit-Forschungen* 5: 7–27.
  (1979) "Il dio Zawalli: Sul culto dei morti presso gli Ittiti," *Altorientalische Forschungen* 6: 81–94.
  (1983) "Die Adad-Hymne ins Hethitische übersetzt," *Orientalia*, N. S. 52: 20–30.
  (1986) "Die ersten zehn Könige von Ebla," *Zeitschrift für Assyriologie und vorderasiatische Archäologie* 76: 213–17.
  (1988) "The cult of the ancestors and the tutelary god at Ebla," in *FUCUS: A Semitic/Afrasian Gathering in Remembrance of Albert Ehrman*, ed. Y. L. Arbeitman. Amsterdam Studies in the Theory and History of Linguistic Science 58. Amsterdam and Philadelphia. 103–12.
  (1990) "The names of the Primeval Gods," *Orientalia*, N. S. 59: 114–29.
  (1999) "Aleppo in the Ebla age." *Les Annales Archéologiques Arabes Syriennes* 43: 131–6.
  (2000) "Nawar-taḫe, king of Puruš ḫanda," *NABU: Nouvelles Assyriologiques Brèves et Utilitaires*: 67.
  (2001a) "The king-lists from Ebla," in *Proceedings of the XLVe Rencontre Assyriologique Internationale*. Volume I: *Historiography in the Cuneiform*

World, ed. T. Abusch, P.-A. Beaulieu, J. Huehnergard, P. Machinist and P. Steinkeller. Bethesda, Md. 1–14.

(2001b) "Star of Ebla, Megi," *NABU: Nouvelles Assyriologiques Brèves et Utilitaires*: 14–15.

(2001c) "Text forms and levels of comparison: The rituals of Emar and the Syrian tradition," in *Kulturgeschichten: Altorientalistische Studien für Volkert Haas zum 65. Geburtstag*, ed. T. Richter, D. Prechel and J. Klinger. Saarbrücken. 19–28.

(2002a) "Ea and the Beast: A song related to the Kumarpi cycle," in *Silva Anatolica: Anatolian Studies Presented to Maciej Popko on the Occasion of his 65th Birthday*, ed. P. Taracha. Warsaw. 1–10.

(2002b) "Formation of the west Hurrian pantheon: The case of Išḫara," in *Recent Developments in Hittite Archaeology and History: Papers in Memory of Hans G. Güterbock*, ed. A. Yener and H. A. Hoffner, Jr. Winona Lake, Ind. 21–33.

(2004a) "The singer of Kaneš and his gods," in *Offizielle Religion, lokale Kulte und individuelle Religiosität: Akten des religionsgeschichtlichen Symposiums "Kleinasien und angrenzende Gebiete vom Beginn des 2. bis zur Mitte des 1. Jahrtausends v. Chr." (Bonn, 20.-22. Februar 2003)*, ed. M. Hutter and S. Hutter-Braunsar. Alter Orient und Altes Testament 318. Münster. 11–26.

(2004b) "Translation of gods: Kumarpi, Enlil, Dagan/NISABA, Ḫalki," *Orientalia*, N. S. 73: 319–36.

(2007a) "The cult of royal ancestors at Hattusa and the Syrian practices," in *VITA: Belkıs Dinçol ve Ali Dinçol'a Armağan, Festschrift in Honor of Belkıs Dinçol and Ali Dinçol*, ed. M. Alparslan, M. Doğan-Alparslan and H. Peker. Istanbul. 49–55.

(2007b) "Transmission of recitative literature by the Hittites," *Altorientalische Forschungen* 34: 185–203.

(2009) "Orality, direct speech, and the Kumarbi cycle." *Altorientalische Forschungen* 36: 209–29.

(2010) "When did the Hittites begin to write in Hittite?," in *Pax Hethitica: Studies on the Hittite and Their Neighbours in Honour of Itamar Singer*, ed. Y. Cohen, A. Gilan and J. L. Miller. Studien zu den Boğazköy-Texten 51. Wiesbaden. 37–46.

Archi, A. and M. G. Biga (2003) "A victory over Mari and the fall of Ebla," *Journal of Cuneiform Studies* 55: 1–44.

Ardzinba, V. G. (1982) *Ritualy i mify drevnei Anatolii*. Moscow.

Arnott, R. (1996) "Healing and medicine in the Aegean Bronze Age," *Journal of the Royal Society of Medicine* 89: 265–70.

Aro, S. (2003) "Art and architecture," in *The Luwians*, ed. H. C. Melchert. Handbuch der Orientalistik 1.68. Leiden. 281–337.

(2009) "The origins of the artistic interactions between the Assyrian empire and north Syria revisited," in *Of God(s), Trees, Kings, and Scholars: Neo-Assyrian and Related Studies in Honour of Simo Parpola*, ed. M. Luukko, S. Svärd and R. Mattila. Helsinki. 9–17.

Arslan, N. (2003) "Zur Frage der Kolonisation Kilikiens anhand der griechischen Importkeramik," in *Griechische Keramik im kulturellen Kontext: Akten des Internationalen Vasen-Symposions in Kiel vom 24.–28.9.2001 veranstaltet durch das Archäologische Institut der Christian-Albrechts-Universität zu Kiel*, ed. B. Schmalz and M. Söldner. Münster. 258–61.

Aslan, C. C. (2002) "Ilion before Alexander: Protogeometric, Geometric, and Archaic pottery from D9," *Studia Troica* 12: 81–130.

(2009a) "End or beginning? The Late Bronze Age to Iron Age transformation at Troia," in *Forces of Transformation: The End of the Bronze Age in the Mediterranean: Proceedings of an International Symposium Held at St. John's College, University of Oxford 25–6th March 2006*, ed. C. Bachhuber and R. G. Roberts. Oxford. 144–51.

(2009b) "Gray ware at Troy in the Protogeometric through Archaic periods," in *Pontic Grey Wares, International Conference, Bucarest – Constantza, September 30th – October 3rd 2008*, ed. A. Avram. Pontica XLII Supplement I. Constanța. 267–83.

(2009c) "New evidence for a destruction at Troia in the mid 7th century B. C.," *Studia Troica* 18: 33–58.

(2011) "A Place of Burning: Hero or ancestor cult at Troy," *Hesperia* 80: 381–429.

Aslan, C. C., L. Kealhofer and P. Grave (2014) "The Early Iron Age at Troy reconsidered," *Oxford Journal of Archaeology* 33: 275–312.

Aslan, C. C. and C. B. Rose (2013) "City and citadel at Troy from the Late Bronze Age through the Roman period," in *Cities and Citadels in Turkey: From the Iron Age to the Seljuks*, ed. S. Redford and N. Ergin. Leuven, Paris and Walpole, Mass. 7–38.

Assmann, J. (2003) "Cultural memory: Script, recollection and political identity in early civilizations," *Historiography East and West* 2: 154–77.

(2008) "Communicative and cultural memory," in *Cultural Memory Studies: An International and Interdisciplinary Handbook*, ed. A. Erll and A. Nünning. Berlin and New York. 109–18.

Astour, M. C. (1964) "Second millennium B. C. Cypriot and Cretan onomastica reconsidered," *Journal of the American Oriental Society* 84: 240–54.

(1965) *Hellenosemitica: An Ethnic and Cultural Study in West Semitic Impact on Mycenaean Greece*. 2nd edn. Leiden.

(1992) "The date of the destruction of Palace G at Ebla," in *New Horizons in the Study of Ancient Syria*, ed. M. W. Chavalas and J. L. Hayes. Bibliotheca Mesopotamica 25. Malibu. 23–39.

(2002) "A reconstruction of the history of Ebla (Part 2)," in *Eblaitica: Essays on the Ebla Archives and Eblaite Language*. Volume IV, ed. C. H. Gordon and G. A. Rendsburg. Winona Lake, Ind. 57–196.

Åström, P. and E. Masson (1982) "A silver bowl with Canaanite inscription from Hala Sultan Tekké," *Report of the Department of Antiquities, Cyprus*: 72–6.

Attinger, P. (1984) "Enki et Ninḫursaĝa," *Zeitschrift für Assyriologie und vorderasiatische Archäologie* 74: 1-52.
Attridge, H. W. and R. A. Oden, Jr. (1981) *Philo of Byblos: The Phoenician History: Introduction, Critical Text, Translation, Notes*. Washington, D.C.
Aupert, P. (1975) "Chronique des fouilles et découvertes archéologiques en Grèce en 1974," *Bulletin de correspondance hellénique* 99: 589-694.
Aura Jorro, F. (1985, 1993) *Diccionario micénico*. Madrid.
Bachvarova, M. R. (1997) "The literary use of dialects: Ancient Greek, Indic and Sumerian," in *CLS 33: Papers from the Panels on Linguistic Ideologies in Contact, Universal Grammar, Parameters and Typology, the Perception of Speech and Other Acoustic Signals*, ed. K. Singer, R. Eggert and G. Anderson. Chicago. 7-22.
  (2001) "Successful birth, unsuccessful marriage: Using Near Eastern birth incantations to interpret Aeschylus' *Suppliants*," *NIN* 2: 49-90.
  (2004) "Topics in Lydian verse: Accentuation and syllabification," *Journal of Indo-European Studies* 32: 227-47.
  (2005a) "The eastern Mediterranean epic tradition from *Bilgames and Akka* to the *Song of Release* to Homer's *Iliad*," *Greek, Roman and Byzantine Studies* 45: 131-53.
  (2005b) "Relations between god and man in the Hurro-Hittite Song of Release," *Journal of the American Oriental Society* 125: 45-58.
  (2006) "Divine justice across the Mediterranean: Hittite *arkuwars* and the trial scene in Aeschylus' *Eumenides*," *Journal of Ancient Near Eastern Religions* 6: 123-54.
  (2007a) "Oath and allusion in Alcaeus fr. 129," in *Horkos: The Oath in Greek Society*, ed. A. H. Sommerstein and J. Fletcher. Exeter. 179-88, 258-64.
  (2007b) "Suffixaufnahme and genitival adjectives as an Anatolian areal feature in Hurrian, Tyrrhenian and Anatolian languages," in *Proceedings of the 18th Annual UCLA Indo-European Conference, Los Angeles, November 3-4, 2006*, ed. K. Jones-Bley, M. E. Huld, A. Della Volpe and M. R. Dexter. Journal of Indo-European Studies Monograph Series 53. Washington, D.C. 169-89.
  (2008a) "The poet's point of view and the prehistory of the *Iliad*," in *Anatolian Interfaces: Hittites, Greeks and Their Neighbors. Proceedings of an International Conference on Cross-Cultural Interaction, September 17-19, 2004, Emory University, Atlanta, Ga.*, ed. B. J. Collins, M. R. Bachvarova and I. C. Rutherford. Oxford. 93-106.
  (2008b) "Sumerian gala priests and Eastern Mediterranean returning gods: Tragic lamentation in cross-cultural perspective," in *Lament: Studies in the Ancient Mediterranean and Beyond*, ed. A. Suter. Oxford and New York. 18-52.
  (2009) "Hittite and Greek perspectives on travelling poets, festivals and texts," in *Wandering Poets in Ancient Greek Culture: Travel, Locality and Pan-Hellenism*, ed. R. Hunter and I. C. Rutherford. Cambridge. 23-45.

(2010) "The manly deeds of Hattusili I: Hittite admonitory history and didactic epic," in *Epic and History*, ed. K. Raaflaub and D. Konstan. Waltham, Mass. 66–85.

(2011) "The meter of Hurrian narrative song," *Altorientalische Forschungen* 38: 285–308.

(2012a) "From 'kingship in heaven' to king lists: Syro-Anatolian courts and the history of the world," *Journal of Ancient Near Eastern Religions* 12: 97–118.

(2012b) "The transmission of liver divination from East to West," *Studi Micenei ed Egeo-Anatolici* 54: 143–64.

(2013a) "Adapting Mesopotamian myth in Hurro-Hittite rituals at Hattuša: IŠTAR, the underworld, and the legendary kings," in *Beyond Hatti: A Tribute to Gary Beckman*, ed. B. J. Collins and P. Michalowski. Atlanta, Ga. 23–44.

(2013b) "CTH 767.7: The birth ritual of Pittei: Its occasion and the use of Luwianisms," in *Luwian Identities: Culture, Language and Religion between Anatolia and the Aegean*, ed. A. Mouton, I. C. Rutherford and I. Yakubovich. Leiden and Boston. 135–57.

(2013c) "Io and the Gorgon: Ancient Greek medical and mythical constructions of the interactions between women's experiences of sex and birth," *Arethusa* 46: 415–46.

(2014) "Hurro-Hittite narrative song as a bilingual oral-derived genre," in *Proceedings of the Eighth International Congress of Hittitology, Warsaw, Poland, Sept. 5–9, 2011*, ed. M. Kapełus and P. Taracha. Warsaw. 77–109.

(2015) "Migrations in the Anatolian epic tradition," in *Nostoi: Indigenous Culture, Migration and Integration in the Aegean Islands and Western Anatolia during the Late Bronze and Early Iron Ages, March 18, 2011, Koç University, Istanbul*, ed. K. Kopanias, Ç. Maner and N. C. Stampolidis. Istanbul. 117–55.

Badalì, E. (1989) "Beziehungen zwischen Musik und kultischen Rufen innerhalb der hethitischen Feste," in XXIII. *Deutscher Orientalistentag vom 16. bis 20. September 1985 in Würzburg, ausgewählte Vorträge*, ed. E. von Schuler. Zeitschrift der deutschen morgenländischen Gesellschaft, Supplement 7. Stuttgart. 282–92.

(1991) *Strumenti musicali, musici e musica nella celebrazione delle feste ittite.* Texte der Hethiter 14. Heidelberg.

Badalì, E., C. Zinko and M. Ofitsch (1994) *Der 16. Tag des AN.TAḪŠUM-Festes: Text, Übersetzung, Glossar.* 2nd edn. Scientia 20. Graz.

Bader, F. (1989) *La langue des dieux, ou l'hermétisme des poètes indo-européens.* Pisa.

Baldriga, R. (1994) "Mopso tra Oriente e Grecia: Storia di un personaggio di frontiera," *Quaderni Urbinati di Cultura Classica*, N. S. 46: 35–71.

Bammer, A. (1990) "A *peripteros* of the Geometric Period in the Artemision of Ephesus," *Anatolian Studies* 40: 137–60.

Bammer, A. and U. Muss (2007) "Ein frühes Quellheiligtum am Ayasolukhügel in Ephesos," *Anatolia Antiqua* 15: 95–101.

Barbujani, G. (2005) "Die Etrusker – eine populationsgenetische Studie," in *Gene, Sprachen und ihre Evolution: Wie verwandt sind die Menschen – wie verwandt sind ihre Sprachen?*, ed. G. Hauska. Regensburg. 185–96.

Barjamoviç, G. (2010) "Sites, routes and historical geography in central Anatolia," in *Ipamati kistamati pari tumatimis: Luwian and Hittite Studies Presented to J. David Hawkins on the Occasion of his 70th Birthday*, ed. I. Singer Tel Aviv. 10–25.

Barjamovic, G., T. Hertel and M. T. Larsen (2012) *Ups and Downs at Kanesh: Chronology, History and Society in the Old Assyrian Period*. PIHANS 120. Leiden.

Barnes, T. (2011) "Homeric ἀνδροτῆτα καὶ ἥβην," *Journal of Hellenic Studies* 131: 1–13.

Barnett, R. D. (1948) "Early Greek and Oriental ivories," *Journal of Hellenic Studies* 68: 1–25.

Barré, M. L. (1978) "^{d}LAMMA and Rešep at Ugarit: The Hittite connection," *Journal of the American Oriental Society* 98: 465–7.

Bartoněk, A. (1966) *Development of the Long-Vowel System in Ancient Greek Dialects*. Brno.

(2003) *Handbuch des mykenischen Griechisch*. Heidelberg.

Basedow, M. (2006) "What the blind man saw: New information from the Iron Age at Troy," in *Common Ground: Archaeology, Art, Science, and Humanities. Proceedings of the xvıth International Congress of Classical Archaeology, August 23–26, 2003*, ed. C. C. Mattusch, A. A. Donohue and A. Brauer. Oxford and Oakville, Conn. 18–22.

(2007) "Troy without Homer: The Bronze Age–Iron Age transition in the Troad," in *Epos: Reconsidering Greek Epic and Aegean Bronze Age Archaeology. Proceedings of the 11th International Aegean Conference/ 11e Rencontre égénne internationale, Los Angeles, UCLA – The J. Paul Getty Villa, 20–23 April 2006*, ed. S. P. Morris and R. Laffineur. Aegaeum 28. Liège and Austin, Tx. 49–58.

(2009) "The Iron Age transition at Troy," in *Forces of Transformation: The End of the Bronze Age in the Mediterranean. Proceedings of an International Symposium Held at St. John's College, University of Oxford 25–6th March 2006*, ed. C. Bachhuber and R. G. Roberts. Oxford. 131–42.

Bass, G. F. (1967) "Cape Gelidonya: A Bronze Age ship wreck," *Transactions of the American Philosophical Society* 57, part 8.

Baumgarten, A. I. (1981) *The Phoenician History of Philo of Byblos, A Commentary*. Leiden.

Baurain, C. (1997) *Les Grecs et la Méditerranée orientale*. Paris.

Bawanypeck, D. (2005a) "Arzawäische Ritualpraktiken – Informationen aus Ḫattuša," in *Motivation und Mechanismen des Kulturkontaktes in der späten Bronzezeit*, ed. D. Prechel. Eothen 13. Florence. 1–18.

(2005b) *Die Rituale der Auguren*. Texte der Hethiter 25. Heidelberg.

Beal, R. H. (1986) "The history of Kizzuwatna and the date of the Šunaššura treaty," *Orientalia*, N. S. 55: 424–45.

(1992) *The Organisation of the Hittite Military*. Texte der Hethiter 20. Heidelberg.

(2002) "Dividing a god," in *Magic and Ritual in the Ancient World*, ed. P. Mirecki and M. Meyer. Leiden. 197–208.

(2003) "The predecessors of Ḫattušili I," in *Hittite Studies in Honour of Harry A. Hoffner, Jr.: On the Occasion of his 65th Birthday*, ed. G. M. Beckman, R. H. Beal and J. G. McMahon. Winona Lake, Ind. 13–35.

Beaulieu, P.-A. (2000) "The descendants of Sîn-lēqi-unninni," in *Assyriologica et Semitica: Festschrift für Joachim Oelsner anläßlich seines 65. Geburtstags am 18. Februar 1997*, ed. J. Marzahn and H. Neumann. Münster. 1–16.

Beckman, G. (1982) "The Anatolian myth of Illuyanka," *Journal of the Ancient Near Eastern Society* 14: 11–25.

(1983a) *Hittite Birth Rituals*. 2nd edn. Studien zu den Boğazköy-Texten 29. Wiesbaden.

(1983b) "Mesopotamians and Mesopotamian learning at Hattuša," *Journal of Cuneiform Studies* 35: 97–114.

(1986) "Proverbs and proverbial allusions in Hittite," *Journal of Near Eastern Studies* 45: 19–30.

(1998) "Ištar of Nineveh reconsidered," *Journal of Cuneiform Studies* 50: 1–10.

(1999a) "The goddess Pirinkir and her ritual from Ḫattuša (CTH 644)," *Ktema* 24: 25–39.

(1999b) *Hittite Diplomatic Texts*. 2nd edn. Writings from the Ancient World 7. Atlanta, Ga.

(2001a) "The Hittite Gilgamesh," in *The Epic of Gilgamesh: A New Translation, Analogs, Criticism*, ed. B. R. Foster. New York and London. 157–65.

(2001b) "Sargon and Naram-Sin in Ḫatti: Reflections of Mesopotamian antiquity among the Hittites," in *Die Gegenwart des Altertums: Formen und Funktionen des Altertumsbezugs in den Hochkulturen der Alten Welt*, ed. D. Kuhn and H. Stahl. Heidelberg. 85–91.

(2002) "Babyloniaca Hethitica: The '*babilili*-ritual' from Boğazköy (CTH 718)," in *Recent Developments in Hittite Archaeology and History: Papers in Memory of Hans G. Güterbock*, ed. K. A. Yener and H. A. Hoffner, Jr. Winona Lake, Ind. 35–41.

(2003) "Gilgamesh in Ḫatti," in *Hittite Studies in Honor of Harry A. Hoffner, Jr.: On the Occasion of his 65th Birthday*, ed. G. Beckman, R. Beal and G. McMahon. Winona Lake, Ind. 37–57.

(2005) "Hittite and Hurrian epic," in *A Companion to Ancient Epic*, ed. J. M. Foley. Oxford. 255–63.

(2007) "A Hittite ritual for depression (CTH 432)," in *Tabularia Hethaeorum: Hethitologische Beiträge Silvin Košak zum 65. Geburtstag*, ed.

D. Groddek and M. Zorman. Dresdner Beiträge zur Hethitologie 25. Wiesbaden. 69–81.
Beckman, G., T. R. Bryce and E. Cline (2011) *The Ahhiyawa Texts. Writings from the Ancient World* 28. Atlanta, Ga.
Becks, R. (2003) "Troia VII: The transition from the Late Bronze Age to the Early Iron Age," in *Identifying Changes: The Transition from Bronze to Iron Ages in Anatolia and Its Neighboring Regions*, ed. B. Fischer, H. Genz, É. Jean and K. Köroğlu. Istanbul. 41–53.
Beekes, R. S. P. (2003a) "Luwians and Lydians," *Kadmos* 42: 47–9.
  (2003b) "The origin of Apollo," *Journal of Ancient Near Eastern Religions* 3: 1–21.
  (2003c) *The Origin of the Etruscans*. Amsterdam.
  (2010) *Etymological Dictionary of Greek*. Leiden and Boston.
Beer, C. (1984) "Quelques aspects des contacts de Chypre aux VIIIe et VIIe siècles avant nôtre ère," *Opus* 3: 253–76.
Benda-Weber, I. (2005) *Lykier und Karer: Zwei autochthone Ethnien Kleinasiens zwischen Orient und Okzident*. Bonn.
Bendall, L. M. (2004) "Fit for a king? Hierarchy, exclusion, aspiration and desire in the social structure of Mycenaean banqueting," in *Food, Cuisine and Society in Prehistoric Greece*, ed. P. Halstead and J. C. Barrett. Oxford. 105–35.
  (2007) *Economics of Religion in the Mycenaean World: Resources Dedicated to Religion in the Mycenaean Palace Economy*. Oxford.
Benzi, M. (1988) "Rhodes in the LH IIIC period," in *Problems in Greek Prehistory: Papers Presented at the Centenary Conference of the British School of Archaeology at Athens, Manchester, April 1986*, ed. E. B. French and K. A. Wardle. Bristol. 253–62.
  (2013) "The southeast Aegean in the age of the Sea Peoples," in *The Philistines and Other "Sea Peoples" in Text and Archaeology*, ed. A. E. Killebrew and G. Lehmann. Atlanta, Ga. 509–42.
Berg, N. (1978) "Parergon metricum: Der Ursprung des griechischen Hexameters," *Münchener Studien zur Sprachwissenschaft* 37: 11–36.
Berg, N. and D. T. Haug (2000) "Innovations vs. tradition in Homer – an overlooked piece of evidence," *Symbolae Osloenses* 75: 5–23.
Berg, N. and F. O. Lindeman (1992) "The etymology of Greek αὖος and Od. 19.327 αυσταλέος: Homeric metrics and linguistics – a question of priority," *Glotta* 70: 181–96.
Berges, D. and J. Nollé (2000) *Tyana: Archäologisch-historische Untersuchungen zum südwestlichen Kappadokien. Teil II*. Inschriften Griechischer Städte aus Kleinasien 55.2. Bonn.
Bergoffen, C. J. (2005) *The Cypriot Bronze Age Pottery from Sir Leonard Woolley's Excavations at Alalakh (Tell Atchana)*. Vienna.
Bernabé, A. (1987) *Poetae epici Graeci: Testimonia et fragmenta*. Pars I. Leipzig.
  (ed.) (2004) *Poetae epici Graeci: Testimonia et fragmenta. Pars II: Orphicorum et Orphicis similium testimonia et fragmenta, fasc. 1*. Munich and Leipzig.

(ed.) (2005) *Poetae epici Graeci: Testimonia et fragmenta. Pars II: Orphicorum et Orphicis similium testimonia et fragmenta, fasc. 2*. Munich and Leipzig.

Berndt-Ersöz, S. (2004) "In search of a Phrygian male superior god," in *Offizielle Religion, lokale Kulte und individuelle Religiosität: Akten des religionsgeschichtlichen Symposiums "Kleinasien und angrenzende Gebiete vom Beginn des 2. bis zur Mitte des 1. Jahrtausends v. Chr." (Bonn, 20.–22. Februar 2003)*, ed. M. Hutter and S. Hutter-Braunsar. Alter Orient und Altes Testament 318. Münster. 47–56.

(2006) *Phrygian Rock-Cut Shrines: Structure, Function, and Cult Practice*. Leiden and Boston.

(2008) "The chronology and historical context of Midas," *Historia* 57: 1–37.

Betancourt, P. B. (1977) *The Aeolic Style in Architecture: A Survey of Its Development in Palestine, the Halikarnassos Peninsula, and Greece, 1000–500 B.C.* Princeton, N. J.

Betegh, G. (2004) *The Derveni Papyrus: Cosmology, Theology, and Interpretation*. Cambridge.

Bielefeld, E. (1962) "Ein altanatolisches Motiv bei Kanachos?," *Istanbuler Mitteilungen* 12: 18–43.

Bittel, K. (1975) *Das hethitische Felsheiligtum Yazılıkaya*. Boğazköy-Ḫattuša: Ergebnisse der Ausgrabungen 9. Berlin.

Bittel, K., W. Herre, H. Otten, M. Rohrs and J. Schaeuble (1958) *Boğazköy-Ḫattuša: Ergebnisse der Ausgrabungen des Deutschen Archäologischen Instituts und der Deutschen Orient-Gesellschaft*. Volume II: *Die Hethitischen Grabfunde von Osmankayası*. Wissenschaftliche Veröffentlichung der Deutschen Orient-Gesellschaft 71. Berlin.

Black, J. A., G. Cunningham, E. Robson and G. Zólyomi (2004) *The Literature of Ancient Sumer*. Oxford and New York.

Blakely, S. (2006) *Myth, Ritual, and Metallurgy in Ancient Greece and Recent Africa*. Cambridge and New York.

Blümel, R. (1926) "Homerisch ταρχύω," *Glotta* 15: 78–84.

Boardman, J. (1990) "Al Mina and history," *Oxford Journal of Archaeology* 9: 169–90.

(1999) *The Greeks Overseas: Their Early Colonies and Trade*. 4th edn. London.

(2002) *The Archaeology of Nostalgia: How the Greeks Re-created Their Mythical Past*. London.

(2006) "Greeks in the east Mediterranean (South Anatolia, Syria, Egypt)," in *Greek Colonisation: An Account of Greek Colonies and Other Settlements Overseas*. Volume I, ed. G. R. Tsetskhladze. Leiden and Boston. 507–34.

Bodi, D. (2003) "Outraging the resident alien: King David, Uriah the Hittite, and an El-Amarna parallel," *Ugarit-Forschungen* 35: 29–56.

Boedeker, D. (2001a) "Heroic historiography: Simonides and Herodotus on Plataea," in *The New Simonides: Contexts of Praise and Desire*, ed. D. Boedeker and D. Sider. Oxford. 120–34.

(2001b) "Paths to heroization at Plataea," in *The New Simonides: Contexts of Praise and Desire*, ed. D. Boedeker and D. Sider. Oxford. 148–63.

Boehringer, D. (2001) *Heroenkulte in Griechenland von der geometrischen bis zur klassischen Zeit: Attika, Argolis, Messenien*. Berlin.

Bol, R., U. Höckmann and P. Schollmeyer (eds.) (2008) *Kult(ur)kontakte: Apollon in Milet/Didyma, Histria, Myus, Naukratis und auf Zypern: Akten der Table Ronde in Mainz vom 11.-12. März 2004*. Rahden.

Bonatz, D. (2000a) *Das syro-hethitische Grabdenkmal: Untersuchungen zur Entstehung einer neuen Bildgattung in der Eisenzeit im nordsyrisch-südanatolischen Raum*. Mainz.

(2000b) "Syro-Hittite funerary monuments: A phenomenon of tradition or innovation?," in *Essays on Syria in the Iron Age*, ed. G. Bunnens. Ancient Near Eastern Studies Supplement 7. Leuven. 189–210.

(2007a) "The divine image of the king: Religious representation of political power in the Hittite empire," in *Representations of Political Power: Case Histories from Times of Change and Dissolving Order in the Ancient Near East*, ed. M. Heinz and M. H. Feldman. Winona Lake, Ind. 111–36.

(2007b) "The iconography of religion in the Hittite, Luwian, and Aramean kingdoms," in *Iconography of Deities and Demons in the Ancient Near East*, ed. J. Eggler and C. Uehlinger. www.religionswissenschaft.uzh.ch/idd/prepublications/e_idd_anatolia_north_syria.pdf, accessed July 12, 2009.

Bonechi, M. (2001) "The dynastic past of the rulers of Ebla," *Ugarit-Forschungen* 33: 53–64.

Bordreuil, P. and D. Pardee (2004) "Ougarit-Adana, Ougarit-Damas: Voyage outremer, voyage outremont vers 1200 av. J.-C.," in *Antiquus Oriens: Mélanges offerts au Professeur René Lebrun*, Volume I, ed. M. Mazoyer and O. Casabonne. Collection KUBABA, Série Antiquité 5. Paris. 115–24.

Börker-Klähn, J. (1993) "Lykien zur Bronzezeit – eine Skizze," in *Akten des II. Internationalen Lykien-Symposions, Wien, 6.-12. Mai 1990, Band I*, ed. J. Borchhardt and G. Dobesch. Österreichische Akademie der Wissenschaften, philosophisch-historische Klasse, Denkschriften 231. Vienna. 53–62.

Bowie, A. M. (1981) *The Poetic Dialect of Sappho and Alcaeus*. Salem, N.H.

Bowie, E. L. (2001) "Ancestors of historiography in early Greek elegaic and iambic poetry?," in *The Historian's Craft in the Age of Herodotus*, ed. N. Luraghi. Oxford and New York. 45–66.

Breitenberger, B. (2007) *Aphrodite and Eros: The Development of Erotic Mythology in Early Greek Poetry and Cult*. New York and London.

Bremmer, J. N. (1996) "The status and symbolic capital of the seer," in *The Role of Religion in the Early Greek Polis: Proceedings of the Third International Seminar on Ancient Greek Cult, Organized by the Swedish Institute at Athens, 16–18 October 1992*, ed. R. Hägg. Skrifter Utgivna av Svenska Institutet i Athen, 8° 14. Stockholm. 97–109.

(2006) "The myth of the Golden Fleece," *Journal of Ancient Near Eastern Religions* 6: 9–38.

(2008) *Greek Religion and Culture, the Bible, and the Ancient Near East*. Leiden.

Brown, B. (2010) "Kingship and ancestral cult in the Northwest Palace at Nimrud," *Journal of Ancient Near Eastern Religions* 10: 1–53.

Brown, E. L. (2004) "In search of Anatolian Apollo," in *ΧΑΡΙΣ: Essays in Honor of Sara A. Immerwahr*, ed. A. P. Chapin. Hesperia Supplement 33. Princeton, N.J. 243–57.

Brown, J. P. (1995) *Israel and Hellas*. Berlin and New York.

Brügger, C., M. Stoevesandt and E. Visser (2003) *Homers Ilias: Gesamtkommentar*. Volume II.2. Munich and Leipzig.

Brumfield, A. C. (1981) *The Attic Festivals of Demeter and Their Relation to the Agricultural Year*. Salem, N.H.

Bruneau, P. and J. Ducat (2005) *Guide de Délos*. 4th edn. Paris.

Bryce, T. R. (1983) "The arrival of the goddess Leto in Lycia," *Historia* 32: 1–13.

(1986) *The Lycians*. Volume 1: *The Lycians in Literary and Epigraphic Sources*. Copenhagen.

(1989) "The nature of Mycenaean involvement in western Anatolia," *Historia* 38: 1–21.

(1996) "The gods and oracles of ancient Lycia," in *Religion in the Ancient World: New Themes and Approaches*, ed. M. Dillon. Amsterdam. 41–50.

(1999) "Anatolian scribes in Mycenaean Greece," *Historia* 48: 257–64.

(2002) *Life and Society in the Hittite World*. Oxford and New York.

(2003a) "History," in *The Luwians*, ed. H. C. Melchert. Handbuch der Orientalistik 1.68. Leiden and Boston. 27–127.

(2003b) *Letters of the Great Kings of the Ancient Near East: The Royal Correspondence of the Late Bronze Age*. London and New York.

(2005) *The Kingdom of the Hittites*. New edn. Oxford and New York.

(2006) *The Trojans and Their Neighbours: An Introduction*. London and New York.

(2012) *The World of the Neo-Hittite Kingdoms: A Political and Military History*. Oxford.

Brysbaert, A. (2008) *The Power of Technology in the Bronze Age Eastern Mediterranean: The Case of Painted Plaster*. London and Oakville, Conn.

Buccellati, G. (2005) "The monumental urban complex at Urkesh," in *General Studies and Excavations at Nuzi 11/1*, ed. D. I. Owen and G. Wilhelm. Studies on the Civilization and Culture of Nuzi and the Hurrians 15. Bethesda, Md. 3–28.

Buccellati, G. and M. Kelly-Buccellati (eds.) (1998) *Urkesh and the Hurrians: Studies in Honor of Lloyd Cotsen*. Bibliotheca Mesopotamica 26. Malibu, Calif.

(2004) "Der monumentale Palasthof von Tall Mozan/Urkeš und die stratigraphische Geschichte des *ābi*," *Mitteilungen der deutschen Orient-Gesellschaft* 136: 13–39.

(2009) "The Great Temple Terrace at Urkesh and the lions of Tish-atal," in *General Studies and Excavations at Nuzi 11/2 in Honor of David I. Owen on the Occasion of his 65th Birthday, October 28, 2005*, ed. G. Wilhelm. Studies on the Civilization and Culture of Nuzi and the Hurrians 18. Bethesda, Md. 33–70.

Buck, C. D. (1955) *The Greek Dialects: Grammar, Select Inscriptions, Glossary.* Chicago and London.

Budin, S. L. (2002) "Creating a goddess of sex," in *Engendering Aphrodite: Women and Society in Ancient Cyprus,* ed. D. Bolger and N. Serwint. Boston, Mass. 315-24.

(2003) *The Origin of Aphrodite.* Bethesda, Md.

(2004) "A reconsideration of the Aphrodite-Ashtart syncretism," *Numen* 51: 95-145.

Bunnens, G. (ed.) (2000) *Essays on Syria in the Iron Age.* Ancient Near Eastern Studies Supplement 7. Leuven.

(2004) "The Storm-God in Northern Syria and Southern Anatolia from Hadad of Aleppo to Jupiter Dolichenus," in *Offizielle Religion, lokale Kulte und individuelle Religiosität: Akten des religionsgeschichtlichen Symposiums "Kleinasien und angrenzende Gebiete vom Beginn des 2. bis zur Mitte des 1. Jahrtausends v. Chr." (Bonn, 20.-22. Februar 2003),* ed. M. Hutter and S. Hutter-Braunsar. Alter Orient und Altes Testament 318. Münster. 57-81.

(2006) *A New Luwian Stele and the Cult of the Storm-god at Til Barsip-Masuwari.* Tell Ahmar 2. Leuven, Paris and Dudley, Mass.

Burgess, J. (2001) *The Tradition of the Trojan War in Homer and the Epic Cycle.* Baltimore and London.

Burke, B. (2005) "Materialization of Mycenaean ideology and the Ayia Triada sarcophagus," *American Journal of Archaeology* 109: 403-22.

(2007) "Gordion of Midas and the Homeric age," in *Epos: Reconsidering Greek Epic and Aegean Bronze Age Archaeology. Proceedings of the 11th International Aegean Conference/ 11e Rencontre égénne internationale, Los Angeles, UCLA - The J. Paul Getty Villa, 20-23 April 2006,* ed. S. P. Morris and R. Laffineur. Aegaeum 28. Liège and Austin, Tx. 151-6.

Burkert, W. (1975) "Apellai und Apollon," *Rheinisches Museum für Philologie* 118: 1-21.

(1976) "Das hunderttorige Theben und die Datierung der Ilias," *Wiener Studien* 89: 5-21. Reprinted in Riedweg (ed.) 2001, pp. 59-71.

(1979a) "Kynaithos, Polycrates, and the Homeric Hymn to Apollo," in *Arktouros: Hellenic Studies Presented to B. M. W. Knox,* ed. G. W. Bowersock, W. Burkert and C. J. Putnam. Berlin. 53-62. Reprinted in Riedweg (ed.) 2001, pp. 189-97.

(1979b) *Structure and History in Greek Mythology and Ritual.* Sather Classical Lectures 47. Berkeley, Los Angeles and London.

(1983a) *Homo Necans: The Anthropology of Ancient Greek Sacrifical Ritual and Myth,* trans. by P. Bing. Berkeley, Los Angeles and London.

(1983b) "Itinerant diviners and magicians: A neglected element in cultural contacts," in *The Greek Renaissance of the Eighth Century B. C.: Tradition and Innovation. Proceedings of the Second International Symposium at the Swedish Institute in Athens, 1-5 June, 1981,* ed. R. Hägg. Skrifter Utgivna av Svenska Institutet i Athen 4º, 30. Stockholm. 115-19.

(1983c) "Oriental myth and literature in the Iliad," in *The Greek Renaissance of the Eighth Century B. C.: Tradition and Innovation, Proceedings of the Second International Symposium at the Swedish Institute in Athens, 1–5 June, 1981*, ed. R. Hägg. Skrifter Utgivna av Svenska Institutet i Athen, 4° 30. Stockholm. 51–6.

(1985) *Greek Religion*, trans. by J. Raffan. Cambridge, Mass.

(1987a) "The making of Homer in the sixth century B. C.: Rhapsodes versus Stesichoros," in *Papers on the Amasis Painter and His World: Colloquium Sponsored by the Getty Center for the History of Art and the Humanities and Symposium Sponsored by the J. Paul Getty Museum*. Malibu, Calif. 43–62. Reprinted in Riedweg (ed.) 2001, pp. 198–217.

(1987b) "Oriental and Greek mythology: The meeting of parallels," in *Interpretations of Greek Mythology*, ed. J. Bremmer. London. 10–40.

(1992) *The Orientalizing Revolution: Near Eastern Influence on Greek Culture in the Early Archaic Age*, trans. by M. E. Pinder and W. Burkert. Cambridge and London.

(1993) "Kronia-Feste und ihr altorientalischer Hintergrund," in *Karnevaleske Phänomene in antiken und nachantiken Kulturen und Literaturen*, ed. S. Döpp. Bochumer Altertumswissenschaftliches Colloquium 13. Trier. 11–30.

(1995) "Lydia between east and west or how to date the Trojan War," in *The Ages of the Homer: A Tribute to Emily Townsend Vermeule*, ed. J. B. Carter and S. P. Morris. Austin, Tx. 139–48. Reprinted in Riedweg (ed.) 2001, pp. 218–32.

(1999) "Artemis der Epheser: Wirkungsmacht und Gestalt einer Großen Göttin," in *100 Jahre österreichische Forschungen in Ephesos: Akten des Symposions Wien 1995*, ed. H. Friesinger and F. Krinzinger. Österreichische Akademie der Wissenschaften, philosophisch-historische Klasse, Denkschriften 260. Vienna. 59–70.

(2004) *Babylon, Memphis, Persepolis: Eastern Contexts of Greek Culture*. Cambridge, Mass. and London.

Burns, B. E. (2010) *Mycenaean Greece, Mediterranean Commerce, and the Formation of Identity*. Cambridge.

Büyükkolancı, M. (2000) "Excavations on Ayasuluk Hill in Selçuk/Turkey. A contribution to the early history of Ephesus," in *Die Ägäis und das westliche Mittelmeer: Beziehungen und Wechselwirkungen 8. bis 5. Jh. v. Chr. Akten des Symposions Wien 1999*, ed. F. Krinzinger. Österreichische Akademie der Wissenschaften, Philosophisch-Historische Klasse, Denkschriften 288. Vienna. 39–43.

(2007) "Apaša, das alte Ephesos und Ayasoluk," in *Frühes Ionien: Eine Bestandsaufnahme: Panionion-Symposion Güzelçamlı*, ed. J. Cobet, V. von Graeve, W.-D. Niemeier and K. Zimmermann. Milesische Forschungen 5. Mainz am Rhein. 21–6.

Calame, C. (2003) *Myth and History in Ancient Greece: The Symbolic Creation of a Colony*, trans. by D. W. Berman. Princeton, N. J. and Oxford.

Calligas, P. G. (1988) "Hero-cult in Early Iron Age Greece," in *Early Greek Cult Practice: Proceedings of the Fifth International Symposium at the Swedish Institute at Athens, 26–29 June, 1986*, ed. R. Hägg, N. Marinatos and G. C. Nordquist. Skrifter Utgivna av Svenska Institutet i Athen 4°, 38. Stockholm. 229–34.

Çambel, H. (1999) *Corpus of Hieroglyphic Luwian Inscriptions*. Volume II: *Karatepe-Aslantaş*. Untersuchungen zur indogermanischen Sprach- und Kulturwissenschaft 8.2. Berlin and New York.

Çambel, H. and A. Özyar (2003) *Karatepe – Aslantaş: Azatiwataya: Die Bildwerke*. Mainz am Rhein.

Campbell, D. A. (1987) *Greek Lyric*. Volume I: *Sappho and Alcaeus*. Cambridge and London.

(1988) *Greek Lyric*. Volume II: *Anacreon, Anacreontea, Choral Lyric from Olympus to Alcman*. Cambridge and London.

Campbell, D. R. M. (2007) *Mood and Modality in Hurrian*. Ph.D. Thesis, University of Chicago.

Carlier, P. (1984) *La royauté en Grèce avant Alexandre*. Strasburg.

(1995) "*qa-si-re-u* et *qa-si-re-wi-ja*," in *Politeia: Society and State in the Aegean Bronze Age, Proceedings of the 5th International Aegean Conference/ 5e Rencontre égéenne internationale, University of Heidelberg, Archäologisches Institut, 10–13 April 1994*, ed. R. Laffineur and W.-D. Niemeier. Aegaeum 12. Liège and Austin, Tx. 355–64.

Carruba, O. (1996) "Neues zur Frühgeschichte Lykiens," in *Fremde Zeiten: Festschrift für Jürgen Borchhardt zum sechzigsten Geburtstag am 25. Februar 1996 dargebracht von Kollegen, Schülern und Freunden*, ed. F. Blakolmer, K. R. Krierer and F. Krinzinger. Vienna. 25–39.

(2006) "Il nome della Lidia e altri problemi lidii," in *Studi linguistici in onore di Roberto Gusmani*, Volume I, ed. R. Bombi, G. Cifoletti, F. Fusco, L. Innocente and V. Orioles. Alessandria. 393–411.

(2008) *Annali etei del Medio Regno*. Studia Mediterranea 18. Pavia.

Carstens, A. M. (2008a) "Huwasi rocks, baityloi, and open air sanctuaries in Karia, Kilicia, and Cyprus," *Olba* 16: 73–93.

(2008b) "Tombs of the Halikarnassos peninsula – the Late Bronze and Early Iron Age," in *Halikarnassian Studies V*, ed. P. Pedersen. Odense. 52–118.

Carter, C. W. (1962) *Hittite Cult-Inventories*. Ph.D. Thesis, University of Chicago.

(1988) "Athletic contests in Hittite religious festivals," *Journal of Near Eastern Studies* 47: 185–7.

Carter, J. (1995) "Ancestor cult and the occasion of Homeric performance," in *The Ages of Homer*, ed. J. Carter and S. P. Morris. Austin, Tx. 285–312.

Casabonne, O. (2004a) *La Cilicie à l'époque achéménide*. Paris.

(2004b) "Rhodes, Cyprus and southern Anatolia during the Archaic and Achaemenid periods: The Ionian question," *Colloquium Anatolicum* 3: 1–14.

Casabonne, O. and A. Marcinkowski (2004) "Apollon-aux-Loups et Persée à Tarse," in *Antiquus Oriens: Mélanges offerts au Professeur René Lebrun*, Vol. I, ed. M. Mazoyer and O. Casabonne. Collection KUBABA, Série Antiquité 5. Paris. 141–73.

Casabonne, O. and A. Porcher (2003) "Notes ciliciennes." *Anatolia Antiqua* 11: 131–4.

Cassio, A. C. (1994) "ΚΕΙΝΟΣ, ΚΑΛΛΙΣΤΕΦΑΝΟΣ, e la circolazione dell'epica in area euboica," *Annali di Archeologia e Storia Antica*, N. S. 1: 55–67.

(1998) "La cultura euboica e la sviluppo dell'epica greca," in *Euboica: L'Eubea e la presenze euboica in Calcidica e in Occidente. Atti del Convegno Internazionale di Napoli 13–16 novembre 1996*, ed. M. Bats and B. d'Agostino. Naples. 11–22.

(2002) "Early editions of the Greek epics and Homeric textual criticism in the sixth and fifth centuries BC," in *Omero tremila anni dopo: Atti del Congresso di Genova 6–8 luglio 2000*, ed. F. Montanari. Rome. 105–36.

Catling, H. W. (1984) "Workshop and heirloom: Prehistoric bronze stands in the east Mediterranean," *Report of the Department of Antiquities, Cyprus*: 69–91.

(1995) "Heroes returned?: Subminoan burials from Crete," in *The Ages of Homer: A Tribute to Emily Townsend Vermeule*, ed. J. Carter and S. P. Morris. Austin, Tx. 123–36.

Catling, R. W. V. (1998) "The typology of the Protogeometric and Subprotogeometric pottery from Troia and its Aegean context," *Studia Troica* 8: 151–87.

Cavanagh, W. and C. Mee (1998) *A Private Place: Death in Prehistoric Greece*. Studies in Mediterranean Archaeology 125. Jonsered.

Cavigneaux, A. (2005) "Les soirées sargoniques des marchands assyriens," in κορυφαίῳ ἀνδρί: *Mélanges offerts à André Hurst*, ed. A. Kolde, A. Lukinovich and A.-L. Rey. Geneva. 595–602.

Cerri, G. (2002) "Teoria dell'oralità e analisi stratigrafica del testo omerico: Il concetto di 'poema tradizionale'," *Quaderni Urbinati di Cultura Classica*, N. S. 70: 7–34.

Çevik, N. (2000) "A dead-cult place in Simena: Lycian open-air rock-cut sanctuaries and their Anatolian aspects," in *Studien zur Religion und Kultur Kleinasiens und des ägäischen Bereiches: Festschrift für Baki Öğün zum 75. Geburtstag*, ed. C. Işık. Asia Minor Studien 39. Bonn. 37–50.

Chadwick, J. (1990) "The descent of Greek epic," *Journal of Hellenic Studies* 110: 174–7.

(1996–1997) "Three temporal clauses," *Minos* 31–32: 293–301.

Chantraine, P. (1958) *Grammaire Homérique*. Volume I: *Phonétique et morphologie*. 3rd edn. Paris.

(2009) *Dictionnaire étymologique de la langue grecque: histoire des mots*. New edn. Paris.

Charpin, D. (1998) "La version Mariote de l' 'Insurrection Générale contre Narâm-Sîn'," in *Florilegium Marianum III: Recueil d'études à la mémoire de Marie-Thérèse Barrelet*, ed. D. Charpin and J.-M. Durand. Paris. 9–17.

Chavalas, M. (1994) "Genealogical history as 'charter': A study of Old Babylonian period historiography and the Old Testament," in *Faith, Tradition, and History: Old Testament Historiography in Its Near Eastern Context*, ed. A. R. Millard, J. K. Hoffmeier and D. W. Baker. Winona Lake, Ind. 103–28.

(ed.) (2006) *The Ancient Near East: Historical Sources in Translation*. Malden, Mass., and Oxford.

(ed.) (2013) *Women in the Ancient Near East: A Sourcebook*. London and New York.

Chiai, G. F. (2006) "Völker, Sprachen und Kulturen der Troas in der archaischen Zeit (9.–8. Jh. v. Chr.)," in *"Troianer sind wir gewesen": Migrationen in der antiken Welt. Stuttgarter Kolloquium zur Historischen Geographie des Altertums 8, 2002*, ed. E. Olshausen and H. Sonnabend. Stuttgart. 276–90.

Christiansen, B. (2006) *Die Ritualtradition der Ambazzi: Eine philologische Bearbeitung und entstehungsgeschichtliche Analyse der Ritualtexte CTH 391, CTH 429 und CTH 463*. Studien zu den Boğazköy-Texten 48. Wiesbaden.

(2012) *Schicksalbestimmende Kommunikation: Sprachliche, gesellschaftliche und religiöse Aspekte hethitischer Fluch-, Segens-und Eidesformeln*. Studien zu den Boğazköy-Texten 53. Wiesbaden.

Christol, A. (1997) "Épopée homérique, épopée caucasienne: Parallèles narratifs," in *Hommage à Milman Parry: Le style formulaire de l'épopée homérique et la théorie de l'oralité poétique*, ed. F. Létoublon. Amsterdam. 355–67.

Clay, J. S. (2006) *The Politics of Olympus: Form and Meaning in the Major Homeric Hymns*. 2nd edn. London and New York.

(2009) "How to be a hero: The case of Sarpedon," in Ἀντιφίλησις: *Studies on Classical, Byzantine and Modern Greek Literature and Culture in Honour of John-Theophanes A. Papademetriou*, ed. E. Karamalengou and E. Makrygianni. Stuttgart. 30–8.

Cline, E. H. (1994) *Sailing the Wine-Dark Sea: International Trade and the Late Bronze Age Aegean*. BAR international Series 591. Oxford.

(1996) "Aššuwa and the Achaeans: the 'Mycenaean' sword at Hattuša and its possible implications," *Annual of the British School at Athens* 91: 137–51.

Cline, E. H. and S. M. Stannish (2011) "Sailing great green sea? Amenhotep III's 'Aegean list' from Kom el-Hetan, once more," *Journal of Ancient Egyptian Interconnections* 3: 6–16.

Clinton, K. (1992) *Myth and Cult: The Iconography of the Eleusinian Mysteries*. Skrifter Utgivna av Svenska institutet i Athen 8°, 11. Stockholm.

Cohen, A. C. (2005) *Death Rituals, Ideology, and the Development of Early Mesopotamian Kingship: Toward a New Understanding of Iraq's Royal Cemetery of Ur*. Leiden and Boston.

Cohen, M. E. (1988) *The Canonical Lamentations of Ancient Mesopotamia*. Potomac, Md.

(1993) *The Cultic Calendars of the Ancient Near East*. Bethesda, Md.

Colarusso, J. (2002) *Nart Sagas from the Caucasus: Myths and Legends from the Circassians, Abazas, Abkhaz, and Ubykhs*. Princeton, N. J.

Colburn, C. S. (2007) "The symbolic significance of distance in the Homeric epics and the Bronze Age Aegean," in *Epos: Reconsidering Greek Epic and Aegean Bronze Age Archaeology. Proceedings of the 11th International Aegean Conference/ 11e Rencontre égénne internationale, Los Angeles, UCLA – The J. Paul Getty Villa, 20–23 April 2006*, ed. S. P. Morris and R. Laffineur. Aegaeum 28. Liège and Austin, Tx. 203–11.

Coldstream, J. N. (1976) "Hero-cults in the age of Homer," *Journal of Hellenic Studies* 96: 8–17.

(1977) *Deities in Aegean Art before and after the Dark Age*. London.

(1989a) "Early Greek visitors to Cyprus and the eastern Mediterranean," in *Cyprus and the East Mediterranean in the Iron Age: Proceedings of the Seventh British Museum Classical Colloquium, April 1988*, ed. V. Tatton-Brown. London. 90–6.

(1989b) "Status symbols in Cyprus in the eleventh century BC," in *Early Society in Cyprus*, ed. E. Peltenburg. Edinburgh. 325–35.

(1998) *Light from Cyprus on the Greek "Dark Age"?* Oxford.

(2006) "'The long, pictureless hiatus'. Some thoughts on Greek figured art between Mycenaean pictorial and Attic Geometric," in *Pictorial Pursuits: Figurative Painting on Mycenaean and Geometric Pottery. Papers from Two Seminars at the Swedish Institute at Athens in 1999 and 2001*, ed. E. Rystedt and B. Wells. Stockholm. 159–63.

(2007) "Foreigners at Lefkandi?," in *Oropos and Euboea in the Early Iron Age: Acts of an International Round Table, University of Thessaly, June 18–20, 2004*, ed. A. Mazarakis Ainian. Volos. 135–9.

Coldstream, J. N. and H. W. Catling (1996) *Knossos North Cemetery: Early Greek Tombs*. London.

Cole, T. (1988) *Epiploke: Rhythmic Continuity and Poetic Structure in Greek Lyric*. Cambridge, Mass.

Collins, B. J. (1990) "The puppy in Hittite ritual," *Journal of Cuneiform Studies* 42: 211–26.

(1998) "Hattušili I, the Lion King," *Journal of Cuneiform Studies* 50: 15–20.

(2002) "Necromancy, fertility and the dark earth: The use of ritual pits in Hittite cult," in *Magic and Ritual in the Ancient World*, ed. P. Mirecki and M. Meyer. Leiden, Boston and Cologne. 224–41.

(2006) "Pigs at the gate: Hittite pig sacrifice in its eastern Mediterranean context," *Journal of Ancient Near Eastern Religions* 6: 155–88.

(2007a) "The Bible, the Hittites, and the construction of the 'other'," in *Tabularia Hethaeorum: Hethitologische Beiträge Silvin Košak zum 65. Geburtstag*, ed. D. Groddek and M. Zorman. Dresdner Beiträge zur Hethitologie 25. Wiesbaden. 153–61.

(2007b) *The Hittites and Their World*. Atlanta, Ga.

(2010) "Hittite religion and the west," in *Pax Hethitica: Studies on the Hittite and Their Neighbours in Honour of Itamar Singer*, ed. Y. Cohen, A. Gilan and J. L. Miller. Studien zu den Boğazköy-Texten 51. Wiesbaden. 54–66.

Collon, D. (1987) *First Impressions: Cylinder Seals in the Ancient Near East.* Chicago.
   (2001) *Catalogue of the Western Asiatic Seals in the British Museum. Cylinder Seals v: Neo-Assyrian and Neo-Babylonian Periods.* London.
Constantinidou, S. (1989) "*Xenia* and *Lekhestroterion*: Two Mycenaean festivals," *Dodone "Philologia"* 18: 9–26.
Cook, E. (1995) *The Odyssey in Athens: Myths of Cultural Origins.* Ithaca, N.Y.
Cook, J. M. (1973) *The Troad: An Archaeological and Topographical Study.* Oxford.
Cook, R. M. and P. Dupont (1998) *East Greek Pottery.* London and New York.
Cooper, J. S. (1971) "Bilinguals from Boghazköi. 1." *Zeitschrift für Assyriologie und vorderasiatische Archäologie* 61: 1–22.
Cornelius, I. (1994) *The Iconography of the Canaanite Gods Reshef and Ba'al: Late Bronze and Iron Age I Periods (c. 1500–1000 BCE).* Orbis Biblicus and Orientalis 140. Fribourg and Göttingen.
Corti, C. (2007) "The so-called 'Theogony' or 'Kingship in Heaven': The name of the song," *Studi Micenei ed Egeo-Anatolici* 49: 109–21.
Crielaard, J. P. (1995) "Homer, history and archaeology: Some remarks on the date of the Homeric world," in *Homeric Questions: Essays in Philology, Ancient History and Archaeology, Including the Papers of a Conference Organized by the Netherlands Institute at Athens (15 May 1993),* ed. J. P. Crielaard. Amsterdam. 201–88.
   (1998) "Surfing on the Mediterranean web: Cypriot long-distance communications during the eleventh and tenth centuries B.C.," in *Eastern Mediterranean: Cyprus–Dodecanese–Crete 16th – 6th cent. B.C.,* ed. V. Karageorghis and N. Stampolidis. Athens. 187–204.
   (2006) "*Basileis* at sea: Elites and external contacts in the Euboaean Gulf region from the end of the Bronze Age to the beginning of the Iron Age," in *Ancient Greece: From the Mycenaean Palaces to the Age of Homer,* ed. S. Deger-Jalkotzy and I. S. Lemos. Edinburgh. 271–97.
   (2009) "The Ionians in the Archaic period: Shifting identities in a changing world," in *Ethnic Constructs in Antiquity: The Role of Power and Tradition,* ed. T. Derks and N. Roymans. Amsterdam. 37–84.
Crouwel, J. (2006a) "Late Mycenaean pictorial pottery," in *Lefkandi IV: The Bronze Age: The Late Helladic IIIC Settlement at Xeropolis,* ed. D. Evely. London. 233–55.
   (2006b) "Late Mycenaean pictorial pottery: A brief review," in *Pictorial Pursuits: Figurative Painting on Mycenaean and Geometric Pottery: Papers from Two Seminars at the Swedish Institute at Athens in 1999 and 2001,* ed. E. Rystedt and B. Wells. Stockholm. 15–22.
Cryer, F. H. (1994) *Divination in Ancient Israel and Its Near Eastern Environment.* Sheffield.
Cunningham, G. (1997) *'Deliver Me from Evil': Mesopotamian Incantations 2500–1500 BC.* Studia Pohl: Series Maior 17. Rome.
Czichon, R. M. (2008) "Die hethitische Kultur im Mittleren Schwarzmeergebiet unter besonderer Berücksichtigung der Umgebung von Verzirköprü," in

Ḫattuša-Boğazköy: Das Hethiterreich im Spannungsfeld des Alten Orients: 6. Internationales Colloquium der Deutschen Orient-Gesellschaft, 22.–24. März 2006 in Würzburg, ed. G. Wilhelm. Wiesbaden. 256–76.

Czichon, R. M., J. Klinger, P. Breuer, J. Eerbeek, S. Fox, E. Marinova-Wolff, H. Marquardt, H. von der Osten-Woldenburg, S. Reichmuth, S. Riehl and T. Johannsen (2011) "Archäologische Forschungen am Oymaağaç Höyük/ Nerik (?) in den Jahren 2007–2010." *Mitteilungen der deutschen Orient-Gesellschaft zu Berlin* 143: 169–250.

Dakoronia, F. (2006) "Bronze Age pictorial tradition on Geometric pottery," in *Pictorial Pursuits: Figurative Painting on Mycenaean and Geometric Pottery. Papers from Two Seminars at the Swedish Institute at Athens in 1999 and 2001*, ed. E. Rystedt and B. Wells. Stockholm. 171–5.

Dale, A. (2011) "Alcaeus on the career of Myrsilos: Greeks, Lydians and Luwians at the east Aegean–west Anatolian interface," *Journal of Hellenic Studies* 131: 15–24.

Dalley, S. (1989) *Myths from Mesopotamia: Creation, the Flood, Gilgamesh and Others.* Oxford and New York.

(1998a) "Occasions and opportunities: 2. Persian, Greek, and Parthian overlords," in *The Legacy of Mesopotamia*, ed. S. Dalley. Oxford and New York. 35–55.

(1998b) "The Sassanian period and early Islam, c. AD 224–651," in *The Legacy of Mesopotamia*, ed. S. Dalley. Oxford and New York. 163–81.

(2000) "Shamshu-Ilu, language and power in the western Assyrian empire," in *Essays on Syria in the Iron Age*, ed. G. Bunnens. Ancient Near Eastern Studies Supplement 7. Leuven. 79–88.

Dalley, S. and A. T. Reyes (1998) "Mesopotamian contact and influence in the Greek world: 1. To the Persian conquest," in *The Legacy of Mesopotamia*, ed. S. Dalley. Oxford and New York. 85–106.

Dardano, P. (2006) *Die hethitischen Tontafelkataloge aus Hattusa (CTH 276–282).* Studien zu den Boğazköy-Texten 47. Wiesbaden.

(2010) "La veste della sera: Echi di fraseologia indoeuropea in un rituale ittito-luvio," *Quaderni di Vicino Oriente* 5: 75–84.

Davies, J. K. (2007) "The origins of the festivals, especially Delphi and the Pythia," in *Pindar's Poetry, Patrons, and Festivals: From Archaic Greece to the Roman Empire*, ed. S. Hornblower and C. Morgan. Oxford and New York. 47–69.

(2009) "*Pythios* and *Python*: The spread of a cult title," in *Greek and Roman Networks in the Mediterranean*, ed. I. Malkin, C. Constantakopolou and K. Panagopoulou. London and New York. 57–69.

Davis, J. L. and J. Bennet (1999) "Making Mycenaeans: Warfare, territorial expansion, and representations of the other in the Pylian kingdom," in *Polemos: Le contexte guerrier en Égée à l'âge du bronze: Actes de la 7e Rencontre égéenne internationale. Université de Liège, 14–17 avril 1998*, ed. R. Laffineur. Aegaeum 19. Liège. 105–20.

Day, J. W. (1989) "Rituals in stone: Early Greek grave epigrams and monuments," *Journal of Hellenic Studies* 109: 16–28.

de Hoz, M. P. (1999) *Die lydischen Kulte im Lichte der griechischen Inschriften.* Asia Minor Studien 36. Bonn.

de Jong, I. J. F. (1987) "Paris/Alexandros in the *Iliad*," *Mnemosyne* 40: 124–8.

de Jong, T. (2012–2013) "Astronomical fine-tuning of the chronology of the Hammurabi age," *Jaarbericht van het Vooraziatisch-Egyptisch Genootschap: Ex Oriente Lux* 44: 147–67.

de Jong, T. and V. Foertmeyer (2010) "A new look at the Venus observations of Ammisaduqa: Traces of the Santorini eruption in the atmosphere of Babylon?," *Jaarbericht van het Vooraziatisch-Egyptisch Genootschap: Ex Oriente Lux* 42: 141–57.

de Martino, S. (1989) *La danza nella cultura ittita.* Eothen 2. Florence.

(1992) *Die mantischen Texte.* Corpus der hurritischen Sprachdenkmäler 1/7. Rome.

(1993) "KUB XXVII 38: Ein Beispiel kultureller und linguistischer Überlagerung in einem Text aus dem Archiv von Boğazköy," *Studi Micenei ed Egeo-Anatolici* 31: 121–34.

(1998) "Le Accuse di Muršili II alla Regina Tawananna Secondo il Testo KUB XIV 4," in *Studi e Testi 1,* ed. S. de Martino and F. Imparati. Eothen 9. Florence. 19–48.

(1999) "Problemi di traduzione per antichi scribi ittiti: La redazione bilingue del 'Canto della liberazione'," *Hethitica* 14: 7–18.

(2000) "Il 'Canto della liberazione': Composizione letteraria bilingue hurrico-ittita sulla distruzione di Ebla," *La Parola del Passato* 55: 296–320.

(2003) *Annali e res gestae antico ittiti.* Studia Mediterranea 12. Pavia.

(2008) "Relations between Ḫatti and Alašiya according to textual and archaeological evidence," in *Ḫattuša – Boğazköy: Das Hethiterreich im Spannungsfeld des Alten Orients. 6. Internationales Colloquium der Deutschen Orient-Gesellschaft 22.–24. März 2006, Würzburg,* ed. G. Wilhelm. Colloquien der Deutschen Orient-Gesellschaft 6. Wiesbaden. 247–63.

de Polignac, F. (1995) *Cults, Territory, and the Origins of the Greek City-State,* trans. by J. Lloyd. Chicago.

de Vet, T. (1996) "The joint role of orality and literacy in the composition, transmission, and performance of the Homeric texts: A comparative view," *Transactions of the American Philological Association* 126: 43–76.

(2005) "Parry in Paris: Structuralism, historical linguistics, and the oral theory," *Classical Antiquity* 24: 257–84.

De Vries, B. (1967) *The Style of Hittite Epic and Mythology.* Ph.D. Thesis, Brandeis University. Boston.

Deger-Jalkotzy, S. (1991a) "Diskontinuität und Kontinuität: Aspekte politischer und sozialer Organisation in mykenischer Zeit und in der Welt der Homerischen Epen," in *La transizione dal miceneo all'alto arcaismo: Dal palazzo alla città. Atti del Convegno Internazionale, Roma, 14–19 marzo 1988*, ed. D. Musti, A. Sacconi, L. Rocchetti, M. Rocchi, E. Scafa, L. Sportiello and M. E. Giannotta. Rome. 53–66.

(1991b) "Die Erforschung des Zusammenbruchs der sogenannten mykenischen Kultur und der sogenannten dunklen Jahrhunderte," in *Zweihundert Jahre Homer-Forschung: Rückblick und Ausblick*, ed. J. Latacz. Colloquium Rauricum 2. Stuttgart and Leipzig. 127–54.

(1994) "The post-palatial period of Greece: An Aegean prelude to the 11th century B.C. in Cyprus," in *Cyprus in the 11th Century B.C.*, ed. V. Karageorghis. Nicosia. 11–30.

(1995) "Mykenische Herrschaftsformen ohne Paläste und die griechische Polis," in *Politeia: Society and State in the Aegean Bronze Age. Proceedings of the 5th International Aegean Conference/ 5e Rencontre égéenne internationale, University of Heidelberg, Archäologisches Institut, 10–13 April 1994*, ed. R. Laffineur and W.-D. Niemeier. Aegaeum 12. Liège and Austin, Tx. 367–77.

(1998a) "The Aegean islands and the breakdown of the Mycenaean palaces around 1200 B.C.," in *Eastern Mediterranean: Cyprus–Dodecanese–Crete 16th – 6th cent. B.C.*, ed. V. Karageorghis and N. Stampolidis. Athens. 105–19.

(1998b) "*The Last Mycenaeans and Their Successors* updated," in *Mediterranean Peoples in Transition Thirteenth to Early Tenth Centuries BCE: In Honor of Professor Trude Dothan*, ed. S. Gitin, A. Mazar and E. Stern. Jerusalem. 114–28.

(1998–1999) "Working for the palace: PY An 261," in *A-na-qo-ta: Studies Presented to J. T. Killen*, ed. J. Bennet and J. Driessen. Minos 33–34. Salamanca. 65–81.

(1999) "Military prowess and social status in Mycenaean Greece," in *Polemos: Le contexte guerrier en Égée à l'âge du bronze. Actes de la 7e Rencontre égéenne internationale, Université de Liège, 14–17 avril 1998*, ed. R. Laffineur. Aegaeum 19. Liège. 121–31.

(2002) "Innerägäische Beziehungen und auswärtige Kontakte des mykenischen Griechenland in nachpalatialer Zeit," in *Die nahöstlichen Kulturen und Griechenland an der Wende vom 2. zum 1. Jahrtausend v. Chr.: Kontinuität und Wandel von Strukturen und Mechanismen kultureller Interaktion. Kolloquium des Sonderforschungsbereiches 295 "Kulturelle und sprachliche Kontakte" der Johannes Gutenberg-Universität Mainz, 11.–12. Dezember 1998*, ed. E. Braun-Holzinger and H. Matthäus. Möhnesee. 47–74.

Deighton, H. J. (1982) *The 'Weather-God' in Hittite Anatolia: An Examination of the Archaeological and Textual Sources*. BAR International Series 143. Oxford.

del Monte, G. F. (1992a) "Epopea ittita," in *La saga di Gilgamesh*, ed. G. Pettinato. Milan. 285–99, 382–97.

(1992b) *Die Orts-und Gewässernamen der hethitischen Texte, Supplement*. Répertoire Géographique des Textes Cunéiformes 6.2. Wiesbaden.

del Monte, G. F. and J. Tischler (1978) *Die Orts- und Gewässernamen der hethitischen Texte*. Répertoire Géographique des Textes Cunéiformes 6. Wiesbaden.

del Olmo Lete, G. (1999) *Canaanite Religion according to the Liturgical Texts of Ugarit*, trans. by W. G. E. Watson. Bethesda, Md.

del Valle Muñoyerro, M. (1999) "Troy and Ilios in Homer: Region and city," *Glotta* 75: 68–81.

Delnero, P. (2012) "Memorization and the transmission of Sumerian literary compositions," *Journal of Near Eastern Studies* 71: 189–208.

Deoudi, M. (1999) *Heroenkulte in homerischer Zeit*. BAR International Series 806. Oxford.

Derakhshani, J. (1998) *Die Arier in den nahöstlichen Quellen des 3. und 2. Jahrtausends v.Chr.* Teheran.

Dercksen, J. G. (2005) "Adad is king! The Sargon text from Kültepe (with an appendix on MARV 4, 138 and 140)," *Jaarbericht van het Vooraziatisch-Egyptisch Genootschap: Ex Oriente Lux* 39: 107–29.

des Courtils, J. (2001) "L'archéologie du peuple lycien," in *Origines gentium*, ed. V. Fromentin and S. Gotteland. Bordeaux. 123–33.

Descat, R. (2001) "Les traditions grecques sur les Lélèges," in *Origines gentium*, ed. V. Fromentin and S. Gotteland. Bordeaux. 169–77.

Descoeudres, J.-P. (2002) "Al Mina across the great divide," *Mediterranean Archaeology* 15: 49–72.

Desideri, P. and A. M. Jasink (1990) *Cilicia: Dall'età di Kizzuwatna alla conquista macedone*. Florence.

Deubner, L. (1966) *Attische Feste*. Berlin.

Devecchi, E. (2005) *Gli annali di Ḫattušili I nella versione accadica*. Studia Mediterranea 16. Pavia.

Devine, A. M. and L. D. Stephens (1985) "Stress in Greek?," *Transactions of the American Philological Association* 115: 125–52.

(1994) *The Prosody of Greek Speech*. New York and Oxford.

DeVries, K. (1980) "Greeks and Phrygians in the Early Iron Age," in *From Athens to Gordion: The Papers of a Memorial Symposium for Rodney S. Young Held at the University Museum, the Third of May, 1975*, ed. K. DeVries. Philadelphia. 33–49.

(2007) "The date of the destruction level at Gordion: Imports and the local sequence," in *Anatolian Iron Ages 6: The Proceedings of the Sixth Anatolian Iron Ages Colloquium Held at Eskişehir, 16–20 August 2004*, ed. A. Çilingiroğlu and A. Sagona. Leuven, Paris and Dudley, Mass. 79–101.

Di Martino, S. (2005) "Tell Mozan/Urkesh: Archeozoologia della struttura sotterranea in A12," *Studi Micenei ed Egeo-Anatolici* 47: 67–80.

Dickinson, O. T. P. K. (1977) *The Origins of Mycenaean Civilisation*. Studies in Mediterranean Archaeology 49. Göteborg.

Dickson, K. (1995) *Nestor: Poetic Memory in Greek Epic*. New York and London.

Dietrich, B. C. (1978) "Some evidence from Cyprus of Apolline cult in the Bronze Age," *Rheinisches Museum für Philologie* 121: 1–18.

Dietrich, M. and O. Loretz (1999) "The Hurrian and Hittite texts," in *Handbook of Ugaritic Studies*, ed. W. G. E. Watson and N. Wyatt. Handbuch der Orientalistik 1.29. Leiden, Boston and Cologne. 58–75.

(2004) "Hund im *ap* des königlichen 'Mausoleums' nach dem ugaritischen Keret-Epos," in *Šarnikzel: Hethitologische Studien zum Gedenken an Emil Orgetorix Forrer (19.02.1894–10.01.1986)*, ed. D. Groddek and S. Rößle. Dresdener Beiträge zur Hethitologie 10. Dresden. 253–62. Reprinted in Dietrich (ed.) 2008, *Orbis Ugariticus: Ausgewählte Beiträge von Manfried Dietrich und Oswald Loretz zu Fest-und Gedenkschriften. Anläßlich des 80. Geburtstages von Oswald Loretz*. Alter Orient und Altes Testament 343. Münster, pp. 109–17.

Dietrich, M. and W. Mayer (1994) "Hurritische Weihrauch-Beschwörungen in ugaritischer Alphabetschrift." *Ugarit-Forschungen* 26: 73–112.

(1995) "Sprache und Kultur der Hurriter in Ugarit," in *Ugarit: Ein ostmediterranes Kulturzentrum im Alten Orient*. Volume I: *Ugarit und seine altorientalische Umwelt*, ed. M. Dietrich and O. Loretz. Abhandlungen zur Literatur Alt-Syrien-Palästinas 7. Münster. 7–42.

(1997a) "Das hurritische Pantheon von Ugarit," *Ugarit-Forschungen* 29: 161–82.

(1997b) "Ein hurritisches Totenritual für 'Ammistamru III. (KTU 1.125)," in *Ana šadî Labnāni lū allik: Beiträge zu altorientalischen und mittelmeerischen Kulturen. Festschrift für Wolfgang Röllig*, ed. B. Pongratz-Leisten, H. Kühne and P. Xella. Alter Orient und Altes Testament 247. Kevelaer and Neukirchen-Vluyn. 79–90.

Dijkstra, M. (2005) "The myth of apši 'the (sea)dragon' in the Hurrian tradition: A new join (KBo 27, 180)," *Ugarit-Forschungen* 37: 315–29.

(2008) "New joins in the Hurrian Epic of Kešši and their ramifications." *Ugarit-Forschungen* 40: 205–23.

Dillon, M. (1997) *Pilgrims and Pilgrimage in Ancient Greece*. London and New York.

Doherty, L. E. (1995) *Siren Songs: Gender, Audiences, and Narrators*. Ann Arbor.

Donbaz, V. (1992) "The 'House of Kings' in the city of Aššur," in *Hittite and Other Anatolian and Near Eastern Studies in Honour of Sedat Alp*, ed. H. Otten, E. Akurgal, H. Ertem and A. Süel. Ankara. 119–25.

Dué, C. (2002) *Homeric Variations on a Lament by Briseis*. Lanham, Md.

Duhoux, Y. (2008) "Mycenaean anthology," in *A Companion to Linear B: Mycenaean Greek Texts and their World*, Volume I, ed. Y. Duhoux and A. Morpurgo Davies. Leuven. 243–393.

Dumézil, G. (1965) *Le livre des héros: Légendes sur les Nartes*. Paris.

Dunkel, G. E. (1993) "Periphrastica Homerohittitovedica," in *Comparative-historical Linguistics: Indo-European and Finno-Ugric Papers in Honor of Oswald Szemerényi III*, ed. B. Brogyanyi and R. Lipp. Current Issues in Linguistic Theory 97. Amsterdam and Philadelphia. 103–18.

(2008) "Luvian -tar and Homeric τ' ἄρ," *Studies in Slavic and General Linguistics* 32: 137–49.

Durand, J.-M. (1993) "Le mythologème du combat entre le Dieu de l'orage et la Mer en Mésopotamie," *MARI: Annales de Recherches Interdisciplinaires* 7: 41–61.

Durand, J.-M. and M. Guichard (1997) "Les rituels de Mari," in *Florilegium marianum III: Recueil d'études à la mémoire de Marie-Thérèze Barrelet*, ed. D. Charpin and J.-M. Durand. Paris. 18–77.

Durante, M. (1971, 1976) *Sulla preistoria della tradizione poetica greca*. Rome.

Durnford, S. P. B. (1971) "Some evidence for syntactic stress in Hittite," *Anatolian Studies* 21: 69–75.

(2008) "Is *Sarpedon* an early Anatolian personal name or a job description?," *Anatolian Studies* 58: 103–13.

(2010) "How old was the Ankara Silver Bowl when its inscriptions were added?," *Anatolian Studies* 60: 51–70.

Easton, D. F., J. D. Hawkins, A. D. Sherratt and E. S. Sherratt (2002) "Troy in recent perspective," *Anatolian Studies* 52: 75–109.

Ebach, J. and U. Rütersworden (1977) "Unterweltsbeschwörung im Alten Testament: Untersuchungen zur Begriffs- und Religionsgeschichte des *'ōb*. Teil III," *Ugarit-Forschungen* 12: 205–20.

Ebeling, E. (1931) *Tod und Leben nach den Vorstellungen der Babylonier*. Berlin and Leipzig.

(1952) "Kultische Texte aus Assur," *Orientalia*, N. S. 21: 129–48.

Edel, E. (1994) *Die ägyptisch-hethitische Korrespondenz aus Boghazköi in babylonischer und hethitischer Sprache*. Abhandlungen der Rheinisch-Westfälischen Akademie der Wissenschaften 77. Opladen.

Edel, E. and M. Görg (2005) *Die Ortsnamenlisten im nördlichen Säulenhof des Totentempels Amenophis' III*. Wiesbaden.

Eder, B. (1998) *Argolis, Lakonien, Messenien vom Ende der mykenischen Palaszeit bis zur Einwanderung der Dorier*. Vienna.

(2006) "The world of Telemachus: Western Greece 1200–700 BC," in *Ancient Greece: From the Mycenaean Palaces to the Age of Homer*, ed. S. Deger-Jalkotzy and I. S. Lemos Edinburgh. 549–80.

Edzard, D. O. (1993) *"Gilgameš und Huwawa": Zwei Versionen der sumerischen Zedernwaldepisode nebst einer Edition von Version "B"*. Bayerische Akademie der Wissenschaften, Philosophisch-historische Klasse, Sitzungsberichte 4. Munich.

(1994) "Sumerian epic: Epic or fairy tale?," *Bulletin of the Canadian Society for Mesopotamian Studies*: 7–14.

Egetmeyer, M. (1992) *Wörterbuch zu den Inschriften im kyprischen Syllabar*. Kadmos Supplement 3. Berlin and New York.

(2007) "Lumière sur les loups d'Apollon," *Res Antiquae* 4: 205–20.

(2009) "The recent debate on Eteocypriote people and language," *Pasiphae: Rivista di filologia e antichità egee* 3: 69–90.

Ehringhaus, H. (2005) *Götter, Herrscher, Inschriften: Die Felsreliefs der hethitischen Grossreichszeit in der Türkei.* Mainz am Rhein.

Eichner, H. (1993) "Probleme von Vers und Metrum in epichorischer Dichtung Altkleinasiens," in *Die epigraphische und altertumskundliche Erforschung Kleinasiens: Hundert Jahre Kleinasiatische Kommission der Österreichischen Akademie der Wissenschaften. Akten des Symposiums vom 23. bis 25. Oktober 1990,* ed. G. Dobesch and G. Rehnböck. Österreichische Akademie der Wissenschaften, philosophisch-historische Klasse, Denkschriften 236. Vienna. 97–169.

Eidem, J. (1992) *The Shemshāra Archives 2: The Administrative Texts.* Copenhagen.

Eidem, J. and J. Læssøe (2001) *The Shemshara Archives 1: The Letters.* Copenhagen.

Eliade, M. (1963) *Myth and Reality,* trans. by W. R. Trask. New York and Evanston.

Elsner, J. and I. C. Rutherford (2005) "Introduction," in *Pilgrimage in Graeco-Roman and Early Christian Antiquity: Seeing the Gods,* ed. J. Elsner and I. C. Rutherford. Oxford and New York. 1–38.

Evans, A. J. (1901) "Mycenaean tree and pillar cult and its Mediterranean relations," *Journal of Hellenic Studies* 21: 99–204.

Falkenstein, A. (1939) "Sumerische Beschwörungen aus Boğazköy," *Zeitschrift für Assyriologie und vorderasiatische Archäologie* 45: 8–41.

Faraone, C. A. (1992) *Talismans and Trojan Horses: Guardian Statues in Ancient Greek Myth and Ritual.* New York and Oxford.

(1996) "Taking the 'Nestor's Cup' inscription seriously: Erotic magic and conditional curses in the earliest inscribed hexameters," *Classical Antiquity* 15: 77–112.

Faraone, C. A. (forthcoming) "Did the Chryses episode in Iliad I begin its life as a Homeric *Hymn to Sminthean Apollo*?," in *Persistent Forms: Explorations in Historical Poetics,* ed. B. Maslov and I. Kliger. New York.

Farber, W. (2001) "Das Püppchen und der Totengeist (KBo. 36,29 ii 8–53 u. Dupl.)," *Zeitschrift für Assyriologie und vorderasiatische Archäologie* 91: 253–63.

Faulkner, A. (2008) *The Homeric Hymn to Aphrodite: Introduction, Text, and Commentary.* Oxford and New York.

Fauth, W. (1995) *Helios Megistos: Zur synkretischen Theologie der Spätantike.* Leiden, New York and Cologne.

Feldman, M. H. (2006) *Diplomacy by Design: Luxury and an "International Style" in the Ancient Near East, 1400–1200 BCE.* Chicago and London.

Felson-Rubin, N. and W. M. Sale (1983) "Meleager and Odysseus: A structural and cultural study of the Greek hunting-maturation myth," *Arethusa* 16: 137–71.

Ferrari, G. (2008) *Alcman and the Cosmos of Sparta.* Chicago and London.

Fick, S. M. E. (2004) "Zur Bedeutung der Baityloi in der Hoch-und Volksreligion," in *Offizielle Religion, lokale Kulte und individuelle Religiosität: Akten des religionsgeschichtlichen Symposiums "Kleinasien und angrenzende Gebiete vom Beginn des 2. bis zur Mitte des 1. Jahrtausends v. Chr."* (Bonn, 20.–22.

Februar 2003), ed. M. Hutter and S. Hutter-Braunsar. Alter Orient und Altes Testament 318. Münster. 157–71.

Fiedler, G. (2005) "Les Phrygiens en Tyanide et le problème des Muskis," *Res Antiquae* 2: 389–98.

Finet, A. (1966) "La place du devin dans la société de Mari," in *La divination en Mésopotamie ancienne et dans les régions voisines. 14e Rencontre assyriologique internationale, Strasbourg, 2–6 juillet 1965*. Paris. 87–93.

Fink, A. S. (2007) "Where was the statue of Idrimi actually found? The later temples of Tell atchana (Alalakh) revisited," *Ugarit-Forschungen* 39: 161–245.

Finkelberg, M. (2005) *Greeks and Pre-Greeks: Aegean Prehistory and Greek Heroic Tradition*. Cambridge and New York.

Finkelstein, J. J. (1966) "The genealogy of the Hammurapi dynasty," *Journal of Cuneiform Studies* 20: 95–118.

Finnegan, R. (1988) *Literacy and Orality: Studies in the Technology of Communication*. Oxford.

Fleming, D. E. (1996) "The Emar festivals: City unity and Syrian identity under Hittite hegemony," in *Emar: the History, Religion and Culture of a Syrian Town in the Late Bronze Age*, ed. M. W. Chavalas. Malibu, Calif. 81–122.

(1999) "Chroniques bibliographiques: 1. Recent work on Mari," *Revue d'Assyriologie* 93: 157–74.

(2000) *Time at Emar: The Cultic Calendar and the Rituals from the Diviner's Archive*. Mesopotamian Civilizations 11. Winona Lake, Ind.

Fleming, D. E. and S. J. Milstein (2010) *The Buried Foundation of the Gilgamesh Epic: The Akkadian Huwawa Narrative*. Leiden and Boston.

Foley, J. M. (1988) *The Theory of Oral Composition: History and Methodology*. Bloomington and Indianapolis.

(1990) *Traditional Oral Epic*. Berkeley

(1997) "Oral tradition and Homeric art: The *Hymn to Demeter*," in *New Light on a Dark Age: Exploring the Culture of Geometric Greece*, ed. S. Langdon. Columbia and London. 144–53.

(1999) *Homer's Traditional Art*. University Park, Pa.

Fontenrose, J. (1959) *Python: A Study of Delphic Myths and Its Origins*. Berkeley. Reprinted in 1980.

(1988) *Didyma: Apollo's Oracle, Cult, and Companions*. Berkeley and Los Angeles.

Forlanini, M. (1996a) "Awariku, un nom dynastique dans le mythe et l'histoire." *Hethitica* 13: 13–15.

(1996b) "Un coin de Phrygie à l'époque hittite: Continuité toponomique et religieuse," *Hethitica* 13: 5–12.

(2005) "Un peuple, plusiers noms: Le problème des ethniques au Proche Orient ancien. Cas connus, cas à découvrir," in *Ethnicity in Ancient Mesopotamia: Papers Read at the 48th Rencontre Assyriologique Internationale, Leiden, 1–4 July 2002*, ed. W. H. van Soldt, R. Kalvelagen and D. Katz. 111–19. Leiden.

Forrer, E. (1924a) "Die Griechen in den Boghazköi-Texten," *Orientalistische Literaturzeitung* 27: 113–18.

(1924b) "Vorhomerische Griechen in den Keilschrifttexten von Boghazköi," *Mitteilungen der Deutschen Orient-Gesellschaft* 63: 1–22.

Forstenpointner, G., G. E. Weissengruber and A. Galik (2005) "Tierreste aus früheisenzeitlichen Schichten des Artemisions von Ephesos. Analyse und funktionelle Interpretation," in *Synergia: Festschrift für Friedrich Krinzinger*, ed. B. Brandt, V. Gassner and S. Ladstätter. Vienna. 85–91.

Foster, B. R. (2005) *Before the Muses: An Anthology of Akkadian Literature*. 3rd edn. Bethesda, Md.

Fowler, R. L. (2013) *Early Greek Mythography*. Volume II: *Commentary*. Oxford and New York.

Frame, D. (2009) *Hippota Nestor*. Washington, D.C.

Franke, S. (1989) *Königsinschriften und Königsideologie: Die Könige von Akkade zwischen Tradition und Neuerung*. Münster and Hamburg.

Frankfurter, D. (1995) "Narrating power: The theory and practice of the magical *historiola* in ritual spells," in *Ancient Magic and Ritual Power*, ed. M. Meyer and P. Mirecki. Leiden, New York and Cologne. 457–76.

Franklin, J. C. (2006) "Lyre gods of the Bronze Age musical koine," *Journal of Ancient Near Eastern Religions* 6: 39–70.

(2008) "'A feast of music': The Greco-Lydian musical movement on the Assyrian periphery," in *Anatolian Interfaces: Hittites, Greeks and Their Neighbors. Proceedings of an International Conference on Cross-Cultural Interaction, September 17–19, 2004, Emory University, Atlanta, Ga.*, ed. B. J. Collins, M. R. Bachvarova and I. C. Rutherford. Oxford. 191–201.

(forthcoming) "Kinyras and the musical stratigraphy of early Cyprus," in *Musical Traditions in the Middle East: Reminiscences of a Distant Past*, ed. G. van den Berg and T. Krispijn.

Frayne, D. (1993) *Sargonic and Gutian Periods (2334–2113 BC)*. The Royal Inscriptions of Mesopotamia – Early Periods, Volume 2. Toronto, Buffalo, and London.

Frei, P. (1993a) "Die Bellerophontessage und das Alte Testament," in *Religionsgeschichtliche Beziehungen zwischen Kleinasien, Nordsyrien und dem Alten Testament. Internationales Symposium Hamburg 17.–21. März 1990*, ed. B. Janowski, K. Koch and G. Wilhelm. Orbis Biblicus et Orientalis 129. Freiburg and Göttingen. 39–65.

(1993b) "Solymer – Milyer – Lykier. Ethnische und politische Einheiten auf der lykischen Halbinsel," in *Akten des II. Internationalen Lykien-Symposions, Wien, 6.–12. Mai 1990*, Band I, ed. J. Borchhardt and G. Dobesch. Österreichische Akademie der Wissenschaften, philosophisch-historische Klasse, Denkschriften 231. Vienna. 87–97.

French, E. B. (2013) "Cilicia," in *The Philistines and Other "Sea Peoples" in Text and Archaeology*, ed. A. E. Killebrew and G. Lehmann. Atlanta, Ga. 479–83.

Freu, J. (2001) "De l'independance a l'annexion: Le Kizzuwatna et le Hatti aux XVIe et XVe siècles avant notre ère," in *La Cilicie: Éspaces et pouvoirs locaux (2e millénaire av. J.-C. – 4e siècle ap. J.-C.). Actes de la Table Ronde Internationale d'Istanbul, 2–5 novembre 1999*, ed. É. Jean, A. M. Dinçol and S. Durugönül. Paris. 13–36.

(2005) "Les Phrygiens en Tyanide et le problème des Muskis: Des Grands Rois de Tarhuntassa aux Grands Rois de Tabal," *Res Antiquae* 2: 389–418.

(2006) *Histoire politique du royaume d'Ugarit*. Paris.

Friedrich, J. (1926) *Staatsverträge des Ḫatti-Reiches in hethitischer Sprache, 1. Teil*. Mitteilungen der Vorderasiatisch-Aegyptischen Gesellschaft 31/1. Leipzig.

(1930a) "Die hethitischen Bruchstücke des Gilgameš-Epos," *Zeitschrift für Assyriologie und vorderasiatische Archäologie* 5: 1–82.

(1930b) *Staatsverträge des Ḫatti-Reiches in hethitischer Sprache, 2. Teil*. Mitteilungen der Vorderasiatisch-Aegyptischen Gesellschaft 34/1. Leipzig.

Fuchs, A. (1994) *Die Inschriften Sargons II. aus Khorsabad*. Göttingen.

Gabeskiria, S. (2005) "On the etymology of Hatti and Hattusa," in *v. Uluslararası Hititoloji Kongresi bildirileri: Çorum, 02-08 Eylül 2002 (Acts of the 5th International Congress of Hittitology: Çorum, September 02–08, 2002)*, ed. Y. Hazırlayan and A. Süel. Ankara. 345–57.

Gallou, C. (2005) *The Mycenaean Cult of the Dead*. BAR International Series 1372. Oxford.

Gallou, C. and M. Georgiadis (2006) "Ancestor worship, tradition and regional variation in Mycenaean culture," in *The Archaeology of Cult and Death: Proceedings of the Session "The Archaeology of Cult and Death" Organized for the 9th Annual Meeting of the European Association of Archaeologists, 11th September 2003, St. Petersburg, Russia*, ed. C. Gallou and M. Georgiadis. Budapest. 125–49.

Gander, M. (2012) "Aḫḫiyawa – Ḫiyawa – Que: Gibt es Evidenz für die Anwesenheit von Griechen in Kilikien am Übergang von der Bronze- zur Eisenzeit?," *Studi Micenei ed Egeo-Anatolici* 54: 281–309.

Gantz, T. (1993) *Early Greek Myth: A Guide to Literary and Artistic Sources*. Baltimore and London.

García Trabazo, J. V. (1996) "Ullikummi und Vṛtra: Zwei Ungeheuer in der hethitischen und in der indischen Mythologie," *Studia Iranica, Mesopotamica & Anatolica* 2: 251–73.

(2002) *Textos religiosos hititas: Mitos, plegarias y rituales: Edición bilingue*. Madrid.

(2005) *Hethitische Texte in Transkription: KUB 58*. Dresdener Beiträge zur Hethitologie 18. Wiesbaden.

(2010) "CTH 419, Ritual de sustitución real: edición crítica y traducción," *Historiae* 7: 27–49.

Gaster, T. H. (1950) *Thespis: Ritual, Myth and Drama in the Ancient Near East*. New York.

Gates, C. (2010) "Greeks in the east: A view of Cilicia," in *Archaic Greek Culture: History, Archaeology, Art and Museology*, ed. S. Solovyov. Oxford. 41–5.

Gelb, I. J. and B. Kienast (1990) *Die altakkadischen Königsinschriften des dritten Jahrtausends v. Chr.* Freiburger Altorientalische Studien 7. Stuttgart.

Geller, M. J. (1989) "A new piece of witchcraft," in *DUMU-E$_2$-DUB-BA-A: Studies in Honor of Åke W. Sjöberg*, ed. H. Behrens, D. Loding and M. T. Roth. Occasional Publications of the Samuel Noah Kramer Fund 11. Philadelphia. 193–205.

Gentili, B. (1988) *Poetry and Its Public in Ancient Greece: From Homer to the Fifth Century*, trans. by A. T. Cole. Baltimore and London.

Gentili, B. and P. Giannini (1977) "Preistoria e formazione dell'esametro," *Quaderni Urbinati di Cultura Classica* 26: 7–51.

Gentili, B. and L. Lomiento (2008) *Metrics and Rhythmics: History of Poetic Forms in Ancient Greece*, trans. by E. C. Kopff. Pisa and Rome.

George, A. R. (1990) "The day the earth divided: A geological aetiology in the Babylonian Gilgameš epic," *Zeitschrift für Assyriologie und vorderasiatische Archäologie* 80: 214–19.

(1999) *The Epic of Gilgamesh: The Babylonian Epic Poem and Other Texts in Akkadian and Sumerian*. London.

(2003) *The Babylonian Gilgamesh Epic: Introduction, Critical Edition and Cuneiform Texts*. Oxford and New York.

(2007) "The Gilgameš epic at Ugarit," *Aula Orientalis* 25: 237–54.

(2009) *Babylonian Literary Texts in the Schøyen Collection*. Bethesda, Md.

Georges, P. (1994) *Barbarian Asia and the Greek Experience: From the Archaic Period to the Age of Xenophon*. Baltimore.

Georgiadis, M. (2003) *The South-Eastern Aegean in the Mycenaean Period: Islands, Landscape, Death and Ancestors*. Oxford.

(2009) "The east Aegean-western Anatolia in the Late Bronze Age III: What do the tombs tell us about memory, tradition and identity?," in *The Past in the Past: The Significance of Memory and Tradition in the Transmission of Culture*, ed. M. Georgiadis and C. Gallou. Oxford. 28–42.

Ghirotto, S., F. Tassi, E. Fumagalli, V. Colonna, A. Sandionigi, M. Lari, S. Vai, E. Petiti, G. Corti, E. Rizzi, G. De Bellis, D. Caramelli and G. Barbujani (2013) "Origins and evolution of the Etruscans' mtDNA," *PLoS ONE* 8 (2): 1–11.

Gilan, A. (2000) *Sargon in Anatolia: The "King of Battle" in a Hittite Context*. M.A. Thesis, Mainz.

(2001) "Kampfspiel in hethitischen Festritualen – eine Interpretation," in *Kulturgeschichten: Altorientalistische Studien für Volkert Haas zum 65. Geburtstag*, ed. T. Richter, D. Prechel and J. Klinger. Saarbrücken. 113–24.

(2004a) "Der Puḫanu-Text – theologischer Streit und politische Opposition in der althethitischen Literatur," *Altorientalische Forschungen* 31: 263–96.

(2004b) "Sakrale Ordnung und politische Herrschaft im hethitischen Anatolien," in *Offizielle Religion, lokale Kulte und individuelle Religiosität: Akten des religionsgeschichtlichen Symposiums "Kleinasien und angrenzende Gebiete vom Beginn des 2. bis zur Mitte des 1. Jahrtausends v. Chr." (Bonn, 20.–22. Februar 2003)*, ed. M. Hutter and S. Hutter-Braunsar. Alter Orient und Altes Testament 318. Münster. 189–205.

(2010) "Epic and history in Hittite Anatolia – in search of a local hero," in *Epic and History*, ed. K. Raaflaub and D. Konstan. Waltham, Mass. 51–65.

Gilibert, A. (2011) *Syro-Hittite Monumental Art and the Archaeology of Performance: The Stone Reliefs at Carchemish and Zincirli in the Earlier First Millennium BCE.* Berlin and New York.

Gimbutas, M. (1982) *The Goddesses and Gods of Old Europe 6500–3500 BC: Myths and Cult Images.* Berkeley, Los Angeles and New York.

(1991) *The Civilization of the Goddess: World of Old Europe.* New York.

Giorgieri, M. (2001) "Die hurritische Fassung des Ullikummi-Lieds und ihre hethitische Parallele," in *Akten des IV. Internationalen Kongresses für Hethitologie. Würzburg, 4.–8. Oktober 1999*, ed. G. Wilhelm. Wiesbaden. 134–55.

(2004) "Das Beschwörungsritual der Pittei," *Orientalia* N. S. 35: 409–26.

(2009) "Hurritisch *arni tidibadoḫḫa*, das Öl und der Löwe in dem mythologischen Text KBo 27.217 (ChS I/6 Nr. 10)," in *General Studies and Excavations at Nuzi 11/2 in Honor of David I. Owen on the Occasion of his 65th Birthday, October 28, 2005*, ed. G. Wilhelm. Studies on the Civilization and Culture of Nuzi and the Hurrians 18. Bethesda, Md. 249–58.

Glassner, J.-J. (1985) "Sargon 'Roi du combat'," *Revue Assyriologique* 79: 115–26.

(2004) *Mesopotamian Chronicles.* Writings from the Ancient World 19. Atlanta, Ga.

Goetze, A. (1938) *The Hittite Ritual of Tunnawi.* American Oriental Series 14. New Haven, Conn.

(1962) "Cilicians," *Journal of Cuneiform Studies* 16: 48–58.

Goldman, H. (1963) *Excavations at Gözlü Kule, Tarsus.* Volume III: *The Iron Age. Text.* Princeton, N. J.

Gonnella, J., W. Khayyata and K. Kohlmeyer (2005) *Die Zitadelle von Aleppo und der Tempel des Wettergottes. Neue Forschungen und Entdecken.* Münster.

Gonnet, H. (1995) "Le culte des ancêtres en Anatolie hittite au IIe mill. avant notre ère," *Anatolica* 21: 189–95.

González, J. M. (2010) "The *Catalogue of Women* and the end of the heroic age (Hesiod fr. 204.94–103 M-W)," *Transactions of the American Philological Association* 140: 375–422.

Gordon, C. (1998) "Personal names of the 'verb + deity' type from Ebla," in *XXXIV. Uluslararası Assiriyiloji Kongresi*, ed. H. Erkanal, V. Donbaz and A. Uğuroğlu. Ankara. 341–4.

Gordon, E. I. (1967) "The meaning of the ideogram ᵈKASKAL.KUR = 'underground watercourse' and its significance for Bronze Age historical geography," *Journal of Cuneiform Studies* 21: 70–88.

Goren, Y., S. Bunimovitz, I. Finkelstein, and N. Na'aman (2003) "The location of Alashiya: New evidence from petrographic investigation of Alashiyan tablets from El-Amarna and Ugarit," *American Journal of Archaeology* 107: 233–55.

Goren, Y., I. Finkelstein and N. Na'aman (2004) *Inscribed in Clay: Provenance Study of the Amarna Tablets and Other Ancient Near Eastern Texts*. Tel Aviv.

Gorman, V. B. (2001) *Miletos, the Ornament of Ionia*. Ann Arbor.

Götze, A. (1933) *Die Annalen des Muršiliš*. Mitteilungen der Vorderasiatisch-Ägyptischen Gesellschaft 38. Darmstadt. Reprinted 1967.

Grabbe, L. L. (1995) *Priests, Prophets, Diviners, Sages: A Socio-Historical Study of Religious Specialists in Ancient Israel*. Valley Forge, Pa.

Graf, F. (1979) "Apollon Delphinios," *Museum Helveticum* 36: 2–22.

  (1985) *Nordionische Kulte: Religionsgeschichtliche und epigraphische Untersuchungen zu den Kulten von Chios, Erythrai, Klazomenai und Phokaia*. Rome.

Grave, P., L. Kealhofer, P. Hnila, B. Marsh, C. C. Aslan, D. Thumm-Doğrayan and W. Rigter (2013) "Cultural dynamics and ceramic resource use at Late Bronze Age/Early Iron Age Troy, northwestern Turkey," *Journal of Archaeological Science* 40: 1760–77.

Grayson, A. K. (2000) "Murmuring in Mesopotamia," in *Wisdom, Gods and Literature: Studies in Assyriology in Honour of W. G. Lambert*, ed. A. R. George and I. L. Finkel. Winona Lake, Ind. 301–8.

Grayson, A. K. and J. Novotny (2012) *The Royal inscriptions of Sennacherib, King of Assyria (704–681 BC)*. The Royal Inscriptions of the Neo-Assyrian Period 3/1. Winona Lake, Ind.

Graziosi, B. (2002) *Inventing Homer: The Early Reception of Epic*. Cambridge and New York.

Graziosi, B. and J. Haubold (2005) *Homer: The Resonance of Epic*. London.

Greaves, A. M. (2002) *Miletos: A History*. London and New York.

  (2010) *The Land of Ionia: Society and Economy in the Archaic Period*. Malden, Mass.

Green, D. J. (2010) *"I Undertook Great Works": The Ideology of Domestic Achievements in West Semitic Royal Inscriptions*. Tübingen.

Greenewalt, C. H., Jr. (1978) *Ritual Dinners in Early Historic Sardis*. Berkeley, Los Angeles and London.

Greenfield, J. C. (1998) "Arameans and Aramaic in Anatolia," in XXXIV. *Uluslararası Assiriyoloji Kongresi*, ed. H. Erkanal, V. Donbaz and A. Uğuroğlu. Ankara. 199–207.

Grethlein, J. (2007) "Epic narrative and ritual: The case of the funeral games in Iliad 23," in *Literatur und Religion: Wege zu einer mythisch-rituellen Poetik bei den Griechen*, ed. A. Bierl, R. Lämmle and K. Wesselmann. Berlin and New York. 151–77.

  (2008) "Memory and material objects in the *Iliad* and the *Odyssey*," *Journal of Hellenic Studies* 128: 27–51.

(2010) "From 'imperishable glory' to history: The *Iliad* and the Trojan War," in *Epic and History*, ed. K. Raaflaub and D. Konstan. Waltham, Mass. 122–44.

Groddek, D. (2001) "'Mausoleum' (É.NA₄) und 'Totentempel' (ᴱḫištā) im Hethitischen," *Ugarit-Forschungen* 33: 213–18.

(2004a) *Eine althethitische Tafel des KI.LAM-Festes*. Munich.

(2004b) *Hethitische Texte in Transkription. KBo 39*. Dresdner Beiträge zur Hethitologie 11. Dresden.

(2004c) *Hethitische Texte in Transkription. KUB 20*. Dresdner Beiträge zur Hethitologie 13. Dresden.

(2007) *Hethitische Texte in Transkription. IBoT 4*. Dresdner Beiträge zur Hethitologie 23. Wiesbaden.

(2008) *Hethitische Texte in Transkription. KBo 22*. Dresdner Beiträge zur Hethitologie 24. Wiesbaden.

(2010a) *Hethitische Texte in Transkription. KBo 54*. Dresdner Beiträge zur Hethitologie 31. Wiesbaden.

(2010b) "Die 10. Tafel des ḫišuu̯a-Festes," *Res Antiquae* 7: 357–98.

(2011a) *Hethitische Texte in Transkription. KBo 47*. Dresdner Beiträge zur Hethitologie 33. Wiesbaden.

(2011b) *Hethitische Texte in Transkription: KBo 57*. Dresdner Beiträge zur Hethitologie 36. Wiesbaden.

Grottanelli, C. (1982) "Healers and saviours of the eastern Mediterranean in pre-Classical times," in *La soteriologia dei culti orientali nell'impero romano: Atti del Colloquio Internazionale, Roma 24–28 Settembre 1979*, ed. U. Bianchi and M. J. Vermaseren. Leiden. 649–70.

Guardata, F. B. (1995) "La necropoli reale di Ebla nel periodo paleosiriano," in *Ebla: Alle origini della civiltà urbana: Trent'anni di scavi in Siria dell'Università di Roma "La Sapienza"*, ed. P. Matthiae, F. Pinnock and G. S. Matthiae. Rome. 180–7.

Gurney, O. R. (1986) "Hittite fragments in private collections," in *Kaniššuwar: A Tribute to Hans G. Güterbock on his 75th Birthday*, ed. H. A. Hoffner, Jr. and G. M. Beckman. Assyriological Studies 23. Chicago. 59–68.

Güterbock, H. G. (1938) "Die historische Tradition und ihre literarische Gestaltung bei Babyloniern und Hethitern bis 1200. Zweiter Teil: Hethiter," *Zeitschrift für Assyriologie und vorderasiatische Archäologie* 44: 45–149.

(1951) "The Song of Ullikummi: Revised text of the Hittite version of a Hurrian myth," *Journal of Cuneiform Studies* 5: 135–65.

(1952) "The Song of Ullikummi: Revised text of the Hittite version of a Hurrian myth (continued)," *Journal of Cuneiform Studies* 6: 8–42.

(1960) "An outline of the Hittite AN.TAḪ.ŠUM festival," *Journal of Near Eastern Studies* 19: 80–9. Reprinted in Hoffner and Diamond (eds.) 1997, pp. 91–110.

(1964) "Sargon of Akkad mentioned by Ḫattušili I of Ḫatti," *Journal of Cuneiform Studies* 18: 1–6.

(1967) "The Hittite conquest of Cyprus reconsidered," *Journal of Near Eastern Studies* 26: 73–81. Reprinted in Hoffner and Diamond (eds.) 1997, pp. 191–8.

(1969) "Ein neues Bruchstück der Sargon-Erzählung 'König der Schlacht'," *Mitteilungen der deutschen Orient-Gesellschaft zu Berlin* 101: 14–26.

(1983) "The Hittites and the Aegean world: Part 1. The Ahhiyawa problem reconsidered." *American Journal of Archaeology* 87: 133-8, reprinted in Hoffner and Diamond (eds.) 1997, pp. 199–205.

(1984) "Hittites and Akhaeans: A new look," *Proceedings of the American Philosophical Society* 128: 114–22. Reprinted in Hoffner and Diamond (eds.) 1997, pp. 205–10.

(1986) "Troy in Hittite texts? Wilusa, Ahhiyawa, and Hittite history," in *Troy and the Trojan War: A Symposium Held at Bryn Mawr College, October 1984*, ed. M. Mellink. Bryn Mawr, Pa. 33–44. Reprinted in Hoffner and Diamond (eds.) 1997, pp. 223–8.

Güterbock, H. G. (1989) "Hittite *kursa* 'hunting bag'," in *Essays in Ancient Civilization Presented to Helene J. Kantor*, ed. A. Leonard, Jr. and B. B. Williams. Studies in Ancient Oriental Civilization 47. Chicago. 113–19. Reprinted in Hoffner and Diamond (eds.) 1997, pp. 137–46.

(1992) "A new look at one Ahhiyawa text," in *Hittite and Other Anatolian and Near Eastern Studies in Honour of Sedat Alp*, ed. H. Otten, E. Akurgal, H. Ertem and A. Süel. Ankara. 235–43. Reprinted in Hoffner and Diamond (eds.) 1997, pp. 217–22.

(2003) "Bull jumping in a Hittite text," in *Hittite Studies in Honour of Harry A Hoffner, Jr.: On the Occasion of his 65th Birthday*, ed. G. M. Beckman, R. H. Beal and J. G. McMahon. Winona Lake, Ind. 127–9.

Haas, V. (1970) *Der Kult von Nerik: Ein Beitrag zur hethitischen Religionsgeschichte.* Rome.

(1975) "Jasons Raub des goldenen Vliesses im Lichte hethitischer Quellen," *Ugarit-Forschungen* 7: 227–33.

(1977) "Bemerkungen zu $^{\text{GIŠ}}eja(n)$-," *Altorientalische Forschungen* 5: 269–71.

(1978) "Medea und Jason im Lichte hethitischer Quellen," *Acta Antiqua Academiae Scientarum Hungaricae* 26: 241–53.

(1979) "Remarks on the Hurrian Ištar/Šawuška of Nineveh in the second millennium B. C.," *Sumer* 35: 397–401.

(1981) "Zwei Gottheiten aus Ebla in hethitischer Überlieferung," *Oriens Antiquus* 20: 251–7.

(1982) *Hethitische Berggötter und hurritische Steindämonen: Riten, Kulte und Mythen; Eine Einführung in die altkleinasiatischen religiösen Vorstellungen.* Mainz am Rhein.

(1984) *Die Serien itkaḫi und itkalzi des AZU-Priesters, Rituale für Tašmišarri und Tatuḫepa sowie weitere Texte mit Bezug auf Tašmišarri.* Corpus der hurritischen Sprachdenkmäler I/1. Rome.

(1988a) "Betrachtungen zur Rekonstruktion des hethitischen Frühjahrsfestes (EZEN *purulliyaš*)." *Zeitschrift für Assyriologie und vorderasiatische Archäologie* 78: 284–98.

(1988b) "Die hurritisch-hethitischen Rituale der Beschwörerin Allaiturah(h)i und ihr literarhistorischer Hintergrund," in *Hurriter und Hurritisch*, ed. V. Haas. Xenia 21. Konstanz. 117–43.

(1993) "Eine hethitische Weltreichsidee: Betrachtungen zum historischen Bewußtsein und politischen Denken in althethitischer Zeit," in *Anfänge politischen Denkens in der Antike: Die nahöstlichen Kulturen und die Griechen*, ed. K. Raaflaub. Munich. 135–44.

(1994) *Geschichte der hethitischen Religion*. Handbuch der Orientalistik 1.15. Leiden and New York.

(1998) *Die hurritischen Ritualtermini in hethitischem Kontext*. Corpus der hurritischen Sprachdenkmäler I/9. Rome.

(2002) "Der Schicksalsstein: Betrachtungen zu KBo 32.10 Rs. III." *Altorientalische Forschungen* 29: 234–7.

(2003a) "Betrachtungen zu CTH 343, einem Mythos des Hirschgottes," *Altorientalische Forschungen* 30: 296–303.

(2003b) *Materia Magica et Medica Hethitica: Ein Beitrag zur Heilkunde im Alten Orient*. Berlin and New York.

(2003c) "Siduri – Nahmezuli. Ein kleiner Beitrag zur Gilgameš-Forschung," *Studi Micenei ed Egeo-Anatolici* 45: 129–30.

(2005) "Die Erzählungen von den zwei Brüdern, vom Fischer und dem Findelkind sowie vom Jäger Kešše," *Altorientalische Forschungen* 32: 360–74.

(2006) *Die hethitische Literatur: Texte, Stilistik, Motive*. Berlin and New York.

(2007a) "Beispiele für Intertextualität im hethitischen rituellen Schrifttum," in *Tabularia Hethaeorum: Hethitologische Beiträge Silvin Košak zum 65. Geburtstag*, ed. D. Groddek and M. Zorman. Dresdner Beiträge zur Hethitologie 25. Wiesbaden. 341–51.

(2007b) "Hittite rituals against threats and other diseases and their relationship to the Mesopotamian traditions," in *Disease in Babylonia*, ed. I. L. Finkel and M. J. Geller. Cuneiform Monographs 36. Leiden: 100–19.

Haas, V. and H. J. Thiel (1978) *Die Beschwörungrituale der Allaiturah(h)i und verwandte Texte*. Alter Orient und Altes Testament 31. Kevelaer and Neukirchen-Vluyn.

Haas, V. and M. Wäfler (1976) "Bemerkungen zu ^{É}heštī/ā- (1. Teil)," *Ugarit-Forschungen* 8: 65–99.

(1977) "Bemerkungen zu ^{É}heštī/ā- (2. Teil)," *Ugarit-Forschungen* 9: 87–122.

Haas, V. and I. Wegner (1988) *Die Rituale der Beschwörerinnen* ^{SAL}ŠU.GI. Corpus der hurritischen Sprachdenkmäler I/5. Rome.

(1991) Review of H. Otten and C. Rüster (1990) *Keilschrifttexte aus Boghazköi* 32. *Orientalistische Literaturzeitung* 86: 384–91.

(1992) "Betrachtungen zum hethitischen Festkalender: Die Kulthandungen des 11. und des 22. bis 26. Tages des AN.TAḪŠUM^{SAR}-Festes," in *Hittite and Other Anatolian and Near Eastern Studies in Honour of Sedat Alp*, ed. H. Otten, E. Akurgal, H. Ertem and A. Süel. Ankara. 245–57.

(1997) "Literarische und grammatikalische Betrachtungen zu einer hurritischen Dichtung," *Orientalistische Literaturzeitung* 92: 437–55.

Haas, V. and G. Wilhelm (1974) *Hurritische und luwische Riten aus Kizzuwatna*. Alter Orient und Altes Testament Sonderreihe 3. Kevelaer and Neukirchen-Vluyn.

Hadzisteliou-Price, T. (1973) "Hero-cult and Homer," *Historia* 22: 129–44.

Hagenbuchner, A. (1989) *Die Korrespondenz der Hethiter, Teil 2*. Texte der Hethiter 16. Heidelberg.

Hägg, R. (1983) "Funerary meals in the Geometric necropolis at Asine?," in *The Greek Renaissance of the Eighth Century B. C.: Tradition and Innovation. Proceedings of the Second International Symposium at the Swedish Institute in Athens, 1–5 June, 1981*, ed. R. Hägg. Skrifter Utgivna av Svenska Institutet i Athen 4º, 30. Stockholm. 189–93.

(2001) "Religious processions in Mycenaean Greece," in *Contributions to the Archaeology and History of the Bronze and Iron Ages in the Eastern Mediterranean: Studies in Honour of Paul Åström*, ed. P. M. Fischer. Vienna. 143–7.

Haider, P. W. (1988) *Griechenland – Nordafrika: Ihre Beziehungen zwischen 1500 und 600 v.Chr*. Darmstadt.

(1997) "Troia zwischen Hethitern, Mykenern und Mysern: Besitzt der Troianische Krieg einen historischen Hintergrund?," in *Troia: Mythen und Archäologie*, ed. H. D. Galter. Graz. 97–140.

(2005) "Von Baal Zaphon zu Zeus und Typhon: Zum Transfer mythischer Bilder aus dem vorderorientalischen Raum in die archaisch-griechische Welt," in *Von Sumer bis Homer: Festschrift für Manfred Schretter zum 60. Geburtstag am 25. Februar 2004*, ed. R. Rollinger. Münster. 303–37.

Hainsworth, J. B. (1993) *The Iliad: A Commentary*. Volume III: *Books 9–12*. Cambridge.

Hajnal, I. (2003) *Troia aus sprachwissenschaftlicher Sicht: Die Struktur einer Argumentation*. Innsbruck.

(2007) "Die Vorgeschichte der griechischen Dialekte: Ein methodischer Rück-und Ausblick," in *Die altgriechischen Dialekte: Wesen und Werden. Akten des Kolloquiums Freie Universität Berlin 19.–22. September 2001*, ed. I. Hajnal. Innsbruck. 131–56.

(2011) "Namen und ihre Etymologien — als Beweisstücke nur bedingt tauglich?," in *Lag Troia in Kilikien? Der aktuelle Streit um Homers Ilias*, ed. C. Ulf and R. Rollinger. Darmstadt. 241–63.

Hall, J. M. (2002) *Hellenicity: Between Ethnicity and Culture*. Chicago and London.

Hallo, W. W. (1988) "Texts, statues and the cult of the divine king," in *Congress Volume: Jerusalem 1986*, ed. J. A. Emerton. Supplements to Vetus Testamentum 40. Leiden. 54–66.

(1992) "Royal ancestor worship in the biblical world," in *"Sha'arei Talmon": Studies in the Bible, Qumran, and the Ancient Near East Presented to Shemaryahu Talmon*, ed. M. Fishbane and E. Tov. Winona Lake, Ind. 381–401.

Hallo, W. W. and K. L. Younger, Jr. (eds.) (1997) *The Context of Scripture*. Volume I: *Canonical Compositions from the Biblical World*. Leiden, New York and Cologne.

(eds.) (2000) *The Context of Scripture*. Volume II: *Monumental Inscriptions from the Biblical World*. Leiden, Boston and Cologne.

(eds.) (2002) *The Context of Scripture*. Volume III: *Archival Documents from the Biblical World*. Leiden, Boston and Cologne.

Halstead, P. (1999) "Towards a model of Mycenaean palatial mobilization," in *Rethinking Mycenaean Palaces: New Interpretations of an Old Idea*, ed. M. L. Galaty and W. A. Parkinson. Los Angeles. 35–41.

Halstead, P. and J. C. Barrett (eds.) (2004) *Food, Cuisine and Society in Prehistoric Greece*. Oxford.

Hamilakis, Y. (1998) "Eating the dead: Mortuary feasting and the politics of memory in the Aegean Bronze Age societies," in *Cemetery and Society in the Aegean Bronze Age*, ed. K. Branigan. Sheffield. 115–32.

Hanfmann, G. M. A. (1983) *Sardis from Prehistoric to Roman Times: Results of the Archaeological Exploration of Sardis 1958-1975*. Cambridge, Mass. and London.

Hannah, R. (2005) *Greek and Roman Calendars: Constructions of Time in the Classical World*. London.

Hansen, W. F. (1997) "Homer and the folktale," in *A New Companion to Homer*, ed. I. Morris and B. Powell. Leiden, New York and Cologne. 442–62.

Harmanşah, Ö. (2007) "Upright stones and building narratives: Formation of a shared architectural practice in the ancient Near East," in *Ancient Near Eastern Art in Context: Studies in Honor of Irene J. Winter by Her Students*. Leiden and Boston. 69–99.

(2011) "Monuments and memory: Architecture and visual culture in ancient Anatolian history," in *Oxford Handbook of Ancient Anatolia (10,000–323 BCE)*, ed. S. R. Steadman and G. McMahon. Oxford. 623–51.

(2013) *Cities and the Shaping of Memory in the Ancient Near East*. New York and Cambridge.

Haslam, M. (1978) "The versification of the new Stesichorus (P.Lille 76abc)," *Greek, Roman, and Byzantine Studies* 19: 29–57.

Haubold, J. (2002) "Greek epic: A Near Eastern genre?," *Proceedings of the Cambridge Philological Society* 48: 1–19.

(2007) "Xerxes' Homer," in *Cultural Responses to the Persian Wars: Antiquity to the Third Millennium*, ed. E. Bridges, E. Hall and P. J. Rhodes. Oxford. 47–63.

Haug, D. T. (2002) *Les phases de l'évolution de la langue épique: Trois études de linguistique homérique*. Hypomnemata 142. Göttingen.

Haug, D. T. and E. Welo (2001) "The proto-hexameter hypothesis: Perspectives for further research," *Symbolae Osloenses* 76: 130–6.

Haviaras, N. K. (2007) "The poet and the place: A modern Chian perspective on Ion of Chios and his home island," in *The World of Ion of Chios*, ed. V. Jennings and A. Katsaros. Leiden and Boston. 64–72.

Hawkins, J. D. (1986) "Writing in Anatolia: Imported and indigenous systems," *World Archaeology* 17: 363–76.

(1990) "The new inscription from the Südburg of Boğazköy-Ḫattuša," *Archäologischer Anzeiger*: 305–14.

(1992) "The inscriptions of the Kizildag and the Karadag in the light of the Yalburt inscription," in *Hittite and Other Anatolian and Near Eastern Studies in Honour of Sedat Alp*, ed. H. Otten, E. Akurgal, H. Ertem and A. Süel. Ankara. 259–75.

(1994) "The end of the Bronze Age in Anatolia: New light from recent discoveries," in *Anatolian Iron Ages 3, Anadolu Demir Çağları 3: The Proceedings of the Third Anatolian Iron Ages Colloquium Held at Van, 6–12 August 1990*, ed. A. Çilingiroğlu and D. H. French. Ankara. 91–4.

(1995a) "'Great Kings' and 'Country Lords' at Malatya and Karkamiš," in *Studio Historiae Ardens: Ancient Near Eastern Studies Presented to H. J. Houwink ten Cate on the Occasion of his 65th Birthday*, ed. T. P. J. van den Hout and J. de Roos. Istanbul. 73–85.

(1995b) *The Hieroglyphic Inscription of the Sacred Pool Complex at Hattusa (SÜDBURG) With an Archaeological Introduction by Peter Neve*. Studien zu den Boğazköy-Texten, Beiheft 3. Wiesbaden.

(1997) "A Hieroglyphic Luwian inscription on a silver bowl in the Museum of Anatolian Civilizations, Ankara," *Anadolu Medeniyetleri Müzesi* 1996 Yilliği: 7–24.

(1998) "Tarkasnawa king of Mira: 'Tarkondemos', Boğazköy sealings and Karabel," *Anatolian Studies* 48: 1–31.

(2000) *Corpus of Hieroglyphic Luwian Inscriptions*. Volume I: *Inscriptions of the Iron Age*. Untersuchungen zur indogermanischen Sprach-und Kulturwissenschaft 8. Berlin and New York.

(2002) "Anatolia: The end of the Hittite empire and after," in *Die nahöstlichen Kulturen und Griechenland an der Wende vom 2. zum 1. Jahrtausend v. Chr.: Kontinuität und Wandel von Strukturen und Mechanismen kultureller Interaktion: Kolloquium des Sonderforschungsbereiches 295 "Kulturelle und sprachliche Kontakte" der Johannes Gutenberg-Universität Mainz, 11.–12. Dezember 1998*, ed. E. Braun-Holzinger and H. Matthäus. Möhnesee. 143–51.

(2011a) "Early recognisable hieroglyphic signs(?) in Anatolia," in *Anatolia's Prologue: Kültepe Kanesh Karum: Assyrians in Istanbul*, ed. F. Kulakoğlu and S. Kangal. Kayseri. 96–97, figs. 1–3.

(2011b) "The inscriptions of the Aleppo temple," *Anatolian Studies* 61: 35–54.

Hazenbos, J. (2003) *The Organization of the Anatolian Local Cults during the Thirteenth Century B.C.* Leiden and Boston.

(2004) "Die lokalen Herbst- und Frühlingsfeste in der späten hethitischen Großreichszeit," in *Offizielle Religion, lokale Kulte und individuelle Religiosität: Akten des religionsgeschichtlichen Symposiums "Kleinasien und angrenzende Gebiete vom Beginn des 2. bis zur Mitte des 1. Jahrtausends v. Chr." (Bonn, 20.–22. Februar 2003)*, ed. M. Hutter and S. Hutter-Braunsar. Alter Orient und Altes Testament 318. Münster. 241–8.

Healey, J. (2007) "From Ṣapānu/Ṣapunu to Kasion. The sacred history of a mountain," in *"He Unfurrowed His Brow and Laughed": Essays in Honour of Professor Nicolas Wyatt*, ed. W. G. E. Watson. Alter Orient und Altes Testament 299. Münster. 141–51.

Heinhold-Krahmer, S. (1977) *Arzawa: Untersuchungen zu seiner Geschichte nach den hethitischen Quellen.* Texte der Hethiter 8. Heidelberg.

Held, W. (2009) "Die Karer und die Rhodische Peraia," in *Die Karer und die Anderen: Internationales Kolloquium an der Freien Universität Berlin 13. bis 15. Oktober 2005*, ed. F. Rumscheid. Bonn. 121–34.

Helm, R. W. O. (1956) *Die Chronik des Hieronymus.* 2nd edn. Berlin.

Helms, M. W. (1988) *Ulysses' Sail: An Ethnographic Odyssey of Power, Knowledge, and Geographic Distance.* Princeton, N.J.

Hemberg, B. (1954) "Τριπάτωρ und τρίσηρως. Grieschischer Ahnenkult in klassischer und mykenischer Zeit," *Eranos* 52: 172–90.

Herda, A. (1998) "Der Kult des Gründerheroen Neileos und die Artemis Kithone in Milet," *Jahreshefte des Österreichischen Archäologischen Institutes in Wien* 67: 1–48.

(2006a) *Der Apollon-Delphinios-Kult in Milet und die Neujahrsprozession nach Didyma: Ein neuer Kommentar der sog. Molpoi-Satzung.* Milesische Forschungen 4. Mainz am Rhein.

(2006b) "Panionion-Melia, Mykalessos-Mykale, Perseus und Medusa: Überlegungen zur Besiedlungsgeschichte der Mykale in der frühen Eisenzeit," *Istanbuler Mitteilungen* 56: 43–101.

(2008) "Apollon Delphinios – Apollon Didymeus: Zwei Gesichter eines milesischen Gottes und ihr Bezug zur Kolonisation Milets in archaischer Zeit," in *Kult(ur)kontakte: Apollon in Milet/Didyma, Histria, Myus, Naukratis und auf Zypern: Akten der Table Ronde in Mainz vom 11.–12. März 2004*, ed. R. Bol, U. Höckmann and P. Schollmeyer. Rahden. 13–86.

(2009) "Karkiša-Karien und die sogenannte Ionische Migration," in *Die Karer und die Anderen: Internationales Kolloquium an der Freien Universität Berlin 13. bis 15. Oktober 2005*, ed. F. Rumscheid. Bonn. 27–108.

(2011) "How to run a state cult: The organization of the cult of Apollo Delphinius in Miletos," in *Current Approaches to Religion in Ancient Greece: Papers Presented at a Symposium at the Swedish Institute at Athens, 17–19*

April 2008, ed. M. Haysom and J. Wallensten. Skrifter Utgivna av Svenska Institutet i Athen, 8°, 21. Stockholm. 57–93.

Hertel, D. (2003a) *Die Mauern von Troia: Mythos und Geschichte im antiken Ilion.* Munich.

(2003b) "Protogeometrische, subprotogeometrische und geometrische Keramik Troias aus den Grabungen Schliemanns und Dörpfelds," in *Probleme der Keramikchronologie des südlichen und westlichen Kleinasiens in geometrischer und archaischer Zeit*, ed. B. Rückert and F. Kolb. Bonn. 91–138.

(2008) *Das frühe Ilion: Die Besiedlung Troias durch die Griechen (1020–650/25 v. Chr.).* Munich.

Hertel, D. and F. Kolb (2003) "Troy in clearer perspective," *Anatolian Studies* 53: 71–88.

Heubeck, A. and A. Hoekstra (1989) *A Commentary on Homer's Odyssey.* Volume II: *Books IX–XVI.* Oxford.

Hiller, S. (1983) "Possible historical reasons for the rediscovery of the Mycenaean past in the age of Homer," in *The Greek Renaissance of the Eighth Century B.C.: Tradition and Innovation. Proceedings of the Second International Symposium at the Swedish Institute in Athens, 1–5 June, 1981*, ed. R. Hägg. Skrifter Utgivna av Svenska Institutet i Athen 4º, 30. Stockholm. 9–14.

(1999) "Scenes of warfare and combat in the arts of the Aegean Late Bronze Age: Reflections on typology and development," in *Polemos: Le contexte guerrier en Égée à l'âge du bronze. Actes de la 7e Rencontre égéenne internationale, Université de Liège, 14–17 avril 1998*, ed. R. Laffineur. Aegaeum 19. Liège. 319–28.

(2006) "Some minor observations concerning the new Thebes tablets," in *Die neuen Linear B-Texte aus Theben: Ihr Aufschlusswert für die mykenische Sprache und Kultur. Akten des internationalen Forschungskolloquiums an der Österreichischen Akademie der Wissenschaften, 5.–6. Dezember 2002*, ed. S. Deger-Jalkotzy and O. Panagl. Österreichische Akademie der Wissenschaften, philosophisch-historische Klasse, Denkschriften 338. Vienna. 71–8.

Hitchcock, L. A. (2005) "'Who will personally invite a foreigner, unless he is a craftsman?': Exploring interconnections in Aegean and Levantine architecture," in *Emporia: Aegeans in the Central and Eastern Mediterranean. Proceedings of the 10th International Aegean Conference/ 10e Rencontre égéenne internationale, Athens, Italian School of Archaeology, 14–18 April 2004*, ed. R. Laffineur and E. Greco. Aegaeum 25. Liège and Austin, Tx. 691–9.

Hitchcock, L. A., R. Laffineur and J. L. Crowley (eds.) (2008) *Dais: The Aegean Feast. Proceedings of the 12th International Aegean Conference/ 12e Rencontre égéenne internationale, University of Melbourne, Centre for Classics and Archaeology, 25–29 March 2008.* Aegaeum 29. Liège and Austin, Tx.

Hodot, R. (1990) *Le dialecte éolien d' Asie: La langue des inscriptions VIIe s. a. C.–IVe s. p. C.* Mémoire 88. Paris.

(2001) "Un point de vue sur le lesbien," in *Peuplements et genèses dialectales dans la Grèce antique*, ed. C. Brixhe and G. Vottéro. Nancy. 155–79.

Hoekstra, A. (1965) *Homeric Modifications of Formulaic Prototypes: Studies in the Development of Greek Epic Diction*. Verhandelingen der Koninglijke Nederlande Akademie van Wetenschappen, N. S. 71. Amsterdam.

(1981) *Epic Verse before Homer: Three Studies*. Amsterdam, Oxford and New York.

Hoffmann, I. (1984) *Der Erlaß Telipinus*. Texte der Hethiter 11. Heidelberg.

Hoffmann, O. (1893) *Die Griechischen Dialekte in ihrem historischen Zusammenhang. Volume II: Der nord-achäische Dialekt*. Göttingen.

Hoffner, H. A., Jr. (1967) "Second millennium antecedents to the Hebrew ʾôḇ," *Journal of Biblical Literature* 86: 385–401.

(1968a) "A Hittite analogue to the David and Goliath contest of champions?," *Catholic Biblical Quarterly* 30: 220–5.

(1968b) "A Hittite text in epic style about merchants," *Journal of Cuneiform Studies* 22: 34–45.

(1970) "Remarks on the Hittite version of the Naram-Sin legend," *Journal of Cuneiform Studies* 23: 17–22.

(1981) "The Hurrian story of the Sungod, the Cow and the Fisherman," in *Studies on the Civilization and Culture of Nuzi and the Hurrians 1*, ed. M. A. Morrison and D. I. Owen. Winona Lake, Ind. 189–94.

(1988) "The Song of Silver: A member of the Kumarbi Cycle of 'songs'," in *Documentum Asiae Minoris Antiquae: Festschrift für Heinrich Otten zum 75. Geburtstag*, ed. E. Neu and C. Rüster. Wiesbaden. 143–66.

(1998a) *Hittite Myths*. 2nd edn. Writings from the Ancient World 2. Atlanta, Ga.

(1998b) "Hurrian civilization from a Hittite perspective," in *Urkesh and the Hurrians: Studies in Honor of Lloyd Cotsen*, ed. G. Buccellati and M. Kelly-Buccellati. Bibliotheca Mesopotamica 26. Malibu, Calif. 167–200.

(2007) "A brief commentary on the Hittite Illuyanka myth (CTH 321)," in *Studies Presented to Robert D. Biggs*, ed. M. T. Roth, W. Farber, M. Stolper and P. von Bechtolsheim. Assyriological Studies 27. Chicago. 119–40.

(2009) *Letters from the Hittite Kingdom*. Writings from the Ancient World 15. Atlanta, Ga.

Hoffner, H. A., Jr. and I. L. Diamond (eds.) (1997) *Perspectives on Hittite Civilization: Selected Writings of Hans Gustav Güterbock*. Assyriological Studies 26. Chicago.

Hoffner, H. A., Jr. and H. C. Melchert (2008) *A Grammar of the Hittite Language: Part 1: Reference Grammar*. Winona Lake, Ind.

Hogarth, D. G. (1914) *Carchemish: Report on the Excavations at Djerabis on Behalf of the British Museum, Conducted by C. Leonard Woolley, M.A. and T. E. Lawrence, B. A.: Part I, Introductory*. London.

Högemann, P. (2000) "Zum Iliasdichter – Ein anatolischer Standpunkt," *Studia Troica* 10: 183–98.

(2002) "Ist der Mythos von Troia nur ein Mythos und die 'ionische Kolonisation' nur eine wahre Geschichte?," in *Mauerschau: Festschrift für Manfred Korfmann*, ed. R. Aslan, S. Blum, G. Kastl, F. Schweizer and D. Thumm. Remshalden-Grumbach. 1123–38.

Högemann, P. and N. Oettinger (2008) "Die Seuche im Heerlager der Achäer vor Troia. Orakel und magische Rituale im Hethiterzeitlichen Kleinasien und im archaischen Griechenland," *Klio* 90: 7–26.

Honko, L. (2000a) "Text as process and practice: the textualization of oral epics," in *Textualization of Oral Epics*, ed. L. Honko. Berlin and New York. 3–54.

(ed.) (2000b) *Textualization of Oral Epics*. Berlin and New York.

Hooker, J. T. (1977) *The Language and Text of the Lesbian Poets*. Innsbruck.

Hope Simpson, R. (2003) "The Dodecanese and the Ahhiyawa question," *Annual of the British School at Athens* 98: 203–37.

Hornblower, S. and C. Morgan (2007) "Introduction," in *Pindar's Poetry, Patrons, and Festivals: From Archaic Greece to the Roman Empire*, ed. S. Hornblower and C. Morgan. Oxford and New York. 1–43.

Horowitz, W. (1998) *Mesopotamian Cosmic Geography*. Winona Lake, Ind.

Horrocks, G. C. (1980) *Space and Time in Homer: Prepositional and Adverbial Particles in the Greek Epic*. New York.

(1987) "The Ionian epic tradition; was there an Aeolic phase in its development?," *Minos* 20–22: 269–94.

(1997) "Homer's dialect," in *A New Companion to Homer*, ed. I. Morris and B. Powell Leiden. New York and Cologne. 193–217.

Householder, F. W. and G. Nagy (1972) *Greek: A Survey of Recent Work*. Janua Linguarum, Series Practica 211. The Hague.

Houwink ten Cate, P. H. J. (1961) *The Luwian Population Groups of Lycia and Cilicia Aspera during the Hellenistic Period*. Leiden.

(1988) "Brief comments on the Hittite cult calendar: The main recension of the outline of the nuntarriyašḫaš festival, especially days 8–12 and 15'–22'," in *Documentum Asiae Minoris Antiquae: Festschrift für Heinrich Otten zum 75. Geburtstag*, ed. C. Rüster and E. Neu. Wiesbaden. 167–94.

(1992) "The Hittite Storm God: His role and his rule according to Hittite cuneiform sources," in *Natural Phenomena: Their Meaning, Depiction and Description in the Ancient Near East*, ed. D. J. W. Meijer. Amsterdam. 83–148.

Hülden, O. (2006) *Gräber und Grabtypen im Bergland von Yavu (Zentrallykien): Studien zur antiken Grabkultur in Lykien, Teil 1*. Antiquitas 3, 45. Bonn.

Hutter, M. (1988) *Behexung, Entsühnung und Heilung: Das Ritual der Tunnawiya für ein Königspaar aus mittelhethitischer Zeit (KBo xxi 1 – KUB ix 34 – KBo xxi 6)*. Orbis Biblicus et Orientalis 82. Freiburg.

(1991) "Bemerkungen zur Verwendung magischer Rituale in mittelhethischer Zeit," *Altorientalische Forschungen* 18: 32–43.

(1993) "Kultstelen und Baityloi: Die Ausstrahlung eines syrischen religiösen Phänomens nach Kleinasien und Israel," in *Religionsgeschichtliche Beziehungen zwischen Kleinasien, Nordsyrien und dem Alten Testament. Internationales Symposium Hamburg 17.-21. März 1990*, ed. B. Janowski, K. Koch and G. Wilhelm. Orbis Biblicus et Orientalis 129. Freiburg and Göttingen. 87-108.

(1995) "Der luwische Wettergott *piḫaššašši* und der griechische Pegasos," in *Studia onomastica et indogermanica: Festschrift für Fritz Lochner von Hüttenbach*, ed. C. Zinko. Graz. 79-97.

(1996) "Das Ineinanderfließen von luwischen und aramäischen religiösen Vorstellungen in Nordsyrien," in *Religionsgeschichte Syriens: Von der Frühzeit bis zur Gegenwart*, ed. P. Haider, M. Hutter and S. Kreuzer. Stuttgart, Berlin and Cologne. 116-22.

(2001) "Luwische Religion in den Traditionen von Arzawa," in *Akten des IV. Internationalen Kongresses für Hethitologie. Würzburg, 4.-8. Oktober 1999*, ed. G. Wilhelm. Studien zu den Boğazköy-Texten 45. Wiesbaden. 224-34.

(2003) "Aspects of Luwian religion," in *The Luwians*, ed. H. C. Melchert. Handbuch der Orientalistik 1.68. Leiden and Boston. 211-80.

(2006) "Die phrygische Religion als Teil der Religionsgeschichte Anatoliens," in *Pluralismus und Wandel in den Religionen im vorhellenistischen Anatolien: Akten des religionsgeschichtlichen Symposiums in Bonn (19.-20. Mai 2005)*, ed. M. Hutter and S. Hutter-Braunsar. Alter Orient und Altes Testament 337. Münster. 79-96.

(2011) "Sammeltafeln – Zufallsprodukt von Schreibern oder Ausdruck von hethitischem Literaturverständnis?," in *Hethitische Literatur: Überlieferungsprozesse, Textstrukturen, Ausdrucksformen und Nachwirken. Akten des Symposiums vom 18. bis 20. Februar 2010 in Bonn*, ed. M. Hutter and S. Hutter-Braunsar. Alter Orient und Altes Testament 391. Münster. 115-28.

Hutter-Braunsar, S. (2008) "Sport bei den Hethitern," in *Antike Lebenswelten: Konstanz – Wandel – Wirkungsmacht: Festschrift für Ingomar Weiler zum 70. Geburtstag*, ed. J. Hengstl, T. Mattern, R. Rollinger, K. Ruffing and O. Witthuhn. Philippika: Marburger altertumskundliche Abhandlungen 25. Wiesbaden. 25-37.

Huxley, G. L. (1960) *Achaeans and Hittites*. Oxford.

(1966) *The Early Ionians*. London.

Iacovou, M. (1988) *The Pictorial Pottery of Eleventh Century BC Cyprus*. Göteborg.

(1999) "The Greek exodus to Cyprus," *Mediterranean Historical Review* 14: 1-28.

(2003) "The Late Bronze Age origins of Cypriot Hellenism and the establishment of the Iron Age kingdoms," in *From Ishtar to Aphrodite: 3200 Years of Cypriot Hellenism: Treasures from the Museums of Cyprus*, ed. S. Hadjisavvas. New York. 79-87.

(2006) "From the Mycenaean *qa-si-re-u* to the Cypriote *pa-si-le-wo-se*: The *basileus* in the kingdoms of Cyprus," in *Ancient Greece: From the Mycenaean*

Palaces to the Age of Homer, ed. S. Deger-Jalkotzy and I. S. Lemos. Edinburgh. 315–35.

(2008) "Cultural and political configurations in Iron Age Cyprus: The sequel to a protohistoric episode," *American Journal of Archaeology* 112: 625–57.

(2013) "Aegean-style material culture in Late Cypriot III: Minimal evidence, maximal interpretation," in *The Philistines and Other "Sea Peoples" in Text and Archaeology*, ed. A. E. Killebrew and G. Lehmann. Atlanta, Ga. 585–618.

Iakovides, S. (1980) *Excavations of the Necropolis at Perati*. Los Angeles.

Ikeda, Y. (1984) "Hittites and Aramaeans in the Land of Bit-Adini," in *Monarchies and Socio-Religious Traditions in the Ancient Near East*, ed. T. Mikasa. Bulletin of the Middle Eastern Culture Center in Japan 1. Wiesbaden. 27–36.

Immerwahr, S. A. (1990) *Aegean Painting in the Bronze Age*. University Park, Pa., and London.

(1995) "Death and the Tanagra Larnakes," in *The Ages of Homer*, ed. J. Carter and S. P. Morris. Austin, Tx. 109–21.

Instone, S. (2007) "Origins of the Olympics," in *Pindar's Poetry, Patrons, and Festivals: From Archaic Greece to the Roman Empire*, ed. S. Hornblower and C. Morgan. Oxford and New York. 71–82.

Işık, F. (2000) "Der karische Bergherrscher und sein heiliger Stein in Kbide," in *Studien zur Religion und Kultur Kleinasiens und des ägäischen Bereiches: Festschrift für Baki Öğün zum 75. Geburtstag*, ed. C. Işık. Asia Minor Studien 39. Bonn. 117–34.

Ivantchik, A. I. (1993) *Les Cimmériens au Proche-Orient*. Orbis Biblicus et Orientalis 127. Freiburg and Göttingen.

Izre'el, S. (1997) *The Scholarly Amarna Tablets*. Groningen.

Jablonka, P. (2002) "Troia – Geschichte, Archäologie, Mythos und Polemik: Zu einem Buch von Dieter Hertel," in *Mauerschau: Festschrift für Manfred Korfmann*, ed. R. Aslan, S. Blum, G. Kastl, F. Schweizer and D. Thumm. Remshalden-Grumbach. 259–73.

Jablonka, P. and C. B. Rose (2004) "Late Bronze Age Troy: A response to Frank Kolb," *American Journal of Archaeology* 108: 615–30.

(2011) "Troy," in *The Homer Encyclopedia*, ed. M. Finkelberg. Chichester, UK and Malden, Mass. 896–905.

Jacquet, A. (2002) "Lugal-meš et *malikum*: Nouvel examen du *kispum* à Mari," in *Florilegium marianum VI: Recueil d'études à la mémoire d'André Parrot*, ed. D. Charpin and J.-M. Durand. Antony, France. 51–68.

Jakobson, R. (1966) "Slavic epic verse: Studies in comparative metrics," in *Selected Writings*, 4. The Hague. 414–63 (orig. pub. 1952).

James, P. and M. A. van der Sluijs (2012) "'Silver': A Hurrian Phaethon," *Journal of Ancient Near Eastern Religions* 10: 237–51.

James, S. A. (2002–2003) "The Thebes tablets and the Fq series: A contextual analysis," *Minos* 37–8: 397–417 (published in 2006).

Jameson, M. H. (1994) "Theoxenia," in *Ancient Greek Cult Practice from the Epigraphical Evidence: Proceedings of the Second International Seminar on Ancient Greek Cult, Organized by the Swedish Institute at Athens, 22–24 November 1991*, ed. R. Hägg. Skrifter Utgivna av Svenska Institutet i Athen 8°, 13. Stockholm. 35–57.

Jameson, M. H., D. R. Jordan and R. D. Kotansky (1993) *A Lex Sacra from Selinous*. Durham, N.C.

Jamison, S. W. (1994) "Draupadi from the walls of Troy: *Iliad* 3 from an Indic perpective," *Classical Antiquity* 13: 5–16.

(1997) "A *gāndharva* marriage in the Odyssey: Nausicaa and her imaginary husband," in *Studies in Honor of Jaan Puhvel. Part Two: Mythology and Religion*, ed. J. Greppin and E. C. Polomé. Journal of Indo-European Studies Monograph 21. Washington, D.C. 151–60.

(1999) "Penelope and the pigs: Indic perspectives on the *Odyssey*," *Classical Antiquity* 18: 227–72.

Janda, M. (2005) *Elysion: Entstehung und Entwicklung der griechischen Religion*. Innsbruck.

Janko, R. (1982) *Homer, Hesiod, and the Hymns: Diachronic Development in Epic Diction*. Cambridge.

(1992) *The Iliad: A Commentary*. Volume IV: Books 13–16. Cambridge.

(1998) Review of I. Morris and B. Powell (1997), *A New Companion to Homer*. *Bryn Mawr Classical Review*. http://bmcr.brynmawr.edu/1998/98.5.20.html, accessed January 21, 2010.

Jasink, A. M. (1994) "Il medio Eufrate: Continuità e innovazioni tra il secondo e il primo millennio a.C.," *Mesopotamia* 29: 3–88.

(2001a) "Kizzuwatna and Tarḫuntašša: Their historical evolution and interactions with Ḫatti," in *La Cilicie: Éspaces et pouvoirs locaux (2e millénaire av. J.-C. – 4e siècle ap. J.-C.). Actes de la Table Ronde Internationale d'Istanbul, 2–5 novembre 1999*, ed. É. Jean, A. M. Dinçol and S. Durugönül. Paris. 47–56.

(2001b) "Presenze micenee e greche nella Cilicia preclassica," in *ΠΟΙΚΙΛΜΑ: Studi in onore di Michele R. Cataudella in occasione del 60° Compleanno*, ed. S. Bianchetti, E. Galvagno, A. Magnelli, G. Marasco, G. Mariotta and I. Mastrorosa. La Spezia. 599–620.

(2001c) "Šuppiluliuma and Hartapu: Two 'Great Kings' in conflict?," in *Akten des IV. Internationalen Kongresses für Hethitologie. Würzburg, 4.–8. Oktober 1999*, ed. G. Wilhelm. Studien zu den Boğazköy-Texten 45. Wiesbaden. 235–40.

Jasink, A. M. and L. Bombardieri (2008) "Assyrians, Phoenicians, Cypriots and Greeks: The co-existence of foreign cultural influences in the Çukurova plain during the Iron Age," *Olba* 16: 23–56.

Jasink, A. M. and M. Marino (2007) "The West-Anatolian origins of the Que kingdom dynasty," *Studi Micenei ed Egeo-Anatolici* 49: 407–26.

Jean, É. (2003) "From Bronze to Iron Ages in Cilicia: The pottery in its stratigraphic context," in *Identifying Changes: The Transition from Bronze to Iron Ages in Anatolia and Its Neighboring Regions. Proceedings of the International Workshop, Istanbul, November 8–9, 2002*, ed. B. Fischer, H. Genz, É. Jean and K. Köroğlu. Istanbul. 79–91.

Jean, É., A. M. Dinçol and S. Durugönül (eds.) (2001) *La Cilicie: Éspaces et pouvoirs locaux (2e millénaire av. J.-C. – 4e siècle ap. J.-C.). Actes de la Table Ronde Internationale d'Istanbul, 2–5 novembre 1999*. Paris.

Jensen, M. S. (1980) *The Homeric Question and the Oral-Formulaic Theory*. Copenhagen.

(2011) *Writing Homer: A Study Based on Results from Modern Fieldwork*. Scientia Danica. Series H, Humanities 8 4. Copenhagen.

Johnston, S. I. (1999) *Restless Dead: Encounters Between the Living and the Dead in Ancient Greece*. Berkeley, Los Angeles and London.

(2008) *Ancient Greek Divination*. Malden, Mass.

Jones, B. N. (2008) *Relative Chronology and the Language of Epic*. Ph.D. Thesis, Cornell University. Ann Arbor.

(2010) "Relative chronology within (an) oral tradition," *Classical Journal* 105: 289–318.

(2011) "Relative chronology and an 'Aeolic phase' of epic," in *Relative Chronology and Early Greek Epic Poetry*, ed. Ø. Andersen and D. Haug. Cambridge. 44–64.

Jonker, G. (1995) *The Topography of Remembrance: The Dead, Tradition and Collective Memory in Mesopotamia*. Leiden, New York, and Cologne.

Kammenhuber, A. (1967) "Die hethitische und hurritische Überlieferung zum 'Gilgameš-Epos'," *Münchener Studien zur Sprachwissenschaft* 21: 45–58.

Kämmerer, T. (1993) "Das Sintflutfragment aus Ugarit (RS 22.421)," *Ugarit-Forschungen* 25: 189–200.

Kapelus, M. (2007) "La 'maison (le palais) des ancêtres' et les tombeaux des rois hittites," *Res Antiquae* 4: 221–9.

Kaptan, D. (2000) "Perseus, Ketos, Andromeda and the Persians," in *Studien zur Religion und Kultur Kleinasiens und des ägäischen Bereiches: Festschrift für Baki Öğün zum 75. Geburtstag*, ed. C. Işık. Asia Minor Studien 39. Bonn. 135–44.

Karageorghis, J. and V. Karageorghis (2002) "The Great Goddess of Cyprus or the genesis of Aphrodite in Cyprus," in *Sex and Gender in the Ancient Near East: Proceedings of the 47th Rencontre Assyriologique International, Helsinki, July 2–6, 2001*, ed. S. Parpola and R. M. Whiting. Helsinki. 263–82.

Karageorghis, V. (1982) *Cyprus from the Stone Age to the Romans*. London.

(1983) *Palaepaphos-Skales: An Iron Age Cemetery in Cyprus*. Volume I: *Text*. Alt-Paphos 3. Konstanz.

(1990) *The End of the Late Bronze Age in Cyprus*. Nicosia.

(ed.) (1994a) *Cyprus in the 11th Century B.C.* Nicosia.

(1994b) "The prehistory of an ethnogenesis," in *Cyprus in the 11th Century B.C.*, ed. V. Karageorghis. Nicosia. 1-9.

(2003) "Heroic burials in Cyprus and other Mediterranean regions," in *ΠΛΟΕΣ. Sea Routes: Interconnections in the Mediterranean 16th - 6th Centuries BC. Proceedings of the International Symposium Held at Rethymnon, Crete September 29th - October 2nd 2002*, ed. N. C. Stampolidis and V. Karageorghis. Athens. 339-51.

Karantzali, E. (2001) *The Mycenaean Cemetery at Pylona on Rhodes*. Oxford.

Kassian, A. S., A. Korolëv and A. Sidel'tsev (2002) *Hittite Funerary Ritual, šališ waštaiš*. Alter Orient und Altes Testament 288. Münster.

Katz, D. (1987) "Gilgamesh and Akka: Was Uruk ruled by two assemblies?," *Revue d'Assyriologie* 81: 105-14.

Katz, J. (1998) "How to be a dragon in Indo-European: Hittite *illuyankaš* and its linguistic and cultural congeners in Latin, Greek, and Germanic," in *Mír Curad: Studies in Honor of Calvert Watkins*, ed. J. Jasanoff, H. C. Melchert and L. Oliver. Innsbrucker Beiträge zur Sprachwissenschaft 92. Innsbruck. 317-34.

(2005) "The Indo-European context," in *A Companion to Ancient Epic*, ed. J. M. Foley. Malden, Mass. 20-30.

(2007) "The epic adventures of an unknown particle," in *Greek and Latin from an Indo-European Perspective*, ed. C. George, M. McCullagh, B. Nielsen, A. Ruppel and O. Tribulato. Proceedings of the Cambridge Philological Society, Supplement 32. Cambridge. 65-79.

Kealhofer, L. (ed.) (2005) *The Archaeology of Midas and the Phrygians: Recent Work at Gordion*. Philadelphia.

Keen, A. G. (1996) "The identification of a hero-cult centre in Lycia," in *Religion in the Ancient World*, ed. M. Dillon. Amsterdam. 229-43.

Keen, A. G. (1998) *Dynastic Lycia: A Political History of the Lycians and Their Relations with Foreign Powers c.545-362 B.C.* Mnemosyne, Supplement 178. Leiden, Boston and Cologne.

Kelder, J. (2010) *The Kingdom of Mycenae: A Great Kingdom in the Late Bronze Age Aegean*. Bethesda, Md.

Kelly-Buccellati, M. (2002) "Ein hurritischer Gang in die Unterwelt," *Mitteilungen der deutschen Orient-Gesellschaft* 134: 131-48.

(2005) "Introduction to the archaeo-zoology of the *ābi*," *Incunabula Graeca* 48: 61-6.

(2006) "Gilgamesh at Urkesh? Literary motifs and iconographic identifications," in *Les éspaces syro-mésopotamiens: Dimensions de l'expérience humaine au proche-orient ancien. Volume d'hommage offert à Jean-Claude Margueron*, ed. P. Butterlin, M. Lebeau, J.-Y. Monchambert, J. L. Montero Fenollós and B. Muller. Subartu 17. Brussels. 403-14.

Kerschner, M. (2003) "Zum Kult im früheisenzeitlichen Ephesos: Interpretation eines protogeometrischen Fundkomplexes aus dem Artemisheiligtum," in

Griechische Keramik im kulturellen Kontext: Akten des Internationalen Vasen-Symposions in Kiel vom 24.–28.9.2001 veranstaltet durch das Archäologische Institut der Christian-Albrechts-Universität zu Kiel, ed. B. Schmalz and M. Söldner. Münster. 246–50.

(2006) "Die ionische Wanderung im Lichte neuer archäologischer Forschungen in Ephesos," in *"Troianer sind wir gewesen": Migrationen in der antiken Welt. Stuttgarter Kolloquium zur Historischen Geographie des Altertums 8, 2002*, ed. E. Olshausen and H. Sonnabend. Stuttgart. 364–82.

Kerschner, M., M. Lawall, P. Scherrer and E. Trinkl (2000) "Ephesos in archaischer und klassischer Zeit. Die Ausgrabungen in der Siedlung Smyrna," in *Die Ägäis und das westliche Mittelmeer: Beziehungen und Wechselwirkungen 8. bis 5. Jh. v. Chr. Akten des Symposions Wien 1999*, ed. F. Krinzinger. Österreichische Akademie der Wissenschaften, philosophisch-historische Klasse, Denkschriften 288. Vienna. 45–54.

Kestemont, G. (1986) "Les dieux néo-hittites," in *Archaéologie et philologie dans l'étude des civilisations orientales*, ed. A. Théodoridès, P. Naster and J. Ries. Acta Orientalia Belgica 4. Leuven. 111–38.

Keswani, P. S. (1996) "Hierarchies, heterarchies, and urbanization processes: The view from Bronze Age Cyprus," *Journal of Mediterranean Archaeology* 9: 211–50.

(2004) *Mortuary Ritual and Society in Bronze Age Cyprus*. London and Oakville, Conn.

Kilian, K. (1980) "Zur Darstellung eines Wagenrennens aus spätmykenischer Zeit," *Mitteilungen des Deutschen Archäologischen Instituts, Athenische Abteilung* 95: 21–31.

(1988) "The emergence of *wanax* ideology in the Mycenaean palaces," *Oxford Journal of Archaeology* 7: 291–302.

Killebrew, A. E. (2005) *Biblical Peoples and Ethnicity: An Archaeological Study of Egyptians, Canaanites, Philistines, and Early Israel, 1300–1100 B.C.E.* Leiden and Boston.

Killebrew, A. E. and G. Lehmann (eds.) (2013) *The Philistines and Other "Sea Peoples" in Text and Archaeology*. Atlanta, Ga.

Killen, J. T. (1992) "Observations on the Thebes sealings," in *Mykenäika: Actes du IXe Colloque international sur les textes mycéniens et égéens organisé par le Centre de l'Antiquité Grecque et Romaine de la Fondation Hellénique des Recherches Scientifiques et l'École française d'Athènes (Athènes, 2–6 octobre 1990)*, ed. J.-P. Olivier. Bulletin de Correspondance Hellénique, Supplément 25. Paris. 365–80.

(1994) "Thebes sealings, Knossos tablets and Mycenaean state banquets," *Bulletin of the Institute of Classical Studies* 39: 67–84.

(1996) "Thebes sealings and Knossos tablets," in *Atti e memorie del Secondo Congresso Internazionale di Micenologia (Roma–Napoli, 14–20 ottobre 1991)*, ed. E. De Miro, L. Godart and A. Sacconi. Rome. 71–82.

(2001) "Religion at Pylos: The evidence of the Fn tablets," in *Potnia: Deities and Religion in the Aegean Bronze Age: Proceedings of the 8th International Aegean Conference/8e Rencontre égéenne internationale, Göteborg, Göteborg University, 12–15 April 2000*, ed. R. Laffineur and R. Hägg. Aegaeum 22. Liège and Austin, Tx. 435–43.

(2004) "Wheat, barley, flour, olives and figs in Linear B tablets," in *Food, Cuisine and Society in Prehistoric Greece*, ed. P. Halstead and J. C. Barrett. Oxford. 155–73.

(2006) "Thoughts on the functions of the new Thebes tablets," in *Die neuen Linear B-Texte aus Theben: Ihr Aufschlusswert für die mykenische Sprache und Kultur. Akten des internationalen Forschungskolloquiums an der Österreichischen Akademie der Wissenschaften, 5.–6. Dezember 2002*, ed. S. Deger-Jalkotzy and O. Panagl. Österreichische Akademie der Wissenschaften, philosophisch-historische Klasse, Denkschriften 338. Vienna. 79–110.

Kirk, G. S. (1960) "Objective dating criteria in Homer," *Museum Helveticum* 17: 189–205. Reprinted in Kirk (ed.) 1964, pp. 174–90.

(1962) *The Songs of Homer*. Cambridge.

(ed.) (1964) *The Language and Background of Homer*. Cambridge.

(1985) *The Iliad: A Commentary*. Volume I: *Books 1–4*. Cambridge.

(1990) *The Iliad: A Commentary*. Volume II: *Books 5–8*. Cambridge.

Kirk, G. S., J. E. Raven and M. Schofield (1983) *The Presocratic Philosophers: A Critical History with a Selection of Texts*. 2nd edn. Cambridge.

Kitchen, K. A. (2003) *Ramesside Inscriptions Translated and Annotated: Translations*. Volume IV: *Merenptah and the Late Nineteenth Dynasty*. Malden, Mass., and Oxford.

(2007) "Some thoughts on Egypt, the Aegean and beyond of the 2nd millennium BC," in *Moving across Borders: Foreign Relations, Religion and Cultural Interactions in the Ancient Mediterranean*, ed. P. Kousoulis and K. Magliveras. Leuven, Paris and Dudley, Mass. 3–14.

(2008) *Ramesside Inscriptions Translated and Annotated: Translations*. Volume V: *Setnakht, Ramesses III, and Contemporaries*. Malden, Mass., and Oxford.

Klein, J. (1976) "Šulgi and Gilgameš: Two brother-peers (Šulgi O)," in *Kramer Anniversary Volume: Cuneiform Studies in Honor of Samuel Noah Kramer*, ed. B. L. Eichler. Alter Orient und Altes Testament 25. Kevelaer and Neukirchen-Vluyn. 271–92.

(1981) *Three Šulgi Hymns: Sumerian Royal Hymns Glorifying King Šulgi of Ur*. Ramat-Gan.

(1989) "From Gudea to Šulgi: Continuity and change in Sumerian literary tradition," in *DUMU-E2-DUB-BA-A: Studies in Honor of Åke W. Sjöberg*, ed. H. Behrens, D. Loding and M. T. Roth. Occasional Publications of the Samuel Noah Kramer Fund 11. Philadelphia. 289–301.

(1999) "'The Ballad about Early Rulers' in eastern and western traditions," in *Languages and Cultures in Contact: At the Crossroads of Civilizations in the Syro-Mesopotamian Realm: Proceedings of the 42th RAI*, ed. K. van Lerberghe and G. Voet. Orientalia Lovaniensia Analecta 96. Leuven. 203–16.

Klengel, H. (1992) *Syria: 3000 to 300 B.C.: A Handbook of Political History*. Berlin.

Klengel, H., F. Imparati, V. Haas and T. P. J. van den Hout (1999) *Geschichte des hethitischen Reiches*. Handbuch der Orientalistik. Erste Abteilung, der Nahe und Mittlere Osten 34. Leiden, Boston and Cologne.

Kling, B. (1984) "Mycenaean IIIC:1b Pottery in Cyprus: Principal Characteristics and Historical Context," in *Cyprus at the Close of the Late Bronze Age*, ed. V. Karageorghis and J. D. Muhly. Nicosia. 29–38.

Klinger, J. (1996) *Untersuchungen zur Rekonstruktion der hattischen Kultschicht*. Studien zu den Boğazköy-Texten 37. Wiesbaden.

(1998) "'Wer lehrte die Hethiter das Schreiben?' Zur Paläographie früher Texte in akkadischer Sprache aus Boğazköy: Skizze einiger Überlegungen und vorläufiger Ergebnisse," in *III. Uluslararası Hititoloji Kongresi Bildirileri: Çorum 16–22 Eylül 1996 – Acts of the IIIrd International Congress of Hittitology: Çorum, September 16–22, 1996*, ed. S. Alp and A. Süel. Ankara. 365–75.

(2001a) "Historiographie als Paradigma. Die Quellen zur hethitischen Geschichte und ihre Deutung," in *Akten des IV. Internationalen Kongresses für Hethitologie. Würzburg, 4.–8. Oktober 1999*, ed. G. Wilhelm. Studien zu den Boğazköy-Texten 45. Wiesbaden. 272–91.

(2001b) "Die hurritische Tradition in Ḫattuša und das Corpus hurritischer Texte," in *Kulturgeschichten: Altorientalistische Studien für Volkert Haas zum 65. Geburtstag*, ed. T. Richter, D. Prechel and J. Klinger. Saarbrücken. 197–208.

(2003) "Zur Paläographie akkadischsprachiger Texte aus Ḫattuša," in *Hittite Studies in Honour of Harry A. Hoffner, Jr.: On the Occasion of his 65th Birthday*, ed. G. M. Beckman, R. H. Beal and J. G. McMahon. Winona Lake, Ind.: 237–48.

(2005) "Die hethitische Rezeption mesopotamischer Literatur und die Überlieferung des Gilgameš-Epos in Ḫattuša," in *Motivation und Mechanismen des Kulturkontaktes in der späten Bronzezeit*, ed. D. Prechel. Eothen 13. Munich. 103–27.

(2007) "Hattisch," in *Sprachen des Alten Orients*, ed. M. Streck. Darmstadt. 128–34.

(2009) "The cult of Nerik – revisited," in *Central-North Anatolia in the Hittite Period: New Perspectives in Light of Recent Research. Acts of the International Conference Held at the University of Florence (7–9 February 2007)*, ed. F. Pecchioli Daddi, G. Torri and C. Corti. Studia Asiana 5. Rome. 97–107.

Kloekhorst, A. (2012) "The language of Troy," in *Troy: City, Homer and Turkey*, ed. J. Kelder, G. Uslu and Ö. F. Şerifoğlu. Zwolle. 46–50.

Knapp, A. B. (1985) "Alashiya, Caphtor/Keftiu, and eastern Mediterranean trade: Recent studies in Cypriote archaeology and history," *Journal of Field Archaeology* 12: 231–50.

(ed.) (1996) *Sources for the History of Cyprus.* Volume II: *Near Eastern and Aegean Texts from the Third to the First Millennia* BC. Altamont, N.Y.

(2008) *Prehistoric and Protohistoric Cyprus: Identity, Insularity, and Connectivity.* Oxford and New York.

(2013) *The Archaeology of Cyprus: From Earliest Prehistory through the Bronze Age.* Cambridge and New York.

Koehl, R. B. (1995) "The Silver Stag '*BIBRU*' from Mycenae," in *The Ages of Homer: A Tribute to Emily Townsend Vermeule*, ed. J. B. Carter and S. P. Morris. Austin, Tx. 61–6.

Koenen, L. (1994) "Greece, the Near East, and Egypt: Cyclic destruction in Hesiod and the *Catalogue of Women*," *Transactions of the American Philological Association* 124: 1–34.

Koenig, Y. (2007) "The image of the foreigner in the magical texts of ancient Egypt," in *Moving across Borders: Foreign Relations, Religion and Cultural Interactions in the Ancient Mediterranean*, ed. P. Kousoulis and K. Magliveras. Leuven, Paris, and Dudley, Mass. 223–38.

Koitabashi, M. (1998) "Music in the texts from Ugarit," *Ugarit-Forschungen* 30: 363–96.

Kolb, F. (2004) "Troy VI: A trading center and commercial city?," *American Journal of Archaeology* 108: 577–613.

Koller, H. (1968) "Πόλις Μερόπων Ἀνθρόπων," *Glotta* 46: 18–26.

Kolsti, J. (1990) *The Bilingual Singer: A Study in Albanian and Serbo-Croatian Oral Epic Traditions.* New York and London.

Korfmann, M. (1998) "Troia – Ausgrabungen 1997," *Studia Troica* 8: 1–70.

(2002) "Ilios, *ca.* 1200 BC – Ilion *ca.* 700 BC: Report on findings from archaeology," in *Omero tremila anni dopo: Atti del Congresso di Genova 6–8 luglio 2000*, ed. F. Montanari. Rome. 209–26.

Košak, S. (2003) "A note on 'The Tale of the Merchants'," in *Hittite Studies in Honor of Harry A. Hoffner, Jr. on the Occasion of His 65th Birthday*, ed. G. Beckman, R. H. Beal and G. McMahon. Winona Lake, Ind. 249–52.

Kowalzig, B. (2005) "Mapping out *communitas*: Performances of *theōria* in their sacred and political context," in *Pilgrimage in Graeco-Roman and Early Christian Antiquity: Seeing the Gods*, ed. J. Elsner and I. C. Rutherford. Oxford and New York. 41–72.

Kozal, E. (2010) "Cypriot Pottery," in *Tell Atchana, Ancient Alalakh.* Volume I: *The 2003–2004 Excavation Seasons*, ed. K. A. Yener. Istanbul. 67–80.

Kraus, W. (ed.) (1966) *Albin Lesky: Gesammelte Schriften: Aufsätze und Reden zu antiker und deutscher Dichtung und Kultur.* Bern and Munich.

Kretschmer, P. (1924) "Alakšanduš, König von Viluša," *Glotta* 13: 205–13.

Kuhrt, A. (1995) *The Ancient Near East c. 3000–330 BC.* London and New York.
  (2002) "Greek contact with the Levant and Mesopotamia in the first half of the first millennium BC: A view from the east," in *Greek Settlements in the Eastern Mediterranean and the Black Sea*, ed. G. R. Tsetskhladze and A. Snodgrass. Oxford. 17–25.

Kullmann, W. (1995) "The two Nekyiai of the *Odyssey* and their oral sources," in *ΕΥΧΗΝ ΟΔΥΣΣΕΙ. Από τα Πρακτικά του Ζ' Συνεδρίου για την Οδύσσεια (3–8 Σεπτεμβρίου 1993)*, ed. M. Päisi-Apostolopoulou. Ithaca, N.Y. 41–52. Reprinted in Rengakos (ed.) 2002, pp. 147–55.
  (1999a) "Homer and historical memory: Some theoretical considerations," in *Signs of Orality: The Oral Tradition and Its Influence in the Greek and Roman World*, ed. E. A. Mackay. Mnemosyne Supplement 188. Leiden, Boston and Cologne. 95–113. Reprinted in Rengakos (ed.) 2002, pp. 44–59.
  (1999b) "Homer und Kleinasien," in *Euphrosyne: Studies in Ancient Epic and Its Legacy in Honor of Dimitris N. Maronitis*, ed. J. N. Kazazis and A. Rengakos. Stuttgart. 189–201. Reprinted in Rengakos (ed.) 2002, pp. 60–74.

Kümmel, H. M. (1967) *Ersatzrituale für den hethitischen König*. Studien zu den Boğazköy-Texten 3. Wiesbaden.

Labov, W. (2001) *Principles of Linguistic Change*. Volume II: *Social Factors*. Oxford and Cambridge, Mass.

Lackenbacher, S. and F. Malbran-Labat (2005) "Ugarit et les Hittites dans les archives de la 'Maison d'Urtenu'," *Studi Micenei ed Egeo-Anatolici* 47: 227–40.

Laffineur, R. (1991) "À propos du sarcophage d'Aghia Triada: Un rituel de nécromancie à l'époque protohistorique?" *Kernos* 4: 277–85.
  (2005) "Imports/exports in the eastern Mediterranean: For a specific methodology," in *Emporia: Aegeans in the Central and Eastern Mediterranean. Proceedings of the 10th International Aegean Conference/ 10e Rencontre égéenne internationale, Athens, Italian School of Archaeology, 14-18 April 2004*, ed. R. Laffineur and E. Greco. Aegaeum 25. Liège and Austin, Tx. 53–8.

Lam, J. (2006) "The Hurrian section of the Ugaritic ritual text RS 24.643 (KTU 1.148)," *Ugarit-Forschungen* 38: 399–413.

Lambert, S. D. (1993) *The Phratries of Attica*. Ann Arbor.

Lambert, W. G. (1957) "Ancestors, authors, and canonicity," *Journal of Cuneiform Studies* 11: 1–14.
  (1960) "Gilgameš in religious, historical and omen texts and the historicity of Gilgameš," in *Gilgameš et sa légende: Comptes Rendues de la VIIe Rencontre Assyriologique Internationale (Paris–1958)*, ed. P. Garelli. Paris. 39–56.
  (1962) "A catalogue of texts and authors," *Journal of Cuneiform Studies* 16: 59–77.
  (1989) "Notes on a work of the most ancient Semitic literature," *Journal of Cuneiform Studies* 41: 1–33.

Lambert, W. G. and A. R. Millard (1969) *Atra-Ḫasīs: The Babylonian Story of the Flood*. Reprint of 1969 edn. Winona Lake, Ind.

Lancellotti, M. G. (2002) *Attis between Myth and History: King, Priest and God*. Leiden and Boston.

Landsberger, B. and R. T. Hallock (1955) "Das Vokabular Sᵃ," in *Materialen zum Sumerischen Lexikon III*. Rome. 47–87.

Lane Fox, R. (2009) *Travelling Heroes in the Epic Age of Homer*. New York.

Lanfranchi, G. B. (2000) "The ideological and political impact of the Assyrian imperial expansion on the Greek world in the 8th and 7th centuries BC," in *The Heirs of Assyria: Proceedings of the Opening Symposium of the Assyrian and Babylonian Intellectual Heritage Project Held in Tvärminne, Finland, October 8–11, 1998*, ed. S. Aro and R. M. Whiting. Helsinki. 7–34.

(2001–2002) "The Cimmerians at the entrance of the netherworld: Filtration of Assyrian cultural and ideological elements into archaic Greece," *Atti e memorie dell'Accademia Galileiana di Scienze Lettere ed Arti in Padova* 114: 75–112.

(2005) "The Luwian-Phoenician bilingual of Çineköy and the annexation of Cilicia to the Assyrian empire," in *Von Sumer bis Homer: Festschrift für Manfred Schretter zum 60. Geburtstag am 25. Februar 2004*, ed. R. Rollinger. Alter Orient und Altes Testament 325. Münster. 481–96.

(2007) "The Luwian-Phoenician bilinguals of ÇİNEKÖY and KARATEPE: An ideological dialogue," in *Getrennte Wege? Kommunikation, Raum und Wahrnehmung in der alten Welt*, ed. R. Rollinger, A. Luther and J. Wiesehöfer. Frankfurt. 179–217.

(2009) "A happy son of the king of Assyria: Warikas and the Çineköy bilingual (Cilicia)," in *Of Gods(s), Trees, Kings, and Scholars: Neo-Assyrian and Related Studies in Honour of Simo Parpola*, ed. M. Luukko, S. Svärd and R. Mattila. Helsinki. 127–50.

Lang, M. L. (1969) *The Palace of Nestor at Pylos in Western Messenia*. Volume II: *The Frescoes*. Princeton, N. J.

Laroche, E. (1960) "Koubaba, déesse anatolienne, et le problème des origines de Cybèle," in *Éléments orientaux dans la religion grecque ancienne. Colloque de Strasbourg 1958*, Paris. 113–28.

(1965, 1968) "Textes mythologiques en transcription," *Revue Hittite et Asianique* 23, 26: 61–178, 5–90, continuous pagination (1–204) used.

(1970) "Sur le vocabulaire de l'haruspicine hittite," *Revue d'Assyriologie* 64: 127–39.

(1973) "Contacts linguistiques et culturels entre la Grèce et l'Asie Mineure au deuxième millénaire," *Revue des Études Grecques* 86: xvii–xix.

Larson, S. (2000) "Boiotia, Athens, the Peisistratids, and the *Odyssey*'s Catalogue of Heroines," *Greek, Roman and Byzantine Studies* 41: 193–222.

Latacz, J. (1996) *Homer: His Art and His World*, trans. by J. P. Holoka. Ann Arbor.

(2004) *Troy and Homer: Towards a Solution of an Old Mystery*. 4th edn., trans. by K. Windle and R. Ireland. Oxford.

(2005) *Troia und Homer: Der Weg zur Lösung eines alten Rätsels*. 5th edn. Leipzig.

Lateiner, D. (2002) "Pouring bloody drops (*Iliad* 16.459): The grief of Zeus," *Colby Quarterly* 38: 42–61.

Laumonier, A. (1958) *Les cultes indigènes en Carie*. Paris.

Lawergren, B. (1998) "Distinctions among Canaanite, Philistine, and Israelite lyres, and their global lyrical contexts." *Bulletin of the American School of Oriental Research* 309: 41-68.

Leaf, W. (1923) *Strabo on the Troad: Book XIII, Cap. 1*. Cambridge.

Lebedynsky, I. (2004) *Les Cimmériens*. Paris.

Lebrun, R. (1982) "Maliya, une divinité anatolienne mal connue," in *Studia Paulo Naster oblata*. Volume II: *Orientalia antiqua*, ed. J. Quaegebeur. Leuven. 123–30.

(1987) "Problèmes de religion anatolienne," *Hethitica* 8: 241–62.

(1992) "De quelques cultes lyciens et pamphyliens," in *Hittite and Other Anatolian and Near Eastern Studies in Honour of Sedat Alp*, ed. H. Otten, E. Akurgal, H. Ertem and A. Süel. Ankara. 357–63.

(1995) "Continuité culturelle et religieuse en Asie Mineure," in *Atti del II Congresso Internazionale di Hittitologia*, ed. O. Carruba, M. Giorgieri and C. Mora. Studia Mediterranea 9. Pavia. 249–56.

(1998a) "L'identité des Troyens," in *Quaestiones Homericae: Acta Colloquii Namurcensis habiti diebus 7-9 mensis Septembris anni 1995*, ed. L. Isebaert and R. Lebrun. Collection d'Études Classiques 9. Leuven and Namur. 149–61.

(1998b) "Panthéons locaux de Lycie, Lykaonie et Cilicie aux deuxième et premier millénaires av. J.-C.," *Kernos* 11: 143–55.

(2001) "Kummanni et Tarse, deux centres ciliciens majeurs," in *La Cilicie: Éspaces et pouvoirs locaux (2e millénaire av. J.-C. – 4e siècle ap. J.-C.). Actes de la Table Ronde Internationale d'Istanbul, 2–5 novembre 1999*, ed. É. Jean, A. M. Dinçol and S. Durugönül. Paris. 87–94.

Lebrun, R. and J. De Vos (2006) "À propos de l'inscription bilingue de l'ensemble sculptural de Çineköy," *Anatolica Antiqua* 14: 45–64.

Lefèvre-Novaro, D. and A. Mouton (2008) "Aux origines de l'ichthyomancie en Anatolie ancienne," *Anatolica* 34: 7–52.

Leichty, E. (2011) *The Royal Inscriptions of Esarhaddon, King of Assyria (680–669 BC)*. The Royal Inscriptions of the Neo-Assyrian Period 4. Winona Lake, Ind.

Lejeune, M. (1972) *Phonétique historique du Mycénien et du Grec ancien*. Paris.

(1997) "Anatomie de la série thébaine Gp," in *Mémoires de philologie mycéniene. Quatrième Série (1969–1996)*, ed. L. Godart and A. Sacconi. Rome. 285–92.

Lemaire, A. (2006) "La maison de Mopsos en Cilicie et en Pamphylie à l'époque du Fer (XIIe–VIe s. av. J.-C.)," *Res Antiquae* 3: 99–107.

Lemos, I. S. (1998) "Euboea and its Aegean koine," in *Euboica: L'Eubea e la presenze euboica in Calcidica e in Occidente. Atti del Convegno Internazionale di Napoli 13-16 novembre 1996*, ed. M. Bats and B. d'Agostino. Naples. 45-58.

(2002) *The Protogeometric Aegean: The Archaeology of the Late Eleventh and Tenth Centuries BC*. Oxford and New York.

(2006) "Athens and Lefkandi: A tale of two sites," in *Ancient Greece: From the Mycenaean Palaces to the Age of Homer*, ed. S. Deger-Jalkotzy and I. S. Lemos. Edinburgh. 505-30.

Lesky, A. (1950) "Hethitische Texte und griechischer Mythos," *Anzeiger der Österreichischen Akademie der Wissenschaften in Wien, Philosophisch-Historische Klasse* 57: 137-60. Reprinted in Kraus (ed.) 1966, pp. 356-71.

(1955) "Griechischer Mythos und vorderer Orient," *Saeculum* 6: 35-52. Reprinted in Kraus (ed.) 1966, pp. 379-400.

Levaniouk, O. (2011) *Eve of the Festival: Making Myth in Odyssey 19*. Washington, D.C.

Levine, B. A. and J.-M. de Tarragon (1985) "Dead kings and rephaim: The patrons of the Ugaritic dynasty," *Journal of the American Oriental Society* 104: 649-59.

Lewis, B. (1980) *The Sargon Legend: A Study of the Akkadian Text and the Tale of the Hero who was Exposed at Birth*. Cambridge, Mass.

Lipiński, E. (1985) "Phoenicians in Anatolia and Assyria 9th-6th Centuries B.C.," *Orientalia Lovaniensia Periodica* 16: 81-90.

(1991) "The Cypriot vassals of Esarhaddon," in *Ah, Assyria...: Studies in Assyrian History and Ancient Near Eastern Historiography Presented to Hayim Tadmor*, ed. M. Cogan and I. Eph'al. Scripta Hierosolymitana 33. Jerusalem. 58-64.

(1995) *Dieux et déesses de l'univers phénicien et punique*. Orientalia Lovaniensia Analecta 64. Leuven.

(2000) "The linguistic geography of Syria in Iron Age II (c. 1000-600 B.C.)," in *Essays on Syria in the Iron Age*, ed. G. Bunnens. Ancient Near Eastern Studies Supplement 7. Leuven. 125-42.

(2004) *Itineraria Phoenicia*. Leuven.

Liverani, M. (1993) "Model and actualization: The kings of Akkad in the historical tradition," in *Akkad, the First World Empire: Structure, Ideology, Traditions*, ed. M. Liverani. Padua. 41-67.

Lloyd, J. B. (1990) "The banquet themes in Ugaritic narrative," *Ugarit-Forschungen* 22: 169-93.

Longman, T., III (1991) *Fictional Akkadian Autobiography: A Generic and Comparative Study*. Winona Lake, Ind.

López-Ruiz, C. (2006) "Some oriental elements in Hesiod and the Orphic cosmogonies," *Journal of Ancient Near Eastern Religions* 6: 71-104.

(2009) "Mopsos and cultural exchange between Greeks and locals in Cilicia," in *Antike Mythen, Medien, Transformationen, Konstruktionen (Fritz Graf Festschrift)*, ed. U. Dill and C. Walde. Berlin and New York. 487–501.

(2010) *When the Gods Were Born: Greek Cosmogonies and the Near East*. Cambridge, Mass.

(2013) *Ancient Mediterranean Myths: Primary Sources from Ancient Greece, Rome, and the Near East*. New York and Oxford.

Lord, A. B. (1960) *The Singer of Tales*. Cambridge, Mass.

(1995) *The Singer Resumes the Tale*. Ithaca, N.Y. and London.

Lorenz, G. (1996) "Die griechische Heroenvorstellung in früharchaischer Zeit zwischen Tradition und Neuerung," in *Wege zur Genese griechischer Identität: Die Bedeutung der früharchaischen Zeit*, ed. C. Ulf. Berlin. 20–58.

Lorenz, J. and E. Rieken (2010) "Überlegungen zur Verwendung mythologischer Texte bei den Hethitern," in *Festschrift für Gernot Wilhelm anlässlich seines 65. Geburtstages am 28. Januar 2010*, ed. J. C. Fincke. Dresden. 217–34.

Lorenz, U. (2008) "Sonnengöttin der Erde – Ereškigal – Allani: Einige Bemerkungen zu den hethitischen Unterweltsgöttinnen in der Ritualliteratur," *Studi Micenei ed Egeo-Anatolici* 50: 501–11.

Loretz, O. (1993) "Nekromantie und Totenevokation in Mesopotamien, Ugarit und Israel," in *Religionsgeschichtliche Beziehungen zwischen Kleinasien, Nordsyrien und dem Alten Testament: Internationales Symposium Hamburg 17.–21. März 1990*, ed. B. Janowski, K. Koch and G. Wilhelm. Orbis Biblicus et Orientalis 129. Freiburg and Göttingen. 285–318.

(1994) "'Ugaritic and Biblical literature': Das Paradigma des Mythos von den *rpum – Rephaim*," in *Ugarit and the Bible: Proceedings of the International Symposium on Ugarit and the Bible, Manchester, September 1992*, ed. G. J. Brooke, A. H. W. Curtis and J. F. Healey. Münster. 175–224.

(2001) "Der ugaritische architektonische Begriff ḫšt 'Totenheiligtum'," *Ugarit-Forschungen* 33: 377–85.

(2002) "Ugaritisch âp (III) und syllabisch-keilschriftlich *abi/apu* als Vorläufer von hebräisch *âb/'ôb* (Kult/Nekromantie-)Grube, Ugarit: Ein Beitrag zu Nekromantie und Magie in Ugarit, Emar, und Israel," *Ugarit-Forschungen* 34: 481–519.

Lorimer, H. L. (1950) *Homer and the Monuments*. London.

Lowenstam, S. (1997) "Talking vases: The relationship between the Homeric poems and archaic representations of epic myth," *Transactions of the American Philological Association* 127: 21–76.

Luce, J. V. (2003) "The case for historical significance in Homer's landmarks at Troia," in *Troia and the Troad: Scientific Approaches*, ed. G. A. Wagner, E. Pernicka and H.-P. Uerpmann. Berlin. 9–30.

Luckenbill, D. D. (1968) *Ancient Records of Assyria and Babylonia*. Volume II: *Historical Records of Assyria*. New York.

Ludwig, M.-C. (1990) *Untersuchungen zu den Hymnen des Išme-Dagan von Isin.* Wiesbaden.

Luke, C. and C. H. Roosevelt (forthcoming) "Memory and meaning in Bin Tepe, the Lydian cemetery of the 'thousand mounds'," in *Tumulus as Sema: Proceedings of an International Conference on Space, Politics, Culture, and Religion in the First Millennium BC*, ed. O. Henry and U. Kelp. Berlin.

Luke, J. (2003) *Ports of Trade, Al Mina and Geometric Greek pottery in the Levant.* Oxford.

Maier, F. G. (1989) "Priest kings in Cyprus," in *Early Society in Cyprus*, ed. E. Peltenburg. Edinburgh. 376–91.

(1999) "Palaipaphos and the transition to the Early Iron Age: Continuities, discontinuities and location shifts," in *Cyprus: The Historicity of the Geometric Horizon. Proceedings of an Archaeological Workshop, University of Cyprus, Nicosia, 11th October 1998*, ed. M. Iacovou and D. Michaelides. Nicosia. 79–93.

Malbran-Labat, F. (1999) "Nouvelles données épigraphiques sur Chypre et Ougarit," *Report of the Department of Antiquities, Cyprus*: 121–3.

Malkin, I. (1987) *Religion and Colonization in Ancient Greece.* Leiden and New York.

(1998) *The Returns of Odysseus: Colonization and Ethnicity.* Berkeley, Los Angeles and London.

Manning, S. W. (2010) "Chronology and terminology," in *The Oxford Handbook of The Bronze Age Aegean (ca. 3000–1000 BC)*, ed. E. H. Cline. Oxford and New York. 11–28.

Manning, S. W. and B. Kromer (2011) "Radiocarbon dating archaeological samples in the eastern Mediterranean, 1730 to 1480 BC: Further exploring the atmospheric radiocarbon calibration record and the archaeological implications," *Archaeometry* 53: 413–39.

Maran, J. (2004) "Architektonische Innovation im spätmykenischen Tiryns – Lokale Bauprogramme und fremde Kultureinflüsse," in *Althellenische Technologie und Technik von der prähistorischen bis zur hellenistischen Zeit mit Schwerpunkt auf der prähistorischen Epoche.* Weilheim. 261–93.

(2006) "Coming to terms with the past: Ideology and power in the Late Helladic IIIC," in *Ancient Greece: From the Mycenaean Palaces to the Age of Homer*, ed. S. Deger-Jalkotzy and I. S. Lemos. Edinburgh. 123–50.

(2011) "Contested pasts – the society of the 12th c. B.C.E. Argolid and the memory of the Mycenaean palatial period," in *Our Cups Are Full: Pottery and Society in the Aegean Bronze Age: Papers Presented to Jeremy B. Rutter on the Occasion of his 65th Birthday*, ed. W. Gauß, M. Lindblom, R. A. K. Smith and J. C. Wright. Oxford. 169–78.

Marcovich, M. (ed.) (1995) *Clementis Alexandri Protrepticus.* Leiden.

Marinatos, N. (1984) *Art and Religion in Thera: Reconstructing a Bronze Age Society.* Athens.

(1990) "Celebrations of death and the symbolism of the lion hunt," in *Celebrations of Death and Divinity in the Bronze Age Argolid: Proceedings of the Sixth International Symposium at the Swedish Institute at Athens, 11–13 June, 1988*, ed. R. Hägg and G. C. Nordquist. Stockholm. 143–8.

(1993) *Minoan Religion: Ritual, Image, and Symbol*. Columbia.

(2004) "The character of Minoan epiphanies," *Illinois Classical Studies* 29: 25–42.

Marks, J. (2002) "The junction between the *Kypria* and the *Iliad*," *Phoenix* 56: 1–24.

(2003) "Alternative Odysseys: The case of Thoas and Odysseus," *Transactions of the American Philological Association* 133: 209–26.

Marshall, J. (2004) *Language Change and Sociolinguistics: Rethinking Social Networks*. Houndmills and New York.

Martin, R. P. (2000) "Synchronic aspects of Homeric performance: The evidence of the *Hymn to Apollo*," in *Una nueva visión de la cultura griega antigua hacia el fin del milenio*, ed. A. M. González de Tobia La Plata. 403–32.

Maslov, B. (2011) "The metrical evidence for pre-Mycenaean hexameter epic reconsidered," *Indoevropeiskoe iazykoznanie i klassicheskaia filologiia* 15: 376–89.

(2012) "The real life of the genre of prooimion," *Classical Philology* 107: 191–205.

(2013) "The dialect basis of choral lyric and the history of poetic languages of Archaic Greece," *Symbolae Osloenses* 87: 1–29.

Mason, H. J. (2008) "Hittite Lesbos?," in *Anatolian Interfaces: Hittites, Greeks and Their Neighbors. Proceedings of an International Conference on Cross-Cultural Interaction, September 17–19, 2004, Emory University, Atlanta, Ga.*, ed. B. J. Collins, M. R. Bachvarova and I. C. Rutherford. Oxford. 57–62.

Masson, O. (1962) *Les fragments du poète Hipponax: Édition critique et commentée*. Paris.

(1983) *Les inscriptions Chypriotes syllabiques: Recueil critique et commenté*. Études Chypriotes. Paris.

Mastrocinque, A. (2007) "The Cilician god Sandas and the Greek Chimaera: Features of Near Eastern and Greek mythology concerning the plague," *Journal of Ancient Near Eastern Religions* 7: 197–217.

Matthews, V. J. (1996) *Antimachus of Colophon: Text and Commentary*. Leiden, New York and Cologne.

Matthiae, P. (1979) "Princely cemetery and ancestors cult at Ebla during the Middle Bronze II: A proposal of interpretation," *Ugarit-Forschungen* 11: 563–70.

(1981) *Ebla: An Empire Rediscovered*, trans. by C. Holme. London, Sydney, Auckland, Toronto.

(1990) "A class of Old Syrian bronze statuettes and the sanctuary B2 at Ebla," in *Resurrecting the Past: A Joint Tribute to Adnan Bounni*, ed. P. Matthiae, M. van Loon and H. Weiss. Leiden. 345–62.

(1997) "Where were the early Syrian kings of Ebla buried?" *Altorientalische Forschungen* 24: 268–76.

(2003) "Ishtar of Ebla and Hadad of Aleppo: Notes on terminology, politics, and religion of Old Syrian Ebla," in *Semitic and Assyriological Studies Presented to Pelio Fronzaroli by Pupils and Colleagues*. Wiesbaden. 381–402.

(2006a) "Archaeology of a destruction: the end of MB II Ebla in the light of myth and history," in *Timelines: Studies in Honour of Manfred Bietak*. Volume III, ed. E. Czerny, I. Hein, H. Hunger, D. Melman and A. Schwab. Orientalia Lovaniensia Analecta 149. Leuven, Paris and Dudley, Mass. 39–51.

(2006b) "The archaic palace at Ebla: A royal building between Early Bronze Age IVB and Middle Bronze Age I," in *Confronting the Past: Archaeological and Historical Essays on Ancient Israel in Honor of William G. Dever*, ed. S. Gitin, J. E. Wright and J. P. Dessel. Winona Lake, Ind. 85–104.

(2007) "The destruction of Old Syrian Ebla at the end of Middle Bronze II. New historical data," in *Proceedings of the International Colloquium: From Relative Chronology to Absolute Chronology: The Second Millennium BC in Syria-Palestine (Rome, 29th November–1st December 2001)*, ed. P. Matthiae, F. Pinnock, L. Nigro and L. Peyronel. Rome. 5–32.

(2008) *Gli archivi reali di Ebla: La scoperta, i testi, il significato*. Milan; Rome.

(2010) "The seal of Ushra-Samu, offical of Ebla, and Ishkhara's iconography," in *Opening the Tablet Box: Near Eastern Studies in Honor of Benjamin R. Foster*, ed. S. C. Melville and A. L. Slotsky. Leiden and Boston. 271–90.

(2014) "Materia epica preomerica nell'Anatolia hittita. Il *Canto della liberazione* e la conquista di Ebla," in *Dai pochi ai molti: Studi in onore di Roberto Antonelli*, ed. P. Canettieri and A. Punzi. Rome. 1075–90.

May, H. G. and B. M. Metzger (eds.) (1973) *The New Oxford Annotated Bible: Revised Standard Version*. New York.

Mayer, W. (2002) "Die Stadt *Kumme* als überregionales religiöses Zentrum," in *Ex Mesopotamia et Syria lux*, ed. O. Loretz, K. A. Metzler and H. Schaudig. Alter Orient und Altes Testament 281. Münster. 329–58.

Mazarakis Ainian, A. (1997) *From Rulers' Dwellings to Temples: Architecture, Religion and Society in Early Iron Age Greece (1100–700 B.C.)*. Jonsered.

(1999) "Reflections on hero cults in Early Iron Age Greece," in *Ancient Greek Hero Cult: Proceedings of the Fifth International Seminar on Ancient Greek Cult, Organized by the Department of Classical Archaeology and Ancient History, Göteborg University, 21–3 April 1995*, ed. R. Hägg. Skrifter Utgivna av Svenska Institutet i Athen 8°, 16. Stockholm. 9–36.

(2006) "The archaeology of *basileis*," in *Ancient Greece: From the Mycenaean Palaces to the Age of Homer*, ed. S. Deger-Jalkotzy and I. S. Lemos. Edinburgh. 181–211.

Mazoyer, M. (2003a) "Le ^{GIŠ}eya dans la religion hittite," in *L'Arbre: Symbole et réalité: Actes des Premières Journées universitaires de Hérisson organisées par la ville de Hérisson et les Cahiers KUBABA (Université de Paris I – Panthéon-Sorbonne) les 21 et 22 juin 2002*, ed. M. Mazoyer, J. Pérez Rey, R. Lebrun and F. Malbran-Labat. Paris. 73–80.

(2003b) *Télipinu, le dieu au marécage: Essai sur les mythes fondateurs du royaume hittite.* Paris.

Mazzoni, S. (2008) "Review of Çambel and Özyar (2003)." *American Journal of Archaeology Online Book Review.* www.ajaonline.org/pdfs/book_reviews/ 112.4/04_Mazzoni.pdf, accessed September 9, 2010.

McNeill, I. (1963) "The metre of the Hittite epic," *Anatolian Studies* 13: 237–42.

Mee, C. (1978) "Aegean trade and settlement in Anatolia in the second millennium B.C.," *Anatolian Studies* 28: 121–56.

Meier, G. (1939) "Ein Akkadisches Heilungsritual aus Boğazköy," *Zeitschrift für Assyriologie und vorderasiatische Archäologie* N.S. 11: 195–215.

Meier-Brügger, M. (2006) "Sprachliche Beobachtungen," in *Die neuen Linear B-Texte aus Theben: Ihr Aufschlusswert für die mykenische Sprache und Kultur. Akten des internationalen Forschungskolloquiums an der Österreichischen Akademie der Wissenschaften, 5.-6. Dezember 2002*, ed. S. Deger-Jalkotzy and O. Panagl. Österreichische Akademie der Wissenschaften, philosophisch-historische Klasse, Denkschriften 338. Vienna. 111–18.

Meillet, A. (1923) *Les origines indo-européennes des mètres grecs.* Paris.

Melchert, H. C. (1978) "The Acts of Hattušili I," *Journal of Near Eastern Studies* 37: 1–22.

(1994) *Anatolian Historical Phonology.* Leiden Studies in Indo-European 3. Amsterdam and Atlanta, Ga.

(1998) "Poetic meter and phrasal stress in Hittite," in *Mír Curad: Studies in Honor of Calvert Watkins*, ed. J. Jasanoff, H. C. Melchert and L. Oliver. Innsbrucker Beiträge zur Sprachwissenschaft 92. Innsbruck. 483–94.

(2003a) "The dialectal position of Lydian and Lycian within Anatolian," in *Licia e Lidia prima dell'ellenizzazione. Atti del Convegno Internazionale, Roma, 11–12 ottobre 1999*, ed. M. Giorgieri, M. Salvini, M.-C. Trémouille and P. Vannicelli. Rome. 265–72.

(2003b) "Introduction," in *The Luwians*, ed. H. C. Melchert. Handbuch der Orientalistik 1.68. Leiden and Boston. 1–7.

(2003c) "Language," in *The Luwians*, ed. H. C. Melchert. Handbuch der Orientalistik 1.68. Leiden and Boston. 170–210.

(ed.) (2003d) *The Luwians.* Handbuch der Orientalistik 1.68. Leiden and Boston.

(2003e) "Prehistory," in *The Luwians*, ed. H. C. Melchert. Handbook der Orientalistik 1.68. Leiden and Boston. 8–26.

(2005) "The problem of Luvian influence on Hittite," in *Sprachkontakt und Sprachwandel: Akten der XI. Fachtagung der Indogermanischen Gesellschaft, 17.–23. September 2000, Halle an der Saale*, ed. G. Meiser and O. Hackstein. Wiesbaden. 445–60.

(2007) "Middle Hittite revisited," *Studi Micenei ed Egeo-Anatolici* 49: 525–31.

(2008) "Greek *mólybdos* as a loanword from Lydian," in *Anatolian Interfaces: Hittites, Greeks and Their Neighbors. Proceedings of an International Conference* on *Cross-Cultural Interaction, September 17–19, 2004, Emory University, Atlanta, Ga.*, ed. B. J. Collins, M. R. Bachvarova and I. C. Rutherford. Oxford. 153–7.

(forthcoming) "Translation strategies in the Hurro-Hittite bilingual from Boğazköy," in *Strategies of Translation: Language Contact and Poetic Language*, ed. J. L. García Ramón.

Melena, J. L. (2001) *Textos griegos micénicos comentados*. Vitoria-Gasteiz.

Melena, J. L. and J.-P. Olivier (1991) *Tithemy: The Tablets and Nodules in Linear B from Tiryns, Thebes and Mycenae: A Revised Transliteration*. Suplementos a "Minos" 12. Salamanca and Lejona.

Mellink, M. J. (1963) "An Akkadian illustration of a campaign in Cilicia?," *Anatolia* 7: 101–15.

(1965) "Mita, Mushki and Phrygians," *Jahrbuch für kleinasiatische Forschung/ Anadolu Araştırmaları* 2: 317–25.

(1983) "Comments on a cult relief of Kybele from Gordion," in *Beiträge zur Altertumskunde Kleinasiens: Festschrift für Kurt Bittel*, ed. R. M. Boehmer and H. Hauptmann. Mainz am Rhein. 349–60.

(1995) "Homer, Lycia, and Lukka," in *The Ages of Homer: A Tribute to Emily Townsend Vermeule*, ed. J. B. Carter and S. P. Morris. Austin, Tx. 33–43.

Mellink, M. J. and D. Strahan (1998) "The bronze figurine from Troia VIIa," *Studia Troica* 8: 141–9.

Méndez Dosuna, J. (1993) "Metátesis de cantidad en jónico-ático y heracleota," *Emerita* 61: 95–134.

Menzel, B. (1981) *Assyrische Tempel*. Studia Pohl, Series Maior 10. Rome.

Meriggi, P. (1968) "Die hethitischen Fragmente vom *šar tamhâri*," in *Studien zur Sprachwissenschaft und Kulturkunde. Gedenkschrift für Wilhelm Brandenstein (1898–1967)*, ed. M. Mayrhofer. Innsbruck. 259–67.

Meyer, M. (2011) "Kilikien: Örtliche Gegebenheiten und archäologische Evidenzen," in *Lag Troia in Kilikien? Der aktuelle Streit um Homers Ilias*, ed. C. Ulf and R. Rollinger Darmstadt. 81–114.

Michalowski, P. (1988) "Divine heroes and historical self-representation: From Gilgamesh to Shulgi," *Bulletin of the Canadian Society for Mesopotamian Studies* 16: 19–23.

(1991) "Charisma and control: On continuity and change in early Mesopotamian bureaucratic systems," in *The Organization of Power: Aspects of Bureaucracy in the Ancient Near East*. 2nd edn., ed. M. Gibson and R. D. Biggs. Studies in Ancient Oriental Civilization 46. Chicago. 45–57.

(1992) "Orality and literacy and early Mesopotamian literature," in *Mesopotamian Epic Literature: Oral or Aural?*, ed. M. E. Vogelzang and H. L. J. Vanstiphout. Lewiston, N.Y. 227–45.

(2003) "The mountains and the stars," in *Semitic and Assyriological Studies Presented to Pelio Fronzaroli by Pupils and Colleagues*. Wiesbaden. 403–10.

Middleton, G. D. (2010) *The Collapse of Palatial Society in LBA Greece and the Postpalatial Period*. Oxford.

Milani, C. (2005) "Le nuove tavolette di Tebe: Note su Lacedemoni e Tebani," *Aevum* 79: 3–7.

Miller, D. G. (1982) *Homer and the Ionian Epic Tradition: Some Phonic and Phonological Evidence Against an Aeolic 'Phase'*. Innsbrucker Beiträge zur Sprachwissenschaft 38. Innsbruck.

Miller, J. L. (2001) "Anum-Ḫirbi and his kingdom," *Altorientalische Forschungen* 28: 65–101.

(2004) *Studies in the Origins, Development and Interpretation of the Kizzuwatna Rituals*. Studien zu den Boğazköy-Texten 46. Wiesbaden.

(2005) "A join to the Hittite Atramḫasi myth (KUB 8.63+1718/u)," *NABU: Nouvelles Assyriologiques Brèves et Utilitaires*: 10.

(2010) "Some disputed passages in the Tawagalawa Letter," in *Ipamati kistamati pari tumatimis: Luwian and Hittite Studies Presented to J. David Hawkins on the Occasion of his 70th Birthday*, ed. I. Singer. Tel Aviv. 159–69.

Mommsen, H., D. Hertel and P. Mountjoy (2001) "Neutron activation analysis of the pottery from Troy in the Berlin Schliemann collection," *Archäologischer Anzeiger*: 169–211.

Mommsen, H. and P. Mountjoy (2006) "Neutron activation analysis of Mycenaean pottery from Troy (1988–2003 excavations)," *Studia Troica* 16: 97–123.

Mommsen, H., P. Mountjoy and A. Özyar (2011) "Provenance determination of Mycenaean IIIC vessels from the 1934–1939 excavations at Tarsus-Gözlükule by neutron activation analysis," *Archaeometry* 53: 900–15.

Mondi, R. (1984) "The ascension of Zeus and the composition of Hesiod's Theogony," *Greek, Roman, and Byzantine Studies* 25: 325–44.

Montanari, F. (1979) *Studi di filologia omerica antica*. Volume I. Pisa.

Moortgat, A. (1955) *Tell Halaf. Dritter Band: Die Bildwerke*. Berlin.

Mora, C. and L. d'Alfonso (2012) "Anatolia after the end of the Hittite Empire: New evidence from Southern Cappadocia," *Origini* 34: 385–98.

Moran, W. L. (1992) *The Amarna Letters*. Baltimore and London.

Morgan, C. (1989) *Athletes and Oracles: The Transformation of Olympia and Delphi in the Eighth Century B.C.* Cambridge and New York.

(1996) "From palace to polis? Religious developments on the Greek mainland during the Bronze Age/Iron Age transition," in *Religion and Power in the Ancient Greek World: Proceedings of the Uppsala Symposium 1993*, ed. P. Hellström and B. Alroth. Uppsala. 41–57.

Morris, I. (1986) "The use and abuse of Homer," *Classical Antiquity* 5: 81–138.

(1988) "Tomb cult and the 'Greek renaissance': The past in the present in the 8th century BC," *Antiquity* 62: 750–61.

(2000) *Archaeology as Cultural History: Words and Things in Iron Age Greece*. Malden, Mass.

Morris, I. and J. G. Manning (2005) "Introduction," in *The Ancient Economy: Evidence and Models*, ed. J. G. Manning and I. Morris. Stanford, Calif. 1–44.

Morris, S. P. (1989) "A tale of two cities: The miniature frescoes from Thera and the origins of Greek poetry," *American Journal of Archaeology* 93: 511–35.
  (1992a) *Daidalos and the Origins of Greek Art*. Princeton, N.J.
  (1992b) "Prehistoric iconography and historical sources: Hindsight through texts?," in *EIKΩN: Aegean Bronze Age Iconography: Shaping a Methodology. Proceedings of the 4th International Aegean Conference/ 4e Rencontre égéenne internationale, University of Tasmania, Hobart, Australia, 6–9 April 1992*, ed. R. Laffineur and J. L. Crowley. Aegaeum 8. Liège. 205–12.
  (1997) "Homer and the Near East," in *A New Companion to Homer*, ed. I. Morris and B. Powell. Leiden, New York and Cologne. 599–623.
  (2001a) "Potnia Aswiya: Anatolian contributions to Greek religion," in *Potnia: Deities and Religion in the Aegean Bronze Age. Proceedings of the 8th International Aegean Conference/8e Rencontre égéenne internationale, Göteborg, Göteborg University, 12–15 April 2000*, ed. R. Laffineur and R. Hägg. Aegaeum 22. Liège and Austin, Tx. 423–34.
  (2001b) "The prehistoric background of Artemis Ephesia: A solution to the enigma of her 'breasts'?," in *Der Kosmos der Artemis von Ephesos*, ed. U. Muss. Österreichisches Archäologisches Institut, Sonderschriften 37. Vienna. 135–51.
  (2006) "The view from east Greece: Miletus, Samos and Ephesus," in *Debating Orientalization: Multidisciplinary Approaches to Change in the Ancient Mediterranean*, ed. C. Riva and N. C. Vella. London and Oakville, Conn. 66–84.
Mosca, P. G. and J. Russell (1987) "A Phoenician inscription from Cebel Ires Dağı in Rough Cilicia," *Epigraphica Anatolica* 9: 1–27.
  (2006) "The view from east Greece: Miletus, Samos and Ephesus," in *Debating Orientalization: Multidisciplinary Approaches to Change in the Ancient Mediterranean*, ed. C. Riva and N. C. Vella. London and Oakville, Conn. 66–84.
Moss, M. L. (2005) *The Minoan Pantheon: Towards an Understanding of Its Nature and Extent*. BAR International Series 1343. Oxford.
Most, G. W. (1997) "Hesiod's myth of the five (or three or four) races," *Proceedings of the Cambridge Philological Society* 43: 104–27.
  (ed.) (2006) *Hesiod I: Theogony, Works and Days, Testimonia*. Cambridge, Mass. and London.
Mountjoy, P. A. (1997) "Local Mycenaean pottery at Troia," *Studia Troica* 7: 259–67.
  (1998) "The east Aegean-west Anatolian interface in the Late Bronze Age: Mycenaeans and the kingdom of Ahhiyawa," *Anatolian Studies* 48: 33–67.
  (1999a) *Regional Mycenaean Decorated Pottery*. Rahden.
  (1999b) "Troia VII reconsidered," *Studia Troica* 9: 295–346.
  (2005) "A Trojan Mycenaean pictorial krater revisited," *Studia Troica* 15: 121–6.

Mouton, A. (2007) *Rêves hittites: Contribution à une historie et une anthropologie du rêve en Anatolie ancienne.* Culture and History of the Ancient Near East 28. Leiden and Boston.

Mouton, A. and I. C. Rutherford (2013) "Luwian religion, a research project: The case of 'Hittite' augury," in *Luwian Identities: Culture, Language and Religion between Anatolia and the Aegean,* ed. A. Mouton, I. C. Rutherford and I. Yakubovich. Leiden and Boston. 329–43.

Moyer, I. (2006) "Golden fetters and the economies of cultural exchange," *Journal of Ancient Near Eastern Religions* 6: 225–55.

Muhlbauer, L. (2007) *Lykische Grabarchitektur: Vom Holz zum Stein.* Forschungen in Limyra 3. Vienna.

Muhly, J. D. (2003) "Greece and Anatolia in the Early Iron Age: The archaeological evidence and literary tradition," in *Symbiosis, Symbolism, and the Power of the Past: Canaan, Ancient Israel and Their Neighbors from the Late Bronze Age through Roman Palaestina: Proceedings of the Centennial Symposium, W. F. Albright Institute of Archaeological Research and American Schools of Oriental Research, Jerusalem, May 29–31, 2000,* ed. W. G. Dever and S. Gitin. Winona Lake, Ind. 23–35.

(2005) "Travelling craftsmen: Love 'em or leave 'em," in *Emporia: Aegeans in the Central and Eastern Mediterranean: Proceedings of the 10th International Aegean Conference/ 10ᵉ Rencontre égéenne internationale, Athens, Italian School of Archaeology, 14–18 April 2004,* ed. R. Laffineur and E. Greco. Aegaeum 25. Liège and Austin, Tx. 685–90.

Mullen, E. T., Jr. (1980) *The Assembly of the Gods: The Divine Council in Canaanite and Early Hebrew Literature.* Harvard Semitic Monographs 24. Atlanta, Ga.

Mullins, R. A. (2010) "A comparative analysis of the Alalakh 2003–2004 season pottery with Woolley's levels," in *Tell Atchana, Ancient Alalakh.* Volume 1: *The 2003–2004 Excavation Seasons,* ed. K. A. Yener. Istanbul. 51–66.

Munn, M. (2006) *The Mother of the Gods, Athens, and the Tyranny of Asia: A Study of Sovereignty in Ancient Religion.* Berkeley, Los Angeles and London.

(2008) "Kybele as Kubaba in a Lydo-Phrygian context," in *Anatolian Interfaces: Hittites, Greeks and Their Neighbors. Proceedings of an International Conference on Cross-Cultural Interaction, September 17–19, 2004, Emory University, Atlanta, Ga.,* ed. B. J. Collins, M. R. Bachvarova and I. C. Rutherford. Oxford. 159–64.

Murray, O. (1993) *Early Greece.* 2nd edn. Cambridge, Mass.

(2008) "The *Odyssey* as performance poetry," in *Performance, Iconography, Reception: Studies in Honour of Oliver Taplin,* ed. M. Revermann and P. Wilson. Oxford and New York. 161–76.

(2009) "The culture of the *symposion,*" in *A Companion to Archaic Greece,* ed. K. A. Raaflaub and H. van Wees. Malden, Mass., and Oxford. 508–23.

Muscarella, O. W. (1998) "Relations between Phrygia and Assyria in the 8th century B.C.," in *xxxiv. Uluslararası Assiriyoloji Kongresi*, ed. H. Erkanal, V. Donbaz and A. Uğuroğlu. Ankara. 149–57.

Muss, U. (2007) "Late Bronze Age and Early Iron Age terracottas: Their significance for an early cult place in the Artemision at Ephesus," in *Anatolian Iron Ages 6: The Proceedings of the Sixth Anatolian Iron Ages Colloquium Held at Eskişehir, 16–20 August 2004*, ed. A. Çilingiroğlu and A. Sagona. Leuven, Paris and Dudley, Mass. 167–94.

Nagy, G. (1974) *Comparative Studies in Greek and Indic Meter*. Cambridge, Mass.

(1983) "On the death of Sarpedon," in *Approaches to Homer*, ed. C. A. Rubino and C. W. Shelmerdine. Austin, Tx. 189–217.

(1985) "Theognis and Megara: A poet's vision of his city," in *Theognis of Megara: Poetry and the Polis*, ed. T. J. Figueira and G. Nagy. Baltimore. 22–81.

(1990a) *Greek Mythology and Poetics*. Ithaca, N.Y. and London.

(1990b) *Pindar's Homer: The Lyric Possession of an Epic Past*. Baltimore.

(1992) "Metrical convergences and divergences in early Greek poetry and songs," in *Historical Philology: Greek, Latin, and Romance*, ed. B. Brogyanyi and R. Lipp. Current Issues in Linguistic Theory 87. Amsterdam. 151–86.

(1996a) *Homeric Questions*. Austin, Tx.

(1996b) *Poetry as Performance: Homer and Beyond*. Cambridge.

(1999) *The Best of the Achaeans: Concepts of the Hero in Archaic Greek Poetry*. 2nd revised edn. Baltimore.

(2002) *Plato's Rhapsody and Homer's Music: The Poetics of the Panathenaic Festival in Classical Athens*. Cambridge, Mass. and Athens.

(2004) *Homer's Text and Language*. Urbana and Chicago.

(2009) *Homer the Classic*. Cambridge, Mass.

(2010) *Homer the Preclassic*. Sather Classical Lectures 67. Berkeley and Los Angeles.

(2011) "The Aeolic component in Homeric diction," in *Proceedings of the 22nd Annual UCLA Indo-European Conference*, ed. S. Jamison, H. C. Melchert and B. Vine. Bremen. 133–79.

Nahm, W. (2013) "The case for the lower middle chronology," *Altorientalische Forschungen* 40: 350–72.

Nakamura, M. (2002) *Das hethitische nuntarriyašḫa-Fest*. Leiden.

(2007) "Ein bisher unbekanntes Fragment der hurritischen Fassung des Gilgameš-Epos," in *Tabularia Hethaeorum: Hethitologische Beiträge Silvin Košak zum 65. Geburtstag*, ed. D. Groddek and M. Zorman. Dresdner Beiträge zur Hethitologie 25. Wiesbaden. 557–9.

Nasrabadi, B. M. (1999) *Untersuchungen zu den Bestattungssitten in Mesopotamien in der ersten Hälfte des ersten Jahrtausends v. Chr*. Baghdader Forschungen 23. Mainz am Rhein.

Na'aman, N. (2005) "Resident-alien or residing foreign delegate? On the *ubāru* in some Late Bronze Age texts," *Ugarit-Forschungen* 37: 475–9.

Negbi, O. (1992) "Early Phoenician presence in the Mediterranean islands: A reappraisal," *American Journal of Archaeology* 96: 599–615.

Neu, E. (1970) *Ein althethitisches Gewitterritual*. Studien zu den Boğazköy-Texten 12. Wiesbaden.

(1988a) *Das Hurritische: Eine altorientalische Sprache in neuem Licht*. Abhandlungen der Akademie der Wissenschaften und der Literatur. Geistes- und Sozialwissenschaftliche Klasse 3. Mainz.

(1988b) "Varia hurritica: Sprachliche Beobachtungen an der hurritisch-hethitischen Bilingue aus Hattuša," in *Documentum Asiae minoris antiquae: Festschrift für Heinrich Otten zum 75. Geburtstag*, ed. E. Neu and C. Rüster. Wiesbaden. 235–54.

(1993a) "Kešše-Epos und Epos der Freilassung," *Studi Micenei ed Egeo-Anatolici* 31: 111–20.

(1993b) "Knechtschaft und Freiheit. Betrachtungen über ein hurritisch-hethitisches Textensemble aus Ḫattuša," in *Religionsgeschichtliche Beziehungen zwischen Kleinasien, Nordsyrien und dem Alten Testament. Internationales Symposium Hamburg 17.-21. März 1990*, ed. B. Janowski, K. Koch and G. Wilhelm. Orbis Biblicus et Orientalis 129. Freiburg and Göttingen. 329–61.

(1995a) "Hethiter und Hethitisch in Ugarit," in *Ugarit: Ein ostmediterranes Kulturzentrum im Alten Orient. Volume 1: Ugarit und seine altorientalische Umwelt*, ed. M. Dietrich and O. Loretz. Abhandlungen zur Literatur Alt-Syrien-Palästinas 7. Münster. 115–29.

(1995b) "Mehrsprachigkeit im Alten Orient – bilinguale Texte als besondere Form sprachlicher Kommunikation," in *Kommunikation durch Zeichen und Wort: Stätten und Formen der Kommunikation im Altertum IV*, ed. G. Binder and K. Ehlich. Bochumer Altertumswissenschaftliches Colloquium 23. Trier. 11–39.

(1996) *Das hurritische Epos der Freilassung I: Untersuchungen zu einem hurritisch-hethitischen Textensemble aus Ḫattuša*. Studien zu den Boğazköy-Texten 32. Wiesbaden.

Neumann, G. (1999) "Wie haben die Troer im 13. Jahrhundert gesprochen?" *Würzburger Jahrbücher für die Altertumswissenschaft*, N. F. 23: 15–23.

(2006) "'... Ganz und Hund und ihresgleichen ...'," in *Die neuen Linear B-Texte aus Theben: Ihr Aufschlusswert für die mykenische Sprache und Kultur. Akten des internationalen Forschungskolloquiums an der Österreichischen Akademie der Wissenschaften, 5.–6. Dezember 2002*, ed. S. Deger-Jalkotzy and O. Panagl. Österreichische Akademie der Wissenschaften philosophisch-historische Klasse Denkschriften 338. Vienna. 125–39.

(2007) *Glossar des Lykischen*, revised and prepared for publication by Johann Tischler. Dresdner Beiträge zur Hethitologie 21. Wiesbaden.

Neve, P. (1969–1970) "Eine hethitische Quellgrotte in Boğazköy," *Istanbuler Mitteilungen* 19/20: 97–107.

(1984) "Die Ausgrabungen in Boğazköy-Ḫattuša 1983," *Archäologischer Anzeiger*: 329–72.
(1986) "Die Ausgrabungen in Boğazköy-Ḫattuša 1985," *Archäologischer Anzeiger*: 365–406, 795–6.
(1987) "Boğazköy – Ḫattuša: Ausgrabungen in der Oberstadt," *Anatolica* 14: 41–88.
(1993) *Ḫattuša – Stadt der Götter und Tempel: Neue Ausgrabungen in der Hauptstadt der Hethiter*. Mainz am Rhein.
Niehr, H. (1994) "Zum Totenkult der Könige von Samʾal im 9. und 8. Jh. v. Chr," *Studi epigrafici e linguistici sul Vicino Oriente antico* 11: 57–73.
(2001) "Ein weiterer Aspekt zum Totenkult der Könige von Samʾal," *Studi epigrafici e linguistici sul Vicino Oriente antico* 18: 83–97.
(2006a) "Bestattung und Ahnenkult in den Königshäusern von *Samʾal* (*Zincirli*) und *Guzāna* (*Tell Ḥalāf*) in Nordsyrien," *Zeitschrift des Deutschen Palästina-Vereins* 122: 111–39.
(2006b) "The royal funeral in ancient Syria: A comparative view on the tombs in the palaces of Qatna, Kumidi and Ugarit," *Journal of Northwest Semitic Languages* 32: 1–24.
(2007) "The topography of death in the royal palace of Ugarit: Preliminary thoughts on the basis of archaeological and textual data," in *Le royaume d'Ougarit de la Crète à l'Euphrate: Nouveaux axes de recherche*, ed. J.-M. Michaud. Sherbrooke, Quebec. 219–42.
Niemeier, W.-D. (1998) "The Mycenaeans in western Anatolia and the problem of the origins of the Sea Peoples," in *Mediterranean Peoples in Transition Thirteenth to Early Tenth Centuries BCE: In Honor of Professor Trude Dothan*, ed. S. Gitin, A. Mazar and E. Stern. Jerusalem. 17–65.
(2001) "Archaic Greeks in the Orient: Textual and archaeological evidence," *Bulletin of the American School of Oriental Research* 322: 11–32.
(2007a) "Milet von den Anfängen menschlicher Besiedlung bis zur Ionischen Wanderung," in *Frühes Ionien: Eine Bestandsaufnahme: Panionion-Symposion Güzelçamlı*, ed. J. Cobet, V. von Graeve, W.-D. Niemeier and K. Zimmermann. Milesische Forschungen 5. Mainz am Rhein. 3–20.
(2007b) "Westkleinasien und Ägäis von den Anfängen bis zur Ionischen Wanderung: Topographie, Geschichte und Beziehungen nach dem archäologischen Befund und den hethitischen Quellen," in *Frühes Ionien: Eine Bestandsaufnahme: Panionion-Symposion Güzelçamlı*, ed. J. Cobet, V. von Graeve, W.-D. Niemeier and K. Zimmermann. Milesische Forschungen 5. Mainz am Rhein. 37–96.
(2008) "Ḫattusas Beziehungen zum westlichen Kleinasien und dem mykenischen Griechenland nach den neuesten Forschungen," in *Ḫattuša – Boğazköy: Das Hethiterreich im Spannungsfeld des Alten Orients. 6. Internationales Colloquium der Deutschen Orient-Gesellschaft 22.–24. März 2006, Würzburg*, ed.

G. Wilhelm. Colloquien der Deutschen Orient-Gesellschaft 6. Wiesbaden. 291–349.

(2009) "Milet und Karien vom Neolithikum bis zu den 'Dunklen Jahrhunderten'," in *Die Karer und die Anderen: Internationales Kolloquium an der Freien Universität Berlin 13. bis 15. Oktober 2005*, ed. F. Rumscheid, Bonn. 7–25.

Niemeyer, H. G. (2004) "Phoenician or Greek: Is there a reasonable way out of the Al Mina debate?," *Ancient West & East* 3: 38–50.

Nikolaev, A. (2010) "A new argument against the assumption of an 'Aeolic phase' in the development of Homeric epic diction," *Indoevropeiskoe iazykoznanie i klassicheskaia filologiia* 14.2: 229–45.

Nikoloudis, S. (2008) "Multiculturalism in the Mycenaean world," in *Anatolian Interfaces: Hittites, Greeks and Their Neighbors. Proceedings of an International Conference on Cross-Cultural Interaction, September 17–19, 2004, Emory University, Atlanta, Ga.*, ed. B. J. Collins, M. R. Bachvarova and I. C. Rutherford. Oxford. 45–56.

Nilsson, M. P. (1950) *The Minoan-Mycenaean Religion and Its Survival in Greek Religion*. Lund.

Nissinen, M. (2000) "The socioreligious role of the Neo-Assyrian prophets," in *Prophecy in Its Ancient Near Eastern Context: Mesopotamian, Biblical, and Arabian Perspectives*, ed. M. Nissinen. Atlanta, Ga. 89–114.

Nissinen, M., C. L. Seow and R. K. Ritner (2003) *Prophets and Prophecy in the Ancient Near East*. Leiden and Boston.

Noegel, S. (1998) "The Aegean Ogygos of Boeotia and the Biblical Og of Bashan: Reflections of the same myth," *Zeitschrift für die alttestamentliche Wissenschaft* 110: 411–26.

Nougayrol, J., E. Laroche, C. Virolleaud and C. F. A. Schaeffer (1968) *Ugaritica v.* Mission de Ras Shamra 16. Paris.

Novák, M. (2003) "Divergierende Bestattungskonzepte und ihre sozialen, kulturellen und ethnischen Hintergründe," *Altorientalische Forschungen* 30: 63–84.

(2005) "Arameans and Luwians – processes of an acculturation," in *Ethnicity in Ancient Mesopotamia: Papers Read at the 48th Rencontre Assyriologique Internationale, Leiden, 1–4 July 2002*, ed. W. H. van Soldt, R. Kalvelagen, and D. Katz. Leiden. 252–66.

Oesch, J. (1996) "Die Religion Eblas," in *Religionsgeschichte Syriens: Von der Frühzeit bis zur Gegenwart*, ed. P. W. Haider, M. Hutter, S. Kreuzer. Stuttgart, Berlin, and Cologne. 39–48.

Oettinger, N. (1989–1990) "Die 'dunkle Erde' im Hethitischen und Griechischen." *Die Welt des Orients* 20/21: 83–98.

(1992) "Achikars Weisheitssprüche im Lichte älterer Fabeldichtung," in *Der Äsop-Roman: Motivgeschichte und Erzählstruktur*, ed. N. Holzberg. Tübingen. 3–22.

(2004) "Entstehung von Mythos aus Ritual. Das Beispiel des hethitischen Textes (CTH 390A)," in *Offizielle Religion, lokale Kulte und individuelle Religiosität: Akten des religionsgeschichtlichen Symposiums "Kleinasien und angrenzende Gebiete vom Beginn des 2. bis zur Mitte des 1. Jahrtausends v. Chr." (Bonn, 20.–22. Februar 2003)*, ed. M. Hutter and S. Hutter-Braunsar. Alter Orient und Altes Testament 318. Münster. 347–56.

(2008) "The seer Mopsos as a historical figure," in *Anatolian Interfaces: Hittites, Greeks and Their Neighbors. Proceedings of an International Conference on Cross-Cultural Interaction, September 17–19, 2004, Emory University, Atlanta, Ga.*, ed. B. J. Collins, M. R. Bachvarova and I. C. Rutherford. Oxford and Oakville, Conn. 63–6.

(2010) "Seevölker und Etrusker," in *Pax Hethitica: Studies on the Hittites and Their Neighbours in Honour of Itamar Singer*, ed. Y. Cohen, A. Gilan and J. L. Miller. Studien zu den Boğazköy-Texten 51. Wiesbaden. 233–46.

Ogden, D. (2001) *Greek and Roman Necromancy*. Princeton, N. J. and Oxford.

Oliver, L. (ed.) (1994) *Calvert Watkins: Selected Writings*. Innsbrucker Beiträge zur Sprachwissenschaft 80. Innsbruck.

Olivier, J.-P. (2013) "The development of Cypriot syllabaries, from Enkomi to Kafizin," in *Syllabic Writing on Cyprus and Its Context*, ed. P. M. Steele. Cambridge. 7–26.

Oppenheim, L. (1969) "Divination and celestial observation in the last Assyrian empire," *Centaurus* 14: 97–135.

Oren, E. D. (ed.) (2000) *The Sea Peoples and Their World: A Reassessment*. Philadelphia.

Oreshko, R. (2013a) "'The Achaean hides, caged in yonder beams': The value of Hieroglyphic Luwian sign *429 reconsidered and a new light on the Cilician Ahhiyawa," *Kadmos* 52: 19–33.

(2013b) "Hieroglyphic inscriptions of western Anatolia: Long arm of the empire or vernacular traditions?," in *Luwian Identities: Culture, Language and Religion between Anatolia and the Aegean*, ed. A. Mouton, I. C. Rutherford and I. Yakubovich. Leiden and Boston. 345–420.

(unpublished) "Danu(na) and Aḫḫiyawa. Reconsidering the problem of terms for Greeks in the Late Bronze Age Near Eastern and Egyptian sources."

Ornan, T. (2010) "Humbaba, the Bull of Heaven and the contribution of images to the reconstruction of the Gilgamesh Epic," in *Gilgamesch: Ikonographie eines Helden*, ed. H. U. Steyman. Orbis Biblicus et Orientalis 245. Freibourg. 229–60.

Osborne, R. (1993) "Competitive festivals and the polis: A context for dramatic festivals at Athens," in *Tragedy, Comedy and the Polis: Papers from the Greek Drama Conference, Nottingham, 18–20 July 1990*, ed. A. H. Sommerstein, S. Halliwell, J. Henderson and B. Zimmerman. Bari. 21–38.

Otten, H. (1951) "Die hethitischen 'Königslisten' und die altorientalische Chronologie," *Mitteilungen der Deutschen Orient-Gesellschaft* 83: 47–71.

(1956) "Ein Text zum Neujahrsfest aus Boğazköy," *Orientalische Literaturzeitung* 51: 101–5.

(1958a) "Die erste Tafel des hethitischen Gilgamesch-Epos," *Istanbuler Mitteilungen* 8: 93–125.

(1958b) *Hethitische Totenrituale*. Deutsche Akademie der Wissenschaften zu Berlin, Institut für Orientforschung, Veröffentlichung 37. Berlin.

(1961) "Eine Beschwörung der Unterirdischen aus Boğazköy," *Zeitschrift für Assyriologie und vorderasiatische Archäologie* 54: 114–57.

(1981) *Die Apologie Hattusilis III: Das Bild der Überlieferung*. Studien zu den Boğazköy-Texten 24. Wiesbaden.

(1988a) *Die Bronzetafel aus Boğazköy*. Studien zu den Boğazköy-Texten, Beiheft 1. Wiesbaden.

(1988b) "Ebla in der hurritisch-hethitischen Bilingue aus Boğazköy," in *Wirtschaft und Gesellschaft von Ebla: Akten der Internationalen Tagung Heidelberg 4.-7. November 1986*, ed. H. Waetzoldt and H. Hauptmann. Heidelberger Studien zum Alten Orient 2. Heidelberg. 291–2.

Otto, E. (2001) "*Kirenzi* und *d^{e}rôr* in der hurritisch-hethitischen Serie 'Freilassung' (*parā tarnumar*)," in *Akten des IV. Internationalen Kongresses für Hethitologie. Würzburg, 4.-8. Oktober 1999*, ed. G. Wilhelm. Studien zu den Boğazköy-Texten 45. Wiesbaden. 524–31.

Owen, D. I. and R. Veenker (1987) "MeGum, the First Ur III Ensi of Ebla," in *Ebla 1975-1985: Dieci anni di studi linguistici e filologici: Atti del convegno internazionale (Napoli, 9-11 ottobre 1985)*, ed. L. Cagni. Naples. 263–91.

Page, D. L. (1955) *Sappho and Alcaeus: An Introduction to the Study of Ancient Lesbian Poetry*. Oxford.

(1959) *History and the Homeric Iliad*. Berkeley and Los Angeles.

Palaima, T. G. (1995) "The nature of the Mycenaean *wanax*: Non-Indo-European origins and priestly functions," in *The Role of the Ruler in the Prehistoric Aegean: Proceedings of a Panel Discussion Presented at the Annual Meeting of the Archaeological Institute of America, New Orleans, Louisiana, 28 December 1992 with Additions*, ed. P. Rehak. Aegaeum 11. Liège and Austin, Tx. 119–39.

(1999) "'Kn02 – Tn 316'," in *Floreant studia mycenaea: Akten des X. internationalen mykenologischen Colloquiums in Salzburg vom 1.-5. Mai 1995*, ed. S. Deger-Jalkotzy, S. Hiller and O. Panagl. Vienna. 437–61.

(2000–2001) "Review of Aravantinos, Godart and Sacconi 2001," *Minos* 35–36: 475–86.

(2003a) "Review of Aravantinos, Godart and Sacconi 2001," *American Journal of Archaeology* 107: 113–15.

(2003b) "Reviewing the new Linear B tablets from Thebes," *Kadmos* 42: 31–8.

(2004) "Sacrificial feasting in the Linear B documents," in *The Mycenaean Feast*, ed. J. C. Wright. *Hesperia* 73:2. Princeton, N.J. 97–126.

(2006a) "*65 = FAR? or *ju*? and other interpretative conundra in the new Thebes tablets," in *Die neuen Linear B-Texte aus Theben: Ihr Aufschlusswert für die mykenische Sprache und Kultur. Akten des internationalen Forschungskolloquiums an der Österreichischen Akademie der Wissenschaften, 5.–6. Dezember 2002*, ed. S. Deger-Jalkotzy and O. Panagl. Österreichische Akademie der Wissenschaften, philosophisch-historische Klasse, Denkschriften 338. Vienna. 139–48.

(2006b) "*Wanaks* and related power terms in Mycenaean and later Greek," in *Ancient Greece: From the Mycenaean Palaces to the Age of Homer*, ed. S. Deger-Jalkotzy and I. S. Lemos. Edinburgh. 53–71.

(2007) "Ilios, Tros and Tlos: Continuing problems with *to-ro, to-ro-o, to-ro-wo, to-ro-ja, wi-ro*, and *a-si-wi-ja/a-si-wi-jo*," in ΣΤΕΦΑΝΟΣ ΑΡΙΣΤΕΙΟΣ: *Archäologische Forschungen zwischen Nil und Istros. Festschrift für Stefan Hiller zum 65. Geburtstag*, ed. F. Lang, C. Reinholdt and J. Weilhartner. Vienna. 197–204.

Palmer, L. R. (1963) *The Interpretation of Mycenaean Greek Texts*. Oxford.

Papadopoulos, A. (2009) "Warriors, hunters and ships in the Late Helladic IIIC Aegean: Changes in the iconography of warfare?," in *Forces of Transformation: The End of the Bronze Age in the Mediterranean. Proceedings of an International Symposium Held at St. John's College, University of Oxford 25-6th March 2006*, ed. C. Bachhuber and R. G. Roberts. Oxford. 69–77.

Pardee, D. (1996) "L'ougaritique et le hourrite dans les textes rituels de Ras Shamra – Ougarit," in *Mosaïque de langues, mosaïque culturelle: Le bilingisme dans le Proche-Orient ancien*, ed. F. Briquel-Chatonnet. Paris. 63–80.

(2002) *Ritual and Cult at Ugarit*. Atlanta, Ga.

(2009) "A new Aramaic inscription from Zincirli," *Bulletin of the American Schools of Oriental Research* 356: 51–71.

Parke, H. W. (1977) *Festivals of the Athenians*. Ithaca, N.Y.

Parker, H. N. (2008) "The linguistic case for the Aiolian migration reconsidered," *Hesperia* 77: 431–64.

Parker, R. (1983) *Miasma: Pollution and Purification in Early Greek Religion*. Oxford.

(1996) *Athenian Religion: A History*. Oxford.

(2005) *Polytheism and Society at Athens*. Oxford and New York.

Parker, S. B. (ed.) (1997) *Ugaritic Narrative Poetry*. Writings from the Ancient World 9. Atlanta, Ga.

Parker, V. (1997) *Untersuchungen zum Lelantischen Krieg und verwandten Problemen der frühgriechischen Geschichte*. Historia, Einzelschriften 109. Stuttgart.

Parpola, S. (1970) *Letters from Assyrian Scholars to the Kings Esarhaddon and Assurbanipal: Part I*. Alter Orient und Altes Testament 5/1. Kevelaer and Neukirchen-Vluyn.

(1983) *Letters from Assyrian Scholars to the Kings Esarhaddon and Assurbanipal.* Part II: Commentary and Appendices. *Alter Orient und Altes Testament 5/2.* Kevelaer and Neukirchen-Vluyn.

(1987) *The Correspondence of Sargon II.* Part I: Letters from Assyria and the West. *State Archives of Assyria 1.* Helsinki.

Parry, A. (ed.) (1971) *The Making of Homeric Verse: The Collected Papers of Milman Parry.* Oxford.

Parry, M. (1930) "Studies in the epic technique of oral verse-making. I. Homer and Homeric style," *Harvard Studies in Classical Philology* 41: 73–147, reprinted in A. Parry (1971), pp. 266–324.

Pasquali, J. and P. Mangiarotti (2005) "Il rito dell' 'ipogeo' (a-ba-i) ad Ebla," *NABU: Nouvelles Assyriologiques Brèves et Utilitaires*: 21–3.

Patzek, B. (1992) *Homer und Mykene: Mündliche Dichtung und Geschichtsschreibung.* Munich.

Pavese, C. O. (1980) "L'origine micenea della tradizione epica rapsodica," *Studi Micenei ed Egeo-Anatolici* 21: 341–52.

Pavúk, P. (2005) "Aegeans and Anatolians: A Trojan perspective," in *Emporia: Aegeans in the Central and Eastern Mediterranean. Proceedings of the 10th International Aegean Conference/ 10e Rencontre égéenne internationale, Athens, Italian School of Archaeology, 14–18 April 2004*, ed. R. Laffineur and E. Greco. Aegaeum 25. Liège and Austin, Tx. 269–77.

(2007) "New perspectives on Troia VI chronology," in *The Synchronisation of Civilisations in the Eastern Mediterranean in the Second Millennium B.C. Volume III: Proceedings of the SCIEM 2000 – 2nd EuroConference, Vienna, 28th of May – 1st of June 2003*, ed. M. Bietak and E. Czerny. Vienna. 473–8.

Payne, A. (2008) "Writing systems and identity," in *Anatolian Interfaces: Hittites, Greeks and Their Neighbors. Proceedings of an International Conference on Cross-Cultural Interaction, September 17–19, 2004, Emory University, Atlanta, Ga.*, ed. B. J. Collins, M. R. Bachvarova and I. C. Rutherford. Oxford. 117–22.

Peabody, B. (1975) *The Winged Word: A Study in the Technique of Ancient Greek Oral Composition as Seen Principally through Hesiod's Works and Days.* Albany, N.Y.

Pecchioli Daddi, F. (1987a) "À proposito di CTH 649 (II)," *Oriens Antiquus* 26: 37–57.

(1987b) "Aspects du culte de la divinité hattie Teteshapi," *Hethitica* 8: 361–80.

Pecchioli Daddi, F. and A. M. Polvani (1990) *La mitologia ittita.* Brescia.

Pedley, J. G. (1974) "Carians in Sardis," *Journal of Hellenic Studies* 94: 96–9.

Pellecchia, M., R. Negrini, L. Colli, M. Patrini, E. Milanesi, A. Achilli, G. Bertorelle, L. L. Cavalli-Sforza, A. Piazza, A. Torroni and P. Ajmone-Marsa (2007) "The mystery of Etruscan origins: Novel clues from Bos taurus mitochondrial DNA," *Proceedings of the Royal Society: Biological Sciences* 274: 1175–9.

Penglase, C. (1994) *Greek Myths and Mesopotamia: Parallels and Influence in the Homeric Hymns and Hesiod*. London and New York.

Peschlow-Bindokat, A. (1996) "Der Kult des anatolischen Regen-und Wettergottes auf dem Gipfel des Latmos und das Heiligtum des Zeus Akraios im Tal von Dikiltaş," *Istanbuler Mitteilungen* 46: 217–25.

Peters, M. (1986) "Zur Frage einer 'achäischen' Phase des griechischen Epos," in *o-o-pe-ro-si: Festschrift für Ernst Risch zum 75. Geburtstag*, ed. A. Etter. Berlin and New York. 303–19.

(1998) "Homerisches und Unhomerisches bei Homer und auf dem Nestorbecher," in *Mír Curad: Studies in Honor of Calvert Watkins*, ed. J. Jasanoff, H. C. Melchert and L. Oliver. Innsbrucker Beiträge zur Sprachwissenschaft 92. Innsbruck. 585–602.

Petropoulos, J. C. B. (1994) *Heat and Lust: Hesiod's Midsummer Festival Scene Revisited*. Lanham, Md.

Pettersson, M. (1992) *Cults of Apollo at Sparta: The Hyakinthia, the Gymnopaidiai and Karneia*. Skrifter Utgivna av Svenska Institutet i Athen, 8° 12. Stockholm.

Pettinato, G. (1991) *Ebla: A New Look at History*, trans. by C. F. Richardson. Baltimore and London.

Pfälzner, P. (2005) "Qatna: Ahnenkult im 2. Jahrtausend v. Chr.," *Welt und Umwelt der Bibel* 36: 56–9.

Piazza, A., N. Cerutti, C. D. Gaetano, F. Crobu, A. Kouvatsi, C. Triantaphyllidis, D. Palli, A. Achilli, S. Fornarino, V. Battaglia, A. S. Santachiara-Benerecetti, P. A. Underhill, G. Matullo, L. L. Cavalli-Sforza, A. Torroni and O. Semino (2007) "Origin of the Etruscans: Novel clues from the Y chromosome lineages," *European Journal of Human Genetics* 15, Supplement 1: 19.

Pirenne-Delforge, V. (1994) *L'Aphrodite grecque: Contribution à l'étude de ses cultes et de sa personnalité dans le panthéon archaïque et classique*. Kernos Supplement 4. Athens and Liège.

Poetto, M. (1993) *L'inscrizione luvio-geroglifica di Yalburt*. Studia Mediterranea 8. Pavia.

Polvani, A. M. (1992) "Su alcuni frammenti mitologici ittiti," in *Hittite and Other Anatolian and Near Eastern Studies in Honour of Sedat Alp*, ed. H. Otten, E. Akurgal, H. Ertem and A. Süel. Ankara. 445–54.

(2003) "Hittite fragments on the Atraḫasīs myth," in *Semitic and Assyriological Studies Presented to Pelio Fronzaroli by Pupils and Friends*. Wiesbaden. 532–9.

(2008) "The god Eltara and the Theogony," *Studi Micenei ed Egeo-Anatolici* 50: 617–24.

(1994) *Ina Šulmi Īrub: Die kulttopographische und ideologische Programmatik der akītu-Prozession in Babylonien und Assyrien im 1. Jahrtausend v. Chr.* Baghdader Forschungen 16. Mainz am Rhein.

Popham, M. R. (1980) "The Other Finds," in *Lefkandi I: The Iron Age. The Settlement; the Cemeteries*, ed. M. R. Popham, L. H. Sackett and P. G. Themelis. London. 81–97.

(1994) "Precolonisation: Early Greek contact with the east," in *The Archaeology of Greek Colonisation: Essays Dedicated to Sir John Boardman*, ed. G. R. Tsetskhladze and F. De Angelis. Oxford. 11–34.

Popham, M. R. and I. S. Lemos (1995) "A Euboean warrior trader," *Oxford Journal of Archaeology* 14: 151–7.

Popham, M. R., E. Touloupa and L. H. Sackett (1982) "The hero of Lefkandi," *Antiquity* 56: 169–74.

Popko, M. (1994) *Zippalanda: Ein Kultzentrum im hethitischen Kleinasien*. Texte der Hethiter 21. Heidelberg.

(1995) *Religions of Asia Minor*. Warsaw.

(1998) "Auf der Suche nach den siegreichen Waffen des Wettergottes von Ḫalab in Kleinasien," in *Written on Clay and Stone: Ancient Near Eastern Studies Presented to Krystyna Szarzyńska on the Occasion of Her 80th Birthday*, ed. J. Braun, K. Łyczkowska, M. Popko and P. Steinkeller. Warsaw. 75–8.

(2002) "Zum Tempel des Teššup von Ḫalap in Ḫattuša," *Altorientalische Forschungen* 29: 73–80.

(2003a) *Das hethitische Ritual CTH 447*. Warsaw.

(2003b) "Zur Topographie von Ḫattuša: Tempel auf Büyükkale," in *Hittite Studies in Honour of Harry A. Hoffner, Jr.: On the Occasion of his 65th Birthday*, ed. G. M. Beckman, R. H. Beal and J. G. McMahon. Winona Lake, Ind. 315–23.

(2008) *Völker und Sprachen Altanatoliens*, trans. by C. Brosch. Wiesbaden.

(2009) *Arinna: Eine heilige Stadt der Hethiter*. Studien zu den Boğazköy-Texten 30. Wiesbaden.

Porada, E. (1981–1982) "The cylinder seals found at Thebes in Boeotia," *Archiv für Orientforschung* 28: 1–78.

Porzig, W. (1930) "Illujankas und Typhon," *Kleinasiatische Forschungen* 1: 379–86.

Potts, T. (2001) "Reading the Sargonic 'historical-literary' tradition: Is there a middle course? (Thoughts on *The Great Revolt against Naram-Sin*)," in *Proceedings of the XLVe Rencontre Assyriologique Internationale. Volume I: Historiography in the Cuneiform World*, ed. T. Abusch, P.-A. Beaulieu, J. Huehnergard, P. Machinist and P. Steinkeller. Bethesda, Md. 391–408.

Powell, B. B. (1991) *Homer and the Origin of the Greek Alphabet*. Cambridge.

(2002) *Writing and the Origins of Greek Literature*. Cambridge and New York.

Prechel, D. (1996) *Die Göttin Išḫara: Ein Beitrag zur altorientalischen Religionsgeschichte*. Münster.

(2008) "Hethitische Rituale in Emar?," in *The City of Emar among the Late Bronze Age Empires: History, Landscape, and Society. Proceedings of the Konstanz Emar Conference, 25.–26.04.2006*, ed. L. d'Alfonso, Y. Cohen and D. Sürenhagen. Alter Orient und Altes Testament 349. Münster. 243–52.

Probert, P. (2006) *Ancient Greek Accentuation: Synchronic Patterns, Frequency Effects, and Prehistory*. Oxford and New York.

Pucci, M. (2008) *Functional Analysis of Space in Syro-Hittite Architecture*. Oxford.

Pucci, P. (1988) "Inscriptions archaïques sur les statues des dieux," in *Les savoirs de l'écriture: En Grèce ancienne*, ed. M. Detienne. Lille. 480–97.

Puhvel, J. (1983) "Homeric questions and Hittite answers," *American Journal of Philology* 104: 217–27.

(1988a) "An Anatolian turn of phrase in the *Iliad*," *American Journal of Philology* 109: 591–3.

(1988b) "Hittite athletics as prefigurations of ancient Greek games," in *The Archaeology of the Olympics: The Olympics and Other Festivals in Antiquity*, ed. W. J. Raschke. Madison, Wis. 26–31.

(1991) *Homer and Hittite*. Innsbrucker Beiträge zur Sprachwissenschaft, Vorträge und kleinere Schriften 47. Innsbruck.

(1992) "Shaft-shedding Artemis and mind-voiding ate: Hittite determinants of Greek etyma," *Historische Sprachforschung* 105: 4–8.

(1993) "A Hittite calque in the Iliad," *Historische Sprachforschung* 106: 36–8.

Pulak, C. (1998) "The Uluburun shipwreck: An overview," *International Journal of Nautical Archaeology* 27: 188–224.

(2005) "Who were the Mycenaeans aboard the Uluburun ship?," in *Emporia: Aegeans in the Central and Eastern Mediterranean. Proceedings of the 10th International Aegean Conference/ 10e Rencontre égéenne internationale, Athens, Italian School of Archaeology, 14–18 April 2004*, ed. R. Laffineur and E. Greco. Aegaeum 25. Liège and Austin, Tx. 295–312.

Raaflaub, K. A. (1998a) "A historian's headache: How to read 'Homeric society'?," in *Archaic Greece: New Approaches and New Evidence*, ed. N. Fisher and H. van Wees. London. 169–93.

(1998b) "Homer, the Trojan War, and history," *Classical World* 91: 386–403.

(2003) "Die Bedeutung der Dark Ages: Mykene, Troia und die Griechen," in *Der neue Streit um Troia: Eine Bilanz*, ed. C. Ulf. Munich. 309–29.

(2005) "Epic and history," in *A Companion to Ancient Epic*, ed. J. M. Foley. London. 55–70.

(2006) "Historical approaches to Homer," in *Ancient Greece: From the Mycenaean Palaces to the Age of Homer*, ed. S. Deger-Jalkotzy and I. S. Lemos. Edinburgh. 449–62.

Radner, K. (2010) "The stele of Sargon II of Assyria in Kition: A focus for an emerging Cypriot identity?," in *Interkulturalität in der Alten Welt: Vorderasien, Hellas, Ägypten und die vielfältigen Ebenen des Kontakts*, ed. R. Rollinger, B. Gufler, M. Lang and I. Madreiter. Philippika 34. Wiesbaden. 429–49.

Raimond, É. (2004) "Quelques cultes des confins de la Lycie," in *Studia Anatolica et varia: Mélanges offerts au Professeur René Lebrun*, ed. M. Mazoyer and O. Casabonne. Paris. 293–314.

Ramanujan, A. K. (1991) "Three Hundred Rāmāyaṇas: Five examples and three thoughts on translation," in *Many Rāmāyaṇas: The Diversity of a Narrative Tradition in South Asia*, ed. P. Richman. Berkeley and Los Angeles. 22–49.

Rau, J. (2008) "The origin of the short-vowel ευ-stems in Homer," *Glotta* 84: 171–88.
  (2010) "Greek and Proto-Indo-European," in *A Companion to the Ancient Greek Language*, ed. E. J. Bakker. Malden, Mass. 171–88.
Reade, J. (2005) "The Ishtar Temple at Nineveh," *Iraq* 67: 347–90.
Redfield, J. (1994) *Nature and Culture in the Iliad: The Tragedy of Hector*. 2nd, expanded edn. Durham, N. C.
Redford, D. B. (2005–2006) "The language of Keftiu: The evidence of the Drawing Board and the London Medical Papyrus (BM 10059) in the British Museum," *Revista del Instituto de Historia Antigua Oriental* 12/13: 149–53.
Reece, S. (1993) *The Stranger's Welcome: Oral Theory and the Aesthetics of the Homeric Hospitality Scene*. Ann Arbor.
Reichl, K. (1992) *Turkic Oral Epic Poetry: Traditions, Forms, Poetic Structure*. New York and London.
  (2001) *Das usbekische Heldenepos Alpomish: Einführung, Text, Übersetzung*. Wiesbaden.
Reiner, E. (1960) "Plague amulets and house blessings," *Journal of Near Eastern Studies* 19: 148–55.
Rengakos, A. (ed.) (2002) *Wolfgang Kullmann: Realität, Imagination und Theorie: Kleine Schriften zu Epos und Tragödie in der Antike*. Stuttgart.
Richardson, N. J. (1989) "Homer and Cyprus," in *The Civilizations of the Aegean and Their Diffusion in Cyprus and the Eastern Mediterranean 2000–600 B.C.: Proceedings of an international Symposium, 18–24 September 1989*, ed. V. Karageorghis. Larnaca. 124–7.
  (1993) *The Iliad: A Commentary*. Volume VI: *Books 21–4*. Cambridge.
Richman, P. (1991) "E. V. Ramasami's reading of the *Rāmāyaṇa*," in *Many Rāmāyaṇas: The Diversity of a Narrative Tradition in South Asia*, ed. P. Richman. Berkeley. 175–201.
Richter, T. (2002) "Zur Frage der Entlehnung syrisch-mesopotamischer Kulturelemente nach Anatolien in der vor-und frühen althethitischen Zeit (19.–16. Jahrhundert v. Chr.)," in *Brückenland Anatolien? Ursachen, Extensität und Modi des Kulturaustausches zwischen Anatolien und seinen Nachbarn*, ed. H. Blum, B. Faist and P. Pfälzner. Tübingen. 295–322.
Riedweg, C. (ed.) (2001) *Walter Burkert: Kleine Schriften*, Volume I: *Homerica*. Hypomnemata Supplement-Reihe 2. Göttingen.
Rieken, E. (2001) "Der hethitische *šar-tamḫāri*-Text: Archaisch oder archaisierend?," in *Akten des IV. Internationalen Kongresses für Hethitologie. Würzburg, 4.–8. Oktober 1999*, ed. G. Wilhelm. Studien zu den Boğazköy-Texten 45. Wiesbaden. 576–85.
  (2009) "Die Tontafelfunde aus Kayalıpınar," in *Central-North Anatolia in the Hittite Period: New Perspectives in Light of Recent Research. Acts of the International Conference Held at the University of Florence (7–9 February 2007)*, ed. F. Pecchioli Daddi, G. Torri and C. Corti. Studia Asiana 5. Rome. 119–43.

Riemschneider, K. K. (2004) *Die akkadischen und hethitischen Omentexte aus Boğazköy*. Dresdner Beiträge zur Hethitologie 12. Dresden.

Riley, R. T. (2000) "The saga of an epic: Gilgamesh and the constitution of Uruk," *Orientalia* N. S. 69: 341–67.

Rinchindorji (2001) "Mongolian-Turkic epics: Typological formation and development," *Oral Tradition* 16: 381–401.

Ritner, R. K. (2001) "Medicine," in *The Oxford Encyclopedia of Ancient Egypt*, Volume II: *G–O*, ed. D. B. Redford. New York. 353–6.

Rix, H. (1968) "Eine morphosyntaktische Übereinstimmung zwischen Etruskisch und Lemnisch: Die Datierungsformel," in *Studien zur Sprachwissenschaft und Kulturkunde: Gedenkschrift für Wilhem Brandenstein*, ed. M. Mayrhofer. Innsbruck: 213–22.

(1998) *Rätisch und Etruskisch*. Innsbruck.

Robert, L. (1955) *Hellenica: Recueil d'épigraphie, de numismatique et d'antiquités grecques*, 10. Paris.

(1962) *Villes d'Asie Mineure: Études de géographie ancienne*. Paris.

Robertson, N. (1982) "Hittite ritual at Sardis," *Classical Antiquity* 1: 122–40.

(1992) *Festivals and Legends: The Formation of Greek Cities in the Light of Public Ritual*. Toronto, Buffalo and London.

Roller, L. E. (1994) "The Phrygian character of Kybele: The formation of an iconography and cult ethos in the Iron Age," in *Anatolian Iron Ages 3, Anadolu Demir Çağları 3: The Proceedings of the Third Anatolian Iron Ages Colloquium Held at Van, 6–12 August 1990*, ed. A. Çilingiroğlu and D. H. French. Ankara. 189–98.

(1999) *In Search of God the Mother: The Cult of Anatolian Cybele*. Berkeley, Los Angeles and London.

(2006) "Midas and Phrygian cult practice," in *Pluralismus und Wandel in den Religionen im vorhellenistischen Anatolien: Akten des religionsgeschichtlichen Symposiums in Bonn (19.–20. Mai 2005)*, ed. M. Hutter and S. Hutter-Braunsar. Alter Orient und Altes Testament 337. Münster. 123–35.

Röllig, W. (1985) "Der Mondgott und die Kuh. Ein Lehrstück zur Problematik der Textüberlieferung im Alten Orient," *Orientalia*, N. S. 54: 260–73.

(1992) "Asia Minor as a bridge between east and west: The role of the Phoenicians and Aramaeans in the transfer of culture," in *Greece between East and West: 10th–8th Centuries BC. Papers of the Meeting at the Institute of Fine Arts, New York University March 15–16th, 1990*, ed. G. Kopcke and I. Tokumaru. Mainz. 93–102.

(2000) "Aramäer und Assyrer: Die Schriftzeugnisse bis zum Ende des Assyrerreiches," in *Essays on Syria in the Iron Age*, ed. G. Bunnens. Ancient Near Eastern Studies Supplement 7. Leuven. 177–86.

(2011) "'Und ich baute starke Festungen an allen Enden auf den Grenzen …' Zur Bedeutung der Inschriften und Reliefs vom Karatepe-Aslantaş," in *Lag*

Troia in Kilikien? Der aktuelle Streit um Homers Ilias, ed. C. Ulf and R. Rollinger. Darmstadt. 115–34.

Rollinger, R. (1996) "Altorientalische Motivik in der frühgriechischen Literatur am Beispiel der homerischen Epen. Elemente des Kampfes in der Ilias und in der altorientalischen Literatur (nebst Überlegungen zur Präsenz altorientalischer Wanderpriester im früharchaischen Griechenland)," in *Wege zur Genese griechischer Identität: Die Bedeutung der früharchaischen Zeit*, ed. C. Ulf. Berlin. 156–210.

(1997) "Zur Bezeichnung von 'Griechen' in Keilschrifttexten," *Revue d'Assyriologie* 91: 167–72.

(2001) "The ancient Greeks and the impact of the ancient Near East: Textual evidence and historical perspective (*ca.* 750–650 BC)," in *Mythology and Mythologies: Methodological Approaches to Intercultural Influences. Proceedings of the Second Annual Symposium of the Assyrian and Babylonian Intellectual Heritage Project Held in Paris, France, October 4–7, 1999*, ed. R. M. Whiting. Helsinki. 233–64.

(2007) "Zu Herkunft und Hintergrund der in altorientalischen Texten genannten 'Griechen'," in *Getrennte Wege? Kommunikation, Raum und Wahrnehmung in der alten Welt*, ed. R. Rollinger, A. Luther and J. Wiesehöfer. Frankfurt. 259–330.

Romm, J. S. (1992) *The Edges of the Earth in Ancient Thought*. Princeton, N. J.

Roosevelt, C. H. (2009) *The Archaeology of Lydia, from Gyges to Alexander*. Cambridge and New York.

Rose, C. B. (2008) "Separating fact from fiction in the Aiolian migration," *Hesperia* 77: 399–430.

(2014) *The Archaeology of Greek and Roman Troy*. New York.

Ruijgh, C. J. (1957) *L'élément achéen dans la langue épique*. Assen.

(1985) "Le mycénien et Homère," in *Linear B: A 1984 Survey: Proceeding of the Mycenaean Colloquium of the VIIIth Congress of the International Federation of the Societies of Classical Studies (Dublin, 27 August – 1st September 1984)*, ed. A. Morpurgo Davies and Y. Duhoux. Louvain-la-Neuve. 143–90.

(1995) "D'Homère aux origines proto-mycéniennes de la tradition épique," in *Homeric Questions: Essays in Philology, Ancient History and Archaeology, Including the Papers of a Conference Organized by the Netherlands Institute at Athens (15 May 1993)*, ed. J. P. Crielaard. Amsterdam. 1–96.

(1997) "Les origines proto-mycéniennes de la tradition épique," in *Hommage à Milman Parry: Le style formulaire de l'épopée homérique et la théorie de l'oralité poétique*, ed. F. Létoublon. Amsterdam. 33–46.

(2004) "À propos des nouvelles tablettes de Thèbes, I" *Mnemosyne* 57: 1–44.

(2006) "The three temporal clauses (TH Fq 126; 130; 254)," in *Die neuen Linear B-Texte aus Theben: Ihr Aufschlusswert für die mykenische Sprache und Kultur. Akten des internationalen Forschungskolloquiums an der Österreichischen Akademie der Wissenschaften, 5.–6. Dezember 2002*, ed. S. Deger-Jalkotzy and

O. Panagl. Österreichische Akademie der Wissenschaften, philosophisch-historische Klasse, Denkschriften 338. Vienna. 159–69.

Rüster, C. and E. Neu (1989) *Hethitisches Zeichenlexicon: Inventar und Interpretation der Keilschriftzeichen aus den Boğazköy-Texten*. Studien zu den Boğazköy-Texten, Beiheft 2. Wiesbaden.

Rutherford, I. C. (2000) "Formulas, voice, and death in *Ehoie*-poetry, the Hesiodic *Gunaikon Katalogos*, and the Odysseian *Nekuia*," in *Matrices of Genre: Authors, Canons, and Society*, ed. M. Depew and D. Obbink. Cambridge, Mass. and London. 81–96.

(2001a) *Pindar's Paeans: A Reading of the Fragments with a Survey of the Genre*. Oxford.

(2001b) "The Song of the Sea (ŠA A.AB.BA SÌR): Thoughts on KUB 45.63," in *Akten des IV. Internationalen Kongresses für Hethitologie. Würzburg, 4.–8. Oktober 1999*, ed. G. Wilhelm. Studien zu den Boğazköy-Texten 45. Wiesbaden. 598–609.

(2004a) "Women singers and the religious organisation of Hatti: On the interpretations of CTH 235.1 & 2 and other texts," in *Offizielle Religion, lokale Kulte und individuelle Religiosität: Akten des religionsgeschichtlichen Symposiums "Kleinasien und angrenzende Gebiete vom Beginn des 2. bis zur Mitte des 1. Jahrtausends v. Chr." (Bonn, 20.–22. Februar 2003)*, ed. M. Hutter and S. Hutter-Braunsar. Alter Orient und Altes Testament 318. Münster. 377–94.

(2004b) "χορὸς εἷς ἐκ τῆσδε τῆς πόλεως... (Xen. *Mem*. 3.3.12): Song-Dance and State-Pilgrimage at Athens," in *Music and the Muses: The Culture of "Mousikē" in the Classical Athenian City*, ed. P. Murray and P. Wilson. Oxford and New York. 67–90.

(2005a) "The dance of the wolf-men of Ankuwa: Networks and amphictionies in the KI.LAM festival," in *v. Uluslararası Hititoloji Kongresi bildirileri: Çorum, 02-08 Eylül 2002 / Acts of the vth International Congress of Hittitology: Çorum, September 02-08, 2002*, ed. Y. Hazırlayan and A. Süel. Ankara. 623–39.

(2005b) "Downstream to the Cat-goddess: Herodotus on Egyptian pilgrimage," in *Pilgrimage in Graeco-Roman and Early Christian Antiquity: Seeing the Gods*, ed. J. Elsner and I. C. Rutherford. Oxford and New York. 131–50.

(2007) "Achilles and the sallais wastais ritual: Performing death in Greece and Anatolia," in *Performing Death: Social Analyses of Funerary Traditions in the Ancient near East and Mediterranean*, ed. N. Laneri. Oriental Institute Seminars 3. Chicago. 223–36.

(2008) "The songs of the *Zintuḫis*: Chorus and ritual in Anatolia and Greece," in *Anatolian Interfaces: Hittites, Greeks and Their Neighbors. Proceedings of an International Conference on Cross-Cultural Interaction, September 17–19, 2004, Emory University, Atlanta, Ga.*, ed. B. J. Collins, M. R. Bachvarova and I. C. Rutherford. Oxford. 73–83.

(2009a) "Hesiod and the literary traditions of the Near East," in *Brill's Companion to Hesiod*, ed. F. Montanari, A. Rengakos and C. Tsagalis. Leiden and Boston. 9–35.

(2009b) "Network theory and theoric networks," in *Greek and Roman Networks in the Mediterranean*, ed. I. Malkin, C. Constantakopolou and K. Panagopoulou. London and New York. 24–38.

Rystedt, E. (1986) "The foot-race and other athletic contests in the Mycenaean world. The evidence of the pictorial vases," *Opuscula Atheniensia* 16: 103–16.

(1999) "No words, only pictures. Iconography in the transition between the Bronze Age and the Iron Age in Greece," *Opuscula Atheniensia* 24: 89–98.

Sagona, A. and P. Zimansky (2009) *Ancient Turkey*. London and New York.

Saïd, E. W. (1978) *Orientalism*. New York.

Sakellariou, M. B. (1990) *Between Memory and Oblivion: The Transmission of Early Greek Historical Traditions*. Athens.

Sale, W. M. (1961) "The Hyperborean maidens on Delos," *Harvard Theological Review* 54: 75–89.

(1987) "The formularity of the place-names in the *Iliad*," *Transactions of the American Philological Association* 117: 21–50.

(1989) "The Trojans, statistics, and Milman Parry," *Greek, Roman and Byzantine Studies* 30: 341–410.

(1994) "The government of Troy: Politics in the *Iliad*," *Greek, Roman and Byzantine Studies* 35: 5–102.

Salvini, M. (1977) "Sui testi mitologici in lingua hurrica;" *Studi Micenei ed Egeo-Anatolici* 18: 73–91.

(1988) "Die hurritischen Überlieferungen des Gilgameš-Epos und des Kešši-Erzählung," in *Hurriter und Hurritisch*, ed. V. Haas. Xenia 21. Konstanz. 157–72.

(1994) "Una lettera di Hattušili relativa alla spedizione contro Hahhum," *Studi Micenei ed Egeo-Anatolici* 34: 61–80.

Salvini, M. and I. Wegner (1986) *Die Rituale des AZU-Priesters*. Corpus der hurritischen Sprachdenkmäler i/2. Rome.

(2004) *Die mythologischen Texte*. Corpus der hurritischen Sprachdenkmäler i/6. Rome.

Sanders, S. L. (2001) "A historiography of demons: Preterit-thema, para-myth and historiola in the morphology of genres," in *Proceedings of the xlve Rencontre Assyriologique Internationale. Volume i: Harvard University: Historiography in the Cuneiform World*, ed. T. Abusch, P.-A. Beaulieu, J. Huehnergard, P. Machinist and P. Steinkeller. Bethesda, Md. 429–40.

Saporetti, C. (1976) "Cipro nei testi neoassiri," *Studi Ciprioti e rapporti di scavo* 2: 83–8.

Sasson, J. M. (ed.) (1995) *Civilizations of the Ancient Near East*. New York.

(2004) "The king's table: Food and fealty at Old Babylonian Mari," in *Food and Identity in the Ancient World*, ed. C. Grottanelli and L. Milano. History of the Ancient Near East 9. Padua. 179–215.

Schattner, T. G. (1992) "Didyma: Ein minoisch-mykenischer Fundplatz?," *Archäologischer Anzeiger*: 369–72.

Scheer, T. S. (1993) *Mythische Vorväter: Zur Bedeutung griechischer Heroenmythen im Selbstverständnis kleinasiatischer Städte*. Munich.

Schibli, H. S. (1990) *Pherekydes of Syros*. Oxford.

Schloen, J. D. (2001) *The House of the Father as Fact and Symbol: Patrimonialism in Ugarit and the Ancient Near East*. Winona Lake, Ind.

Schmidt, B. B. (1995) "The 'witch' of En-Dor, 1 Samuel 28, and ancient Near Eastern necromancy," in *Ancient Magic and Ritual Power*, ed. M. Meyer and P. Mirecki. Leiden and New York. 111–29.

Schmitt, R. (1967) *Dichtung und Dichtersprache in indogermanischer Zeit*. Wiesbaden.

Schmitz, P. C. (2009a) "Archaic Greek names in a Neo-Assyrian Cuneiform tablet from Tarsus," *Journal of Cuneiform Studies* 61: 127–31.

(2009b) "Phoenician KRNTRYŠ, Archaic Greek *ΚΟΡΥΝΗΤΗΡΙΟΣ, and the Storm God of Aleppo," in *Kleine Untersuchungen zur Sprache des Alten Testaments und seiner Umwelt 10*, ed. R. G. Lehmann. Waltrop. 119–60.

Schretter, M. K. (1974) *Alter Orient und Hellas: Fragen der Beeinflussung griechischen Gedankgutes aus altorientalischen Quellen. Dargestellt an den Göttern Nergal, Rescheph, Apollon*. Innsbrucker Beiträge zur Kulturwissenschaft, Sonderheft 33. Innsbruck.

Schuol, M. (2000) "Darstellungen von hethitischen Musikinstrumenten unter Berücksichtigung der Schriftzeugnisse," in *Musikarchäologie früher Metallzeiten: Vorträge des 1. Symposiums der International Study Group on Music Archaeology im Kloster Michaelstein, 18.–24. Mai 1998*, ed. E. Hickmann, I. Laufs and R. Eichmann. 2. Rahden. 159–70.

(2004) *Hethitische Kultmusik: Eine Untersuchung der Instrumental-und Vokalmusik anhand hethitischer Ritualtexte und von archäologischen Zeugnissen*. Orient-Archäologie 14. Rahden.

Schuster, H.-S. (1974) *Die ḫattisch-hethitischen Bilinguen*. Volume I: *Einleitung, Text und Kommentar. Teil 1*. Documenta et Monumenta Orientis Antiqui 17.1. Leiden.

(2002) *Die ḫattisch-hethitischen Bilinguen*. Volume II: *Textbearbeitungen. Teil 2 und 3*. Documenta et Monumenta Orientis Antiqui. Leiden, Boston and Cologne.

Schütte-Maischatz, A. and E. Winter (2004) *Doliche – Eine kommagenische Stadt und ihre Götter: Mithras und Iupiter Dolichenus*. Asia Minor Studien 52. Bonn.

Schwemer, D. (1995) "Das alttestamentliche Doppelritual ʿlwt wšlmym im Horizont der hurritischen Opfertermini ambašši und keldi," in *Edith Porada Memorial Volume*, ed. D. I. Owen and G. Wilhelm. Studies on the Civilization and Culture of Nuzi and the Hurrians 7. Bethesda, Md. 81–116.

(1998) *Akkadische Rituale aus Hattusa: Die Sammeltafel KBo XXXVI 29 und verwandte Fragmente*. Texte der Hethiter 23. Heidelberg.

(2001) *Die Wettergottgestalten Mesopotamiens und Nordsyriens im Zeitalter der Keilschriftkulturen: Materialien und Studien nach den schriftlichen Quellen*. Wiesbaden.

(2004) "Ein akkadischer Liebeszauber aus Ḫattuša," *Zeitschrift für Assyriologie* 94: 59–79.

(2007) "The Storm-gods of the ancient Near East: Summary, synthesis, recent studies. Part I," *Journal of Ancient Near Eastern Religions* 7: 121–68.

(2008a) "Fremde Götter in Ḫatti: Die hethitische Religion im Spannungsfeld von Synkretismus und Abgrenzung," in *Ḫattuša – Boğazköy: Das Hethiterreich im Spannungsfeld des Alten Orients. 6. Internationales Colloquium der Deutschen Orient-Gesellschaft 22.–24. März 2006, Würzburg*, ed. G. Wilhelm. Colloquien der Deutschen Orient-Gesellschaft 6. Wiesbaden. 137–58.

(2008b) "The Storm-gods of the ancient Near East: Summary, synthesis, recent studies. Part II." *Journal of Ancient Near Eastern Religions* 8: 1–44.

Scullion, S. (2007) "Festivals," in *A Companion to Greek Religion*, ed. D. Ogden. Malden, Mass. and Cambridge. 190–203.

Scurlock, J. A. (1988) *Magical Means of Dealing with Ghosts in Ancient Mesopotamia*. Ph.D. Thesis, University of Chicago.

(1995) "Magical uses of ancient Mesopotamian festivals of the dead," in *Ancient Magic and Ritual Power*, ed. M. Meyer and P. Mirecki. Leiden and New York: 93–107.

Seaford, R. (1994) *Reciprocity and Ritual: Homer and Tragedy in the Developing City-State*. Oxford.

Seeher, J. (2001) "Die Zerstörung der Stadt Ḫattuša," in *Akten des IV. Internationalen Kongresses für Hethitologie. Würzburg, 4.–8. Oktober 1999*, ed. G. Wilhelm. Studien zu den Boğazköy-Texten 45. Wiesbaden. 623–34.

(2002) *Hattusha Guide: A Day in the Hittite Capital*. 2nd edn. Istanbul.

Selz, G. J. (2000) "Five divine ladies: Thoughts on Inana(k), Ištar, In(n)in(a), Annunītum, and Anat, and the origin of the title 'Queen of Heaven'," *NIN* 1: 29–62.

Serwint, N. (2002) "Aphrodite and her Near Eastern sisters: Spheres of influence," in *Engendering Aphrodite: Women and Society in Ancient Cyprus*, ed. D. Bolger and N. Serwint. Boston, Mass. 325–50.

Shaw, J. W. and M. C. Shaw (eds.) (2000) *Kommos IV: The Greek Sanctuary, Part 1*. Princeton, N. J. and Oxford.

Shear, I. M. (1998) "Bellerophon tablets from the Mycenaean world? A tale of seven bronze hinges," *Journal of Hellenic Studies* 118: 187–9.

Shelmerdine, C. W. (1998) "Where do we go from here? And how can the Linear B tablets help us get there?," in *The Aegean and the Orient in the Second Millennium: Proceedings of the 50th Anniversary Symposium, Cincinnati, 18–20 April 1997*, ed. E. H. Cline and D. Harris-Cline. Liège. 291–301.

(2008) "Host and guest at a Mycenaean feast," in *Dais: The Aegean Feast: Proceedings of the 12th International Aegean Conference/ 12e Rencontre égéenne internationale, University of Melbourne, Centre for Classics and Archaeology, 25–29 March 2008*, ed. L. A. Hitchcock, R. Laffineur and J. L. Crowley. Aegaeum 29. Liège and Austin, Tx. 401–10.

Sherratt, A. and S. Sherratt (1991) "From luxuries to commodities: The nature of Mediterranean Bronze Age trading systems," in *Bronze Age Trade in the Mediterranean: Papers Presented at the Conference Held at Rewley House, Oxford, on December 1989*, ed. N. H. Gale. Studies in Mediterranean Archaeology 90. Jonsered. 351–86.

Sherratt, S. (1990) "'Reading the texts': Archaeology and the Homeric questions," *Antiquity* 64: 807–24.

(2003a) "The Mediterranean economy: 'Globalization' at the end of the second millennium B.C.E.," in *Symbiosis, Symbolism, and the Power of the Past: Canaan, Ancient Israel and Their Neighbors from the Late Bronze Age through Roman Palaestina. Proceedings of the Centennial Symposium, W. F. Albright Institute of Archaeological Research and American Schools of Oriental Research, Jerusalem, May 29–31, 2000*, ed. W. G. Dever and S. Gitin. Winona Lake, Ind. 37–62.

(2003b) "Visible writing: Questions of script and identity in Early Iron Age Greece and Cyprus," *Oxford Journal of Archaeology* 22: 225–42.

(2006) "LH IIIC Lefkandi: An overview," in *Lefkandi IV: The Bronze Age. The Late Helladic IIIC Settlement at Xeropolis*, ed. D. Evely. London. 303–9.

Sherratt, S. and J. H. Crowel (1987) "Mycenaean pottery from Cilicia," *Oxford Journal of Archaeology* 6: 325–52.

Sherratt, S. and A. Sherratt (1993) "The growth of the Mediterranean economy in the early first millennium BC," *World Archaeology* 24: 361–78.

Shortland, A. J. and C. Bronk Ramsey (eds.) (2013) *Radiocarbon and the Chronologies of Egypt*. Oxford.

Sidel'tsev, A. V. (2002) "Inverted Word Order in Middle Hittite," in *Anatolian Languages*, ed. V. V. Shevoroshkin and P. J. Sidwell. Canberra. 137–88.

Siegelová, J. (1971) *Appu-Märchen und Ḫedammu-Mythos*. Studien zu den Boğazköy-Texten 14. Wiesbaden.

Sihler, A. (1995) *New Comparative Grammar of Greek and Latin*. New York.

Simon, Z. (2009) "Die ANKARA-Silberschale und das Ende des hethitischen Reiches," *Zeitschrift für Assyriologie und Vorderasiatische Archäologie* 99: 247–69.

Singer, I. (1981) "Hittites and Hattians in Anatolia in the beginning of the second millennium B.C.," *Journal of Indo-European Studies* 9: 119–34.

(1983) *The Hittite KI.LAM Festival*. Part I: Studien zu den Boğazköy-Texten 27. Wiesbaden.

(1984a) "The AGRIG in the Hittite texts," *Anatolian Studies* 34: 97–127.

(1984b) *The Hittite KI.LAM Festival*: Part II: Studien zu den Boğazköy-Texten 28. Wiesbaden.

(1986) "The ḫuwaši of the Storm-god in Ḫattuša," in IX. *Türk Tarıh Kongresi, Ankara: 21–25 Eylül 1981*. Ankara. 245–53.

(1991) "The title 'Great Princess' in the Hittite empire," *Ugarit-Forschungen* 23: 327–38.

(1994) "'The thousand gods of Hatti': the limits of an expanding pantheon," in *Concepts of the Other in Near Eastern Religions*, ed. I. Alon, I. Gruenwald and I. Singer. Israel Oriental Studies 14. Leiden, New York and Cologne. 81–102.

(1995) "Some thoughts on translated and original Hittite literature," in *Language and Culture in the Near East*, ed. S. Izre'el and R. Drory. Israel Oriental Studies 15. Winona Lake, Ind. 123–8.

(1996) "Great Kings of Tarḫuntašša," *Studi Micenei ed Egeo-Anatolici* 38: 63–71.

(1999) "A political history of Ugarit," in *Handbook of Ugaritic Studies*, ed. W. G. E. Watson and N. Wyatt. Handbuch der Orientalistik 1.29. Leiden, Boston and Cologne. 603–733.

(2000) "New evidence on the end of the Hittite Empire," in *The Sea Peoples and Their World: A Reassessment*, ed. E. D. Oren. Philadelphia. 21–34.

(2002a) "The Cold Lake and its Great Rock," in *Gregor Giorgadze von Kollegen und ehemaligen Studenten zum 75. Geburtstag gewidmet*, ed. L. Gordesiani. Tblisi. 128–32.

(2002b) *Hittite Prayers*. Writings from the Ancient World 11. Atlanta, Ga.

(2006a) "The failed reforms of Akhenaten and Muwatalli," *Phasis* 6: 37–58.

(2006b) "Ships bound for Lukka: A new interpretation of the companion letters RS 94.2530 and RS 94.2523," *Altorientalische Forschungen* 33: 242–62.

(2007) "The origins of the 'Canaanite' myth of Elkunirša and Ašertu reconsidered," in *Tabularia Hethaeorum: Hethitologische Beiträge Silvin Košak zum 65. Geburtstag*, ed. D. Groddek and M. Zorman. Dresdner Beiträge zur Hethitologie 25. Wiesbaden. 631–42.

(2009) "'In Hattuša the royal house declined'. Royal mortuary cult in 13th century Hatti," in *Central-North Anatolia in the Hittite Period: New Perspectives in Light of Recent Research. Acts of the International Conference Held at the University of Florence (7–9 February 2007)*, ed. F. Pecchioli Daddi, G. Torri and C. Corti. Studia Asiana 5. Rome. 169–91.

Skendi, S. (1954) *Albanian and South Slavic Oral Epic Poetry*. Philadelphia. Reprinted 1969.

Smith, D. (2013) "Portentous birds flying west: On the Mesopotamian origin of Homeric bird-divination," *Journal of Ancient Near Eastern Religions* 13: 49–85.

Smith, M. S. (1994) *The Ugaritic Baal Cycle*. Volume 1: *Introduction with Text, Translation and Commentary of KTU 1.1–1.2*. Supplements to Vetus Testamentum 55. Leiden, New York and Cologne.

Smith, M. S. and E. M. Bloch-Smith (1988) "Death and afterlife in Ugarit and Israel." *Journal of the American Oriental Society* 108: 277–84.

Snodgrass, A. (1982) "Les origines du culte des héros dans la Grèce antique," in *La mort, les morts dans les sociétés anciennes*, ed. G. Gnoli and J.-P. Vernant. Paris and Cambridge. 107–19.

(1988) "The archaeology of the hero," *Annali di Archeologia e Storia Antica* 10: 19–26.

Sommer, F. (1932) *Die Aḫḫijavā-Urkunden*. Abhandlungen der Bayerischen Akademie der Wissenschaften. Philosophisch-historische Abteilung 6, N. F. Munich.

(1934) *Aḫḫijavāfrage und Sprachwissenschaft*. Abhandlungen der Bayerischen Akademie der Wissenschaften. Philosophisch-historische Abteilung 9, N. F. Munich.

Sommer, F. and A. Falkenstein (1938) *Die hethitisch-akkadische Bilingue des Ḫattušili I. (Labarna II.)*. Abhandlungen der Bayerischen Akademie der Wissenschaften, N. F. 16. Munich.

Souček, V. and J. Siegelová (1974) "Der Kult des Wettergotts von Ḫalap in Ḫatti," *Archív Orientální* 42: 39–52.

Sourvinou-Inwood, C. (1990) "What is polis religion?," in *The Greek City from Homer to Alexander*, ed. O. Murray and S. Price. Oxford. 295–322.

(1995) *"Reading" Greek Death: To the End of the Classical Period*. Oxford and New York.

(2003) *Tragedy and Athenian Religion*. Lanham, Boulder, New York and Oxford.

(2005) *Hylas, the Nymphs, Dionysos and Others: Myth, Ritual, Ethnicity*. Skrifter Utgivna av Svenska Institutet i Athen 8°, 19. Stockholm.

Soysal, O. (2002) "Zur Herkunft eines gemeinsamen Wortes in Altanatolien: *parninka/i-*," in *Silva Anatolica: Anatolian Studies Presented to Maciej Popko on the Occasion of his 65th Birthday*, ed. P. Taracha. Warsaw. 315–37.

(2003) "Did a Hittite acrobat perform a bull-leaping?," *NABU: Nouvelles Assyriologiques Brèves et Utilitaires*: 105–7.

(2004a) *Hattischer Wortschatz in hethitischer Textüberlieferung*. Leiden and Boston.

(2004b) "A new fragment to Hittite Gilgameš epic," *NABU: Nouvelles Assyriologiques Brèves et Utilitaires*: 9–10.

(2004c) "On Hittite 'bull-leaping' again: With a lexical examination of the verb *watku-* 'to jump'," *NABU: Nouvelles Assyriologiques Brèves et Utilitaires*: 64–5.

(2007) "Zur Lesung des Namens 'Utanapišta' im Boğazköy-Fragment KBo 54.2," *NABU: Nouvelles Assyriologiques Brèves et Utilitaires*: 7.

(2013) "On recent cuneiform editions of Hittite fragments (II)," *Journal of the American Oriental Society* 133: 691–703.

Spencer, N. (1995) "Early Lesbos between east and west: A 'grey area' of Aegean archaeology," *Annual of the British School at Athens* 90: 269–306.

Spronk, K. (1986) *Beatific Afterlife in Ancient Israel and in the Ancient Near East*. Alter Orient und Altes Testament 219. Kevelaer and Neukirchen-Vluyn.

Starke, F. (1985) *Die keilschrift-luwischen Texte in Umschrift*. Studien zu den Boğazköy-Texten 30. Wiesbaden.

(1990) *Untersuchung zur Stammbildung des keilschrift-luwischen Nomens*. Studien zu den Boğazköy-Texten 31. Wiesbaden.

(1997) "Troia im Kontext des historisch-politischen und sprachlichen Umfeldes Kleinasiens im 2. Jahrtausend," *Studia Troica* 7: 447–87.

Steel, L. (2002) "Wine, women and song: Drinking ritual in Cyprus in the Late Bronze and Early Iron Ages," in *Engendering Aphrodite: Women and Society in Ancient Cyprus*, ed. D. Bolger and N. Serwint. Boston, Mass. 105–19.

(2004a) *Cyprus before History: From the Earliest Settlers to the End of the Bronze Age*. London.

(2004b) "A goodly feast ... a cup of mellow wine: Feasting in Bronze Age Cyprus," in *The Mycenaean Feast*, ed. J. C. Wright. Hesperia 73:2. Princeton, N.J. 161–80.

Stefanini, R. (2002) "Toward a diachronic reconstruction of the linguistic map of ancient Anatolia," in *Anatolia Antica: Studi in memoria di Fiorella Imparati*, ed. S. de Martino and F. Pecchioli Daddi. Eothen 11. Florence. 783–806.

Steiner, G. (1971) "Die Unterweltsbeschwörung des Odysseus im Lichte hethitischer Texte," *Ugarit-Forschungen* 3: 265–83.

(1990) "The immigration of the first Indo-Europeans into Anatolia reconsidered," *Journal of Indo-European Studies* 18: 185–214.

(1999) "Syrien als Vermittler zwischen Babylonien und Ḫatti (in der ersten Hälfte des 2. Jahrtausends v. Chr.)," in *Languages and Cultures in Contact: At the Crossroads of Civilizations in the Syro-Mesopotamian Realm: Proceedings of the 42th RAI*, ed. K. van Lerberghe and G. Voet. Orientalia Lovaniensia Analecta 96. Leuven. 425–41.

Stol, M. (2000) *Birth in Babylonia and the Bible: Its Mediterranean Setting*. Cuneiform Monographs 14. Groningen.

Strauss, R. (2006) *Reinigungsrituale aus Kizzuwatna: Ein Beitrag zur Erforschung hethitischer Ritualtradition und Kulturgeschichte*. Berlin and New York.

Struble, E. J. and V. Rimmer Herrmann (2009) "An eternal feast at Sam'al: The new Iron Age mortuary stele from Zincirli in context," *Bulletin of the American Schools of Oriental Research* 356: 15–49.

Süel, A. (1976–1977) "Das in den Urkunden von Boğazköy verwendete Wort $^{LÚ}UBĀRU$," *Anatolia* 20: 131–40.

(2001) "Ortaköy Tabletleri Işığında Batı Anadolu İle İlgili Bazı Konular Üzerine," in *Akten des IV. Internationalen Kongresses für Hethitologie. Würzburg, 4.-8. Oktober 1999*, ed. G. Wilhelm. Studien zu den Boğazköy-Texten 45. Wiesbaden. 670–8.

Sundaram, P. S. (1989) *Kamba Ramayanam*. Thanjavur.

Sürenhagen, D. (1981) "Zwei Gebete Ḫattušilis und der Puduḫepa. Textliche und literaturhistorische Untersuchungen," *Altorientalische Forschungen* 8: 83–168.

Suter, A. (1991a) "Δύσπαρι, εἶδος ἄριστε," *Quaderni Urbinati di Cultura Classica* 39 (68): 7–30.

(1991b) "Language of gods and language of men: The case of Paris/Alexandros," *Lexis* 7/8: 13–25.

(2002) *The Narcissus and the Pomegranate: An Archaeology of the Homeric Hymn to Demeter*. Ann Arbor.

Sutherland, R. K. (1986) *The Political Role of the Assemblies in Ancient Israel*. Ph.D. Thesis, Vanderbilt University.

Svenbro, J. (1993) *Phrasikleia: An Anthropology of Reading in Ancient Greece*, trans. by J. Lloyd. Ithaca. (Originally published in French in 1988.)

Swartz Dodd, L. (2005) "Legitimacy, identity and history in Iron Age Gurgum," in *Anatolian Iron Ages 5: Proceedings of the Fifth Anatolian Iron Ages Colloquium held at Van, 6–10 August 2001*, ed. A. Çilingiroğlu and G. Darbyshire. London. 47–64.

Sweek, J. (2002) "Inquiring for the state in the ancient Near East: Delineating political location," in *Magic and Divination in the Ancient World*, ed. L. Ciraolo and J. Seidel. Leiden, Boston and Cologne. 41–56.

Symington, D. (1991) "Late Bronze Age writing boards and their uses: Textual evidence from Anatolia and Syria," *Anatolian Studies* 41: 111–24.

Szemerényi, O. (1968) "The Attic 'Rückverwandlung' or atomism and structuralism in action," in *Studien zur Sprachwissenschaft und Kulturkunde: Gedenkschrift für Wilhelm Brandenstein (1898–1967)*, ed. M. Mayrhofer. Innsbruck. 139–57.

Tadmor, H. (1977) "Observations on Assyrian historiography," in *Essays on the Ancient Near East in Memory of Jacob Joel Finkelstein*, ed. M. de Jong Ellis. Memoirs of the Connecticut Academy of Arts & Sciences 19. Hamden, Conn. 209–13.

(1997) "Propaganda, literature, historiography: Cracking the code of the Assyrian royal inscriptions," in *Assyria 1995: Proceedings of the 10th Anniversary Symposium of the Neo-Assyrian Text Corpus Project, Helsinki, September 7–11, 1995*, ed. S. Parpola and R. M. Whiting Helsinki. 325–38.

Tadmor, H. and S. Yamada (2011) *The Royal Inscriptions of Tiglath-pileser III (744–727 BC), and Shalmaneser V (726–722 BC), Kings of Assyria*. The Royal Inscriptions of the Neo-Assyrian Period 1. Winona Lake, Ind.

Taggar-Cohen, A. (2005) *Hittite Priesthood*. Texte der Hethiter 26. Heidelberg.

(2006) "The NIN.DINGIR in the Hittite kingdom: A Mesopotamian priestly office in Hatti?" *Altorientalische Forschungen* 33: 313–27.

Tandy, D. W. (1997) *Warriors into Traders: The Power of the Market in Early Greece*. Berkeley, Los Angeles and London.

Taracha, P. (1985) "Zu den hethitischen *taknaz dā-* Ritualen," *Altorientalische Forschungen* 12: 278–82.

(1990) "More about the Hittite *taknaz da* rituals," *Hethitica* 10: 171–84.

(2000) *Ersetzen und Entsühnen: Das mittelhethitische Ersatzritual für den Großkönig Tuthalija (CTH *448.4) und verwandte Texte*. Culture and History of the Ancient Near East 5. Leiden, Boston and Cologne.

(2002) "Bull-leaping on a Hittite vase: New light on Anatolian and Minoan religion," *Archeologia: Rocznik Instytutu Archeologii i Etnologii Polskiej Akademii Nauk* 53: 7–20.

(2004) "More about Hittite bull-leaping," *NABU: Nouvelles Assyriologiques Brèves et Utilitaires*: 53.

(2008) "The Storm-God and the Hittite Great King," *Studi Micenei ed Egeo-Anatolici* 50: 745–51.

(2009) *Religions of Second Millennium Anatolia*. Dresdner Beiträge zur Hethitologie 27. Wiesbaden.

Tassignon, I. (2001) "Les éléments anatoliens du mythe et de la personnalité de Dionysos," *Revue de l'histoire des religions* 218: 307–37.

Tausend, K. and S. Tausend (2006) "Lesbos – Zwischen Griechenland und Kleinasien," in *Altertum und Mittelmeerraum: Die antike Welt diesseits und jenseits der Levante. Festschrift für Peter W. Haider zum 60. Geburtstag*, ed. R. Rollinger and B. Truschnegg. Stuttgart. 89–110.

Teffeteller, A. (2013) "Singers of Lazpa: Reconstructing identities on Bronze Age Lesbos," in *Luwian Identities: Culture, Language and Religion between Anatolia and the Aegean*, ed. A. Mouton, I. C. Rutherford and I. Yakubovich. Leiden and Boston. 567–89.

Tekoğlu, R. and A. Lemaire (2000) "La bilingue royale louvito-phénicienne de Çinekoy," *Comptes Rendues des Séances de l'Académie des Inscriptions & Belles-Lettres (juillet–octobre 2000)* 3: 961–1006.

Tenger, B. (1999) "Zur Geographie und Geschichte der Troas," in *Die Troas: Neue Forschungen III*, ed. E. Schwertheim. Asia Minor Studien 33. Bonn. 103–80.

Thiel, H.-J. and I. Wegner (1984) "Eine Anrufung an den Gott Teššub von Ḫalap in hurritischer Sprache," *Studi micenei ed egeo-anatolici* 24: 187–213.

Thomas, R. (1992) *Literacy and Orality in Ancient Greece*. Cambridge.

(2000) *Herodotus in Context: Ethnography, Science and the Art of Persuasion*. Cambridge.

Thomason, S. G. and T. Kaufman (1988) *Language Contact, Creolization and Genetic Linguistics*. Berkeley, Los Angeles and Oxford.

Thomatos, M. (2006) *The Final Revival of the Aegean Bronze Age: A Case Study of the Argolid, Corinthia, Attica, Euboea, the Cyclades, and the Dodecanese during the LH IIIC Middle*. Oxford.

Tigay, J. H. (1982) *The Evolution of the Gilgamesh Epic*. Philadelphia.

Tonietti, M. V. (1998) "The mobility of the NAR and the Sumerian personal names in the Pre-Sargonic Mari onomasticon," *Subartu* 4: 83–101.

Torri, G. (1999) *Lelwani: Il culto di una dea Ittita*. Rome.

(2009) "Sargon, Anitta, and the Hittite kings against Purushanda," *Altorientalische Forschungen* 36: 110–18.

Trameri, A. (2012) *Il rituale ittita di purificazione CTH 446: Uno scongiuro degli "Antichi Dei" e delle divinità infere. Edizione critica, traduzione, commento*. M.A. Thesis, Università degli Studi di Pavia.

Trémouille, M.-C. (2000) "La religione dei Hurriti," *Parola del Passato* 55: 114–70.

(2001) "Kizzuwatna, terre de frontière," in *La Cilicie: Éspaces et pouvoirs locaux (2e millénaire av. J.-C. – 4e siècle ap. J.-C.). Actes de la Table Ronde Internationale d'Istanbul, 2–5 novembre 1999*, ed. É. Jean, A. M. Dinçol and S. Durugönül. Paris. 57–78.

(2005) *Texte verschiedenen Inhalts*. Corpus der hurritischen Sprachdenkmäler I/8. Rome.

(2006) "Un exemple de continuité religieuse en Anatolie: Le dieu Šarruma," in *Pluralismus und Wandel in den Religionen im vorhellenistischen Anatolien: Akten des religionsgeschichtlichen Symposiums in Bonn (19.–20. Mai 2005)*, ed. M. Hutter and S. Hutter-Braunsar. Alter Orient und Altes Testament 337. Münster. 191–224.

Tropper, J. (1993) *Die Inschriften von Zincirli*. Abhandlungen zur Literatur Alt-Syrien-Palästinas 6. Münster.

Trümpy, C. (1997) *Untersuchungen zu den altgriechischen Monatsnamen und Monatsfolgen*. Heidelberg.

Tsetskhladze, G. R. (1999) "Between west and east: Anatolian roots of local cultures of the Pontus," in *Ancient Greeks West and East*, ed. G. R. Tsetskhladze. Leiden, Boston and Cologne. 469–96.

Tsukimoto, A. (1985) *Untersuchungen zur Totenpflege (kispum) im alten Mesopotamien*. Alter Orient und Altes Testament 216. Kevelaer and Neukirchen-Vluyn.

Ulf, C. (1996) "Griechische Ethnogenese versus Wanderungen von Stämmen und Stammstaaten," in *Wege zur Genese griechischer Identität: Die Bedeutung der früharchaischen Zeit*, ed. C. Ulf. Berlin. 240–80.

Ünal, A. (1996) *The Hittite Ritual of Ḫantitaššu from the City of Ḫurma against Troublesome Years*. Ankara.

(1998) *Hittite and Hurrian Cuneiform Tablets from Ortaköy (Çorum), Central Turkey, with Two Excurses on the "Man of the Storm God" and a Full Edition of KBo 23.27*. Istanbul.

van de Mieroop, M. (1999) *Cuneiform Texts and the Writing of History*. London and New York.
(2000) "Sargon of Agade and his successors in Anatolia," *Studi Micenei ed Egeo-Anatolici* 42: 133–59.
van den Hout, T. P. J. (1991–1992) "Some remarks on the third tablet of the Hittite KI.LAM festival," *Jaarbericht van het Vooraziatisch-Egyptisch Genootschap: Ex Oriente Lux* 32: 101–18.
(1994) "Death as a privilege: The Hittite royal funerary ritual," in *Hidden Futures: Death and Immortality in Ancient Egypt, Anatolia, the Classical, Biblical and Arabic-Islamic World*, ed. J. M. Bremer, T. P. J. van den Hout and R. Peters. Amsterdam. 37–76.
(1998) *The Purity of Kingship: An Edition of CHT 569 and Related Hittite Oracle Inquiries of Tuthaliya IV*. Documenta et Monumenta Orientis Antiqui 25. Leiden, Boston and Cologne.
(2001) "Zur Geschichte des jüngeren hethitischen Reiches," in *Akten des IV. Internationalen Kongresses für Hethitologie. Würzburg, 4.–8. Oktober 1999*, ed. G. Wilhelm. Studien zu den Boğazköy-Texten 45. Wiesbaden. 213–23.
(2002a) "Another view of Hittite literature," in *Anatolia Antica: Studi in memoria di Fiorella Imparati*, ed. S. de Martino and F. Pecchioli Daddi. Eothen 11. Florence. 857–78.
(2002b) "Tombs and memorials: The (divine) Stone-House and Ḫegur reconsidered," in *Recent Developments in Hittite Archaeology and History: Papers in Memory of Hans G. Güterbock*, ed. K. A. Yener and H. A. Hoffner, Jr. Winona Lake, Ind. 73–92.
(2006) "Administration in the reign of Tuthaliya IV and the later years of the Hittite empire," in *The Life and Times of Ḫattušili III and Tuthaliya IV: Proceedings of a Symposium Held in Honour of J. de Roos, 12–13 December 2003, Leiden*, ed. T. P. J. van den Hout. Leiden. 77–106.
(2009a) "A century of Hittite text dating and the origins of the Hittite cuneiform script," *Incontri Linguistici* 32: 11–35.
(2009b) "Reflections on the origins and development of the Hittite tablet collections in Ḫattuša and their consequences for the rise of Hittite literacy," in *Central-North Anatolia in the Hittite Period: New Perspectives in Light of Recent Research. Acts of the International Conference Held at the University of Florence (7–9 February 2007)*, ed. F. Pecchioli Daddi, G. Torri and C. Corti. Studia Asiana 5. Rome. 71–96.
van der Meer, L. B. (2004) "Etruscan origins: Language and archaeology," *Bulletin Antieke Beschaving* 79: 51–7.
van der Toorn, K. (1994) "Gods and ancestors in Emar and Nuzi," *Zeitschrift für Assyriologie und vorderasiatische Archäologie* 84: 38–59.
(1995) "The domestic cult at Emar," *Journal of Cuneiform Studies* 47: 35–49.
van Leuven, J. (1989) "The religion of the Shaft Grave Folk," *Aegaeum: Annales d'archéologie égéenne de l'Université de Liège*: 191–201.

van Loon, M. N. (1991) *Anatolia in the Earlier First Millennium B.C.* Iconography of Religions XV, 13. Leiden.
van Soldt, W. H. (1999) "The syllabic Akkadian texts," in *Handbook of Ugaritic Studies*, ed. W. G. E. Watson and N. Wyatt. Handbuch der Orientalistik 1.29. Leiden, Boston and Cologne. 28–45.
van Wees, H. (1994a) "The Homeric way of war: The *Iliad* and the hoplite phalanx (I)," *Greece and Rome* 41: 1–18.
  (1994b) "The Homeric way of war: The *Iliad* and the hoplite phalanx (II)," *Greece and Rome* 41: 131–55.
  (2000) "The development of the hoplite phalanx: Iconography and reality in the seventh century," in *War and Violence in Ancient Greece*, ed. H. van Wees. London. 125–66.
van Windekens, A. J. (1957–1958) "Note sur la structure phonétique d'un mot câlin micro-asianique," *Archiv für Orientforschung* 18: 366–7.
Vanschoonwinkel, J. (1990) "Mopsos: Légendes et réalité," *Hethitica* 10: 185–211.
  (1991) *L'Égée et la Méditerranée orientale à la fin du deuxième millénaire: Témoignage archéologiques et sources écrites*. Louvain-la-Neuve.
  (2005) "L'achéen Achille est-il l'ancêtre du philistine Goliath? À propos de l'armement et de la technique de combat du Philistin," *Res Antiquae* 2: 347–62.
  (2008) "Les Eubéens, premiers voyageurs grecs en Orient," *Res Antiquae* 5: 405–21.
Vansina, J. (1985) *Oral Tradition as History*. Madison, Wis.
Veldhuis, N. (1991) *A Cow of Sîn*. Library of Oriental Texts 2. Groningen.
Verbrugghe, G. P. and J. M. Wickersham (1996) *Berossus and Manetho, Introduced and Translated: Native Traditions in Ancient Mesopotamia and Egypt*. Ann Arbor.
Vermeule, E. (1972) *Greece in the Bronze Age*. Chicago and London.
Vermeule, E. and V. Karageorghis (1982) *Mycenaean Pictorial Vase Painting*. Cambridge, Mass. and London.
Versnel, H. S. (2002) "The Poetics of the magical charm: An essay on the power of words," in *Magic and Ritual in the Ancient World*, ed. P. Mirecki and M. Meyer. Leiden, Boston and Cologne. 105–58.
Vidal, J. (2000) "King lists and oral transmission: From history to memory," *Ugarit-Forschungen* 32: 555–66.
  (2005) "El culto a las tumbas de los ancestros en el Levante Mediterráneo," *Antiguo Oriente* 3: 55–64.
  (2006) "The origins of the last Ugaritic dynasty," *Altorientalische Forschungen* 33: 168–75.
Vigorita, J. (1976) "The antiquity of Serbo-Croatian verse," *Južnoslovenski Filolog* 32: 205–11.
Vogelzang, M. E. (1990) "Patterns introducing direct speech in Akkadian literary texts," *Journal of Cuneiform Studies* 41: 50–70.

Vogelzang, M. E. and H. L. J. Vanstiphout (eds.) (1992) *Mesopotamian Epic Literature: Oral or Aural?* Lewiston, N.Y., Queenston, Ont. and Lampeter.

Voigt, M. M. (2005) "Old problems and new solutions: Recent excavations at Gordion," in *The Archaeology of Midas and the Phrygians: Recent Work at Gordion*, ed. L. Kealhofer. Philadelphia. 22–35.

Voigt, M. M. and R. C. Henrickson (2000a) "The Early Iron Age at Gordion: The evidence from the Yassıhöyük stratigraphic sequence," in *The Sea Peoples and Their World: A Reassessment*, ed. E. D. Oren. Philadelphia. 327–60.

(2000b) "Formation of the Phrygian state: The Early Iron Age at Gordion." *Anatolian Studies* 50: 37–54.

von Dassow, E. (2008) *State and Society in the Late Bronze Age Alalaḫ under the Mitanni Empire*. Studies on the Civilization and Culture of Nuzi and the Hurrians 17. Bethesda, Md.

(2013) "Piecing together the Song of Release," *Journal of Cuneiform Studies* 65: 127–62.

von Schuler, E. (1965) *Die Kaskäer: Ein Beitrag zur Ethnographie des alten Kleinasien*. Untersuchungen zur Assyriologie und Vorderasiatischen Archäologie 3. Berlin.

Voskos, I. and A. B. Knapp (2008) "Cyprus at the end of the Late Bronze Age: Crisis and colonization or continuity and hybridization?," *American Journal of Archaeology* 112: 659–84.

Voutsaki, S. (1998) "Mortuary evidence, symbolic meanings and social change: comparison between Messenia and the Argolid in the Mycenaean period," in *Cemetery and Society in the Aegean Bronze Age*, ed. K. Branigan. Sheffield. 41–58.

Waal, W. (2011) "They wrote on wood: The case for a hieroglyphic scribal tradition on wooden writing boards in Hittite Anatolia," *Anatolian Studies* 61: 21–34.

Wade-Gery, H. T. (1952) *The Poet of the Iliad*. Cambridge.

Walcot, P. (1966) *Hesiod and the Near East*. Cardiff.

(1984) "Odysseus and the contest of the bow: The comparative evidence," *Studi Micenei ed Egeo-Anatolici* 84: 357–69.

Waldbaum, J. C. (1997) "Greeks *in* the east or Greeks *and* the east? Problems in the definition and recognition of presence," *Bulletin of the American School of Oriental Research* 305: 1–17.

Walker, K. G. (2004) *Archaic Eretria: A Political and Social History from the Earliest Times to 490 BC*. London and New York.

Ward, W. A. and M. S. Joukowsky (eds.) (1992) *The Crisis Years: The 12th Century B.C. from Beyond the Danube to the Tigris*. Dubuque.

Warren, P. (1990) "Of baetyls," *Opuscula Atheniensia* 18: 193–206.

Warren, P. and V. Hankey (1989) *Aegean Bronze Age Chronology*. Bristol.

Wathelet, P. (1970) *Les traits éoliens dans la langue de l'épopée grecque*. Incunabula Graeca 37. Rome.

Watkins, C. (1970) "Language of gods and language of men: Remarks on some Indo-European metalinguistic traditions," in *Myth and Law among the*

Indo-Europeans, ed. J. Puhvel. Berkeley. 1–17. Reprinted in Oliver (ed.) 1994, pp. 456–72.

(1976) "Observations on the 'Nestor's Cup' inscription," *Harvard Studies in Classical Philology* 80: 25–40. Reprinted in Oliver (ed.) 1994, pp. 544–59.

(1986) "The language of the Trojans," in *Troy and the Trojan War*, ed. M. Mellink. Bryn Mawr, Pa. 45–62. Reprinted in Oliver (ed.) 1994, pp. 700–17.

(1987a) "Linguistic and archaeological light on some Homeric formulas," in *Proto-Indo-European: The Archaeology of a Linguistic Problem. Studies in Honor of Marija Gimbutas*, ed. S. N. Skomal and E. C. Polomé. Washington, D.C. 286–98. Reprinted in Oliver (ed.) 1994, pp. 728–40.

(1987b) "Questions linguistiques palaïtes et louvites cunéiformes," *Hethitica* 8: 423–6.

(1987c) "Two Anatolian forms: Palaic *aškumāuwa-*, Cuneiform Luvian *wa-a-ar-ša*," in *Festschrift for Henry Hoenigswald on the Occasion of His 70th Birthday*, ed. G. Cardona and N. Zide. Tübingen. 399–404. Reprinted in Oliver (ed.) 1994, pp. 309–14.

(1992) "Le dragon hittite Illuyankas et le géant grec Typhôeus," *Comptes Rendues des Séances de l'Academie des Inscriptions & Belles-Lettres* 2: 319–30.

(1995) *How to Kill a Dragon: Aspects of Indo-European Poetics*. Oxford.

(1998) "Homer and Hittite revisited," in *Style and Tradition: Studies in Honor of Wendell Clausen*, ed. P. Knox and C. Foss. Stuttgart and Leipzig. 201–11.

(2000a) "L'Anatolie et la Grèce: Résonances culturelles, linguistiques et politiques," *Comptes Rendues des Séances de l'Academie des Inscriptions & Belles-Lettres (juillet–octobre 2000)* 3: 1143–58.

(2000b) "A distant Anatolian echo in Pindar: The origin of the aegis again," *Harvard Studies in Classical Philology* 100: 1–14.

(2001) "An Indo-European linguistic area and its characteristics: Ancient Anatolia. Areal diffusion as a challenge to the comparative method?," in *Areal Diffusion and Genetic Inheritance: Problems in Comparative Linguistics*, ed. A. Y. Aikhenvald and R. M. W. Dixon. Oxford. 44–63.

(2007a) "The golden bowl: Thoughts on the New Sappho and its Asianic background," *Classical Antiquity* 26: 305–25.

(2007b) "Hipponactea quaedam," in *Hesperos: Studies in Ancient Greek Poetry Presented to M. L. West on His Seventieth Birthday*, ed. P. Finglass, C. Collard and N. J. Richardson. Oxford and New York. 118–25.

(2008) "'Hermit crabs', or new wine in old bottles: Anatolian and Hellenic connections from Homer and before to Antiochus I of Commagene and after," in *Anatolian Interfaces: Hittites, Greeks and Their Neighbors. Proceedings of an International Conference on Cross-Cultural Interaction, September 17–19, 2004, Emory University, Atlanta, Ga.*, ed. B. J. Collins, M. R. Bachvarova and I. C. Rutherford. Oxford. 135–41.

Watrous, L. V. (1991) "The origin and iconography of the Late Minoan painted larnax," *Hesperia* 60: 285–307.

Webb, J. M. (1999) *Ritual Architecture, Iconography, and Practice in the Late Cypriot Bronze Age*. Jonsered.

(2002) "Device, image and coercion: The role of glyptic in the political economy of Late Bronze Age Cyprus," in *Script and Seal Use on Cyprus in the Bronze and Iron Ages*, ed. J. Smith. Boston. 111–54.

(2003) "From Ishtar to Aphrodite: The transformation of a goddess," in *From Ishtar to Aphrodite: 3200 Years of Cypriot Hellenism. Treasures from the Museums of Cyprus*, ed. S. Hadjisavvas. New York. 15–20.

(2005) "Ideology, iconography and identity: The role of foreign goods and images in the establishment of social hierarchy in Late Bronze Age Cyprus," in *Archaeological Perspectives on the Transmission and Transformation of Culture in the Eastern Mediterranean*, ed. J. Clarke. Oxford and Oakville, Conn. 176–82.

Wegner, I. (1981) *Gestalt und Kult der Ištar-Šawuška in Kleinasien*. Hurritologische Studien 3. Kevelaer and Neukirchen-Vluyn.

(1995) *Hurritische Opferlisten aus hethitischen Festbeschreibungen*. Teil 1: *Texte für IŠTAR-Ša(w)uška*. Corpus der hurritischer Sprachdenkmäler 1/3-1. Rome.

(2007) *Einführung in die hurritische Sprache*. 2nd edn. Wiesbaden.

Wegner, I. and M. Salvini (1991) *Die hethitisch-hurritischen Ritualtafeln des (H̬)išuwa-Festes*. Corpus der Hurritischen Sprachdenkmäler 1/4. Rome.

Weickert, C. (1959/1960) *Die Ausgrabung beim Athena-Tempel in Milet, 1957*. Istanbul.

Weilhartner, J. (2005) *Mykenische Opfergaben nach Aussage der Linear B-Texte*. Österreichische Akademie der Wissenschaften, philosophisch-historische Klasse, Denkschriften 330. Vienna.

Weissert, E. (1997) "Royal hunt and royal triumph in a prism fragment of Ashurbanipal," in *Assyria 1995: Proceedings of the 10th Anniversary Symposium of the Neo-Assyrian Text Corpus Project, Helsinki, September 7–11, 1995*, ed. S. Parpola and R. M. Whiting. Helsinki. 339–58.

Weißl, M. (2004) "Das Artemision von Ephesos zur Zeit des lydischen Reiches," in *Offizielle Religion, lokale Kulte und individuelle Religiosität: Akten des religionsgeschichtlichen Symposiums "Kleinasien und angrenzende Gebiete vom Beginn des 2. bis zur Mitte des 1. Jahrtausends v. Chr." (Bonn, 20.–22. Februar 2003)*, ed. M. Hutter and S. Hutter-Braunsar. Alter Orient und Altes Testament 318. Münster. 471–89.

Welwei, K.-W. (1992) *Athen: Vom neolithischen Siedlungsplatz zur archaischen Grosspolis*. Darmstadt.

Weniger, B. and R. Jung (2009) "Absolute chronology of the end of the Aegean Bronze Age," in *LH IIIC Chronology and Synchronisms, III: LH IIIC Late and the Transition to the Early Iron Age. Proceedings of the international*

Workshop at the Austrian Academy of Sciences at Vienna, February 23rd and 24th, 2007, ed. S. Deger-Jalkotzy and A. E. Bächle. Vienna. 373–416.

West, M. L. (1966) *Hesiod: Theogony*. Oxford.

(1971a) *Early Greek Philosophy and the Orient*. Oxford.

(1971b) "Stesichorus," *Classical Quarterly*, N. S. 21: 302–14.

(1973) "Greek poetry 2000–700 B.C.," *Classical Quarterly*, N. S. 23: 179–92.

(1978) *Hesiod: Works and Days*. Oxford.

(1985) *The Hesiodic Catalogue of Women: Its Nature, Structure, and Origins*. Oxford.

(1988) "The rise of Greek epic," *Journal of Hellenic Studies* 108: 151–72.

(1992a) *Ancient Greek Music*. Oxford.

(1992b) "The descent of the Greek epic: A reply," *Journal of Hellenic Studies* 112: 173–5.

(1995) "The date of the *Iliad*," *Museum Helveticum* 52: 203–19.

(1997a) *The East Face of Helicon*. Oxford.

(1997b) "Homer's meter," in *A New Companion to Homer*, ed. I. Morris and B. Powell. Leiden, New York, and Cologne. 218–37.

(ed.) (1998) *Homeri Ilias*. Volume I: *Rhapsodias I–XII continens*. Leipzig and Stuttgart.

(1999) "The invention of Homer," *Classical Quarterly* 49: 364–82.

(2000) "Geschichte des Textes," in *Homer Ilias: Gesamtkommentar: Prolegomena*, ed. J. Latacz. Munich and Leipzig. 27–38.

(2002a) "'Eumelos': A Corinthian epic cycle?," *Journal of Hellenic Studies* 122: 109–33.

(2002b) "The view from Lesbos," in *Epea Pteroenta: Beiträge zur Homerforschung. Festschrift für Wolfgang Kullmann zum 75. Geburtstag*, ed. M. Reichel and A. Rengakos. Stuttgart. 207–19.

(ed.) (2003a) *Greek Epic Fragments*. Cambridge, Mass. and London.

(ed.) (2003b) *Homeric Hymns, Homeric Apocrypha, Lives of Homer*. Cambridge, Mass., and London.

(2005) "*Odyssey* and *Argonautica*," *Classical Quarterly* 55: 39–64.

(2007) *Indo-European Poetry and Myth*. Oxford.

(2011) *The Making of the Iliad: Disquisition and Analytical Commentary*. Oxford and New York.

West, S. (1994) "Nestor's bewitching cup," *Zeitschrift für Papyrologie und Epigraphik* 101: 9–15.

Westenholz, A. (1999) "The Old Akkadian period: History and culture," in *Mesopotamien: Akkade-Zeit und Ur III-Zeit*, ed. P. Attinger and M. Wäfler. Orbis Biblicus et Orientalis 160/3. Freiburg and Göttingen. 17–117.

Westenholz, J. G. (1983) "Heroes of Akkad," *Journal of the American Oriental Society* 103: 327–36.

(1992) "Oral traditions and written texts in the Cycle of Akkade," in *Mesopotamian Epic Literature: Oral or Aural?*, ed. M. E. Vogelzang and H. L. J. Vanstiphout. Lewiston, N.Y., Queenston, Ont. and Lampeter. 123–54.

(1993) "Writing for posterity: Naram-Sin and Enmerkar," in *Kinattūtu ša dārâti: Raphael Kutscher Memorial Volume*, ed. A. F. Rainey. Tel Aviv. 205–18.

(1997) *Legends of the Kings of Akkade: The Texts.* Mesopotamian Civilizations 7. Winona Lake, Ind.

(1998) "Relations between Mesopotamia and Anatolia in the age of the Sargonic kings," in *III. Uluslararası Hititoloji Kongresi Bildirileri: Çorum 16–22 Eylül 1996 – Acts of the IIIrd International Congress of Hittitology: Çorum, September 16–22, 1996*, ed. S. Alp and A. Süel. Ankara. 5–22.

(2008) "The memory of Sargonic kings under the Third Dynasty of Ur," in *On the Third Dynasty of Ur: Studies in Honor of Marcel Sigrist*, ed. P. Michalowski. *Journal of Cuneiform Studies*, Supplemental Series 1. Boston. 251–60.

(2010) "Historical events and the process of their transformation in Akkadian heroic traditions," in *Epic and History*, ed. D. Konstan and K. Raaflaub. Malden, Mass. 26–50.

(2011) "The transmission and reception of the Sargonic sagas in the Hittite world," in *Hethitische Literatur: Überlieferungsprozesse, Textstrukturen, Ausdrucksformen und Nachwirken. Akten des Symposiums vom 18. bis 20. Februar 2010 in Bonn*, ed. M. Hutter and S. Hutter-Braunsar. Alter Orient und Altes Testament 391. Münster. 285–303.

Whitley, J. (1988) "Early states and hero-cult: A reappraisal," *Journal of Hellenic Studies* 108: 173–82.

(1995) "Tomb cult and hero cult: The uses of the past in Archaic Greece," in *Time, Tradition and Society in Greek Archaeology: Bridging the 'Great Divide'*, ed. N. Spencer. London and New York. 43–63.

Wijngaarden, G. J. (2002) *Use and Appreciation of Mycenaean Pottery in the Levant, Cyprus and Italy (ca. 1600–1200 BC).* Amsterdam.

Wilcke, C. (1969) *Das Lugalbanda Epos.* Wiesbaden.

(1977) "Die Anfänge der akkadischen Epen," *Zeitschrift für Assyriologie und vorderasiatische Archäologie* 67: 153–216.

(1988) "Die Sumerische Königsleste und erzählte Vergangenheit," in *Vergangenheit in mündlicher Überlieferung*, ed. J. von Ungern-Sternberg and H. Reinau. Stuttgart. 113–40.

(1989) "Genealogical and geographical thought in the Sumerian King List," in *DUMU-E₂-DUB-BA-A: Studies in Honor of Åke W. Sjöberg*, ed. H. Behrens, D. Loding and M. T. Roth. Occasional Publications of the Samuel Noah Kramer Fund 11. Philadelphia. 557–71.

(1997) "Amar-girids Revolte gegen Narām-Suʾen," *Zeitschrift für Assyriologie und vorderasiatische Archäologie* 87: 11–32.

(2001) "Gestaltetes Altertum in antiker Gegenwart: Königslisten und Historiographie des älteren Mesopotamien," in *Die Gegenwart des Altertums: Formen und Funktionen des Altertumsbezugs in den Hochkulturen der Alten Welt*, ed. D. Kuhn and H. Stahl. Heidelberg. 93–116.

Wilhelm, G. (1984) "Zur Paläographie der in Ägypten geschriebenen Keilschriftbriefe," *Studien zur altägyptischen Kultur* 11: 643–53.
  (1988) "Neue akkadische Gilgameš-Fragmente aus Ḫattuša," *Zeitschrift für Assyriologie und vorderasiatische Archäologie* 78: 99–121.
  (1989) *The Hurrians*, trans. by J. Barnes. Warminster, England.
  (1991) *Literarische Texte in sumerischer und akkadischer Sprache.* Keilschrifttexte aus Boğazköi 36. Berlin.
  (1992) "Zum eblaitischen Gott Kura," *Vicino Oriente* 8: 23–31.
  (1994) "Kumme und *Kumar: Zur hurritischen Ortsnamenbildung," in *Beiträge zur Altorientalischen Archäologie und Altertumskunde: Festschrift für Barthel Hrouda zum 65. Geburtstag*, ed. P. Calmeyer, K. Hecker, L. Jakob-Rost and C. B. F. Walker. Wiesbaden. 315–20.
  (1996) "The Hurrians in the western parts of the ancient Near East." *Michmanim* 9: 17–30.
  (1997) "Die Könige von Ebla nach der hurritisch-hethitischen Serie 'Freilassung'," *Altorientalische Forschungen* 24: 277–93.
  (1999) "Kešše," in *Nuzi at Seventy-Five*, ed. D. I. Owen. Studies on the Civilization and Culture of Nuzi and the Hurrians 10. Bethesda, Md. 411–13.
  (2002) "'Gleichsetzungstheologie', 'Synkretismus' und 'Gottesspaltungen' im Polytheismus Anatoliens," in *Polytheismus und Monotheismus in den Religionen des Vorderen Orients*, ed. M. Krebernik and J. van Oorschot. Alter Orient und Altes Testament 298. Münster. 53–70.
  (2003) "König Silber und König Ḫidam," in *Hittite Studies in Honour of Harry A. Hoffner, Jr.: On the Occasion of his 65th Birthday*, ed. G. M. Beckman, R. H. Beal and J. G. McMahon. Winona Lake, Ind. 393–5.
  (2008) "Hurrians in the Kültepe texts," in *Anatolia and the Jazira during the Old Assyrian Period*, ed. J. G. Dercksen. Publications de l'Institut Historique-archéologique néerlandais de Stamboul 111. Istanbul. 181–94.
  (2009) "Die Götter der Unterwelt als Ahnengeister des Wettergottes nach altsyrischen und altanatolischen Quellen," in *JHWH und die Götter der Völker: Symposium zum 80. Geburtstag von Klaus Koch*, ed. F. Hartenstein and M. Rösel. Neukirchen-Vluyn. 59–75.
  (2010a) "Ein Fragment mit hurritischen Gallenomina und der Beginn der hurritischen Überlieferung in Ḫattuša," in *Kulturlandschaft Syrien: Zentrum und Peripherie. Festschrift für Jan-Waalke Meyer*, ed. J. Becker, R. Hempelmann and E. Rehm. Alter Orient und Altes Testament 371. Münster. 623–35.
  (2010b) "Die Lesung des Namens der Göttin IŠTAR-li," in *Investigationes Anatolicae: Gedenkschrift für Erich Neu*, ed. J. Klinger, E. Rieken and C. Rüster. Studien zu den Boğazköy-Texten 52. Wiesbaden. 337–44.
Wilson, P. (2009) "Thamyris the Thracian: The archetypal wandering poet?," in *Wandering Poets in Ancient Greek Culture: Travel, Locality and Pan-Hellenism*, ed. R. Hunter and I. C. Rutherford. Cambridge. 46–79.

Winter, I. J. (1979) "On the problems of Karatepe: The reliefs and their context," *Anatolian Studies* 29: 115–51.

(1995) "Homer's Phoenicians: History, ethnography, or literary trope? [A perspective on early orientalism]," in *The Ages of Homer: A Tribute to Emily Townsend Vermeule*, ed. J. B. Carter and S. P. Morris. Austin, Tx. 247–71.

Wittke, A.-M. (2004) *Mušker und Phryger: Ein Beitrag zur Geschichte Anatoliens vom 12. bis zum 7. Jh. v. Chr.: Kommentar zur TAVO-Karte B IV 8 "Östlicher Mittlemeerraum und Mesopotamien um 700 v. Chr."*. Wiesbaden.

(2007) "Remarks on the early history of Phrygia (twelfth to eighth century BC)," in *Anatolian Iron Ages 6: The Proceedings of the Sixth Anatolian Iron Ages Colloquium Held at Eskişehir, 16–20 August 2004*, ed. A. Çilingiroğlu and A. Sagona. Leuven, Paris and Dudley, Mass. 335–47.

Wolf, A. (2006) "Odysseus im Phaiakenland – Homer in der Magna Graecia," in *"Troianer sind wir gewesen" – Migrationen in der antiken Welt: Stuttgarter Kolloquium zur Historischen Geographie des Altertums 8, 2002*, ed. E. Olshausen and H. Sonnabend. Stuttgart. 20–53.

Woodard, R. D. (ed.) (2004) *The Cambridge Encyclopedia of the World's Ancient Languages*. Cambridge and New York.

Woolley, L. (1952) *Carchemish: Report on the Excavations at Jerablus on Behalf of the British Museum. Part III: The Excavations in the Inner Town*. London.

Wright, J. C. (1994) "The spatial configuration of belief: The archaeology of Mycenaean religion," in *Placing the Gods: Sanctuaries and Sacred Space in Ancient Greece*, ed. S. E. Alcock and R. Osborne. Oxford. 37–78.

(1995a) "Empty cups and empty jugs: The social role of wine in Minoan and Mycenaean societies," in *The Origins and Ancient History of Wine*, ed. P. E. McGovern, S. J. Fleming and S. H. Katz. Amsterdam. 287–309.

(1995b) "From chief to king in Mycenaean Greece," in *The Role of the Ruler in the Prehistoric Aegean: Proceedings of a Panel Discussion Presented at the Annual Meeting of the Archaeological Institute of America, New Orleans, Louisiana, 28 December 1992 with Additions*, ed. P. Rehak. Aegaeum 11. Liège and Austin, Tx. 63–80.

(ed.) (2004a) *The Mycenaean Feast*. Hesperia 73.2. Princeton, N. J.

(2004b) "A survey of evidence for feasting in Mycenaean society," in *The Mycenaean Feast*, ed. J. C. Wright. Hesperia 73:2. Princeton, N. J. 13–58.

Wyatt, N. (1995) "The significance of ṢPN in west Semitic thought: A contribution to the history of a mythological motif," in *Ugarit: Ein ostmediterranes Kulturzentrum im Alten Orient. Volume I: Ugarit und seine altorientalische Umwelt*, ed. M. Dietrich and O. Loretz. Abhandlungen zur Literatur Alt-Syrien-Palästinas 7. Münster. 213–37.

(1996) *Myths of Power: A Study of Royal Myth and Ideology in Ugaritic and Biblical Tradition*. Ugaritisch-Biblische Literatur 13. Münster.

(1998) "Arms and the king: The earliest allusions to the Chaoskampf motif and their implications for the interpretation of the Ugaritic and Biblical traditions," in *'Und Mose schrieb dieses Lied auf...': Studien zum Alten Testament und zum Alten Orient. Festschrift für O. Loretz zur Vollendung seines 70. Lebensjahres mit Beiträgen von Freunden, Schülern und Kollegen*, ed. M. Dietrich and I. Kottsieper. Alter Orient und Altes Testament 250. Münster. 833–82. Reprinted in N. Wyatt 2005, *'There's Such Divinity Doth Hedge a King': Selected Essays of Nicolas Wyatt on Royal Ideology in Ugaritic and Old Testament Literature*, Hants, England and Burlington, Vt., pp. 191–220.

(1999) "The religion of Ugarit: An overview," in *Handbook of Ugaritic Studies*, ed. W. G. E. Watson and N. Wyatt. Handbuch der Orientalistik 1.29. Leiden, Boston and Cologne. 529–85.

(2002) *Religious Texts from Ugarit: The Words of Ilimilku and His Colleagues*. 2nd edn. The Biblical Seminar 53. Sheffield.

(2007) "À la recherche des rephaïm perdus," in *Le royaume d'Ougarit de la Crète à l'Euphrate: Nouveaux axes de recherche*, ed. J.-M. Michaud. Sherbrooke, Quebec. 579–613.

Wyatt, W. F. (1992) "Homer's linguistic forebears," *Journal of Hellenic Studies* 112: 167–73.

Yağcı, R. (2003) "The stratigraphy of Cyprus WS II & Mycenaean cups in Soli Höyük excavations," in *Identifying Changes: The Transition from Bronze to Iron Ages in Anatolia and Its Neighboring Regions. Proceedings of the International Workshop, Istanbul, November 8–9, 2002*, ed. B. Fischer, H. Genz, É. Jean and K. Köroğlu. Istanbul. 93–106.

(2007) "Hittites at Soli (Cilicia)," *Studi Micenei ed Egeo-Anatolici* 49: 797–814.

Yakar, J. (1993) "Anatolian civilization following the disintegration of the Hittite empire: An archaeological appraisal," *Tel Aviv* 20: 3–28.

(2001) "The socio-economic organization of the rural sector in Kizzuwatna – an archaeological assessment," in *La Cilicie: Éspaces et pouvoirs locaux (2e millénaire av. J.-C. – 4e siècle ap. J.-C.). Actes de la Table Ronde Internationale d'Istanbul, 2–5 novembre 1999*, ed. É. Jean, A. M. Dinçol and S. Durugönül. Paris. 37–46.

Yakubovich, I. (2005) "Were Hittite kings divinely anointed? A Palaic invocation to the Sun-god and its significance for Hittite religion." *Journal of Ancient Near Eastern Religions* 5: 107–37.

(2010) *Sociolinguistics of the Luvian Language*. Leiden and Boston.

Yalouris, N. (1989) "Ein Schlachtengemälde im Palast des Nestor," *Mitteilungen des Deutschen Archäologischen Instituts, Athenische Abteilung* 104: 41–8.

Yamauchi, E. (2003) *Foes from the Northern Frontier: Invading Hordes from the Russian Steppes*. Eugene, Ore.

Yasur-Landau, A. (2010) *The Philistines and Aegean Migration at the End of the Late Bronze Age*. New York.

Yener, K. A. (2009) "Acrobats, bulls, and leaping scenes on new Alalakh amphoroid craters," *Near Eastern Archaeology* 72: 48–50.

Yener, K. A., H. Özbal, L. Barnes, R. H. Brill and E. C. Joel (1998) "Anatolian metal trade and lead isotope analysis," in xxxiv. *Uluslararası Assiriyoloji Kongresi*, ed. H. Erkanal, V. Donbaz and A. Uğuroğlu. Ankara. 547–64.

Yon, M. (1980) "'Zeus de Salamine'," in *Recherches sur les religions de l'antiquité classique*, ed. R. Bloch. Geneva and Paris. 85–103.

(1999) "Chypre et Ougarit à la fin du Bronze Récent," *Report of the Department of Antiquities, Cyprus*: 113–19.

Younger, J. G. and P. Rehak (2008) "Minoan culture: Religion, burial customs, and administration," in *The Cambridge Companion to the Aegean Bronze Age*, ed. C. W. Shelmerdine. Cambridge. 165–85.

Younger, K. L. (2009) "The deity Kur(r)a in the first millennium sources," *Journal of Ancient Near Eastern Religions* 9: 1–23.

Zaccagnini, C. (1983) "Patterns of mobility among ancient Near Eastern craftsmen," *Journal of Near Eastern Studies* 42: 245–64.

(1987) "Aspects of ceremonial exchange in the Near East during the late second millennium BC," in *Centre and Periphery in the Ancient World*, ed. M. Rowlands, M. Larsen and K. Kristiansen. Cambridge. 57–65.

Zeeb, F. (2001) *Die Palastwirtschaft in Altsyrien nach den spätaltbabylonischen Getreidelieferlisten aus Alalaḫ (Schlicht VII)*. Alter Orient und Altes Testament 282. Münster.

Ziegler, N. (2006) "Les Musiciens de la cour Mari," *Les Dossiers d'Archéologie* 310: 32–8.

(2007) *Les musiciens et la musique d'après les archives de Mari*. Florilegium Marianum 9. Antony, France.

Zinko, C. (1987) *Betrachtungen zum AN.TAḪŠUM-Fest (Aspekte eines hethitischen Festrituals)*. Scientia 8. Innsbruck.

Zumthor, P. (1987) *La lettre et la voix de la "littérature" médiévale*. Paris.

(1992) *Toward a Medieval Poetics*, trans. by P. Bennett. Minneapolis.

Subject index

1 Kings *See* Bible
1 Samuel *See* Bible
2 Kings *See* Bible
2 Samuel *See* Bible

ᵈA.NUN.NA.KE4 94, 96n83 *Also see* Anunnaki
ᴸᵁ́A.ZU 108, 213n67 *Also see* ᴸᵁ́AZU; exorcist
Ab/p šarrāni 87
Abadu 95n78, 97n86
a-ba-i 87 *Also see* pit rituals
Abantes 435
Abaza myths 25n16, 27n28, 106n122
Abi (Former God) 96 *Also see* āpi
Abkhaz myths 126n58
abu 86, 88 *Also see* pit rituals
Abu, month 85, 87n44, 88, 109
abû 87–8n44
abu festival 79, 87–8
Abu Salabikh 209
Abydenos 392n157
Acem Höyük 172n23
Achaean layer, Homeric dialect 266n1, 427n30
Achaemenids 312, 314n63
Acheles 378
Acheron 100, 106
Achilleid See Achilles, story of
Achilles 193, 282n62, 410, 422, 449–50, 453n134
  Aeolic hero 371, 405–6, 454
  embassy 144–5
  friendship with/mourning for Patroclus 22, 194, 434
  Gilgamesh tradition 1, 13, 22, 107, 194, 434, 454
  playing lyre 144, 276, 298, 415n72
  quarrel, *Song of Release* 33–4, 132, 139–42
  raids in Anatolia 353, 406
  solar myth 107
  story of 406, 432, 438, 454
  tomb 409–10, 412
  wrath 406, 433–4
Achilleum 409–10
Adad 170
  Storm-god of Aleppo 161–2
Adad-Nirari II 390n153

Adalur, Mt. 159
Adana 7, 18, 317–18, 383 *Also see* Danuna
Adanawa 317
Adaniya 260, 313, 317
Adarwan, Mt. 160n48
admonitory history
  epic 124, 158, 166–7, 196
  omens 168
  Testament of Hattusili I 32
  wisdom 196
ådny 313
Adonis 215n77, 325
Aduntarri 96, 98n91
Adyattes 352, 374
  tumulus 376
Aeae 103n112
Aeaean island 102, 103n112
Aegeidae 239
Aegiroessa 451
Aegocoreis 241n111
Aegyptus 215n77
Aelian, *Varia Historia* 12.50 214n69
  8.2 416n76
Aeneas
  Aphrodite, son of 325, 327–8
  birth/conception 328–9, 410
  after fall of Troy 407n41, 410, 436–7
  genealogy 190, 378, 429
Aeneidae 328–9, 407, 410, 412n65, 429, 435–7
Aeolians 234, 236, 359, 409, 435–6
  in *Iliad* 411
Aeolic
  bards, bilingual 429
  base 460
  borrowings/layer, Homeric dialect 357, 396, 402–9, 412n66, 444
  dialect 240, 405, 437 *Also see* Aeolic borrowings/layer
  Dodecapolis 451
  epic 329, 396, 402–10, 412n62, 416, 454
  ethnogenesis 359, 406
  Hera 329
  and Ionic bards, competition 19, 395–6, 402–12, 417

565

Aeolic (cont.)
   migrations 359–60, 403, 406, 409–10n52, 411, 451
   settlement, Troy *See* Troy, Aeolian settlement
Aeolic-Lydian bilingual bards 429
Aeolic-Phrygian bilingual bards 429–31
   Also see Greek-Phrygian bilingual bards
Aeolis 236, 333, 358–9, 409n49
Aeolus 378, 411n58, 441
Aërias 324
Aeschylus
   en de 427n29
   Eumenides 96n80
   Persians 108
   Prometheus Bound 351–2, 255n158
      700–35 215n73
   Seven against Thebes 220 133n2
   Suppliants 215n73
      291–319 214n72
      531–89 214n72
      870 446
Aesop 129n69
Aethiopis 97, 444n97
Aetolia 287
Afrin River 159n47, 177n47
Agagalis *See* Ikinkalis
Agamemnon 146, 330n131, 353, 407, 409, 435, 450
   ancestor, fictional 409, 435–6
   Cuthean Legend of Naram-Sin 193
   of Cyme 435
   dreams 173, 193
   quarrel with Achilles, *Song of Release* 33–4, 132, 139–42
   Sargonic legends 173
   scepter 378, 421–2
Agapenor 324
Agdistis 343
Agenor 215–16n77
Ages of Man *See* Hesiod, *Works and Days*
Agron 376
Ahhiyawa 2–3, 6, 273, 332–41, 344–7 *Also see* Hiyawa
   Anatolia, west, and Cilicia 393
   Anatolian coast 353, 339–40, 341, 358
   Assuwa rebellion 334–5, 341
   connection between Greece and Cilicia 318
   dynastic marriages
      Assuwa 334–5
      Milawatta 339
      Wilusa 347, 351
   Egypt 315
   Greece 315, 333n6
   Hatti, gift exchange 344–5
   Lukka 339, 441 *Also see* Hiyawans, Lukka
   Mycenae 333n6
   Mycenaean settlements 339–40, 358
   Mycenaeans 3
   refuge for Anatolians 338–9
   Sea Peoples 315
   Thebes 333n6
   transfer, gods 202n10, 346
   Wilusa 344, 354, 431–2
Ahiqar 129n69
Ahithophel 134n3
Aidoneus 114
Aigaion 257n166
Ailanuwa 34
aimpa- 31n44
Ajax 141, 144
Akar Çay 337n27
a-ke-ne-u-si 230n58
akītu festival 118, 221, 262
Akka 134, 188
Akkade 166, 169, 174
   destruction 76, 185, 190–2, 348, 354, 431
   The Heroic Deeds of Gurparanzah 21, 34
Akkadian
   bards, bilingual 52
   epic 41–2, 52
   meter 46
   scribes, Hattusa 6, 8–9, 171
   source for NE influence on Greek literature 2–3, 5, 54–5, 200
   texts
      Hattusa 4, 9, 15, 20–1, 32–3, 56, 60–3, 85, 163, 171, 191, 213n67, 213–14n68, 214n72, 317n77, 340, 341n51
   Ugarit *See* Concordance of Tablets from Ugarit
Akkadian Fragments (Naram-Sin) 191n108
Akkadian Incantations 85, 214n68
Akkadian Prescription against Fever 214n68
Aky 304
al-Mina 300n129, 312
ala- 21n4
Alaca Höyük 224
Alaksandu 2, 196, 351, 362–3, 431 *Also see* Alexander; Paris
   fictional ancestor 363
Alaksandu Treaty See Treaty between Muwattalli II and Alaksandu of Wilusa

Alalakh
  bird-faced figurines 323n103
  bull-leaping 227n38
  cremation 284
  Cyprus 323
  Hurrians 10, 162n56
  Idrimi 186n91, 381
  Ishhara 115n10
  script 8
Alalgar 189
Alalu 25, 95, 97n86, 189–90
Alantalli 337
Alashiya 303 *Also see* Cyprus; Iatnana
  Elisha 293–4
  Old Assyrian Sargon Legend 170, 303
Albanian influence, Serbo-Croatian epic 428
Albanian-Serbo-Croatian bilingual bards 13, 47–8, 428
Alcaeus (Heraclid) 376, 378
Alcaeus
  F 42.2 Lobel-Page 406n39
  F 70.6 409n52
  F 70.7 374–5n105
  F 129.6 329n129
  F 130B.14 43n98
  F 130B.17–20 329n129
  F 337 12n48
  hexametric poetry, relation to 329, 406, 416
  Myrsilus 374–5n105
Alcman
  F 1 Page 239n103
  F 52 239n103
  F 74 427n32
  Lydian 214n69, 239–40
  -ske/o- 427n32
Aleppo
  EIA 311
  Hebat 261n190
  Hittites 6, 158
  Hurrians 162n56
  HH rituals 160
Alexander 354, 429 *Also see* Alaksandu; Paris
  meaning 351
  Paris, double name 2, 351–2, 434
Alexander Polyhistor 239n102
  FGrH 680 FF 5 (6), 7c (31) 392n157
Alexander Romance 54n2
Alexandrea 436
Alişar 357
Alizones *See* Halizones
Allaiturahhi 90n53 *Also see Ritual of Allaiturahhi*

Allani 114
  ancestor veneration 128
  (ḫ)išuwa festival 159–60
  hospitality scene, *Song of Release* 113, 124–6, 128–9
  Ishhara 129
  Ritual of Allaiturahhi 155
  Sun-goddess of the Earth 96, 114n9
Allatum 159
Allanzu 159, 184
Alpamysh 34n55, 48n122
alphabet, Greek 295n112, 397n6, 400n17
'althyts 319n86
alu=m=ai=n kad=i=a 42, 174n34
Alulim 189
Alulu 74, 189n100
Alybe 52, 104
am(m)ate=na en=na 94 *Also see* Former Gods
Amanus Gates 313
Amanus Mts. 159, 175n37, 313
Amar-Sin 161n53
Amarna *Also see* Index of Amarna Tablets
  Arzawa 335
  Brotherhood of Great Kings 202n10, 226
  Cyprus 303
  diplomats 226
  gift exchange 202n10, 207n32, 213
  Hittites 7, 207, 213, 335
  IŠTAR of Nineveh, visit from 202n10, 347n78
  Mitanni Letter 9
  Sargon, King of Battle 172–3
  Song of Keshshi 28
a-ma-ru-to 228
Amarynthus 228
Amathus 307
Amazons 105, 374n103, 378, 423
ambašši rituals 81, 83, 84
Amenhotep III 9, 226, 317n78, 335, 347n78
Amisodarus 440, 453
Ammezadu 95n78, 97n86
Ammiditana 197n119
Ammisaduqa xxx.n1, 197n119
Ammuna 313n59
Ammurapi 150n1, 304n13, 315n71
Amorites *See* Amurru
Amphiclus 435
Amphidamas (Cytheran) 282n63
Amphidamas (Euboean) 219, 233, 240, 396n2, 398
Amphilochus 318
Amphimachus 442
Amphinomos 75n98

Subject index

Amunki 95n78, 96, 97n86
Amurru 6, 170, 197n119, 216, 337n31
Amyclae 233
Amyntor 282n63
An 25, 31n44, 58, 68–9, 97, 136, 162, 166,
    185n83, 189, 217, 260, 325
AN.TAḪŠUM festival 151, 152n13, 222,
    223n15
  Storm-god of Aleppo 259
Anacreon 209
anapāš 81, 84
Anat 144n27, 306, 325
Anatolia *Also see* Syro-Anatolia
  continuity 357, 448
    of memory 273
Anatolia, BA
  and Greece, shared feasting etiquette 344
  Mycenaean settlement 320
  post-palatial period 274
Anatolia, EIA
  ancestor veneration 375–6
  Hieroglyphic Luwian inscriptions 3, 343, 350
  king lists 375–8
Anatolia, west
  ancestor statues 375
  and Cilicia, Ahhiyawa 393 *Also see* Hiyawa
    Cilicia
    shared identity
      migration 17–18, 316, 318–19, 382,
      392–3
    continuity 356–9
    of memory 18, 332, 341, 374
Anatolian influence
  Homeric tradition 419
  Odyssey 79, 105–7, 295, 298–9
    journeys, underworld 103–7, 109, 298–9
Anatolians
  in Greece, BA 231–2
    festivals 345–6
  intermediaries 1, 4–5, 14
  shared legendary past with Greeks 19, 332–3
ancestor gods 130, 160
ancestor reliefs 153, 381, 384–6, 390
ancestor statues
  Early Dynastic 186n91
  Ebla 150, 161, 186n91
  Egypt 272
  Enkidu 58, 79
  Gilgamesh tradition 58, 79, 186
  Hittite 151–4, 183, 186, 446
  kispum 150, 186
  Levant 272
  Lugalbanda 58

Mopsus 384
Mycenaean 270–2
Syro-Anatolian 186, 379–81
Ugarit 149–50, 151, 381
ancestor statues/stelae, Karatepe 382n134, 384,
    386
ancestor veneration
  abu-festival 87–8
  Allani 128
  Anatolia, west, EIA 375–6
  Bible 290
  Boeotia, BA 270, 281
  Carchemish, EIA 380–2
  city gate 381–2
  Crete 272
  Cyprus 272
  Emar 150n1, 197n118
  epic 18, 196–7, 218, 264, 271–2, 273, 349–50,
    370–1, 386–92, 438–9, 445–9
    Karatepe 18, 350, 382–6, 391–2
  festivals 87–8, 151, 155–6, 233–4, 264, 350
  genealogies 271–2
  Gilgamesh tradition 14, 51, 58–9, 79–81, 391
  Greece
    post-palatial 276–7
    Protogeometric 279, 281–2, 286–7, 370
  HH narr. song 50, 51
  Israel 150n1
  Lycians 420, 438–9
  magico-medical rituals 218
  Mycenaean 268–73
  Naram-Sin 178–9, 186
  NE, influence on Greece 279, 289–92
  pit rituals 79–80, 87–8
  statues 186
  Storm-god 152, 155, 380, 446
  Syro-Anatolia *See* Syro-Anatolia
  transfer, verbal art 4, 13, 15, 17, 108, 110, 165,
    196–7, 279, 284–5, 289–92, 370–1,
    373, 377–8, 391, 394, 438–9, 445–9
  Troy, EIA 349, 367–70
  Ugarit *See rapa ūma*
  world history 196–7, 350
ancestor veneration, royal 51, 151, 156
  Allani 128
  Ebla 149–50
  Hattusa 152–3
  Hittite 150–3, 156
    cult singers 156
  Lydian 349
  NE 149–53
  nuntarriyašḫaš festival 151, 156
  šarrena ritual 15

Song of Release 14, 51, 110, 119, 122, 129, 149–50, 153, 155, 161, 165
   Storm-god 122–4, 155
   Syria, north, BA 186
   Syria, north, and east Anatolia 149–50, 186, 350, 373–4, 379–91
   Ugarit 149–50, 290, 381–2
      festivals 151
   Yazılıkaya 152–3
ancestors
   divine
      of Enlil 97n87
      healers 17 *Also see m^erappîm*
      rapa ūma 285, 290, 293
      repā 'îm 285, 290
      Song of Keshshi 28
   fictional 14, 80, 186–7, 374, 376–8, 392–3
      Also see kispum
      Agamemnon 409, 435–6
      Alaksandu 363
      Gilgamesh 14, 79–80, 186
      Glaucids 438–9, 440n82
      Homer 416n76
      Manishtushu 186n90
      Mopsus 315, 382–3, 392–3, 448–9
      Naram-Sin 155, 186
      Neileus 413–14
      Nestor 444–5
      Sargon 155, 186
      Sarpedon 438–9
   royal
      curses 129, 153–5
      Former Kings 94
      Gyges 375–6
      Hattusili III 153n21
      Labarna 156
      Mursili I 151
      šarrena 182
      šarru 182n71
      Suppiluliuma I 151
      Tudhaliya I/II 151, 153
      Tudhaliya IV 152
Androclus 360, 444n95
Andromache 330n130, 411, 421n9, 434, 458n2
Andromeda 425n21
andurārum 124n54, 178
Angim 210n52
Ani *See* An
Anitta 6, 8n27, 172–3
Annals of Arnuwanda I 315n71, 334n14

Annals of Hattusili I 33, 123–4, 158, 159, 164, 176–8, 183–4
   Ikinkalis 112, 157, 162n56
   oral performance 179–80
   written object 180
Annals of Tudhaliya I/II 334n14
anniš maššanaššiš 320n91, 447
anointed priest 252
Antandrus 12n48
Anthesteria 88n46, 235
Antigonus 436
Antilochus 440
Antimachus F 99 Matthews 238n100
antiques *See* heirlooms
Antum 88, 325
Anu *See* An
Anumhirbi 160n50
Anunna-gods *See* ^dA.NUN.NA.KE₄; Anunnaki
Anunnaki 85, 94, 97, 136–8 *Also see* Former Gods
Anunuwa 224
Anzili
   DINGIR.MAḪ.MEŠ 65n41, 94
   GAŠAN 96
   HH narr. song 26, 39–40, 127, 327n120
   HH pit rituals 81
   HH rituals 155
   IŠTAR 26, 84, 96
   mugawars 238
Anzu 210 *Also see Epic of Anzu*
'ap, Ugarit 86–7, 382n139 *Also see* pit rituals
Apasa 338, 344 *Also see* Ephesus
Apatouria 235
Apatourion 235
Apeilon 247n128
Aphrodite *Also see Homeric Hymn to Aphrodite*
   Cythereia 325n110, 323n100
   Ashtarte 306, 322–3n100
   birds 323nn102–103
   birth 324
   Crete 324
   Cyprus 323–9
   Cythera 323n100
   Eos 323n102
   Homeric tradition, entry into, storylines 18, 301
   Iliad 139, 325–6
   Inanna 327–8
   Ishtar 139n18, 323, 325–6, 327
   Kommos 322n100
   Lesbos 324
   Nestor's Cup 398

Aphrodite (cont.)
   Odyssey 23, 297
   Ouraniā 323–4n103
   syncretized with NE goddesses 306, 323–9
āpi 86–7, 94 *Also see* pit rituals
āpilu 201n4
a-pi-qo-ro-i 346n74
āpiti 86, 94 *Also see āpi*; pit rituals
Aplahanda 161n53
Apollo *Also see* Appaliuna
   Aeolian Dodecapolis 451–2
   Alasiotas 319
   Amyclaeus 233n77, 243n119
   Anatolia, EIA 234
   birth 25n16, 236–8, 320n91
   Carneus 239, 249
   Chryses 132, 140, 450–1
   Cillaean 451
   Cyprus 243, 249, 301, 313, 319–20
   Delian 398, 452
   Delphinius 241, 249–51, 440
   Didymeus 241–2, 248, 452–3
   Erra 243n119
   etymology 246–7
   festivals 16, 250n136 *Also see below*, Miletus
      Odyssey 453n135
      transfer, verbal art 16, 243–51, 263–4, 420, 440, 444, 450–2, 454
   Iliad 139–40, 142, 193, 243–7, 449–53
      Chryseis episode, hymn to 450
      original subject of 449–50
   Illuyanka 251
   Indo-European 243
   journeys 249
   Keraiātas 249, 319–20
   Keraiītēs 242, 249
   dLAMMA (ŠA LÍL) 243–9, 319–20, 447, 450
   Linear B 247
   Lycian 447, 452–3
   lukeios 447
      Zeus 250n136
   Lykios 447, 452n132
   Miletus 248–9, 444, 452 *Also see* Apollo Delphinius; Didymeus; Philesius; Phylius
      festivals, EIA 220, 241–2, 452–4
   Mopsus, father of 318n81
   Nergal 243n119
   origins 243–9
   Panionia 444, 452
   Panionius 452n131
   Peisistratids 453n135
   Philesius 244–5
   Phylius 242
   plague god *See above*, dLAMMA
   Pythius 249, 398
   Reshep 243n119, 313, 319–20
   Sarpedonius 452n132
   Smintheus 140, 231n63, 450–2
   snake-slayer *See* Pytho
   Sun-god 250n136
   Thargelia 235
   Troy 245–7, 351, 449–50
   Wolf-god 447
Apollodorus
   Bibliotheca 1.6.3 255, 258
      1.7.2–3 293
      2.1.3 215n73
      2.1.4 423n14
      2.2.1 346n71
      2.4.3 425n21
      3.1.1 318n79
      3.1.1–2 423n14
      3.12.5 351n9
      3.18.2 325n110
   Epitome 6.2–4 318n81
      7.38 75n98
Apollonius of Rhodes, *Argonautica* 103, 211
   1.752, Σ 374n105
Apollonius Sophista 143, 9 450n125
Apology of Hattusili III 278n44
Appadurai, Arjun 206
Appaliuna 245–7, 351
Appalu(wa) 246–7, 351
appantan tarna- 124
Appawiya *See* Seha River Land
Appian, *Civil Wars* 4.78–9 446
Appu *See Tale of Appu*
Apsu 29n35
apu 86 *Also see* pit rituals
ʾA-q3-3-jj-w3-3-š3-3 315
Aqhat 42n91, 143n26, 144n27, 325–6 *Also see Concordance of Tablets from Ugarit*
   type scenes, hospitality scenes 143–4
Arab bards 48
Arabia 215
Arabus 216n77
Aramaic inscriptions 311, 380n124, 380n128
Arameans 311
Aranzah River 177n50
a-ra-si-jo 303n5
Aratta 57n13, 210
Arcado-Cypriot
   epic 404, 408 *Also see* Cypriot epic
   forms, Homeric dialect 266n1, 408
   language 308–9n37

Subject index

Archaia Ilias 449–50
Archilochus 399n17
archives and libraries, Hattusa 3–4, 7, 35n61
Arctinus 444n97
ard-, ardāla 31n44
Arduna 253n148
a-re-ka-sa-da-ra 247n128, 351n5
Ares 297, 326, 378
Arete 101
Argadeis 241n111
Arge 238–9
Argos 288
Aribibla 119
Arimaspea 211
Arimoi 255n158
Arinna 164n69, 225
Arisbe/a 359
Aristarchus 396, 450n125
Aristeas 211
Aristophanes *Frogs* 1.308, Σ 393n159
Aristotle
    Constitution of the Athenians 23.4 237n92
    F 611, 37 Rose 435n58
[Aristotle] *Rhetoric to Alexander* 15.1375b30 409n51
Arma 128, 184n76, 358n38 *Also see* Moon-god
Armanum 176n42
Armarik, Mt. 159, 160n48
Armenia 106
Armenian language 357
Arnobius, *Adversus Nationes* 5.5–6 343n59
Arnuwanda I 6, 124, 153, 336
arri 82
Artemis 93, 237, 306, 447
    Ephesus 234, 238, 242, 320n91, 360
    ^{d}LAMMA 447
    Sarpedonius 452n132
Artemision 338n35, 360
Artemon *FGrH* 443 F 2 444n97
Artukka 334n14, 443n93
Arzawa 6, 331, 334n14, 335–7, 447n111
    dynastic marriages 333, 339
    gift exchange 207n32
    Greater 337
    Hatti
        cultural interaction with 342–3
        dependent on 335, 337, 340–1
    invocations from 342
    king 207n32, 338, 339n39
    Sea Peoples, destroyed by 356
Arzawan traditions, Hattusa 213, 243–4, 342, 346–7
Asag 210

Ascanius 407, 410, 436n61, 437
Ashamaz *See Ballad of Ashamaz*
Ashdu 93n67 *Also see Ritual of the Hurrian Woman Ashdu against Witchcraft*
Ashertu *See Elkunirsa and Ashertu*
Ashkelon 324n103
Ashmunikal's Instructions for the Workers of the Stone-House 124, 153
Ashnuri 174
Ashtarte 87–8n44, 163
    Aphrodite 306, 322–3n100
    Cyprus 306, 323–4n103
Ashtata *See* Emar
Āsiā 334n13
Asine 370n91
āšipu 213n67
asīru 118n24
Asius 421
Asius (Hecuba's brother) 430, 453
Assaracus 190
Assarlık 360n45
assemblies
    Bible 133–5
    divine
        Baal Cycle 133n2
        Bible 133n2
        Epic of Creation 29n35
        Epic of Gilgamesh 68–9
        Greek 133n2, 195
        Hittite magico-medical rituals 69
        Hittite prayers 69
        Song of Gilgamesh 65, 68–9, 75
        Song of Hedammu 133n2
        Tale of Appu 133n2
    Epic of Gilgamesh 57, 65, 133n2
    Gilgamesh and Akka 134
    Iliad, Trojan, bribed to not release Helen 139n16
    Song of Gilgamesh 71
    Song of Keshshi 28, 133n2
assembly scenes
    Atrahasis 142, 146–7, 135–9
    Gilgamesh and Akka 134–5
    Song of Release 14, 119–23, 130, 155, 158, 187
        Atrahasis, 137–9, 142, 147
        Bible 134–5
        Gilgamesh and Akka 134–5
        Iliad 33–4, 133, 139–42, 195, 355–6, 450
Assos 334n13, 334–5n14
Assur 57n15, 87n44, 88–90, 311
    akītu festival 263

Assur (god) 377
Assur-sharru-uṣur 392n157
Assurbanipal 377, 389n151, 396n2
Assurbanipal Prism B §§ 909–10 377
Assurnasirpal II 389n151, 390–1
Assuwa 6, 334–5, 341, 354, 443n93
   Ahhiyawa, dynastic marriages 334–5
   Asia 334n13
   lady of *See* Potniya Aswiya
Assyria *Also see* colonies, Old Assyrian merchant
   BA 7, 169, 345n67
   EIA 3, 206n27, 322, 357n34, 376–7, 392
Assyrian Royal Chronicle 10 197n119
   B i 5 290n98
Astarpa River 334n13, 336n27
Astyanax 351n9, 412
Astypalaia 272
ašûm 213n67 *Also see* ^{LÚ}A.ZU; ^{LÚ}AZU
Aswiā 334n13, 346
Atalanta 28
Atalshen 183
Athena
   birth 25n16
   Gigantomachy 262
   Iliad 194, 326, 416n76
   Maliya 447
   Miletus 370n91
   Odyssey 296
      cult 416n76
   Peisistratid temple 262
   peplos 262, 416n76
   Xerxes' sacrifice 418
Athenaeus 8.334b 326n117
   15.682df 327
   15.682e 326n117
Athenian colonization, Sigeum 409
Athenians, in *Iliad* 411n58
Athens *Also see* Peisistratids; Panathenaic recension
   cremation of war dead 399n17
   Delia 237–8
   Delian League 236–7
   Delos 236–8
   Dipylon vase 397–8
   festivals
      Anthesteria 88n46, 235
      Apatouria 235
      Cronia 230n59
      Dionysia 263–4
      Lenaea 235
      Panathenaea 262, 396, 415–16n76

      Skira 230n59
      Thargelia 235
   Grey Ware 365
   Homeric tradition, influence on 406n37, 409n51, 416n76
   Ionian migrations 235, 237, 360, 404n29, 416n76, 444n95
   Peisistratid temple of Athena 263
   Protogeometric 274
   Terpander 213–14
   tri(to)pateres 287n82
   tribes 236, 241n111
   Troad 409–10
Athirat 143n25
athletic competitions *See* festivals; funeral games
Atpa 339
Atrahasis 14, 20, 24, 29–32, 94n72
   OB A I 1 136
   OB A I 39 ff. 136
   OB A I 72–80 145
   OB A I 99–123 136–7
   OB A I 163–7 137
   OB A I 218–9 137
   OB A I 364–412 138
   OB A III iv 16–v 35 138
   Ages of Man 292
   bilinguals 30, 32
   Gilgamesh tradition 29, 31, 58–9, 147
   historiolae 30n40, 216
   Hittite version
      Hittite Fragments with Various Contents 30n40
      Hurrian influence 31
      Kumarbi cycle 31, 94
      variations 30–1
   HH narr. song 13, 20, 30
   Iliad 147, 396–7n2
   song 36
   Song of Release 147
      assembly scene 137–9, 142, 147
      gods like men 135–6
      waking for message 145–6
   Ugarit 31–2, 135
Atreids 409n52
Attarimma 447n111
Attarissiya 336
Attic forms, Homeric dialect 416n76
Attic-Ionic festivals 234–6, 463
Attic-Ionic, $ā > ē$ 55n8, 463
Attis 343n59
Atymnius 440
Atys 376

Audaluma 184, 185n85
[Au]nnamu 95n78
augurs 140, 193, 202n10, 342, 346–7
  Calchas 243–4, 351, 450
augury 244n121
Aulis 219, 406
auloi 240–1n108, 384
Autolycus 282n63
Automedon 144
axes, rituals 90
Ayasoluk 338n35
Ayia Triada
  Harvest Rhyton 231
  sarcophagus 89n47, 91–2, 272
Azatiwatayas 386 *Also see* Karatepe
Azatiwatas 18, 386
Azeri bards 48
LÚAZU 86, 94–5, 98 *Also see* LÚA.ZU; exorcists
āzziri 118n24

Baal 25
  of Aleppo 261
  kr 320n90
  krntryš 320, 386
  of Sapon 261, 305
  Yam 25, 143–4, 257
Baal Cycle 110 *Also see* Concordance of Tablets from Ugarit
  assembly, divine 133n2
  formulas, large numbers 127n63
  ḫiyara festival 261
  kingship 261
  type scenes, hospitality scenes 125, 143–4
Babylon 176n42, 197n119
  akītu festival 262
  capture, by Mursili I xxx.n1, 6, 30n41, 171n19
  flooding by Sennacherib 396–7n2
  source for Akkadian material/scribes at Hattusa 8–9, 30n41
  source of doctors 202n10, 213n67
Babyloniaka See Berossus
Bacchylides 459
baetyls 50, 121, 152n13, 225, 242, 324 *Also see gulloi*
Balaam 202n11
Balaclava 102
balags 397n2
Balak 202n11
Ballad of Ashamaz 27n28
Ballad of Early Rulers
  12 74
  9–13 190

Banihu 380, 393
barathra 92 *Also see* pit rituals
barbarophōnoi 421, 441n86, 442
barbiton 241n108, 384
bard and patron, IE, reciprocity 394n163
bards
  Azeri 48
  bilingual *See* bilingual bards
  Celtic 394
  competition
    funeral games 233, 240
    festivals 17, 239–40
  competitive collaboration 396, 414–15, 417, 437–8, 443, 451–2
  Greco-Anatolian, competitions 432
  Ionic, competitions 412–13
  Karakalpak 49
  nodes 212, 298, 404–5
  transfer, verbal art 21, 41, 110, 199–201, 283, 426–8 *Also see* bilingual bards
  traveling, BA Anatolia 21
  Turkmen 48
  wisdom 187
    transfer, verbal art 16, 166–7
    wandering, transfer, verbal art 16
bārû 201
Bashan 293
basileus 133, 281, 309 *Also see qa-si-re-u*
battles
  chariot 105, 269–70, 386, 429n41
  with mountains, Storm-god 26
  Ninurta, with monster 114
  at sea 114, 229–30, 278, 352, 386–8, 392n157
  in sea, *Epic of Creation* 29n35, 263 *Also see* Tiamat
  with sea, Storm-god 26, 256–7
  with snake *See* snake-slaying stories
    Storm-god *See* Storm-god, battle with snake
  with volcanic monster, Storm-god 26, 255
  with Yam, Storm-god 25, 257
beds, rituals 93n67
Belih River 51n131
Bellerophontes 378, 423–6, 441–3 *Also see* Pegasus
  deadly letter 400n17, 423–4
  dynastic marriages 423–4
  Elkunirsa and Ashertu 34, 424
  epic, Greco-Lycian 426, 429, 439
  Illuyanka 425
  journeys, long-distance 425
  meaning 425
  Potiphar's wife 34, 424

Bellerophontes (cont.)
  Silver 27
  wooden writing tablets 400n17, 424
Belus
  Io 215n77, 376
  Lydian 376
  meaning 215n77, 376
Benteshina 337n31
Benti-Sharruma 315n71
Berossus 392n157
  Babyloniaka FGrH 680 F 1b 188n97
Bible
  1 Kings 12:1–10 134–5
    17–19, 21:17–19 202n11
  1 Samuel 28 89
  2 Kings 1–2, 4–10, 202n11
    2:15–19 203n13
  2 Samuel 11 424
    16:15–17:14 134
  Genesis 292, 376
    6 293
    39 424
  Joshua 12:4 293
  Leviticus 24:10–26 113
  Numbers 22 202n11
  ancestor veneration 290
  assemblies 133–5
    divine 133n2
  deadly letter 424
  flood stories 29, 292–3
  Hittites 7, 311–12
  holocaust rituals 84
  Noah 29
  Og 293
  pit rituals 89
  Potiphar's wife 34, 424
  prophets 201–3
  rᵉpā 'îm 285, 290
  semi-divine heroes 293
  type scenes, assembly scenes 134–5
bibrûs 345
bilingual bards
  Aeolic-Lydian 429
  Akkadian 52
  Carian–Ionic 429
  Central Asian 13, 48–9, 428
  dactylic hexameter 428
  Eteocypriot 52–3
  Homeric dialect 426–8
  Hurrian-Hittite 13, 22, 37–8, 46–8, 76
  Lycian–Greek 426, 438–49
  Lycian–Ionic 429
  Lydian–Aeolic 429
  Mesopotamian 52–3
  Phoenician–Greek 53, 322n100, 326
  Phrygian–Aeolic 429–31
  Phrygian–Greek 328–9, 429–32, 435
  Phrygian–Trojan 420, 429
  Serbo-Croatian-Albanian 13, 47–8, 428
  Song of Release 48–9
  transfer, verbal art 1, 49, 52–3, 55, 200, 283, 326, 372, 420, 428
  west Semitic 52, 53
bilingual households 375n108
  transfer, verbal art 199, 283
bilingual tablets 30–3, 427–8
  Atrahasis 30, 32
  Song of Release 32, 111
bilingualism
  language of gods 427–8
  Lydian–Greek 93n63, 427
Bin Tepe 376
binding image, denoting song 37
bird-faced figurines 323n103
birds, goddesses 323n102
birth incantations 51, 214–15, 238
birth
  Aeneas 328–9, 410
  Aphrodite 324
  Apollo 25n16, 236–8, 320n91
  Athena 25n16
  Attis 343n59
  gods 27, 188n97
  iron 104
  Pegasus 424–5
  silver 52, 104
  Storm-god, HH 25, 162, 185, 261
  Zeus 25n16
Birth, Song of See *Song of Birth*
The Birth of Soseruquo 106n122
Bīt Gabbari 379–80, 383
Bithynia 361n54
Black Sea 14, 103–6, 211, 215n73, 258n171, 298, 300, 371n93, 376
  Greek colonization 103, 238
boar's-tusk helmets 229, 266, 282, 371, 378
boats, in rituals 88–9, 91
Boeotia
  ancestor veneration/mortuary rituals, BA 270, 281
  Hector 365, 405–6, 432, 436
  Homeric tradition 403, 406, 408n44, 454
  Ogygus 293
Boeotians, *Iliad* 352, 406, 411n58
Boğazköy *Also see* Hattusa
  Phrygian 357

Boldavin Üçhöyük 172n23
Book of Enoch 54n2
Boreas (North Wind) 190
Boreis 241
Borus 241n111
bothroi 91, 100 *Also see* pit rituals
Branchidae (clan) 242–3
Branchidae (place) 444
Branchus 242–3
bricolage 79, 99, 107–8
bride-stealing 76n99, 139, 434
Briseis 142, 411
Bronze Tablet Treaty betweenTudhaliya IV and Kurunta/Ulmi-Teshshub of Tarhuntasssa 334n10, 337
Bull of Heaven 58, 61, 69, 175, 325, 390–1, 445
  horns an offering container 61, 79
bull-leaping 227, 269
bulls
  Assurnasirpal II slays 390
  Gilgamesh slays *See* Bull of Heaven
  Gilgamesh wrestles 63
  Naram-Sin slays 174
  Ninurta slays 114
  Panionian sacrifice 413n69, 443–4
  Storm-god 159, 163, 216n77, 320n88, 328n126 *Also see* Sherish; Tauri; Tilla
  Zeus 216n77, 328n126
Buluqiya 54n2
Burkert, Walter 1–3, 5, 41n85, 54–5, 125, 133n2, 138n13, 200–6, 216, 243n119, 247n128, 249, 255n155, 262, 283n67, 290n99, 318n80, 326–7, 343n59, 376–7, 396, 397n6, 398n11, 402n25, 423n15, 424nn19–20, 425n21, 441
Burunkaya 312
Büyükkale, Hattusa 7, 63n35, 151
Büyükkaya, Hattusa 72n76

Cadmus 105n119
Caecus River 337, 359
Calaenus 416n76
Calchas 141, 318
  Arzawan augurs 243–4, 351, 450
Callimachus
  Epigrams 6 Pfeiffer 416n76
  Hymn to Apollo 2.71–96 239n103
    4.304–6 239n102
  Hymn to Artemis 3.204, 240, 238n100
  Iambus IV, F 194.28–31 Pfeiffer 243n118
  Iambi F 217 249

Callinus 318, 392, 416n76
Calydnae islands 353
Calymna 272
Calypso 293n106, 299n126
Campaign against the Sea Peoples: Medinet Habu, Pylon II Presentation Scene 317n77
Candaules 93n63, 374
Cape Gelidonya 316n71
Cappadocia 313n57
Carchemish 6, 7, 160n48, 161n53, 310, 311n52, 337n31, 352n10, 356
  EIA
    ancestor veneration 380–2
    Enkidu 389–90
    monumental art 380–2, 384n141, 389–90, 424n20
    patron deities 27, 306, 358n38
    Song of LAMMA 27, 306
Caria 358n39, 360–1, 439 *Also see* Karkisa
  Leleges 12n48
  Mycenaean settlement 340n44
Carian gods 93n63, 234n81
Carian language 11, 356, 375
Carian–Ionic bilingual bards 429
Carians 12, 435, 439
  and Greeks, shared past 19, 332
  Iliad 421, 442
  Ionian migrations 360
  migrations 19, 442
  Miletus 358n39, 422n13, 440
Carnea 239
Carneus, Apollo 239, 249
Carpathus 272, 353
Carystus 228, 414n69
Casius, Mt. *Also see* Hazzi, Mt.
  Hazzi 259
  landmark 211
  Typhon 259
Casius, Zeus 183
Cassiepeia 216n77
Castor 107
Çatallar Tepe 413n69
Catalog of Ships *See* Homer, *Iliad*, Catalog of Shipss
catalog of Trojan allies
  Demetrius of Scepsis 437
  Iliad 191, 327n121, 441–3
Cattle of the Sun 102
Caucasian myths *Also see* Abaza; Abkhaz; Circassian; Ossetian; Ubykh
  Cyclops 105–6
Caucasus, Io's journey 215

Caucones 438
Cayster River 334n13, 337n27
Cebelıreis Dağ 320n90
Cebron 436
Cedar Forest
    Gilgamesh tradition 57, 60–1, 66–8, 75, 169
        change in location 71n75, 175
    Sargonic legends 166, 170, 172, 175
Celadus 241
Celsus 258n172
Celtic bards 394
Central Asia
    artifacts, Shaft Graves 207
    bilingual bards 13, 48–9, 428
    epic 48–9, 110, 139n17
Ceyhan River 313
Chalcidice 372n95
Chalcis 219
Chalybe *See* Alybe
Chaoskampf
    festivals 256–61
    Hazzi, Mt. 251, 256–9
    kingship 16, 183, 185, 250–61
    Ninurta 210
    transfer, verbal art 425
    Zeus 250
chariot battles 105, 269–70, 386, 429n41
chariot-drivers, Myrtilus 374
chariot-racing 17, 228, 269–70, 275, 278
chariots
    hero cult 286
    hunting 275
    mortuary rituals 270, 278, 281, 286, 322
    processions 222, 304
    sun 27
charismatics 16, 201, 204–5
Cheimerians 106
Chimera 423–5, 440
Chios 358n39, 413
    Crete 435
    Euboea 435
    Hector of 435
    Homer, birthplace of 330n132
    Homeric Hymn to Apollo 239
    Homeric tradition, transfer of 396, 416n76
Chronicle of the Single Monarchy 188–9
    G I 1–9 188–9
    dating 188n96
chronicles, Mesopotamian *See* king lists
chronology
    high middle xxx.n1, 6
    low middle xxx.n1

Chryse 140, 451
Chryseis
    Aeolian 411
    Song of Release 33–4, 133, 139–42, 450
Chryses
    Apollo 132, 140, 450–1
    NE prayer 139n18
Chwadlazhwiya's Tale 27n28
Cilicia
    and Anatolia, west
        Ahhiyawa 393 *Also see* Hiyawa
        shared identity/migration 17–18, 316, 318–19, 382, 392–3
    BA, Luwian-Hurrian 10, 147
    continuity 17, 302, 310, 379–91, 420
    Cyprus 308
    EIA
        Assyrians 392
        Cyprus, shared identity, transfer, verbal art 17–18, 302, 310, 316–17, 319
        Greek settlement 17, 216n77, 274, 302, 310, 313–16, 320, 392
        Javan 293–4
        long-distance elite interactions 268
        Luwians 256, 314n67
        Phoenicians 299, 311
        Phrygians 392
    in *Iliad* 330n130, 411n62, 421n9
    Io 215
    LH IIIC:1b pottery 313–15
    Plain 312–17 *Also see* Adana; Danuna; Hiyawa; Karatepe; Kizzuwatna; Mopsus; Que
        continuity 313
    pre-Greek language 247
    Rough 7, 312, 320n90 *Also see* Tarhuntassa
    Sarpedon 423n14, 446n104, 452n132
    Sea Peoples 274, 314
    source of verbal art 13, 17, 147, 256, 293–5, 299–301, 321, 329–30
    Typhon 255–6
    Zeus 255–6, 313
Cilician Gates 313, 315n69
Cilician painted wares 313
Cilicians, *Iliad* 330n130, 411n62, 421
Cilix 216n77, 318n79, 423n14
Cilla 140, 451
Cimmerian Bosporus 14, 103, 106
Cimmerians 100, 105–7, 435n58
Cinyrades 324
Cinyras 324–5, 330
Circassian myths 27n28, 106n122

Circe 100–3
    daughter of Sun 107
    Old Woman 101
    Shiduri 101n104, 299n126
cithara 325n110
city laments 397n2
clans 17, 232, 240–1, 287n82, 328, 370, 394,
        435, 440, 463 *Also see* phratries;
        tribes
Clarus 318–19, 382, 392, 452n131
classification, formal, of genres *See* genres,
        formal classification
classification, indigenous, of genres *See* genres,
        indigenous
Clazomenae 340, 358n39, 372n95
Clement of Alexandria
    Protrepticus 11 92
    Stromata 5.8.48–9 242–3
clitic doubling *See* HH narr. song, poetic
        features
Cnidos 324, 345
Cocytus 100
code-switching 428
Codrus 438, 444n95
Colchis 103
collective memory *See* memory, collective
Colonae 450
colonies
    founders, Greek heroes 286n76, 317,
        318, 393, 422–3, 435, 438–9, 442,
        444
    Old Assyrian merchant 5–6, 52, 176 *Also see*
        Hahhu; Hassu; Hattusa; Kanesh;
        Purushanda
        Sargonic legends 10, 52, 169–70, 172–3,
            176
colonization *Also see* migrations; settlement
    Athenian, Sigeum 409
    Greek *Also see* migrations; settlement
        Black Sea 103, 238
        Cilicia 314
        legends, *Iliad* 353, 422–3
        Odyssey 296
        westwards 296
    of Miletus 103, 423n14, 436–7
    by Miletus, Scepsis 412n63, 436–7
    Phoenician 322–3n100
Colophon 340, 358n39, 392, 412n66
    Minos 359
Comana 10
Çömbekçi 274n29
Commagene *See* Kummuh
compensatory lengthening 463

competitions
    Aeolic and Ionic bards 19, 395, 396, 402–12,
        417
    athletic *See* festivals; funeral games
    bards
        festivals 17, 239–40
        Greco-Anatolian 432
        Ionic 412–13
    elite 17, 269–70, 275, 281
    Hesiod, at funeral games 233, 240, 396n2
    between Hesiod and Homer 240, 250, 414
    poetry/music, festivals
        Greek, EIA 233, 237–41, 267, 454
        Greek, Mycenaean 267, 269–70
        Homeric tradition 297
        IE 239–40
    polities/courts 6
    rhapsodes, Panathenaea 415
competitive collaboration, bards 396, 414–15,
        417, 437–8, 443, 451–2
competitive display, exotic goods 304–5
competitive emulation
    elite 268, 303, 321, 398
    Homeric dialect 404–5, 407–9
    Homeric tradition 404–5, 412–15, 417
    transfer, verbal art 16–17, 21, 226, 233, 250,
        333, 342–3, 394–5
composition in performance 38, 63, 130, 300
Comprehensive Annals of Mursili II 253n148,
        338
Conon *FGrH* 25 F 1, 44 414n69
Consultation of Ditānu *with a View to Healing*
        290n98
continuity
    Anatolia 357, 448
        west 356–9
    Cilicia 17, 302, 310, 313, 379–91, 420
    Cyprus 301–2, 306–10, 404, 319–21
    Ephesus 357, 360
    Gordion 357
    Greece 233
        epic 267
        Protogeometric 278–9
    Lefkandi 274, 404
    Lesbos 359
    Lycia 446–8
    Lydia 356
    Malatya 257–8, 312
    of memory
        Anatolia 273
        Anatolia, west 18, 332, 341
        dynastic lists 18, 196
        Syro-Anatolia, EIA 349, 373–4

continuity (cont.)
   Miletus 357, 360
   Phrygia 357, 448
   Rhodes 274
   Sardis 357
   Syria, north 17, 302, 310, 379–81
   Syro-Anatolia 7, 17, 302, 310–13
      ancestor veneration 374, 379–81
      dynastic names 373–6
   Troy 357
contraction, adjacent vowels 401, 458–64
copper trade 283n67, 301, 309, 316n71, 441n83
Corcyra 296n115
corvée labor 123, 134–6, 147
Corycian Cave 255–6
Corycus 256, 313
Cos 272, 290n97, 291n102, 340, 353
cosmogonic epic, unity with other forms of epic 22
cosmogonies *Also see* Kumarbi cycle
   eastern Mediterranean 24
   genealogies 15, 185–6, 272, 291–2
   historiolae 213–14, 216–17, 262–3
   king lists 15, 291–2
   long-distance journeys 216–17
   Mesopotamian 29–30
   Orphic 24n14
   snake-slaying stories 251, 257–8
   transfer, verbal art 16, 197, 213–14, 217–18, 262, 292
   west Semitic 291–2
   world history 188–9, 196, 292
councils *See* assemblies
Cow-maiden 213–15
craftsmen
   corvée labor 124
   divine 325n110
   traveling 186n91, 199–203, 205–8, 217, 283, 346
cremation
   Alalakh 284
   Athens 399n17
   Çömbekçi 274n29
   Cyprus 284, 322
   Greece, post-palatial 274
   Hittite 152, 153n16, 284n73, 399n17
   Homeric tradition 284n73, 399n17
   Lefkandi 281
   shared practice 284–5, 321
   Syro-Anatolia 284
      EIA 284–5, 380–1
   Thermon 284n71
   Troy 370

Creophylus, *Oikhalias Halosis* 416n76
Cretan Hieroglyphic 11
Cretan magico-medical incantations 213
Crete
   Anatolia, settlement 273, 359, 423n14
   ancestor veneration 272
   Aphrodite 324
   Apollo Pythius 249
   Chios 435
   Egypt 213, 317n78
   Epimenides 213–14
   "Homeric" culture 321
   Homeric tradition 231n69, 282n63, 422–3, 442
   journeys, long-distance 215, 238
   Miletus 231n69, 422–3, 440n82, 442
   Phoenicians 322–3n100
   Sarpedon 422–3, 438, 442, 452n132
   Theseus 238
   Ugarit 215
Crimea 102, 106
Croesus 209, 377
Cronia 230n59, 291
Cronus 121n44, 291n100
   kingship in heaven 266, 291
Cult Inventories of the Storm-god 343n57
Cult Inventories under Tudhaliya IV 222n5, 224n21, 253n149, 343n57
cult personnel, transfer, Storm-god of Aleppo 162, 261
cult singers *See* singers, cult
cultural interaction
   Arzawa, Hatti 342–3
   Cyprus 303–5
   dynastic marriages 435
   Ephesus 360
   festivals
      Hattusa 4, 9, 224
      Miletus, EIA 220, 242–3, 440
      Mycenaean 229
   Greco-Anatolian, BA 341
   mortuary rituals, Mycenaean 272–3
   transfer, verbal art 1, 3–5, 13, 18
   Troad 358
cultural memory *See* memory, collective
Curse of Akkade 76, 191n106, 431, 433
curses
   Epic of Gilgamesh 58
   HH magico-medical incantations 98, 121n41, 126
   HH narr. song 44–6, 69, 113, 117–18, 121, 126, 129

inscriptions 181
royal ancestors 129, 153–5
Cuthean Legend of Naram-Sin 191–3
  OB 8' 397n2
  SB 1–3 178
  SB 1–30 178–9
  SB 47–50 52
  SB 80–3 194
  SB 90–3, 94–5, 97 195
  –SB 175–80 179
  Agamemnon 193
  dream interpretation 194
  dreams (Hittite) 191
  Epic of Gilgamesh 178
  at Hattusa 20, 171n19, 191
  Homeric tradition, entry into, plotline, 355–6, 419, 432–5, 437–8
  HH narr. song 191
  Iliad See Naram-Sin, Hector
  Silver Mountains 52
  written object 178–9
Cybele 234n81, 328–9, 343n59, 357
Cyclades 238, 274, 281, 358
Cyclops *Also see* Homer, *Odyssey*
  Anatolian origin 78, 105–6, 298–9
  Caucasian origin 105–6
  Gilgamesh tradition 55–6
  Huwawa 55–6
  IE origin 106n122
A Cyclops Bound atop Wash'hamakhwa 106n122
Cycnus 362n59
Cyme 359n41, 411n58, 435–6, 451
Cypria 326–7
  F 1 West 288n87, 301
  FF 5, 6, 7 327
  F 7 327n120
  authorship 326
  opening 138, 288 n87, 301, 325
  Proclus, *Epitome*, §§7, 9 West 406n37
Cypriot epic 322, 324–9 *Also see* Arcado-Cypriot epic
Cypriot syllabary 308
Cypro-Minoan script 304, 309
Cyprus *Also see* Alashiya; Eteo cypriot; Iatnana
  Alalakh 323
  Amarna 303
  ancestor veneration 272
  Aphrodite 323–9
  Apollo 243, 301, 313
    Alasiotas 319
    Keraiātās 249, 319–20

  Ashtarte 306, 323–4n103
  bird-faced figurines 323n103
  Brotherhood of Great Kings 202n10, 226, 303–5
  Cilicia 308, 310, 316–17, 319
    settlement from 308
    shared identity, transfer, verbal art 17–18, 302, 310, 316–17, 319
  competitive display, exotic goods 304–5
  continuity 301–2, 306–10, 319–21, 404
  cremation 284, 322
  cultural contact/mixing 303–5
  Egypt 289, 304–5, 322
  extispicy 201n4
  gods, syncretized, transfer, verbal art 301, 319–20, 323–9
  Greece, shared identity, transfer, verbal art 17–18, 302, 310
  Greek identity 321–2
  Greek settlement 17, 274, 283n67, 302, 316
  Greek-speakers 310, 319
    arrival of 306–10
  Hellenization 307–9, 321
  Hittites 6, 153, 303, 336
  "Homeric" culture 284, 308, 322
  Homeric tradition 330
  Horned God 249n130
  Hurrian epic 306
  Hurrians 304
  intermediaries 1, 13, 17–18, 283–5, 292–5, 298–302, 305–6, 316–17, 324–30, 454
  iron 275, 282–3, 296, 309
  languages, intermediaries 5, 52–3 *Also see* Eteocypriot
  Levant 304–5, 308
  LH IIIC pottery 276n40, 404
  LH IIIC:1b pottery 307
  long-distance elite interactions, EIA 17, 268, 275–6, 280–3, 296, 298, 302, 321
  metal trade 283n67, 296, 309
  Mitanni 304
  Mycenaean vessels 344–5
  Mycenaeans 303
  Naram-Sin 169n10
  north Syrian culture 17, 302, 304
  nostoi 322, 324
  Phoenician–Greek bards 53
  Phoenicians 305, 307, 319n86, 322, 323–4n103, 324
  PG vessels 275–6, 404
  Pytho 321
  qa-si-re-u 309

Cyprus (cont.)
   Reshep 243, 319–20
   Sea Peoples 274, 278, 307, 314, 356
   seals, Mycenaean Thebes 345n67
   Storm-god 321
      syncretism 305–6, 319–20
   Tarsus 314
   transfer, craftsmen, BA 202n10
   Typhon 256, 321
   Ugarit 303–6
   The Valorous Sun 303
   west Semitic 301, 304
      epic 306, 329
      gods, syncretized 305–6
   writing, use of 309
   Zeus 320
Cyrene 239
Cythera 169n10, 282n63, 317n78, 323n100, 324n103, 325n110
Cythereia 322n100, 325n110
Cyzicene 359

d3-jnjw-n3 317, 317n78
D-3-r-d-n-jj 429n41
dactylic hexameter
   bilingual bards 428
   foreign origin/influence 428, 458n3
   history 401–2, 404–5, 458–64
   incantations 398n8
   IE origin 458–9
   inscriptions 397–8, 413n67
Dagan 170, 173n31
   Duddul 51n131, 166
   Kumarbi 51n131
Damu 217
Dan-, Egyptian 317
Danaids 264, 317–18
Danaoi 317–18
Danaus 215n77, 318
Danel 143n26
   rapa 'um 290
danku tekan 43, 68
dankuš daganzipaš 43, 68n59
Danu 317n77
Danuna 18, 319, 383, 386, 392 *Also see* Adana; Cilicia
   Egypt 317
   Greek identity 392
   Sea Peoples 317
Dardanids 429, 430n43
   Phrygians 328, 410
Dardanoi 429
Dardanus 190, 288

Dark Earth 43, 66, 67, 68n59, 90n53, 97, 125n55, 189
Dascylium 357–8, 362
David, King 424
Dawn-goddess 323n102
deadly letter 400n17, 423–4
Death of Gilgamesh 29, 79, 101n105
   Nippur version 8–23, 97n87
Death of Ur-Namma 97n87
Death Rituals (Hittite) 96n84, 156n32
debates 133–7, 140–2, 195, 445 *Also see* assemblies
debt slaves, *Song of Release* 113, 118n24
deer 245–9
Deity List (Ugarit) 261n190
delegates *See* diplomats
Delia 16, 220, 236–9, 261, 398
   supralocal audiences 237
Delian
   Apollo 398, 452
   girls, attendants of Apollo 237
   League 237
   songs 238–9
Delos 211, 236–9, 243, 249–50, 320n91, 413n67, 414 *Also see* Delia
Delphi 240, 249, 262, 435
Delphinius *See* Apollo Delphinius
deltoi 424n19 *Also see* woodeon writing tablets
Deluge *See* floods; flood stories
Demeter 104n115, 230, 263–4 *Also see* Homeric Hymn to Demeter
Demetrius of Scepsis, *On the Trojan Battle Order*
   F 26 Gaede 410
   F 35 410, 437
dēmiourgoi 199, 202–4
Democedes 203n17
Demodocus 23, 297
Dendra 269n8
depas 282n62, 345 *Also see* vessels
Derveni papyrus *See* Orphic cosmogonies
deseterjac 47n117, 428
Deucalion 29, 293
DEUS.VIA.TERRA *See* KASKAL.KUR
Didyma 453 *Also see* Apollo Didymeus; Apollo Keraiítēs; Apollo Philesius
   oracle 241n112
   procession 241–2
   sanctuary 241n112, 242
Dimpiku 97
DINGIR.MAḪ 65
DINGIR.MAḪ.MEŠ 65n41, 94
Diodorus Siculus 32.10.2 452n132

Diogenes Laertius 1.109–10 203n17
Diomedes 120n36, 193, 325, 423
Dionysia 264
Dionysius of Argos *FGrH* 308 F 2 414n72
Dionysius of Halicarnassus 1.25–30 361n54
    1.45.4–48.11 407n41
Dionysus 104n115, 204n19, 263, 264, 343
Dioscuri 107
di-pi-si-je-wi-jo 227n36, 271n15
di-pi-si-jo 227, 271n15
di-pi-si-jo-i 227, 271n15
diplomats 156n33, 219, 225–6, 338–9, 377
Dipylon vase 397–8
Disappearance and Return of Anzili and Zukki 238
disappearing gods 233n77 Also see *mugawars*
Disputation between Heron and Turtle 133n1
Ditanu
    dynastic lists 197n119
    meaning 290n98
    rapa'um 290
    Titans 290–1
divided Mediterranean model 205
divination, liver *See* extispicy
divine ancestors *See* ancestors, divine
Divine Drinking Rite and Blessing (Ugarit) 151n9
diviners *See* seers
di-wi-jo-jo me-no 226
'dn 316n72, 317
dnnym 316n72, 317
Do(m)potās 286
doctors 201–3, 213–14, 217, 290n97 Also see healers
dog dinners, Sardis 92–3
Dolichenus, Zeus 104, 259n181
dolls, rituals 85, 183, 186
dolphins 249
Domuztepe 383
Dorian festivals 233n77, 234, 239
Dorian invasion 403
Doric layer, Homeric dialect 408n44
Doryclus 216n77
double case-marking 362n55
double-naming 2, 10, 351–2, 374, 412, 434
drama, ritual
    festival of the Storm-god Iyarri 224
    (*ḫ*)*išuwa* festival 260–1
    KI.LAM festival 223–4, 343
    purulli festival 254–5
drawing paths rituals 94–5
dream interpretation
    Cuthean Legend of Naram-Sin 194
    Hittite 69, 96, 98n91, 154

Iliad 140
dreams
    Agamemnon 173, 193
    Assurbanipal Prism B 377
    Cuthean Legend of Naram-Sin (Hittite) 191
    Enkidu 43n99, 58, 68–9, 101
    Gilgamesh 28, 57, 60, 61n26, 62–3, 66, 145n30
    Sargon, King of Battle (Hittite) 173
    Song of Keshshi 28, 66, 122n44, 145n30
    waking from *See* type scenes
Drehem 161n53
dressing scenes *See* type scenes
Drink Offerings for the Throne of Hebat 86n32, 163n66 Also see *Fragments of Hurro-Hittite Rituals and Incantations*
ductus, Hittite tablets 8
Duddul 51, 166
düden 89n52
Dumuzi 79, 88n46, 97n87
Duris *FGrH* 76
    F 21 75n98
    F 41 402n25
Dyme 239n102
Dynamis 242
dynastic connections Also see Aeneidae; ancestors, fictional; dynastic lists; king lists
    Agamemnon 409, 435–6
    Hector 328, 407, 435–7
    Troy 328, 407, 430–1, 434–7 Also see Aeneidae; Hector
dynastic lists Also see king lists
    continuity, memory 18, 196
    Ditanu 197n119
    Lydian 350, 375, 376–8, 441n84
    Syria, north, EIA 18, 373–4
    west Semitic 197n119
dynastic marriages
    Ahhiyawa
        Assuwa 334–5
        Miletus, BA 339
        Wilusa 347, 351
    Anatolia, west 336, 337, 347
    Arzawa 333, 339
    Bellerophontes 423–4
    cultural contact/mixing 435
    Io 215
    Kizzuwatna 156–7, 164, 260–1, 347
    long-distance elite interactions 215, 374, 422
    Midas 435
    Pelops 374, 422n10
    Phrygians and Greeks 435

dynastic marriages (cont.)
  transfer
    festivals 260
    verbal art 15, 156–7, 164, 258, 346–7, 377–8, 435
dynastic names
  continuity, Syro-Anatolia 373–6
  Gyges 375, 377, 441n84
  Lydian 350, 352, 374–6
  Midas 357–8
  Mursili 374–5
  Muwattalli 359, 374–5
  Suppiluliuma 373
  Syro-Anatolia, EIA 350
Dzhangar 415

É *ḫuḫḫaš* *See* House of the Grandfathers
É *ma-tim* 150
É.NA4 152, 153n20 *Also see* Stone House
Ea 29n35, 31
  epithet, HH narr. song 43
  HH narr. song 40, 45, 68, 72n76, 73, 123n49
  Iyas 447
  šarrena ritual 184
  Ugarit 261n190
  wisdom 131n77
Ea and the Beast 26–7, 97n89
eagles
  mountain gods 159, 160n48
  omens 34n55
ear models, rituals 95
Eber Lake 172n23
Ebla
  ancestor statues 150, 161, 186n91
  destruction
    historical 111–12, 160–1, 175–6
    Song of Release 33, 113, 116–19
  Gilgamesh tradition 175
  Hassu 160n51
  House of Stars 150
  Hurrians 161
  HH rituals 160
  Ikinkalis 161
  Ishhara 114–15
  king lists 119, 150, 190–1
  Meki 161n53
  Naram-Sin 160–1, 175
  OH historical texts 112n5, 158
  pit rituals 87
  royal ancestor veneration 149–50
  Sargonic legends 160–1, 166, 175
  Storm-god of Aleppo 161, 257

  world history 160–1, 175–6
  Zazalla 161n53
Egypt *Also see* Amarna
  Ahhiyawa 315
  ancestor statues 272
  Bible 134
  Crete 213, 317n78
  Cyprus 289, 304–5, 322
  Danuna 317
  Dardanoi 429
  Hittites 7, 312
  Homeric tradition 330n131, 396
  Io 215, 318
  Karatepe 320n91
  kingship 289
  mortuary rituals 272
  necromancy 101n101
  Perati 275
  Sea Peoples 274, 314–15
  Shaft Graves 207, 345n66
  snake-slaying stories 257
  Thesmophoria 264
Egyptian influence, Homeric tradition 34n55
Egyptian magic 99n95, 213
Ekur 76, 114, 145
El 144n27, 291n101
Eltara 26
Elam 57n13, 184
elders 28, 57, 61, 119n33, 133–5, 142, 287
elegiac couplets 401n23
Eleon 282n63, 352
Eleusinian mysteries 265
Eleusis 242n113, 264, 279
Elijah 202
Elis 422n10
Elisha (Noah's descendant) 293–4
Elisha (prophet) 202–3
elite competition *See* competition, elite
Elkunirsa and Ashertu
  Bellerophontes 34, 424
  historiolae 34, 51, 73, 108, 126, 213, 216
  HH narr. song 21, 34
  Levantine sorcerers 216
  Potiphar's wife 126, 424
  Song of Huwawa 73
  west Semitic 216, 424
Ellerophontes 425
Eltara 26
Emar
  abû 87–8n44
  ancestor veneration 150n1, 197n118
  Ballad of Early Rulers 74n93, 190n102
  Epic of Gilgamesh 57, 60, 72n75

Former Gods 97n86, 189n100
Hittites 6, 115n10
Ishhara 115
pit rituals 87–8
Empedocles 31 B 139 DK 203n17
en de 427
en priests 97n87
Endashuruma 97n87
Endor, witch 93
Endukuga 97n87
ēni mahanahi 320n91, 447
Enki 29, 31, 69, 97n87, 135–6, 138, 140
Enki and Ninhursag 24
Enkidu 57–8, 61, 65–6, 68–9, 72–3, 75, 79, 133n2, 147
  ancestor statues 58, 79
  Ballad of Early Rulers 74, 190
  Carchemish 389–90
  dreams 43n99, 58, 68–9, 101
  Gilgamesh, relationship with 56 *Also see* Gilgamesh tradition, *Iliad*, Achilles
  journeys, underworld *See* Gilgamesh tradition, journeys, underworld
  Karatepe 389
  substitute, ritual 69, 107
Enkomi 249n130, 307
Enlil 58, 97n87, 114, 136–7, 142, 145–6, 166, 170
  ancestors of 97n87, 374
  Former God 95n78, 97n86
  Hamsha 30
  HH narr. song 30, 68–9
  HH rituals 95n78, 97n86
  Ishhara, father of 95n78, 97n86
  Kumarbi 30
Enmebaragesi xxx.n9
Enmerkar 178, 188
Enmerkar and En-suhgir-ana 210n50
Enmeshara 97n87
Enmul 97n87
Enmutula 97n87
Enoch *See* Book of Enoch
ensi 161n53
Enuma Anu Enlil xxx.n1
Enuma Elish See Epic of Creation
Eos 323n102
Epeians 411n58
Ephesus 318, 337n27, 392, 429
  Artemis 234, 238, 242, 320n91, 360
  BA *Also see* Apasa
    Mycenaeans 272, 338, 340
  clans 241n111
  continuity 357, 360

cultural contact/mixing 360
founders 444n95
Iliad 353
Ionian migrations 357, 360, 444n95
Ionians 358n39
Lydia 358n39, 361n52
Panionia 353, 444, 452
pit rituals 93
Ephorus *FGrH* 70 F 119 410n52
  F 127 359n40, 422
  F 223 402n25
Ephyra 441
epic
  Akkadian 41–2, 52
  Albanian 13, 47–8, 428
  ancestor veneration 18, 196–7, 218, 264, 271–2, 273, 349–50, 370–1, 386–92, 438–9
    Karatepe 18, 350, 382–6, 391–2
    transfer, verbal art 445–9
  Arcado-Cypriot 404, 408 *Also see* Cypriot epic
  Central Asian 48–9, 110, 139n17
  Cypriot 322, 324–9
  definition 22, 166, 168
  festivals, performance at *Also see* festivals; HH narr. song, festivals; Milesian stage; Panathenaea; Panionic stage
    modern 415
    serial performance 414–15
  Greco-Aryan 142, 266, 434
  Greco-Lycian 426, 429, 439–41
  Greek *Also see* Homer; Homeric tradition
    continuity 267
    iconography 274–6, 278–9
    Mycenaean 271–2, 273
    Panhellenic 286n76, 355–6n25, 407, 411, 415, 419, 445, 452n132, 453n135
    post-palatial period 275–8
    Protogeometric 279–81, 300
    Trojan War, in BA 352–3, 401, 416–17
  at Hattusa 20–1
  hero cult 186–7, 268, 383, 394 *Also see* Homeric tradition
    Lycians 420
  historiolae 394
  Hurrian 15, 22, 52
    Cyprus 306
  HH *See* HH narr. song
  journeys, underworld 99
  Kalmyk 415
  Karatepe *See above*, ancestor veneration
  Kyrgyz 415

epic (cont.)
   Lesbian 406–7, 410, 412
   Lycian 426, 429, 439
   pit rituals 78, 98–9, 105, 108–9
   Pylian 355
   Serbo-Croatian 47–8, 110, 355, 407, 428
      forked pathway 75n98
      Return Songs, *Odyssey* 75n98
   Sumerian 41–2, 52, 147 *Also see* Enmerkar; Gilgamesh tradition, Sumerian; Lugalbanda
   Ugaritic *See* Ugaritic epic
   west Semitic 52–3 *Also see* Ugaritic epic
      Cyprus 306, 329
   wisdom 187
   world history 3, 111–12
Epic of Anzu OB II 133n2
   SB I 1–12 114
Epic of Creation 24, 29n35, 262
   OB I 122 29n35
   akītu festival 55–6, 262
   assemblies, divine 29n35
   Deception of Zeus 55n8, 327
   read/recited aloud 55–6, 262
   song 36
   Theogony 24
Epic of Gilgamesh Also see Gilgamesh tradition; *Song of Gilgamesh*; *Song of Huwawa*
   MB 56–7, 59
   MB Boğ$_1$ 60–1, 68
   MB Boğ$_2$ 61–4
   MB Boğ$_3$ 60
   MB Emar$_2$ 71n75
   OB 56, 61–3, 65n45, 71n75, 73
   OB Harmal$_1$ 9 63
   OB IM obv. 15 74n92
   OB Ishchali 74n92
   OB Ishchali 31' 175n39
   OB Penn 56n12, 59n17, 61
   OB Schøyen$_2$ 5–12, 62
   OB Schøyen$_2$ 26 175
   OB Yale 56n12, 61
   SB 57–9, 61, 72n75, 74n89
   SB I 6–10 59
   SB I 29 59n17
   SB I 245–300 145n30
   SB II 213–301 172n24
   SB II 260–III 12 133n2
   SB IV 4 175n39
   SB V 6 74n89
   SB V 9 173n26
   SB V 133–4 74n89
   SB V 134 175n39
   SB V 135–6 171n21
   SB VII 1 68
   SB VIII 101
   SB IX 138–71 171n21
   SB IX 172–93 172n25
   SB X 11–12 46n110
   SB XII 79–80
      Gilgamesh, Enkidu, and the Netherworld 57, 59
      Odyssey 105, 299n126
   assemblies 57, 65, 133n2
      divine 68–9
   author *See* Sin-leqi-unninni
   Cuthean Legend of Naram-Sin 178
   formulas, speech introductions 42
   Gilgamesh and Akka 147
   at Hattusa 1, 13, 20, 32, 54, 56, 60–3
   Huwawa 57–8, 61
   opening 59, 64, 178
   oral tradition 63
   oral wisdom 59
   performed at royal funerals 80, 155, 186
   variations 61–3
   wisdom 59
   written object 59, 64, 178
Epigonoi F 4 West 318n81, 393n159
Epimenides 213–14
   FGrH 457 T 1 203n17
Eratosthenes *FGrH* 241 F 1d 402n25
e-re-o-ni 352
Ereshkigal 97n87, 126, 154
Ereshkigal and Nergal 126
Erichthonius 190
Eridu 189
e-ro-e 286n77
Erra 216, 243n119
Erra and Ishum 216n81
Erythrae 438
Esarhaddon 88, 316n75, 386, 392
Esarhaddon No. 1 (*Nineveh A*) v 63–71 322
eschatology 267, 273, 284–5, 447–8
Esharra-hamat 88
Eshuwara 304
Eskişehir 343
esoteric content, *Epic of Gilgamesh* 74n89
esoteric knowledge 16, 209, 211, 217
   transfer, verbal art 4, 14, 211–12
ešuwan 159–60
Etana 74, 188, 190, 191n105
Eteocles 339n41
Eteocypriot 307
   bilingual bards 52–3
   intermediaries 12, 17, 52–3, 309–10, 324, 326

Eternal Rocky Peak 153, 447
e-te-wo-ke-re-we-i-yo- 339n41
Etruscan 361–2
  Trojan language 362
Euboea *Also see* Lefkandi
  Chios 435
  competitive emulation 321
  contact with north Syria 2n2, 295
  Hesiod 219
  intermediaries 2, 13, 283–5, 294
    dating 299
    Odyssey 295–6
  Io 215n73
  Levant 282, 295, 321
  long-distance elite interactions 268, 281
  pendant semi-circle skyphoi 295, 372n95
  Thebes, BA 228
  warrior-trader values 268, 281, 283
    transfer, verbal art 295–8
Euboean *koinē* 281
Eudemus of Rhodes F 150 Wehli 55n8
Eumelus 400n17
  Titanomachy F 3 West 257n166
Euphrates 6, 51n131, 157n36, 177 *Also see* Mala River
Euripides
  Hecuba 467–74 262n195
  F 30 Jouan-van Looy 425n21
Europa 216n77, 318n79, 423n14
Eurylochus 100
Eurytus 203n16
Eusebius 24n14
  Chronicle 392n157
  Chronological Canons 415n76, 444n97
Eustathius *ad Iliad* 16.702 (1082) 378n118
e-u-te-re-u 352
Eutresis 352
Evocation Ritual for dMAḪMEŠ and the Fate-Goddesses 94–5, 98n94
Evocation Rituals 342n53
evri 424
exorcists 86, 94–8, 101, 108–9, 202, 213n67
  Ritual for Mt. Hazzi 108
exotic goods
  competitive display 304–5
  kingship 207–9
  magico-medical rituals 213–15
  Mycenaean vessels 207–8, 344–5
  Shaft Graves 207
exotic knowledge, healers 215
exotic, valorization of, transfer, verbal art 4, 17, 200, 206–7, 213, 297–8

Expansion of the Cult of the Goddess of Night 72n80, 84n24
extispicy 192, 194, 201n4, 244n121
eya trees 104, 246, 252n140

Fate-goddesses 72, 94, 120
feasting etiquette, shared, BA Greece, Anatolia 344
festival calendar, Mycenaean 226–7
festival for Storm-god Iyarri of Gursamassa 224
Festival for the Goddess Teteshapi 254–5
festival of Istanuwa 21, 32, 163, 227, 342, 347, 401n20
festivals
  ancestor veneration 87–8, 151, 155–6, 233–4, 264, 350
  Attic-Ionic 234–6, 463
  Chaoskampf 256–61
  competitions, bards, in Homeric tradition 17, 239–40, 297
  cultural contact/mixing
    Hittite, KI.LAM 224
    Mycenaean 229
    Miletus, EIA 220, 242–3
  modern, epic performance 415
  supralocal audiences, transfer, verbal art 4, 13, 16, 234
  Theogony 250
  transfer
    Greek, EIA 234–6
    from Hattusa 259n178
    to Hattusa *See* (ḫ)išuwa; ḫiyara
    kingship 16, 251, 258–9, 261
    transfer, verbal art 16, 234–6, 239, 250–1, 263–5
  wrestling 57, 79–80, 223n15
festivals, EIA Greek *Also see* Anthesteria; Apatouria; Carnea; Cronia; Delia; Dionysia; Panathenaea; Panionia; Skira; Thargelia
  Aeolian Hera 329
  Apollo 16, 250n136 *Also see below*, Miletus
    transfer, verbal art, 16, 243–9, 264, 420, 440, 444, 450–2, 454
  competitions
    athletic 17, 233, 241, 267, 394
    poetry/music 233, 237–41, 267, 454
  contributions 232
  funeral games 233–4
  hegemony 232
  hero cult 233–4
  Homeric Hymn to Apollo 237, 249–51, 261–2, 263–4

festivals, EIA Greek (cont.)
　musical performances 238–42
　Miletus
　　Apollo 220, 241–2, 452–4
　　processions 232, 241–2
　Panhellenic 232–3, 262, 415, 422n10
　supralocal audiences 234
　supralocal performers 239–40
festivals, Hittite *Also see* festival for Storm-god Iyarri, festival of Istanuwa, (ḫ)išuwa; ḫiyara; KI.LAM; New Year's; nuntarriyašḫaš; purulli
　competitions, athletic 223
　contributions 223
　hegemony 222–4
　HH narr. song 50–1, 256–7
　　Ritual for Mt. Hazzi 25, 50, 108, 183, 256–7
　Kizzuwatna, source 258–60
　Kumarbi cycle 256
　musical performances 222–5, 260
　processions 222
　ritual drama *See* drama, ritual
　Song of Hedammu 51
　supralocal audiences 222, 225–6
festivals, IE, competitions, poetry/music 239–40
festivals, Mycenaean 228–31
　Thebes 220, 228–31
　　Anatolian visitors 231–2, 345–6
　competitions
　　athletic 227–8, 267, 269–70
　　poetry/music 267, 269–70
　contributions 228
　cultural contact/mixing 229
　hegemony 228–30, 233
　musical performances 227, 231
　processions 227–8
　supralocal audiences 227–8, 231–2
festivals, NE, BA *Also see* abu; akītu; ḫiyara
　competitions, athletic 79–80
　kingship 16, 251
　Storm-god 250, 259–61
　supralocal audiences 225–6
fictional ancestors *See* ancestors, fictional
first compensatory lengthening 463
floating gap 287n82, 289, 402
flood stories 29–30 *Also see* Atrahasis; *Epic of Creation*
　Bible 29, 292–3
　Deucalion 29, 293
　HH narr. song 25
　Ogygus 293
　Sumerian chronicles 188

Flood Story (Sumerian) 29
floods
　Gilgamesh tradition 29–30, 58–9, 147
　Illuyanka 255
　imagery 195, 396–7n2
　Poseidon 396n2
folk epic *See* oral poetry
forked pathway
　Gilgamesh and Huwawa 75, 431
　Return Songs 75n98
Former Gods 26, 189n100 *Also see* Anunnaki; Purification Ritual for the Former Gods
　Former Kings 94, 154n24, 185
　HH pit rituals 94–8
　Ishhara 95n78, 97n86, 129
　names 26, 95n78, 96–7
　Song of Birth 50, 94, 96–7
　terminology 94
Former Kings 101
　judges 154
　kingship 130, 149, 152–5
　magico-medical incantations 154–5
　powers 153–5
　Ritual of Allaiturahhi 154–5
　Ritual of Mastigga 154n24
　substitution rituals 154
formulaic templates 42
formulas *See* Hurro-Hittite narrative song
founders
　Dardanus 190
　Ephesus 444n95
　Gabbar/Banihu 379–80, 393
　Greek heroes 286n76, 314n63, 318n79, 393, 435, 442
　　Glaucids 429, 438–9
　　nostoi, Cyprus 322, 324
　　Mopsus 18, 317–19
　　Neleids 241, 413–14, 422n13, 438–9, 444
　　Sarpedon 422–3, 438
　　Tarsus 314n63
Fragments Mentioning Ishtar (Mt. Pishaisha) 26
Fragments Mentioning the Ašuša(tal)la-People 242n114
Fragments Mentioning Ea See Ea and the Beast
Fragments of Akkadian Historical Texts 317n77
Fragments of Akkadian Letters 315n71, 441n83
Fragments of Annals See "The Offenses of Seha River Land"
Fragments of Historical Texts 338–9
Fragments of Hittite Letters 207n32, 344
Fragments of Hurro-Hittite Rituals and Incantations 86n35, 160, 214n72

Fragments of Itkalzi Rituals Mentioning Tashmisharri and Taduhepa 160n48
Fragments of Palace Chronicles 129n69, 158
Fragments of Prayers 338-9
Fragments of Purification Rituals 246
Fragments of Rituals Mentioning Pirinkir 163
Fragments of Royal Letters See Tikunani Letter
Fragments of the Kumarbi Myth 121n42
    Song of the Sea 25n17
Fraktın 153
frescos, Mycenaean, Hattusa 346
funeral games
    competitions
        athletic 282
        bards 233, 240
    festivals 233-4
    Patroclus 282n62, 288
    Theogony 233
A Funerary Ritual in Poetic Form (Ugarit) 150n1
funerary rituals *See* mortuary rituals

Gabbar 379-80, 393
Ganymede 190
GAŠAN 96
Gassuliyawiya 337n31
Ğebel al-Aqra 251, 258n173
Ğebel Seman 159
Geleontes 241n111
Gelidonya, Cape *See* Cape Gelidonya
Geme-Sin 214-15
genealogies *Also see* Hesiod, *Catalog of Women*; dynastic lists; king lists
    Aeneas 190, 378, 429
    ancestor veneration 271-2
    Catalog of Women 190 *Also see below*, world history
    cosmogonies 15, 185-6, 272, 291-2
    Glaucus 378, 423n14, 441-2
    Io 215, 318, 376
    king lists 15, 167, 190, 196, 291, 378
    of objects 282, 378, 422
    Theogony 190, 292
    world history 196, 350, 377-8, 394
        Catalog of Women 377-8
Genesis *See* Bible
genitival adjectives 362
genres
    formal classification 35-6
    indigenous classification 22, 35
Gerçin 380
Gergithes 12
ghost prescriptions 14, 85, 88-9, 101n101

ghosts 79-80, 85, 89, 100, 153, 287n82
giants 290, 293, 346n71 *Also see* Cyclops; Gigantomachy
gift exchange
    Ahhiyawa 344-5
    Amarna 202n10, 207n32, 213
    Arzawa 207n32
gifts 207
    festivals, Hittite 223n17
    guest 296
    vessels 202, 275, 282, 297n117, 317n78, 344-5
Gigantomachy 263
Gilgamesh
    Ballad of Early Rulers 188
    deified 79
    dreams 28, 57, 60, 61n26, 62-3, 66, 145n30
    Epic of See Epic of Gilgamesh
    fictional ancestor 14, 79-80, 186n90
    hero (UR.SAG) 64
    historical figure xxx.n9, 54
    judge/ruler of dead 14, 57, 79, 85-6, 109
    Lugalbanda, son of 58, 79, 80n11, 210n50
    magico-medical incantations 79, 85
    name, GIŠ 390
    Naram-Sin 174-5
    semi-divine 57
    Shulgi 80
    Song of See Song of Gilgamesh
    Tell Halaf 389-90
    Urkesh 72n76
Gilgamesh and Akka 147, 277n43
    1-47 134
    assembly scene 14, 134-5
    Epic of Gilgamesh 147
Gilgamesh and Huwawa 22n9, 56, 175
    A 1-12 175n39
    Cyclops 55-6
    forked pathway 75, 431
    Odyssey 55-6
    Ziusudra 30n38
Gilgamesh and the Bull of Heaven 325n111
Gilgamesh, Enkidu, and the Netherworld 22n9
    Epic of Gilgamesh SB XII 57, 59
Gilgamesh tradition
    ancestor statues 58, 79, 186n91
    ancestor veneration 14, 51, 58-9, 79-81, 391
    Atrahasis 29, 31, 58-9, 147
    Ballad of Early Rulers 190
    bulls 63 *Also see* Bull of Heaven
    Cedar Forest, change in location 71n75, 175
    Cedar Forest/Mountains episode 57, 60, 61n26, 66-8, 75, 169

Gilgamesh tradition (cont.)
  Ebla 175
  Elam 57n13
  eternal life 31, 58, 79, 84, 109, 190
  flood 29–30, 58–9, 147
  historiolae 213, 216
  Homeric tradition, entry into 298, 454
  HH pit rituals 14, 51, 78, 81–6, 98–9, 109
  HH, Hattusa 1, 13, 54 *Also see Song of Gilgamesh*; *Song of Huwawa*
  Iliad
    Achilles 1, 13, 22, 107, 194, 434, 454
    Iliad 5 325–6
    Sarpedon 68, 195, 445
  journeys, edge of world 58, 177, 210–11
    entry into Homeric tradition 218, 298, 300
    Odyssey 22, 268, 298, 299n126
  journeys, underworld 22, 57, 59, 79–80
    Odyssey 78, 101, 105, 109, 216, 298–9
  lions, slain 389, 71
  mortuary offerings 58, 79
  NE 54–6
  Ocean, crossing 58, 99n97
  OB, epic about Huwawa 56n12, 73
  Odyssey 1, 13
    Cyclops 55–6
  oral 54, 60, 76
  Sargonic legends 168–9, 171, 172n21, 173–4, 196
    journey to Cedar Forest 172–3
  Song of Keshshi 28, 66, 145
  Sumerian 55–7, 71n75, 75n94
  writing down 54, 75
  wrestling 57, 61n26, 79
Gimirrāya 106
Glaucids
  fictional ancestors 438–9, 440n82
  founders, Miletus 429, 438–9
Glaucus 423, 439, 448–9, 452–3
  Bay 439
  catalog of Trojan allies 442
  genealogies 378, 423, 441–2
gods
  of the father 130, 160n49
  healing, transfer 248
  shared, transfer, verbal art 250
  syncretism, transfer
    festivals 305–6
    verbal art 301, 319
  transfer 202, 342–3, 346–7
    kingship 164
    transfer, cult personnel 162, 260, 346–7
    transfer, verbal art 4, 13, 15, 110, 346

Göksu River 313
Golden Fleece 103–4, 211, 256n161
Golgoi 324
Gordion 343, 363n63
  continuity 357
Göroglï See Köroglu
grammata Ephesiaka 242
grandmother-goddesses 65n41, 104n115 *Also see* DINGIR.MAḪ
Great Assembly 156, 225
Great Goddess *See* DINGIR.MAḪ
Great Kings
  Ahhiyawa 339, 344
  Brotherhood 177, 184, 196–7, 202–3, 207–8, 225–6, 232, 303–5
  Hartapu 312, 374
  Hattusili I 123, 166, 177
  Kurunta 312
  Muwattalli 331
  Neo-Hittite 310, 312, 374
  Storm-god of Kummi 42–3
  Tawalagawa 339
Great Libyan War Inscription, Karnak, 443n93
Great Revolt against Naram-Sin
  OB 16–20, 178
  Hittite 192nn108–109
  Mari 155, 186
Greco-Anatolian bards, competitions 432
Greco-Anatolian cultural interaction, BA 341
Greco-Aryan epic 142, 266, 434
Greco-Lycian epic 426 *Also see* Bellerophontes; Sarpedon
Greece *Also see* Mycenaean; post-palatial; PG
  ancient history, NE influence 268, 279–81, 291–2
  cultural continuity 233
  Cyprus, shared identity, transfer, verbal art 17–18, 302, 310
  Dan- 317
  NE influence, role of ancestor veneration 279, 289–92
  Tanaya 317n78
Greek
  colonization *See* colonization, Greek
  epic *See* Homeric epic
  festivals *See* festivals, Greek
  migrations *See* migrations, Greek
  settlement *See* settlement, Greek
Greek–Lycian bilingual bards 426, 438–49
Greek–Lydian bilingualism 93n63, 427
Greek–Phoenician bilingual bards 53, 322n100, 326

Greek–Phrygian bilingual bards 328–9, 429–32, 435 *Also see* Aeolic-Phrygian bilingual bards
Greeks
　at Karatepe 392
　and Phrygians, dynastic marriages 435
　shared legendary past with Anatolians 19, 332
Grey and Tan Ware 363
Grey Ware 359, 365, 367, 372, 412n66
groves, sacred 104, 242
Gryneum 451
Gudea Cylinder A 145n30
LÚGUDU₁₂ 252n142
guest friendship 16, 204, 296–8, 351n9, 420, 423
guest-gifts 296
guests 203n16 *Also see* diplomats
Guggu 377
Gula 217
Gula-AN and the Seventeen Kings 30n43
　OB 5' 176n45
Gulla 338n33
gulloi 241–2, 440
Gurgum 374
Gurparanzah *See The Heroic Deeds of Gurparanzah*
Gursamassa 224, 343
Gutians 192, 197n119
Guzana *See* Tell Halaf
Güzelçamlı 413n69, 443
Gygaean Lake 337n28, 376
Gyges 377
　dynastic name 375, 441n84
　monument 375–6, 448
　patron of Greek epic 105
　royal ancestor 375

Habur River 10
Hadad 380n124
　Storm-god of Aleppo 161, 260
　of the Vineyard 380n124 *Also see* Storm-god of the Vineyard
Hagneus 230n58
Hahhu
　colony, Old Assyrian merchant 176
　Hattusili I 123, 176–7, 180
　Naram-Sin 176
　Sargonic legends 170, 176
LÚHAL 86, 95–6, 98n91 *Also see* exorcists
Hala Sultan Tekke 304, 307
Halicarnassus 340, 345, 358
Halizones 52, 104, 374n103

Halki 223, 225
LÚḫalliyariš 162
ḫalmi 21, 162
Halparuntiyas III 374
Hamsha 30 *Also see* Land of Fifty
Handmade Coarse War 362
Haneans 197n119
Hannahanna 65n41, 104n115 *Also see* DINGIR.MAḪ
ḫantawata/i- 374
Hantili II 252
Hantitassu *See Ritual of Hantitassu of Hurma*
ḫapalki 104
Hapalla 336
ḫarki- 52n138
harps 156, 240–1n108, 260
GIŠḫaršandaḫit 31n44
ḫaršantan 31n44
ḫartagga- 421
Hartapu xxx.n17, 312, 374
Harvest Rhyton 231
Hassu 158, 160, 163
　colony, Old Assyrian merchant 176
　Hattusili I 9, 159, 176–7, 258
　Sargonic legends 176
　Storm-god of Aleppo 159, 258
GIŠḫattala- 320
ḫattannaš ḫaršumnaš EN-*aš* 131n77
ḫattātar 131, 158, 187
Hatti 9, 171, 224, 225, 331, 337, 343, 356, 376–7
　Ahhiyawa, gift exchange 207n32, 344–5
　Arzawa, cultural interaction with 342–3
　king/lord of 185, 192n109, 225, 354n19
　meaning 52
　Neo-Hittite 7, 311–12
　in Sargonic legends 170, 184–5, 192n109, 197
　Storm-god of 253n148
Hattians
　KI.LAM festival 223–4
　silver trade 51–2
Hattic
　bilinguals 32–3, 427–8
LÚḫalliyari- 162
　Hittite culture, contribution to 4
　influence, Hittite poetic language 36, 43
　Storm-god, Taru 260
　texts at Hattusa 9
　towns
　　Nerik 252n143
　　Tissaruliya 223–4
　language 9
　lyres 156n32

Hattic (cont.)
  priests, anointed 252n142
  purulli festival 32–3, 252
  voces magicae 242
Hattic Songs, Women of Tissaruliya 32
ḫattuš 52
Hattusa *Also see* Boğazköy
  Akkadian texs 4, 9, 15, 20–1, 32–3, 56, 60–3,
    85, 163, 171, 191, 213n67,
    213–14n68, 214n72, 317n77, 340,
    341n51
  archives and libraries 3–4, 7, 35n61
  Arzawan traditions 213, 243–4, 342, 346–7
  Büyükkale 7, 63n35, 151
  Büyükkaya 72n76
  colony, Old Assyrian merchant 6
  cultural mixing 4, 9
  Cuthean Legend of Naram-Sin 20, 171, 191
  Epic of Gilgamesh 1, 13, 20, 32, 54, 56, 60–3
    Also see Gilgamesh tradition
  epic traditions 20–1
  festivals, transfer from 259n178
  Gilgamesh tradition, HH 1, 13, 54 *Also see*
    Song of Gilgamesh; *Song of Huwawa*
  Hattic texts 9
  Haus am Hang 7
  Hieroglyphic Luwian inscriptions 90, 153
  Hurrian texts 9–10
  Ishhara 115
  KASKAL.KUR 89–92, 153
  Luwian texts 9, 11
  meaning 52
  Mesopotamian wisdom literature 33n51
  Mycenaean frescos 346
  Mycenaean sword 341
  Naram-Sin 21, 191–2
  Oberstadt 32, 111, 153
  oral-derived traditions 1, 15, 38, 179, 182
  pit rituals 89–91, 93–8
  purulli 254
  royal ancestor veneration 152–3
  Sargonic legends 171–4 *Also see* Sargonic
    legends, reception, Hittites
  scribal training 8–9, 60
  scribes
    Akkadian 6, 8–9, 171n19
    Syrian, north 8–9, 171n19
  silver 52, 104
  Storm-god of Aleppo 161–4, 259–60
  Südburg 90, 153
  Sumerian texts 9, 33n51, 85
  Temple 1 7, 63n35, 72nn76–77, 90
  Unterstadt 63n35

Hattusili
  dynastic name 373
  meaning 52
Hattusili I 6, 8–10, 184, 313n59
  ancestor veneration 151
  Ebla 111–12
  Hahhu 123, 176–7, 180
  Hassu 9, 159, 176–7, 258
  Ikinkalis 112, 157
  Sargonic legends 166, 168, 176–80, 196
  Song of Release 111–12, 123–4, 149, 157–61,
    258
  Storm-god of Aleppo 149, 159, 163–4, 184,
    258
  wisdom 158
Hattusili III 7, 186n91, 213n67, 252–3, 312,
    339–40
  ancestor veneration 153n21
  dynastic marriage 337n31
Hattusili's Annals See Annals of Hattusili I
Haus am Hang, Hattusa 7
Hazor 207–8
Hazzi, Mt. *Also see* Casius, Mt.; Sapon, Mt.
  battles
    with Storm-god 26
    between Storm-god and sea 25
    between Storm-god and Yam 257
  Casius, Mt. 258
  Chaoskampf 251, 256–60
  HH rituals 25 *Also see Ritual for*
    Mt. Hazzi
  Ikinkalis 157–8
  landmark 251, 257
  Song of the Sea 25–6
  Song of Ullikummi 39–40, 257n170
healers *Also see* doctors, $m^e rapp\bar{\imath} m$
  ancestors, divine 17
  Dioscuri 107
  esoteric knowledge 217
  Gilgamesh 285
  $m^e rapp\bar{\imath} m$ 285
  Nasatyas 107
  sent for 199, 203, 213–14
  transfer 16, 200, 208, 342
    divine 248
  wandering 205
healing incantations *See* magico-medical
    incantations
Hebat 84, 121n42, 157n34, 159, 184
  Aleppo 261n190
  Carchemish 27
  invocations 10
  Song of LAMMA 27

Hecataeus *FGrH* 1 F 119 438n72
 F 300 257n166
Hecate 93n63, 242
Hector
 Boeotian hero 365, 405–6, 432, 436
 of Chios 435
 dynastic connections 328, 407, 435–7
 hero cult 288, 406, 446
 hero of *Iliad* 193, 433–4, 437, 452
 leadership 33
 Naram-Sin 1, 15, 166–7, 191, 193–5, 355–6, 414, 420, 433, 437, 454
 Trojan hero 432–4, 436, 454
 wedding 458
Hecuba 416n76
Hedammu 184–5, 190 *Also see* Kumarbi cycle, *Song of Hedammu*
 Duddul 51
Hegesias 326n117
heirlooms
 boar's-tusk helmets 229, 282
 connection to past 17, 208, 268, 274–5, 281–2, 284, 321, 373
 display 207–8, 274–5
 scepters 207, 274–5, 378, 422
 vessels 207–8, 274, 281, 345, 367
NA₄*ḫekur* 152–3
Helen
 Paris 326–7, 434
 Song of Release 33, 132, 139, 432, 450
Heliconian bull 413n69, 443–4
Helios 27, 102, 105, 107 *Also see* Sun-god
 Apollo 250n136
Hellado-Cilician pottery 313
Hellanicus *FGrH* 4 F 25b 410n56
 F 31 407, 436n61, 437n65
 F 32 410n52
 F 85a 239n103
 FGrH 323a F 23 241n111
Helms, Mary 196–7, 206, 209–11, 216, 425
Hephaestus 144n29, 282, 297
Hera
 Aeolian, festivals 329
 hērōs 286n76
 Iliad
  Deception of Zeus 327
  Iliad 5 326
  Trojan War 288
 Io 215
 Proetids 204n19
Heraclea See Panyassis

Heracles
 Anatolia 422
 founder, Tarsus 314n63
 Hydra 251
 journeys 210
 Ninurta 210
 Oikhalias Halosis 416n76
 Omphale 377n117, 378
 Tlepolemus 353
Heraclids
 Iliad 353
 Lydian 376–8
 Spartan 377
heralds 203n16
Hermes 44, 93n63, 242, 374n105, 378, 422
 LAMMA 447
Hermus River 337, 360
hero cult *Also see* ancestor veneration
 ancestor veneration 268
 epic 80, 186–7, 268, 383, 394
  Lycians 420
  transfer, verbal art 445–9
 festivals 233–4
 Homeric tradition 287–8
 Lefkandi 281
 Lycians 420, 445–9
 Menelaus 286n76
 Mycenaean 17, 279, 285–6, 291–2
 Protogeometric Greece 286–7
 scholarly discussions 285–6n76, 287n82
Herodorus *FGrH* 31 F 45 423n14
Herodotus 1.1–5 418n1
 1.7 378n118
 1.7.2 374–5n105
 1.7.4 352n11
 1.12 375n108
 1.16–29 416n76
 1.29 209
 1.56ff. 377
 1.57 361n54
 1.70 377
 1.84 352n11
 1.94.5–7 361n54
 1.105 323n100
 1.105.2–3 323–4n103
 1.117 326n117
 1.132.3 216n81
 1.142 358n39, 361n52
 1.142–3 444n95
 1.143.3 235
 1.146.2 237n92, 416n76
 1.147 438, 440n82
 1.147.2 235, 237n92, 416n76

Herodotus 1.1–5 (cont.)
  1.149 451n129
  1.149–50 412n66
  1.149–51 359n41
  1.161–9 416n76
  1.173 443n92
  2.53.2 399n17
  2.145 402n25
  2.171.2–3 264
  3.5 258n173
  3.125, 129–37, 203n17
  4.14.3 211n57
  4.33 238
  4.35 238
  4.35.3 239n102
  4.149 239n103
  5.13 418–19
  5.66 241n111
  5.94 409
  5.94.2 410n55, 411n60
  5.119–21 234n81
  5.122 12n48
  6.54 314n63
  7.33 418n1
  7.42–3 418–19
  7.43 12n48
  9.116–22 418n1
  dialect 295n112
  en de 427n29
  exotic pharmaka, interest in 214
  Homer
    date of 399n17
    Cypria 326n117
  Miletus, founding of 438–9
  Lydian dynasty 376–8
  Panionic League 235, 412n66, 444n95
  -ske/o- 427n32
  Thesmophoria 264
  Troad, competition for 409
  Trojan War
    date of 399n17, 402n25
    and Persian War 196, 418–19, 421
  Tyrsenoi 361
heroes 22 *Also see* m^{e}rappîm; semi-divine figures
  founders *See* founders
  qarrādum 170
  ur.sag 64–5, 75n94, 179
The Heroic Deeds of Gurparanzah 21, 34
heroic values, iconography 404
hērōs 286–7
Hesiod
  dating 398
  dialect 399n14

Euboea 219
hērōs 287
  and Homer, competition 240, 250, 414
  Hurrian–west Semitic influence 147, 290–1, 294, 299–300, 305–6
  NE influence 1
    HH narr. song 23
  sea, journey to/across 219
  west Semitic influence 285, 289–94
Hesiod, *Aegimius* F 230 Most 215n73
Hesiod, *Catalog of Women* F 35 204n18
  F 69 411n58
  FF 72–107 216n77
  F 77 425n21
  FF 79, 80 204n18
  F 89 423n14
  F 90.20 291n102
  FF 155.94–119 288n87
  F 155.98 291n102
  Deucalion 293
  genealogies 190
    world history 377–8
  Io 215–16n77, 376, 394, 423n14
  NE parallels 16
  Odyssey, underworld journey 101–2
  Perseus 425n21
  Sarpedon 423n14
  Theogony 190
Hesiod, *Melampodia* FF 206–15 204n18
  F 212.5 291n102
  F 214 393n159
Hesiod, *Theogony* 207–10 290n99, 291n101
  280–3 425n21
  617–733 262
  805–6 293n106
  820–70 255
  851 291n101
  Chaoskampf 250, 262
  Epic of Creation 24
  festivals 250
  funeral games 233, 240, 396n2
  genealogies 190, 292
  Hurrian–west Semitic influence 147, 290–1
  Illuyanka 285
  Kumarbi cycle 13, 22, 24–5, 147, 285
    Song of Birth 290
    Song of Hedammu 255
    Song of Ullikummi 255
  west Semitic influence 285
Hesiod, *Works and Days* 20–6 395
  27–46 34, 133n2
  55 233
  98–103 233
  109 289n96

109–26 266
111 291
143–4, 180 289n96
636 411n58
650–7 219
654–9 233
656–8 240
Ages of Man 268, 280, 285, 288–93, 373
  kingship 289
  Lefkandi 289
  meropes See meropes
  west Semitic influence 285, 289–92
  against Perses 34, 133n2
Hesiod, F 241 425n21
  F 297 250, 414
ḫešti-house 87n42, 151, 383, 448
  Hittite festivals 151, 253n148
  Mopsou Hestia 382
  Yazılıkaya 152n14
Hesychius s.v. *gullos* 242n113
hexametric narratives, unity of genre 22, 110
Hieroglyphic, Cretan 11
Hieroglyphic Luwian 11
  wooden tablets 11, 424
Hieroglyphic Luwian inscriptions *Also see*
  Index of Hieroglyphic Luwian
  Inscriptions
  Anatolia, west 3, 343, 350
  Çineköy 315, 318
  Gordion 357
  Karatepe 311, 315–17, 320n89, 383, 386
  Panunis 381
  Hattusa 90, 153
  Kanesh 11n40
  silver bowl (Ankara 2) 11n40, 347–8, 400–1, 453
  Soli 314
  Syro-Anatolia, EIA 310–12, 381
  Yalburt 447n111
Hieropythus 436
Hieros Lithos 242n113
"high Troy" 21
"high/steep Wilusa" 21, 400, 453
Hilakku 7, 310, 312, 374, 392n157
Hipparchus 400, 415–16n76
Hippias (Sophist) 349, 378
Hippocleides 415n76
Hippocrates *On the Sacred Disease* 1.4 vi 354
  Littré 204n20
Hippodameia 374, 422n10
Hippolochus 378, 438
Hipponax
  F 2.1 Degani 93n63
  F 7 375n109

F 107.49 235
Lydian–Greek bilingualism 93n63, 427
poetic dialect 399n17
scapegoat ritual 235
Hishmi-Sharruma 352n10
Historical-Mythological Hurrian Texts See HH
  narr. song; Sargonic legends; *šarrena*
  ritual
historiolae 200
  Atrahasis 30n40, 216
  cosmogonies 213–14, 216–17, 262
  epic 394
  Geme-Sin 213–15
  Gilgamesh tradition 213, 216
  HH narr. song 50–2
    Elkunirsa and Ashertu 34, 51, 73, 108, 126, 213, 216
    Song of Birth 50–1, 86n36, 121n44
    Song of Hedammu 50–1
    Song of Keshshi 51
    Song of Kingship 256–7
    Song of LAMMA 50
    Song of Oil 51
    Tale of Appu 50
  HH pit rituals 82
  journeys 263
  magico-medical rituals 262–3
  transfer, verbal art 213
history *Also see* admonitory history; world
  history
  ancient, NE, influence on Greece 268, 279–81, 291–2
(ḫ)išuwa festival 159–60, 260–1
  ešuwan 160n48
  kingship 260–1
  Storm-god of Aleppo 160, 258–61
  transfer 260
  ritual drama 261–2
Hittite
  ancestor statues 151–4, 183, 186n91, 446
  ancestor veneration, royal 150–3, 156
  campaigns, north Syria 6, 8–9, 112n5, 158–9, 163–5, 176–8, 313n59
  court
    kingship 164–5, 258–61
    world history 166–7
  culture 4–11
    Hurrian influence 157, 159–62, 164–5
  cuneiform script 8, 171n19
  empire, fall 7
  festivals *See* festivals, Hittite
  hegemony
    Kizzuwatna 6, 10, 156–7, 164, 258, 303, 313
    north Syria 6, 303, 312

Hittite (cont.)
  king lists 151–2
  language 9
  mortuary rituals, royal *Also see Death Rituals*
    cult singers 156
      Homeric 284n73, 399n17
      supralocal audience 156
  prayers *See* prayers, Hittite
Hittite Fragments with Various Contents,
    Atrahasis 30n40
Hittite-Hurrian, bilingual bards 13, 22, 37–8,
    46–8, 76
Hittites
  Aleppo 6, 158
  Amarna 7, 207, 213, 335
  Cyprus 6, 153, 303, 336
  Egypt 7, 312
  Emar 6, 7, 115
  Hurrians, conflicts with 6, 10, 163
  memories of, EIA west Anatolia 374
ḫiyara festival 258, 261
ḫiyaru, month 151n9, 261
Hiyawa 18, 315, 318n80, 383 *Also see* Adana;
    Ahhiyawa; Cilicia; Danuna; Que
Ḫiyawaniš 315
Hiyawans, Lukka 316n71, 441n83
Hof Building *See* Terrace House
holocaust offerings 81, 83, 84, 99
homārios 240
Homer
  ancestor, fictional 416n76
  birthplace 330n132, 412n66
  date 396–400
  hērōs 287
  Hesiod, competition 240, 250–1, 414
  legendary figure 63n32, 239–40, 396–7
  Melesigenes 379
  oral tradition 63n32, 212, 397, 400
  single poet 396
  Thebaid, author of 416n76
Homer, *Iliad Also see* Homeric tradition;
    Trojan War
  1.8–16 132
  1.17–32 139–40
  1.37–42 140, 451
  1.38 231n63, 450
  1.39, Σ D 450n125
  1.43–100 244
  1.58–67 140
  1.84 42n90
  1.131–9 141
  1.188–92 45
  1.250 291n102

1.595–8 144–5n29
2.1–36 193
2.100–8 422
2.169 461
2.205 412n67
2.366–9 411n62
2.370–2 120n36
2.407 461
2.461 334n13
2.500, 502 352
2.558 409n51
2.591–600 203n16
2.636 461
2.647 231n69, 422
2.653–70 353
2.671–80 353
2.689–91 411n62
2.699 43
2.783 255n158
2.803–4 421n6
2.816–78 334–5n14
2.819–21 327n121
2.838 421n8
2.857 52, 104
2.865–6 376
2.867 421
2.867–75 442
2.876–7 442
3.184–7 430nn43–44
3.204 139n16
3.400–1 430n44
4.1 133n2
4.50–2 288
4.141–2 442n90
4.437–8 421n6
4.438 203n16
5.44 241n111
5.428–30 326
5.471–80 418
5.471–92 439n79
5.639, Σ bT 440–1
5.738–42 427n29
6.63–311 416n76
6.152–4 411n58
6.153–5 378, 441n84
6.155–95 423
6.169 423
6.184–6 378
6.196–206 378
6.198–9 423n14
6.203–4 378
6.327 421n9
6.397 330n130

Subject index 595

6.402–3 412
6.415 330n130
6.415–16 411n62, 421n9
7.9 320
7.47 461
7.85–6 446
7.86–90 288
7.132–57 355
7.138 320
7.334–5 399n17
7.442–64 396n2
8.167–244 193
9.13–15 43
9.54–7 120n36
9.128–31 411n62
9.129, Σ A 329n129
9.129–30 353n15
9.129–30, Σ D 329n129
9.165 203n16
9.184–91 415n72
9.185–219 144
9.186–91 276
9.189 298
9.207–8 427n29
9.270–3 411n62
9.381 396n2
9.664–5 353n15
10.1–179 146
10.137 461
10.261–70 282n63
10.414–16 288n85
10.420 203n16
10.428 442n90
10.429 438n72
11.19–28 330n131
11.122–42 139n16
11.166 288n85
11.200 461
11.371–2 288n85
11.403–4 45–6
11.670–762 355
12.17–33 396n2
12.23 287n84
12.230–43 194
12.310–28 439n76
13.685–6 411n58
13.689 411n58
14.153–15.219 327
14.166–221 327
14.282–93 329
14.319–20 425n21
15.283–4 120n36
16.3–4 43

16.317–29 440
16.328–9 440
16.419–683 445n101
16.431–61 195n114
16.456 453
16.456–7 445–6
16.513–16 452–3
16.666–84 453
16.672, 674 453
16.674–5 445–6
16.682 453
16.698–801 453
16.717–19 430
18.290–1 430n44
18.310–13 194–5
18.483 427n29
19.245–6 411n62
20.4–30 133n2
20.86–96 12n48
20.213–40 190, 378n119
20.306–17 407, 412
20.307–8a1, Σ bT 412n65, 436n61
20.390–1 376n110
20.403–5 413n69
20.404b, Σ bT 413n69
21.86–7 12n48
22.98–107 195
22.108–10 195
22.136 195
22.147–56 90n55
22.167–85 195
23.87 396n2
23.740–9 282n62
24.228–37 282n62
24.340–5 44
24.349 288n85
24.544–6 353
24.602–17 422
24.616b, Σ bT 378n118
24.735b, Σ bT 407n41
Aphrodite 139, 325–6
Apollo 139–40, 142, 193, 243–7, 449–53
assemblies *Also see below, under Song of Release*
   divine 133n2, 195
   Trojan, bribed not to release Helen 139n16
Athenians 411n58
Atrahasis 147, 396–7n2
Boeotians 352, 406, 411n58
Carians 421, 442
Catalog of Ships 191, 352–3, 406, 409n51, 422, 440–2

596 Subject index

Homer, *Iliad* (cont.)
   catalog of Trojan allies 191, 327, 334–5n14,
     441–3
   Lycians 442–3
   Chryseis episode, a hymn to Apollo 450
   Cilicia 330n130, 411n62, 421n9
   colonization legends 353, 422–3
   Cuthean Legend of Naram-Sin See Hector,
     Naram-Sin
   embassy scene 144–5, 147
   Epic of Creation, Deception of Zeus 55n8,
     327
   formulas, weeping 43
   Gilgamesh tradition
     Achilles 1, 13, 22, 107, 194, 434, 454
     Iliad 5, 325–6
     Sarpedon 68, 195, 445
   Ionians 411n58
   Ionic perspective 411–12
   kingship 33–4
   Lesbos 353, 411
   Lycia 418, 442
   Lycian influence 423–6, 432, 438–43, 454
   Lycians 420–1, 423–6 *Also see*
     Bellerophontes; Glaucus; Sarpedon
   Maeonians 241n111, 376, 421, 430,
     442n90
   Miletus 353, 442
   Miletus (Crete) 231n69, 422–3, 442
   Mycenaean origin 401, 416–17
   NE influence, layers of 453–4, 455–7
   Neleids 398, 440, 444–5
   Rhodes 353
   Song of Release, type scenes
     assembly scenes 33–4, 133, 139–42, 195,
       355–6, 450
     hospitality scenes 144–5
     negative reactions 45
     waking for message 146
   Thebes (Egypt) 396n2
   Thebes (Greece) 352
   type scenes
     dressing scenes 327
     messengers 44
Homer, *Ilias Homerica in Cyclum Inclusa*
   Bernabé 449
Homer, *Odyssey Also see* Homeric tradition
   1.1–5 114
   1.85 293n106
   1.178–94 296
   2.403–5 443
   2.409 461n13
   3.130–71 407

3.366 438n72
4.81–5 330n131
4.126–7 396n2
4.614–19 297n117
4.615–9 282
5.44–9 44
5.265–7 427n29
6.162–5 236
8.496–8 297
10.55, 60 411n58
10.138 107
10.488–95 101n103
10.505–40 101n104
10.513–15 100
10.571–2 100
11.3–4 427n29
11.13–50 100
11.100–17 102
11.100–37 101n102
11.118–37 102
11.281–97 204n18
11.298–304 107n130
12.69–72 103n112
12.90–1 427n29
14.288–97 297n117
15.225–42 204n18
15.403–84 297n117
16.476 461n13
17.382–6 199, 203
17.415–44 330n131
18.60 461n13
18.405 461n13
19.134–5 203n16
19.175–6 427n29
20.149–56, 276–8, 453n135
21.101 461n13
21.130 461n13
21.258–68 453n135
22.354 461n13
Alpamysh 34n55
Anatolian influence 79, 105–7, 295,
   298–9
Aphrodite 23, 297
Argonautica 103
Athena 296
   cult 416n76
Caucasian myth 299
colonization 296
Cyclops episode 101, 296 *Also see* Cyclops
   late addition 105–6, 298–300
   oral tradition 55–6
eastern adventures, late addition 14, 102,
   105–6, 296

festivals
    Apollo 453n135
    competitions, poetry/music 297
    supralocal audiences 297
Gilgamesh tradition 1, 13, 556 *Also see above*, Cyclops episode; *below*, journeys, underworld
The Heroic Deeds of Gurparanzah 34n55
hospitality scenes 142–3
HH pit rituals 93, 99–102
intermediaries, Euboea 295–6
journeys through darkness, Sargonic legends 105
journeys, edge of world 99–103, 177, 211, 298–9
    Gilgamesh tradition 22, 268, 298–9
    Sargonic legends 1, 218
journeys, long-distance elite interactions 295–6
journeys, underworld 99–102
    Anatolian influence 103–7, 109, 298–9
    Catalog of Women 101–2
    Gilgamesh tradition 78, 101, 105, 109, 216, 298, 299n126
    late addition 14, 105–6, 298–300
long-distance elite interactions 17, 296–8
NE influence, layers of 268, 295, 298–9, 455–7
Purification Ritual for the Former Gods 78, 95, 99–101, 105, 109
Return Songs 75n98
trading network 296
Trojan War 298
type scenes, messengers 44
westward orientation 296
Homer *Vita* 1 West 240, 414
    1.2 379, 412n66
    2.1–3 412n66
    2.29–32 235n83
"Homeric" culture
    Crete 321
    Cyprus 284, 308, 322
Homeric dialect 407–9, 412–13
    Achaean layer 266n1, 427n30
    Aeolic borrowings/layer 357, 396, 402–9, 412n66, 412–13n67, 444
    Arcado-Cypriot forms 266n1, 408
    Attic forms 416n76
    bilingual bards 426–8
    Doric layer 408n44
    en de 427
    Lesbian dialect 405, 407–9, 411n58
    -ske/o- 427

tar 427
west Ionic forms 295n112, 408
Homeric epic
    Greco-Aryan origin 266
    Mycenaean roots 266, 403–4, 416–17, 461
Homeric Hymn to Aphrodite 18, 239, 265, 323n101, 327–9
    58–69 327
    111–15 421
    113–16 328
    6.19–20 239
    dressing scene 327–9
    Phrygian, Aphrodite's first language 328, 421
    prooimia 239
Homeric Hymn to Apollo 37 411n58
    42 291n102
    146–64 237
    147 411n58
    164–74 239
    172 330n132
    174–5 204n17
    179–83 243
    371 250n136
    Chios 239
    dating 398
    festivals 237, 249–52, 261, 263–4
    Kumarbi cycle 25
    prooimia 24
Homeric Hymn to Demeter 263–4, 449n122
    1–5 114
Homeric meter *See* dactylic hexameter
Homeric mortuary rituals, Hittite 284n73, 399n17
Homeric tradition
    Anatolian influence 419
    Athenian influence 406n37, 409n51, 416n76
    Chios, transfer via 396, 416n76
    cremation 284n73, 399n17
    Crete 231n69, 282n63, 422–3, 442
    Cyprus 330
    date of textualization, 397–400, 416n76
    Egypt 330n131, 396
    Egptian influence 34n55
    entry of
        Aphrodite storylines 18, 301
        Cuthean Legend of Naram-Sin plotline 355–6, 419, 430–5, 437–8, 454
        Cyclops episode 105–6, 298–300
        Gilgamesh tradition 298, 454
        HH narr. song motifs 331, 347
        journeys, edge of world 218, 298, 300
        Pytho story 301, 321
        Sargonic legends 298

Homeric tradition (cont.)
   Song of Release plotline 355–6, 419, 432
   Trojan War legend 373, 400–2, 405,
      416–17, 454
   Typhon story 256, 301, 306, 321
   Ugaritic epic motifs 302, 305–6
  hero cult 287–8
  HH narr. song 4, 15, 22
   formulas and type scenes shared 41, 43–6
    Also see type scenes
  Lefkandi 295n112, 408n44
  Milesian stage 353, 420, 437–45, 452–4
  Neleids 413–14
  Panionic stage 235, 264, 267, 396, 398,
    400n19, 413–15, 419, 441–5, 48–9,
    452
  Phoenicians 282n62, 296–7n117
  Thrace/Thracians 282n62, 297
Homeridae 24n13, 330n132, 416n76, 449, 458n2
homēros 240n105
Hoplethes 241
Horanu and the Mare (Ugarit) 215
Horned God 249
hospitality scenes *See* type scenes
House of Stars 150
House of the Grandfathers 151, 154, 375, 448
House of the Hurrian Priest 150n2
How Sosruquo Brought Fire to His Troops
   106n122
How Sosruquo Was Born 25n16
ḫuḫḫa- 375
Hulaya River Land 447n111
humnos 37
hunting 28, 275, 386, 388–9
ḫunzinar 156
Hupasiya 253–4, 257n171
huph- 37
Hurri 160n48
ḫurri-bird 244n121
Hurrian
  epic 15, 22, 52
   Cyprus 306
  influence
   Hittite culture 4, 157, 159–62, 164–5
   source, Kizzuwatna 10, 86, 156–7, 164
  language 9
  singers 162
  texts
   Hattusa 9–10
   Ugarit 10, 131n77, 261n190, 306n25
Hurrian Fragments 160n48
  Invocation of Teshshub of Aleppo 162,
    185n83, 261

Hurrian Omens 157n34
Hurrian Ritual for the Royal Couple
  (invocation of Teshshub and Hebat)
  10n35, 261n191
Hurrian-Hittite, bilingual bards 13, 22, 37–8,
  46–8, 76
Hurrian-Luwian
  Cilicia, BA 10, 147
Hurrian-west Semitic 301
  influence, Hesiod 294, 299–300, 305–6
  Theogony 147, 290–1
Hurrians 9–10
  Alalakh 10, 162n56
  Aleppo 162n56
  Cyprus 304
  Ebla 161
  Hittites, conflicts with 6, 10, 163
  homeland 27n28, 258
  intermediaries 3, 5
   Mesopotamian culture 4–5, 10
   north Syrian culture 10, 157n34, 186, 257
   Sargonic legends 169, 173n31, 174, 179
  Neo-Hittites 311
  Syria, north 10
HH narr. song 13–15
  ancestor veneration 50–1
  archaisms 35
  Atrahasis 13, 20, 30
  bilingual bards 46–8
  Caucasian myths 25n16, 27n28, 126n58
  curses 44–6, 69, 113, 117–18, 121, 126, 129
  Cuthean Legend of Naram-Sin 191
  dating 35
  epithets 42–3
  festivals 50–1, 256–7
   Ritual for Mt. Hazzi 25, 50, 108, 183, 256–7
  flood stories 25
  formal classification 35–6
  formulas 42–3
   Dark Earth 43
   large numbers 125, 127
   speech introductions 42, 174n34
   weeping 43
  historiolae 50–2 *Also see* historiolae
  Homeric tradition 4, 15, 22
   entry into 331, 347
   formulas and type scenes shared 41, 43–6
    Also see type scenes
  HH rituals 13–15, 51 *Also see individual HH*
   narr. songs
  kingship 50
  members 20–1
  Naram-Sin 15, 182, 190

openings 36, 113
oral-derived 13, 37–9, 46–8, 156–7
performers 36
poetic features 36
prosody 46
Sargonic legends 15, 20, 167, 169, 174, 182, 190, 197
shared vocabulary 31
Song of Gilgamesh 13, 20, 22, 63–4, 71–2, 167, 191
terminology 21
type scenes
    assemblies 133–42, 147
    dressing 327
    hospitality 124–8
    messengers 43–4
    negative reactions 44–6
    Song of Release and Song of Keshshi, shared passage 43
    waking for a message 115, 145–6
unplaced fragments 34–5n57
wisdom 187
HH parables Also see Song of Release
wisdom 131, 187
HH pit rituals 81–4, 86, 93–8
    Former Gods 94–8
    Gilgamesh tradition 14, 51, 78, 81–6, 98–9, 109
    historiolae 82
    juridical scenarios 95–6
    Odyssey 93, 99–102
HH Prayer to Ishtar 214n72
HH rituals
    Aleppo 160
    Ebla 160
    Hazzi, Mt. 25 Also see Ritual for Mt. Hazzi
    HH narr. song 13–15, 51
    Storm-god of Aleppo 161–2
Hurtacus 421
Hushai 134n3
Hutena 72
ḫuwaši See baetyls
Huwawa Also see Gilgamesh and Huwawa; Song of Huwawa
Huwawa
    Ballad of Early Rulers 74, 190
    Carchemish 389–90
    Cyclops 55–6
    Epic of Gilgamesh 57–8, 61
        OB 56n12, 73
    Karatepe 389
    local hero 75–6, 431
    Shulgi O 74–5

Song of Gilgamesh 52, 71–2, 75–6
Tell Halaf 389–90
Huwawa episode
    oral transmission to Homeric tradition 55–6
Hyacinthus 233n77
Hyampolis 93
Hydra 252
Hymn to Ishtar (Akkadian) 25–8, 120n36
Hyperboreans 211, 238–9
Hyperoche 238

Ialysus 273–4
Iapetus 285, 292–4
Iarmutti 166
Iasos 274, 340
Iatnana 18, 316–17, 319 Also see Alashiya; Cyprus
Ibbi-Damu 161n53
Ibbit-Lim 161n53
Ibycus 209
ichthyomancy 447n113
Ida, Mt. 12n48, 18, 327–9, 336n23, 436
Idaean Mother 328
Idalion 322
Idrimi 186n91, 381
Igigi-gods 94, 136–7, 145–7
Ikinkalis
    Annals of Hattusili I 112, 157, 162n56
    Ebla 161
    Hazzi, Mt. 157
    location 157n36
    OH historical texts 157–8
    Song of Release 14, 33, 112–13, 116–19, 121–3, 125n57, 126n58, 130, 141–2, 145, 150, 153, 155–6
Iliou proparoithe(n) 401, 433, 454
Illaya 185
Illuyanka 27, 251–5
    Agdistis 343
    Anatolia, north 257–8n171
    Apollo 251
    Apollodorus 255
    Bellerophontes 425
    dating 253n150
    Jason 103–4
    Malatya 257n171
    Nonnus 255
    Oppian 255–6
    purulli festival 252–5
    sea 257–8n171
    Storm-god's battle with snake 103–4
    Typhon 255

Illuyanka (cont.)
   Theogony 285
   Zeus 251, 255
Ilus 190, 287
ᵈIM 162 *Also see* Storm-god
Immashku 184
Inanna 210, 327–8 *Also see* Ishtar
Inanna and Shukaletuda 26
Inanna's Descent 126n58
ᴳᴵˢ ᵈINANNA GAL 156
Inara 253–5, 257n171
Incantation against a Mote (Akkadian) 217n82
Incantation against Infant Illness (Akkadian) 217n82
Incantation against Toothache (Akkadian) 217n82
incantations *Also see* magico-medical incantations
   dactylic hexameter 398n8
Incantations with Luwianisms 214n72
Incense Prayers (Ugarit) 131n77
İncirli 311
indigenous classification of genres *See* genres, indigenous classification
IE (Indo-European)
   Apollo 243
   chariot racing 270n10
   culture, study of 2–3
   Cyclops 106n122
   Dark Earth 43
   dawn goddess 323n102
   deseterjac 428n37
   festivals, competitions, poetry/music, 239–40
   Hittite culture, contribution to 4
   incantations, Tunnawiya 90n53
   invocations 453n133
   languages of gods and men 427–8
   meter 458, 461
   poetic craft, metaphors for 37
   Pytho 258n174
   reciprocity, bard and patron 394n163
   snake-slaying stories 251
   solar myth 107
   Typhon 258n174
Ingira 392n157
Ini-Teshshub 337n31
Inscription of Suppiluliuma II Concerning the Conquest of Alashiya 153, 303n7
intermediaries *Also see* transfer, verbal art
   Anatolians 1, 4–5, 14
   colonies, Old Assyrian merchant *See* colonies, Old Assyrian merchant

Cyprus 1, 13, 17–18, 283–5, 292–5, 298–302, 305–6, 316–17, 324–30, 454
   languages of 5, 52–3
   Eteocypriot 12, 17, 52–3, 309–10, 324, 326
   Euboea 2, 13, 283–5, 294
   dating 299
   Odyssey 295–6
   Hurrian 3, 5
   Mesopotamian culture 4–5, 10
   north Syrian culture 10, 157n34, 186, 258
   Sargonic legends 169, 173n31, 174, 179
   Levant 326
   Luwian 3n7, 4, 11
   Luwic 11, 53
   Lydian 11, 53
   Phoenician 17, 268, 305, 311n52, 322n100, 423n15 *Also see* Phoenician-Greek bards
   Phrygians
      Anatolian narr. song 53, 419
      Trojan War legend 19, 419–20, 429–32, 454
   Syria, north 289–95, 299, 321, 329–30
   west Semitic 4–5
International Style 207, 218
inūma ilū awīlum 136n7
Inventory of Clothing and Fabric 344n61
inverted word order *See* HH narr. song, poetic features
Invocation of Teshshub and Hebat *See* Hurrian Ritual for the Royal Couple
Invocation of Teshshub of Aleppo 162, 185n83, 260
invocations 10, 162, 185n83, 192, 239, 260, 324, 342, 451n127, 452–3 *Also see* pit rituals; *šarrena* ritual
Io
   birth incantations 214–15
   community of Greek-speakers 318
   genealogies 215, 318, 376, 423n14
   journeys 215, 314n63, 318n79
Ion (hero) 293–4
Ion of Chios *FGrH* 115 F 276 435
Ionia 333, 360n46
   Lydia 358
Ionian
   ethnogenesis 332, 360, 414
   migrations 237n92, 359–61, 401, 411, 414, 416, 427, 438
   Athens 235, 237, 360, 404, 416, 444
   Ephesus 357, 360, 444,
   Pylos 404, 422, 438, 444

Subject index

Smyrna 359n41, 412n66
mode 241n108
scale 241n108
Ionians
   Assyrian term 319, 392
   in *Iliad* 411n58
      Phaeacians 296n115
Ionic bards
   and Aeolic bards, competition 19, 395, 396,
      402–12, 417
   ascendant 300
   competitions 412–13
Ionic dialect *Also see* Homeric dialect
   $ā > ē$ 55n8, 463
Ionic, west, forms, Homeric dialect 295n112,
   408
Ionic–Carian bilingual bards, 429
Ionic–Lycian bilingual bards 429 *Also see*
   Greek–Lycian bilingual bards
iron, birthplace of 104
Iron Age
   beginning, dating 267n3
   myth of *See* Ages of Man
iron-working 205, 289, 292, 321
   Cyprus, 275–6, 282–3, 296, 309
Irpitiga 96
Irri[b- 72–3
Isander 378
išḫai-/išḫiya- 37
išḫamāi- 21, 37
Ishhara
   Alalakh 115n10, 323
   Allani 129
   Ebla 114–15
   Emar 115
   Former Gods 95n78, 97n86, 129
   Hattusa 115
   Ishtar 114–15, 139n18, 323
   parents 95, 97
   Shawushka 114–15
   Song of Release 113, 115–16, 129, 131, 139,
      145, 187
   wisdom 113, 131, 187
išḫoni 52n138
^dIŠKUR 162n56 *Also see* Storm-god
Ishtar 120n36, 170, 173–4 *Also see* Anzili,
   Inanna, IŠTAR, Shawushka
   Alalakh 115n10, 323
   Aphrodite 139n18, 323, 325–6, 327
   Cuthean Legend of Naram-Sin 76, 192
   Dumuzi 88n46
   Epic of Gilgamesh 58, 61, 71n75, 325
   Inanna 327

Ishhara 114–15, 139n18, 323
Shawushka 26, 114–15, 213
Israel 134n3, 202–3
   ancestor veneration 150n1
Istaea 435
Istanu *See* Sun-god
Istanuwa 21, 342 *Also see* festival of Istanuwa
IŠTAR *Also see* Ishtar
   Anzili 26, 84, 96
   Elkunirsa and Ashertu 34, 73
   epithet, HH narr. song 43
   HH narr. song, rape of, parallel to *Inanna*
      and Shukaletuda 26
   Song of Gilgamesh 68
   Song of Release 117n22
   IŠTAR of Nineveh 114, 213 *Also see*
      Shawushka
   visit to Amarna 202n10, 347n78
ištarrazil 43
Isthmian games 232–3
iśvaraḥ 304
Ithaca 286n76, 296
itkaḫi/itkalzi rituals 160n48, 162
   Song of Birth 51, 86n36
Itla 81, 82
İvriz 311
Iyandu 95n78
Iyarri 224
Iyas 447

Japeth 293–4, 376
Jason
   Golden Fleece 103–4, 211, 256n161
   Illuyanka 103–4
   journeys 103, 211
Javan 293–4
Jeroboam 134
Jerome
   Chronicle 415n76, 444n97
   Commentary on Ezekiel 38:2 376n113
Josephus, *Antiquities* 1.123 376n113
Joshua *See* Bible
journeys through darkness, Sargonic legends
   171
   Odyssey 105
journeys to edge of world
   Argonautica 103, 211
   Gilgamesh tradition 58, 177, 210–11
      Homeric tradition, entry into 218, 298,
         300
      Odyssey 22, 268, 298, 299n126
   magico-medical rituals 102, 107
   Odyssey 99–103, 103, 177, 211, 298–9

journeys to edge of world (cont.)
  Sargonic legends
    Homeric tradition, entry into 298
    Odyssey 1, 218
  šarrena ritual 185
  solar myth 107
  underworld journeys, equated with 102, 107–8
journeys, long-distance
  Apollo 249
  Arimaspea 211
  Bellerophontes 425
  cosmogonies 216–17
  Crete 215, 238
  Delos 238
  Enmerkar 210n50
  Heracles 210
  historiolae 263
  Io 215, 314n63, 318n79
  Lugalbanda 210
  magico-medical incantations 213, 215
  Ninurta 210
  Shulgi 210n50
  Theseus 238
  valorization, transfer, verbal art 16–17, 107, 167, 200, 209–12, 217–18, 284, 295–9, 425
journeys, long-distance elite interactions, *Odyssey* 295–6
journeys for power 207, 209–10, 216, 295–6
journeys to/across Ocean/sea
  Gilgamesh tradition 58, 69, 99n97
  Hesiod 219
  Io 215
  Odyssey 100, 103
  real-life *Also see* Sea Peoples
    diplomats, 338–9, 377
    theōriai 234, 238
    Tanaya 317
  Sargon 166
  Trojan War 219, 355n25
  The Valorous Sun 209, 303
journeys across space, across time 109, 210–11, 216–18, 284, 295–6
journeys, underworld
  epic, connection to 99
  Gilgamesh tradition 22, 57, 59, 79–80
    Odyssey 101, 216, 298–9
  magico-medical rituals 79–80, 88, 107
  Odyssey
    Anatolian influence 103–7, 109, 298–9
    late addition 14, 105–6, 298–300
  Purification Ritual for the Former Gods 78
jubilee 125n57, 130n70

judge/ruler of dead
  Dumuzi 79
  Gilgamesh 14, 57, 79, 85–6, 109
judges
  Former Kings 154
  šarrena 184
  Sun-god 85, 133, 154
juridical scenarios
  Hittite prayers 69
  HH pit rituals 95–6
  Song of Gilgamesh 68–9
  substitution rituals 69, 154

Kadashman-Enlil I 226
Kadashman-Enlil II 186n91, 213n67
Kadesh 7, 429n41
Kalabaktepe 370n91
Kalipodi 233
Kalkal 145
Kalmyk epic 415
kalû priest 80n12, 397n2
kandaulos 93n63
Kanesh xxx.n1, 5–6, 8, 10, 161n53, 163, 345n66
  Anitta 8n27
  Hieroglyphic Luwian inscriptions 11n40
  Naram-Sin 192n109
  Sargonic legends 169–70, 172, 173n27
Kanesh Eponym Lists xxx.n1
Kantuzzili 10
Kantuzzili's Prayer to the Sun-god 140n20
Karabel pass 336, 343n56
Kara Dağ 159n47, 312n57
Karakalpak bards 49
Karasu River 159n47
Karatepe *Also see* Mopsus
  ancestor stelae 382n134, 384, 386
    Mopsus 384
  ancestor veneration, epic 18, 350, 382–6, 391–2
  Azatiwatayas 386
  battle scenes 384, 386–9
  dating 315–16, 317n76
  Egypt 320n91
  Enkidu 389
  Greeks 392
  HL inscriptions 311, 320, 383, 386
    (A)hiyawa 315–17
  ᵈLAMMA 384, 386 *Also see* Runzas, *below*
  Neo-Hittite polity 7
  nursing goddess 320n91
  orthostats, dating 383–4n141
  Phoenician influence 320n91, 383, 383–4n141, 386

Phoenician inscriptions
   Danuna 315–17
   krntryš 320
   Reshep *ṣprm* 313n61, 249n131
   Phoenician warship 386
   Runzas 249n131, 313, 320
   Storm-god 320, 392
Karkisa 334, 342, 360–1 *Also see* Caria
Karkiya 342
karūiliēš 94, 96n83, 97n88, 154n26 *Also see*
      Former Gods; Former Kings
ka-ru-to 228
Kaska 6, 123, 278n44
   Nerik 252
KASKAL.KUR
   Hattusa 89–92, 153
   Troy 90n55
Kastama 258n171
katabasis See journeys, underworld
Katakekaumene 343
Kayalıpınar 7n21
Kaymançı 337n28
Kazanlı 314
Keftiu 317n78
   magico-medical incantations 213
Kel Dağ 258n173
Kella 252
Keret, *rapa ʾum* 290
Keret 87n42, 290, 382n139 *Also see*
      Concordance of Tablets at Ugarit
   type scenes, hospitality scenes 143n26
KEŠDA, song 37
ke-se-ni-wi-jo 271
Keshshi 28 *Also see Song of Keshshi*
Keteioi 374n103
khalups 104
Khorsabad Annals 392n157
KI.LAM festival 151n8, 220, 222–5, 229
   cultural contact/mixing 224
   ritual drama 223–4, 343
kibisis 425n21
Kiklipatalli 184
Kilamuwa/Kulamuwa 380
Kili-Teshshub 352n10
Kilise Tepe 319n85
kināru 156n32, 324
Kinet Höyük 319n85
king lists
   Anatolia, west 375–8
   cosmogonies 15, 291–2
   Ebla 119, 150, 190–1
   genealogies 15, 167, 190, 196, 291, 378
   Hittite 151–2

kispum 188n95
Mari 186
Mesopotamian 188–9, 197n119, 290
Song of Release 119, 150, 190–1
Ugarit 150n2, 290
world history 167
King Lists 151n10, 156n31
kings, deified
   šarrena ritual 183–7
   stars 150
kingship
   Baal Cycle 261
   Chaoskampf 16, 183, 185, 250–61
   Egypt 289
   exotic goods 207–9
   Former Kings 130, 149, 152–5
   (*ḫ*)*išuwa* festival 260–1
   Hittite court 164–5, 258–61
   HH narr. song 50
   Iliad 33–4
   International Style 207, 218
   scepters 207, 422
   Song of Release 33–4, 135, 138–9, 160
   Storm-god 16, 152, 155, 259–60, 261n191
   Storm-god of Aleppo 162–5, 251–2, 259–61
   transfer
      festivals 16, 251, 259–60, 261
      gods 164
      verbal art 4, 16, 218, 251, 260, 391
   Works and Days, Ages of Man 289
   Zeus 250n136, 422
kingship in heaven 188–9, 266, 291–2
   Storm-god 24–7, 97n89, 127, 184–5, 260, 292
   Zeus 290–2
ki-ni-di-ja 345
LÚ*kinirtallaš* 36
kinor 156n32
Kirua 392n157
Kish
   Gilgamesh 134
   Sargonic legends 167, 178
Kiskilussa 254, 257n171
kispum 149–50, 152, 155, 186, 197
   ancestor statues 150, 186
   king lists 188n95
Kition 307n28, 322, 323n103
Kizzuwatna 313 *Also see* Cilicia, Plain
   dynastic marriages 156–7, 164, 258, 260, 347
   Hittite hegemony 6, 10, 156–7, 164, 258, 303, 313
   Luwian-Hurrian blend 10, 147, 157, 260
   Mittani 313
   Qode 356n26

Kizzuwatna (cont.)
  source
    festivals 260–1
    Hurrian influence 10, 86, 156–7, 164
    rituals 10, 86, 213
Kızıl Irmak 6, 311 *Also see* Halys River
Kızıldağ 312, 374
Klopedi 359n42
Knobbed Ware 362
Knossos
  BA 230, 242, 286, 462
    festivals 228–9
  EIA 281n55, 282, 284, 321
knot, denoting song 37
Kom el Hetan 317n78
Kommos 322–3n100
Köroğlu 48
korunētērios 320, 392
Kothar 143n26, 325n110
Kouklia 276, 314n63
Kourion 169n10, 319
ko-wa 230
Kreophyleioi 416n76
krntryš 320, 386
KUB 8.62 78, 81–5, 98–9
  Purification Ritual for the Former Gods 79, 95, 98–9
Kubaba 234n81, 328, 358n38
Kukkunni 362
Kültepe *See* Kanesh
Kululu 311, 374, 381
Kumarbi *Also see* Kumarbi cycle
  Atrahasis (Hittite) 31
  Dagan 51n131
  Enlil 30
  epithet, HH narr. song 43
  HH pit rituals 81, 84
  mother of Storm-god 162, 185n83
  šarrena 185
  Song of Birth 25, 45, 121n44, 131n77
  Song of Hedammu 25–6, 40, 123n49, 127–8
  Song of Ullikummi 26
  wisdom 131n77
Kumarbi cycle 1, 24–7 *Also see* cosmogonies; Song of Birth; Song of Hedammu; Song of Ullikummi
  Atrahasis 31
  dating 35
  festivals 256–7
  Hattusa, arrival at 258
  historiolae 51
  Homeric Hymn to Apollo 25
  Homeric Hymns 24

  HH narr. song 13
  HH rituals 51
  kingship 260
  Lake Van 258
  linguistic differences between members 25n15
  Sargonic legends 167, 184–5
  šarrena ritual 184–6
  Song of Huwawa 73
  Theogony 13, 22, 24–5, 147, 285
Kummani 10, 162n57
Kummi
  location 25n16
  Teshshub, home of 25n16
Kummuh 7, 373
kumra priest 252
kunkunuzzi stone 50, 117, 121
Kupanta-Kurunta 336, 337, 340
  Sapinuwa 339n39
ku-pi-ri-jo 303n5
Kura 159, 320n90
kurša 246
  Golden Fleece 103–4, 211
  kibisis 425n21
  purulli 252n140
Kurşunlu Tepe 437
Kurunta (god) 249 *Also see* Runzas
Kurunta (person) 213n67, 312, 312–13n57, 337
Kuşaklı 7
Kushuh 28, 183–4
Kutamuwa 380n124
Kutiladu 121n42
Kuwaliya *See* Mira
kuwayaralla 261
Kuzi-Teshshub (king) 310
Kuzi-Teshshub (scribe) 157n34
Kyrgyz epic 415

Labarna 156
Lacedaemonian's son 231
ladders, HH pit rituals 81, 94–5
Laestrygonians 79, 102, 299n127
lagar priests 97n87
Lagash 188
Lake Gygaea *See* Gygaean Lake
Lake Urmia 117n21
Lake Van 258
lallarum 184n81
lamaštu 425n21
Lament for Sumer and Ur 191n105
lamentation-priests 80n12, 184, 397n2
laments, city 397n2

ᵈLAMMA 245 *Also see Song of LAMMA*
   Apollo 243–9, 319–20, 447, 450
   Artemis 447
   Carchemish 27, 306
   Hermes 447
   Karatepe 384, 386
   Kurunta 250
   Miletus, BA 248–9, 341
   Reshep 313, 319–20
   Runzas 249, 313, 319–20
ᵈLAMMA ŠA *kurša* 244n121
ᵈLAMMA ŠA LÍL 45
Lamus River 312, 313
Land of Fifty 30n43 *Also see* Hamsha
Lane Fox, Robin 2n2, 199n1, 209n48, 256, 257n167, 258n173, 295n112, 300n129, 312n55, 315n71, 382, 423n15
languages of gods and men 427–8
Laodameia 378, 423n14
Laodice 238
Larissa 359n43, 405, 451
larnakes 91–2, 269, 270n10, 272
Latacz, Joachim 3, 266n1, 333n6, 335n15, 339n41, 352–4, 399n16, 401n22, 406n37
LH IIIC pottery
   Cyprus 276n40, 404
   Troy 362
LH IIIC:1b pottery
   Cilicia 313–15
   Cyprus 307
   Sea Peoples 307, 313–15
   Tarsus 314
Late New Hittite 8
Latmus, Mt. 234n81, 442n87
Lazpa 338n37, 359 *Also see* Lesbos
   transfer, gods 202, 346–7
Lebanon, Mt. 58, 74n89, 175n39
Lefkandi *Also see* Euboea
   contact with/interest in east 268, 280–3
   continuity 274, 404
   Grey Ware 365, 372
   heirlooms, connection to past 268, 281–2
   hero cult 281
   Homeric burials 281–2, 284
   Homeric tradition 295n112
   Troy 372
   Works and Days, Ages of Man 289
Legend of Kosovo 47
Legend of the Queen of Kanesh 20
legends, definition 168n7
Lelantine War 398, 414n69

Leleges 12, 360, 422n13, 438n72
Lelwani 151, 154
   purulli 253
Lemnian language 361–2
Lemnos 297, 345, 361, 372n95
Lenaea 235
Leodamas 413–14n69
Lesbian
   dialect 405–9, 411 *Also see* Aeolic dialect
   epic 406–7, 410, 412
   poetry 329
Lesbians, Troad 409
Lesbos *Also see* Lazpa; Lesches; Terpander
   Aeolian 329, 359
   Aphrodite 324
   continuity 359
   Hera 329
   Iliad 353, 411
   Mycenaeans 272, 340n44
   Myrsilus 374
   transfer, verbal art 325, 329
   Trojan War legend 406–7
Lesches of Pyrrha, *Little Iliad* F 30 West 407n41
Leto 236, 237, 288, 320n91, 447
Letter from Amenhotep III to Tarhuntaradu of Arzawa 335
Letter from Ammurapi to the King of Alashiya (Ugarit) 303n5
Letter from an Official in Alashiya to Ammurapi (Ugarit) 305–6
Letter from Arzawa to Amenhotep III 335
Letter from Benti-Sharruma to Ammurapi (Ugarit) 315n71
Letter from Eshuwara, Pidduri of Alashiya, to Ammurapi (Ugarit) 304n13
Letter from Hattusili III to Kadashman-Enlil 186n91, 213n67
Letter from Kadashman-Enlil I to Amenhotep III (Amarna) 226
Letter from Ramses II to Hattusili III 213n67
Letter from Ramses II to Kupanta-Kurunta of Mira-Kuwaliya 340
Letter from Suppiluliuma II to Ammurapi (Ugarit) 315n71
Letter from the King of Ahhiyawa to the Hittite King 335
Letter from the King of Alashiya to Amenhotep III (Amarna)
   EA 37 303n5
   EA 39 303n9
Letter from the King of Alashiya to Ammurapi (Ugarit) 303n5

Levant *Also see* Syria, north; west Semitic
  ancestor statues 272
  Cyprus 304–5, 308
  Euboea 282, 295, 321
  intermediaries 326
  mortuary feasting 150n1, 274n33
  Mycenaean vessels 207–8
  necromancy 101n101
  Sea Peoples 274, 315
  trade 295, 300n129
Levantine
  goods, Shaft Graves 207
  Javan, term for westerners 293
  sorcerers, *Elkunirsa and Ashertu* 216
Leviticus *See* Bible
Libya 207, 215
Libya (heroine) 215n77
Libyan War Stele from Kom el-Ahmar (Menuf) 315n70
Liluri 159, 160n48
Linear B *Also see* Index of Linear B Inscriptions
  dialect 308–9n37, 462
'lion', Walmu 362
lion gate, Mycenae 346
lions
  Chimera 424
  fear of
    Cuthean Legend of Naram-Sin 195
    Ritual of Allaiturahhi 51, 155
  Gurgum 374
  predators 270
  Pylos 228
  Sandas 424
  similes
    Cuthean Legend of Naram-Sin 194
    Epic of Gilgamesh 62
    Hattusili I 176
    Homeric 418
    Sargon 176 *Also see* Sargon the Lion
  slaying
    Assurnasirpal II 391
    Carchemish 390
    Gilgamesh tradition 71, 389
    Song of Oil 34
lists
  Ballad of Early Rulers 190
  dynastic *See* dynastic lists
  šarrena ritual 187–8
  world history 187–91, 196
Lithophoros 242n113
liver divination *See* extispicy
Liver Oracles 162n57, 260, 346
living rock 152–3, 447–8 *Also see* baetyls

local courts
  competition 6
  world history 15, 174, 185, 196–7, 394
local history, world history 196
Locrians 411n58
London Medical Papyrus (BM 10059) 213
long-distance elite interactions
  dynastic marriages 215, 374, 422
  Euboea 268, 281
  Melampous 204
  Odyssey 17, 296–8
    journeys 295–6
  Protogeometric Greece 17, 268, 281, 283–5
  transfer, performers 200
  valorization, post-palatial Greece 275
  verbal art 16, 280–1, 296–8, 302
long-distance journeys *See* journeys, long-distance
Lord, Albert 39, 42n87
Lower Land (Hittite) 310, 447n111
LÚ.DINGIR.RA 32–3
Lugal-e 210n52
Lugalbanda and the Anzud Bird 210n50
Lugalbanda
  ancestor statues 58
  ancestor veneration 58, 79
  Ballad of Early Rulers 188
  fairy tale motifs 22n9
  Gilgamesh, father of 58, 79, 80n11, 210n50
  journeys 210
  Shulgi 80n11
Lugalzagesi 177n48
Lukka *Also see* Lycia
  Ahhiyawa 339, 441
  area 334, 447
  Assuwa confederation 334–5n14, 443n93
  Hiyawans 316n71, 441n83
Lullu
  HH rituals 160n49, 184
  location 117n21
  Sargonic legends 184
  šarrena ritual 184
  Song of Release 117
Luwian
  bilingual bards 52
  Hieroglyphic *See* Hieroglyphic Luwian
  incantations 21, 90n53
  songs 21, 32, 163, 363, 400, 453
  texts, at Hattusa 9, 11
Luwian Moon Incantation 21n4
Luwian-Hurrian, BA Cilicia 10, 147

Luwians
  BA 5, 11
  Cilicia, EIA 256, 314
  intermediaries 3n7, 11, 44
Luwic 11n43, 11–12n44
  intermediaries 11, 53
Lycaon 443n93
Lycaonia 447n111
Lycia *Also see* Lukka; Ulu Burun
  continuity 446–8
  Homeric Hymn to Apollo 243
  Iliad 418, 442
  Rhodes 429, 440–1
  yanar 424n20
Lycian
  ancestor veneration 420, 438–9
  Apollo 447, 452–3
  epic *See* Bellerophontes; Sarpedon
  giants, Tiryns 346n71
  gods 446–7
  hero cult 445–9
    epic 420
  Iliad, influence 423–6, 432, 438–43, 454
  language 11, 356
  migrations 19, 440n82, 441, 443
  poets, Olen 238–9
  tombs 446, 448
  Zeus 446
Lycian–Greek bilingual bards 426, 438–49
Lycian–Ionic bilingual bards 429
Lycians
  ethnonyms 443n92
  Iliad 420–1, 423–6 *Also see* Bellerophontes; Glaucus; Sarpedon
    catalog of Trojan allies 442–3
    Zeleians 443
  Sea Peoples 443n93
  shared legendary past with Greeks 19, 332
Lycophron 772, Σ; 806, Σ 75n98
Lydia
  continuity 356
  Ephesus 358n39, 361n52
  Ionia 358
  Magog 376
  Seha River Land 336–7, 358
  Typhon 343
Lydian
  ancestor veneration, royal 375–6
  dynastic lists 350, 375, 376–8, 441n84
  dynastic names 350, 352, 374–6
  kandaulos 93n63
  meter 428n38

  mode 241n108
  necropolis 376
  poets, Olympus 250
  scale 241n108
  Pelops 422
  Tantalus 422, 430
  Trojan language 361–2, 430
Lydian–Aeolic bilingual bards 429
Lydian–Greek bilingualism 93n63, 427
Lydians
  Amazons, epics 105
  destroy Ionian cities 416n76
  Ephesus 360
  intermediaries 11, 53
  migrations 361
  shared past with Greeks 332
Lydus 376
Lykios, Apollo 447, 452n132
lyres 36, 144, 156, 227, 240, 276, 279, 325n110, 384, 415n72
  divinized 324
Lyrnessus 411n62
Lysimachus 436

mace, Storm-god of Aleppo 257, 320
Maddunassa 361n54
Madduwatta 337
Madduwatta Indictment 318, 336
mādi 131, 187
madōli 184
Maeonia 243, 361n54 *Also see* Lydia
  Lydia 358, 430
Maeonians, *Iliad* 241n111, 376, 421, 430, 442n90
Magan 166
magic, Late Antique 99, 214
magico-medical incantations *Also see* birth incantations; ghost prescriptions; historiolae; incantions
  Branchus hymn 242–3
  Cretan 213
  Former Kings 154–5
  Gilgamesh 79, 85
  HH, curses 98, 121n41, 126
  journeys, long-distance 213, 215
magico-medical rituals *Also see* pit rituals; purification rituals; scapegoat rituals; substitution rituals
  Anatolian 89, 90n53
  ancestor veneration 218
  cosmogonies 213–14, 216–17, 262
  exotic goods 213–15
  historiolae 262–3

magico-medical rituals (cont.)
   HH *See ambašši* rituals; *Elkunirsa and Ashertu*; *itkaḫi/itkalzi* rituals; pit rituals; *Ritual of Allaiturahhi*; *Ritual of Mastigga*; *Ritual of Shalashu*; *Ritual of the Hurrian Woman Ashdu*
   journeys to edge of world 102, 107
   Luwian *See Ritual of Hantitassu*; *Ritual of Puriyanni*; *Ritual of Tunnawiya*
   Mesopotamian *See* Cow-Maiden; Dumuzi; Gilgamesh; maqlû
   solar myth 107
   transfer, verbal art 4, 13–14, 200, 213–18, 248, 450–1
   underworld journeys 79–80, 88, 107
Magna Graecia 296n115
Magna Mater 328
Magnes 105
Magnesia 438, 451n130
Magog 376
magoi 216n81, 418
Maharastri 407n43
maiden songs 32–3 *Also see* Delian girls
ma-ka 230
Makar 411n58
Mala River 66, 177n47 *Also see* Euphrates
Malatya 7, 310, 382n134
   continuity 257, 312
   Storm-god, snake 257, 259
Malaziti 338n33
Maliya 447
Mallus 318
Mami 114
Man of the Staff 254
Manas 415
ma-na-sa 286
Manishtushu 185
   fictional ancestor 186n90
mantis 199 *Also see* augurs; seers
Manuzzi, Mt. 160n48, 260
Map of the World 210
   obv. 10′ 171n21
maqlû ritual 85
Maraş 380n126
Marat Su River 177n50
Marduk 29n35
Marhashi 173n27
Mari 10, 161n53, 166, 170, 175, 176n42
   abu festival 87
   diplomats 156n33, 226
   kispum 155, 186
   muštawûm 37
   nārum 37
   performers, imported 209
   prophets 201n4, 202–3
   šarru 182n71
   Storm-god's battle with sea 257
Mari Eponym Chronicle xxx.n1, 155, 186
Maris 440
Marmara Gölü 376
Masa 224, 334, 342, 343
   Maeonia 361n54
   Mysia 334n8
Maşat 7
Masduri 337
   Sapinuwa 339n39
Mashuiluwa 337
mašmaššu priest 80
Massanuzzi 337
Mastigga *See Ritual of Mastigga against Family Quarrel*
māt Gugi 376
Matar Kubeleya 234n81, 328n127
ma-te-re te-i-ja 346
materia magica, silver 52
Meander River 336, 338, 442
medicine *See* doctors; healers; magico-medical rituals; pharmaka
Medusa 425n21
Megarians 409n51
Megiddo 57
Meki *Also see Song of Release*, assembly
   Ebla 161n53
   meaning 161n53
   purification ritual 155
   Song of Release 122
      historical king 355
      star of Ebla 116n17, 120, 150, 161
      tenth king of Ebla 118–19
Melampous 202, 204, 212
Meleager 28
Meles 355
Melesigenes 379
Melia/Melite 413n69
Melian War 413–14n76, 444n97
melku 161n53
memiškiwan daiš 42, 81, 174n33
memories of Hittites, EIA west Anatolia 374
memory, collective 17, 197n119, 268, 332, 347
memory, continuity
   Anatolia, west 18, 332, 341
   dynastic lists 18, 196
   Syro-Anatolia, EIA 349, 373–4
Men 358n38
Menander Rhetor 334.31–2 Spengel 324n104

Menelaus 146, 282, 297n117, 330, 407
  hero cult 286n76
Mentes 296
m^erappîm 17, 285, 290, 302
merchants *See* traders
The Merchants' Tale 172n25
Meriones 282, 378
Mermnads 352, 375, 430n43
Merneptah 315, 443n93
Merope 291n102
meropes 266, 289–92
Meropie 290n97, 291n102
Merops 290n96, 291n102
merops (bird) 291n102
Mersin 319n85
Mesopotamian
  bilingual bards 52–3
  cosmogonies 29–30
  culture, Hurrians, intermediaries 4–5, 10
  festivals *See abu*; *akītu*
  Hittite culture, contribution to 4
  king lists, 188–9, 197n119, 290
  oral tradition 42
  scribal training 32, 60, 181, 196
  seers 192, 196, 201, 205
  wisdom literature, at Hattusa 33
messenger scenes *See* type scenes
metal trade *See* copper; iron
meter *Also see* dactylic hexameter
  Aeolic 458–9
  HH narr. song 46
  IE 458, 461
  isomoraic 401–2, 458–9, 461–2 *Also see* dactylic hexameter
  isosyllabic 458–60 *Also see* dactylic hexameter
  Mesopotamian epic 46
  Sappho 458n2
  Stesichorus 458n2
me-tu-wo ne-wo 227n36
Mezzulla 159
Midas 105n119, 240n108, 328, 357, 435
  dynastic name 357–8
Midas I and II 435n58
middle chronology xxx.n1, 6
Middle Hittite 6, 7–8
Middle Script 8
Midea 269, 274–5
midwives 51, 184n76 *Also see* birth incantations
migrations *Also see* colonization; settlement
  at end of BA 12, 393 *Also see* Sea Peoples
  Carians 19, 442

Greek
  to Anatolia 234–5, 242, 267, 352–3, 419, 421, 432, 454 *Also see* Aeolian migrations; Ionian migrations
  to Cilicia *See* Cilicia
  to Cyprus *See* Cyprus
  Protogeometric period 278, 356–7, 402, 463 *Also see* Aeolian migrations; Ionian migrations
  Lycians 19, 440n82, 441, 443
  Lydians 361
  Phrygians 357–8, 361, 362–3, 423
Milawanda *See* Miletus, BA
Milawatta *See* Miletus, BA
Milawatta Letter 340–1
Milesian author, *Argonautica* 103
Milesian stage 353, 420, 437–45, 452–4
Milesians
  in LB tablets 231
  at Thebes, BA, festival 231, 346
Miletus
  Apollo 248–9, 444, 452 *Also see* Apollo Didymeus, Philesius, Phylius
  Carians 358n39, 422n13, 440
  continuity 357, 360
  cross-cultural contact 360
Miletus, BA
  dynastic marriages, Ahhiyawa 339
  ^dLAMMA 248–9, 341
  Mycenaeans 231, 272–4, 337–41, 344, 353, 358
Miletus, EIA
  Black Sea colonies 103
  festivals *See* festivals, EIA Greek
  founders
    Glaucids 429, 438–9
    Neleids 241, 338, 413–14, 422n13, 438–9, 444
    Sarpedon 422–3, 438
  Greco-Anatolian bards 429
  Homeric Hymn to Apollo 243
  Iliad 353, 442
  Minoans 423n14, 440n82
  Minos 359, 423n14
  Panionia 353, 413–14n76, 444
  destroyed by Persians 444
  Scepsis 412n63, 436–7
  stone circles 370
  temple of Athena 370n91
Miletus (Crete), *Iliad* 231n69, 422–3, 442
Miletus (hero) 423n14
Milyans 11, 443n92
Mimnermus F 9.6 West 412n66

Minki 95n78, 96, 97n86
Minoan settlement 340n44, 423n14, 440n82
Minos 273, 359, 423n14
Mira(-Kuwaliya) 343
mi-ra-ti-jo 346
Misis *See* Mopsou Hestia
Mita 357, 435
Mita of Pahhuwa 357–8n35
Mitanni 6, 10
   Cyprus 304
   Indic names 304, 352n10
   Kizzuwatna 313
   seal in Euboea 275
Mitanni Letter 9
Moab 202n11
Molpoi decree 241, 440
molpoi procession 241–2
Molus 282n63
month names
   EIA Greek 234–5
   Mycenaean 226–7
Moon Omen Compendium 157n34
Moon-god *Also see* Arma, Kushuh
   HH narr. song 28, 71, 125n55
   Ugarit 163
The Moon-god and the Cow 214n72
Mopsou Hestia 382–3
Mopsus
   ancestor, fictional 315, 382–3, 392–3, 448–9
   ancestor stelae 384
   ancestor veneration 384, 448–9
   father
      Apollo 318n81
      Rhacius 318n81
   founder 18, 317–19
   Greco-Anatolian hero 18, 350, 379, 382, 420
mo-qo-so 318
morphological stretching 460
Morris, Sarah P. 2, 3n6, 34n55, 229, 234n81, 238n100, 243n119, 249n130, 272, 296n117, 320n91, 322–3n100, 334–5n14, 345n68, 346nn73–75, 346n77, 352, 360n47, 397
mortuary feasting, Levant 274n33
   Funerary Ritual in Poetic Form (Ugarit) 150n1
mortuary offerings, Gilgamesh tradition 58, 79
mortuary rituals *Also see* cremation
   Boeotia, BA 270, 281
   chariots 270, 278, 281, 286, 322
   Cyprus, EIA, "Homeric" 308, 321–2
   Egypt 272

Epic of Gilgamesh, performance of 80, 155, 186
Hittite, royal
   Homeric 284n73, 399n17
   supralocal audience 156
Mycenaean 269–70
   cultural contact/mixing 272–3
   post-palatial Greece 274
   transfer, verbal art 267
mother goddess 234
Mother of the Gods 447 *Also see ma-te-re te-i-ja*
mountain god, eagle 159, 160n48
mountains *See* Adalur; Adarwan; Amanus; Armarik; Casius; Ğebel al-Aqra; Ğebel Seman; Hazzi; Ida; Latmus; Lebanon; Manuzzi; Namni; Olympus; Parnassus; Pishaisha; Sapon; Silver; Sipylus; Sirara; Sirion; Taurus; Tmolus
   battle with Storm-god 26
   home of gods 74
   landmarks 74
   rain 255
mouvance 39
mugawars 82, 93, 192, 238, 246 *Also see* disappearing gods
   formulas, HH narr. song 43
   Jason 103–4
muhhû(tu) 201
Mujo and Halil 47–8
Mukish 86, 90n53, 160n48
Mukishanu 51, 128
Muksus 318 *Also see* Mopsus
Mursili, dynastic name 374–5
Mursili I
   ancestor 151
   Babylon, capture xxx.n1, 6, 30n41, 171n19
   Ebla 112, 165n71
Mursili II 6, 253, 336–9, 346
Mursili II concerning the Tawananna Affair 115n10
Mursili III 312, 312–13n57, 352n10, 374
Müsgebi 272, 274, 340
Mushki 357, 435
musical performances, festivals
   Greek, EIA 238–42
   Hittite 222–5, 260
   Mycenaean 227, 231
musical scores, Ugarit 306n25
muštawûm 37
Muttallu 374
Muwattalli
   dynastic name 359, 374–5
Mytilene 359

Muwattalli II 7, 253, 312, 335, 337, 340, 352n10
Muwatti 337
Mycale, Mt. 442, 444
Mycenae
   BA 269–70, 272, 274–6, 346
      Ahhiyawa 333n6
      lion gate 346
      Shaft Graves 207, 345
   Geometric period 370n91
   Iliad 288
Mycenaean Greece 231, 345–6 *Also see*
      Index of Linear B Texts
   Anatolians in
   ancestor statues 270–2
   ancestor veneration 268–73
   epic 271–2, 273
      Homeric 266, 403–4, 461
      Trojan War 352–3, 401, 416–17
   festivals *See* festivals, Mycenaean
   frescos, at Hattusa 346
   hero cult 17, 279, 285–6, 291–2
   month names 226–7
   mortuary rituals 269–70, 272–3
   pit rituals 91–2
   ruins, cult sites 287–8, 369–70
   settlements
      Ahhiyawa 339–40, 358
      Anatolia, west 320, 340
   sword, Hattusa 341
   vessels, exotic goods 207–8, 344–5
Mycenaeans
   Ahhiyawa 3
   Ephesus 272, 338n35, 340
   Lesbos 272, 340n44
   Miletus 272–4, 337–41, 344, 353, 358
   Rhodes 272–3, 340
   Smyrna 340
   Troy 274, 340, 344–5
   Ulu Burun 316n71
Mylasa 234n81
Myrina 451
Myrsilus (Lesbian) 374
Myrsilus (Lydian) 352, 375n105
Myrsus 352, 375n105
Myrtilus 374
Mysia 334n8
Mysians 406
Mytalis, dynastic name 375
Mythological Fragments 35
   battle between Storm- god and mountains 26
   Hurrian *Song of Birth* 25n16, 51
Mytilene 359, 409–10

nābûm 201n4
Nagar 169n10 *Also see* Nawar
Nagy, Gregory 23n10, 37, 63n32, 107n130,
      201n7, 212, 233, 235n83, 237n93,
      238n97, 240n105, 247n128, 251n137,
      262n195, 264, 266n1, 286n76,
      297n119, 298n121, 323n102,
      329n129, 351n9, 379n122, 398n11,
      400, 401n22, 403n26, 406n37,
      407n41, 408n43, 408n45, 409n48,
      409n51, 410nn53–57, 411nn59–62,
      412nn63–64, 412n66, 413n69,
      414–15n72, 415, 416, 428n38,
      436n61, 444n95, 445n102, 446,
      449–50, 451, 458nn1–2, 458–9n3,
      459, 460n6, 461n9, 462n14
Nahma/izule 71n73, 73–4
Namni, Mt. 26, 183
Namshara 95n78, 96
Namtar 97n87, 138, 142
^LÚNAR (Hittite) 36–7, 162–3
   Song of Release 36, 111
Nara 95n78, 96
Naram-Sin *Also see Gula-AN and the Seventeen
      Kings*; Sargonic legends
   Akkade, destruction of 76, 185n86, 191n106,
      354 *Also see* Curse of Akkade;
      Cuthean Legend of Naram-Sin
   ancestor, fictional 186
   ancestor veneration 178–9, 186
   bull, slays 174
   Cedar Forest 175
   Chronicle of the Single Monarchy 188
   Curse of Akkade 76, 191n106, 431, 433
   Cyprus 169n10
   Cythera 169n10
   Ebla 160–1, 175
   Gilgamesh 174–5
   Hahhu 176n45
   Hattusa 21, 191–2
   Hector 1, 15, 166–7, 191, 193–5, 355–6, 414,
      420, 433, 437, 454
   historical omens 168
   HH narr. song 15, 182, 190
   kispum 155, 186n90
   Nagar 169n10
   rivers, crossing 177n48
   šarrena ritual 184
   Sargon
      foil for 167–8, 185n86
      son of 185n86
   Silver Mountain 52
Naram-Sin 2 ii 7–15 177n48

Naram-Sin 23.9–14 174n36
Naram-Sin 25.1–16 175n37
Naram-Sin 26 175n40, 180n60
   i 21–9 175n37
Naram-Sin 27 175n40
Naram-Sin 29 rev. 3′–7′ 177n48
   rev. 8′–10′ 175n38
Naram-Sin 1001 180n60
Naram-Sin 1004 175n40
Naram-Sin 2005 175n40
Naram-Sin and the Enemy Hordes
   191n108
Naram-Sin in Asia Minor 21, 178n52, 192n109
Naram-Sin inscription, OB copy ix 32–x 14
   178n52
Naram-Sin legends
   Anatolian influence/focus 192
   --Hittite 191
   Homeric tradition, entry into 355–6, 419,
      430–5, 437–8, 454
nārum 37, 263n198 *Also see* ᴸᵁNAR
narûs 168, 178–9, 191–2n108
Nasatyas 107
Nastes 442–3
nāvî 201n4
Nawar 173n31, 183
Nawar-tahe 173n31, 183n74
Naxos 274, 287, 413n67
necromancy 89, 98n94, 99–102, 105, 108
necropolis, Lydian 376
negative reactions *See* type scenes
Neileus 438, 439n73, 444n95
   fictional ancestor 413–14
Neleids
   founders, Miletus 241, 413–14, 422n13, 438,
      439n73, 444
   Homeric tradition 413–14
   Iliad 398, 440, 444–5
   Sarpedon 440, 453
Neleus 204 *Also see* Neileus; Neleids
Nemean games 232
Neo-Hittite, Hatti 7, 311–12
Neo-Hittites 7, 294, 393
Neon Ilion 410, 437, 451
Neon Teichos 451
Neoptolemus 406, 407n41
Nerak 252n143
Nergal 126, 152, 243n119
Nerik
   Kaska 252
   Oymaağaç 7n21
   purulli festival 252–4, 257–8n171
   Storm-god 93n68, 121n42, 252–3

Nerikkil 252n143
Nesa *See* Kanesh
nešili 5
Nestor
   ancestor, fictional 444–5
   in Homeric epic 120n36, 291n102, 355,
      397–9, 407, 413–14, 444–5
   Pylian epic 355
   solar myth 107n130
   waking for message 146
Nestor's Cup 397–8
Neti 97n87
New Hittite 6–8
New Script 8
New Year's festival *Also see* akītu; purulli
   Apollo 250n136 *Also see below*, Miletus
   Miletus, EIA 241–3, 440
   Ugarit 151n9
New Year's Festival 152n13
Nicandre inscription 413n67
Nichoria 370n91
Nicias 238n96
Nicolaus of Damascus *FGrH* 90 FF 46–7, 374
   FF 52–3 413–14n69
   F 62 105
Nimion 442
Nimrud 390–1
NIN.DINGIR 255
Ninatu 183
Nindashuruma 97n87
Nindukuga 97n87
Nineveh 10, 191, 215, 377, 389n151
   performers, imported 209
   Shawushka 114, 174, 202n10, 213, 215,
      323n102, 347n78
   Song of Release 113, 116
Ningishzida 79, 97n87
Ninki 97n87
Ninmul 97n87
Ninsun 57, 65, 80n11
Ninurta
   battle with monster 114
   bull, slays 114
   Chaoskampf 210
   Heracles 210
   journeys 210
Ninurta's Exploits 210n52
Ninurta's Return to Nibru 210n52
Ninus 376
Niobe 422, 430
Nippur 56, 76, 185n86, 186n90
Niqmaddu III 303
Nişantepe 153, 448

Noah 29, 292–3
Nonnus, *Dionysiaca* 1.137–2.569 255
   18.289–305 314n63
North Wind 190
nostoi 273, 422
   Cyprus 322, 324
Nostoi 318n81, 379
Nostoi arg. 2 West 393n159
Notium 451
Nuhashshe 113, 157n34, 158
nuntarriyašḫaš festival 259
   hegemony 222
   KI.LAM festival 222n11, 223n18
Nur-Dagan 171n21, 173n31, 179
Nur-daggal 171n21, 172, 173, 210n53
Nurdahhi 173 n31
nursing goddess 320n91
Nusku 30, 137, 145–6
Nuzi 10, 182n71, 197n118
Nymphaeus 214n69
nymphs 242, 376, 435 *Also see* springs

Oannes 188n97
oath gods 447n113
'ôb 86, 89 *Also see* pit rituals
Oberstadt, Hattusa 32, 111, 153
Ocean
   Cimmerians 106
   crossing, Gilgamesh tradition 58, 99n97
   god 55n8 *Also see* Pontus; Sea; Tiamat
   journey to, *Odyssey* 100, 103
Odysseus 286n76 *Also see* Odyssey
   Iliad
      embassy scene 144
         waking for message 146
      Penelope killed by 75n98
      Zeus, descended from 101n103, 146
Oechalia 203n16, 416n76
Oenoanda 447n111
Oenomaus 374n105, 422n10
Oenopes 241, 435
Oenopion 435
"The Offenses of Seha River Land"
   335n17, 341
Offering and Prayer for the Storm-god of Nerik
   93n68
Offerings for Royal Statues 151n10, 152n12
Og 293
Ōgugios 292–3
Ogygia 293n106
Ogygus 293
Oikhalias Halosis 416n76
oimē 37

oimos 37
Old Assyrian Sargon Legend 169–70, 173n27,
   303
   41–3 171n21
   51 184n80
   62 176, 184n80
Old Assyrian trading colonies *See* colonies, Old
   Assyrian merchant
Old Babylonian Catalog from Nippur (N2)
   75n97
Old Babylonian Catalog from Urim (U1) 75n97
Old Babylonian Catalog from Urim (U2) 75n97
Old Babylonian Catalog in the Louvre (L)
   75n97
Old Hittite 8
Old Kingdom, Hittite 6
Old Script 8
Old Women 86, 90n53, 93n67, 182, 238
   Circe 101
Olen 238–9, 263
Olympian games 232–3, 422n10
Olympianization 449n122
Olympus (poet) 240, 250, 263
Olympus, Mt. 27, 144n29
Omen Compendium Concerning the "Presence"
   157n34
omens 9, 28, 33–4, 34, 60, 98, 140–2, 154, 157,
   167–8, 191–4, 196, 244, 434 *Also see*
   dreams; extispicy
   historical 168
Omphale 377n117, 378
One Thousand and one Arabian Nights 54n2
openings *Also see* prooimia
   Cypria 138, 288n87, 301, 325
   Epic of Gilgamesh 59, 64–5, 178
   HH narr. song 36, 65, 113
      Song of Birth 50, 96–7
      Song of Gilgamesh 36n66, 54, 64–5
      Song of Release 113–14
      Song of Silver 20, 27, 36n66, 187n94
      Song of Ullikummi 36n66, 65
Opheltas 308–9
Opis 238–9
o-po-re-i 230
Oppian, *Haleutica* 3.8, 208–9, 256n160
   3.15 255n158
   3.15–25 255
Oracle Concerning the Celebration of Various
   Festivals 222n11, 223n18
Oracle for an Itinerary in the Kaska Territory
   253n147
oracles, Didyma 241n112
oral and written traditions, interaction 55, 181–2

oral formulaic theory 42
oral performance of written texts, Greece 181
oral performance vs. written transmission, NE
    179–82
oral poetry
    definition 38
    formulas 42
oral recitation, *Epic of Creation* 55–6, 263
oral traditions
    Epic of Gilgamesh 63
    Gilgamesh tradition 54, 60, 76
    at Hattusa 1, 15, 38, 179, 182
    Homer 63, 212, 397, 400
    Mesopotamia 42
    Sargonic legends 15, 167–9, 171, 174, 179,
        181–2, 185n86
oral transmission
    to Homeric tradition, Huwawa episode 55–6
    Shulgi 180
    transfer, verbal art 1, 5, 167, 197–8
oral wisdom, *Epic of Gilgamesh* 59
oral-derived
    definition 38–9
    HH narr. song 13, 37–9, 46–8, 156–7
    Song of Gilgamesh 63–4, 65, 66–72
    variations 39
orality *See* oral literature
Orestes 409–10n52
Orientalizing period 3, 5, 101n101, 200, 201n4,
    268, 295, 397, 423n15
Orpheus 103n112
Orphic cosmogonies 24n14
Orphic, opening to *Archaia Ilias* 450n123
Ortaköy 7 *Also see* Sapinuwa
Osmankayası 153n16
Ossetian myths 106n122
Ouraniā, Aphrodite 323–4n103
Ovid, *Metamorphoses* 10.270–502 325n110
Oymaağaç 7n21

Paeonians 419n3
Pahhuwa 357–8
Paibibla 119
pa-ki-ja 286
pa-ki-ja-ni-jo-jo 227
Palace Chronicles 129n69, 158
Palaepaphos *See* Kouklia; Paphos
Palaescepsis 436
Palaic 9
Palermo 324
Palestine 307 *Also see* Levant
palm trees 236, 320n91
Pamba 192n109

Pan 75n98
Panamuwa I 380n124
Panathenaea 262, 396, 415–16n76
    rhapsodic competitions 415
Panathenaic recension 396, 400n19, 415
Pancatantra 129n69
Pandarus 421, 443n93
Panhellenic
    epic 286n76, 355–6n25, 407, 411, 415n76,
        419, 445, 452n132, 453n135
    festivals 232–3, 262, 415n76, 422n10 *Also see*
        Panathenaea
Panionia 235 *Also see* Panionic stage
    Apollo 444, 452
    Ephesus 353, 444, 452
    Miletus 353, 413–14n76, 444
Panionian sacrifice, bulls 413n69, 443–4
Panionic League 235–6, 413–14, 436n60, 444
Panionic stage 235, 264, 267, 396, 398,
    400n19, 413–15, 419, 441–5, 448–9,
    452
Panionium 413–14n69, 435, 443–4
Panionius, Apollo 452n131
Panunis 381
Panyassis, *Heraclea* 377n117
    F 20 Bernabé 378
Paphlagonia 9
Paphos 276, 297, 307, 322–5, 327
parā tarna- 111, 123–4
parables, *Song of Release* 34, 113, 118, 129–31
    type scenes, negative reactions 44
Parian Marble *FGrH* 239 §24 402n25
Paris 33, 433–4 *Also see* Alaksandu
    Alexander, double name 2, 351–2, 434
    fall of Troy, alternate tellings 434
pariššan 121n39
pariya- 351–2
Pariyamuwa 351
Parnassus, Mt. 255n158
Parry-Lord "oral formulaic" theory 42
path image, denoting song 37n74
Patroclus
    Achilles, friendship with/mourning 22, 194,
        434
    death 453
        death of Sarpedon 442, 445, 452
    embassy scene 144, 276, 415n72
    funeral 281n56, 284n73
    funeral games 282n62, 288
    substitute, ritual 107
    weeping formula 43n100
patronymic adjectives 362, 427
patteššar 96 *Also see* pit rituals

Pausanias 221n4
  1.18.5 239n102
  3.21.1 323n100
  4.35.9 425n21
  5.7.8 239n102
  5.8.7 412n66
  6.20.17 374n105
  7.2.1–6 438–9
  7.2.5 359n40
  7.2.6 242
  7.2.8 360n47
  7.3.1 359n40
  7.4.8–10 435
  8.5.2 324
  8.10.3 234n81
  8.12.6 75n98
  8.21.3 239n102
  9.9.5 416n76
  9.27.2 239n102
  10.5.7–8 239n102
Pazzanikarri 120, 121
Pedasa, -us 12n48, 336n23
peer polity interactions 233n75, 333
  transfer, gods 342–3
  Wilusa 333, 342–6
Pegasa, -us 27, 424–5
Peisistratean recension 415
Peisistratid temple of Athena 262
Peisistratids
  Apollo 453n135
  Delos 236–7
  Panathenaea 415
Peisistratus 409, 415n76
Pelasgians 12, 438n72
Pelopidae 104n119
Peloponnese 317n78, 422n10, 438n72
Pelops 374, 422
Penelope 75n98, 203n16
Penthelidae 409n52
Penthilus 409n52
peplos, Athena 262, 416n76
Peramos 406
Perati 274, 275
performers *See* bards; singers
Periclymenus 107n130
Perimedes 100
Perramos 406
Persephone 100, 101n103, 126n58
Perses 34, 133n2
Perseus 215n77, 424–5
  Persians 314n63
  snake-slaying stories 425n21
Persian War and Trojan War 196, 418–19, 421

Persians 216n81, 314n63, 430n44 *Also see* Achaemenids
  conquest of Anatolia 413n69, 416n76, 444
Pessinus 343
Phaeacians 286n76, 296n115, 297, 299 *Also see* Scheria
Phaethon 27
phalanx warfare 399n17
pharmaka 52, 214
pharmakos 235n87 *Also see* scapegoat rituals
Pherecydes of Athens *FGrH* 3 F 2 415n76
  F 11 425n21
  F 21 216n77
  F 33 204n18
  F 37 374n105
  F 82 378
  F 86 216n77
  F 114 204n18
  F 155 12n48, 360n47, 422n13, 444n95
Pherecydes of Syros 24, 258–9
Philinna spell 99
Philistines 314n66, 315
Philo of Byblos, *Phoenician History* 24, 291n101
Philochorus *FGrH* 328 F 212 415n72
Philodemus, *de Musica* 18.36.9 203n17
Phineus 216n77
Phocaea 358n39
Phoenicia, Io 215, 318n79
Phoenician
  alphabet 400n17
  colonization 322–3n100
  epics 324
  gods *See* Ashtarte; Baal kr; Baal krntys; nursing goddess; Reshep
  Greek use of term 311n51
  inscriptions 311–12, 319n86, 320n90, 380n125 *Also see* Index of Phoenician Inscriptions
  Çineköy 315
  Karatepe 311, 313n61, 315–17, 320, 383, 386
  intermediaries 17, 268, 305, 311n52, 322n100, 423n15 *Also see* Phoenician-Greek bards
  Karatepe
    influence 320n91, 383, 386
    warship 386
  scribes 311n52
  Skales, goods 322
  theogonies 24, 147 *Also see* Pherecydes of Syros; Sanchuniathon
  trade 296–7n117
  wooden tablets 424n19

Phoenician History See Philo of Byblos
Phoenician–Greek, bilingual bards 53,
 322n100, 326
Phoenicians
 Cilicia 299, 311
 Cyprus 305, 307, 319n86, 322, 323–4n103,
  324
 Cythera 322n100
 Homeric tradition 282, 296–7n117
 Kommos 322n100
 Syro-Anatolia 311–12
 Tarsus 311
Phoenix (Europa's brother) 215–16n77, 318n79
Phoenix, *Iliad* 144
phorminx 241n108, 243, 276
phratries 235, 287n82 *Also see* clans; tribes
Phrygia 310
 continuity 357, 448
 Tantalus 422
Phrygian
 gods *Also see* Cybele; Idean Mother; Magna
  Mater; Matar Kubeleya
  "Young Male God" 328n126
 Homeric Hymn to Aphrodite, influence,
  328–9, 410, 431, 435
 ladle, Karatepe 384
 language 11, 357
 migrations 357–8, 361, 362–3, 423
 mode 241n108
 music, influence on Greece 240–1n108
 Niobe 422
 poets, Olympus 240
 scale 241n108
Phrygian–Trojan bilingual bards 420, 429
Phrygian–Aeolic bilingual bards 429–31
Phrygian–Greek bilingual bards 328–9,
 429–32, 435
Phrygians
 Assyria, in conflict with 357n34, 392
 at Boğazköy 7, 357
 in Cilicia 392
 Dardanids 328, 410
 and Greeks
  dynastic marriages 435
  shared legendary past with Greeks 19, 332–3
 Iliad 353, 421
 intermediaries
  Anat. narr. song 53, 419
  Trojan War legend 19, 419–20, 429–32,
   454
 migrations 361, 362–3, 423
 Mushki 357n34
 Troad 11, 357–8

Troy 19, 362–3, 419, 454
Tyana 357n34
Phthia 371, 411n58
Phthires/Phthiron, Mt. 442
phulai See tribes, clans
Phylace 204
physicians *See* doctors
^{LÚ}*pidduri* 304n13
piḫaššaššiš 331, 425
pillar tombs 448
Pinali 447n111
Pinara 443n93, 447n111
Pindar 221n4, 459
 Isthmian 7.43–8 27n28
 Nemean 2.1–3 449n122
  2.1d, Σ 250, 414n72
  2.3 24n13
  10.5–59 107n130
  11.33, Σ 410n52
 Olympian 1 374n105, 422n10
 Pythian 1.31–2 255n158
  5.72–81, 99 239n103
  8.21 255n158
 F 264 330n132
Pirinkir 163
Pishaisha 26, 108
Pisidian 11, 356
pit rituals *Also see* āpi; underworld entrances
 ancestor veneration 79 80, 87–8
 Bible 89
 Ebla 87
 Emar 87–8n44
 Ephesus 93
 epic, connection to 78, 98–9, 105, 108–9
 Hattusa 89–91, 93–8
 Homeric 99–102
 HH 81–4, 86, 93–8
 Hyampolis 93
 Mycenaean Greece 91–2
 NE 86–92
 NA 87, 89
 Sardis 93
 Ugarit 86, 87n42, 382
 Urkesh 87, 89, 90n55, 92
Pitane 451
Pitassa 336–7
Pithecusae 397
Pittacus 405
Piyama-Kurunta 338, 339n39
Piyamaradu 339, 354n19
Piyassili 352n10
Pizikarra 113, 115n12, 116, 117, 278
Plain Cilicia *See* Cilicia, Plain

Plato
  Hippias Maior 285d 349
  Ion 530d 416n76
  Laws 642d 203n17
  Republic 364b 204n20
  Timaeus 21b 235n83
[Plato] *Hipparchus* 228b 415n76
Pliny *Natural History* 34.75 245
Plutarch
  Moralia 301f–302a 234n81
  Nicias 3.4–6 238n96
  Septem sapientium convivium 153f 398n12
  Solon 12.4 203n17
[Plutarch] *de Musica* 1131d 240n107
  1132b 458n2
  1136c 240n107
  1146c 203n17
Podarces 351n9
Poem of the Righteous Sufferer (Akkadian) 141n20
Policha 436
Polis cave 286n76
Pollux 9.83 435n58
Polycrates 209, 236, 398
Polydamas 194–5
Polydeuces 107
Pontus 257n166
pools, sacred 90, 376
po-re-no-zo-te-ri-ja 227n36
Poseidāheiā 286
Poseidon
  Chios, father of 435
  Heliconius 443–4
  Iliad 396n2, 407, 412
  Mycenaean 286
  Odyssey 101n102, 443
  Panionia 443–4, 452
Posidonius FF 169.31, 172 Theiler 394n163
post-palatial Greece 273–8
  and Anatolia, west 274
  ancestor veneration 276–7
  epic 275–8
  long-distance elite interactions, valorization 275
  mortuary rituals 274
Potiphar's wife 34, 424
  Elkunirsa and Ashertu 126, 424
Potnia 286
Potniya Aswiya 346
A Prayer for Well-Being (Ugarit) 382n139
Prayer of Arnuwanda I and Ashmunikal for the Sun-goddess of Arinna 123, 162n61
Prayer of Hattusili III and Puduhepa for the Sun-goddess of Arinna 121n42

Prayer to Adad 98n91
prayer, NE, Chryses 139n18
prayers, Hittite 9, 93, 121n42, 123, 140n20, 162n61, 214, 260, 338–9
  juridical scenarios 69
  parallels to Sappho 397, 453n133
pre-Greek language 246–7
Priam 33, 105n119, 139, 353, 433
  name 351, 406
    double-naming 351n9
Priene 358n39
priest, anointed 253
Proclamation of Anitta 8n27, 172n23, 389n151
Proclus 326, 406n37
Proconessus 211n57
proems *See* openings, epic; prooimia
Proetus 204n19, 423
Proetids 204n19
Prometheus 138, 215n73, 293
prooimia 24n13, 239, 264, 449, 451
prophets *Also see* seers
  Biblical 120n33, 201–3
  west Semitic 201
PG
  ancestor veneration 279, 281–2, 286–7, 370
  continuity 278–9
  dating 267n3
  east, fascination with 281–3, 373
  epic 279–81
  hero cult 286–7, 300
  long-distance elite interactions 17, 268, 281, 283–5
  nostalgia 17, 268, 279–82, 300, 373
  pottery
    Cyprus 275–6, 404
    Ephesus 360
    Smyrna 412n66
    Troy 365, 370–2
  social structures 278
  values 277–8, 283–5
PU-Sharruma 157n34
Puduhepa 153n21
Puhanu Chronicle 163–4
puppies, ritual use 87, 92–3
purapši man 261
Purattu River 177n47
Purification Ritual for the Former Gods 95–8, 121n41
  Ea and the Beast 97n89
  KUB 8.62 79, 95, 98–9
  Odyssey 78, 95, 99–101, 105, 109

Purification Ritual for the Former Gods (cont.)
   Song of Birth 94, 96–8
purification rituals *Also see* magico-medical rituals; ghost prescriptions
   Song of Release 155
Puriyanni *See* Ritual of Puriyanni against Impurity of a House
Purra
   Sapinuwa 117n20
   Song of Release 117–19, 121, 123, 141
purulli festival 32, 252–5
   Golden Fleece 256n161
   Hattic 32–3, 252
   ḫešti-house 151n8, 253
   ritual drama 254–5
Purushanda
   Anitta 173
   colony, Old Assyrian merchant 172
   Cuthean Legend of Naram-Sin 52
   location 172n23
   Sargonic legends 52, 171n21, 172–3, 180
   Silver Mountains 52
puthikos nomos 240, 261–2
Pyanopsion 235
Pylian epic 355
Pylos
   BA 228–31, 271, 285, 345–6
      festivals 228–9
      Ionian migrations 404n29, 422n13, 438, 444n95
   Melampous 204
Pyriphlegethon 100
Pythian games 232, 261–2
Pythius, Apollo 249, 398
Pytho 16, 221, 240, 243, 250n136, 261–2
   entry into Homeric tradition 301, 321
   etymology 258n174

qarrādum 170
qa-si-re-u 273, 283n67 *Also see basileus*
Qatna 381
Qode 356
quantitative metathesis 412
Que 7, 310, 316, 383, 386, 388, 392, 435n58
   Also see Adana; Cilicia; Danuna; Hiyawa
Qumran 54n2

racing
   chariot 17, 228, 269–70, 275, 278
   foot 223
Radaman 143
Raetic language 361–2

ragginu/raggintu 201
rain
   mountains 254
   Storm-god 242n115, 254, 259
Ramayana 76n99
ra-mi-ni-ja 345
Ramses II 7, 213n67, 340
Ramses III 317, 356
rapa ʾūma
   divine ancestors 285, 290, 293
   Ugarit 150n1, 151n9, 285, 290
Recurring Festival 223n18
Rehoboam 134–5
re-ke-to-ro-te-ri-jo 227n36
Release, Song of *See* Song of Release
reliefs, ancestors 153, 381, 384–6, 390
$r^e p\bar{a}\ \hat{\imath}m$, divine ancestors 285, 290
Res Gestae of Hattusili I 112n5, 158n39
Reshep
   'althyts 319n86
   Apollo 243n119, 313, 319–20
   LAMMA 313, 319–20
   Runzas 313, 319–20
   ṣprm 249n131, 313n61, 320
Return Songs
   forked pathway 75n98
   Odyssey 75n98
returning gods *See* mugawars
Rhacius 318
rhapsodes *Also see* rhapsōidos
   Apatouria 235n83
   Panathenaea 415
rhapsōidos, etymology 37, 414–15
Rhegium 209
Rhodes
   continuity 274
   Iliad 353
   Lycia 429, 440–1
   Mycenaeans 272–3, 340
   post-palatial 441
   PG 321
Rites Involving the Royal Shades of the Dead (Ugarit) 150n2, 151n9
Ritual against Depression 214n68
Ritual against Underworld Powers 98n94
ritual drama *See* drama, ritual
Ritual for a Single Month (Ugarit) 151n9, 290n98
Ritual for Ishtar of Nineveh 95n76
Ritual for Ishtar/Pirinkir, with Babilili Incantations 163, 214n68
Ritual for Mt. Hazzi 25n17, 50, 108, 183, 256
   Also see Hazzi, Mt.

Ritual for the Sun-goddess of the Earth 154
Ritual Mentioning the Former Gods 95, 97, 129n67
Ritual of Allaiturahhi 33n51, 84n22, 90n53, 154–5
 Song of Oil 51, 108
Ritual of Hantitassu of Hurma 94n71
Ritual of Mastigga against Family Quarrel 93n66, 154n24
Ritual of Puriyanni against Impurity of a House 21
Ritual of Shalashu 32, 51n136, 214n72
Ritual of the Hurrian Woman Ashdu against Witchcraft 93n67, 95n78
Ritual of Tunnawiya 90n53, 93n67
ritual substitutes *See* substitutes, ritual
rituals *Also see* magico-medical rituals
 Anatolian, indigenous 90n53, 94n71
 "drawing paths" 94–5
 "take from the earth" 93n67, 95n78
Rituals for Two Months (Ugarit) 151n9, 262
rivers
 crossing, heroic deed 66, 68, 177
 roads, underworld *See* KASKAL.KUR
 underworld entrances 89–90, 96, 99, 106–7
rock *See* stone
Room of the Chariot Tablets 462
royal ancestor veneration *See* ancestor veneration, royal
Royal Chronicle of Lagash 188
ruins, BA, cult sites 287–8, 367–71
Runzas
 Karatepe 249n131, 313, 320
 ᵈLAMMA 249, 313, 319–20
 Reshep 313, 319–20
Rusa I 106

Sa Vocabulary 36n68
Sadyattes 374
šahhan 123–4
Salamis (Cyprus) 306, 307n28, 320–2
Salamis (island) 409n51
šalli aššeššar 156, 225
Sam'al *See* Zincirli
sāman 37n74
samaryam 240
Same 228
sa-me-we 228
Sammeltafeln 35n61, 168n5, 175n37, 180n60, 214n72
Samos 209, 228, 235n83, 237–8, 272, 340, 358n39, 416n76
Samsuditana xxx.n1

Samuel 89
Samuha 7n21, 84n24
Sanchuniathon 24
Sandas 358n38, 424
Sangarius River 21n4, 430n44
Santorini *See* Thera
Sapinuwa 86, 342
 Arzawan names 339n39
 Hittite texts 7, 8
 Purra 117n20
Sapon, Mt. *Also see* Hazzi, Mt.
 Baal, home of 25
 Typhon 258
Sappho F 2 Lobel-Page 324n104
 F 16.2 43
 F 17 407
 F 35 324n104
 F 44 458n2
 F 44.16 406n39
 F 71 409n52
 T 47 324n104
 Hittite prayers, parallels to 397, 453n133
 hexametric poetry, relations to 329, 406–7, 416, 458n2
 meter 458n2
Sardis 106, 209, 337n27, 374, 376
 continuity 357
 cross-cultural contact/mixing 358
 pit rituals 93
Sargon the Great
 Anatolia, journeys to 168–73, 210, 218
 historical omens 168
 kispum 155, 186
 Naram-Sin, paired with 167–8
 šarrena 184–5
 west, activities in 168n4, 169 *Also see* Sargon, King of Battle
Sargon I 169n12
Sargon II 310, 316n75, 319n84, 392n157
Sargon 1.23–31 177n48
Sargon 11.1–42 166
 11.20–6 175n37
 11.20–8 170, 175n40
Sargon 12.13′ –18′ 175n40
 12.13′ –21′ 175n37
Sargon 14 180n60
Sargon and Ur-Zababa 424n17
Sargon Geography 210n53
 12, 34, 35 184n80
Sargon II 1.1.21 392n157
Sargon II 2.3.117–18 392n157
Sargon II, SAA 1.1, 251 392n157
 SAA 1.30–32 106

Sargon in Foreign Lands 171n20, 173n27
   i 12' –15' 171n21
   ii 21 177n50
   iv 9' –11' 171n21
Sargon, King of Battle 21, 170–4, 177, 183n74, 210n53
   Amarna 171n21, 172–3
      rev. 4' 177n50
   Hittite 173–4
      KBo 13.46 ii 8' 171n21
      KBo 22.6 iv 11' –12' 179–80
   HH narr. song 174
   Late Assyrian 4' 45n109
Sargon Letters 168n9, 173n27
Sargon the Conquering Hero 171nn20–21, 173n27
   48–9 176n45
   58 171n21
   59–64 171n21
   120–3 177
Sargon the Lion 171n20
   obv. 16' –17' , rev. 9' 176n46
Sargonic legends
   Agamemnon 173
   Cedar Forest 166, 170, 172, 175
   Chronicle of the Single Monarchy 188
   Ebla 160–1, 166, 175
   Elam 184
   Gilgamesh tradition 168–9, 171, 172n21, 196
      journey to Cedar Forest 172–3
      Song of Release 176
   Hahhu 170, 176–7
   Hassu 176
   Hatti 170, 184–5, 192n109, 197
   Hattusa 171–4 *Also see* Sargonic legends, reception, Hittites
      source, north Syria 169, 171n19
   Hattusili I 166, 168, 176–80, 196
   historical omens 168
   Homeric tradition, entry into 298
   Hurrian intermediaries 171, 173–4, 179
   HH narr. song 15, 20, 167, 169, 174, 182, 190, 197
   HH rituals *See šarrena* ritual
   journeys, through darkness 171–2
      Odyssey 105
   journeys, edge of world, *Odyssey* 1, 218
   Kanesh 169–70, 172, 173n27
   Kish 167, 178
   Kumarbi cycle 167, 184–5
   Lullu 184n80
   Map of the World See Map of the World
   oral traditions 15, 167–9, 171, 174, 179, 181–2, 185n86

   Purushanda 52, 171n21, 172–3, 180
   reception
      Hittites 15, 21, 166–7, 169, 171–4, 179, 378 *Also see* above, Hattusili I
      Syria, north 171n19 *Also see* above, Hurrian mediation
   Old Assyrian kings 169n12
   Old Assyrian merchant colonies 169–70, 173, 298
   rivers, crossing 177
   šarrena ritual *See šarrena* ritual
   scribal training/transmission 9, 15, 60, 168, 171–2, 173n27, 174, 181–2, 185n86, 192n108, 196
   Silver Mountains 52, 166, 170
   Song of Gilgamesh 172–3, 177
   Tukrish 184n80
Sarissa 7–8
Sarpedon
   ancestor, fictional 438–9
   Carian name 375n108, 439
   Cilicia 423n14, 446n104, 452n132
   Crete 422–3, 438, 442, 452n132
   epic, Greco-Lycian 429, 439–41
   Gilgamesh tradition 68, 195, 445
   Iliad
      catalog of Trojan allies 442
      death 445–6
      Tlepolemos 429, 440–1
      Trojan ally 418
      wrong generation 423n14, 439, 445n102
   Lycia, migration to 443
   Lycian hero 420, 445–9
   Miletus, founder 422–3, 438
   Neleids 440, 453
Sarpedoneum 446
Sarpedonius, Apollo and Artemis 452n132
šarrašiya 183, 261
šarrena 182 *Also see* Former Kings; *šarrena* ritual
šarrena ritual 15–16, 160n49, 167, 174
   Kumarbi cycle 184–6
   lists 187–8
   wisdom 183–4, 187
šarri, deified kings 185n85
šarru, royal ancestors 182n71
Sasruquo's Sorrow 126n58
Satnioeis River 12n48
Saul, King 89, 93
Scamandrius 407, 410, 436–7
   name 351n9, 412
Scandeia 282n63
scapegoat rituals 104n115, 235
Scepsis 410, 412n63, 435–7

scepters
  heirlooms 207, 274–5, 378, 422
  kingship 207, 422
Scheria 297 Also see Phaeacians
scribal training
  Hattusa 8–9, 32, 60
  Mesopotamia 32, 60, 181, 196
  Ugarit 32
  wisdom literature 32–3, 60
scribal training/transmission, Sargonic legends 9, 15, 60, 168, 171–2, 173n27, 174, 181–2, 185, 192, 196
scribes
  Hattusa
    Akkadian 6, 8–9, 30n41, 171
    north Syrian 8–9, 171n19
  transfer, verbal art 54–5, 200
  transmission from Sumerian to Akkadian 55
  wisdom 59
Scythia 215n73
Scythians 105–6
sea
  battles See battles
  journeys to/across See journeys to edge of world; journeys to/across Ocean/sea
Sea Also see Ocean; Tiamat; Yam
  daughter of See Shertapshururi
  šarrena ritual 183
  Song of Gilgamesh 69
  Song of Hedammu 25–6, 41, 127–8
Sea, Song of See Song of the Sea
Sea of Azov 105–6
Sea of Marmara 357
Sea Peoples 7, 356–7
  Aegean 17, 274, 314–15
  Ahhiyawans 315
  Arzawa 356
  Cilicia 274, 314
  Cyprus 274, 278, 307, 314, 356
  Danuna 317
  LH IIIC:1b pottery 307, 313–15
  Levant 274, 315
  Lycians 443n93
  Philistines 315
  Troy 354
Sea People's Campaign, Medinet Habu: Great Inscription of Year 8 317n77
second compensatory lengthening 463
seers Also see augurs; prophets
  divine 96, 98, 101
  Greek 101, 199, 203, 213–14 Also see Calchas; Melampous; Mopsus; Polydamas; Teiresias

^{LÚ}HAL 98n91
  Mesopotamian 192, 196, 201, 205
  transfer, verbal art 217, 262
Seha River 337
Seha River Land 336–7, 339n39, 343 Also see "The Offenses of Seha River Land"
  Lydia 336–7, 358, 376
Seleucus II 451n130
Selinous 287n82
semi-divine figures
  Bible 293
  Gilgamesh 57
  heroes 287
  Illuyanka 27, 254
  Phaethon 27
  Silver 27
Semitic, west See west Semitic
Semonides 399n17
Sennacherib 106, 392, 396n2
Sennacherib 17 iv 61–91, 392n157
Seraglio 340
Serbo-Croatian epic 47–8, 110, 355, 407, 428
  forked pathway 75n98
  Return Songs, Odyssey 75n98
  Turkish influence 428
Serbo-Croatian-Albanian bilingual bards 13, 47–8, 428
šērum 37n70
Seth 257n166
settlement Also see colonization; migrations
  Anatolia, from Crete 273, 359, 423n14, 440n82
  Greek, Cyprus 17, 274, 302, 316
  Mycenaean, west Anatolia 320
sewing image, denoting song 37
Seyhan River 313
Shalashu See Ritual of Shalashu
Shalmaneser V 392n157
Shamash 57–8, 62–3, 85, 140–1n20, 209, 303n4
  Also see Sun-god
Shamhat 57, 65,
Shamshi-Adad I xxx.n1, 161n53, 186n90, 197n119
Shangashu 65
Sharkalisharri 185, 189
Sharri-Kushuh 352n10
Sharri-Teshshub 352n10
Sharruma 152, 157n34, 183
Shattahamo 125n56
Shattiwaza 352n10
Shauraseni 407n43
Shawushka 183
  epithet, HH narr. song 43
  HH narr. song 26, 28, 34, 73, 174

Shawushka (cont.)
   HH rituals 86, 96
   Ishhara 115
   Ishtar 115, 213
   IŠTAR 26
   Nineveh 114, 174, 202n10, 213, 215, 347n78
      doves 323n102
Sherish 45, 160n48
Shertapshuruhi 26, 127
*sh₂ey 37
Shiduri 58, 73, 172, 190 Also see Ziduri; Nahmazule
   Circe 101n104, 299n126
   meaning 73–4
Shimige 28, 73, 185 Also see Sun-god
Shimmurra 121n42, 173
Shinda(li)meni 28, 51, 184n76
Shulgi
   Gilgamesh 80
   journeys 210
   Lugalbanda 80n11
   Ninsun 80n11
   oral transmission 180
Shulgi A 210n50
Shulgi B 270–80 180n62
Shulgi O 50 80n11
   95,100 75n94
   139 80n11
Shulgi P C.22–3, 38 80n11
Sidetic 11, 356
Sidon 282, 297n117
šiduri 73–4, 159n45, 184
Sigeum 409–10, 412n66
silver
   birthplace of 52, 104
   Hattusa 52, 104
   materia magica 52
   terminology 52
   trade 52, 209
Silver, hero 28, 51–2, 184–5, 187n94
      Also see Song of Silver
   Bellerophontes 27
   Phaethon 27
   šarrena ritual 184–5
Silver Mountains
   Naram-Sin 52
   Sargon 52, 166, 170
   Taurus Mountains 170n13
si-mi-te-u 346
Simonides F 8.1 West 330n132
Sin 214–15 *Also see* Moon-god
Sin-leqi-unninni 57n15, 80

Sinbad 54n2, 106
singers, cult 162–3
   Delian girls 237
   for specific gods 162–3, 224
   Hittite royal ancestor veneration 156
   transfer, verbal art 162–3, 306
singers
   Hittite *See* ᴸᵁNAR
   Hurrian 162
   NE 36–7, 162–3, 263n198
single combat 278, 454
sinkholes, rituals 89 *Also see* KASKAL.KUR
Sippar 87n44, 190n102
Sipylus, Mt. 422
SIR₃
   definition 37
   išḫamāiš 21
SIR₃ *parā tarnumaš See* Song of Release
šir tag.tag 37n74
širadili 25n17, 37
Sirara, Mt. 58, 74n89, 175n39 *Also see* Sirion, Mt.
Sirens 103n112
šīri 37
Sirion, Mt. 175n39 *Also see* Mt. Sirara
Sirkeli 153, 319n85
Sisyphus 378, 411n58, 423, 441
Sito 231n60
si-to-ko[-wo] 231
šiuneš linkiyaš 447n113
Skales 322n99
-*ske/o*- 427
Skira 230n59
skyphoi, pendant semi-circles 295, 372n95
Skyros 372
Smintheus 231, 345
   Apollo 140, 231n63, 450–2
Sminthia 231n63, 346, 450n125
Smyrna 451n130
   Aeolian and Ionian 359n41, 412n66
   Homer 330n132, 412n66
   Magnes 105
   Mycenaeans 340
   Protogeometric pottery 412n66
snake-slaying stories 250–8
   Apollo *See* Pytho
   cosmogonies 251, 257–8
   Egypt 258
   Heracles 251
   Hittite *See* Illuyanka
   IE 251
   Perseus 425n21
   Song of Hedammu 251, 255

Storm-god *See* Storm-god, battle with snake
Ugarit 18, 257
Zeus *See* Typho
solar myth 107
Soli (Cilicia) 314
Soli (Cyprus) 322
Solomon 134
Solymi 378, 423, 443n92
song
   images denoting 37
   versus speech 37
Song of Birth 25, 31n43
   Agdistis 343
   Berossus, *Babyloniaka* 188n97
   Chronicle of the Single Monarchy 188–9, 196, 292
   curses 45
   dating 35
   Former Gods 50, 94, 96–7
   historiolae 50–1, 86
   Hurrian version 25
   HH narr. song 20, 24, 31n44
   Invocation of Teshshub of Aleppo 162, 185n83, 260
   itkalzi rituals 51, 86n36
   kingship in heaven 188–9
   Kumarbi cycle 24
   kunkunuzzi stone 121n44
   opening 50, 96–7
   Purification Ritual for the Former Gods 94, 96–8
   Theogony 290
   type scenes, negative reactions 45
Song of Emergence See Song of Birth
Song of Freedom See Song of Release
Song of Gilgamesh 63–72, 75, 445 *Also see* Gilgamesh tradition; *Song of Huwawa*
   Anatolian audience, caters to 29, 71–2
   dating 35, 63–4
   differences, Hurrian and Hittite versions 29, 73
   find spots 63n35
Song of Gilgamesh, Hittite version
   assemblies 71
      divine 65, 68–9, 75
   dreams 28, 43n99, 66, 68–9, 122
   Epic of Gilgamesh, differences from 29, 65–6, 69, 72
   Hurrian influence 73
   HH formulas
      epithets 42
      large numbers 127n63

speech introductions 42n90
weeping 43
HH narr. song 13, 20, 22, 63–4, 71–2, 167, 191
Huwawa 52, 71–2, 75–6
juridical scenarios 68–9
opening 36n66, 54, 64–5
oral-derived 63–72
Sargonic legends 172–3, 177
substitutes, ritual, Enkidu 69
not a translation of *Epic of Gilgamesh* 13, 63–4, 74
not a translation of the Hurrian version 64, 74
type scenes, hospitality scenes 69
variations 63–4, 66–72
Song of Gilgamesh, Hurrian version 42, 72–3
Song of Going Out See Song of Birth
Song of Hedammu 25–6, 123n49
   assemblies, divine 133n2
   festivals 50–1
   historiolae 50–1
   Hurrian version 26
   HH formulas
      large numbers 127
      weeping 43
   HH narr. song 20
   Kumarbi cycle 24, 256
   Malatya 257n171
   šarrena ritual 184–5
   snake-slaying stories 251, 255
   Theogony 255
   type scenes, hospitality scenes 127–8
   Typhon 251, 255
   variations 40–1
   versions "X" and "Y" 40–1
Song of Huwawa 74–6
   Anatolian audience, caters to 75–6
   Elkunirsa and Ashertu 73
   Epic of Gilgamesh, differences from 73
   Kumarbi cycle 73
Song of Keshshi 20, 28, 184n76
   Akkadian version 28
   Amarna 28
   ancestors, divine 28
   assemblies 28, 133n2
   dating 35
   dreams 28, 66, 122n44, 145
   formulas, speech introductions 42n90
   Gilgamesh tradition 28, 66, 145n30
   historiolae 51
   kunkunuzzi stone 122n44
   Meleager 28

Song of Keshshi (cont.)
   Song of Release 43
   variations 28
Song of Kingship 183, 256–7, 261
   historiolae 256–7
Song of Kingship in Heaven, correct title 25n16, 257n165
Song of Kumarbi, correct title 25n16
Song of LAMMA 27, 31n44
   Carchemish 27, 306
   historiolae 50
   Kumarbi cycle 27
Song of Liberation See Song of Release
Song of Oil 34
   historiolae 51
   HH narr. song 34
   Ritual of Allaiturahhi 51, 108
Song of Release 14–15, 32, 111–31 *Also see* Allani; Meki; Pizikarra; Purra; Storm-god; Zazalla
   ancestor veneration, royal 14, 51, 110, 119, 122, 129, 149–50, 153, 161, 165
      Storm-god 122–4, 155
   assembly scene 14, 119–23, 130, 155, 158, 187
      Atrahasis 137–9, 142, 147
      Bible 134–5
      Gilgamesh and Akka 134–5
      Iliad 33–4, 133, 139–42, 195, 355–6, 450
   Atrahasis, gods like men 135–6
   Biblical prophets 120n33
   bilingual bards 48–9
   bilingual tablets 32, 111
   Caucasian myths 126n58
   curses 117–19
   dating 32
   debt slaves 113, 118n24
   Ebla
      destruction 33, 113, 116–19
      historical destruction 111–12, 160–1
   find spot 32, 111
   Gilgamesh tradition, Sargonic legends 174–5
   Hattusili I 111–12, 123–4, 149, 157–61, 258
   Helen 33, 132, 139, 432, 450
   Homeric tradition, entry into, plotline 355–6, 419, 432
   HH formulas, large numbers 125, 127n63
   HH narr. song 13, 20
   Ishhara 113, 115–16, 129, 131, 139n18, 145, 187
   king lists 119, 150, 190–1
   kingship 33–4, 135, 138–9, 160
   length 111
   Leviticus 113
   opening 113–14
   parables 34, 113, 118, 129–31
      type scenes, negative reactions 44
   performed by singer 36, 111
   plot 33–4, 113
   purification ritual 155
   releasing prisoners 116–19, 121–2
   Song of Keshshi 43
   speaker in assembly 120–1
   Storm-god *See* Storm-god, *Song of Release*; *above*, *under* ancestor veneration
   Storm-god of Aleppo 149, 159, 161–5, 259
   substitutes, ritual 126
   Telipinu Myth (Mugawar) 121n42
   transfer in Old Kingdom 157–65
   type scenes
      hospitality scenes 124–9, 143–5
      waking for message 115, 145–6
   variations 122, 129–30
   war captives 118n24
   wisdom 113, 131, 158, 187
   writing down 130, 164–5
Song of Silver 27 *Also see* Silver
   Caucasian myths 27n28
   dating 35
   formulas, speech introductions 42n90
   historiolae 52
   HH song 20
   Kumarbi cycle 27
   opening 20, 27, 36n66, 187n94
   Urkesh 27
   wisdom 187n94
Song of the Sea
   historiolae 50
   Hittite version 25n17
   Hurrian version 25n17
   HH narr. song 20
   Kumarbi cycle 24–6, 257
   Ritual for Mt. Hazzi 25, 50, 108, 183, 256
Song of Ullikummi 26
   Agdistis 343
   differences between Hittite and Hurrian versions 26
   Hazzi, Mt. 39–40, 257n170
   Hurrian version 26, 34n57
   HH formulas
      epithets 42–3
      large numbers 127n63
      speech introductions 42
      weeping 43
   HH narr. song 20, 31n44
   Kumarbi cycle 24, 26
   Luwianisms 25n15, 31n44, 35n60
   opening 36n66, 65

saw 31n44
Song of Release 117, 118n28
Theogony 256
type scenes
  dressing scenes 327n120
  hospitality scenes 126–7
Typhon 255
variations 39–40
song-making as a craft 37
Songs of Thunder 21, 163
Sosruquo 25n16, 106n122, 126n58
Sparta 203n17, 213–14, 234, 240, 288, 349, 377
speaker in assembly 120–1
spinning image, denoting song 37
springs, sacred 90n53, 98, 242n115, 338n35, 360n49, 447 *Also see* nymphs
ṣprm, Reshep 249n131, 313n61, 320
šr, Ugarit 37n70
stag *bibrû* 208, 245–7, 345
star of Ebla 116n17, 120, 150, 161
stars, deified kings 150
Stasinus 326
Statius, *Thebaid* 4.443–72 98n94
statues
  ancestor *See* ancestor statues
  ancestor veneration 186
  divine 162–3, 245, 248, 249n130, 319–20, 369
  Ephesus 338n35, 360n49
  Mycenaean 227
  votive 168, 180–1
Stesichorus 458n2, 459, 461n9
stone *See* baetyls; Eternal Rocky Peak; *kunkunuzzi* stone; living rock; tombs
stone circles 369–70
Stone House 124, 151n8, 152, 153n20, 448
Storm-god *Also see* Adad; Baal; Hadad; ᵈIM; ᵈIŠKUR; Kumarbi Cycle; Tarhun; Taru; Teshshub; ᵈU
  Adalur, Mt. 159
  ancestor veneration 152, 155, 380, 446
  Annals of Hattusili I 177
  Armaruk, Mt. 159
  baetyls 50, 121, 152n13, 225
  battle with mountains 26
  battle with sea
    Hazzi, Mt. 256–7
    HH narr. song 26 *Also see* Song of the Sea
    Titanomachy 257n166
  battle with snake 16, 257–8
    Hedammu 25–6, 255
    Illuyanka 103–4, 251, 425
    Zeus *See* Typhon, Zeus
  battle with volcanic monster 26, 255
  battle with Yam 25, 257
  birth, HH, 25, 162, 185n83, 260
  bull 159, 163, 216n77, 320n88, 328n126
  Chaoskampf 16, 251–7
  Cyprus 306, 321
  Elkunirsa and Ashertu 34, 126
  epithet, HH narr. song 42–3
  festivals 250, 259–61
  Former Kings 154–5
  Hattic name 259
  Hittite name 259
  Hurrian invocations 10, 162, 185n83, 261
  Hurrian name 259
  HH narr. song (fragment) 72n76
  HH parables 44
  HH rituals 34, 97–8, 126, 154–5
  Illuyanka 104, 252–5
  importation of Kumarbi cycle 258
  Iyarri 224
  Kanesh 163
  Karatepe 320
  kingship 16, 152, 155, 259–61
    in heaven 24–7, 97n89, 127, 184–5, 259, 292
  Luwian name 259
  Malatya 249, 257, 259, 312
  Manuzzi, Mt. 160n48
  mugawars 93, 104n115
  musician of 163
  NE 162n56, 259
  rain 242n115, 254, 259
  Ritual for Mt. Hazzi 256–7
  Semitic name 162n56, 259
  song of 163 *Also see* Songs of Thunder
  Song of Birth 24, 25
  Song of Gilgamesh
    Hittite 72
    Hurrian 72–3
  Song of Hedammu 26, 40, 123n49, 127
  Song of Huwawa 73
  Song of Kingship 256–7
  Song of LAMMA 50
  Song of Release 33–4, 111, 113, 115–16, 118–26, 128–9, 136–40, 145, 152, 162–5, 450
    royal ancestor veneration 122–4, 155
  Song of the Sea 25–6, 256
  Song of Ullikummi 39–40, 127
  syncretism, Cyprus 305–6, 319–20
  Taru 259
  Yazılıkaya 152n13, 225
Storm-god of Aleppo
  AN.TAḪŠUM festival 259
  Ebla 161, 257
  Hassu 159, 258

Storm-god of Aleppo (cont.)
   Hattusa 161–4, 258–60
   Hattusili I 149, 159, 163–4, 184, 258
   (ḫ)išuwa festival 160n48, 260–1
   ḫiyara festival 258, 261
   HH rituals 161–2
   kingship 162–5, 251, 259–61
   mace 257, 320
   name 162n56
   nuntarriyašḫaš festival 259
   Song of Release 149, 159, 161–5, 258
   Teshshub of Kummi 161–2, 185n83, 260
   transfer
      cult personnel 162, 258, 260
      verbal art 16, 149, 159, 162–5, 221, 251, 258, 260
Storm-god of Hatti 253n148
Storm-god of Heaven 177, 252
Storm-god of Kummi 25 *Also see* Teshshub of Kummi
Storm-god of Mt. Manuzzi 160n48, 260
Storm-god of Nerik 93n68, 121n42, 252–3
Storm-god of the Vineyard 163
Storm-god of Ziplanda 253n148
Storm-god *piḫaššaššiš* 331, 425
Strabo 5.2.4 361n54
   8.6.11 346n71
   8.7.2 413n69
   9.1 409n51
   9.2.3 410n52
   9.10 409n51
   10.4.14 231n69
   12.3.24 104n119
   12.8.3 363n63
   12.8.4 441n85
   12.8.5 422n13
   12.8.19 343n58
   12.44.4 358n37
   13.1.3 359, 410n52, 435n57
   13.1.8 409n49
   13.1.25 410n57
   13.1.35–6 410n57
   13.1.38 410
   13.1.38–9 409n49, 409n51, 410n55
   13.1.40 363
   13.1.40–2 407n41, 437n65
   13.1.42 410n56
   13.1.45 437
   13.1.48 231n63
   13.1.50–1 12n48
   13.1.52 436
   13.1.52–3 410n57
   13.1.53 437
   13.1.58–9 12n48
   13.1.62 451n130
   13.3.5 451n129
   13.4.6 255n158
   14.1.3 12n48, 353n17, 360n47, 422n13, 438–9n72, 444n95
   14.1.4 412n66
   14.1.6 359n40, 422
   14.1.21 359n40
   14.1.27 393n159
   14.1.37 412n66
   14.2.2 439n75
   14.2.23 234n81
   14.2.28 421n5
   14.3.5 443n93
   14.4.3 318
   14.5 255n158
   14.5.12 314n63
   14.5.16 318
   14.5.19 452n132
   14.5.28 104n119
   16.2.28 425n21
Straits of Kerch *See* Cimmerian Bosporus
Styx 100, 293
MUNUSŠU.GI *See* "Old Women"
Subarian incantations 213
Subartu 10
Submycenaean phase, definition 267n3
substitutes, ritual 97n89, 154
   Enkidu 69, 107
   Patroclus 107
   Song of Release 126
substitution rituals 88–9, 97n89
   juridical scenarios 69, 154
Substitution Rituals for the King 154
Südburg, Hattusa 90, 153
Suffixaufnahme 362n55
Suhis II 381
Suidas
   Arktinos (Adler A 3960) 444n97
   Magnēs (M 21) 105n120
   meta Lesbion ōidon (M 701) 214n69
   Puthia kai Dēlia (Π 3128) 398n11
   Ōlēn (Ω 71) 239n102
Sumerian
   epic 41–2, 52, 147 *Also see* Enmerkar; Lugalbanda
      Gilgamesh tradition 55–7, 75
   meter 46
   texts
      Hattusa 9, 33n51, 85
      Ugarit 31–2
Sumerian Incantations 85

Sumerian King List See Chronicle of the Single Monarchy
Sumerian Sargon Legend 191n105, 424
Šumma Ālu 244n121
Sun *Also see* Helios
    Cattle 102
    chariot 27
    father of Circe 107
Sun-god *Also see* Istanu; Shamash; Shimige; Utu
    Annals of Hattusili I 177
    Apollo 250n136
    at Hattusa 90
    Hittite prayers 140–1n20
    HH narr. song 34, 40, 50, 117, 127, 128, 133
    judge 85, 133, 154
    pit ritual with Gilgamesh 84
    Song of Gilgamesh 65–7, 69
    Song of Release 115n12, 117, 129
    substitution rituals 154
    title of Hittite king 164n69
The Sun-god, the Cow, and the Fisherman 214n72
Sun-goddess of Arinna 124, 152n10, 164n69, 180–1
Sun-goddess of the Earth *Also see* Ritual for the Sun-goddess of the Earth
    Allani 96, 114n9
    Purification Ritual for the Former Gods 124
    Song of Release 124–6
Suppiluliuma
    dynastic name 373
    meaning 90
Suppiluliuma I 6, 90, 310, 337n31
    ancestor 151
Suppiluliuma II xxx.n15, 7, 48, 153, 303, 310, 312n57, 315n71
suppliants 203
supralocal audiences
    festivals
        Greece, EIA 234, 237
        Hittite 222, 225–6
        Mycenaean 227–8, 231–2
        NE, BA 225–6
        transfer, verbal art 234
    Hittite royal mortuary rituals 156
supralocal performers, EIA Greek festivals 239–40, 250–1
Susa 72
Susarwa 81, 84
Sutean, Ishtar's lover 71–2n75
sūtra, etymology 37
Suwaliyat 115–16, 124–5, 145
    ritual substitute, *Song of Release* 126
Suwasuna 21n4

sword, Mycenaean, Hattusa 341
Syme 353
symposia 398
syncretism, gods
    Cyprus 305–6, 319–20, 323–4
    transfer, verbal art 110, 161–2
Syria, north *Also see* Alalakh; Aleppo; Carchemish; Ebla; Emar; Hazzi, Mt.; Neo-Hittite; Ugarit
    Abu 87n44
    ambašši ritual 84
    ancestor veneration, royal, BA 186
    Aphrodite 324
    Cedar Forest 175
    continuity 17, 302, 310, 379–81
    culture, in Cyprus 17, 302, 304
    dynastic lists, EIA, 18, 373–4
    Euboea, contact with 2n2, 295
    festivals *See ḫiyara* festival; *(ḫ)išuwa* festival; *Ritual for Mt. Hazzi*
    Gilgamesh tradition 64
        Huwawa 75–6
    Hittite campaigns 6, 8–9, 112n5, 158–9, 163–5, 176–8, 313n59
    Hittite hegemony 6, 303, 312
    Hittite tablets 7
    Hurrian intermediaries 10, 157, 169, 171n19, 186, 257
    Hurrians 10
    reception, Sargonic legends 171n19 *Also see* Sargonic legends, Hurrian mediation
    scribes 8–9, 171n19
    source 289–95, 299, 321, 329–30
        Hittite cuneiform script 8, 171n19
        Sargonic legends, Hattusa 169, 171n19
    wooden writing tablets 424
Syro-Anatolia
    ancestor statues 186, 379–81
    ancestor veneration
        continuity 374, 379–81
        royal 149–50, 186, 350, 373–4, 379–91
    continuity 7, 17, 302, 310–13
        dynastic names 373–6
        memory 349, 373–4
    EIA
        cremation 284
        dynastic names 350
        Hieroglyphic Luwian inscriptions 310–12, 381

T[a-.. .] (god) 81, 84
Tabal 7, 310, 312, 374, 381
Tablet Catalog, DUB.x.KAM Type 25n17

Tablet Catalog, x DUB UMMA/mān Type
　151n8
Tablet of Lallupiya 227n38
Tablet of the Pardon by the Storm-god of Nerik
　253n149
tablets, wooden *See* wooden writing tablets
Tacitus, *Histories* 2.3 324
Tadizuli 34
Tajik bards 48–9
"take from the earth" rituals 93, 95n78
Takidu 84, 121n44, 183
taknaz dā- See "take from the earth" rituals
Talawa 447n111
Tale of Appu 34
　debate 133n2
　formulas, speech introductions 42n90
　HH narr. song 21
　opening 50
　The Sun-god, the Cow and the Fisherman
　　214n72
　type scenes, hospitality scenes 126–7
Talmi-Teshshub 310
Tamassos 296n117, 319
Tanagra 270
Tanaya 317n78
Tanipiya 258n171
Tantalus 104n119, 422, 430
Tapalazunauli 338
Taphos 296
Tapikka 7–8, 342
tapiš 345
tapišana 345
tar 427
Tar(a)iu 348n83
Tara/i-wa/i-za 347
Tarchon 362
Tarhun *Also see* Storm-god; Teshshub
　HH narr. song 25
　syncretized with Teshshub 25, 259
Tarhun(t), 'overcome' 256, 362, 446
Tarhunnaradu 335n17, 341
Tarhunt
　Cilicia, EIA 256
　　Corycus 313
　Lycia, EIA 446
　Luwian Storm-god 259
　Tarquinius 362
Tarhuntaradu 335
Tarhuntassa 7, 312, 334n10, 337, 339, 447n111
　Also see Cilicia, Rough
Tarkasnawa 337n27, 341
tarkhu- 446
tarlā-bird 81, 82

tarna-, appantan 124
tarna-, parā 111, 123–4
tarnaš, waštul 121n42
tarpalli- 97n89, 108n130 *Also see* substitutes,
　ritual
Tarquinius 362
Tarsus
　Achaemenids 314n63
　Assyrians 392n157
　Cyprus 314
　founders 314n63
　Greek names at 314n67
　Hittites 260, 314
　LH IIIC:1b pottery 314
　Persians 314n63
　Phoenicians 311
Tartarus 290
Taru 260
Taruisa 334, 334–5n14, 348n83
Tarukka 257n171
tārumaki-bird 81, 82
Tarwiza 347, 400–1, 453
Tashmisharri 10, 352n10
Tashmishu 84, 127
tatinzi maššaninzi 94 *Also see* Former Gods
Taureon 241n109
Tauri 45
Taurus Mountains 160, 163, 313
　Silver Mountains 170n13
Tawagalawa 335, 339, 441n83
　etymology 339n41
Tawagalawa Letter 339, 341n50, 344, 354,
　441n83
Tāwatu See Tiamat
Teiresias 100–2, 105
Telemachus 282, 296
　hexametric formula 461
Telephus 406
Telepylus 102
Telipinu
　Delphinius 249
　myth 82, 104n115, 252n140
　purulli festival 254
Telipinu Myth (Mugawar)
　formulas, speech introduction 42n90
　Song of Release 121n42
Telipinu Proclamation 33, 171n19, 313
Tell Brak *See* Nagar; Nawar
Tell el Fakhariya 10
Tell Halaf 284, 380, 382n135, 384n141
　Gilgamesh 389–90
Tell Mardikh *See* Ebla
Tell Mozan *See* Urkesh

Tell Tayinat 380n126
Temesa 296
Temnus 451
Temple 1, Hattusa 7, 63n35, 72nn76–77, 90
Temple aux Rhytons 207
Ten-Year Annals of Mursili II 338n35
Tenedos 140, 231n63, 359n41, 450–1
te-o-po-ri-ja 227n36
Teos 209, 358n39
te-qa-jo 228
Termilae 443n92, 447n111
Terpander 213–14, 239, 241n108, 263
   TT 7, 9 214n69
Terrace House, Troy 367–9
tesēti 447n113
Teshshub *Also see* Storm-god; Tarhun
   HH narr. song 25
   invocations 10, 162, 185n83, 260
   of kingship 261n191
   of Kummi 25
   Storm-god of Aleppo 161–2, 185n83, 259–60
   Tarhun, syncretized with 259
Teshshub Cycle 35n57
Testament of Hattusili I 32, 42n90, 158
Teteshapi 254–5
Tethys 55n8
Teucrians 419n3
textualization, definition 38n76
Thaletas 203n17, 214n69
thamuris 240
Thamyris 203n16, 240
Thargelia 235
Thargelion 236
Thasos 372n95
Thebaid, Homeric 393n159, 416n76
Thebe 411, 421n9
Thebes (Egypt), *Iliad* 396n2
Thebes (Greece)
   Hector 406
   Iliad 352
Thebes, BA
   Ahhiyawa 333n6
   ancestor veneration 269–70
   athletic competitions 270
   festivals 220, 228–31
      Anatolian visitors 231–2
   NE seals 345n67
Theocritus 5.83, Σ 239n103
theogonies 24 *Also see* cosmogonies; Hesiod, *Theogony*
   Phoenician 24, 147
Theopompus *FGrH* 115 F 103 382n137
   F 354 75n98

theōriai 234, 238
theoxeniā 271n16
Thera 229–30, 239, 352
   volcanic eruption xxx.n1
Therapne 285n76
therapon, tarpalli- 107n130
Thermon 284n71, 287
Theseus 238
Thesmophoria 264
Thessaloniki 372n95
Thessaly 262n194, 281, 462
   Achilles 371, 406n37
   Hector 406
   Homeric epic 403, 408n44, 454
   Troy, connections to 371–2
Thetis 142
thirsty ones 227, 271
Thoas 120n36, 282n62
Thrace 104n119, 238
   Ares 297
   Homeric tradition 282n62, 297
   Phrygian emigration 362–3, 432
   Thamyris 240
Thracian immigrants, Troy 362–3, 372, 432
Thrasymedes 440
Thucydides 1.3.3 421n5
   1.9.2 422n10
   1.95–7 237n92
   3.104 24n13, 237n94
   4.109 361n54
   5.18 234n80
   en de 427n29
Thunder Songs 21, 163
Thutmose I, annals 317n78
Thyestes 422
Tiamat 29n35, 55n8
Tiawatu *See* Tiamat
Tidnum 290n98
Tiglath-Pileser I 350n1, 389n151
Tiglath-Pileser III 316, 392
Tiglath-Pileser 11.8', 14.11, 27.4, 32.3, 35 iii 8, 47 rev. 7 316n73
Tigris River 27, 177n48, 177n50, 215 *Also see* Aranzah
Tikunani Letter 8–9
Tilla 160n48
Tilmun 166
Timaeus of Tauromenium *FGrH* 566 F 129 410n55
timeri eže 43
ti-ri-se-ro-e 285
Tiryns 228n45, 269n9, 274–5, 346n71, 423
Tissaruliya 223–4

Titanomachy 257n166, 290–1
Titans 257n166, 285, 290–5
Ditanu 290–1
tj-n3-jj-w 317–18n78
Tlepolemus 353, 429, 441
Tlos 231n64, 346, 447n111
Tmolus, Mt. 376
to-no-e-ke-te-ri-jo 227n36
to-ro-o 231n64
to-ro-wo 231n64, 346
toggle switch 147
tombs, Lycian 420, 446, 448
Tous 375
traders
   heroes/characters in legend 45n109, 172, 209–10, 298, 303
   warrior-traders 17
trading network, *Odyssey* 296
transfer, craftsmen, BA 202n10, 346
transfer, cult personnel
   transfer, gods 260, 346–7
      Storm-god of Aleppo 162, 261
transfer, festivals
   Apatouria 235
   Carnea 239
   dynastic marriages 260, 262
   gods, syncretism 305–6
   Greek, EIA 234–6
   from Hattusa 259n178
   (ḫ)išuwa festival 260
   ḫiyara festival 259, 261
   kingship 16, 251, 259, 261
   Thargelia 235
   Zeus 251, 264
transfer, gods *Also see* Storm-god of Aleppo
   Ahhiyawa 202
   kingship 164
   Lazpa 202, 346–7
   peer polity interactions 342–3
transfer, healers 16, 200, 208, 342
transfer, Homeric tradition, Chios 396, 416n76
transfer, performers
   long-distance elite interactions, 200
   transfer, verbal art 16
transfer, verbal art *Also see* intermediaries
   ancestor veneration 4, 13, 15, 17, 108, 110, 165, 196–7, 279, 284–5, 289–92, 370–1, 373, 377–8, 391, 394, 438–9
   epic 445–9
   bards 21, 41, 110, 199–201, 426–8 *Also see* bilingual bards
   nodes 212, 298
   wisdom 16, 166–7

bilingual bards 1, 49, 52–3, 55, 200, 283, 326, 372, 420, 428
bilingual households 199, 283
BA 232, 342–3, 347
Chaoskampf 425
Cilicia, west Anatolia, shared identity 17–18
competitive emulation 16–17, 21, 226, 233, 250–1, 333, 342–3, 394–5
cosmogonies 16, 197, 213–14, 217–18, 262, 292
cross-cultural interaction 1, 3–5, 13, 18
cult singers 162–3, 306
Cyprus
   Cilicia, shared identity 17–18, 302, 310, 316–17, 319
   Greece, shared identity 17–18, 302, 310
dynastic marriages 15, 156–7, 164, 258, 346–7, 435
esoteric knowledge 4, 14, 211–12
exotic, valorization of 4, 17, 200, 206–7, 213, 297–8
festivals 16, 234–6, 239, 250–1, 262–5
   Apollo 16, 243–51, 265, 420, 440, 444, 450–2, 454
   supralocal audiences 4, 13, 16, 234
gods 4, 13, 15, 110, 346
   shared 251
   Storm-god of Aleppo 16, 149, 159, 162–5, 221, 251, 258, 260–1
   syncretism 110, 161–2, 301, 305–6, 319–20, 323–9
   transfer 4, 13, 15, 110, 162–5, 323–9, 346
hero cult, NE influence 17, 81, 197, 267, 279, 284–5, 291–2
historiolae 213
journeys, long-distance, valorization of, 16–17, 107, 167, 200, 209–12, 217–18, 284, 295–9, 425
kingship 4, 16, 218, 251, 260–1, 391
Lesbos 325, 329
long-distance elite interactions 16, 280–1, 296–8, 302
magico-medical rituals 4, 13–14, 200, 213–18, 248, 450–1
mortuary rituals 267
oral transmission 1, 5, 167, 197–8
scribes 54–5, 200
seers 217, 262
transfer, performers 16
wandering bards/seers/healers 16
warrior-trader values, 295–8
   Euboea 295–8
world history 4, 15, 166–7, 196–7

Subject index 631

transitional texts 39
translation literature, Hittite 36
transmission *See* oral transmission; transfer
Treaty between Arnuwanda I and the Kaska 115n10
Treaty between Mursili II and Kupanta-Kurunta of Mira-Kuwaliya 336n27, 337n30
Treaty between Muwattalli II and Alaksandu of Wilusa 2, 90, 245, 247, 331, 337, 351
Treaty between Suppiluliuma I and Sharri-Kushuh of Carchemish 160n48
Treaty between Tudhaliya IV and Kurunta/Ulmi-Teshshub of Tarhuntassa 334n10, 337
trees, sacred 104, 228, 236, 246, 252n140, 320n91, 416n76
tri(to)pateres 287n82
tribes, Greek 236, 239n103, 241n111
    Also see clans; phratries
tripods 219, 233, 274, 286n76
Triptolemus 314n63
tris(h)ērōs 285–7
Tr̃mmili 443n92, 447n111
Troad
  Aeolic inscriptions 359, 405
  Apollo, worship of 451
  Athens 409–10
  competition for 409–10
    Trojan War legend 332, 356, 405, 409–12, 415–17, 432, 434–5, 437–8
  cultural contact/mixing 358
  Greek settlement 356, 359
  Leleges 12n48
  Lesbians 409
  Lycians 443
  Lydians 362
  Phrygians 11, 358
Troia VIIb1 362
Troia VIIb2 362–5
Troia VIIb3 365
Trōilios 362
Trojan language
  Etruscan 362
  Lydian 361–2, 430
Trojan-Phrygian bilingual bards 420, 429
Trojan War
  epic
    Mycenaean 352–3, 401, 416–17
    popular, dating 298
  heroic age, end of 288
  historical event 2–3, 354–5
  legend
    date 347, 371, 400–1, 453
    Homeric tradition, entry into 373, 400–2, 405, 416–17, 454
    Lesbos 406–7
    Phrygians, intermediaries 19, 419–20, 429–32, 454
    and Persian War 196, 418–19, 421
Trojans
  at Mycenaean festivals 231, 346
  Paeonians, descendants 419n3
  Persians, equated with 430n44
Tros 190
Troy *Also see* Taruisa, West Sanctuary, Wilusa
  Apollo 245–8, 351, 449–50
  continuity 357
  D9 363, 371–2n95
  dating of layers 354n20, 362–5
  divine statues 369
  "high Troy" 21
  Phrygians 19, 362–3, 419, 454
  Thracian immigrants 362–3, 372, 432
  West Sanctuary 365–72
Troy, BA
  in Anatolian legends 345–8
  contested space 354, 356, 363, 371–3, 454
  KASKAL.KUR 90n55
  language 361–2
  LH IIIC pottery 362
  Mycenaeans 274, 340, 344–5
  Wilusa 2–3, 334, 410
Troy, EIA
  Aeolian settlement 365, 405–6, 410, 437
  ancestor veneration 349, 367–70
  cult site
    BA ruins 367–71
    Greek 369–71, 373
  dynastic connections 328, 407, 430–1, 434–7
    Also see Aeneidae; Hector
  Greek settlement 365
  memories of BA 196, 351, 363
  Lefkandi 372
  Protogeometric pottery 365, 370–2
  Scepsis 410, 412n63, 435–7
  stone circles 369–70
  Terrace House 367–9
  Thessaly, connections with 371–2
Trqqñt 446
trty 261n190
Tudhaliya I or II? 6n15
Tudhaliya I/II 6, 313, 340–1, 334–5, 347–8, 453
  ancestor 151, 153
  Song of Release 164–5

Subject index

Tudhaliya III 10n37, 352n10
Tudhaliya IV 7, 213n67, 340–1, 343, 352n10
    ancestor veneration 152–3
Tukrish 184
Tukulti-Ninurta I xxx.n15, 345
Tukulti-Ninurta II 390n153
Tunip-Teshshub 8
Tunnawiya 90n53, 93n67
Turkic epic *See* epic, Central Asian
Turkish influence, Serbo-Croatian epic 428
Turkmen bards 48
Tushratta 9
tutelary deity *See* LAMMA
Tuttul *See* Duddul
Tyana 310–11, 357n34
tympanon 384
type scenes
    assembly scenes 133–42, 147
    dressing 327–9
    hospitality 124–8, 142–5
    messengers 43–4
    negative reactions 44–6
    waking for a message 115, 145–6
Typhoeus *See* Typhon
Typhon 221
    Agdistis 343
    Casius, Mt. 258
    Corycus 256, 313
    Cyprus 256, 321
    etymology 258 n174
    Illuyanka 256
    IE 258n174
    Sapon 258
    Seth 257n166
    Song of Hedammu 251, 255
    Song of Ullikummi 255
Tyrrhenian 12, 361–2
Tyrsenoi 361
Tyrtaeus 214n69

ᵈU/10 162n56 *Also see* Storm-god
ubārum 225
Ubykh myths 106n122
Udibsharri 28
Ugarit
    Adaniya 313
    Akkadian *See* Concordance of tablets from Ugarit
    ancestor statues 149–50, 151, 381
    Atrahasis 31-2, 135
    Baal of Aleppo 261
    Baal of Sapon 261, 305
    Ballad of Early Rulers 74n93, 190n102
    birth incantations 214
    Crete 215
    Cypro-Minoan script 304
    Cyprus 303–6
    Ditanu 290
    Epic of Gilgamesh 57, 59n17
    ḫešti-house 382
    Hittite texts 7
    Hittite vassal state 6, 303
    ḫiyara festival 261
    ḫiyaru, month 151n9, 262
    Hiyawa 315–16n71, 441n83
    House of Stars 150
    House of the Hurrian Priest 150n2
    Hurrian texts 10, 131n77, 261n190, 306n25
    incense prayers 131n77
    king lists 150n2, 290
    Kothar 143n26, 325n110
    LÚ.DINGIR.RA 32–3
    lyre deity 324
    musical scores 306n25
    Mycenaean vessels 208
    New Year's festival 151n9
    pit rituals 86–7, 382n139
    rapa ūma 150n1, 151n9, 285, 290
    Reshep 313n61
    royal ancestor veneration 149–50, 290, 381–2
    festivals 151
    Sapon, Mt. 256–8
    šarrašiya 261
    scribal training 32
    Sea Peoples 315
    singers for specific gods 163
    snake-slaying stories 18, 257
    šr 37n70
    Sumerian texts 31–2
    Temple aux Rhytons 207
    theogonies, Ages of Man 291n101
    transfer of craftsmen 202n10
Ugaritic epic 3, 14, 41, 52, 132, 146 *Also see* Aqhat; Baal Cycle; Keret
    formulas, speech introductions 42n90
    Homeric tradition, entry into 302, 305–6
    type scenes, hospitality scenes 143–4
Ugaritic literature *See* Concordance of tablets from Ugarit
Ugljanin, Salih 47–8
Uhhamuwa 375
Uhhaziti 338, 375n108
Uighur bards 48
Ullikummi *Also see Song of Ullikummi*
    kunkunuzzi stone 121n44
    meaning 26

Ullu 69, 71, 72–3, 74, 81–3, 94
   meaning 71
Ulmi-Teshshub 312
Ulu Burun 316n71, 424n19
underworld entrances 89–92, 153 *Also see* rivers, underworld entrances
underworld journeys *See* journeys, underworld
underworld, queen *See* Allani; Ereshkigal; Lelwani; Sun-goddess of Arinna; Sun-goddess of the Earth
Unterstadt, Hattusa 63n35
Upoyo Potniya 87n39
Upper Land (Mesopotamia) 166
Ur 57, 87, 173n27
Ur III period 10, 54, 74–5, 80, 87, 97n87, 161n53, 180–1, 183, 186, 210n50
   Also see Shulgi
Ur-Namma 97n87
Ur-Namma A 97n87
ur.sag 64–5, 75n94, 179
Uranus 290–1
Urartian, language 9
Urartians 106, 392
Urartu 348n83
Urhi-Teshshub 312, 352n10
Uriah 424
Urikki 316
Urkesh 10
   āpi 87, 89–90, 92
   Atalshen 183
   Gilgamesh 72n76
   Hurrians 10, 27, 87, 89
   Kumarbi, home of 27
   Song of Silver 27
Urshanabi 58, 69, 71
Urshu 158
Uruk
   Epic of Gilgamesh 57–8
      assemblies 57, 61
      monument 59
   Gilgamesh 54
   Lugalbanda 210
   Sargon 178
   Sin-leqi-unninni 80n12
   Song of Gilgamesh 65, 71
Urymaeg et le géant borgne 106n122
^dÚS 136n6
UŠ.KU 80n12
Ushas 323n102
ušḫoni See išḫoni
Ušpilulume 373
ušt- 184n82
uštawûm 37

Uta-rapashtim 171–2n21
Utnapishtim 29–31, 58–9, 74, 211
   HH rituals 84
   Sargonic legend 171–2n21, 210n53
   Song of Gilgamesh 69–71, 73–4 *Also see* Ullu
Utruna 253
Utu 175n39 *Also see* Sun-god
Utu-hegal 188n96
Uzbek bards 48–9

The Valorous Sun 298
   16–21 209–10
   vii 1 303
variations
   Atrahasis (Hittite) 30–1
   Epic of Gilgamesh 61–3
   oral-derived 39
   Song of Gilgamesh 63–4, 66–72
   Song of Hedammu 40–1
   Song of Keshshi 28
   Song of Release 122, 129–30
   Song of Ullikummi 39–40
Various Tablet Catalogs 151n8
vessels
   Baal Cycle 143
   Cyprus
      Aky 304
      LH IIIC 276, 404
      PG 275–6, 404
   Dipylon vase 397–8
   festivals, Mycenaean 227–8
   gifts 202, 275, 282, 297n117, 317n78, 344–5
   Harvest Rhyton 231
   heirlooms 207–8, 274, 281, 345, 367
   Lefkandi 281
   Mycenaean
      Cyprus 344–5
      exotic goods 207–8, 344–5
      Levant 207–8
      Troy 344–5
      Ugarit 208
   Nestor's Cup 397–8
   offerings 286
   pendant semi-circle skyphoi 295, 372
   prizes 219, 233, 282n62
   silver bowl (ANKARA 2) 11n40, 347–8, 400–1, 453
   Song of Release 125
   stag *bibrûs* 245–7, 345
Vitruvius 4.1.4–6 413n69
   4.1.5 452n131
voces magicae 94, 214, 242–3
voyages *See* journeys

Wahisi 224
wailing-priest 184
waking for a message *See* type scenes
Walmu 340–1, 362
wa-na-se-wi-ja 227n36
wa-na-se-wi-jo 227
wanassa 227n36, 309
wanax 228n45, 309
wandering bards/seers/healers 200–1, 203–5
　transfer, verbal art 16
wanizas 242n114
Warikas 315–16, 318
warrior graves 17, 275n38, 308, 321
warrior-trader values, Euboea 268, 281, 283
　transfer, verbal art 295–8
Warsama xxx.n1
warship, Phoenician, Karatepe 386
Wash'hamakhwa 106n122
Washukanni 10
waštul tarnaš 121
Wasusarmas 374
ᵐ*Wa-tar-ra-ḫa-ši-iš* 30
water *See* ocean; pools, sacred; rain; rivers; sea; sinkholes; springs, sacred
Watis 381
Watkins, Calvert 3, 21, 36n62, 52n141, 90n53, 224, 243n119, 251n139, 253n150, 255n155, 255n158, 258n174, 330n133, 334n13, 334–5n14, 345n65, 346n73, 351n5, 351n7, 351n9, 362n55, 362n59, 394n163, 398n8, 421n6, 421n8, 427nn29–30, 427n32, 428n33, 430n44, 446n106, 447n112, 448, 461n12
weaving image, denoting song 37
West, M. L., 1–2, 3n7, 22n6, 24n14, 29n36, 41n85, 46n110, 55nn8–10, 78n2, 90n53, 101n104, 102–3, 106n122, 106n127, 113n7, 127n63, 129n68, 133n2, 139n18, 141n20, 143n24, 145n30, 190n104, 193n110, 194n112, 195n114, 200–1n2, 203n15, 215n73, 215n77, 240n105, 240–1n108, 251n139, 257n166, 262n194, 263n198, 266nn1–2, 289n96, 293n106, 293n109, 295, 299n126, 323n100, 325n110, 326, 327n119, 327nn121–123, 396–7, 398n12, 399n14, 399n17, 400n17, 401n22, 403, 406, 407, 408, 423n15, 425n21, 426n27, 427n30, 428n33, 433, 441nn85–86, 445n102, 446n106, 450n125, 453n133, 458n2, 458–9n3, 459, 460n6, 461n11

West Sanctuary, Troy 365–72
west Semitic *Also see* Amurru; Phoenician; Ugarit
　ancestors, divinized *See* mᵉrappîm
　bilingual bards 52, 53
　cosmogonies 291–2
　Cyprus 301, 304
　dynastic lists 197n119
　Elkunirsa and Ashertu 216, 424
　epic 52–3 *Also see* Ugaritic epic
　　Cyprus 306, 329
　gods, syncretized on Cyprus 305–6
　　transfer, verbal art 301, 319–20
　Hittite culture, contribution to 4, 294
　Iapetus 292–4
　incantations, Egypt 213n66
　influence 2
　　Hesiod 285, 289–94
　　Theogony 285
　　Works and Days, Ages of Man 285, 289–92
　intermediaries 4–5
　legendary founders 393
　lyre 324–5
　melku 161n53
　meropes 289–90, 292
　Neo-Hittite 294, 311
　Ogygus 292–3
　prophets 201
　Storm-god *See* Adad; Hadad
　Titans 290–2
west Semitic-Hurrian *See* Hurrian-West Semitic
wife-stealing 142, 434, 454
Wilusa *Also see* Alaksandu; Troy
　Ahhiyawa 344, 354, 431–2
　　dynastic marriages 347, 351
　Arzawa 331, 333, 337
　Assuwa 334
　EIA memories 333, 347, 351, 354
　"high/steep Wilusa" 21, 400, 453
　Milawatta Letter 340–1
　node of contact 333, 347
　peer polity interaction 333–4
　supralocal gods invoked from 342
　Troy 2–3, 334, 410
Wilusiad 21, 363, 400, 453
Wilusiya 334
wisdom *Also see* ḫattātar; mādi
　admonitory history 196
　Ballad of Early Rulers 190
　bards, transfer, verbal art 16, 166–7
　Ea 131n77
　epic 187

Epic of Gilgamesh 59
Hattusili I 158
HH narr. song 187
HH parables 131, 187
Ishhara 113, 131, 187
knowledge of past, 59, 187, 190
Kumarbi 131n77
oral, *Epic of Gilgamesh* 59
šarrena ritual 183–4, 187
scribes 59
Song of Release 113, 131, 158, 187
Song of Silver 187n94
wisdom literature
   Mesopotamian, Hattusa 33n51
   scribal training 32–3, 60
Wiyanawanda 447n111
wo-de-wi-jo-jo me-no 227
Wolf-god, Apollo 447
wooden writing tablets 11, 12n45, 400n17, 424
world history 196
   ancestor veneration 196–7, 350
   cosmogonies 188–9, 196, 292
   Ebla 160–1, 175–6
   epic 3, 111–12
   genealogies 196, 350, 394
      Catalog of Women 377–8
   Hittite court 166–7
   king lists 167
   lists 187–91, 196
   local courts 15, 174, 185, 196–7, 394
   local history 196
   transfer, verbal art 4, 15, 166–7, 196–7
wrestling
   festivals 57, 79–80, 223n15
   Gilgamesh tradition 57, 61n26, 79
writing *Also see* oral performance; scribes
   Cypriot syllabary 308
   Cypro-Minoan script 304, 309
   Cyprus 309
      use of 309
   Greek alphabet 295n112, 397n6, 400n17
writing tablets, wooden *See* wooden writing
      tablets
written object
   Annals of Hattusili I 180
   Cuthean Legend of Naram-Sin 178–9
   Epic of Gilgamesh 59, 64, 178

Xanthus (city) 239, 426, 446
Xanthus of Lydia *FGrH* 765 F 13a 343n58
   F 4 378
Xanthus River 418, 442
Xerxes 418–19

Yakapınar 382
Yalburt 447n111
Yam, battle with Baal 25, 257
   victory celebration, 143–4
Yamhad 158, 162n56
yanar 424n20
Yarim-Lim III 158
Yasmah-Addu 161n53, 186n90
Yaw(a)naya 319n84
Yawan 319n84
Yazılıkaya
   ancestor veneration 152–3
   baetyl 152n13, 225
   festivals 152, 225
   ḫešti-house 152
   Storm-god with mace 320
Ygrš 257
Yigris-Halab 257
Ykhd 304
Yugoslav *See* Serbo-Croatian

Zagros mountains 117n21, 175n39
Zaliyanu, Mt. 254, 258n171
Zalpa(r) 158
zamāru 36
zandanatar 81, 84
zatraš 81, 84
zawalli 153
Zazalla 120–2, 130, 137–8, 140–2, 150, 195
   at Ebla 161n53
Zeleian Lycians 443
Zenobius of Athos 1.62 398n11
Zephyrus 345
ze-pu₃-ra₃ 345
Zeus
   Agamemnon's scepter 422
   Ages of Man 266, 288–9, 291
   Anatolia, EIA 234, 255–6
   Anatolian Storm-god 234, 251, 255–6, 313, 446
   Apollo *lukeios* 250n136
   Argonautica 104
   battle with snake
      Illuyanka 251, 255
      Typhon 221, 251, 255–8, 321
      entry into Homeric tradition 256, 301, 306, 321
   birth 25n16
   bulls 216n77, 328n126
   Carian 234n81
   Chaoskampf 251
   Casius 183
   Cilicia 255–6, 313

Zeus (cont.)
   Cypria 288n87, 301
   Cyprus 306
   Dolichenus 104, 259n181
   Europa 216n77, 318n79
   festivals, transfer 250, 265
   heroes, destruction of race of 266, 288, 291, 301
   hexametric formula 461
   Homeric Hymn to Aphrodite 327
   Homeric Hymn to Demeter 114, 449n122
   Iliad
      Apollo, father of 132, 139
      Dardanus, father of 190
      Ganymede 190
      Iliad 5 325
      omens, sends 193–4, 434
      Sarpedon, death of 445, 453
      Sarpedon, father of 423n14, 439
      Thetis 142
      Troy 288
      wise 146
   Io 215, 318n79
   kingship 250n136, 422
      in heaven 290–2
   Kumarbi cycle 255, 290
   Lycian 446
   Mycenaean festival 227, 229
   nostoi 407
   Odysseus 101n103, 146
   Pegasus 425
   Phrygian "Young Male God" 328n126
   prooimia
      Homeridae 24n13
      Iliad 449–50
   Tarhunt 255–6, 446
   Titanomachy 257n166, 290–1
Ziduri 69, 71 *Also see* Shiduri; Nahmazule
   meaning 73–4
Ziggarata 257n171
Zincirli 7, 284, 379–80, 381n134, 384n141, 384n144, 389n151, 393, 424n20
Zipani 192n109
Ziplanda
   priests at KI.LAM 225
   purulli 252n140, 253n148
   Storm-god 253n148
Ziusudra 29–30, 190
Zukki 94, 238
Zulki 96, 98n91

List of Hittite texts by *CTH* number

CTH Number	Title
1	*Proclamation of Anitta*
4	*Annals of Hattusili I*
6	*Testament of Hattusili I*
8	*Palace Chronicles*
9	*Fragments of Palace Chronicles*
14	*Res Gestae of Hattusili I*
16	*Puhanu Chronicle*
19	*Telipinu Proclamation*
50	*Treaty between Suppiluliuma I and Sharrikushuh of Carchemish*
61	*(Ten-Year/ Comprehensive) Annals of Mursili II*
68	*Treaty between Mursili II and Kupanta-Kurunta of Mira-Kuwaliya*
70	*Mursili II Concerning the Tawananna Affair*
76	*Treaty between Muwatalli II and Alaksandu of Wilusa*
81	*Apology of Hattusili III*
106	*Bronze Tablet Treaty: between Tudhaliya IV and Kurunta/Ulmi-Teshshub of Tarhuntasssa*
121	*Inscription of Suppiluliuma II Concerning the Conquest of Alashiya*
139	*Treaty between Arnuwanda I and the Kaska*
142	*Annals of Tudhaliya I/II*
143	*Annals of Arnuwanda I*
146	*Midas of Pahhuwa*
147	*Madduwatta Indictment*
151	*Letter from Amenhotep III to Tarhuntaradu of Arzawa*
152	*Letter from Arzawa to Amenhotep III*
163	*Letter from Ramses II to Hattusili III*
166	*Letter from Ramses II to Kupanta-Kurunta of Mira-Kuwaliya*

172	*Letter from Hattusili III to Kadashman-Enlil*
181	*Tawagalawa Letter*
182	*Milawatta Letter*
183	*Letter from the King of Ahhiyawa to the Hittite King*
187	*Fragments of Royal Letters* (includes *Tikunani Letter*)
208	*Fragments of Akkadian Letters*
209	*Fragments of Hittite Letters*
211	*Fragments of Annals* (includes "The Offenses of Seha River Land")
214	*Fragments of Historical Texts*
216	*Fragments of Akkadian Historical Texts*
243	*Inventory of Clothing and Fabric*
252	*Ashmunikal's Instructions for the Workers of the Stone-House*
276	*Tablet Catalog, DUB.x.KAM Type*
278	*Tablet Catalog, x DUB UMMA/mān Type*
282	*Various Tablet Catalogs*
299	*Sa Vocabulary*
310	*Sargon, King of Battle*
311	*Naram-Sin in Asia Minor*
313	*Prayer to Adad*
321	*Illuyanka*
324	*Telipinu Myth (Mugawar)*
333	*Disappearance and Return of Anzili and Zukki*
341	*Song of Gilgamesh*
342	*Elkunirsa and Ashertu*
343	*Song of LAMMA*
344	*Song of Birth*
345	*Song of Ullikummi*
346	*Fragments of the Kumarbi Myth* (includes *Song of the Sea*)
347	*Atrahasis*
348	*Song of Hedammu*
349	*Teshshub Cycle*
350	*Fragments Mentioning Ishtar (Mt. Pishaisha)*
351	*Fragments Mentioning Ea (Ea and the Beast)*
360	*Tale of Appu*

361	*Song of Keshshi*
362	*Heroic Deeds of Gurparanzah*
363	*The Sun-god, the Cow, and the Fisherman*
364	*Song of Silver*
370	*Mythological Fragments (includes Hurrian Song of Birth)*
373	*Kantuzzili's Prayer to the Sun-god*
375	*Prayer of Arnuwanda I and Ashmunikal for the Sun-goddess of Arinna*
383	*Prayer of Hattusili III and Puduhepa for the Sun-goddess of Arinna*
389	*Fragments of Prayers*
395	*Ritual of Hantitassu of Hurma*
404	*Ritual of Mastigga against Family Quarrel*
409	*Ritual of Tunnawiya*
419	*Substitution Rituals for the King*
432	*Ritual against Depression*
446	*Purification Ritual for the Former Gods*
447	*Ritual against Underworld Powers*
448	*Ritual for the Sun-goddess of Earth*
449	*Rituals Mentioning the Former Gods*
450	*Death Rituals*
456	*Fragments of Purification Rituals*
481	*Expansion of the Cult of the Goddess of Night*
483	*Evocation Rituals*
484	*Evocation Ritual for DINGIR.MAḪ.MEŠ and the Fate-Goddesses*
490	*Ritual of the Hurrian Woman Ashdu against Witchcraft*
509	*Cult Inventories of the Storm-god*
525	*Cult Inventories under Tudhaliya IV*
533	*Moon Omen Compendium*
549	*Omen Compendium Concerning the "Presence"*
562	*Oracle for an Itinerary in the Kaska Territory*
568	*Oracle Concerning the Celebration of Various Festivals*
570	*Liver Oracle*
600	*New Year's Festival*
604	*AN.TAḪ.ŠUM Festival, Outline*

609	AN.TAḪŠUM Festival, Eleventh Day
612	AN.TAḪŠUM Festival, Sixteenth Day: Temple of Ziparwa, Sun-goddess of the Earth
626	Nuntarriyašḫaš Festival
627	KI.LAM Festival
628	(Ḫ)išuwa Festival
629	Recurring Festival
644	Fragments of Rituals Mentioning Pirinkir
660	Offerings for Royal Statues
661	King Lists
665	Fragments Mentioning the Ašuša(tal)la-People
671	Offering and Prayer for the Storm-god of Nerik
673	Tablet of the Pardon by the Storm-god of Nerik (-> CTH 525.7)
674	Purulli Festival
701	Drink Offerings for the Throne of Hebat (also see CTH 790)
716	Ritual for Ishtar of Nineveh
717	Hurro-Hittite Prayer to Ishtar
718	Ritual for Ishtar/Pirinkir with Babilili Incantations
738	Festival for the Goddess of Teteshapi
742	Hattic Songs, Women of Tissaruliya
758	Ritual of Puriyanni against Impurity of a House
766	Luwian Moon Incantation
767	Incantations with Luwianisms
771	Tablet of Lallupiya
772	Festival of Istanuwa
774	Hurrian Omens
775	Historical-Mythological Hurrian Texts (includes šarrena ritual and a song fragment naming Sargon)
777	Itkahi/Itkalzi Ritual
778	Fragments of Itkalzi Rituals Naming Tashmisharri and Taduhepa
780	Ritual of Allaturahhi
784	Hurrian Ritual for the Royal Couple (includes Invocation of Teshshub and Hebat)
785	Ritual for Mt. Hazzi

788	*Ritual of Shalashu*
789	*Song of Release*
790	*Fragments of Hurro-Hittite Rituals and Incantations*
791	*Hurrian Fragments* (includes *Invocation of Teshshub of Aleppo*)
800	*Sumerian Incantations*
810	*The Moon-god and the Cow*
811	*Akkadian Prescription against Fever*
812	*Akkadian Incantations*
819	*Akkadian Fragments* (includes *Naram-Sin*)
822	*The Merchants' Tale*
832	*Hittite Fragments with Varying Content*

Index of tablets and inscriptions

Hittite tablets

(Note: Unpublished fragments are cited by their excavation numbers.)

ABoT 1.14 iii 8–24 223n18
ABoT 1.14 iii 12–13 222n11
ABoT 1.48 133n2
Bo 69/546 41n84
Bo 69/546 iii 5′–18′ 128
Bo 5700 4′ 82
Bo 6404 41n84
Bo 8617 123n50
FHG 21 i 9 160n48
Gurney 5 83n19
HFAC 12 i 4 187n94
HFAC 12 i 7 27, 36n66
HFAC 12 i 7–8 20
HFAC 12 i 8 187n94
HT 10 2′–15′ 67
IBoT 2.1 vi 8′–14′ 151n8
IBoT 2.17 2′–5′ 151n8, 252n141
IBoT 2.128 rev. 2′–7′ 98
IBoT 2.135 41n84
IBoT 4.7 192n108
KBo 1.10 rev. 34–48 213n67
KBo 1.10 rev. 58–61 186n91
KBo 1.52 i 15′–16′ 36n68
KBo 2.1 343
KBo 2.3 iv 26–31 154n24
KBo 2.5 iii 13′–24′ 253n148
KBo 2.9 i 1′–13′ 342n53
KBo 2.9 iv 12 95n76
KBo 2.11 rev. 11′–14′ 207n32, 344
KBo 2.16 343
KBo 3.1 i 30–1 171n19
KBo 3.1 ii 1–4 313n59
KBo 3.4 ii 15–32 338n35
KBo 3.4 ii 50–2 338
KBo 3.4 iii 2–4 338
KBo 3.6 ii 22–4 278n44
KBo 3.7 i 1–8 252

KBo 3.7 ii 15′–26′ 254
KBo 3.9, 10 173n29
KBo 3.13 192n108
KBo 3.13 obv. 11′ 192n109
KBo 3.16 192n108
KBo 3.16 iii 5–13 192
KBo 3.17, 18 192n108
KBo 3.18 iii 9–17 192
KBo 3.19 192n108
KBo 3.19 iii 9–17 192
KBo 3.40 rev. 8′–11′ 163–4
KBo 3.41 obv. 1–14 164n69
KBo 4.9 iii 11–12 151n6
KBo 4.11 rev. 46 21
KBo 5.13 i 29′–34′ 336n27
KBo 7.45 i 5′–6′ 160n48
KBo 7.57 95n79
KBo 7.70 6′ 184n76
KBo 8.35 ii 10′ 115
KBo 8.86 obv. 5′, rev. 4′ 256–7
KBo 8.88 obv. 8 256–7
KBo 8.144 i 4′, iv 22′ 74n90
KBo 8.144 l. edge 73
KBo 10.1 obv. 8 157
KBo 10.1 obv. 32–3 159n47
KBo 10.1 obv. 37–8, 43–4 159
KBo 10.1 rev. 14 124n51
KBo 10.1 rev. 18–25 176–7
KBo 10.2 i 15–18 162n56
KBo 10.2 i 17–18 157
KBo 10.2 ii 18 176n46
KBo 10.2 ii 26–8, 38–40 159
KBo 10.2 iii 1 176n46
KBo 10.2 iii 15–20 123–4
KBo 10.2 iii 21–2 180
KBo 10.2 iii 29–42 176–7
KBo 10.7 157n34

KBo 10.20 i 19–23 223n15
KBo 10.20 ii 11–13 151n8
KBo 10.20 iii 19 259n182
KBo 10.23+ vi 1–8 224n23
KBo 10.25 v 2′–3′ 224n25
KBo 10.45 i 32′–5′ 96
KBo 10.45 i 39′–45′ 96
KBo 10.45 i 45′–52′ 98
KBo 10.45 ii 21–5 98
KBo 10.45 ii 36 96n81
KBo 10.45 ii 36–8 98n94
KBo 10.45 iv 13–15 121n41
KBo 10.47a i 65
KBo 10.47a iv 16–32 67
KBo 10.47b 65
KBo 10.47b i 65
KBo 10.47c iv 66
KBo 10.47c iv 20 68n59
KBo 10.47c iv 1–7 66
KBo 10.47c iv 8–30 66
KBo 10.47d iv 66
KBo 10.47d iv 1–7 66
KBo 10.47d iv 20 68n59
KBo 10.47e i 65
KBo 10.47f ii 65
KBo 10.47g iii 1′–3′ 65
KBo 10.47g iii 2′ 177n50
KBo 10.47g iii 4′–28′ 66
KBo 10.47g iii 12′–14′ 173n26
KBo 10.47h iv 66
KBo 10.47h iv 8–30 66
KBo 10.47h iv 16–32 67
KBo 11.14 iii 5′–31′ 94n71
KBo 11.42 l. col. 2′ 224n25
KBo 12.1 173n29
KBo 12.13 158
KBo 12.38 303n7
KBo 12.38 ii 17′–21′ 153n17
KBo 12.83 i 1–5 252
KBo 13.46 173n29
KBo 13.46 ii 8′ 171n21
KBo 13.78 rev. 6′–10′ 163–4
KBo 13.241 214n72
KBo 13.257 223n18
KBo 15.29 iii 12′ 72n80
KBo 15.52 v 1″–2″ 260–1
KBo 17.94 iii 29′–32′ 95
KBo 18.117 341n48
KBo 18.181 rev. 33′ 344
KBo 19.98 191n108
KBo 19.99 171n19, 191–2n108
KBo 19.102, 108 133n2
KBo 19.109 + 109a, 110, 111 41n84
KBo 19.112 rev.? 1′–15′ 127

KBo 19.112 rev.? 18′ 43n99
KBo 19.114 66
KBo 19.115 65n47
KBo 19.116 69, 70
KBo 19.124 72
KBo 20.60 v 4′–11′ 260–1
KBo 20.114 i 5′–6′ 160n48
KBo 21.90 23′ 255n154
KBo 22.6+ 173n29
KBo 22.6 i 6′ 173n30
KBo 22.6 i 9′ 174n33
KBo 22.6 i 16′–20′ 177n50
KBo 22.6 i 17′ 174n33
KBo 22.6 i 21′–8′ 173–4
KBo 22.6 i 22′ 173n31
KBo 22.6 iv 11′–12′ 180
KBo 22.6 iv 19′, 22′ 174n33
KBo 22.51 41n84
KBo 22.85 192n108
KBo 22.87 26
KBo 22.91 70, 71
KBo 22.125 i 9′, 10′ 246
KBo 23.15 iii 17′–18′ 163n66
KBo 23.103 iv 14′–19′ 252n140
KBo 25.48 iii 6′–9′ 254–5
KBo 26.58 iv 33′–36′ 117n23
KBo 26.58 iv 51′–4′ 127n64
KBo 26.64 ii 5′–12′ 327n120
KBo 26.65 ii 18′ 31n44
KBo 26.65+ 25n15
KBo 26.71 41n84
KBo 26.71 iii 5′–18′ 128
KBo 26.72, 73, 74, 75 41n84
KBo 26.82 51
KBo 26.85 133n2
KBo 26.88 iv 1–3 121n42
KBo 26.101 65
KBo 26.105 25n17
KBo 26.112 41n84
KBo 26.112 iii 5′–18′ 128
KBo 26.117 51n131
KBo 27.42 ii 21–67 225n27
KBo 27.117 214n72
KBo 27.176 10′ 51
KBo 27.217 34
KBo 28.24 317n77
KBo 28.25 rev. 7″ 317n77
KBo 28.30 213n67
KBo 31.31 151n8
KBo 31.95+ 27
KBo 32.10 115n12, 117
KBo 32.11 115, 129–31
KBo 32.11 i 1–3 111
KBo 32.11 i 1–13 113

KBo 32.11 i 5-6 131
KBo 32.11 i 8 116
KBo 32.11 i 9 158
KBo 32.11 iv 6', 7', 9', 12'-22' 116
KBo 32.12 129-31
KBo 32.13 118n26, 144, 170n15
KBo 32.13+ 124-6, 128-9
KBo 32.13 i/ii 10 43n95
KBo 32.13 bott. edge 2 37n69
KBo 32.14 129-31
KBo 32.14 i/ii 55-60 118n28
KBo 32.14 ii 9-14 44
KBo 32.14 ii 50-6 44
KBo 32.14 iii 1 136
KBo 32.14 iii 1-5 130n76
KBo 32.14 l. edge 1-3 44n104
KBo 32.14 rev. 44-6 44
KBo 32.15 118n26, 120-2
KBo 32.15 i 12' 136n6
KBo 32.15 i 20'-iv 6 141
KBo 32.15 ii 13', 17' 135
KBo 32.15 l. edge 111n3
KBo 32.16 122
KBo 32.16 ii 6-13, ii 17-iii 18' 120
KBo 32.16 iii 4' 37n69
KBo 32.17, 18 116n17
KBo 32.19 117-19, 122n45
KBo 32.19 i 1-31 118
KBo 32.19 ii 1-31, 45 118
KBo 32.19 iii 27'-51' 118n26
KBo 32.20 118n 26, 119
KBo 32.22 118n26
KBo 32.24 118n26
KBo 32.26 l. col. 5' 119n31
KBo 32.29 118n26
KBo 32.31 115n12
KBo 32.32 115n12
KBo 32.37 4'-19' 115
KBo 32.54 6'-9' 120n36
KBo 32.63 115n12
KBo 32.65 125n55
KBo 32.66 2' 37n69
KBo 32.67 115n12
KBo 32.72, 82, 105 125n55
KBo 32.107 43n94
KBo 32.121 32
KBo 32.126+ 126a 32
KBo 32.128-33 32, 61
KBo 32.129 2', 6', 9' 68
KBo 32.208, 209 115n12
KBo 32.214 i 8'-11' 43n94
KBo 32.215 116n17
KBo 32.216 118n26

KBo 33.8 ii$^?$ 4', 9' 160n48
KBo 33.10 72
KBo 33.115 i 5', iv 2' 86
KBo 33.119 13' 84n22
KBo 33.178 rev. 2'-10' 260n186
KBo 35.43 i 7' 184n76
KBo 36.7a iv 51'-4' 127n64
KBo 36.26 30
KBo 36.29 iv 7' 85
KBo 36.13 r. col. 15' 85
KBo 39.8 ii 26-54 93n66
KBo 39.90 152n12
KBo 39.273 157
KBo 45.10 iii 41-8 97
KBo 47.147 30n40
KBo 51.38 95n79
KBo 52.10 iv 28' 25n16
KBo 53.5 30
KBo 53.232 73
KBo 54.1 173n29
KBo 54.2 69, 71n73
KBo 56.6 41n84
KBo 57.15 145n30
KBo 57.269 173n29
KBo 62.54 157n34
KUB 1.16 iii 56 42n90
KUB 3.23+ 340
KUB 3.67 213n67
KUB 4.12 61
KUB 4.12 i 13'-19' 62
KUB 5.6 ii 57'-64' 346
KUB 5.6 iv 9 162n57
KUB 7.41 95n79
KUB 7.41 i 1-2 95
KUB 8.29 iv 1'-3' 157n34
KUB 8.47 157n34
KUB 8.48 69, 70
KUB 8.48 i 18-19 43n99
KUB 8.49 69, 70
KUB 8.50 70, 71
KUB 8.51 ii 65
KUB 8.51 iii 1'-12' 66
KUB 8.51 iii, iv 66
KUB 8.52 68
KUB 8.53 iii, iv 66
KUB 8.53 iv 6' 67
KUB 8.53 iv 13'-31' 66
KUB 8.54 i 3 68
KUB 8.55 65
KUB 8.56 65
KUB 8.57 65
KUB 8.57 i 1-2 36n66, 54, 65
KUB 8.57 i 7-9 127n63

KUB 8.58 68
KUB 8.59 69
KUB 8.60 72
KUB 8.60 l. edge 72
KUB 8.61 73
KUB 8.61 i 4′ 74n90
KUB 8.61 iv 22′ 74n90
KUB 8.62 78, 81–5, 98–9
KUB 8.62 iv 13′ 78
KUB 8.63 30
KUB 8.63 i 14′ 31n44
KUB 8.65 41n84
KUB 8.66 41n84
KUB 8.67 iv 4′ 51n131
KUB 9.13 obv. 6′, rev. 13–18 154
KUB 11.8 151n10
KUB 11.8 iv 20′–5′ 156n31
KUB 11.9 151n10
KUB 11.9 iv 20′–5′ 156n31
KUB 12.11 ii? 29′–31′ 163n66
KUB 12.58 i 12′–14′ 90n53
KUB 12.61 iii 126n59
KUB 12.65 41n84
KUB 12.65 iii 5′–18′ 128
KUB 12.66 iv 8′–17′ 253n147
KUB 13.8 obv. 1–9 124
KUB 14.1+ 336
KUB 14.1 rev. 75 318
KUB 14.2 rev. 4–6 338–9
KUB 14.3 339
KUB 14.3 i 1–4 441n83
KUB 14.3 i 53–5 344
KUB 14.3 iv 7–9 354n19
KUB 14.4 iv 17–18 115n10
KUB 14.7 iv 3–4 121n42
KUB 14.15 i 24′–26′ 338n33
KUB 15.31 i 1–2 94n74
KUB 15.31 ii 10–21 95
KUB 15.32 ii 4′–16′ 95
KUB 15.34 i 52–65 342n53
KUB 15.35 i 25′–7′ 342n53
KUB 17.1 iii 145n30
KUB 17.2 65
KUB 17.3 70, 71
KUB 17.3 iii 9′ 74n90
KUB 17.7 iii 10′–11′ 43n101
KUB 17.7 iii 32′ 43n92
KUB 17.10 iii 24–5 121n42
KUB 17.21 i 9′–27′ 123n50
KUB 17.21 ii 10′–11′ 162n61
KUB 17.35 343
KUB 17.35 iii 9–15 224n21

KUB 19.27 obv. 8′ 160n48
KUB 19.55 rev. 32′–44′ 340–1
KUB 19.55 rev. 45′ 341n50
KUB 20.52 i 17′, 21′ 260n187
KUB 21.1 iv 27 247n123
KUB 21.1 iv 28 90n55
KUB 21.2 i 1–12 331
KUB 21.5 i 1–9 331
KUB 21.5 i 18 362n59
KUB 22.25 obv. 19′–21′ 253n147
KUB 23.9 68
KUB 23.9 7 177n50
KUB 23.11 ii 14′–19′ 334n14
KUB 23.13 341
KUB 23.21 obv. 6′ 315–16n71
KUB 23.21 rev. 16′–23′ 334n14
KUB 23.125 iii 5′–7′ 338
KUB 24.5 obv. 6′, rev. 13–18 154
KUB 24.8 i 1–6 50
KUB 24.8 i 27 42n88
KUB 24.8 ii 14–18 127
KUB 25.27 223n18
KUB 26.91 335
KUB 27.34 iii 12′–14′ 86
KUB 27.38 183–90
KUB 27.38 iii 8–9 159n45
KUB 27.42 10
KUB 27.42 rev. 15′ 261n91
KUB 30.1–4 85n29
KUB 30.25 rev. 19–20 156n32
KUB 30.43 iii 2′–3′ 25n17
KUB 30.68 ii 3″–9″ 151n8
KUB 31.1 192n108
KUB 31.3 174
KUB 31.4 obv. 1–14 164n69
KUB 31.29 339
KUB 31.124 i 5′–7′ 123n50
KUB 32.46 obv. 15′–17′ 86
KUB 32.46 obv. 20′ 86
KUB 33.7a iv 44′–8′ 127
KUB 33.84, 85, 86, 88 41n84
KUB 33.92 iii 18′–22′ 117n23
KUB 33.92 iv 3′–19′ 39–40
KUB 33.93 iii 25′ 118–19n28
KUB 33.93 iii 32′ 43n92
KUB 33.93 iv 33′–6′ 117n23
KUB 33.93 iv 44′–8′ 127
KUB 33.96 i 4 36n66
KUB 33.96 iv 44′–8′ 127
KUB 33.98 i 15–16 127n63
KUB 33.100 41n84
KUB 33.100 iii 8′–16′ 123n49

KUB 33.103 41n84
KUB 33.103 obv. ii 1–8 123n49
KUB 33.106 iii 52′ 31n44
KUB 33.108 26
KUB 33.109 i 7–8 127n63
KUB 33.110 ii 5′ 133n2
KUB 33.112 iv 10′ 31n44
KUB 33.113 i 10′ 257n170
KUB 33.113 i 15′–23′ 39–40
KUB 33.113 i 16′–17′ 43n99
KUB 33.116 41n84
KUB 33.116 ii 1′–8′ 123n49
KUB 33.120 i 1–4 50
KUB 33.120 i 1–5 97
KUB 33.120 i 7–19 189
KUB 33.120 i 12–15 97
KUB 33.120 i 30, 34 31n44
KUB 33.120 ii 5 131n77
KUB 33.120 ii 42–73 121n44
KUB 33.120 iii 15′ 131n77
KUB 33.120 iii 19′–21′ 45n109
KUB 33.120 iii 67′–72′ 45
KUB 33.120 iv 28′ 25n16
KUB 33.121 145n30
KUB 33.121 iii 7′ 122n44
KUB 33.122 41n84
KUB 33.122 ii 6′–9′ 128
KUB 33.123 66
KUB 33.124 70, 71
KUB 34.65 i 23″ 96n84
KUB 34.116 v 1″–2″ 260–1
KUB 35.54 iii 18 21n4
KUB 35.103 iii 11 21n4
KUB 35.132 iii 1 227n38
KUB 35.133 i 15′–17′ 242n114
KUB 35.135 iv 16′–17′ 21n4
KUB 36.7a iii 39′–41′ 43n101
KUB 36.8 i 15–16 127n63
KUB 36.10 iii 18′–22′ 117n23
KUB 36.12 i 15′–23′ 39–40
KUB 36.12 ii 5′–12′ 327n120
KUB 36.12 iii 7′ 31n44
KUB 36.16 41n84
KUB 36.16 iii 8′–16′ 123n49
KUB 36.31 5′–7′ 45
KUB 36.55 ii 10′–11′ 97n89
KUB 36.56 41n84
KUB 36.57 41n84
KUB 36.62 145n30
KUB 36.65 71n73
KUB 36.65 3′ 74n90
KUB 36.72 ii 65

KUB 36.72 iii 66
KUB 36.73 3′ 67
KUB 36.73 4′ 68n59
KUB 36.74 30n41
KUB 36.74 iii 2′ 31n44
KUB 36.89 93n68
KUB 36.95 41n84
KUB 36.97 152n13
KUB 37.108–10 85n29
KUB 37.128 60
KUB 39.4 obv. 13 96n84
KUB 39.4 rev. 19–20 156n32
KUB 39.8 iii 29″–36″ 154n23
KUB 40.4 158
KUB 40.4 ii 6′ 112n5
KUB 41.8 iv 12–14 121n41
KUB 42.94 iv$^?$ 15′–25′ 154
KUB 42.100 iv 12′–21′ 253n149
KUB 44.4 214n72
KUB 44.7 25n17
KUB 44.7 i 11′–12′, vi 3′ 256
KUB 44.7 i 11′–14′ 108
KUB 45.21 rev. 29′ 108
KUB 45.63 25n17
KUB 45.73 6′ 160n48
KUB 45.84 obv. 16′, 18′ 160n49
KUB 47.2 133n2
KUB 47.2 l. edge 9–11 28n31
KUB 47.4 i 4″ 184n76
KUB 47.5 i 6′ 184n76
KUB 47.5 iv 13–15 43n94
KUB 47.9 72
KUB 47.10 72n76
KUB 47.15 73
KUB 47.16 72n76
KUB 47.19 214n72
KUB 47.56 25n16, 51
KUB 47.78 i 12′–14′ 185n83
KUB 47.78 i 12′–15′ 162n58
KUB 48.90 rev. 32′–44′ 340–1
KUB 48.90 rev. 45′ 341n50
KUB 48.95 i 1–12 331
KUB 58.48 iv 2′–16′ 223n19
KUB 58.74 ii$^?$ 13–16 90n53
KUB 59.75 i 22′ 95n78
KUB 60.14 65
StBoTB 1 i 14–ii 20 334n10
StBoTB 1 iv 31 337n31
StBoTB 1 iv 32 337
StBoTB iv 36 337n31
TC-4F5h 73
VBoT 1 335

VBoT 2 14–25 335
VBoT 13 4′–6′, 14′ 159
VBoT 59 25n17
VBoT 120 ii 5′–22′ 155

Amarna tablets

EA 3.18–20 226
EA 31 335
EA 32 335
EA 34 226n30
EA 37 303n5
EA 39 303n9
EA 151.49–55 317n77
EA 349 rev. 5′ 172–3
EA 359 171–3
EA 359 rev. 4′ 177n50
EA 375 172n22

Egyptian inscriptions

KRI 4.2 443n93
KRI 4.4 §22 315n70
KRI 5.8 §37.1 317n77
KRI 5.9 §39 356n26
KRI 5.9 §40 317n77

Hieroglyphic Luwian inscriptions

ANKARA 2 §§2–3 11n40, 347–8, 400–1, 453
BURUNKAYA 312n57
KARADAĞ 1–2 312n57
KARATEPE 1 §II, 10
 §III, 14 316n72
KARATEPE 1 §XL, 212 313n61
KIZILDAĞ 1–3 312n57
KULULU 2 A4 381
MARAŞ 1 374
NIŞANTEPE 153

Linear B tablets

KN De 1381.B 318
KN E 842.3 247
KN Fp 5 226
KN Ga 953-955 227
KN Ga 1058 227n36
KN Sc 244 286n77
MY V 659 247n148
MY V 659.2 351n5
PY Aa 61, 792 345n68
PY Ab 186.B, 189.B 345n68
PY An 292 231n60
PY An 654.8–9 339n41
PY Aq 64.15 339n41
PY Fn 187.8 87n39
PY Fr 343, 1202 227n36
PY Fr 1202a 346n75
PY Fr 1204 286n77
PY Fr 1205 346n74
PY Fr 1206 346n73
PY Fr 1215 227
PY Fr 1217 227n36
PY Fr 1218 227n36, 271n15
PY Fr 1221, 1222 227n36
PY Fr 1224 227
PY Fr 1225 87n39
PY Fr 1231 227n36, 271
PY Fr 1236 87n39
PY Fr 1240 227, 271n15
PY Sa 774 318
PY Tn 316 286
PY Tn 316.5 286n77
PY Un 443 227n36
TH Av 104[+]191.1 231
TH Av 106.3 231n63
TH Fq 126, 130 230n51
TH Fq 177.2, 198.5, 214.[12], 244.2 231n62
TH Fq 254[+]255 230n51
TH Fq 254[+]255.10, 269.3, 276.6 231n62
TH Ft 140 352
TH Gp 164 231n64
TH Wu 47, 55, 58, 59 228

Mesopotamian tablets

A 842 87n44
BAM 323 36–8 89n50
BM 10059 213
BM 80328 38–43 197n119
CT 23.15–22+ i 33′–9′ 89n51
K 649 85n30
K 164 88–9
K 9717.10 57n15

KAR 146 iii 10′–29′, iv 23′–30′ 89n47
KAR 227 iii 14, 25–50 85
Msk. 74.224, obv. 10′ 115n10
VAT 13657 iii 50–1 85
YOS 11.5 1–8 217
YOS 12.345 87n44

Phoenician inscriptions

KAI 24.1–4 380n125
KAI 214 380–1n128
Karatepe Ph/A I 2, 4 316n72
Karatepe Phu/A II, 10–11 313n61
Karatepe Phu/A II 19, III 2–3, 4; Pho/B 6, 8; PhSt/c III 16, 17, 19 320n89

Ugaritic tablets

KTU 1.2 i 15–49 133n2
KTU 1.3 i 2–19 143–4
KTU 1.4 i 27–43 127n63
KTU 1.4 iv 29 144n27
KTU 1.4 v 46–7 145n29
KTU 1.15 iii 2–4, 13–15 290n98
KTU 1.15 iv 1 vi 8 143n26
KTU 1.16 i 3 87n42, 382n139
KTU 1.16 i 17, ii 39 87n42, 382n139
KTU 1.17 ii 11 144n27
KTU 1.17 v 14-31 143n26
KTU 1.17 vi 8–1.19 i 19 325–6
KTU 1.19 iii 13 42n91
KTU 1.100 215
KTU 1.105, 108, 112 151n9
KTU 1.113 150n2, 151n9
KTU 1.114 290n98
KTU 1.123 30′ 382n139
KTU 1.124 290n98
KTU 1.148 rev. 28 261n190
KTU 1.161 150n1
KTU 1.161 3, 10 290
L.1 303n5
RS 18.113A + B 305–6
RS 20.18 304n13
RS 20.238 303n5
RS 22.421 31
RS 24.285.4 131n77
RS 25.421 32
RS 92.2004 obv. 8 261n190
RS 94.2523 315n71
RS 94.2523 rev. 36–7 441n83
RS 94.2530 315n71
RS 94.2530 rev. 33–9 441n83

Concordance of tablets from Ugarit

Ugaritic texts

Epics

KTU 1.2 *Baal Cycle*
KTU 1.3 *Baal Cycle*
KTU 1.4 *Baal Cycle*
KTU 1.15 *Keret*
KTU 1.16 *Keret*
KTU 1.17 *Aqhat*
KTU 1.19 *Aqhat*

Rituals

RS 24.244 *KTU* 1.100 *Horanu and the Mare*
RS 24.249 *KTU* 1.105 *Rituals for Two Months*
RS 24.252 *KTU* 1.108 *A Divine Drinking Rite and Blessing*
RS 24.256 *KTU* 1.112 *Ritual for a Single Month*
RS 24.257 *KTU* 1.113 *Rites involving the Royal Shades of the Dead*
RS 24.248 *KTU* 1.114 *Ritual for a Single Month*
RS 24.271 *KTU* 1.123 *A Prayer for Well-Being*
RS 24.272 *KTU* 1.124 *Consultation of* Ditānu *with a View to Healing*
RS 24.643 *KTU* 1.148 *Rituals for Two Months*
RS 34.126 *KTU* 1.161 *A Funerary Ritual in Poetic Form*
RS 94.2518 *KTU* 1.113 *Rites involving the Royal Shades of the Dead*

Texts in other languages

Akkadian

RS L.1 *Letter from King of Alashiya to Ammurapi*
RS 18.113A + B *Letter from an Official in Alashiya to Ammurapi*
RS 20.18 *Letter from Eshuwara, Pidduri of Alashiya, to Ammurapi*
RS 20.238 *Letter from Ammurapi to King of Alashiya*
RS 22.421 *Atrahasis*
RS 92.2004 *Deity List*
RS 94.2523 *Letter from Benti-Sharruma to Ammurapi* = *CTH* 208
RS 94.2530 *Letter from Suppiluliuma II to Ammurapi* = *CTH* 208

Trilingual: Sumerian, Akkadian, Hittite

RS 25.421 LÚ.DINGIR.RA

Hurrian

RS 24.285 *Incense Prayer*

649

Printed by Printforce, United Kingdom